Eleventh Edition

Encyclopedia
of
Careers
and
Vocational Guidance

Holli R. Cosgrove

Editor-in-Chief

Volume 4

Career Articles

Ferguson Publishing Company
Chicago, Illinois

Library of Congress Cataloging-in-Publication Data

Encyclopedia of Careers and Vocational Guidance / Holli R. Cosgrove,
    editor-in-chief — 11th Edition
        p. cm.
    Includes indexes.
    ISBN 0-89434-274-6
    1. Vocational guidance—Handbooks, manuals, etc. 2. Occupations—Handbooks, manuals, etc.
    I. Cosgrove, Holli, 1964-.
    HF5381.E52 1999
    331.7'02--dc21

                                                                    99-16438
                                                                    CIP

Copyright © 2000 by Ferguson Publishing Company
    Published and Distributed by
    Ferguson Publishing Company
    200 West Jackson Street, Suite 700
    Chicago, Illinois 60606
    www.fergpubco.com

Printed in the United States of America

W-8

Contents

Volume 4: **Career Articles**

Packaging Designers

■ Overview

Package designers, or *graphic artists* or *visual artists,* design product packaging and related materials. They often work with *packaging engineers, product managers,* and *marketing and sales personnel* to design packages that not only protect the product but also present the project in a manner that is visually pleasing and adds to its marketability.

■ History

Art has been around since before the first drawings on cave walls. Historically, there has been a need for people to express themselves creatively through the use of pictures, graphics, and words. This means of expression remains a vital part of today's manufacturing and marketing.

Wherever there is a product in the marketplace, the elements of design have been involved at some point. From the first automobile that was developed to today's luxury vehicles, designers have helped create "the look." They are responsible for the corporate logos that we recognize at a glance. Their designs and graphics build brand-name recognition and consumer loyalty.

Although computers aid many of today's artists and designers, creativity, imagination, and ingenuity must still drive the artistic process. Artists today are a diverse group, usually with their own specialties. Some designers use their artistic talents to design packages, furniture, floral arrangements, appliances, or fashions. Other fine artists use the medium of oils and watercolors to create the masterpieces we see in homes and museums.

Many artists and graphic designers today are self-employed, while others work for design studios, manufacturing facilities, and corporate communications firms.

■ The Job

Package designers usually work in packaging plants of various industries or for a company that contracts for package design services. They usually work with a team of employees involved with the product to be packaged.

Typically, the designer meets with the product manager, the packaging engineer, the copywriter, and the marketing person to determine the type of package to be produced, safety and storage issues, and intended market. It is up to the designer to consider all of the factors that determine the final package, such as product weight and size; packaging production methods; design elements that must be included, such as logo, product pictures, instructions; labeling requirements, such as ingredients or warnings; and the method of shipment and storage. The designer

then designs the packaging and graphics by using computer software, through more traditional design methods, or both. These packaging ideas are usually presented to the product manager or before a committee for feedback. Prototypes may be developed and analyzed.

When a packaging design is agreed upon, the package designer develops the final layout and works with the production people and product manager to produce the package.

■ Requirements

High School

In high school, students should take classes in art and computers, including computer-aided design and graphics, if available. Voc-tech classes such as electrical shop, machine shop, and mechanical drawing will also be helpful when working with the manufacturing industry as a packaging designer. In addition to developing artistic abilities, students should also develop communication skills through English and writing classes. Foreign language skills are also beneficial.

Postsecondary Training

Educational requirements vary, but competition in this field is so fierce, postsecondary education is recommended. Some design occupations require a bachelor's degree or a degree from a design school. Some formal training for design artists is usually required. There are two- and three-year design schools that award certificates or associate's degrees upon completion. A bachelor of fine arts degree is also available at colleges and universities. College courses that are recommended in addition to art classes include computer-aided design, business administration, basic engineering, computerized design, mechanical drawing, psychology, sales, and marketing.

Other Requirements

Persons interested in this field should have highly creative skills, be imaginative, have mechanical aptitudes and manual dexterity, and have good verbal and visual com-

PACKAGING DESIGNERS	
SCHOOL SUBJECTS	Art Computer science
PERSONAL SKILLS	Artistic Mechanical/manipulative
WORK ENVIRONMENT	Primarily indoors Primarily one location
MINIMUM EDUCATION LEVEL	Some postsecondary training
SALARY RANGE	$20,000 to $36,400 to $43,000
CERTIFICATION OR LICENSING	None available
OUTLOOK	Faster than the average
DOT	141
O*NET	34035C

DO YOU HAVE GRAPHIC DESIGN SKILLS?

Graphic designers are able to...

- Visualize the finished design.
- Use graphics and layout software.
- Work quickly and accurately.
- Work well with other people's ideas.
- Use words to generate ideas.
- Learn new technology.
- Organize projects.
- Generate new ideas.

munication skills. In addition, they should have analytical and problem-solving skills. They also must be familiar with computers and their use in the design and manufacturing fields. They should have the ability to work well under pressure.

Employers

Various packaging and manufacturing industries employ packaging designers. In addition, employment opportunities are available with companies who contract out package design services. Package designers usually work with a team of employees and managers involved with the product to be packaged.

Packaging is one of the largest industries in the United States so jobs are plentiful across the country, in small towns and large cities; however, the field of graphic design is highly competitive because there are many talented people attracted to this career. Fortunately, there are many areas of employment for designers. In addition, many prefer to be self-employed as freelancers.

Opportunities in the packaging field can be found in almost any company that produces and packages a product. Food, chemicals, cosmetics, electronics, pharmaceuticals, automotive parts, hardware, plastics, and almost any products you can think of need to be packaged before reaching the consumer market. Because of this diverse industry, jobs are not restricted to any geographic location or plant size.

Starting Out

Students in a graphic arts program may be able to get job leads through their schools' job placement services. Many jobs in packaging are unadvertised and are learned about through contacts with professionals in the industry. Students may learn about openings from teachers, school administrators, and industry contacts they may have acquired during training.

Applicants can also apply directly to machinery manufacturing companies or companies with packaging depart-

ments. Employment opportunities may also be available with design studios that specialize in packaging designs.

Advancement

Graphic artists who work with a design firm usually begin in entry-level positions and work their way up as they gain design experience and build their portfolio. Packaging designers who work for a manufacturing company may advance within the company to other positions either in the packaging area, such as product manager, or in the corporate communications and marketing areas.

Some packaging designers pursue additional education to qualify as design engineers. Others may pursue business, economics, and finance degrees and use these additional skills in other areas of the manufacturing or design industries.

Earnings

Earnings for graphic designers vary with the skill level of the employee, the size of the company and the type of industry. Salaries for graphic designers usually begin around $20,000 a year. The mid-salary range is about $36,400, with some salaries reaching $43,000 or more. A designer who has established an excellent reputation can earn considerably more.

Benefits vary and depend upon the company, but generally include paid holidays, vacations, sick days, and medical and dental insurance. Some companies also offer tuition assistance programs, pension plans, profit sharing, and 401(k) plans. Graphic designers who are freelancers usually have to provide their own insurance and savings plans.

Work Environment

Packaging designers who work in a manufacturing setting usually work in a studio or office that is well lighted and ventilated. However, they may be subjected to odors from glues, paint, and ink when paste-up procedures are used. Also, as computers are used more and more, designers are often sitting in front of a computer monitor for a considerable amount of time.

Occasionally, they may have to be in the noisy factory floor environment when observing product packaging and production. Most plants are clean and well ventilated although actual conditions vary based on the type of product manufactured and packaged. Certain types of industries and manufacturing methods can pose special problems. For example, plants involved in paperboard and paper manufacturing may have dust created from paper fibers. Workers in food plants may be exposed to strong smells from the food being processed, although most workers usually get accustomed to this. Pharmaceutical and electronic component manufacturers may require special conditions to ensure that the manufacturing environments are free from dirt, contamination, and static. In general, most plants have no unusual hazards.

Most designers work 40 hours a week, although overtime may be required, especially during the introduction of a new product line.

■ Outlook

Packaging designers are in high demand, however, there is tough competition for the jobs available. Persons who have little or no formal education and limited experience may find it difficult to find a job. The plus side is that there are many designers who choose to freelance or work for design firms so that may give the person seeking a staff position in a manufacturing environment an edge.

With packaging one of the largest industries in the United States, jobs can be found across the country, in small towns and large cities, in small companies or multi-plant international corporations. The jobs are not restricted to any one industry or geographical location—wherever there is industry, there is some kind of packaging going on.

■ For More Information

For information on graphic design careers, contact:

The American Institute of Graphic Arts
164 Fifth Avenue
New York, NY 10010
Tel: 202-807-1990
Web: http://www.aiga.org

Industrial Designers Society of America
1142 East Walker Road
Great Falls, VA 22066
Tel: 703-759-0100
Web: http://www.idsa.org

■ Related Articles

Advertising and Marketing
Packaging
Visual Arts
Advertising Account Executives
Advertising Workers
Art Directors
Desktop Publishing Specialists
Graphic Designers
Illustrators
Packaging Engineers
Packaging Machinery Technicians

Packaging Engineers

■ Overview

The *packaging engineer* designs, develops, and specifies containers for all types of goods, such as food, clothing, medicine, housewares, toys, electronics, appliances, and computers. In creating these containers, some of the packaging engineer's activities include product and cost analysis, management of packaging personnel, development and operation of packaging filling lines, and negotiations with customers or sales representatives.

Packaging engineers may also select, design, and develop the machinery used for packaging operations. They may either modify existing machinery or design new machinery to be used for packaging operations.

■ History

Certain packages, particularly glass containers, have been used for over 3,000 years; the metal can was developed to provide food for Napoleon's army. However, the growth of the packaging industry developed during the Industrial Revolution, when shipping and storage containers were needed for the increased numbers of goods produced. As the shipping distance from producer to consumer grew, more care had to be given to packaging so goods would not be damaged in transit. Also, storage and safety factors became important with the longer shelf life required for goods produced.

Modern packaging methods have developed since the 1920s with the introduction of cellophane wrappings. Since World War II, early packaging materials such as cloth and wood have been largely replaced by less expensive and more durable materials such as steel, aluminum, and plastics such as polystyrene. Modern production methods have also

PACKAGING ENGINEERS	
SCHOOL SUBJECTS	**Mathematics** **Physics**
PERSONAL SKILLS	**Mechanical/manipulative** **Technical/scientific**
WORK ENVIRONMENT	**Primarily indoors** **Primarily one location**
MINIMUM EDUCATION LEVEL	**Bachelor's degree**
SALARY RANGE	**$35,000 to $45,000 to $60,000+**
CERTIFICATION OR LICENSING	**Required by certain states**
OUTLOOK	**Faster than the average**
DOT	**019**
GOE	**05.03.09**
NOC	**2148**
O*NET	**22199**

allowed for the low-cost, mass production of traditional materials such as glass and paperboard. Both government agencies and manufacturers and designers are constantly trying to improve packaging so that it is more convenient, safe, and informative.

Today, packaging engineers must also consider environmental factors when designing packaging because the disposal of used packages has presented a serious problem for many communities. The United States uses more than 500 billion packages yearly; 50 percent of these are used for food and beverages, and another 40 percent for other consumer goods. To help solve this problem, the packaging engineer attempts to come up with solutions such as the use of recyclable, biodegradable, or less bulky packaging.

■ The Job

Packaging engineers plan, design, develop, and produce containers for all types of products. When developing a package, they must first determine the purpose of the packaging and the needs of the end-user and their clients. Packaging for a product may be needed for a variety of reasons: for shipping, storage, display, or protection. A package for display must be attractive as well as durable and easy to store; labeling and perishability are important considerations, especially for food, medicine, and cosmetics. If the packaging purpose is for storage and shipping, then ease of handling and durability have to be considered. Safety factors may be involved if the materials to be packaged are hazardous, such as toxic chemicals or explosives. Finally, the costs of producing and implementing the packaging have to be considered, as well as the packaging material's impact on the environment.

After determining the purpose of the packaging, the engineers study the physical properties and handling requirements of the product in order to develop the best kind of packaging. They study drawings and descriptions of the product or the actual product itself to learn about its size, shape, weight, and color, the materials used, and the way it functions. They decide what kind of packaging material to use and with the help of *designers* and *production workers*, they make sketches, draw up plans, and make samples of the package. These samples, along with lists of materials and cost estimates, are submitted to management or directly to the customer. Computer design programs and other related software may be used in the packaging design and manufacturing process.

When finalizing plans for packaging a product, packaging engineers contribute additional expertise in other areas. They are concerned with efficient use of raw materials and production facilities as well as conservation of energy and reduction of costs. For instance, they may use materials that can be recycled, or they may try to cut down on weight and size. They must keep up with the latest developments in packaging methods and materials and often recommend innovative ways to package products. Once all the details for packaging are worked out, packaging engineers may be involved in supervising the filling and packing operations, operating production lines, or drawing up contracts with customers or *sales representatives*. They should be knowledgeable about production and manufacturing processes, as well as sales and customer service.

After a packaging sample is approved, packaging engineers may supervise the testing of the package. This may involve simulation of all the various conditions a packaged good may be subjected to, such as temperature, handling, and shipping.

This can be a complex operation involving several steps. For instance, perishable items such as food and beverages have to be packaged to avoid spoilage. Electronic components have to be packaged to prevent damage to parts. Whether the items to be packaged are food, chemicals, medicine, electronics, or factory parts, considerable knowledge of the properties of these products is often necessary to make suitable packaging.

Design and marketing factors also need to be considered when creating the actual package that will be seen by the consumer. Packaging engineers work with *graphic designers* and *packaging designers* to design effective packaging that will appeal to consumers. For this task, knowledge of marketing, design, and advertising are essential. Packaging designers consider color, shape, and convenience as well as labeling and other informative features when designing packages for display. Very often, the consumer is able to evaluate a product only from its package.

The many different kinds of packages require different kinds of machinery and skills. For example, the beverage industry produces billions of cans, bottles, and cardboard containers. Often packaging engineers are involved in selecting and designing packaging machinery along with other engineers and production personnel. Packaging can be manufactured either at the same facility where the goods are produced or at facilities that specialize in producing packaging materials.

The packaging engineer must also consider safety, health, and legal factors when designing and producing packaging. Various guidelines apply to the packaging process of certain products and the packaging engineer must be aware of these regulations. Labeling and packaging of products are regulated by various federal agencies such as the Federal Trade Commission and the Food and Drug Administration. For example, the Consumer Product Safety Commission requires that safe packaging materials be used for food and cosmetics.

■ Requirements

High School

During high school, students planning to enter a college engineering or packaging program should take college algebra, trigonometry, physics, chemistry, computer science, mechanical drawing, economics, and accounting classes. Speech, writing, art, computer-aided design, and graphic arts classes are also recommended.

Postsecondary Training

Several colleges and universities offer a major in packaging engineering. These programs may be offered through an engineering school or a school of packaging within a university. Both bachelor of science and master of science degrees are available. It generally takes four or five years to earn a bachelor's degree and two additional years to earn a master's degree. A master's degree is not required to be a packaging engineer, although many professionals pursue advanced degrees, particularly if they plan to specialize in a specific area or do research. Many students take their first job in packaging once they have earned a bachelor's degree, while other students earn a master's degree immediately upon completing their undergraduate studies.

Students interested in this field often structure their own programs. In college, if no major is offered in packaging engineering, students can choose a related discipline, such as mechanical, industrial, electrical, chemical, materials, or systems engineering. It is useful to take courses in graphic design, computer science, marketing, and management.

Students enrolled in a packaging engineering program will usually take the following courses during their first two years: algebra, trigonometry, calculus, chemistry, physics, accounting, economics, finance, and communications. During the remaining years, classes focus on core packaging subjects such as packaging materials, package development, packaging line machinery, and product protection and distribution. Elective classes include topics concentrating on packaging and the environment, packaging laws and regulation, and technical classes on specific materials. Graduate studies, or those classes necessary to earn a master's degree, include advanced classes in design, analysis, and materials and packaging processes.

Certification or Licensing

Special licensing is required for engineers whose work affects the safety of the public. Much of the work of packaging engineers, however, does not require a license even though their work affects such factors as food and drug spoilage, protection from hazardous materials, or protection from damage. Licensing laws vary from state to state, but, in general, states have similar requirements. They

WHAT GOES INTO MAKING A PACKAGE?

There are many questions to ask when designing and manufacturing packaging. These are just a few.

- Does it have an appealing design?
- Is it easy to open and close?
- Does the package meet government and industry safety regulations?
- Is it made out of nontoxic materials?
- Is it packaged so it can be handled safely?
- Does the package protect the product?
- Is it environmentally safe?
- Does the package complement the product?
- Is the packaging material recyclable?
- Is the package labeled appropriately?
- Is the package secure?
- Is the package durable?
- Can the package be transported and handled easily?

require that an engineer must be a graduate of an approved engineering school, have four years of engineering experience, and passes the state licensing examination. A state board of engineering examiners administers the licensing and registration of engineers.

Professional societies offer certification to engineers instead of licensing. Although certification is not required, many professional engineers obtain it to show that they have mastered specified requirements and have reached a certain level of expertise.

For those interested in working with the specialized field of military packaging technology, the U.S. Army offers courses in this field. Generally, a person earns a bachelor of science degree in packaging engineering before taking these specialized courses. The National Institute of Packaging, Handling, and Logistic Engineers has information about the field of military packaging.

Other Requirements

Packaging engineers should have the ability to solve problems and think analytically and creatively. They must work well with people, both as a leader and as a team player. They should also be able to write and speak well in order to deal effectively with other workers and customers, and in order to document procedures and policies. In addition, a packaging engineer should have the ability to manage projects and people.

■ Exploring

To get firsthand experience in the packaging industry, students can call local manufacturers to see how they handle and package their products. Often, factories will allow visitors to tour their manufacturing and packaging facilities.

IT TAKES A TEAM TO PRODUCE A PACKAGE

Some of the people who may be involved in producing a package are:

Chemical engineer
Consumer
Copywriter
Government inspector
Manufacturing engineer
Marketing personnel
Materials engineer
Packaging designer
Packaging engineer
Packaging technician
Packing operator
Product testing engineer
Product manager
Safety engineer
Sales representative
Shipper

Another way to learn about packaging is by observing the packaging that we encounter every day, such as containers for food, beverages, cosmetics, and household goods. Visit stores to see how products are packaged, stored, or displayed. Notice the shape and labeling on the container, its ease of use, durability for storage, convenience of opening and closing, disposability, and attractiveness.

Students may also explore their aptitude and interest in a packaging career through graphic design courses, art classes that include construction activities, and computer-aided design classes. Participating in hobbies that include designing and constructing objects from different types of materials can also be beneficial. Students may also learn about the industry by reading trade publications, such as *Packaging* and *Packaging Digest*.

■ Employers

Packaging engineers are employed by almost every manufacturing industry. Pharmaceutical, beverage, cosmetics, and food industries are major employers of packaging engineers. Some packaging engineers are hired to design and develop packaging while others oversee the actual production of the packages. Some companies have their own packaging facilities while other companies subcontract the packaging to specialized packing firms. Manufacturing and packaging companies can be large, multinational enterprises who manufacture, package, and distribute numerous products or they can be small operations that are limited to the production of one or two specific products. Specialized packaging companies hire employees for all aspects of the packaging design and production process. Worldwide manufacturing offers career opportunities

around the world. The federal government and the armed services also have employment opportunities for packaging engineers.

■ Starting Out

College graduates with a degree in packaging or a related field of engineering should find it easy to get jobs as the packaging industry continues its rapid growth. Many companies send recruiters to college campuses to meet with graduating students and interview them for positions with their companies. Students can also learn about employment possibilities through their schools' placement services, job fairs, classified advertisements in newspapers and trade publications, and referrals from teachers. Students who have participated in an internship or work-study program through a college may learn about employment opportunities through contacts with industry professionals.

Students can also research companies they are interested in working for and apply directly to the person in charge of packaging or the personnel office.

■ Advancement

Beginning packaging engineers generally do routine work under the supervision of experienced engineers and may also receive some formal training through their company. As they become more experienced, they are given more difficult tasks and more independence in solving problems, developing designs, or making decisions.

Some companies provide structured programs in which packaging engineers advance through a sequence of positions to more advanced packaging engineering positions. For example, an entry-level engineer might start out by producing engineering layouts to assist product designers, advance to a product designer, and ultimately move into a management position.

Packaging engineers may advance from being a member of a team to a project supervisor or department manager. Qualified packaging engineers may advance through their department to become a manager or vice president of their company. To advance to a management position, the packaging engineer must demonstrate good technical and production skills and managerial ability. After years of experience, a packaging engineer might wish to become self-employed as a packaging consultant.

To improve chances for advancement, the packaging engineer may wish to get a master's degree in another branch of engineering or in business administration. Many executives in government and industry began their careers as engineers. Some engineers become patent attorneys by combining a law degree with their technical and scientific knowledge.

Many companies encourage continuing education throughout one's career and provide training opportunities in the form of in-house seminars and outside workshops. Taking advantage of any training offered helps one to develop new skills and learn technical information that can increase chances for advancement. Many companies also encourage their employees to participate in professional association activities. Membership and involvement in professional associations are valuable ways to stay current on new trends within the industry, to familiarize oneself with what other companies are doing, and to make contacts with other professionals in the industry. Many times, professionals learn about opportunities for advancement in new areas or at different companies through the contacts they have made at association events.

■ Earnings

Currently, the average starting salary for a packaging engineer with a bachelor's degree is about $35,000 per year. The mid-range salary is $45,000, with packaging engineers easily earning $60,000 or more as they gain experience and advance within a company.

Benefits vary from company to company but can include any of the following: medical, dental, and life insurance; paid vacations, holidays, and sick days; profit sharing; 401(k) plans; bonus and retirement plans; and educational assistance programs. Some employers pay fees and expenses for participation in professional associations.

■ Work Environment

The working conditions for packaging engineers vary with the employer and with the tasks of the engineer. Those who work for companies that make packaging materials or who direct packaging operations might work around noisy machinery. Generally, they have offices near the packaging operations where they consult with others in their department, such as packaging machinery technicians and other engineers.

Packaging engineers also work with nontechnical staff such as designers, artists, and marketing and financial people. Packaging engineers must be alert to keeping up with new trends in marketing and technological developments.

Most packaging engineers have a five-day, 40-hour workweek, although overtime is not unusual. In some companies, particularly during research and design stages, product development, and the start up of new methods or equipment, packaging engineers may work 10-hour days or longer and work on weekends.

Some travel may be involved, especially if the packaging engineer is also involved in sales. Also, travel between plants may be necessary to coordinate packaging operations. At various stages of developing packaging, the packaging engineer will probably be engaged in hands-on activities. These activities may involve handling objects, working with machinery, carrying light loads, and using a variety of tools, machines, and instruments.

The work of packaging engineers also involves other, social concerns such as consumer protection, environmental pollution, and conservation of natural resources. Packaging engineers are constantly searching for safer, tamper-proof packaging, especially because harmful substances have been found in some food, cosmetics, and drugs. They also experiment with new packaging materials and utilize techniques to conserve resources and reduce the disposal problem. Many environmentalists are concerned with managing the waste from discarded packages. Efforts are being made to stop littering; to recycle bottles, cans, and other containers; and to use more biodegradable substances in packaging materials. The qualified packaging engineer, then, will have a broad awareness of social issues.

■ Outlook

The packaging industry, which employs more than a million people, offers almost unlimited opportunities for packaging engineers. Packaging engineers work in almost any industry because virtually all manufactured products need one or more kinds of packaging. Some of the industries with the fastest growing packaging needs are food, drugs, and cosmetics.

The demand for packaging engineers is expected to increase faster than the average for all occupations as newer, faster ways of packaging are continually being sought to meet the needs of economic growth, world trade expansion, and the environment. Increased efforts are also being made to develop packaging that is easy to open for the growing aging population and those persons with disabilities.

■ For More Information

The following sources can provide information on educational programs and the packaging industry.

Institute of Electrical and Electronics Engineers
1828 L Street NW, Suite 1202
Washington, DC 20036-5104
Tel: 202-785-0017
Web: http://www.ieee.org/usab

Institute of Packaging Professionals
481 Carlisle Drive
Herndon, VA 22070-4823
Tel: 703-318-8970
Web: http://www.pakinfo-world.org/iopp/

National Institute of Packaging, Handling, and Logistic Engineers
6902 Lyle Street
Lanham, MD 20706
Tel: 301-459-9105

This Web site lists U.S. and international associations related to the packaging industry.

NAPCO Packaging Association Links from North American Publishing Co.
Web: http://www2.packageprinting.com/
packaginglinks.html

■ Related Articles

Packaging Machinery Technicians

■ Overview

Packaging machinery technicians work with automated machinery that packages products into bottles, cans, bags, boxes, cartons, and other containers. The machines perform various operations, such as forming, filling, closing, labeling, and marking. The systems and technologies that packaging machinery technicians work with are diverse. Depending on the job, packaging machinery technicians may work with electrical, mechanical, hydraulic, or pneumatic systems. They also may work with computerized controllers, fiber-optic transmitters, robotic units, and vision systems.

■ History

Packaging has been used since ancient times, when people first wrapped food in materials to protect it, or devised special carriers to transport items over long distances. One of the oldest packaging materials, glass, was used by Egyptians as early as 3000 BC. Packaging as we know it, though, has its origins in the Industrial Revolution. Machinery was used for mass production of items, and manufacturers needed some way to package products and protect them during transport. Packages and containers were developed that not only kept goods from damage during shipment, but also helped to increase the shelf life of perishable items.

Initially, packaging was done by hand. Workers at manufacturing plants hand-packed products into paper boxes, steel cans, glass jars, or other containers as they were produced. As manufacturing processes and methods improved, equipment and machines were developed to provide quicker and less expensive ways to package products. Automated machinery was in use by the 19th century and was used not only to package products but to create packaging materials. The first containers produced through automated machinery were glass containers created by Michael Owens in Toledo, Ohio, in 1903.

The use of new packaging materials, such as cellophane in the 1920s and aluminum cans in the early 1960s, required updated machinery to handle the new materials and to provide faster, more efficient production. Semiautomatic machines and eventually high-speed, fully automated machines were created to handle a wide variety of products, materials, and packaging operations. Today, packaging engineers, packaging machinery technicians, and other engineering professionals work to develop new equipment and techniques that are more time-, material-, and cost-efficient. Advanced technologies, such as robotics, are allowing for the creation of increasingly sophisticated packaging machinery.

■ The Job

Packaging machinery technicians work in packaging plants of various industries or in the plants of packaging machinery manufacturers. Their jobs entail building machines, installing and setting up equipment, training operators to use the equipment, and maintaining, troubleshooting, and repairing machines. Machines of today are computer-controlled and may include robotic or vision-guided applications.

Machinery builders, also called *assemblers,* assist engineers in the development and modification of new and existing machinery designs. They build different types of packaging machinery following engineering blueprints, wiring schematics, pneumatic diagrams, and plant layouts. Beginning with a machine frame that has been welded in another department, they assemble electrical circuitry, mechanical components, and fabricated items that they may have made themselves in the plant's machine shop. They may also be responsible for bolting on additional elements of the machine to the frame. After the machinery is assembled, they perform a test run to make sure it is performing according to specifications.

Field service technicians, also called *field service representatives,* are employed by packaging machinery manufacturers. They do most of their work at the plants where the packaging machinery is being used. In some companies, assemblers may serve as field service technicians; in others, the field service representative is a technician other than the assembler. In either case, they install new machinery at customers' plants and train in-plant machine operators and maintenance personnel on its operation and maintenance.

When a new machine is delivered, the field service technicians level it and anchor it to the plant floor. Then, following engineering drawings, wiring plans, and plant layouts, they install the system's electrical and electro-mechanical components. They also regulate the controls and setup for the size, thickness, and type of material to be processed and ensure the correct sequence of processing stages. After installation, the technicians test-run the machinery and make any necessary adjustments. Then they teach machine operators the proper operating and maintenance procedures for that piece of equipment. The entire installation process, which may take a week, is carefully documented. Field service representatives may also help the plant's in-house mechanics troubleshoot equipment already in operation, including modifying equipment for greater efficiency and safety.

Automated packaging machine mechanics, also called *maintenance technicians,* perform scheduled preventive maintenance as well as diagnose machinery problems and make repairs. Preventive maintenance is done on a regular basis following the manufacturer's guidelines in the service manual. During routine maintenance, technicians do such things as change filters in vacuum pumps, grease fittings, change oil in gearboxes, and replace worn bushings, chains, and belts. When machines do break down, maintenance technicians must work quickly to fix them so that production can resume as soon as possible. The technician might be responsible for all the machinery in the plant, one or more packaging lines, or a single machine. In a small plant, a single technician may be responsible for all the duties required to keep a packaging line running, while in a large plant a team of technicians may divide the duties.

■ Requirements

High School

Although a high school diploma is not required, it is preferred by most employers who hire packaging or engineering technicians. In high school, students should take geometry, and voc-tech classes such as electrical shop, machine shop, and mechanical drawing. Computer classes, including computer-aided design, are also helpful. In addition to developing mechanical and electrical abilities, students should develop communication skills through English and writing classes.

Postsecondary Training

Many employers prefer to hire technicians who have completed a two-year technical training program. Completing a machinery training program or packaging machinery program can provide students with the necessary knowledge and technical skills for this type of work. Machinery training programs can be found in community colleges, trade schools, and technical institutes throughout the country, but there are only a few technical colleges specializing in packaging machinery programs. These programs award either a degree or certificate in automated packaging machinery systems. You may get a list of these technical colleges by writing to the Packaging Machinery Manufacturers Institute.

Packaging machinery programs generally last two years and include extensive hands-on training as well as classroom study. Students may learn to use simple hand tools such as hacksaws as well as drill presses, lathes, mills, and

PACKAGING MACHINERY TECHNICIANS	
SCHOOL SUBJECTS	**Mathematics** **Technical/Shop**
PERSONAL SKILLS	**Mechanical/manipulative** **Technical/scientific**
WORK ENVIRONMENT	**Primarily indoors** **Primarily multiple locations**
MINIMUM EDUCATION LEVEL	**High school diploma**
SALARY RANGE	**$20,200 to $32,700 to $54,800**
CERTIFICATION OR LICENSING	**Voluntary**
OUTLOOK	**Faster than the average**
DOT	**638**
GOE	**05.05.05**
NOC	**7311**
O*NET	**92974**

Technicians need many talents to succeed, including:

Mechanical aptitude
Problem-solving skills
Writing skills
Manual dexterity
Electrical aptitude
People skills
Communication skills
Analytical skills

grinders. Other technical courses cover sheet metal and welding work, power transmission, electrical and mechanical systems, maintenance operations, industrial safety, and hazardous materials handling.

Classes in packaging operations include bag making, loading, and closing; case loading; blister packaging; palletizing, conveying, and accumulating; and labeling, and bar coding. There are also classes in form fill, seal wrap, and carton machines as well as packaging quality control and package design and testing. Courses especially critical in an industry where technology is increasingly sophisticated are PLC (programmable logic control), CAD/CAM (computer-aided design and manufacturing), fiber optics, robotics, and servo controls.

Certification or Licensing

Although employers may not require certification, it can provide a competitive advantage when seeking employment. A voluntary certification program is available for engineering technicians through the National Institute for Certification in Engineering Technologies (NICET). Certification is available at various levels and in different specialty fields. Most programs require passing a written exam and possessing a certain amount of work experience.

Union membership may be a requirement for some jobs, depending on union activity at a particular company. Unions are more likely found in large-scale national and international corporations. Field service technicians are usually not unionized. Maintenance technicians and assemblers may be organized by the International Brotherhood of Teamsters or the International Association of Machinists and Aerospace Workers. In addition, some technicians may be represented by the International Longshoremen's and Warehousemen's Union.

Other Requirements

Persons interested in this field should have mechanical and electrical aptitudes, manual dexterity, and the ability to work under time pressure. In addition, they should have analytical and problem solving skills. The ability to communicate effectively with people from varying backgrounds is especially important as packaging machinery technicians work closely with engineers, plant managers, customers, and machinery operators. They need to be able to listen to workers' problems as well as to explain things clearly. They frequently have to provide written reports, so good writing skills are beneficial.

■ Exploring

Students can test their interest for this type of work by engaging in activities that require mechanical and electrical skills, such as building a short-wave radio, taking appliances apart, and working on cars, motorcycles, and bicycles. Participating in science clubs and contests can also provide opportunities for working with electrical and mechanical equipment and building and repairing things. Taking vocational shop classes can also help students explore their interests and acquire useful skills.

Students may also visit a plant or manufacturing company to observe packaging operations and see packaging machinery technicians at work. Many plants provide school tours, and you may be able to arrange a visit through a school counselor or teacher. Reading trade publications can also familiarize students with the industry.

■ Employers

Packaging machinery technicians are usually employed by companies who manufacture packaging machinery or by companies who package the products they produce. Packaging is one of the largest industries in the United States so jobs are plentiful across the country; in small towns and large cities. Opportunities in the packaging field can be found in almost any company that produces and packages a product. Food, chemicals, cosmetics, electronics, pharmaceuticals, automotive parts, hardware, plastics, and almost any products you can think of need to be packaged before reaching the consumer market. Because of this diversity, jobs are not restricted to any product, geographic location, or plant size.

■ Starting Out

Students in a technical program may be able to get job leads through their schools' job placement services. Many jobs in packaging are unadvertised and are learned about through contacts with professionals in the industry. Students may learn about openings from teachers, school administrators, and industry contacts they acquired during training.

Applicants can also apply directly to machinery manufacturing companies or companies with manufacturing departments. Local employment offices may also list job openings. Sometimes companies hire part-time or summer help in other departments, such as the warehouse or shipping. These jobs may provide an opportunity to move into other areas of the company.

■ Advancement

Technicians usually begin in entry-level positions and work as part of an engineering team. They may advance from a maintenance technician to an assembler, and then move up to a supervisory position in production operations or packaging machinery. They can also become project managers and field service managers.

Workers who show an interest in their work, who learn quickly and have good technical skills, can gradually take on more responsibilities and advance to higher positions. The ability to work as part of a team and communicate well with others, plus self-motivation and the ability to work well without a lot of supervision, are all helpful traits for advancement. People who have skills as a packaging machinery technician can usually transfer those skills to engineering technician positions in other industries

Some packaging machinery technicians pursue additional education to qualify as an engineer and move into electrical engineering, mechanical engineering, packaging engineering, or industrial engineering positions. Other technicians pursue business, economics, and finance degrees and use these credentials to obtain positions in other areas of the manufacturing process, in business development, or in areas such as importing or exporting.

■ Earnings

Earnings vary with geographical area and the employee's skill level and specific duties and job responsibilities. Other variables that may affect salary include the size of the company and the type of industry, such as the food and beverage industry or the electronics industry. Technicians who work at companies with unions generally, but not always, earn higher salaries.

In general, technicians earn approximately $20,000 a year to start, and with experience can increase their salaries to about $33,000. Seasoned workers with two-year degrees who work for large companies may earn between $50,000 and $70,000 a year, particularly those in field service jobs or in supervisory positions.

Benefits vary and depend upon company policy, but generally include paid holidays, vacations, sick days, and medical and dental insurance. Some companies also offer tuition assistance programs, pension plans, profit sharing, and 401(k) plans.

■ Work Environment

Packaging machinery technicians work in a variety of environments. They may work for a machinery manufacturer or in the manufacturing department of a plant or factory.

Most plants are clean and well ventilated, although actual conditions vary based on the type of product manufactured and packaged. Certain types of industries and manufacturing methods can pose special problems. For example, plants involved in paperboard and paper manufacturing may have dust created from paper fibers. Workers in food plants may be exposed to strong smells from the food being processed, although most workers usually get accustomed to this. Pharmaceutical and electronic component manufacturers may require special conditions to ensure that the manufacturing environments are free from dirt, contamination, and static. Clean-air environments may be special rooms that are temperature- and moisture-controlled, and technicians may be required to wear special clothing or equipment when working in these rooms.

In general, most plants have no unusual hazards, although safety practices need to be followed when working on machinery and using tools. The work is generally not strenuous, although it does involve carrying small components and hand tools, and some bending and stretching.

Most workers work 40 hours a week, although overtime may be required, especially during the installation of new machinery or when equipment malfunctions. Some technicians may be called in during the evening or on weekends to repair machinery that has shut down production operations. Installation and testing periods of new equipment can also be very time-intensive and stressful when problems develop. Troubleshooting, diagnosing problems, and repairing equipment may involve considerable time as well as trial-and-error testing until the correct solution is determined.

Technicians who work for machinery manufacturers may be required to travel to customers' plants to install new machinery or to service or maintain existing equipment. This may require overnight stays or travel to foreign locations.

■ Outlook

Packaging machinery technicians are in high demand both by companies that manufacture packaging machinery and by companies that use packaging machinery. With the growth of the packaging industry, which grosses over $80 billion a year, a nationwide shortage of trained packaging technicians has developed over the last 20 years. There are far more openings than there are qualified applicants.

The packaging machinery industry is expected to continue its growth into the 21st century. American-made packaging machinery has earned a worldwide reputation for high quality and is known for its outstanding control systems and electronics. According to the Packaging Machinery Manufacturers Institute's Fourth Annual Packaging Machinery Shipments and Outlook Study, U.S.

shipments of packaging machinery increased by 8.1 percent in 1997 to an estimated $4.5 billion. U.S. shipments of packaging machinery are forecast to grow at a cumulative annual rate of 4.0 percent over the next three years, to $4.9 billion by 2000. Continued success in global competition will remain important to the packaging machinery industry's prosperity and employment outlook.

The introduction of computers, robotics, fiber optics, and vision systems into the industry has added new skill requirements and job opportunities for packaging machinery technicians. There is already widespread application of computer-aided design and computer-aided manufacturing (CAD/CAM). The use of computers in packaging machinery will continue to increase, with computers communicating with other computers on the status of operations and providing diagnostic maintenance information and production statistics. The role of robotics, fiber optics, and electronics will also continue to expand. To be prepared for the jobs of the future, packaging machinery students should seek training in the newest technologies.

With packaging one of the largest industries in the United States, jobs can be found across the country, in small towns and large cities, in small companies or multiplant international corporations. The jobs are not restricted to any one industry or geographical location—wherever there is industry, there is some kind of packaging going on.

■ For More Information

For career and industry information and educational programs, contact the following organizations.

Institute of Electrical and Electronics Engineers
1828 L Street, NW, Suite 1202
Washington, DC 20036-5104
Tel: 202-785-0017
Web: http://www.ieee.org/usab

Institute of Packaging Professionals
481 Carlisle Drive
Herndon, VA 22070-4823
Tel: 703-318-8970
Web: http://www.pakinfo-world.org

National Institute of Packaging, Handling, and Logistic Engineers
6902 Lyle Street
Lanham, MD 20706
Tel: 301-459-9105

Packaging Education Forum
481 Carlisle Drive
Herndon, VA 22070-4823
Tel: 703-318-8970
Web: http://www.packagingeducation.org

Packaging Machinery Manufacturers Institute
4350 North Fairfax Drive, Suite 600
Arlington, VA 22203
Tel: 703-243-8555
Web: http://www.packnet.com
Web: http://www.packexpo.com

■ Related Articles

Machining and Machinery
Manufacturing
Packaging
General Maintenance Mechanics
Industrial Engineering Technicians
Industrial Machinery Mechanics
Mechanical Engineering Technicians
Millwrights
Packaging Engineers
Quality Control Engineers and Technicians
Robotics Engineers and Technicians

Pad Cutters

■ **See Plastics Products Manufacturing Workers**

Painters and Paperhangers

■ Overview

For both practical purposes and aesthetic appeal, building surfaces are often painted and decorated with various types of coverings. Although painting and paperhanging are two separate skills, many building trades craftsworkers do both types of work. *Painters* apply paints, varnishes, enamels, and other types of finishes to decorate and protect interior and exterior surfaces of buildings and other structures. *Paperhangers* cover interior walls and ceilings with decorative paper, fabric, vinyls, and other types of materials.

■ History

The history of the skilled house painter's occupation in this country begins in the 18th century, when American colonists made their own paints for use on their homes. There were few people in the business of manufacturing paint in the colonies, and it was unusual to order materials from other countries because the shipping and transport industries were not as sophisticated as they are today.

Instead, builders and owners depended on local products for making paint. Milk, for example, was often used as a base. Soil from land that had traces of iron was burned to make paint with a red pigment, or colored tint. Material called lampblack, which is black soot, was also used to make pigmented paint. In 1867, manufacturers made available the first prepared paints. After this, machines were invented to enable manufacturers to produce paint in large amounts.

Paperhanging as an occupation probably began around the 16th century. Although the Chinese invented decorative paper, it was the Europeans who first used it to cover walls. Wealthy homeowners often decorated the walls of their rooms with tapestries and velvet hangings (which was often done for warmth as well as decoration); those who could not afford such luxuries would imitate the rich by hanging inexpensive, yet decorative, wallpaper in their homes.

Paperhangers and painters were in great demand as building construction developed on a large scale in the early part of the 20th century. Since the middle of the 20th century, there have been great advancements in the materials and techniques used by these skilled trades workers.

■ The Job

Workers in the painting and paperhanging trades often perform both functions; painters may take on jobs that involve hanging wallpaper, and paperhangers may work in situations where they are responsible for painting walls and ceilings. However, although there is some overlap in the work, each trade has its own characteristic skills.

Painters must be able to apply paint thoroughly, uniformly, and rapidly to any type of surface. To do this, they must be skilled in handling brushes and other painting tools and have a working knowledge of the various characteristics of paints and finishes—their durability, suitability, and ease of handling and application.

Preparation of the area to be painted is an important duty of painters, especially when repainting old surfaces. They first smooth the surface, removing old, loose paint with a scraper, paint remover (usually a liquid solution), wire brush, or paint-removing gun (similar in appearance to a hairdryer) or a combination of these items. If necessary, they remove grease and fill nail holes, cracks, and joints with putty, plaster, or other types of filler. Often, a prime coat or sealer is applied to further smooth the surface and make the finished coat level and well blended in color.

Once the surface is prepared, painters select premixed paints or prepare paint by mixing required portions of pigment, oil, and thinning and drying substances. (For purposes of preparing paint, workers must have a thorough knowledge of the composition of the various materials they use and of which materials mix well together.) They then paint the surface using a brush, spray gun, or roller; choosing the most appropriate tool for applying paint is one of the most important decisions a painter must make because using incorrect tools often slows down the work and produces unacceptable results. Spray guns are used generally for large surfaces or objects that do not lend themselves to brush work, such as lattices, cinder and concrete block, and radiators.

Many painters specialize in working on exterior surfaces only, painting house sidings and outside walls of large buildings. When doing work on tall buildings, scaffolding (raised supportive platforms) must be erected to allow the painter to climb to his or her position at various heights above the ground; workers also might use swinglike and chairlike platforms hung from heavy cables.

The first task of the paperhanger is similar to that of the painter: to prepare the surface to be covered. Rough spots must be smoothed, holes and cracks must be filled, and old paint, varnish, and grease must be removed from the surface. In some cases, old wallpaper must be removed by brushing it with solvent, soaking it down with water, or steaming it with portable steamer equipment. In new work, the paperhangers apply sizing, which is a prepared glazing material used as filler to make the plaster less porous and to ensure that the paper sticks well to the surface.

After erecting any necessary scaffolding, the paperhangers measure the area to be covered and cut the paper to size. They then mix paste and apply it to the back of the paper, which is then placed on the wall or ceiling and smoothed into place with brushes or rollers. In placing the paper on the wall, paperhangers must make sure that they match any design patterns at the adjacent edges of paper strips, cut overlapping ends, and smooth the seams between each strip.

■ Requirements

High School

Although a high school education is not essential, it is preferred that workers have at least the equivalent of a high school diploma (i.e., a GED). Shop classes can help prepare you for the manual work involved in painting and paperhanging, while art classes will help develop an eye for color and design. Chemistry classes should prove useful in dealing with the paints, solvents, and other chemicals used in this work.

PAINTERS AND PAPERHANGERS	
SCHOOL SUBJECTS	Mathematics Technical/Shop
PERSONAL SKILLS	Artistic Following instructions
WORK ENVIRONMENT	Indoors and outdoors Primarily multiple locations
MINIMUM EDUCATION LEVEL	Apprenticeship
SALARY RANGE	$12,000 to $24,000 to $38,000
CERTIFICATION OR LICENSING	None available
OUTLOOK	Faster than the average
DOT	840
GOE	05.10.07
O*NET	87402A

House painters at work

Postsecondary Training

To qualify as a skilled painter or paperhanger, a person must complete either an apprenticeship or an on-the-job training program. The apprenticeship program, which often combines painting and paperhanging, consists of three years of carefully planned activity, including work experience and related classroom instruction (approximately 144 hours of courses each year). During this period, the apprentice becomes familiar with all aspects of the craft: use of tools and equipment, preparation of surfaces as well as of paints and pastes, application methods, coordination of colors, reading of blueprints, characteristics of wood and other surfaces, cost-estimating methods, and safety techniques. Courses often involve the study of mathematics as well as practice sessions on the techniques of the trade.

On-the-job training programs involve learning the trade while working for two to three years under the guidance of experienced painters or paperhangers. The trainees usually begin as helpers until they acquire the necessary skills and knowledge for more difficult jobs. Workers without formal apprenticeship training are more easily accepted in these crafts than in most of the other building trades.

Other Requirements

Basic skills requirements are the same for both painters and paperhangers. Most employers prefer to hire applicants in good physical condition, with manual dexterity and a good sense of color. For protection of their own health, applicants should not be allergic to paint fumes or other materials used in the trade.

■ Exploring

You can explore the work of painters and paperhangers by reading trade journals and watching instructional videos or television programs. Those who already have some experience in the trade should keep up with the news by reading such publications as the monthly *Painters and Allied Trades Journal*, available to members of the International Brotherhood of Painters and Allied Trades union. Look for educational books and videos at your local library. The projects tackled on television home improvement shows almost always feature the work of painters or paperhangers to some extent.

Certainly, painting and paperhanging in one's own home or apartment provide valuable firsthand experience, often impossible to obtain in other fields. Also valuable is the experience gained with a part-time or summer job as a helper to skilled workers who are already in the trade. Those who have done satisfactory part-time work sometimes go to work full time for the same employer after a certain period of time.

■ Employers

Painters and paperhangers are, of course, usually employed by painting and paperhanging contractors. Some find work with other construction contractors and many go into business for themselves.

■ Starting Out

If they wish to become an apprentice, you should contact employers, the state employment service bureau, the state apprenticeship agency, or the appropriate union headquarters (International Brotherhood of Painters and Allied Trades). You must, however, have the approval of the joint labor-management apprenticeship committee before you can enter the occupation by this method. If the apprentice program is filled, you may wish to enter the trade as an on-the-job trainee. In this case, you usually should contact employers directly to begin work as a helper.

■ Advancement

Successful completion of one of the two types of training programs is necessary before individuals can become qualified, skilled painters or paperhangers. If workers have management ability and good planning skills, and if they work for a large contracting firm, they may advance to the following positions: supervisor, who supervises and coordinates activities of other workers; painting and decorating contract estimator, who computes material requirements and labor costs; and superintendent on a large contract painting job.

Some painters and paperhangers, once they have acquired enough capital and business experience, go into business for themselves as painting and decorating contractors. These self-employed workers must be able to take care of all standard business affairs, such as bookkeeping, insurance and legal matters, advertising, and billing.

■ Earnings

Painters and paperhangers tend to earn more per hour than many other construction workers, but their total annual incomes may be less because of work time lost due to poor weather and periods of layoffs between contract assignments. The average annual beginning salary for painters and paperhangers is about $12,000; for more experienced workers, $24,000; and for the top wage earners, $38,000. Wages often vary depending on the geographic location of the job. Apprentices tend to earn starting wages that are about 50 percent less than those of more experienced workers.

■ Work Environment

Most painters and paperhangers have a standard 40-hour workweek, and they usually earn extra pay for working overtime. Their work requires them to stand for long periods of time, to climb, and to bend. Painters work both indoors and outdoors, because their job may entail painting interior surfaces as well as exterior siding and other areas; paperhangers work exclusively indoors. Because these occupations involve working on ladders and often with electrical equipment such as power sanders and paint sprayers, workers must adhere to safety standards.

■ Outlook

In the 1990s, there were about 465,000 painters and paperhangers employed in the United States; most of them were painters and trade union members. About 40 percent of these workers were self-employed. Jobs are found mainly with contractors who work on projects such as new construction, remodeling, and restoration; others are found as maintenance workers for such establishments as schools, apartment complexes, and high-rise buildings.

Employment of painters and paperhangers is expected to grow faster than the average for all occupations through the next decade. Most job openings will occur as other workers retire, transfer, or otherwise leave the occupation. Turnover is very high in this trade. Openings for paperhangers will be fewer than those for painters, however, because this is a smaller specialized trade.

Increased construction will generate a need for more painters to work on new buildings and industrial structures. However, this will also lead to increased competition among self-employed painters and painting contractors for the better jobs. Newer types of paint have made it easier for inexperienced persons to do their own painting, but this does not affect the employment outlook much because most painters and paperhangers work on industrial and commercial projects and are not dependent on residential work.

■ For More Information

International Brotherhood of Painters and Allied Trades
United Unions Building
1750 New York Avenue, NW
Washington, DC 20006
Tel: 202-637-0700

National Association of Home Builders
15th and M Streets, NW
Washington, DC 20005
Tel: 202-822-0200

National Joint Painting, Decorating, and Drywall Apprenticeship and Training Committee
1750 New York Avenue, NW
Washington, DC 20006
Tel: 202-783-7770

Painting and Decorating Contractors of America
3913 Old Lee Highway, Suite 33B
Fairfax, VA 22030
Tel: 703-359-0826

■ Related Articles

Construction

Drywall Installers and Finishers

Plasterers

Painters and Sculptors

■ Overview

Painters use watercolors, oils, acrylics, and other substances to paint pictures or designs onto flat surfaces. *Sculptors* design and construct three-dimensional artwork from various materials, such as stone, concrete, plaster, and wood.

■ History

Painting and sculpture are probably as old as human civilization. At their essence, painting and sculpture represent attempts to bring order and focus to life and society, and the earliest known artworks were probably created for functional purposes rather than for artistic or aesthetic reasons. For example, the cave paintings of France and Spain, which date from 15,000 BC, were probably ceremonial in nature, meant to bring good luck to the hunt. From an earlier period, around 21,000 to 25,000 BC, the Venus of Willendorf, a figure carved from limestone, which along with other figures from the same time might have formed a part of fertility rites and rituals and prehistoric relief sculptures, that is, sculptures carved into the walls of caves in France.

Painting and sculpture have ranged from purely decorative to narrative (art that tells a story), from symbolic to realistic. Much of early visual art was religious in nature, reflecting the beliefs and myths with which people tried to understand their place in the world and in life. Art was also used to glorify society or the leaders of society. The immense sculptures of Ramses II (?-1225 BC) of ancient Egypt, and much of Roman art, served to glorify their rulers and reinforce their stature in society. Often, the main subject of a painting or sculpture would appear out of proportion to the other figures in the work, symbolizing his or her importance or dominance. While this use of artists and their art continues today, the independence we typically associate with modern artists also has its roots in ancient times, as ancient artists sought to create art based on more immediately personal concerns.

The art of Greece and Rome exerted a profound influence on much of the history of Western art. The sculptural ideals developed by the ancient Greeks, particularly with their perfection of anatomical forms, continued to dominate Western sculpture until well into the 19th century. In painting, artists sought methods to depict or suggest a greater realism, experimenting with techniques of lighting, shading, and others to create an illusion of depth.

The rise of the Christian era brought a return to symbolism over realism. Illuminated manuscripts, which were written texts, usually religious in content, and decorated with designs and motifs meant to provide further understanding of the text, became the primary form of artistic expression for nearly a millennium. The artwork for these manuscripts often featured highly elaborate and detailed abstract designs. The human figure was absent in much of this work, reflecting religious prohibition of the creation of idols.

Artists returned to more naturalistic techniques during the 14th century with the rise of Gothic art forms. The human figure returned to art; artists began creating art not only for rulers and religious institutions, but also for a growing wealthy class. Portrait painting became an increasingly important source of work and income for artists. New materials, particularly oil glazes and paints, allowed artists to achieve more exact detailing and more subtle light, color, and shading effects.

During the Renaissance, artists rediscovered the art of ancient Greece and Rome. This brought new developments not only in artists' techniques but also in their stature in society. The development of perspective techniques in the 14th and 15th centuries revolutionized painting. Perspective allowed the artists to create the illusion of three dimensions, so that a spectator felt that he or she looked not merely at a painting but into it. Advances in the study of anatomy enabled artists to create more dramatic and realistic figures, whether in painting or sculpture, providing the illusion of action and fluidity and heightening the naturalism of their work. The role of the artist changed from simple artisan or craftsworker to creative force. They were sought out by the wealthy, the church, and rulers for their talent and skill, receiving commissions for new work or being supported by patrons as they worked.

The work of Giotto (1266-1337), Michelangelo (1475-1564), Raphael (1483-1520), Leonardo da Vinci (1452-1519), Titian (1477-1576), and other Renaissance artists continue to fascinate people today. Artists developed new concerns for the use of line, color, contour, shading, setting, and composition, presenting work of greater realism and at the same time of deeper emotional content. The style of an artist became more highly individualized, more a personal reflection of the artist's thoughts, beliefs, ideas, and feelings. The fantastic, nightmare-like paintings of Hieronymus Bosch (1450?-1516) opened new areas of thematic and subjective exploration. In the late Renaissance, new styles began to emerge, such as the mannerist style of El Greco (1541?-1614?) of Spain and the northern styles of Albrecht Durer (1471-1528) and Pieter Bruegel the Elder (1525?-69), and the subject matter of painting was extended to depict common scenes of ordinary life.

Artists continued to influence one another, but national and cultural differences began to appear in art as the Catholic church lost its dominance and new religious movements took hold. Art academies, such as the Academie Royale de Peinture et de Sculture in Paris, were established and sought to codify artistic ideals. The works of the Flemish painter Peter Paul Rubens (1577-1640), the Dutch

PAINTERS AND SCULPTORS	
SCHOOL SUBJECTS	Art History
PERSONAL SKILLS	Artistic Communication/ideas
WORK ENVIRONMENT	Indoors and outdoors One location with some travel
MINIMUM EDUCATION LEVEL	High school diploma
SALARY RANGE	$10,000 or less to $20,000 to $40,000
CERTIFICATION OR LICENSING	None available
OUTLOOK	About as fast as the average
DOT	144
GOE	01.02.02
O*NET	34035A, 34035E

painters Vermeer (1632-75) and Rembrandt (1606-69), and the French painter Nicolas Poussin (1594-1665) highlight the different techniques, styles, and concerns rising during the baroque period of the 17th century.

The next two centuries would see profound changes in the nature of art, leading to the revolutionary work of the impressionists of the late 19th century and the dawn of the modern era in art. Sculpture, which had remained largely confined to the Greek and Roman ideals, found new directions beginning with the work of Rodin (1840-1917). The individual sensibility of the artist himself took on a greater importance and led to a greater freedom of painting techniques, such as in the work of John Constable (1776-1837) and J. M. W. Turner (1775-1851) of England. In France, Gustave Courbet (1819-77) challenged many of the ideals of the French academy, leading to the avant-garde work of the early French impressionists. Artists began to take on a new role by challenging society with new concepts, ideas, and visions, and radical departures in style. Artists no longer simply reflected prevailing culture, but adopted leadership positions in creating culture, often rejecting entirely the artistic principles of the past. The revolutionary works of Edouard Manet (1832-83), Edgar Degas (1834-1917), Claude Monet (1840-1926),

Georges Seurat (1859-91), Paul Cezanne (1839-1906), and others would in turn be rejected by succeeding generations of artists intent on developing new ideas and techniques. The image of the artist as cultural outsider, societal misfit, or even tormented soul took hold, with painters such as Paul Gauguin (1848-1903), Edvard Munch (1863-1944), and Vincent van Gogh (1853-90). Artists working in the avant garde achieved notoriety, if not financial reward, and the "misunderstood" or "starving" artist became a popular 20th-century image.

The 20th century witnessed an explosion of artistic styles and techniques. Art, both in painting and sculpture, became increasingly abstracted from reality, and purely formal concerns developed. Impressionism and postimpressionism gave way to futurism, expressionism, Henri Matisse's (1869-1954) fauvism, the cubism developed by Pablo Picasso (1881-73) and Georges Braque (1882-1963), the nonobjective paintings of Wassily Kandinsky (1866-1944), Piet Mondrian (1874-1944) and Salvadore Dali's (1904-89) surrealism, and others.

American art, which had largely followed the examples set by European artists, came into its own during the 1940s and 1950s, with the rise of abstract expressionism lead by Willem de Kooning (born 1904) and Jackson Pollock (1912-56). During the 1950s, a new art form, pop art, reintroduced recognizable images. The work of Richard Hamilton, Andy Warhol (1927-87), Roy Lichtenstein (born 1923), and others used often mundane objects, such as

A wood sculptor at work in his studio

Warhol's Campbell soup cans, to satirize and otherwise comment on cultural and societal life.

More recent trends in art have given the world the graffiti-inspired works of Keith Haring and the "non-art" sculpture of Jeff Koons, as well as the massive installations of Christo. Artists today work in a great variety of styles, forms, and media. Many artists combine elements of painting, sculpture, and other art forms, such as photography, music, and dance, into their work. The rise of video recording techniques, and especially of three-dimensional computer animations has recently begun to challenge many traditional ideas of art.

■ The Job

Painters and sculptors use their creative abilities to produce original works of art. They are generally classified as fine artists rather than commercial artists because they are responsible for selecting the theme, subject matter, and medium of their artwork.

Painters use a variety of media to paint portraits, landscapes, still lifes, abstracts, and other subjects. They use

GLOSSARY: PAINTING

Broken color: Colors laid next to each other and blended by the eye of the viewer; thus instead of mixing red and blue on a palette to produce purple, red and blue are placed next to each other on the canvas

Drybrush: A technique in which paint of a thick consistency is stroked lightly over a dry surface; it produces a broken or mottled effect

Glaze: A film of transparent paint applied over a solid color, producing a luminous, rich effect

Grisaille: A monochromatic painting, usually in shades of gray; it may be a finished painting or an underpainting

Impasto: A thick application of paint to a canvas or panel; the marks of the brush or palette knife can be seen plainly

Imprimatura: A toned ground created by a thin wash or glaze of transparent color

Scumble: An application of opaque paint over a different color of paint; the original color is not covered entirely, giving an uneven effect

Stippling: The technique of applying small dots of paint to a surface to build up tonal areas or textures

Underpainting: A preliminary painting on the painting surface; using tones of one color, the artist makes an underpainting to establish the basic shapes, values, and overall composition of a painting

Wash: A thin layer of paint spread evenly over a broad area

Wet-in-wet: A technique in which fresh paint is applied on top of or into wet paint already on the support; used with watercolors and oils and can produce both distinctive contrasts of color and softly blended effects

brushes, palette knives, and other artist's tools to apply color to canvas or other surfaces. They work in a variety of media, including oil paint, acrylic paint, tempera, watercolors, pen and ink, pencil, charcoal, crayon, pastels, but may also use such nontraditional media as earth, clay, cement, paper, cloth, and any other material that allows them to express their artistic ideas. Painters develop line, space, color, and other visual elements to produce the desired effect. They may prefer a particular style of art, such as realism or abstract, and they may be identified with a certain technique or subject matter. Many artists develop a particular style and apply that style across a broad range of techniques, from painting to etching to sculpture.

Sculptors use a combination of media and methods to create three-dimensional works of art. They may carve objects from stone, plaster, concrete, or wood. They may use their fingers to model clay or wax into objects. Some sculptors create forms from metal or stone, using various masonry tools and equipment. Others create works from found objects, such as car parts or tree branches. Like painters, sculptors may be identified with a particular technique or style. Their work can take monumental forms, or they may work on a very small scale.

There is no single way to become or to be an artist. As with other areas of the arts, painting and sculpting usually are intensely personal endeavors. If it is possible to generalize, most painters and sculptors are people with a desire and need to explore visual representations of the world around them or the world within them, or both. Throughout their careers, they seek to develop their vision and the methods and techniques that allow them to best express themselves. Many artists work from or within a tradition or style of art. They may develop formal theories of art or advance new theories of visual presentation. Painters and sculptors are usually aware of the art that has come before them as well as the work of their contemporaries.

Every painter and sculptor has his or her own way of working. Many work in studios, often separate from their homes, where they can produce their work in privacy and quiet. Many artists, however, work outdoors. Most artists probably combine both indoor and outdoor work during their careers. Some artists may choose complete solitude in order to work; others thrive on interaction with other artists and people. Artists engaged in monumental work, particularly sculptors, often have helpers who assist in the creation of a piece of art, working under the artist's direction. They may contract with a foundry in order to cast the finished sculpture in bronze, iron, or another metal. As film, video, and computer technology has developed, the work of painters and sculptors has expanded into new forms of expression. The recently developed three-dimensional computer animation techniques in particular often blur the boundaries between painting, sculpture, photography, and cinema.

■ Requirements

There are no educational requirements for becoming a painter or sculptor. However, most artists benefit from training, and many attend art schools or programs in colleges and universities. There are also many workshops and other ways for artists to gain instruction, practice, and exposure to art and the works and ideas of other artists. The artist should learn a variety of techniques, be exposed to as many media and styles as possible, and gain an understanding of the history of art and art theory. By learning as much as possible, the artist is better able to choose the appropriate means for his or her own artistic expression.

An important requirement for a career as a painter or sculptor is artistic ability. Of course, this is entirely subjective, and it is perhaps more important that artists believe in their own ability and in their own potential. Apart from being creative and imaginative, painters and sculptors should exhibit such traits as patience, persistence, determination, independence, and sensitivity.

Both painters and sculptors should be good at business and sales if they intend to support themselves through their art. As small-business people, they must be able to market and sell their products to wholesalers, retailers, and the general public.

Artists who sell their works to the public may need special permits from the local or state tax office. In addition, artists should check with the Internal Revenue Service for laws on selling and tax information related to income received from the sale of artwork.

Many artists join professional organizations that provide informative advice and tips as well as opportunities to meet with other artists.

■ Exploring

Experience in drawing, painting, and even sculpting can be had at a very early age, even before formal schooling begins. Most elementary, middle, and high schools offer classes in art. Aspiring painters and sculptors can undertake a variety of artistic projects at school or at home. Many arts associations and schools also offer beginning classes in various types of art for the general public.

Students interested in pursuing art as a career are encouraged to visits museums and galleries to view the work of other artists. In addition, they can learn about the history of art and artistic techniques and methods through books, videotapes, and other sources. The New York Foundation for the Arts sponsors a toll-free hotline (800-232-2789) that offers quick information on programs and services and answers to specific questions on visual artists. The hotline is open Monday through Friday, between 2 and 5 PM Eastern Standard Time.

■ Employers

Because earning a living as a fine artist is very difficult, especially when one is just starting out, many painters and sculptors work at another job. With the proper training and educational background, many painters and sculptors are able to work in art-related positions as art teachers, art directors, or graphic designers, while pursuing their own art activities independently. For example, many art teachers hold classes in their own studios.

Sculptors creating large works, especially those that will be placed outdoors and in public areas, usually work under contract or commission. Most artists, however, create works that express their personal artistic vision and then hope to find someone to purchase them.

GLOSSARY: SCULPTURE

Bronzing: The process of coloring a plaster cast in imitation of bronze

Cast: A work of sculpture that has been produced from a mold

Cast stone: A mixture of cement or concrete and stone that is cast from a mold

Dry lacquering: A technique in which a modeled clay form is covered with many layers of lacquer-soaked cloth; when the cloth is dry, the clay is removed and the hollow form is finished with gesso (a fine plaster) and painted

Mold: The shell-like impression into which a casting material is poured or pressed. A *piece mold* is made in several sections, or pieces; it can easily be pulled off the cast and used again. A *waste mold* has to be broken, or "wasted," to remove the cast.

Plastic: A sculpture that was produced by the modeling technique; it is the opposite of *glyptic*, a sculpture that was produced by carving. Any material that can be shaped by modeling is also referred to as plastic.

Repoussé: A term used in sculpture to describe a sculpture that has been hammered, or beaten, from a sheet of metal into the desired shape

Stucco: A blend of gypsum or cement and pulverized marble used as a medium for relief sculpture

■ Starting Out

Artists interested in exhibiting or selling their products should investigate potential markets. Reference books, such as *Artist's Market*, may be helpful, as well as library books that offer information on business laws, taxes, and related issues. Local fairs and art shows often provide opportunities for new artists to display their work. Art councils are a good source of information on upcoming fairs in the area.

Some artists sell their work on consignment. When a painter or sculptor sells work this way, a store or gallery displays an item; when the item is sold, the artist gets the price of that item minus a commission that goes to the store or gallery. Artists who sell on consignment should read contracts very carefully.

■ Advancement

Because most painters and sculptors are self-employed, the channels for advancement are not as well defined as they are at a company or firm. An artist may become increasingly well known, both nationally and internationally, and as an artist's reputation increases, he or she can command higher prices for his or her work. The success of the fine artist depends on a variety of factors, including talent, drive, and determination. However, luck often seems to play a role in many artists' success, and some artists do not achieve recognition until late in life, if at all. Artists with business skills may open their own galleries to display their own and others' work. Those with the appropriate educational backgrounds may become art teachers, agents, or critics.

■ Earnings

The amount of money earned by painters and sculptors varies greatly. Self-employed painters and sculptors set their own hours and prices. Artists often work long hours and earn little, especially when they are first starting out. The price they charge is up to them, but much depends on the value the public places on their work. A particular item may sell for a few dollars or tens of thousands of dollars, or at any price in between. Often, the value of an artwork may increase considerably after it has been sold. An artwork that may have earned an artist only a few hundred dollars may earn many thousands of dollars the next time it is sold.

Some artists obtain grants that allow them to pursue their art; others win prizes and awards in competitions. Most artists, however, have to work on their projects part-time while holding down a regular, full-time job. Many artists teach in art schools, high schools, or out of their studios. Artists who sell their products must pay social security and other taxes on any money they receive.

■ Work Environment

Most painters and sculptors work out of their homes or in studios. Some work in small areas in their apartments; others work in large, well-ventilated lofts. Occasionally, painters and sculptors work outside. In addition, artists often work at fairs, shops, museums, and other places where their work is being exhibited.

Artists often work long hours, and those who are self-employed do not receive paid vacations, insurance coverage, or any of the other benefits usually offered by a company or firm. However, artists are able to work at their own pace, set their own prices, and make their own decisions. The energy and creativity that go into an artist's work brings feelings of pride and satisfaction. Most artists genuinely love what they do.

■ Outlook

The employment outlook for painters and sculptors is difficult to predict. Because they are usually self-employed, much of their success depends on the amount and type of work created, the drive and determination in selling the artwork, and the interest or readiness of the public to appreciate and purchase the work.

Success for an artist, however, is difficult to quantify. Individual artists may consider themselves successful as their talent matures and they are better able to present their vision in their work. This type of success goes beyond financial considerations. Few artists enter this field for the money. Financial success depends on a great deal of factors, many of which have nothing to do with the artist or his or her work. Artists with good marketing skills will likely be the most successful in selling their work. Although artists should not let their style be dictated by market trends, those interested in financial success can attempt to determine what types of artwork are wanted by the public.

It often takes several years for an artist's work and reputation to be established. Many artists have to support themselves through other employment. There are numerous employment opportunities for commercial artists in such fields as publishing, advertising, fashion and design, and teaching. Painters and sculptors should consider employment in these and other fields. They should be prepared, however, to face strong competition from others who are attracted to these fields.

■ For More Information

For general information on ceramic arts study, contact:

National Art Education Association
1916 Association Drive
Reston, VA 22091-1590
Tel: 703-860-8000
Web: http://www.cedarnet.org/emig

The following organization helps artists market and sell their art. It offers marketing tools, a newsletter, a directory of artists, and reference resources.

National Association of Fine Artists
ArtNetwork
PO Box 1360
Nevada City, CA 95959
Tel: 530-470-0862
Web: http://www.artmarketing.com

The following organization provides an information exchange and sharing of professional opportunities.

Sculptors Guild
110 Greene Street
New York, NY 10012
Tel: 212-431-5669

■ Related Articles

Advertising and Marketing

Fashion

Photography

Publishing

Visual Arts

Art Directors

Ceramic Artists

Fashion Designers

Fashion Illustrators and Photographers

Graphic Designers

Illustrators

Jewelers and Jewelry Repairers

Medical Illustrators and Photographers

Photo Stylists

Photographers

Paleontologists

■ Overview

Paleontologists study the fossils of ancient life-forms, including human life, found in sedimentary rocks on or within the earth's crust. Paleontological analyses range from the description of large, easily visible features to biochemical analysis of incompletely fossilized tissue. The observations are used to infer relationships between past and present groups of organisms (taxonomy), to investigate the origins of life, and to investigate the ecology of the past (paleoecology), from which implications for the sustainability of life under present ecological conditions can be drawn. Paleontology is usually considered a subspecialty of the larger field of geology.

■ History

During Europe's Renaissance, the artist and scientist Leonardo da Vinci, among others, established that fossils were the natural remains of organic creatures, and in the middle of the 17th century, Nicolaus Steno of Denmark wrote a treatise proposing that sedimentary rocks were laid down in layers, with the oldest at the bottom. The physical description of fossils was permissible as long as it did not lead to dissonant conclusions regarding the age of the Earth. As an example, the early 17th century saw the naming and characterization of the trilobites, an extinct but very large group of marine arthropods once abundant everywhere in the seas and, as a group, of far greater longevity than the dinosaurs. When fossil evidence was used to advance a history of Earth at variance with a literal reading of the Bible, however, the penalties were severe.

The Age of Enlightenment in Europe sped up religion's waning grip on the interpretation of science, and paleontology as a scientific discipline may be considered to have started in the early 1800s. In the young republic of the United States, Thomas Jefferson, then vice president, in 1797 published one of the first papers on American fossil vertebrates; he also named a gigantic ground sloth that once roamed over much of the United States *Megalonyx jeffersonii*. At this time there was considerable congress between natural historians in Europe, Great Britain, and the United States, each eager to learn of the other's latest findings and theories. The 19th century was also the age of the quintessential "gentleman explorer," whose travels overlapped in time with government-sponsored exploring expeditions to all parts of the globe. The number of specimens returned from these expeditions led to the founding of many of the great natural history museums. In the middle of this activity—and part of it—Charles Darwin boarded the *Beagle* for a multiyear voyage of exploration and natural observation, resulting in his writing *On the Origin of Species*

by Means of Natural Selection in 1859, a major contribution to the blossoming of paleontology.

Contemporary paleontology is modeled on an understanding of life-forms as related in extended family trees, some of very ancient origin. In detailing ancestral and modern lineage, paleontologists want to know the precise physical, chemical, and nutritional environment that supported life, and what changes in this environment forced some creatures into extinction while allowing others to thrive.

■ The Job

Paleontologists broadly classify themselves according to the life-form studied. *Palynologists* study tiny to submicroscopic life-forms, such as pollen or plankton. Microfossils may be of plant or animal origin and are extremely abundant. *Paleobotanists* study macroscopic fossil plants. In the animal kingdom, *invertebrate paleontologists* study animals without a backbone, such as the classes insects, sponges, corals, and trilobites. *Vertebrate paleontologists* study animals with a backbone, among them the classes fishes, birds, reptiles, and mammals. Each area of specialization requires extensive knowledge of the anatomy, ecology, and habits of modern representatives of the class.

When conducting paleontolgoical research, your analysis begins with careful measurement and anatomical description of a fossil, accompanied, if possible, by a drawing showing what the three-dimensional creature may have looked like in life. The fossils then are dated and placed in a physical context. Dating may entail both laboratory analyses and comparisons with fossil beds of known age, or a comparison with stratigraphic layers of rock in different formations around the world. In the third step, the fossils and the formations in which they occurred are used to construct a history of Earth on either a small, local scale or a large scale. Large-scale events that can be reconstructed from fossil evidence

PALEONTOLOGISTS	
SCHOOL SUBJECTS	Biology Earth science
PERSONAL SKILLS	Helping/teaching Technical/scientific
WORK ENVIRONMENT	Indoors and outdoors One location with some travel
MINIMUM EDUCATION LEVEL	Doctoral degree
SALARY RANGE	$40,000 to $60,000 to $90,000
CERTIFICATION OR LICENSING	None available
OUTLOOK	Little change or more slowly than the average
DOT	024
GOE	02.01.01
NOC	2113
O*NET	24111A

This paleontologist is extracating a Tyrannosaurus Rex fossil.

include the uplift, tilting, and erosion of mountain ranges, the rise and subsidence of seas, and movements of land masses over geological time. In the fourth step, fossils are used as evidence of life to fill in missing links in the fossil record, to revise taxonomic classifications, and to construct the biology of descent of living organisms.

To teach at the college level, you must have a doctorate or be a candidate for a doctorate. Your primary educational responsibilities will be divided between teaching undergraduate courses in earth science and advanced seminars in paleontology. In addition to in-class duties, you must also prepare lessons and curriculum, make tests, meet with students during office hours, and attend department meetings. You'll also conduct personal research, focusing on any area of the field that interests you.

Invertebrate paleontologists are especially useful to the oil industry, for fossil plankton taken from drilling cores are an indication of the age of the rocks and of the formations in which oil reservoirs are likely to be concentrated. The mining and minerals industry also hires *stratigraphers* and *petrographers,* who study the distribution and content of rock layers to identify subsurface mineral deposits. These scientists helped to discover quarries of oolitic limestone in Indiana. This limestone, composed of the skeletal remains of tiny fossilized creatures, has provided impressive amounts of building material. However, the mining and minerals industry has few positions for paleontologists.

Museum curators are linked to the fourth phase of paleontological analysis, for virtually all contemporary geology curators are evolutionists. Museum curators typically hold a doctorate and have done considerable independent research; these positions are highly competitive. Geology curators must raise grant funding to support themselves and a work crew in the field, and some have teaching responsibilities in joint programs of study with universities as well. *Collection managers* in geology usually have a minimum of a master's degree; some have doctorates. Collection managers study, catalogue, and maintain the museum's collection, ship specimens to external researchers for study, and sometimes participate in fieldwork. Ordinarily there is one collection manager for the geology holdings, but occasionally there is more than one. In that case, the duties may be divided among vertebrate mammals, invertebrate mammals, fossil amphibians and reptiles, fossil birds, and fossil plants. Collection managers are generalists and work as colleagues with curators.

Although the preponderance of paleontological research is carried out on land, marine fossil beds are of great interest. The cost of mounting an expedition to extract samples of sedimentary rock from the deep-sea floor usually means that the sponsoring institution must procure sizable support from industry or the government. Some paleontologists work in the oil industry to develop off-shore wells; a few find employment with oceanographic institutes.

■ Requirements

High School

Supplement your high school's college prep program with additional courses in the sciences and mathematics. Paleontologists rely a great deal on computer programs and databases, so take courses in computers and programming. You'll be preparing your findings for publication and presentation, so take English and speech classes. Foreign language classes will also be valuable, as you may be conducting research in other countries.

Postsecondary Training

Paleontology is a subspecialty of geology or, less commonly, of botany, zoology, or physical anthropology. In college, you'll major in geology or biology. The college curriculum for a geology major includes mathematics through calculus, chemistry, physics, and life sciences, with additional seminars in the specialty area and in the history of science.

Because paleontology is a specialty area encountered only briefly during the undergraduate curriculum, you should anticipate graduate training. In fact, most scientists in the field find that a doctorate is necessary simply to have time to gain the substantial knowledge base and independent research skills necessary in their field.

Other Requirements

You should be inquisitive, with a natural curiosity about the world and its history. A desire to read and study is also important, as you'll be spending many years in school. It's important to have a respect for other cultures, as you may be working closely with professionals from other countries. Good organizational skills will help you in your work with fossils and museum collections. People skills are also very important, as you'll be relying on personal contacts in your pursuit of work and funding.

■ Exploring

An estimated 55,000 amateur "rock hounds" belong to organized clubs in the United States, and an untold additional number with no formal group membership also delight in fossil hunting in areas open to the public. You should locate and join one of these clubs and/or take fossil-hunting expeditions and visits to museums on your own. Local museums with a strong geology component frequently conduct field trips that are open to the public.

The Midwest and Great Plains states are especially rich in fossil beds, owing to the inland sea that once overlay these areas and whose sediments protected the skeletal remains of creatures from predation or being moved about. Professional geology societies publish brochures on fossil hunting and the kinds of fossils available in different locales. State geological societies, often housed on the main campus of state universities, are excellent sources of information. Earthwatch is an organization that involves people with various environmental projects, including the mammoth-fossil excavation site of Hot Springs, South Dakota.

■ Employers

Most paleontologists work in colleges and universities as faculty of paleontology and geology programs. They also find work in museums and with government research projects. The petroleum industry was once a great source of jobs for paleontologists, but these jobs, though still available, are fewer in number. Some paleontologists are self-employed, offering their expertise as consultants.

PALEONTOLOGY MEETS PHARMACOLOGY

In the 19th century, some Chinese pharmacists made regular trips to a limestone hill near Beijing to dig for fossils—not for the purposes of research, but to collect the fossils for grinding into medicine. These bones were eventually recognized as "near-human," dating from about a half-million years before. In 1929, part of a skull was discovered, as well as a new species: Peking Man, a species that preceded Homo sapiens in the evolutionary chain.

■ Starting Out

As an undergraduate, you may be able to work as an intern or volunteer in the geology department of a local museum. You may be able to participate in fieldwork as a paying member of an expedition. Such an arrangement is usually worked out personally with the expedition leader. These entry-level positions may lead to admission to graduate programs and even to employment after advanced degrees are earned. The American Geological Institute (AGI) and the Geological Society of America offer some internship and scholarship opportunities.

You'll rely mostly on personal contacts when seeking a job after receiving a graduate degree. Networking with others in paleontology, especially your college professors, can allow you to meet those who can direct you to job openings and research opportunities.

■ Advancement

Advancement depends on where the paleontologist is employed. Universities and museums follow a typical assistant, associate, and senior (or full) professorial or curatorial track, with the requirements for advancement very similar: research and publishing, education, and service to the institution. Advancement in museum work may also depend on the acquisition of a doctorate. Advancement in state and federal surveys requires research and publishing. In federal employment and in industry, mechanisms for advancement are likely to be spelled out by the employer. Government-sponsored research and term positions are the least stable avenues of work, because of their temporal nature and dependence on a source of funding that may not be renewed.

Many paleontologists remain active in the field beyond the date of formal retirement, procuring independent research funds to support their activities or developing an unpaid association with a neighboring university to gain access to collections and laboratory facilities. The low-tech nature of geological fieldwork allows basic field studies to be conducted fairly inexpensively. Others become consultants to geoscientific firms.

■ Earnings

AGI estimates that an experienced professional with a bachelor's degree in the geological sciences can make about $40,000 a year; those with doctorates can average as high as $77,000 a year. According to the American Association of University Professors (AAUP) 1998 salary survey, professors in doctoral institutions made an average of $61,816 a year, compared to $50,243 for those in graduate institutions and $45,163 for those in four-year institutions. A 1997 survey by the American Association of Petroleum Geologists found that those professionals in the petroleum industry with only a few years' experience averaged $51,300 a year. Those with 10 to 20 years experience averaged between $78,000 and $90,000 annually.

Once these highly trained scientists have entered the field, they usually receive excellent benefits packages and ample vacation time and sick leave. In addition, paleontologists who travel to various locations for their research have their travel and accommodations paid for and receive travel stipends from their employer or funding source.

■ Work Environment

The day-to-day activities of a paleontologist vary but, in the course of a year, usually involve some mix of fieldwork, laboratory analysis, library research, and grant writing or teaching. In industry, a paleontologist's duties may be defined by the project the company has developed. In academia and in museum work, a paleontologist may be able to define a personal course of research but may have less time for that research because of teaching or administrative responsibilities.

Paleontological study is international in scope and impressive in the sweep of time it commands. Because the fossil-bearing strata of interest to paleontologists occur in widely separated localities, U.S. paleontologists may undertake extensive correspondence or joint fieldwork with colleagues throughout the world. In addition, paleontology is a living science, with new plant and animal species extracted from the rocks every year and corresponding new biological relationships waiting to be explored. The depth and breadth of paleontological study and its ever-clearer relationship to contemporary ecological concerns make it an attractive profession for those interested in a larger view of life.

■ Outlook

More paleontologists graduate each year than there are available positions, and consequently many paleontologists are unemployed or underemployed. Educational opportunities are also diminishing: with decreasing enrollment in all of the physical sciences and increasing pressure to contain costs, colleges and universities are eliminating entire science departments, including geology.

Economics is a determining factor in employment outside of the university as well. An increasing amount of the United States's daily oil needs are being imported. As the energy sector moves overseas, fewer jobs are available in the domestic fossil fuels industry. Federal and state surveys absorb a small number of new graduates with baccalaureate or master's degrees but cannot accommodate all those seeking work.

To increase the likelihood of employment, students will find it helpful to pursue high academic standards, including, if possible, independent research and publication during the advanced degree years; cross-training in a related field, such as zoology or botany; and planning a broad-based career that combines knowledge of government activities, industry experience, and teaching and research.

■ For More Information

For a brochure on careers in the geological sciences, as well as information about scholarships and internships, contact:

American Geological Institute
4220 King Street
Alexandria, VA 22302
Tel: 703-379-2480
Web: http://www.agiweb.org

Geological Society of America
3300 Penrose Place
PO Box 9140
Boulder, CO 80301-9140
Tel: 303-447-2020
Web: http://www.geosociety.org

For career information, contact:

Paleontological Research Institution
1259 Trumansburg Road
Ithaca, NY 14850
Tel: 607-273-6623
Web: http://www.englib.cornell.edu/pri

■ Related Articles

Education
Mining
Museums and Cultural Centers
Anthropologists
Archaeologists
Biologists
College Professors
Ecologists
Geologists
Mining Engineers
Museum Attendants and Teachers
Museum Directors and Curators
Naturalists
Petroleum Engineers
Surveying and Mapping Technicians

Paper Processing Occupations

■ Overview

In papermaking, wood, recycled paper, and a small amount of vegetable fibers are turned into pulp, which is spread in a very thin layer, pressed, and dried. The mass-production processes in which large quantities of paper are made involve the use of highly complicated machinery. *Paper processing occupations* employ many skilled and semiskilled production workers to complete this process. Also included in paper processing occupations are research, technical, and supervisory personnel, who play various roles in the production of the end product.

■ History

We use it every day. In fact, you're probably within an arm's reach of some kind of paper product right now. But how often do you stop to think about where paper comes from and what processes it goes through? Although you may take it for granted, the process of turning pulp into a finished paper product is an interesting and ancient one.

Wood-based paper as we know it today can be traced to China around AD 100. The craft of papermaking spread to the Middle East in the 8th century, and eventually, as a result of expeditions made during the Crusades, to Europe. Until the Industrial Revolution, all paper was made by hand, using a laborious process that produced a single sheet at a time. In the 18th and 19th centuries, the first papermaking machines were invented; however, these were simple contraptions that also made only one sheet of paper at a time by dipping a framed screen into a vat of pulp and allowing the sheet to dry. In the early 1800s, Henry and Sealy Fourdrinier patented a machine that improved upon the early equipment and used a cylindrical mechanism to produce continuous rolls of paper (even today, some papermaking machines are called fourdrinier machines). In later years, machines were invented that chemically processed or ground pulpwood into pulp for papermaking. This made possible the mass production of paper and the development of pulp and paper processing as a major industry.

The main source of fiber for making paper used to be rags, or cloth that was converted to pulp; other sources have been straws and grasses. Beginning in the mid- to late-1800s, however, most paper began to be made from wood fiber. Although the materials have changed and the machinery has become very mechanized within the last several hundred years, the essential principles used in making paper are still the same. These principles involve separating and wetting the fibers, creating the pulp, filtering the pulp, squeezing out excess water, and allowing the pulp to dry and be compressed.

As environmental issues have become increasingly important in our society, the paper processing industry has witnessed certain changes concerning the reuse of used paper. Recycling of waste paper has become an industry in itself, as environmental concerns have underscored the potential problems in disposing of our nation's trash. New occupations will continue to be formed as the recycling industry struggles to solve technical problems, such as methods for refining and purifying used paper, and general problems, such as how to encourage the public to be more aware of waste paper issues.

■ The Job

The U.S. Department of Labor has cataloged nearly 250 distinct job titles for the skilled and semiskilled workers who operate pulp and paper processing machinery. These workers perform a wide variety of duties, throughout the entire spectrum of the pulp and papermaking process.

Pulpmaking and papermaking are two separate processes. Some mills produce only pulp, some only paper, and still others—called integrated mills—produce both. Daishowa Forest Products, Limited, of Quebec City, Quebec, Canada, owns both pulp mills and paper mills. Mark Turcotte, human resources manager for Daishowa, says that the mills' main product is newsprint—the kind of paper used in newspapers everywhere. Daishowa's mills are highly computerized, according to Mark. "The mills are run by operators, who work on computers," he says. "They follow the process through on the computer, starting with wood chips and continuing all the way until the pulp is transported, in tanks, to the paper mill." Mark says that the only employees who actually work hands-on with the machinery are maintenance and repair workers.

The pulping process truly begins at the barker. The *barker operator* con-

PAPER PROCESSING OCCUPATIONS	
SCHOOL SUBJECTS	Chemistry
	Technical/Shop
PERSONAL SKILLS	Mechanical/manipulative
	Technical/scientific
WORK ENVIRONMENT	Primarily indoors
	Primarily one location
MINIMUM EDUCATION LEVEL	High school diploma
SALARY RANGE	$18,000 to $44,000 to $76,906
CERTIFICATION OR LICENSING	None available
OUTLOOK	Decline
DOT	534
GOE	06.04.14
NOC	9234
O*NET	92953

PAPERMAKING BY HAND

Handmade papers have become very fashionable. They are frequently used in stationery, invitations, and various craft projects. Although there are a number of kits available to teach you how to make handmade paper, below is a brief outline of the process.

The pulp: To make pulp, plant fibers and water must be beaten together. This process works the water molecules deep into the structure of the fiber. The thickness and hardness of the paper will depend upon how much water is beaten into the pulp. The more water that is used, the more translucent the paper will be after it has dried.

Forming the sheet: Each sheet of paper is formed by dipping a mold into the vat of pulp. The mould is, basically, a very fine mesh of wire, supported by underlying wooden ribs. After the mold is dipped into the pulp, the papermaker holds the mold level and shakes it from side to side and front to back as the water drains through. This action helps lock the fibers into a smooth surface.

Couching: While still damp, the freshly formed sheet of paper is *couched,* or transferred onto a piece of wool. Another sheet of wool is then placed on top of the paper sheet. Each additional sheet of paper is stacked, between sheets of wool, on top of each other.

Pressing: When a sufficient number of sheets of paper have been formed and stacked, they are pressed until all the water is squeezed out. After pressing, the sheets are strong enough to be lifted out of the stack by hand.

trols the movement of cut logs into and out of machines that clean and strip the bark. Several types of machines may be used in this step of the papermaking process, but all operate on the same principle. The logs are fed into the barker on a conveyor belt. In the barker, they are tumbled against a revolving drum that strips off the bark, while a jet of water, controlled by the barker operator, washes off dirt and other impurities. If logs become jammed in a machine, the barker operator breaks up the jam with a pike pole and chain hoist. The cleaned and stripped logs are carried on a conveyor belt to the chipping machine.

The *chipper* operates a machine that cuts logs into one-inch-square chips in preparation for their conversion into pulp. He or she regulates the flow of the logs according to their size. At Daishowa, these jobs are performed in the wood yard, according to Mark. The work of the pulp mill begins when the chips arrive at the mill.

Mark's mill uses a thermomechanical process to make pulp. In this process, the chips are fed into machines that grind them into smaller fibers. After this, the fiber is placed into a large vat and mixed with water and other chemical products. During this process, the color of the pulp is lightened. "The operator of the mill basically has the responsi-

bility of running all the machinery for a 12-hour shift," Mark says. "He sits in a booth, with the whole process in front of him on a computer."

In another method of pulping, chemical pulping, wood chips are cooked along with soda, ash, acid, or other chemicals in a high-pressure vat, or digester. The *digester operator,* a skilled worker who supervises one or more helpers, operates controls that regulate the temperature and pressure inside the digesters and the flow of steam into these machines. This worker tests samples of the digester liquid to determine when the pulp has been cooked to the proper degree. When the process is completed, the pulp, which has the consistency of wet cotton, is mechanically blown or dumped into a blow tank where it is washed to remove traces of chemicals and other impurities. Pulp to be used for white paper is then bleached in a chemical process.

The papermaking process begins where the pulping process ends. In its first step, the *beater engineer* controls the process that mixes the pulp with sizing, fillers, and dyes to produce a liquid pulp solution. The beater engineer starts the pumps of the beater engines and controls the flow of pulp into the vat by regulating the opening and closing of valves. "Again, everything is controlled by computer in this operation," Mark says. After the liquid pulp solution has been mixed, the beater engineer draws samples of it for testing in the laboratory and uses sophisticated computer equipment to make sure the desired consistency and fiber size have been reached.

The *paper-machine operator* is largely responsible for the quality of the finished paper. As the liquid pulp enters one end (called the wet end) of the huge paper machine, it flows over a continuously moving belt of fine wire screen, which causes the fibers to adhere and form a thin sheet of paper as the liquid from the pulp drains out. The paper-machine operator regulates the flow of pulp and the speed and pitch of the machine's wire belt to produce paper of desired thickness, width, and strength. This operator uses a computerized process control system to monitor the quality of the paper being produced and also draws samples to be sent to the lab. In addition, the operator may supervise other workers on the machine crew.

Backtenders work at the opposite end (that is, the dry end) of the paper machine, usually under the supervision of the paper-machine operator. They operate the machinery that dries, calendars (smooths), and finishes the paper and winds it onto rolls. Backtenders control the temperature of the drying and calendaring rolls, adjust their tension level, and control the speed of the continuous sheet of paper through an automated control system. They inspect the paper for spots, holes, and wrinkles, and they mark defective sections for removal. The backtenders also operate the machinery that cuts the rolls of paper into smaller rolls for shipment.

Process engineers work in the mills to help establish schedules to ensure maximum use of equipment, employees, tools, and capacity. They are responsible for coordinating production operations to meet delivery dates of finished product. *Quality control engineers* install and oversee product inspecting and testing procedures within the mills that are used to establish and maintain quality standards.

Pulp-and-paper lab testers use standard testing equipment and chemical analyses to monitor and control the quality of paper products. Testers determine the liquid content of cooked pulp and measure its acidity with a pH meter. Using a wire screen, a press, and a drying oven similar to those used in the days when all paper was made by hand, they make a single sheet of paper from the pulp. They then examine it under a microscope and use automated equipment to count the number of dirt specks in a unit area. They test the sample sheet for bursting, tearing, and folding strength on an apparatus specially developed for this purpose. They also perform these tests on samples of paper from the huge rolls produced by the paper machine. The pulp-and-paper tester also tests paper samples for brightness, using a reflectance meter, and for weight, thickness, and bulk, using scales and a micrometer. All test data are recorded and reported to the machine operators, with instructions to correct variations from the standard specifications. Some paper mills put their lab data on a computer database so it can be used by both machine operators and customers.

Other paper processing occupations include *pulp plant supervisors,* who coordinate all the activities of workers who are responsible for the cooking, bleaching, and screening of pulp in preparation for use in making paper; *cylinder-machine operators,* who operate cylinder-type equipment for making paper, cardboard, insulation board, and other types of fiber sheets; and *control inspectors,* who inspect pulpwood boards (such as ceiling tiles, insulation panels, and siding) that are used in construction.

■ Requirements

Mark says that all the machine operators in Daishowa's paper and pulp mills have college degrees in papermaking. Other companies are less rigorous in their educational requirements. As a rule, however, paper companies generally require at least a high school diploma for skilled and semiskilled production positions.

High School

If you are considering a career in paper processing, high school courses in chemistry, physics, and mathematics are valuable. Because the industry is heavily computerized, basic computer skills are vital. You should take classes in computers whenever possible. If you are interested in

installing and repairing paper processing machinery, courses in shop, mechanical drawing, and blueprint reading may also prove helpful.

Postsecondary Training

A bachelor's degree is strongly recommended for those who are interested in this industry. Such degrees as wood science and technology, papermaking, engineering, or business are good options. Courses in mathematics, chemistry, computer, and wood science are important. Applicants with degrees from junior colleges or technical institutes may be hired as laboratory technicians.

Other Requirements

According to Mark, the ability to work on a team is key to success in this career. "Each person has a specific responsibility, and it's important that everyone really pull together," he says. "To make a good product, you need everyone from the top job to the bottom job doing their best." Communication skills are also important, Mark says, especially during shift changes. "Because our shifts are long, people on the outgoing shift really need to make sure that the new shift knows what's going on."

Because of the highly automated machinery in pulp and paper plants, few production jobs in this field require great physical strength. However, manual dexterity and a certain degree of mechanical aptitude are necessary for success in these jobs. Alertness, attention to detail, and good vision and hearing are also very important for the skilled workers who tend complicated control panels and check the quality of the product.

■ Exploring

If you live in a state that has forested areas, you might try to get a summer job on a logging crew that works for a paper company. Those who work for such crews can often transfer their knowledge and skills to jobs in the company's plant. Summer jobs in plant maintenance and as machine helpers are also sometimes available.

You might also arrange to tour a pulp or paper plant and talk with some of the workers there. Often, employees who have experience in the field can provide a full and detailed picture of what the work is like.

There are many books that explain the paper processing industry in greater detail than outlined here. Check your local library to see what is available. Performing a simple keyword search using an Internet search engine may also yield interesting information. Industry groups, such as the ones listed at the end of this article, may also have pamphlets or brochures about the industry.

Finally, to get a feel for the mechanics of papermaking, you might buy a kit that teaches you how to make your own sheets of paper. These kits are available in many art shops and can provide valuable hands-on experience in learning about the properties and functions of paper.

Employers

In 1997, the paper and allied industries employed 681,000 people. This employment is scattered throughout the United States and among a number of mills of different sizes. However, there are three key pulp and paper manufacturers who are larger and employ substantially more people than any of the others. The largest, International Paper, is headquartered in Purchase, New York, and operates 29 pulp, paper, and paperboard mills in the United States. It employs approximately 80,000 people worldwide. Kimberly-Clark, which operates manufacturing facilities in 35 countries, employs 55,000 worldwide. And Georgia-Pacific, headquartered in Atlanta, Georgia, has 47,000 employees in the United States alone.

Although their number is decreasing, there are still many smaller mills throughout the United States. The distribution of pulp and paper mills tends to be heaviest where there are a lot of logging and sawmill operations.

Starting Out

Persons who are interested in jobs in the paper processing industry should apply directly to any companies that they are interested in. Many pulp and paper companies have Web sites—and some post their job openings online.

Another method is to check local library reference materials for a listing of pulp and paper mills and manufacturers operating in the United States and apply to the personnel departments of any that are promising.

Paper production workers usually begin as laborers or helpers and move up to more skilled jobs as they gain experience and skill. Competition for these more highly skilled jobs, which tend to pay better than comparable jobs, is intense.

Advancement

Job progress in pulp and paper plants usually takes the form of promotion from routine, semiskilled jobs to positions requiring considerable technical skill and independent judgment, such as that of the paper-machine operator. However, as the papermaking process becomes more automated, even entry-level positions may require computer literacy and good math skills.

Traditionally, advancement in this industry has been limited to specific work areas. For example, a worker involved in the pulping stage of operations could not easily transfer to the papermaking stage without starting over at an entry-level position.

After gaining several years' experience, workers are often given the opportunity to advance within their area of expertise. Such positions as production supervisor, paper final inspector, paper testing supervisor, pulp plant supervisor,

and control inspector are examples of advancement possibilities. Workers with exceptional competence and supervisory ability may become supervisors of plant sections or of an entire phase of operations. Also, production workers who continue their educations and receive degrees in science may obtain positions as laboratory and testing technicians or engineers.

Earnings

According to a survey by the Technical Association of the Pulp and Paper Industry (TAPPI), the median income for all pulp and paper industry workers was $76,906 in 1997. The median income for new employees in the industry was $44,000. You should note, however, that the respondents to this survey were primarily graduates of either bachelor's or master's degree programs. It is safe to say that with less education, workers in this industry would be earning considerably lower salaries—probably between $18,000 and $30,000 annually.

Workers in this industry almost always receive fringe benefits such as medical insurance and paid vacation and sick time.

Work Environment

Most pulp and paper plants operate 24 hours a day, 7 days a week, and the days are divided into three shifts. Production workers with seniority are usually assigned to the day shift, but they also may have to work nights and weekends in certain situations.

These jobs, like many other production jobs, can consist of doing the same thing over and over again. Workers may have to battle tedium and boredom. In addition, some areas of the plant may be hot, humid, and noisy. The chemicals used in papermaking produce unpleasant odors. However safety regulations exist and, if followed, the chance of injury is minimal.

Few jobs in this field require heavy physical labor, although some may require that workers be on their feet for most of the day.

Outlook

Even though the demand for paper products is increasing, employment in the pulp and paper industries has been decreasing for several years. This decrease will likely continue, although at a slow rate. Perhaps the most important reason for the decreasing number of jobs is the trend toward computerization. As the industry has increasingly used technology to run the pulp and papermaking process, the need for workers has decreased.

Fortunately, however, this factor has been offset somewhat by an increase in the amount of paper products the United States is exporting to foreign markets. Because of the growing foreign market, as well as more relaxed international trade regulations, U.S. paper exports have grown substantially in the last decade. In addition, the domestic market for paper products is strong. Between 1982 and 1997, production of printing and writing papers increased by 60 percent. The sale of newspapers and books has also grown. This increased demand for paper has counterbalanced, to a large degree, the trend toward computerization and the resulting need for fewer workers.

Employment prospects in this industry are better for college-educated individuals with scientific or technical backgrounds. Most of the jobs lost in the mechanization of the industry have been those that require semiskilled or skilled laborers. Opportunities in marketing may also be good, due to the expansion of the international paper market and the push for new product development. Finally, the growing demand for recycled paper products is creating job opportunities in recycling collection and recycled paper distribution. According to the September 1997 *Monthly Labor Review,* employment in recycling-related jobs has shown a steady and increasing rate of growth since 1990.

■ For More Information

For up-to-date information on forestry, paper, wood products, recycling, environmental issues, and government policies that pertain to the pulp and paper industry, contact:

American Forest and Paper Association
1111 19th Street, NW, Suite 800
Washington, DC 20036
Tel: 202-463-2700
Web: http://www.afandpa.org

For a history of pulp and paper in Canada, current news, and other facts about the Canadian pulp and paper industry, contact:

Canadian Pulp and Paper Association
1155 Metcalfe Street, 19th Floor
Montreal, Quebec H3B 4T6 Canada
Tel: 514-866-6621
Web: http://www.open.doors.cppa.ca

For educational programs on pulp and paper, information on local and student chapters, and a pulp and paper industry jobline, contact:

Technical Association of the Pulp and Paper Industry (TAPPI)
15 Technology Parkway South
Norcross, GA 30092
Tel: 800-291-3145
Web: http://www.tappi.org

■ Related Articles

Printing

Pulp and Paper

Wood

Bindery Workers

Foresters

Forestry Technicians

Industrial Engineers

Industrial Machinery Mechanics

Instrumentation Technicians

Logging Industry Workers

Mechanical Engineering Technicians

Mechanical Engineers

Operating Engineers

Printing Press Operators and Assistants

Quality Control Engineers and Technicians

Recycling Coordinators

Wood Science and Technology Workers

Paper-Machine Operators

■ See Paper Processing Occupations

Paraeducators

■ See Teacher Aides

Paralegals

■ Overview

Paralegals, also known as *legal assistants,* assist in trial preparations, investigate facts, prepare documents such as affidavits and pleadings, and, in general, do work customarily performed by lawyers. More than 113,000 paralegals work in law firms, businesses, and government agencies all over the United States; the majority work with lawyers and legislators.

■ History

The U.S. legal system has undergone many changes over the past few decades as more people turn to lawyers for help in settling disputes. This increase in litigation has placed greater demands on lawyers and other legal professionals. To help meet these demands, lawyers have hired legal assistants to help provide legal services to more people at a lower cost.

The first paralegals were given a limited number of routine duties; many started as legal secretaries who were gradually given more responsibilities. Today, however, the work of the paralegal has grown and expanded and formal training programs have been established.

Since this occupation developed in the late 1960s, paralegals have taken on much of the routine work that lawyers once did themselves, such as researching, investigating, and preparing legal briefs, allowing lawyers to concentrate on the more skilled aspects of providing legal services. The paralegal profession continues to grow as paralegals gain wider acceptance as professionals.

Computers play an important role in the research conducted by paralegals today. A paralegal must be proficient at using the computer to find information and to create reports.

■ The Job

A paralegal's main duty is to do everything a lawyer needs to do but doesn't have time to do. Paralegals assist lawyers in a variety of ways to accomplish this goal. Although the lawyer assumes responsibility for the paralegal's work, the paralegal may take on all the duties of the lawyer except for setting fees, appearing in court, accepting cases, and giving legal advice.

Paralegals spend much of their time in law libraries, researching laws and previous cases and compiling facts to help lawyers prepare for trial. Paralegals often interview witnesses as part of their research as well. After analyzing the laws and facts that have been compiled for a particular client, the paralegal often writes a report that the lawyer may use to determine how to proceed with the case. If a case is brought to trial, the paralegal helps prepare legal arguments and draft pleadings to be filed in court. They also organize and store files and correspondence related to cases.

Not all paralegal work centers on trials. Many paralegals work for corporations, agencies, schools, and financial institutions. Paralegals working in business create and maintain contracts, mortgages, affidavits, and other documents. They assist with corporate matters, such as shareholder agreements, contracts, and employee benefit plans. Another important part of a *corporate paralegal's* job is to stay on top of new laws and regulations to make sure the company is operating within those parameters.

Some paralegals work for the government. They may prepare complaints or talk to employers to find out why health or safety standards are not being met. They often analyze legal documents, collect evidence for hearings, and prepare explanatory material on various laws for use by the public. For example, a *court administrator paralegal* is in charge of keeping the courthouse functioning—tasks include monitoring personnel, handling the case load for the court, and general administration.

Other paralegals are involved in community or public-service work. They may help specific groups, such as poor or elderly members of the community. They may file forms, research laws, and prepare documents. They may represent clients at hearings, although they may not appear in court on behalf of a client.

Many paralegals work for large law firms, agencies, and corporations and specialize in a particular area of law. Some work for smaller firms and have a general knowledge of many areas of law. Paralegals have varied duties, and an increasing number use computers in their work.

■ Requirements

Requirements for paralegals vary by employer. Some paralegals start out as legal secretaries or clerical workers and gradually are given more training and responsibility. The majority, however, choose formal training and education programs.

High School

High school students should take a broad range of subjects, including English, social studies, computer science, and languages, especially Spanish and Latin. Because legal terminology is used constantly, word origins and vocabulary should be a focus.

Postsecondary Training

Formal training programs usually range from 1 to 3 years and are offered in a variety of educational settings: 4-year colleges and universities, law schools, community and junior colleges, business schools, proprietary schools, and paralegal associations. Admission requirements vary, but good grades in high school and college are always an asset. There are over 800 paralegal programs, about 200 of which have been approved by the American Bar Association.

Some paralegal programs require a bachelor's degree for admission; others do not require any college. In either case, those who have a college degree usually have an edge over those who do not.

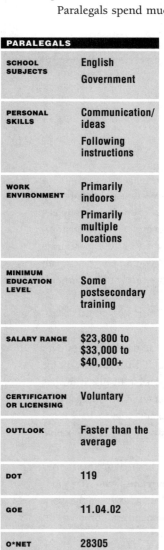

PARALEGALS	
SCHOOL SUBJECTS	English Government
PERSONAL SKILLS	Communication/ ideas Following instructions
WORK ENVIRONMENT	Primarily indoors Primarily multiple locations
MINIMUM EDUCATION LEVEL	Some postsecondary training
SALARY RANGE	$23,800 to $33,000 to $40,000+
CERTIFICATION OR LICENSING	Voluntary
OUTLOOK	Faster than the average
DOT	119
GOE	11.04.02
O*NET	28305

Certification or Licensing

Paralegals are not required to be licensed or certified. Instead, when lawyers employ paralegals, they often follow guidelines designed to protect the public from the practice of law by unqualified persons.

Paralegals may, however, opt to be certified. To do so, they may take and pass an extensive two-day test conducted by the National Association of Legal Assistants Certifying Board. Paralegals who pass the test may use the title Certified Legal Assistant (CLA) after their names. In 1996, the National Federation of Paralegal Associations established the Paralegal Advanced Competency Exam, a means for paralegals with bachelor's degrees and at least two years' experience to acquire professional recognition. Paralegals who pass this exam may use the designation Registered Paralegal (RP).

Other Requirements

Communication skills, both verbal and written, are vital to working as a paralegal. The paralegal must be able to turn research into reports that a lawyer or corporate executive can use. A paralegal must be able to think logically and learn new laws and regulations quickly. Research skills, computer skills, and people skills are necessary for success as a paralegal.

■ Exploring

If you're interested in a career as a paralegal, but you aren't positive yet, don't worry. There are several ways you can explore the career of a paralegal. Colleges, universities, and technical schools have a wealth of information available for the asking. Elizabeth Houser, a practicing paralegal, says "Contact schools that have paralegal programs and ask questions; they are helpful and will give you a lot of information about being a paralegal."

Look for summer or part-time employment as a secretary or in the mailroom of a law firm to get an idea of the nature of the work. If paid positions aren't available, offer yourself as a volunteer to the law offices in town. Ask your guidance counselor to help you set up a volunteer/internship agreement with a lawyer.

Talk to your history or government teacher about organizing a trip to a lawyer's office and a courthouse. Ask your teacher to set aside time for you to talk to paralegals working there and to their supervising attorneys.

If you have access to a computer, search the World Wide Web for information on student organizations that are affiliated with the legal profession. You can also write to the organizations listed at the end of this article for general information.

A paralegal doing research in a law library

■ Employers

A majority of paralegals work for lawyers in law offices or in law firms. Other paralegals work for the government, namely for the Federal Trade Commission, Justice Department, Treasury, Internal Revenue Service, Department of the Interior, and many other agencies and offices. Paralegals are also found in the business community. Anywhere legal matters are part of the day-to-day work, paralegals are usually handling them. Paralegals fit in well in business because many smaller corporations must deal with legal regulations but don't necessarily need an attorney or a team of lawyers.

Paralegals in business can be found all over the country. Larger cities employ more paralegals who focus on the legal side of the profession, and government paralegals will find the most opportunities in state capitals and Washington, DC.

Paralegals can be found all over corporate America—but they often aren't called paralegals. Although these professionals deal with laws and regulations, they do not work under lawyers and attorneys; in fact, some paralegals work for themselves. Check out this short list of just a few of the different jobs you can set your sights on as a paralegal:

Health care paralegals use medical experience or knowledge to compile information to be used in medical malpractice hearings.

Real estate paralegals work with leases and negotiate their terms.

Housing law paralegals help protect the housing rights of the poor.

Freelance paralegals can work from home for various lawyers or corporations; they hire their services out on contract.

Compliance paralegals work to ensure that their company is following the guidelines and regulations in whatever area of business they are in.

■ Starting Out

Although some law firms promote legal secretaries to paralegal status, most employers prefer to hire individuals who have completed paralegal programs. To have the best opportunity at getting a quality job in the paralegal field, you should attend a paralegal school. In addition to providing a solid background in paralegal studies, most schools help graduates find jobs. Even though the job market for paralegals is expected to grow rapidly over the next 10 years, those with the best credentials will get the best jobs.

For Elizabeth, the internship program was the springboard to her first paralegal position, "The paralegal program of study I took required an internship. I was hired directly from that internship experience."

The National Federation of Paralegal Associations recommends using job banks that are sponsored by paralegal associations across the country. For paralegal associations that may be able to help, see the addresses listed at the end of this article.

Many jobs for paralegals are posted on the Internet as well. Search on the phrase "paralegals and jobs" to see what positions are available.

■ Advancement

There are no formal advancement paths for paralegals; paralegals usually do not become lawyers or judges. There are, however, some possibilities for advancement, as large firms are beginning to establish career programs for paralegals.

For example, a person may be promoted from a paralegal to a head legal assistant who supervises others. In addition, a paralegal may specialize in one area of law, such as environmental, real estate, or medical malpractice. Many paralegals also advance by moving from small to large firms.

Expert paralegals who specialize in one area of law may go into business for themselves. Rather than work for one firm, these freelance paralegals often contract their services to many lawyers. Some paralegals with bachelor's degrees enroll in law school to train to become lawyers.

Paralegals can also move horizontally by taking their specialized knowledge of the law into another field, such as insurance, occupational health, or law enforcement.

■ Earnings

Salaries vary greatly for paralegals. The size and location of the firm and the education and experience of the employee are some factors that determine the annual earnings of paralegals.

According to 1997 statistics from the National Federation of Paralegal Associations, beginning paralegals average about $23,800 a year. Paralegals with 7 to 10 years' experience earn about $32,900. Top paralegals in large offices can earn as much as $40,000 a year, and paralegal supervisors, $40,000 to $50,000. Many paralegals receive year-end bonuses, some averaging $1,900 or more.

Paralegals employed by the federal government averaged $44,000 annually in 1997, as reported by the U.S. Department of Labor.

■ Work Environment

Paralegals often work in pleasant and comfortable offices. Much of their work is performed in a law library. Some paralegals work out of their homes in special situations. When investigation is called for, paralegals may travel to gather information. Most paralegals work a 40-hour week, although long hours are sometimes required to meet court-imposed deadlines. Longer hours—sometimes as much as 90 hours per week—are usually the normal routine for paralegals starting out in law offices and firms.

Many of the paralegal's duties involve routine tasks, so they must have a great deal of patience. However, paralegals may be given increasingly difficult assignments over time. Paralegals are often unsupervised, especially as they gain experience and a reputation for quality work. Elizabeth does much of her work unsupervised. "You get to put a lot of yourself into what you do and that provides a high level of job satisfaction," she says.

■ Outlook

In 1997, there were about 113,000 paralegals employed in the United States; most were employed by private law firms. The employment outlook for paralegals through 2006 is excellent, representing one of the fastest-growing professions in the country. One reason for the expected growth in the profession is the financial benefits of employing paralegals. The paralegal, whose duties fall between those of the legal secretary and those of the attorney, helps make the delivery of legal services more cost effective to clients. The growing need for legal services among the general population and the increased popularity of prepaid legal plans is creating a tremendous demand for paralegals in private law firms. In the private sector, paralegals can work in banks, insurance companies, real estate firms, and corporate legal departments. In the public sector, there is a growing need for paralegals in the courts and community legal service programs, government agencies, and consumer organizations.

The growth of this occupation, to some extent, is dependent on the economy. Businesses are less likely to pursue litigation cases when profit margins are down, thus curbing the need for new hires.

■ For More Information

For information regarding accredited educational facilities, contact:

American Association for Paralegal Education
2965 Flowers Road South, Suite 105
Atlanta, GA 30341
Tel: 770-452-9877
Web: http://www.aafpe.org

For general information about careers in the law field, contact:

American Bar Association
750 North Lake Shore Drive
Chicago, IL 60611
Tel: 312-988-5000
Web: http://www.abanet.org

For information about educational and licensing programs, contact:

National Association of Legal Assistants
1516 South Boston Avenue, Suite 200
Tulsa, OK 74119
Tel: 918-587-6828
Web: http://www.nala.org

For brochures about almost every aspect of becoming a paralegal, contact:

National Federation of Paralegal Associations
PO Box 33108
Kansas City, MO 64114-0108
Tel: 816-941-4000
Web: http://www.paralegals.org

For information about employment networks and school listings, contact:

National Paralegal Association
PO Box 406
Solebury, PA 18963
Tel: 215-297-8333
Email: admin@nationalparalegal.org
Web: http://www.nationalparalegal.org

For various career information, contact:

Association of Legal Administrators
175 East Hawthorn Parkway, Suite 325
Vernon Hills, IL 60061-1428
Tel: 847-816-1212
Web: http://www.alanet.org

■ Related Articles

Business
Government
Law
Intellectual Property Lawyers
Lawyers and Judges
Legal Secretaries
Process Servers

Park Rangers

■ Overview

Park rangers enforce laws and regulations in national, state, and county parks. They help care for and maintain parks as well as inform, guide, and ensure the safety of park visitors.

■ History

The National Park System in the United States was begun by Congress in 1872 when Yellowstone National Park was created. The National Park Service (NPS), a bureau of the U.S. Department of the Interior, was created in 1916 to preserve, protect, and manage the national, cultural, historical, and recreational areas of the National Park System. At that time, the park system contained less than 1 million acres. Today, the country's national parks cover more than 80 million acres of mountains, plains, deserts, swamps, historic sites, lakeshores, forests, rivers, battlefields, memorials, archaeological properties, and recreation areas.

PARK RANGERS	
SCHOOL SUBJECTS	Earth science Geography
PERSONAL SKILLS	Helping/teaching Leadership/management
WORK ENVIRONMENT	Primarily outdoors Primarily multiple locations
MINIMUM EDUCATION LEVEL	Bachelor's degree
SALARY RANGE	$20,000 to $30,000 to $37,000+
CERTIFICATION OR LICENSING	None available
OUTLOOK	Little change or more slowly than the average
DOT	169
GOE	04.02.03
NOC	2224
O*NET	63014A

A park ranger at Muir Woods in California gives a young boy a nature lesson.

All NPS areas are given one of the following designations: National Park, National Historical Park, National Battlefield, National Battlefield Park, National Battlefield Site, National Military Site, National Memorial, National Historic Site, National Monument, National Preserve, National Seashore, National Parkway, National Lakeshore, National Reserve, National River, National Wild and Scenic River, National Recreation Area, or just Park. (The White House in Washington, DC, for example, which is administered by the NPS, is officially a Park.)

To protect the fragile, irreplaceable resources located in these areas, and to protect the millions of visitors who climb, ski, hike, boat, fish, and otherwise explore them, the National Park Service employs park rangers. State and county parks employ rangers to perform similar tasks.

■ The Job

Park rangers have a wide variety of duties that range from conservation efforts to bookkeeping. Their first responsibility is, however, safety. Rangers who work in parks with treacherous terrain, dangerous wildlife, or severe weather must make sure hikers, campers, and backpackers follow outdoor safety codes. They often require visitors to register at park offices so that rangers will know when someone does not return from a hike or climb and may be hurt. Rangers often participate in search-and-rescue missions for visitors who are lost or injured in parks. In mountainous or forested regions, they may use helicopters or horses for searches.

Rangers also are concerned with protecting parks from inappropriate use and other threats from humans. They register vehicles and collect parking and registration fees, which are used to help maintain roads and facilities. They enforce the laws, regulations, and policies of the parks,

patrolling to prevent vandalism, theft, and harm to wildlife. Rangers may arrest and evict people who violate these laws. Some of their efforts to conserve and protect park resources include keeping jeeps and other motorized vehicles off sand dunes and other fragile lands. They make sure visitors do not litter, pollute water, chop down trees for firewood, or start unsafe campfires that could lead to catastrophic forest fires. When forest fires do start, rangers often help with the dangerous, arduous task of putting them out.

Park rangers carry out various tasks associated with the management of the natural resources within our National Park System. An important aspect of this responsibility is the care and management of both native and exotic animal species found within the boundaries of the parks. Duties may include conducting basic research, as well as disseminating information about the reintroduction of native animal populations and the protection of the natural habitat that supports the animals.

Rangers also help with conservation, research, and ecology efforts that are not connected to visitors' use of the park. They may study wildlife behavior patterns, for example, by tagging and following certain animals. In this way, they can chart the animals' migration patterns, assess the animals' impact on the park's ecosystem, and determine whether the park should take measures to control or encourage certain wildlife populations.

Some rangers study plant life and may work with conservationists to reintroduce native or endangered species. They measure the quality of water and air in the park to monitor and mitigate the effects of pollution and other threats from sources outside park boundaries.

In addition, park rangers help visitors enjoy and experience parks. In historical and other cultural parks, such as the Alamo in San Antonio, Independence Hall in Philadelphia, and the Lincoln Home in Springfield, Illinois, rangers give lectures and provide guided tours explaining the history and significance of the site. In natural parks, they may lecture on conservation topics, provide information about plants and animals in the park, and take visitors on interpretive walks, pointing out the area's flora, fauna, and geological characteristics. At a Civil War battlefield park, such as Gettysburg National Military Park in Pennsylvania or Vicksburg National Military Park in Mississippi, they explain to visitors what happened at that site during the Civil War and its implications for our country.

Park rangers are also indispensable to the management and administration of parks. They issue permits to visitors and vehicles and help plan the recreational activities in parks. They are involved with planning and managing park budgets. They keep records and compile statistics concerning weather conditions, resource conservation activities, and the number of park visitors.

Many rangers supervise other workers in the parks—those who build and maintain park facilities, work part time or seasonally, or operate concession facilities. Rangers often have their own park maintenance responsibilities, such as trail building, landscaping, and caring for visitor centers.

In some parks, rangers are specialists in certain areas of park protection, safety, or management. For example, in areas with heavy snowfalls and a high incidence of avalanches, experts in avalanche control and snow safety are designated *snow rangers*. They monitor snow conditions and patrol park areas to make sure visitors are not lost in snowslides.

■ Requirements

High School

High school students should take courses in earth science, mathematics, English, and speech. Any classes or activities that deal with plant and animal life, the weather, geography, and interacting with others will be helpful.

Postsecondary Training

Employment as a federal or state park ranger requires either a college degree or a specific amount of education and experience. Approximately 200 colleges and universities offer bachelor's degree programs in park management and park recreation. To meet employment requirements, students in other relevant college programs must accumulate at least 24 semester hours of academic credit in park recreation and management, history, behavioral sciences, forestry, botany, geology, or other applicable subject areas.

Without a degree, applicants need three years of experience in parks or conservation and must show they understand what is required in park work. In addition, they must demonstrate good communications skills. A combination of education and experience can also fulfill job requirements, with one academic year of study equalling nine months of experience. Also, the orientation and training a ranger receives on the job may be supplemented with formal training courses.

Rangers need skills in protecting forests, parks, and wildlife and in interpreting natural or historical resources. Law enforcement and management skills are also important. Rangers who wish to move into management positions may need graduate degrees. Approximately 50 universities offer master's degrees in park recreation and management and 16 have doctoral programs.

Other Requirements

The right kind of person to fill a park ranger position believes in the importance of the country's park resources and the mission of the park system. People who enjoy working outdoors—independently and with others—may enjoy park ranger work. Rangers need self-confidence, patience, and the ability to stay levelheaded during emergencies. Those who participate in rescues need courage, physical stamina, and endurance, while those who deal with visitors need tact, sincerity, personable natures, and a sense of humor. A sense of camaraderie among fellow rangers also can add to the enjoyment of being a park ranger.

■ Exploring

Persons interested in exploring park ranger work may wish to apply for part-time or seasonal work in national, state, or county parks. Such workers usually perform maintenance and other unskilled tasks, but they have opportunities to observe park rangers and talk with them about their work. Interested persons also may wish to work as volunteers. Many park research activities, study projects, and rehabilitation efforts are conducted by volunteer groups affiliated with universities or conservation organizations, and these activities can provide insight into the work done by park rangers.

■ Employers

Park rangers in the National Park Service are employed by the U.S. Department of the Interior. Other rangers may be employed by other federal agencies or by state and county agencies in charge of their respective parks.

■ Starting Out

Many workers enter national park ranger jobs after working part time or seasonally at different parks. These workers often work at information desks or in fire control or law enforcement positions. Some help maintain trails, collect trash, or perform forestry activities. Persons interested in applying for park ranger jobs with the federal government should contact their local Federal Job Information Center or the Federal Office of Personnel Management in Washington, DC, for application information. Those people seeking jobs in state parks should write to the appropriate state departments for information.

■ Advancement

Nearly all rangers start in entry-level positions, which means that nearly all higher-level openings are filled by the promotion of current workers. Entry-level rangers may move into positions as district ranger or park manager, or they may become specialists in resource management or park planning. Rangers who show management skills and become park managers may move into administrative positions in the district, regional, or national headquarters.

The orientation and training a ranger receives on the job may be supplemented with formal training courses. Training for job skills unique to the National Park Service is available at the Horace M. Albright Training Center at Grand Canyon National Park in Arizona, and the Stephen T. Mather Training Center at Harpers Ferry, West Virginia. In addition, the NPS makes use of training facilities at the Federal Law Enforcement Training Center in Brunswick, Georgia.

■ Earnings

Rangers in the National Park Service are usually hired at the GS-5 grade level, with a salary of around $20,000. More experienced or educated rangers may enter the Park Service at the GS-9 level, which pays approximately $30,000 to start. The government may provide housing to rangers who work in remote areas.

Rangers in state parks work for the state government. They receive comparable salaries and benefits, including paid vacations, sick leave, paid holidays, health and life insurance, and pension plans.

■ Work Environment

Rangers work in parks all over the country, from the Okefenokee Swamp in Florida to the Rocky Mountains of Colorado. They work in the mountains and forests of Hawaii, Alaska, and California and in urban and suburban parks throughout the United States.

National park rangers are hired to work 40 hours per week, but their actual working hours can be long and irregular, with a great deal of overtime. They may receive extra pay or time off for working overtime. Some rangers are on call 24 hours a day for emergencies. During the peak tourist seasons, rangers work longer hours. Although many rangers work in offices, many also work outside in all kinds of climates and weather, and most work in a combination of the two settings. Workers may be called upon to risk their own health to rescue injured visitors in cold, snow, rain, and darkness. Rangers in Alaska must adapt to long daylight hours in the summer and short daylight hours in the winter. Working outdoors in beautiful surroundings, however, can be wonderfully stimulating and rewarding for the right kind of worker.

■ Outlook

Park ranger jobs are scarce, and competition for them is fierce. The U.S. Park Service has reported that the ratio of applicants to available positions is sometimes as high as 100 to 1. As a result, applicants should attain the greatest number and widest variety of applicable skills possible. They may wish to study subjects they can use in other fields: forestry, land management, conservation, wildlife management, history, and natural sciences, for example.

The scarcity of openings is expected to continue indefinitely. Job seekers, therefore, may wish to apply for outdoor work with agencies other than the National Park Service, including other federal land and resource management agencies and similar state and local agencies. Such agencies usually have more openings.

■ For More Information

for more information about careers in the park service, contact the following:

National Association of State Park Directors
9894 East Holden Place
Tucson, AZ 85748
Tel: 520-298-4924

National Recreation and Park Association
22377 Belmont Ridge Road
Ashburn, VA 20148-4510
Tel: 703-858-0784
Web: http://www.nrpa.org

National Parks and Conservation Association
1776 Massachusetts Avenue, NW
Washington, DC 20036
Tel: 202-223-6722
Web: http://www.npca.org/npca

Student Conservation Association
PO Box 550
Charlestown, NH 03603-0550
Tel: 603-543-1700
Web: http://www.sca-inc.org

■ Related Articles

Earth Sciences

The Environment

Parks and Public Lands

Adventure Travel Specialists

Ecologists

National Park Service Employees

Parking Attendants

■ See Amusement Park Workers

Parole Officers

■ Overview

Parole is the conditional release of a prisoner who has not served out a full sentence. A long-standing practice of the U.S. justice system, parole is granted for a variety of reasons, including the "good behavior" of a prisoner, as well as overcrowding in prisons.

Prisoners on parole, or parolees, are assigned to a parole officer upon their release. It is the job of the *parole officer* to meet periodically with the parolee; to ensure that the terms of the release are followed; to provide guidance and counseling; and to help the parolee find a job, housing, a therapist, or any other means of support. Parolees who break the release agreement may be returned to prison. There are approximately 60,000 parole officers in the United States.

■ History

The use of parole can be traced at least as far back as the 18th century, when England, awash in the social currents of the Enlightenment and Rationalism, began to cast off its reliance on punishment by death. Retribution as the primary legal goal was increasingly challenged by the idea that reform of prisoners was not only possible but also desirable. At first, this new concern took the form of a conditional pardon from a death sentence. Instead of being executed, felons were sent away to England's foreign possessions, initially to the American colonies to fill their acute labor shortage. Although this practice actually began in the 1600s, it was not until the next century that a majority of condemned convicts were pardoned and transported across the ocean. After the American colonies gained independence in the late 18th century, England began to ship felons to Australia.

An important next step in the history of parole is the "ticket of leave," first bestowed upon transported convicts in Australia. Taking various forms, this system eventually allowed a convict to be released from government labor but only after a designated number of years and only as a result of good conduct or behavior.

In the mid-19th century, the English Penal Servitude Act abolished the practice of transporting convicts to colonies and replaced it with the sentence of imprisonment. The use of the ticket of leave, however, was kept, and prisoners with good conduct could be freed after serving a designated part of the sentence. If another crime was committed, the prisoner would be required to complete the full term of the original sentence.

Although aspects of parole were tried as early as 1817 in New York State, a complete system of conditional and early release did not emerge in the United States until the 1870s. This program, begun in New York, included a method of grading prisoners, compulsory education, and supervision by volunteers called guardians, with whom the released prisoner was required to meet periodically. By 1916, every state and the District of Columbia had established a comparable program. This system of early release from prison came to be called parole—French for word, promise, or speech—because prisoners were freed on their word, or parole, of honor.

Since its beginning, parole has been linked with the idea of rehabilitation. Those on parole were given counseling and assistance in finding job training, education, and housing, but, unlike prisoners released without parole,

they were also monitored. It was hoped that supervision, assistance, and the threat of being confined again would lessen the chance that released prisoners would commit another crime. Parole, however, has come to have other important functions. Prison overcrowding has commonly been solved by releasing inmates who seem least likely to return to crime. Inequities in sentencing have sometimes been corrected by granting early release to inmates with relatively long prison terms. Parole has also been used effectively as a means of disciplining disruptive prisoners while encouraging passive prisoners to good behavior. Without the incentive of parole, a prisoner would have to serve out the entire term of his or her sentence.

■ The Job

Parole officers play an important role in protecting society from crime. By helping, guiding, and supervising parolees, parole officers can reduce the chance that these individuals will again break the law and thus return to prison.

The regulations concerning parole differ from state to state. In some places, prisoners are given what are called indeterminate, or variable, sentences; if convicted of robbery, for example, an offender may be sentenced to no less than three years in prison but no more than seven. In this case, the prisoner would become eligible for parole after three years. In other places, an offender is given a definite sentence, such as seven years, but according to law may be paroled after completing a certain percentage of the sentence. Particularly heinous crimes may be excluded from the parole system.

Not all prisoners eligible for parole are released from prison. Parole is generally granted for good behavior, and those who successfully complete a drug or alcohol rehabilitation program, finish their GED (general equivalency diploma), or show other signs that they will lead a productive, crime-free life are considered good candidates for parole. In a few cases, such

PAROLE OFFICERS	
SCHOOL SUBJECTS	Government Psychology
PERSONAL SKILLS	Helping/teaching Leadership/management
WORK ENVIRONMENT	Primarily indoors One location with some travel
MINIMUM EDUCATION LEVEL	Bachelor's degree
SALARY RANGE	$20,000 to $30,000 to $41,000
CERTIFICATION OR LICENSING	Voluntary
OUTLOOK	Faster than the average
DOT	195
GOE	10.01.02
NOC	4155
O*NET	27305C

as prison overcrowding, prisoners might be released before they are technically eligible. The parole decision is made by a parole board or other government oversight committee.

The work of a parole officer begins when a prisoner becomes eligible for parole. A parole officer working inside the correctional institution is given the job of writing a report on the prisoner. To help determine the risks involved in releasing the prisoner, the report might discuss the prisoner's family background, lifestyle before entering prison, personality, skills, and job prospects, as well as the crime for which the prisoner was incarcerated and any other crimes committed. The parole board or other oversight body reviews the report; conducts interviews with the prisoner, the prisoner's family, and others; and then decides whether the prisoner is suitable for release. In some cases, the parole officer might be called to testify or may help the prisoner prepare for the meeting with the parole board.

If released, the prisoner is assigned to another parole officer outside of the correctional institution. The initial meeting between the prisoner and this parole officer, however, may take place inside the prison, and it is there that the parole officer explains the legal conditions that the prisoner must follow. Beyond refraining from criminal activity, common conditions are attending school, performing community service, avoiding drug or alcohol abuse, not possessing a gun, and not associating with known criminals.

At this point, the parole officer tries not only to help the parolee find housing, employment, job training, or formal education but also to provide counseling, support, and advice. The parole officer may try to help by referring the parolee to other specialists, such as a psychologist or a drug rehabilitation counselor, or to a halfway house, where the parolee can live with other former prisoners and may be assisted by drug therapists, psychologists, social workers, and other professionals. Parolees with financial problems may be referred to welfare agencies or social service organizations, and the parole officer may help arrange welfare or other public assistance. This is especially important for a parolee who has a family. The parole officer also sets up periodic meetings with the parolee.

An important part of the parole officer's job may be to contact and talk with businesses that might employ former prisoners. The parole officer tries to alleviate the concerns of business leaders reluctant to hire parolees and to highlight the role of the business community in helping former prisoners begin a new life.

Much of the parole officer's work is directed toward ensuring that the parolee is upholding the release agreement. The parole officer might interview the parolee's teachers, employers, or family and might conduct other types of investigations. Records must be kept of the parolee's employment or school status, finances, personal activities, and mental health. If the parolee does not follow the release agreement, the parole officer must begin proceedings for returning the parolee to a correctional institution. In some places, the parole officer is charged with arresting a parolee who is violating the agreement.

Parole officers often have a heavy caseload, and it is not unusual for 50 to 300 parolees to be assigned to a single parole officer. With so many parolees to monitor, little time may be spent on any single case. Some parole officers are helped by parole aides or parole officer trainees. A job with similar responsibilities is the *probation officer,* and some officers handle both parolees and those on probation. As the title suggests, probation officers work with offenders who are given probation, which is the conditional suspension of a prison sentence immediately after conviction. Probation is often given to first-time offenders. Like parolees, those on probation must follow strict guidelines, and failure to do so can result in incarceration. Probation officers, like parole officers, monitor the offenders; assist with finding employment, training, or education; make referrals to therapists and other specialists; help arrange public assistance; interview family, teachers, and employers; and provide advice and guidance. Those who work with children may be called *juvenile court workers.*

■ Requirements

High School

High school students take a courses in English, history, and the social sciences, as well as civics, government, and psychology. Knowledge of a foreign language, particularly those spoken by larger immigrant and minority populations, will be especially helpful to a prospective parole officer. Some parole officer positions require fluency in specific foreign languages.

Postsecondary Training

The minimum educational requirement for becoming a parole officer is usually a bachelor's degree in criminal justice, criminology, corrections, social work, or a related subject. A degree in public administration, law, sociology, or psychology may also be accepted. A master's degree, as well as experience in social work or in a correctional institution, may be required for some positions.

Other Requirements

Essential personal qualities for a parole officer include patience, good communications skills, and the ability to work well with and motivate other people.

■ Exploring

The best way to gain exposure to the field is to volunteer for a rehabilitation center or other social service organization. Some agencies offer internship programs for students interested in the field. It may also be helpful to call a local government agency handling parole and to arrange an informational interview with a parole officer.

Employers

There are approximately 60,000 parole officers in the United States. Most are employed by state or county correctional departments. Other parole officers are federal employees. Probation officers generally work for the courts. Halfway houses and work release centers also hire parole and probation officers.

Starting Out

After fulfilling the necessary requirements, many enter the field by directly contacting local civil service offices or county, state, or federal parole boards. In some areas, applicants are required to take a civil service examination. Job listings are also found in the placement offices of colleges and universities and in the classified section of newspapers. Contacts leading to employment are sometimes made during internships at a rehabilitation center or other organization. Greater opportunities exist for applicants with a master's degree and for those who are willing to relocate. Many parole officers are former police and corrections officers who have gained additional training.

Advancement

Some people enter the field as a parole officer trainee before assuming the title of parole officer. New employees are given on-the-job training to learn the specifics of their job.

There are a number of higher-level positions. Beyond the job of parole officer, there are opportunities as supervisors, administrators, and department heads. Some parole officers are promoted to director of a specialized unit.

Earnings

Starting salaries for parole officers range from about $20,000 to $28,000 a year. The average annual salary ranges from $25,000 to $35,000. Earnings vary by location and by level of government. Parole officers working for the federal government receive the highest salaries, with an average of $41,000 per year. Educational level also affects salary. Parole officers with advanced degrees generally earn more than those with only bachelor's degrees.

Like most government workers, parole officers are given a good benefits package. Benefits include vacation days, health insurance, and a pension plan.

Work Environment

Parole officers usually work out of a clean, well-lighted office in a government building, courthouse, correctional institution, or social service agency. Those who work in the field must travel to various settings, such as private homes, businesses, or schools, in order to conduct interviews and investigations.

Parole officers typically have a 40-hour workweek, although overtime, as well as evening and weekend work, may be necessary. Because of potential emergencies, some may be on call 24-hours per day, 7 days a week.

The job can bring a considerable amount of stress. Many parole officers have workloads that are too heavy, sometimes approaching 300 cases at once. Frustration over not having enough time to do an effective job is a common complaint. In addition, many parolees commit new crimes despite efforts by the parole officer to provide assistance. Others may be angry or violent and thus difficult to help or counsel. The job, in fact, can be dangerous. Despite the drawbacks, many people are attracted to the field and remain in it because they want to be challenged and because they know that their work has a positive impact on public safety.

Outlook

The employment outlook for parole officers is good through the year 2006, according to the U.S. Department of Labor. The number of prisoners has increased dramatically during the past decade, and many of these will become eligible for parole. Overcrowding of prisons across the United States, combined with heightening concerns over the high cost of incarceration, has prompted the early release of many convicts who will require supervision. New programs replacing prison as a method of punishment and rehabilitation are being instituted in many states, and these programs will require additional parole officers. However, public outcry over perceived leniency toward convicted criminals, particularly repeat offenders, has created demand and even legislation for stiffer penalties and the withdrawal of the possibility of parole for many crimes. This development may ultimately decrease the demand for parole officers, as more and more criminals sit out their full sentences.

For More Information

Contact the ACA for information on job openings and for a list of colleges that offer degree programs in corrections:

The American Correctional Association
4380 Forbes Boulevard
Lanham, MD 20706-5646
Tel: 800-222-5646
Web: http://www.corrections.com

For a list of accredited bachelor's and master's degree programs in social work, please contact:

Council on Social Work Education
1600 Duke Street, Suite 300
Alexandria, VA 22314-3421
Tel: 703-683-8080
Web: http://www.cswe.org/

For information on careers in social work, please contact:

National Association of Social Workers
750 First Street, NE, Suite 700
Washington, DC 20002-4241
Tel: 202-408-8600
Web: http://www.naswdc.org/

■ Related Articles
Government
Law
Public Safety
Corrections Officers
Detectives
FBI Agents
Human Services Workers
Lawyers and Judges
Paralegals
Police Officers
Psychologists
Social Workers

Passenger Rate Clerks
■ See Billing Clerks

Passport-Application Examiners
■ See Health and Regulatory Inspectors

Paste-Up Workers
■ See Prepress Workers

Pastry Cooks
■ See Cooks, Chefs, and Bakers

Pathologists

■ Overview
Pathologists are physicians who analyze tissue specimens to identify abnormalities and diagnose diseases.

■ History
During the late Middle Ages, the earliest known autopsies were performed to determine cause of death in humans. As these autopsies were documented, much information about human anatomy was gathered and studied. In 1761, the culmination of autopsy material resulted in the first textbook of anatomy by Giovanni Batista Morgagni.

Many developments in pathology occurred during the 19th century, including the discovery of the relationship between clinical symptoms and pathological changes. In 1958, Ruldolf Virchow revealed the significance of the microscopic analysis of cells. Louis Pasteur and Robert Koch later developed the bacteriologic theory, which was fundamental to understanding disease processes. By the late 19th century, pathology was a recognized medical specialty.

Technological advances of the 20th century, from electron microscopes to computers, have led to further growth and developments in the field of pathology.

■ The Job
Pathologists provide information that helps physicians care for patients; because of this, the pathologist is sometimes called the "doctor's doctor." When a patient has a tumor, an infection, or symptoms of a disease, a pathologist examines tissues from the patient to determine the nature of the patient's condition. Without this knowledge, a physician would not be able to make an accurate diagnosis and design the appropriate treatment. Because many health conditions first manifest themselves at the cellular level, pathologists are often able to identify conditions before they turn into serious health problems.

Many people associate pathologists only with the performing of autopsies. In fact, while pathologists do perform autopsies, much of their work involves living patients. Pathologists working in hospital laboratories examine the blood, urine, bone marrow, stools, tissues, and tumors of patients. Using a variety of techniques, pathologists locate the causes of infections and determine the nature of unusual growths. Pathologists consult with a patient's physician to determine the best course of treatment. They may also talk with the patient about his or her condition. In a sense, the work of pathologists is much like detective work. It is often through the efforts of pathologists that health conditions are recognized and properly treated.

■ Requirements

Postsecondary Training

Like any medical specialist, a pathologist must earn an M.D. degree and become licensed to practice medicine (See *Physicians*), after which begins a four-year pathology residency. Residents may choose to specialize in anatomical pathology or clinical pathology. Many pathologists, however, prefer to specialize in both anatomical and clinical pathology; licensing as an AP/CP pathologist requires a five-year residency. Various subspecialties require further training beyond the residency.

Certification and Licensing

A pathologist can pursue certification along three primary paths—an anatomic pathology program, a clinical pathology program, or a combined anatomic and clinical pathology program. Once a pathologist has completed certification, he or she can choose to specialize in a particular area of pathology. Gaining certification in a specialty generally requires an additional one to two years of training, although there is a potential for combining this training with the standard pathology residency program.

Other Requirements

Successful pathologists should have an eye for detail and be able to concentrate intently on work, work well and communicate effectively with others, and be able to accept a great deal of responsibility. They need to perform well under pressure, be patient, thorough, and confident in decisions.

■ Earnings

According to a 1998 survey conducted by the American Medical Association, the average net pay for a pathologist is about $212,200, but salaries may range from $169,138 to $232,432. Several factors influence earnings, including years of experience, geographic region of practice, and reputation.

■ Outlook

According to the *Occupational Outlook Handbook,* physicians' careers are expected to grow faster than the average through 2006. The outlook for careers in pathology is particularly good. New medical tests are constantly being developed and refined, making it possible to detect an increasing number of diseases in their early stages. The medical community depends on pathologists to analyze results from these tests. Another factor favorably affecting the demand for pathologists is the shifting of health care to cost-consciousness managed care services. Testing for, diagnosing, and treating a disease or other health condition

A pathologist at work in the laboratory

in its early stages is much less expensive than treating a health condition in its advanced stages.

■ For More Information

Following are organizations that provide information on pathology careers, accredited schools, and employers.

American Board of Pathology
PO Box 25915
Tampa, FL 33622
Tel: 813-286-2444
Web: http://www.abpath.org

College of American Pathologists
325 Waukegan Road
Northfield, IL 60093
Tel: 847-832-7000
Web: http://www.cap.org

Intersociety Committee on Pathology Information
4733 Bethesda Avenue, Suite 730
Bethesda, MD 20814
Tel: 301-656-2944
Web: http://www.pathologytraining.org

United States and Canadian Academy of Pathology
3643 Walton Way Extension
Augusta, GA 30909
Tel: 706-733-7550
Web: http://www.uscap.org

■ Related Articles

Alternative Health Care

Health Care

Allergists/Immunologists

Anesthesiologists

Cardiologists

Dermatologists

Ear, Nose, and Throat Specialists

Epidemiologists

Gastroenterologists

General Practitioners

Patient Activity Therapists

■ **See Child Life Specialists**

Patient-Care Technicians

■ **See Dialysis Technicians**

Patrol Conductors

■ **See Corrections Officers**

Patternmakers

■ **See Computer-Aided Design Drafters and Technicians**

PBX Installers and Repairers, and Technicians

■ **See Communications Equipment Technicians**

PC Set Up Specialists

■ **See Systems Set Up Specialists**

Pediatric Dentists

■ **See Dental Care**

Pediatricians

■ **Overview**

Pediatricians are physicians who provide health care to infants, children, and adolescents. Typically, a pediatrician meets a new patient soon after birth, and takes care of that patient through his or her teenage years.

■ **History**

Children became the focus of separate medical care during the 18th century in Europe. Children's health care became a recognized medical specialty during the early 19th century, and by the middle of the 19th century, pediatrics was taught separately in medical schools. The first pediatric clinic in the United States opened in New York City in 1862. About that same time, several children's hospitals opened in Europe.

Studies focused on developing treatments for infectious diseases of childhood such as measles and scarlet fever. By the beginning of the 20th century, pediatricians began promoting the normal growth and development of children. Well-child clinics began to open around the United States.

Some of the most significant breakthroughs in children's health care have been in disease prevention. By the middle of the 20th century, the development of vaccines and antibiotics greatly decreased the threat of infectious diseases.

■ **The Job**

A significant part of a pediatrician's job is preventive medicine—what is sometimes called "well care." This involves periodically seeing a patient for routine health checkups. During these checkups, the doctor examines the child to make sure he or she is growing at a normal rate and to look for symptoms of illness. The physical examination includes testing reflexes, listening to the heart and lungs, checking eyes and ears, and measuring height and weight.

During the checkup, the pediatrician also assesses the child's mental and behavioral development. This is done both by observing the patient's behavior and by asking the parents questions about their child's abilities.

Immunizing children against certain childhood diseases is another important part of preventive medicine. Pediatricians administer routine immunizations for such diseases as rubella, polio, and smallpox, as children reach certain ages. Yet another part of preventive medicine is family education. Pediatricians council and advise parents on the care and treatment of their children. They provide information on such parental concerns as safety, diet, and hygiene.

In addition to practicing preventive medicine, pediatricians also treat sick infants and children. When a sick or injured patient is brought into the office, the doctor examines him or her, makes a diagnosis, and orders treatment. Common ailments include ear infections, allergies, feeding difficulties, viral illnesses, respiratory illnesses, and gastrointestinal upsets. For these and other illnesses, pediatricians prescribe and administer treatments and medications.

If a patient is seriously ill or hurt, a pediatrician arranges for hospital admission and follows up on the patient's progress during the hospitalization. In some cases, a child may have a serious condition, such as cancer, cystic fibrosis, or hemophilia, that requires the attention of a specialist. In these cases, the pediatrician, as the primary care physician, will refer the child to the appropriate specialist.

Some pediatric patients may be suffering from emotional or behavioral disorders or from substance abuse. Other patients may be affected by problems within their families, such as unemployment, alcoholism, or physical abuse. In these cases, pediatricians may make referrals to such health professionals as psychiatrists, psychologists, and social workers.

Some pediatricians choose to pursue pediatric subspecialties, such as the treatment of children who have heart disorders, kidney disorders, or cancer. Subspecialization requires a longer residency training than does general practice. A pediatrician practicing a subspecialty typically spends a much greater proportion of his or her time in a hospital or medical center than does a general practice pediatrician. Subspecialization permits pediatricians to be involved in research activities.

■ Requirements

Postsecondary Training

After earning an M.D. degree and becoming licensed to practice medicine (See *Physicians*), pediatricians must complete a three-year residency program in a hospital. The pediatric residency provides extensive experience in ambulatory pediatrics, the care of infants and children who are not bedridden. Residents also spend time working in var-

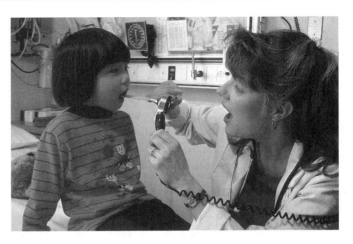

A pediatrician examines a young patient.

ious specialized pediatric units, including neonatology, adolescent medicine, child development, psychology, special care, intensive care, and outpatients.

Some of the other subspecialties a pediatrician might acquire training for include adolescent medicine, pediatric cardiology (care of children with heart disease), pediatric critical care (care of children requiring advanced life support), pediatric endocrinology (care of children with diabetes and other glandular disorders), pediatric neurology (care of children with nervous system disorders), pediatric hematology/oncology (care of children with blood disorders and cancer), and neonatology.

Certification or Licensing

Certification by the American Board of Pediatrics (ABP) is recommended. A certificate in General Pediatrics is awarded after three years of residency training and the successful completion of a two-day comprehensive written examination. A pediatrician who specializes in cardiology, infectious diseases, or other areas must complete an additional three-year residency in the subspecialty before taking the certification examination. To remain board-certified, pediatricians must pass an examination every seven years.

Other Requirements

To be a successful pediatrician, you should like children and adolescents; have patience, compassion, and a good sense of humor; be willing to continually learn; have a desire to help others; and be able to withstand stress and make sound decisions.

■ Earnings

Pediatricians, while at the low end of the earning scale for physicians, still have among the highest earnings of any occupation in the United States.

According to a 1998 survey conducted by the American Medical Association, the average net pay for pediatricians is about $140,600, but salaries may range from $105,375 to $142,595. The earnings of pediatricians are partly dependent upon the types of practices they choose. Those who are self-employed tend to earn more than those who are salaried. Geographic region, hours worked, number of years in practice, professional reputation, and personality are other factors which can impact a pediatrician's income.

■ Outlook

According to the *Occupational Outlook Handbook,* physician's jobs are expected to grow faster than the average through the year 2006. The employment prospects for pediatricians—along with other general practitioners, such as family physicians—are especially good. This is because of the increasing use of managed care plans which stress preventive care.

■ For More Information

Following are organizations that provide information on pediatric careers, accredited schools, and employers.

> **American Academy of Pediatrics**
> 141 Northwest Point Boulevard
> Elk Grove Village, IL 60007
> Tel: 847-228-5005
> Web: http://www.aap.org

> **American Pediatric Society**
> 3400 Research Forest Drive, Suite B7
> The Woodlands, TX 77381
> Tel: 281-296-0244
> Web: http://www.aps-spr.org

> **Ambulatory Pediatric Association**
> 6728 Old McLean Village Drive
> McLean, VA 22101
> Tel: 703-556-9222
> Web: http://www.ambpeds.org

■ Related Articles

Alternative Health Care
Health Care
Allergists/Immunologists
Anesthesiologists
Cardiologists
Dermatologists
Ear, Nose, and Throat Specialists
Epidemiologists
Gastroenterologists
General Practitioners
Geriatricians
Holistic Physicians
Neurologists
Obstetricians/Gynecologists
Oncologists
Ophthalmologists
Osteopaths
Pathologists
Podiatrists
Psychiatrists
Sports Physicians
Surgeons
Urologists

Pedodontists

■ See Dentists

Pedorthists

■ Overview

Pedorthists design, manufacture, fit, and modify shoes and other devices aimed at lessening pain or correcting foot problems as prescribed by a *physician*. This process involves making clay impressions of the patient's feet, modifying the mold to make special footwear, choosing the correct materials, and, finally, creating the custom footwear. Pedorthists must also evaluate current and future footwear to find out if it fits properly and performs as intended.

■ History

Foot disorders and problems have plagued people throughout history. However, until recently, most people were forced to seek relief from pain and discomfort at shoe stores. Because of the limited amount of knowledge concerning pedorthics in the past, most people could find little help for their problems.

Recently, though, there has been more and more information and research available about the possibilities for correcting foot problems. Shoe stores that previously employed inexperienced employees began hiring people with a pedorthic background, giving customers suffering from foot disorders the opportunity to get the kind of help and information they had been looking for all along.

Today, pedorthists are an important part of the skilled medical team that works together to find solutions to foot disorders. Pedorthists have become a great source for teaching people how to prevent foot problems and how to recognize initial symptoms.

■ The Job

Pedorthists examine a doctor's prescription for a patient and then design and fit therapeutic footwear to treat the problem. This involves first discussing the prescription with the patient and examining the patient's feet.

Pedorthists begin the task of further evaluation by making impressions of the patient's feet to get the exact measurements and contours correct. Next, a plaster mold is created from the impression to be used as a model in choosing or creating the footwear or device.

If the foot problem can be corrected by using footwear that has already been created, pedorthists will make minor adjustments to this ready-made device to fit the patient's needs. Sometimes, pedorthists must design new footwear that meets the specific needs of the patient. Usually, pedorthists will request that the specific design be made by the technicians in the lab.

After pedorthists have followed this process, they must evaluate the footwear or device to make sure it was made correctly and will function as it was intended. They try the footwear or device on the patient to make sure it fits. If the fit is not correct, changes must be made, since improperly fitting footwear may cause further damage to the patient. Often, pedorthists must oversee several trial fittings, making numerous adjustments to be sure the footwear is absolutely correct.

At this point, pedorthists must instruct the patient in how to properly use the new footwear or device. They answer questions the patient may have about the device, referring certain questions to other members of the medical team.

Pedorthists will conduct follow-up visits to track the patient's progress and to gauge how well the footwear is working. Frequently, changes must be made after the patient has had a chance to try out the footwear on a daily basis.

Pedorthists maintain precise records of their patients' footwear needs and problems. They must be very detailed in these records, since many adjustments are minor. Also, these final records are used to create a report for the doctors to inform them of the treatment applied.

Many pedorthists specialize in certain areas. These include adult foot deformities, amputations, arthritis, congenital deformities, diabetes, geriatrics, overuse injuries, pediatrics, sports-related injuries, and trauma. These more specialized pedorthists focus on one or two of these conditions and create comprehensive treatments, which include preventive, corrective, and accommodative measures. Pedorthists create treatments that try to prevent the condition from developing, but when it does, they then attempt to correct the disorder. Finally, they try to accommodate the condition to alleviate as much pain as possible from the patient.

Pedorthists don't just work in the patient care segment of medicine. Some work on creating new, innovative techniques, materials, and treatments to be used in their field. They may research how to make better shoe inserts or ankle braces. Or, they may try to find the cause of certain conditions so that preventive treatment can be developed.

Finally, pedorthists who are researchers use tests to improve the products and treatments being currently used.

Pedorthists may incorporate computer-based techniques when designing footwear and devices. They may use computers to create three-dimensional models instead of the traditional methods of model creation.

Some pedorthists may take their skills to places where the demand is high. For example, nursing homes tend to have a high number of residents with foot conditions that a pedorthist can treat. Also, pedorthists may conduct clinics at hospitals to heighten public awareness about foot care and possible treatments.

Pedorthists have a wide range and variety of footwear and devices to select from or modify to suit their patients' needs. Some of these include arch supports, ankle supports, lifts, inserts, walking shoes, brace shoes, surgical boots, and custom-made shoes.

■ Requirements

High School

High school students should take courses that relate to health, the human body, and movement. Courses like anatomy, biology, physics, and health will provide a good basis for work in pedorthics. Also, communications courses will prepare the student for dealing with a team of medical professionals and patients on a day-to-day basis. Some areas may only require a high school diploma and related experience to enter the field of pedorthics; however, most employers will require at least some college or university training.

Postsecondary Training

Pedorthists must have a either an associate's or bachelor's degree in a health- or science-related field from an accredited college or university in order to qualify for the certification examination. Another option is to accumulate 300 points from one or a combination of the following: completing science courses at an accredited college or university (20 points per credit hour); performing an internship under the direction of a board-certified pedorthist (points awarded for hours worked); and completing

PEDORTHISTS	
SCHOOL SUBJECTS	Biology Technical/Shop
PERSONAL SKILLS	Helping/teaching Mechanical/manipulative
WORK ENVIRONMENT	Primarily indoors Primarily one location
MINIMUM EDUCATION LEVEL	Some postsecondary training
SALARY RANGE	$20,000 to $28,000 to $65,000
CERTIFICATION OR LICENSING	Recommended
OUTLOOK	Much faster than the average

Board of Certified Pedorthists-accredited courses and seminars (points vary).

Certification or Licensing

After completing one of the above education requirements, the beginning pedorthist should take the certification examination, although it is not required. The exam is multiple choice and lasts about three-and-a-half hours. Once certification has been awarded, the certified pedorthist must participate in a program of continuing education to keep the certification from year to year.

Other Requirements

Even if a beginning pedorthist does not choose to become certified, he or she should get hands-on experience as an intern in a hospital, clinic, or agency with opportunities in pedorthics. Shoe stores that sell custom-fit and therapeutic shoes are another option for practical experience.

■ Exploring

Students interested in the field of pedorthics should try to get summer jobs in medical facilities, podiatrists' offices, shoe stores, and clinics to get a feel for what the field entails. Students can also arrange to speak to a certified pedorthist or visit a hospital, clinic, or shoe store to get an idea of what the pedorthist does during a typical day. Make sure to take a full day for each visit to really get a feel for each job in its unique setting. Be sure to ask a lot of questions and get a tour of the facilities that relate to pedorthics.

■ Employers

Employment opportunities in the field of pedorthists are found in nursing homes, hospitals, foot and ankle clinics, podiatrists' offices, and other medical facilities. Some pedorthists do research in labs or operate specialty shoe stores.

■ Starting Out

The most direct way to enter this field is to earn at least a two-year degree with summer internships built in. Most likely, the internships will turn into jobs or into leads to other possible job opportunities. Although certification is important, it's not necessary to break into the field.

If a four-year degree is chosen, there is even more opportunity to gain hands-on experience through internships and summer jobs. Many college and university campuses have abundant student jobs in all areas. When choosing a college or university, be sure to select one with an on-campus hospital so you'll have opportunities to learn in a health care setting.

The Pedorthic Footwear Association sponsors several national and regional seminars each year. These seminars focus on specialty areas within pedorthics, such as diabetes, sports-related injuries, and geriatrics. These events provide many educational opportunities for the beginning pedorthist and allow the beginner to meet and talk with experienced pedorthists.

■ Advancement

The more skills a pedorthist gains, the easier it is to advance in the field. For example, a pedorthist who has experience in creating certain footwear and devices may be able to get a higher-level position in a foot clinic that specializes in making its own footwear. Other pedorthists may become the head of research in the pedorthic area at a college, university, or laboratory.

Since there are many areas in pedorthics to specialize in, skilled pedorthists can use their experience to advise shoe companies or any business that relies on proper footwear. Some pedorthists will advance to manage therapeutic shoe stores or run a foot and ankle clinic.

■ Earnings

Pedorthists just entering the field will usually start out making $20,000 to $28,000 a year. With certification and hands-on experience, pedorthists can make $30,000 to $35,000 a year. Those at the top of their field may earn up to $65,000. These amounts depend on the type of facility and the location. Those working in hospitals and research labs may have a set salary that is very close to the numbers previously cited, while earnings vary at shoe stores and clinics.

Pedorthists working in shoe stores and clinics usually receive paid sick days, holidays, vacation days, and some level of insurance. Retirement savings plans are usually offered as well. Most hospitals provide insurance and other benefits, but usually don't offer as many days off. However, some hospitals offer discounted or free medical services to their employees.

■ Work Environment

Pedorthists may work in a variety of settings. Some work in hospitals and clinics, while others do research in labs or operate specialty shoe stores. Those working in labs and shoe stores usually have a set 40-hour week. Pedorthists in hospitals and clinics may be called on to work evening hours to meet the needs of patients.

Still other pedorthists may make home visits to people who are unable to come in to the clinic or hospital. Nursing homes are a prime example.

All of these settings are generally pleasant, although the research lab setting differs greatly from the specialty store setting. All require the pedorthist to work with many other people on a day-to-day basis. Because of this, the pedorthist's day is filled with activity that includes consulting with other medical personnel and talking to patients.

Pedorthists may spend some time taking notes and keeping records, but this is definitely not a desk job.

In order to work with patients, the pedorthist may be kneeling, sitting, or standing several times every day. If pedorthists are designing and creating footwear, they will work with special tools and materials.

■ Outlook

Jobs are abundant for pedorthists for many reasons. Two of the main reasons for the high demand for pedorthists are the popularity of sports and fitness and the fact that as the population ages, people tend to have foot problems.

The sports and fitness boom shows no signs of declining. Many people involved in different sports activities will need special braces, inserts, and devices to maintain a high level of activity. Also, sports-related injuries are increasingly common, so skilled pedorthists able to treat such injuries will be in high demand.

Advancing age brings many chronic conditions such as arthritis and bone disease that require the help of a pedorthist. Many of these people will require special equipment and advice from the pedorthist. The growing elderly population has created a great need for pedorthists. As a result of these factors, the future of pedorthics is stable and ever-growing.

■ For More Information

For information about the pedorthist profession and free brochures, contact:

Pedorthic Footwear Association
9861 Broken Land Parkway, Suite 255
Columbia, MD 21046-1151
Tel: 800-673-8447

For certification information, and a free certification handbook, contact:

Board for Certification in Pedorthics
9861 Broken Land Parkway, Suite 255
Columbia, MD 21046-1151
Tel: 800-560-2025

■ Related Articles

Health Care
Industrial Safety and Health Technicians
Orthotic and Prosthetic Technicians
Orthotists and Prosthetists
Podiatrists

Perforator Typists

■ **See Typists and Word Processors**

Perfusionists

■ Overview

Although *perfusionists,* formerly known as *cardiovascular perfusionists,* are not well known to the general public, they play a crucial role in the field of cardiovascular surgery by operating what is known as the "heart-lung machine." The perfusionist is responsible for all aspects of the heart-lung machine whenever it becomes necessary to interrupt or replace the functioning of the heart by circulating blood outside of a patient's body.

■ History

When open-heart surgery began in 1953, surgeons found it was virtually impossible to operate on the heart while at the same time expecting the heart to maintain its normal functions. Heart-lung machines were developed to circulate the patient's blood outside the body and to maintain certain body temperatures during surgery. These machines solved the problem of maintaining stable bodily functions during the operation so that the heart could resume its normal functioning following the operation. Those who operated the early heart-lung machines were not specifically trained for this subspecialty but, rather, came from the ranks of respiratory therapists, operating room technologists, biomedical and laboratory technologists, and nurses. These early heart-lung machine operators were often called pump technicians, perfusion technicians, extracorporeal technologists, and extracorporeal perfusionists.

From the mid-1950s until 1968, perfusionists were trained primarily by apprenticing under existing practitioners. In 1968, the American Society of Extracorporeal Technology (AmSECT) instituted a program of perfusionists' certification that the American Medical Association recognized with formal status in the 1970s. Also at this time, the American Board of Cardiovascular Perfusion (ABCP) was established. In

PERFUSIONISTS	
SCHOOL SUBJECTS	Biology Mathematics
PERSONAL SKILLS	Helping/teaching Technical/scientific
WORK ENVIRONMENT	Primarily indoors Primarily one location
MINIMUM EDUCATION LEVEL	Bachelor's degree
SALARY RANGE	$42,000 to $55,000 to $125,000
CERTIFICATION OR LICENSING	Recommended
OUTLOOK	Faster than the average
DOT	078
GOE	10.03.02
NOC	3214
O*NET	32925

THE HEART OF THE MATTER

Considering the age of humankind and the evolution of the medical sciences, heart surgery is still in its infancy. The first bypass operation was performed in 1944 by Dr. John Blalok, whose patient was a newborn infant with oxygen-poor blood. The baby was born with a bluish tint because blood was not circulating correctly. Dr. Blalock operated on the baby, bypassing a blocked blood vessel.

The most significant breakthrough in open heart surgery occurred 10 years later, when Dr. John Gibbon used a machine to pump blood and supply oxygen to an 18-year-old patient, giving the surgeon needed time for delicate heart surgery. The machine was the heart-lung machine, which is now a standard fixture in cardiac operating rooms.

1980, the American Board of Cardiovascular Perfusion established formal requirements for the education and accreditation of perfusionists.

Reflecting the increased sophistication and specialization of open-heart surgery, perfusionism has grown more complex. The job of the perfusionist now includes putting together and operating the heart-lung machine, the artificial heart, blood transfusion devices, the intra-aortic balloon pump, and various ventricular-assist devices.

■ The Job

Perfusionists perform one of the most delicate and crucial services for patients during open-heart surgery, coronary bypass, or any other procedure that involves the heart or the lungs. The perfusionist operates equipment that literally takes over the functioning of the patient's heart and lungs during surgery. Such equipment may also be used in emergency cases of respiratory failure.

When *surgeons* pierce the patient's breast bone and the envelope surrounding the heart, which is known as the pericardial sac, they must transfer the functions of the patient's heart and lungs to the heart-lung machine before any surgery can begin on the heart itself. This process is known as establishing extracorporeal bypass, or outside heart and lung functions. The heart-lung machine is activated by inserting two tubes into the heart, one circulates blood from the heart to the machine and the other circulates blood from the machine back into the heart. It is necessary during this procedure not only to maintain circulation and pumping action but also to maintain the appropriate oxygen, carbon dioxide, and other blood gas levels. In addition, perfusionists must effectively control the body temperature of patients who are undergoing extracorporeal bypass circulation because the flow of blood through the body greatly influences body temperature. To slow metabolism and reduce the stress on the heart and other bodily systems, perfusionists often reduce the body temperature of patients during open-heart surgery to 70

degrees Fahrenheit or below. Perfusionists use various probes within the body to monitor body temperature, blood gases, kidney functioning, electrolytes, and blood pressure.

Although the ultimate responsibility for open-heart surgery and for decisions concerning blood circulation, temperature, and other matters rests with the surgeon in charge of the operation, surgeons tend to rely heavily upon the judgment of perfusionists, who are regarded as specialists in their own right. Although the perfusionist may never have a discussion with the patient, perfusionists almost always have preoperative conferences with surgeons to discuss the patient's condition and other characteristics, the nature of the operation, and the equipment to be used.

Because of the nature of their work, perfusionists work in hospitals in cardiac operating rooms. They are members of a cardiac surgery team, and it is not uncommon for perfusionists to work through several successive operations in a row as well as to work on emergency cases. Because open-heart surgery cannot be performed without these specialists, perfusionists are usually on call a great deal of the time.

■ Requirements

High School
High school students interested in perfusion technology should prepare by taking all available science, mathematics, and health science courses. The American Society of Extracorporeal Technology offers some financial aid and scholarships, and a number of schools offer work-study programs as well as financial aid.

Postsecondary Training
Upon the completion of instruction from an accredited school of perfusion technology, perfusionists may take a written test administered by the American Board of Cardiovascular Perfusion. Those who pass it are then qualified to take an oral examination. The written and oral examinations are given once a year, and candidates are permitted to take these tests three times; candidates who are not able to pass the tests become ineligible for further examinations.

To work as a cardiovascular perfusionist requires formal training from one of over 25 schools throughout the United States accredited by the Accreditation Committee for Perfusion Education. As a prerequisite to admission, these schools generally require a bachelor of science degree, although in some cases they accept applicants who have trained at nursing schools and other technical schools and have experience as nurses or health technicians. Accredited perfusion technology programs range in length from one and one-half to two years. Several accredited schools offer a combined undergraduate degree and a degree in perfusion technology, but more often perfusionists are trained once they have completed a bachelor's degree or other training.

Those desiring entry to an accredited perfusion technology program can expect intense competition as only 10 to 20 percent of applicants are accepted into such programs. The accredited schools carefully examine academic record, character, and even personal temperament before accepting new students. The admissions officers at these schools realize that it takes a special individual to function under the kind of pressure and long hours perfusionists frequently encounter.

A strong background in biology, mathematics, and other sciences is recommended for applicants to perfusion technology programs as these programs are designed to convey a great deal of technical information as well as clinical training over a one-and-one-half- to two-year period. The perfusion technology program includes courses in physiology, cardiology, respiratory therapy, pharmacology, and heart surgery. Classroom experience is combined with extensive clinical experience where students learn about extracorporeal circulation, respiratory therapy, general surgical procedures, anesthesia, and other operating room procedures. Nearly all of the accredited perfusion technology programs attempt to involve students as early and as much as possible in clinical experience, as the practice of extracorporeal circulation relies so much upon actual operating room experience.

Certification or Licensing

Certification currently is not an absolute requirement for perfusionists, but it is rapidly becoming a practical requirement as more than two-thirds of perfusionists nationally are now certified. Certified perfusionists pay an annual $75 fee to maintain their certification. At present, perfusionists do not need separate state licenses to practice their profession. Students who graduate from a school accredited by the Accreditation Committee for Perfusion Education have a definite advantage.

To maintain their certification, perfusionists are expected to engage in continuing education programs to remain abreast of the latest techniques. The cardiovascular surgery field is constantly changing, and open-heart surgery, bypass surgery, heart transplants, and other complicated operations are becoming increasingly common throughout the health care system. Therefore, the field of perfusion technology will become increasingly more complex in the future.

■ Exploring

As with any technical medical field, one of the best ways to learn about the work of perfusionists is to talk with an existing practitioner. All hospitals performing open-heart

---

GLOSSARY

Blood salvaging: Using as much of the patient's blood as possible so as not to depend on donated blood. Some patients donate their own blood supply prior to their surgery.

Cardiac: Relating to the heart

Cardiologist: Heart surgeon

Cardiopulmonary: Relating to the heart and lungs

Cell savers: Machines that separate plasma, damaged platelets, and saline from blood that should not be returned to the patient's body

Extracorporeal circulation: Circulation of the patient's blood outside the body

Heart-lung machine: A machine used to take over the function of the patient's heart and lungs during surgery or respiratory failure. The machine draws blood from the patient's body, reoxygenates it, and pumps it back into the patient's body.

Induced hypothermia: A condition that the perfusionist may inflict on the patient to reduce body temperature to 70 degrees or below; this slows the patient's metabolism and reduces stress on the heart.

Pulmonary circulation: Blood flow to and from the lungs

---

surgery have perfusionists on staff who may be available for interviews with students. AmSECT offers a list of accredited perfusion technology programs, and those interested in such programs can talk to the professors, instructors, and admissions officers in those respective schools.

■ Employers

Roughly half of all perfusionists are directly employed by hospitals, and the other half are independent contractors or practitioners who make themselves available by contract to one or more hospitals. Independent contractors are responsible for their own business affairs including medical health insurance, uniforms, liability insurance, and other items.

■ Starting Out

The most important prerequisite for entering the field of perfusion technology is acceptance at an accredited school that offers such a program. Once students have entered a program they should begin to investigate the field first through their professors and teachers and then through AmSECT. This professional society of perfusion technologists, has an active student membership division that hosts meetings and conferences and is a good source of advice and information concerning various job openings in the field.

■ Advancement

Because there are relatively few perfusionists nationwide and the field of extracorporeal technology (open-heart surgery) is growing rapidly, perfusionists have advancement opportunities in terms of both high salaries and the opportunities to perform more complicated work. However, the field of perfusion technology is so specialized and so small that the concept of advancement is related more to improving one's technical skills through experience than to administering large departments or large numbers of people. Qualified perfusionists, however, can advance into management or to the technological side of the field. The practicing perfusionist advances through gaining higher pay, better working conditions, and the ability to be involved in more complicated procedures as well as to train less-experienced perfusionists. Perfusionists may also obtain teaching positions in one of the accredited schools or conduct research funded by educational institutions, foundations, or professional societies.

■ Earnings

Salaries for perfusion technologists compare favorably with those of other health technicians. The national range of salaries in the mid-1990s starts at about $42,000 per year for entering perfusionists and rises to an average of $55,000 per year for more experienced professionals. Some perfusionists annually earn as much as $125,000, but those earning higher salaries are generally employed directly by a physician or are self-employed.

■ Work Environment

Perfusionists typically work in operating rooms of hospitals. They work alongside the operating table as part of the surgical team; it is the responsibility of the perfusionist to see that the equipment is properly assembled and maintained at all times.

Perfusionists frequently must spend long hours in operating rooms, often under stressful conditions. Although most perfusionists average 125 procedures a year, some of these procedures can be quite lengthy, and they may occur at odd hours as well as under emergency conditions.

■ Outlook

The perfusion field is highly specialized and employs approximately 2,500 individuals nationwide. These professionals work in approximately 750 hospitals with open-heart surgery departments. Employment in this area is expected to grow at a rate faster than the average for all occupations through the year 2006. As with many medical fields, advancing technology calls for additional professionals as these procedures are performed on a more regular basis. The field of open-heart surgery and the expanded scope of extracorporeal technology grew dramatically during the 1980s and are expected to continue to expand, so that the job opportunities and job stability for perfusionists are expected to be excellent.

■ For More Information

For information about perfusionists, contact:

American Society of Extracorporeal Technology
503 Carlisle Drive, Suite 125
Herndon, VA 20170
Tel: 703-435-8556
Web: http://www.amsect.org

For information about certification, contact:

American Board of Cardiovascular Perfusion
207 North 25th Avenue
Hattiesburg, MS 39401
Tel: 601-582-3309

For information on medical careers, contact:

American Medical Association
515 North State Street
Chicago, IL 60610
Tel: 312-464-5000
Web: http://www.ama-assn.org

For accreditation information, contact:

Accreditation Committee for Perfusion Education
7108-C South Alton Way
Englewood, CO 80112-2106
Tel: 303-741-3598

■ Related Articles

Health Care
Biomedical Equipment Technicians
Cardiovascular Technologists
Diagnostic Medical Sonographers
Dialysis Technicians
Electroneurodiagnostic Technologists
Medical Laboratory Technicians
Medical Technologists
Orthotic and Prosthetic Technicians
Phlebotomy Technicians
Radiologic Technologists
Respiratory Therapists and Technicians
Surgical Technologists

Periodontists

■ Overview

Periodontists are *dentists* who specialize in the diagnosis and treatment of diseases affecting the gums and bone that support the teeth. They perform thorough clinical examinations, measuring the depth of gum pockets and checking for gingival bleeding, and may do tests to find out which types of bacteria are involved. Periodontal surgery may be needed in more severe cases of periodontitis. Some periodontists also insert dental implants to replace lost teeth.

■ History

Although the field of periodontology was formalized in the early 20th century, periodontal disease and treatment have been recognized throughout history. For thousands of years, it was thought that build-ups of calculus, or tartar, were responsible for periodontal disease. Many old civilizations documented periodontal diseases or treatment methods.

In the late 1800s, periodontal surgery techniques were developed and diagnosis was improved by the use of X rays. In recent years, digital radiography and superimposed X-ray images have enhanced the effectiveness of X rays. Surgical methods have also been refined, and lasers are now used in place of scalpels in certain procedures. About 20 to 25 years ago, a multitude of diagnostic procedures were established. Periodontal researchers have developed methods to regenerate lost bone in recent years.

In recent years it has been confirmed that bacterial infection, not calculus build-up, causes periodontal disease. Periodontists now use antibiotics, either in pill form or placed inside the periodontal pocket.

When treatment fails and a tooth must be extracted, dental implants offer a new way of replacing the tooth; artificial teeth or dentures may be attached to implants.

An intensive area of periodontal research today is the relationship between gum disease and medical conditions, including heart disease and premature births. Chronic exposure to periodontal bacteria and inflammation may make people more susceptible to other diseases.

Future research may provide a vaccine to prevent periodontal infections.

■ The Job

Periodontists perform thorough clinical examinations, using calibrated periodontal probes to measure periodontal pocket depths and the "attachment level" of periodontal tissues. They check for gingival bleeding, evaluate the amount of plaque and calculus, and assess tooth stability. They also take X rays to see if the patient has bone loss from past periodontal disease. Periodontists may do tests to find out which types of bacteria are involved.

Meticulous removal of calculus below the gum line, or scaling, remains an important part of treatment. Root planing is a more intensive form of scaling that involves removing infected cementum from root surfaces. When their periodontal disease has been stabilized, patients enter the maintenance phase of treatment and return every few months for scaling and root planing.

Periodontists also prescribe antibiotics to eliminate bacteria in the periodontal pockets. Increasingly, antibiotics are placed directly in the pocket in the form of fibers, gels, or chips.

Periodontal surgery may be needed in more severe cases of periodontitis. Periodontics has been one of the most surgically oriented dental specialties, but this may change as more effective antibiotic treatments become available.

Periodontists also can surgically insert bone-regenerating materials into areas with bone loss to grow new bone. This process is known as guided tissue regeneration.

When periodontal disease is left untreated or treatment fails, tooth loss may occur. Periodontists and other dentists can replace lost teeth with dental implants, which are metal or ceramic-metal devices surgically inserted into the jawbone. Artificial teeth or dentures are attached to the implants to restore normal function.

Periodontists may also perform cosmetic procedures, such as reshaping the gum line to make the teeth appear longer in patients with "gummy" smiles.

Those who manage their own practices must hire, train, and supervise employees, including office staff and *dental hygienists*.

■ Requirements

Postsecondary Training

To enter dental school, applicants generally need significant college course work in the sciences, a bachelor's degree, and a good score on the Dental Admissions Test, or DAT. After completing four years of dental school, dentists who want to specialize in periodontics attend a three-year graduate training program.

Certification or Licensing

Before entering practice, dentists must pass a licensing examination. Qualified candidates may also seek certification by the American Board of Periodontology.

Other Requirements

Periodontists, like other dentists, must have excellent hand-eye coordination and the ability to do finely detailed work. As procedures and technology change, practicing periodontists must continue life-long learning. They stay up to date on advances in their specialty by

PERIODONTISTS	
SCHOOL SUBJECTS	Chemistry Health
PERSONAL SKILLS	Helping/teaching Technical/scientific
WORK ENVIRONMENT	Primarily indoors Primarily one location
MINIMUM EDUCATION LEVEL	Medical degree
SALARY RANGE	$119,000 to $130,000 to $145,000
CERTIFICATION OR LICENSING	Required by all states
OUTLOOK	About as fast as the average
DOT	072
GOE	02.03.02
NOC	3113
O*NET	32105B

GLOSSARY

Alveolar bone: The bone that contains tooth sockets and supports the teeth

Anaerobic bacteria: Bacteria that exist in the absence of oxygen; associated with periodontal infections

Bone loss: Loss of alveolar bone as a result of periodontal disease

Calculus: Mineral deposits on the teeth; tartar

Dental implant: A metal or ceramic-metal device surgically inserted into the jawbone to support an artificial tooth

Gingiva: The oral tissue that is covered by a mucous membrane and surrounds the teeth; the gums

Gingivitis: Inflammation of the gingiva, or gums

Guided tissue regeneration: The use of bone replacement materials and barrier membranes to regenerate alveolar bone

Inflammation: The body's response to an injury, marked by pain, redness, heat, and swelling

Periodontal pocket: The space between the tooth and gingiva, when deepened by periodontal disease

Periodontics: The branch of dental practice involving examination, prevention, diagnosis, and treatment of periodontal diseases

Periodontitis: Inflammation of the periodontium that can progress and lead to tooth loss

Periodontium: The tissues that support the teeth, including the gingiva, cementum, periodontal ligament, and alveolar bone

Periodontology: The branch of dental science concerning the study of the periodontium and periodontal diseases

Plaque: The sticky substance that forms on tooth surfaces, made up principally of bacteria; responsible for starting tooth decay and gingivitis

Probing depth: The depth of a periodontal pocket, measured by a probe calibrated in 1-millimeter increments; probing depths greater than 3 millimeters indicate periodontal disease, especially if probing causes bleeding

Root planing: A more intense form of scaling, it involves removal of cementum contaminated by bacteria; root planing is a basic treatment for all forms of periodontal disease

Scaling: Removal of calculus and other deposits from tooth surfaces

taking continuing education courses each year. Also, because many dentists own their own practices, knowledge of business practices is beneficial.

■ Employers

Like general dentists, more than 90 percent of periodontists are in private practice. They may have a solo practice or work in a group practice with other dentists. Dentists serving in the military treat members of the military and their families. The U.S. Public Health Service also employs dentists to provide care or conduct research. Periodontists may also teach full-time or part-time in dental schools. Hospitals employ dentists to treat hospitalized patients.

Periodontists may work in scientific research or administration at universities, private or government research institutes, and dental product manufacturers.

■ Starting Out

After completing dental school and an advanced training program in periodontology, most periodontists either start their own practices or join an established practice. While many dentists choose to have their own practices, start-up costs can be steep: new dentists often need to borrow money to buy or lease office space and buy expensive equipment.

■ Advancement

Periodontists in private practice advance their careers by building their reputation among the general dentists who refer patients to specialists. To establish a good reputation, it is important to communicate effectively and coordinate treatment with general dentists.

Periodontists who teach at dental schools may advance in academic rank and eventually chair the department of periodontology.

Experienced periodontists and periodontal researchers can become more prominent through professional activities such as writing scientific books and articles and being active in professional organizations such as the American Academy of Periodontology.

■ Earnings

According to the American Dental Association Survey Center, periodontists under age 40 have an average net salary of about $119,000. This represents the lower end of the salary range. Periodontists who have been in practice for some time generally have higher earnings; the average net salary for periodontists over age 40 is $145,000.

Salaries also vary by geographic region and are influenced by the number of other periodontists practicing in a community.

Benefits vary by place of employment. Self-employed periodontists often arrange their own benefits through their dental practices.

■ Work Environment

Most periodontists work in private dental practices. The hours worked vary; some practitioners work only part-time, perhaps because they also teach part-time or are nearing retirement. Others work full-time and may treat some patients in the evening or on weekends.

While many dentists wear comfortable business attire underneath a laboratory coat, some opt to wear surgical scrubs when treating patients.

Periodontists may travel from time to time to attend continuing education courses or meetings held by professional organizations.

■ Outlook

The demand for periodontists is expected to remain relatively steady, but the procedures that they perform may change over time. As Americans retain more teeth and live longer, they have more teeth at risk for periodontal disease. Furthermore, as the possible links between chronic periodontal infection and medical diseases become more widely known, people may be more motivated to receive regular periodontal care.

Periodontal surgery is expected to be less common as more patients are managed with antibiotics and preventive care. This is good news for patients because periodontal surgery is expensive, but may mean reduced income for periodontists.

Lasers allow periodontists to perform some surgical procedures with less bleeding, pain, and scarring. Periodontists who use lasers in their practices may attract patients who prefer laser surgery to conventional procedures.

Some periodontists treat tooth loss with dental implants. Many patients are willing to pay out-of-pocket for implants because they want an alternative to wearing a conventional denture or bridge.

■ For More Information

This professional organization for specialists in periodontics sponsors the Journal of Periodontology, *scientific workshops, continuing education programs, and annual meetings. It has more than 7,000 members.*

American Academy of Periodontology
737 North Michigan Avenue
Chicago, IL 60611
Tel: 312-787-5518
Web: http://www.perio.org

This primary professional organization for dentists promotes dental health and the dental profession through education, research, and advocacy. It publishes the Journal of the American Dental Association *and* ADA News *and holds an annual conference. It has 120,000 members.*

American Dental Association
Department of Career Guidance
211 East Chicago Avenue
Chicago, IL 60611
Tel: 312-440-2500
Web: http://www.ada.org/tc-educ.html

■ Related Articles

Dental Care
Health Care
Dental Assistants
Dental Hygienists
Dental Laboratory Technicians
Dentists
Endodontists

Personal Chefs

■ Overview

Personal chefs prepare menus for individuals and their families, purchase the ingredients for the meals, then cook, package, and store the meals in the clients' own kitchens. Approximately 3,000 personal chefs work across the United States and Canada, cooking for busy families, seniors, people with disabilities, and others who don't have the time or the ability to prepare meals for themselves.

■ History

Though royalty, the famous, and the wealthy have long hired private chefs to work in their kitchens, personal chefs have only recently come onto the scene. Within the last 10 years, experienced cooks, either looking to expand their catering and restaurant businesses, or burnt-out from working as chefs, have begun meeting the demand for quick, easy meals that taste homemade. Men and women are holding down demanding, time-consuming jobs, and looking for alternatives to microwave dinners, fast food, and frozen pizzas. David MacKay founded the first professional association for personal chefs, the United States Personal Chef Association (USPCA), in 1991, and helps to establish over 400 new businesses every year. The American Personal Chef Institute (APCI), founded by Candy Wallace, has also developed in recent years, offering training materials and certification to experienced cooks wanting to set up their own businesses.

■ The Job

What will you be cooking for dinner tonight? Spice-rubbed lamb chops with roasted tomatoes? Tarragon chicken with West Indian pumpkin soup? Or maybe turkey parmesan on a bed of red-pepper linguini? If you're rolling up your sleeves and ready to take on a variety of cooking challenges, then a personal chef service may be in your future. People without the time to cook, or without the ability, or those who just plain don't care to cook, are calling upon the services of chefs who will come into their kitchens, throw together delicious meals, then stack the meals in their freezers. A complete meal prepared according to the client's specifications is then only a few minutes of re-heating away.

A personal chef is usually someone with a great deal of cooking experience who, for a per-meal fee, will prepare enough meals to last a few days, or a few weeks, for individuals and their families. As a personal chef, you first meet with a new client to discuss special dietary needs and food preferences. Some clients require vegetarian and low-fat cooking; others have diabetes, or swallowing disorders that require special consideration. (If you have to do a great deal of research into a special diet plan, you might charge an additional consultation fee.) From these specifications, you prepare a menu. On the day that you'll be cooking the meals, you visit the grocery store to purchase fresh meats, fish, fruits, and vegetables. At the home of your client, you prepare the meals, package them, label them, and put them in the freezer. Depending on the number of meals, you'll spend anywhere from 3 to 8 hours in your client's kitchen. You then clean up after yourself, and move onto your next client. Personal chefs are able to control their work hours by limiting the number of clients they take on. You'll need between 5 and 10 regular clients to earn a full-time wage.

Most personal chefs prepare the meals in the kitchens of the clients, thereby avoiding the requirements of licensing their own kitchens for commercial use. Greg Porter, a personal chef in South Carolina, is an exception to this norm. As the owner of Masterchef Catering, he is able to prepare meals for his clients in his own commercial kitchen. He had been catering for four years when he began reading articles about personal cheffing. "I researched it on the Internet," he says, "and realized that I was already set up to do it."

Greg pursued training from the APCI and branched out into the business of personal chef. An article about him in an area newspaper resulted in five new clients. "I don't know of anyone else doing this in South Carolina," Greg says. He prepares upscale, gourmet meals for his clients.

But cooking isn't the only talent called upon for success in the personal chef business. You must also know meals and ingredients that can be easily frozen and reheated without hurting taste and appearance. You should have an understanding of nutrition, health, and sanitation. Good business sense is also important, as you'll be keeping financial records, marketing your service, and scheduling and billing clients. You'll be testing recipes, experimenting with equipment, and looking for the most cost-effective ways to purchase groceries.

Most personal chefs try to confine their services to their local areas, or neighborhoods, to keep travel from kitchen to kitchen at a minimum. Sometimes, a good personal chef's services become so valuable to a client, the chef will be invited along on a family's vacation.

■ Requirements

High School

A home economics course can give you a good taste of what it's like to be a personal chef. You'll learn something about cooking, budgeting for groceries, and how to use various cooking equipment and appliances. A course in health will teach you about nutrition and a proper diet. Take a business course that offers lessons in bookkeeping and accounting to help you prepare for the record-keeping aspect of the job. A composition or communications course can help you develop the writing skills you'll need for self-promotion. Join a business organization for the chance to meet with small business owners, and to learn about the fundamentals of business operation.

Postsecondary Training

Both the APCI and the USPCA offer self-study courses and seminars on the personal chef business. These courses are not designed to teach people how to cook, but rather how to start a service, how to market it, how much to charge for services, and other concerns specific to the personal chef business. These courses also offer recipes for foods that freeze and store well. The USPCA has begun to accredit community colleges that offer personal chef courses as part of a culinary curriculum.

A formal education isn't required of personal chefs, but a good culinary school can give you valuable cooking experience. "You must be well trained," Greg advises. Greg holds an associate degree in the culinary arts from the Johnson and Wales Culinary Institute, one of the highest ranked cooking schools in the country. With a degree, you can pursue work in restaurants, hotels, health care facilities, and other industries needing the expertise of professional cooks. Culinary programs include courses in vegetarian cooking, menu design, food safety and sanitation, along with courses like economics and math. "But what will teach you more," Greg says, "is working part-time for a restaurant, or a caterer, to learn the business. I've sold food, catered, managed, owned a restaurant—I've done it all, to learn the whole business inside out."

Certification or Licensing

To become a Certified Personal Chef (CPC) with the USPCA, you must work for at least three months as a personal chef. You're required to complete written and practical exams, and submit testimonial letters from at least five different clients. The APCI also offers certification to those who complete their special training course. One quarter to one half of the personal chefs working in the United States and Canada are certified, but certification isn't required to work in the business.

Because you'll be working in the kitchens of your clients, you won't need licensing, or to adhere to the health department regulations of commercial kitchens. A few states, however, do charge permit fees, and require some inspections of the vehicle in which you carry groceries and cooking equipment.

Other Requirements

"Customer service is the most important thing," Greg says. "If you're not people-oriented, you can just hang it up." A strong work ethic and an ambition to succeed are also very important—you'll be promoting your business, building a client list, and handling administrative details all yourself. You'll need patience, too, not only as you prepare quality meals, but as you wait for your business to develop and your client list to grow. You should be a creative thinker, capable of designing interesting menus within the specifications of the client. And, of course, keep in mind that you'll be cooking several meals a day, every day. So it may not be enough to just "like" cooking; you'll need a passion for it.

■ Exploring

The most valuable exploration you can do is to spend time in the kitchen. Learn how to properly use the cooking appliances and utensils. Experiment with recipes. This way you'll learn what meals would work best in a personal chef service. Cook for friends and family, and volunteer to work at school or church events. Contact the professional associations for names of personal chefs in your area. Some chefs participate in mentoring programs to help people learn about the business. Look into part-time work with a restaurant or caterer. Many caterers hire assistants on a temporary basis to help with large events.

■ Employers

As a personal chef, you'll be in business for yourself. Nearly all personal chef services are owned and operated by individuals, though some well-established chefs serving a largely populated, affluent area may hire assistants. If you live in one of these areas and have some cooking experience and education, you may be able to hire on as a cook with a big personal chef operation. But you'll most likely be in business for yourself and will promote your services in areas near your home.

The majority of people who use the services of personal chefs are working couples who have household incomes of over $70,000. Most of these couples have children. Personal chefs also work for people with disabilities and senior citizens.

■ Starting Out

David MacKay, Executive Director and Founder of USPCA, emphasizes that personal cheffing is really for those who have tried other careers and have some experience in the food and service industry. The new personal chef courses being offered by USPCA-accredited community colleges may eventually change this and may attract people with little cooking experience into the business. For now, though, a personal chef course and seminar isn't really enough to get you started unless you also have a culinary education, or a great deal of knowledge about cooking.

If you feel confident that you have the cooking knowledge necessary to prepare good-tasting, well-balanced meals for paying customers, then you should consider training through either APCI or USPCA. Once you have a good sense of the requirements and demands of the job, you can start seeking out clients. Because you'll be cooking with the stoves and appliances of your clients, you don't need to invest much money into starting up your business. An initial investment of about $1,000 will buy you some quality cookware and utensils. But you'll also need a reliable vehicle, as you'll be driving to the grocery store and to the homes of your clients every day.

Volunteer your services for a week or two to friends and neighbors who you think might be interested in hiring you. Print up some fliers and cards, and post your name on community bulletin boards. You may have to offer a low, introductory price to entice clients to try your services.

■ Advancement

Most personal chefs only cook for 1 or 2 clients every day, so maintaining between 5 and 10 clients will keep you pretty busy. If you're able to attract many more customers than you can handle, it may benefit you to hire assistants and to raise your prices. As you advance in the business, you may choose to expand into other areas, like catering large events, writing food-related articles for a local newspaper or magazine, or teaching cooking classes. You may also meet with owners of grocery stores and restaurants, consulting with them about developing their own meal take-out services.

■ Earnings

According to the USPCA, salaries for personal chefs range from about $35,000 annually on the low end to $50,000 on the high end. Some chefs with assistant cooks and a number of clients can make much more than that, but businesses composed of a single owner/operator average about $40,000 per year.

Personal chefs usually sell their services as a package deal-typically $250 to $300 for 10 meals for 2 people, with a fee of $10 to $15 for each additional meal. A complete package may take a full day to prepare. This may seem like a very good wage, but it's important to remember that you're also paying for the groceries. Though you'll be able to save some money by buying staples in bulk, and by planning your menus efficiently, you'll also be spending a lot on fresh meat, fish, and vegetables. One-third or less of your 10-meal package fee will go toward the expense of its ingredients.

■ Work Environment

Greg likes the "personal" aspect of working as a personal chef. "My customers become friends," he says. He appreciates being able to prepare meals based on the individual tastes of his customers, rather than "the 300 people coming into a restaurant." Many personal chefs enter the business after burning out on the demands of restaurant work. As a personal chef, you can make your own schedule, avoiding the late nights, long hours, and weekends of restaurant service.

Though you won't be working in your own home, there isn't much travel involved. You will have to visit a grocery store every morning for fresh meats and produce, but most of the hours of each work day will be spent in one kitchen. Freezer space, pantries, and stoves obviously won't be as large as those in a commercial kitchen, but your work spaces will be much more inviting and homey than those in the back of a restaurant. Your work will be done entirely on your own, with little supervision by your clients.

■ Outlook

The personal chef industry is growing in leaps and bounds, and will continue to do so. The career has become recognized by culinary institutes, and some schools are beginning to include personal chef courses as part of their curriculums. The USPCA predicts that the personal chef industry will contribute over $100 million a year to the U.S. economy by the early 21st century. The national publications *Entrepreneur Magazine, Business Start-ups, US News and World Report,* and others have listed personal chef services as one of the hottest new businesses.

Though the basics of the job will likely remain the same in future years, it is subject to some trends. You will need to keep up with diet fads and new health concerns, as well as trends in gourmet cooking. As the career gains prominence, states may regulate it more rigorously, requiring certain health inspections and permits. Some states may also begin to require special food safety and sanitation training.

■ For More Information

The USPCA offers training courses, certification, and mentorship:

United States Personal Chef Association
3615 Highway 528, Suite 107
Albuquerque, NM 87114-8919
Tel: 505-899-4223 and 800-995-2138
Web: http://www.uspca.com

The APCI holds seminars, offers a self-study course, and maintains an informative Web site with a personal chef message board:

American Personal Chef Institute
4572 Delaware Street
San Diego, CA 92116
Tel: 800-644-8389
Web: http://www.personalchef.com

■ Related Articles

Business, Personal, and Consulting Services

Entrepreneurs

Cooks, Chefs, and Bakers

Franchise Owners

Restaurant and Food Service Managers

Personal Secretaries

■ See Secretaries

Personal Shoppers

■ Overview

People who don't have the time or the ability to go shopping for themselves use the services of *personal shoppers.* Personal shoppers shop department stores, look at catalogs, and surf the Internet for the best buys and most appropriate items for their clients. Relying on a sense of style and an ability to spot a bargain, a personal shopper helps clients develop a wardrobe and find gifts. Though personal shoppers work all across the country, their services are in most demand in large, metropolitan areas.

■ History

For decades, American retailers have been working to create easier ways to shop. Mail-order was an early innovation—catalog companies like Montgomery Wards and Sears and Roebuck started business in the late 19th century to meet the shopping needs of people living in rural areas and small towns. Many consumers relied on mail-order for everything from suits and dresses to furniture and stoves; Sears even sold automobiles through the mail. Shopping for food, clothes, and gifts was considered a household chore, a responsibility that belonged to women. By the late 1800s, shopping had developed into a popular past-time in metropolitan areas. Wealthy women of leisure turned downtown shopping districts into the busiest sections of their cities, as department stores, boutiques, tea shops, and cafes evolved to serve them.

As more women joined the work force after World War II, retailers worked to make their shopping areas more convenient. Supermarkets, shopping centers and malls became popular. Towards the end of the 20th century, shoppers began looking for even more simplicity and convenience. In the 1990s, many companies began to market their products via the Internet. In addition to Internet commerce, overworked men and women are turning to personal shoppers, professional organizers, and personal assistants to fulfill their shopping needs.

■ The Job

Looking for a job where you get to shop all the time, tell people what to wear, and spend somebody else's money? Though this may seem to describe the life of the personal shopper, it's not quite accurate. For one thing, you don't get to shop all the time—you will be spending some time in stores and browsing catalogs, but you're often looking for something very specific, and working as quickly as you can. And you're not so much telling people what to wear, as teaching them how to best match outfits, what colors suit them, and what styles are most appropriate for their workplaces. And, yes, you're spending someone else's money, but it's all for someone else's closet.

So, if you're not too disillusioned, read on: working as a personal shopper may still be right for you. As a personal shopper, you help people who are unable or uninterested in doing their own shopping. You'll be hired to look for that perfect gift for a difficult-to-please aunt. You'll be hired by senior citizens, or people with disabilities, to do their grocery shopping and run other shopping errands. You'll help professionals create a nice, complete wardrobe. All the while, you'll rely on your knowledge of the local marketplace in order to do the shopping quickly and efficiently.

Some personal shoppers use their backgrounds in other areas to assist clients. Someone with a background in real estate may serve as a personal shopper for houses, working for a buyer rather than a seller. These house shoppers inspect houses and do some of the client's bargaining. Those with a background in cosmetology may work as *image consultants*, advising clients on their hair, clothes, and makeup. Another shopper may have some experience in dealing antiques, and will help clients locate particular items. An interior decorator may shop for furniture and art to decorate a home.

If you're offering wardrobe consultation, you'll need to visit the client's home and evaluate his or her clothes. You'll help your clients determine what additional clothes and accessories they'll need, and you'll advise them on what jackets to wear with what pants, what skirt to wear with what blouse. Together with the client, you'll determine what additional clothes are needed to complete the wardrobe, and you'll come up with a budget. Then it's off to the stores.

Irene Kato owns I Kan Do It, a personal shopping service. She offers a variety of services, including at-home wardrobe consultation, closet organization, and gift-shopping. "Most of my shopping so far has been for clothes," Irene says. "I have a fairly good idea of what I'm looking for so I don't spend too much time in any one store if I don't see what I want right away. I can usually find two or three choices for my client and rarely have to shop another day." Irene spends about two to three hours every other day shopping, and spends about two hours a day in her office working on publicity, her budget, and corresponding with clients. Shopping for one client can take about three hours. "I have always enjoyed shopping," Irene says, "and

especially like finding bargains. Waiting in lines, crowds, etc. do not bother me."

As a personal shopper, you'll likely cater to professionals needing business attire and wardrobe consultation. A smaller part of your business will be shopping for gifts. You may even supplement your business by running non-shopping errands, such as purchasing theater tickets, making deliveries, and going to the post office. Many personal shoppers also work as *professional organizers:* they go into homes and offices to organize desks, kitchens, and closets.

In addition to the actual shopping, you'll have administrative responsibilities. You'll do record-keeping, make phone calls, and schedule appointments. Self-promotion will be very important; because personal shopping is a fairly new endeavor, you have the added burden of educating the public about the service. "A personal shopper has no commodity to sell," Irene says, "only themselves. So it is twice as hard to attract clients." To publicize her business, Irene maintains a Web site that lists the services she provides and testimonials from clients. She also belongs to two professional organizations that help her network and develop her business: Executive Women International (EWI) and Giving Referrals to Other Women (GROW).

■ Requirements

High School

Take classes in home economics to develop budget and consumer skills, as well as learn about fashion and home design. If the class offers a sewing unit, you'll learn about tailoring, and can develop an eye for clothes sizes. Math, business, and accounting courses will prepare you for the administrative details of the job. English composition and speech classes will help you develop the communication skills you'll need for promoting your business, and for advising clients about their wardrobes.

PERSONAL SHOPPERS	
SCHOOL SUBJECTS	Business Family and Consumer Science
PERSONAL SKILLS	Following instructions Helping/teaching
WORK ENVIRONMENT	Primarily indoors Primarily multiple locations
MINIMUM EDUCATION LEVEL	High school diploma
SALARY RANGE	$10,000 to $22,000 to $38,000
CERTIFICATION OR LICENSING	None available
OUTLOOK	Faster than the average
DOT	296
GOE	09.04.02
O*NET	4999C

Postsecondary Training

Many people working as personal shoppers have had experience in other areas of business. They've worked as managers in corporations or have worked as salespeople in retail stores. But because of the entrepreneurial nature of the career, you don't need any specific kind of education or training. A small-business course at your local community college, along with classes in design, fashion, and consumer science, can help you develop the skills you'll need for the job. If you're unfamiliar with the computer, you should take some classes to learn desktop publishing programs for creating business cards and other publicity material.

Other Requirements

"I seem to have an empathy for people," Irene says. "After talking with a client I know what they want and what they're looking for. I am a very good listener." In addition to these people skills, a personal shopper should be patient, and capable of dealing with the long lines and customer service of department stores. You should be creative, and able to come up with a variety of gift ideas. A sense of style is important, along with knowledge of the latest brands and designers. You'll need a good eye for colors and fabrics. You should also be well-dressed and organized so that your client will know to trust your wardrobe suggestions.

■ Exploring

If you've spent any time at the mall, you probably already have enough shopping experience. And if you've had to buy clothes and gifts with limited funds, then you know something about budgeting. Irene advises future personal shoppers to work a few years at a retail clothing store. "This way," she says, "you can observe the way people dress, what shapes and sizes we all are, how fashion trends come and go and what stays."

■ Employers

Most of your clients will be professional men and women with high incomes and busy schedules. You'll be working with people with new jobs requiring dress clothes, but also with people who need to perk up an old wardrobe. You may work for executives in corporations who need to buy gifts for large staffs of employees. Some of your clients may be elderly or have disabilities and have problems getting out to do their shopping.

■ Starting Out

The start-up costs can be very low; you may only have to invest in a computer, business cards, and a reliable form of transportation. But it could take you a very long time to develop a regular clientele. You'll want to develop the business part-time while still working full-time at another, more reliable job. Some of your first clients may come from your

workplace—offer free introductory services to a few people and encourage them to spread the word around and hand out your business card. You'll also need to become very familiar with the local retail establishments and the discount stores with low-cost, high-quality merchandise.

"My friends and colleagues at work," Irene says, "were always complimentary on what I wore and would ask where I bought my clothes, where they could find certain items, where were the best sales." Irene was taking the part-time approach to developing her personal shopping service, when downsizing at her company thrust her into the new business earlier than she'd planned. She had the opportunity to take an entrepreneur class at a local private university which helped her devise a business plan and taught her about the pros and cons of starting a business.

■ Advancement

The first few years of your personal shopper business will likely be lean. After a few years of working part-time, you may be able to turn it into a well-paying, full-time job for yourself. As more people learn about your business, you'll take on more clients. Eventually, you may be able to hire an assistant to help you with the administrative work, such as client billing and scheduling.

■ Earnings

Personal shoppers bill their clients in different ways: you'll set a regular fee for services, charge a percentage of the sale, or charge an hourly rate. You might use all these methods in your business; your billing method may depend on the client and the service. For example, when offering wardrobe consultation and shopping for clothes, you may find it best to charge by the hour; when shopping for a small gift, it may be more reasonable to only charge a percentage. Personal shoppers charge anywhere from $25 to $125 an hour; the average hourly rate is about $75. Successful shoppers living in a large city can make between $1,500 and $3,000 a month.

■ Work Environment

You'll have all the advantages of owning your own business, including setting your own hours, and keeping a flexible schedule. But you'll also have all the disadvantages, such as job insecurity and lack of benefits. "I have a bad habit of thinking about my business almost constantly," Irene says. Though you won't have to deal with the stress of a full-time office job, you will have the stress of finding new clients and keeping the business afloat entirely by yourself.

Your office will be in your home, but you'll be spending a lot of time with people, from clients to salespeople. You'll obviously spend some time in department stores; if you like to shop, this can be enjoyable even when you're not buying anything for yourself. In some cases, you'll be visiting client's homes to advise them on their wardrobe. You can expect to do a lot of traveling, driving to a department store after a meeting with a client, then back to the clients with the goods.

■ Outlook

Personal shopping is a new business development, so anyone embarking on the career will be taking some serious risks. There's not a lot of research available about the career, no national professional organization specifically serving personal shoppers, and no real sense of the career's future. The success of Internet commerce will probably have a big effect on the future of personal shopping. If purchasing items through the Internet becomes more commonplace, personal shoppers may have to establish places for themselves on the World Wide Web. Some personal shoppers currently with Web sites offer consultation via email and help people purchase products online.

It may be in your best interest to offer as expansive a service as you can. Professional organizing is being recognized as one of the top home businesses for the future; the membership for the National Association of Professional Organizers (NAPO) has doubled every year since 1985. *Personal assistants,* those who run errands for others, have also caught the attention of industry experts, and there are programs to help you get started as an assistant.

■ For More Information

To learn about the career of professional organizer, contact:

National Association of Professional Organizers
1033 La Posada, Suite 220
Austin, TX 78752
Tel: 512-206-0151
Web: http://www.napo.net

To learn about a program that can help you establish a business as a personal assistant, contact:

Personal Assistants International
1800 30th Street, Suite 220C
Boulder, CO 80301
Tel: 303-443-7646
Web: http://www.personalassistants.com

■ Related Articles

Business, Personal, and Consulting Services
Retail Managers
Retail Sales Workers
Wedding/Party Planners

Personal Trainers

■ Overview

Personal trainers, often known as *fitness trainers,* assist health-conscious people with exercise, weight training, weight loss, diet and nutrition, and medical rehabilitation. During one training session, or over a period of several sessions, trainers teach their clients how to achieve their health and fitness goals. They train in the homes of their clients, their own studio spaces, or in health clubs. Approximately 55,000 personal trainers work in the United States, either independently or on the staff of a fitness center.

■ History

For much of the last half of the 20th century, "98-pound weaklings" were tempted by the Charles Atlas' comic book ads to buy his workout plan and to bulk up. Atlas capitalized on a concern for good health that developed into the fitness industry after World War II. The videotape revolution of the 1980s went hand in hand with a new fitness craze, as Jane Fonda's workout tape became a bestseller and inspired a whole industry of fitness tapes and books. Now most health clubs offer the services of fitness trainers to attend to the personal health concerns of its members.

■ The Job

If you have worked with a personal trainer, then you've learned a great deal about your own health and fitness: you've learned how to properly use weight machines; you've learned about calisthenics and cardiovascular exercise; you've developed a proper diet for yourself. If you've reached your own workout goals, then you may be ready to help others reach theirs. "You have to believe in working out and eating healthy," advises Emelina Edwards, a personal trainer in New Orleans. For 12 years she's been in the business of personal training, a career she chose after whipping herself into great shape at the age of 46. Now, at 58, she has a lot of first-hand experience in

PERSONAL TRAINERS	
SCHOOL SUBJECTS	Health Physical education
PERSONAL SKILLS	Communication/ideas Helping/teaching
WORK ENVIRONMENT	Primarily indoors Primarily multiple locations
MINIMUM EDUCATION LEVEL	Some postsecondary training
SALARY RANGE	$17,000 to $30,000 to $45,000
CERTIFICATION OR LICENSING	Voluntary
OUTLOOK	Faster than the average
DOT	153
O*NET	34058B

training, nutrition, aerobic exercise, and stress management. Emelina says, "You have to practice what you preach."

And practice, Emelina does. Not only does she devote time every day to her own weight training, jogging, and meditation, but she works with 3 to 5 clients in the workout facility in her home. She has a total of about 20 clients, some of whom she assists in one-on-one sessions, and others in small groups. Her clients have included men and women from the ages of 20 to 80 who are looking to improve their general physical conditions, or to work on specific ailments. When meeting with a client for the first time, Emelina gets a quick history of physical problems and medical conditions. "If the problems are serious," she says, "I check with their doctor. If mild, I explain to them what I believe will help." When she discovered that 4 out of 5 people seeking her help suffered from back problems, she did a research on back pain and how to alleviate it through exercise. "I teach people how to do for themselves," she says. "Sometimes I see a person once, or for 3 or 4 sessions, or forever."

In addition to working directly with clients, Emelina is active promoting her line of "Total Body Rejuvenation" products. These products, consisting of audio tapes and books, are based on her years of experience and the many articles she has written for fitness publications. A recent appearance on the popular Spanish talk show has resulted in a number of calls that she has had to handle herself. When she's not training clients, writing articles, and selling products, she's reading fitness publications to keep up on the business, as well as speaking at public events. "When I realized I loved training," she says, "I thought of all the things I could relate to it. So along with the training, I began to write about it, and to give talks on health and fitness."

To have a successful career as a personal trainer, you don't necessarily have to keep as busy as Emelina. You may choose to specialize in certain areas of personal training. You may work as an *athletic trainer,* helping athletes prepare for sports activities. You may specialize in helping with the rehabilitation treatment of people with injuries and other physical problems. Yoga, dance, martial arts, boxing, water fitness: these have all become aspects of special training programs. People call upon the aid of personal trainers to help them quit smoking, to assist with healthy pregnancies, and to maintain mental and emotional stability. Whatever the problem, whether mental or physical, people are turning to exercise and nutrition to help them deal with it.

Many personal trainers have their own studios or home gyms where they train their clients; others go into the homes of their clients. Because of the demands of the workplace, many personal trainers also work in offices and corporate fitness centers. Though most health clubs hire their own trainers to assist with club members, some hire freelance trainers as independent contractors. These indepen-

dent contractors are not considered staff members and don't receive employee benefits. (IDEA, a fitness professional association, found that 30 percent of the personal trainers hired by the fitness centers surveyed were independent contractors.)

■ Requirements

High School

If you're interested in health and fitness, you're probably already taking physical education classes and involved in sports activities. It's also important to take health and family and consumer sciences, which include lessons in diet and nutrition. Business courses can help you prepare for the management aspect of running your own personal training service. Science courses such as biology, chemistry, and physiology are important for your understanding of muscle groups, food and drug reactions, and other concerns of exercise science. If you're not interested in playing on sports teams, you may be able to volunteer as an assistant—you'll learn about athletic training, as well as rehabilitation treatments.

Postsecondary Training

A college education isn't required to work as a personal trainer, but you can benefit from one of the many fitness-related programs offered at colleges across the country. Some relevant college programs are: health education, exercise and sports science, fitness program management, and athletic training. These programs include courses in therapeutic exercise, nutrition, aerobics, and fitness and aging. IDEA recommends a bachelor's degree from a program that includes at least a semester each in anatomy, kinesiology, and exercise physiology. IDEA has some scholarships available to students seeking careers as fitness professionals.

If you're not interested in a full four-year program, many schools offer shorter versions of their bachelor's programs. Upon completing a shorter program, you'll receive either an associate's degree or certification from the school. Once you've established yourself in the business, continuing education courses are important for you to keep up with the advances in the industry. IDEA is one of many organizations that offer independent study courses, conferences, and seminars.

Certification or Licensing

There are so many schools and organizations that offer certification to personal trainers that it has become a concern in the industry. Without more rigid standards, the profession could suffer at the hands of less experienced, less skilled trainers. Some organizations only require membership fees and short tests for certification.

Some health clubs look for certified trainers when hiring independent contractors. If you are seeking certification, you should choose an certifying board that offers scientifically based exams and requires continuing education credits. American Council on Exercise (ACE), the National Federation of Professional Trainers (NFPT), and American Fitness Professionals and Associates (AFPA) are just a few of the many groups with certification programs.

Other Requirements

Physical fitness and knowledge of health and nutrition are the most important assets of personal trainers. "The more intelligently you can speak to someone," Emelina says, "the more receptive they'll be." Your clients will also be more receptive to patience and friendliness. "I'm very enthusiastic and positive," Emelina says. You should be capable of explaining things clearly and recognizing progress and encouraging it. You should be comfortable working one-on-one with people of all ages and in all physical conditions. An interest in reading fitness books and publications is important to your continuing education.

■ Exploring

Your high school may have a weight-training program, or some other extracurricular fitness program; in addition to signing up for the program, assist the faculty who manage it. That way, you can learn about what goes into developing and maintaining such a program. If your school doesn't have a fitness program, seek one out at a community center, or join a health club. You should also try the services of a personal trainer. Stay in good condition and eat a healthy diet. Any number of books and magazines address issues of health and nutrition and offer weight training advice. A magazine specifically for personal trainers is published 10 times a year by IDEA. Seek out part-time work at a gym or health club, and you'll meet trainers and learn about weight machines and certification programs.

■ Employers

As a personal trainer, you'll find opportunities to work for all age groups. Individuals hire the services of trainers, as do companies for the benefit of its employees. Though most health clubs hire personal trainers full-time, a large percentage of clubs hire trainers on an independent contractor basis. Sports and exercise programs at community colleges hire trainers part-time to conduct classes.

Personal trainers can find clients in most major cities in all regions of the country. In addition to health clubs and corporate fitness centers, trainers find work at YMCAs, aerobics studios, and hospital fitness centers.

■ Starting Out

Most people who begin personal training do so after successful experiences with their own training. Once you've developed a good exercise regimen and healthy diet plan

for yourself, you may feel ready to help others. Emelina had hit a low point in her life and had turned to weight training to help her get through the difficult times. "I didn't have a college degree," she says, "and I needed something to do. All I had was weight training." She then called up all the women she knew, promoting her services as a personal trainer. Through word-of-mouth, she built up a clientele.

Some trainers begin by working part-time or full-time for health clubs and, after making connections, they go into business for themselves. As with most small businesses, personal trainers must promote themselves through classified ads, fliers posted in community centers, and other forms of advertisement. Many personal trainers have published guides on how to establish businesses. IDEA offers a package called "The Business of Personal Training," which includes a textbook and audio cassettes with advice on selling and marketing services, developing networking skills, and creating partnerships with retailers, medical professionals, and others.

■ Advancement

After you've taken on as many individual clients as you need to maintain a business, you may choose to lead small group training sessions or conduct large aerobics classes. Some trainers join forces with other trainers to start their own fitness centers. Emelina has advanced her business by venturing out into other areas of fitness instruction, such as publishing books and speaking to groups.

■ Earnings

A compensation survey conducted by IDEA in 1997 listed the wages of personal trainers who worked as independent contractors for health clubs and other fitness centers. Over one-half of the trainers earned an hourly wage of $20 to $29.99, with 26 percent receiving $30 or over. As for average yearly salary, 57 percent received $20,000 to $29,999, 29 percent received $15,000 to $19,999, and 14 percent received $40,000 and over. Most independent contractors are paid by the hour, according to the survey, and the top three factors determining pay are certification, continuing education, and years in the industry. Working with your own clients in your own home, you can charge a higher hourly rate. The average hourly fee for the services of personal trainers is $40 to $50.

■ Work Environment

Personal training is obviously a physically demanding job; but, if you're in good shape and eating the right foods, you should be able to easily handle the demands. Because you'll be working out of your home, your work environment and comfort is under your control. Working in a gym as an independent contractor will also provide a comfortable workplace. Most good gyms maintain a cool temperature.

Whether in a gym or at home, you'll be working directly with your clients, usually in one-on-one training sessions. In this teaching situation, you'll want to keep the workplace quiet and conducive to learning. Exercise as stress management is what many of your clients will be seeking, so most of your training will be calm and soothing.

Sustaining your own business can be both rewarding and difficult. Many trainers appreciate being able to keep their own hours, and to work as little, or as much, as they care to. By setting their own schedules, they can arrange time for their personal workout routines. But, without an employer, there's less security, no benefits, and no steady paycheck. You also have to regularly promote your services and take on new clients.

■ Outlook

IDEA estimates that there was a 100 percent growth in the business of fitness training between 1997 and 1998. This growth will likely continue, and it's why *Working At Home Magazine* listed fitness training as one of the "Best Businesses for Unique Talents" in their ranking of the top 20 home businesses.

As the baby boomers grow older, so will the clientele of personal trainers. Boomers have long been interested in health and fitness, and they'll carry this into their old age. A knowledge of special weight training, stretching exercises, and diets for seniors will be necessary for personal trainers in the years to come.

■ For More Information

For information about the fitness industry in general, and personal training specifically, contact IDEA. IDEA conducts surveys, provides continuing education, and publishes a number of books and magazines relevant to the business.

IDEA Health and Fitness Source
6190 Cornerstone Court East, Suite 204
San Diego, CA 92121-3773
Tel: 800-999-4332, ext. 7
Email: member@ideafit.com
Web: http://www.ideafit.com

For general health and fitness topics, and to learn about certification, contact:

American Council on Exercise (ACE)
5820 Oberlin Drive, Suite 102
San Diego, CA 92121-3787
Tel: 619-535-8227
Web: http://www.acefitness.org

■ Related Articles

Business, Personal, and Consulting Services
Entrepreneurs
Aerobics Instructors and Fitness Trainers
Franchise Owners

Personnel and Labor Relations Specialists

■ Overview

Personnel specialists, also known as *human resources professionals,* formulate policy and organize and conduct programs relating to all phases of personnel activity. *Labor relations specialists* may work with both union and nonunion employees. They represent management during the collective-bargaining process, when contracts with employees are negotiated. They also represent the company at grievance hearings, in which an employee feels management has not fulfilled the requirements of the contract.

■ History

The concept of personnel work developed as businesses grew in size from small owner-operated affairs to large corporate structures with many employees. As these small businesses became large ones, it became increasingly difficult for owners and managers to stay connected and in touch with all their employees—and still run the day-to-day operations of the business. Smart business owners and managers, however, were aware that the success of their company depended upon attracting good employees, matching them to jobs they were suited for, and motivating them to do their best. To meet these needs, the personnel department was established, with a specialist or staff of specialists whose job was to oversee all aspects of employee relations.

The field of personnel, or human resources, grew as business owners and managers became more aware of the importance of human psychology in managing employees. The development of more sophisticated business methods, the rise of labor unions, and the enactment of government laws and regulations concerned with the welfare and rights of employees have all created an even greater need for personnel specialists who can balance the needs of both employees and employers for the benefit of all.

The development and growth of labor unions in the late 1700s and early 1800s created the need for a particular kind of personnel specialist—one who could work as a liaison between a company's management and its unionized employees. Labor relations specialists often try to arbitrate, or settle employer-employee disagreements. One of the earliest formal examples of this sort of arbitration in the United States was the first arbital tribunal created by the New York Chamber of Commerce in 1768. Although arbitration resolutions were often ignored by the courts in preindustrial United States, by the end of World War I, the court system was overwhelmed by litigation—and in 1925 the Federal Arbitration Act was passed, which enforced arbitration agreements reached independent of the courts.

■ The Job

Personnel and labor relations specialists are the liaison between the management of an organization and its employees. They see that management makes effective use of employees' skills, while at the same time improving working conditions for employees and helping them find fulfillment in their jobs. Most positions in this field involve heavy contact with people, at both management and non-management levels.

Both personnel specialists and labor relations specialists are experts in employer-employee relations, although the labor relations specialists concentrate on matters pertaining to union members. Personnel specialists interview job applicants and select or recommend those who seem best suited to the company's needs. Their choices for hiring and advancement must follow the guidelines for equal employment opportunity and affirmative action established by the federal government. Personnel specialists also plan and maintain programs for wages and salaries, employee benefits, and training and career development.

In small companies, one person often handles all the personnel work. This is the case for Susan Eckerle, human resources manager for Crane Federal Credit Union. Susan is responsible for all aspects of personnel management for 50 employees who work at 3 different locations. "I handle all hiring, employee relations counseling, corrective action, administration of benefits, and termination," she says. When Susan started working for the credit union, there was no specific human resources department. Therefore, much of her time is spent establishing policies and procedures to ensure that personnel matters run smoothly and consistently. "I've had to write job descriptions, set up interview procedures, and write the employee handbook," she says. "In addition, we don't have a long-term disability plan, and I think we need one. So I've been researching that."

Although Susan handles all phases of the human resources process, this is not always the case. The personnel department of a large organization may be staffed by many specialists, including recruiters, interviewers, job analysts, and specialists in charge of benefits, training, and labor relations. In addition, a large personnel department might include *personnel clerks* and assistants who issue forms, maintain files, compile statistics, answer inquiries, and do other routine tasks.

Personnel managers and *employment managers* are concerned with the overall functioning of the personnel department and may be involved with hiring, employee orientation, record keeping, insurance reports, wage surveys, budgets, grievances, and analyzing statistical data and reports. *Industrial relations directors* formulate the policies to be carried out by the various department managers.

Of all the personnel specialists, the one who first meets new employees is often the recruiter. Companies depend on *personnel recruiters* to find the best employees available. To do this, recruiters develop sources through contacts within the community. In some cases, they travel extensively to other cities or to college campuses to meet with college placement directors, attend campus job fairs, and conduct preliminary interviews with potential candidates.

Employment interviewers interview applicants to fill job vacancies, evaluate their qualifications, and recommend hiring the most promising candidates. They sometimes administer tests, check references and background, and arrange for indoctrination and training. They must also be familiar and current with guidelines for equal employment opportunity (EEO) and affirmative action.

In very large organizations, the complex and sensitive area of EEO is handled by specialists who may be called *EEO representatives, affirmative-action coordinators,* or *job development specialists.* These specialists develop employment opportunities and on-the-job training programs for minority or disadvantaged applicants; devise systems or set up representative committees through which grievances

PERSONNEL AND LABOR RELATIONS SPECIALISTS	
SCHOOL SUBJECTS	**Business** **Psychology**
PERSONAL SKILLS	**Communication/ideas** **Leadership/management**
WORK ENVIRONMENT	**Primarily indoors** **One location with some travel**
MINIMUM EDUCATION LEVEL	**Bachelor's degree**
SALARY RANGE	**$19,500 to $52,900 to $106,100+**
CERTIFICATION OR LICENSING	**Recommended**
OUTLOOK	**About as fast as the average**
DOT	**166**
GOE	**11.05.02**
NOC	**1223**
O*NET	**21511F**

can be investigated and resolved as they come up; and monitor corporate practices to prevent possible EEO violations. Preparing and submitting EEO statistical reports is also an important part of their work.

Job analysts are sometimes also called *compensation analysts.* They study all of the jobs within an organization to determine job and worker requirements. Through observation and interviews with employees, they gather and analyze detailed information about job duties and the training and skills required. They write summaries describing each job, its specifications, and the possible route to advancement. Job analysts classify new positions as they are introduced and review existing jobs periodically. These job descriptions, or "position classifications," form a structure for hiring, training, evaluating, and promoting employees, as well as for establishing an equitable pay system.

Occupational analysts conduct technical research on job relationships, functions, and content; worker characteristics; and occupational trends. The results of their studies enable business, industry, and government to utilize the general workforce more effectively.

Developing and administering the pay system is the primary responsibility of the *compensation manager.* With the assistance of other specialists on the staff, compensation managers establish a wage scale designed to attract, retain, and motivate employees. A realistic and fair compensation program takes into consideration company policies, government regulations concerning minimum wages and overtime pay, rates currently being paid by similar firms and industries, and agreements with labor unions. The compensation manager is familiar with all these factors and uses them to determine the compensation package.

Training specialists prepare and conduct a wide variety of education and training activities for both new and existing employees. Training programs may cover such special areas as apprenticeship programs, sales techniques, health and safety practices, and retraining displaced workers. The methods chosen by training specialists for maximum effectiveness may include individual training, group instruction, lectures, demonstrations, meetings, or workshops, using such teaching aids as handbooks, demonstration models, multimedia programs, and reference works. These specialists also confer with management and supervisors to determine the needs for new training programs or revision of existing ones, maintain records of all training activities, and evaluate the success of the various programs and methods. Training instructors may work under the direction of an education and training manager. *Coordinators of auxiliary personnel* specialize in training nonprofessional nursing personnel in medical facilities.

Training specialists may help individuals establish career development goals and set up a timetable in which to strengthen job-related skills and learn new ones. Sometimes this involves outside study paid for by the company or rotation to jobs in different departments of the organization. The extent of the training program and the responsibilities of the training specialists vary considerably, depending on the size of the firm and its organizational objectives.

Benefits programs for employees are handled by *benefits managers* or *employee-welfare managers.* The major part of such programs generally involves insurance and pension plans. Since the enactment of the Employee Retirement Income Security Act (ERISA), reporting requirements have become a primary responsibility for personnel departments in large companies. The retirement program for state and local government employees is handled by *retirement officers.* In addition to regular health insurance and pension coverage, employee benefit packages have often grown to include such things as dental insurance, accidental death and disability insurance, automobile insurance, homeowner's insurance, profit sharing and thrift/savings plans, and stock options. The expertise of benefits analysts and administrators is extremely important in designing and carrying out the complex programs. These specialists also develop and coordinate additional services related to employee welfare, such as car pools, child care, cafeterias and lunchrooms, newsletters, annual physical exams, recreation and physical fitness programs, and counseling. Personal and financial counseling for employees close to retirement age is growing especially important.

LEARN MORE ABOUT IT

Want to know more about the personnel and labor relations management? Check out some of the books written for professionals in the field!

Beam, Burton and John McFadden. *Employee Benefits.* Chicago: Dearborn Trade, 1998.

Boyle, Daniel. *Secrets of a Successful Employee Recognition System.* Portland, OR: Productivity Press, 1995.

Connolly, Walter. *A Practical Guide to Equal Employment, Opportunity.* Law Journal Seminars Press, 1982.

Kaplan, Victoria. *The A to Z Book of Managing People.* New York: Berkley Publishing Group, 1996.

Mathis, Robert and John Jackson. *Human Resource Management.* Belmont, CA: West/Wadsworth Publishing Company, 1996.

Mornell, Pierre. *45 Effective Ways for Hiring Smart!: How to Predict Winners and Losers in the Incredibly Expensive People-Reading Game.* Berkeley, CA: Ten Speed Press, 1998.

Stone, Florence. *Coaching, Counseling & Mentoring : How to Choose & Use the Right Tool to Boost Employee Performance.* New York: AMACOM, 1998.

Tracy, Diane. *10 Steps to Empowerment: A Common-Sense Guide to Managing People.* New York: Quill, 1992.

In some cases—especially in smaller companies—the personnel department is responsible for administering the occupational safety and health programs. The trend, however, is toward establishing a separate safety department under the direction of a safety engineer, industrial hygienist, or other safety and health professionals.

Personnel departments may have access to resources outside the organization. These resources include:

Employer relations representatives who promote the use of public employment services and programs among local employers.

Employee-health maintenance program specialists who help set up local government-funded programs among area employers to provide assistance in treating employees with alcoholism or behavioral medical problems.

In companies where employees are covered by union contracts, labor relations specialists form the link between union and management. Prior to negotiation of a collective-bargaining agreement, *labor relations managers* counsel management on their negotiating position and provide background information on the provisions of the current contract and the significance of the proposed changes. They also provide reference materials and statistics pertaining to labor legislation, labor market conditions, prevailing union and management practices, wage and salary surveys, and employee benefit programs. This work requires that labor relations managers be familiar with sources of economic and wage data and have an extensive knowledge of labor law and collective-bargaining trends. In the actual negotiation, the employer is usually represented by the director of labor relations or another top-level official, but the members of the company's labor relations staff play an important role throughout the negotiations.

Specialists in labor relations, or union-management relations, usually work for unionized organizations, helping company officials prepare for collective-bargaining sessions, participating in contract negotiations, and handling day-to-day labor relations matters. A large part of the work of labor relations specialists is analyzing and interpreting the contract for management and monitoring company practices to ensure their adherence to the terms. Of particular importance is the handling of grievance procedures. To investigate and settle grievances, these specialists arrange meetings between workers who raise a complaint, managers and supervisors, and a union representative. A grievance, for example, may concern seniority rights during a layoff. Labor relations disputes are sometimes investigated and resolved by professional conciliators or mediators. Labor relations work requires keeping up to date on developments in labor law, including arbitration decisions, and maintaining close contact with union officials.

Government personnel specialists do essentially the same work as their counterparts in business, except that they deal with public employees whose jobs are subject to civil service regulations. Much of government personnel work concentrates on job analysis, because civil service jobs are strictly classified as to entry requirements, duties, and wages. In response to the growing importance of training and career development in the public sector, however, an entire industry of educational and training consultants has sprung up to provide similar services for public agencies. The increased union strength among government workers has resulted in a need for more highly trained labor relations specialists to handle negotiations, grievances, and arbitration cases on behalf of federal, state, and local agencies.

■ Requirements

Most employers require personnel specialists and labor relations specialists to have a college degree. After high school, Susan attended a four-year college and received a bachelor's degree in retail management, with a minor in psychology. She says that if she was starting over now, however, she would get a degree in human resources instead.

High School

To prepare for a career as a personnel or labor relations specialist, you should take high school classes that will help prepare you for college. A good solid background of the basics—math, science, and English—should be helpful in transitioning into college-level work. You might especially focus on classes that will help you understand and communicate easily with people. Psychology, English, and speech classes are all good choices. Business classes can help you understand the fundamental workings of the business world, which is also important. Finally, foreign language skills could prove very helpful, especially in areas where there are large numbers of people who speak a language other than English.

Postsecondary Training

Although most employers demand a college education even for beginning positions in this field, there is little agreement as to what type of undergraduate training is preferable for personnel and labor relations work. Some employers favor college graduates who have majored in personnel administration or industrial and labor relations, while others prefer individuals with a general business background. Another opinion is that personnel specialists do best with a well-rounded liberal arts education, with a degree in psychology, sociology, counseling, or education. A master's degree in business administration (MBA) is also considered suitable preparation. Students interested in personnel work with a government agency may find it an asset to have a degree in personnel administration, political science, or public administration.

Many colleges and universities offer programs leading to a degree in the field of personnel and labor relations. Some schools have programs in personnel administration or personnel management, while others offer degree or certificate programs in training and development. Preparation for a career in human resource development may also be obtained in departments of business administration, education, instructional technology, organizational development, human services, communication, or public administration.

There are many phases of personnel work, for which a varied educational background would be useful. For example, a combination of courses in the social sciences, behavioral sciences, business, and economics would be entirely appropriate. Individuals preparing for a career as a personnel specialist would also benefit from courses in the principles of management, organization dynamics, and human relations. Other relevant courses might include business administration, public administration, psychology, sociology, political science, economics, and statistics. For prospective labor relations specialists, valuable courses include labor law, collective bargaining, labor economics, labor history, and industrial psychology.

Work in labor relations may require graduate study in industrial or labor relations. While not required for entry-level jobs, a law degree is a must for those who conduct contract negotiations, and a combination of industrial relations courses and a law degree is especially desirable. For a career as a professional arbitrator, a degree in industrial and labor relations, law, or personnel management is required.

Certification or Licensing

Some organizations for human resources professionals offer certification programs, which usually consist of a series of classes and a test. For example, the International Foundation of Employee Benefits Plans offers the Certified Employee Benefits Specialist certification to candidates who complete a series of college-level courses and pass exams on employee benefits plans. The Society for Human Resources Management has two levels of certification, both of which require experience and the passing of a comprehensive exam. Although these certification programs are voluntary, they are worth undertaking for human resources specialists who want to advance in their careers.

Other Requirements

Personnel and labor relations specialists must be able to communicate effectively and clearly both in speech and in writing and deal comfortably and easily with people of different levels of education and experience. "You've got to be people oriented," says Susan. "You have to love people and like working with them. That is huge." Objectivity and fair-mindedness are also necessary in this job, where you often need to consider matters from both the employee's and the employer's point of view. "Being the liaison between management and employees can put you in a tough spot sometimes," Susan says. "You're directly between the two poles, and you have to be able to work with both sides."

These workers cooperate as part of a team; at the same time, they must be able to handle responsibility individually. It is important to be organized because you are often responsible for tracking many different things regarding many different people. "You can't be sloppy in your work habits," Susan says, "because you're dealing with a lot of important information and it all has to be processed correctly."

■ Exploring

High school students who enjoy working with others will find helpful experience in managing school teams, planning banquets or picnics, working in the dean's or counselor's office, or reading books about personnel practices in businesses. You might also contact and interview the personnel director of a local business to find out more about the day-to-day responsibilities of this job. Part-time and summer employment in firms that have a personnel department are very good ways to explore the personnel field. Large department stores usually have personnel departments and should not be overlooked as a source of temporary work.

■ Employers

In 1996, there were approximately 544,000 personnel specialists working in the United States. More than 85 percent of them worked in the private sector. Fourteen percent held jobs in the federal, state, and local governments, and the remainder were self-employed. Of those specialists who worked in the private sector, 40 percent worked in the service industries, including health, business, social services, management, and educational services. Twenty percent worked in manufacturing, and 10 percent worked in the fields of finance, insurance, and real estate. The companies that are most likely to hire personnel specialists are the larger ones, which have more employees to manage.

■ Starting Out

Colleges and universities have placement counselors who can help graduates find employment. Also, large companies often send recruiters to campuses looking for promising job applicants. Otherwise, interested individuals may apply directly to local companies. High school graduates may apply for entry-level jobs as personnel clerks and assistants. Private employment agencies and local offices of the state employment service are other possible sources for work. In addition, newspaper want ads often contain listings of many personnel jobs.

Beginners in personnel work are trained on the job or in formal training programs, where they learn how to classify jobs, interview applicants, or administer employee benefits. Then they are assigned to specialized areas in the personnel department. Some people enter the labor relations field after first gaining experience in general personnel work, but it is becoming more common for qualified individuals to enter that field directly.

■ Advancement

After trainees have mastered the basic personnel tasks, they are assigned to specific areas in the department to gain specialized experience. In time they may advance to supervisory positions or to manager of a major part of the personnel program, such as training, compensation, or EEO/affirmative action. Advancement may also be achieved by moving into a higher position in a smaller organization. A few experienced employees with exceptional ability ultimately become top executives with titles such as director of personnel or director of labor relations. As in most fields, employees with advanced education and a proven track record are the most likely to advance in human resources positions.

■ Earnings

Jobs for personnel and labor relations specialists pay salaries that vary widely depending on the nature of the business and the size and location of the firm, as well as on the individual's qualifications and experience.

According to a survey conducted by the National Association of Colleges and Employers, an entry-level human resources specialist with a bachelor's degree might expect to earn around $25,300 annually. With a master's degree, he or she might make around $39,900. Median salaries for selected occupations at an experienced level are as follows: industrial and labor relations directors, $106,100; training directors, $86,600; compensation and benefits directors, $90,500; recruitment and interviewing managers, $63,800; safety specialists, $42,500; and EEO/affirmative action specialists, $38,200.

The federal government offers new graduates with a bachelor's degree starting salaries of about $19,500 a year. With a master's degree, new workers start at about $29,600; with a doctorate in a personnel field, about $35,800. The average salary for all personnel specialists in the federal government was $52,900 in 1997. Personnel managers in the federal government averaged $44,400.

■ Work Environment

Personnel employees work under pleasant conditions in modern offices. Personnel specialists are seldom required to work more than 35 or 40 hours per week, although they may do so if they are developing a program or special pro-

ject. The specific hours you work as a personnel specialist may depend upon which company you work for. "I work Monday through Friday," says Susan, "but if you work for a company that has weekend hours, you'll probably have to work some weekends too. If you never work weekends, you won't know your employees."

Labor relations specialists often work longer hours, especially when contract agreements are being prepared and negotiated. The difficult aspects of the work may involve firing people, taking disciplinary actions, or handling employee disputes.

■ Outlook

The U.S. Department of Labor predicts that there will be average growth through the year 2006 for personnel, training, and labor relations specialists. Competition for jobs will continue to be strong, however, as there will be an abundance of qualified applicants. Opportunities will be best in the private sector as businesses continue to increase their staffs as they begin to devote more resources to increasing employee productivity, retraining, safety, and benefits. Employment should also be strong with consulting firms who offer personnel services to business that cannot afford to have their own extensive staffs. Job growth in this field may be slowed slightly by the increasing use of computers, which speed up work and make workers more productive.

■ For More Information

For information on personnel careers in the health care industry, contact:

American Society for Healthcare Human Resources Administration
One North Franklin Street
Chicago, IL 60606
Tel: 312-422-3720
Web: http://www.aha.org

For information on careers in training, related industry links, and other resources, contact:

American Society for Training and Development
1640 King Street, Box 1443
Alexandria, VA 22313-2043
Tel: 703-683-8100
Web: http://www.astd.org

For a list of U.S. and Canadian schools offering degrees in industrial relations and human resources, contact:

Industrial Relations Research Association
4223 Social Sciences Building
University of Wisconsin
1180 Observatory Drive
Madison, WI 53706-1373
Web: http://www.irra.ssc.wisc.edu/

For information on training, job opportunities, human resources publications, or online discussions, contact:

International Personnel Management Association
1617 Duke Street
Alexandria, VA 22314
Tel: 703-549-7100
Email: ipma@ipma-hr.org
Web: http://www.ipma-hr.org/

■ Related Articles

Business

Human Resources

Career and Employment Counselors and Technicians

Employment Firm Workers

Ergonomists

Management Analysts and Consultants

Occupational Safety and Health Workers

Personnel Directors

■ See Sports Facility Managers

Pest Control Workers

■ Overview

Pest control workers treat residential and commercial properties with chemicals and mechanical traps to get rid of rodents, insects, and other common pests. They may work for a pest control company, lawn or landscaping firms, or own and operate their own company. In 1996 there were approximately 60,000 pest control workers in the United States. Pest control workers make periodic visits to their clients' properties to make sure they remain pest-free. They may also use chemicals to control diseases and pests that attack lawns, shrubs, and other outdoor vegetation.

■ History

Pest control as an industry is a fairly recent development. In earlier times, fumigators were often brought into houses where someone had suffered a highly contagious disease, such as smallpox to rid the house of germs. The most common method of banishing germs was to burn a large amount of an antiseptic, but highly corrosive, substance such as sulfur. However, this practice was dangerous to humans and often damaged furniture and household goods.

As scientists researched and tested chemicals, it was discovered that the application of certain chemicals as a method of controlling pests in the homes and offices was effective. Chemical research in the 20th century has made possible the use of a variety of substances that are toxic to pests but not harmful to people, pets, or household furnishings, when they are used in the proper quantities.

The use of specially trained pest control technicians arose from this need for precision and knowledge in the application of treatments, and today, the pest control industry does more than $2 billion a year in business.

■ The Job

The majority of pest control workers are employed as *exterminators* or *pest control technicians*. These workers travel to homes, restaurants, hotels, food stores, warehouses and other places where pests are likely to live and breed. Before starting on their route, they load their truck with pesticides, sprayers, and other necessary equipment, and obtain route slips from company offices showing the customers' names and addresses, services to be performed, and inspection comments. Once at the residence to be serviced, they inspect the premises for rodent droppings, physical damage from insects, and other signs of infestation. They then apply chemical sprays for flies, roaches, beetles, silverfish, and other household insects in cracks in floors and walls, under sinks, and in other places that provide shelter for these pests. Mechanical traps are set for rodents, and poisonous bait is left for them in areas where it will not contaminate food supplies or endanger children or pets.

Sometimes the pest infestation in a house requires the pest control worker to resort to fogging, which involves using a vapor that contains a very small amount of pesticide. This fog penetrates the different places where pests hide. Before fogging, the homeowners must leave for a short while, taking any pets with them. The pest control worker then begins to spray a fine pesticide mist that will not leave deposits on fabrics or flat surfaces. The worker wears a mask or respirator and protective clothing during this procedure. This mist is applied starting in the rear of the house and continuing until the worker exits through the front door. After a certain amount of time, the residents can safely return.

Many commercial establishments have service contracts with an exterminating company that sends workers on a biweekly, monthly, or quarterly basis to make sure the premises remain free of pests. Workers often use a concept known as "integrated pest management" with these customers, which involves advising them on housekeeping and home repair methods to keep pests from returning.

A smaller percentage of pest control workers are *termite technicians,* and they perform a more extensive and complicated job than other workers in the industry do.

Termites are particularly destructive pests. Their appetite for wood causes more than $800 million a year in property damage. Termite technicians treat termites, which live in underground colonies and eat away the foundations and structural members of wooden houses, by laying down a chemical barrier between the termite colony and the structure. This barrier traps the termites either underground, where there is no wood to eat, or in the walls, where they cannot find water. Eventually, the colony dies of either starvation or dehydration. Another method of treating termite infestation involves pumping gaseous pesticides into buildings that have been sealed or covered by tarpaulins.

Termite exterminators must sometimes make structural changes to the buildings they service. Holes may have to be drilled in basement floors to pump chemicals into the soil under the house. To keep termites from returning, exterminators must sometimes raise foundations or replace infested wood. If this alteration work is very extensive, however, the homeowner usually calls in building contractors and carpenters. Once termites have been thoroughly eradicated from a building, they are not likely to return soon. For this reason, termite exterminators work on a single-visit rather than a contract basis. The work of several exterminators may be directed and coordinated by an *extermination supervisor.*

In addition to the above duties, pest control workers must keep records of the dates each account is serviced, the type and strength of pesticides used, and any reported pest problems. They may also be responsible for collecting payment on accounts.

■ Requirements

High School
The minimum requirement for pest control occupations is a high school diploma. A college degree is not required, although nearly half of all pest controllers have attended college or earned a degree. High school classes such as voc-tech, earth science, math, writing, and chemistry would be beneficial to this profession.

Postsecondary Training
Pest controllers usually begin as apprentices when they learn pesticide safety and use. At this time they also train in one or more of several pest control categories, such as nuisance pest control. Wood preservation and treatment, termite control, fumigation, and ornamental and turf control. Training includes approximately 10 hours in the classroom and 60 hours on the job for each specialty. Apprentices have up to one year to prepare for and pass the written examinations, after which they become licensed technicians.

Certification or Licensing
Under the Federal Insecticide, Fungicide, and Rodenticide Act, all pesticide products are classified by the degree of hazard they pose to people and the environment. Therefore, pest control workers must be licensed in many states. Some of these states also require the applicant to pass a written examination. Because many pest control workers have access to residences and businesses, most exterminating companies require that their employees be bonded. This means an employee must be at least 18 years of age and have no criminal record.

Other Requirements
Pest control technicians should be able to use good judgment, and follow oral and written instructions well. These workers should also be very conscientious and responsible, because any mistakes they make applying or handling chemicals could result in serious injury or even death for either themselves or their clients.

Pest control workers should be in good general health and able to lift fairly heavy objects. Because route workers usually make service calls alone, they need a driver's license, a safe driving record, and the ability to work well alone. Manual dexterity and mechanical ability are also important for pest control workers. Termite exterminators will also find knowledge of carpentry valuable.

■ Exploring
The student who is interested in becoming a pest control worker might want to talk to someone already working in the field to get a good perspective on what the job is like. Students who have held part-time and summer jobs as drivers or helpers on milk, bakery, dry-cleaning, or other routes will find the experience helpful if they plan to enter this field. Also working part-time in the landscaping and lawn products business would be a good experience. An interest in chemistry or, in the case of termite extermina-

PEST CONTROL WORKERS	
SCHOOL SUBJECTS	Chemistry Mathematics
PERSONAL SKILLS	Following instructions Technical/scientific
WORK ENVIRONMENT	Indoors and outdoors Primarily multiple locations
MINIMUM EDUCATION LEVEL	High school diploma
SALARY RANGE	$12,300 to $25,000 to $32,000
CERTIFICATION OR LICENSING	Required by certain states
OUTLOOK	Little change or more slowly than the average
DOT	383
GOE	05.10.09
NOC	7444
O*NET	67008

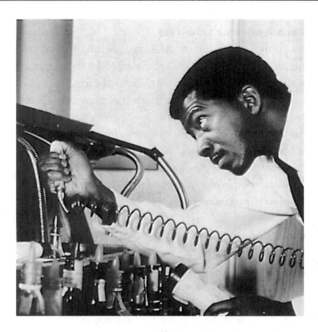

A pest control worker sprays pesticides around a bar. He must be careful not to touch any of the bottles with chemicals.

tors, in woodworking and carpentry is also an asset. More information regarding this profession can be obtained by contacting your local library or the sources at the end of this article.

■ Employers

Pest control jobs are available across the country, but most workers are employed in large, high-density population areas. Pest control companies and landscaping and lawn services may employ pest control workers. Some government agencies and large manufacturing or processing companies may hire their own pest control workers as part of their routine maintenance. Some pest control workers operate their own businesses.

■ Starting Out

Pest control workers usually obtain their jobs through newspaper ads or leads from friends. Job seekers can also apply directly to local pest control firms listed in the Yellow Pages. Owners of firms who use the services of a pest control company may be able to provide job seekers with names of pest control firms. State and local employment offices may have job opportunities with pest control firms.

■ Advancement

Skilled pest control workers may be promoted to higher-paying jobs, such as route manager. Those with job experience and sales aptitude may become pest control salespersons that contact prospective customers to inform

them of the firm's services. They might also become employees of firms that make pesticides or equipment for the industry. Other workers may get jobs as service managers and act as liaisons between the company and its customers. Some may advance to owning their own exterminating businesses. Termite exterminators who are skilled at structural work may become carpenters.

■ Earnings

Salaries vary according to geographic area and company. Beginning technicians can earn between $5 and $6 per hour. More experienced workers can earn up to $10 hourly, which translates into $20,800 annually for a 40-hour a week job. According to the *Occupational Outlook Quarterly*, the lowest 10 percent of pest controllers earn $12,300 annually. The middle 50 percent earn about $25,000 and the top 10 percent earn more than $32,000. Some technicians receive commission based on a percentage of the service charge to the customer, and others receive a percentage of the route income.

Most pest control companies give their full-time workers regular vacations, health insurance, pension plans, and other benefits.

■ Work Environment

Most pest control workers are employed in urban areas, where older buildings provide easy access and good shelter for roaches, rats, and other pests. Termite exterminators tend to work in suburbs and small towns, where there are many wood frame buildings. They usually work a 40-hour week, but may work longer hours in the spring and summer when insects and rodents are most active. Sometimes they have to work nights if an establishment such as a restaurant does not want spraying to occur in front of their customers.

Most pest control technicians work alone, driving to each individual client's property. They must often carry equipment and supplies weighing as much as 50 pounds. The job requires them to work both indoors and outdoors, in all kinds of weather, and they usually spend a large amount of time walking and driving. Termite exterminators may have to crawl under buildings and work in dirty or damp cellars. Therefore, people with a strong aversion to dirt, and who are sensitive to unpleasant odors, or who have strong allergies are not well suited to this field. In addition, because the nature of the job requires workers to spend time in pest-infested houses, anyone who is disturbed or frightened by the various bugs or rodents that might be encountered is not a good candidate.

Most of the chemicals used in exterminating are not harmful to humans if handled properly, although some may be injurious if inhaled in large quantities or left on the skin. Pest control workers wear rubber gloves when mixing the pesticides, in addition to other protective clothing. To make certain that workers are safe, some companies routinely take blood samples to test for any residual amounts of the pesticides they use.

■ Outlook

Approximately 60,000 pest control workers are employed in the United States, and the demand for exterminating services is expected to grow faster than the average for all occupations through the year 2006. This growth will be due to increased environmental and health concerns, greater numbers of dual income households, and newer insulation materials that have made certain homes more susceptible to pest infestation. Although steady advances in science are resulting in safer and more effective pesticides, pest control will always be needed, since most vermin breed rapidly and develop an immunity to pesticides over time. The high turnover rate among employees will also provide a certain number of job openings.

Pest control jobs are concentrated in warmer climates. In 1996, more than half of all pest control workers worked in California, Florida, Georgia, North Carolina, Tennessee, and Texas.

■ For More Information

These two organizations offer information on correspondence courses in pest control:

Center for Urban and Industrial Pest Management
Department of Entomology, Purdue University
1158 Entomology Hall
West Lafayette, IN 47907
Tel: 765-494-4566
Web: http://www.agry.purdue.edu

University of Florida, Department of Independent Study
Independent Study, Correspondence & Distance Education
2209 NW 13th Street, Suite D
Gainesville, FL 32609
Tel: 800-327-4218

For information on education and careers in the pest control industry, contact:

National Pest Control Association
8100 Oak Street
Dunn Loring, VA 22027
Tel: 703-573-8330
800-678-6722
Web: http://www.pestworld.org

■ Related Articles

Business, Personal, and Consulting Services
Construction
Carpenters
Construction Inspectors
Health and Regulatory Inspectors
Janitors and Cleaners

Personnel Managers

■ See Personnel and Labor Relations Specialists

Personnel Recruiters

■ See Employment Firm Workers, Personnel and Labor Relations Specialists

Pet Groomers

■ Overview

Pet groomers comb, cut, trim, and shape the fur of all types of dogs and cats. They comb out the animal's fur and trim the hair to the proper style for the size and breed. They also trim the animal's nails, bathe it, and dry its hair. In the process, they check for flea or tick infestation and any visible health problems. In order to perform these grooming tasks, the pet groomer must be able to calm the animal down and gain its confidence.

■ History

As long as dog has been man's best friend, humans have been striving to keep their animal companions healthy and happy. Pets are often considered members of the family and are treated as such. Just as parents take their children to the doctor for vaccinations and to the barber for haircuts, pets are often treated to regular veterinarian visits and grooming services.

An increasingly urban society and higher standards of living can both be considered significant factors in the grow-

PET GROOMERS	
SCHOOL SUBJECTS	Business Health
PERSONAL SKILLS	Artistic Helping/teaching
WORK ENVIRONMENT	Indoors and outdoors Primarily one location
MINIMUM EDUCATION LEVEL	High school diploma
SALARY RANGE	$14,300 to $20,000 to $26,000+
CERTIFICATION OR LICENSING	Voluntary
OUTLOOK	Faster than the average
DOT	418
GOE	03.03.02
NOC	6483
O*NET	79017C

A pet groomer towels off a now clean golden retriever.

ing number of professional grooming establishments in this country. City-dwellers who live in small apartments have less space to groom their pets than their farm-dwelling forebears had. Many busy professionals have neither the time nor the inclination to learn the proper techniques and purchase the tools needed for grooming. Additionally, many apartment and condominium buildings have regulations to which pet owners must adhere in order to ensure the safety and comfort of tenants. In compact living quarters, people don't want to encounter smelly pups in the hallway. Also, the rise of multiple-income families and an increased standard of living gives animal aficionados the disposable income to pamper their pets with professional grooming services.

Groomers are also called upon to tend to more exotic pets these days, such as ferrets, birds, and reptiles. New developments in animal grooming include high performance clippers and cutting tools and more humane restraining devices. Current trends toward specialized services include perfuming, powdering, styling, and even massage, aromatherapy, and tattooing for pets!

■ The Job

Although all dogs and cats benefit from regular grooming, shaggy, longhaired dogs give pet groomers the bulk of their business. Some types of dogs need regular grooming for their standard appearance; among this group are poodles, schnauzers, cocker spaniels, and many types of terriers. Show dogs, or dogs that are shown in competition, are groomed frequently. Before beginning grooming, the dog groomer talks with the owner to find out the style of cut that the dog is to have. The dog groomer also relies on experience to determine how a particular breed of dog is supposed to look.

The dog groomer places the animal on a grooming table. To keep the dog steady during the clipping, a nylon collar or noose, which hangs from an adjustable pole attached to the grooming table, is slipped around its neck. The dog groomer talks to the dog or uses other techniques to keep the animal calm and gain its trust. If the dog doesn't calm down but snaps and bites instead, the groomer may have to muzzle it. If a dog is completely unmanageable, the dog groomer may ask the owner to have the dog tranquilized by a veterinarian before grooming.

After calming the dog down, the groomer brushes it and tries to untangle its hair. If the dog's hair is very overgrown or is very shaggy such as an English sheepdog's, the groomer may have to cut away part of its coat with scissors before beginning any real grooming. Brushing the coat is good for both longhaired and shorthaired dogs as brushing removes shedding hair and dead skin. It also neatens the coat so the groomer can tell from the shape and proportions of the dog how to cut its hair in the most attractive way. Hair that is severely matted is actually painful to the animal because the mats pull at the animal's skin. Having these mats removed is necessary to the animal's health and comfort.

Once the dog is brushed, the groomer cuts and shapes the dog's coat with electric clippers. Next, the dog's ears are cleaned and its nails are trimmed. The groomer must take care not to cut the nails too short because they may bleed and cause the dog pain. If the nails do bleed, a special powder is applied to stop the bleeding. The comfort of the animal is an important concern for the groomer.

The dog is then given a bath, sometimes by a worker known as a dog bather. The dog is lowered into a stainless steel tub, sprayed with warm water, scrubbed with a special shampoo, and rinsed. This may be repeated several times if the dog is very dirty. The dog groomer has special chemicals that can be used to deodorize a dog that has encountered a skunk or has gone for a swim in foul water. If a dog has fleas or ticks, the dog groomer treats them at this stage by soaking the wet coat with a solution to kill the insects. This toxic solution must be kept out of the dog's eyes, ears, and nose, which may be cleaned more carefully with a sponge or washcloth. A hot oil treatment may also be applied to condition the dog's coat.

The groomer dries the dog after bathing, either with a towel, hand-held electric blower, or in a drier cage with electric blow driers. Poodles and some other types of dogs have their coats fluff-dried, then scissored for the final pattern or style. Poodles, which at one time were the mainstay of the dog grooming business, generally take the longest to groom because of their intricate clipping pattern. Most dogs can be groomed in about 90 minutes, although grooming may take several hours for shaggier breeds whose coats are badly matted and overgrown.

More and more cats, especially longhaired breeds, are now being taken to pet groomers. The procedure for cats is the same as for dogs, although cats are not dipped when bathed. As the dog or cat is groomed, the groomer checks to be sure there are no signs of disease in the animal's eyes, ears, skin, or coat. If there are any abnormalities, such as bald patches or skin lesions, the groomer tells the owner and may recommend that a veterinarian check the animal. The groomer may also give the owner tips on animal hygiene.

Pet owners and those in pet care generally have respect for pet groomers who do a good job and treat animals well. Many people, especially those who raise show dogs, grow to rely on particular pet groomers to do a perfect job each time. Pet groomers can earn satisfaction from taking a shaggy, unkempt animal and transforming it into a beautiful creature. On the other hand, some owners may unfairly blame the groomer if the animal becomes ill while in the groomer's care or for some malady or condition that is not the groomer's fault.

Because they deal with both the pets and their owners, pet groomers can find their work both challenging and rewarding. One owner of a grooming business asserts, "Nothing feels better than developing a relationship with pets and their owners. It's almost like they become an extended part of the family. When working with living animals you accept the responsibility of caring for them to the best of your ability, and the rewards are great. I don't think that can be said of a mechanic or furnace repairman."

■ Requirements

High School

A high school diploma generally is not required for people working as pet groomers. A diploma or GED certificate, however, can be a great asset to people who would like to advance within their present company or move to other careers in animal care that require more training, such as *veterinary technicians*. Useful courses include English, business math, general science, anatomy and physiology, health, zoology, psychology, bookkeeping, office management, typing, art, and first aid.

Postsecondary Training

A person interested in pet grooming can be trained for the field in one of three ways: enrolling in a pet grooming school; working in a pet shop or kennel and learning on the job; or reading one of the many books on pet grooming and practicing on his or her own pet.

To enroll in most pet grooming schools, a person must be at least 17 years old and fond of animals. Previous experience in pet grooming can sometimes be applied for course credits. Students study a wide range of topics including the basics of bathing, brushing, and clipping, the care of ears and nails, coat and skin conditions, animal anatomy terminology, and sanitation. They also study customer relations, which is very important for those who plan to operate their own shops. During training, students practice their techniques on actual animals, which people bring in for grooming at a discount rate.

Students can also learn pet grooming while working for a grooming shop, kennel, animal hospital, or veterinarian's office. They usually begin with tasks such as shampooing dogs and cats, and trimming their nails, then gradually work their way up to brushing and basic haircuts. With experience, they may learn more difficult cuts and use these skills to earn more pay or start their own business.

The essentials of pet grooming can also be learned from any of several good books available on grooming. These books contain all the information a person needs to know to start his or her own pet grooming business, including the basic cuts, bathing and handling techniques, and type of equipment needed. Still, many of the finer points of grooming, such as the more complicated cuts and various safety precautions, are best learned while working under an experienced groomer. There still is no substitute for on-the-job training and experience.

Certification or Licensing

Presently, state licensing or certification is not required, and there are no established labor unions for pet groomers. To start a grooming salon or other business, a license is needed from the city or town in which a person plans to practice.

Other Requirements

The primary qualification for a person who wants to work with pets is a love of animals. Animals can sense when someone does not like them or is afraid of them. A person needs certain skills in order to work with nervous, aggressive, or fidgety animals. They must be patient with the animals, able to gain their respect, and enjoy giving the animals a lot of love and attention. Persistence and endurance are also helpful as grooming one animal can take several hours of strenuous work. Groomers should enjoy working with their hands and have good eyesight and manual dexterity to accurately cut a clipping pattern.

■ Exploring

To find out if they are suited for a job in pet grooming, students should familiarize themselves with animals as much as possible. This can be done in many ways, starting with the proper care of the family pet. Students can also offer to tend to the pets of friends and neighbors to see how well they handle unfamiliar animals. Youth organizations such as the Boy Scouts, Girl Scouts, and 4-H Clubs sponsor projects that give members the chance to raise and care for animals. Students also may do part-time or volunteer work caring for animals at an animal hospital, kennel, pet shop, animal shelter, nature center, or zoo.

■ Employers

Grooming salons, kennels, pet shops, veterinary practices, animal hospitals, and grooming schools employ pet groomers. The pet business is thriving all over the country, and the opportunities for groomers are expected to increase steadily in the coming years. Although most employers can offer attractive benefits packages, many pet groomers choose to go into business for themselves rather than turn over 40 to 50 percent of their fees to their employers. Graduates of accredited pet grooming schools benefit from the schools' job placement services, which can help students find work in the kind of setting they prefer.

■ Starting Out

The best ways for most people to gain a thorough knowledge of dog grooming is through hands-on experience and enrollment in an accredited pet grooming course or a pet grooming school. The National Dog Groomers Association of America (NDGAA) provides a referral listing of approximately 40 dog grooming schools throughout the United States to persons who send a stamped, self-addressed envelope. Three schools of dog grooming are recognized by the National Association of Trade and Technical Schools (NATTS): the Pedigree Professional School of Dog Grooming, the New York School of Dog Grooming (three branches), and the Nash Academy of Animal Arts. Many other dog grooming schools advertise in dog and pet magazines. It is important for students to choose an accredited, licensed school in order to increase both their employment opportunities and professional knowledge.

Graduates from dog grooming schools can take advantage of the school's job placement services. Generally, there are more job openings than qualified groomers to fill them, so new graduates may have several job offers to consider. These schools learn of job openings in all parts of the United States and are usually happy to contact prospective employers and write letters of introduction for graduates.

The NDGAA also promotes professional identification through membership and certification testing throughout the United States and Canada. The NDGAA offers continuing education, accredited workshops, certification testing, seminars, insurance programs, a job placement program, membership directory, and other services and products. Other associations of interest to dog groomers are the Humane Society of the United States and the United Kennel Club. Because dog groomers are concerned with the health and safety of the animals they service, membership in groups that promote and protect animal welfare is very common.

Other sources of job information include the classified ads of daily newspapers and listings in dog and pet magazines. Job leads may be available from private or state employment agencies or from referrals of salon or kennel owners. People looking for work should phone or send letters to prospective employers, inform them of their qualifications, and, if invited, visit their establishments.

■ Advancement

Pet groomers who work for other people may advance to a more responsible position such as office manager or dog trainer. If dog groomers start their own shops, they may become successful enough to expand or to open branch offices or area franchises. Skilled groomers may want to work for a dog grooming school as an instructor, possibly advancing to a job as a school director, placement officer, or other type of administrator.

The pet industry is booming, so there are many avenues of advancement for groomers who like to work with pets. With more education, a groomer may get a job as a veterinary technician or assistant at a shelter or animal hospital. Those who like to train dogs may open obedience schools, train guide dogs, work with field and hunting dogs, or even train stunt and movie dogs. People can also open their own kennels, breeding and pedigree services, gaming dog businesses, or pet supply distribution firms. Each of these requires specialized knowledge and experience, so additional study, education, and work is often needed.

■ Earnings

Groomers charge either by the job or the hour. If they are on the staff of a salon or work for another groomer, they get to keep 50 to 60 percent of the fees they charge. For this reason, many groomers branch off to start their own businesses. "I would never want to go back to working for someone else or giving up a commission on my groomings," says one owner-operator of a grooming business.

According to the 1998 edition of the *O*Net Dictionary of Occupational Titles*, animal groomers can expect to earn $14,300 per year, while the Bureau of Labor Statistics suggests that the top 10 percent of workers in the field earned more than $500 per week ($26,000 per year) in 1996. Those who own and operate their own grooming services can earn significantly more, depending on how hard they work, the clientele they service, and the economy of the area in which they work.

Groomers generally buy their own clipping equipment, including barber's shears, brushes, and clippers. A new set of equipment costs around $325; used sets cost less. Groomers employed full time at salons, grooming schools, pet shops, animal hospitals, and kennels often get a full range of benefits, including paid vacations and holidays, medical and dental insurance, and retirement pensions.

■ Work Environment

Salons, kennels, and pet shops, as well as gaming and breeding services, should be clean and well lighted, with modern equipment and clean surroundings. Establishments that do not meet these standards endanger the health of the animals that are taken there and the owners of these establishments should be reported. Groomers who are self-employed may work out of their homes. Some groomers buy vans and convert them into grooming shops. They drive them to the homes of the pets they work on, which many owners find very convenient. Those who operate these groommobiles may work on 30 or 40 dogs a week, and factor their driving time and expenses into their fees.

Groomers usually work a 40-hour week and may have to work evenings or weekends. Those who own their own shops or work out of their homes, like other self-employed people, work very long hours and may have irregular schedules. One groomer points out that, "You can't just decide to call in sick when you have seven dogs scheduled to be groomed that day. We have had midnight emergency calls from clients needing immediate help of one kind or another with their pet." Many groomers/business owners believe that the occasionally hectic schedule of the field is not always a negative aspect, since they take great pride in being able to offer personal service and care to both critters and clients.

Groomers are on their feet much of the day, and their work can get very tiring when they have to lift and restrain large animals. They must wear comfortable clothing that allows for freedom of movement, but they should also be presentable enough to deal with pet owners and other clients.

When working with any sort of animal, a person may encounter bites, scratches, strong odors, fleas, and other insects. They may have to deal with sick or bad-tempered animals. The groomer must regard every animal as a unique individual and treat it with respect. Groomers need to be careful while on the job, especially when handling flea and tick killers, which are toxic to humans (as well as the pests!).

■ Outlook

The demand for skilled dog groomers has grown faster than average, and is expected to continue through the year 2006. The NDGAA estimates that more than 30,000 dog groomers are currently employed, and expects that more than 3,000 new groomers will be needed every year during the next decade.

Every year more people are keeping dogs and cats as pets. They are spending more money to pamper their animals, but often don't have enough free time or the incli-

nation to groom their pets themselves. Grooming is not just a luxury for pets, however, because regular attention makes it more likely that any injury or illness will be noticed and treated.

Also, as nontraditional pets become more mainstream, innovative groomers will need to take advantage of new techniques and facilities for bringing animals other than dogs and cats into the pet salon.

■ For More Information

The National Dog Groomers Association of America (NDGAA) publishes a newsletter for dog groomers that includes information on shows, new grooming products and techniques, and workshop and certification test sites and dates. For information and/or list of dog grooming schools across the country, send a stamped, self-addressed #10 envelope to:

National Dog Groomers Association of America, Inc.
PO Box 101
Clark, PA 16113
Tel: 724-962-2711
Web: http://www.nauticom.net/www/ndga/index.html

For information on pet grooming schools and certification, contact:

New York School of Dog Grooming
248 East 34th Street
New York, NY 10016
Tel: 212-685-3776

California School of Dog Grooming
727 West San Marcos Boulevard, Suite 105A
San Marcos, CA 92069
Tel: 760-471-0787 or 800-949-3746
Email: csdg@pacbell.net
Web: http://www.csdg.net/index1a.htm

Nash Academy of Animal Arts
857 Lane Allen Plaza
Lexington, KY 40504
Tel: 606-276-5301

For more information about grooming and related professions, contact:

Intergroom
250 East 73rd Street, Suite 4-F
New York, NY 10021-4311
Tel: 212-628-3537
Email: intergroom@aol.com
Web: http://www.intergroom.com/

■ Related Articles

Animals
Animal Caretakers
Animal Handlers
Animal Shelter Employees
Animal Trainers
Pet Shop Workers
Pet Sitters
Veterinary Technicians

Pet Shop Workers

Larger pet stores may employ a sizeable staff, including cashiers, managers, bookkeepers, pet groomers, animal caretakers, and animal trainers. Smaller stores may employ a few individuals trained to perform a variety of responsibilities. Regardless of the size of the store or the duties of its staff, employees of pet stores all should be knowledgeable about animals and products and friendly and helpful to customers. All members of the pet shop staff contribute to the running of the shop through their various responsibilities, such as stocking shelves, ordering products, assisting customers, cleaning cages and aquariums, and maintaining records. Some pet shops offer specialized services such as grooming, training, and boarding. Most shops sell smaller animals such as birds, fish, and hamsters. Some shops do sell larger animals like cats and dogs, but most buyers will turn to breeders or shelters for these pets. Pet shop workers are in the retail business, so people skills may be more important for this type of work than for some other careers in animal care.

While a high school diploma is the minimum educational requirement for most positions in a pet shop, those aspiring to management or ownership would do well to pursue degrees in business. A background in accounting, marketing, math, and the sciences will be an important component of the education of anyone interested in a career with a pet shop. Some pet shops also like to hire people with veterinary technician training.

The outlook for pet shop workers is good. The pet retail industry is expected to grow through the year 2006. Larger pet stores will take over much of the business of smaller "mom and pop" shops. The smaller stores that survive will be those that successfully promote and provide a more personalized approach and more knowledgeable assistance than are available at the large operations.

■ Related Articles

Animals
Animal Caretakers
Animal Shelter Employees
Animal Trainers
Horse Grooms
Pet Groomers
Pet Sitters
Veterinary Technicians

Pet Sitters

■ Overview

When pet owners are on vacation or working long hours, they hire *pet sitters* to come to their homes and visit their animals. During short, daily visits, pet sitters feed the animals, play with them, clean up after them, give them medications when needed, and let them in and out of the house for exercise. *Dog walkers* may be responsible only for taking their clients' pets out for exercise. Pet sitters may also be available for overnight stays, looking after the houses of clients as well as their pets.

■ History

Animals have been revered by humans for centuries, as is evidenced by early drawings on the walls of caves and tombs-cats were even considered sacred by the ancient Egyptians. Though these sacred cats may have had their own personal caretakers, it has only been within the last 10 years that pet sitting has evolved into a successful industry and a viable career option. Before groups such as the National Association of Professional Pet Sitters (NAPPS), which formed in the early 1980s, and Pet Sitters International (PSI) were developed, pet sitting was regarded as a way for people with spare time to make a little extra money on the side. Like babysitting, pet sitting attracted primarily teenagers and women; many children's books over the last century have depicted the trials and tribulations of young entrepreneurs in the business of pet sitting and dog walking. Patti Moran, the founder of both NAPPS and PSI, and author of *Pet Sitting for Profit*, is credited with helping pet sitters gain recognition as successful small business owners. Though many people still only pet sit occasionally for neighbors and friends, others are developing long lists of clientele and proving strong competition to kennels and boarding facilities.

Pet shop workers show off a toy fox terrier.

The Job

If you live in a big city, you've seen them hit the streets with their packs of dogs. Dragged along by four or five leashes, the pet sitter walks the dogs down the busy sidewalks, allowing the animals their afternoon exercise while the pet owners are stuck in the office. You may not have realized it, but those dog walkers are probably the owners of thriving businesses. Though a hobby for some, pet sitting is for others a demanding career with many responsibilities. Michele Finley is one of these pet sitters, in the Park Slope neighborhood of Brooklyn, New York. "A lot of people seem to think pet sitting is a walk in the park (pun intended)," she says, "and go into it without realizing what it entails (again)."

For those who can't bear to leave their dogs or cats at kennels or boarders while they are away, pet sitters offer peace of mind to the owners, as well as their pets. With a pet sitter, pets can stay in familiar surroundings, as well as avoid the risks of illnesses passed on by other animals. The pets are also assured routine exercise and no disruptions in their diets. Most pet sitters prefer to work only with cats and dogs, but pet sitters are also called upon to care for birds, reptiles, gerbils, fish, and other animals.

With their own set of keys, pet sitters let themselves into the homes of their clients and care for their animals while they're away at work or on vacation. Pet sitters feed the animals, make sure they have water, and give them their medications. They clean up any messes the animals have made and clean litter boxes. They give the animals attention, playing with them, letting them outside, and taking them for walks. Usually, a pet sitter can provide pet owners with a variety of personal pet care services—they may take a pet to the vet, offer grooming, sell pet-related products, and give advice. Some pet sitters take dogs out into the country, to mountain parks, or to lakes, for exercise in wide-open spaces. "You should learn to handle each pet as an individual," Finley advises. "Just because Fluffy likes his ears scratched doesn't mean Spot does."

Pet sitters typically plan one to three visits (of 30 to 60 minutes in length) per day, or they may make arrangements to spend the night. In addition to caring for the animals, pet sitters also look after the houses of their clients. They bring in the newspapers and the mail; they water the plants; they make sure the house is securely locked. Pet sitters generally charge by the hour or per visit. They may also have special pricing for overtime, emergency situations, extra duties, and travel.

Most pet sitters work alone, without employees, no matter how demanding the work. Though this means getting to keep all the money, it also means keeping all the responsibilities. A successful pet sitting service requires a fair amount of business management. Finley works directly with the animals from 10:00 AM until 5:00 or 6:00 PM,

with no breaks; upon returning home, she will have five to 10 phone messages from clients. Part of her evening then consists of scheduling and rescheduling appointments, offering advice on feeding, training, and other pet care concerns, and giving referrals for boarders and vets. But despite these hours, and despite having to work holidays, as well as days when she's not feeling well, Michele appreciates many things about the job. "Being with the furries all day is the best," she says. She also likes not having to dress up for work and not having to commute to an office.

Requirements

As a pet sitter, you'll be running your own business all by yourself; therefore you should take high school courses such as accounting, marketing, and office skills. Computer science will help you learn about the software you'll need for managing accounts and scheduling. Join a school business group that will introduce you to business practices and local entrepreneurs.

Science courses such as biology and chemistry, as well as health courses, will give you some good background for developing animal care skills. As a pet sitter, you'll be overseeing the health of the animals, their exercise, and their diets. You'll also be preparing medications and administering eye and ear drops.

As a high school student, you can easily gain hands-on experience as a pet sitter. If you know anyone in your neighborhood with pets, volunteer to care for the animals whenever the owners go on vacation. Once you've got experience and a list of references, you may even be able to start a part-time job for yourself as a pet sitter.

Many pet sitters start their own businesses after having gained experience in other areas of animal care. Vet techs and pet shop workers may promote their animal care skills to develop a clientele for more profitable pet sitting careers. Graduates from a business college may recognize pet sitting as a great way to start a business with little overhead. But neither a vet tech qualification nor a business degree is required to become a successful pet sitter. And the only special training you need to pursue is actual

PET SITTERS	
SCHOOL SUBJECTS	**Business** **Family and Consumer Science**
PERSONAL SKILLS	**Helping/teaching** **Following instructions**
WORK ENVIRONMENT	**Indoors and outdoors** **Primarily multiple locations**
MINIMUM EDUCATION LEVEL	**High school diploma**
SALARY RANGE	**$5,000 to $20,000 to $40,000**
CERTIFICATION OR LICENSING	**Voluntary**
OUTLOOK	**Faster than the average**

A pet sitter gives her customer's dog his daily walk.

experience. A local pet shop or chapter of the ASPCA may offer seminars in various aspects of animal care; the NAPPS offers a mentorship program, as well as a newsletter, while PSI sponsors correspondence programs. There are many publications devoted to pet care, such as *Dog Fancy* and *Cat Watch*, which can educate you about pet health and behavior.

PSI offers accreditation on four levels: *Pet Sitting Technician*, *Advanced Pet Sitting Technician*, *Master Professional Pet Sitter*, and Accredited Pet Sitting Service. Pet sitters receive accreditation upon completing home study courses in such subjects as animal nutrition, office procedures, and management. Because the accreditation program was developed only within the last few years, PSI estimates that less than 10 percent of pet sitters working today are accredited. That number is likely to increase, though there are no plans for any kind of government regulation that would require accreditation. "I really don't think such things are necessary," Michele says. "All you

need to know can be learned by working for a good sitter and reading pet health and behavioral newsletters."

Though there is no particular pet-sitting license required of pet sitters, insurance protection is important. Liability insurance protects the pet sitter from lawsuits; both NAPPS and PSI offer group liability packages to its members. Pet sitters must also be bonded. Bonding assures the pet owners that if anything is missing from homes after a pet sitting appointment, they can receive compensation immediately.

You must love animals and animals must love you. But this love for animals can't be your only motivation—keep in mind that, as a pet sitter, you'll be in business for yourself. You won't have a boss to give you assignments, and you won't have a secretary or bookkeeper to do the paperwork. You also won't have employees to take over on weekends, holidays, and days when you're not feeling well. Though some pet sitters are successful enough to afford assistance, most must handle all the aspects of their businesses by themselves. You should be self-motivated and as dedicated to the management of your business as you are to the animals.

Pet owners are entrusting you with the care of their pets and their homes, so you must be trustworthy and reliable. You should also be organized and prepared for emergency situations. And not only must you be patient with the pets and their owners, but also with the development of your business: it will take a few years to build up a good list of clients.

As a pet sitter, you must also be ready for the dirty work—you'll be cleaning litter boxes and animal messes within the house. On dog walks, you'll be picking up after them on the street. You may be giving animals medications. You'll also be cleaning aquariums and bird cages.

"Work for an established pet sitter to see how you like it," Finley advises. "It's a very physically demanding job and not many can stand it for long on a full-time basis." Pet sitting isn't for those who just want a nine-to-five desk job. Your day will be spent moving from house to house, taking animals into backyards, and walking dogs around the neighborhoods. Though you may be able to develop a set schedule for yourself, you really will have to arrange your work hours around the hours of your clients. Some pet sitters start in the early morning hours, while others only work afternoons or evenings. To stay in business, a pet sitter must be prepared to work weekends, holidays, and long hours in the summertime.

■ Exploring

There are many books, newsletters, and magazines devoted to pet care. *Pet Sitting for Profit*, by Patti Moran, and *The Professional Pet Sitter* by Lori and Scott Mangold, are a few of the books that can offer insight into pet sitting as a career. Magazines such as *Cat Fancy* can also teach you about the requirements of animal care. And there are any number of books discussing the ins and outs of small business ownership.

Try pet sitting for a neighbor or family member to get a sense of the responsibilities of the job. Some pet sitters hire assistants on an independent contractor basis; contact an area pet sitter listed in the phone book or with one of the professional organizations, and see if you can "hire on" for a day or two. Not only will you learn firsthand the duties of a pet sitter, but you'll also see how the business is run.

■ Employers

Nearly all pet sitters are self-employed, although a few may work for other successful pet sitters who have built up a large enough clientele to require help. It takes most pet sitters an appreciable period of time to build up a business substantial enough to make a living without other means of income. However, the outlook for this field is excellent and start-up costs are minimal, making it a good choice for animal lovers who want to work for themselves. For those who have good business sense and a great deal of ambition, the potential for success is good.

■ Starting Out

You're not likely to find job listings under "pet sitter" in the newspaper. Most pet sitters schedule all their work themselves. However, you may find ads in the classifieds or in weekly community papers, from pet owners looking to hire pet sitters. Some people who become pet sitters have backgrounds in animal care—they may have worked for vets, breeders, or pet shops. These people enter the business with a client list already in hand, having made contacts with many pet owners. But, if you're just starting out in animal care, you need to develop a list of references. This may mean volunteering your time to friends and neighbors, or working very cheaply. If you're willing to actually stay in the house while the pet owners are on vacation, you should be able to find plenty of pet sitting opportunities in the summertime. Post your name, phone number, and availability on the bulletin boards of grocery stores, colleges, and coffee shops around town. Once you've developed a list of references, and have made connections with pet owners, you can start expanding, and increasing your profits.

■ Advancement

Your advancement will be a result of your own hard work; the more time you dedicate to your business, the bigger the business will become. The success of any small business can be very unpredictable. For some, a business can build very quickly, for others it may take years. Some pet sitters start out part-time, perhaps even volunteering, then may find themselves with enough business to quit their

full-time jobs and to devote themselves entirely to pet sitting. Once your business takes off, you may be able to afford an assistant, or an entire staff. Some pet sitters even have franchises across the country. You may even choose to develop your business into a much larger operation, such as a dog day care facility.

■ Earnings

Pet sitters set their own prices, charging by the visit, the hour, or the week. They may also charge consultation fees, and additional fees on holidays. They may have special pricing plans in place, such as for emergency situations or for administering medications. Depending on the kinds of animals (sometimes pet sitters charge less to care for cats than dogs), pet sitters generally charge between $8 and $15 a visit (with a visit lasting between 30 and 60 minutes). PSI conducted a recent salary survey and discovered that the range was too great to determine a median. Some very successful pet sitters have annual salaries of over $100,000, while others only make $5,000 a year. Though a pet sitter can make a good profit in any area of the country, a bigger city will offer more clients. Pet sitters in their first five years of business are unlikely to make more than $10,000 a year; pet sitters who have had businesses for eight years or more may make more than $40,000 a year.

■ Work Environment

Some pet sitters prefer to work close to their homes; Michele only walks dogs in her Brooklyn neighborhood. In a smaller town, however, pet sitters have to do a fair amount of driving from place to place. Depending on the needs of the animals, the pet sitter will let the pets outside for play and exercise. Although filling food and water bowls and performing other chores within the house is generally peaceful work, walking dogs on the busy city sidewalks can be stressful. And in the wintertime, you'll spend a fair amount of time out in the inclement weather. "Icy streets are murder," Finley says. "And I don't like dealing with people who hate dogs and are always yelling to the get the dog away from them."

Though you'll have some initial interaction with pet owners when getting house keys, taking down phone numbers, and meeting the pets and learning about their needs,

SPECIAL PROTECTION

Professional pet sitters do more than just take care of pets; they also help protect homes from theft. How? By:

*Turning on different lamps at different times

*Opening and closing curtains and blinds

*Arriving in unmarked cars

*Wearing everyday attire

*Bringing in newspapers and mail

most of your work will be alone with the animals. But you won't be totally isolated; if dog walking in the city, you'll meet other dog owners and other people in the neighborhood.

■ Outlook

Pet sitting as a small business is expected to skyrocket in the coming years. Most pet sitters charge fees comparable to kennels and boarders, but some charge less. And many pet owners prefer to leave their pets in the house, rather than take the pets to unfamiliar locations. This has all made pet sitting a desirable and cost-effective alternative to other pet care situations. Pet sitters have been successful in cities both large and small. In the last few years, pet sitting has been featured in the *Wall Street Journal* and other national publications; last year, *Woman's Day* magazine listed pet sitting as one of the top-grossing businesses for women. Pet Sitters International has grown 500 percent in the last four years.

Because a pet sitting business requires little money to start up, many more people may enter the business hoping to make a tidy profit. This could lead to heavier competition; it could also hurt the reputation of pet sitting if too many irresponsible and unprepared people run bad businesses. But if pet owners remain cautious when hiring pet sitters, the unreliable workers will have trouble maintaining clients.

■ For More Information

For career and small business information, as well as general information about pet sitting, contact these organizations:

Pet Sitters International
418 East King Street
King, NC 27021-9163
Tel: 336-983-9222
Web: http://www.petsit.com

National Association of Professional Pet Sitters
1200 G Street, NW, Suite 760
Washington, DC 20005
Tel: 202-393-3317
Web: http://www.petsitters.com

■ Related Articles

Animals
Animal Caretakers
Animal Handlers
Animal Shelter Employees
Animal Trainers
Pet Groomers
Pet Shop Workers
Veterinary Technicians

Petroleum Engineers

■ Overview

Petroleum engineers apply the principles of geology, physics, and the engineering sciences to the recovery, development, and processing of petroleum. As soon as an exploration team has located an area that could contain oil or gas, petroleum engineers begin their work, which includes determining the best location for drilling new wells, as well as the economic feasibility of developing them. They are also involved in operating oil and gas facilities, monitoring and forecasting reservoir performance, and utilizing enhanced oil recovery techniques that extend the life of wells.

■ History

Within a broad perspective, the history of petroleum engineering can be traced back hundreds of millions of years to when the remains of plants and animals blended with sand and mud and transformed into rock. It is from this ancient underground rock that petroleum is taken, for the organic matter of the plants and animals decomposed into oil during these millions of years and accumulated into pools deep underground.

In primitive times, people did not know how to drill for oil; instead, they collected the liquid substance after it had seeped to above ground surfaces. Petroleum is known to have been used at that time for caulking ships and for concocting medicines.

Petroleum engineering as we know it today was not established until the mid-1800s, an incredibly long time after the fundamental ingredients of petroleum were deposited within the earth. In 1859, the American Edwin Drake was the first person to ever pump the so-called rock oil from under the ground, an endeavor that, before its success, was laughed at and considered impossible. Forward-thinking investors, however, had believed in the operation and thought that underground oil could be used as inexpensive fluid for lighting lamps and for lubricating machines (and therefore could make them rich). The drilling of that first well, in Titusville, Pennsylvania (1869), ushered in a new worldwide era—the oil age.

At the turn of the century, petroleum was being distilled into kerosene, lubricants, and wax. Gasoline was considered a useless by-product and was run off into rivers as waste. However, this changed with the invention of the internal combustion engine and the automobile. By 1915 there were more than half a million cars in the United States, virtually all of them powered by gasoline.

Edwin Drake's drilling operation struck oil 70 feet below the ground. Since that time, technological advances have been made, and a professional field of petroleum engineering has been established. Today's operations drill as far down as six miles. Because the United States began to rely so much on oil, the country contributed significantly to creating schools and educational programs in this engineering discipline. The world's first petroleum engineering curriculum was devised in the United States in 1914; today there are 30 U.S. universities that offer petroleum engineering degrees.

The first schools were concerned mainly with developing effective methods of locating oil sites and with devising efficient machinery for drilling wells. Over the years, as sites have been depleted, engineers have been more concerned with formulating methods for extracting as much oil as possible from each well. Today's petroleum engineers focus on issues such as computerized drilling operations; however, because usually only about 40 to 60 percent of each site's oil is extracted, engineers must still deal with designing optimal conditions for maximum oil recovery.

■ The Job

Petroleum engineer is a rather generalized title that encompasses several specialties, each one playing an important role in ensuring the safe and productive recovery of oil and natural gas. In general, petroleum engineers are involved in the entire process of oil recovery, from preliminary steps such as analyzing cost factors to the last stages such as monitoring the production rate and then repacking the well after it has been depleted.

Petroleum engineering is closely related to the separate engineering discipline of geoscience engineering. Before petroleum engineers can begin work on an oil reservoir, prospective sites must first be sought by geological engineers, along with geologists and geophysicists. These scientists determine whether a site has potential oil. Petroleum engineers develop plans for drilling. Drilling is usually unsuccessful, with eight out of 10 test wells being "dusters" (dry wells) and only one of the remaining two test wells having enough oil to be commercially producible. When a significant amount of oil is discovered, engineers can begin their work of maximizing oil production at the site. The development company's engineering manager oversees the activities of the various petroleum engineering specialties, including *reservoir engineers, drilling engineers,* and *production engineers.*

Reservoir engineers use the data gathered by the previous geoscience studies and estimate the actual amount of oil that will be extracted from the reservoir. It is the reservoir engineers who determine whether the oil will be taken by primary methods (simply pumping the oil from the field) or by enhanced methods (using additional energy such as water pressure to force the oil up). The reservoir engineer is responsible for calculating the cost of the recovery process relative to the expected value of the oil produced, and simulates future performance using sophisticated computer models. Besides performing studies of existing company-owned oil fields, reservoir engineers also evaluate fields the company is thinking of buying.

Drilling engineers work with geologists and drilling contractors to design and supervise drilling operations. They are the engineers involved with the actual drilling of the well. They ask, What will be the best methods for penetrating the earth? It is the responsibility of these workers to supervise the building of the derrick (a platform, constructed over the well, that holds the hoisting devices), choose the equipment, and plan the drilling methods. Drilling engineers must have a thorough understanding of the geological sciences so that they can know, for instance, how much stress to place on the rock being drilled.

Production engineers determine the most efficient methods and equipment to optimize oil and gas production. For example, they establish proper pumping unit configuration and perform tests to determine well fluid levels and pumping load. They plan field workovers and well stimulation techniques such as secondary and tertiary recovery (for example, injecting steam, water, or a special recovery fluid) to maximize field production.

Various research personnel are involved in this field; some are more specialized than others. They include the *research chief engineer,* who directs studies related to the design of new drilling and production methods, and the *oil-well equipment research engineer,* who directs research to design improvements in oil-well machinery and devices; and the *oil-field equipment test engineer,* who conducts experiments to determine the effectiveness and safety of these improvements.

In addition to all of the above, sales personnel play an important part in the petroleum industry. *Oil-well equipment and services sales engineers* sell various types of equipment and devices

PETROLEUM ENGINEERS	
SCHOOL SUBJECTS	Mathematics Physics
PERSONAL SKILLS	Helping/teaching Technical/scientific
WORK ENVIRONMENT	Indoors and outdoors One location with some travel
MINIMUM EDUCATION LEVEL	Bachelor's degree
SALARY RANGE	$42,000 to $53,000 to $67,000
CERTIFICATION OR LICENSING	Recommended
OUTLOOK	Decline
DOT	010
GOE	05.01.08
NOC	2145
O*NET	22111

used in all stages of oil recovery. They provide technical support and service to their clients, including oil companies and drilling contractors.

■ Requirements

High School

High school students can prepare for college engineering programs by taking courses in mathematics, physics, chemistry, geology, and computer science; economics, history, and English are also highly recommended because these subjects improve communications and management skills. Mechanical drawing and foreign languages will also be helpful. Students should try for courses that are taught at the honors level.

Postsecondary Training

A bachelor's degree in engineering is the minimum requirement. In college, one can follow either a specific petroleum engineering curriculum or a program in a closely related field, such as geophysics or mining engineering. In the United States, there are about 30 universities and colleges that offer programs that concentrate on petroleum engineering; many of these are located in California and Texas. The first two years toward the bachelor of science degree involve the study of many of the same subjects taken in high school, only at an advanced level, as well as basic engineering courses. In the junior and senior years, students take more specialized courses: geology, formation evaluation, properties of reservoir rocks and fluids, well drilling, properties of reservoir fluids, petroleum production, and reservoir analysis.

Because the technology changes so rapidly, many petroleum engineers continue their education to receive a master's degree and then a doctorate. Both command higher salaries and often result in better advancement opportunities. Those who work in research and teaching positions usually need these higher credentials.

Students considering an engineering career in the petroleum industry should be aware that the industry uses all kinds of engineers. Those with chemical, electrical, geoscience, mechanical, environmental, and other engineering degrees are also employed in this field.

Certification or Licensing

Many jobs require that the engineer be licensed as a professional engineer (P.E.), which is often needed on certain public projects. To be licensed, candidates must have a degree from an engineering program accredited by the Accreditation Board for Engineering and Technology. Additional requirements for obtaining the P.E. license vary from state to state, but all applicants must take an exam and

have several years of related experience on the job or in teaching.

Other Requirements

Students thinking about this career need to enjoy science and math. You need to be creative problem-solvers who like to come up with new ways to get things done and try them out. They need to be curious, wanting to know why and how things are done. You also need to be logical thinkers with a capacity for detail, and you must be good communicators who can work well with others.

■ Exploring

One of the most satisfying ways to explore this occupation is to participate in Junior Engineering Technical Society (JETS) programs. JETS participants enter engineering design and problem-solving contests and learn team development skills, often with an engineering mentor. Science fairs and clubs also offer fun and challenging ways to learn about engineering.

Certain students are able to attend summer programs held at colleges and universities that focus on material not traditionally offered in high school. For example, Worcester Polytechnic Institute offers the Frontiers program, a 13-day residential session for high school seniors. The American Indian Science and Engineering Society (AISES) also sponsors two- to six-week mathematics and science camps that are open to American Indian students and held at various college campuses.

Talking with someone who has worked as a petroleum engineer would also be a very helpful and inexpensive way of exploring this field, as would tours of oilfields or corporate sites (contact the public relations department of oil companies) and summer and other temporary jobs in the petroleum industry on drilling and production crews. Trade journals, high school guidance counselors, the placement office at technical or community colleges, and the associations listed at the end of this article are other helpful resources.

■ Employers

Petroleum engineers are employed by oil companies. They work in oil exploration and production. Some petroleum engineers are employed by consulting companies and equipment suppliers. The government is also an employer of engineers.

■ Starting Out

The most common and perhaps the most successful way to obtain a petroleum engineering job is to apply with the student placement services department at the college that you attend. Oil companies often have recruiters who seek potential graduates while they are in their last year of engineering school.

Applicants are also advised to simply check the job sections of major newspapers and apply directly to companies seeking employees; they should also keep informed of the general national employment outlook in this industry by reading trade and association journals, such as the Society of Petroleum Engineers' *Journal of Petroleum Technology.*

Engineering internships or co-op programs where students attend classes for a portion of the year and then work in an engineering-related job for the remainder of the year allow students to graduate with valuable work experience sought by employers. Many times these students are employed full time after graduation at the place where they had their internship or co-op job.

As in most engineering professions, entry-level petroleum engineers first work under the supervision of experienced professionals for a number of years. New engineers usually are assigned to a field location where they learn different aspects of field petroleum engineering. Initial responsibilities may include well productivity, reservoir and enhanced recovery studies, production equipment and application design, efficiency analyses, and economic evaluations. Field assignments are followed by other opportunities in regional and headquarters offices.

■ Advancement

After several years of working under professional supervision, engineers can begin to move up to higher levels. Workers often formulate a choice of direction during their first years on the job. In the operations division, petroleum engineers can work their way up from the field to district, division, and then operations manager. Some engineers work through various engineering positions from field engineer to staff, then division, and finally chief engineer on a project. Some engineers may advance into top executive management. In any position, however, continued enrollment in educational courses is usually required to keep abreast of technological progress and changes. After about four years of work experience, engineers tend to apply for a P.E. license so they can be certified to work on a larger number of projects.

Others get their master's or doctorate so they can advance to more prestigious research engineering, university-level teaching, or consulting positions. There are also opportunities for petroleum engineers to transfer to many other occupations, such as economics, environmental management, and groundwater hydrology. Finally, there are the workers with entrepreneurial spirit who become independent operators of their own oil companies.

■ Earnings

Salaries for entry-level engineers with a bachelor's degree are often higher than for workers in any other field. Furthermore, petroleum engineers tend to make the highest starting salaries of all engineers. According to the *American Almanac of Jobs and Salaries,* entry level petroleum engineers earn an average of $42,000; those with some experience earn an average of $53,000; and those with extensive experience earn an average of $67,000.

Salary increases tend to reflect changes in the petroleum industry as a whole. When the price of oil is high, salaries can be expected to grow; low oil prices often result in stagnant wages.

Fringe benefits are good. Most employers provide health and accident insurance, sick pay, retirement plans, profit-sharing plans, and paid vacations. Education benefits are also competitive.

■ Work Environment

Petroleum engineers work all over the world—the high seas, remote jungles, vast deserts, plains, and mountain ranges. In the United States, oil or natural gas is produced in 33 states, with most sites located in Texas, Alaska, Louisiana, California, and Oklahoma, plus offshore regions. Many other U.S. engineers work in other oil-producing areas such as the Arctic Circle, China's Tarim Basin, and Saudi Arabia. Assignments to remote foreign locations can make family life difficult. Those working overseas may live in company-supplied housing.

Some petroleum engineers, such as drilling engineers, work primarily out in the field at or near drilling sites in all kinds of weather and environments. The work can be dirty and dangerous. Responsibilities such as making reports, conducting studies of data, and analyzing costs are usually tended in offices either away from the site or in temporary work trailers.

Other engineers work in offices in cities of varying sizes, with only occasional visits to an oil field. Research engineers work in laboratories much of the time, while those who work as professors spend most of their time on campuses and at other teaching areas. Workers involved in economics, management, consulting, and government service tend to spend their work time exclusively in indoor offices.

■ Outlook

The opportunity for employment in this field directly depends on the world price for oil and gas. Conditions at the beginning of 1996 included a worldwide surplus of oil, which is expected to continue. At the same time, domestic conservation of oil by industry and the public has reduced the demand for oil. The surplus has resulted in low oil prices. For these reasons, the number of job openings for petroleum engineers is expected to decline through

2006. Even so, some opportunities for petroleum engineers will exist because the number of degrees granted in petroleum engineering is low.

The challenge for petroleum engineers in the past decade has been to develop technology that lets drilling and production be economically feasible even in the face of low oil prices. For example, engineers had to rethink how they worked in deep water. They used to believe deep wells would collapse if too much oil was pumped out at once. But the high costs of working in deep water plus low oil prices made low volumes uneconomical. So engineers learned how to boost oil flow by slowly upping the quantities wells pumped by improving valves, pipes, and other equipment used. Engineers have also cut the cost of deepwater oil and gas production in the Gulf of Mexico, predicted to be one of the most significant exploration hot spots in the world for the next decade, by placing wellheads on the ocean floor instead of on above-sea production platforms.

Cost-effective technology that permits new drilling and increases production will continue to be essential in the profitability of the oil industry. Therefore, petroleum engineers will continue to have a vital role to play, even in this age of streamlined operations and company restructurings.

■ For More Information

This trade association represents employees in the petroleum industry. Free videos, fact sheets, and informational booklets are available to educators.

American Petroleum Institute
1220 L Street, NW
Washington, DC 20005
Tel: 202-682-8000
Web: http://www.api.org

For a petroleum engineering career brochure, a list of petroleum engineering schools, and scholarship information, contact:

Society of Petroleum Engineers
PO Box 833836
Richardson, TX 75083-3836
Tel: 972-952-9393
Web: http://www.spe.org

For information about JETS programs, products, and engineering career brochures (all disciplines), contact:

Junior Engineering Technical Society, Inc.
1420 King Street, Suite 405
Alexandria, VA 22314-2715
Tel: 703-548-5387
Web: http://www.jets.org

For a Frontiers program brochure and application, write :

Worcester Polytechnic Institute
100 Institute Road
Worcester, MA 01609-2280
Tel: 508-831-5514

For information on AISES precollege programs and scholarships, contact:

American Indian Science & Engineering Society
5655 Airport Road
Boulder, CO 80301
Tel: 303-939-0023

For Opportunities for Performance, *a booklet describing professional jobs at Phillips Petroleum Company, contact:*

Phillips Petroleum Company
Employment & College Relations
180 Plaza Office Building
Bartlesville, OK 74004
Tel: 918-661-6385

For Oil, *a booklet describing all phases of the oil industry, and information on careers with Shell, contact:*

Shell Oil Company
External Affairs
PO Box 2463
Houston, TX 77252-2463
Tel: 713-241-6161
Web: http://www.shell.com

■ Related Articles

Energy
The Environment
Petroleum
Chemical Engineers
Environmental Engineers
Geological Technicians
Geologists
Geophysicists
Metallurgical Engineers
Mining Engineers
Paleontologists
Petroleum Technicians
Petrologists

Petroleum Refining Workers

■ Overview

Crude oil and gas are of little use. The value of the crude lies in the refined oils, fuels, and thousands of other products that can be created from it. *Petroleum refining workers* design, test, operate, and maintain equipment and processes that purify crude petroleum into useful, marketable products.

■ History

Petroleum comes from ancient rock under the ground, where the organic matter of plants and animals has accumulated over millions of years and, through pressure and heat, changed into oil. In early times, petroleum was obtainable only after it had seeped through the earth's surface into aboveground pools. The first oil well was drilled in 1859 because people were looking for a replacement for whale oil, which was difficult to get, to light their lamps. For this they needed kerosene, which they got by boiling the crude in a kind of still. Other products of this early refining were regarded as waste and thrown away including the gasoline we now depend on to fuel our cars.

By the early 1900s the advent of the internal combustion engine to propel "horseless carriages" provided a use for gasoline, as automakers adapted engines to use this practical fuel. And petroleum eventually replaced coal as the major energy source for heating.

Besides motor and heating fuels, petrochemicals that are used in making dyes, cosmetics, plastics, synthetic rubber, and thousands of other products are produced through refining, thanks to a conversion process developed in 1913 by chemists William M. Burton and Robert E. Humphreys.

The rise of the industry was greatly accelerated by World War II. The suddenly increased demand for high-octane aviation gasoline led to a surge in refinery capacity. Also, the need for synthetic rubber required the development of a large-scale technology for producing benzene, butylenes, and other petroleum derivatives. The war also created a demand for many other petrochemical products, including nylon for parachutes and polyethylene to protect electric cables in radar equipment. At the end of the war, pent-up consumer demand kept plants running and petrochemical sales growing at more than 10 percent for the next 20-odd years.

By the late 1960s, Europe and Japan's industrial growth had narrowed the U.S. lead in petrochemicals. In the 1970s, oil-rich nations such as Saudi Arabia, Canada, and Iran began building their own petrochemical plants. By the early 1980s, world trade in petrochemicals had greatly expanded, and today most countries have some petrochemical production facilities.

Though updated, some basic processes and jobs have been performed since petroleum was first refined, while other jobs have been created as a result of the development of new processes; for example, the position of catalytic cracking unit operator was born with the development of this conversion process in the 1930s. Many processes and people are involved in the refining of crude oil, with changes and advances being made as researchers develop new methods.

■ **The Job**

The refining world is a highly technical one that, to the untrained eye, appears to be a strange maze of towers, pipes, and tanks. Actually, it is an organized and coordinated arrangement of manufacturing processes designed to produce physical and chemical changes in crude oil and gas, resulting in saleable products.

The types of crude to be processed and the requirements of the market determine the techniques used in a refinery. More than a hundred different types of crudes are internationally traded, and a modern refinery may process as many as twenty grades in the course of a year.

Three basic refining procedures are separation, conversion, and treatment. The first procedure separates the crude oil into different parts, or fractions, and is usually accomplished by distillation in tall tanks called fractionating columns. In this process, the oil is heated in pipes in a huge furnace. The heated oils produce vapors, which pass into the fractionating column, where they condense into materials with different properties. Pipes that are set at different levels in the towers draw off the various fractions, which rise to different heights depending on their weight and other characteristics. Distillation is continuous, with hot crude oil flowing in near the base of the column and the separate fractions flowing out at each level. The lighter fractions, like liquefied petroleum gases (LPG), gasoline, and naphtha, a major feedstock for the chemical industry, are tapped off from the top of the tower. Heavier fractions, like kerosene (jet fuel), diesel fuel, and heating oil, are drawn off around the midsection of the towers; very heavy materials, such as fuel oils or residues, remain in the bottom sections.

Products from the fractionating columns are straight-run products. They may be ready for the market, or they may be treated to remove impurities. Often they go through conversion techniques to chemically change their makeup. For example, fuel oil, one of the heaviest fractions, may account for between one-third and one-half of the yield from distillation, whereas demand from customers is predominantly for the lighter fractions, such as gasoline.

PETROLEUM REFINING WORKERS	
SCHOOL SUBJECTS	Chemistry Technical/Shop
PERSONAL SKILLS	Following instructions Mechanical/manipulative
WORK ENVIRONMENT	Indoors and outdoors Primarily one location
MINIMUM EDUCATION LEVEL	High school diploma
SALARY RANGE	$35,000 to $43,000 to $100,000+
CERTIFICATION OR LICENSING	None available
OUTLOOK	Little change or more slowly than the average
DOT	549
GOE	06.02.12
NOC	9212
O*NET	98999A

A refinery worker inspects the equipment on his daily rounds.

This is especially so in the United States, with all its cars. Heavy oil fractions can be converted to high-octane gasoline through a heat and pressure process called cracking to help meet market demand.

Distillation and cracking also produce petrochemicals. At petrochemical plants, which may be separate facilities or, increasingly, part of the refinery complex, these first-stage petrochemicals are changed via conventional chemistry into secondary petrochemicals, which in turn are transformed into the medicines, fabrics, cosmetics, detergents, and other everyday products used at home and work.

In recent years, many refineries have invested considerably in conversion facilities, installed computers to process refinery operations, and introduced energy management plans. At the beginning of 1996, there were about 165 operating refineries in the United States, employing 101,600 workers in a wide range of jobs. In general, those jobs can be classified into 4 broad categories: operations, maintenance, engineering and scientific support, and supervision. Following are a number of examples of jobs in each category.

Operations workers run the variety of machines that refine petroleum. Control panel operators work the gauges that regulate the temperature, pressure, rate of flow, and tank level in petroleum refining and petrochemical processing units. They observe and regulate meters and instruments to process petroleum under specified conditions. When the fractionating process is complete, treaters are responsible for controlling the equipment that removes impurities and improves the quality of gasoline, kerosene,

and lubricants; to perform their jobs, treaters use steam, clay, hydrogen, solvents, and chemicals. Clay roasters use a kiln to clean and treat clay that has been used to treat oil.

Certain refined oils are blended to achieve specific qualities or make specific fuels. Various types of workers are needed for such operations. Compounders add antioxidants, corrosion inhibitors, detergents, and other additives to enhance lubricating oils. Blenders mix gasoline with chemicals, lead, or distilled crude oil to make specified commercial fuel. Grease makers heat oils with fat, soda, water, dye, and mineral oils to produce various grades of lubricating grease.

Involved in the operation of petrochemical processing plants are paraffin plant operators, who work with filter presses to separate paraffin oil distillate from paraffin wax. Paraffin plant sweater operators operate tanks that heat and cool substances to separate liquid from processed paraffin distillate. Lead recoverers at naphtha-treating plants operate centrifuge machines that separate lead compounds from a naphtha solution used to treat gasoline.

Other operations workers include *oil-recovery-unit operators,* who separate recoverable oil from refinery sewage systems, and *refinery laborers,* who prepare work sites, load and unload equipment, dump ingredients for mixing into machines, and perform many other tasks. In addition, the industry employs many workers to load and drive delivery trucks.

Maintenance workers make up more than half of all refinery employees. They keep the workplaces safe and the machinery in working condition. *Fire marshals* are needed because of the flammable nature of petroleum and its by-products. *Refinery marshals* coordinate firefighters' activities, inspect equipment and workplaces to make sure they meet fire regulations, order fire drills, and direct fire fighting and rescues in the event of a refinery fire. *Mechanical inspectors* inspect tanks, pipes, pipe fittings, stills, towers, and pumps for defects and report the need for repairs. They use special instruments to measure the thickness of tower walls and pipes and to determine rates of corrosion and decay. *Line walkers* patrol pipelines to look for leaks. *Salvagers* are responsible for fixing defective valves and pipe fittings.

Other maintenance workers include *gas-regulator repairers,* who fix and install equipment that controls the pressure of gases used in petroleum refining; *meter testers,* who ensure the correct functioning of the meters that indicate the flow and pressure of gases, steam, and water; and *electricians,* who repair and maintain refineries' electrical systems, including motors, transformers, wiring, switches, and alarms. Other workers, including *tube cleaners,* keep equipment clean so it will perform at required standards. *Tankcar inspectors* examine the wheels, bearings, brakes, and safety equipment of refining tank cars to prevent catastrophic accidents. *Construction and maintenance inspectors* inspect petroleum-dispensing equipment at distribution plants.

Engineers, chemists, and other scientific support staff are involved in tasks that require more theoretical knowledge than those done by operations and maintenance workers. These workers are often responsible for the actual design and development of refining plants. They also devise ways to treat and improve products, and they develop, improve, and test refinery processes.

There is also a variety of managers and supervisors who work in the petroleum refining industry. *Contract managers* negotiate the purchase and delivery of crude oil, and they negotiate sales of refinery products. *Purchasing managers* procure chemicals, catalysts, piping, valves, motors, pumps, and many other commodities for use in the refinery complex. Services include contracting for construction work, waste disposal, janitorial, catering, photography, and transportation. *Bulk plant managers* manage storage and distribution facilities for petroleum products. *Dispatchers* regulate the flow of products through processing, treating, and shipping departments. In addition, most operations at refineries are headed by supervisors, who coordinate workers' activities, plan production schedules, and oversee processes.

■ Requirements

High School

Because of the diversity of functions, qualifications differ greatly. Petroleum refining workers who are involved in operations and maintenance need at least a high school diploma, and a year or two at college or a technical school is very helpful and highly desirable to most employers. Maintenance workers may also be required to have special training in repairing certain kinds of equipment.

Operations workers learn most of their skills on the job. High school and college-level courses in chemistry, physics, and mathematics, however, should help them understand and learn these skills more readily. As computers are now widely used in refinery operations, those who take computer science classes will discover that computer skills are not only valuable, but essential for some jobs.

Postsecondary Training

Engineers and scientists need college degrees from accredited institutions. Chemical and laboratory technicians may be graduates of a two-year program, but engineers and scientists must have a minimum of a bachelor's degree, and many also have a master's degree and doctorate. High school students preparing for such college study should take math, chemistry, physics, biology, drafting, and computer applications, as well as English classes.

Other Requirements

Most work in refineries requires a high degree of precision and accuracy, and many positions require knowledge of intricate machine operations. Workers should be alert, attentive, and quick-thinking, and able to work under pressure.

■ Exploring

Talking with someone who has worked in a refinery would be a very helpful and inexpensive way of exploring this field. One good way to find an experienced person to talk to is through online computer services.

Another way to learn about petroleum refining occupations is checking school or public libraries for books on the petroleum refining and petrochemical industries. Industry unions, to which most operations and maintenance refinery workers belong, are also good sources of information about this type of work; one of the largest such unions is the Oil, Chemical and Atomic Workers International Union. Other resources include trade journals, high school guidance counselors, the placement office at technical or community colleges, and the associations listed at the end of this article.

Most refineries are very open to high schoolers taking free plant tours and provide information to students. Contact the public relations department of a nearby refinery to arrange a tour or to request information.

Some summer and other temporary jobs in refineries are available, and they provide a very good way of finding out about this field. Because refineries are in operation 24 hours a day, late-shift work may also be available to those exploring the industry. Temporary workers can learn firsthand the basics of oil refining operations, equipment maintenance, safety, and other aspects of the work.

■ Employers

Refining workers can find employment at large and small refineries and petrochemical companies.

■ Starting Out

High school or technical school graduates should fill out applications at employment offices of refineries. State employment offices and local offices of trade unions such as the Oil, Chemical and Atomic Workers International can also be contacted for employment information. Apprenticeships are often available to teach workers specialized skills. These programs may take as many as four to five years to complete, and they combine formal classroom instruction with practical experience.

College and university students may interview on campus with companies that have recruitment programs. In addition, college placement offices usually have information on positions and internships.

All job seekers can increase their chances of success by familiarizing themselves with the concerns and activities of potential employers. Many companies make their annual reports available, which can be found in the business section at many libraries, along with trade and professional magazines and journals.

■ Advancement

Advancement in the petroleum refining industry depends on experience, type of position, and place of employment (larger refineries tend to have greater advancement opportunities). Seniority plays a large role in promotions for operations and maintenance workers, since they belong to unions. Operations workers may move to a more responsible, higher-paying position such as grease maker, which requires long experience and specialized knowledge. They may also move up to supervisory jobs.

An advancement path for a maintenance worker might be machinist, to machinery assistant supervisor, to maintenance mechanic superintendent with responsibility for planning and budgeting repairs. With additional engineering and business administration schooling, the worker could further advance to senior machinery reliability specialist, responsible for finding the best, most cost-effective way to improve refinery equipment reliability, designing and installing new refinery equipment, and training supervisors on that equipment.

Engineers and scientists may be promoted to positions involving management and supervision, in which they are responsible for supervising many workers and taking charge of entire refining processes. Someone with a bachelor's in chemistry, for example, might start out as a junior research chemist, then move up to senior research chemist, to product, process, and environmental quality chemist, with responsibility for sampling and analyzing products, processes, and environmental effects of refining. From there the chemist could progress to chief plant chemist.

This person could also be an industrial hygiene chemist, performing occupational health, air, and water pollution control sampling and analyses, continuing on to industrial hygienist, with responsibility for industrial hygiene programs including performing safety investigations and recommending and designing controls to maintain healthful working conditions. Ultimately, an industrial hygienist could be supervisor of safety and industrial hygiene, managing an entire department. For this career path, certification in hazardous materials and industrial hygiene would be necessary, as well as additional schooling in safety engineering.

In general, persons with good judgment, who can act effectively in emergencies, and who are willing to learn new skills and obtain additional schooling when neces-

sary, should be in a good position to receive promotions as they become available.

■ Earnings

Because of the diversity of jobs, salaries differ greatly. Salaries also vary with geographic location, experience, education, and employer. In 1995, refinery maintenance and operations workers in nonsupervisory positions earned an average of $19 per hour, according to the Oil, Chemical and Atomic Workers International Union, although salaries are dependent on the worker's job type and level of experience. These workers also receive premium pay for evening and night shifts as well as overtime pay.

Salaries for engineering and scientific support positions are higher. Entry-level mechanical engineers earn about $35,000 to $40,000 per year; experienced engineers, up to $80,000, according to an industry source. A 1995 salary survey from the American Chemical Society gave a mean salary of $39,799 for chemical engineers with a bachelor of science degree and two to four years of experience, ranging up to $81,255 for four or more years of experience. For chemical engineers with a master's, mean salaries ranged from $49,747 to $86,766, depending on experience; with a doctorate, from $59,010 to $110,410, depending on experience. The same salary survey showed mean salaries for petroleum industry chemists of $38,560 to $105,864, depending on experience and education. Entry-level chemical technicians had a mean salary of $24,430, going up to $43,292 for 30 or more years of experience.

Workers in this industry have paid vacations, pensions, and health and life insurance.

■ Work Environment

Plants operate 24-four hours a day, year-round, resulting in an air of urgency that is a permanent part of the job. Overtime is often involved, and workers may be requested to work nights, evenings, weekends, or holidays, depending on seniority. Extreme pressure occurs during shutdown of selected operating units for maintenance overhaul.

Many refinery operations are located in fairly remote areas. Conditions in locations such as Alaska and the North Sea can be quite rugged during winter months. Refinery work often takes workers outside to check equipment. Those who work indoors usually encounter clean, modern conditions, usually some distance away from the equipment or the operations.

■ Outlook

Although domestic production of oil has declined, the United States continues to import much crude oil. In addition, demand for petroleum products, while not growing much, is holding steady, employment of refinery workers is expected to be steady. A few thousand jobs will open up each year as workers retire, transfer, or otherwise leave the industry.

However, the refining industry is much leaner than it used to be. Due to less domestic oil production and environmental regulations, close to half of the petroleum refineries operating in 1982 have since closed. U.S. refiners have had to reevaluate their operations closely in light of federal and state environmental regulations. Large companies with multiple refining operations have had to commit substantial resources to plant additions and reconfigurations, product reformulations, and research and development of processing technologies to comply with regulations. The required investments are greater on a per-barrel basis for smaller refineries, many of which didn't have the resources to meet new environmental standards and were forced to shut down. Older refineries too were particularly hard hit.

Refining operations and capital investment will continue to be affected by pending technological standards to reduce emissions. The increases in environmental costs come at a time of little growth in overall demand for petroleum products. Therefore, the trend for certain refineries to close down partially or entirely rather than upgrade facilities to meet the new standards is likely to continue.

Besides considering the industry overall, those contemplating a career in petroleum refining need to be aware of what individual companies are doing. Some companies are hiring workers, while many others are downsizing. The discrepancy is due to some companies moving away from domestic refining operations, while others are concentrating on that side of the business. In the past, it was common for oil companies to be involved in all areas of the industry—exploration, drilling and production, transportation, refining, and distribution/marketing—in both the domestic and worldwide arena. Now companies are trying to narrow their place in the market based on their strengths instead of trying to do it all.

Closely linked to the oil industry is the petrochemical industry, which is currently the fastest-growing industrial chemical field and produces the largest number of new chemicals. Because most of its products are considered hazardous at some stage in their manufacture, the petrochemical industry has also been profoundly affected by government environmental regulations.

Automation and computerization are changing the face of the refinery employment population. Refinery personnel recruiters are more attracted to applicants with computer, chemistry, engineering, and mechanical backgrounds than they are to unskilled workers. While automation may be decreasing the number of jobs for operations workers, jobs will open up for maintenance workers such as pipefitters, electricians, machinists, and repair personnel.

Employment will remain fairly static among professional, technical, and administrative workers.

■ For More Information

This trade association represents employees in the petroleum industry. Free videos, fact sheets, and informational booklets are available to educators.

American Petroleum Institute
1220 L Street, NW
Washington, DC 20005
Tel: 202-682-8000
Web: http://www.api.org

For information about careers, salaries, and employment trends, contact:

American Chemical Society
Department of Career Services
1155 16th Street, NW
Washington, DC 20036
Tel: 800-227-5558
Web: http://www.acs.org

For information about JETS programs, products, and engineering career brochures (all disciplines), contact:

Junior Engineering Technical Society, Inc.
1420 King Street, Suite 405
Alexandria, VA 22314-2715
Tel: 703-548-5387
Email: jets@nae.edu
Web: http://www.jets.org

For Opportunities for Performance, a booklet describing professional jobs at Phillips Petroleum Company, contact:

Phillips Petroleum Company
Employment & College Relations
180 Plaza Office Building
Bartlesville, OK 74004
Tel: 918-661-6385
Web: http://www.phillips66.com

For Oil, a booklet describing all phases of the oil industry, and information on careers with Shell, contact:

Shell Oil Company
External Affairs
PO Box 2463
Houston, TX 77252-2463
Tel: 713-241-6161
Web: http://www.shell.com

■ Related Articles

Energy

The Environment

Mining

Petroleum

Biochemists

Biomedical Engineers

Boilermakers and Mechanics

Chemical Engineers

Chemical Technicians

Chemists

Environmental Engineers

General Maintenance Mechanics

Industrial Chemicals Workers

Industrial Engineering Technicians

Industrial Engineers

Industrial Machinery Mechanics

Occupational Safety and Health Workers

Petroleum Engineers

Petroleum Technicians

Petroleum Technicians

■ Overview

Petroleum technicians work in a wide variety of specialties. Many kinds of *drilling technicians* drill for petroleum from the earth and beneath the ocean. *Loggers* analyze rock cuttings from drilling and measure characteristics of rock layers. Various types of *production technicians* "complete" wells (prepare wells for production), collect petroleum from producing wells, and control production. *Engineering technicians* help improve drilling technology, maximize field production, and provide technical assistance. *Maintenance technicians* keep machinery and equipment running smoothly.

PETROLEUM TECHNICIANS	
SCHOOL SUBJECTS	Mathematics Physics
PERSONAL SKILLS	Helping/teaching Technical/scientific
WORK ENVIRONMENT	Indoors and outdoors Primarily multiple locations
MINIMUM EDUCATION LEVEL	High school diploma
SALARY RANGE	$18,000 to $33,000 to $50,000+
OUTLOOK	About as fast as the average
DOT	222
GOE	05.07.05
NOC	2212
O*NET	24511E

■ History

In the 1950s and 1960s, the oil industry was relatively stable. Oil was cheap and much in demand. The international oil market was dominated by the "seven sisters"—Shell, Esso, BP, Gulf, Chevron, Texaco, and Mobil. However, by the end of the 1960s, Middle Eastern countries became more dominant. Many nationalized the major oil companies' operations or negotiated to control oil production. To promote and protect their oil production and revenues gained, Iran, Iraq, Kuwait, Saudi Arabia, and Venezuela formed OPEC (the Organization of Petroleum Exporting Countries). The Arab producers' policies during the Arab/Israeli War of 1973-1974 and the Iranian Revolution in 1978 disrupted oil supplies and skyrocketed oil prices, indicating just how powerful OPEC had become.

By the early 1980s, economic recession and energy conservation measures had resulted in lower oil prices. There was and still is worldwide surplus production capacity. OPEC, which expanded membership to countries in the Far East and Africa, tried to impose quotas limiting production, with little success. In 1986, prices, which had once again risen, plummeted.

The events of the 1970s and 1980s significantly altered the nation's attitude toward the price and availability of petroleum products. Domestic oil companies came to realize that foreign sources of oil could easily be lost through regional conflicts or international tensions. The drop in prices during the mid-1980s, however, reinforced the need for domestic producers to continue to find economical oil-producing methods to remain competitive with foreign-produced oil.

These developments have fostered great changes in the technology of oil drilling, in the science related to oil exploration, and in the management of existing oil fields. In many old abandoned fields, scientists found that they still had nearly as much oil as had been produced from them by older methods. New technology is constantly being developed and used to find ways of extracting more of this remaining oil economically from old and new fields alike.

The petroleum technician occupation was created to help the industry meet such challenges. Technological changes require scientifically competent technical workers as crewmembers for well-drilling and oil field management. Well-prepared technicians are essential to the oil industry and will continue to be in the future.

■ The Job

Before petroleum technicians can begin work on an oil reservoir, prospective sites must first be sought by geological exploration teams. These crews perform seismic surveying, in which sound waves are created and their reflection from underground rocks recorded by seismographs, to help locate potential sources of oil. Other team members collect and examine geological data or test geological samples to determine petroleum and mineral content. They may also use surveying and mapping instruments and techniques to help locate and map test holes or the results of seismic tests.

It is the drill bit, however, that ultimately proves whether or not there is oil. Drilling for oil is a highly skilled operation involving many kinds of technicians: *rotary drillers*, *derrick operators*, *engine operators*, and *tool pushers*.

In the most common type of drilling, a drill bit with metal or diamond teeth is suspended on a drilling string consisting of 30-foot pipes joined together. The string is added to as the bit goes deeper. The bit is turned either by a rotary mechanism on the drill floor or, increasingly, by a downhole motor. As drilling progresses, the bit gets worn and has to be replaced. The entire drilling string, sometimes weighing more than 100 tons must be hauled to the surface and dismantled section by section, the bit replaced, then the string reassembled and run back down the well. Known as a "round trip," this operation can take the drilling crew most of a 12-hour shift in a deep well. Until recently, drill strings were mostly manually handled; however, mechanized drill rigs that handle pipe automatically have been introduced to improve safety and efficiency.

The *driller* directs the crew and is responsible for the machinery operation. The driller watches gauges and works throttles and levers to control the hoisting and rotation speed of the drill pipe and the amount of weight on the bit. Special care is needed as the bit nears oil and gas to avoid a "blow-out." Such "gushers" were common in the early days of the oil industry, but today's drilling technicians are trained to prevent them. Drillers also are responsible for recording the type and depth of strata penetrated each day and materials used.

Derrick operators are next in charge of the drilling crew. They work on a platform high up on the derrick and help handle the upper end of the drilling string during placement and removal. They also mix the special drilling "mud" that is pumped down through the pipe to lubricate and cool the bit as well as help control the flow of oil and gas when oil is struck.

Engine operators run engines to supply power for rotary drilling machinery and oversee their maintenance. They may help when the *roughnecks* pull or add pipe sections.

Tool pushers are in charge of one or more drilling rigs. They oversee erection of the rig, the selection of drill bits, the operation of drilling machinery, and the mixing of drilling mud. They arrange for the delivery of tools, machinery, fuel, water, and other supplies to the drilling site.

One very specialized drilling position is the *oil-well fishing-tool technician.* These technicians analyze conditions at wells where some object, or "fish," has obstructed the borehole. They direct the work of removing the obstacle (lost equipment or broken drill pipes, for example), choosing from a variety of techniques.

During drilling, *mud test technicians*, also called *mud loggers*, use a microscope at a portable laboratory on-site to analyze drill cuttings carried out of the well by the circulating mud for traces of oil. After final depth is reached, technicians called *well loggers* lower measuring devices to the bottom of the well on cable called wireline. Wireline logs examine the electrical, acoustic, and radioactive prop-

Petroleum technicians at work on an oil rig

erties of the rocks and provide information about rock type and porosity, and how much fluid (oil, gas, or water) it contains. These techniques, known as formation evaluation, help the operating company decide whether enough oil exists to warrant continued drilling.

The first well drilled is an exploration well. If oil is discovered, more wells, called appraisal wells, are drilled to establish the limits of the field. Then the field's economic worth and profit are evaluated. If it is judged economically worthwhile to develop the field, some of the appraisal wells may be used as production wells. The production phase of the operation deals with bringing the well fluids to the surface and preparing them for their trip through the pipeline to the refinery.

The first step is to complete the well—that is, to perform whatever operations are needed to start the well fluids flowing to the surface—and is performed by *well-servicing technicians.* These technicians use a variety of well-completion methods, determined by the oil reservoir's characteristics. Typical tasks include setting and cementing pipe (called production casing) so that the oil can come to the surface without leaking into the upper layers of rock. Well-servicing technicians may later perform maintenance work to improve or maintain the production from a formation already producing oil. These technicians bring in smaller rigs similar to drilling rigs for their work.

After the well has been completed, a structure consisting of control valves, pressure gauges, and chokes (called a Christmas tree because of the way its fittings branch out) is assembled at the top of the well to control the flow of oil and gas. Generally, production crews direct operations for several wells.

Well fluids are often a mixture of oil, gas, and water and must be separated and treated before going into the storage tanks. After separation, *treaters* apply heat, chemicals, electricity, or all three to remove contaminants. They also control well flow when the natural pressure is great enough to force oil from the well without pumping.

Pumpers operate, monitor, and maintain production facilities. They visually inspect well equipment to make sure it's functioning properly. They also detect and perform any routine maintenance needs. They adjust pumping cycle time to optimize production and measure the fluid levels in storage tanks, recording the information each day for entry on weekly gauge reports. Pumpers also advise oil haulers or purchasers when a tank is ready for sale.

Gaugers ensure that other company personnel and purchasers comply with the company's oil measurement and sale policy. They spotcheck oil measurements and resolve any discrepancies. They also check pumpers' equipment for accuracy and arrange for the replacement of malfunctioning gauging equipment.

Once a field has been brought into production, good reservoir management is needed to ensure that as much oil as possible is recovered. Production engineering technicians work with the production engineers to plan field workovers and well stimulation techniques such as secondary and tertiary recovery (for example, injecting steam, water, or a special recovery fluid) to maximize field production. *Reservoir engineering technicians* provide technical assistance to reservoir engineers. They prepare spreadsheets for analyses required for economic evaluations and forecasts. They also gather production data and maintain well histories and decline curves on both company-operated and outside-operated wells.

The petroleum industry has a need for other kinds of technicians as well, including *geological technicians, chemical technicians,* and *civil engineering technicians.*

■ Requirements

All petroleum technician jobs require at least a high school diploma, and a few specialties require at least a bachelor's degree.

High School

If you are interested in this field, you should begin preparing in high school by taking math, algebra, geometry, trigonometry, and calculus classes. Earth science and physics are other useful subjects. High school courses in drafting, mechanics, or auto shop are also valuable preparation, especially for drilling and production technicians. Computer skills are particularly important for engineering technicians, as are typing and English courses.

Postsecondary Training

As mentioned above, postsecondary training is required for only a few petroleum technician positions. For example, a mud test technician must have at least a bachelor's degree in geology. Although postsecondary training is not usually required for drilling, production, or engineering technicians, these workers can gain familiarity with specified basic processes through special education in technical or community colleges. Postsecondary training can also help entry-level workers compete with experienced workers.

Petroleum technology programs, located primarily at about 10 schools in the West and Southwest, are helpful both for newcomers to the field and for those trying to upgrade their job skills. An associate's degree in applied science can be earned by completing a series of technical and education courses.

Petroleum technology programs provide training in drilling operations, fluids, and equipment; production methods; formation evaluation along with the basics of core analysis; and well completion methods and petroleum property evaluation, including evaluation of production history data and basic theories and techniques of economic analysis. These programs emphasize practical applications in the laboratory, field trips, and summer employment, as available.

Specialized training programs designed for oil company employees are offered by the suppliers of the special materials, equipment, or services.

Other Requirements

Petroleum technicians must be able to work with accuracy and precision; mistakes can be costly or hazardous to the technician and to others in the workplace. You should also be able to work both independently and as part of a team, display manual dexterity, mathematical aptitude, and be willing to work irregular hours.

Much of the work in the petroleum industry involves physical labor and is potentially dangerous. Field technicians must be strong and healthy, enjoy the outdoors in all weather, and be flexible and adaptable about working conditions and hours. Drilling crews may be away from their home base for several days at a time, while technicians on offshore rigs must be able to deal with a restricted environment for several days at a time. Petroleum technicians must also like working with machinery, scientific equipment and instruments, and computers. In addition, petroleum technicians must have good eyesight and hearing and excellent hand, eye, and body coordination.

Some petroleum technicians require additional safety training, including hazardous materials training and first-aid training. In some cases, special physical examinations and drug testing are required. Testing and examinations generally take place after technicians are hired.

■ Exploring

You may want to investigate petroleum technician occupations further by checking your school or public libraries for books on the petroleum industry. Other resources include trade journals, high school guidance counselors, the placement office at technical or community colleges, and the associations and Web sites listed at the end of this article. If you live near an oil field, you may be able to arrange a tour by contacting the public relations department of oil companies or drilling contractors.

Summer and other temporary jobs on drilling and production crews are excellent ways of finding out about this field. Temporary work can provide you with firsthand knowledge of the basics of oil field operations, equipment maintenance, safety, and other aspects of the work. You may also want to consider entering a two-year training program in petroleum technology to learn about the field.

■ Employers

Although drilling for oil and gas is conducted in a large number of states, the vast majority of workers are employed in eight states: Texas, Louisiana, Oklahoma, California, Colorado, Wyoming, Alaska, and New Mexico. Employers in the crude petroleum and natural gas industry include major oil companies and independent producers. The oil and gas field services industry, which includes drilling contractors, logging companies, and well servicing contractors, is the other major source of employment.

■ Starting Out

You may enter the field of petroleum drilling or production as a laborer or general helper if you have completed high school. From there, you can work your way up to highly skilled technical jobs, responsibilities, and rewards.

Engineering technicians might start out as engineering or production secretaries and advance to the position of technician after two to five years of on-the-job experience and demonstrated competency in the use of computers.

As mentioned above, other technicians, such as mud test loggers or well loggers, will need a geology degree first.

Upon obtaining your degree, you may start out as assistants to experienced geologists or petroleum engineers.

Generally speaking, industry recruiters from major companies and employers regularly visit the placement offices of school with petroleum technology programs and hire technicians before they finish their last year of technical school or college.

Because many graduates have little or no experience with well drilling operations, new technicians work primarily as assistants to the leaders of the operations. They may also help with the semiskilled or skilled work in order to become familiar with the skills and techniques needed.

It is not uncommon, however, for employers to hire newly graduated technicians and immediately send them to a specialized training program. These programs are designed for oil company employees and usually are offered by the suppliers of the special materials, equipment, or services. After the training period, technicians may be sent anywhere in the world where the company has exploratory drilling or production operations.

■ Advancement

In oil drilling and production, field advancement comes with experience and on-the-job competency. Although a petroleum technology degree is generally not required, it is helpful in today's competitive climate. On a drilling crew, the usual job progression is as follows: from roughneck or rig builder to derrick operator, rotary driller, to tool pusher, and finally, oil production manager. In production, pumpers and gaugers may later become oil company production foremen or operations foremen; from there, they may proceed to operations management, which oversees an entire district. Managers who begin as technicians gain experience that affords them special skills and judgment.

Self-employment also offers interesting and lucrative opportunities. For example, because many drilling rigs are owned by small, private owners, technicians can become independent owners and operators of drilling rigs. The rewards for successfully operating an independent drill can be very great, especially if the owner discovers new fields and shares in the royalties for production.

Working as a consultant or a technical salesperson can lead to advancement in the petroleum industry. Success is contingent upon an excellent record of field success in oil and gas drilling and production.

In some areas, advancement requires further education. Well loggers who want to analyze logs are required to have at least a bachelor's degree in geology or petroleum engineering, and sometimes they need a master's degree. With additional schooling and a bachelor's degree, an engineering technician can become an engineer. For advanced level engineering, a master's degree is the minimum requirement and a doctorate is typically required. Upper-level researchers also need a doctorate.

During periods of rapid growth in the oil industry, advancement opportunities are plentiful for capable workers. However, downsizing in recent years has made advancement more difficult, and in many cases technicians, geologists, engineers, and others have accepted positions for which they are overqualified.

■ Earnings

Because of their many work situations and conditions, petroleum technicians' salaries vary widely. Salaries also vary according to geographic location, experience, and education. Graduates of two-year petroleum technology programs are usually hired in a salary range from $18,000 to $30,000. Hourly salaries for some selected production positions include a range of $12.15 to $13.65 an hour for pumpers and $14.15 for gaugers according to one industry source, while a 1994 Bureau of Labor Statistics report listed a higher hourly salary of $17.85. The same report listed a yearly salary of more than $50,000 for tool pushers. According to industry sources, entry-level engineering technicians start at $26,400, with a top end of $36,000. Entry-level salaries for mud test technicians who are petroleum geologists range from $35,700 to $48,400.

In general, technicians working in remote areas and under severe weather conditions usually receive higher rates of pay, as do technicians who work at major oil companies and companies with unions.

Fringe benefits are good. Most employers provide health and accident insurance, sick pay, retirement plans, profit-sharing plans, and paid vacations. Education benefits are also competitive.

■ Work Environment

Petroleum technicians' workplaces and conditions vary as widely as their duties. They may work on land or offshore, at drilling sites or in laboratories, in offices or refineries.

Field technicians do their work outdoors, day and night, in all kinds of weather. Drilling and production crews work all over the world, often in swamps, deserts, or in the mountains. The work is rugged and physical, and more dangerous than many other kinds of work. Safety is a big concern. Workers are subject to falls and other accidents on rigs, and blowouts can injure or kill workers if well pressure is not controlled.

Drilling crews often move from place to place because work in a particular field may be completed in a few weeks or months. Technicians who work on production wells usually remain in the same location for long periods. Hours are often long for both groups of workers.

Those working on offshore rigs and platforms can experience strong ocean currents, tides, and storms. Living quarters are usually small, like those on a ship, but they are adequate and comfortable. Workers generally live and work on the drilling platform for days at a time and then get several days off away from the rig, returning to shore by helicopter or crewboat.

Engineering technicians generally work indoors in clean, well-lit offices, although some may also spend part of their time in the field. Regular, 40-hour workweeks are the norm, although some may occasionally work irregular hours.

■ Outlook

Although overall employment of technicians in most other fields is expected to increase about as fast as the average, employment of most petroleum technicians is expected to grow slower than average as a result of reduced exploration and falling production in the domestic oil industry.

Companies are likely to continue to restructure and reduce costs in an effort to conserve more money for exploration and drilling abroad and offshore in the Gulf of Mexico, predicted by experts to be one of the most significant exploration hot spots in the world for the next decade.

Besides looking for new fields, companies are also expending much effort to boost production in existing fields. New cost-effective technology that permits new drilling and increases production will continue to be important in helping the profitability of the oil industry.

Continued low oil prices, a worldwide surplus, and anticipated low global demand (partly due to the growing use of more energy-efficient cars and other equipment) mean conditions will continue to be tough for the oil industry for the next several years. However, the anticipated pattern could change. For example, legislation passed at the end of 1995 that lifted a 22-year export ban of Alaskan oil to Japan, South Korea, and other Asian countries could produce 25,000 jobs, according to an Energy Department study. In addition, technological advances have renewed interest in drilling in the Gulf of Mexico. Economic recoveries abroad could also help brighten the picture.

Despite its difficulties, the oil industry still plays an important role in the economy and employment. Oil and gas will continue to be primary energy sources well into the next century. Most job openings will be due to retirements and job transfer. The outlook is best for those with specialized training.

■ For More Information

For information on careers in geology, contact:

American Association of Petroleum Geologists
PO Box 979
Tulsa, OK 74101
Tel: 918-584-2555

For facts and statistics about the petroleum industry, contact:

American Petroleum Institute
1220 L Street, NW
Washington, DC 20005
Tel: 202-682-8118

For information on well-servicing careers, contact:

Association of Oilwell Servicing Contractors
6060 North Central Expressway, Suite 428
Dallas, TX 75206
Tel: 214-692-0771

For information about JETS programs, products, and engineering career brochures (all disciplines), contact:

Junior Engineering Technical Society, Inc.
1420 King Street, Suite 405
Alexandria, VA 22314-2715
Tel: 703-548-5387
Email: jets@nas.edu
Web: http://www.jets.org

For Oil, a booklet describing all phases of the oil industry, contact:

Shell Oil Company
External Affairs
PO Box 2463
Houston, TX 77252-2463
Tel: 713-241-6161

For a list of petroleum technology schools and careers in petroleum engineering, contact:

Society of Petroleum Engineers
PO Box 833836
Richardson, TX 75083
Tel: 214-952-9393
Web: http://www.spe.org

For a training catalog listing publications, audiovisuals, and short courses, including correspondence courses, contact:

The University of Texas at Austin
Petroleum Extension Service
J.J. Pickle Research Campus
Austin, TX 78712-1100
Tel: 512-471-5940

■ Related Articles

Energy

Mining

Petroleum

Chemical Technicians

Civil Engineering Technicians

Energy Conservation Technicians

Geological Technicians

Geologists

Petroleum Engineers

Petroleum Refining Workers

Petrologists

Roustabouts

Petrologists

■ Overview

Geologists study the overall formation of the earth and its history, the movements of the earth's crust, and the mineral compositions and other natural resources. *Petrologists* focus specifically upon the analysis of the composition, structure, and history of rocks and rock formations. Petrologists are also interested in the formation of particular types of rocks that contain economically important materials such as gold, copper, and uranium. They also study the formation and composition of metals, precious stones, minerals, and meteorites, and they analyze a wide variety of substances, ranging from diamonds and gold to petroleum deposits that may be locked in rock formations beneath the earth's surface.

■ History

The field of petrology began to emerge in the early part of the 20th century as a subspecialty within geology. During this period, the mining of oil, coal, precious metals, uranium, and other substances increased rapidly. With the development of the gasoline engine in the mid-1950s, oil was the most significant raw material produced in the world, and the study of the earth's rock formations became invaluable to the mining of petroleum. In fact, the petroleum industry is the largest employer of petrologists; most are employed by one segment or another of the mining industry. Petrologists are also used in many other areas of mining and mineral extraction, and they are employed by numerous government agencies.

■ The Job

The major goal of petrology is to study the origin, composition, and history of rocks and rock formations. Because petrologists are intimately involved in the mining industry, they may

PETROLOGISTS	
SCHOOL SUBJECTS	Chemistry Earth science
PERSONAL SKILLS	Helping/teaching Technical/scientific
WORK ENVIRONMENT	Indoors and outdoors Primarily multiple locations
MINIMUM EDUCATION LEVEL	Bachelor's degree
SALARY RANGE	$20,000 to $25,000 to $62,000
CERTIFICATION OR LICENSING	Required by certain states
OUTLOOK	About as fast as the average
DOT	024
GOE	02.01.01
NOC	2113
O*NET	24111A

A petrologist extracts residue from air-sensitive catalysts.

work closely with the following types of scientists: geologists, who study the overall composition and structure of the earth as well as mineral deposits; geophysicists, who study the physical movements of the earth including seismic activity and physical properties of the earth and its atmosphere; hydrologists, who study the earth's waters and water systems; mineralogists, who examine and classify minerals and precious stones; and paleontologists, who study the fossilized remains of plants and animals found in geological formations.

Depending upon the type of work they do, petrologists may work frequently in teams with the many specialists mentioned above. For example, in oil drilling they may work with geologists and geophysicists. The petrologist is responsible for analyzing rocks from bored samples beneath the earth's surface to determine the oil-bearing composition of rock samples as well as to determine whether certain rock formations are likely to have oil or natural gas content. In precious metal mining operations, petrologists may work closely with mineralogists. They may analyze core samples of mineral rock formations, called "mineral ore," while the mineralogists analyze in detail the specific mineral or minerals contained in such samples.

Because the surface of the earth is composed of thousands of layers of rock formations shaped over several billion years, the contents of these layers can be revealing depending upon the rock and mineral composition of each respective layer. Each layer, or "stratum," of rock beneath the earth's surface tells a story of the earth's condition in the past and can reveal characteristics such as weather patterns, temperatures, the flow of water, the movement of glaciers, volcanic activity, and numerous other characteristics. These layers can also reveal the presence of minerals, mineral ores, and extractable fossil fuels such as petroleum and natural gas.

Petrologists spend time both in the field gathering samples and in the laboratory analyzing those samples. They use physical samples, photographs, maps, and diagrams to describe the characteristics of whatever rock formation or formations they are analyzing. They use chemical compounds to break down rocks and rock materials to isolate certain elements. They use X rays, spectroscopic examination, electron microscopes, and other sophisticated means of testing and analyzing samples to isolate the specific components of various minerals or elements within the samples, in order to draw conclusions from their analysis.

■ Requirements

Most professional positions in the field of petrology require a master's degree or a doctorate. Although individuals without these degrees can technically become petrologists, advances in the field and the profession's requirements will make it extremely difficult to enter the field without a graduate degree.

High School

If you are interested in petrology, you should focus your high school studies in the sciences and in mathematics.

Postsecondary Training

In college, you should concentrate your studies on the earth and physical sciences, geology, paleontology, mineralogy, and, of course, physics, chemistry, and mathematics. Because petrologists frequently analyze large volumes of data and write reports on such data, courses in computer science and English composition are advisable. Many students begin their careers in petrology by first majoring in geology or paleontology as an undergraduate and then, as graduate students, enter formal training in the field of petrology.

Certification or Licensing

Although no special certification exists for the field of petrology, several states require the registration of petrologists, and government petrologists may be required to take the civil service examination. The two major professional associations that provide information and continuing education to petrologists are the Geological Society of America (GSA) and the American Association of Petroleum Geologists (AAPG). The American Geological Institute (AGI) directory can provide information concerning educational requirements for petrologists as well as schools offering formal training in this area.

Other Requirements

Requirements for this profession will depend in large part upon the segment or subspecialty of the profession you choose. In some cases, petrologists work within a confined geographic area and spend most of their time in laboratories. In other instances, petrologists are called upon to travel throughout the United States and even overseas. Extensive travel is often required if you are working for multinational oil companies or other mining operations where you need to be available on short notice to analyze samples in various localities. Where important mining operations are undertaken, petrologists may be required to analyze rocks, ore, core samples, or other materials on short notice and under deadline pressure.

As with other scientific disciplines, teamwork is often an essential part of the job. Petrologists must be able to understand and relate to geologists, paleontologists, mineralogists, and other scientific experts; they must also be able to relate to and communicate their findings to supervisory personnel who may lack a strong technical background.

If you are considering petrology, you must be able to work well with others, as well as independently on various projects. You should also enjoy travel and the outdoors.

■ Exploring

If you are interested in pursuing this field, you may wish to meet and interview petrologists to find out more about the field. Petrologists may be found in universities and colleges that offer courses in geology and petrology, in certain government offices and field offices, and especially throughout the mining, oil, and natural gas industries.

Both geologists and petrologists require assistance in their work, and it is possible to obtain summer jobs and part-time employment in certain parts of the country where mining or oil exploration activities are taking place. For further information about the field of petrology and about various conferences in the geological professions, contact the American Geological Institute, the American Association of Petroleum Geologists, or the Geological Society of America.

■ Employers

Because much of the practice of petrology relates to the extraction of minerals, fossil fuels, metals, or natural resources, most petrologists work for petroleum and mining companies. Their work includes mining on the earth's surface, beneath the earth's surface, and under the ocean floor (in the case of off-shore oil drilling, for example). Other petrologists work for federal, state, or local governments. In the federal branch, petrologists are often employed by the Environmental Protection Agency, the Department of Agriculture, the Department of Energy, the Department of Defense, and the Department of Commerce, or the Department of the Interior. In fact, the largest government employer is the U.S. Geological Survey, a branch of the U.S. Department of the Interior. Other petrologists teach earth science in high schools or teach geology and petrology courses in colleges and universities or work as consultants. In fact, the consulting industry is the most active employer, and will probably remain so.

The field of petrology is open to a number of activities and subspecialties, and during their careers petrologists normally specialize in one area or another.

■ Starting Out

If you are seeking to pursue petrology as a career, you must obtain either a master's degree or a doctorate at a qualified college or university. This requirement is especially necessary in light of the U.S. oil industry's slump during the 1980s, which has affected the fields of geology, paleontology, mineralogy, and petrology.

Both the federal government and state governments employ petrologists in various agencies. Thus, if you are undertaking graduate programs in petrology, you should contact both state civil service agencies in your respective state and the federal Office of Personnel Management (OPM). Federal agencies generally notify the OPM when they wish to fill vacancies in various positions and when new positions are created. The OPM has job information centers located in major cities throughout the United States. You can also obtain job information concerning employment with the states through your state's capital.

Although industrial firms do engage in campus recruiting, particularly for master's and doctoral level job applicants, less recruiting is occurring now because of the U.S. oil industry slump. Thus, job seekers should not hesitate to contact oil exploration companies, mining companies, and other organizations directly. It is always a good idea to contact geologists and petrologists directly in various companies to learn about opportunities.

Part-time employment is available to geologists and petrologists from both private industry and various federal and state agencies. In some cases, agencies use volunteer students and scientists and pay only some expenses rather than a full salary. This arrangement may still be a good way to gain experience and to meet professionals in the field.

If you wish to teach petrology, you should consult college and university employment listings. For graduate students in the field, a limited number of part-time jobs as well as instructor-level jobs are available.

Note that junior high schools and high schools generally need more instructors in petrology than do colleges. This new reality reflects the fact that many high schools are beginning to offer a broader than ever range of science courses. Individuals with a master's or doctoral degree are likely to be qualified to teach any one of a variety of science courses at the high school level, including earth science, physics, chemistry, mathematics, or biology.

■ Advancement

Because the level of competition in this field is keen and the oil industry is subject to fluctuation, those wishing to enter the petrology profession must think seriously about obtaining the highest level of education possible.

Advancement in the field generally involves spending a number of years as a staff scientist and then taking on supervisory and managerial responsibilities. The ability to work on a team, the ability to perform accurate and timely research, and the ability to take charge of projects are all important for advancement in this field.

Because petrology, geology, and mineralogy are sciences that overlap, especially in industry, it is possible for petrologists to become mineralogists or geologists under the right circumstances. The fact that the three disciplines are intimately related can work to a career person's advantage, particularly in changing economic times.

■ Earnings

Earnings as a petrologist will vary according to a person's educational attainment, experience, and ability. In 1997, according to a report by the National Association of Colleges and Employers, graduates holding a bachelor's degree in geology received salary offers averaging $31,100 a year. Those with a master's degree averaged $40,000, and those with a doctorate averaged $62,000. Petrologists with a bachelor's degree working for local or state government averaged about $26,000 a year.

Petrologists employed by oil companies or consulting firms will generally start at somewhat higher salaries, but private industry favors those with master's or doctoral degrees. According to a survey conducted by the American Association of Petroleum Geologists in the mid-1990s, geoscientists working in the oil and gas industry with fewer than two years of experience averaged $42,500.

Many petrologists are eligible to receive fringe benefits, such as life and health insurance, paid vacations, and pension plans.

■ Work Environment

Because the field of petrology involves a considerable amount of testing of rocks, ores, and other materials at mining sites and other types of geological sites, petrologists can expect to travel a considerable amount. In some cases, petrologists must travel back and forth from a field site to a laboratory several times while conducting a series of tests. If petrologists are working on exploratory investigations of a potential site for fuel, they may be at a remote location for weeks or months, until the data collected are sufficient to return to the laboratory. The conditions may be arduous, and leisure time may provide little to do on-site.

The hours and working conditions of petrologists vary, but petrologists working in the field can generally expect long hours. Petrologists, geologists, and mineralogists frequently work in teams, and petrologists may work under the supervision of a head geologist, for example. In private industry, they are also frequently working with mining engineers, mine supervisors, drilling supervisors, and others who are all part of a larger mining or drilling operation.

■ Outlook

Oil and gas exploration has decreased in the past several years because of reduced prices for oil. As a result, the number of new jobs in this field has dropped, and the number of students who graduate with degrees in petrology or geology has declined. Eventually, new sources of oil and gas must be found. When exploration activities resume, the outlook for petrologists will improve. A worldwide increase in oil prices, which will spur oil drilling and exploration, is inevitable.

Despite the setbacks in the oil industry, the Bureau of Labor Statistics reports that employment opportunities for geologists, petrologists, and geophysicists will grow about as fast as the average for all occupations through the year 2006. Increased environmental regulations will create a need for these scientists in environmental protection and reclamation work.

■ For More Information

For information on geology careers, contact:

American Association of Petroleum Geologists
Communications Department
PO Box 979
Tulsa, OK 74101
Tel: 918-584-2555

For information on geology careers, contact:

American Geological Institute
4220 King Street
Alexandria, VA 22302
Tel: 703-379-2480
Web: http://www.agiweb.org

For career information and job listings, contact:

Association of Engineering Geologists
Department of Geology
Texas A&M University, MS-3115
College Station, TX 77843-3115
409-845-0142
Web: http://aegweb.org

For career information and job listings, contact:

Geological Society of America
PO Box 9140
3300 Penrose Place
Boulder, CO 80301
Tel: 303-447-2020
Web: http://www.geosociety.org

■ **Related Articles**

Pharmaceutical Industry Workers

■ **Overview**

Pharmaceutical industry workers are involved in many aspects of the development, manufacture, and distribution of pharmaceutical products. *Pharmaceutical operators* work with machines that perform such functions as filling capsules and inspecting the quality and weight of tablets. *Pharmaceutical supervisors* and *managers* oversee research and development, production, and sales and promotion workers. *Pharmaceutical sales representatives* sell and distribute pharmaceutical products and introduce new items to pharmacists, retail stores, and medical practitioners.

■ **History**

The oldest known written records relating to pharmaceutical preparations—5,000 years old—come from the ancient Sumerians. Other ancient cultures, such as the Indians and Chinese, used primitive pharmaceutical applications to eradicate evil spirits, which they believed to cause evil in the body. The Babylonians, Assyrians, Greeks, and Egyptians also compounded early pharmaceuticals in hope that they would rid the body of disease (which they believed was caused primarily by sinful thoughts and deeds).

Professions in pharmacy began to be established in the 17th century, after the first major list of drugs and their

applications and preparations was compiled. The discoveries of the anesthetics, morphine (first used in 1806), ether (1842), and cocaine (1860), were among the first pharmaceutical advancements to significantly benefit humankind. Since then, numerous vaccines have cured sickness and disease and in effect have helped people live longer, healthier lives.

In 1852 in the United States, the American Pharmaceutical Association was formed to help those in the pharmaceutical field organize their professional, political, and economic goals (the Pharmaceutical Manufacturers Association replaced the APA in 1958). Government intervention in the pharmaceutical industry began in 1848, and in 1931 the Food and Drug Administration (FDA) was formed to provide legal regulation and monitoring of the pharmaceutical industry. As the industry became increasingly regulated and organized, qualified, trained workers were sought to professionally develop, produce, package, and market pharmaceutical products. These workers, known collectively as pharmaceutical industry workers, possess a variety of skills, responsibilities, and education levels and continue to actively work to improve the quality and length of our lives.

PHARMACEUTICAL INDUSTRY WORKERS	
SCHOOL SUBJECTS	**Business** **Mathematics** **Technical/Shop**
PERSONAL SKILLS	**Following instructions** **Mechanical/manipulative**
WORK ENVIRONMENT	**Primarily indoors** **Primarily one location**
MINIMUM EDUCATION LEVEL	**High school diploma**
SALARY RANGE	**$18,000 to $33,000 to $75,000+**
CERTIFICATION OR LICENSING	**None available**
OUTLOOK	**Faster than the average**
DOT	**559**
GOE	**06.04.19**
NOC	**9232**

Pharmaceutical industry workers must pay strict attention to each task.

■ The Job

The pharmaceutical, or simply, the drug industry, has four main divisions: research and development, production, administration, and sales.

Research and development professionals create new drug products and improve existing ones. For more information about research and development, see the chapters on *Drug Developers, Pharmacists,* and *Pharmacologists.* These products designed by the research and development professionals are manufactured by production workers called, as a whole, pharmaceutical operators. Many of these employees work on production lines, tending equipment that measures, weighs, mixes, and granulates various chemical ingredients and components, which are then manufactured into such forms as pills and capsules. Often these employees inspect the finished goods, looking for such inconsistencies as broken tablets and unfilled capsules.

There are a number of specific job designations in the realm of production.

Capsule filling machine operators run machines that fill gelatin capsules with medicine. They scoop empty capsules into a loading hopper and medicine into a filling hopper. After the filled and sealed capsules are ejected by the machinery, these operators inspect the capsules for proper filling and for evidence of breakage. They may also spot-check individual capsules or lots by comparing their weight with standardized figures on a weight specification sheet. This process is used for certain antihistamines, vitamins, and general pain relievers, for example.

Ampule and vial fillers work with glass tubes and plastic and glass containers with rubber stopules that are filled with medicine and then sealed. The process for filling is similar to that for the capsule filler; however, the operator must adjust gas flames to the appropriate temperature so that the tubes are completely sealed. They also count and

pack readied ampules and vials for shipment. (Vials and syringes have recently become the primary containers for liquid drug production in the United States.)

Ampule and vial inspectors use magnifying glasses to check for cracks, leaks, and other damage. They keep records of inspected cartons, as well as damaged or flawed products.

Granulator machine operators operate mixing and milling machines that are equipped with fine blades that mix ingredients and then crush or mill them into powdered form so that they can be formed into tablets. They are responsible for weighing and measuring each batch, blending the ingredients with the use of machinery, and adding alcohol, gelatins, or starch pastes to help the pill keep its form. They then spread the mixture on trays which they place into an oven or steam dryer set at a predetermined temperature. At the conclusion of the heating process, they check each batch for dryness levels, size, weight, and texture.

Coaters operate machines that cover pills and tablets with coatings that flavor, color, or preserve the contents.

Fermenter operators oversee fermenting tanks and equipment, which produce antibiotics and other drugs. Operators start the mixing tanks, add ingredients, such as salt, yeast, and sugar, and transfer the mixture to a fermenting tank when it is ready. They are responsible for monitoring the temperature in the tanks, for adding precise amounts of liquid antibiotic, water, and foam-preventive oil, and for measuring the amount of solution so that it may be transferred to another tank for additional processing.

There are also a vast number of laborer professions involved in the production area of the pharmaceutical industry. *Hand packers and packagers* remove filled cartons from conveyor belts and transport other finished pharmaceutical products to and from shipping departments. *Industrial machinery mechanics* ensure that all machinery is working properly and at optimum production capacity.

The third major branch of this industry comprises administrative positions. *Production managers* direct workers in the manufacturing field by scheduling projects and deadlines. These employees also oversee factory operations and enforce safety and health regulations, monitor efficiency, and plan work assignments. They also direct and schedule assignments for the shipping department, which packs and loads the pharmaceutical products for distribution.

The finished products are marketed by the sales branch. *Service and sales representatives* supply pharmaceutical drugs and related products to hospitals, independent medical practitioners, pharmacists, and retail stores. Telephone calls and office visits allow the representatives to keep in contact with buyers, monitor supplies, and introduce new products. Often, reps supplement free samples of new products with printed literature when available. Sales reps may choose to promote, for example, certain vitamins and other nutritional supplements, pain relievers, and general health care supplies. Jim Batastini works as a sales representative for the pharmaceutical industry; much of his work entails calling on physicians within a certain geographic area. "The purpose of my visits with these physicians," he says, "is to provide the latest clinical information relevant to our products and how they can best be used to manage different disease states."

■ Requirements

High School

To prepare for a job in sales or administration, you should take courses in speech and English, to develop your communication skills. You should also take science courses, including biology and chemistry, so that you'll have some insight into pharmaceutical research and development. If you're interested in a job as a production worker, take courses in math and science. You should also take courses, such as voc-tech, that will give you some background in machine work and engineering.

Postsecondary Education

Most employers offering production jobs require at least a high school diploma or the equivalent. Certain labor positions also require technical or vocational training.

Some pharmaceutical companies offer on-the-job training to nonprofessional workers. Employees in sales may be required to have sufficient training or a background in pharmacology as well as in sales and marketing, whereas certain administrative positions require course work in liberal arts, data processing, and business administration. Various types of pharmaceutical training are also available in the military. Information about pharmaceutical careers in the armed forces can be obtained by contacting your nearest military recruitment office.

Other Requirements

Pharmaceutical industry workers on the whole must be alert, dependable, and possess good communications skills, both oral and written. Workers can expect to interact with all divisions and levels of employees—strong communications skills promote faster and more accurate production. Production workers must be physically fit, mentally alert to oversee production lines and processes, and have the temperament to work at sometimes repetitive tasks. Administrative and managerial workers must be decisive leaders with empathy for workers at all levels of education and responsibility. Sales and marketing workers need good people and persuasive skills in order to effectively promote products. "You should have the ability to learn a large

volume of technical material," Jim says, "and have the ability to assimilate the information and concisely communicate it to medical professionals."

■ Exploring

If your high school has a vocational training program, look into taking a class that will prepare you for production work; a local community college may also have such a course. You should consider contacting trade organizations such as the American Foundation for Pharmaceutical Education, whose objective is to improve pharmaceutical educational programs and student performance. In addition, science-related clubs and social organizations often schedule meetings and professional lectures and offer career guidance as well.

To prepare for a sales career, you might be able to find part-time work in a pharmacy. Working for a pharmacy, you can learn about the drug manufacturers, the most-prescribed drugs, and other information about the industry. You may also meet sales representatives, and have the opportunity to read the promotional materials distributed by drug companies.

■ Employers

Production workers and sales representatives work for pharmaceutical companies that manufacture prescription and over-the-counter products. These companies include Johnson & Johnson and Bristol-Myers Squibb. A small percentage of industry workers are employed with companies that make the biological products that are used by manufacturers in the production of drugs.

■ Starting Out

College-trained applicants often benefit from placement services provided by the student services division of their schools. Applicants can also apply directly to pharmaceutical companies or through school contacts with professional organizations. In addition, newspapers and professional trade publications list job opportunities that are offered in each division and level of the industry.

THE PHARMACEUTICAL INDUSTRY ONLINE

At http://www.pharmaceuticalonline.com, you can read about new products, pharmaceutical sales trends, and new technology and equipment. Recent articles featured on the site have included news about sales increases in biotech drugs, new cancer treatments, and pharmaceutical manufacturer mergers. The site also includes a "Career Center" that allows you to search for jobs and apply for them online. The Career Center also spotlights major employers.

"If you're interested in pharmaceutical sales," Jim says, "a strong science background with good academic standing will probably be required in the future. And networking with people in the industry is a great way to get your foot in the door."

■ Advancement

There are many advancement opportunities for pharmaceutical industry workers. Production workers may advance to managerial positions and learn how to operate more sophisticated machinery. Laboratory assistants and research assistants may prepare for advancement with additional education and be promoted to new research projects and duties. Administrators may become supervisors, executives, sales managers, or marketing executives.

There are always possibilities for advancement for employees who are willing to develop new skills and take on more responsibilities. Many positions, however, require additional, formal training. "The industry maintains a high level of continuing education requirements," Jim says.

■ Earnings

Because the pharmaceutical industry is a large field, earnings vary tremendously and depend on the worker's position, educational background, and amount of work experience. However, some generalizations can be made about certain wages.

Production workers average approximately $14 per hour, though the wage range for these employees is broad, depending on the size of the firm, the shift to which the worker is assigned, years at the company, and the geographic location of the plant. Overtime compensation is usually equal to time and a half or double time.

According to *The National Business Employment Weekly,* those in pharmaceutical sales make between $34,000 a year and $55,000, depending on the position. The median is about $43,000 a year.

All full-time workers, regardless of their work specialty, receive paid vacations, medical and dental insurance, paid sick and personal days, pension plans, and life insurance. Some workers may also be offered profit-sharing, savings plans, and reimbursement for job-related education.

■ Work Environment

Production workers average 45-hour work weeks and 8 hours per shift; at some pharmaceutical firms, however, shifts may run round the clock, meaning that some employees work a variety of shifts. Production workers often work in chemicals factories, which are well ventilated and offer good lighting but may be noisy and crowded. These workers may have to package products and load them onto trucks or docks by hand or with forklifts. Machinery operators may stand much of their shift. Laborers and pack-

agers frequently walk, stand, bend, and lift in the course of their day. They may be required to operate machinery to lift heavy or bulky material. Ampule and vial fillers wear special clothing, such as complete face and body coverings, to maintain sterile conditions. Safety equipment is required for hazardous tasks of all types.

Administrators work in office environments that are often modern, neat, and have good lighting and ample work spaces. They often bring work home with them or have late meetings with other staff members.

Advertising and sales workers travel considerable distances to hospitals, pharmacies, and physician's offices. They may go to other cities or even other countries to promote their product line. Jim says the work sometimes requires 80 hours per week. "But it's an ever evolving field," he says, "so you never get bored with the subject matter."

■ Outlook

As the U.S. population continues to include increasing numbers of older people, the pharmaceutical industry is expected to grow to accommodate medical needs. In addition, technological developments continue to be pursued in many scientific endeavors, including the creation of new drugs for the treatment of such widespread diseases as AIDS and cancer. The overall employment outlook for workers in the pharmaceutical industry is thus considered very good and is anticipated to continue at a growing pace at least through the first years of the 21st century.

Many pharmaceutical manufacturing companies are investigating growth in health-related areas, such as cosmetics, veterinary products, agricultural chemicals, and medicinals and botanicals. Dietary supplements account for $12 billion a year in sales, and the demand for herbal products grew from about $1.6 billion a year to more than $3 billion a year in 1998.

In production positions there will be a decline for machine operators as more machinery becomes automated. Inspectors, testers, and graders may also see a decline in jobs as a result of downsizing. Expected increases in production positions include industrial machinery mechanics, hand packers and packagers, and granulator machine operators. Sales and marketing personnel will be needed to educate buyers about newly approved over-the-counter medications, generics, biopharmaceuticals, and other new products. Some companies have experimented with selling products directly in magazines, which has increased sales for some drugs. But these increased sales may not be enough to account for the expense of advertising.

■ For More Information

For more information about the pharmaceutical industry, contact:

American Foundation for Pharmaceutical Education
One Church Street, Suite 202
Rockville, MD 20850
Tel: 301-738-2160

National Association of Pharmaceutical Manufacturers
320 Old Country Road
Garden City, NY 11530-1752
Tel: 516-741-3699
Web: http://www.napmnet.org

For information about student membership and publications, and for news about the industry, visit the APhA Web site, or contact:

American Pharmaceutical Association
2215 Constitution Avenue, NW
Washington, DC 20037-2985
Tel: 202-628-4410
Web: http://www.aphanet.org

■ Related Articles

Chemicals
Health Care
Pharmaceuticals
Biochemists
Chemical Technicians
Chemists
Drug Developers
Industrial Machinery Mechanics
Laboratory Testing Technicians
Pharmacists
Pharmacologists
Pharmacy Technicians
Toxicologists

Pharmaceutical Operators

■ See Pharmaceutical Industry Workers

Pharmaceutical Sales Representatives

■ See Pharmaceutical Industry Workers

Pharmacists

■ Overview

Pharmacists are health professionals responsible for the dispensation of prescription and nonprescription medications. They act as consultants to health practitioners and the general public concerning possible drug adverse reactions and interactions, and may also give advice relating to home medical supplies and durable health care equipment. The role of the pharmacist has evolved into that of consultant and medicinal expert, because of the expanded duties of pharmacy technicians and the increasing time restrictions placed on health maintenance organization physicians. There are over 180,000 pharmacists practicing in the United States.

■ History

The word pharmacist itself can be traced to the early Greeks. During the time of Aristotle (384-322 BC), those who compounded drugs were called *pharmakons*. The word has changed little from its original form and still means approximately the same thing: one who compounds drugs, medicines, or poisons.

Pharmacy as a profession grew slowly in the United States. It is said that one of our earliest pharmacists was Governor John Winthrop (1588-1649) of the Massachusetts Bay Colony. He learned to compound drugs because there were no other sources in the colony for obtaining medicines. The first school established to teach pharmacy in this country was the Philadelphia College of Pharmacy, founded in 1821. It is still in operation today.

In 1906, the Federal Pure Food and Drug Act was passed. The Food and Drug Administration (FDA), created in 1931, approves all pharmaceuticals sold in the United States. The work of the pharmacist has become increasingly important because of the complexity

PHARMACISTS	
SCHOOL SUBJECTS	Chemistry Mathematics
PERSONAL SKILLS	Following instructions Technical/scientific
WORK ENVIRONMENT	Primarily indoors Primarily one location
MINIMUM EDUCATION LEVEL	Doctorate
SALARY RANGE	$52,100 to $64,800 to $81,400
CERTIFICATION OR LICENSING	Required by all states
OUTLOOK	About as fast as the average
DOT	074
GOE	02.04.01
NOC	3131
O*NET	32517

A pharmacist carefully counts pills to fill a prescription.

and potential side effects of the thousands of medications now on the market.

■ The Job

As a pharmacist, you'll need a thorough knowledge of drug products. Most importantly, you'll need an understanding of how drugs work for people who are sick. In addition to dispensing drugs according to orders from physicians, dentists, and other health care practitioners, you advise the professionals on the appropriate selection and use of medications. You inform and caution patients about medications and how to use them properly, answer questions from customers or patients about symptoms, and discuss nonprescription products such as headache remedies, vitamins, and cough syrups. You also keep records of drugs and medications dispensed to each person in order to identify duplicate drugs or combinations of drugs that can cause adverse reactions or side effects.

In conjunction with these duties, you're required to maintain your license through continuing education, though type and requirements vary. Some states may require this education in the form of correspondence (written responses to educational material), or conferences and sem-

inars. Some states may also require continuing education in particular disease topics and treatment.

You'll have a variety of other duties depending on where you are employed. Most pharmacists practice in community pharmacies, but some practice in hospitals and other health care facilities or in pharmaceutical manufacturing companies. Some pharmacists teach. Others conduct research. You may be employed in a laboratory, as a manufacturer's representative, or with the armed forces. Many practice with some branch of government, such as the U.S. Public Health Service. Others may work for Health Maintenance Organizations (HMOs) or for insurance companies. An increasing number of pharmacists work in nursing homes, monitoring drug therapy of the elderly.

You must be diligent in maintaining a clean and ordered work area. You must be exceedingly accurate and precise in your calculations, and possess a high degree of concentration, in order to reduce the risk of error as you compound and assemble prescriptions. You must be proficient with a variety of technical devices and computer systems. However, more and more drug products are shipped in finished form by the pharmaceutical manufacturer. The actual compounding of prescription medications, therefore, is taking a smaller amount of time.

In addition to pharmaceutical duties, pharmacists in community pharmacies buy and sell merchandise unrelated to health, hire and supervise other workers, and oversee the general operation of the pharmacy.

Pharmacists in hospitals and other health care facilities provide pharmaceutical services to aid physicians, nurses, and other health care personnel. They dispense prescription medicines, make sterile solutions or special mixtures, buy medical supplies, and perform administrative duties. They counsel patients at discharge about their continuing drug therapy, monitor drug regimens, and review drug use. If the hospital is large, there may be the need for a large staff of pharmacists.

Shreen Beshures works as a *consultant pharmacist*, which involves reviewing patient charts in nursing homes. She accesses patient information with a laptop computer. "I print recommendations to the doctors," she says, "for a reduction in the number of medications, a more cost-effective medication, and a reduction in the amount of psych meds a patient is on—so that nursing home patients aren't over-sedated." She also consults directly with doctors, nurse practitioners, and physician assistants on medications. Other days are spent in the pharmacy, preparing medications for the nursing home and supervising pharmacy technicians.

Many pharmacists are employed by large pharmaceutical manufacturers. They may work in one of several capacities. Some engage in research to help develop new drugs or to improve or find new uses for old ones. Others supervise the preparation of ingredients that go into the tablets, capsules, ointments, solutions, or other dosage forms produced by the manufacturer. Others test or standardize the raw or refined chemicals that eventually will go into the finished drug. Some may assist with advertising the company's products, to make sure that nothing untruthful or misleading is said about a product in professional literature. Some pharmacists may prepare literature on new products for pharmaceutical or technical journals. Others write material for package inserts.

Pharmacists employed by government agencies may work in a number of different kinds of positions. They may be *inspectors* who monitor drug manufacturing firms, hospitals, wholesalers, or community pharmacies. They may work with agencies involved with narcotics and other controlled substances.

Some pharmacists write or edit reports for journals or draft technical papers, teach in pharmacy programs, or work in advertising. Others are staff members in professional associations. A few are patent attorneys or experts in pharmaceutical law.

■ Requirements

High School

If you're going to enroll in a college of pharmacy, you should take college preparatory courses and concentrate in the areas of mathematics and science, especially chemistry. You should take speech courses, because good communications skills will be important as you progress through college, job interviews, and eventual employment as a pharmacist. You should also consider business and accounting courses; some pharmacists own their own drugstores or buy into pharmacy franchises.

Postsecondary Training

The federal government has mandated that pharmacy schools lengthen their degree programs to six years by 2001. Though the six-year doctor of pharmacy (Pharm. D.) degree has long been an option, some pharmacists currently working hold only a four-year Bachelor's of Science degree.

The first one or two years of your college education may be obtained in a four-year undergraduate college or in a junior college. Pre-pharmacy courses typically include mathematics, physics, biology, and two years of chemistry. Some pharmacy colleges require applicants to take the Pharmacy College Admissions Test (P-CAT).

The top pharmacy graduate programs include (as ranked by *U.S. News and World Report*): the University of California-San Francisco, University of Texas-Austin, University of Kentucky, and University of Minnesota. In graduate school, you'll take courses in the principles of

THE FAMOUS WALL DRUG OF SOUTH DAKOTA

If you're planning a cross-country road trip this summer, mark the small town of Wall, South Dakota, on your Rand McNally. There, at the edge of the Badlands, stands Wall Drug, possibly the most famous drug store in the country. (Second only, perhaps, to Schwab's Drug Store, the Hollywood pharmacy where many a starlet was fabled to have been discovered.) Wall Drug's owners, Ted and Dorothy Hustead, struggled to succeed during the Depression by posting billboards promoting free ice water to weary travelers. Since then, the store has evolved into a tourist trap par excellence, selling everything from stuffed jackalope wall mounts to Mount Rushmore toothpick holders to 5-cent cups of coffee.

pharmacology, biochemistry, pharmacy law and ethics, and pharmaceutical care. Most states require some form of internship, which is completed during school and summer hours.

Certification or Licensing

When you receive a degree, you are then required to take a state board examination to be licensed to practice. You'll need a license to practice in all states and the District of Columbia. Applicants for a license must have graduated from an accredited pharmacy program and have passed a state board examination. You must also be over the age of 21, be of good character, and have a specified amount of practical experience or have served an internship.

Other Requirements

You'll need good people skills in dealing with patients and assistants. A good "bed-side" manner (a kind, comforting approach), like that required of doctors, will help you in a hospital or nursing home setting, particularly as pharmacists' responsibilities expand to include counseling and advising. You should also be very organized, and have an eye for detail—doctors, nurses, and patients will all be relying on you to keep accurate drug records.

■ Exploring

"Get a part-time job in a drug store," Shreen advises, "or volunteer at a pharmacy in a hospital to see if its really what you want to do." In a drug store, you can get part-time work as a stock clerk, salesperson, or delivery person. In these positions, you'll have the opportunity to observe first-hand the kind of work that pharmacists do and gain experience dealing with customers. If you've demonstrated responsibility, you may even have the opportunity to assist in the pharmacy—entering data in customer computer records, taking inventory on pharmaceuticals, bottles, and vials, and preparing labels. Working in a nutrition and vitamin store, you can also learn a great deal about dietary supplements and herbal alternatives to pharmaceuticals.

Employers

Three out of five pharmacists work in community pharmacies—there are more than 30,000 pharmacies operated by traditional chain pharmacy companies and supermarkets, and another 20,000 independent pharmacies. One-fourth of the pharmacists in the United States work in hospitals. Pharmacists can also find work in clinics, pharmaceutical companies, and with the government. Some pharmacists are self-employed and fill-in as "temps" at a number of different community pharmacies.

Starting Out

While in high school, Shreen got a part-time job as a pharmacy technician in a neighborhood drugstore. "I had always wanted to go to medical school," Shreen says, "but wasn't sure. I took pre-med classes in college, which were also pre-pharmacy, and decided to transfer to a pharmacy school in New York."

After receiving your degree and license, you'll begin your career by accepting a salaried position in a community pharmacy or a hospital. Though the level of work is the same for beginning pharmacists as it is for experienced pharmacists, you may have to work long hours, evenings, and weekends until you've gained some seniority with the pharmacy.

Advancement

Community pharmacists may enjoy advancement to supervisory positions. The hospital pharmacist may advance to the position of chief pharmacist or director of pharmacy services after accumulating several years of experience.

Pharmacists who are employed by drug manufacturing firms may anticipate increases in both salary and responsibility as they gain experience and increase their value to their firms.

There are many new areas of pharmacy, which may offer increases in salary, responsibility, or creativity. *Pharmacoeconomists* research cost versus benefit of new therapies. *Radiopharmacists* prepare and dispense radioactive pharmaceuticals. *Pharmacotherapists* work with physicians to determine proper drug therapies.

Pharmacists who acquire advanced degrees and education may become *pharmacologists* (who study the effects of drugs on the body), educators and researchers, or pharmacy administrators.

Earnings

The earnings of salaried pharmacists are largely determined by the location, size, and type of employer as well as by the duties and responsibilities of the individual pharmacist. Pharmacists who own or manage pharmacies often earn considerably more than other pharmacists.

According to a salary survey published by *Drug Topics* magazine in 1997, the average annual salary of pharmacists in community drugstores is $52,000 to $60,000. A pharmacist in a hospital earns about $61,300 a year. A pharmacist working for a pharmaceutical company can make considerably more, with an average yearly salary of $81,000.

Pharmacists, in addition to salary, enjoy fringe benefits such as paid vacation, medical and dental insurance, overtime, and sometimes bonuses and profit-sharing, depending on the size and type of employer. Because of the high demand for pharmacists who will work odd hours in community drugstores, temp pharmacists can often negotiate for benefits, as well.

Work Environment

A pharmacy is usually a pleasant place to work. It is usually a neighborhood institution and often a health information center. Most pharmacies are well lighted, well ventilated, and kept in a clean and orderly fashion. Many chain-owned pharmacies now provide 18- or 24-hour operations.

Hospital pharmacies are efficient, orderly, and busy with a variety of important activities. The physicians, nurses, technicians, and other medical personnel with whom the pharmacist works are usually intelligent and concerned people.

The two most unfavorable conditions of the pharmacist's practice are long hours and the necessity to stay on one's feet. It is not unusual to be on duty at least 48 hours a week. Most state laws covering the practice of pharmacy require that there be a pharmacist on duty at all times when the pharmacy is open. Most pharmacies employ at least 2 pharmacists because it is customary to remain open at least 12 hours a day. Many pharmacies are also open at least part of the time on Sundays. Despite the requirements of the job, most pharmacists appreciate being involved in health care. "I'm an integral part of the health care system," Shreen says, "preventing medication errors and aiding nurses and physicians with medications."

Pharmacists who operate their own pharmacies have financial responsibilities. Many pharmacies do better than one to two million dollars in gross sales each year in business. They must hire employees, maintain an adequate inventory, and keep records. They must make rent or mortgage payments and pay insurance premiums and taxes. The growing influence of third-party prescription programs has forced pharmacists to spend considerable amounts of time processing claims, maintaining government records, and explaining benefit plans to customers. Many community pharmacy owners complain of restrictions placed on them by government agencies, insurance companies, and

HMOs that they claim hinders their ability to compete with chain competitors.

Outlook

In 1995, the Pew Health Professions Commission published a report that proved controversial in the industry. The report predicted an upcoming surplus of 40,000 pharmacists, and suggested that many pharmacy schools be closed. Industry experts were skeptical of these predictions, and the current marketplace has supported that skepticism. In the late 1990s, there was a shortage of pharmacists in every state but New York and New Jersey. The expanded education requirements demanded by the federal government is expected to result in even fewer pharmacists, as many students may be put off by the additional expense of an extra few years of college. The U.S. Bureau of Labor Statistics predicts a job growth rate of 12.9 percent for all sectors of the industry: 11.5 percent for retail trade, and 7.4 percent for hospitals. According to a report published by *Drug Topics* magazine in 1998, hospitals are expected to have trouble competing with retail stores for pharmacists. Retail stores can better afford to offer higher salaries and good benefit packages.

The National Association of Chain Drug Stores predicts, with fewer qualified pharmacists, a health care crisis. With the prescription volume expected to increase to 4 billion by 2006, more pharmacists will be needed to staff the expanding chain stores and stores open 24-hours. Furthermore, a growing and aging population will require more pharmacists, especially in retirement-heavy areas such as California, the Southwest, and the Southeast.

The role of the pharmacist is expected to expand. Pharmacists will be more involved in counseling patients and advising physicians on the drugs to prescribe. They will make house calls and see patients in doctor's offices. They will also be studying more complex medications, and sorting out drug information on the Internet.

For More Information

For information about student membership and publications, and for news about the industry, visit the APhA Web site, or contact:

American Pharmaceutical Association
2215 Constitution Avenue, NW
Washington, DC 20037-2985
Tel: 202-628-4410
Web: http://www.aphanet.org

For information on careers in pharmacy, and for industry facts, visit the NACDS Web site, or contact:

National Association of Chain Drug Stores
413 North Lee Street
Alexandria, VA 22313-1480
Tel: 703-549-3001
Web: http://www.nacds.org

For facts about consultant pharmacists, visit the ASCP Web site, or contact:

American Society of Consultant Pharmacists
1321 Duke Street
Alexandria, VA 22314-3563
Tel: 703-739-1300
Web: http://ascp.com

Related Articles

Pharmaceuticals
Drug Developers
Pharmaceutical Industry Workers
Pharmacologists
Pharmacy Technicians
Toxicologists

Pharmacologists

Overview

Pharmacologists play an important role in medicine and in science by studying the effects of drugs, chemicals, and other materials on humans and animals. These highly educated specialists perform research designed to identify the effects of drugs and other substances on living organs and tissues and on the vital life processes of humans and animals. The goals of pharmacological research are to determine how drugs and other chemicals act at the cellular level; to discover how drugs should be most effectively used; to standardize drug dosages; to analyze chemicals, food additives, poisons, insecticides, and other substances to determine their effects; and to identify dangerous substances as well as dangerous levels of chemicals.

History

Pharmacology is not the same as pharmacy. Pharmacology is the science concerned with the interactions between chemicals and biological

PHARMACOLOGISTS	
SCHOOL SUBJECTS	Chemistry Mathematics
PERSONAL SKILLS	Communication/ideas Technical/scientific
WORK ENVIRONMENT	Primarily indoors Primarily one location
MINIMUM EDUCATION LEVEL	Doctorate
SALARY RANGE	$43,680 to $69,316 to $111,379+
CERTIFICATION OR LICENSING	Recommended
OUTLOOK	Much faster than the average
DOT	041
GOE	02.02.01
NOC	2121
O*NET	24311

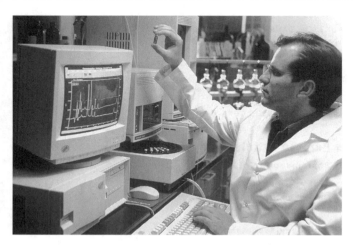

A pharmacologist inspects a vial of medication in a laboratory.

systems. Pharmacy is the health profession responsible for preparation and dispensing of drugs to patients.

Past civilizations, especially the cultures of ancient Greece and China, compiled the earliest written pharmacological knowledge, identifying certain diseases and the recommended "prescriptions" for these ailments. It was not until thousands of years later that crude organized experiments in pharmacology began. Many credit Francois Magendie, an early 19th-century French physiologist, with the birth of experimental pharmacology. The research of Magendie and his student, Claude Bernard, regarding poisons such as strychnine and carbon monoxide, and on curare as a muscle relaxant, helped to establish many of the principles of modern pharmacology. In 1847, a German, Rudolf Bucheim, established the first institute of pharmacology at the University of Dorpat, aiding the emergence of pharmacology as a singular discipline. A student of Bucheim, Oswald Schmiedeberg, became professor of pharmacology at Strasbourg, passing on his knowledge to students from all over the world. One of these students, John Jacob Abel, eventually brought experimental pharmacology to the United States.

The medical achievements and discoveries of pharmacologists are numerous. They include involvement in the development of antibiotics, anesthetics, vaccines, tranquilizers, vitamins, and many other substances in wide use today. Pharmacologists have been instrumental in the development of ether and other anesthetics that have modernized surgical procedures; of lifesaving substances such as penicillin, the tetanus and polio vaccines, antimalaria drugs, and countless other lifesaving compounds; and of drugs to treat heart disease, cancer, and psychiatric illnesses.

With the scientific advances of the early 20th century, especially experimental use of drugs in Europe and the introduction of antibacterial drugs into medicine in the early 1900s, pharmacology gained recognition as a distinct

discipline. Also, the Federal Food, Drug, and Cosmetic Act of 1938 required rigorous studies of drugs before they could be marketed. Those regulations continue today with the Food and Drug Administration (FDA).

Unlike early pharmacologists who were strictly devoted to developing new drugs, modern pharmacologists perform a much broader range of activities, including the testing of pesticides, the identification of poisons and their effects, the analysis of industrial pollutants, the analysis of food preservatives and food colorings, and the study of other substances and their effects upon the environment as well as upon humans. Their research includes all aspects of modern molecular and cellular biology as well as effects of drugs in animals and humans.

■ The Job

To become a pharmacologist, you'll train and study extensively in order to design the chemical agents that cure, lessen, or prevent disease. Once you've achieved this training, you'll continue to study as an important part of your career. You'll perform your research in laboratories using cultured cells, laboratory animals, plants, and human tissues to study the effects of drugs, chemicals, or other substances. In some cases, you'll inject chemicals, radioactive and nonradioactive isotopes, or other substances into laboratory animals. You may also culture these substances with live tissue samples from animals or from human donors. Recently, the field of pharmacology has branched beyond pure medical and drug research into toxicological research involving substances used in the environment, agriculture, and industry. Pharmacologists have identified toxic substances, such as lead, mercury, and ammonia, in the workplace, in pesticides, in food preservatives and colorings, and even in common household items such as paints, aerosol sprays, and cleaning fluid.

Your main duties will include developing and testing new drugs for use in medicine and testing chemicals, pollutants, poisons, and other materials to determine their effects upon animals and humans. Most pharmacologists specialize in a particular type of research. Those specializing in drug research use animals and humans to study the effects of drugs and medical compounds upon specific organs or bodily systems as well as to study potentially harmful side effects. By identifying the positive and negative aspects of a drug, pharmacologists are better able to predict usefulness against specific diseases and to recommend proper dosages as well as to advise the medical community as to the circumstances in which the drug should be administered.

As a pharmacologist, you may specialize in a particular part of the human body. *Neuropharmacologists* focus on drugs relating to the nervous system, including the brain, spinal cord, and nerves. Those specializing upon the effect of drugs relating to the cardiovascular and circulatory systems are called *cardiovascular pharmacologists. Endocrine pharmacologists* study the effects of drugs relating to the hormonal balance of the body. *Molecular pharmacologists* study the biochemical and biophysical interactions between drug molecules and cells.

Other types of pharmacologists include *biochemical pharmacologists* who use biochemistry, cell biology, and physiology to determine how drugs interact and influence the chemical machinery within an organism, and *veterinary pharmacologists,* experts on the use and study of drugs for the health problems and diseases of animals. Within the past 20 years, there has been a widespread use of psychotropic drugs, or drugs that influence mood and behavior patterns. *Behavioral pharmacologists* identify and develop drugs relating to human and animal behavior.

Some pharmacologists specialize strictly in testing various drugs and compounds on human subjects, and these specialists are known as *clinical pharmacologists.* It is not uncommon for teams of pharmacologists to work together, especially in the development of complex drugs as well as drugs and compounds that are capable of treating numerous diseases.

Dr. Dennis Mungall is the Director of Clinical Pharmacology and Anticoagulation Services at TMRMC Family Practice Residency. His clinical research involves cardiovascular medicine and coagulation disorders. He also works as a teacher, helping physicians-in-training, pharmacy students, and general health care providers to understand therapies and side effects. "I teach how to streamline care," he says, "so that it's cost-effective and easy for the patients. I teach them how to pick the best therapy that fits the patient's pathology. Drug-drug interactions can cause adverse effects—I teach how to understand these and how to avoid them." He says this work is a science of tailoring drug therapy to the individual patient.

In addition to the teaching and clinical responsibilities, Dennis also does a lot of multi-media work. He has developed software programs for teaching that capture clinical experience. "It is the experience of seeing patients face-to-face," he says, "but using computer technology." Dennis has also published in many journals including *Clinical Pharmacology and Therapeutics.*

■ Requirements

High School
You should take science courses, such as physics, physical chemistry, biology, molecular biology, and organic and physical chemistry. You should also take advanced math courses (including calculus), computer science, and statistics. Courses in English and speech are essential in order to be able to write and present intelligent research reports.

ASPIRIN AND ITS MANY USES

Just as pharmacologists are involved in new therapies and treatments, so are they involved in discovering new uses for drugs that have long been on the market. Aspirin, which was introduced into medical use over 100 years ago, has proven a very effective treatment for strokes, heart attacks, and arthritis. When recommended and monitored by a physician, aspirin can prevent cardiovascular attacks. But only aspirin, and not ibuprofen or acetaminophen, has demonstrated these beneficial effects.

Postsecondary Training
Nearly all pharmacologists earn a Ph.D. The Ph.D. in pharmacology is usually earned at an accredited medical school or at an accredited school of pharmacy. Because pharmacology is so intimately related with the practice of medicine, many pharmacologists are also medical doctors (M.D.s), and some pharmacologists who specialize in animal pharmacology are doctors of veterinary medicine (D.V.M.s). It is not uncommon for the course in pharmacology to resemble closely many aspects of the training for M.D.s, and in some cases pharmacologists become M.D.s, while in other cases M.D.s become pharmacologists. In either case, the best places to study pharmacology are large university medical centers that offer degrees for a variety of medical disciplines. Certain veterinary schools offer degrees in veterinary pharmacology as well.

During the last two years of college, you should evaluate graduate programs in pharmacology, making certain to apply only to accredited institutions. The major professional organization of pharmacologists, American Society for Pharmacology and Experimental Therapeutics (ASPET), can provide a list of accredited pharmacology graduate programs as well as other relevant information. Once you've been accepted to such an institution, the Ph.D. program requires from four to five years of study. This study involves intensive courses in cellular and molecular biology, physiology, neuroscience, basic and molecular pharmacology, chemotherapy, toxicology, and statistics and research. The major portion of the Ph.D. program will require you to undertake independent and supervised research, and successfully complete an original laboratory research project as well as writing a doctoral thesis on that project.

Many pharmacologists who receive their Ph.D. complete two to four additional years of research training assisting a scientist on a second research project in order to gain further research skills, experience, and maturity.

Certification or Licensing
You may choose to become certified within your special area of study. Through the American College of Clinical Pharmacology, you can obtain certification from the Board of Clinical Pharmacology. Applicants are judged individu-

ally, based on training and experience. A doctoral degree is required, along with five years post-doctoral experience in clinical pharmacology.

Other Requirements

"Communication is the most important part of the job," says Dennis. "You'll be organizing patients, administrators, people in business, and others—bringing people together for projects." Dennis also emphasizes creativity. "Being creative," he says, "adds to your ability to be a good researcher, to be a good thinker." You must be creative, curious, and flexible in order to entertain new ideas or investigative strategies. You need to be patient and willing to work long hours in order to master research that does not provide quick or easy answers. You should have above average intelligence and should be decisive. You must also be able to work alone or with similarly dedicated and driven colleagues to the conclusion of a project.

■ Exploring

The best way for you to learn about pharmacology is to interview pharmacologists. Your high school counselor or science teacher may be able to arrange a talk by a qualified pharmacologist or even a tour of a pharmacological facility.

Medical and other laboratories frequently employ part-time personnel to assist with various tasks, and it is sometimes possible to secure a part-time job in a pharmacological laboratory. Information regarding summer or part-time opportunities can be obtained by contacting work-study or student research programs and student placement services. But you need to keep in mind that you may be competing with pharmacological graduate students for such positions.

The American Society for Pharmacology and Experimental Therapeutics also provides information concerning accredited pharmacology educational programs and academic institutions, the various subspecialties of pharmacology, and information relating to laboratories, drug companies, and other branches of the profession that employ pharmacologists. Some of these subspecialties have organizations and professional societies, such as the American Society of Pharmacognosy (the study of natural drugs), the American College of Neuropsychopharmacology, the American Society for Clinical Pharmacology and Therapeutics, the American Association of Pharmaceutical Sciences, the American Society of Veterinary Physiologists and Pharmacologists, and the American Academy of Clinical Toxicology.

■ Employers

Pharmacologists are employed as faculty in medical, dental, veterinary medicine, or pharmacy schools or as researchers in industry or research institutes. They work for private research foundations, as well as government organizations such as the National Institutes of Health, the Environmental Protection Agency, and the FDA.

■ Starting Out

Drug companies, research organizations, medical, dental, and pharmacy schools and universities, and other organizations, including the federal and state governments, often recruit pharmacologists who are in the process of earning their doctorates. Most pharmacologists have a pretty good idea of what subspecialty they would like to pursue by the second year of their doctoral program, and organizations representing and employing members in that subspecialty should be sought out.

Graduates looking to break into pharmacology should consult the placement office of the school they attended or consider sending a resume and cover letter to large pharmaceutical or chemical firms or research institutes. Pharmacological journals also provide a list of employment opportunities.

■ Advancement

Most beginning pharmacologists start out in academics at the assistant professor level or in laboratories at a junior level working for more advanced pharmacologists. They learn proper laboratory procedures, how to work with the FDA and various other government agencies, and learn about the testing of drugs and other substances with animal and human subjects. In private industry and in academic laboratories, including drug companies, advancement in the field of pharmacology usually means supervising a number of people in a laboratory setting and heading up major research projects. Government pharmacology workers may obtain similar types of promotions, although civil service regulations and tenure characteristics do come into play. Some pharmacologists who are teachers may become department heads, supervise research laboratories at universities, present public papers, and speak at major conferences.

Many pharmacologists envision their advancements in terms of successful research projects. Dennis is looking forward to branching out into other areas, combining his interests in pharmacology, writing, and the Internet. "I have a grant from the American Heart Association to do just that," he says, "using the Internet to improve health care communication with patients."

■ Earnings

According to the Hospital Salary and Benefits Report published in 1997, directors of pharmacy (positions frequently held by pharmacologists) have annual salaries ranging from $43,680 to $111,379, with a national average of $69,316. A survey by the American Association of Pharmaceutical Scientists place average salaries at $70,000 a year for those working in industry, $66,400 for those in academia, and $62,500 for those in government. Normally, higher-salaried pharmacologists are those who supervise teams of people in larger laboratory or university settings, or are senior faculty in academic departments of pharmacology. Other benefits include health and dental insurance and paid vacation and sick days.

■ Work Environment

You'll work in academic settings or laboratories and have a regular workweek of approximately 40 hours, though you may sometimes be required to work extra hours to monitor experiments that need special attention. Most laboratories associated with academic or major research institutions are clean, well-lit, pleasant workplaces equipped with the sophisticated instruments necessary for modern research. Because pharmacologists perform such a vital role with respect to drug and chemical research, their laboratories tend to be fairly up-to-date.

You must be prepared to work on projects that require months of effort and seemingly slow progress; the average FDA drug approval time is 10 years. You must be able to deal with stress associated with working in close quarters with other similarly involved professionals.

In some cases, you'll be called upon to work with forensic biologists, coroners, or others involved in attempting to determine causes of death under specific circumstances. You may also be asked to travel to other research institutions to share your findings.

■ Outlook

Health care and health care-related industries in general are expected to continue to expand, and this means that the activities of drug companies, hospitals, medical, dental, and pharmacy schools, and the government in pharmacological research will continue to be strong. The growing elderly population will also mean more drug production and development. A number of medical conditions and diseases will require the continuing and increasing expertise of the pharmacologist. Further study will be necessary regarding drug addiction and the effect of chemical substances on the environment. Herbal pharmacology is also being taken more seriously, as the public interest in the medicinal values of plants has inspired interest from biomedical scientists. More teachers of pharmacology will also be needed to train prospective students, and the expanding field of gene therapy will offer qualified pharmacologists increased opportunity. Pharmacologists with the most advanced and updated education will best prosper in future expanding and specialized job markets.

■ For More Information

The ASPET Web site features sections on student news, research fellowship opportunities, and other information. ASPET also offers a free booklet on pharmacology careers. Contact:

American Society for Pharmacology and Experimental Therapeutics
9650 Rockville Pike
Bethesda, MD 20814-3995
Tel: 301-530-7060
Web: http://www.faseb.org/aspet

For information about student chapters, news releases, and publications, contact:

American Association of Pharmaceutical Sciences
1650 King Street, Suite 200
Alexandria, VA 22314-2747
Tel: 703-548-3000
Web: http://www.aaps.org

■ Related Articles

Pharmaceuticals

Biochemists

Biologists

Chemical Engineers

Chemists

Drug Developers

Genetic Scientists

Medical Laboratory Technicians

Pharmacists

Pharmacy Technicians

Toxicologists

Pharmacy Technicians

■ Overview

Pharmacy technicians provide technical assistance for registered pharmacists and work under their direct supervision. They usually work in chain or independent drug stores, hospitals, community ambulatory care centers, home health care agencies, nursing homes, and the pharmaceutical industry. They perform a wide range of technical support functions and tasks related to the pharmacy profession. They maintain patient records; count, package, and label medication doses; prepare and distribute sterile products; and fill and dispense routine orders for stock supplies such as over-the-counter products. There are over 33,000 pharmacy technicians certified by the Pharmacy Technician Certification Board (PTCB).

PHARMACY TECHNICIANS	
SCHOOL SUBJECTS	Biology Chemistry
PERSONAL SKILLS	Following instructions Technical/scientific
WORK ENVIRONMENT	Primarily indoors Primarily one location
MINIMUM EDUCATION LEVEL	Some postsecondary training
SALARY RANGE	$15,600 to $21,000 to $30,000
CERTIFICATION OR LICENSING	Required by certain states
OUTLOOK	About as fast as the average
DOT	074
GOE	10.03.02
NOC	3414
O*NET	32518

■ History

Professionally trained pharmacy technicians have assisted pharmacists since the 1950s. In recent years, the role of the pharmacist has shifted and evolved away from standard dispensing to consultation, restricting the time actually spent dispensing medication. Pharmacy technicians have filled this gap, enjoying a significant increase in duties and responsibilities, and becoming an even more integral part of the pharmaceutical health care team.

■ The Job

The roles of the pharmacist and pharmacy technician expanded greatly in the 1990s. The pharmacist's primary responsibility is to ensure that medications are used safely and effectively through clinical patient counseling and monitoring. In order to provide the highest quality of pharmaceutical care, pharmacists now focus on providing clinical services. As a result, pharmacy technicians' duties have evolved into a more specialized role known as pharmacy technology. As a pharmacy technician, you'll perform more of the manipulative functions associated with dispensing prescriptions. Your primary duties are drug-product preparation and distribution, but you're also concerned with the control of drug products. You assemble, prepare, and deliver requested medication. You are responsible for record keeping and you record drug-related information on specified forms. Depending on your experience, you'll order pharmaceuticals and take inventory of controlled substances, such as Valium and Ritalin.

Technicians who work in hospitals have the most varied responsibilities of all pharmacy technicians. In a hospital, you'll fill total parenteral nutrition (TPN) preparations and standard and chemotherapy IVs (intravenous solutions) for patients under doctors' orders. You may be required to fill "stat," or immediate, orders and deliver them. You prepare special emergency carts stocked with medications and monitor defibrillators and resuscitation equipment. In an emergency, you'll respond with doctors and nurses, rushing the cart and other equipment to the emergency site. You'll also keep legal records of the events that occur during an emergency. You'll work in the hospital's outpatient pharmacy, which is similar to a commercial drugstore, and assist the pharmacist in dispensing medication.

Tamara Britton works as a technician in a hospital. Because the hospital pharmacy is open 24 hours a day, Tamara has worked all 3 shifts. Her work involves using a computer to create labels for large IV bags and "piggybacks" (small-volume IV bags). She stacks the IVs on carts, then delivers them to the appropriate nurse stations. She also delivers medications through a process known as "tubing and shagging." Two "tubes," or lines, (similar to those at a bank's drive-through) run through the entire hospital to every nurse unit. "Shagging" is the process of placing the nurse unit's medications in baggies; the meds are then shot through the tubes to the proper units. Tamara also prepares drug carts with the aid of a RxOBOT; this robotic arm is in a glassed-off room, and fills the drawers of the carts with the correct medication for individual patients. Tamara places coded labels on the drawers of the carts. She explains, "I put the drawers with labels facing Robota (we named her) and a conveyor belt takes them in the room for Robota to fill with all of the patients' existing meds for the day. The tray, after filling, drops down to a lower conveyor belt that brings the drawer back to me, which I replace in the cart."

As their roles increase, trained technicians have become more specialized. Some specialized types of pharmacy technicians include narcotics control pharmacy technicians, operating room pharmacy technicians, emergency room pharmacy technicians, nuclear pharmacy technicians, and home health care pharmacy technicians. Specially trained pharmacy technicians are also employed as *data entry technicians, lead technicians, supervisors,* and *technician managers.*

■ Requirements

High School

You should take courses in mathematics and science, especially chemistry and biology. Health classes can help you get a basic understanding of the healthcare industry and various medical treatments. Take English and speech classes to help you develop your writing and communication skills. You'll be using the computer a lot to maintain records and prepare labels, so take courses in computer fundamentals.

Postsecondary Training

In the past, pharmacy technicians received most of their training on the job in hospital and community pharmacy-training programs. Since technician functions and duties have changed greatly in recent years, most pharmacy technicians today receive their education through formal training programs offered through community colleges, vocational/technical schools, hospital community pharmacies, and government programs throughout the United States. Program length usually ranges from six months to two years, and leads to a certificate, diploma, or associate's degree in pharmacy technology. Pharmacy technicians must possess a specific core of knowledge and skills that can be applied in the pharmacy setting. Training programs provide this knowledge to pharmacy technician students. A high school diploma usually is required for entry into a training program. The Pharmacy Technology Educators Council is working toward implementing a standardized curriculum in all pharmacy technician training programs throughout the country and provides a guide to pharmacy technician training programs throughout Canada and the United States (see address at end of this article).

In a pharmacy technician training program, you'll receive classroom instruction and participate in supervised clinical apprenticeships in health institutions and community pharmacies. Courses include introduction to pharmacy and health care systems, pharmacy laws and ethics, medical terminology, chemistry and microbiology. Most pharmacy technicians continue their education even after their formal training ends by reading professional journals and attending training or informational seminars, lectures, review sessions, and audiovisual presentations.

Certification or Licensing

At least 3 states license pharmacy technicians and all 50 states have adopted a written, standardized test for voluntary certification of technicians. Some states, including Texas and Louisiana, require certification of pharmacy tech-

WEIGHTS AND MEASURES
Apothecary weights:
20 grains = 1 scruple
3 scruples = 1 dram
8 drams = 1 ounce
12 ounces = 1 pound
Apothecary fluid measures:
60 minims = 1 fluidram
8 fluidram = 1 fluid ounce
16 fluid ounce = 1 pint

nicians. To receive certification from the PTCB, you'll be tested on such subjects as the top 200 drugs in use by the medical profession. After receiving certification, you'll be required to complete 20 hours of continuing education hours every 2 years.

Other Requirements

You must be precision-minded, honest, and mature as you are depended on for accuracy and high levels of quality control, especially in hospitals. "I pay attention to details," Tamara says, "and try to catch all my own mistakes before a pharmacist checks my work." You need good communications skills in order to successfully interact with pharmacists, supervisors, and other technicians. You must be able to precisely follow written or oral instructions as a wide variety of people, including physicians, nurses, pharmacists, and patients rely on your actions. You also need some computer aptitude in order to effectively record pharmaceutical data.

■ Exploring

Volunteering at a local hospital or nursing home may provide opportunities to meet and talk with pharmacy technicians. Jobs at a local retail pharmacy also can provide relevant experience. Students may be able to arrange a talk by a trained pharmacy technician or a tour of a hospital pharmacy with the help of their guidance or career counselors.

■ Employers

Most opportunities for pharmacy technicians are in retail—there are more than 30,000 pharmacies operated by traditional chain pharmacy companies and supermarkets, and another 20,000 independent pharmacies. Technicians also work in hospitals and long-term care facilities, and clinics at military bases, prisons, and colleges. Technicians are also finding work with home health care agencies.

■ Starting Out

In some cases you may be able to pursue education and certification while employed as a pharmacy technician. Some chain drugstores are paying the certification fees for their techs, and are also rewarding certified techs with higher hourly pay. This practice will probably increase—industry experts predict a shortage of pharmacists and technicians as more chain drugstores open across the country, and more pharmacies offer 24-hour service.

Pharmacy technicians often are hired by the hospital or agency where they interned. If employment is not found this way, aspiring technicians can use employment agencies or newspaper ads to help locate job openings. Tamara found her hospital job in the classifieds. "There was an ad that said 'use your data entry skills and become a pharmacy technician.' They tested me on data entry and then interviewed me and gave me the job. They trained me on all I needed to know to do the job."

■ Advancement

Depending on where you're employed, you may direct or instruct newer pharmacy technicians, make schedules, or move to purchasing or computer work. Some hospitals have a variety of tech designations, based on experience and responsibility, with an according increase in pay. Some pharmacy techs return to school to pursue a degree in pharmacy.

■ Earnings

Most technicians are paid by the hour, and certified technicians can expect to make more than those without certification. In 1997, the Hospital and Healthcare Report found that pharmacist assistants made between $5.90 and $15.41 an hour, with a national average of $9.54 an hour. The highest averages were in the Mid Atlantic and Pacific regions of the country. Richland College, a Dallas County community college that offers allied health certificate programs, estimates the entry level salary for a technician is $6.25 to $7.00 an hour in retail; $7.50 to $8.50 in hospitals; $9.00 to $10.00 in home healthcare.

Benefits generally include medical and dental insurance, retirement savings plans, and paid sick, personal, and vacation days.

■ Work Environment

You'll work in clean, well-lit, pleasant, and professional surroundings. You may wear scrubs or other uniforms in hospitals, especially in the IV room. In a retail drugstore, you may only be required to wear casual clothing, or a smock. Most pharmacy settings are extremely busy, especially hospital and retail. "I feel like I'm part of a system," Tamara says, "to help the sick get better and maybe keep people from dying." The job of pharmacy technician, like any other occupation that demands skill, speed, and accuracy, can be stressful. Because most hospitals, nursing homes, health care centers, and retail pharmacies are open between 16 and 24 hours a day, multiple shifts, weekend, and holiday hours usually are required.

■ Outlook

As the role of the pharmacist shifts to consultation, more technicians will be needed to assemble and dispense medications. Furthermore, new employment avenues and responsibilities will mirror that of the expanding and evolving role of the pharmacist. A strong demand for technicians with specialized training has emerged. Because of more complex medications and new drug therapies on the market, more education may be necessary for certification in the future. The clinical pharmacy technician is a new specialization that involves interpreting lab results of blood test levels. Mechanical advances in the pharmaceutical field, such as robot-picking devices and automatic counting equipment, may eradicate some of the duties pharmacy technicians previously performed, yet there will remain a need for skilled technicians to clean and maintain such devices. Traditionally, pharmacists have been required to check the work of technicians; in some states, hospitals are allowing techs to check the work of other techs.

■ For More Information

To learn more about certification and training, contact:

Pharmacy Technician Certification Board
2215 Constitution Avenue, NW
Washington, DC 20037-2985
Tel: 202-429-7576
Web: http://www.ptcb.org

To obtain a copy of The Journal of Pharmacy Technology, *which lists opportunities for pharmacy technicians and developments in technology, and the* PTEC Directory, *which lists pharmacy tech training programs in the United States and Canada, contact:*

Pharmacy Technology Educators Council
Harvey Whitney Book Publishing
PO Box 42696
Cincinnati, OH 45242
Tel: 513-793-3555

To learn about membership, contact:

Association of Pharmacy Technicians
PO Box 1447
Greensboro, NC 27402
Tel: 336-275-1700
Web: http://pharmacytechnician.com

■ Related Articles

Health Care
Pharmaceuticals
Chemical Technicians
Medical Laboratory Technicians
Pharmaceutical Industry Workers
Pharmacists
Pharmacologists

Pharmakineticists

■ **See Drug Developers**

Phlebotomy Technicians

■ **Overview**

Phlebotomy technicians draw blood from patients or donors in hospitals, blood banks, clinics, physicians' offices, or other facilities. They assemble equipment, verify patient identification numbers, and withdraw blood either by puncturing a person's finger, or by extracting blood from a vein or artery with a needle syringe. They label, transport, and store blood for analysis or for other medical purposes.

■ **History**

Ancient people did not understand the role of blood, but they knew it was vital. Some believed that it might even be the home of the soul. Early Egyptians bathed in blood, hoping this act would cure illness or reverse the aging process. Some Romans drank the blood of dying gladiators in order to acquire the athletes' strength and bravery. Over time, scientists began to understand how blood functioned and they searched for ways to collect it or transfer it from one person to another. The methods they used, the lack of sterile procedures, and their limited knowledge sometimes resulted in the death of the donor as well as the patient.

Modern techniques of blood collection, typing, and transfusion developed only within this century. Today, professionals, called phlebotomy technicians, draw blood and work in clean, well-lighted laboratories, hospitals, and clinics.

■ **The Job**

The first step a phlebotomy technician performs when drawing blood is to take the patient's medical history, temperature and pulse, and match the physician's testing order with the amount of blood to be drawn. Next, the site of the withdrawal is located. Typically, the large vein that is visible on the underside of the arm near the elbow is used.

Finding a suitable vein, however, is not always easy because there are a great many anatomical differences among people. Once a suitable site is located, a tourniquet is wrapped high on the patient's upper arm. The phlebotomy technician checks the site for lesions, other needle marks, and any skin disorders that might interfere with the collection process. Then the site is cleansed by swabbing with a sterile solution. The technician positions the patient's arm in order to make a proper puncture. The needle is inserted almost horizontal to the vein and as parallel to the skin as possible. Then the hub of the needle is raised and the angle toward the skin increased so that the needle can pierce the wall of the vein. After the needle is advanced slightly into the vein, blood may be withdrawn. Generally this is done by releasing a clamp attached to the blood collection device or to the tubing. When the required amount of blood is collected, the needle is removed and sealed, the site covered, and the tourniquet removed.

After collection, the phlebotomy technician labels the blood, coordinates its number with the worksheet order, and transports the blood to a storage facility or to another laboratory worker. The phlebotomy technician also checks to make sure that the patient is all right, notes any adverse reactions, and administers first aid or other medical assistance when necessary.

■ **Requirements**

High School

Biology, health, and other science courses are helpful if you wish to become a phlebotomy technician after graduation. Computer science, English, and speech classes are also important. In addition, if you plan on entering formal phlebotomy training programs, you should take the courses that fulfill the entrance requirements for the program you plan to attend.

Postsecondary Training

Until recently, on-the-job training was the norm for phlebotomy technicians. Now, formal programs are offered through independent training schools, community colleges, or hospitals. Most programs last from 10 weeks to one year. They include both in-class study and supervised, clinical practice. Course work includes anatomy, physiology, introduction to laboratory practices, communication, medical terminology, phlebotomy techniques, emergency situations, and CPR training.

PHLEBOTOMY TECHNICIANS	
SCHOOL SUBJECTS	**Biology** **Chemistry**
PERSONAL SKILLS	**Helping/teaching** **Technical/scientific**
WORK ENVIRONMENT	**Primarily indoors** **Primarily one location**
MINIMUM EDUCATION LEVEL	**Some postsecondary training**
SALARY RANGE	**$16,000 to $25,000 to $38,000**
CERTIFICATION OR LICENSING	**Required by certain states**
OUTLOOK	**About as fast as the average**
DOT	**079**
GOE	**02.04.02**

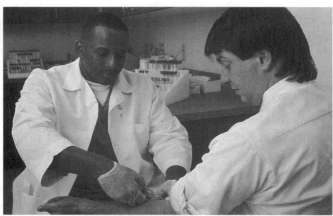

A phlebotomy technician draws blood from a patient.

Certification or Licensing

Certification for phlebotomy technicians varies according to state and employer. Several agencies grant certification. To be eligible to take the qualifying examination from the American Society of Phlebotomy Technicians, or from the Board of Registry of the American Society of Clinical Pathologists, there are several criteria. You must have worked as a full-time phlebotomist for six months or as a part-time phlebotomist for one year, or have completed an accredited phlebotomy training program.

Other Requirements

To be a successful phlebotomy technician, you should enjoy working with people and be an effective communicator and a good listener. You should also be attentive to detail and be able to work under pressure. In addition, you should have patience and good manual dexterity.

■ Employers

Phlebotomy technicians work in a variety of health care settings. The majority work in hospitals or in outpatient settings such as clinics, physicians' offices, reference laboratories, or blood banks. A few are hired by private industry or by insurance companies. The greatest need for phlebotomy technicians is in small hospitals (fewer than 100 beds).

■ Starting Out

Many of the publications serving health care professionals list job advertisements, as do daily newspapers. In addition, some employers actively recruit employees by contacting students who are graduating from accredited programs. Some programs offer job placement assistance as well.

■ Advancement

At some hospitals, phlebotomy technicians advance through several different levels of responsibility and pay, depending on their training and experience.

One of the most common career paths for phlebotomy technicians is to work for a few years in a hospital or laboratory and then return to school to study medical laboratory technology or some other branch of clinical laboratory medicine.

There may also be supervisory advancement opportunities within blood bank centers. For example, you can return to school, obtain a bachelor's degree, attend a specialized fifth-year program, and become a certified specialist in blood bank technology.

■ Earnings

Experience, level of education, employer, and work performed determine the salary ranges for phlebotomy technicians. Beginning full-time phlebotomy technicians have median annual salaries of around $16,000. The median annual salary for more experienced workers is around $18,000. Pay rates are highest in the Northeast and West. They are lowest in the central United States.

A specialist in blood bank technology with a bachelor's degree and advanced training can usually expect a starting salary of approximately $38,000 a year.

Benefits such as vacation time, sick leave, insurance, and other fringe benefits vary by employer, but are usually consistent with other full-time health care workers.

■ Work Environment

Most phlebotomy technicians are supervised by other laboratory personnel and work in hospitals, clinics, doctors' offices, reference laboratories, and blood banks. Some technicians may be required to work shifts. If you work for a blood bank, you may be required to travel to other sites for a blood drive.

■ Outlook

The demand for phlebotomy technicians in the United States is highest in small hospitals. As the percentage of our population aged 65 or older continues to rise, the demand for all kinds of health care professionals will increase as well. There is a demand for workers who are qualified to draw blood at the bedside of patients. The growing number of patients with certain diseases, such as HIV and AIDs, also increases the need for phlebotomy technicians.

■ For More Information

The following organizations provide information on phlebotomy technician careers, accredited schools and scholarships, and employment opportunities.

American Association of Blood Banks
8101 Glenbrook Road
Bethesda, MD 20814
Tel: 301-907-6977

American Medical Association
515 North State Street
Chicago, IL 60610
Tel: 312-464-5000
Web: http://www.ama-assn.org

American Society of Phlebotomy Technicians, Inc.
1109 2nd Avenue, SW
Hickory, NC 28602-2545
Tel: 704-322-1334

■ **Related Articles**

Biology

Health Care

Cytotechnologists

Emergency Medical Technicians

Histologic Technicians

Medical Assistants

Medical Technologists

Psychiatric Technicians

Surgical Technologists

Transplant Coordinators

Photo Stylists

■ **Overview**

Photo styling is actually an all-encompassing term for the many and varied contributions that a *photo stylist* brings to the job. Primarily, the photo stylist works with a photographer to create a particular image, using props, backgrounds, accessories, clothing, costumes, food, linens, and other set elements. Much of the work exists within the print advertising industry, although stylists are also called to do film and commercial shoots. There are many specialties that can be included on a photo stylist's resume, from fashion to food, bridal to bathrooms, hair and makeup styling to prop shopping and location searches. Some stylists may focus on one specialty; others may seek to maintain a wide repertoire of skills. While photo styling may seem like a vague and nebulous profession, it is an increasingly vital part of the photography and advertising industries.

■ **History**

Photo styling has existed since the first photographs were taken. Someone, maybe the photographer, an assistant, a studio worker, designer, or editor, had to make sure all the elements within the frame were arranged in a certain way. Hair and makeup stylists in the film and publishing industries were probably the first to gain recognition (and credit lines). In fact, most people still associate "styling" exclusively with hair and makeup work, without fully appreciating the contribution of other stylists to the finished photo or film. To this day, photo styling credit is only occasion-

ally listed in fashion and advertising spreads, but that trend is changing. Society is becoming more visually oriented, and the contributions made by stylists are becoming more important. Stylists are gaining the respect of people within the industry. Some photographer/stylist teams are as well-known for their collaborative work as are actors and directors. After toiling in relative obscurity for many years, photo stylists are emerging as powerful voices in industry and in society.

■ **The Job**

The photo stylist is a creative collaborator, working with photographers, art directors, models, design houses, and clients to produce a visual image, usually for commercial purposes. It is both a technical and artistic occupation. The kind of work a photo stylist performs depends upon, among other things, the nature of the photography; the needs of the photographer, studio, and art director; and the requests of the client. Because these vary from one situation to another, it is impossible to list all the aspects of a photo stylist's job. In simple terms, what a stylist does is help to create a "look." The specifics of how it is done are far more complicated. These depend on the stylist's skill, resourcefulness, ingenuity, artistic sense, and collaborative relationship with the rest of the crew. Moreover, "photo styling" itself is a very general term-there are many kinds of styling, almost as many as there are reasons for taking a photograph.

Prop gathering and set decoration are the most common assignments in photo styling, but there are many subspecialties within the field, each requiring different skills and experience. For example, fashion, wardrobe, and portrait shoots often require a number of professional stylists on hand to scout locations, prepare the set, acquire clothes and accessories, dress the models, and style hair and makeup.

Food stylists employ a variety of techniques, from painting to glazing, to make everything from a bowl of cereal to a crawfish etouffee appear especially appetizing.

Home furnishings and domestic items specialists often intro-

PHOTO STYLISTS	
SCHOOL SUBJECTS	Art Business
PERSONAL SKILLS	Artistic Communication/ideas
WORK ENVIRONMENT	Indoors and outdoors Primarily multiple locations
MINIMUM EDUCATION LEVEL	High school diploma
SALARY RANGE	$15,000 to $35,000 to $90,000
CERTIFICATION OR LICENSING	None available
OUTLOOK	Faster than the average
NOC	5243

A photo stylist carefully arranges shirts in an attractive stack for maximum eye appeal in a catalog.

duce various props to give a natural look to the photographic set.

On-figure stylists fit the clothes to the model, and *off-figure stylists* arrange the clothes in attractive stacks or against an interesting background.

Soft-goods stylists introduce appropriate fabric, linens, and clothing into a shoot. The *tabletop stylist* may use anything from glue to Vaseline to give an added allure to a set of socket wrenches. *Hair and makeup stylists* are almost invariably cosmetic specialists, and are usually present on any set that employs live models.

Casting stylists locate modeling talent. Others specialize in set design, child photography, bedding, bridal, and catalogs. Many stylists are adept in more than one area, making them difficult to categorize.

Stylists may also bring special talents to the set, like floral design, gift wrapping, model building, or antiquing. They usually have a "bag of tricks" that will solve problems or create certain effects (a stylist's work kit might include everything from duct tape and cotton wadding to C-clamps and salt shakers). Sometimes a photo stylist is called upon to design and build props, perform on-set last-minute tailoring, even coordinate the entire production from the location search to crew accommodations. The most successful stylists will adapt to the needs of the job, and if they can't produce something themselves, they will know in an instant how and where to find someone who can. Versatility and flexibility are key attributes no matter what the stylist's specialty.

Being prepared for every possible situation is simply part of the photo stylist's job. For example, knowledge of photographic techniques, especially lighting, lenses, and filters, can help a stylist communicate better with the photographer. An understanding of the advertising industry and familiarity with specific product lines and designers, are also good tools for working with clients.

Organization is another vital aspect of the photo stylist's job. Before the shoot, the stylist must be sure that everything needed has been found and will arrive on time at the studio or location. During the shoot, even while working on a model or set, the stylist must be sure that all borrowed material is being treated with care and that preparations for the next shot are underway. Afterwards, he or she must return items and maintain receipts and records, so as to keep the project within budget. The freelance stylist does all this while also rounding up new assignments and maintaining a current portfolio.

Only part of the stylist's time is spent in photo studios or on location. Much of the work is done on the phone and on the street, preparing for the job by gathering props and material, procuring clothes, contacting models, or renting furniture. For the freelancer, lining up future employment can be a job in itself. A senior stylist working in-house at a magazine may have additional editorial duties, including working with art directors to introduce concepts and compose advertising narratives.

Even during downtime, the stylist must keep an eye out for ways to enhance his or her marketability. The chance discovery of a new boutique or specialty shop on the way to the grocery store can provide the stylist with a valuable new resource for later assignments. Maintaining a personal directory of resources is as essential as keeping a portfolio. Staying abreast of current trends and tastes through the media is also important, especially in the areas of fashion and life-style.

What a stylist does on the job depends largely upon his or her unique talents and abilities. Photo stylists with the most experience and creative resources will make the greatest contribution to a project. As a premier stylist, that contribution extends beyond the set to the society as a whole—shaping its tastes, making its images, and creating art that defines the era.

■ Requirements

There is no specific training or schooling to become a photo stylist. However, there are ways to prepare for entry into the business. Formal education in the visual arts can help train one's eye for design and composition, even if it does not lead to a degree. Manual dexterity is important, so building things, from models to sculptures, can be a good exercise, as is painting, be it on walls or canvas. Skill with fabric is a must, so pressing and steaming clothes, doing minor alterations, and needlework are important skills to cultivate. The specialties employed for certain shoots require a familiarity with, for instance, food preparation, home decorating, children, formal attire, bedding, and any number of other potential subjects. A photo stylist, like any artist, draws from his or her own experience for inspiration, so exposure to a wide variety of experiences will benefit anyone entering the field.

Postsecondary Training

For hair and makeup styling, classes in cosmetology are recommended. Experience on a retail level, in a department store or boutique, is a good place to gain knowledge and experience designing displays, while also developing interpersonal skills.

Knowledge of photography, even the basics, will be an invaluable asset on the job. A general understanding of the advertising industry will also be helpful. Basic business procedures and terminology are an important foundation for anyone starting out on a freelance career.

Other Requirements

The personal qualities most sought in a photo stylist are creativity, taste, resourcefulness, good instincts, patience, a calm, supportive personality, a good sense of humor, and flexibility. Stylists must possess an even temperament in order to professionally respond to changing deadlines and other high pressure situations. Being "easy to work with" is recommended in this field.

■ Exploring

Students interested in photography and styling can team up and, with a camera, a location (inside or outside), and some props or costumes, conduct a photo shoot. At a professional level, these are known as "test shots," used to build up the portfolios of photographers, models, and stylists. But a backyard photo shoot can be a good way to appreciate the elements involved with this career. Obviously, any opportunity to visit a real photographer's set can be an invaluable learning experience; perhaps a teacher can arrange such a field trip. Watching someone prepare a display in a department store window can also provide a good demonstration-a lot of stylists start out as window dressers.

■ Employers

There are relatively few positions available for full-time, salaried photo stylists. They are employed by ad agencies and companies that sell their merchandise through catalogs. Magazines that conduct regular photo shoots may also have a photo stylist on staff. Most photo stylists, however, work as freelancers. They are hired for individual assignments by photographers, ad agencies, design firms, catalog houses, and any other enterprise that uses photographic services.

■ Starting Out

A person can enter the field of photo styling at any point in life, but there is as yet no clear-cut way to go about it. Some people, if they have the resources, hire photographers to shoot a portfolio with them, then shop it around to production houses and other photographers. However, most prospective employers prefer that a stylist has previous on-set experience. The best path is to find work as a stylist's assistant. Production houses and photo studios that employ full-time stylists usually keep a directory of assistants. Most cities have a creative directory of established stylists who may need assistants. It is important to always leave a name and number (they may have no work available immediately, but might be desperate next month). Assisting provides one with important on-set experience, while showing the nuts and bolts of the job, including the drudgery, as well as the rewards. Building a reputation is the most important thing to do at any stage of this career, since most photographers find stylists by word of mouth and recommendations, in addition to reviewing portfolios. Assistants will also be introduced to the people who may hire them down the road as full-fledged stylists, giving them an opportunity to make a good impression. Eventually, one can seek out a photographer who needs a stylist and work together on test shots. Once a portfolio has been established, it can be shown to agents, editors, and photographers. Agency representation is an enormous aid to the freelancer. An agent finds work for the stylist and pays him or her on a regular basis (after extracting an average commission of 20 percent). The benefits of representation include the fact that while a stylist is working one job, the agent is lining up the next. Some agencies represent stylists exclusively; others also handle models, photographers, and actors.

Finally, as photo styling grows in recognition, the avenues for entry should become more clearly defined.

■ Advancement

Advancement in this field can be measured by the amount of bookings a stylist obtains, the steadiness of work, and a regularly increasing per diem pay rate. It can also be determined by the quality of stylist's clients, the reputation of the photographer, and the nature of the assignments. Some stylists start out with lower-end catalogs and work their way up If the goal is to do high-fashion, then the steps along the way will be readily apparent in the quality of the merchandise and the size of the client. The opportunity to work with highly regarded photographers is also a step up, even if the stylist's pay rate remains the same. In a career built on reputation, experience with the industry's major players is priceless. Senior stylists at magazines often help in ad design and planning. Some stylists advance to become art directors and fashion editors. Ultimately, each stylist has his or her own goals in sight. The "rare-air" of high fashion and celebrity photography may not be the end-all of a stylist's career; a good steady income and the chance to work regularly with friendly, creative people may, in fact, be the only pinnacle that matters.

■ Earnings

Like almost everything else in this field, earning potential varies from one stylist to the next. Salaries at production houses can start as low as $8 an hour, but usually include fringe benefits like health insurance, not to mention a regular paycheck. The freelancer has enormous earning potential. An experienced fashion or food stylist can demand as much as $800 a day and more, depending on his or her reputation and the budget of the production. Regular bookings at this level, along with travel and accommodation costs (almost always paid for), translate into a substantial income. On the average, though, stylists earn around $350 to $500 per day as freelancers; assistants earn around $100 to $150. The stylist can request that an assistant be written into the budget, though this may affect his or her rate.

■ Work Environment

Work conditions for a photo stylist are as varied as the job itself. Preparation for a shoot may involve hours on the telephone, calling from the home or office, and more hours shopping for props and material to use on set. Much of the work is done inside comfortable photo studios or at other indoor locations, but sometimes, especially in fashion and catalog photography, outdoor locations are also used. If the merchandise is of a seasonal nature, this could mean long days working in a cold field photographing winter parkas against a snowy background, or it could mean flying down to Key West in January for a week shooting next summer's line of swimwear. Travel, both local and long-distance, is part of the job. Days can be long, from dawn to dusk, or they may require the stylist's presence for only a few hours on the set. Hours vary, but a stylist must always be flexible, especially the freelancer who may be called in on a day's notice.

There are numerous financial outlays to contend with, whether one keeps a personal inventory of props or rents the material. Most clients and studios budget for these expenses and reimburse the stylist, but the initial funds must sometimes come from the stylist's own pocket. Maintaining a portfolio, purchasing equipment, and paying agents' fees may also add to the cost of doing business.

Photo styling can be an extremely lucrative career, but there is no assurance that a stylist will find steady employment. It is wise to establish an emergency fund in the event that work disappears for a time. Busy periods often correspond to seasonal advertising campaigns and film work, and between them there can be slow periods. A stylist might have a great year followed by a disappointing one. Freelancers must file their own quarterly tax returns and purchase their own health insurance.

Stress levels vary from one assignment to the next. Some shoots may go smoothly, others may have a crisis occur every minute. Stylists must be able to remain calm and resilient in the face of enormous pressure. Personality clashes may also occur despite every effort to avoid them, adding to the stress of the job. For the freelancer, the pressure to find new work and maintain proper business records are still further sources of stress. Photo stylists will also spend considerable time on their feet, stooping and kneeling in uncomfortable positions, trying to get something aligned just right. They also may need to transport heavy material and merchandise to and from the studio or location, or move these elements around the set during the shoot. Reliable transportation is essential.

The irregular hours of a photo stylist can be an attraction for people who have other commitments and enjoy variety in their lives. Work conditions are not always that strenuous—they can also be pleasant and fun, as the crew trades jokes and experiences, solves problems together, and shares the excitement of a sudden inspiration. The rewards of working with a team of professionals on an interesting, creative project is a condition of the job that most stylists treasure.

■ Outlook

The value of a good photo stylist is becoming more and more apparent to photographers and advertising clients. The outlook for employment, once again, depends on the perseverance and reputation of the stylist. Larger cities are the most fertile places to find work, but there are photo studios in nearly every community. The fortunes of the stylist are intrinsically related to the health of the advertising, film, video, and commercial photography industries, and these appear to be in good shape. Stylists should try, however, to maintain a wide client base, so they can be assured of regular work in case one source dries up.

Technological advances, especially in the areas of digital photography and photo enhancement, may transform, but not eliminate, the role of the photo stylist in the future. Someday there may be educational avenues for the stylist to enter into the field, and this may increase the amount of competition for styling assignments. Ultimately, though, maintaining the quality of work is the best insurance for continued employment.

■ For More Information

Association of Stylists and Coordinators
125 Washington Place, #4B
New York, NY 10014
Tel: 718-278-6160

Photocomposing-Keyboard and Perforator Machine Operators

■ **See Typists and Word Processors**

Photographers

■ Overview

Photographers take and sometimes develop and print pictures of people, places, objects, and events, using a variety of cameras and photographic equipment. They work in publishing, advertising, public relations, science, and business, as well as provide personal photographic services. They may also work as fine artists.

■ History

The word photograph means, literally, "to write with light." Although the art of photography goes back only about 150 years, the two Greek words that were chosen and combined to refer to this skill quite accurately describe what it does.

The discoveries that led eventually to photography began early in the 18th century when a German scientist, Dr. Johann H. Schultze, experimented with the action of light on certain chemicals. He found that when these chemicals were covered by dark paper they did not change color, but when they were exposed to sunlight, they darkened. A French painter named Louis Daguerre (1787-1851) became the first photographer in 1839, when he perfected the process of using silver-iodide-coated plates inside a small box. He then developed the plates by means of mercury vapor. The daguerreotype, as these early photographs came

to be known, took minutes to expose and the developing process was directly to the plate. There were no prints made.

Although the daguerreotype was the sensation of its day, it was not until George Eastman (1854-1932) invented a simple camera and flexible roll film that photography began to come into widespread use in the late 1800s. With exposure to the negative, light-sensitive paper was used to make positive multiple copies of the image.

■ The Job

Photography is both an artistic and technical occupation. There are many variables in the process that a knowledgeable photographer can manipulate to produce a precise documentation or a work of fine art. First, photographers know how to use cameras and can adjust focus, shutter speeds, aperture, lenses, and filters. They know about the types and speeds of films. Photographers know about light and shadow, how to use available light and how to set up artificial lighting to achieve desired effects.

Some photographers send their film to laboratories, but some develop their own negatives and make their own prints. These processes require knowledge about chemicals such as developers and fixers and how to use enlarging equipment. They are familiar with the large variety of papers available for printing photographs. Most photographers continually experiment with photographic processes to improve their technical proficiency or to bend the rules to create special effects.

Digital photography is a relatively new development. Film is replaced by microchips which record pictures in digital format. They can then be downloaded onto a computer's hard drive and the photographer uses special software to manipulate the images on screen. Digital photography is used primarily for electronic publishing and advertising.

Photographers usually specialize in one of several areas:

PHOTOGRAPHERS	
SCHOOL SUBJECTS	Art Chemistry
PERSONAL SKILLS	Artistic Communication/ideas
WORK ENVIRONMENT	Indoors and outdoors Primarily multiple locations
MINIMUM EDUCATION LEVEL	Some postsecondary training
SALARY RANGE	$16,500 to $30,700 to $38,900+
CERTIFICATION OR LICENSING	None available
OUTLOOK	Faster than the average
DOT	143
GOE	01.02.02
NOC	5221
O*NET	34023A

Three photographers take aim on a bear in Tongass National Forest in Alaska.

portraiture, commercial and advertising photography, photojournalism, fine art, educational photography, or scientific photography. (See *Photography*) There are subspecialties within each of these categories. A scientific photographer, for example, may specialize in aerial or underwater photography. A commercial photographer may specialize in food or fashion photography.

Some photographers write for trade and technical journals, teach photography in schools and colleges, act as representatives of photographic equipment manufacturers, sell photographic equipment and supplies, produce documentary films, or do freelance work.

■ Requirements

High School

High school students should take classes in art and photography. Chemistry is useful for understanding developing and printing processes. You can learn about photo manipulation software and digital photography in computer classes, and business classes will help if you are considering a freelance career.

Postsecondary Training

Formal educational requirements depend upon the nature of the photographer's specialty. For instance, photographic work in scientific and engineering research generally requires an engineering background with a degree from a recognized college or institute.

A college education is not required to become a photographer, although college training probably offers the most promising assurance of success in fields such as industrial, news, or scientific photography. In the 1990s, 103 community and junior colleges offer associate degrees in

photography, more than 160 colleges and universities offer bachelor's degrees, and 38 offer master's degrees. Many of these schools offer courses in cinematography, although very few have programs leading to a degree in this specialty. Many men and women, however, become photographers with no formal education beyond high school.

Prospective photographers should have a broad technical understanding of photography plus as much practical experience with cameras as possible. Take many different kinds of photographs with a variety of cameras and subjects. Learn how to develop photographs and, if possible, build your own darkroom or rent one. Experience in picture composition, cropping prints (cutting to desired size), enlarging, and retouching are all valuable.

Other Requirements

Students who hope to become photographers should possess manual dexterity, good eyesight and color vision, and artistic ability. You need an eye for form and line, an appreciation of light and shadow, and the ability to use imaginative and creative approaches to photographs or film, especially in commercial work. In addition, you should be patient and accurate and enjoy working with detail.

Self-employed, or freelance, photographers need good business skills. They must be able to manage their own studios, including hiring and managing assistants and other employees, keeping records, and maintaining photographic and business files. Marketing and sales skills are also important to a successful freelance photography business.

■ Exploring

Photography is a field that almost every person with a camera can explore. Students can join high school camera clubs, yearbook or newspaper staffs, photography contests, and community hobby groups to gain experience. Students also may seek a part-time or summer job in a camera shop or work as a developer in a laboratory or processing center.

■ Employers

About 90,000 photographers were employed in the 1990s. About half were salaried employees; the rest were self-employed. Most jobs for photographers are provided by photographic or commercial art studios; other employers include newspapers and magazines, radio and TV broadcasting, government agencies, and manufacturing firms. Colleges, universities, and other educational institutions employ photographers to prepare promotional and educational materials.

■ Starting Out

Some photographers enter the field as apprentices, trainees, or assistants. As a trainee, you may work in a darkroom, camera shop, or developing laboratory. You may move lights and arrange backgrounds for a commercial or portrait photographer or motion picture photographer. You may spend many months learning this kind of work before you move into a job behind a camera.

In many large cities, there are schools of photography, which may be a good way to start in the field. A press photographer may work for one of the many newspapers and magazines published in the United States and abroad. Some employers require a probationary period of 30 to 90 days before a new employee attains full job security. On publications where there is a full Newspaper Guild shop, a photographer will be required to join the guild.

Some go into business for themselves as soon as they have finished their formal education. Setting up a studio may not require a large capital outlay, but beginners may find that success does not come easily.

■ Advancement

Because photography is such a diversified field, there is no usual way in which to get ahead. Those who begin by working for someone else may advance to owning their own businesses. Commercial photographers may gain prestige as more of their pictures are placed in well-known trade journals or popular magazines. Press photographers may advance in salary and the kinds of important news stories assigned to them. A few photographers may become celebrities in their own right by making contributions to medical science, engineering science, or natural or physical science.

■ Earnings

The earnings of photographers in private industry vary according to the level of responsibility. In the 1990s, those who handle routine work earn an average of about $24,800 a year. Photographers who do difficult or challenging work earn approximately $37,200 a year.

In the 1990s, beginning photographers working for newspapers that had contracts with the Newspaper Guild earn a median salary of about $19,000 a year. Most earn between $16,500 and $22,500, with the top 10 percent receiving $26,500 or more. Experienced newspaper photographers earn a median of $30,700 a year; most earn from $26,300 to $35,700 a year. The top 10 percent of experienced newspaper photographers earn in excess of $38,900.

Photographers in government service earn an average salary of about $29,500 a year. Self-employed photographers often earn more than salaried photographers, but their earnings depend on general business conditions. In addition, self-employed photographers do not have the benefits that a company provides its employees.

Photographers who combine scientific training and photographic expertise, as do scientific photographers, usu-

PROFILE: ANSEL ADAMS (1902-1984)

U.S. photographer Ansel Adams was known for his dramatic scenes of the American West and for his contributions to photographic technology. His zone system is a method of exposure and development that controls the range of dark and light tones in black and white prints.

Adams was born in San Francisco. He studied music and photography and was a concert pianist until 1930. In 1932 he joined Edward Weston and others in forming Group f/64, photographers who helped establish photography as a fine art. Adams was cofounder of the photography department at the Museum of Modern Art (1940) and founder of the Friends of Photography (1966). He was also an active conservationist and served on the board of directors of the Sierra Club, 1934-71. His photos were published in more than 35 books and portfolios. He also wrote many books on photographic techniques.

ally start at higher salaries than other photographers. They also usually receive consistently larger advances in salary than do others, so that their income, both as beginners and as experienced photographers, place them well above the average in their field. Photographers in salaried jobs usually receive benefits such as paid holidays, vacations, and sick leave and medical insurance.

■ Work Environment

Work conditions vary based on the job and employer. Many photographers work a 35- to 40-hour workweek, but freelancers and news photographers often put in long, irregular hours. Commercial and portrait photographers work in comfortable surroundings. Photojournalists seldom are assured physical comfort in their work and may in fact face danger when covering stories on natural disasters or military conflicts. Some photographers work in research laboratory settings; others work on aircraft; and still others work underwater. For some photographers, conditions change from day to day. One day, they may be photographing a hot and dusty rodeo; the next they may be taking pictures of a dog sled race in Alaska.

In general, photographers work under pressure to meet deadlines and satisfy customers. Freelance photographers have the added pressure of continually seeking new clients and uncertain incomes.

For specialists in fields such as fashion photography, breaking into the field may take years. Working as another photographer's assistant is physically demanding when carrying equipment is required.

For freelance photographers, the cost of equipment can be quite expensive, with no assurance that the money spent will be recouped through income from future assignments. Freelancers in travel-related photography, such as travel and tourism, and photojournalism, have the added cost of transportation and accommodations. For all photographers, flexibility is a major asset.

■ Outlook

Employment of photographers will increase about as fast as the average for all occupations through the year 2006, according to the *Occupational Outlook Handbook*. The demand for new images should remain strong in education, communication, entertainment, marketing, and research. As more newspapers and magazines turn to electronic publishing, it will increase the need for photographs.

Photography is a highly competitive field. There are far more photographers than positions available. Only those who are extremely talented and highly skilled can support themselves as self-employed photographers. Many photographers take pictures as a sideline while working another job.

■ For More Information

The ASMP promotes the rights of photographers, educates its members in business practices, and promotes high standards of ethics.

American Society of Media Photographers
14 Washington Road, Suite 502
Princeton Junction, NJ 08550-1033
Tel: 609-799-8300
Web: http://www.asmp.org

The NPPA maintains a job bank, provides educational information, and makes insurance available to its members. It also publishes News Photographer *magazine.*

National Press Photographers Association
3200 Croasdaile Drive, Suite 306
Durham, NC 27705
Tel: 800-289-6772
Email: nppa@mindspring.com
Web: http://metalab.unc.edu/nppa/index.html

The PPA provides training, publishes its own magazine, and offers various services for its members.

Professional Photographers of America
229 Peachtree Street, NE, No. 2200
Atlanta, GA 30303-2206
Tel: 404-522-8600
Email: membership@ppa.world.org
Web: http://www.ppa-world.org

■ Related Articles

Film
Photography
Visual Arts
Camera Operators
Cinematographers and Directors of Photography
Medical Illustrators and Photographers
Photo Stylists
Photojournalists
Photographic Equipment Technicians
Photographic Laboratory Workers

Photographic Equipment Technicians

■ Overview

Photographic equipment technicians, sometimes called *camera technicians,* maintain, test, disassemble, and repair cameras and other equipment used to take still and motion pictures. They are responsible for keeping the equipment in working order.

Photographic equipment technicians use a variety of hand tools (such as screwdrivers, pliers, and wire cutters) for maintenance and repair of the complex cameras used by motion picture and still photographers.

As hobbyists' cameras and equipment become more convenient to use, they become more complicated to maintain and repair. Professionals' cameras as well—especially those of filmmakers—have become increasingly more complicated and expensive. In both cases, photographic equipment is too valuable to entrust to the care of anyone but a trained photographic equipment technician. Today, there are thousands of these technicians working in the United States, providing services that range from quick and simple adjustments to complicated repairs requiring specialized equipment.

■ History

Although the first permanent photographs were made in the 1820s, it was the introduction of the Kodak camera in 1888 that brought photography within reach of the amateur. This hand-held, roll-film camera developed by George Eastman (1854-1932) replaced the earlier bulky cameras and complicated dry-plate developing processes that had restricted photography to professionals. The Leica camera, the first 35-millimeter "miniature" camera, was introduced in 1924. It immediately created an immense interest in candid photography and had a great impact on both everyday American life and on the use of photography as an art form, as an entertainment medium, and as an influential advertising tool.

The early development of motion pictures was also tied to a series of inventions-flexible celluloid film, Thomas Edison's (1847-1931) kinetoscope (in which motion pictures were viewed by looking through a peephole at revolving reels of film), and his later projecting kinetoscope, the immediate forerunner of the modern film projector. In 1876, Edison presented the first public exhibition of motion pictures projected on a screen.

Further improvements in cameras, projectors, lighting equipment, films, and prints have contributed to making still and motion picture photography one of the most popular hobbies. Early cameras were completely mechanical. Now they are computerized, with internal light meters, and automatic focus and film advancement. Photographic equipment technicians must be able to repair both the mechanics and the electronics of modern cameras. Digital cameras are the newest development in photographic technology. Film has been replaced by microchips that record a picture in digital format, which can then be downloaded onto a computer.

■ The Job

Technicians diagnose a camera's problem by analyzing the camera's shutter speed and accuracy of focus through the use of sophisticated electronic test equipment. Once the problem is diagnosed, the camera is opened and checked for worn, misaligned, or defective parts. At least half of all repairs are done without replacing parts. All tests and adjustments are done to manufacturer's specifications, using blueprints, specification lists, and repair manuals.

Most repairs and adjustments can be made using small hand tools. A jeweler's loupe (magnifying glass) is used to examine small parts for wear or damage. Electronic and optical measuring instruments are used to check and adjust focus, shutter speed, operating speed of motion picture cameras, and light readings of light meters.

Many modern cameras designed for amateur use include built-in light meters as well as automatic focus and aperture (lens opening) settings. These features are convenient for the user, but the mechanisms require careful adjustment by a skilled technician when they malfunction.

Cameras must be kept clean and well lubricated to operate properly. Photographic equipment technicians use vacuum and air pressure devices to remove tiny dust particles and ultrasonic cleaning equipment to dislodge and remove hardened dirt and lubricant. Lenses are cleaned with a chemical solvent and soft tissue paper. Very fine lubricants are applied, often with the aid of a syringe or fine cotton swab.

Occasionally technicians, especially those employed by manufacturers or shops servicing professional studios, fabricate replacement parts. They employ small instrument-makers' lathes, milling machines, grinders, and other tools.

Technicians must be able to discuss a camera's working problems with a customer in order to extract the necessary information to diagnose the problem.

■ Requirements

High School

To prepare for this career, high school students should take classes in computer science, shop, and mathematics.

Postsecondary Training

Because their work is highly technical, photographic equipment technicians need specialized training, which is available through either classroom instruction or a correspondence course. The training provides basic technical background information to work with cameras as well as a thorough understanding and working knowledge of electronics. Not all camera models can be covered in the training course. More specialized training on additional models is obtained on the job or through specialized seminars.

Camera manufacturers and importers provide training for their technicians. This training usually covers only the technical aspects of the manufacturer's own products.

Other Requirements

In order to work with extremely small parts, photographic equipment technicians need excellent vision, manual dexterity, and mechanical aptitude. Those who work directly with the public must be able to communicate easily with people.

■ Exploring

Larger camera stores often have an on-site employee who does limited camera adjustment and repair. This person can be a good source of information about opportunities in this field. Information may also be obtained from technical schools and institutes offering photographic equipment courses. In addition, many schools and community centers

PHOTOGRAPHIC EQUIPMENT TECHNICIANS	
SCHOOL SUBJECTS	Mathematics Technical/Shop
PERSONAL SKILLS	Mechanical/manipulative Technical/scientific
WORK ENVIRONMENT	Primarily indoors Primarily one location
MINIMUM EDUCATION LEVEL	Some postsecondary training
SALARY RANGE	$13,500 to $25,000 to $35,000+
CERTIFICATION OR LICENSING	None available
OUTLOOK	About as fast as the average
DOT	714
GOE	05.05.11
O*NET	34026

A photographic equipment technician must have good manual dexterity skills to work with small camera parts.

have photography clubs, some with their own darkrooms, that offer an excellent chance to explore the general field of photography.

■ Employers

Many photographic equipment technicians work in shops specializing in camera adjustment and repair or in the service departments of large camera stores. Quite a few technicians work for camera manufacturers, repairing cameras and photographic equipment that customers have returned to the factory. Some camera dealers have their own in-house repair departments and sometimes hire technicians to adjust cameras on site. Technicians specializing in motion picture cameras and equipment may work for motion picture or television studios or companies renting such equipment to studios.

■ Starting Out

Individual shops looking for technicians usually notify schools in their area or advertise through national photographic service publications. Manufacturers hire technicians through their personnel departments. The placement counselor of a student's training institute can help locate openings for graduates.

■ Advancement

Advancement in a photographic equipment repair facility is usually from trainee to experienced worker to a supervisory position. Many manufacturer's technicians also open their own shops, perhaps starting part time on weekends

and evenings. Although technicians who have worked for a manufacturer usually know only one line of cameras well, they can learn other manufacturers' models on their own.

Independent technicians advance as their reputation grows for doing quality work. They must become familiar with all the major brands and models of camera equipment. In recent years, major camera manufacturers have been offering more training courses and seminars to inform independent technicians about their newer models—particularly those repairs that can be done efficiently in their shops and the types of repairs that need to be handled at the factory. Because of this increased cooperation, technicians who decide to open independent businesses are now much better able to provide quality services for the cameras they service.

Some independent technicians expand their activities into selling small "add-ons" such as film, accessories, and used equipment. Some photographic equipment technicians also work as professional photographers during their off-hours.

■ Earnings

Photographic equipment technicians employed by camera and equipment manufacturers and repair shops can expect to earn starting salaries in the range of $13,500 to $15,500 a year. The average salary for an experienced technician working for a manufacturer is often between $19,500 and $26,500 a year. A skilled and experienced technician working on commission in a busy repair shop can make over $35,000 a year. Self-employed technicians have earnings that vary widely. In the right location, independent technicians can build up businesses that give them earnings higher than those of technicians who work for manufacturers or shops.

■ Work Environment

Photographic equipment technicians work in clean, well-lighted shop conditions. They are usually seated at a bench for much of the time, working with hand tools. Eyestrain and stiffness from long hours of sitting are common physical complaints. Tedium can be a problem for some technicians.

Photographic equipment technicians work alone most of the time, concentrating on their work. Patience and steadiness are required to work successfully with the small mechanisms of modern camera equipment.

■ Outlook

The *Occupational Outlook Handbook* predicts a faster than average employment growth for this occupation through 2006. In recent years there have been some geographical areas where the demand for well-qualified technicians has greatly exceeded the supply. This suggests that technicians who are flexible about location will probably have the best job opportunities.

In general, the low price of many of today's point-and-shoot cameras and the high cost of labor make it uneconomical to do extensive service on these cameras. Cameras that incorporate more sophisticated electronics will require technicians with more extensive training. Technicians whose training has covered a wide variety of equipment brands and models will be in greatest demand.

■ For More Information

For career information, contact:

National Association of Photo Equipment Technicians
3000 Picture Place
Jackson, MI 49201
Tel: 517-788-8100
Web: http://www.pmai.org/sections/napet.html

Society of Photo-Technologists
367 Windsor Highway, Suite 404
New Windsor, NY 12553
Tel: 914-782-4248

■ Related Articles

Computers

Film

Photography

Photographers

Photographic Laboratory Workers

Watch and Clock Repairers

Photographic Laboratory Workers

■ Overview

Photographic laboratory workers develop black-and-white and color film, using chemical baths or printing machines. They mount slides, and sort and package finished photographic prints. Some of these laboratory workers are known as *darkroom technicians, film laboratory technicians,* and *developers.*

■ History

The first permanent photographs were taken in the early 19th century. The size and awkwardness of early cameras and their accessories, the long exposure time needed, and the necessity of developing the photographic plate before the chemical solution on it dried, made photography largely the province of professional technicians in its early years.

The Kodak camera, introduced in 1888 by George Eastman (1854-1932), brought photography within the reach of amateurs. This hand-held snapshot camera contained a roll of film capable of producing 100 negatives. The camera with the exposed film in it had to be returned to Eastman Kodak in Rochester, New York, for processing.

Further technical developments in photography included the invention of celluloid-based film, light-sensitive photographic paper, and faster methods of developing film. Today, photography has become so popular that there are few U.S. households without at least one camera. Professional photographers are constantly experimenting with new ways of creating interesting pictures. While many professional photographers develop their own film in home darkrooms, the vast majority of amateur photographers bring their film to film centers, drugstores, or camera stores for development. Photographic laboratories have continued to expand their operations to serve this ever-increasing number of amateur photographers.

■ The Job

Film process technicians develop exposed film or paper in a series of chemical or water baths. They mix developing and fixing solutions. They immerse exposed film in developer, stop bath, and fixer which causes the negative image to appear. The developer may vary the immersion time in each solution, depending on the qualities desired in the

PHOTOGRAPHIC LABORATORY WORKERS	
SCHOOL SUBJECTS	Chemistry Mathematics
PERSONAL SKILLS	Following instructions Technical/scientific
WORK ENVIRONMENT	Primarily indoors Primarily one location
MINIMUM EDUCATION LEVEL	High school diploma
SALARY RANGE	$13,500 to $16,500 to $40,000+
CERTIFICATION OR LICENSING	None available
OUTLOOK	Little change or more slowly than the average
DOT	976
GOE	05.10.05
O*NET	89914D

A technician attaches a roll of film to an automatic film developing machine.

finished print. After the film is washed with water to remove all traces of chemical solutions, it is placed in a drying cabinet.

The developer may be assisted by a *projection printer*, who uses a projection printer to transfer the image from a negative to photographic paper. Light passing through the negative and a magnifying lens projects an image on the photographic paper. Contrast may be varied or unwanted details blocked out during the printing process.

Most semiskilled workers, such as those who simply operate photofinishing machinery, are employed in large commercial laboratories that process color snapshot and slide film for amateur photographers. Often, they work under the supervision of a developer.

Automatic print developers tend machines that automatically develop film and fix, wash, and dry prints. These workers attach one end of the film to a leader in the machine; they also attach sensitized paper for the prints. While the machine is running, workers check temperature controls and adjust them as needed. The developers check prints coming out of the machine and refer those of doubtful quality to quality control workers.

Color-printer operators control a machine that makes color prints from negatives. Under darkroom conditions, they load the machine with a roll of printing paper. Before loading the negative film, they examine it to determine what machine setting to use to produce the best color print from it. After the photographic paper has been printed, they remove it from the machine and place it in the developer. The processed negatives and finished prints are inserted into an envelope to be returned to the customer.

Automatic mounters operate machines that cut apart rolls of positive color transparencies and mount them as slides.

After trimming the roll of film, the mounter places it on the cutting machine, takes each cut frame in turn, and places it in a press that joins it to the cardboard mount. *Paper process technicians* develop strips of exposed photographic paper. *Takedown sorters* sort processed film.

Photo checkers and assemblers inspect prints, mounted transparencies, and negatives for color shading, sharpness of image, and accuracy of identifying numbers, using a lighted viewing screen. They mark any defective prints, indicating the corrective action to be taken, and return them with the negatives for reprocessing. Satisfactory prints and negatives are assembled in the proper order, packaged, and labeled for delivery to the customer.

Digital imaging technicians use computer images of traditional negatives and special software to vary the contrast, remove distracting backgrounds, or superimpose photos on top of one another. *Precision photographic process workers* work directly on negatives. These workers include *airbrush artists*, who restore damaged and faded photographs, *colorists*, who apply oil colors to portrait photographs to create natural, lifelike appearances, and *photographic spotters*, who spot out imperfections on photographic prints.

Laboratories that specialize in custom work may employ a *retoucher* to alter negatives or prints in order to improve their color, shading, or content. The retoucher uses artists' tools to smooth features on faces, for example, or to heighten or eliminate shadows. (Some retouchers work in art studios or advertising agencies; others work as freelancers for book or magazine publishers.)

Other photographic process specialists include *print controllers, photograph finishers, hand mounters, print washers, splicers, cutters, print inspectors, automatic developers,* and *film processing utility workers.*

■ Requirements

High School

High school graduates are preferred for photographic laboratory jobs. Courses in chemistry and mathematics are recommended.

Postsecondary Training

Many two-year colleges and technical institutes offer programs in photographic technology. Graduates of these programs can obtain jobs as developers and supervisors in photo labs.

Other Requirements

An interest in photography and an understanding of its basic processes are natural assets for those applying for jobs in this field. Manual dexterity, good vision with no defects in color perception, and mechanical aptitude are also important. Students who plan to pursue careers as darkroom technicians for professional photographers need to have experience with developing procedures. Film convenience stores and camera stores are good places to get this experience.

■ Exploring

Many high schools and colleges have photography clubs, which can provide valuable experience for those interested in careers in this field. Evening courses in photography are offered in many technical schools and adult education programs. The armed forces also train personnel as photographic technicians.

There are several magazines that may be both interesting and helpful for prospective photographic laboratory workers. These include *American Photo, Darkroom Photography,* and *Photographic Processing.* Local libraries often have large collections of photography books as well.

■ Employers

Photographic process workers held about 63,000 jobs in 1996. Photofinishing laboratories and one-hour minilabs employed almost 70 percent. Developers are employed mainly in portrait studios; photo studios of newspapers, magazines, and advertising agencies; commercial laboratories that process the work of professional photographers; and retail stores that provide developing and printing services. They are highly skilled workers who can control the light contrast, surface finish, and other qualities of the photographic print by their mastery of the steps in the developing process. They perform many of their tasks in well-equipped darkrooms.

■ Starting Out

After receiving a high school diploma or its equivalent, prospective photographic laboratory workers usually apply for jobs at photofinishing laboratories. New employees in photographic laboratories begin as helpers to experienced technicians, moving into specialized jobs, such as printing and developing, as they gain more experience. Semiskilled workers usually receive a few months of on-the-job training, while developers may take three or four years to become thoroughly familiar with their jobs.

■ Advancement

Advancement in this field is usually from technical jobs, such as developer, to supervisory and managerial positions. Semiskilled workers who continue their education in film processing techniques may move up to developer, all-around darkroom technician, and supervisory jobs.

Aspiring young photographers often take jobs in photo labs to provide themselves with a source of income while they attempt to establish themselves as professionals. There they can learn the most basic techniques of color, black and white, and slide reproduction. Those who accumulate sufficient capital may open their own commercial studios.

■ Outlook

According to the *Occupational Outlook Handbook,* employment is expected to increase more slowly than the average in this field through the year 2006. Most openings will occur as a result of the need to replace workers, especially machine operators.

Although digital photography is now used by advanced amateurs and professionals, it is likely to coexist rather than compete with traditional film photography. In the future, however, as digital cameras and image manipulation software become cheaper, the need for photographic lab workers will decrease.

■ Earnings

In the 1990s, the median annual salary for photo process workers is about $16,500. Weekly wages range from $10,500 for the lowest 10 percent to $32,000 for the top 5 percent. Hourly wages for photofinishing laboratory workers range from minimum wage for entry-level workers to $10 for experienced machine operators. The average entry-level salary for darkroom technicians is $16,600 per year. Those employees who go on to managerial positions can expect to earn $40,000 or more a year. Most employees worked a 40-hour week, with premium pay for overtime.

Most photographic workers are eligible for benefits such as medical insurance.

■ Work Environment

Photographic laboratories are usually clean, well lighted (except for darkroom areas), and air-conditioned. There is usually no heavy physical labor. Many of the jobs performed by semiskilled workers are limited and repetitive and may become monotonous. The jobs often entail sitting or standing for a considerable amount of time in one place. Employees in these jobs need patience and ability to concentrate on details.

Some employees, such as printer operators, photo checkers, and assemblers who examine small images very closely, may be subject to eyestrain. Process workers may be exposed to chemicals and fumes, requiring safety precautions.

Photographic laboratory work has peak seasons: school graduation, weddings, summer vacation, and the December-January holiday season.

The work of developers and darkroom technicians calls for good judgment, ability to apply specialized technical knowledge, and an appreciation of the aesthetic qualities of photography. Their contributions to the clarity and beauty of the finished photographs can be a great source of satisfaction.

■ For More Information

For information about photographic laboratory careers, contact these organizations.

Association of Professional Color Laboratories
3000 Picture Place
Jackson, MI 49201
Tel: 517-788-8146

Photo Marketing Association International
3000 Picture Place
Jackson, MI 49201
Tel: 517-788-8100
Web: http://www.pmai.org

Professional Photographers of America
229 Peachtree Street, NE, No. 2200
Atlanta, GA 30303-2206
Tel: 404-522-8600
Web: http://www.ppa-world.org

■ Related Articles

Film
Photography
Camera Operators
Photographers
Photographic Equipment Technicians

Photographic Technicians

■ **See Optics Technicians**

Photojournalists

Photojournalists shoot photographs that capture news events. Their job is to tell a story with pictures. They may cover a war in central Africa, the Olympics, a national election, or a small town Fourth of July parade. In addition to shooting pictures, they also write captions or other supporting text. Photojournalists may also develop and print photographs or edit film. More and more photojournalists are using digital photography, particularly for foreign assignments, since the electronic images can be sent instantly by computer modem.

To prepare for a career in photojournalism, high school students can work on school newspapers or yearbooks. Try a job shadowing experience with a photojournalist at a local paper.

Some colleges and universities offer photojournalism majors, while others offer a journalism major with three to four photography courses. Although a journalism degree is not required for becoming a photojournalist, experience is mandatory. A four-year degree is recommended, but sometimes an associate's degree with the right experience is sufficient. There are internship opportunities available to undergraduates in journalism programs, and in fact many programs require students to complete an internship. This experience also helps the student build a portfolio.

In addition to experience and an outstanding portfolio, photojournalists need people skills, an eye for art and photography, and a working knowledge of camera and developing equipment. They must be able to work flexible hours, handle pressure, write well, and perform research.

Photojournalists are employed by newspapers, magazines, and other print publications. Many work as freelancers who research their own stories, document them, and sell them to various print media.

According to the Inland Press Association's 1997 Newspaper Compensation Survey, newspaper photojournalist salaries range from a low of $10,400 to a median of $26,343 to a high of $94,707. Larger newspapers can offer their staff photojournalists larger salaries and better benefits. Freelance rates for magazine photojournalists are dependent on both the experience of the photographer and the size of the magazine, but can sometimes be as high as $800 per day.

Photojournalism is a highly competitive field, but employment of photographers is expected to increase as fast as the average for all occupations through the year 2006, according to the *Occupational Outlook Handbook*.

■ For More Information

The following organization offers a job bank, a network for professionals, and a list of schools that have photojournalism programs.

The National Press Photographers Association
3200 Croasdaile Drive, Suite 306
Durham, NC 27705
Tel: 800-289-6772
Email: nppa@mindspring.com
Web: http://metalab.unc.edu/nppa/index.html

For information about photojournalism, contact:

American Society of Magazine Photographers
14 Washington Road, Suite 502
Princeton Junction, NJ 08550-1033
Tel: 609-799-8300

■ Related Articles

Film
Photography
Television
Camera Operators
Photo Stylists
Photographers

Photonics Technicians

■ See Optics Technicians

Photo-Optics Technicians

■ See Optics Technicians

Physical Science Technicians and Aides

■ See Soil Conservationists and Technicians

Physical Therapists

■ Overview

Physical therapists, formerly called *physiotherapists,* are health care specialists who restore mobility, alleviate pain and suffering, and work to prevent permanent disability for their patients. They test and measure the functions of the musculoskeletal, neurological, pulmonary, and cardiovascular systems, and treat problems in these systems caused by illness, injury, or birth defect. Physical therapists practice preventive, restorative, and rehabilitative treatment for their patients.

■ History

The practice of physical therapy has developed as our knowledge of medicine and our understanding of the functions of the human body have grown. During the first part of the 20th century, there were tremendous strides in medical practice in general. The war-time experiences of medical teams who had to rehabilitate seriously injured soldiers contributed to the medical use and acceptance of physical therapy practices. The polio epidemic in the 1940s, which left many victims paralyzed, also led to the demand for improved physical therapy.

A professional association was organized in 1921, and physical therapy began to achieve professional stature. The American Physical Therapy Association (APTA) now serves a membership of more than 67,000 physical therapists, physical therapy assistants, and students.

Today the use of physical therapy has expanded beyond hospitals, where it has been traditionally practiced. Physical therapists now are working in private practices, nursing homes, sports facilities, home health agencies, public and private schools, academic institutions, hospices, and in industrial physical therapy programs-a reflection of their versatility of skills and the public's need for comprehensive health care.

■ The Job

To initiate a program of physical therapy, the physical therapist consults the individual's medical history, examines the patient and identifies problems, confers with the physician or other health care professionals involved in the patient's care, establishes objectives and treatment goals that are consistent with the patient's needs, and determines the methods for accomplishing the objectives.

Treatment goals established by the physical therapist include preventing disability, relieving pain, and restoring function. In the presence of illness or injury, the ultimate goal is to assist the patient's physical recovery and reentry into the community, home, and work environment at the highest level of independence and self-sufficiency possible.

To aid and maintain recovery, the physical therapist also provides education to involve patients in their own care. The educational program may include exercises, posture reeducation, and relaxation practices. In many cases, the patient's family is involved in the educational program to provide emotional support or physical assistance as needed. These activities evolve into a continuum of self-care when the patient is discharged from the physical therapy program.

The care physical therapists provide for many types of patients of all ages includes working with burn victims to

PHYSICAL THERAPISTS	
SCHOOL SUBJECTS	Biology Health
PERSONAL SKILLS	Helping/teaching Mechanical/manipulative
WORK ENVIRONMENT	Primarily indoors Primarily one location
MINIMUM EDUCATION LEVEL	Bachelor's degree
SALARY RANGE	$20,000 to $38,000 to $68,000
CERTIFICATION OR LICENSING	Required by all states
OUTLOOK	Much faster than the average
DOT	076
GOE	10.02.02
NOC	3142
O*NET	32308

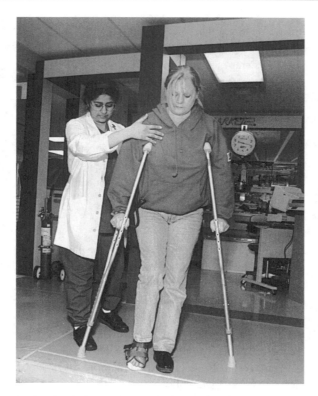

A physical therapist assists a patient as she gets used to walking with crutches.

prevent abnormal scarring and loss of movement, with stroke victims to regain movement and independent living, with cancer patients to relieve discomfort, and with cardiac patients to improve endurance and achieve independence. Physical therapists also provide preventive exercise programs, postural improvement, and physical conditioning to individuals who perceive the need to promote their own health and well-being.

Physical therapists should have a creative approach to their work. No two patients respond the same way to exactly the same kind of treatment. The challenge is to find the right way to encourage the patient to make progress, to respond to treatment, to feel a sense of achievement, and to refuse to become discouraged if progress is slow.

Many physical therapists acquire specialized knowledge through clinical experience and educational preparation in specialty areas of physical therapy practice, such as cardiopulmonary, clinical electrophysiologic, neurologic, orthopedic, pediatric, geriatric, and sports.

■ Requirements

High School

High school students who plan to become physical therapists should have a strong background in the physical and biological sciences.

Postsecondary Training

Physical therapists attain their professional skills through extensive educational and clinical training. Either a bachelor's degree or a master's degree in physical therapy is necessary to practice physical therapy. Entry-level professional accredited education is offered in more than 45 bachelor's degree programs, and more than one hundred master's degree programs. All accredited physical therapy programs will be at the master's level or higher by the year 2001.

Certification or Licensing

Upon graduating from an accredited physical therapy educational program, physical therapists must successfully complete a licensure examination and comply with the legal requirements of the jurisdiction in which they practice. These qualifications are required in all 50 states, the District of Columbia, the Virgin Islands, and the commonwealth of Puerto Rico.

Specialist certification of physical therapists, while not a requirement for employment, is a desirable advanced credential. The American Board of Physical Therapy Specialties, an appointed group of the American Physical Therapy Association, certifies physical therapists who demonstrate specialized knowledge and advanced clinical proficiency in a specialty area of physical therapy practice and who pass a certifying examination. The seven areas of specialization are cardiopulmonary, clinical electrophysiology, neurology, orthopedics, pediatrics, geriatrics, and sports physical therapy. In 1995, there were 1,348 certified specialists.

■ Exploring

Students interested in exploring a career as a physical therapist might work as a counselor in a summer camp for the disabled or as an orderly or a physical therapy aide in a hospital. Students also may interview or visit physical therapists at their work.

■ Employers

Hospitals employ about two-thirds of physical therapists. Nursing homes, outpatient rehabilitation centers, and home health care agencies are other employers. Veterans Administration hospitals and other government agencies also hire physical therapists.

■ Starting Out

Physical therapy graduates may obtain jobs through their college placement offices or by answering ads in any of a variety of professional journals. They can apply in person or send letters and resumes to hospitals, medical centers, rehabilitation facilities, and other places that hire physical therapists. Some find jobs through the American Physical Therapy Association.

■ Advancement

In a hospital or other health care facility, one may rise from being a staff physical therapist to being the chief physical therapist and then director of the department. Administrative responsibilities are usually given to those physical therapists who have had several years of experience, plus the personal qualities that prepare them for undertaking this kind of assignment.

After serving in a hospital or other institution for several years, some physical therapists open up their own practices or go into a group practice, with both often paying higher salaries.

■ Earnings

Salaries for physical therapists depend on experience and type of employer. Physical therapists earned an annual average salary of $39,364 in 1996. Fifty percent averaged between $30,004 and $54,860; the top 10 percent earned over $67,288 a year. According to the American Physical Therapy Association, hospital-employed therapists earned an average of $48,000 annually.

Federally employed physical therapists are paid starting salaries of about $20,000 a year, while supervisory therapists average about $38,700. The average for all therapists working in the federal government is about $26,400 per year.

■ Work Environment

The average physical therapist works approximately 40 to 50 hours each week, including Saturdays. Patient sessions may be brief or may last an hour or more. Usually, treatment is on an individual basis, but occasionally therapy may be given in groups when the patients' problems are similar.

■ Outlook

Physical therapy is one of the fastest-growing professions in the United States. In 1996, 115,000 physical therapists were employed in the United States; about 25 percent worked part time. The Bureau of Labor Statistics projects an occupational growth of about 75 percent through the year 2006.

One reason for this rapid growth is the fact that the median age of the American population is rising, and this older demographic group develops a higher number of medical conditions that cause physical pain and disability. Also, advances in medical technology save more people, who then require physical therapy. For example, as more trauma victims and newborns with birth defects survive, the need for physical therapists will rise. Another reason is the public's growing interest in physical fitness, which has resulted in an increasing number of athletic injuries requiring physical therapy. In industry and fitness centers, a growing interest in pain and injury prevention also has created new opportunities for physical therapists.

Employment prospects for physical therapists should continue to be excellent into the next century. If enrollment in accredited physical therapy programs remains at the current level, there will be more openings for physical therapists than qualified individuals to fill them.

■ For More Information

The American Physical Therapy Association offers a brochure entitled "A Future in Physical Therapy" as well as other general career information.

American Physical Therapy Association
1111 North Fairfax Street
Alexandria, VA 22314
Tel: 800-999-2782
Web: http://www.apta.org

■ Related Articles

Alternative Health Care
Health Care
Creative Arts Therapists
Kinesiologists
Massage Therapists
Occupational Therapists
Occupational Therapy Assistants
Physical Therapy Assistants
Psychologists
Recreational Therapists
Rehabilitation Counselors
Social Workers

Physical Therapy Assistants

■ Overview

Physical therapy assistants are skilled health care workers who assist *physical therapists* in a variety of techniques (such as exercise, massage, heat, and water therapy) to help restore physical function in people with injury, birth defects, or disease.

Physical therapy assistants work directly under the supervision of physical therapists. They teach and help patients improve functional activities required in their daily lives, such as walking, climbing, and moving from one place to another. The assistants observe patients during treatments, record the patients' responses and progress, and report these to the physical therapist, either orally or in writing. They fit patients for and teach them to use braces, artificial limbs, crutches, canes, walkers, wheelchairs, and other devices. They may make physical measurements to assess the effects of treatments or to evaluate patients' range of motion, length and girth of body parts, and vital signs. Physical therapy assistants act as members of a team and regularly confer with other members of the physical therapy staff.

■ History

The practice of treating ailments with heat and exercise is very old. For many centuries, people have known of the therapeutic value of hot baths, sunlight, and massage. The ancient Greeks and the Romans used these methods, and there is a long tradition of them in the far northern part of Europe.

Two factors spurred the development of physical therapy techniques during this century: the world wars and epidemic poliomyelitis. These catastrophes created large numbers of young but seriously disabled patients.

World War I brought about great strides in medicine and in our understanding of how the human body functions. Among these was the realization that physical therapy could help shorten the recovery time of the wounded. A Reconstruction Aide corps in the U.S. Army was organized to perform physical therapy in military hospitals, and the Army organized the first department of physical therapy in 1916. Training programs were hastily started to teach physiotherapy, as physical therapy used to be called, to those administering services.

The American Physical Therapy Association was organized in 1921, thus establishing physical therapy's professional stature. In 1925, the association took on the responsibility of identifying approved training programs for physical therapy personnel.

During World War II, physical therapy's benefits were recognized. Because medical teams in the armed forces were able to rehabilitate seriously injured patients, this field gained acceptance from the medical world.

Between the wars, polio became a major health problem, especially because it left many of its victims paralyzed. In 1944, the United States suffered the worst polio epidemic in its history. Public demand for improved physical therapy services led to more therapists and improved techniques. As knowledge grew and the number of people in the field grew, physical therapy services were redefined and expanded in scope. Physical therapy is now available in many settings outside the hospital. Currently there is preventive musculoskeletal screening for children in pediatric clinics and public schools, therapy in industrial settings for workers recovering from injuries on the job, therapy for the elderly in nursing homes and in community health agencies, and therapy for people with athletic injuries in sports medicine clinics.

The physical therapy assistant's occupation is rather new—it was developed in 1967 to help meet this greatly expanded interest in physical therapy services. Physical therapy assistants and physical therapy aides (another new occupational category, requiring less education than an assistant) specialize in some of the less complex treatments that were formerly administered by the physical therapist.

■ The Job

Physical therapy personnel work to prevent, diagnose, and rehabilitate, to restore physical function, prevent permanent disability as much as possible, and help people achieve their maximum attainable performance. For many patients, this objective involves daily living skills, such as eating, grooming, dressing, bathing, and other basic movements that unimpaired people do automatically without thinking.

Physical therapy may alleviate conditions such as muscular pain, spasm, and weakness, joint pain and stiffness, and neuromuscular incoordination. These conditions may be caused by any number of disorders, including fractures, burns, amputations, arthritis, nerve or muscular injuries, trauma, birth defects, stroke, multiple sclerosis, and cerebral palsy. Patients of all ages receive physical therapy services; they may be severely disabled or they may need only minimal therapeutic intervention.

Physical therapy assistants always work under the direction of a qualified physical therapist. Other members of the health team may be a *physician* or *surgeon, nurse, occupational therapist, psychologist,* or *vocational counselor.* Each of these practitioners helps establish and achieve realistic goals consistent with the patient's individual needs. Physical therapy assistants help perform tests to evaluate disabilities and determine the most suitable treatment for the patient; then, as the treatment progresses, they routinely report the patient's condition to the physical therapist. If they observe a patient having serious problems during treatment, the assistants notify the therapist as soon as possible. Physical therapy assistants generally perform complicated therapeutic procedures decided by the physical therapist; however, assistants may initiate routine procedures independently.

PHYSICAL THERAPY ASSISTANTS	
SCHOOL SUBJECTS	Biology Health
PERSONAL SKILLS	Helping/teaching Mechanical/manipulative
WORK ENVIRONMENT	Primarily indoors Primarily one location
MINIMUM EDUCATION LEVEL	Associate's degree
SALARY RANGE	$20,000 to $25,000 to $30,000
CERTIFICATION OR LICENSING	Required by certain states
OUTLOOK	Much faster than the average
DOT	076
GOE	10.02.02
NOC	6631
O*NET	66017

These procedures may include physical exercises, which are the most varied and widely used physical treatments. Exercises may be simple or complicated, easy or strenuous, active or passive. Active motions are performed by the patient alone and strengthen or train muscles. Passive exercises involve the assistant moving the body part through the motion, which improves mobility of the joint but does not strengthen muscle. For example, for a patient with a fractured arm, both active and passive exercise may be appropriate. The passive exercises may be designed to maintain or increase the range of motion in the shoulder, elbow, wrist, and finger joints, while active resistive exercises strengthen muscles weakened by disuse. An elderly patient who has suffered a stroke may need guided exercises aimed at keeping the joints mobile, regaining the function of a limb, walking, or climbing stairs. A child with cerebral palsy who would otherwise never walk may be helped to learn coordination exercises that enable crawling, sitting balance, standing balance, and, finally, walking.

Patients sometimes perform exercises in bed or immersed in warm water. Besides its usefulness in alleviating stiffness or paralysis, exercise also helps to improve circulation, relax tense muscles, correct posture, and aid the breathing of patients with lung problems.

Other treatments that physical therapy assistants may administer include massages, traction for patients with neck or back pain, ultrasound and various kinds of heat treatment for diseases such as arthritis that inflame joints or nerves, cold applications to reduce swelling, pain, or hemorrhaging, and ultraviolet light.

Physical therapy assistants train patients to manage devices and equipment that they either need temporarily or permanently. For example, they instruct patients how to walk with canes or crutches using proper gait and maneuver well in a wheelchair. They also teach patients how to apply, remove, care for, and cope with splints, braces, and artificial body parts.

Physical therapy personnel must often work on improving the emotional state of patients, preparing them psychologically for treatments. The overwhelming sense of hopelessness and lack of confidence that afflict many disabled patients can reduce the patients' success in achieving improved functioning. The health team must be attuned to both the physical and nonphysical aspects of patients to assure that treatments are most beneficial. Sometimes physical therapy personnel work with patients' families to educate them on how to provide simple physical treatments and psychological support at home.

In addition, physical therapy assistants may perform office duties: they schedule patients, keep records, handle inventory, and order supplies.

A physical therapy assistant uses water therapy to help a patient suffering from severe arthritis.

■ Requirements

High School

While still in high school, prospective physical therapy assistants should take courses in health, biology, mathematics, psychology, social science, physical education, computer data entry, English, and other courses that develop communications skills.

Postsecondary Training

A degree from an accredited physical therapy assistant program is required; programs are usually offered in community and junior colleges. These programs, typically two years long, combine academic instruction with a period of supervised clinical practice in a physical therapy setting. Students can expect to study anatomy, physiology, biology, history and philosophy of rehabilitation, human growth and development, psychology, and physical therapist assistant procedures such as massage, therapeutic exercise, and heat and cold therapy. Other courses in mathematics and applied physical sciences help students understand the physical therapy apparatus and the scientific principles on which therapeutic procedures are based.

In recent years, admission to accredited programs has been fairly competitive, with three to five applicants for each available opening.

Some physical therapy assistants begin their careers while in the armed forces, which operate training programs. While these programs are not sufficient for state licensure and do not award degrees, they can serve as an excellent introduction to the field for students who later enter more complete training programs.

GLOSSARY

Disassociation: Passive exercises performed on the patient by the physical therapist or PTA that involve stretching parts of the body in order to loosen rigid or locked joints

Iontophoresis: Using electrical impulses to introduce anti-inflammatory medication through the skin into an inflamed area

Traction: A therapy that uses mechanical equipment to stretch, pull, or hold a part of the patient's body into position. It is used for fractures, muscle spasms, or other injuries to aid proper healing and to relieve pain caused by physical pressure

Ultrasound: Ultrasound is commonly used in physical therapy to relieve pain and swelling of joints and to improve muscle condition

Vestibular stimulation: The vestibular nerve in the ear affects a person's balance; some patients require therapy to restore their sense of balance

Certification or Licensing

Licensure for physical therapy assistants is currently mandatory in 44 states. Licensure requirements vary from state to state, but all require graduation from an American Physical Therapy Association-accredited two-year associate degree program and passing a written examination administered by the state. Conditions for renewing the license also vary by state. For information about licensing requirements, candidates should consult their schools' career guidance offices or the state licensure boards.

Other Requirements

Physical therapy assistants must have stamina, patience, and determination, but at the same time they must be able to establish personal relationships quickly and successfully. They should genuinely like and understand people, both under normal conditions and under the stress of illness. An outgoing personality is highly desirable as is the ability to instill confidence and enthusiasm in patients. Much of the work of physical retraining and restoring is very repetitive, and assistants may not perceive any progress for long periods of time. At times patients may seem unable or unwilling to cooperate. In such cases, assistants need boundless patience, to appreciate small gains and build on them. When restoration to good health is not attainable, physical therapist assistants must help patients adjust to a different way of life and find ways to cope with their situation. Creativity is an asset to devising methods that help disabled people achieve greater self-sufficiency. Assistants should be flexible and open to suggestions offered by their co-workers and willing and able to follow directions closely.

Because the job can be physically demanding, physical therapy assistants must be reasonably strong and enjoy physical activity. Manual dexterity and good coordination are needed to adjust equipment and assist patients. Assistants should be able to lift, climb, stoop, and kneel.

■ Exploring

While still in high school, students can get experience through summer or part-time employment or by volunteering in the physical therapy department of a hospital or clinic. Also, many schools, both public and private, have volunteer assistance programs for work with disabled students. Students can also gain direct experience by working with disabled children in a summer camp.

These opportunities provide prospective physical therapy workers with direct job experience that helps them determine whether they have the personal qualities necessary for this career. Students who have not had such direct experience should make an effort to talk to a physical therapist or physical therapy assistant during career-day programs, if available. It may also be possible to arrange to visit a physical therapy department, watch the staff at work, and ask questions.

■ Employers

Physical therapy assistants are employed in hospitals, rehabilitation centers, schools for the disabled, nursing homes, community and government health agencies, physicians' or physical therapists' offices, and facilities for the mentally disabled.

■ Starting Out

The student's school placement office is probably the best place to find a job. Alternatively, assistants can apply to the physical therapy departments of local hospitals, rehabilitation centers, extended-care facilities, and other potential employers. Openings are listed in the classified ads of newspapers, professional journals, and with private and public employment agencies. In locales where training programs have produced many physical therapy assistants, competition for jobs may be keen. In such cases, assistants may want to widen their search to areas where there is less competition, especially suburban and rural areas

■ Advancement

With experience, physical therapy assistants are often given greater responsibility and better pay. In large health care facilities, supervisory possibilities may open up. In small institutions that employ only one physical therapist, the physical therapist assistant may eventually take care of all the technical tasks that go on in the department, within the limitations of his or her training and education.

Physical therapy assistants with degrees from accredited programs are generally in the best position to gain advancement in any setting. They sometimes decide to earn a bachelor's degree in physical therapy and become fully qualified physical therapists.

■ Earnings

Salaries for physical therapy assistants vary considerably depending on geographical location, employer, and level of experience. The yearly income for a recently graduated assistant is usually between $20,000 and $24,000 a year, while experienced physical therapist assistants usually earn between $25,000 and $30,000. Fringe benefits vary, although they usually include paid holidays and vacations, health insurance, and pension plans.

■ Work Environment

Physical therapy is generally administered in pleasant, clean, well-lighted, and well-ventilated surroundings. The space devoted to physical therapy services is often large, in order to accommodate activities such as gait training and exercises and procedures requiring equipment. Some procedures are given at patients' bedsides.

In the physical therapy department, patients come and go all day, many in wheelchairs, on walkers, canes, crutches, or stretchers. The staff tries to maintain a purposeful, harmonious, congenial atmosphere as they and the patients work toward the common goal of restoring physical efficacy.

The work can be exhausting. Physical therapy assistants may be on their feet for hours at a time, and they may have to move heavy equipment, lift patients, and help them to stand and walk. Most assistants work daytime hours, five days a week, although some positions require evening or weekend work. Some assistants work on a part-time basis.

The combined physical and emotional demands of the job can exert a considerable strain. Prospective assistants would be wise to seek out some job experience related to physical therapy so that they have a practical understanding of their psychological and physical capacities. By checking our their suitability for the work, they can make a better commitment to the training program.

Job satisfaction can be great for physical therapy assistants as they can see how their efforts help to make people's lives much more rewarding.

■ Outlook

Employment prospects are very good for physical therapy assistants, with job growth projected around 80 percent through the year 2006. Demand for rehabilitation services is expected to continue to grow much more rapidly than the average for all occupations, and the rate of turnover among workers is relatively high. Many new positions for physical therapy assistants are expected to open up as hospital programs that aid the disabled expand and as long-term facilities seek to offer residents more adequate services.

A major contributing factor is the increasing number of Americans aged 65 and over. This group tends to suffer a disproportionate amount of the accidents and chronic illnesses that necessitate physical therapy services. Many from the baby boom generation are reaching the age common for heart attacks, thus creating a need for more cardiac and physical rehabilitation. Legislation that requires appropriate public education for all disabled children also may increase the demand for physical therapy services. As more adults engage in strenuous physical exercise, more musculoskeletal injuries will result, thus increasing demand for physical therapy services.

■ For More Information

For career information, contact:

American Physical Therapy Association
1111 North Fairfax Street
Alexandria, VA 22314
Tel: 800-999-2782
Web: http://www.apta.org

■ Related Articles

Alternative Health Care
Health Care
Creative Arts Therapists
Kinesiologists
Massage Therapists
Occupational Therapists
Occupational Therapy Assistants
Physical Therapists
Psychologists
Recreational Therapists
Rehabilitation Counselors
Social Workers

Physician Assistants

■ Overview

Physician assistants practice medicine under the supervision of licensed doctors of medicine or osteopathy, providing various health care services to patients. Much of the work they do was formerly limited to physicians.

■ History

Physician assistants are fairly recent additions to the health care profession. The occupation originated in the 1960s when many medical corpsmen received additional education enabling them to help physicians with various medical tasks. Since then, the work of the physician assistant has grown and expanded; in addition, the number of physician assistants in the United States has greatly increased. Fewer than 100 PAs were practicing in 1970; today there are more than 24,000.

■ The Job

Physician assistants, also known as PAs, help physicians provide medical care to patients. PAs may be assigned a variety of tasks; they may take medical histories of patients, do complete routine physical examinations, order laboratory tests, draw blood samples, give injections, decide on diagnoses, choose treatments, and assist in surgery. Although the duties of PAs vary by state, they always work under the supervision and direction of a licensed *physician*. The extent of the PA's duties depends on the specific laws of the state and the practices of the supervising physician, as well as the experience and abilities of the PA. PAs work in a variety of health care settings, including hospitals, clinics, physician's offices, and federal, state, and local agencies.

About 50 percent of all PAs specialize in primary care medicine, such as family medicine, internal medicine, pediatrics, obstetrics and gynecology, and emergency medicine. Nineteen percent of all PAs work in surgery or surgical subspecialties. In 1998, 41 states and the District of Columbia allowed PAs to prescribe medicine to patients. In California, prescriptions written by PAs are referred to as written prescription transmittal orders. Physician assistants may be known by other occupational titles such as *child health associates, MEDEX, physician associates, anesthesiologist's assistants,* or *surgeon's assistants.*

PAs are skilled professionals who assume a great deal of responsibility in their work. By handling various medical tasks for their physician employers, PAs allow physicians more time to diagnose and treat more severely ill patients.

PHYSICIAN ASSISTANTS	
SCHOOL SUBJECTS	Biology Health
PERSONAL SKILLS	Helping/teaching Technical/scientific
WORK ENVIRONMENT	Primarily indoors Primarily multiple locations
MINIMUM EDUCATION LEVEL	Some postsecondary training
SALARY RANGE	$30,000 to $62,000 to $100,000
CERTIFICATION OR LICENSING	Required by all states
OUTLOOK	Faster than the average
DOT	079
GOE	10.02.01
NOC	3123
O*NET	32511

■ Requirements

Postsecondary Training

Most states require that PAs complete an educational program approved by the Commission on Accreditation of Allied Health Education Programs (CAAHEP). In 1998, there were 104 fully accredited PA programs, and 24 programs with provisional accreditation. Admissions requirements vary, but two years of college courses in science or health, and some health care experience, are usually the minimum requirements. More than half of all students accepted, however, have their bachelor's or master's degrees. Most educational programs last 24 to 25 months, although some last only one year and others may last as many as three years.

The first six to 24 months of most programs involve classroom instruction in human anatomy, physiology, microbiology, clinical pharmacology, applied psychology, clinical medicine, and medical ethics. In the last nine to 15 months of most programs, students engage in supervised clinical work, usually including assignments, or rotations, in various branches of medicine, such as family practice, pediatrics, and emergency medicine.

Graduates of these programs may receive a certificate, an associate's degree, a bachelor's degree, or a master's degree; most programs, however, offer graduates a bachelor's degree. The one MEDEX program that presently exists lasts only 18 months. It is designed for *medical corpsmen, registered nurses,* and others who have had extensive patient-care experience. MEDEX students usually obtain most of their clinical experience by working with a physician who will hire them after graduation.

PA programs are offered in a variety of educational and health care settings, including colleges and universities, medical schools and centers, hospitals, and the armed forces. State laws and regulations dictate the scope of the PA's duties, and, in all but a few states, PAs must be graduates of an approved training program.

Certification or Licensing

Currently, all states—except Mississippi—require that PAs be certified by the National Commission on Certification of Physician Assistants (NCCPA). To become certified, applicants must be graduates of an accredited PA program and pass the Physician Assistants National Certifying Examination. The examination consists of three parts: the first part tests general medical knowledge, the second section tests the PA's specialty—either primary care or surgery—and the third part tests for practical clinical knowledge. After successfully completing the examination, physician assistants can use the credential "Physician Assistant-Certified (PA-C)."

Once certified, PAs are required to complete 100 hours of continuing medical education courses every two years, and in addition must pass a recertification examination every six years. Besides NCCPA certification, most states also require that PAs register with the state medical board. State rules and regulations vary greatly concerning the work of PAs, and applicants are advised to study the laws of the state in which they wish to practice.

■ Exploring

Those interested in exploring the profession should talk with school guidance counselors, practicing PAs, PA students, and various health care employees at local hospitals and clinics. Students can also obtain information by contacting one of the organizations listed at the end of this chapter. Serving as a volunteer in a hospital, clinic, or nursing home is a good way for students to get exposure to the health care profession. In addition, while in college, students may be able to obtain summer jobs as hospital *orderlies, nurse assistants,* or *medical clerks.* Such jobs can help students assess their interest in and suitability for work as PAs before they apply to a PA program.

■ Employers

PAs work in a variety of health care settings. Most PAs, about 36 percent, are employed by single physicians, or group practices; three out of 10 are employed by hospitals. PAs also work in clinics and medical offices. They are employed by nursing homes, long-term care facilities, and prisons. Many areas lacking quality medical care personnel, such as remote rural areas and the inner city, are hiring PAs to meet their needs.

■ Starting Out

PAs must complete their formal training programs before entering the job market. Once their studies are completed, the placement services of the schools may help them find jobs. PAs may also seek employment at hospitals, clinics, medical offices, or other health care settings. Information about jobs with the federal government can be obtained by contacting the Office of Personnel Management.

■ Advancement

Since the PA profession is still quite new, formal lines of advancement have not yet been established. There are still several ways to advance. Hospitals, for example, do not employ head PAs. Those with experience can assume more responsibility at higher pay, or they move on to employment at larger hospitals and clinics. Some PAs go back to school for additional education to practice in a specialty area, such as surgery, urology, or ophthalmology.

■ Earnings

According to the American Academy of Physician Assistants, 80 percent of PA graduates find employment as a PA in less than a year. Salaries of PAs vary according to experience, specialty, and employer. In 1998, PAs earned a starting average of $62,294 annually. Those working in hospitals and medical offices earn slightly more than those working in clinics. Experienced PAs have the potential to earn close to $100,000 a year. PAs working for the military averaged $50,320 a year. PAs are well compensated compared with other occupations that have similar training requirements. Most PAs receive health and life insurance among other benefits.

■ Work Environment

Most work settings are comfortable and clean, although, like physicians, PAs spend a good part of their day standing or walking. The workweek varies according to the employment setting. A few emergency room PAs may work 24-hour shifts, twice a week; others work 12-hour shifts, three times a week. PAs who work in physicians' offices, hospitals, or clinics may have to work weekends, nights, and holidays. PAs employed in clinics, however, usually work five-day, 40-hour weeks.

■ Outlook

There were approximately 64,000 physician assistants employed in the United States in 1998. Employment for PAs, according to the U.S. Department of Labor, is expected to increase much faster than the average for all occupations. A 46.4 percent increase in the number of new jobs is projected through the year 2006. In fact, job growth is expected to outpace the number of potential employees entering this occupation by as much as 9 percent. This field was also mentioned in *U.S. News & World Report*'s 1998 article, "Best Jobs for the Future."

The role of the PA in delivering health care has also expanded over the past decade. PAs have taken on new duties and responsibilities, and they now work in a variety of health care settings.

■ For More Information

The following organizations have information on physician assistant careers, education, and certification.

American Academy of Physician Assistants
950 North Washington Street
Alexandria, VA 22314
Tel: 703-836-2272
Web: http://www.aapa.org

Association of Physician Assistant Programs
950 North Washington Street
Alexandria, VA 22314
Tel: 703-548-5538
Web: http://www.apap.org

National Commission on Certification of Physician Assistants
6849-B2 Peachtree Dunwoody Road
Atlanta, GA 30328
Tel: 404-493-9100
Web: http://www.social.com/health/nhicdata/
hr1300/hr1334.html

■ Related Articles

Physician Associates

■ See Physician Assistants

Physicians

■ Overview

Physicians diagnose, prescribe medicines for, and otherwise treat diseases and disorders of the human body. A physician may also perform surgery and often specializes in one aspect of medical care and treatment. Physicians hold either a doctor of medicine (M.D.) or osteopathic medicine (D.O.) degree. (See *Osteopaths.*)

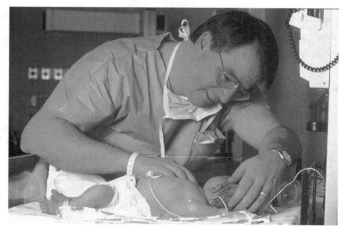

A physician examines a newborn.

■ History

The first great physician was Hippocrates, a Greek who lived almost 2,500 years ago. He developed theories about the practice of medicine and the anatomy of the human body, but Hippocrates is remembered today for a set of medical ethics that still influences medical practice. The oath that he administered to his disciples is administered to physicians about to start practice. His 87 treatises on medicine, known as the "Hippocratic Collection," are believed to be the first authoritative record of early medical theory and practice. Hippocratic physicians believed in the theory that health was maintained by a proper balance of four "humors" in the body: blood, phlegm, black bile, and yellow bile.

Another Greek physician, Galen (130?-201?) influenced medical thought for more than a thousand years. During the Middle Ages, his works were translated into Arabic and Syriac.

The great civilizations of Egypt, India, and China all developed medical theories of diagnosis and treatment that influenced later cultures of their own countries and those of other countries. The school of medicine at Alexandria, Egypt, for example, incorporated the theories of the ancient Greeks as well as those of the Egyptians. This great medical school flourished and was influential for several hundred years. Research specialists there learned more about human anatomy than had ever been learned before.

The theories and practices of medicine were kept alive almost entirely during the Middle Ages by monks in monasteries. Few new theories were developed during this period, but the medical records of most of the great early civilizations were carefully preserved and copied.

The Renaissance saw a renewal of interest in medical research. Swiss physician Parcelsus (1493-1541) publicly burned the writings of Galen and Avicena, signifying a break with the past. Concepts of psychology and psychiatry were introduced by Juan Luis Vives (1492-1540), a Spanish humanist and physician.

In the 17th century English physician William Harvey discovered that the blood, propelled by the pumping action of the heart, circulates through the body. Many inventions in other fields helped the progress of medicine. Anton van Leeuwenock (1632-1723), a Dutch lens grinder, made instruments that magnified up to 270 times. He also studied blood circulation and composition, and was the first to see bacteria and protozoans.

During the 18th century the Dutch physician Hermann Boerhaave introduced clinical instruction (teaching at the bedside of patients). Edward Jenner discovered a vaccination against smallpox. Specialization grew rapidly, as did the growth of medical schools, hospitals, and dispensaries.

The 19th century saw advances in more precise instruments, such as the stethoscope, the ophthalmoscope, and

X rays. Doctors began to use anesthetics like ether and nitrous oxide and antiseptics. Knowledge of the cell, digestion, metabolism, and the vasomotor system increased.

Among the 20th century discoveries and developments have been the identification of four blood types, the discovery of insulin, development of antibiotics, and immunizations such as the polio vaccine. Technological advances have included the electron microscope, pacemakers, ultrasound, heart-lung machines, dialysis machines, and prostheses, to name only a few. Medical research and practice made giant strides toward the relief of human distress and the prolonging of human life. Every day brings new discoveries and the possibility of major breakthroughs in the areas that have long plagued humans.

■ The Job

The greatest number of physicians are in private practice. They see patients by appointment in their offices and examining rooms, and visit patients who are confined to the hospital. In the hospital, they may perform operations or give other kinds of medical treatment. Some physicians also make calls on patients at home if the patient is not able to get to the physician's office or if the illness is an emergency.

Approximately 15 percent of physicians in private practice are *general practitioners* or *family practitioners*. They see patients of all ages and both sexes and will diagnose and treat those ailments that are not severe enough or unusual enough to require the services of a specialist. When special problems arise, however, the general practitioner will refer the patient to a specialist.

Not all physicians are engaged in private practice. Some are in academic medicine and teach in medical schools or teaching hospitals. Some are engaged only in research. Some are salaried employees of health maintenance organizations or other prepaid health care plans. Some are salaried hospital employees.

Some physicians, often called *medical officers,* are employed by the federal government, in such positions as public health, or in the service of the Department of Veterans Affairs. State and local governments also employ physicians for public health agency work. A large number of physicians serve with the armed forces, both in this country and overseas.

Industrial physicians or *occupational physicians* are employed by large industrial firms for two main reasons: to prevent illnesses that may be caused by certain kinds of work and to treat accidents or illnesses of employees. Although most industrial physicians may roughly be classified as general practitioners because of the wide variety of illnesses that they must recognize and treat, their knowledge must also extend to public health techniques and to

understanding such relatively new hazards as radiation and the toxic effects of various chemicals, including insecticides.

A specialized type of industrial or occupational physician is the *flight surgeon.* Flight surgeons study the effects of high-altitude flying on the physical condition of flight personnel. They place members of the flight staff in special low-pressure and refrigeration chambers that simulate high-altitude conditions and study the reactions on their blood pressure, pulse and respiration rate, and body temperature.

Another growing specialty is the field of nuclear medicine. Some large hospitals have a nuclear research laboratory, which functions under the direction of a *chief of nuclear medicine,* who coordinates the activities of the lab with other hospital departments and medical personnel. These physicians perform tests using nuclear isotopes and use techniques that let physicians see and understand organs deep within the body.

M.D.s may become specialists in any of the 40 different medical care specialties. Many of these specialties are discussed elsewhere in this encyclopedia.

■ Requirements

High School

The physician is required to devote many years to study before being admitted to practice. Interested high school students should enroll in a college preparatory course, and take courses in English, languages (especially Latin), the humanities, social studies, and mathematics, in addition to courses in biology, chemistry, and physics.

Postsecondary Training

The student who hopes to enter medicine should be admitted first to a liberal arts program in an accredited undergraduate institution. Some colleges offer a "premedical" course, and it is advisable for the student to take such a course where it is offered. A good general education, however, with as many courses as possible in science and perhaps a major in biology, is considered ade-

PHYSICIANS	
SCHOOL SUBJECTS	Biology Health
PERSONAL SKILLS	Helping/teaching Technical/scientific
WORK ENVIRONMENT	Primarily indoors Primarily multiple locations
MINIMUM EDUCATION LEVEL	Medical degree
SALARY RANGE	$44,400 to $160,000 to $250,000
CERTIFICATION OR LICENSING	Required by all states
OUTLOOK	Faster than the average
DOT	070
GOE	02.03.01
NOC	3112
O*NET	32102A

quate preparation for the study of medicine. Courses should include physics, biology, inorganic and organic chemistry, English, mathematics, and the social sciences.

College freshmen who hope to apply to a medical school early in their senior year should have adequate knowledge of the requirements for admission to one of the 125 accredited schools of medicine or 17 accredited schools of osteopathic medicine in the country. They should consult a copy of *Medical School Admission Requirements, U.S. and Canada*, available from the Association of American Medical Colleges. It is also available in college libraries. If students read carefully the admissions requirements of the several medical schools to which they hope to apply, they will avoid making mistakes in choosing a graduate program.

THE OATH OF HIPPOCRATES

Ancient Version

I SWEAR by Apollo the physician and Aesculapius, and Health, and All-heal, and all the gods and goddesses, that, according to my ability and judgment,

I will keep this Oath and this stipulation—to reckon him who taught me this Art equally dear to me as my parents, to share my substance with him, and relieve his necessities if required; to look upon his offspring in the same footing as my own brothers, and to teach them this art, if they shall wish to learn it, without fee or stipulation; and that by precept, lecture, and every other mode of instruction,

I will impart a knowledge of the Art to my own sons, and those of my teachers, and to disciples bound by a stipulation and oath according to the law of medicine, but to none others.

I will follow that system of regimen which, according to my ability and judgement, I consider for the benefit of my patients, and abstain from whatever is deleterious and mischievous.

I will give no deadly medicine to any one if asked, nor suggest any such counsel; and in like manner I will not give to a woman a pessary to produce abortion. With purity and with holiness I will pass my life and practice my Art.

I will not cut persons labouring under the stone, but will leave this to be done by men who are practitioners of this work. Into whatever houses I enter, I will go into them for the benefit of the sick, and will abstain from every voluntary act of mischief and corruption; and, further, from the seduction of females or males, of freemen and slaves. Whatever, in connection with my professional service, or not in connection with it, I see or hear, in the life of men, which ought not to be spoken of abroad.

I will not divulge, as reckoning that all such should be kept secret. While I continue to keep this Oath unviolated, may it be granted to me to enjoy life and the practice of the art, respected by all men, in all times. But should I trespass and violate this Oath, may the reverse be my lot.

Students who do not enter a premedical program may find it possible to change to a major in biology or chemistry after they have enrolled. Such majors may make them eligible for consideration to be admitted to many medical schools.

Some students may be admitted to medical school after only three years of study in an undergraduate program. There are a few medical schools that will award the bachelor's degree at the end of the first year of medical school study. This practice is becoming less common as more students seek admission to medical schools. Most premedical students plan to spend four years in an undergraduate program and to receive the bachelor's degree before entering the four-year medical school program.

During the second or third year in college, undergraduates should arrange with an advisor to take the Medical College Admission Test (MCAT). This test is given each spring and each fall at certain selected sites. The student's advisor should know the date, place, and time; or the student may write for this information to the Association of American Medical Colleges. All medical colleges in this country require this test for admission, and a student's MCAT score is one of the factors that is weighed in the decision to accept or reject any applicant. Because the test does not evaluate medical knowledge, most college students who are enrolled in liberal arts programs should not find it to be unduly difficult. The examination covers four areas: verbal facility, quantitative ability, knowledge of the humanities and social sciences, and knowledge of biology, chemistry, and physics.

Students who hope to be admitted to medical school are encouraged to apply to at least three institutions to increase their chances of being accepted by one of them. Approximately one out of every two qualified applicants to medical schools will be admitted each year. To facilitate this process, the American Medical College Application Service (AMCAS) will check, copy, and submit applications to medical schools specified by the individual student. More information about this service may be obtained from AMCAS, premedical advisers, and medical schools.

In addition to the traditional medical schools, there are several schools of basic medical sciences that enroll medical students for the first two years (preclinical experience) of medical school. They offer a preclinical curriculum to students similar to that which is offered by a regular medical school. At the end of the two-year program, the student will then apply to a four-year medical school for the final two years of instruction.

Although high scholarship is a determining factor in admitting a student to a medical school, it is actually only one of the criteria considered. By far the greatest number of successful applicants to medical schools are "B" students. Because admission is also determined by a number of other factors, including a personal interview, other qualities in addition to a high scholastic average are considered desirable for a prospective physician. High on the list of desirable qualities are emotional stability, integrity, reliability, resourcefulness, and a sense of service.

The average student enters medical school at age 21 or 22. The student then begins another four years of formal schooling. During the first two years of medical school, the student learns human anatomy, biochemistry, physiology, pharmacology, psychology, microbiology, pathology, medical ethics, and laws governing medicine. Most instruction in the first two years is given through classroom lectures, laboratories, seminars, independent research, and the reading of textbook material and other types of literature. Students also learn to take medical histories, examine patients, and recognize symptoms.

During the last two years in medical school, the student becomes actively involved in the treatment process. Students spend a large proportion of the time in the hospital as part of a medical team headed by a teaching physician who specializes in a particular area. Others on the team may be interns or residents. Students are closely supervised as they learn techniques such as how to take a patient's medical history, how to make a physical examination, how to work in the laboratory, how to make a diagnosis, and how to keep all the necessary records.

Students rotate from one medical specialty to another, to obtain a broad understanding of each field. They are assigned to duty in internal medicine, pediatrics, psychiatry, obstetrics and gynecology, and surgery. Students may be assigned to other specialties, too.

In addition to this hospital work, students continue to take coursework. They are expected to be responsible for assigned studies and also for some independent study.

Most states require all new M.D.s to complete at least one year of postgraduate training, and a few require an internship plus a one-year residency. Physicians wishing to specialize spend from three to seven years in advanced residency training plus another two or more years of practice in the specialty. Then they must pass a specialty board examination to become a board-certified M.D. The residency years are stressful: residents often work 24-hour shifts and put in 80 hours or more per week.

For a teaching or research career, physicians may also earn a master's degree or a Ph.D. in biochemistry or microbiology.

Certification or Licensing

After receiving the M.D. degree, the new physician is required to take an examination to be licensed to practice. Every state requires such an examination. It is conducted through the board of medical examiners in each state. Some states have reciprocity agreements with other states so that

THE OATH OF GENEVA

The Declaration of Geneva was one of the first and most important actions of the General Assembly of the World Medical Association at Geneva in 1948. It was amended by the 22nd World Medical Assembly at Sydney in 1968. The declaration was intended to update the Oath of Hippocrates, which was no longer suited to modern conditions.

At the time of being admitted as a member of the medical profession:

I solemnly pledge myself to consecrate my life to the service of humanity;

I will give to my teachers the respect and gratitude which is their due;

I will practice my profession with conscience and dignity;

The health of my patient will be my first consideration;

I will respect the secrets which are confided in me, even after the patient has died;

I will maintain by all the means in my power, the honor and the noble traditions of the medical profession;

My colleagues will be my brothers;

I will not permit considerations of religion, nationality, race, party politics or social standing to intervene between my duty and my patient;

I will maintain the utmost respect for human life from the time of conception; even under threat, I will not use my medical knowledge contrary to the laws of humanity.

I make these promises solemnly, freely and upon my honor.

-*World Medical Journal 3* (1956), Supplement, pp. 10-12

a physician licensed in one state may be automatically licensed in another without being required to pass another examination. Because this is not true throughout the United States, however, the wise physician will find out about licensing procedures before planning to move.

Other Requirements

Prospective physicians must have some plan for financing their long and costly education. They face a period of at least eight years after college when they will not be self-supporting. While still in school, students may be able to work only during summer vacations, because the necessary laboratory courses of the regular school year are so time consuming that little time is left for activities other than the preparation of daily lessons. Some scholarships and loans are available to qualified students.

Physicians who work directly with patients need to have great sensitivity to their needs. Interpersonal skills are required by all physicians, even in isolated research laboratories, since they must work and communicate with other scientists. Since new technology and discoveries happen at such a rapid rate, physicians must continually pursue further education to keep up with new treatments, tools, and medicines.

■ Exploring

One of the best introductions to a career in health care is to volunteer at a local hospital, clinic, or nursing home. In this way it is possible to get a feel for what it's like to work around other health care professionals and patients and possibly determine exactly where your interests lie. As in any career, reading as much as possible about the profession, talking with a high school counselor, and interviewing those working in the field are other important ways to explore your interest.

■ Employers

Physicians can find employment in a wide variety of settings, including hospitals, nursing homes, managed-care offices, prisons, schools and universities, research laboratories, trauma centers, clinics, and public health centers. Some are self-employed in their own or group practices. In the past, many physicians went into business for themselves, either by starting their own practice or by becoming a partner in an existing one. Very few physicians—about 6 percent—are choosing to follow this path today. There are a number of reasons for this shift. Often, the costs of starting a practice or buying into an existing practice are too high. Most are choosing to take salaried positions with hospitals or groups of physicians.

Jobs for physicians are available all over the world, although licensing requirements may vary. In Third World countries, there is great demand for medical professionals of all types. Conditions, supplies, and equipment may be poor and pay is minimal, but there are great rewards in terms of experience. Many doctors fulfill part or all of their residency requirements by practicing in other countries.

Physicians interested in teaching may find employment at medical schools or university hospitals. There are also positions available in government agencies such as the Centers for Disease Control, the National Institutes of Health, and the Food and Drug Administration.

Pharmaceutical companies and chemical companies hire physicians to research and develop new drugs, instruments, and procedures.

■ Starting Out

There are no shortcuts to entering the medical profession. Requirements are an M.D. degree, a licensing examination, a one- or two-year internship, and a period of residency that may extend as long as five years.

Upon completing this program, which may take up to 15 years, physicians are then ready to enter practice. They may choose to open a solo private practice, enter a partnership practice, enter a group practice, or take a salaried job with a managed care facility or hospital. Salaried positions are also available with federal and state agencies, the military, including the Department of Veterans Affairs, and private companies. Teaching and research jobs are usually obtained after other experience is acquired.

The highest ratio of physicians to patients is in the Northeast and West. The lowest ratio is in the South. Most M.D.s practice in urban areas near hospitals and universities.

■ Advancement

Physicians who work in a managed-care setting or for a large group or corporation can advance by opening a private practice. The average physician in private practice does not advance in the accustomed sense of the word. Their progress consists of advancing in skill and understanding, in numbers of patients, and in income. They may be made a fellow in a professional specialty or elected to an important office in the American Medical Association or American Osteopathic Association. Teaching and research positions may also increase a physician's status.

Some physicians may become directors of a laboratory, managed-care facility, hospital department, or medical school program. Some may move into hospital administration positions.

A physician can achieve recognition by conducting research in new medicines, treatments, and cures, and publishing their findings in medical journals. Participation in professional organizations can also bring prestige.

A physician can advance by pursuing further education in a subspecialty or a second field such as biochemistry or microbiology.

■ Earnings

Physicians have among the highest average earnings of any occupational group. The level of income for any individual physician depends on a number of factors, such as region of the country, economic status of the patients, and the physician's specialty, skill, experience, professional reputation, and personality. Income tends to vary less across geographic regions, however, than across specialties. The median income after expenses for all physicians in 1995, according to the American Medical Association, was $160,000 per year. The median income of radiologists was $230,000; general surgeons, $225,000; family practitioners, $124,000; anesthesiologists, $203,000, and emergency medicine physicians, $170,000.

In 1996-97, the average first year resident received a stipend of about $32,789 a year, depending on the type of residency, the size of the hospital, and the geographic area. Sixth year residents earned about $40,849 a year. If the physician enters private practice, earnings during the first year may not be impressive. As the patients increase in number, however, earnings will also increase.

Physicians who complete their residencies but have no other experience begin work with the Department of Veterans Affairs at salaries of about $44,400 in addition to other cash benefits of up to $13,000.

Salaried doctors usually earn fringe benefits such as health and dental insurance, paid vacations, and the opportunity to participate in retirement plans.

■ Work Environment

The offices and examining rooms of most physicians are well equipped, attractive, well lighted, and well ventilated. There is usually at least one nurse-receptionist on the physician's staff, and there may be several nurses, a laboratory technician, one or more secretaries, a bookkeeper, or receptionist.

Physicians usually see patients by appointments that are scheduled according to individual requirements. They may reserve all mornings for hospital visits and surgery. They may see patients in the office only on certain days of the week.

Physicians spend much of their time at the hospital performing surgery, setting fractures, working in the emergency room, or visiting patients.

Physicians in private practice have the advantages of working independently, but most put in long hours—an average of 58 per week in 1994. Also, they may be called from their homes or offices in times of emergency. Telephone calls may come at any hour of the day or night. It is difficult for physicians to plan leisure-time activities, because their plans may change without notice. One of the advantages of group practice is that members of the group rotate emergency duty.

The areas in most need of physicians are rural hospitals and medical centers. Because the physician is normally working alone, and covering a broad territory, the workday can be quite long with little opportunity for vacation. Because placement in rural communities has become so difficult, some towns are providing scholarship money to students who pledge to work in the community for a number of years.

Physicians in academic medicine or in research have regular hours, work under good physical conditions, and often determine their own workload. Teaching and research physicians alike are usually provided with the best and most modern equipment.

■ Outlook

In the late 1990s, there were about 560,000 M.D.s and D.O.s working in the United States. Others are involved in research, teaching, administration, and consulting for insurance or pharmaceutical companies. About 70 percent of all physicians practice in offices. Others are on the staff of hospitals, or work in a variety of other health care facilities and in schools, prisons, and business firms.

This field is expected to grow faster than the average through the year 2006. Population growth, particularly among the elderly, is a factor in the demand for physicians. Another factor contributing to the predicted increase is the widespread availability of medical insurance, through both private plans and public programs. More physicians will also be needed for medical research, public health, rehabilitation, and industrial medicine. New technology will allow physicians to perform more procedures to treat ailments once thought incurable.

Employment opportunities will be good for family practitioners and internists, geriatric and preventive care specialists, as well as general pediatricians. Rural and low-income areas are in need of more physicians, and there is a short supply of general surgeons and psychiatrists.

The shift in health care delivery from hospitals to outpatient centers and other nontraditional settings to contain rising costs may mean that more and more physicians will become salaried employees. In 1994, for example, 39 percent of employed physicians were considered employees, rather than self-employed, up from 36 percent the previous year.

There will be considerable competition among newly trained physicians entering practice, particularly in large cities. Physicians willing to locate to inner cities and rural areas—where physicians are scarce—should encounter little difficulty.

The issue of physician oversupply has been addressed by groups such as the National Academy of Sciences Institute of Medicine and the Pew Health Professions Commission. They suggest limiting the number of future residency positions available to reduce the number of doctors vying for positions in the medical field.

■ For More Information

For career information, contact:

American Academy of Family Physicians
8880 Ward Parkway
Kansas City, MO 64114
Tel: 816-333-9700
Web: http://www.aafp.org

American Medical Association
515 North State Street
Chicago, IL 60610
Tel: 312-464-5000
Web: http://www.ama-assn.org

For a list of accredited U.S. and Canadian medical schools and other education information, contact:

Association of American Medical Colleges
2450 N Street, NW
Washington, DC 20037
Tel: 202-828-0400
Web: http://www.aamc.org

Physicists

■ Overview

Physics is a science dealing with the interaction of matter and energy, and *physicists* conduct research on the principles that surround this phenomena. They study the behavior and structure of matter, the ways that energy is generated and transferred, and the relationships between matter and energy. Physicists perform experiments and analyze the products or results of those experiments. They may teach, oversee scientific projects, or act as consultants in a laboratory. They investigate and attempt to understand the fundamental laws of nature and how these laws may be formulated and put to use.

■ History

About 330 BC, when Aristotle (384-322 BC) was writing *Physics,* physics was considered a branch of philosophy. From the time of Galileo, 1,000 years later, physics evolved into a mathematically based science.

Galileo (1564-1642) is often called the first modern physicist. His most famous experiment may be the one in which he is said to have proved that all weights fall at the same speed by dropping a ten-pound weight and a one-pound weight from the Leaning Tower of Pisa. They hit the ground simultaneously. Galileo's work in astronomy, with the aid of a telescope, proved that the moon was not smooth; by mathematical calculations, he proved that the moon reflects the light of the sun.

In the four centuries since Galileo demonstrated the value of conducting experiments to determine whether or not scientific theory may be valid, scholars have made great strides. Michael Faraday (1791-1867) conducted experiments that made the modern age of electricity possible. A generation later, Thomas Edison (1847-1931) took advantage of his studies to produce more than a thousand inventions, including the incandescent light and the motion picture. Marie (1867-1934) and Pierre (1859-1906) Curie discovered radium; Sir J. J. Thomson (1856-1940) discovered the electron. Niels Bohr (1885-1962) proposed a theory of atomic structure; Albert Einstein (1879-1955) developed the mathematical theories that have led us into the atomic age.

Physicists have made great progress in recent years in probing the depths of the ocean and research into nuclear energy, communications, and aerospace.

■ The Job

Physics is the most comprehensive of the natural sciences because it includes the behavior of all kinds of matter from the smallest particles to the largest galaxies.

Basic, or *pure,* physics extends human knowledge of the behavior of the universe and organizes this knowledge into a series of related laws. The work in basic physics is done from two points of view—experimental and theoretical. A physicist may work from one, or the other, or both of these points of view. The experimental physicist performs experiments to gather information. The results of the experiments may support or contradict existing theories or the experiments may be in a field where no theories exist.

The *theoretical physicist* tries to construct theories that will explain the experimental results. If the theories are to stand, they must also predict the results of future experiments. Both the experimental physicist and the theoretical physicist try to extend the limits of what is known.

Not all physicists are concerned with testing or developing new theories. Some physicists work in *applied physics,* the purpose of which is to develop useful devices and procedures. Various types of engineers, such as electrical and mechanical engineers, are trained in physics. Applied physics and engineering have led to the development of such devices as television sets, airplanes, washing machines, satellites, and elevators.

Physicists rely heavily on mathematics. Mathematical statements are more precise than statements in words alone. Moreover, the results of experiments can be accurately compared with the various theories only when mathematical techniques are used.

The various laws of physics are attempts by physicists to explain the behavior of nature in a simple and general way. Even the most accepted laws of physics, however, are subject to change. Physicists continually subject the laws of physics to new tests to see if, under new conditions, they still hold true. If they do not hold true, changes must be made in the laws or entirely new theories must be proposed. New theories must explain not only all phenomena that the old laws explained but also results of the new tests.

At the beginning of the 20th century, the laws of physics were tested extensively and were found to be too narrow to explain many of the new discoveries. A new body of theories was started. The older body of laws is called classical physics; the new is called modern physics.

Classical physics is usually divided into several branches, each of which deals with a group of related phenomena. *Mechanics* is the study of forces and their effect on matter. *Hydromechanics* is the mechanics of fluids; that is, of liquids and gases. *Optics* is the study of the behavior of light. Physicists in this field study such things as lasers, liquid crystal displays, or light emitting diodes. *Thermodynamics* is the study of heat. *Acoustics* is the study of sound, such as in recording studio acoustics, underwater sound waves, and electroacoustical devices like loudspeakers. The study of electricity and magnetism also forms a branch of classical physics. Research in this area includes microwave propagation, the magnetic properties of matter, and electrical devices for science and industry.

Modern physics is also broken up into various fields of study. *Atomic physics* is the study of the structure of atoms and the behavior of electrons, one of the kinds of particles that make up the atom. *Nuclear physics* is the study of the structure of the nucleus, or center, of the atom and of the forces that hold the nucleus together. *High-energy physics*, or *particle physics*, is the study of the production of subatomic particles from other particles and from energy. The characteristics of the various particles, including the antiparticles associated with antimatter, are also studied. Particle accelerators, popularly called atom smashers, are important tools in high-energy physics.

Solid-state physics is the study of the behavior of solids, particularly crystalline solids. *Cryogenic*, or low-temperature, techniques are often used in research into the solid state. Research in solid state physics has produced transistors, integrated circuits, and masers that have improved computers, radios, televisions, and navigation and guidance systems for satellites. *Plasma physics* is the study of the properties of highly ionized gases. Physicists in this field are concerned with the generation of thermonuclear power.

Although such sciences as biology and geology have their own viewpoints and experimental procedures, the viewpoint and procedures of physics can also be directly applied to them. Where this application has been made, a new series of sciences has developed. To separate them from their parent sciences, they are known by such names as *biophysics* (the physics of living things) and *geophysics* (the physics of the earth). The sciences of chemistry and physics sometimes overlap in subject matter as well as in viewpoint and procedure. The result is *physical chemistry*. In *astrophysics*, the techniques of physics are applied to astronomical observations to determine the properties of celestial objects.

Most physicists are engaged in research, and some combine their research with teaching at the university level. Some physicists are employed in industries, such as petroleum, communications, manufacturing, and medicine.

■ Requirements

High School

High school students who are interested in becoming physicists should take college preparatory courses. You should take as much mathematics as is offered in your school, and as many of the sciences as possible. English skills are important as you must write up their results, communicate with other scientists, and lecture on your findings. High school students interested in becoming physicists should also get as much experience as possible working with computers.

Postsecondary Training

After high school, you should enroll in a four-year college or university. Physicists may have one, two, or three degrees. The physicist at the doctoral level will probably command the jobs with the greatest responsibility. Those at the master's level will secure good jobs, but with less responsibility, and those at the bachelor's level will compete intensely for positions that hold the least challenge.

Some positions in industry are available for graduates with a bachelor's degree. The firm

PHYSICISTS	
SCHOOL SUBJECTS	**Mathematics** **Physics**
PERSONAL SKILLS	**Communication/ ideas** **Technical/ scientific**
WORK ENVIRONMENT	**Primarily indoors** **Primarily one location**
MINIMUM EDUCATION LEVEL	**Bachelor's degree**
SALARY RANGE	**$35,000 to $67,000 to $76,000+**
CERTIFICATION OR LICENSING	**None available**
OUTLOOK	**Decline**
DOT	**023**
GOE	**02.01.01**
NOC	**2111**
O*NET	**24102A**

Two physicists adjust a superconcentrating solar collector.

will often encourage its research employees to obtain advanced training. Sometimes, employers in industry are interested in taking young people who have had a broad background of training and teaching them the specialty in which the firm operates, as, for instance, the manufacture of electrical devices. When the young employees have developed competency in the special field, they may then return to graduate school to concentrate their study in this particular field.

A master's degree is usually required for a teaching position in a junior college. Some secondary schools, too, prefer to employ those with a master's degree.

Physicists with a master's degree may obtain a job as an assistant in a physics department in a university while working toward a doctorate in physics. A doctorate is usually required for employment as a college teacher. A master's degree is usually required for a teaching position in a junior college. Some secondary schools, too, prefer to employ those with a master's degree.

Physicists with a master's degree may obtain a job as an assistant in a physics department in a university while working toward a doctorate in physics. A doctorate is usually required for employment as a college teacher.

Approximately one-third of all physicists have doctorates. Students who are interested in going to a graduate school that offers the doctor's degree in physics should write to the American Institute of Physics for a list of such graduate institutions. In the 1990s, there were approximately 250 colleges and universities offering advanced degrees in physics.

Certification or Licensing

Those who plan to teach at the secondary school level may be able to obtain a teaching position with a bachelor's degree if they also meet the certification requirements for teach-ing (established by the state department of education in each state). Because different states have different certification requirements, undergraduates are wise to discover the requirements for the state in which they hope to teach.

Other Requirements

Physicists are detail-oriented and precise. They must have patience, perseverance, and be self-motivated. Physicists should be able to work alone or on research teams.

■ Exploring

If you are interested in a career in physics you can gain at least a working acquaintance with various aspects of physics through talks with your science teachers and through the use of the school library. Other possibilities are membership in the various organizations that specialize in one aspect of physical science, such as science clubs, astronomy clubs, and so forth.

Participation in science fair projects will give you invaluable knowledge into theory, experimentation, and the scientific process. If your school does not sponsor science fairs, you may find fairs sponsored by your school district, state, or a science society.

■ Employers

Many physicists are employed by large research and development facilities in industrial areas. In private industry physicists work in applied research in areas including electrical electronics and aerospace technology. Physicists also work in colleges in universities where they teach and do research. Some physicists work for federal government agencies.

■ Starting Out

The placement office of the college or university from which you obtain a degree will often have listings of jobs available. Many industries send personnel interviewers to the campuses of universities that have programs in physics to seek out and talk to students who are about to receive degrees. Students should also attend industry, career, and science-society fairs to find out about job openings and interview opportunities.

Those who are interested in teaching in public schools should apply to several school systems in which they may want to work. There are occasionally some positions available for science teachers. Some of the larger school systems also send personnel interviewers to campuses to talk with students who are about to receive degrees in science and who also have acquired the necessary courses in education.

Teaching jobs in universities are often obtained either through the contacts of the student's own faculty members in the degree program or through the placement office of the university.

Jobs with an agency of the federal government are gained through taking a civil service examination. Notices of such examinations may be obtained through the local post office or by writing to the Office of Personnel Management, Washington DC 20415.

■ Advancement

High school teachers will advance in salary and possibly in degree of responsibility as they acquire experience. This advancement is also likely to be facilitated by the attaining of advanced degrees. The college or university teacher, who should have a doctorate to secure a staff appointment, will advance from assistant to full professor, and perhaps to head of department, provided that the professor publishes the amount of research required by the institution for promotion. Higher rank also carries with it additional income and responsibilities.

The research physicist who is employed by a university may be given greater responsibility for planning and carrying through research programs. The salary level may also increase with experience in research over a period of years.

Physicists in federal government agencies advance in rank and salary as they gain experience. They may also reach positions in which they are asked to make decisions vital to the defense effort or to the safety and welfare of the country.

Scientists employed by industry are usually the highest paid in the profession. They may advance to positions in which they direct the research efforts of the total organization.

■ Earnings

Starting salaries for physicists average about $35,000 a year. An average mid-range salary is $67,000, and the highest physicists earn an average of $76,000. Those who earn the highest salaries have doctoral degrees and many years experience in the field.

As highly trained and respected scientists, physicists usually receive excellent benefits packages, including health plans, vacation and sick leave, and other benefits. The average earnings for physicists (nonsupervisory, supervisory, and managerial) employed by the federal government was $71,800 in 1997.

■ Work Environment

Most physicists work a 40-hour week under pleasant circumstances. Laboratories are usually well equipped, clean, well lighted, temperature controlled, and functional. Adequate safety measures are taken when there is any sort of physical hazard involved in the work. Often, a group of scientists will work together as a team. Their association

will be a close one and may last over a period of many years.

Physicists who teach at the high school, college, or university level have the added benefit of the academic calendar which gives them ample time away from teaching and meeting with students in order to pursue their own research, studies, or travel.

■ Outlook

About 32,000 physicists worked in the United States in 1990s, most of them in industry and research and development laboratories. Approximately 14,000 physicists worked in research at colleges and universities. Nearly one-fifth of all physicists worked for the federal government, mostly in the Departments of Defense, Energy, and Commerce.

While the demand for physicists has been slower than the average in the early 1990s, opportunities in the field are expected to decline through the year 2006 due to reductions in defense related research as well as civilian physics-related research. Job candidates with doctoral degrees have the best outlook for finding work.

Graduates with only a bachelor's degree are generally underqualified for most physicist jobs. They may find better employment opportunities as engineers, technicians, or computer specialists. With a suitable background in education, they may teach physics at the high school level.

FYI

The department of Energy has its own research and development facilities operated by academic institutions and private firms, through contracts with the government.

Brookhaven National Laboratory in Upton, Long Island, New York, is mainly involved in studies of nuclear physics, but research is also conducted in the chemical, biological, electronic, and medical fields.

Fermi National Accelerator Laboratory in Batavia, Illinois, conducts research in high-energy physics.

Lawrence Berkeley National Laboratory in Berkeley, California, conducts research in a wide variety of fields, including high-energy particle physics, nuclear fusion, computer-aided engineering, earth sciences, chemical sciences, and biological sciences.

Los Alamos National Laboratory in Los Alamos, New Mexico, conducts research in nuclear weaponry and energy, cryogenic physics, space sciences, molecular biology, and metallurgy.

For More Information

For employment statistics and information on jobs and career planning, contact:

American Institute of Physics
Division of Careers Placement
One Physics Ellipse
College Park, MD 20740
Tel: 301-209-3100
Email: aipinfo@aip.org
Web: http://www.aip.org

For employment information, contact:

Canadian Association of Physicists
Suite 112, MacDonald Building
150 Louis Pasteur Priv.
Ottawa, ON Canada K1N 6N5
Tel: 613-562-5614
Email: cap@physics.uottawa.ca
Web: http://www.cap.ca/

Fermilab offers internships, employment opportunities, and general information about their laboratory. Friends of Fermilab is a nonprofit organization that supports pre-college education programs.

Fermi National Accelerator Laboratory
PO Box 500
Batavia, IL 60510
Tel: 630-840-8258
Web: http://www.fnal.gov

Related Articles

Computers

Defense

Energy

Mathematics and Physics

Astronomers

Chemists

College Professors

Geologists

Geophysicists

Mathematicians

Operations Research Analysts

Optical Engineers

Physiotherapists
■ See Physical Therapists

Piano Technicians and Tuners
■ See Musical Instrument Repairers and Tuners

Pilling-Machine Operators
■ See Plastics Products Manufacturing Workers

Pilots

Overview

Pilots perform many different kinds of flying jobs. In general, pilots operate an aircraft for the transportation of passengers, freight, mail, or for other commercial purposes.

History

The age of modern aviation is generally considered to have begun with the famous flight of Orville and Wilbur Wright's heavier-than-air machine on December 17, 1903. On that day, the Wright brothers flew their machine four times and became the first airplane pilots. In the early days of aviation, the pilot's job was quite different from that of the pilot of today. As he flew the first plane, for instance, Orville Wright was lying on his stomach in the middle of the bottom wing of the plane. There was a strap across his hips, and to turn the plane, Wright had to tilt his hips from side to side.

Aviation developed rapidly as designers raced to improve upon the Wright brothers' design. During the early years of flight, many aviators earned a living as "barnstormers," entertaining people with stunts and by taking passengers on short flights around the countryside. Airplanes were quickly adapted to military use. Pilots soon became famous for their war exploits and for feats of daring and endurance as improvements in airplane designs allowed them to make transcontinental, transoceanic, or transpolar flights. As airplanes grew more complex and an entire industry developed, pilots were joined by copilots and flight engineers to assist in operating the plane.

The airline industry originated from the United States government-run air mail service. Pilots who flew for this service were praised in newspapers and their work in this new, advanced industry made their jobs seem glamorous. But during the Great Depression, pilots faced the threat of losing their high pay and status. The Air Line Pilots Association stepped in and won federal protection for the airline pilot's job. In 1978, when the airline industry was deregulated, many expected the pay and status of pilots to decrease. However, the steady growth of airlines built a demand for good pilots and their value remained high.

Today, pilots perform a variety of services. Many pilots fly for the military services. Pilots with commercial airlines fly millions of passenger and cargo flights each year. Other pilots use airplanes for crop-dusting, pipeline inspection, skydiving, and advertising. Many pilots provide instruction for flight schools. A great many pilots fly solely for pleasure, and many people own their own small planes.

■ The Job

The best known pilots are the commercial airline pilots who fly for the airlines. Responsible, skilled professionals, they are among the highest paid workers in the country. The typical pilot flight deck crew includes the captain, who is the pilot in command, and the copilot, or first officer. In larger aircraft, there may be a third member of the crew, called the flight engineer, or second officer. The captain of a flight is in complete command of the crew, the aircraft, and the passengers or cargo while they are in flight. In the air, the captain also has the force of law. The aircraft may hold 30 people or 300 or be completely loaded with freight, depending on the airline and type of operations. The plane may be fitted with either turbojet, turboprop (which have propellers driven by jet engines), or reciprocating propeller engines. An aircraft may operate near the speed of sound and at altitudes as high as 40,000 feet.

In addition to actually flying the aircraft, pilots must perform a variety of safety-related tasks. Before each flight, they must determine weather and flight conditions, ensure that sufficient fuel is on board to complete the flight safely, and verify the maintenance status of the aircraft. The captain briefs all crew members, including the flight attendants, about the flight. Pilots must also perform system operation checks to test the proper functioning of instrumentation, controls, and electronic and mechanical systems on the flight deck. Pilots coordinate their flight plan with airplane dispatchers and air traffic controllers. Flight plans include information about the airplane, the passenger or cargo load, and the air route the pilot is expected to take.

Once all preflight duties have been performed, the captain taxis the aircraft to the designated runway and prepares for takeoff. Takeoff speeds must be calculated based on the aircraft's weight. The aircraft systems, levers, and switches must be in proper position for takeoff. After takeoff, the pilots may engage an electrical device known as the autopilot. This device can be programmed to maintain the desired course and altitude. With or without the aid of the autopilot, pilots must constantly monitor the aircraft's systems.

Because pilots may encounter turbulence, emergencies, and other hazardous situations during a flight, good judgment and ability are extremely important. Pilots also receive periodic training and evaluation on their handling of in-flight abnormalities and emergencies and on their operation of the aircraft during challenging weather conditions. As a further safety measure, airline pilots are expected to adhere to checklist procedures in all areas of flight operations.

During a flight, pilots monitor aircraft systems, keep a watchful eye on local weather conditions, perform checklists, and maintain constant communication with the air traffic controllers along the flight route. The busiest times for pilots are during takeoff and landing. The weather conditions at the aircraft's destination must be obtained and analyzed. The aircraft must be maneuvered and properly configured to make a landing on the runway. When the cloud cover is low and visibility is poor, pilots rely solely on the instruments on the flight deck. These instruments include an altimeter and an artificial horizon. Pilots select the appropriate radio navigation frequencies and corresponding course for the ground-based radio and microwave signals that provide horizontal, and in some cases vertical, guidance to the landing runway.

After the pilots have safely landed the aircraft, the captain taxis it to the ramp or gate area where passengers and cargo are off-loaded. Pilots then follow "afterlanding and shutdown" checklist procedures, and inform maintenance crews of any discrepancies or other problems noted during the flight.

Pilots must also keep detailed logs of their flight hours, both for payroll purposes and to comply with Federal Aviation Administration (FAA) regulations. Pilots with major airlines generally have few nonflying duties. Pilots with smaller airlines, charter services, and other air service companies may be responsible for loading the aircraft, refueling, keeping records, performing minor repairs and maintenance, and arranging for more major repairs.

The chief pilot directs the operation of the airline's flight department. This individual is in charge of training new pilots, preparing schedules and assigning flight personnel, reviewing their performance, and improving their morale and

PILOTS	
SCHOOL SUBJECTS	Mathematics Physics
PERSONAL SKILLS	Leadership/management Technical/scientific
WORK ENVIRONMENT	Primarily indoors Primarily multiple locations
MINIMUM EDUCATION LEVEL	High school diploma
SALARY RANGE	$26,290 to $76,800 to $200,000
CERTIFICATION OR LICENSING	Required by all states
OUTLOOK	About as fast as the average
DOT	196
GOE	05.04.01
NOC	2271
O*NET	97702C

The cockpit of a jet airliner

efficiency. Chief pilots make sure that all legal and government regulations affecting flight operations are observed, advise the airline during contract negotiations with the pilots' union, and handle a multitude of administrative details.

In addition to airline pilots, there are various other types of pilots. *Business pilots*, or executive pilots fly for businesses that have their own planes. These pilots transport cargo, products, or executives and maintain the company's planes as well. *Test pilots*, though there are not many, are very important. Combining knowledge of flying with an engineering background, they test new models of planes and make sure they function properly. *Flight instructors* are pilots who teach others how to fly. They may teach in classrooms or provide inflight instruction, or both. Other pilots work as examiners, or check pilots. They may fly with experienced pilots as part of their periodic review; they may also give examinations to pilots applying for licenses.

Some pilots are employed in the following specialties: *photogrammetry pilots* fly planes or helicopters over designated areas and photograph the earth's surface for mapping and other purposes. *Facilities-flight-check pilots* fly specially equipped planes to test air navigational aids, air traffic controls, and communications equipment and to evaluate installation sites for such equipment. This testing is directed by a supervising pilot.

■ Requirements

High School

All prospective pilots must complete high school. A college-preparatory curriculum is recommended because of the need for pilots to have at least some college education. Science and mathematics are two important subjects to prospective pilots, who should also take advantage of any computer courses offered. As explained below, students can start pursuing their pilot's license while in high school.

Postsecondary Training

Most companies that employ pilots require at least two years of college training; many require applicants to be college graduates. Courses in engineering, meteorology, physics, and mathematics are helpful in preparing for a pilot's career. Flying can be learned in either military or civilian flying schools. There are approximately one thousand FAA-certified civilian flying schools, including some colleges and universities that offer degree credit for pilot training. Pilots leaving the military are in great demand.

Certification or Licensing

To become a pilot, certain rigid training requirements must be met. Although obtaining a private pilot's license is not difficult, it may be quite difficult to obtain a commercial license. Any student who is 16 or over and who can pass the rigid mandatory physical examination may apply for permission to take flying instruction. When the training is finished, a written examination must be taken. If prospective pilots pass the examination, they may apply for a private pilot's license. To qualify for it, a person must be at least 17 years of age, successfully fulfill a solo flying requirement of 20 hours or more, and check out in instrument flying and cross-country flying. Student pilots are restricted from carrying passengers; private pilots may carry passengers but may not receive any payment or other compensation for the piloting activities.

All pilots and copilots must be licensed by the FAA before they can do any type of commercial flying. An applicant who is 18 years old and has 250 hours of flying time can apply for a commercial airplane pilot's license. In applying for this license, a candidate must pass a rigid physical examination and a written test given by the FAA covering safe flight operations, federal aviation regulations, navigation principles, radio operation, and meteorology. The applicant also must submit proof that the minimum flight-time requirements have been completed and, in a practical test, demonstrate flying skill and technical competence to a check pilot. Before pilots or copilots receive an FAA license, they must also receive a rating for the kind of plane they can fly (single-engine, multi-engine, or seaplane) and for the specific type of plane, such as Boeing 707 or 747.

An instrument rating by the FAA and a restricted radio telephone operator's permit by the Federal Communications Commission (FCC) are required. All airline captains must have an air transport pilot license. Applicants for this license must be at least 23 years old and have a minimum of 1,500 hours of flight time, including night flying and instrument time. All pilots are subject to two-year flight reviews, regular six-month FAA flight checks, simulator tests, and medical exams. The FAA also makes unannounced spot check inspections of all pilots.

Jet pilots, helicopter pilots, and agricultural pilots all have special training in their respective fields.

Other Requirements

Sound physical and emotional health are essential requirements for aspiring pilots. Emotional stability is necessary because the safety of other people depends upon a pilot remaining calm and level-headed, no matter how trying the situation. Physical health is equally important. Vision and hearing must be perfect; coordination must be excellent; heart rate and blood pressure must be normal.

■ Exploring

High school students who are interested in flying may join the Explorers (Boy Scouts of America) or a high school aviation club. At 16 years of age, they may start taking flying lessons. One of the most valuable experiences for high school students who want to be a pilot is to learn to be a ham radio operator. By so doing, they meet one of the qualifications for commercial flying.

■ Employers

The commercial airlines, including both passenger and cargo transport companies, are the primary employers of pilots. Pilots also work in general aviation, and many are trained and employed by the military.

■ Starting Out

A large percentage of commercial pilots have received their training in the armed forces. A military pilot who wants to apply for a commercial airplane pilot's license is required to pass only the Federal Aviation Regulations examination if application is made within a year after leaving the service.

Pilots possessing the necessary qualifications and license may apply directly to a commercial airline for a job. If accepted, they will go through a company orientation course, usually including both classroom instruction and practical training in company planes.

Those who are interested in becoming business pilots will do well to start their careers in mechanics. They may also have military flying experience, but the strongest recommendation for a business pilot's job is an airframe and powerplant (A and P) rating. They should also have at least 500 hours flying time and have both commercial and instrument ratings on their license. They apply directly to the firm for which they would like to work.

■ Advancement

Many beginning pilots start out as copilots. Seniority is the pilot's most important asset. If pilots leave one employer and go to another, they must start from the bottom again, no matter how much experience was gained with the first employer. The position of captain on a large airline is a high-seniority, high-prestige, and high-paying job. Pilots may also advance to the position of check pilot, testing other pilots for advanced ratings; chief pilot, supervising the work of other pilots; or to administrative or executive positions with a commercial airline (ground operations). They may also become self-employed, opening a flying business, such as a flight instruction, agricultural aviation, air-taxi, or charter service.

■ Earnings

Airline pilots are among the highest paid workers in the country. The 1996 average starting salary for airline pilots was about $15,000 at small turboprop airlines and $26,290 at larger, major airlines. Pilots with six years of experience made $28,000 a year at turboprop airlines and nearly $76,800 at the largest airlines. Senior captains on the largest aircraft earned as much as $200,000 a year. Salaries vary widely depending on a number of factors, including the specific airline, type of aircraft flown, number of years with a company, and level of experience. Airline pilots are also paid more for international and nighttime flights.

Pilots with the airlines receive life and health insurance and retirement benefits; if they fail their FAA physical exam during their career, they are eligible to receive disability benefits. Some airlines give pilots allowances for buying and cleaning their uniforms. Pilots and their families may usually fly free or at reduced fares on their own or other airlines.

■ Work Environment

Airline pilots work with the best possible equipment and under highly favorable circumstances. They command a great deal of respect. Although many pilots regularly fly the same routes, no two flights are ever the same. FAA regulations limit airline pilots to no more than 100 flying hours per month, and most work around 75 hours per month, with few nonflying duties. This is because the pilot's job may be extremely stressful. During flights, they must maintain constant concentration on a variety of factors. They must always be alert to changes in conditions and to any problems that may occur. They are often responsible for hundreds of lives besides their own, and they are always aware that flying contains an element of risk. During emergencies, they must react quickly, logically, and decisively. Pilots often work irregular hours, may be away from home a lot, and are subject to jet lag and other conditions associated with flying. Pilots employed with smaller airlines may also be required to perform other, nonflying duties, which increase the number of hours they work each month.

For other pilots who handle small planes, emergency equipment, and supply delivery or routes to remote and isolated areas, the hazards may be more evident. Dropping medical supplies in Somalia, flying relief supplies into war zones, or delivering mail to northern Alaska are more difficult tasks than most pilots face. Business pilot schedules may be highly irregular and they must be on call for a great portion of their off-duty time. Business pilots and most private and small plane pilots are also frequently called upon to perform maintenance and repairs.

■ Outlook

The employment prospects of airline pilots look very good into the next century. The airline industry expects passenger travel to grow by as much as 60 percent, and airlines will be adding more planes and more flights to accommodate passengers. The outlook is less favorable, however, for business pilots. The recession of the early 1990s caused a decrease in the numbers of business and executive flights as more companies chose to fly with smaller and regional airlines rather than buy and operate their own planes and helicopters. The position of flight engineer is slowly being phased out as more and more airlines install computerized flight engineering systems.

Competition is expected to diminish as the many pilots who were hired during the boom of the 1960s reach mandatory retirement age. In addition, because the military has increased its benefits and incentives, many pilots choose to remain in the service, further reducing the supply of pilots for civilian work. These factors are expected to create a shortage of qualified pilots.

The aviation industry remains extremely sensitive to changes in the economy. When an economic downswing causes a decline in air travel, airline pilots may be given furlough. Business flying, flight instruction, and testing of new aircraft are also adversely affected by recessions.

■ For More Information

Contact the following organizations for information on a career as a pilot:

Air Line Pilots Association, International
PO Box 1169
Herndon, VA 22070
Tel: 703-689-2270
Web: http://www.alpa.org/

Air Transport Association of America
1709 New York Avenue, NW
Washington, DC 20006
Tel: 202-626-4000

Federal Aviation Administration
Flight Standards Division
Fitzgerald Federal Building
John F. Kennedy International Airport
Jamaica, NY 11430

Future Aviation Professionals of America
4291 J Memorial Drive
Atlanta, GA 30032
Tel: 800-JET-JOBS

■ Related Articles

Airlines
Military Services
Transportation
Agricultural Pilots
Astronauts
Helicopter Pilots
Public Transportation Operators

Pipefitters
■ **See Plumbers and Pipefitters**

Plainclothes Investigators
■ **See Border Patrol Officers**

Planetologists
■ **See Geophysicists**

Planimeter Operators
■ **See Statistical Clerks**

Plant Protection Inspectors
■ **See Fire Safety Technicians**

Plasterers

■ Overview

Plasterers apply coats of plaster to interior walls, ceilings, and partitions of buildings to produce fire-resistant and relatively soundproof surfaces. They also work on exterior building surfaces and do ornamental forming and casting work. Their work is similar to that of *drywall workers,* who use drywall rather than plaster to build interior walls and ceilings.

■ History

Plastering is one of the most ancient crafts in the building trades. Before current plasters were invented, primitive people used damp clay, sand, grasses, or reeds. They used their hands, stones, and early tools to smooth the surfaces of the walls of their dwellings. The trade has evolved into a highly skilled type of work through the development and use of many new and improved materials and techniques.

■ The Job

Plasterers work on building interiors and exteriors. They apply plaster directly to masonry, wire, wood, metal, or lath. (Lath is a supportive reinforcement made of wood or metal that is attached to studs to form walls and ceilings.) These surfaces are designed to hold the plaster in position until it dries. After checking the specifications and plans made by the builder, architect, or foreman, plasterers put a border of plaster of the desired thickness on the top and bottom of the wall. After this border has hardened sufficiently, they fill in the remaining portion of the wall with two coats of plaster. The surface of the wall area is then leveled and smoothed with a straightedged tool and darby (a long flat tool used for smoothing). They then apply the third or finishing coat of plaster, which is the last operation before painting or paperhanging. This coat may be finished to an almost velvet smoothness or into one of a variety of decorative textures used in place of papering.

When plastering cinder block and concrete, plasterers first apply what is known as a brown coat of gypsum plaster as a base. The second coat, called the white coat, is lime-based plaster. When plastering metal lath foundations, they first apply a scratch coat with a trowel, spread it over the lath, and scratch the surface with a rake-like tool to make ridges before it dries so that the next coat—the brown coat—will bond tightly. Next, the plasterer sprays or trowels the plaster for the browncoat and smooths it. The finishing coat is either sprayed on or applied with a hawk and trowel. Plasterers also use brushes and water for the finishing coat. The final coat is a mix of lime, water, and plaster of Paris that sets quickly and is smooth and durable.

The plasterer sometimes works with plasterboard or sheetrock, which are types of wallboard that come ready for installation. When working with such wallboard, the plasterer cuts and fits the wallboard to the studding and joists of ceilings and interior walls. When installing ceilings, workers perform as a team.

Plasterers who specialize in exterior plastering are known as *stucco masons.* They apply a weather-resistant decorative covering of Portland cement plaster to lath in the same manner as interior plastering or with the use of a spray gun. In exterior work, however, the finish coat usually consists of a mixture of white cement and sand or a patented finish material that may be applied in a variety of colors and textures.

Decorative and ornamental plastering is the specialty of highly skilled *molding plasterers.* This work includes molding or forming and installing ornamental plaster panels and trim. Some molding plasterers also cast intricate cornices and recesses used for indirect lighting. Such work is rarely used today because of the great degree of skill involved and the high cost.

In recent years, most plasterers began using machines to spray plaster on walls, ceilings, and structural sections of buildings. Machines that mix plaster have been in general use for many years.

■ Requirements

High School

Although a high school or trade school education is not mandatory, it is highly recommended. In high school or vocational school, students should take mechanical drawing, drafting, woodwork, and other shop courses. Classes in mathematics will sharpen their skills in the applied mathematics of layout work.

Postsecondary Training

To qualify as a journeyworker plasterer, a person must complete either an apprenticeship or on-the-job training program. The apprenticeship program consists of three to four years of carefully planned activity combined with approximately 6,000 to 8,000 hours of work experience and an annual 144 hours of related classroom instruction. An apprenticeship is usually

PLASTERERS	
SCHOOL SUBJECTS	Art Technical/Shop
PERSONAL SKILLS	Artistic Mechanical/manipulative
WORK ENVIRONMENT	Primarily indoors Multiple locations
MINIMUM EDUCATION LEVEL	Apprenticeship
SALARY RANGE	$17,772 to $29,300 to $39,180
CERTIFICATION OR LICENSING	None available
OUTLOOK	Little change or more slowly than the average
DOT	840
GOE	05.05.04
NOC	7284
O*NET	87317

A plasterer uses his trowel to smooth plaster on a ceiling. This is the first of three coats of plaster.

the best start, since it includes on-the-job training as well as formal instruction.

On-the-job training consists of working for four or more years under the supervision of experienced plasterers. The trainee usually begins as a helper or laborer and learns the trade informally by observing or being taught by other plasterers.

Other Requirements

Most employers prefer to hire applicants who are at least 17 years old, in good physical condition, and have a high degree of manual dexterity.

■ Exploring

To observe the plasterer at work, field trips to construction sites may be arranged by a school counselor or students can arrange an interview on their own. An excellent first-hand experience in this trade would be to obtain a part-time or summer job as a plasterer's helper or laborer.

■ Employers

Most plasterers work for independent plastering contractors and are members of unions, either the Operative Plasterers' and Cement Masons' International Association of the United States and Canada or the Bricklayers and Allied Craftsmen International Union.

■ Starting Out

Those who wish to become apprentices usually contact local plastering contractors, the state employment service bureau, or the appropriate union headquarters. In most places, the local branch of the Operative Plasterers' and Cement Masons' International Association of the United States and Canada is the best place to inquire about appren-

ticeships. The Bureau of Apprenticeship and Training, U.S. Department of Labor, and the state employment office are also good places to contact for information.

If the apprenticeship program is filled, applicants may wish to enter the field as on-the-job trainees. In this case, they usually contact a plastering contractor directly and begin work as helpers or laborers. They learn about the work by mixing the plaster, helping plasterers with scaffolding, and carrying equipment.

■ Advancement

Most plasterers learn the full range of plastering skills. They develop expertise in finish plastering as well as rough coat plastering. They also learn the spray gun technique and become proficient spray gun plasterers. With additional training, they may specialize in exterior work as stucco masons or in ornamental plastering as molding plasterers.

If they have certain personal characteristics such as the ability to deal with people and good judgment and planning skills, plasterers may progress to become supervisors or job estimators. Many plasterers become self-employed, and some eventually become contractors.

■ Earnings

The median annual salary for plasterers is about $29,300. However, the minimum wage rate varies considerably according to geographic regions. Hourly wages vary from lows of $4.50 and $5.00 to $23.00 for experienced plasterers in certain areas. Average monthly wages range from $1,481 to $3,265. Plasterers may receive traditional fringe benefits, such as health insurance and paid vacation days.

■ Work Environment

Most plasterers have a regular 40-hour workweek with occasional overtime when necessary to meet a contract deadline. Overtime work is usually compensated at the rate of one and a half times the regular hourly wage. The workday may start earlier than most (7:00 AM), but it also usually ends earlier (3:00 PM). Some plasterers face layoffs between jobs, while others may work with drywall or ceiling tile as required by their contractors when there is no plastering work to be done.

Most of the work is performed indoors, plastering walls and ceilings and forming and casting ornamental designs. Plasterers also work outdoors, doing stucco work and EIFS. They often work with other construction workers, including carpenters, plumbers, and pipe-fitters. Plasterers must do a considerable amount of standing, stooping, and lifting. They often get plaster on their work clothes and dust in their eyes and noses.

Plasterers take pride in seeing the results of their work—something they have helped to build that will last a long time. Their satisfaction with progress on the job, day by day, may be a great deal more than in jobs where the worker never sees the completed product or where the results are less obvious.

As highly skilled workers, plasterers have higher earnings, better chances for promotion, and more opportunity to go into business for themselves than other workers. They also can usually find jobs in almost any part of the United States.

■ Outlook

There are approximately 32,000 plasterers employed in the United States. Employment opportunities for plasterers are expected to increase slowly during the remainder of the decade and beyond, because of the trend toward wider use of drywall construction. Plasterers' employment prospects usually rise and fall with the economy, and especially with the health of the construction industry.

However, recent improvements in both plastering materials and methods of application are expected to increase the scope of the craft and create more job opportunities. To name a few such developments: more lightweight plasters are being used because of excellent soundproofing, acoustical, and fireproofing qualities; machine plastering, insulating, and fireproofing are becoming more widespread; and the use of plaster veneer or high-density plaster in creating a finished surface is being used increasingly in new buildings. Plaster veneer is a thin coat of plaster that can be finished in one coat. It is made of lime and plaster of Paris and can be mixed with water at the job site. It is often applied to a special gypsum base on interior surfaces. Exterior systems have also changed to include Styrofoam insulation board and two thin coats of polymer and acrylic modified materials, called Exterior Insulated Finish Systems, or EIFS.

■ For More Information

Contact the following organizations for more information about a career as a plasterer.

Foundation of the Wall and Ceiling Industry
307 East Annandale Road, Suite 200
Falls Church, VA 22042
Tel: 703-534-1703

International Institute for Lath and Plaster
820 Transfer Road
St. Paul, MN 55114
Tel: 612-645-0208

Operative Plasterers' and Cement Masons' International Association of the United States and Canada
1125 17th Street, NW
Washington, DC 20036
Tel: 202-393-6569

■ Related Articles

Construction
Bricklayers and Stonemasons
Drywall Installers and Finishers

Plaster-Sheet Cutters

■ **See Plastics Products Manufacturing Workers**

Plastic Form Makers

■ **See Plastics Products Manufacturing Workers**

Plastic Patternmakers

■ **See Plastics Products Manufacturing Workers**

Plastics Engineers

■ Overview

Plastics engineers engage in the manufacture, fabrication, and end use of existing materials, as well as with the development of new materials, processes, and equipment. The term plastics engineer encompasses a wide variety of applications and manufacturing processes. Depending on the processes involved, plastics engineers develop everything from the initial part design to the processes and automation required to produce and finish the production parts.

■ History

Thermoplastics, plastics that soften with heat and harden when cooled, were discovered in France in 1828. In the United States in 1869, a printer, John Wesley Hyatt, created celluloid in the process of attempting to create an alternate material to supplement ivory in billiard balls. His invention, patented in 1872, brought about a revolution in production and manufacturing. By 1892, over 2,500 articles were being produced from celluloid. Among these inventions were frames for eyeglasses, false teeth, the first movie film, and, of course, billiard balls. Celluloid did have its drawbacks. It could not be molded and it was highly flammable.

It was not until 1909 that the Belgian-American chemist Leo H. Baekeland (1863-1944) produced the first synthetic plastic. This product replaced natural rubber in electrical insulation and was used for phone handsets and automobile distributor caps and rotors, and is still used today. Other plastics materials have been developed steadily. The greatest variety of materials and applications, however, came during World War II, when the war effort brought about a need for changes in clothing, consumer goods, transportation, and military equipment.

Today, plastics manufacturing is a major industry whose products play a vital role in many other industries and activities around the world. It is difficult to find an area of our lives where plastic does not play some role. Plastics engineers apply their skills to a vast array of professional fields. For example, plastics engineers assisting those in the medical field may help to further develop artificial hearts, replacement limbs, artificial skin, implantable eye lenses, and specially designed equipment that will aid surgeons and other health professionals in the operating room.

PLASTICS ENGINEERS	
SCHOOL SUBJECTS	Chemistry Computer science
PERSONAL SKILLS	Mechanical/manipulative Technical/scientific
WORK ENVIRONMENT	Primarily indoors Primarily one location
MINIMUM EDUCATION LEVEL	Bachelor's degree
SALARY RANGE	$30,000 to $46,500 to $87,750
CERTIFICATION OR LICENSING	Required for certain positions
OUTLOOK	Faster than the average
DOT	019
NOC	2134
O*NET	22105D

■ The Job

Plastics engineers perform a wide variety of duties depending on the type of company they work for and the products it produces. Plastics engineers, for example, may develop ways to produce clear, durable plastics to replace glass in areas where glass cannot be used. Others design and manufacture lightweight parts for aircraft and automobiles, or create new plastics to replace metallic or wood parts that have come to be too expensive or hard to obtain. Others may be employed to formulate less-expensive, fire-resistant plastics for use in the construction of houses, offices, and factories. Plastics engineers may also develop new types of biodegradable molecules that are friendly to the environment, reducing pollution and increasing recyclability.

Plastics engineers perform a variety of duties. Some of their specific job titles and duties include: *application engineers,* who develop new processes and materials in order to create a better finished product; *process engineers,* who oversee the production of reliable, high quality, standard materials; and *research specialists,* who use the basic building blocks of matter to discover and create new materials.

In the course of their day, plastics engineers must solve a wide variety of internal production problems. Duties include making sure the process is consistent to insure creation of accurate and precise parts and making sure parts are handled and packaged efficiently, properly, and cheaply. Each part is unique in this respect.

Computers are increasingly being used to assist in the production process. Plastics engineers use computers to calculate part weight and cycle times; for monitoring the process on each molding press; for designing parts and molds on the CAD system; for tracking processes and the labor in the mold shop; and to transfer engineering files over the Internet.

Plastics engineers also help customers solve problems that may emerge in part design—finding ways to make a part more moldable or to address possible failures or inconsistencies in the final design. Factors that may make a part difficult to mold include: thin walls, functional or cosmetic factors, sections that are improperly designed that will not allow the part to be processed efficiently, or inappropriate material selection which results in an improperly created part.

Plastics engineers also coordinate mold-building schedules and activities with tool vendors. Mold-building schedules consist of the various phases of constructing a mold, from the development of the tool and buying of materials (and facilitating their timely delivery), to estimating the roughing and finishing operations. Molds differ depending on the size of the tool or product, the complexity of the work orders, and the materials required to build the mold.

Most importantly, plastics engineers must take an application that is difficult to produce and make it (in the short period of time allowed) profitable to their company, while still satisfying the needs of the customer.

■ Requirements

High School

Follow your school's college prep program by taking classes in English, government, foreign language, and history. You should take additional classes in mathematics and the sciences, particularly chemistry and physics. Computer classes are also important. You should also take voc-tech, drafting, and other classes that involve you directly with design and manufacture.

Postsecondary Training

The level of education required beyond high school varies greatly depending on the types of plastics processes involved. Most plastic companies do not require a bachelor's degree in plastics engineering. Companies that design proprietary parts usually require a bachelor's or advanced degree in mechanical engineering. The field of plastics engineering, overall, is still a field where people with the proper experience are scarce—experience is a key factor in qualifying a person for an engineering position.

To pursue an associate's or bachelor's degree in plastics engineering, you should contact the Society of the Plastics Industry (SPI) or the Society of Plastics Engineers (SPE) for information about two-year and four-year programs. Plastics programs are sometimes listed under polymer science, polymer engineering, materials science, and materials engineering. The Society of Plastics Engineers offers scholarships to some students enrolled in engineering programs. Awards range up to $4,000 annually, and are renewable for up to three additional years. Certain branches of the military also provide training in plastics engineering.

Certification or Licensing

Some states may require that engineers be licensed. Though national certification isn't required, SPE has established The Institute for Plastics Certification. To receive this certification, technologists and engineers with the required amount of education and experience can receive certification after passing an exam.

Other Requirements

You need to have good mechanical aptitude, in order to develop the plastics parts and the tooling necessary to develop these parts. You must have thorough knowledge of the properties of plastic and of the processes which occur. There are thousands of different materials which you may encounter in the course of your workday. You also must be imaginative and creative in order to be able to solve any problems which might arise from new applications or in the transition/transformation of a mechanical metal part to that of a plastic one.

■ Exploring

You can gain some insight into plastics careers by looking at the industry publications *Plastics Engineering* and *Plastics Industry News*. SPI also publishes a careers brochure. *Opportunities in Plastics Careers,* by Jan Bone, is a useful overview of the plastics industry. There are numerous chapters which focus on job-finding skills and financial aid opportunities.

High school students may seek to join JETS (Junior Engineering Technical Society), a program which provides organized engineering-related activities. Students, through

A plastics engineer compares the specifications of a new product on a blueprint and a work order.

group activities, can gain practice in problem solving, scientific reasoning, and actual real life experience with the real world of engineering.

A high school counselor, science, or shop teacher may be able to arrange a presentation or question-and-answer session with a plastics engineer, or even a tour of a local plastics manufacturer. There are also student chapters of SPI and SPE which provide opportunities to gain valuable experience and contacts with similarly interested people. You may also be able to find a summer job at a plastics-processing plant to learn the basics and experience the varied areas involved with producing plastics parts.

■ Employers

Plastics engineers work for the manufacturers of plastic products, materials, and resins. Major plastics employers in the United States include DuPont, General Motors, and Owens-Corning. Some of the top thermoforming companies are in Illinois: Tenneco Packaging, Solo Cup Company, and Ivex Packaging Corporation are a few of them. Michigan has some of the top injection molding companies, including Textron, Lear Corporation, UT Automotive, and Venture Industries Corporation. But large plastics companies are located all across the country. According to the SPI, the top plastics industry states ranked by employment are California, Ohio, Michigan, Illinois, and Texas.

Starting Out

To get a job as a plastics engineer, you'll need considerable experience in the plastics industry or a college degree. A variety of starting points exist within the industry. Experienced plastics setup and process technicians can use their skills to advance to engineering responsibilities. Many plastics engineers start out as tool and die makers or mold-makers before they move into engineering positions.

School placement centers are good sources of job leads. Also, many major companies recruit plastics engineers on college campuses. SPE's Web site features the "online plastics employment network," a database of job openings.

Advancement

The advanced training, expertise, and knowledge of experienced plastics engineers allows them the luxury of migrating to almost any position within the plastics industry. Engineers may also advance to supervisory or management positions, for example, becoming director of engineering for their entire plant or division. Further advancement may come in the form of employment at larger companies.

Experienced plastics engineers, as a result of their expertise in materials and matching products to applications, are good candidates for sales and marketing jobs. They may also train the engineers of tomorrow by becoming teachers at technical schools or colleges or by writing for a technical trade journal.

Earnings

According to a survey by the Institute of Industrial Engineers, the median annual salary for engineers working for rubber and plastics products manufacturers is $46,500. Those starting out may make less than $30,000, but those with more education and experience can make well over $50,000. In a 1998 industry report, the American Association of Engineering Societies stated that engineers with 10 years' experience in the plastics industry made an average of $64,000 a year. Those with 14 years' experience made $69,800, and those with 25 years' experience made $87,750.

Benefits for plastics engineers usually include paid vacations and sick days, pension plans, and health and dental insurance. Depending on the size of the company, engineers may be offered production bonuses, stock options, and paid continuing education.

Work Environment

Plastics engineers are constantly busy as they deal with people at all levels and phases of the manufacturing process. Dress codes may be formal since plastics engineers interact with customers frequently during the course of a day. Engineers may be required to work more than a standard eight-hour day and also some Saturdays when a specific project is on a deadline.

As a plastics engineer, you may work directly with design materials in a laboratory, or sit at a computer in an office. You may spend some hours working alone, as well some hours working as part of a team. You may only be involved in certain aspects of a project, or you may work on a project from the original design to final testing of a product.

Outlook

The future of plastics engineering is very bright. Three or four new plastics materials are being discovered every day. Most industries are less likely to lay off plastics engineers than other types of workers. More industries are incorporating plastics into their product lines, which will create more opportunities for qualified plastics engineers. As more plastics products are substituted for glass, paper, and metal products and parts, plastics engineers will be needed to oversee design and production processes. An example of this change is in the automotive industry, where a high percentage of engine parts will eventually be made of plastic. Plastics engineers will increasingly be required to develop environmentally friendly products and processes, and play a role in developing easily recyclable products for certain industries.

Many opportunities exist in smaller companies, such as plastics parts suppliers. Many openings will come as a result of experienced engineers who advance to sales, management, or other related occupations within the plastics industry. Those with the most advanced skills and experience, as always, will enjoy the best future career outlook.

For More Information

For information on obtaining a copy of Plastics Engineering *and information on college scholarships, contact:*

Society of Plastics Engineers
PO Box 403
Brookfield, CT 06804-0403
Tel: 203-775-0471
Web: http://www.4spe.org

For a career brochure and information about college programs, contact:

Society of the Plastics Industry
1801 K Street, NW, Suite 600K
Washington, DC 20006-1301
Tel: 202-974-5200
Web: http://www.socplas.org

For information on membership and programs, contact:

Junior Engineering Technical Society, Inc.
1420 King Street, Suite 405
Alexandria, VA 22314-2794
Tel: 703-548-5387
Web: http://www.jets.org

■ Related Articles

Chemicals

Plastics

Chemical Engineers

Chemists

Engineers

Plastics Products Manufacturing Workers

Plastics Technicians

Plastics Products Manufacturing Workers

■ Overview

Plastics products manufacturing workers mold, cast, and assemble products made of plastics materials. The objects they make are almost without number. They include dishes, signs, toys, insulation, appliance parts, automobile parts, combs, gears, bearings, and many others.

■ History

Thermoplastics, plastics that soften with heat and harden when cooled, were discovered in France in 1828. In the United States in 1869, a printer named John Wesley Hyatt attempted to create an alternative material to supplement ivory in billiard balls. He experimented with a mixture of cellulose nitrate and camphor, creating what he called celluloid. His invention, patented in 1872, brought about a revolution in production and manufacturing. By 1892, over 2,500 hundred articles were being produced from celluloid. Among these inventions were piano keys, false teeth, and the first movie film. Celluloid did have its drawbacks. It could not be molded and it was highly flammable.

It was not until 1909, however, that the Belgian-American chemist Leo H. Baekeland produced the first synthetic plastic. This product replaced natural rubber in electrical insulation and was used for phone handsets, and automobile distributor caps and rotors, and is still used today. Other plastics materials have been developed steadily. The greatest variety of materials and applications, however, came during World War II, when the war effort brought about a need for innovation in clothing, consumer goods, transportation, and military equipment.

Today, plastics manufacturing is a major industry whose products play a vital role in many other industries and activities around the world. It is difficult to find an area of our lives where plastics do not play some role. Major users of plastics include the electronics, packaging, aerospace, medical, and housing and building industries. The plastics industry also provides the makings for a large variety of consumer goods. Appliances, toys, dinnerware, luggage, and furniture are just a few products that require plastics.

Plastics products manufacturing workers have always been needed in the production of plastic. Their job responsibilities and skills have changed and grown more specialized as new productions processes and materials have come into widespread use.

PLASTICS PRODUCTS MANUFACTURING WORKERS	
SCHOOL SUBJECTS	Mathematics Technical/Shop
PERSONAL SKILLS	Following instructions Mechanical/manipulative
WORK ENVIRONMENT	Primarily indoors Primarily one location
MINIMUM EDUCATION LEVEL	High school diploma
SALARY RANGE	$19,000 to $28,000 to $40,000
CERTIFICATION OR LICENSING	Voluntary
OUTLOOK	Faster than the average
DOT	553
GOE	06.02.10
NOC	9214
O*NET	91902

Workers sort through plastic bits that will later be used in production.

■ The Job

Plastics are usually made by a process called polymerization, in which many molecules of the same kind are combined to make networks of giant particles. All plastics can be formed or shaped; some become pliable under heat, some at elevated room temperatures. When treated, some plastics become hard, some incredibly strong, some soft like putty.

Plastic objects are formed using several different methods. Each method produces a different type of plastic. In compression molding, plastics compounds are compressed and treated inside a mold to form them. In injection molding, liquid plastic is injected into a mold and hardened. Blow molding is like glass blowing-air is forced into plastic to make it expand to the inner surface of a mold. In extrusion, hot plastic is continuously forced through a die to make products like tubing. Laminating involves fusing together resin-soaked sheets, while the calender process forms sheets by forcing hot plastic between rollers. Finally, in fabrication, workers make items out of solid plastic pieces by heating, sawing, and drilling.

Marvin Griggs works for a company called Centro, in Springdale, Arkansas. "We're a rotational molder for plastic products," Marvin says. "We make custom parts for companies like John Deere. We don't produce our own product. They send the mold, we build the parts." Marvin is part of a four-person crew running one of the machines—the *machine operator* and *assistant operator* pour resin into the molds, which is then placed into the oven, and then the cooler. They open the molds and remove and inspect the part for warping, or some other defect. The *trimmer* then trims the line, cutting off the plastic flange. "If the part needs holes cut into it, or fixtures put in it," Marvin says, "they pass it down to me." The tools he uses include pneumatic hand tools, routers, and a large tank. "The parts are dunk-tested to make sure they're sealed, and there are no holes. We have a tight quality control system."

While plastics compounds may be mixed in plastics-materials plants, plastics fabricators sometimes employ *blenders,* or *color mixers,* and their helpers to measure, heat, and mix materials to produce or color plastic materials. *Grinding-machine operators* run machines that grind particles of plastics into smaller pieces for processing. *Pilling-machine operators* take plastics powder and compress it into pellets or biscuits for further processing. Other workers are responsible for making the molds (*plastic form makers*) and patterns (*plastics patternmakers*) that are used to determine the shape of the finished plastics items. Foam-machine operators spray thermoplastic resins into conveyor belts to form plastic foam.

Many plastics products plants make goods according to clients' specifications. When this is the case, *job setters,* using their knowledge of plastics and their properties, adjust molding machines to clients' instructions. They make such adjustments as changing the die through which the plastic flows, adjusting the speed of the flow, and replacing worn cutting tools when necessary. Then the machine is ready to accept the plastic and produce the object.

Injection molders operate machines that liquefy plastic powders or pellets, inject liquid plastic into a mold, and eject a molded product. Compact discs, toys, typewriter keys, and many other common products are made by injection molding. Injection workers set and observe gauges to determine the temperature of the plastic and examine ejected objects for defects.

One common plastic is polystyrene, which when molded using heat and pressure makes cast foam products such as balls, coolers, and packing nests. *Polystyrene-bead molders* operate machines that expand these beads and mold them into sheets of bead board. *Polystyrene-molding-machine tenders* run machines that mold pre-expanded beads into objects. At the end of the molding cycle, they lift the cast objects from the molds and press a button to start the machine again.

Extruder operators and their helpers set up and run machines that extrude thermoplastics to form tubes, rods, and film. They adjust the dies and machine screws through which the hot plastic is drawn, adjust the machine's cooling system, weigh and mix plastics materials, empty them into the machine, set the temperature and speed of the machine, and start it.

Blow-molding-machine operators run machines that mold objects such as bleach bottles and milk bottles by puffing air into plastic to expand it. *Compression-molding-machine operators* and *tenders* run machines that mold thermosetting plastics into hard plastic objects. Thermosetting plastics are those that harden because of a chemical reaction rather than by heating and cooling.

Casters make similar molded products by hand. *Strippers* remove molded items from molds and clean the molds. Some molded products must be vacuum cured. *Baggers* run machines that perform this task.

Plastic sheeting is formed by *calender operators,* who adjust the temperature, speed, and roller position of machines that draw plastic between rollers to produce sheets of specified thickness. *Stretch-machine operators* stretch plastic sheets to specified dimensions. *Preform laminators* press fiberglass and resin-coated fabrics over plaster, steel, or wooden forms to make plastic parts for boats, cars, and airplanes.

Other common plastics products are fiberglass poles and dowels. *Fiberglass-dowel-drawing-machine operators* mount dies on machines, mix and pour plastics compounds, draw fiberglass through the die, and soak, cool, cure, and cut dowels. *Fiberglass tube molders* make tubing used in fishing rods and golf club shafts.

Plastics that are not molded may be cut into shapes. *Shaping-machine operators* cut spheres, cones, blocks, and other shapes from plastic foam blocks. *Pad cutters* slice foam rubber blocks to specified thicknesses for such objects as seat cushions and ironing board pads.

Many products undergo further processing to finish them. *Foam-gun operators* reinforce and insulate plastic products such as bathtubs and auto body parts by spraying them with plastic foam. *Plastic-sheet cutters* use power shears to cut sheets, following patterns glued to the sheets by pattern hands. *Sawyers* cut rods, tubes, and sheets to specified dimensions. *Trimmers* trim plastic parts to size using a template and power saw. Machine finishers smooth and polish the surface of plastic sheets. And *plastics heat welders* use hot-air guns to fuse together plastic sheets.

Hand finishers trim and smooth products using hand tools and sandpaper. *Buffers* remove ridges and rough edges from fiberglass or plastic castings. *Sponge buffers* machine-buff the edges of plastic sponges to round them, and *pointing-machine operators* round the points on the teeth of plastic combs. *Edge grinders* tend machines that square and smooth edges of plastic floor tile.

Some plastics workers (assemblers) and *laminated plastics assemblers-and-gluers* assemble pieces to form certain products. These may include skylights (*skylight assemblers*) and wet suits (*wet suit gluers*). Other workers are lacquerers, embossers, printers, carvers, or design inserters. *Plastics inspectors* inspect and test finished products for strength, size, uniformity, and conformity to specifications.

Experienced workers supervise plastics-making departments, and the industry also employs unskilled workers such as laborers to help haul, clean, and assemble plastics materials, equipment, and products.

■ Requirements

High School

You should take courses in mathematics, chemistry, physics, computer science, shop, drafting, and mechanical drawing. English and speech classes will help build good communications and interpersonal skills.

Postsecondary Training

You'll need a high school diploma to enter the field, and you'll learn most of your skills on the job. In extrusion plants, trainees can become Class I extruders after about 3 months. Other jobs require training from 1 to 12 months.

Applicants with some knowledge of chemistry, mathematics, physics, drafting, industrial technology, or computer science have a better chance of being hired. Some colleges offer associate's or bachelor's degrees in plastics technology. Job seekers with these degrees have a definite competitive edge and may also advance more quickly.

Another training option is to participate in an apprenticeship program. Apprenticeships provide experience and a chance to explore the field. Apprenticeships in tool and die making for plastics last four or five years and teach through classroom instruction and on-the-job training. A high school education is normally a prerequisite for an apprenticeship.

Certification or Licensing

Certification isn't required of plastics technicians, but it is available through the Society of the Plastics Industry (SPI). As industry equipment becomes more complex, employers may prefer to hire only certified technicians. To become an NCP Certified Operator, you'll take an exam in one of four areas: blow molding, extrusion, injection molding, or thermoforming. The exam is open to anyone seeking a career in the plastics industry, but you'll likely need at least two years of plastics experience to pass the exam.

Other Requirements

You must have mechanical aptitude and manual dexterity to work well with tools and various materials. Lifting equipment and materials takes some strength, and workers who operate machines stand much of the time. You must be

Howards Grove High School in Wisconsin is one of the first schools to establish a youth apprenticeship program for students interested in plastics manufacturing. The four-semester course for junior and senior high school students includes the courses Introduction to Manufacturing, Plastics Manufacturing Materials and Processes, and Plastics Technology. Graduates of the course receive a Certificate of Occupational Proficiency.

able to work well with others and follow oral and written directions. You must be precise and organized in your work.

"I'm really particular about my work from being in construction for six years," Marvin says. "I pay really close attention to detail."

■ Exploring

Many high schools are beginning to offer vocational programs, and other apprenticeship opportunities, for those interested in becoming technicians; some of these programs have courses geared specifically towards preparation for the plastics industry. SPI is currently involved in providing career direction to young people interested in the plastics industry. Contact SPI for career and industry information. You can also learn about the industry by reading trade magazines such as *Modern Plastics*. *Plastics News* (http://www.plasticsnews.com) publishes many informative articles on the Web, including rankings of plastics manufacturers.

■ Employers

Major plastics employers in the United States include DuPont, General Motors, and Owens-Corning. Some of the top thermoforming companies are in Illinois: Tenneco Packaging, Solo Cup Company, and Ivex Packaging Corporation are a few of them. Michigan has some of the top injection molding companies, including Textron, Lear Corporation, UT Automotive, and Venture Industries Corporation. But large plastics companies are located all across the country. According to the SPI, the top plastics industry states ranked by employment are California, Ohio, Michigan, Illinois, and Texas.

■ Starting Out

After receiving a high school diploma, you should apply directly to the personnel departments of plastics plants in the area in which you wish to work. Newspaper ads may list openings in the industry, and state employment agencies may also provide leads. The Web site http://www.polysort.com features a "virtual job fair" which offers free access to job listings in the plastics industry. The Plastics Molders and Manufacturers Association, a divi-

sion of the Society of Manufacturing Engineers (http://www.sme.org/), also maintains a job database for members.

■ Advancement

In the plastics industry, advancement comes with experience, skill, and education. Because plants like to teach workers their own methods, and because skilled plastics workers are scarce, most plastics companies promote workers from within to fill more responsible and higher-paying jobs. Plastics workers who understand machine setup and the properties of plastics will advance more quickly than those limited to machine operations.

Workers who pursue bachelor's or associate's degrees in plastics technology have the best chances for advancement. With advanced training and experience some plastics workers may become plastics engineers or mold designers. Others may move into supervisory, management, or sales and marketing positions. Apprenticeships, such as in tool and die manufacturing, may also lead to more highly paid production work.

■ Earnings

According to wage surveys conducted by SPI, material handlers in the plastics industry earn about $19,000 to $21,000 a year. In entry-level, or apprenticeship, positions, moldmakers earn between $20,000 and $28,000 a year. Experienced moldmakers earn $31,000 to $40,000 a year.

In addition to salary, many employers offer medical and dental benefits, life insurance, paid sick leave, personal and vacation days, and retirement plans. Employees may also be able to participate in profit-sharing plans.

■ Work Environment

Most plastics industry workers work 40 hours per week. Because plants operate on 3 shifts, entry-level workers may work nights and move to day shifts as they gain experience and seniority.

Plastics plants are generally safe, well lighted and ventilated, and modern. Workers must observe safety precautions when working around hot machines and plastics, sharp machine parts, and electrical wiring, and when sawing, cutting, or drilling plastics parts. Plastics work, however, is not usually strenuous. Workers use machines to lift heavy dies and other equipment.

As with most production work, jobs in the plastics industry often demand a fair amount of repetition. Workers who need great variety in their jobs may not enjoy production work. Plastics plants tend to be smaller than many other types of factories so a sense of teamwork often develops among the production workers. Such camaraderie can lead to increased job satisfaction and enjoyment.

■ Outlook

Increased opportunities in foreign markets, the development of new compounds, and increased competition will likely spur the industry as a whole to new economic heights. As a result, the employment of many types of plastics products manufacturing workers is expected to increase faster than the average for all occupations through the year 2006. As more plastics products are substituted for paper, glass, and metal products, more plastics workers will be needed. Molding machine operators, which constitute a large percentage of the workforce, will enjoy a 30 percent increase in growth. Other growth occupations include managers and executives, industrial machine operators, assemblers and fabricators, tool and die makers, extruding and forming machine operators, and cutters and trimmers. Occupations which may experience a decline in employment include grinding-machine operators (due to automation), blenders, and color mixers.

■ For More Information

For a career brochure and information about education and certification, contact:

Society of the Plastics Industry
1801 K Street, NW, Suite 600K
Washington, DC 20006-1301
Tel: 202-974-5200
Web: http://www.socplas.org

The APC is a trade industry that offers a great deal of information about the plastics industry, and maintains an informative Web site:

American Plastics Council
1801 K Street, NW, Suite 701-L
Washington, DC 20006-1301
Tel: 800-243-5790
Web: http://www.plastics.org

For information about scholarships, seminars, and training, contact:

Plastics Institute of America
University of Massachusetts-Lowell
333 Aiken Street
Lowell, MA 01854
Tel: 978-934-3130
Web: http://www.eng.uml.edu/dept/PIA/index.html

■ Related Articles

Plastics
Chemical Technicians
Coremakers
Industrial Chemicals Workers
Molders
Petroleum Refining Workers
Plastics Engineers
Plastics Technicians
Rubber Goods Production Workers

Plastics Heat Welders

■ **See Plastics Products Manufacturing Workers**

Plastics Technicians

■ Overview

Plastics technicians are skilled professionals who help design engineers, scientists, research groups, and manufacturers develop, manufacture, and market plastics products.

Most commonly, plastics technicians work in research and development or manufacturing. In these settings, they function at a level between the engineer or scientist in charge of a job, and the production or laboratory workers who carry out most of the tasks. Other plastics technicians handle mold and tool making, materials and machinery, sales and services, and related technical tasks.

■ History

The plastics industry traces its commercial beginnings to 1869. A billiard ball manufacturer in New York offered a prize of $10,000 to anyone who could create an alternative material to ivory for the production of their billiard balls (balls had been made from elephant tusks, which grew increasingly rare and expensive to obtain). A printer named John Wesley Hyatt experimented with a mixture of cellulose nitrate and camphor, creating what he called celluloid. Although he didn't win the prize, his invention, patented in 1872, brought about a revolution in production and manufacturing. By 1892, over 2,500

PLASTICS TECHNICIANS	
SCHOOL SUBJECTS	Chemistry Mathematics
PERSONAL SKILLS	Mechanical/manipulative Technical/scientific
WORK ENVIRONMENT	Primarily indoors Primarily one location
MINIMUM EDUCATION LEVEL	High school diploma Apprenticeship
SALARY RANGE	$16,000 to $31,000 to $39,500
CERTIFICATION OR LICENSING	Voluntary
OUTLOOK	Much faster than the average
DOT	754
GOE	06.01.04
NOC	2233
O*NET	92197

articles were being produced from celluloid. Among these inventions were piano keys, false teeth, the first movie film, frames for eyeglasses, flexible windows, and, of course, billiard balls. Celluloid did have its drawbacks. It could not be molded and was highly flammable.

In the years that followed, many tried to overcome these shortcomings. In 1909, Leo Hendrik Baekeland developed phenolic plastic. This product replaced natural rubber in electrical insulation, and was used for pot handles, phone handsets, chemical ware, and automobile distributor caps and rotors, and it is still used today. Other plastics materials were developed steadily. The greatest variety of materials and applications, however, came during World War II, when the war effort accelerated major changes in transportation, clothing, military equipment, and consumer goods.

Today, plastics manufacturing is a major industry whose products play a vital role in many other industries and activities around the world, including the electronics, aerospace, medical, and housing industries. Plastic is used in the production of computers, radar equipment, modern aircraft, medical tubing, food packaging, plumbing, paint and adhesives, home appliances, and thousands of other items. The position of plastics technician is relatively new in the industrial workforce. It was created by technological developments in the plastics industry that required people with some technical background, but not an engineering degree.

■ The Job

The duties of plastics technicians can be grouped into five general categories: research and development, mold and tool making, manufacturing, sales and service, and related technical tasks. In research and development, technicians work in laboratories to create new materials or to improve existing ones. In the laboratory, technicians monitor chemical reactions, test, evaluate test results, keep records, and submit reports. A wide variety of chemical apparatus is used. Technicians also use testing equipment to conduct standardized routine tests to determine properties of materials. They set up, calibrate, and operate devices to obtain test data for interpretation and comparison. John Haan is a Quality Control Layout Technician for a Japanese company called TRMI in Michigan. "I'm responsible for the verification of dimensions of assembled product that we ship to our customer," John says. "This audit is done on an annual basis of all parts that we make." The tools he uses in his job include calipers, micrometers, radius gauges, and thread gauges. "But mostly the Coordinate Measuring Machine (CMM), Optical Comparator, and granite surface plate with height gauge and dial indicator are used." Most of his career has been spent in machining of steel, cast iron, and aluminum, so he finds working with plastics to be an interesting challenge. "I have found that plastics present their own unique problems when it comes to inspecting parts," he says. "The parts are very flexible and any pressure on them seems to change their shape."

As new product designs are conceived, *research and development technicians* work on prototypes, assist in the design and manufacture of specialized tools and machinery, and monitor the manufacturing process. To be good at these tasks, plastics technicians must have a mechanical aptitude, thorough knowledge of a variety of materials, and the ability to solve problems.

Mold and tool making is a specialized division of plastics manufacturing. Plastics technicians with drafting skills are employed as mold and tool designers or as drawing detailers. They may also become involved in product design.

Technicians in plastics manufacturing work in molding, laminating, or fabricating. Molding requires the technician to install molds in production machines, establish correct molding cycles, monitor the molding process, maintain production schedules, test incoming raw materials, inspect goods in production, and ensure that the final product meets specifications.

Laminating technicians are trained to superimpose materials in a predetermined pattern. This process is used to make aircraft, aerospace and mass-transit vehicles, boats, satellites, surfboards, recreational vehicles, and furniture. Laminating entails bench work for small parts, and teamwork for large parts. A reinforced plastics item the size of a shoe box can be built by one person, while a large motorized vehicle for a Disney World ride requires the work of several technicians.

Technicians employed as *fabricators* work with plastic sheets, rods, and tubes, using equipment similar to that used in woodworking. Aircraft windshields and canopies, solariums, counter displays, computer housings, signs, and furniture are some of the products made by fabricators.

Basic machine shop methods combined with heat-forming, polishing, and bonding are skills used by technicians in this area.

Sales and service work encompasses a wide variety of jobs for plastics technicians. These technicians are needed in the sales departments of materials suppliers, machinery manufacturers, molding companies, laminators, and fabricators.

Sales representatives for materials suppliers help customers select the correct grade of plastic. They provide a liaison between the customer and the company, assist in product and mold design, and solve problems that may arise in manufacturing.

Sales representatives for machinery manufacturers help customers select the proper equipment for their needs. *Sales technicians* are able to apply scientific training to arrive at the best selection. They are familiar with hydraulic systems and electrical circuitry in the machines they sell, and are knowledgeable about the customer's manufacturing processes.

Molding companies employ technicians to contact customers that require plastics products. Technicians help them choose the correct plastic for the job, discuss the best design, determine the optimum mold size for cost-effectiveness, and provide follow-up services.

Technicians employed in sales capacities by laminators call on the United States Air Force, Navy, Army, and Coast Guard, as well as aircraft companies and commercial businesses. They constantly update their specialized knowledge and training to keep up with the rapid technological advances in this field.

Plastics technicians are also important and valued employees in certain related fields. For example, companies that make computers, appliances, electronic devices, aircraft, and other products that incorporate plastics components rely heavily on plastics technicians to specify, design, purchase, and integrate plastics in the manufacture of the company's major product line.

■ Requirements

High School

A high school diploma is the minimum educational requirement for a career as a plastics technician, but this will only qualify applicants for the most basic positions. While in high school, you should take subjects designated as college preparatory. These subjects will provide a solid foundation for the specialized knowledge required of a plastics technician. Courses should include mathematics, including one year each of algebra, geometry, and trigonometry, and courses in the laboratory sciences, preferably organic chemistry and physics. English and speech classes

will also help you to hone your communications skills. Mechanical drawing and shop will also be useful.

Postsecondary Training

While still in high school, you should investigate programs offered by community colleges, technical institutes, and vocational-technical schools. Some schools include plastics courses as part of mechanical or chemical technicians programs. Also, an increasing number of colleges offer bachelor's degrees in plastics technology.

A typical two-year curriculum for plastics technicians at a community college includes class, laboratory, and, sometimes, work experience. In the first year, courses typically include introduction to plastics, applied mathematics, compression molding procedures, fabrication of plastics, properties of thermo-plastics, injection molding, and extrusion molding.

Second-year courses typically include reinforced plastics procedures, applied chemistry of plastic materials, dies and molds, thermo-forming, synthetic elastomers, foamed plastics procedures, test procedures, and basic employment information.

Another training option for students is to participate in apprenticeship programs or in-plant training programs while earning a degree. Many companies operate on a three-shift basis; hours can be arranged around students' class schedules. As part of the learning experience, it is possible to participate in cooperative education or work-study programs. This is a joint venture between the school and the industry where students can work a limited number of hours per month and often receive college credit.

Students who plan to enter the military should investigate branches of service that offer training in plastics. The United States Air Force, Navy, Coast Guard, and Army publish procurement specifications, operate repair facilities, and carry on their own research and development.

In the plastics industry, each process requires a specific knowledge. For example, injection molding skills are completely different from those required for laminating. The technician who specializes in compression molding has skills not common to other processes. Certain bodies of knowledge, however, are common to all areas of the plastics industry.

Certification and Licensing

Certification isn't required of plastics technicians, but is available through the Society of the Plastics Industry (SPI). As industry equipment becomes more complex, employers may prefer to hire only certified technicians. To become an NCP Certified Operator, you'll take an exam in one of four areas: blow molding, extrusion, injection molding, or thermoforming. The exam is open to anyone seeking a career in the plastics industry, but you'll likely need at least two years plastics experience to pass the exam.

Other Requirements

You should have good hand-eye coordination and manual dexterity to perform a variety of tasks, especially building laminated structures. You must have normal eyesight; color blindness could be a limitation for those whose work requires color matching or keen color perception. You should also have good communications skills since you must interact with a variety of coworkers including various engineers, chemists, supervisors, designers, estimators, and other technicians. You must be able to follow both oral and written instructions in order to be able to create a product according to precise specifications and demands.

■ Exploring

Films about plastics can be obtained free of charge directly from the materials or machinery manufacturers, from lending libraries, and from professional organizations within the industry.

Through your high school counselor, you can arrange visits to community colleges, vocational-technical schools, and universities that offer technical programs. Tours of laboratories, shops, and classrooms can provide firsthand information on the nature of the courses. Part-time or summer employment at a plastics-production factory is also an option.

■ Employers

Primary plastics producers employ the majority of plastics technicians. A smaller number of technicians will find employment with manufacturers who have in-house plastics departments. Some major employers of plastics technicians in the United States include DuPont, Monsanto, and General Motors. In Canada, most plastics employers are located in Ontario, Quebec, British Columbia, and Alberta.

■ Starting Out

Personnel managers maintain contact with schools that have ongoing plastics programs. Recruiting agents visit graduating technicians to acquaint them with current opportunities.

Experts in various fields are regularly invited to lecture at technical schools and colleges. Their advice and information can provide good ideas about finding entry-level employment.

Student chapters of the Society of Plastics Engineers maintain close ties with the parent organization. Student members receive newsletters and technical journals, and they attend professional seminars. These contacts are invaluable when seeking employment.

Field trips are an important part of the technician's education. Visits to plants and laboratories give students a broad overview of the many manufacturing processes. During these tours, students can observe working conditions and discuss employment possibilities.

■ Advancement

There are excellent opportunities for advancement for well-prepared technicians. Some manufacturers conduct in-plant training programs, and many provide incentives for technicians to continue their education at accredited schools. An employee with sales or customer service potential is trained in various manufacturing aspects before joining the sales or service division. Those with advanced education may become involved in supervisory or management capacities, quality control, purchasing, or cost estimating. Others may become owners of a plastic manufacturing enterprise. Technicians who are especially creative may work hand in hand with customers as designers of products and molds, or as plastics engineers.

Advancement within a company is earned by demonstrating increased technical skill or supervisory ability, together with a willingness to accept added responsibility. In molding plants, technicians advance to positions as supervisors, department heads, assistant managers, and managers. Laboratory technicians advance to positions as supervisors and managers. In the field of reinforced plastics, advanced positions are shop supervisors, quality control supervisors, and training supervisors.

Some of the other positions to which technicians can advance are described as follows:

Product designers create designs for products to be produced from plastics materials. They investigate the practicability of designs in relation to the limitations of plant equipment, cost, probable selling price, and industry specifications. *Plastics engineers* engage in the manufacture, fabrication, and use of existing materials, as well as the development of new materials, processes, and equipment. (For more information on this career, see the article, *Plastics Engineers.*)

Production managers direct the work of various production departments, either directly or through subordinate supervisors. They provide information on new production methods and equipment, problems, and the need for maintenance of all plant machinery and equipment. Production managers work closely with union representatives. *Research and development department managers* direct research studies in the development of new products and manufacturing methods. They are usually in charge of specialized testing and analytical services and of test methods to evaluate conformance to national standards.

Purchasing agents are responsible for overall direction and coordination of buyers who secure raw materials, components, packaging material, office equipment, supplies, machinery, and services for a production complex.

■ Earnings

According to 1997 wage surveys conducted by SPI, machine operators in the plastics industry earn between $16,000 and $22,000 a year. Quality assurance inspectors make around $21,000 a year. Computer-aided design (CAD) specialists earn between $31,000 and $39,500 a year.

Benefits often include paid vacations, health and dental insurance, pension plans, credit union services, production bonuses, stock options, and industry-sponsored education. These benefits will vary with the size and nature of the company.

■ Work Environment

Working conditions that technicians encounter in the plastics field vary greatly. Research or test laboratories are clean, quiet, air-conditioned, and well lighted. Normal business hours are usually observed, although some overtime may be necessary. Some companies operate more than one shift. No more than normal physical strength is required for most of the work in this profession. High safety standards are uniformly observed. Equipment is well maintained to prevent accidents to machine operators. Cleanliness in the workplace is mandatory.

Injection-molding plants are quiet to moderately noisy. Extrusion plants are quiet, clean, and efficient. Machine-heating zones are protected and product take-off or wind-up devices are guarded. Laminating procedures range from clean to extremely messy. Catalysts, solvents, and resins present hazards unless strict precautionary measures are taken to prevent accidents. Compression-molding shops are quiet, safe places to work. Temperatures during the summer can be uncomfortable; molds must be maintained at 300 degrees Fahrenheit.

■ Outlook

The plastics industry encompasses so many employment categories that employment is virtually assured for any qualified graduate of a technical program. Worldwide expansion of this industry is expected to continue through the year 2006. This expansion is expected to create a strong demand for technicians who can meet the challenges of this changing industry. Those who pursue advanced education and who acquire a variety of skills and talents will have the best employment opportunities. More plastics technicians will be needed because of the increasing focus on cheaper and more effective ways of recycling and making other types of plastics biodegradable. Other jobs will arise from the automobile industry changing over many of its

metal parts to plastics. SPI ranks the top plastics industry states by employment: in 1996, the top five states were California, Ohio, Michigan, Illinois, and Texas.

■ For More Information

For a career brochure and information about education and certification, contact:

Society of the Plastics Industry
1801 K Street, NW, Suite 600K
Washington, DC 20006-1301
Tel: 202-974-5200
Web: http://www.socplas.org

The APC is a trade industry that offers a great deal of information about the plastics industry, and maintains an informative Web site:

American Plastics Council
1801 K Street, NW, Suite 701-L
Washington, DC 20006-1301
Tel: 800-243-5790
Web: http://www.plastics.org

For information about scholarships, seminars, and training, contact:

Plastics Institute of America
University of Massachusetts-Lowell
333 Aiken Street
Lowell, MA 01854
Tel: 978-934-3130
Web: http://www.eng.uml.edu/dept/PIA/index.html

For information on student membership, contact:

Society of Plastics Engineers
PO Box 403
Brookfield, CT 06804-0403
Tel: 203-775-0471
Web: http://www.4spe.org

■ Related Articles

Plastics
Chemical Engineers
Chemical Technicians
Chemists
Industrial Engineering Technicians
Industrial Engineers
Metallurgical Engineers
Metallurgical Technicians
Plastics Engineers
Plastics Products Manufacturing Workers

Platemakers

■ **See Prepress Workers**

Play Therapists

■ See Child Life Specialists

Playwrights

■ See Screenwriters

Plumbers and Pipefitters

■ Overview

Plumbers and pipefitters assemble, install, alter, and repair pipes and pipe systems that carry water, steam, air, or other liquids and gases for sanitation and industrial purposes as well as other uses. Plumbers also install plumbing fixtures, appliances, and heating and refrigerating units.

PLUMBERS AND PIPEFITTERS	
SCHOOL SUBJECTS	Chemistry Physics
PERSONAL SKILLS	Following instructions Mechanical/manipulative
WORK ENVIRONMENT	Primarily indoors Primarily multiple locations
MINIMUM EDUCATION LEVEL	Apprenticeship
SALARY RANGE	$19,740 to $28,900 to $38,800
CERTIFICATION OR LICENSING	Required by certain states
OUTLOOK	About as fast as the average
DOT	862
GOE	05.05.03
NOC	7251
O*NET	87502A

■ History

Although the early Egyptians are known to have used lead pipes to carry water and drainage into and out of buildings, the use of plumbing in a citywide system was first achieved in the Roman Empire. In Renaissance times, the techniques of plumbing were revived and used in some of the great castles and monasteries. But, the greatest advances in plumbing were made in the 19th century, when towns grew into cities and the need for adequate public sanitation was recognized.

■ The Job

Because little difference exists between the work of the plumber and the pipefitter in most cases, the two are often considered to be one trade. However, some craftsworkers specialize in one field or the other, especially in large cities.

The work of pipefitters differs from that of plumbers mainly in its location and the variety and size of pipes used. Plumbers work primarily in residential and commercial buildings, whereas pipefitters are generally employed by large industrial concerns—such as oil refineries, refrigeration plants, and defense establishments—where more complex systems of piping are used. Plumbers assemble, install, and repair heating, water, and drainage systems, especially those that must be connected to public utilities systems. Some of their jobs include replacing burst pipes and installing and repairing sinks, bathtubs, water heaters, hot water tanks, garbage disposal units, dishwashers, and water softeners. Plumbers also may work on septic tanks, cesspools, and sewers. During the final construction stages of both commercial and residential buildings, plumbers install heating and air-conditioning units and connect radiators, water heaters, and plumbing fixtures.

Most plumbers follow set procedures in their work. After inspecting the installation site to determine pipe location, they cut and thread pipes, bend them to required angles by hand or machines, and then join them by means of welded, brazed, caulked, soldered, or threaded joints. To test for leaks in the system, they fill the pipes with water or air. Plumbers use a variety of tools, including hand tools such as wrenches, reamers, drills, braces and bits, hammers, chisels, and saws; power machines that cut, bend, and thread pipes; gasoline torches; and welding, soldering, and brazing equipment.

Specialists include *diesel engine pipefitters, steamfitters, ship and boat building coppersmiths, industrial-gas fitters, gas-main fitters, prefab plumbers,* and *pipe cutters.*

■ Requirements

High School

A high school diploma is especially important for getting into a good apprenticeship program. High school preparation should include courses in mathematics, chemistry, and physics, as well as some shop courses.

Postsecondary Training

To qualify as a plumber, a person must complete either a formal apprenticeship or an informal on-the-job training program. To be considered for the apprenticeship program, individuals must pass an examination administered by the state employment agency and have their qualifications approved by the local joint labor-management apprenticeship committee.

The apprenticeship program for plumbers consists of four years of carefully planned activity combining direct training with at least 144 hours of formal classroom instruction each year. The program is designed to give apprentices diversified training by having them work for several different plumbing or pipe-fitting contractors.

On-the-job training, on the other hand, usually consists of working for five or more years under the guidance of an experienced craftsworker. Trainees begin as helpers until they acquire the necessary skills and knowledge for more difficult jobs. Frequently, they supplement this practical training by taking trade (or correspondence) school courses.

Certification or Licensing

A license is required for plumbers in many places. To obtain this license, plumbers must pass a special examination to demonstrate their knowledge of local building codes as well as their all-around knowledge of the trade. To become a plumbing contractor in most places, a master plumber's license must be obtained.

Other Requirements

Those who would be successful and contented plumbers should like to solve a variety of problems and should not object to being called on during evenings, weekends, or holidays to perform emergency repairs. As in most service occupations, plumbers should be able to get along well with all kinds of people. The plumber should be a person who works well alone, but who can also direct the work of helpers and enjoy the company of those in the other construction trades.

■ Exploring

Although opportunities for direct experience in this occupation are rare for those in high school, there are ways to explore the field. Speaking to an experienced plumber or pipefitter will give you a clearer picture of day-to-day work in this field. Pursuing hobbies with a mechanical aspect will help you determine how much you like such hands-on work.

■ Employers

Plumbers generally start out working at local plumbing firms or large industrial facilities. Many plumbers gain experience this way before going into business for themselves.

■ Starting Out

Applicants who wish to become apprentices usually contact local plumbing, heating, and air-conditioning contractors who employ plumbers, the state employment service bureau, or the local branch of the United Association of Journeymen and Apprentices of the Plumbing and Pipe Fitting Industry of the United States and Canada. Individual contractors or contractor associa-

A pipefitter welds two pipes together.

tions often sponsor local apprenticeship programs. Apprentices very commonly go on to permanent employment with the firms with which they apprenticed.

■ Advancement

If plumbers have certain qualities, such as the ability to deal with people and good judgment and planning skills, they may progress to such positions as supervisor or job estimator for plumbing or pipefitting contractors. If they work for a large industrial company, they may advance to the position of job superintendent. Many plumbers go into business for themselves. Eventually they may expand their activities and become contractors, employing other workers.

■ Earnings

The annual median salary for plumbers who are not self-employed is $28,900. Wages vary, however, according to location. Monthly wages for plumbers range from $1,600 to $3,200. Hourly pay rates for apprentices usually start at 50 percent of the experienced worker's rate, and increase by 5 percent every six months until a rate of 95 percent is reached. Benefits for union workers usually include health insurance, sick time, and vacation pay, as well as pension plans.

■ Work Environment

Most plumbers have a regular 40-hour workweek with extra pay for overtime. Unlike most of the other building trades, this field is little affected by seasonal factors. The work of the plumber is active and strenuous. Standing for prolonged periods and working in cramped or uncomfortable positions are often necessary. Possible risks include falls from ladders, cuts from sharp tools, and burns from hot pipes or steam. Working with clogged pipes and toilets can also be smelly.

Outlook

Approximately 30,000 plumbers were employed in the mid-1990s. Employment opportunities for plumbers are expected to increase as fast as the average for all jobs through the year 2006. There are several reasons for this outlook. First and most important is the anticipated increase in construction activity. Second, plumbing and heating work in new homes is expected to include the installation of sprinkler systems, more bathrooms per house, washing machines, waste disposals, air-conditioning equipment, and solar heating devices. Third, because pipework is becoming more important in large industries, more workers will be needed for installation and maintenance work, especially where refrigeration and air-conditioning equipment are used. Fourth, thousands of job openings each year are created by those who leave the field.

For More Information

National Association of Plumbing-Heating-Cooling Contractors
PO Box 6808
180 South Washington Street
Falls Church, VA 22040
Tel: 703-237-8100

United Association of Journeymen and Apprentices of the Plumbing and Pipe Fitting Industry of the United States and Canada
901 Massachusetts Avenue, NW
Washington, DC 20001
Tel: 202-628-5823
Web: http://www.ua.org/

Related Articles

Construction

Heating and Cooling Technicians

Sprinkler Fitters

Podiatrists

Overview

Podiatrists, or doctors of podiatric medicine, are specialists in diagnosing and treating disorders and diseases of the foot and lower leg. The most common problems that they treat are bunions, calluses, corns, warts, ingrown toenails, heel spurs, arch problems, and ankle and foot injuries. Podiatrists also treat deformities and infections. A podiatrist may prescribe treatment by medical, surgical, and mechanical or physical means.

The human foot is a complex structure, containing 26 bones plus muscles, nerves, ligaments, and blood vessels. The 52 total bones in your feet make up about one-fourth of all the bones in your body. Because of the foot's relation to the rest of the body, it may be the first body part to show signs of serious health conditions, such as diabetes or cardiovascular disease. Podiatrists may detect these problems first, making them an important part of the health care team.

History

Doctors who treat feet first began making rounds in larger U.S. cities in the early 1800s. During that century, podiatrists were called chiropodists, after the Greek word "chiropody." Chiropody refers to the study of the hand and foot. Most other physicians and surgeons of that era ignored the treatment of foot disorders.

The first offices devoted exclusively to foot care were established in 1841. The chiropodists of this period had difficulty competing with physicians in the care of ingrown toenails. The law read that a chiropodist had no right to make incisions involving the structures below the true skin. Treatments included removal of corns, warts, calluses, bunions, abnormal nails, and general foot care.

The term *chiropody* was eventually replaced by *podiatry,* likely because chiropody dealt mainly with the foot.

Modern podiatric medicine emerged in the early 1900s. More recently, surgery has become a necessary part of podiatric care. Today, the skills of podiatric physicians are in increasing demand, because foot disorders are among the most common and most often neglected health problems affecting people in the United States.

The Job

Podiatrists provide foot care in private offices, hospitals, ambulatory surgical centers, skilled nursing facilities, and treatment centers or clinics. They also work in the armed forces, government health programs, and on the faculty in health professional schools.

To diagnose a foot problem, the podiatrist may take X rays, perform blood tests, or prescribe other diagnostic tests. A main concern of the podiatrist is to keep people walking by eliminating pain and deformities. The ability to recognize other body disorders is a requirement for a podiatrist, as arthritis or diabetes may first appear in the feet. Circulation problems may also affect the feet first because they are farthest away from the heart's blood supply.

Treatment may involve fitting corrective devices, prescribing drugs and medications, ordering physical therapy, performing surgery, and prescribing corrective footgear.

■ Requirements

High School

High school students should take as many courses in biology, zoology, and inorganic and organic chemistry, and as much physics and math as possible to determine whether they have an interest in this field. The profession requires a scientific aptitude, manual dexterity, a good business sense, and an ability to put patients at ease.

Postsecondary Training

A minimum of 90 semester hours of prepodiatry education is required for entrance into a college of podiatric medicine. Over 90 percent of podiatric students have a bachelor's degree. Undergraduate work should include courses in English, chemistry, biology or zoology, physics, and mathematics.

There are seven accredited colleges offering the four-year course leading to a Doctor of Podiatric Medicine (D.P.M.). All colleges of podiatric medicine require the Medical College Admission Test (MCAT) as part of the application procedure. There is no schooling available in Canada, but an educational packet is available for students by writing to the Ontario Podiatric Medical Association.

The first two years in podiatry school are spent in classroom and laboratory work in anatomy, bacteriology, chemistry, pathology, physiology, pharmacology, and other basic sciences. In the final two years, students gain clinical experience in addition to their academic studies.

To practice in a specialty, podiatrists need an additional one to three years of postgraduate education, usually in the form of an office- or hospital-based residency.

Certification or Licensing

Podiatrists must be licensed in all 50 states, the District of Columbia, and Puerto Rico. A state board examination must be passed to qualify for licensing. Some states allow the exams to be taken during medical podiatric college, from the National Board of Podiatric Examiners, as a substitute for the state boards. About two-thirds of the states require applicants to serve an additional residency of at least one year.

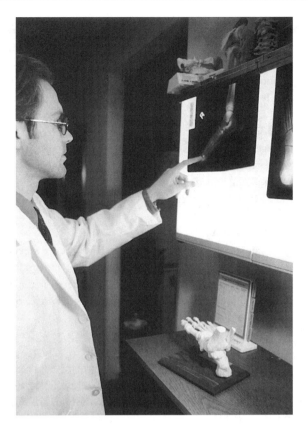

A podiatrist checks an X ray of a patient's foot for a fracture.

Podiatrists may gain certification in one of three specialties: orthopedics, primary medicine, or surgery.

Other Requirements

The podiatrist must have a capacity to understand and apply scientific findings, the skill to manipulate delicate instruments, and, for those with their own practices, good business skills. Most importantly, they should like all kinds of people and have a sincere desire to help those needing care and attention.

■ Exploring

Students interested in podiatric medicine should arrange an interview with a trained podiatrist. To gain experience, they may obtain a summer job or volunteer their time in a clinic specializing in podiatric medicine.

■ Employers

A newly licensed podiatrist might begin working in a multispecialty group, a clinic, a hospital, or in an established solo or group podiatric medical practice. There are jobs for podiatrists in the armed forces, too. Most offices are found in large cities. The majority of podiatrists set up practices in the seven states where the colleges of podiatry are located (California, Florida, Illinois, Iowa, New York, Pennsylvania, and Ohio). Other states with a high number of podiatrists are New Jersey, Massachusetts, Michigan, and Texas.

■ Starting Out

College placement offices are usually the place to start the job search. Checking the classifieds in professional journals and applying directly to area clinics and practices are other ways to uncover job leads.

■ Advancement

Most podiatrists provide all types of foot care. However, some specialize in such areas as surgery (foot and ankle), orthopedics (bone, muscle, and joint disorders), podopediatrics (children's foot ailments), or podogeriatrics (foot disorders of the elderly).

■ Earnings

Podiatrists in well-established practices have incomes comparable to those earned by other well-paid professionals. For newly licensed podiatrists who have been in full-time practice for at least two years, the average income in 1997 was $61,000, according to the American Podiatric Medical Association. The association reported that median net income of podiatrists with 10 to 15 years of experience was $135,000.

■ Work Environment

Most podiatrists work independently in their own offices or in a group practice. The workweek is generally 40 to 44 hours per week. Podiatrists usually can set their own hours to coordinate office hours with hospital staff time or teaching schedules.

■ Outlook

In 1996, there were approximately 13,000 practicing podiatrists in the United States, according to the American Podiatric Medical Association.

Demand for podiatrists' skills is rapidly increasing, as the profession gains recognition as a health care specialty and as foot disorders become more widespread. More people are involved in sports and fitness programs, which can cause foot problems or make existing foot problems more apparent or unbearable. Also, a rapidly growing aging population, many of whom may have neglected their feet, will seek podiatric care. The demand for podiatric services is expected to grow even more as health insurance coverage for such care becomes widespread. Although foot care is not ordinarily covered by health insurance, Medicare and private insurance programs frequently cover acute medical and surgical foot services, as well as diagnostic X rays, frac-

ture casts, and leg braces. Many HMOs and other prepaid plans provide routine foot care as well.

The outlook for podiatrists through the year 2006 is favorable throughout the country, but especially in the South and Southwest, where a shortage of practitioners exists.

Competition for residency positions is strong. If a state's licensing board requires residency, as two-thirds of the states currently do, it must be done before a podiatrist can begin practicing. With the heavy competition for these posts, it is unlikely that students with average grades will be able to secure employment in those states.

■ For More Information

For education and career information, contact the following organizations.

American Association of Colleges of Podiatric Medicine
1350 Piccard Drive, Suite 322
Rockville, MD 20850-4307
Tel: 301-990-6882
Web: http://www.aacpm.org

American Board of Podiatric Surgery
1601 Dolores Street
San Francisco, CA 94110-4906
Tel: 415-826-4640

American Podiatric Medical Association
9312 Old Georgetown Road
Bethesda, MD 20814-1621
Tel: 301-571-9200
Web: http://www.apma.org

Medical College Admission Test Program Office
PO Box 4056
2255 North Dubuque Road
Iowa City, IA 52243-4056
Tel: 319-337-1357

Canadian Podiatric Medical Association
45 Sheppard Avenue East, Suite 900
North York, ON M2N 5W9 Canada
Tel: 416-927-9111 or 888-220-3338

■ Related Articles

Health Care
Chiropractors
Dentists
Orthotists and Prosthetists
Physical Therapists
Physicians

Poets

■ **See Literary Arts, Writers**

Pointing-Machine Operators

■ See Plastics Products Manufacturing Workers

Police Clerks

■ See Office Clerks

Police Officers

■ Overview

Police officers perform many duties relating to public safety. Their responsibilities include not only preserving the peace, preventing criminal acts, enforcing the law, investigating crimes, and arresting those who violate the law but also directing traffic, community relations work, and controlling crowds at public events. Police officers are employed at the federal, state, county, and city level.

State police officers patrol highways and enforce the laws and regulations that govern the use of those highways, in addition to performing general police work. Police officers are under oath to uphold the law 24-hours a day.

■ History

People have historically sought some form of protection for their lives and property and to help preserve their welfare. The true origins of police work, however, are virtually unknown. In medieval times, feudal lords employed retainers who made sure taxes were paid. These employees may have attempted to maintain some kind of law and order among the people, but at the same time, they were employed by the lords and often merely enforced their employers' wishes.

Colonial America followed the British form of police organization. A sheriff, appointed by the governor of a colony, enforced laws, collected taxes, and maintained public property throughout the colony. Constables performed similar duties in the cities and towns. Night watchmen protected the cities from fires and crime. However, as cities grew rapidly during the 19th century, a larger, more organized police service was needed to control growing problems with crimes and public disturbances.

In 1829 in London, Sir Robert Peel established the first modern, nonmilitary police force. The British police became known as *bobbies* after Sir Robert's name. The police force in New York City was established in 1844. These new police forces wore uniforms, worked 24-hours a day, and often carried guns. They patrolled the streets and soon became a fixture in many cities. On the American frontier, however, laws were often enforced by volunteer police officers until regular police forces were established. Many areas of the West were guarded by a sheriff and the sheriff's deputies. An early effort to create a statewide police force resulted in the creation of the Texas Rangers in 1835. In 1905, Pennsylvania formed the first official state police departments. Soon, almost every state had a state police department as well as those police units that worked for individual cities or towns.

These early police efforts were often notoriously inadequate. Many police departments were seats of corruption and abuse of authority. Police officers were generally untrained and were often appointed as agents serving the political machine of their city, rather than the people. Efforts to clean up the police departments began in the early decades of the 20th century. Police were expected to be professionals. Higher selection standards and special training programs were instituted, and efforts were made to eliminate the influence of politics on the police department. Command of the police department soon became more centralized, with a chief of police supervising the operations of the entire department. Other ranks were created, such as sergeant and detective. At the same time, scientists working with the police were developing scientific advances in crime detection and prevention, such as fingerprinting.

Today, every state has uniformed police. About one-fourth of the states restrict their officers to the enforcement of laws and regulations governing the operation of motor vehicles and the use of highways. State police operations are customarily confined to unincorporated areas as a matter of policy, although a few states restrict them by statute. In addition, police operate at the federal level in such agencies as the Federal Bureau of Investigation, the Immigration and Naturaliza-

POLICE OFFICERS	
SCHOOL SUBJECTS	Physical education Psychology
PERSONAL SKILLS	Leadership/ management
WORK ENVIRONMENT	Indoors and outdoors Primarily multiple locations
MINIMUM EDUCATION LEVEL	High school diploma
SALARY RANGE	$19,200 to $34,700 to $58,500+
CERTIFICATION OR LICENSING	None
OUTLOOK	About as fast as the average
DOT	375
GOE	04.01.02
NOC	6261
O*NET	271998

A police officer writes up a field report on her laptop computer.

tion Service, and the Drug Enforcement Agency. While the many types of police forces operate independently, they often cooperate to provide more effective law enforcement.

■ The Job

If police officers patrol a beat or work in small communities, their duties may be many and varied. In large city departments, their work may be highly specialized.

Depending on the orders they receive from their commanding officers, police may direct traffic during the rush-hour periods and at special events when traffic is unusually heavy. They may patrol public places such as parks, streets, and public gatherings to maintain law and order. Police are sometimes called upon to prevent or break up riots and to act as escorts at funerals, parades, and other public events. They may administer first aid in emergency situations, assist in rescue operations of various kinds, investigate crimes, issue tickets to violators of traffic or parking laws or other regulations, or arrest drunk drivers. Officers in small towns may have to perform all these duties and administrative work as well.

As officers patrol their assigned beats, either on foot, bicycle, horseback, or in cars, they must be alert for any situations that arise and be ready to take appropriate action. Many times they must be alert to identify stolen cars, identify and locate lost children, and identify and apprehend escaped criminals and others wanted by various law enforcement agencies. While on patrol, they keep in constant contact with headquarters and their fellow officers by calling in regularly on two-way radios. Although their profession may at times be dangerous, police officers are trained not to endanger their own lives or the lives of ordinary citizens. If they need assistance, they radio for additional officers.

In large city police departments, officers usually have more specific duties and specialized assignments. The police departments generally are comprised of special work divisions such as communications, criminal investigation, firearms identification, fingerprint identification and forensic science, accident prevention, and administrative services. In very large cities, police departments may have special work units such as the harbor patrol, canine corps, mounted police, vice squad, fraud or bunco squad, traffic control, records control, and rescue units. A few of the job titles for these specialties are identification and records commanders and officers, narcotics and vice detectives or investigators, homicide squad commanding officers, detective chiefs, traffic lieutenants, sergeants, parking enforcement officers, public safety officers, accident-prevention squad officers, safety instruction police officers, and community relations lieutenants.

In very large city police departments, officers may fill positions as police chiefs, precinct sergeants and captains, desk officers, booking officers, police inspectors, identification officers, complaint evaluation supervisors and officers, crime prevention police officers. Some officers work as plainclothes detectives in criminal investigation divisions. *Internal affairs investigators* are employed to police the police. Other specialized police officers include police reserves commanders; *police officer commanding officers III,* who act as supervisors in missing persons and fugitive investigations; and *police officers III,* who investigate and pursue nonpayment and fraud fugitives. Many police departments employ *police clerks,* who perform administrative and community-oriented tasks.

A major responsibility for state police officers (sometimes known as *state troopers* or *highway patrol officers*) is to patrol the highways and enforce the laws and regulations of those traveling on them. Riding in patrol cars equipped with two-way radios, they monitor traffic for troublesome or dangerous situations. They write traffic tickets and issue warnings to drivers who are violating traffic laws or otherwise not observing safe driving practices. They radio for assistance for drivers who are stopped because of breakdowns, flat tires, illnesses, or other reasons. They direct traffic around congested areas caused by fires, road repairs, accidents, and other emergencies. They may check the weight of commercial vehicles to verify that they are within allowable limits, conduct driver examinations, or give safety information to the public.

In case of a highway accident, officers take charge of the activities at the site by directing traffic, giving first aid to any injured parties, and calling for emergency equipment such as ambulances, fire trucks, or tow trucks. They write up a report to be used by investigating officers who attempt to determine the cause of the accident.

In addition to these responsibilities, state police officers in most states do some general police work. They are often the primary law-enforcement agency in communities or counties that have no police force or a large sheriff's department. In those areas, they may investigate such crimes as burglary and assault. They also may assist municipal or county police in capturing lawbreakers or control civil disturbances.

Most police officers are trained in the use of firearms and carry guns. Police in special divisions, such as chemical analysis and handwriting and fingerprint identification, have special training to perform their work. Police officers often testify in court regarding cases with which they have been involved. Police personnel are required to complete accurate and thorough records of their cases.

■ Requirements

High School

The majority of police departments today require that applicants have a high school education. Although a high school diploma is not always required, related work experience is generally required.

High school students who are interested in pursuing this career will find the subjects of psychology, sociology, English, law, mathematics, U.S. government and history, chemistry, and physics most helpful. Because physical stamina is very important in this work, sports and physical education are also valuable. Knowledge of a foreign language is especially helpful, and bilingual officers are often in great demand. High school students interested in specialized and advanced positions in law enforcement should pursue studies leading to college programs in criminology, criminal law, criminal psychology, or related areas.

Postsecondary Training

The best chance for advancement, however, is for officers with some postsecondary education, and many police departments now require a 2-year or 4-year degree, especially for more specialized areas of police work. There are more than 800 junior colleges and universities offering 2-year and 4-year degree programs in law enforcement. The armed forces also offer training and opportunities in law enforcement that can be applied to civilian police work.

Newly recruited police officers must pass a special training program. After training, they are usually placed on a probationary period lasting from three to six months. In small towns and communities, training may be given on the job by working with an experienced officer. Inexperienced officers are never sent out on patrol alone but are always accompanied by veteran officers.

Large city police departments give classroom instruction in laws, accident investigation, city ordinances, and traffic

GLOSSARY

Adam codes: Codes used by some during radio communications to describe types of calls. For example, A1 means arrest, A20 means assistance rendered, and A63 means pursuit.
Probable cause: Information developed by an officer to give a reason to arrest, search, or stop and detain a person.
Reasonable suspicion: The reasons an officer believes a person should be stopped and detained.

control. These departments also give instruction in the handling of firearms, methods of apprehension and arrest, self-defense tactics, and first-aid techniques. Both state and municipal police officers are trained in safe driving procedures and maneuvering an automobile at high speeds.

Other Requirements

Police job appointments in most large cities and in many smaller cities and towns are governed by local civil service regulations. Applicants are required to pass written tests designed to measure the candidates' intelligence and general aptitude for police work. Physical examinations are required and usually include tests of physical agility, dexterity, and strength. Candidates' personal histories, backgrounds, and character undergo careful scrutiny because honesty and law-abiding characteristics are essential traits for law-enforcement officers. An important requirement is that the prospective police officer has no arrest record.

Applicants must be at least 21 years of age (or older for some departments), and some municipalities stipulate an age limit of not more than 35 years. Candidates must have, in most cases, 20/20 uncorrected vision, good hearing, and weight proportionate to their height. Applicants must meet locally prescribed weight and height rules for their gender. Most regulations require that applicants be U.S. citizens, and many police departments have residency requirements.

Prospective police officers should enjoy working with people and be able to cooperate with others. Because of the stressful nature of much police work, police officers must be able to think clearly and logically during emergency situations, have a strong degree of emotional control, and be capable of detaching themselves from incidents.

Physical fitness training is a mandatory, continuing activity in most police departments, as are routine physical examinations. Police officers can have no physical disabilities that would prevent them from carrying out their duties.

■ Exploring

A good way to explore police work is to talk with various law enforcement officers. Most departments have community outreach programs and many have recruiting programs as well. Students may also wish to visit colleges offering programs in police work or write for information on their training programs.

In some cases, high school graduates can explore this occupation by seeking employment as police cadets in large city police departments. These cadets are paid employees who work part time in clerical and other duties. They attend training courses in police science on a part-time basis. When they reach the age of 21, they are eligible to apply for regular police work. Some police departments also hire college students as interns.

■ Employers

Most police officers work for local governments, with some finding employment with a state department, and a small percentage working for a federal agency. The United States has more than 18,000 municipal police agencies, 3,000 county sheriff departments, and 1,200 state and federal police agencies. In the 1990s, local police departments employed about 604,000 full-time sworn police officers with general arrest powers. Large cities each employ thousands of police officers. In 1997, New York had 31,000 police officers, and Chicago employed nearly 13,000 police officers.

■ Starting Out

Applicants interested in police work should apply directly to local civil service offices or examining boards to qualify as a candidate for police officer. In some locations, written examinations may be given to groups at specified times. In smaller communities that do not follow civil service methods, applicants should apply directly to the police department or city government offices in the communities where they reside. Those interested in becoming state police officers may apply directly to their state civil service commissions or state police headquarters, which are usually located in the state capital.

■ Advancement

Advancement in these occupations is determined by several factors. An officer's eligibility for promotion may depend on a specified length of service, job performance, formal education and training courses, and results of written examinations. Those who become eligible for promotion are listed on the promotional list along with other qualified candidates. Promotions generally become available from six months to three years after starting, depending on the department. As positions of different or higher rank become open, candidates are promoted to fill them according to their position on the list. Lines of promotion usually begin with officer third grade and progress to grade two and grade one. Other possible promotional opportunities include the ranks of detective, sergeant, lieutenant, or captain. Many promotions require additional training

and testing. Advancement to the very top-ranking positions, such as division, bureau, or department director or chief, may be made by direct political appointment. Most of these top positions are held by officers who have come up through the ranks.

Large city police departments offer the greatest number of advancement opportunities. Most of the larger departments maintain separate divisions, which require administration workers, line officers, and more employees in general at each rank level. Officers may move into areas that they find challenging, such as criminal investigation or forensics.

Most city police departments offer various types of in-service study and training programs. These programs allow police departments to keep up-to-date on the latest police science techniques and are often required for those who want to be considered for promotion. Training courses are provided by police academies, colleges, and other educational institutions. Some of the subjects offered are civil defense, foreign languages, and forgery detection. Some municipal police departments share the cost with their officers or pay all educational expenses if the officers are willing to work toward a college degree in either police work or police administration. Independent study is also often required.

Intensive 12-week administrative training courses are offered by the National Academy of the Federal Bureau of Investigation in Washington, DC. A limited number of officers are selected to participate in this training program.

Advancement opportunities on police forces in small communities are considerably more limited by the rank and number of police personnel needed. Other opportunities for advancement may be found in related police, protective, and security service work with private companies, state and county agencies, and other institutions.

■ Earnings

According to the U.S. Department of Labor, police officers in 1996 earned an annual average salary of $34,700; the lowest 10 percent earned less than $19,200 a year, while the highest 10 percent earned over $58,500 annually. Police officers in supervisory positions earned median salaries of $41,200 a year in 1996, with a low of $22,500 and a high of over $64,500. Sheriffs and other law enforcement officers earned median annual salaries of $26,700 in 1996. Salaries for police officers range widely based on geographic location. Police departments in the West and North generally pay more than those in the South.

Most police officers receive periodic and annual salary increases up to a limit set for their rank and length of service. Police departments generally pay special compensation to cover the cost of uniforms. They usually provide any equipment required such as firearms and handcuffs.

Overtime pay may be given for certain work shifts or emergency duty. In these instances, officers are usually paid straight or time-and-a-half pay, while extra time off is sometimes given as compensation.

Because most police officers are civil service employees, they receive generous benefits, including health insurance and paid vacation and sick leave, and enjoy increased job security. In addition, most police departments offer retirement plans and retirement after 20 or 25 years of service, usually at half pay.

■ Work Environment

Police officers work under many different types of circumstances. Much of their work may be performed outdoors, as they ride in patrol cars or walk the beats assigned to them. In emergency situations, no consideration can be made for weather conditions, time of day or night, or day of the week. Police officers may be on call 24 hours a day; even when they are not on duty, they are usually required by law to respond to emergencies or criminal activity. Although they are assigned regular work hours, individuals in police work must be willing to live by an unpredictable and often erratic work schedule. The work demands constant mental and physical alertness as well as great physical strength and stamina.

Police work generally consists of an eight-hour day and a five-day week, but police officers may work night and weekend shifts and on holidays. Emergencies may add many extra hours to an officer's day or week. The occupation is considered dangerous. Some officers are killed or wounded while performing their duties. Their work can involve unpleasant duties and expose them to sordid, depressing, or dangerous situations. They may be called on to deal with all types of people under many types of circumstances. While the routine of some assigned duties may become boring, the dangers of police work are often stressful for the officers and their families. Police work in general holds the potential for the unknown and unexpected, and most people who pursue this work have a strong passion for and commitment to police work.

■ Outlook

Employment of police officers is expected to increase about as fast as the average for all occupations through the year 2006. Federal "tough-on-crime" legislation passed in the mid-1990s has created a short-term increase of new jobs in police departments at the federal, state, and local levels.

The opportunities that become available, however, may be affected by technological, scientific, and other changes occurring today in police work. Automation in traffic control is limiting the number of officers needed in this area, while the increasing reliance on computers throughout society is creating demands for new kinds of police work.

New approaches in social science and psychological research are also changing the methodology used in working with public offenders. These trends indicate a future demand for more educated, specialized personnel.

This occupation has a very low turnover rate. However, new positions will open as current officers retire, leave the force, or move into higher positions. Retirement ages are relatively low in police work compared to other occupations. Many officers retire while in their forties and then pursue a second career. In response to increasing crime rates, some police departments across the country are expanding the number of patrol officers; however, budget problems faced by many municipalities may limit growth.

In the past decade, private security firms have begun to take over some police activities such as patrolling airports and other public places. Some private companies have even been contracted to provide police forces for some cities. Many companies and universities also operate their own police forces.

■ For More Information

The educational arm of the American Federation of Police and the National Association of Chiefs of Police, the American Police Academy compiles statistics, operates a placement service and a speaker's bureau, and offers home study programs.

American Police Academy
1000 Connecticut Avenue, NW, Suite 9
Washington, DC 20036
Tel: 202-293-9088

NPOAA maintains a speaker's bureau, conducts educational programs, and offers both recognition and scholarship awards. For more information, contact:

National Police Officers Association of America
PO Box 22129
Louisville, KY 40252-0129
Tel: 800-467-6762

NULEOA compiles statistics, operates a hotline, hall of fame, and speaker's bureau, offers children's services, and sponsors competitions and scholarships:

National United Law Enforcement Officers Association
256 East McLemore Avenue
Memphis, TN 38106
Tel: 800-533-4649

■ Related Articles

Law

Public Safety

Bodyguards

Border Patrol Officers

Bounty Hunters

Corrections Officers

Crime Analysts

Cryptographic Technicians

Customs Officials

Deputy U.S. Marshals

Detectives

FBI Agents

Forensic Experts

Health and Regulatory Inspectors

Intelligence Officers

National Park Service Employees

Occupational Safety and Health Workers

Park Rangers

Parole Officers

Polygraph Examiners

Process Servers

Secret Service Special Agents

Security Consultants and Technicians

Political Consultants

■ See Press Secretaries

Political Scientists

■ Overview

Political scientists study the structure and theory of government, usually as part of an academic faculty. They are constantly seeking both theoretical and practical solutions to political problems. They divide their responsibilities between teaching and researching. After compiling facts, statistics, and other research, they present their analysis in reports, lectures, and journal articles.

■ History

Political science is the oldest of the social sciences and is currently one of the most popular subjects of undergraduate study. In your first political science courses, you'll learn about some of the people who influenced current political theories: Machiavelli, the 16th-century Italian statesman and philosopher, believed that politics and morality are two entirely different spheres of human activity and that they should be governed by different standards and different laws; in the 17th century, Thomas Hobbes thought of government as a police force which prevented people from plundering their neighbors; John Locke was a 17th-century Englishman from whom we get the philosophy of "the greatest good for the greatest number." Some people call him the originator of "beneficent paternalism," which

means that the state or ruler acts as a kindly leader to citizens, deciding what is best for them, then seeing that the "best" is put into effect, whether the citizens like it or not.

Common among theorists today is the assumption that politics is a process, the constant interaction of individuals and groups in activities that are directly or indirectly related to government. By 1945, political science in the United States was much more than the concern for institutions, law, formal structures of public government, procedures, and rules. It had expanded to include the dynamics of public governance. Instead of studying the rules of administrative procedure in a political group, for example, political scientists had begun to study the actual bureaucratic processes at work within the group. This signified a turning from formality and the start of what would become systems theory in political science.

■ The Job

If pursuing a career in political science, you'd better be prepared to hit the books. While many government careers involve taking action that directly effects political policy, political scientists study and discuss the results of these actions. "You can look into just about anything that interests you," says Chris Mooney, an associate professor and director of graduate studies for the political science department of West Virginia University, "but you have to be able to argue that it's relevant to some basic theory in political science." In addition to his teaching responsibilities, Mooney is currently researching the reasons why some states have the death penalty. You may choose to research political lyrics in rock music, or study how teenagers form their political ideas. You may research the history of women in politics, the role of religion in politics, and the political histories of other countries. Many political scientists specialize in one area of study, such as public administration, history of political ideas, political parties, public law, American government, or international relations.

About 80 percent of all political scientists are employed as college and university professors. Depending on the institution for which you work, you'll be dividing your time between teaching and researching. Mooney estimates that 45 percent of his time is devoted to teaching, 45 percent to research, and the remaining time is for service to the university, such as committee work. Though he works for a research-oriented university, "teaching drives everything," he says.

In addition to teaching and researching, you'll be writing books and articles based on your studies. A number of political science associations publish journals, and there are small presses devoted to publishing political theory. Mooney has published two books, and many scholarly articles in such journals as *Policy Studies Journal, Health Economics*, and the *American Journal of Political Science.*

His area of study is behavioral political science. For his current study of the death penalty, he is compiling economic, social, and demographic facts. This data is then fed into the computer, and Mooney attempts to draw some conclusions. Sometimes graduate students are involved with the research; they assist with the collection of data, computer work, and copy editing.

In researching policy issues, you'll use a variety of different methods. You'll work with historians, economists, and policy analysts. You'll work with demographers and statisticians. The Internet has become a very important resource tool for political scientists. The federal government has been dedicated to expanding the World Wide Web; this has included making available full text of legislation, recent Supreme Court decisions, and access to the Library of Congress. You'll also use the data found in yearbooks and almanacs, material from encyclopedias, clippings from periodicals or bound volumes of magazines or journals. You'll refer to law books, to statutes, to records of court cases, to the *Congressional Record*, and to other legislative records. You'll consult census records, historical documents, personal documents such as diaries and letters, and statistics from public opinion polls. You'll use libraries and archives to locate rare and old documents and records. For other information, you'll use the "participant observer" method of research. In this method, you become part of a group and participate in its proceedings, while carefully observing interaction. You may also submit questionnaires. Questions will be carefully worded to elicit the facts needed, and the questionnaire will be administered to a selected sample of people.

When conducting research, you must avoid letting your own biases distort the way in which you interpret the gathered facts. Then, you must compare your findings and analysis with those of others who have conducted similar investigations. Finally, you must present the data in an objective fashion, even though the findings may not reveal the kinds of facts you anticipated.

Those political scientists who are not employed as teachers work for labor unions, political organizations, or political interest groups. Political scientists working for government may study organizations ranging in scope from the United Nations to local city councils. They may study the politics of a large city like New York or a small town in the Midwest. Their research findings may be used by a city's mayor and city council to set public policy concerning waste management or by an organization, such as the National Organization for Women, to decide where to focus efforts on increasing the participation of women in local politics. Political scientists who work for the U.S. Department of State in either this country or in the foreign service use their analyses of political structures to make recommendations to the U.S. government concerning foreign policy.

Political scientists may also be employed by individual members of Congress. In this capacity, they might study government programs concerned with low-income housing and make recommendations to help the member of Congress write new legislation. Businesses and industries also hire political scientists to conduct polls on political issues that affect their operations. A tobacco company might want to know, for example, how the legislation restricting advertising by tobacco companies affects the buying habits of consumers of tobacco products.

■ Requirements

High School

Take courses in government, American history, and civics to gain insight into politics. Math is also important because, as a political scientist, you'll be evaluating statistics, demographics, and other numerical data. English and composition classes will help you develop the writing and communication skills you'll need for teaching, publishing, and presenting papers. Take a journalism course and work for your high school newspaper to develop research, writing, and editing skills. On a speech and debate team, you'll be researching current events, analyzing data, and presenting the information to others.

Postsecondary Training

Though you'll be able to find some government jobs with a bachelor's degree in political science, you won't be able to pursue work in major academic institutions without a doctorate. The American Political Science Association (APSA) publishes directories of undergraduate and graduate political science programs. An undergraduate program requires general courses in English, economics, statistics, and history, as well as courses in American politics, international politics, and political theory. Look for a

POLITICAL SCIENTISTS	
SCHOOL SUBJECTS	Government Sociology
PERSONAL SKILLS	Communication/ideas Helping/teaching
WORK ENVIRONMENT	Primarily indoors Primarily one location
MINIMUM EDUCATION LEVEL	Doctorate
SALARY RANGE	$39,000 to $47,000 to $85,000
CERTIFICATION OR LICENSING	None available
OUTLOOK	Little change or more slowly than the average
DOT	051
GOE	11.03.02
NOC	4169

school with a good internship program that can involve you with the U.S. Congress or state legislature.

U.S. News and World Report publishes an annual ranking of graduate schools; top-ranked political science departments include Harvard, University of Michigan-Ann Arbor, University of Chicago, and Duke University. Your graduate study will include courses in political parties, public opinion, comparative political behavior, and foreign policy design. You'll also assist professors with research, attend conferences, write articles, and teach undergraduate courses.

Other Requirements

Because you'll be compiling information from a number of different sources, you must be well-organized. You should also enjoy reading, and possess a curiosity about world politics. "You have to really enjoy school," Mooney says, "but it should all be fairly fascinating. You'll be studying and telling people about what you're studying." People skills are important, as you'll be working closely with students and other political scientists.

■ Exploring

Write to college political science departments for information about their programs. You can learn a lot about the work of a political scientist by looking at college course lists and faculty bios. Political science departments also have Web pages with information, and links to the curriculum vitae of faculty. A *curriculum vitae*, or c.v., is an extensive resume including lists of publications, conferences attended, and other professional experience. A c.v. can give you an idea of a political scientist's career and education path.

Contact the office of your state's senator or representative in the U.S. Congress about applying to work as a page. Available to students at least 16 years old, and highly competitive, these page positions allow students to serve members of Congress, running messages across Capitol Hill in Washington, DC. This experience would be very valuable to you in learning about the workings of government.

■ Employers

Political science is one of the most popular majors among undergraduates, so practically every college and university has a political science department. You'll find work at public and private universities, and at community colleges. You'll be teaching in undergraduate, master's, and doctoral programs. The teaching jobs at doctoral institutions are usually better-paying and more prestigious. The *U.S. News and World Report* ranking can give you an idea of the most respected schools in the country. The most sought-after positions are those that offer tenure.

■ Starting Out

"Go to the best school you can," Mooeny advises, "and focus on getting into a good graduate school." Most graduate schools accept a very limited number of applicants every semester, so there's a lot of competition for admittance into some of the top programs. Applicants are admitted on the basis of grade point averages, test scores, internships performed, awards received, and other achievements. Once you're in graduate school, you'll begin to perform the work you'll be doing in your career; you'll teach undergraduate classes, attend conferences, present papers, and submit articles to political science journals. Your success as a graduate student will help you in your job search. After completing a graduate program, you'll teach as an adjunct professor or visiting professor at various schools until you can find a permanent "tenure-track" position. Membership in APSA and other political science associations entitles you to job placement assistance. APSA can also direct you to a number of fellowship and grant opportunities. Michigan State University posts job openings on its H-Net (Humanities and Social Sciences Online) Web page at http://www.matrix.msu.edu/jobs. Due to the heavy competition for these jobs, you'll need an impressive curriculum vitae, including a list of publications in respected political science journals, a list of conferences attended, and good references attesting to your teaching skills.

■ Advancement

In a "tenure-track" position, you'll work your way up through the ranks from assistant professor, to associate professor, to full professor. You'll probably have to work a few years in temporary, or visiting, faculty positions before you can join the permanent faculty of a political science department. You can then expect to spend approximately seven years working toward tenure. Tenure provides job security and prominence within your department, and is awarded on the basis of publications, research performed, student evaluations, and teaching experience.

■ Earnings

Both the *Chronicle of Higher Education* and the American Association of University Professors (AAUP) conduct annual surveys of the salaries of college professors. With the 1998 survey, the *Chronicle* found that full professors at public universities received an average of $69,924 a year, while professors at private universities received $84,970 a year. Associate professors received an average of $50,186 annually at public universities, and $56,517 at private. For assistant professors, the average salaries were $42,335 public and $47,387 private.

The AAUP's 1998 survey found that salary levels had increased from the previous year, but remain 4.4 percent lower than 25 years ago, when figures are adjusted for inflation. And professors earn 42 percent less than those in comparable professions. The AAUP survey found that professors in doctoral institutions made an average of $61,816 a year, compared to $50,243 for those in master's institutions, and $45,163 for those in four-year institutions. Professors working in the Western Pacific states, such as California and Oregon, earned the most, followed by those working in New England. The survey found the average pay to be the lowest in such southern states as Alabama, Kentucky, and Mississippi.

■ Work Environment

As a faculty member in a tenured position, you'll work in pleasant surroundings. Depending on the size of the department, you'll have your own office and be provided with a computer, Internet access, and research assistants. With good teaching skills, you'll earn the respect of your students and colleagues. Political science professors are also well-respected in their communities.

You'll work a fairly flexible schedule, teaching two or three courses a semester. The rest of your 40- to 50-hour workweek will be spent meeting individually with students, conducting research, writing, and serving on committees. Some travel may be required, as you attend a few conferences a year on behalf of your department, or as you take short-term assignments at other institutions. You may teach some courses in the summer, or have the summer off. You'll also have several days off between semesters.

■ Outlook

The survival of political science departments depends on continued community and government support of education. The funding of humanities and social science programs is often threatened, resulting in budget cuts and hiring freezes. This makes for heavy competition for the few graduate assistantships and new faculty positions avail-

able. Also, there's not a great deal of mobility within the field; professors who achieve tenure generally stay in their positions until retirement.

The pay inequity between male and female professors is of some concern. In the workplace in general, women are paid less than men, but this inequity is even greater in the field of academics. The American Association of University Professors is fighting to correct this, and female professors are becoming more cautious when choosing tenure-track positions.

More and more professors are using computers and the Internet, not just in research, but in conducting their classes. According to an annual survey conducted by the Campus Computing Project, computer and CD-ROMs are used increasingly in the lecture hall, and many professors use Web pages to post class materials and other resources.

■ For More Information

The American Political Science Association has over 13,000 members. For more information on a political science career, contact:

American Political Science Association
1527 New Hampshire Avenue, NW
Washington, DC 20036
Tel: 202-483-2512
Web: http://www.apsanet.org

■ Related Articles

Government

Ambassadors

Congressional Aides

Federal and State Officials

Foreign Service Officers

Lobbyists

Press Secretaries

Regional and Local Officials

Pollution Control Technicians

■ Overview

Pollution control technicians, also known as *environmental technicians,* conduct tests and field investigations to obtain samples and data required by engineers, scientists, and others to clean up, monitor, control, or prevent pollution. They apply principles and methods of engineering, chemistry, meteorology, agriculture, or other disciplines in their work. A pollution control technician usually specializes in air, water, or soil pollution.

■ History

Stricter pollution control regulations of the mid-1960s to early 1970s created a job market for pollution control technicians. As regulations on industry have become more stringent, the job of pollution control technician has grown both in number and in scope. For centuries, the biosphere—the self-regulating "envelope" of air, water, and land in which all life on earth exists—was generally able to scatter, break down, or adapt all the wastes and pollution produced by people.

This began to change drastically with the Industrial Revolution. Begun in England in the 1750s, the Industrial Revolution was the shift from a farming society to an industrialized society. Although it had many economic benefits, it took a terrible toll on the environment. Textile manufacturing and then iron processing spread through England, and coal-powered mills, machines, and factories spewed heavy black smoke into the air. Rivers and lakes became open sewers as factories dumped their wastes anywhere. By the 19th century, areas with high population density and clusters of factories were experiencing markedly higher death and disease rates than areas with little industrial development.

The Industrial Revolution spread all over the world, including France in the 1830s, Germany in the 1850s, the

United States after the Civil War, Asia (especially Japan), beginning at the turn of the century, and Russia, beginning after the Russian Revolution of 1917. Wherever industry took hold, there were warning signs that the biosphere could not handle the resulting pollution. Smog hung over large cities with many factories. Residents experienced more respiratory and other health problems. Manufacturing wastes and untreated sewage poisoned surface waters and underground sources of water, affecting drinking-water supplies and increasing disease. Wastes and pollution also seeped into soil, affecting crops.

After World War II, the development of new synthetic materials including plastics, pesticides, and other substances that were more toxic or more difficult to degrade (break down) worsened pollution problems. So did vehicle exhaust. Fish and wildlife were dying; rivers and lakes were choked with chemicals and wastes. Scientists documented connections between pollution and birth defects, cancer, fertility problems, genetic damage, and many other serious problems.

Not until the mid-1960s to early 1970s did public outcry, environmental activism, and political and economic necessity force the passage of stricter pollution control laws. Federal environmental legislation mandated cleanups of existing air, water, and soil pollution, and began to limit the type and amount of polluting substances that industry could release to the environment. Manufacturers began to be required to operate within strict guidelines for air emissions, process-wastewater treatment and disposal, and other polluting activities. States and municipalities also were given increasing responsibilities for monitoring and working to reduce levels of auto, industrial, and other pollution. Out of the need to meet these new requirements, the U.S. pollution control industry was born—and with it, the job of pollution control technician.

■ The Job

Technicians usually specialize in one aspect of pollution control and are categorized as water pollution control technicians, air pollution control technicians, or soil pollution control technicians. Sampling, monitoring, and testing are the major activities of the job. No matter what the specialty, pollution control technicians work largely for or with government agencies that regulate pollution by industry.

Increasingly, pollution control technicians input their data into computers. Instruments used to collect water samples or monitor water sources may be highly sophisticated electronic devices. Technicians usually do not analyze the data they collect. However, they may report on what they know to scientists or engineers, either verbally or in writing.

Water pollution control technicians monitor both industrial and residential discharge, such as from wastewater

POLLUTION CONTROL TECHNICIANS	
SCHOOL SUBJECTS	Biology Chemistry
PERSONAL SKILLS	Mechanical/manipulative Technical/scientific
WORK ENVIRONMENT	Indoors and Outdoors One location with some travel
MINIMUM EDUCATION LEVEL	Some postsecondary training
SALARY RANGE	$17,400 to $28,500 to $49,500+
CERTIFICATION OR LICENSING	Required for certain positions
OUTLOOK	About as fast as the average
DOT	029
GOE	05.03.08
NOC	2231
O*NET	24199B

treatment plants. Soil pollution technicians may work in rural areas, where the concern is how substances in the soil enter into crops for human consumption. Water pollution control technicians help to determine the presence and extent of pollutants in water. They collect water samples from lakes, streams, rivers, or other surface waters; groundwater (the water under the earth); industrial or municipal wastewater; or other sources. Samples are brought to labs, where chemical and other tests are performed to analyze them. If the samples contain harmful substances, remedial (cleanup) actions will need to be taken. Technicians also may perform various field tests, such as checking the pH, oxygen, and nitrate level of surface waters.

Some water pollution control technicians set up monitoring equipment to obtain information on water flow, movement, temperature, pressure, or other factors and record readings from these devices. To trace flow patterns, they may introduce dyes into the water.

Water pollution control technicians have to be careful not to contaminate their samples, stray from the specific testing procedure, or otherwise do something to ruin the sample or cause faulty or misleading results.

Depending on the specific job, water pollution control technicians may spend a good part of their time outdoors, in good weather and bad, aboard boats, and sometimes near unpleasant smells or potentially hazardous substances. Field sites may be scattered or remote places; in some cases it may be necessary to fly to a different part of the country (especially if the technician works for a private consulting firm), perhaps staying away from home for a long period of time. Water pollution control technicians play a big role in industrial wastewater discharge monitoring, treatment, and control. Nearly every manufacturing process produces wastewater, but U.S. manufacturers today must be more careful about what they discharge with their wastewater.

Some water technicians specialize in groundwater, ocean water, or other types of natural waters. Estuarine resource technicians, for example, specialize in estuary waters, or coastal areas where fresh water and salt water come together. These bays, salt marshes, inlets, and other tidal water bodies support a wide variety of plant and animal life with ecologically complex relationships. They are vulnerable to destructive pollution from adjoining industries, cities and towns, and other sources. Estuarine resource technicians aid scientists in studying the resulting environmental changes. They may work in laboratories or aboard boats, or clad in diving gear in the water. They operate, maintain, and calibrate instruments; collect and analyze water samples; record observations; and perform other tasks that are part of investigating estuarine habitats and their organisms.

A pollution control technician takes water samples to test for harmful chemicals.

Air pollution control technicians collect and test air samples, such as from stacks or chimneys of industrial manufacturing plants; record data on atmospheric conditions, such as to help a city determine levels of airborne substances from auto or industrial emissions; and supply data to scientists and engineers for further testing and analysis. In labs, air pollution control technicians may help test air samples or re-create contaminants. They may use atomic absorption spectrophotometers, flame photometers, gas chromatographs, and other instruments for analyzing samples.

In the field, air pollution control technicians may utilize rooftop sampling devices or operate mobile monitoring units or stationary trailers. The trailers may be equipped with elaborate, continuously operating automatic testing systems, including some of the same devices found in laboratories. Outside air is pumped into various chambers in the trailer where it is analyzed for the presence of pollutants. The results may be recorded by machine on 30-day rolls of graph paper or fed into a computer at regular intervals. Technicians may set up and maintain the sampling devices, replenish the chemicals used in tests, replace worn parts, calibrate instruments, and record results. Some air pollution control technicians specialize in certain pollutants or pollution sources. For example, engine emission technicians focus on exhaust from internal combustion engines.

Soil or land pollution control technicians collect soil, silt, or mud samples so they can be checked for contamination. Soil can become contaminated when polluted water seeps into the earth, such as when liquid waste (leachate) leaks from a landfill or other source into surrounding ground. Soil pollution control technicians work for federal, state, and local government agencies, for private consulting firms, and elsewhere. (Some soil conservation technicians perform pollution control work.)

EPA LAWS

As late as the 1950s, there were few pollution control technicians. Environmental laws passed in the 1960s and later created the need for professionals to monitor and regulate pollution of soil, water, and air.

One such law was the Clean Air Act, passed in 1970. This law is the comprehensive federal law that regulates air emissions from factories and other sources. The law set maximum pollutant standards, applicable mainly to industry. For example, if smokestacks at a factory were found to emit pollutants beyond the maximum allowed, the government enforced sanctions, such as fines, and required the factory to reduce emissions by installing scrubbers, changing their processes, or other solutions. Another law that pollution control technicians should be familiar with is the Pollution Prevention Act, passed in 1990. This law focused industry, government, and public attention on reducing the amount of pollution by making better use of raw materials. This law advocates source reduction, i.e., reducing the amount of waste or pollution produced in the first place, rather than trying to treat it after the fact. Practices encouraged by this law include recycling, source reduction, and sustainable agriculture. For more information on the comprehensive laws that support the EPA's authority, visit the EPA Web site (http://www.epa.gov).

A position sometimes grouped with other pollution control technicians is that of noise pollution control technician. Noise pollution control technicians use rooftop devices and mobile units to take readings and collect data on noise levels of factories, highways, airports, and other locations in order to determine noise exposure levels for workers or the public. Some test noise levels of construction equipment, chain saws, snow blowers, lawn mowers, or other equipment.

■ Requirements

High School

In high school, key courses include biology, chemistry, and physics. Conservation or ecology courses also will be useful. Math classes should include at least algebra and geometry. English, speech, communications, or other language arts classes will help sharpen written and oral communications skills, necessary in any job. Computer classes are also helpful.

Postsecondary Training

Some technician positions call for a high school degree plus employer training. As pollution control becomes more technical and complex, more positions are going to technicians with at least an associate's degree. To meet this need, many community colleges across the country have developed appropriate programs for pollution control technicians. Areas of study include environmental engineering technologies, pollution control technologies, air pollution control technologies, conservation, ecology, and others. A future air pollution control technician, for example, might take courses in meteorology, toxicology, source testing, sampling and analysis, air quality management, technical math, chemistry, communications skills, physics, air pollution instrumentation, sources of air pollution, air pollution control, biology, environmental science, computers, and statistics. The exact degree or other training required varies by employer. Some experts advise attending school in the part of the country where you'd like to begin your career so you can start getting to know local employers before you graduate.

Certification or Licensing

Certification or licensing is required for some positions in pollution control, especially those in which sanitation, public health, a public water supply, or a sewage treatment system is involved.

Other Requirements

Pollution control technicians should be patient, detail-oriented, capable of following instructions, and curious. Basic manual skills are a must for collecting samples and performing similar tasks. Today, often-complex environmental regulations drive technicians' jobs; therefore, it's crucial to be able to read and understand technical materials and to follow to the letter any written guidelines for sampling or other procedures. Computer skills, as well as skills in reading and interpreting maps, charts, and diagrams are also a help.

Technicians must make accurate and objective observations, maintain clear and complete records of data, and do certain types of computations. Good physical conditioning is a requirement for some activities, such as climbing up smokestacks to take emission samples.

■ Exploring

Students who want to learn about jobs in pollution control can begin by visiting a large library and reading technical and general-interest publications in environmental science. This will give you an idea of the technologies being used and issues being discussed. You also can visit a municipal health department or pollution control agency in your community. Many agencies are pleased to explain their work to visitors.

School science clubs, local community groups, and naturalist clubs may help broaden your understanding of various aspects of the natural world and allow you to take an in-depth look at a few specific areas of interest. Most schools have recycling programs that enlist student help.

A tour of a local manufacturing plant using an air- or water-pollution abatement system also might be arranged.

Many plants offer tours of their operations to the public. This would provide an excellent opportunity to see the equipment and conditions technicians work with.

As a high school student, it may be difficult to obtain summer or part-time work as a technician, due to the extensive operations and safety training required for some of these jobs. However, it is worthwhile to check with a local environmental agency, nonprofit environmental organizations, or private consulting firms to learn of volunteer or paid support opportunities. Any hands-on experience you can get will be of value to a future employer.

■ Employers

Many jobs for pollution control technicians are with the government agencies that monitor the environment, such as the Environmental Protection Agency, and Departments of Agriculture, Energy, and Interior.

Water pollution control technicians may be employed by manufacturers that produce wastewater; municipal wastewater treatment facilities; consultants or other private firms hired to monitor or control pollutants in water or wastewater; pollution control equipment and supply manufacturers that make filters, chemicals, or other products to eliminate or reduce the level of harmful substances in water or wastewater; or government regulatory agencies responsible for protecting water quality, including monitoring local water and wastewater.

Air pollution control technicians work for government agencies, including regional EPA offices, as well as private manufacturers producing airborne pollutants; consultants; research facilities; air pollution control equipment manufacturers; and other employers.

Soil pollution control technicians may work for federal or state departments of agriculture, federal or regional EPA offices, or for private agricultural groups that monitor soil quality for pesticide levels.

Noise pollution control technicians are employed by private companies and by government agencies such as OSHA (Occupational Safety and Health Administration).

■ Starting Out

Graduates of two-year pollution control technology or related programs are often employed during their final term by recruiters who visit their schools. Specific opportunities will vary depending on the part of the country, the segment of the environmental industry, the specialization of the technician (air, water, land), the economy, and other factors. When they first start out, technicians may find the greatest number of positions available in state or local government agencies. One career path is to start out working for a state or local government agency, and then move on to higher-paying jobs in the private sector.

PHYTOREMEDIATION

The job of pollution control technician is one that works within the rigid laws of science. But the field also allows for some creativity in helping other professionals find solutions to pollution control. One such creative solution that pollution control technicians have helped others make possible is phytoremediation. Phytoremediation is the use of plants and trees to clean up contaminated soil and water. This solution is cost-effective, saving thousands of dollars by using plants instead of expensive equipment and chemicals, as well as environmentally friendly, in some cases creating esthetically pleasing areas such as ponds and gardens. Plants can break down organic pollutants or stabilize metal contaminants by acting as filters or traps. Methods vary, but basically, over time, plants absorb contaminants from the soil or water by soaking them up in their root system. One example of how phytoremediation is succeeding is in Chernobyl (site of a 1986 nuclear accident), where sunflowers floating on rafts with their roots dangling in water are being used to remove the contaminants cesium 137 and strontium 90 from a pond. In the eastern United States, where acid mine drainage is a problem, the Bureau of Mines encourages the planting of wetlands using the common cattail to soak up mining contaminants from streams. On a smaller scale, the Indian Creek Nature Center in Cedar Rapids, Iowa, used phytoremediation when its septic system became overloaded. The center built a wetlands area, surrounded by attractive native plants. Waste from the center first goes to a conventional septic system, then it flows to three basins, two of which are filled with pea gravel. Water doesn't extend to the surface, but the plants extend their roots down into the dirty water. The water, now clean, flows into the third basin—a pond that itself has become a popular attraction at the nature center.

Most schools can provide job-hunting advice and assistance. Direct application to state or local environmental agencies, employment agencies, or potential employers can also be a productive approach. Students hoping to find employment outside their current geographic area may get good results by checking with professional organizations or by reading advertisements in technical journals, many of which have searchable job listings on the Internet.

■ Advancement

The typical hierarchy for pollution control work is technician (two years of postsecondary education or less), technologist (two years or more of postsecondary training), technician manager (perhaps a technician or technologist with many years of experience), and scientist or engineer (four-year bachelor of science degree or more, up to Ph.D. level).

In some private manufacturing or consulting firms, technician positions are used for training newly recruited professional staff. In such cases, workers with four-year degrees in engineering or physical science are likely to be promoted before those with two-year degrees. Employees of government agencies usually are organized under civil service systems that specify experience, education, and other criteria for advancement. Private industry promotions are structured differently and will depend on a variety of factors.

■ Earnings

Pay for pollution control technicians varies widely depending on the nature of the work they do, training and experience required for the work, type of employer, geographic region, demand for technicians compared to available supply, and other factors. Public-sector positions tend to pay less than private-sector positions.

Government entry-level salaries for pollution control technicians are about $15,500 to $19,500 per year, depending on education and experience. The average is $28,500 per year. Technicians who move up to become managers or supervisors can make up to $49,500 per year or more. Technicians who further their education to secure teaching positions can also expect to earn higher than the average.

No matter which area they specialize in, pollution control technicians generally enjoy fringe benefits such as paid vacation, holidays and sick time, and employer paid training. Technicians who work full-time (and some who work part-time) often have employer-paid health insurance benefits. Technicians who are employed by the federal government may get additional benefits, which may or may not be paid by private employers, such as pension and retirement benefits.

■ Work Environment

Conditions range from clean and pleasant indoor offices and laboratories to outdoor hot or cold, wet, bad-smelling, noisy, even hazardous situations. Anyone planning a career in pollution control technology should realize the possibility of exposure to unpleasant conditions at least occasionally in his or her career. Employers often can minimize these negatives through special equipment and procedures. Most laboratories and manufacturing companies have safety procedures for potentially dangerous situations.

Some jobs involve vigorous physical activity (for example, handling a small boat or climbing ladders on smokestacks). For the most part, technicians need only be able to do moderate activity. Travel may be required. It may be necessary to go to urban, industrial, or rural settings for sampling.

Because technicians' jobs can involve a considerable amount of repetitive work, patience and the ability to handle routine are important. Yet, particularly when they are working in the field, pollution control technicians also have to be ready to use their resourcefulness and ingenuity to find the best ways of responding to new situations.

Technicians need to be able to communicate with others-including fellow technicians, supervisors, scientists, and engineers, and, in some positions, clients, the public, regulatory officials, and others as well. They should work well alone or as part of a team.

■ Outlook

Demand for technicians is expected to increase about as fast as the average through 2006. Those trained to handle increasingly complex technical demands will have the upper hand. All science technicians (including medical science, agricultural, pollution control) held about 228,000 jobs in 1996. While other technicians were employed by manufacturing (largely the chemical industry), the federal government employed 16,000 science technicians, largely pollution control technicians, in 1996. The government predicts that 258,000 science technicians will be employed in 2006, a 12.9 percent increase for all science technicians.

Demand will be higher in some areas of the country than others depending on specialty; for example, air pollution control technicians will be especially in demand in large cities facing pressure to comply with national air quality standards (Los Angeles, New York). Amount of industrialization, stringency of state and local pollution control enforcement, local economy, and other factors also will affect demand by region and specialty. Perhaps the single greatest factor affecting all pollution control work is continued mandates for pollution control by the federal government. As long as the federal government is supporting pollution control, the pollution control industry will continue to grow and technicians will be needed.

■ For More Information

The following organizations' members work in air pollution control, hazardous waste management, and groundwater quality control:

Air and Waste Management Association
One Gateway Center, Third Floor
Pittsburgh, PA 15222
Tel: 412-232-3444
Web: http://www.awma.org

National Ground Water Association
601 Dempsey Road
Westerville, OH 43081
Tel: 614-898-7791
Web: http://www.ngwa.org

ASCET is affiliated with the National Society of Professional Engineers and is a source of technician certification:

American Society of Certified Engineering Technicians
PO Box 1348
Flowery Branch, GA 30542-1348
Tel: 770-967-9173

Following is the national organization. For your state's Environmental Protection Agency, check the government listings in your phone book:

Environmental Protection Agency
401 M Street, SW
Washington, DC 20460
Tel: 202-260-2090
Web: http://www.epa.gov

The following organization is an environmental careers resource for high school and college students:

Environmental Careers Organization
179 South Street
Boston, MA 02111
Tel: 617-426-4375
Web: http://www.eco.org

Water Environment Federation
601 Wythe Street
Alexandria, VA 22314-1994
Tel: 703-684-2452
Web: http://www.wef.org

■ Related Articles

Hazardous Waste Management Specialists

Hazardous Waste Management Technicians

Recycling Coordinators

Wastewater Treatment Plant Operators and Technicians

Polygraph Examiners

■ Overview

Polygraph examiners use polygraph equipment and techniques to determine whether individuals have answered questions truthfully or dishonestly. Polygraphs, often called "lie detectors," are instruments that measure and record certain nonvoluntary body responses that are affected by the individual's emotional state. To judge whether the subject has answered all the questions truthfully, the examiner compares the reactions recorded for questions that are not likely to cause stress with the reactions recorded for other questions.

■ History

Automatic body functions such as breathing and blood circulation are the basis for measuring individuals' truthfulness. Even though there is no one physiological response that reveals a lie, the rates of these nonvoluntary processes change in response to stress, and stress is likely to increase when an individual is lying. One of the first attempts to use this knowledge to detect deception was made in 1898, when suspected criminals were interrogated while their pulse rates and blood volumes were monitored. Tests conducted in 1914 worked by measuring the volume of the air that test subjects breathed, and tests performed in 1917 showed that changes in blood pressure also could indicate whether the subjects were telling the truth.

The first modern lie detector was invented in 1921 by John A. Larson, a medical student who worked with a local police department. Larson's instrument continuously recorded blood pressure, pulse rate, and respiration, and it was called a polygraph, which means "many writings," because it recorded all these processes simultaneously. Later polygraphs incorporated galvanic skin reflex (GSR) testing, which recorded the changes in the electrical conductivity of the skin resulting from changes in perspiration levels.

Polygraphs have been used in police intelligence and security investigations since 1924. Lie detector testing has sparked a great deal of controversy. Many people object to such testing as an invasion of privacy and a violation of civil liberties. The validity of polygraph tests has often been questioned, and test results are generally inadmissible in court unless the defense, prosecution, and judge agree to their use. While studies have rated the validity of polygraph examinations at 87.2 to 96.2 percent, their reliability depends on the skill and experience of the examiner.

This controversy resulted in federal legislation. In 1988, the federal government placed strict controls on the use of polygraph testing by private employers. This meant that businesses were prohibited from requiring polygraph testing of employees or job applicants, except businesses engaged in security services, or when an individual is suspected of committing a finance-related crime. Government agencies, however, were exempt from this legislation.

■ The Job

Although polygraph examiners often test suspects and witnesses in criminal cases, the applications of the polygraph are not limited to police work. For example, the armed forces government

POLYGRAPH EXAMINERS	
SCHOOL SUBJECTS	Biology Psychology
PERSONAL SKILLS	Technical/scientific
WORK ENVIRONMENT	Primarily indoors One location with some travel
MINIMUM EDUCATION LEVEL	Some postsecondary training
SALARY RANGE	$18,000 to $30,000 to $60,000
CERTIFICATION OR LICENSING	Recommended
OUTLOOK	About as fast as the average
DOT	199
GOE	02.04.02
NOC	6465
O*NET	39999G

A polygraph examiner tests a subject.

agencies employ polygraph examiners to screen prospective civilian employees.

Before polygraph examiners meet the subject they will test, they gather information about the individual and the circumstances involved. They try to learn about the subject's childhood, medical history, and any police record; whether the subject has a history of emotional illness or drug or alcohol abuse; and whether the subject is taking any medication. In criminal cases, they may visit the police station, the crime scene, or the morgue for information.

After gathering this information, polygraph examiners spend at least an hour with the test subject to obtain information about background, current health, and knowledge of the circumstances that led to the polygraph examination. They try to calm the subject's fears about the test by explaining how the polygraph instrument works and explaining the test procedure.

Next, polygraph examiners develop test questions that are easy to understand and not ambiguous. Before they actually give the test, they read the questions to the subject and assure the person there will be no surprise questions. Then the examiners attach the apparatus to the

individual to measure changes in certain nonvoluntary body responses.

The examiner fastens a tube around the subject's chest; this tube measures the rate of the subject's respiration. A cuff similar to that found on a blood pressure meter is wrapped around the subject's arm in order to record cardiovascular activity. Special sensors are placed on the subject's skin to measure the subject's galvanic skin reflex. These sensors are connected to the polygraph machine, which contains pens that respond to changes in the subject's breathing, heart rate, and perspiration. An electric motor moves a roll of graph paper while the pens record the subject's responses on the paper.

The actual testing session is rather brief; a 10-question test takes about 4 minutes. The test may consist of control questions, which are not likely to cause stress, and key questions, which are likely to produce a strong reaction if the subject is lying. Another form of the test includes a number of similar questions, with only one question that contains the correct details. Because only the guilty person knows which question has the right details, the subject's reaction to that question can indicate guilt or innocence.

Some people believe they can affect their reactions by taking drugs. But a drug that reduces an individual's reactions to key questions also will reduce the individual's reactions to control questions. Thus the test results will still show a difference between the subject's reactions when answering truthfully and when lying.

After administering the test, polygraph examiners evaluate the subject's recorded responses and then discuss the results with the individual. If it appears that the subject has been untruthful, examiners try to give individuals a chance to explain the reasons for their reactions and may even retest them later.

In addition to administering and evaluating polygraph tests, polygraph examiners keep records and make reports on test results. They may appear in court as witnesses on matters dealing with polygraph examinations, and some also teach classes in polygraph operation and interrogation techniques.

Polygraph examiners are also employed by government agencies and by some private security employers who test potential employees for security clearance.

■ Requirements

High School

High school students interested in becoming polygraph examiners should take courses that help them understand how the body functions and how it is affected by stress. Courses in psychology, physiology, and biology will be especially useful. In general, students should take courses that will prepare them for college.

Postsecondary Training

College students should major in science or criminal justice. In addition, classes in English and writing will help prepare them to write reports, and classes in public speaking will help them develop the self-confidence they will need when testifying in court.

Candidates for lie-detection schools usually need four-year college degrees, but applicants with two years of college courses in criminal investigation plus five years of investigative experience may be accepted. Polygraph training in an approved school usually takes from six to eight weeks.

Students must take polygraph tests upon entering a lie-detection school to ensure they have the good moral character this field requires. During their training, students learn how to operate the polygraph, how to develop and ask questions, how to interpret polygraph charts, the legal aspects of polygraph testing, and about the physical responses the polygraph measures. They observe polygraph tests administered by others, administer the tests themselves, and hear and see audiotapes and videotapes of their own performances. When they complete lie-detection school, students go on to internships of at least six months before becoming fully qualified as polygraph examiners.

Certification or Licensing

Although many states license polygraph examiners, their requirements vary. Typical requirements include a high school diploma or the equivalent, either a bachelor's degree or five years of experience as a detective, completion of polygraph training at a state-approved school, a six month internship, and successful completion of a state-administered test.

National standards for training, and also for polygraph equipment, are established by the American Polygraph Association (APA), which also conducts research and publishes information. The American Association of Police Polygraphists offers the Certified Forensic Law Enforcement Examiner designation to its members.

Other Requirements

Polygraph examiners must show good moral character and cannot have police records. They should speak and write well, have self-confidence, be alert, and be able to maintain objectivity and self-control. They also must be comfortable working with strangers and relate well to all kinds of people, and they should not be influenced by such factors as economic status, race, or sex.

In addition, polygraph examiners must be willing to work under pressure and under a variety of conditions and should not be shocked by distressing sights. Finally, they must understand the importance of protecting their subjects' rights and maintaining confidentiality.

Exploring

Because polygraph examiners must obtain cooperation from their test subjects, activities that offer you contact with people can provide valuable experience. Such activities include summer work as a camp counselor and volunteer or part-time work in a hospital or nursing home. Students at some colleges can volunteer for campus security patrols, which provide opportunities to develop their observation and investigative skills.

If you live near a large population center you may be able to visit lie-detection schools and talk with staff members. You also may be able to visit courts and tour police facilities. Take advantage of any opportunities you get to talk with people who conduct police or private investigations.

Employers

Polygraph examiners are employed in many types of organizations, and their surroundings and the type of people they work with are determined by the nature of the organization. Many examiners are involved in law enforcement and may work for criminal or civil courts, police or sheriff departments, the FBI, or the Secret Service. Some work for the armed forces, and many others work for private businesses, such as retail stores, drug firms, companies that have their own security forces, and firms that provide testing services for other business organizations.

Starting Out

Lie-detection schools often provide placement assistance for their graduates, and graduates also may learn about job openings from contacts they make during their internships. Professional groups may be a source of job leads, and periodicals that specialize in law enforcement and criminal justice may list job openings. In addition, qualified polygraph examiners can apply to courts and crime laboratories. They also can apply to federal agencies, which may require them to take civil service examinations. Generally, polygraph examiners at the federal level are required to have several years of investigative service before training in polygraph techniques.

In some cases, people who are already involved in investigative work, such as police and private investigators, criminologists, and particularly military intelligence staff members, add to their skills by earning polygraph examiner certificates.

Advancement

Polygraph examiners in civil service positions can advance through various job levels and eventually hold management jobs, and examiners who work for private security agencies can advance to such executive positions as director of operations. Polygraph examiners who are employed by business and industry in security positions may become supervisors and eventually head their department. In addition, some experienced polygraph examiners start their own agencies or work as security consultants or security systems specialists.

■ Earnings

Polygraph examiners beginning their internships may earn from $18,000 to $30,000 a year, and experienced examiners earn as much as $60,000 a year or more. Examiners who are paid employees often receive such benefits as sick leave, paid vacations, medical and dental insurance, retirement plans, and bonuses.

■ Work Environment

Most polygraph examiners work 40-hour weeks, although some work longer and irregular hours, including nights and weekends. Examiners usually work indoors, but may travel to their appointments, often carrying their polygraph equipment, which weighs about 25 pounds.

■ Outlook

In the late 1990s, the American Polygraph Association listed about 2,000 members. Because of the 1988 legislation, there are fewer positions for private polygraph examiners than there were a decade ago. However, there is increasing need for law enforcement examiners, especially in the federal government.

The growing population and increasing crime rate may create more openings for polygraph examiners in the future. Courts in at least 30 states allow the use of polygraph test results as evidence, and public pressure for reducing court backlogs may increase the use of polygraph tests.

■ For More Information

The following organization compiles statistics, operates a speaker's bureau, publishes a journal, offers awards to outstanding polygraphists, offers certification, and conducts specialized education and research. For more information, contact:

American Association of Police Polygraphists
18160 Cottonwood Road, # 503
Sunriver, OR 97707
Tel: 888-743-5479
Email: bobheard@prodigy.net
Web: http://www.wordnet.net/aapp/

For general information on polygraph testing, as well as information on licensing and accredited polygraph schools and training, contact:

American Polygraph Association
PO Box 8037
Chattanooga, TN 37414-0037
Tel: 800-APA-8037
Web: http://www.polygraph.org/

■ Related Articles

Government
Military Services
Public Safety
Border Patrol Officers
Crime Analysts
Detectives
FBI Agents
Forensic Experts
Insurance Claims Representatives
Police Officers
Security Consultants and Technicians

Polystyrene-Bead Molders and Molding-Machine Tenders

■ See Plastics Products Manufacturing Workers

Pop/Rock Musicians

■ Overview

Pop/rock musicians perform in nightclubs, concert halls, on college campuses, and at live events such as festivals and fairs. They also record their music for distribution on CDs and audio cassettes. A pop/rock musician usually performs as a member of a band comprising instrumentalists and vocalists. The band may perform original music or music composed and recorded by other artists.

■ History

Since the term "rock 'n' roll" was first coined by radio disc jockey Alan Freed in the 1950s, rock music has been a significant part of teenage culture. Rock music has always been marketed to teens, purchased by teens, and stirred controversy with parents. Though much of rock music has appealed to all ages, it was the teen culture that evolved in the 1950s that brought the doo wop and boogie woogie music of the South to audiences all across the country. Teens, for the first time in U.S. history, were spending their own money, and they were spending it on the records they heard spun on the radio. What had previously been music appreciated primarily by black audiences, was brought to white audiences by the success of Chuck Berry, Little Richard, and Fats Domino; then, later, Elvis Presley and Jerry Lee Lewis.

To capitalize on this popularity, recording companies hired songwriters, singers, and musicians to produce rock songs for the masses. Girl groups, such as the Ronettes, were formed in the 1960s. Later that decade, rock took on more diverse sounds, as Motown artists, the Beatles, and other performers experimented with the genre. Though this experimentation led to a variety of musical forms in the 1970s—folk, heavy metal, disco, punk—record sales slipped, but not for long. The 1980s saw the huge popularity of the music video and MTV, a cable network that brought music back to the teen culture and revived the music industry.

■ The Job

You hear a lot about the lives of rock musicians—the limousines, the groupies, the multimillion dollar record deals. Though most pop/rock musicians do long for this kind of success, many have very successful careers on a much smaller scale. You don't have to live in a major city, tour the world, or record top-selling CDs in order to be a rock musician. According to the Recording Workshop, a school for the recording arts in Ohio, most cities of over 25,000 have at least one audio production studio. These studios cater to the many rock musicians writing songs, performing them, and promoting their music to regional and national audiences. You probably have music ambitions of your own and have written songs or learned to play an instrument. If you stick with it and make contacts, over time you may develop a life for yourself that involves performing your music on a regular basis.

Julia Greenberg is a rock musician in New York who has devoted years to the pursuit of a career in the music industry. With her new CD, "Past Your Eyes," she's getting attention that should propel her to even greater success. "I started my own band, using all original music, in 1993," Julia says. "I hired musicians and old friends to arrange the songs to play on my first demo. I used the demo to get gigs at clubs." Her band was very well received, and she has managed to get gigs all around Manhattan ever since. She's played at clubs, such as Mercury Lounge, Fez, and Brownie's, that are famous for promoting new and established acts. "My music is in the singer/songwriter vein," she says. "I'm very much focused on the writing. But we're also a straight-ahead rock band." Her work is influenced by roots rock, as well as the New Wave music—Blondie, Elvis Costello—with which she grew up.

In order to be truly successful as a rock musician, you'll need original material to perform. Some regional rock bands, however, do make careers for themselves playing the music of other bands, performing at local clubs, dances,

wedding receptions, and private parties. They may specialize in a specific period of music, such as music of the 1980s, or Motown hits of the 1960s. But A&R (artist and repertoire) coordinators for record companies, managers, producers, and other professionals in the recording industry are looking for musicians who write and perform their own music.

As a rock musician, you'll write music and practice performing it with a band. Rehearsal and commitment to the band is extremely important to a rock musician. In order for the band to sound as good as it possibly can, all the instrumentalists and vocalists must develop a sense of each other's talents and styles. You'll put together a tape (called a "demo") demonstrating the band's talent, which you will then submit to club managers and music producers. When making a demo, or recording a CD for a record company, you'll record in a studio, and work with recording professionals. Audio engineers, producers, and mixing engineers help to enhance your performance, and to make your music sound as good as it possibly can.

When booked by a club, the club's promotional staff may advertise your upcoming appearance. For the most part, however, you'll have to scare up an audience on your own. This involves distributing fliers, sending press releases to area newspapers and arts weeklies, and sending announcements to those on your mailing list. Your mailing list is composed of the names and addresses of people who have attended previous performances and have expressed interest in hearing about future gigs. You may also maintain a Web site listing your performance schedule. Of course, if you're very successful and have a well established fan-base, your record company or promoter will handle all the advertising.

On the date of the performance, you'll arrive early to prepare the stage. This involves setting up instruments and sound systems, checking for sound quality, and becoming familiar with the stage and facil-

POP/ROCK MUSICIANS	
SCHOOL SUBJECTS	Business Music
PERSONAL SKILLS	Artistic Communication/ ideas
WORK ENVIRONMENT	Indoors and outdoors Primarily multiple locations
MINIMUM EDUCATION LEVEL	High school diploma
SALARY RANGE	$1,000 to $25,000 to $1,000,000+
CERTIFICATION OR LICENSING	None available
OUTLOOK	About as fast as the average
DOT	152
GOE	01.04.04
NOC	5133
O*NET	34047A

ity. Together, your band will go over the list of songs to be performed.

Your audience will likely effect your performance. If you're playing to a small crowd in a club, you'll have a much different experience than playing to an auditorium full of hundreds of people. Regardless of your audience, you'll play each song to the best of your ability, with the intention of entertaining and enlightening your listeners and developing a strong base of devoted fans.

■ Requirements

High School

High school classes that will help you become a pop/rock musician include English, business, mathematics, and, of course, music, specifically voice or instrument training. Playing in your high school band will give you an idea of what it is like to interact with fellow musicians as well as perform in front of an audience.

Postsecondary Training

A college education isn't necessary for becoming a pop/rock musician, but it can help you learn about music, recording, and writing. In general, you should have a background in music theory and an understanding of a variety of styles of music. Learning to play one or more instruments, such as the piano or guitar, will be especially helpful in writing songs. You can pursue this education at a community college, university, or trade school. There are a number of seminars, conferences, and workshops available that will involve you with songwriting, audio recording, and producing.

Other Requirements

You need to be able to work closely with other artists and to have patience with the rehearsal and recording process. You'll also need persistence to proceed with your ambitions in the face of much rejection. "You have to have a really strong personality," Julia says. "You have to be able to get up on stage and command a room. You have to be really starved for attention!"

■ Exploring

Talk to your music teachers at school about opportunities in music. Try to attend as many musical performances as possible—they don't all have to be in the pop/rock genre. Many clubs and other concert facilities offer all-ages shows where you can see musical artists perform firsthand. Depending on the size of the venue, you may have a chance to approach a musician after the show to ask a few questions about the field.

The best way to get experience is to learn to play an instrument or take voice lessons. Once you've mastered the basics, you can get together with friends or classmates and experiment with different musical styles. Don't forget the writing aspect of pop/rock music. Keep a journal of your thoughts and ideas. Read the lyrics of your favorite songs and try to figure out what makes them so appealing. Try to create the lyrics to a song of your own by combining this knowledge with your journal entries or other creative writing.

■ Employers

You may work for another member of the band, who pays you to rehearse and perform. But in most cases, you'll work on a freelance basis, taking on gigs as they come. You'll be hired to play at clubs, concert halls, and for community events. You may also play private gigs, for weddings and other celebrations. Many musicians also maintain flexible "day jobs" which help to support them as they perform on the evenings and weekends.

■ Starting Out

Many bands form when a group of friends get together to collaborate on the writing and performing of original songs. However, openings for band members are frequently advertised in the classifieds of local and college newspapers and arts weeklies. You may have to audition for many bands before you find one with which you fit, or you may have to put together your own group of musicians. If part of a new band, you'll have to put a lot of time into rehearsal, as well as gaining a following. This may involve playing a lot of gigs for free until a club owner can rely on you to bring in a crowd.

■ Advancement

The sky's the limit when it comes to advancing in the music industry. Once you've made the right connections, you may find yourself with a record deal, national concert dates, awards, and a great deal of media attention. Julia dreams of success that will allow her to perform and write music full time. Through the help of independent investors, Julia has been able to finance a new demo. "I'm shopping the CD to industry people, and putting the CD out myself," she says. "A lot of people are doing this these days. Industry people are looking for artists who can get their own following." The new music, available at http://www.cropduster.com, has already sparked a great deal of interest, including a write-up in *New York* magazine.

■ Earnings

Even when you're in the business, with regular club dates, it's difficult to predict how much you'll make from one year to the next. When starting out, you'll likely play clubs and events for free; later you may get a percentage of the club's cover charge or drink receipts. Even if you're paid for a club date, you may end up losing money once you pay all your band members, and figure in the expense of promotion. On the other end of the scale, there's potential for successful pop/rock musicians to make millions in the business. According to *Forbes* Magazine's 1999 edition of "The Celebrity 100," the Rolling Stones ranked the highest of any rock group, with an income of $57 million the previous year.

■ Work Environment

Creative people can be a temperamental bunch, so you may be working closely with band members who are difficult to get along with. But the opportunity to perform with talented musicians will be inspiring. Rehearsal may require a great deal of time and late hours, but can result in work that you're proud of. You may be performing in dark, smoky bars, or in open-air auditoriums; you'll have to be prepared to perform in a variety of settings. To play as many gigs as you can may involve a great deal of travel.

■ Outlook

There will always be thousands more rock musicians than there are record contracts. But there will also always be opportunities for new performers with record companies and clubs. Record companies are always on the lookout for original sounds and talents. Even with a record deal, however, there are no guarantees of success—the music industry, and the CD-buying public, have fickle tastes. Often rock musicians are dropped by their label when record sales fail to meet expectations.

With the recording studios becoming more sophisticated, artists can more effectively promote themselves with quality CDs. Record companies will be paying close attention to these independently produced CDs when scouting for new talent.

■ For More Information

For information about the professional associations that serve songwriters, contact:

American Society of Composers, Authors, and Publishers
One Lincoln Plaza
New York, NY 10023
Tel: 212-621-6000
Web: http://www.ascap.org

National Academy of Songwriters
6255 Sunset Boulevard, Suite 1023
Hollywood, CA 90028
Tel: 800-826-7287
Web: http://www.nassong.org

■ Related Articles

Music

Music and Recording Industry

Radio

A&R Workers
Audio Recording Engineers
Composers
Music Producers
Musical Directors and Conductors
Musicians
Singers
Songwriters

Portraitists

■ See Cartoonists and Animators

Postal Clerks

■ Overview

Postal clerks are employees of the United States Postal Service (USPS). The equivalent employees at package delivery companies have different titles but perform many of the same duties; at Federal Express they are called *service agents,* at United Parcel Service, *administrative assistants* and *account executives.* Their job duties may be diversified, depending upon the size of the post office or company in which they are employed. Among their duties are working at the public service windows in post offices, answering telephone inquiries, handling packages, and sorting incoming and outgoing mail. About 297,000 postal clerks work for the United States Postal Service.

■ History

The public mail system had its beginning during the 1400s, when King Edward IV of England established a series of post houses for transporting official mail. The

POSTAL CLERKS	
SCHOOL SUBJECTS	Computer science Speech
PERSONAL SKILLS	Following instructions Mechanical/manipulative
WORK ENVIRONMENT	Primarily indoors Primarily one location
MINIMUM EDUCATION LEVEL	High school diploma
SALARY RANGE	$24,599 to $31,000 to $36,551+
CERTIFICATION OR LICENSING	None available
OUTLOOK	Little change or more slowly than the average
DOT	243
GOE	07.03.01
NOC	1461
O*NET	57308

A postal clerk helps a girl buy stamps.

American postal system dates back to 1639, when Richard Fairbanks was granted permission to receive and dispatch mail at his home for the Massachusetts Bay Colony. In 1775, the Second Continental Congress appointed Benjamin Franklin as the first Postmaster General and established the postal system in the American colonies. Franklin completely reorganized the service, making improvements in efficiency, speed, and service.

Since the days of the early American Postal Service, technology has moved forward; the mail system has taken advantage of advances in automation and the speed of the jet age to improve mail delivery. The ZIP code system and the use of computer sorting, coding, and stamp canceling are among the many innovations put in place in recent years.

■ The Job

Postal clerks may perform numerous duties. Those who work in large city post offices, however, usually perform more specialized tasks as either postal window clerks or distribution clerks. In small post offices, clerks may perform both types of work, sorting mail for distribution when business at the customer windows is slow. Wherever they are employed, all postal clerks must know how to sort mail.

Window clerks deal directly with the public at the post office service windows. They sell stamps, accept and weigh parcel post packages, and advise customers regarding parcel post regulations and foreign mail postal fees. They also sell and cash money orders, register mail, rent post office boxes, accept deposits for postal savings accounts, and sell U.S. Savings Bonds. When customers come to the post office to pick up a special package or letter, postal clerks examine the customers' notice and retrieve the items. In addi-

tion, they may answer customer questions about postal rates and rules.

In large city post offices, postal window clerks may specialize in only one or two of these services, such as working a window for money orders, savings bonds, and registered mail only, or working at a window at which only stamps are sold and parcel post accepted. Still other clerks may work general delivery windows. Service agents at Federal Express and administrative assistants and account executives at UPS offer customers assistance and follow up on complaints. Service agents, like postal clerks, also handle packages, so they must do some heavy lifting.

Distribution clerks begin their work as the carriers and delivery drivers who have collected mail and bring it back to the post office. The mail from route boxes and mail carriers' bags is dumped onto long work tables. Usually, the *new distribution clerks,* also known as *mail handlers,* perform the first rough separation of the mail into parcel post, paper mail, and letter mail. The mail is then "faced" (placed with stamps down and facing the same direction) so that it can be fed into canceling machines. These machines mark each piece of mail with the date, time, and the city and state in which the post office is located. Once the mail is canceled, it is moved to different work sections where distribution clerks sort the mail according to its destination.

Clerks operating electronic letter-sorting machines push keys corresponding to the ZIP code of the local post office to which each letter will be delivered. The machine then sends the letter to the proper slot or bin. A growing number of clerks operate optical character readers (OCRs) and bar code sorters, which are machines that can "read" the address and sort a letter according to a code printed on the envelope. Other clerks sort odd-sized letters, magazines, and newspapers by hand. Finally, the mail is sent to local post offices for sorting according to delivery route.

Parcel post sorting is performed in a similar manner using conveyor belts, slides, and chutes. These packages require even finer separating and routing before they are sent to local post offices to be delivered by the mail carrier.

Duties similar to those described above are performed by mail clerks in the mail rooms of business firms. With the rise of private mail delivery services, *mail clerks* are also employed by letter and package delivery services. They take payment, label packages, assist customers in packing, and route mail to the delivery system.

All distribution clerks must be able to perform their duties accurately and efficiently so that the mail may be transported to its correct destination as soon as possible. A related occupation includes *transfer clerks,* who are responsible for moving the mail being carried to and from train stations and airports with the greatest speed possible.

■ Requirements

Although a high school education is not required for most entry-level positions in the post office, the trend has been to give preference to high school graduates. Federal Express service agents must be at least 18 years old and possess a high school diploma (or GED); UPS account executives usually have at least some college education.

High School

High school classes that will help you in this career include speech, English, computer science, and geography.

Other Requirements

Applicants for postal clerk positions must be citizens of the United States or have permanent alien residence status, and they must meet the necessary minimum age requirement (usually 18).

Applicants for USPS postal clerk positions are given a written examination that measures their speed and accuracy at checking names and numbers and their ability to memorize mail distribution procedures. Because jobs in the post office are becoming increasingly automated, applicants must also pass a special examination that includes a machine aptitude test. Information on the testing dates and locations can be found at your local post office.

Those who have scored successfully on the examinations are listed on a register in the order of their scores. When a vacancy occurs, the appointing postal officer chooses one of the top three applicants; the rest of the names remain on the list to be considered for future openings until their eligibility expires, usually two years after the examination date.

Because they must memorize many postal regulations, operational rules, and distribution schemes, people in these positions must have a good memory. They must also be able to read rapidly and accurately, as well as possess good hand-eye coordination. Physical stamina is required for both window and distribution clerks and for service agents. Window clerks must stand for many hours at a time, while distribution clerks and service agents must do a great deal of reaching, lifting, walking, bending, and handling packages and heavy sacks of mail.

Postal clerks need to have an even temperament and a pleasant disposition. They frequently work under pressure to meet time and schedule deadlines, and their work is often performed with others in close physical spaces. Window clerks must have a neat appearance and a pleasant manner and must be able to deal with all types of people because they are in constant contact with the public.

The majority of postal employees are members of the American Postal Workers Union, National Association of Letter Carriers, National Postal Mail Handlers Union, or National Rural Letter Carriers Association. UPS employees

---

STAMPS. ENVELOPES. LOONEY TUNES?

Postal clerks sell more than just stamps, envelopes, and other mailing necessities these days. Most post offices are now the proud marketers of everything from Pony Express T-shirts to Bugs Bunny neckties. The availability of all items depends on the size of the post office and its location. Smaller offices tend to only stock a few big-selling items, such as Bugs Bunny caps and shirts. Larger offices may have it all: Superman apparel, Framed Stamp Art, Just Delivered baby clothes, and don't forget the suede fringed jacket like the ones worn by the Pony Express riders of yesteryear. If you can't find what you want at your post office, you can order from the postal service Web site (http://www.usps.gov). It's clear that the post office isn't just about stamps anymore.

Source: Postmark America brochure, USPS

---

are unionized by the International Brotherhood of Teamsters 1991.

■ Exploring

If you are interested in one of these positions you can explore this type of work by seeking part-time work during vacations and summer periods, especially the rush holiday periods when many more jobs become available. Related jobs, such as store or office clerk, stock clerk, shipping clerk, or others that require sorting and distributing materials or dealing with the public, might also be beneficial when looking for a position in this area. Also check out the information about postal clerk jobs on the USPS Web site (http://www.usps.gov) and talk to your local post office clerk to get an insider viewpoint.

■ Employers

Postal clerks work for the USPS in the over 38,000 post offices all over the country. Smaller towns and cities employ fewer postal clerks than large metropolitan areas, but every town with a post office has a postal clerk or two. Even very small towns usually have a post office. Clerks are also employed by commercial delivery companies such as FedEx, UPS, and Airborne Express.

■ Starting Out

All new USPS employees serve a one-year probationary period during which their job performance and general conduct are closely observed. New employees generally spend a considerable amount of time memorizing postal regulations and operational procedures so that they may become proficient, accurate workers as quickly as possible.

After they have met the general job requirements and received a job appointment, most postal employees begin their careers as substitutes. These substitutes, who are listed on a roster in order of examination scores or by veterans' preference, may be called in as replacements for regular workers or to supplement the workforce. Vacancies in the permanent staff are filled by promoting the substitutes to regular employment according to seniority. The number of vacancies that occur depends on the size of the post office and the number of employees needed, as well as on the economic growth and population increases in the postal area served.

Package delivery companies prefer to promote employees from within the company, so the best way to enter is to start with an entry-level job, as a package sorter or package driver. To advance to the level of account executive at UPS, prospective employees should have some college experience or a bachelor's degree in any field of study.

■ Advancement

Although the advancement opportunities for postal clerks are considered better than for mail carriers, they are still rather limited. Large numbers of postal clerks do not move up to higher-level positions; however, as they accrue seniority, individuals may bid (by written request) for more preferable assignments, such as window jobs or other work on the day shift. Assignments to any higher-level positions are based on merit, with consideration given to the employee's education, experience, training, and aptitude on written examinations.

Employees of UPS who want to advance to the position of account executive will most likely first hold a job as an administrative assistant to gain experience assisting customers.

■ Earnings

Most USPS postal employees are paid under the Postal Field Service Compensation Act. Salaries are established for different job grade levels, which depend upon each position's responsibilities and the amount of knowledge, experience, and skills required.

In 1996, full-time postal clerks began at an average annual base salary of $24,599 and could advance to $35,683 after 14 years. Entry-level window clerks started at $26,063; those with 14 years of service earned $36,551 a year. Part-time clerks started at about $12.82 an hour, depending on their work schedule and experience on the job. Clerks working night shifts receive 10 percent above base pay. Those who work more than 8 hours a day or 40 hours a week receive one-and-one-half times base pay. When substitute workers receive appointments as regular postal clerks, they are given credit for their years of work as substitutes.

Fringe benefits for USPS postal clerks and substitute workers are generally the same as for all postal employees. Benefits include 13 days of annual vacation for each of the first 3 years of service and 20 days each year thereafter until 15 years of service are completed. Thereafter, postal clerks receive 26 days annually. Additional benefits include retirement benefits, disability benefits, health and life insurance, and paid sick leave.

■ Work Environment

The majority of regular postal employees work eight-hour days and five-day weeks, and the physical surroundings in the post office are usually pleasant. The closeness of the work areas gives employees the opportunity to develop a spirit of cooperation and friendship among themselves.

In most cases, the position of window clerk is considered a preferred job among postal workers. The work is often more interesting and varied than that of the distribution clerk, because the job requires continual direct contact with the public, more mental activity, and less physical exertion.

Distribution clerks must do considerable walking, throwing, lifting, and other types of physical labor. Most of their job tasks are repetitive and routine, with little or no contact with the public. Behind the scenes at the post office, these employees work in close contact with each other, often in teams. Their primary challenge is to increase their speed, accuracy, and overall efficiency.

As departments within the Postal Service adopt new automatic and electronic equipment and as greater technological advances are introduced, the work of distribution clerks continues to involve more labor-saving techniques. Working conditions vary with the equipment used, the size of the postal operation, and the clerk's area of specialization.

■ Outlook

About 297,000 postal clerks work for the U.S. Postal Service. Most of these clerks work in mail processing centers rather than in local post offices, and about three-fourths work full-time. Some new workers will be needed in the next decade to replace workers who retire or leave the profession. The number of clerk positions, however, is expected to increase more slowly than the average for all other occupations because of technological developments, including automation and electronic sorting and canceling devices, which allow clerks to handle greater volumes of mail. UPS expects the number of administrative positions, including account executives, to decline as the company consolidates to keep costs down.

■ For More Information

The following union organizations offer information about employment:

National Postal Mail Handlers Union
1101 Connecticut Avenue, NW, Suite 500
Washington, DC 20036
Tel: 202-833-9095
Web: http://www.npmhu.org/

American Postal Workers Union
Research and Education Department
1300 L Street, NW, Suite 525
Washington, DC 20005
Tel: 202-842-4200
Web: http://www.apwu.org

For information about eligibility and qualifying examinations for the U.S. Postal Service, consult your local post office or state employment service. Current information on the Postal Service also is summarized annually in the U.S. Government Manual. For general information on postal employment and information about Inspection Service employment, contact:

U.S. Postal Service
c/o Chief Postal Inspector
Headquarters Personnel Division
475 L'Enfant Plaza, SW, Room 1813
Washington, DC 20260-4261
Tel (HR INFORMATION LINE): 800-474-7195
Web: http://www.usps.gov/hrisp/ (job listings)

The following commercial delivery companies also offer employment opportunities:

United Parcel Service of America
Human Resources
55 Glenlake Parkway, NE
Atlanta, GA 30328
Tel: 888-WORK-UPS
Web: http://www.careermosaic.com/cm/ups/home.html

Airborne Freight Corporation
Human Resources
3101 Western Avenue
Seattle, WA 98121
Tel: 202-285-4600
Web: http://www2.airborne.com/HRWeb/

For a free Student Information packet, contact:

Federal Express
Student Info Pack
PO Box 727
Memphis, TN 38194
Tel: 901-395-4555
Web: http://www.fedex.com/us/careers/

■ Related Articles

Letter and Package Delivery

Cashiers

Counter and Retail Clerks

Data Entry Clerks

Mail Carriers

Route Drivers

Shipping and Receiving Managers and Clerks

Stock Clerks

Traffic Agents and Clerks

Postal Inspectors

■ See Health and Regulatory Inspectors

Postal Window Clerks

■ **See Postal Clerks**

Power Plant Occupations

■ Overview

In general, *power plant operators* control the machinery that generates electricity. *Power distributors* and *power dispatchers* oversee the flow of electricity through substations and a network of transmission and distribution lines to individual and commercial consumers. The generators in these power plants may produce electricity by converting energy from a nuclear reactor; burning oil, gas, or coal; or harnessing energy from falling water, the sun, or the wind.

■ History

The first permanent, commercial electric power-generating plant and distribution network was set up in New York City in 1882 under the supervision of the inventor Thomas Edison (1847-1931). Initially, the purpose of the network was to supply electricity to Manhattan buildings equipped with incandescent light bulbs, which had been developed just a few years earlier by Edison. Despite early problems in transmitting power over distance, the demand for electricity grew rapidly. Plant after plant was built to supply communities with electricity, and by 1900 incandescent lighting was a well-established part of urban life. Other uses of electric power were developed as well, and by about

POWER PLANT OCCUPATIONS	
SCHOOL SUBJECTS	Mathematics Technical/Shop
PERSONAL SKILLS	Mechanical/manipulative Technical/scientific
WORK ENVIRONMENT	Primarily indoors Primarily one location
MINIMUM EDUCATION LEVEL	High school diploma
SALARY RANGE	$28,000 to $40,000 to $60,000
OUTLOOK	Little change or more slowly than the average
DOT	952
GOE	05.06.01
NOC	7352
O*NET	95021

An electrical power plant control room operator uses a touchscreen monitor to adjust power settings.

1910 electric power became common in factories, public transportation systems, businesses, and homes.

Many early power plants generated electricity by harnessing water, or hydro, power. In hydroelectric plants, which are often located at dams on rivers, giant turbines are turned by falling water, and that energy is converted into electricity. Until the 1930s, hydroelectric plants supplied most electric power because hydro plants were less expensive to operate than plants that relied on thermal energy released by burning fuels such as coal. Afterwards, various technological advances made power generation in thermal plants more economical. Burning fossil fuels (coal, oil, or gas) creates heat, which is used to make steam to turn turbines and generate power. During the last several decades, many plants that use nuclear reactors as heat sources for making steam have been in operation.

Today, energy from all these sources—burning fossil fuels, nuclear reactors, and hydro power—is used to generate electricity. Large electric utility systems may generate power from different sources at multiple sites. While the essentials of generating, distributing, and utilizing electricity have been known for a century, the techniques and the equipment have changed. Over the years the equipment used in power generation and distribution has become much more sophisticated, efficient, and centralized, and the use of electric power exceeds the demand for workers.

■ The Job

Workers in power plants monitor and operate the machinery that generates electric power and sends power out to users in a network of distribution lines. Most employees work for electric utility companies or government agencies that produce power, but there are a small number who work for private companies that make electricity for their own use.

In general, *power plant operators* who work in plants fueled by coal, oil, or natural gas operate boilers, turbines, generators, and auxiliary equipment such as coal crushers. They also operate switches that control the amount of power created by the various generators and regulate the flow of power to outgoing transmission lines. They keep track of power demands on the system and respond to changes in demand by turning generators on and off and connecting and disconnecting circuits.

Operators must also watch meters and instruments and make frequent tests of the system to check power flow and voltage. They keep records of the load on the generators, power lines, and other equipment in the system, and they record switching operations and any problems or unusual situations that come up during their shifts.

In older plants, *auxiliary equipment operators* work throughout the plant monitoring specific kinds of equipment, such as pumps, fans, compressors, and condensers.

In newer plants, however, these workers have been mostly replaced by automated controls located in a central control room. *Central control room operators* and their assistants work in these nerve centers. Central control rooms are complex installations with many electronic instruments, meters, gauges, and switches that allow skilled operators to know exactly what is going on with the whole generating system and to quickly pinpoint any trouble that needs repairs or adjustments. In most cases, mechanics and maintenance workers are the ones who repair the equipment.

The electricity generated in power plants is sent through transmission lines to users at the direction of *load dispatchers*. Load dispatcher workrooms are command posts, where the power generating and distributing activities are coordinated. Pilot boards in the workrooms are like automated maps that display what is going on throughout the entire distribution system. Dispatchers operate converters, transformers, and circuit breakers, based on readings given by monitoring equipment.

By studying factors, such as weather, that affect power use, dispatchers anticipate power needs and tell control room operators how much power will be needed to keep the power supply and demand in balance. If there is a failure in the distribution system, dispatchers redirect the power flow in transmission lines around the problem. They also operate equipment at substations, where the voltage of power in the system is adjusted.

■ Requirements

High School

Most employers prefer to hire high school graduates for positions in this occupational field, and often college-level training is desirable. High school students should take all of the courses needed to obtain a standard high school diploma, but should focus on obtaining a solid background in mathematics and science.

Postsecondary Training

Beginners in this field may start out as helpers or in laborer jobs, or they may begin training for duties in operations, maintenance, or other areas. Those who enter training for operator positions undergo extensive training by their employer, both on the job and in formal classroom settings. The training program is geared toward the particular plant in which they work, and usually lasts several years. Even after they are fully qualified as operators or dispatchers, most employees will be required to take continuing education refresher courses.

Certification or Licensing

Power plants that generate electricity using nuclear reactors are regulated by the Nuclear Regulatory Commission (NRC). Operators in nuclear plants must be licensed by the NRC, as only NRC-licensed operators are authorized to control any equipment in the plant that affects the operation of the nuclear reactor. *Nuclear reactor operators* will also be required to undertake regular drug testing.

Other Requirements

Although union membership is not necessarily a requirement for employment, many workers in power plants are members of either the International Brotherhood of Electrical Workers or the Utility Workers Union of America. Union members traditionally have been paid better than non-union members.

■ Exploring

There is little opportunity for part-time or summer work experience in this field. However, many power plants (both nuclear and nonnuclear) have visitor centers where interested members of the public are welcome to observe some of the power plant operations and to learn about the various processes for converting energy into electricity. High school students interested in this field should also take advantage of information available in libraries about generating electric power.

■ Employers

Employees in the power plant field work in several types of power-generating plants, including those that use natural gas, oil, coal, nuclear, hydro, solar, and wind energies. Because electric utility companies have dominated the energy field, most power plant workers work in electrical utilities. Government agencies that produce power are also employers, as are private companies that make electricity for their own use. Employment opportunities are available

PROFILE: THOMAS ALVA EDISON (1847-1931)

Edison invented the incandescent lightbulb and then played a major role in creating an electricity-generating network for the City of New York. The first central electric power plant opened on Pearl Street, New York City, in 1882. Despite start-up and transmission problems, the demand for electricity continued to grow and incandescent lighting was part of most American homes by 1900.

This prolific inventor was also responsible for inventing many other items, including an electric vote counting machine, the phonograph, storage batteries, dictating machines, the fluoroscope, and the mimeograph duplicating machine.

in any part of the country, as power plants are scattered nationwide.

■ Starting Out

People interested in working in electric power plants can contact local electric utility companies directly. Local offices of utility worker unions may also be sources of information about job opportunities. Leads for specific jobs may be found in newspaper classified ads and through the local offices of the state employment service. Graduates of technical training programs can often get help locating jobs from the placement office of their school.

■ Advancement

After they have completed their training, power plant operators may move into supervisory positions, such as the position of a shift supervisor. Most opportunities for promotion are within the same plant or at other plants owned by the same utility company. With experience and appropriate training, nuclear power plant operators may advance to become *senior reactor operators* and shift supervisors. Workers in this field do not usually move from one company to another.

■ Earnings

Salaries for workers in the utilities industry are relatively high, but they do depend on skills and experience, geographical location, union status, and other factors. Most operators in conventional (nonnuclear) power plants earn more than $31,000 a year. Operators who are union members earn from $28,000 to over $40,000 a year, with senior operators earning between $30,000 and $47,000 a year. Operators in nuclear power plants average between $40,000 and $60,000 a year. In many cases, employee salaries are supplemented significantly by overtime pay, which becomes necessary during power outages and under severe weather conditions.

Since power plants operate around the clock, employees work multiple shifts, which can last anywhere from four to 12 hours. In general, workers on night shifts are paid higher salaries than workers on day shifts. In addition to their regular earnings, most of these workers receive benefits, such as paid vacation days, paid sick leave, health insurance, and pension plans.

■ Work Environment

Most areas of power plants are clean and well lighted and ventilated. Some areas of the plant may be quite noisy. The work of power plant workers is not physically strenuous; workers usually sit or stand in one place as they perform their duties. Risk of falls, burns, or electric shock increases for those who work outside of the control room. Workers must follow strict safety regulations and sometimes wear protective clothing, such as hard hats and safety shoes, to ensure safety and avoid serious accidents.

Electricity is needed 24 hours a day, every day of the year, so power plants must be staffed at all times. Most workers will work some nights, weekends, and holidays, usually on a rotating basis so that all employees share the stress and fatigue of working the more difficult shifts.

■ Outlook

In the next 10 to 15 years, employment in this field is expected to grow more slowly than the average for other occupations. Consumer demand for electric power will surely continue to increase, but power-generating plants will install more automatic control systems and more efficient equipment, which will reduce the growth of operating staffs.

It is unlikely that new nuclear power plants will be ordered in the coming decade and many of the ones now in operation are shutting down. However, some additional operators may be needed to work in existing plants because of regulatory requirements for increased staffing.

Most job openings will develop when experienced workers retire or leave to go into other occupations. Jobs in electric power plants are seldom affected by ups and downs in the economy, so employees in the field have rather stable jobs.

■ For More Information

This national trade association represents more than 2,000 municipal, state, and local government-owned electric utilities.

American Public Power Association
2301 M Street, NW
Washington, DC 20037
Tel: 202-467-2900
Web: http://www.appanet.org/cgi-bin/wwwais

This trade association represents shareholder-owned electric utilities, with 180 member companies. It conducts meetings and expos, and provides lighting solutions to residential, commercial, and industrial areas. A publications catalog is available.

Edison Electric Institute
701 Pennsylvania Avenue, NW
Washington, DC 20004-2696
Tel: 202-508-5000
Web: http://www.eei.org

IBEW serves approximately 750,000 members who work primarily, in the utility, construction, electrical, and manufacturing areas. Some written information is available.

International Brotherhood of Electrical Workers
1125 15th Street, NW
Washington, DC 20005
Tel: 202-833-7000
Web: http://www.ibew.org

This union consists of approximately 45,000 members working in the gas, water, electric, and nuclear industries.

Utility Workers Union of America
815 16th Street, NW
Washington, DC 20006
Tel: 202-347-8105

■ Related Articles

Energy

Machining and Machinery

Nuclear Power

Petroleum

Boilermakers and Mechanics

Electricians

Nuclear Engineers

Nuclear Reactor Operators and Technicians

Stationary Engineers

Precision Assemblers

■ **See Sporting Goods Production Workers**

Precision Machinists

■ Overview

Precision machinists use machine tools such as lathes, drill presses, and milling machines to produce precision metal parts. They combine their knowledge of the working properties of metals and their skill with machine tools to plan and carry out the operations needed to make precisely specified machined products.

History

The modern era of producing metal parts accurately and according to specifications began with the invention of the steam engine by James Watt in the latter part of the 18th century. During this same period, John Wilkinson invented the boring machine, which enabled the precise cutting of cylinders for Watt's engine. Also in this period, Henry Maudslay developed a lathe to precisely cut screw threads.

Many new methods of production were eventually developed during the Industrial Revolution. In Great Britain, metal molds and energy-powered engines were used to produce items that had originally been handcrafted. They lowered costs and speeded up production schedules. At about the same time in the United States, Eli Whitney was using tools and machines to make gun parts with such accuracy that they were interchangeable.

The interchangeability of machine-produced parts became the basis for modern mass production. Throughout the 19th century, more specialized and refined metal-working machines were designed. The electric motor became widely used as a source of power, which also spurred further improvements.

The workers who used these machines to create parts—machinists and machine tool operators—developed into a specialized group who combined machining knowledge with skillful handiwork. By 1888, there were enough machinists in various industries to organize a machinists' union.

In the 20th century, the automobile industry was probably the largest single force in the development of machinery and the increased demand for machinists. Technological developments, such as numerical control machinery and CAD (computer-aided design) applications, have continued to spur progress in machining operations.

These developments have also changed the jobs of machinists. Now workers set manual, conventional machines to cut at extremely close tolerances and program computer-controlled machine tools to cut and contour metal into intricate shapes. They use lasers and coordinate measuring machines and modern imaging equipment to check dimensions. Though machinists still use their hands, their profession has evolved into much more of a science than a craft.

The Job

Precision machinists are trained to operate most types of machine tools that shape pieces of material—usually metal—to specifications. The work done by machine tools can be classified into one of the following categories: cutting, drilling, boring, turning (lathe), milling, planing (shaper, slotter, broach), and grinding.

After receiving a job assignment, the machinist's first task is to review the blueprints or written specifications for the piece to be made. Next, the machinist decides which machining operations should be used, plans their sequence, and calculates how fast to feed the metal into the machine. When this is complete, the machinist sets up the machine with the proper shaping tools and marks the metal stock (a process called layout work) to indicate where cuts should be made.

Once the layout work is done, the machinist performs the necessary machining operations. The metal is carefully positioned on the tool, the controls are set, and the cuts are made. During the shaping operation, the machinist constantly monitors the metal feed and the machine speed. If necessary, the machinist adds coolants and lubricants to the workpiece.

At times, machinists produce many identical machined products by working at a single machine; at other times, they produce one item by working on a variety of machines. After completing the machining operations, they might finish the work by hand, using files and scrapers, for example, and then assemble the finished parts with hand tools.

A high degree of accuracy is required in all work performed by machinists. Some specifications call for accuracy within one-ten-thousandth of an inch. To achieve this precision, machinists must use measuring instruments such as scribers, micrometers, calipers, verniers, scales, and gauges.

In the past, machinists had direct control of their machines. However, the increasing use of numerically controlled machines and, in particular, computer numerically controlled machines, has changed the nature of the work. Machinists may now work alone or with tool programmers to program the machines that make the parts. They may also be responsible for checking computer programs to ensure that they run the machinery properly.

Some machinists, often called *production machinists,* may produce large quantities of one part. Others produce relatively small numbers of each item they make. Finally, some specialize in repairing

PRECISION MACHINISTS	
SCHOOL SUBJECTS	**Computer science** **Mathematics** **Technical/Shop**
PERSONAL SKILLS	**Mechanical/manipulative** **Technical/scientific**
WORK ENVIRONMENT	**Primarily indoors** **Primarily one location**
MINIMUM EDUCATION LEVEL	**Apprenticeship**
SALARY RANGE	**$26,200 to $40,000 to $70,000**
CERTIFICATION OR LICENSING	**None available**
OUTLOOK	**Decline**
DOT	**600**
GOE	**05.05.07**
NOC	**7221**
O*NET	**89108**

A precision machinist works on a gear hob with a lathe.

machinery or making new parts for existing machinery. In repairing a broken part, the machinist might refer to existing blueprints and perform the same machining operations that were used to create the original part.

■ Requirements

High School

For trainee or apprentice jobs, most companies prefer high school or vocational school graduates. Courses in algebra, geometry, mechanical drawing, blueprint reading, machine shop, drafting, and computer applications are very helpful. Classes in electronics and hydraulics are also useful.

Postsecondary Training

To qualify as a precision machinist, a worker must complete either an apprenticeship or an on-the-job training program. Apprenticeships, which most employers prefer, generally consist of four to five years of carefully planned activity combining shop training with related classroom instruction. In shop training, apprentices learn filing, handtapping, and dowel fitting, as well as the operation of various machine tools. The operation and programming of computer-controlled tools are also covered. The classroom instruction, usually offered in the evenings, includes industrial math, blueprint reading, precision machining, computer numerical control concepts, machine tool technology, and manufacturing processes.

The other method of becoming a machinist, on-the-job training, involves working for four or more years under the supervision of experienced machinists, progressing from one machine to another. Trainees usually begin as machine operators. Then, as they show the necessary aptitude, they are given additional training on the machines they are operating. Further instruction in the more technical aspects of machine shop work is obtained through studying manuals and, occasionally, classroom instruction. The amount of progress depends on the skill of the worker.

Other Requirements

A precision machinist must have an aptitude for using mechanical principles in practical applications. A knowledge of mathematics is important. In addition, the ability to understand and visualize spatial relationships is needed to read engineering drawings.

Machinists must have excellent manual dexterity, good vision and hand-eye coordination, and the concentration and diligence necessary to do highly accurate work. Because their work requires a great deal of standing and moving, good physical condition and stamina are important. Finally, it is necessary for machinists to be able to work independently in an organized, systematic way.

■ Exploring

To observe machinists at work, ask a school counselor or teacher to arrange a field trip to a machine shop. Another excellent opportunity to explore this occupation could be a part-time job in a machine shop, perhaps during the summer months. Talk to someone already working as a machinist to learn the pros and cons of the job.

■ Employers

Most precision machinists work in small machining shops or in manufacturing firms that produce durable goods, such as metalworking and industrial machinery, aircraft, or motor vehicles. Maintenance machinists work in most of the industries that use production machinery. Although machinists work in all parts of the country, jobs are most plentiful in areas where manufacturing is concentrated.

■ Starting Out

If you want to become an apprentice, contact potential employers directly to ask about opportunities. Other sources of information are state employment offices, the U.S. Labor Department's Bureau of Apprenticeship and Training, and an appropriate union headquarters (e.g., the International Association of Machinists and Aerospace Workers or the International Union, United Automobile, Aerospace, and Agricultural Implement Workers of America). School counselors or trade school job placement offices may also have information.

If you enter the field through on-the-job training, you will generally be required to start with a less-skilled job, such as machine shop helper or machine tool operator. You will eventually work up to the position of machinist. In order to find an entry-level job, contact potential employers directly. Check job listings at state employment offices and local newspaper ads.

■ Advancement

Workers must successfully complete a training program before becoming qualified machinists. After several years, when machinists have increased their skill level and have taken additional training, many advancement opportunities may become available. For instance, they may specialize in niches such as tool and die design or fabrication, sales, or instrument repairing. In large production shops, machinists have the opportunity to become setup operators and layout workers.

Those who have good judgment, excellent planning skills, and the ability to deal well with people may progress to supervisory positions, such as shop supervisor or even plant manager. With additional education, some machinists may become tool engineers. Finally, some exceptionally skilled and experienced workers eventually go into business for themselves.

■ Earnings

The average annual wage for precision machinists is at least $40,000, according to the U.S. Bureau of Labor Statistics. Industry trade associations put the pay closer to $55,000 annually. At the top end of the pay scale, industry sources say workers can earn $70,000 or more. Overtime has become quite common in the industry, and machinists are paid for overtime work. Benefits that generally are available to machinists include paid holidays and vacations; life, medical, and accident insurance; and retirement plans.

■ Work Environment

Machinists work indoors in machine shops that are fairly clean, with proper lighting and ventilation; however, noise levels are often quite high because of the nature of power-driven machinery. Although machining work is not physically strenuous, machinists are usually on their feet for most of the day. Often, they must wear special shoes to reduce foot fatigue. Safety glasses are required as cutting tools, moving machine parts, and flying metal chips can cause eye injuries.

Because machinists can set up and operate almost every machine in the shop, their work may vary with the production needs of the company. They are often challenged by the needs of each job, and their accuracy and patience is tested by the precise demands of production. Machinists play an important role in the world of complex machinery and they have the satisfaction of knowing that their contributions are valuable and seeing the results of their efforts.

■ Outlook

Employment of machinists is expected to decline slightly through the year 2006. Automation is contributing to this slight decline. The increased use of computer-controlled machine tools improves machine efficiency. Therefore, fewer machinists are needed to accomplish the same amount of work.

Even so, many openings will arise from the need to replace machinists who retire or transfer to other jobs. In recent years, employers have reported difficulty in attracting workers to machining occupations. If this trend continues, good employment possibilities should exist for candidates with the necessary skills.

Layoffs are often a factor affecting employment of machinists. When the demand for products declines, workers' hours may be either shortened or reduced completely for days, weeks, even months at a time. There is somewhat more job security for maintenance machinists because machines must be cared for even when production is slow.

■ For More Information

For information on apprenticeships for machinists, contact:

International Union, United Automobile, Aerospace, and Agricultural Implement Workers of America
Skilled Trades Department
8000 East Jefferson Avenue
Detroit, MI 48214
Tel: 313-926-5000
Web: http://www.uaw.org

For information about opportunities in the metalworking industry, contact:

National Tooling & Machining Association
9300 Livingston Road
Fort Washington, MD 20744
Tel: 301-248-6200 or 800-248-6862
Web: http://www.ntma.org

For information about training and opportunities in the metalworking industry, contact:

Precision Machined Products Association
6700 West Snowville Road
Brecksville, OH 44141
Tel: 440-526-0300
Web: http://www.pmpa.org

For literature on careers and training in the machine tools trades, contact:

Tooling and Manufacturing Association
1177 South Dee Road
Park Ridge, IL 60068
Tel: 847-825-1120
Web: http://www.tmanet.com

■ Related Articles

Machining and Machinery

Manufacturing

Metals

Fluid Power Technicians

Forge Shop Workers

Heat Treaters

Industrial Machinery Mechanics

Precision Metalworkers

■ Overview

Precision metalworkers are skilled craftsworkers who produce the tools, dies, molds, cutting devices, and guiding and holding devices used in the mass production of a variety of products. *Tool makers* produce precision tools for cutting, shaping, and forming metal and other materials. They also produce jigs and fixtures—the devices for holding the tools and metal while it is being worked—and various gauges and other measuring devices. *Die makers* make precision metal forms, or dies, used in stamping and forging metal. *Mold makers* design and make metal molds for molding plastics, ceramics, and composite materials. In some cases, the term *tool and die maker* is used generically, referring to any or all of these job categories.

■ History

The modern machine tool industry came into existence around the beginning of the 19th century. One of the most important early contributors was Eli Whitney, the American inventor and manufacturer who is credited with the first successful use of standardized, interchangeable parts in manufacturing. When Whitney received an order from the U.S. government in 1798 for thousands of muskets, he envisioned a new work method. He realized that he could design machines that would allow unskilled workers to turn out many identi-

PRECISION METALWORKERS	
SCHOOL SUBJECTS	Mathematics Technical/Shop
PERSONAL SKILLS	Mechanical/manipulative Technical/scientific
WORK ENVIRONMENT	Primarily indoors Primarily one location
MINIMUM EDUCATION LEVEL	Apprenticeship
SALARY RANGE	$20,000 to $36,500 to $70,000
CERTIFICATION OR LICENSING	None available
OUTLOOK	Decline
DOT	601
GOE	05.05.07
NOC	7232

cal copies of each part in a musket. In carrying out his plan, he invented *jigs* (tool-guiding patterns) and *fixtures* (devices that clamp workpieces in place). They were the first versions of devices that are very important in today's tool and die making.

Another significant invention of the 19th century was the power press, which could be fitted with presswork dies, or stamping dies, to cut and form items out of sheet metal. Today, the fabrication of presswork dies remains an important part of tool and die making. Other significant developments in the field have included methods for die-casting metals and injection-molding materials, such as plastics.

The rapid growth of mass-production techniques in the late 19th century spurred the development of tool and die shops, mostly small, independent contractors, who today employ the majority of precision metalworkers in the United States. Also, as manufacturing industries came to use more kinds of precision tools and dies, the workers who fabricate them have become increasingly specialized. So, even though today's tools and dies make hundreds of thousands of mass-produced parts, they themselves must be custom made by highly skilled craftsworkers. Today's tooling shops typically perform a few very sophisticated types of tasks, rather than a broad range of tool making and die making.

■ The Job

Tool, die, and mold makers are among the most highly skilled production workers in the economy. They possess a broad knowledge of machining operations, can read complex blueprints, and are able to do complicated mathematical calculations. They may produce many different kinds of devices or they may specialize in just one item. In a small shop, a single worker is typically responsible for all the steps necessary to complete a device from start to finish, while in a larger shop, specialized production tasks are allocated among several workers, with the tool maker or die maker acting as a job supervisor.

Many types of machine shops and workers are covered under the tool and die category. They include tool and die shops that produce dies, punches, die sets and components, sub-presses, jigs and fixtures, and special checking devices. Also included are companies that manufacture molds for die-casting and foundry casting, and shops that make metal molds for plastics, rubber, plaster, and glass working.

In general, pressworking dies are used to cut and shape sheet metals with electrical or hydraulic presses. Composed of two units, the upper part attaches to a press ram and the lower part attaches to a press bed. Molding dies, used to form both metals and plastics, consist of two units which when closed form a cavity into which molten material is poured.

No matter what the shop produces, however, when a job first arrives, the tool and die makers must analyze instructions, blueprints, sketches, or models of the finished product. Using such information, they decide how to go about making the device. After the dimensions are computed, the tool and die makers plan the layout and assembly processes and decide on a sequence of operations for machining the metal.

When the plan is clear, workers select and lay out metal stock, measuring and marking the metal, and if necessary, cutting it into pieces of the approximate size needed for the project. They set up the machine tools, such as lathes, drill presses, and grinders, and carefully cut, bore, and drill the metal according to their predetermined plan. In the machining process, they closely monitor the dimensions of the workpiece since their work must have a high degree of accuracy—frequently within ten-thousandths of an inch. Measuring equipment, such as micrometers, gauge blocks, and dial indicators, is used to ensure precision.

When satisfied that the parts are accurately machined in accordance with the original specifications, tool and die makers fit the pieces together to make the final product. They may need to do finishing work on the product, such as filing and smoothing surfaces. Depending on the size and complexity of the device, the production process may take weeks or months to complete.

Modern technology is changing the way tools are developed and produced. Firms now commonly use computer-aided design (CAD) to develop products and parts, and to design the tooling to make the parts. These tool drawings are then processed by a computer program to calculate cutting paths and the sequence of operations. Once these instructions are developed, computer numerically controlled machines are usually used to produce the individual components of the tool. Often, these programs are stored for future use.

■ Requirements

High School

Applicants for jobs in this field need to have at least a high school or vocational school education. Courses in mathematics, blueprint reading, drafting, computers, metalworking, and machine shop are very useful.

Postsecondary Training

Precision metalworkers can learn their trade either through informal on-the-job training or formal apprenticeships, which most employers prefer because of the thoroughness of the training. Lasting four to five years, apprenticeships combine a planned and supervised on-the-job training program with class work in related fields. On the job, apprentices learn how to set up and operate machine tools, such

Precision metalworkers must pay close attention at all times when operating dangerous machinery.

as lathes, milling machines, grinders, and jig borers. They also learn to use other mechanical equipment, gauges, and various hand tools. In addition, they receive classroom instruction in blueprint reading, mechanical drawing, tool programming, shop theory, shop mathematics, properties of various metals, and tool design.

Workers who become on-the-job trainees are initially assigned simple tasks that usually involve operating machines; later they are given increasingly more complex work. They pick up skills gradually. One drawback to this method is that it may take many years to learn all the necessary skills.

Tool and die makers or mold makers may start out as machinists. They supplement their metalworking experience with additional training, which may include layout work, shop mathematics, blueprint reading, heat treating, and the use of precision tools, through vocational or correspondence schools.

Other Requirements

Precision metalworkers have a mechanical aptitude and the ability to work with careful attention to detail. To ensure the absolute precision of their work, they are very method-

" I'm always looking for young people who want to learn mold making," says Richard H. Burman, president of Graphic Tool Corporation in Itasca, Illinois. "We work with the machine shop program in a local high school to encourage students to consider becoming an apprentice."

The image of a "greasy, old system" in a machine shop is a hard one to break, according to Rich. Modern mold-making shops are anything but, he goes on to say. At Graphic Tool, they use a computer-aided design (CAD) system to make the mold drawings, and in production they have electronic discharge machines do some of the grinding and numeric control machines for most of the processing. The equipment is expensive and the technology advanced.

Graphic Tool specializes in making molds for the manufacture of plastic parts. Since this process involves injecting molten plastic into the cavity of a mold to form a part and then within seconds ejecting the fully formed and cooled part, each mold has an elaborate web of water lines to remove heat from the part. Their mold makers are responsible for designing and producing molds that are efficient and cost-effective in production.

"A good mold design can shave seconds off each machine cycle," says Rich. This is important to their clients, most of whom are high-volume manufacturers of plastic parts.

Each project at Graphic Tool is lead by a journeyman mold maker who knows and coordinates all the steps that must be done. No two projects are exactly the same, and experienced mold makers relish the challenges. When a mold is up and running, Rich says there is much satisfaction in a job well done.

ical and continuously check measurements of the workpiece throughout the job. Workers also need to be able to work as efficiently as possible, with a minimum waste of time or materials. Good eyesight is a must, and in some jobs, workers must to be able to lift moderately heavy objects.

Because they often work without close supervision, tool and die makers need to be self-motivated and organized in their work habits. In addition, they need good communication skills to help them work in cooperation with other workers.

■ Exploring

There are several ways to learn about precision metalworking. Hobbies such as tinkering with cars, making models, and assembling electronic equipment may be helpful in testing patience, accuracy, and mechanical ability, all of which are important qualities for both tool and die makers. A field trip to a mold shop or tool and die shop can give you a glimpse of the work in this field and may offer the opportunity to talk to experienced workers. Even better is a part-time or summer job in such a setting. Although your work would probably be basic labor, such as sweep-

ing floors, the experience could provide a valuable opportunity to observe firsthand the day-to-day activities in a machine shop.

■ Employers

Most precision metalworkers are employed in independent job shops where tools and dies are tailor-made for a variety of manufacturers. These shops are generally located in the Midwest as well as Pennsylvania, California, New York, and New Jersey. The largest concentration is in Michigan. Precision metalworkers also work in industries that manufacture machines and equipment for metalworking, automobiles, and other motor vehicles, aircraft, and plastics products. Among large manufacturers, such as automakers, however, there seems to be a trend to close in-house shops.

■ Starting Out

There are various sources for information about apprentice programs and job openings for prospective precision metalworkers. These include the state employment offices; local employers, such as tool and die shops and manufacturing firms; various metalworking trade associations; and the local offices of unions, such as the United Auto Workers or the International Association of Machinists and Aerospace Workers. Additionally, high school, vocational school, and technical institute students may get help from their teachers or the placement office at their schools.

■ Advancement

After completing apprenticeship training, workers often need several more years' experience to learn the most difficult and specialized skills. Well-qualified, experienced workers may have several avenues of advancement open to them. There is a shortage of precision metalworkers so opportunities are plentiful for those who have good experience. Some may choose to move into a larger shop for more pay or accept a supervisory position. Others may decide to become a tool designer or specialist in programming computer numerical-controlled machine tools.

Another possibility for some tool makers is to become a tool inspector in an industry that requires a particularly high degree of accuracy in components. Many workers go into business for themselves, opening their own independent job shops to make items for manufacturing firms that do not maintain their own tool-making or die-making department.

■ Earnings

Earnings for tool and die makers are generally good. According to the U.S. Bureau of Labor Statistics, the average annual wage in 1997 was $36,500. Entry-level workers in this field make about $20,000, while those in the highest paid positions can make $70,000.

Salary levels vary somewhat in different areas of the country, with workers in the western and midwestern states earning more than workers in the northeastern and southern states. The size of the employer is also a factor in salary level. Tool and die makers who work for larger establishments tend to have proportionally higher wages.

In addition to regular earnings, most precision metalworkers receive benefits such as health insurance, paid vacation days, and retirement plans.

■ Work Environment

Precision metalworkers typically work 40 hours per week, although overtime is not unusual. Most plants that employ these workers operate only one shift per day. They usually work in shops that are adequately lighted, temperature-controlled, and well ventilated. Their work areas are not typically very noisy, as opposed to production departments. There are exceptions, however—tool and die departments that are near production areas or heat-treating or casting areas may be hot and noisy. Workers spend much of the day standing and moving about, and they may occasionally have to lift moderately heavy objects.

To avoid injury from machines and flying bits of metal, workers must follow good safety practices and use appropriate protective gear, including safety glasses and hearing protectors. In some settings, workers are exposed to smoky conditions, and they may get oil, coolants, and other irritating substances on their skin.

Since most precision metalworkers work on a variety of projects, their work is seldom routine. In some cases, workers are completing several jobs at once. Many who choose this field find the work to be very satisfying. They typically work with little supervision. They also have the pleasure of seeing a project through from start to finish and knowing that they have done a precise and skillful job.

■ Outlook

Although employers report difficulty in finding skilled workers for their jobs, the employment of precision metalworkers is expected to decline in the near future, according to the U.S. Bureau of Labor Statistics. More numerically controlled machine tools and other automated equipment are being used, so fewer operations are being done by hand, resulting in fewer workers being needed. Furthermore, some products that are mass-produced using tools and dies are being imported from abroad, as are some tools and dies. China, for example, is becoming a competitor in the tool and die making field although their technology is not yet at the level of shops here.

Despite the expected decline in employment, there are still openings for new workers each year. Many of the work-

ers presently employed in these occupations are approaching retirement, which will result in job openings. Many more openings will occur due to individuals advancing into other fields. Employers in almost every area of the country are experiencing significant trouble filling positions, according to several trade associations. Highly skilled workers can continue to expect to have very good job opportunities if the shortage grows more acute.

These craftsworkers play a key role in the operation of many firms. As firms continue to invest in new equipment and modify production techniques, they will continue to rely heavily on skilled tool and die makers for retooling. This, coupled with the growing demand for products that use machined parts, should help to moderate employment decline.

■ For More Information

For information on training and apprenticeships in precision metalworking, contact:

American Mold Builders Association
701 East Irving Park Road, Suite 207
Roselle, IL 60172
Tel: 630-980-7667
Web: http://www.amba.org

International Union of Electronic, Electrical, Salaried, Machine, and Furniture Workers
Skilled Trades Department
1126 16th Street, NW
Washington, DC 20036
Tel: 202-785-7200
Web: http://iue.org

National Tooling & Machining Association
9300 Livingston Road
Fort Washington, MD 20744
Tel: 301-248-6200
Web: http://ntma.org

Precision Machined Products Association
6700 West Snowville Road
Brecksville, OH 44141
Tel: 216-526-0300
Web: http://www.pmpa.org

Tooling and Manufacturing Association
1177 South Dee Road
Park Ridge, IL 60068
Tel: 847-825-1120
Web: http://www.tmanet.com

■ Related Articles

Machining and Machinery

Metals

Plastics

Iron and Steel Industry Workers

Job and Die Setters

Lathers

Layout Workers

Numerical Control Tool Programmers

Precision Machinists

Precision-Lens Technicians

■ See Ophthalmic Laboratory Technicians, Optics Technicians

Pre-Flight Technicians

■ See Prepress Workers

Preform Laminators

■ See Plastics Products Manufacturing Workers

Prep Cooks

■ See Cooks, Chefs, and Bakers

Prepress Workers

■ Overview

Prepress is the first stage in the printing process. It is where a printed product is prepared for the printing press. This initial phase of production involves multiple steps, including creating pages from text and graphics and making printing plates. Computerized processes have replaced many of the traditional processes, eliminating a number of prepress jobs but opening up new opportunities as well.

According to the U.S. Bureau of Labor Statistics, prepress jobs employed more than 150,000 people in the late 1990s.

■ History

The history of modern printing began with the invention of movable type in the 15th century. For several centuries before that, books had been printed from carved wooden blocks or laboriously copied by hand. These painstaking methods of production where so expensive that books were chained to prevent theft.

In the 1440s, Johannes Gutenberg invented a form of metal type that could be used over and over. The first known book to be printed with this movable type was a Bible in 1455—the now-famous Gutenberg Bible. Gutenberg's revolutionary new type greatly reduced the time and cost involved in printing, and books soon became plentiful.

Ottmar Mergenthaler, a German immigrant to the United States, invented the Linotype machine in 1886. Linotype allowed the typesetter to set type from a keyboard that used a mechanical device to set letters in place. Before this, printers were setting type by hand, one letter at a time, picking up each letter individually from their typecases as they had been doing for more than 400 years. At about the same time, Tolbert Lanston invented the Monotype machine, which also had a keyboard but set the type as individual letters. These inventions allowed compositors to set type much faster and more efficiently.

With these machines, newspapers advanced from the small two-page weeklies of the 1700s to the huge editions of today's metropolitan dailies. The volume of other periodicals, advertisements, books, and other printed matter also proliferated.

In the 1950s, a new system called photocomposition was introduced into commercial typesetting operations. In this system, typesetting machines used photographic images of letters, which were projected onto a photosensitive surface to compose pages. Instructions to the typesetting machine about which letters to project and where to project them were fed in through a punched-paper or magnetic tape, which was, in turn, created by an operator at a keyboard.

Most recently, typesetting has come into the home and office in the form of desktop publishing. This process has revolutionized the industry by enabling companies and individuals to do their own type composition and graphic design work.

■ The Job

Prepress work involves a variety of tasks, most of which are now computer-based. The prepress process is typically broken down into the following areas of responsibility: compositor and typesetter, paste-up worker, desktop publishing specialist, pre-flight technician, output technician, scanner operator, camera operator, lithographic artist, film stripper, and platemaker.

Compositors and typesetters are responsible for setting up and arranging type by hand or by computer into galleys for printing. This is done using "cold type" technology (as opposed to the old "hot type" method, which involved using molten lead to create letters and lines of text). A common method is phototypesetting, in which type is entered into a computer and output on photographic film or paper. Typesetting in its traditional sense requires a *paste-up worker* to then position illustrations and lay out columns of type. This manual process is quickly being phased out by desktop publishing.

Most often today, desktop publishing is the first step in the production process. The *desktop publisher* designs and lays out text and graphics on a personal computer according to the specifications of the job. This involves sizing text, setting column widths, and arranging copy with photos and other images. All elements of the piece are displayed on the computer screen and manipulated using a keyboard and mouse. In commercial printing plants, jobs tend to come from customers on computer disk, eliminating the need for initial desktop publishing work on the part of the printing company.

The entire electronic file is reviewed by the *pre-flight technician* to ensure that all of its elements are properly formatted and set up. At small print shops—which account for the majority of the printing industry—a *job printer* is often the person in charge of typesetting, page layout, proofing copy, and fixing problems with files.

Once a file is ready, the *output technician* transmits it through an imagesetter onto paper, film, or directly to a plate. The latter method is called digital imaging, and it bypasses the film stage altogether. Direct-to-plate technology has been adopted by only a small percentage of printing companies nationwide, but it is expected to be universal within the next decade.

If a file is output onto paper or provided camera-ready, the *camera operator* photographs the material and develops film negatives, either by hand or by machine. Because the bulk of commercial printing today is done using lithography, most camera operators can also be called *lithographic photographers*.

Often it is necessary to make corrections, change or reshape images, or lighten or darken the film negatives. This is the job of the *lithographic artist,* who, depending on the area of specialty, might have the title *dot etcher, retoucher,* or *letterer.* This film retouching work is highly specialized and is all done by hand using chemicals, dyes, and special tools.

The *film stripper* is the person who cuts film negatives to the proper size and arranges them onto large sheets called flats. The pieces are taped into place so that they are in proper position for the plate to be made.

The *platemaker*—also called a *lithographer* because of the process used in most commercial plants—creates the printing plates. This is done using a photographic process. The film is laid on top of a thin metal plate treated with a light-sensitive chemical. It is exposed to ultraviolet light, which "burns" the positive image into the plate. Those areas are then chemically treated so that when ink is applied to the plate, it adheres to the images to be printed and is repelled by the non-printing areas.

Lithography work traditionally involved sketching designs on stone, clay, or glass. Some of these older methods are still used for specialized purposes, but the predominant method today is the one previously described, which is used in offset printing. In offset printing, a series of cylinders are used to transfer ink from the chemically treated plate onto a rubber cylinder (called a blanket), then onto the paper. The printing plate never touches the paper but is "offset" by the rubber blanket.

If photos and art are not provided electronically, the *scanner operator* scans them using a high-resolution drum or flatbed scanner. In the scanning process, the continuous color tone of the original image is interpreted electronically and converted into a combination of the four primary colors used in printing: cyan (blue), magenta, yellow, and black—commonly called CMYK. A screening process separates the image into the four colors, each of which is represented by a series of dots called a halftone. These halftones are recorded to film from which printing plates are made. During the printing process, ink applied to each of the plates combines on paper to recreate the color of the original image.

■ Requirements

Educational requirements for prepress workers vary according to the area of responsibility, but all require at least a high school diploma, and most call for a strong command of computers.

High School

Those interested in prepress work are advised to take courses in computer science, mathematics, and electronics.

Postsecondary Training

The more traditional jobs, like camera operator, film stripper, lithographic artist, and platemaker, require longer, more specialized preparation. This might involve an apprenticeship or a two-year associate's degree. But

PREPRESS WORKERS	
SCHOOL SUBJECTS	Computer science Mathematics Technical/Shop
PERSONAL SKILLS	Artistic Technical/scientific
WORK ENVIRONMENT	Primarily indoors Primarily one location
MINIMUM EDUCATION LEVEL	High school diploma
SALARY RANGE	$11,000 to $25,000 to $60,000+
CERTIFICATION OR LICENSING	None available
OUTLOOK	Decline
DOT	979
GOE	01.06.01
NOC	9472
O*NET	92998

A GROWING SLICE OF THE PIE

The electronic prepress segment of the printing industry is experiencing phenomenal growth—9.5 percent sales growth during the first quarter of 1998, compared with -2.8 percent sales growth in the traditional prepress segment for the same period.

Prepress services overall account for about a fifth of sales revenue among printers:

Average Composition of Printers' Sales Revenue

Printing, 54 percent

Prepress Services, 20 percent

Binding, 20 percent

Ancillary Services, 6 percent

these jobs now are on the decline as they are replaced by computerized processes.

Postsecondary education is strongly encouraged for most prepress positions and a requirement for some jobs, including any managerial role. Graphic arts programs are offered by community and junior colleges as well as four-year colleges and universities. Postsecondary programs in printing technology are also available.

Any programs or courses that give students exposure to the printing field will be an asset. Courses in printing are often available at vocational-technical institutes and through printing trade associations.

Other Requirements

Prepress work requires strong communications skills, attention to detail, and the ability to perform well in a high-pressure, deadline-driven environment. Physically, prepress workers should have good manual dexterity and good eyesight and overall visual perception. Artistic skill is an advantage in nearly any prepress job.

■ Exploring

A summer job or internship doing basic word processing or desktop publishing is one way to get a feel for what prepress work involves. Such an opportunity could even be found through a temporary agency. Of course, a knowledge of computers and certain software will be needed.

You also can volunteer to do desktop publishing or design work for your school newspaper or yearbook. This would have the added benefit of exposing you to the actual printing process.

■ Employers

The U.S. Bureau of Labor Statistics reported there were over 150,000 prepress jobs in the late 1990s. Of these, 30,000 were desktop publishing jobs. The majority of pre-press work is in firms that do commercial or business printing and in newspaper plants. Other jobs are at companies that specialize in certain aspects of the prepress process—for example, platemaking or outputting of film.

Because printing is so widespread, prepress jobs are available in almost any part of the country. However, according to the *Occupational Outlook Handbook*, prepress work is concentrated in large printing centers like New York, Chicago, Los Angeles, Philadelphia, Dallas, and Washington, DC.

■ Starting Out

Information on apprenticeships and training opportunities is available through state employment services and local chapters of printing industry associations.

Those who wish to start working first and learn their skills on the job should contact potential employers directly, especially if they want to work in a small nonunion print shop. Openings for trainee positions may be listed in newspaper want ads or with the state employment service. Trade school graduates may find jobs through their school's placement office. And industry association offices often run job listing services.

■ Advancement

Some prepress work, such as typesetting, can be learned fairly quickly; other jobs, like film stripping or platemaking, take years to master. Workers often begin as assistants and move into on-the-job training programs. Entry-level workers are trained by more experienced workers and advance according to how quickly they learn and prove themselves.

In larger companies, prepress workers can move up the ranks to take on supervisory roles. Prepress and production work is also a good starting point for people who aim to become a customer service or sales representative for a printing company.

■ Earnings

Pay rates vary for prepress workers, depending on their level of experience and responsibility, type of company, where they live, and whether or not they are union members. The *Occupational Outlook Handbook* reports that the median earnings of lithographers and photoengravers were $497 a week. Typesetters and compositors earned a reported $424 a week. The Handbook quoted 1996 wages of $22.05 an hour for scanner operators and $18.88 an hour for film strippers. According to the book *Careers in Graphic Communications* (Graphic Arts Technical Foundation, 1998), some jobs, such as color scanner operator, pay up to $18 per hour. And high-tech color specialists, who manipulate color in a document before it goes to press, are paid in the range of $40,000 to $60,000.

■ Work Environment

Generally, prepress workers work in clean, quiet settings away from the noise and activity of the pressroom. Prepress areas are usually air-conditioned and roomy. Desktop publishers and others who work in front of computer terminals can risk straining their eyes, as well as their backs and necks. Film stripping and other detail-oriented work also can be tiring to the eyes. The chemicals used in platemaking can irritate the skin.

An eight-hour day is typical for most prepress jobs, but frequently workers put in more than eight hours. Prepress jobs at newspapers and financial printers often call for weekend and evening hours.

■ Outlook

Overall employment in the prepress portion of the printing industry is expected to decline through the year 2006, according to the U.S. Bureau of Labor Statistics. While it is anticipated that the demand for printed materials will increase, prepress work will not, mainly because of new innovations.

The Bureau projects that almost all prepress operations will be computerized by 2006. This will phase out many of the traditional jobs that involved highly skilled hand work: film strippers, paste-up workers, photoengravers, camera operators, and platemakers.

However, the computer-oriented aspects of prepress work are another story. Desktop publishing specialists, for example, will be in heavy demand in the near future. And specialized computer skills will increasingly be needed to handle direct-to-plate and other new technology.

Given the increasing demand for rush print jobs, printing trade service companies should offer good opportunities for prepress workers. Larger companies and companies not equipped for specialized prepress work will continue to turn to these specialty shops to keep up with their workload.

■ For More Information

GATF offers information, services, and training related to printing, electronic prepress, electronic publishing, and other areas of the graphic arts industry.

Graphic Arts Technical Foundation
200 Deer Run Road
Sewickley, PA 15143-2600
Tel: 412-741-6860
Web: http://www.gatf.org

GCCC serves as a clearinghouse, resource center, and coordinator of programs promoting career awareness, training, and a positive industry image.

Graphic Communications Career Center
1899 Preston White Drive
Reston, VA 22091
Tel: 703-648-1768
Web: http://www.npes.org/edcouncil/index.htm

GCIU represents U.S. and Canadian workers in all craft and skill areas of the printing and publishing industries. It offers education and training through local union schools.

Graphic Communications International Union
1900 L Street, NW
Washington, DC 20036
Tel: 202-462-1400
Web: http://www.gciu.org

NAPL is a graphic arts trade association is a good source of general information.

National Association of Printers and Lithographers
75 West Century Road
Paramus, NJ 07652
Tel: 201-634-9600
Web: http://www.napl.org

■ Related Articles

Book Publishing

Newspapers and Magazines

Printing

Art Directors

Graphic Designers

Printing Press Operators and Assistants

Preschool Teachers

■ Overview

Preschool teachers promote the education of children under age five in all areas. They help students develop physically, socially, and emotionally, work with them on language and communications skills, and help cultivate their cognitive abilities. They also work with families to support parents in raising their young children and reinforcing skills at home. They plan and lead activities developed in accordance with the specific ages and needs of the children. It is the goal of all preschool teachers to help students develop the skills, interests, and individual creativity that they will use for the rest of

PRESCHOOL TEACHERS	
SCHOOL SUBJECTS	Art English
PERSONAL SKILLS	Communication/ideas Helping/teaching
WORK ENVIRONMENT	Primarily indoors Primarily one location
MINIMUM EDUCATION LEVEL	Apprenticeship
SALARY RANGE	$12,000 to $19,000 to $21,000
CERTIFICATION OR LICENSING	Recommended
OUTLOOK	Faster than the average
DOT	092
O*NET	31303

A preschool teacher works with a group of her students.

their lives. Many schools and districts consider *kindergarten teachers,* who teach students five years of age, to be preschool teachers. For the purposes of this article, kindergarten teachers will be included in this category. According to 1998 reports from the Bureau of Labor Statistics, there were over 380,000 kindergarten and prekindergarten teachers in the United States.

■ History

Friedrich Froebel, a German educator, founded the first kindergarten ("child's garden" in German) in 1837 in Blankenburg, Germany. He also taught adults how to be kindergarten teachers. One of his adult students, Mrs. Carl Schurz, moved to the United States and started the first kindergarten of this country in Watertown, Wisconsin, in the mid-1800s. By 1873, St. Louis added the first American public kindergarten, and preschools for students under age five began to spring up in Europe around this same time. Preschools were introduced into the United States in the 1920s.

Preschool programs expanded rapidly in the United States during the 1960s, due in large part to the government instituting the Head Start program, designed to help preschool-aged children from low-income families receive educational and socialization opportunities and therefore be better prepared for elementary school. This program also allowed the parents of the children to work during the day. Around the same time, many U.S. public school systems began developing mandatory kindergarten programs for five-year-olds, and today many schools, both preschool and elementary, both public and private, are offering full-day kindergarten programs.

■ The Job

As a preschool teacher, you'll plan and lead activities that build on children's abilities and curiosity and aid them in developing skills and characteristics that help them grow.

Because the children in your class will be at varying skill levels as well as have differing temperaments, you'll need to develop a flexible schedule with time allowed for music, art, playtime, academics, rest, and other activities.

You'll plan activities that encourage children to develop skills appropriate to their developmental needs. For example, you should plan activities based on the understanding that a three-year-old child has different motor skills and reasoning abilities than a child of five years of age. You'll work with the youngest students on learning the days of the week and the recognition of colors, seasons, and animal names and characteristics; you'll help older students with number and letter recognition and even simple writing skills. You'll help children with such simple, yet important, tasks as tying shoelaces and washing hands before snack time. Attention to the individual needs of each child is vital; you'll need to be aware of these needs and capabilities, and when possible, adapt activities to the specific needs of the individual child. Self-confidence and the development of communication skills are encouraged in preschools. For example, you may give children simple art projects, such as finger painting, and have children show and explain their finished projects to the rest of the class. Show and tell, or "sharing time" as it is often called, gives students opportunities to speak and listen to others.

"A lot of what I teach is based on social skills," says June Gannon, a preschool teacher in Amherst, New Hampshire. "During our circle time, we say hello to one another, sing songs, have show and tell, talk about the weather and do calendar events. We then move on to language arts, which may include talking to children about rules, good listening, helping, sharing, etc., using puppets, work papers, games, and songs."

You'll adopt many parental responsibilities for the children. You greet the children in the morning and supervise them throughout the day. Often these responsibilities can be quite demanding and complicated. In harsh weather, for example, you'll contend not only with boots, hats, coats, and mittens, but with the inevitable sniffles, colds, and generally cranky behavior that can occur in young children. For most children, preschool is their first time away from home and family for an extended period of time. A major portion of your day will be spent helping children adjust to being away from home and encouraging them to play together. This is especially true at the beginning of the school year. You may need to gently reassure children who become frightened or homesick.

In both full-day and half-day programs, you'll supervise snack time, helping children learn how to eat properly and clean up after themselves. Proper hygiene, such as hand washing before meals, is also stressed. Other activities include storytelling, music, and simple arts and crafts projects. Full-day programs involve a lunch period and at least one nap time. Programs usually have exciting activities interspersed with calmer ones. Even though the children get nap time, you must be energetic throughout the day, ready to face with good cheer the many challenges and demands of young children.

You'll also work with the parents of each child. It is not unusual for parents to come to preschool and observe a child or go on a field trip with the class, and preschool teachers often take these opportunities to discuss the progress of each child as well as any specific problems or concerns. Scheduled meetings are available for parents who cannot visit the school during the day. Solutions to fairly serious problems are worked out in tandem with the parents, often with the aid of the director of the preschool, or in the case of an elementary school kindergarten, with the principal or headmaster.

Kindergarten teachers usually have their own classrooms, made up exclusively of five-year-olds. Although these teachers don't have to plan activities for a wide range of ages, they need to consider individual developmental interests, abilities, and backgrounds represented by the students. Kindergarten teachers usually spend more time helping students with academic skills than do other preschool teachers. While a teacher of a two-, three-, and four-year-old classroom may focus more on socializing and building confidence in students through play and activities, kindergarten teachers often develop activities that help five-year-olds acquire the skills they will need in grade school, such as introductory activities on numbers, reading, and writing.

■ Requirements

High School

You should take child development, home economics, and other classes that involve you with child care. You'll also need a fundamental understanding of the general subjects you'll be introducing to preschool students, so take English, science, and math. Also, take classes in art, music, and theater to develop creative skills.

Postsecondary Training

Specific education requirements for preschool and kindergarten teachers vary from state to state and also depend on the specific guidelines of the school or district. Many schools and child care centers require preschool teachers to have a bachelor's degree in education or a related field, but others accept adults with a high school diploma and some childcare experience. Some preschool facilities offer on-the-job training to their teachers, hiring them as assistants or aides until they are sufficiently trained to work in a classroom alone. A college degree program should include coursework in a variety of liberal arts subjects, including

English, history, and science as well as nutrition, child development, psychology of the young child, and sociology.

Several groups offer on-the-job training programs for prospective preschool teachers. For example, the American Montessori Society offers a career program for aspiring preschool teachers. This program requires a three-month classroom training period followed by one year of supervised on-the-job training.

Certification or Licensing

In some states, licensure may be required. Many states accept the Child Development Associate (CDA) credential or an associate or bachelor's degree as sufficient requirements for work in a preschool facility. Individual state boards of education can provide specific licensure information. Kindergarten teachers working in public elementary schools almost always need teaching certification similar to that required by other elementary school teachers in the school. Other types of licensure or certification may be required, depending upon the school or district. These may include first-aid or cardiopulmonary resuscitation (CPR) training.

Other Requirements

Because young children look up to adults and learn through example, it is especially important that a preschool teacher be a good role model. "Remember how important your job is," June says. "Everything you say and do will affect these children." June also emphasizes being respectful of the children and keeping a sense of humor. "I have patience and lots of heart for children," June says. "You definitely need both."

■ Exploring

Preschools, day care centers, and other childcare programs often hire high school students for part-time positions as aides. There are also many volunteer opportunities for working with kids—check with your library or local literacy program about tutoring children and reading to preschoolers. Summer day camps or Bible schools with preschool classes also hire high school students as counselors or counselors-in-training. Discussing the field with preschool teachers and observing in their classes are other good ways to discover specific job information and explore one's aptitude for this career.

■ Employers

Six of every ten mothers of children under the age of six are in the labor force, and the number is rising. Both government and the private sector are working to fill the enormous need for quality childcare. As a preschool teacher, you'll find many job opportunities in private and public preschools, including day care centers, government-funded learning programs, churches, and Montessori schools. You

Here are some recent books for preschool-age children, each addressing a basic aspect of development:

Colors: *Hello, Red Fox* by Eric Carle (Simon and Schuster, 1998). This story concerns a party tossed by Mama Frog, and her confusion over the changing colors of her guests. The book instructs readers to participate in Mama's confusion by staring for ten seconds at the brightly colored animal on the page, then looking immediately at a blank white page to see an optical illusion—a shadowy image of the animal in your vision has changed to the complementary color.

Senses: *What Do You See When You Shut Your Eyes?* by Cynthia Zarin and Sarah Durham (Houghton Mifflin, 1998). Along with the title, the book asks "What do you hear when you listen hard?", "What do you yell when you yell really loud?" and other imagination-provoking questions that invite children to consider their senses and sensibilities.

Counting: *My Little Sister Ate One Hare* by Bill Grossman and Kevin Hawkes (Random House, 1998). Though a bit disgusting (the little sister only begins with the hare...she eventually moves on to devour nine lizards), the sing-song rhyming helps children learn their numbers with humorous and colorful illustrations.

may find work in a small center, or with a large preschool with many students and classrooms. Preschool franchises, like Primrose Schools and Kids 'R' Kids International, are also providing more opportunities for preschool teachers.

Starting Out

Before becoming a preschool teacher, June gained a lot of experience in child care. "I have worked as a special education aide and have taken numerous classes in childhood education," she says. "I am a sign language interpreter and have taught deaf children in a public school inclusion program."

You can contact child care centers, nursery schools, Head Start programs, and other preschool facilities to identify job opportunities. Often jobs for preschool teachers are listed in the classified section of newspapers. In addition, many school districts and state boards of education maintain job listings of available teaching positions. If no permanent positions are available at preschools, you may be able to find opportunities to work as a substitute teacher. Most preschools and kindergartens maintain a substitute list and refer to it frequently.

Advancement

Many teachers advance by becoming more skillful in what they do. Skilled preschool teachers, especially those with additional training, usually receive salary increases as they become more experienced. A few preschool teachers with administrative ability and an interest in administrative work advance to the position of director. Administrators need to have at least a master's degree in child development or a related field and have to meet any state or federal licensing regulations. Some become directors of Head Start programs or other government programs. A relatively small number of experienced preschool teachers open their own facilities. This entails not only the ability to be an effective administrator but also the knowledge of how to operate a business. Kindergarten teachers sometimes have the opportunity to earn more money by teaching at a higher grade level in the elementary school. This salary increase is especially true when a teacher moves from a half-day kindergarten program to a full-day grade school classroom.

Earnings

Although there have been some attempts to correct the discrepancies in salaries between preschool teachers and other teachers, salaries in this profession tend to be lower than teaching positions in public elementary and high schools. Because some preschool programs are only in the morning or afternoon, many preschool teachers work only part time. As part-time workers, they often do not receive medical insurance or other benefits and may get paid minimum wage to start.

According to the Bureau of Labor Statistics, preschool teachers made about $404 a week in 1998. Kindergarten teachers, on average, have the highest salaries in this field, earning about the same as elementary school teachers. A 1997 report from the National Education Association estimated the annual average teacher salary to be $38,611.

Work Environment

You'll spend much of your work day on your feet in a classroom or on a playground. Facilities vary from a single room to large buildings. Class sizes also vary; some preschools serve only a handful of children, while others serve several hundred. Classrooms may be crowded and noisy, but if you love children, you will enjoy all the activity. "The best part about working with children," June says, "is the laughter, the fun, the enjoyment of watching the children grow physically, emotionally, and intellectually."

Many children do not go to preschool all day, so work may be part-time. Part-time employees generally work between 18 and 30 hours a week, while full-time employees work 35 to 40 hours a week. Part-time work gives the employee flexibility, and for many, this is one of the advantages of the job. Some preschool teachers teach both morning and afternoon classes, going through the same schedule and lesson plans with two sets of students.

Outlook

Employment opportunities for preschool teachers are expected to increase through 2006. Specific job opportunities vary from state to state and depend on demographic characteristics and level of government funding. Jobs should be available at private child care centers, nursery schools, Head Start facilities, public and private kindergartens, and laboratory schools connected with universities and colleges. In the past, the majority of preschool teachers were female, and although this continues to be the case, more males are becoming involved in early childhood education.

One-third of all childcare workers leave their centers each year, often because of the low pay and lack of benefits. This will mean plenty of job openings for preschool teachers and possibly improved benefit plans, as centers attempt to maintain qualified preschool teachers.

For More Information

For information about certification, contact:

Council for Early Childhood Professional Recognition
2460 16th Street, NW
Washington, DC 20009
Tel: 800-424-4310
Web: http://www.cdacouncil.org

For information on training programs, contact:

American Montessori Society
281 Park Avenue South, 6th Floor
New York, NY 10010-6102
Tel: 212-358-1250
Web: http://www.amshq.org

For general information on preschool teaching careers, contact:

National Association for the Education of Young Children
1509 16th Street, NW
Washington, DC 20036
Tel: 800-424-2460
Web: http://www.naeyc.org

For information about student memberships and training opportunities, contact:

National Association of Child Care Professionals
304-A Roanoke Street
Christiansburg, VA 24073
Tel: 800-537-1118
Web: http://www.naccp.org

Related Articles

Education

Child Care Workers

Elementary School Teachers

School Administrators

Special Education Teachers

Teacher Aides

Press Mold Operators

■ See Glass Manufacturing Workers

Press Secretaries

Overview

Press secretaries, political consultants, and other media relations professionals help politicians promote themselves and their issues among voters. They advise politicians on how to address the media. Sometimes considered "spin doctors," these professionals use the media to either change or strengthen public opinion. Press secretaries work for candidates and elected officials, while political consultants work with firms, contracting their services to politicians. The majority of press secretaries and political consultants work in Washington, DC; others work all across the country, involved with local and state government officials and candidates.

History

Using the media for political purposes is nearly as old as the U.S. government itself. The news media developed right alongside the political parties, and early newspapers served as a battleground for the Federalists and the Republicans. The first media moguls of the late 1800s often saw their newspapers as podiums from which to promote themselves—George Hearst bought the *San Francisco Examiner* in 1885 for the sole purpose of helping him campaign for Congress. The latter half of the 20th century introduced whole other forms of media, which were quickly exploited by politicians seeking offices. Many historians mark the Kennedy-Nixon debate of 1960 as the moment when television coverage first became a key factor in the election process. Those who read of the debate in the next day's

PRESS SECRETARIES	
SCHOOL SUBJECTS	English Government Journalism
PERSONAL SKILLS	Communication/ideas Leadership/management
WORK ENVIRONMENT	Primarily indoors One location with some travel
MINIMUM EDUCATION LEVEL	Bachelor's degree
SALARY RANGE	$47,000 to $150,000 to $200,000+
CERTIFICATION OR LICENSING	None available
OUTLOOK	About as fast as the average

newspapers were under the impression that Nixon had easily won, but it was Kennedy's composure and appeal on camera that made the most powerful impression. Negative campaigning first showed its powerful influence in 1964, when Democratic presidential candidate Lyndon Johnson ran ads featuring a girl picking a flower while a nuclear bomb burst in the background, which commented on Republican Barry Goldwater's advocacy of strong military action in Vietnam.

Bill Clinton is probably the first president to benefit from the art of "spin," as his press secretaries and political managers were actively involved in dealing with his scandals and keeping his approval ratings high among the population. James Carville and George Stephanopolis, working for Clinton's 1992 campaign, had the task of playing up Clinton's strengths as an intelligent, gifted politician, while down-playing his questionable moral background. Their efforts were portrayed in the documentary *The War Room*, and their success earned them national renown as "spin doctors."

■ The Job

If you were to manage a political campaign, how would you go about publicizing the candidate to the largest number of voters? You'd use TV, of course. The need for TV and radio spots during a campaign is the reason it costs so much today to run for office. And it's also the reason many politicians hire professionals with an understanding of media relations to help them get elected. Once elected, a politician continues to rely on media relations experts, such as press secretaries, political consultants, and political managers, to use the media to portray the politician in the best light. In recent years, such words as "spin," "leak," and "sound-bite" have entered the daily vocabulary of news and politics to describe elements of political coverage in the media.

Political consultants usually work independently, or as members of consulting firms, and contract with individuals. As a political consultant, you're involved in producing radio and TV ads, writing campaign plans, and developing "themes" for these campaigns. A theme may focus on a specific issue or on the differences between your client and the opponent. Your client may be new to the political arena or someone established looking to maintain an office. You conduct polls and surveys to gauge public opinion and to identify your client's biggest competition. You advise your clients in the best ways to use the media. In addition to TV and radio, the Internet has proven important to politicians. Consultants launch campaign Web sites and also chase down rumors that spread across the Internet. A consultant may be hired for an entire campaign, or may be hired only to produce an ad, or to come up with a "sound-bite"—or catchy quote—for the media.

Though voters across the country complain about negative campaigning, or "mud-slinging," such campaigns have proven effective. In his 1988 presidential campaign, George Bush ran TV ads featuring the now notorious Willie Horton, a convict who was released from prison only to commit another crime. The ad was intended to draw attention to what Bush considered his opponent's "soft" approach to crime. It proved very effective in undermining the campaign of Michael Dukakis and putting him on the defensive. Many consultants believe they must focus on a few specific issues in a campaign, emphasizing their client's strengths as well as the opponent's weaknesses.

Press secretaries serve on the congressional staffs of senators and representatives and on the staffs of governors and mayors. The president also has a press secretary. Press secretaries and their assistants write press releases and opinion pieces to publicize the efforts of the government officials for whom they work. They also help prepare speeches and prepare their employers for press conferences and interviews. They maintain Web sites, posting press releases and the results of press conferences.

Media relations experts are often called *spin doctors* because of their ability to manipulate the media, or put a good spin on a news story to best suit the purposes of their clients. Corporations also rely on spin for positive media coverage. Media relations experts are often called upon during a political scandal, or after corporate blunders, for "damage control." Using the newspapers and radio and TV broadcasts, spin doctors attempt to downplay public relations disasters, helping politicians and corporations save face. In highly sensitive situations, they must answer questions selectively and carefully, and they may even be involved in secretly releasing, or leaking, information to the press. Because of these manipulations, media relations professionals are often disrespected. They're sometimes viewed as people who conceal facts and present lies, prey on the emotions of voters, or even represent companies responsible for illegal practices. However, many political consultants and media representatives are responsible for bringing public attention to important issues and good political candidates. They also help organizations and nonprofit groups advocate for legislative issues and help develop support for school funding, environmental concerns, and other community needs.

■ Requirements

High School

Take journalism courses, and work with your school newspaper, radio station, or TV station—you'll recognize how important reporters, editors, and producers are in putting together newspapers and shaping news segments. English composition, drama, and speech classes will help you develop good communication skills, while government, history, and civics classes will teach you about the structure of local, state, and federal government. Join your speech and debate team, and you'll gain experience in research and in persuasive argument. Take math, economics, and accounting courses to prepare you for poll-taking and for analyzing statistics and demographics.

Postsecondary Training

Most people in media relations have bachelor's degrees, and some also hold master's degrees, doctorates, and law degrees. As an undergraduate, you should enroll in a four-year college and pursue a well-rounded education; press secretaries and political consultants need a good understanding of the history and culture of the United States and foreign countries. Some of the majors you should consider as an undergraduate are journalism, political science, English, marketing, and economics. You'll also take courses in government, psychology, statistics, history of western civilization, and a foreign language. You might then choose to pursue a graduate degree in journalism, political science, public administration, or international relations.

Seek a college with a good internship program. You might also pursue internships with local and state officials and your congress members in the Senate and House of Representatives. Journalism internships will involve you with local and national publications, or the news departments of radio and TV stations.

The American Association of Political Consultants (AAPC) does have a code of conduct for consultants, but there is no established training or licensing process.

Other Requirements

You'll need to be very organized and capable of juggling many different tasks—from quickly writing ads and press releases to developing budgets and expense accounts. You'll need good problem-solving skills and some imagination when putting a positive spin on negative issues. Good people skills are important so that you can develop contacts within government and the media. You should feel comfortable with public speaking as you'll be leading press conferences and speaking on behalf of your employers and clients. You should also enjoy competition. You can't be intimidated by people in power or by journalists questioning the issues addressed in your campaigns.

■ Exploring

Get involved with your school government as well as with committees and clubs that have officers and elections. You can also become involved in local, state, and federal elections by volunteering for campaigns; though you may just be making phone calls and putting up signs, you may also have the opportunity to write press releases and schedule

---

LEARN MORE ABOUT IT

Here are some books about politics and the media:

Train Fever: Spin Doctors, Rented Strangers, and Thumb Wrestlers on the Road to the White House by Michael Lewis (Vintage Books, 1998).

Soundbites and Spin Doctors: How Politicians Manipulate the Media and Vice Versa by Nicholas Jones (Trafalgar Square, 1996).

All's Fair: Love, War, and Running for President by Mary Matalin and James Carville (Simon and Schuster, 1995).

Political Consultants and Negative Campaigning: The Secrets of the Pros by Kerwin C. Swint (University Press of America, 1998).

Spin Cycle: Inside the Clinton Propaganda Machine by Howard Kurtz (Free Press, 1998).

---

press conferences and interviews, and you'll see first-hand how a campaign operates.

Working for your school newspaper will help you learn about conducting research, interviews, and opinion polls, which all play a part in managing media relations. You may be able to get a part-time job or an internship with your city's newspaper or broadcast news station, where you'll gain experience with election coverage and political advertising. Visit the Web sites of U.S. Congress members; many sites feature lists of recent press releases. By reading the press releases, you'll get a sense of how a press office publicizes the efforts and actions of Congress members. You should also read some of the many books examining recent political campaigns and scandals, and read magazines like *Harper's*, *Atlantic Monthly*, *George*, and the online magazine *Salon*, for political commentary.

■ Employers

Press secretaries work for local, state, and federal government officials. Political consultants are generally self-employed, or work for consulting firms that specialize in media relations. You might also find work with public relations agencies, and the press offices of large corporations. Celebrities, and others in the public eye also hire press agents to help them control rumors and publicity. Political consultants contract with politicians, corporations, non-profit groups, and trade and professional associations. They participate in the campaigns of mayors, governors, and Congress members as well as in the political campaigns of other countries. Someone like the president will keep in close contact with many different media advisors, including his or her current and former press secretaries, consultants, speechwriters, and political managers.

■ Starting Out

Media relations jobs aren't advertised, and there's no pre-determined path to success. You'll find your way in the field by making connections with people in both politics and the media. Volunteer for political campaigns, and also advocate for public policy issues of interest to you. You can make good connections, and gain valuable experience, working or interning in the offices of your state capitol. You might also try for an internship with your one of your state's members of Congress; contact their offices in Washington, DC, for internship applications. If you're more interested in the writing and producing aspects of the career, work for local newspapers or the broadcast news media; or work as a producer for a television production crew or for an ad agency that specializes in political campaigns. A political consulting firm may hire assistants for writing and for commercial production. Whereas some people pursue the career directly by working in the press offices of political candidates, others find their way into political consulting after having worked as lawyers, lobbyists, or journalists.

■ Advancement

A press secretary who has worked closely with a successful government official may advance into a higher staff position, like chief of staff or legislative director. Political consultants, after winning many elections and establishing credentials, will begin to take on more prominent clients and major campaigns. Network TV, cable, and radio news departments also hire successful media relations experts to serve as political analysts on the air. Some consultants also write columns for newspapers and syndicates and publish books about their insights into politics.

■ Earnings

Press secretaries working in the U.S. Congress can make between $42,000 and $60,000 a year, according to the Congressional Management Foundation, a consulting firm in Washington, DC. The incomes of political consultants vary greatly; someone contracting with local candidates, or with state organizations and associations, may make around $40,000 a year; someone consulting with high-profile candidates may bring in hundreds of thousands of dollars a year. In 1998, the Pew Research Center released the results of one of the first comprehensive studies of political consultants. More than half of its respondents reported family incomes of more than $150,000 a year; one-third reported annual incomes of more than $200,000.

■ Work Environment

Representing politicians can be thankless work. You may have to speak to the press about sensitive, volatile issues and deal directly with the frustrations of journalists unable to get the answers they want. When working for prominent politicians, you may become the subject of personal attacks.

Despite these potential conflicts, your work can be exciting and fast-paced. You'll see the results of your efforts in the newspapers and television, and you'll have the satisfaction of influencing voters and public opinion. If working on a campaign as a consultant, your hours will be long and stressful. In some cases, you'll have to scrap unproductive media ads and start from scratch with only hours to write, produce, and place new commercials. You'll also have to be available to your clients around the clock.

Though a majority of press secretaries and political consultants work in Washington, DC, others work in state capitols and major cities all across the country.

■ Outlook

Consultants and media representatives will become increasingly important to candidates and elected officials. Television ads and Internet campaigns have become necessary to reach the public. The work of press secretaries will expand as more news networks and news magazines closely follow the decisions and actions of government officials.

The Pew Research Center, which surveys public opinion on political issues, has found that most Americans are concerned about negative campaigning, while most political consultants see nothing wrong with using negative tactics in advertising. Despite how the general public may feel about negative campaigning, it remains a very effective tool for consultants. In some local elections, candidates may mutually agree to avoid the mud-slinging, but the use of negative ads in general is likely to increase.

This negative campaigning may be affected somewhat by developing technology. Voters will soon be able to access more information about candidates and issues via the Internet. Also, the increase in the number of channels available to cable TV watchers will make it more difficult for candidates to advertise to a general audience. However, the greater number of outlets for media products will employ more writers, TV producers, and Web designers in the process of creating a political campaign.

■ For More Information

Visit the Web sites of the House and the Senate for links to the Web sites of individual members of Congress. At the Web sites, you can read press releases:

Office of Senator (Name)
United States Senate
Washington, DC 20510
Tel: 202-224-3121
Web: http://www.senate.gov

U.S. House of Representatives (Name)
Washington, DC 20515
Tel: 202-224-3121
Web: http://www.house.gov

For general information about careers in broadcast media, contact:

National Association of Broadcasters
1771 N Street, NW
Washington, DC 20036
Tel: 202-429-5335
Web: http://www.nab.org/

The Pew Research Center is an opinion research group that studies attitudes toward press, politics, and public policy issues. To read some of their survey results, visit their Web site, or write:

The Pew Research Center for the People and the Press
1150 18th Street, NW, Suite 975
Washington, DC 20036
Tel: 202-293-3126
Web: http://www.people-press.org

■ Related Articles

Government

Ambassadors

Campaign Workers

Congressional Aides

Federal and State Officials

Lobbyists

Political Scientists

Regional and Local Officials

Pressers

■ **See Apparel Industry Workers**

Pressworkers

■ **See Glass Manufacturing Workers**

Priests

■ **See Roman Catholic Priests**

Print Shop Stenographers

■ **See Stenographers**

Printing Customer Service Representatives

■ Overview

Customer service representatives are the people who see a print job through all phases of production, from prepress to delivery. They act as go-between for the sales representatives and the employees in the plant, ensuring that each print job goes smoothly and that the customer is happy with the end result. Most printing customer service representatives are employed by large commercial printers.

■ History

The history of commercial printing dates back centuries, but a job devoted solely to customer service in printing is a development of this century, and the title customer service representative is a relatively new phenomenon. Older job titles include *project manager* and *production coordinator.*

■ The Job

In many industries, customer service representatives simply field inquiries from customers, handling simple matters themselves and channeling more involved problems to another person within the company. In printing, the duties of customer service representatives go beyond that.

"Customer service in printing is not just answering the phone," says Kathy Jahnke, a customer service and client services representative for Wicklander Printing Corporation in Chicago, Illinois. "You are largely responsible for the

PRINTING CUSTOMER SERVICE REPRESENTATIVES	
SCHOOL SUBJECTS	Business Speech
PERSONAL SKILLS	Communication/ideas Following instructions
WORK ENVIRONMENT	Primarily indoors Primarily one location
MINIMUM EDUCATION LEVEL	High school diploma
SALARY RANGE	$25,000 to $35,000 to $50,000
CERTIFICATION OR LICENSING	None available
OUTLOOK	About as fast as the average

outcome of your company's product." Customer service representatives, commonly called CSRs, typically work under one or more sales representatives and act as the conduit between that person and the employees in the printing plant. It is the responsibility of the CSR to see a print job from start to finish: meeting with the salesperson and establishing the job's specifications; tracking the job through each phase of production, including prepress, press, and finishing; coordinating the delivery and/or mailing of the piece; and handling any necessary follow-up work.

A CSR's day-to-day duties might include attending production meetings, arranging for outside vendors to handle parts of a job—such as a specialized type of binding—that the printing company is not equipped for, filling out and submitting work orders, checking and routing proofs, and updating and advising clients.

■ Requirements

The minimum educational requirement for a printing customer service representative is a high school diploma, but many employers consider only college graduates for their customer service positions. This is because the job is demanding and calls for people who are quick thinkers and effective communicators.

The tasks of a printing customer service representative are varied but all require the same fundamental skills: close attention to detail, the ability to work on multiple projects simultaneously, and strong communication skills, both verbal and written. CSRs in printing must also function well as part of a team and perform effectively in pressure situations. Because printing customer service representatives must have a solid grasp of the printing process, a background in printing is ideal.

■ Employers

Printing customer service jobs are mostly with large commercial or business printers, trade shops, and binderies. Because printing is so widespread, customer service jobs are available in most parts of the country. However printing work is concentrated in large printing centers like New York, Chicago, Los Angeles, Philadelphia, Dallas, and Washington, DC.

■ Starting Out

Customer service reps in printing must have a thorough understanding of printing processes and technology to be successful. A summer or part-time job in a printing plant can provide the exposure and experience needed for this career. Young people looking for a customer service position with a printer should check newspaper want ads and job placement listings with local chapters of printing associations. Approaching a printing company directly also can

be effective. Many companies employ a number of CSRs and frequently have openings.

■ Advancement

Because the printing industry is so technical, many companies choose to promote staff from within rather than investing in the training of a new person. Often, working as a customer service representative or prepress specialist can be a stepping stone to a print sales job. Some companies reward their successful CSRs by giving them nominal sales responsibilities, if not a full-time sales job.

■ Earnings

According to the book *Careers in Graphic Communications* (Graphic Arts Technical Foundation, 1998), customer service representatives typically earn between $25,000 and $50,000 a year. They are usually eligible for fringe benefits, including medical insurance, paid vacation and sick days, and retirement plans.

■ Work Environment

Customer service representatives in printing typically work in an office or cubicle, but they do a lot of running back and forth between the office and the plant, coordinating various aspects of the print jobs they are in charge of. While at their desk, printing CSRs might spend a quarter of their time on the phone talking to customers or outside vendors. The rest of the time is spent working on the computer, filling out forms, and doing other paperwork. On average, printing customer service representatives work about 40 hours a week, but many log more than that. It's not unusual for a CSR to put in 60 hours weekly.

■ Outlook

The U.S. Bureau of Labor Statistics does not publish employment projections for printing customer service representatives, but in general the career looks promising. Despite predictions of a "paperless society," the demand for printed products is increasing rather than decreasing. Another good sign is that with the stiff competition in printing today, companies are placing more emphasis on building and maintaining client relationships. This means that there will be a growing need for printing customer service representatives, at least in the near future. In fact, many companies today report they are having a hard time filling sales and customer service representative positions.

■ For More Information

GATF offers information, services, and training related to printing, electronic prepress, electronic publishing, and other areas of the graphic arts industry. It also sponsors the National Scholarship Trust Fund of the Graphic Arts, which awards scholarships to undergraduate and gradu-

ate students preparing to enter the field of graphic communications. (Scholarship applications may be downloaded from the GATF Web site listed below.) NSTF also publishes a directory of technical schools, colleges, and universities that offer courses in graphic communications.

Graphic Arts Technical Foundation
200 Deer Run Road
Sewickley, PA 15143-2600
Tel: 412-741-6860
Web: http://www.gatf.org

GCCC serves as a clearinghouse, resource center, and coordinator of programs promoting career awareness, training, and a positive industry image.

Graphic Communications Career Center
1899 Preston White Drive
Reston, VA 22091
Tel: 703-648-1768
Web: http://www.npes.org/edcouncil/index.htm

NAPL is a graphic arts trade association is a good source of general information.

National Association of Printers and Lithographers
75 West Century Road
Paramus, NJ 07652
Tel: 201-634-9600
Web: http://www.napl.org

■ Related Articles

Book Publishing

Business

Newspapers and Magazines

Printing

Sales

Customer Service Representatives

Printing Sales Representatives

Services Sales Representatives

Printing Press Operators and Assistants

■ Overview

Printing press operators and printing press operator assistants prepare, operate, and maintain printing presses. Their principal duties include installing and adjusting printing plates, loading and feeding paper, mixing inks and controlling ink flow, and ensuring the quality of the final printed piece.

According to the U.S. Bureau of Labor Statistics, there were over 240,000 printing press operators in the United States in the late 1990s. They were mostly employed by newspaper plants and commercial and business printers.

■ History

The forerunners of today's modern printing presses were developed in Germany in the 15th century. They made use of the new concept of movable type, an invention generally credited to Johannes Gutenberg. Before Gutenberg's time, most books were copied by hand or printed from carved wooden blocks. Movable type used separate pieces of metal that could be easily set in place, locked into a form for printing, and then used again for another job.

The first presses consisted of two flat surfaces. Once set in place, the type was inked with a roller, and a sheet of paper was pressed against the type with a lever. Two people working together could print about 300 pages a day.

In the early 19th century, Friedrich Konig, another German, developed the first cylinder press. With a cylinder press, the paper is mounted on a large cylinder that is rolled over a flat printing surface.

The first rotary press was developed in the United States in 1865 by William Bullock. On this kind of press, the inked surface is on a revolving cylinder called a plate cylinder. The plate cylinder acts like a roller and prints onto a continuous sheet of paper (called a web) coming off a giant roll.

The speed and economy of the web press was improved by the discovery of offset printing in the early 20th century.

PRINTING PRESS OPERATORS AND ASSISTANTS	
SCHOOL SUBJECTS	Computer science Mathematics Technical/Shop
PERSONAL SKILLS	Mechanical/manipulative Technical/scientific
WORK ENVIRONMENT	Primarily indoors Primarily one location
MINIMUM EDUCATION LEVEL	High school diploma
SALARY RANGE	$11,000 to $25,000 to $43,000+
CERTIFICATION OR LICENSING	Voluntary
OUTLOOK	Little change or more slowly than the average
DOT	651
GOE	05.05.13
NOC	7381
O*NET	92998

A press operator runs a six-color press.

In this process, the raised metal type used in earlier processes was substituted with a flexible plate that could be easily attached to the plate cylinder. The ink is transferred from the plate onto a rubber cylinder (called a blanket), then onto the paper. The printing plate never touches the paper but is "offset" by the rubber blanket.

Offset printing uses the process of lithography, in which the plate is chemically treated so that ink sticks only to the parts that are to be printed and is repelled by the nonprint areas.

Offset lithography is the most common form of printing today and is used on both web-fed and sheet-fed presses. Web-fed presses are used for newspapers and other large-volume, lower-cost runs. The fastest web presses today can print about 150,000 complete newspapers in an hour. Sheet-fed presses, which print on single sheets of paper rather than a continuous roll, are used for smaller, higher-quality jobs.

Other forms of printing are gravure (in which depressions on an etched plate are inked and pressed to paper), flexography (a form of rotary printing using flexible rubber plates with raised image areas and fast-drying inks), and letterpress (the most traditional method, in which a plate with raised, inked images is pressed against paper).

■ The Job

The duties of press operators and their assistants vary according to the size of the printing plant in which they work. Generally, they are involved in all aspects of making the presses ready for a job and monitoring and operating the presses during the print run. Because most presses now are computerized, the work of press operators involves both electronic and manual processes.

In small shops, press operators usually handle all of the tasks associated with running a press, including cleaning and oiling the parts and making minor repairs. In larger shops, press operators are aided by assistants who handle most maintenance and cleanup tasks.

Once the press has been inspected and the printing plate arrives from the platemaker, the "makeready" process begins. In this stage, the operators mount the plates into place on the printing surface or cylinder. They mix and match the ink, fill the ink fountains, and adjust the ink flow and dampening systems. They also load the paper, adjust the press to the paper size, feed the paper through the cylinders and, on a web press, adjust the tension controls. When this is done, a proof sheet is run off for the customer's review.

When the proof has been approved and final adjustments have been made, the press run begins. During the run, press operators constantly check the quality of the printed sheets and make any necessary adjustments. They look to see that the print is clear and properly positioned and that ink is not offsetting (blotting) onto other sheets. If the job involves color, they make sure that the colors line up properly with the images they are assigned to (this is called registration). Operators also monitor the chemical properties of the ink and correct temperatures in the drying chamber, if the press has one.

On a web press, the feeding and tension mechanisms must be continually monitored. If the paper tears or jams, it must be rethreaded. As a roll of paper runs out, a new one must be spliced onto the old one. According to *Careers in Graphic Communications* (Graphic Arts Technical Foundation, 1998), some web presses today can print up to 50,000 feet an hour. At this rate, the press might run through a giant roll of paper every half hour. In large web printing plants, it takes an entire crew of specialized operators to oversee the process.

Most printing plants now have computerized printing presses equipped with sophisticated instrumentation. Press operators work at a control panel that monitors the printing processes and can adjust each variable automatically.

■ Requirements

High School

The minimum educational requirement for printing press operators and assistants is a high school diploma. Students interested in this field should take courses that offer an introduction to printing and color theory, as well as chemistry, computer science, electronics, mathematics, and physics—any course that develops mechanical and mathematical aptitude.

Postsecondary Training

Postsecondary training in a vocational-technical or graphic arts program is also recommended. And computer training is essential.

With today's rapid advances in technology, "students need all the computer knowledge they can get," advises John Smotherman, press operator and shift supervisor at Busch and Schmidt Company in Broadview, Illinois.

Certification or Licensing

The National Council for Skill Standards in Graphic Communications offers the designation of National Council Certified Operator. See the sidebar, "Press Operators Put to the Test" for more information.

Other Requirements

Strong communication skills—both verbal and written—are a must for press operators and assistants. They also must be able to work well as a team, both with each other and with others in the printing company. Any miscommunication during the printing process can be costly if it means re-running a job or any part of it. Working well under pressure is another requirement since most print jobs run on tight deadlines.

■ Exploring

High school is a good time to begin exploring the occupation of printing press operator. Some schools offer print shop classes, which provide the most direct exposure to this work. Working on the high school newspaper or yearbook is another way to gain a familiarity with the printing process. A delivery job with a print shop or a visit to a local printing plant will offer you the chance to see presses in action and get a feel for the environment in which press operators work. You also might consider a part-time, temporary, or summer job as a cleanup worker or press feeder in a printing plant.

■ Employers

There were over 240,000 press operator jobs in the United States in the late 1990s, according to the U.S. Bureau of Labor Statistics. The bulk of these were with newspapers and commercial and business printers. Companies range from small print shops, where one or two press operators handle everything, to large corporations that employ teams of press operators to work around the clock.

Other press operator jobs are with in-plant operations—that is, in companies and organizations that do their own printing in-house.

Because printing is so geographically diverse, press operator jobs are available in almost any city or town in the country. However, according to the *Occupational Outlook Handbook,* press work is concentrated in large printing centers like New York, Chicago, Los Angeles, Philadelphia, Dallas, and Washington, DC.

PRESS OPERATORS PUT TO THE TEST

The National Council for Skill Standards in Graphic Communications is putting America's press operators to the test, according to an article in *American Printer* magazine. A nonprofit organization borne out of a federal movement to boost industry competitiveness, the Council has developed a national certification exam for press operators.

In the *American Printer* piece (September 1998), Katherine O'Brien reported that 30 sheet-fed and 35 web press operators had passed the test and earned the title National Council Certified Operator. The sheet-fed and the web exam each include 175 multiple-choice questions in 3 skill areas: applied math, operating functions, and supporting functions.

For more information about the National Council for Skill Standards in Graphic Communications, call 207-985-9898.

■ Starting Out

Traditionally, press operators learned their craft through apprenticeship programs ranging from two to five years. Apprenticeships are still available, but they are being phased out by postsecondary programs in printing equipment operation offered by technical and trade schools and community and junior colleges. Information on apprenticeships is often available through state employment services and local chapters of printing industry associations.

In addition to classroom education, on-the-job training is needed. Openings for trainee positions may be listed in newspaper want ads or with the state employment service. Trade school graduates may find jobs through their school's placement office. And industry association offices often run job listing services.

John notes that many young people entering the field start out in a part-time position while still in school. "I think students should pursue all the classroom education they can, but many intricacies of the printing process, like how certain inks and papers work together, need to be learned through experience," he says.

■ Advancement

Most printing press operators, even those with some training, begin their careers doing entry-level work, such as loading, unloading, and cleaning the presses. In large print shops, the line of promotion is usually as follows: press helper, press assistant, press operator, press operator-in-charge, press room supervisor, superintendent.

Press operators can advance in salary and responsibility level by learning to work more complex printing equipment—for example by moving from a one-color press to a four-color press. Printing press operators should be prepared to continue their training and education throughout their careers. As printing companies upgrade their equipment and buy new, more computerized presses, retraining will be essential.

Press operators who are interested in other aspects of the printing business also may find advancement opportunities elsewhere in their company. Those with business savvy may be successful in establishing their own print shops.

■ Earnings

Pay rates vary for press operators, depending on their level of experience and responsibility, type of company, where they live, and whether or not they are union members. The *Occupational Outlook Handbook* reported that the median weekly earnings of press operators were about $484 in 1996. The salary ranges cited in *Careers in Graphic Communications* (Graphic Arts Technical Foundation, 1998): minimum wage for entry-level workers to $21 an hour for veteran operators.

■ Work Environment

Pressrooms are well-ventilated, well-lit, and humidity-controlled. They are also noisy. Often press operators must wear ear protectors. Press work can be physically strenuous and requires a lot of standing. Press operators also have considerable contact with ink and cleaning fluids that can cause skin and eye irritation.

Working around large machines can be hazardous, so press operators must constantly observe good safety habits.

An eight-hour day is typical for most press operators, but some work longer hours. Smaller plants generally have only a day shift, but many larger plants and newspaper printers run around the clock. At these plants, like in hospitals and factories, press operator shifts are broken into day, afternoon/evening, and "graveyard" hours.

■ Outlook

Through the year 2006, the U.S. Department of Labor predicts that employment of press operators will grow more slowly than the average for all occupations. An increased demand for printed materials—advertising, direct mail pieces, computer software packaging, books, and magazines—will be offset by the use of larger, more efficient machines.

Newcomers to the field are likely to encounter stiff competition from experienced workers or workers who have completed retraining programs to update their skills. Opportunities are expected to be greatest for students who have completed formal apprenticeships or postsecondary training programs.

Jobs in letterpress printing will continue to decline, while opportunities are expected grow in offset lithography, gravure, and flexography printing.

"If you're not afraid of work or learning, you can do well in this industry," John says.

■ For More Information

For more information on the National Council Certified Operator designation, contact:

National Council for Skill Standards in Graphic Communications
Kennebunk, Maine 04043
Tel: 207-985-9898

GATF offers information, services, and training. It also sponsors the National Scholarship Trust Fund (NSTF) of the Graphic Arts, which awards scholarships to undergraduate and graduate students preparing to enter the field of graphic communications. (Applications may be downloaded from the GATF Web site.) NSTF also publishes a directory of technical schools, colleges, and universities that offer courses in graphic communications.

Graphic Arts Technical Foundation
200 Deer Run Road
Sewickley, PA 15143-2600
Tel: 412-741-6860
Web: http://www.gatf.org

GCCC serves as a clearinghouse, resource center, and coordinator of programs promoting career awareness, training, and a positive industry image.

Graphic Communications Career Center
1899 Preston White Drive
Reston, VA 22091
Tel: 703-648-1768
Web: http://www.npes.org/edcouncil/index.htm

GCIU represents U.S. and Canadian workers in all craft and skill areas of the printing and publishing industries and offers education and training through local union schools.

Graphic Communications International Union
1900 L Street, NW
Washington, DC 20036
Tel: 202-462-1400
Web: http://www.gciu.org

NAPL is a graphic arts trade association is a good source of general information.

National Association of Printers and Lithographers
75 West Century Road
Paramus, NJ 07652
Tel: 201-634-9600
Web: http://www.napl.org

■ Related Articles

Book Publishing

Newspapers and Magazines

Printing

Bindery Workers

General Maintenance Mechanics

Industrial Machinery Mechanics

Packaging Machinery Technicians

Paper Processing Occupations

Prepress Workers

Printing Sales Representatives

■ Overview

A *printing sales representative* is a printing company's front-line operator, the person in charge of visiting companies and other prospective clients to solicit their print business. A salesperson in printing may represent a commercial printer, a business printer, a magazine and book printer, or a company that specializes in one aspect of the industry, such as binding.

■ History

The concept of employees dedicated full-time to selling print is fairly modern. Traditionally, most owners of printing companies did the selling themselves. This is still true at some small print shops, although many small shops use brokers or simply market themselves and let the customers come to them. There was a time when the plant manager often acted as salesperson. When a prospective customer requested a presentation, the plant manager would quickly put on a tie and sport coat and make the call.

Today most printing sales representatives are devoted entirely to selling, although many also manage a multiple-member sales team.

■ The Job

Printing sales representatives are the lifeblood of the companies they represent. They are responsible for identifying prospective customers and securing their printing business. As with nearly any sales job, this process is ongoing, both in the search for new clients and in maintaining relationships with clients they already have.

There are several ways salespeople find customers. One is researching companies they think are a good fit with the specific printing services they offer and making "cold calls." Another is following up on referrals they get from existing clients or other sources. As in any business, networking is crucial.

Once they have leads, printing reps then make sales calls. These calls might be general, letting the prospective customer know what services their printing company can offer, or they might be in response to a specific job a customer needs printed. If a specific job is being discussed, the sales rep helps the client determine the job's parameters and then provides an estimate of how much it will cost to be printed. Most companies request bids from two or three different print vendors.

Once a job is procured, the role of the sales representative is by no means over. Printing salespeople are assisted by customer service representatives, who oversee much of the production work, but the salesperson continues to be the main conduit between the customer and the company. They must communicate with both parties every step of the way to make sure that the customer is satisfied with the quality of the job. This means establishing good relationships with not only the customers, but with the staff in the printing plant who do the hands-on work.

■ Requirements

High School

In printing, a person with only a high school diploma is likely to get a job as a sales representative only if he or she has a history of work in the printing industry. High school courses that will be helpful include business, speech, mathematics, and computer science.

Postsecondary Training

Most often, a college degree is the minimum educational requirement for printing sales representatives. Four-year college programs in graphic arts or marketing and finance are recommended.

Other Requirements

Printing sales representatives must have strong written and verbal communication skills and the ability to interact well with people.

"It is important for sales representatives to be team players," says Jim Reinhardt, a sales representative for Wicklander Printing Corporation in Chicago, Illinois. "There are lots of people involved in the process, so you have to be flexible and communicative."

PRINTING SALES REPRESENTATIVES	
SCHOOL SUBJECTS	Business Speech
PERSONAL SKILLS	Communication/ideas
WORK ENVIRONMENT	Primarily indoors Primarily multiple locations
MINIMUM EDUCATION LEVEL	Bachelor's degree
SALARY RANGE	$30,000 to $50,000 to $100,000+
CERTIFICATION OR LICENSING	None available
OUTLOOK	Much faster than the average

Successful salespeople are also persuasive, have an outgoing and enthusiastic personality, are highly energetic and motivated, and perform well under pressure.

■ Employers

The U.S. Bureau of Labor Statistics reported that service sales representatives held more than 694,000 wage and salary jobs in 1996. Of these, some 20,000 were in mailing, reproduction, and stenographic fields, including printing.

Printing sales jobs may be with commercial or business printers, magazine or book printers, trade shops, or binderies. Because printing is so widespread, sales jobs are available in most parts of the country. However printing work is concentrated in large printing centers like New York, Chicago, Los Angeles, Philadelphia, Dallas, and Washington, DC.

■ Starting Out

Traditionally, most printing sales reps started in entry-level production jobs and rose through the ranks to sales. This is still a common way to move into the job of sales representative. Often, working as a customer service representative or prepress specialist can be a stepping stone.

Today it is possible to get a job as printing sales representative directly out of school, with a business-related degree like marketing or a degree in graphic arts. But printing is a highly technical industry, and a salesperson must have a solid understanding of printing processes and technology to be successful. That is why many companies choose to promote staff from within.

Young people looking for jobs in print sales should check newspaper want ads and job placement listings through local chapters of printing associations.

■ Advancement

Often printing sales representatives will start out with a few of a company's smaller accounts and take on more as they prove their success.

Sales representatives at printing companies with a large sales force have the opportunity to advance to the position of *sales manager*. In that capacity, they oversee the work of the entire sales team, establishing goals, setting quotas and territories, arranging for training the sales force in new technology and techniques, and analyzing marketing and sales statistics to improve policies and practices.

■ Earnings

The salary of printing sales representatives can vary greatly, depending on how they are compensated and how successful they are. According to the book *Careers in Graphic Communications* (Graphic Arts Technical Foundation, 1998), some sales reps are paid straight commission, and others might be paid a mix of salary and bonuses.

Newcomers and trainees might expect to be placed on straight salary until they are up and running.

Printing sales reps typically earn between $30,000 to $75,000 annually, but the most successful salespeople can make more than $100,000 a year.

■ Work Environment

Most industry sources say that printing sales reps spend about 70 percent of their time out of the office, traveling locally, regionally, or nationally to visit clients and make sales calls. A sales rep might report to the office in the morning, check in on the jobs he or she is currently overseeing, handle any problems or other matters that need attending to, make calls or write letters, and then head out for the bulk of the day. No day is the same as the next, which means there really is no typical work environment or structure.

Hours vary as well, although most veteran print salespeople put in well over 40 hours a week. On average, printing sales reps work about 50 hours, but some log as many as 80 hours in a week.

"This is not a career for people who are never willing to put in more than 40 hours a week," Jim Reinhardt says.

■ Outlook

According to the U.S. Bureau of Labor Statistics, employment of services sales representatives, as a group, is expected to grow much faster than the average for all occupations through the year 2006, in response to growth of the services industries employing them.

Despite recent predictions of a "paperless society," the demand for printed products is increasing rather than decreasing. This means that there will be a growing need for printing sales representatives in the near future. In fact, many companies today are having a hard time filling sales and customer service representative positions.

Because of the competitive nature of the printing industry, the role of the salesperson is critical to a company's success and offers much opportunity.

■ For More Information

GATF offers information, services, and training. It also sponsors the National Scholarship Trust Fund (NSTF) of the Graphic Arts, which awards scholarships to undergraduate and graduate students preparing to enter the field of graphic communications. (Applications may be downloaded from the GATF Web site.) NSTF also publishes a directory of technical schools, colleges, and universities that offer courses in graphic communications.

Graphic Arts Technical Foundation
200 Deer Run Road
Sewickley, PA 15143-2600
Tel: 412-741-6860
Web: http://www.gatf.org

GCCC serves as a clearinghouse, resource center, and coordinator of programs promoting career awareness, training, and a positive industry image.

Graphic Communications Career Center
1899 Preston White Drive
Reston, VA 22091
Tel: 703-648-1768
Web: http://www.npes.org/edcouncil/index.htm

NAPL is a good source of general information.

National Association of Printers and Lithographers
75 West Century Road
Paramus, NJ 07652
Tel: 201-634-9600
Web: http://www.napl.org

■ Related Articles
Book Publishing
Business
Newspapers and Magazines
Printing
Sales
Printing Customer Service Representatives
Real Estate Agents and Brokers
Sales Representatives
Services Sales Representatives
Wireless Sales Workers

Printmakers
■ See Visual Arts

Private Branch Exchange Advisers
■ See Telephone Operators

Private Investigators
■ See Detectives

Probation Officers
■ See Parole Officers

Process Control Programmers
■ See Computer Programmers

Process Engineers
■ See Paper Processing Occupations, Plastics Engineers

Process Servers

■ Overview
Process servers are licensed by the courts to serve legal papers, such as summonses, subpoenas, and court orders, to the parties involved in legal disputes. People served may include witnesses, defendants in lawsuits, or the employers of workers whose wages are being garnished by court order. Corporations can be served through their statutory agents (representatives), and unknown parties can be served as John or Jane Doe, with their true names being substituted when learned by the court. Process servers work independently or as employees of law firms and other companies.

■ History
Modern-day process servers owe their lineage to the English bailiff, whose powers included the serving and enforcement of common law decrees such as *writs of attainder* (a notice of outlawry, the loss of civil rights, or sentence of death), or *habeas corpus* (a call for one in custody to be brought to court). The bailiff was considered a minor court official with authority to serve the court in several ways, one of which included handling legal documents. In English literature, the most notable char-

PROCESS SERVERS	
SCHOOL SUBJECTS	English Government
PERSONAL SKILLS	Following instructions
WORK ENVIRONMENT	Indoors and outdoors Primarily multiple locations
MINIMUM EDUCATION LEVEL	High school diploma
SALARY RANGE	$10,000 to $27,000 to $45,000+
CERTIFICATION OR LICENSING	Recommended
OUTLOOK	About as fast as the average
DOT	249
GOE	07.07.02
NOC	1227
O*NET	55347

GLOSSARY

Affidavit: Written statement made under oath to an officer of the court

Ex parte: In behalf of

Garnishment: This order of the court calls for the served person to bring certain property before the court

Injunction: A judge's ruling to stop someone from doing something

Process: A formal writing issued by authority of law.

Subpoena: A writ authorized by the court that demands a witness to appear in court.

acterizations of bailiffs can be found in the works of the 19th century writer Charles Dickens.

In the United States, these duties were carried out by the constables until the 1930s, when the term private process server was coined to describe an official who could serve legal documents, but who had no law enforcement powers. The heavy burden of serving all the legal papers fell on the court officials and law enforcement personnel until the process server position was born. Although all criminal process service is still carried out by many sheriff and marshal office's, much of the civil process service is now handled by independent process servers.

■ The Job

Process servers are responsible for assuring that people are notified in a timely and legal fashion that they are required to appear in court. Their clients may include attorneys, government agencies (such as a state's attorney general's office), or any person who files a lawsuit, seeks a divorce, or begins a legal action. As private individuals, process servers occupy a unique position in the legal system: They are court officers, but not court employees; they cannot give legal advice, or practice as attorneys.

A process server's duties are also distinct from that of the sheriff's because process servers serve papers only in civil matters, although the sheriff and constable serve in both civil and criminal matters. Criminal arrest warrants, for example, or papers ordering the seizure of property, are served exclusively by sheriffs, constables, and other law enforcement officials. To ensure that private process servers aren't mistaken for law enforcement officials, most jurisdictions forbid process servers to wear uniforms and badges or to place official-looking emblems on their vehicles.

Process servers use their knowledge of the rules of civil procedure on a daily basis as they carry out their duties. Certain types of papers—for example, a summons or court orders—expire if not served within a certain number of days. Others, such as subpoenas, must be served quickly to allow a witness time to plan or to make travel arrangements. Eviction notices and notices of trustee sales can be posted on the property in certain situations, and writs of garnishments (order to bring property to the court) require the process server to mail papers as well as serve them.

Besides being aware of the time limits on serving a paper, process servers must know who they are allowed to serve in a given situation. A summons, for example, can be served directly to the person named or to a resident of the household, provided they are of a suitable age. A court order or a subpoena, on the other hand, can only be served to the person named. Special circumstances also exist for serving minors, people judged to be mentally incompetent, or people who have declared bankruptcy. Many such rules and exceptions exist, and the process server is responsible for making sure that every service is valid by following these rules. An invalid service can cause excessive delays in a case, or even cause a case to be dismissed due to procedural mistakes on the part of the process server. In light of this, many process servers, or the companies they work for, are bonded and carry malpractice insurance.

A process server's job is further complicated by the fact that many people do not want to be served and go to great lengths to avoid it. Much of a process server's time is spent skip-tracing—that is, attempting to locate an address for a person who has moved or who may be avoiding service. The client may provide the process server with some information about the person, such as a last known address, a place of business, or even a photograph of the person, but occasionally process servers have to gather much of this information on their own. Questioning neighbors or co-workers is a common practice, as is using the public information provided by government offices such as the assessor's office, voter's registration, or the court clerk to locate the person. Sometimes, process servers even stake out a home or business to serve papers.

Tony Klein, from the Process Server Institute, says the clientele and the people who are served vary according to the type of work the process server does: "Some servers have clients that send primarily collection lawsuits. The defendants are generally of low to moderate income, live in low to moderate income neighborhoods, and might be evasive. Some servers specialize in the high end, same day, special-handling assignments involving lawsuits over substantial amounts of money."

The actual service of the paper is a simple, often anticlimactic process. The process server identifies himself or herself as an officer of the court and tells the person that he or she is being served, then hands the person the documents. If the person won't accept service, or won't confirm his or her identity, the process server will drop papers or simply leave the documents. In the eyes of the court, the person is considered served whether or not they actually touch the papers, sign for them, or even acknowledge the process server's presence.

Requirements

High School

High school students should take courses in English, political science, communications, law, and business. Training in a foreign language can also be extremely helpful because process servers may encounter non-English speakers.

Postsecondary Training

Although college is not required, advanced courses in psychology, communication, and business would be of great benefit to a potential process server. You won't find many, if any, college or university majors called "process serving." However, any college level work in legal studies will prepare you for work in this field. The Process Server Institute (see their contact information at the end of this article) holds training seminars that focus directly on process serving. This type of specific training will help a new process server more than the general legal studies approach.

Certification or Licensing

According to the National Association of Investigating Specialists, any U.S. citizen who is not party to the case and is over the age of 18 and who resides in the state where the matter is to be tried may serve due process (that is, be a process server for a specific legal matter). However, people who serve papers on a regular basis usually must register with their particular state. The courts take the licensing of process servers seriously, and many jurisdictions require applicants to take a written exam; some even require an interview with the presiding judge. Alvin Esper, a process server in Indiana, recommends that all new servers obtain private detective status with their particular state: "This is not a requirement in most state or the federal courts," Alvin adds, "but it can protect you when you must perform stakeouts to locate a person to be served." Because most states differ on their requirements, you should get more information from your local office of the Clerk of the Superior Court.

Other Requirements

Because process serving is a face-to-face job, people who excel in this field are usually bold, confident, and skilled at working with people. Gaining a reputation as reliable and responsible will go a long way with prospective clients who want someone that won't give up on serving papers to someone. Because process servers often serve papers to people who don't want them, a certain element of danger is involved. Process servers must be willing to take that risk in some situations. Alvin says, "Depending on the individual to be served, serving can be dangerous. I usually try to serve papers during daylight hours depending on whether the neighborhood seems safe or unsafe."

Exploring

Because you have read this far into the field of process serving, maybe you think this is the job for you. The hard part is finding out for sure before you make a commitment to doing this particular work. A first step is to check the National Association of Professional Process Servers Web site for process servers in your state. Contact some of these people who are working in the field now and ask for information. Speaking to attorneys, or to a local constable or sheriff's deputy, could also be helpful. Since most court records are public, an interested person could look at actual files of court cases to familiarize themselves with the types of papers served and examine affidavits filed by process servers.

Employers

Most process servers are independent contractors. They set up their own service business and provide process serving to individuals, lawyers, and courts. Other process servers may work for small law firms, attorney's offices, or law enforcement agencies on a full-time or part-time basis. Because courts are located throughout the country, process servers will find opportunities just about everywhere. Larger cities will have more opportunities, of course, simply due to the higher concentration of people.

Starting Out

Most process serving companies train their new employees and encourage them to travel with licensed process servers to familiarize them with the job. Often, the employer will assist in preparing the employee for the examination by providing them with copies of the local rules or even a study guide. Because of the flexible hours and hands-on experience with legal papers and cases, process serving is a popular job with college students, especially those who are interested in becoming attorneys themselves.

Firms specializing in attorney services will frequently train messengers and other office personnel as process servers, because they are already familiar with legal terms and documents.

You won't see many advertisements in newspapers for process servers. Instead the key to landing this job is to network with people in the legal profession. If you or someone in your family knows a lawyer, ask him or her to refer you to someone who may be interested in training a new process server.

Advancement

A process server may start out as a *legal messenger,* delivering documents to law offices and filing papers with the city, state, or federal courts. In most jurisdictions, subpoenas don't need to be served by a licensed process server, so an employee of an attorney service can begin a career in process serving in this manner.

Once licensed, a process server can expect to work for a firm as either a salaried employee or a private contractor. As process servers gain experience, they typically serve more papers, and perhaps acquire bigger or more lucrative territory in which to work. In this way, advancement is also tied to the papers themselves.

In a sense, the papers that a process server delivers or serves are actually worth money, but only to the process server who delivers them. Just as private delivery companies charge for their services, process serving companies or individuals also charge for their services. The difference is that the rates are determined by the courts with the amount any given paper is worth legally fixed by law. Usually, the pricing is set in terms of the location of the delivery, the number of miles from the courthouse, and so on, but anything that makes delivery more difficult or time-consuming can add to the cost. For example, papers to be served on someone living 50 miles from the courthouse are worth more because it takes more time and money to drive 50 miles out of town. The value of those particular papers increases if they must be served within a day and the person being served has moved, forcing the process server to spend considerable time, money, and effort learning the new address. Because most process servers are independent contractors, they are rewarded for their seniority and long service with a company by being assigned to the most lucrative territories, or those areas in which the papers are worth the most.

Some process servers use the knowledge and experience they gain working for a firm to start their own businesses. Process servers who operate their own companies are responsible for all aspects of the business, from supervising and training personnel to advertising, accounting, and tax preparation.

■ Earnings

Salaries are extremely difficult to predict. Earnings vary according to the number and type of papers served. If a process server is working as an employee of a firm, or as a private contractor, he or she can expect to earn approximately 25 to 40 percent of the total amount the firm charges the client to serve the paper. The average cost a firm charges to serve a paper is $25, but this number can vary wildly, depending on the mileage traveled to serve the paper, the number of attempts made, or any special efforts required to effect service. When taking into consideration skip-tracing, stakeout time, and other investigative efforts, the fee can be much higher.

A salaried employee who works part-time as a process server can expect to make approximately $27,000, although a salaried, full-time process server can expect almost twice

as much, approximately $45,000 to $50,000. These figures can be misleading, however. A process server can work all day and not serve any papers. The next day, he or she could make almost $600. A non-salaried process server who hustles and has a decent territory can make good money, too. "The rate depends on the type of work and the need for it," Tony Klein says. "You can make a living doing this type of work. If you work for someone, you make less than working for yourself. Every market is different; for example, in California independent servers make $2,000 to $4,000 per month."

Employees may receive such benefits as health insurance and paid vacation time.

■ Work Environment

Being a process server requires a certain amount of hustle. The job requires that the person be part investigator, part process server, and part legal messenger. The successful process server will enjoy the more tedious aspects of sleuthing, such as tracking down routine information about someone's life.

Considering the process server's position as the bearer of bad news, it is not surprising that the job can be stressful at times. Defendants who have been avoiding service may become angry when finally served. Violence against process servers is rare but does occur. Subsequently, process servers need to remain clearheaded in stressful situations and be able to use their communication skills to their best advantage.

Process servers may work at any hour of the day in most jurisdictions, and many choose to work weekends or holidays as well. This allows for an extremely flexible work schedule, because the process server is usually the one who decides when to attempt service on a given paper. In scheduling an attempted service, the process server's main considerations are serving the paper as quickly as possible with the fewest number of attempts; if the party is not home, the process server must return later.

Many large process serving companies assign their employees fixed areas to work in, allowing a process server to become familiar with a certain section of a large city, for example, or several small towns in a given area. Even if a process server has a fixed territory, he or she can still expect to travel to a wide variety of locations. "Process serving is a lot of driving," Alvin Esper says. "Most often you are searching for the address of the person to be served." In the course of a year, a process server might serve at hospitals, prisons, schools, and any number of private offices.

When not serving papers, process servers spend much of their time working closely with attorneys, judges, and other court personnel. For this reason, many process servers dress in a professional manner. When serving, however, a process server may wear whatever he or she prefers, and many choose to dress casually. Some dress casually to appear unobtrusive, hoping that potentially evasive parties will be caught off guard, and therefore served more easily.

■ Outlook

Employment opportunities for process servers will grow as the number of legal matters grow. The rising number of civil lawsuits bodes well for process servers, since a single case can produce anywhere from one service to dozens, when taking into account subpoenas, supporting orders, writs of garnishment, and the like.

Some sheriff's departments (long mandated by law to serve civil papers) are now beginning to rely solely on private process servers, since they cannot effectively compete with the faster and more inexpensive private process serving companies. Other jurisdictions, increasingly under pressure to justify serving civil papers at a loss, are likely to revise their laws as well.

From time to time, various jurisdictions experiment with service by registered mail, but these experiments are limited and usually not long-lasting, since the most efficient way to ensure that a person has been notified is to notify him or her in person.

■ For More Information

For a listing of current process servers, contact:

United States Process Server Association
1 West Old Capitol Plaza, Suite 502
Springfield, IL 62701
Tel: 217-525-0364
Web: http://www.usprocessservers.com

For information about training seminars and to request a free newsletter, contact:

Process Server Institute
667 Folsom Street, 2nd floor
San Francisco, CA 94107
Tel: 415-495-3850
Web: http://www.psinstitute.com/

To learn more about membership, contact:

National Association of Professional Process Servers
PO Box 4547
Portland, OR 97208
Tel: 800-477-8211
Web: http://napps.org/

■ Related Articles

Information Services

Law

Detectives

Lawyers and Judges

Legal Secretaries

Paralegals

Procurement Coordinators

■ **See Transplant Coordinators**

Producers

■ Overview

Producers organize and secure the financial backing for the production of motion pictures. They decide which scripts will be used or which books will be adapted for film. Producers also raise money to finance the filming of a motion picture; hire the director, screenwriter, and cast; oversee the budget and production schedule; and monitor the distribution of the film.

■ History

Motion picture cameras were invented in the late 1800s. The two earliest known films—made in 1888 by French-born Louis Le Prince—showed his father-in-law's garden and traffic crossing an English bridge.

More advanced cameras and motion picture techniques quickly followed. In 1903 American director Edwin Porter and inventor Thomas Edison made *The Great Train Robbery*, one of the first movies in which scenes were filmed out of sequence; when the filming was completed, the scenes were edited and spliced together. By 1906 feature-length films were being made and many talented and financially savvy individuals were making their livings as producers. The first woman to become a producer was Alice Guy, who started the Solax Company in New York in 1910.

In 1911 the Centaur Company, which had been

PRODUCERS	
SCHOOL SUBJECTS	Business English
PERSONAL SKILLS	Communication/ideas Leadership/management
WORK ENVIRONMENT	Primarily indoors Primarily one location
MINIMUM EDUCATION LEVEL	High school diploma
SALARY RANGE	$17,000 to $70,000 to $200,000+
CERTIFICATION OR LICENSING	None available
OUTLOOK	Faster than the average
DOT	187
GOE	01.03.01
NOC	5121
O*NET	34056G

trying to film westerns in New Jersey, moved to California and became the first studio to settle in Hollywood. Many film companies followed the lead of Centaur and moved their operations to southern California where there was abundant sunshine and a variety of terrain.

The film industry began to consolidate in the late 1920s after the introduction of sound films and the 1929 stock market crash. Small and marginally profitable producers were forced out of business, leaving the largest companies, which controlled most of the first-run theaters, to dominate the market. Major studios produced their films in a factory-like fashion. With their permanent staff of cameramen and other technical workers, a major studio could produce 40 or more films annually. And because many of the larger studios also owned their own network of theaters throughout the United States, they had a guaranteed market to which they could distribute their films. This stable, mass-produced system gave some studios the encouragement to produce commercially risky art films as well.

The introduction of television after World War II brought mixed fortunes to motion picture producers. Television was partly responsible for a decline in the number of theater goers, causing financial difficulties for the studios. An antitrust court judgment against the studios also eliminated their dominance of the movie theater market. But with the emergence and growth of television, and a steady need for new shows and made-for-TV films, television broadened employment opportunities for producers.

The major studios experienced financial difficulties in the 1950s, which because of studio downsizing and other pressures, led to a growth in the number of independent producers. Changes in the U.S. tax code made independent producing even more profitable. In response to their financial difficulties, studios began to reduce the number of films produced each year and to rely more on expensive "blockbuster" films to attract audiences.

In the early 1970s the industry again went through a major reorganization. The staggering expense of producing blockbusters had drained the major studios of their profits, and these financially strapped companies began to make films under strict cost-containment measures. Film projects, moreover, were increasingly initiated by independent producers.

Technical innovations have had great influence on motion picture producing. Portable lights, cameras, and other equipment allow films to be made anywhere and reduce the dependence on studio sets. More recently, the emergence of cable television and the ensuing demand for new shows has opened a new market for film producers. In recent years, the traditional distinctions between television and movie production, as well as between American and foreign films, have become increasingly blurred. Many foreign-made films are now financed by Americans, and a number of American motion picture companies are owned by foreigners.

■ The Job

The primary role of a producer is to organize and secure the financial backing necessary to undertake a motion picture project. The director, by contrast, creates the film from the screenplay. Despite this general distinction, the producer often takes part in creative decisions, and occasionally one person is both the producer and director. On some small projects, such as a nature or historical documentary for a public television broadcast, the producer might also be the writer and cameraman.

The job of a producer generally begins in the preproduction stage of filmmaking with the selection of a movie idea from a script, or other material. Some films are made from original screenplays, while others are adapted from books. If a book is selected, the producer must first purchase the rights from the author or his or her publishing company, and a writer must be hired to adapt the book into a screenplay format. Producers are usually inundated with scripts from writers and others who have ideas for a movie. Producers may have their own ideas for a motion picture and will hire a writer to write the screenplay. Occasionally a studio will approach a producer, typically a producer who has had many commercially or artistically successful films in the past, with a project.

After selecting a project, the producer will find a director, the technical staff, and the star actor or actors to participate in the film. Along with the script and screenwriter, these essential people are referred to as the "package." Packaging is sometimes arranged with the help of talent agencies. It is the package that the producer tries to sell to an investor to obtain the necessary funds to finance the salaries and cost of the film.

There are three common sources for financing a film: major studios, production companies, and individual investors. A small number of producers have enough money to pay for their own projects. Major studios are the largest source of money and finance most of the big budget films. Although some studios have full-time producers on staff, they hire self-employed, or *independent producers*, for many projects. Large production companies often have the capital resources to fund projects which they feel will be commercially successful. On the smaller end of the scale, producers of documentary films commonly approach individual donors; foundations; art agencies of federal, state, and local governments; and even family members and churches. The National Endowment for the Humanities and the National Endowment for the Arts are major federal benefactors of cinema.

Raising money from individual investors can occupy much of the producer's time. Fund-raising may be done on the telephone, as well as in conferences, business lunches, and even cocktail parties. The producer may also look for a distributor for the film even before the production begins.

Obtaining the necessary financing does not guarantee a film will be made. After raising the money, the producer takes the basic plan of the package and tries to work it into a developed project. The script may be rewritten several times, the full cast of actors is hired, salaries are negotiated, and logistical problems, such as the location of the filming, are worked out; on some projects it might be the director who handles these tasks, or the director may work with the producer. Most major motion film projects do not get beyond this complicated stage of development.

During the production phase, the producer tries to keep the project on schedule and the spending within the established budget. Other production tasks include the review of dailies, which are prints of the day's filming. As the head of the project, the producer is ultimately responsible for resolving all problems, including personal conflicts such as those between the director and an actor and the director and the studio. If the film is successfully completed, the producer monitors its distribution and may participate in the publicity and advertising of the film.

To accomplish the many and varied tasks that the position requires, producers hire a number of subordinates, such as associate producers, sometimes called coproducers, line producers, and production assistants. Job titles, however, vary from project to project. In general, associate producers work directly under the producer and oversee the major areas of the project, such as the budget. *Line producers* handle the day-to-day operations of the project. Production assistants may perform substantive tasks, such as reviewing scripts, but others are hired to run errands. Another title, *executive producer*, often refers to the person who puts up the money, such as a studio executive, but it is sometimes an honorary title with no functional relevance to the project.

■ Requirements

There is no minimum educational requirement for becoming a producer. Many producers, however, are college graduates, and many also have a business degree or other previous business experience. They must not only be talented salespeople and administrators but also have a thorough understanding of films and motion picture technology.

High School

High school courses that will be of assistance to you in your work as a producer include speech, mathematics, business, psychology, and English.

Postsecondary Training

Formal study of film, television, communications, theater, writing, English literature, or art are helpful, as the producer must have the background to know whether an idea or script is worth pursuing. Many entry-level positions in the film industry are given to people who have studied liberal arts, cinema, or both.

In the United States there are more than a 1,000 colleges, universities, and trade schools that offer classes in film or television studies; more than 120 of these offer undergraduate programs, and more than 50 grant master's degrees. A small number of Ph.D. programs also exist.

Graduation from a film or television program does not guarantee employment in the industry. Some programs are quite expensive, costing more than $50,000 in tuition alone for three years of study. Others do not have the resources to allow all students to make their own films.

Programs in Los Angeles and New York City, the major centers of the entertainment industry, may provide the best opportunities for making contacts that can be of benefit when seeking employment.

Other Requirements

Producers come from a wide variety of backgrounds. Some start out as magazine editors, business school graduates, actors, or secretaries, messengers, and production assistants for a film studio. Many have never formally studied film.

Most producers, however, get their position through several years of experience in the industry, perseverance, and a keen sense for what projects will be artistically and commercially successful.

■ Exploring

There are many ways to gain experience in filmmaking. Some high schools have film and video clubs or courses on the use of motion picture equipment. Experience in theater can also be useful. One of the best ways to get experience is to volunteer for a student or low-budget film project; positions on such projects are often advertised in local trade publications. Community cable stations also hire volunteers and may even offer internships.

■ Employers

Many producers in the field are self-employed. Others are salaried employees of film companies, television networks, and television stations. The greatest concentration of motion picture producers is in Hollywood and New York City. Hollywood alone has more than 2,000 producers.

■ Starting Out

Becoming a producer is similar to becoming president of a company. Unless a person is independently wealthy and can finance whichever projects he or she chooses, prior experience in the field is necessary. Because there are so few positions, even with experience it is extremely difficult to become a successful producer.

Most motion picture producers have attained their position only after years of moving up the industry ladder. Thus, it is important to concentrate on immediate goals, such as getting an entry-level position in a film company. Some enter the field by getting a job as a production assistant. An entry-level production assistant may Xerox copies of the scripts for actors to use, assist in setting up equipment, or may perform other menial tasks, often for very little or even no pay. While a production assistant's work is often tedious and of little seeming reward, it nevertheless does expose one to the intricacies of filmmaking and, more importantly, creates an opportunity to make contacts with others in the industry.

Those interested in the field should approach film companies, television stations, or the television networks about employment opportunities as a production assistant. Small television stations often provide the best opportunity for those who are interested in television producing. Positions may also be listed in trade publications.

■ Advancement

There is little room for advancement beyond the position, as producers are at the top of their profession. Advancement for producers is generally measured by the types of projects, increased earnings, and respect in the field. At television stations, a producer can advance to program director. Some producers become directors or make enough money to finance their own projects.

■ Earnings

Producers are generally paid a percentage of the project's profits or a fee negotiated between the producer and a studio. Average yearly earnings range from about $25,000 to $70,000. Producers of highly successful films can earn as much as $200,000 or more, while those who make low-budget, documentary films might earn considerably less than the average. In general, producers in the film industry earn more than television producers. A producer for a large market news program can average from about $24,000 to $40,000 a year. Smaller markets pay less, about $17,000 a year. Entry-level production assistants can earn from less than minimum wage to $15,000 per year.

■ Work Environment

Producers have greater control over their working conditions than most other people working in the motion picture industry. They may have the autonomy of choosing their own projects, setting their own hours, and delegating duties to others as necessary. The work often brings considerable personal satisfaction. But it is not without con-

straints. Producers must work within a stressful schedule complicated by competing work pressures and often daily crises. Each project brings a significant financial and professional risk. Long hours and weekend work are common. Most producers must provide for their own health insurance and other benefits.

■ Outlook

Employment for producers is expected to grow faster than the average through the year 2006, according to the U.S. Department of Labor. The occupation of TV news producer was recently listed as a runner-up in *U.S. News & World Report*'s annual compilation of 20 hot track careers. Though opportunities may increase with the expansion of cable television and news programs, video rentals, and an increased overseas demand for American-made films, competition for jobs will be high. Live theater and entertainment will also provide job openings. Some positions will be available as current producers leave the workforce.

■ For More Information

Visit the PGA Web site to read an online version of Point of View *magazine, which focuses on the role of producers in the motion picture and television industries:*

Producers Guild of America
400 South Beverly Drive
Beverly Hills, CA 90212
Web: http://www.producersguild.com/

■ Related Articles

Broadcasting
Film
Television
Actors
Art Directors
Cinematographers and Directors of Photography
Film and Television Directors
Fund-Raisers
Marketing Research Analysts
Music Producers
Screenwriters
Talent Agents and Scouts
Writers

Product Designers

■ **See Plastics Technicians**

Production Assistants

■ Overview

The *production assistant* performs a variety of tasks for the producer and other staff members. He or she must be prepared to help out everywhere, ensuring that daily operations run as smoothly as possible. Some production assistants may perform substantive jobs, such as reviewing scripts, but others may primarily run errands. They must be willing to work hard and keep long hours at times, since tight production schedules require full days. An agreeable temperament and willingness to follow instructions and perform simple tasks are very important skills.

■ History

In the early 20th century, as motion pictures were first developing, the roles of director and producer were combined in one person. European filmmakers such as Georges Melies and Leon Gaumont and New Yorker Edwin S. Porter directed, filmed, and produced very short movies. The first woman to become a director and producer was Alice Guy, who started the Solax Company in New York in 1910.

The film industry settled in Hollywood and began to consolidate in the first two decades of this century, as jobs were differentiated. Major studios assembled large staffs, so all stages of production from conception to financing and directing could be performed within a single studio. Twentieth Century Fox, for example, would have producers, writers, directors, and actors on staff to choose from for each film. Small producers were forced out of business as major studios grew to have a monopoly on the industry.

In the 1950s the dominance of major studios in film production was curbed by an antitrust court decision, and more independent producers were able to find projects. Changes in the United States tax code made independent producing more profitable. At the same time, the growth of television provided new opportunities for producers. The industry is becoming increasingly international; many foreign-made films are now financed by Americans, and a number of American motion picture companies are under foreign ownership.

Currently many producers work on a project-by-project basis. The independent producer must be a good salesperson to market a project to a studio and to other financial backers. He or she will try to involve popular actors and actresses with the project from its inception in order to attract a studio's interest. Studios hire production assistants to facilitate the work of the producer and other staff members.

■ The Job

The work of a production assistant is not glamorous, but production is the best place to learn about the film and television industries. All hiring, casting, and decision making is done by members of production; they are involved with a project from the very beginning through its final stages. The *producer* is in charge—he or she is responsible for coordinating the activities of all employees involved in a production. Producers oversee the budget, and they have the final word on most decisions made for a film or television show.

Your responsibilities as a production assistant (PA) will range from making sure the star has coffee in the morning to stopping street traffic so a director can film a scene. You'll photocopy the script for actors, assist in setting up equipment, and perform other menial tasks. The best PAs know where to be at the right time to make themselves useful. Production can be stressful; time is money and mistakes can be very costly. You must be prepared to handle unforeseen problems and smooth out difficulties, and prepared to help out as quickly as possible.

Duties may include keeping production files in order. These files will include contracts, budgets, page changes (old pages from a script that has been revised), and other records. The documents must be kept organized and accessible for whenever the producer may need them.

You may also have to keep the producer's production folder in order and up-to-date. The production folder contains everything the producer needs to know about the production at a glance. It is particularly useful for times when a producer is on location away from the studio and cannot access the office files. You must ensure that the folder includes the following: the shooting schedule, the most recent version of the budget, cast and crew lists with phone numbers, a phone sheet detailing all production-related phone calls the producer needs to make, and the up-to-date shooting script. As new versions of these forms are created,

PRODUCTION ASSISTANTS	
SCHOOL SUBJECTS	**Business** **Theater/Dance**
PERSONAL SKILLS	**Communication/ ideas** **Following instructions**
WORK ENVIRONMENT	**Indoors and outdoors** **Primarily multiple locations**
MINIMUM EDUCATION LEVEL	**High school diploma**
SALARY RANGE	**$500 to $20,000 to $65,000**
CERTIFICATION OR LICENSING	**None available**
OUTLOOK	**About as fast as the average**
DOT	**962**
GOE	**01.03.01**
NOC	**5227**
O*NET	**98999B**

GLOSSARY

Breakdown script: A list of cast members and items, such as production equipment and props, required for that day's shoot.
Call sheet: A list of the actors needed for each scene.
Craft service: Working with the caterer, craft service provides snacks for cast and crew during a production.
Hot set: The set on which filming is currently taking place.
Swing gang: The construction team that builds and breaks down a set.

you'll update the producer's folder and file the older versions for reference.

You may also be in charge of making sure that the producer gets the dailies, the film shot each day. You will have to schedule an hour or so in a producer's schedule to watch the dailies and to make related calls to discuss them with other staff members.

■ Requirements

High School

To work in the film industry, you should have an understanding of both the artistic and technical aspects of production, as well as knowledge of the movie marketplace. Take courses in photography, broadcast journalism, and media to learn about cameras and sound equipment. You should also take courses in art and art history to learn about visual composition, and English to develop communication skills. Business and accounting can help you prepare for the bookkeeping requirements of office work.

Postsecondary Training

There are no formal education requirements for production assistants. Most people in the industry consider the position a stepping stone into other careers in the industry. You'll learn much of what you'll need to know on the set of a film, following the instructions of crew members and other assistants. Though a film school education can't guarantee entry into the business, it can give you an understanding of the industry and help you make some connections. A listing of film schools is available from the American Film Institute (AFI). You may choose to major in English or theater as an undergraduate, then apply to graduate film schools. However, many people break into the business without formal training—they volunteer on as many film productions as they can, getting to know professionals in the business and making valuable connections in the industry.

Other Requirements

As a production assistant, you'll need an agreeable personality and willingness to follow instructions and perform simple tasks. You'll need to catch on quickly to the things you're taught. Organizational skills will help you keep track of the many different aspects of a production. Great ambition and dedication are very important, as getting paying jobs on a production will require persistence. Also, you won't get a great deal of recognition for your hours of work, so you'll need an individual sense of purpose. A love of movies and a fascination with the industry, particularly an interest in the technical aspects of filmmaking, will help you keep focused. Though you'll need an outgoing personality for making connections on a production, you should be capable of sitting quietly on the sidelines when not needed.

■ Exploring

There are many ways to gain experience with filmmaking. Some high schools have film clubs and classes in film or video. Experience in theater can also be useful. To learn more, you can work as a volunteer for a local theater or a low-budget film project; these positions are often advertised in local trade publications. You may also be able to volunteer with your state's film commission, helping to solicit production companies to do their filming in the state.

Students interested in production work should read as much as possible about the film and television industry. Two of the most prominent trade journals are *Hollywood Reporter* and *Daily Variety*. These resources will have information about production studios that will prove very useful for prospective PAs.

■ Employers

Production assistants are hired by production companies for individual film projects. Some assistants are employed full time, however, working in the main offices of a production company or serving as a personal assistant to a producer or executive.

■ Starting Out

You should seek out internships, which may offer course credit if they are unpaid, by looking in trade journals and contacting film and television studios. You can also find production opportunities listed on the Internet or through your state's film commission. To gain experience, you may have to work for free on some of your first productions to make contacts within the industry. Since this is an entry-level position, opportunities will open as other assistants advance.

■ Advancement

By performing your work efficiently and enthusiastically, you can make contacts on the job that may help you advance into other jobs, such as that of *line producer*. A line producer works closely with the producer; he or she signs checks, advises on union rules, and negotiates deals with studio personnel. An associate producer performs similar work. To become a producer or director requires years of experience and hard work. To advance in the film industry, you'll have to be of assistance to everyone on a film set, including cast and crew members.

■ Earnings

Salaries for production assistants are nearly impossible to gauge. Because working as a production assistant is the starting point for most professionals and artists in the film industry, many people volunteer their time until they make connections and move up into paid positions. Those assistants who can negotiate payment may make between $200 and $400 a week, but they may only have the opportunity to work on a few projects a year. Production assistants working full time in an office may start at around $20,000 a year, but with experience can make around $65,000. If working full time, you may belong to the Office and Professional Employees International Union which negotiates salaries. Experienced script supervisors, production office coordinators, and continuity coordinators have the opportunity to join Local #161 of the International Alliance of Theatrical Stage Employees (IATSE). As a member, you may be entitled to over $180 a day when working for a production company.

There are unwritten rules that should be followed. A production assistant who works for the producer or for the studio can be seen as an outsider in the eyes of the director and the creative team, so the PA should be respectful and well-behaved. This means you should be quiet, stay out of the way, and avoid touching sets and equipment. If you behave as a guest, but remain helpful when needed, you will earn a good reputation that will be valuable for advancing your career.

Those working on a project-to-project basis won't receive any fringe benefits, but those employed full time with a production company can expect health coverage and retirement benefits.

■ Work Environment

A film set is an exciting environment, but the production assistant may be treated poorly there. With a positive attitude, energy, and a desire to be useful, the PA will earn respect from the production department.

The work environment will vary—the PA may be required on location, or may work mainly in the studio. Production assistants must be willing to work long, demanding hours. Film productions are typically off schedule and over-budget, requiring dedication from all those involved. Production assistants and other crew members often go days without seeing family members.

■ Outlook

There will always be a need for assistants in film and television production. However, since it is such a good entry-level position for someone who wants to make connections and learn about the industry, competition for jobs can be tough. Production assistants will find employment anywhere a motion picture or television show is being filmed, but significant opportunities exist in Los Angeles and New York City—the production hubs of the industry.

■ For More Information

For information about colleges with film and television programs of study, and to read interviews with filmmakers, visit the AFI Web site:

American Film Institute
2021 North Western Avenue
Los Angeles, CA 90027
Tel: 323-856-7600
Email: info@afionline.org
Web: http://www.afionline.org

Visit the ASC Web site for a great deal of valuable insight into the industry, including interviews with award-winning cinematographers, information about film schools, multimedia presentations, and the American Cinematographer *online magazine:*

American Society of Cinematographers
1782 North Orange Drive
Hollywood, CA 90028
Tel: 323-969-4333
Web: http://www.cinematographer.com

■ Related Articles

Broadcasting

Film

Television

Visual Arts

Advertising Workers

Cinematographers and Directors of Photography

Producers

Production Control Technicians

■ **See Apparel Technicians**

Production Engineers

■ **See Electrical and Electronics Engineers**

Production Managers

■ **See Pharmaceutical Industry Workers, Plastics Technicians**

Production Test Supervisors

■ **See Electronics Engineering Technicians**

Professional Athletes— Individual Sports

■ Overview

In contrast with amateur athletes who play or compete in amateur circles for titles or trophies only, *professional athletes* participate in individual sports such as tennis, figure-skating, golf, running, or boxing, competing against others to win prizes and money.

Tiger Woods makes an eagle putt.

■ History

The origin of the first recreational activity—or sport—is not known. It can be assumed, however, that the notion of sport was born the first time anyone attempted to fish, hunt, or wrestle, simply for the pleasure of it or to compete against another person, rather than for self-preservation.

The Olympic Games are generally credited as being the first instance of organized sports. Historians believe that they actually began as early as two centuries before the first written mention of them in 776 BC. In AD 394 the Olympic Games were abolished and weren't revived until 1896.

In the interim, popular support for organized sports developed slowly. Tennis rose to popularity in France in the 1400s; historical records indicate that a track-and-field competition was held in England in 1510; Mary, Queen of Scots loved to play golf and popularized the sport during her reign from 1542 to 1567; Her son, James I of England, lifted a ban on football (soccer); and the first sweepstakes in horse racing was introduced in England in 1714.

The difference in the nature of sports before and after the 19th century largely has to do with organization. Prior to the 19th century, most sports were not officially organized; there were no official rules, competitions, or standards of play. During the 19th century, however, many sports underwent a transition from invented pastime to official sport. Rules governing play, the field of play, and competitions were agreed upon. The first modern track-and-field meet, for example, was held in England in 1825.

Baseball, basketball, golf, tennis, and then boxing began to attract large crowds of people in the years before World War II. As these sports and others grew in popularity, governing bodies and organizations were created to oversee the fair play of each sport. Gradually, coverage of sporting events on radio and in newspapers began to grow until sports quite literally became the national pastime for Americans. Sports stars became as renowned as movie stars or politicians, sometimes even more so.

Today, athletes who compete in individual sports at the professional level earn hundreds of thousands of dollars in salaries or prize money at professional competitions. The top players or athletes in each individual sport earn as much or more in endorsements and advertising, usually for sports-related products and services, but increasingly for products or services completely unrelated to their sport.

■ The Job

Professional athletes participate in individual sports such as tennis, figure-skating, golf, running, or boxing, competing against others to win prizes and money.

Depending on the nature of the specific sport, most athletes compete against a field of individuals. The field of competitors can be as small as one (tennis, boxing) or as large as the number of qualified competitors, anywhere from 6 to 30 (figure skating, golf, cycling). In certain individual events, such as the marathon or triathlon, the field may seem excessively large—often tens of thousands of runners compete in the New York Marathon—but for the professional runners competing in the race, only a handful of other runners represent real competition.

The athletic performances of those in individual sports are evaluated according to the nature and rules of each specific sport. For example, the winner of a foot race is whoever crosses the finish line first; in tennis the winner is the one who scores the highest in a set number of games; in boxing and figure skating, the winners are determined by a panel of judges. Competitions are organized by local, regional, national, and international organizations and associations whose primary functions are to promote the sport and sponsor competitive events. Within a professional sport there are usually different levels of competition based on age, ability, and gender. There are often different designations and events within one sport. Tennis, for example, consists of doubles and singles, while track-and-field contains many different events, from field events such as the javelin and shot putt, to track events such as the 110-meter dash and the two-mile relay race.

Athletes train year-round, on their own or with a coach, friend, parent, or trainer. In addition to stretching and exercising the specific muscles used in any given sport, athletes concentrate on developing excellent eating and sleeping habits that will help them remain in top condition throughout the year. Although certain sports have a particular season, most professional athletes train rigorously all year, varying the type and duration of their workouts to develop strength, cardiovascular ability, flexibility, endurance, speed, and quickness, as well as to focus on technique and control. Often, an athlete's training focuses less on the overall game or program that the athlete will execute, than on specific areas or details of that game or program. Figure skaters, for example, won't simply keep going through their entire long programs from start to finish but instead will focus on the jumps, turns, and hand movements that refine the program. Similarly, sprinters don't keep running only the sprint distances they race in during a meet; instead, they vary their workouts to include some distance work, some sprints, a lot of weight training to build strength, and maybe some mental exercises to build control and focus while in the starter's blocks. Tennis players routinely spend hours just practicing their forehand, down-the-line shots.

Athletes often watch videotapes or films of their previous practices or competitions to see where they can improve their performance. They also study what the other competitors are doing in order to prepare strategies for winning.

■ Requirements

High School

A high school diploma will provide you with the basic skills that you will need in your long climb to becoming a professional athlete. Business and mathematics classes will teach you how to manage money wisely. Speech classes will help you become a better communicator. Physical education classes will help you build your strength, agility, and competitive spirit. You should, of course, participate in every organized sport that your school offers and that interests you.

Some individual sports such as tennis and gymnastics have professional competitors who are high school students. Teenagers in this situation often have private coaches with whom they practice both before and after going to school, and others are home-schooled as they travel to competitions.

Postsecondary Training

There are no formal education requirements for sports, although certain competitions and training opportunities are only available to those enrolled in four-year colleges and universities. Collegiate-level competitions are where most athletes in this area hone their skills; they may also compete in international or national competitions outside

PROFESSIONAL ATHLETES—INDIVIDUAL SPORTS	
SCHOOL SUBJECTS	Health Physical education
PERSONAL SKILLS	Following instructions
WORK ENVIRONMENT	Indoors and outdoors Primarily multiple locations
MINIMUM EDUCATION LEVEL	High school diploma
SALARY RANGE	$10,000 to $40,000 to $1,000,000+
CERTIFICATION OR LICENSING	None available
OUTLOOK	About as fast as the average
DOT	153
GOE	12.01.03
NOC	5251
O*NET	34058C

of college, but the chance to train and receive an education isn't one many serious athletes refuse. In fact, outstanding ability in athletics is the way many students pay for their college educations. Given the chances of striking it rich financially, an education (especially a free one) is a wise investment and one fully supported by most professional sports organizations.

Other Requirements

There is so much competition to be among the world's elite athletes in any given sport that talent alone isn't the primary requirement. Diligence, perseverance, hard work, ambition, and courage are all essential qualities to the individual who dreams of making a career as a professional athlete. "If you want to be a pro, there's no halfway. There's no three-quarters way," says Eric Roller, a former professional tennis player who competed primarily on the Florida circuit. Other, specific requirements will vary according to the sport. Jockeys, for example, are usually petite men and women.

■ Exploring

If you are interested in pursuing a career in professional sports you should start participating in that sport as much and as early as possible. With some sports, an individual who is 15 may already be too old to realistically begin pursuing a professional career. By playing the sport and by talking to coaches, trainers, and athletes in the field, you can ascertain whether you like the sport enough to make it a career, determine if you have enough talent, and gain new insight into the field. You can also contact professional organizations and associations for information on how to best prepare for a career in their sport. Sometimes there are specialized training programs available, and the best way to find out is to get in contact with the people whose job it is to promote the sport.

■ Employers

Professional athletes who compete in individual sports are not employed in the same manner as most workers. They do not work for employers, but choose the competitions or tournaments they wish to compete in. For example, a professional runner may choose to enter the Boston Marathon and then travel to Atlanta for the Peachtree Road Race.

■ Starting Out

Professional athletes must meet the requirements established by the organizing bodies of their respective sport. Sometimes this means meeting a physical requirement, such as age, height, or weight; and sometimes this means fulfilling a number of required stunts, or participating in a certain number of competitions. Professional organizations usually arrange it so that athletes can build up their skills

and level of play by participating in lower-level competitions. College sports, as mentioned above, are an excellent way to improve one's skills while pursuing an education.

■ Advancement

Professional athletes advance into the elite numbers of their sport by working and practicing hard, and by winning. Professional athletes usually obtain representation by *sports agents* in the behind-the-scenes deals that determine for which teams they will be playing and what they will be paid. These agents may also be involved with other key decisions involving commercial endorsements, personal income taxes, and financial investments of the athlete's revenues.

A college education can prepare all athletes for the day when their bodies can no longer compete at the top level, whether because of age or an unforeseen injury. Every athlete should be prepared to move into another career, related to the world of sports or not.

■ Earnings

Salaries, prize monies, and commercial endorsements will vary from sport to sport; a lot depends on the popularity of the sport and its ability to attract spectators, or on the sport's professional organization and its ability to drum up sponsors for competitions and prize money. Still other sports, like boxing, depend on the skill of the fight's promoters to create interest in the fight. An elite professional tennis player who wins Wimbledon, for example, usually earns over half a million dollars in a matter of several hours. Add to that the incredible sums a Wimbledon-champion can make in endorsements and the tennis star is earning over one million dollars a year. This scenario is misleading, however; to begin with, top athletes usually cannot perform at such a level for very long, which is why a good accountant and investment counselor comes in handy. Secondly, for every top athlete who earns millions of dollars in a year, there are hundreds of professional athletes who earn less than $40,000. The stakes are incredibly high, the competition fierce.

Perhaps the only caveat to the financial success of an elite athlete is the individual's character or personality. An athlete with a bad temper or prone to unsportsmanlike behavior may still be able to set records or win games, but he or she won't necessarily be able to cash in on the commercial endorsements. Advertisers are notoriously fickle about the spokespeople they choose to endorse products; some athletes have lost million-dollar accounts because of their bad behavior on and off the field of play.

Other options exist, thankfully, for professional athletes. Many go into some area of coaching, sports administration, management, or broadcasting. The professional athlete's unique insight and perspective can be a real asset in careers in these areas. Other athletes have been simultaneously pursuing other interests, some completely unrelated to their sport, such as education, business, social welfare, or the arts. Many continue to stay involved with the sport they have loved since childhood, coaching young children or volunteering with local school teams.

■ Work Environment

Athletes compete in many different conditions, according to the setting of the sport (indoors or outdoors) and the rules of the organizing or governing bodies. Track-and-field athletes often compete in hot or rainy conditions, but at any point, organizing officials can call off the meet, or postpone competition until better weather. Indoor events are less subject to cancellation. However, since it is in the best interests of an organization not to risk the athletes' health, any condition which might adversely affect the outcome of a competition is usually reason enough to cancel or postpone it. An athlete, on the other hand, may withdraw from competition if he or she is injured or ill. Nerves and fear are not good reasons to default on a competition and part of ascending into the ranks of professional athletes means learning to cope with the anxiety that competition brings. Some athletes actually thrive on the nervous tension.

In order to reach the elite level of any sport, athletes must begin their careers early. Most professional athletes have been working at their sports since they were small children; skiers, figure skaters, and gymnasts, for example, begin skiing, skating, and tumbling as young as age two or three. Athletes have to fit hours of practice time into an already full day, usually several hours before school, and several hours after school. To make the situation more difficult, competitions and facilities for practice are often far from the young athlete's home, which means they either commute to and from practice and competitions with a parent, or they live with a coach or trainer for most of the year. Separation from a child's parents and family is an especially hard and frustrating element of the training program. When a child has demonstrated uncommon excellence in a sport, the family often decides to move to the city in which the sports facility is located, so that the child doesn't have to travel or be separated from a normal family environment.

The expenses of a sport can be overwhelming, as can the time an athlete must devote to practice and travel to and from competitions. In addition to specialized equipment and clothing, the athlete must pay for a coach, travel expenses, competition fees and, depending on the sport, time at the facility or gym where he or she practices. Tennis, golf, figure skating, and skiing are among the most expensive sports to enter.

Even with the years of hard work, practice, and financial sacrifice that most athletes and their families must endure, there is no guarantee that an athlete will achieve the rarest of the rare in the sports world—financial reward. An athlete needs to truly love the sport at which he or she excels, and also have a nearly insatiable ambition and work ethic.

■ Outlook

Again, the outlook will vary depending on the sport, its popularity, and the number of professional athletes currently competing. On the whole, the outlook for the field of professional sports is healthy, but the number of jobs will not increase dramatically. Some sports, however, may experience a rise in popularity, which will translate into greater opportunities for higher salaries, prize monies, and commercial endorsements.

■ For More Information

Individuals interested in becoming professional athletes should contact the professional organizations for the sport in which they would like to compete, such as the National Tennis Association, the Professional Golf Association, or the National Bowling Association. Ask for information on requirements, training centers, coaches, et cetera. The following organization may also be able to provide further information:

American Alliance for Health, Physical Education, Recreation, and Dance
1900 Association Drive
Reston, VA 20191
Tel: 703-476-3400
Web: http://www.aahperd.org/

For a free brochure and information on the Junior Olympics and more, contact:

Amateur Athletic Union
c/o The Walt Disney World Resort
PO Box 10000
Lake Buena Vista, FL 32830-1000
Tel: 407-828-4394
Web: http://www.aausports.org/

■ Related Articles

Recreation

Sports

Jockeys

Professional Athletes—Team Sports

Professional Athletes—Team Sports

■ Overview

Professional athletic teams compete against one another to win titles, championships, and series; team members are paid salaries and bonuses for their work. Team sports include football, basketball, hockey, baseball, and soccer.

■ History

The origin of the first recreational activity—or sport—is not known. It can be assumed, however, that the notion of sport was born the first time anyone attempted to fish, hunt, or wrestle, simply for the pleasure of it or to compete against another person, rather than for self-preservation.

The Olympic Games are generally credited as being the first instance of organized sports. Historians believe that they actually began as early as two centuries before the first written mention of them in 776 BC. In AD 394 the Olympic Games were abolished and weren't revived until 1896.

In the interim, popular support for organized sports developed slowly. Tennis rose to popularity in France in the 1400s; historical records indicate that a track-and-field

PROFESSIONAL ATHLETES—TEAM SPORTS	
SCHOOL SUBJECTS	**Health** **Physical education**
PERSONAL SKILLS	**Following instructions**
WORK ENVIRONMENT	**Indoors and outdoors** **Primarily multiple locations**
MINIMUM EDUCATION LEVEL	**High school diploma**
SALARY RANGE	**$20,000 to $100,000 to $1,000,000+**
CERTIFICATION OR LICENSING	**None available**
OUTLOOK	**About as fast as the average**
DOT	**153**
GOE	**12.01.03**
NOC	**5251**

competition was held in England in 1510; Mary, Queen of Scots loved to play golf and popularized the sport during her reign from 1542 to 1567; Her son, James I of England, lifted a ban on football (soccer); and the first sweepstakes in horse racing was introduced in England in 1714.

The difference in the nature of sports before and after the 19th century largely has to do with organization. Prior to the 19th century, most sports were not officially organized; there were no official rules, competitions, or standards of play. During the 19th century, however, many sports underwent a transition from invented pastime to official sport. Rules governing play, the field of play, and competitions were agreed upon. The first modern track-and-field meet, for example, was held in England in 1825.

Baseball, basketball, golf, tennis, and then boxing began to attract large crowds of people in the early 20th century. As these sports and others grew in popularity, governing bodies and organizations were created to oversee the fair play of each sport. Gradually, coverage of sporting events on radio and in newspapers began to grow until sports quite literally became the national pastime for Americans. Sports stars became as renowned as movie stars or politicians, sometimes even more so.

Today, the number of professional team sports is growing, but the numbers still favor male athletes. Only a few professional teams exist for female athletes, none of which are currently promoted or supported by the media and public to the degree that are male teams. The performance of women athletes in the 1996 Olympic Games held in Atlanta, Georgia, such as the women's softball team, and the creation of a women's professional basketball league, the Women's National Basketball Association (WNBA) in the late-1990s, may indicate the tide is turning.

■ The Job

Unlike amateur athletes who play or compete in amateur circles for titles or trophies only, *professional athletic teams* compete against one another to win titles, championships, and series; team members are paid salaries and bonuses for their work.

The athletic performances of individual teams are evaluated according to the nature and rules of each specific sport: usually the winning team compiles the highest score, as in football, basketball, and soccer. Competitions are organized by local, regional, national, and international organizations and associations whose primary functions are to promote the sport and sponsor competitive events. Within a professional sport there are usually different levels of competition based on age, ability, and gender. There are often different designations and divisions within one sport. Professional baseball, for example, is made up of the two major leagues (American and National) each made up of three divisions, East, Central, and West; and the minor leagues (single-A, double-A, triple-A). All of these teams are considered professional because the players are compensated for their work, but the financial rewards are the greatest in the major leagues.

Whatever the team sport, most team members specialize in a specific area of the game. In gymnastics, for example, the entire six-member team trains on all of the gymnastic apparatuses—balance beam, uneven bars, vault, and floor exercise—but usually each of the six gymnasts excels in only one or two areas. Those gymnasts who do excel in all four events are likely to do well in the individual, all-around title which is a part of the team competition. Team members in football, basketball, baseball, soccer, and hockey all assume different positions, some of which change depending on whether or not the team is trying to score a goal (offensive positions) or prevent the opposition from scoring one (defensive positions). During team practices, athletes focus on their specific role in a game, whether that is defensive, offensive, or both. For example, a pitcher will spend some time running bases and throwing to other positions, but the majority of his or her time will most likely be spent practicing pitches.

Professional teams train for most of the year, but unlike athletes in individual sports, the athletes who are members of a team usually have more of an off-season. The training programs of professional athletes differs according to the season. Following an off-season, most team sports have a training season, in which they begin to focus their workouts after a period of relative inactivity to develop or maintain strength, cardiovascular ability, flexibility, endurance, speed, and quickness, as well as to focus on technique and control. During the season, the team coach, physician, trainers, and physical therapists will organize specific routines, programs, or exercises to target game skills as well as individual athletic weaknesses, whether skill-related or from injury.

These workouts also vary according to the difficulty of the game schedule. During a playoff or championship series, the coach and athletic staff realize that a rigorous workout in between games might tax the athletes' strength, stamina, or even mental preparedness, jeopardizing the outcome of the next game. Instead, the coach might prescribe a mild workout followed by intensive stretching. In addition to stretching and exercising the specific muscles used in any given sport, athletes concentrate on developing excellent eating and sleeping habits that will help them remain in top condition throughout the year. Abstaining from drinking alcoholic beverages during a season is a practice to which many professional athletes adhere.

The coaching or training staff often films the games and practices so that the team can benefit from watching their individual exploits, as well as their combined play. By watching their performances, team members can learn how

Sammy Sosa hits another home run.

to improve their techniques and strategies. It is common for professional teams to also study other teams' moves and strategies in order to determine a method of coping with the other teams' plays during a game.

■ Requirements

High School
Most professional athletes demonstrate tremendous skill and interest in their sport well before high school. High school offers student athletes the opportunity to gain experience in the field in a structured and competitive environment. Under the guidance of a coach, high school students can begin developing suitable training programs for themselves and learn about health, nutrition, and conditioning issues.

High school also offers the opportunity to experiment with a variety of sports and a variety of positions within a sport. Most junior varsity and some varsity high school teams allow players to try out different positions and begin to discover whether they have more of an aptitude for the defensive dives of a goalie or for the forwards' front-line action. High school coaches are there to help you learn to expand upon your strengths and abilities and develop yourself more fully as an athlete. High school is also an excellent time to begin developing the concentration powers, leadership skills, and good sportsmanship necessary for success in the field.

People who hope to become professional athletes should take a full load of high school courses including four years of English, math, and science as well as health and physical education. A solid high school education will help ensure success in college (often the next step in becoming a professional athlete) and may help you in earning a college athletic scholarship. A high school diploma will certainly give you something to fall back on if an injury, a change in career goals, or other circumstance prevents you from earning a living as an athlete.

Postsecondary Training

College is important for future professional athletes for several reasons. It provides the opportunity to gain skill and strength in your sport before you try to succeed in the pros, and it also offers you the chance of being observed by professional scouts.

Perhaps most importantly, however, a college education arms you with a valuable degree that you can use if you do not earn a living as a professional athlete or after your performance career ends. College athletes major in everything from communications to pre-med and enjoy careers as coaches, broadcasters, teachers, doctors, actors, and business people to name a few. As with high school sports, college athletes must maintain certain academic standards in order to be permitted to compete in intercollegiate play.

Other Requirements

If you want to be a professional athlete you must be fully committed to succeeding. You must work almost nonstop to improve your conditioning and skills and not give up when you don't succeed as quickly or as easily as you had hoped. And even then, because the competition is so fierce, the goal of earning a living as a professional athlete is still difficult to reach. For this reason, professional athletes must not get discouraged easily. They must have the self-confidence and ambition to keep working and keep trying. Professional athletes must also have a love for their sport that compels them to want to reach their fullest potential.

■ Exploring

Students interested in pursuing a career in professional sports should start playing that sport as much and as early as possible. Most junior high and high schools have well-established programs in the sports that have professional teams.

If a team sport does not exist in your school, that doesn't mean your chances at playing it have evaporated. Petition your school board to establish it as a school sport and set aside funds for it. In the meantime, organize other students into a club team, scheduling practices and unofficial games. If the sport is a recognized team sport in the United States or Canada, contact the professional organization for the sport for additional information; if anyone would have helpful tips for gaining recognition, the professional organization would. Also, try calling the local or state athletic board to see what other schools in your area recognize it as a team sport; make a list of those teams and try scheduling exhibition games with them. Your goal is to show that other students have a definite interest in the game and that other schools recognize it.

To determine if you really want to commit to pursuing a professional career in your team sport, talk to coaches, trainers, and any athletes who are currently pursuing a professional career. You can also contact professional organizations and associations for information on how to best prepare for a career in their sport. Sometimes there are specialized training programs available, and the best way to find out is to get in contact with the people whose job it is to promote the sport.

■ Employers

Professional athletes are employed by private and public ownership groups throughout the United States and Canada. At the highest male professional level, there are 31 National Football League franchises, 30 Major League Baseball franchises; 29 National Basketball Association franchises, 27 National Hockey League franchises, and 12 Major League Soccer franchises. The Women's National Basketball Association has 12 franchises.

■ Starting Out

Most team sports have some official manner of establishing which teams acquire which players; often, this is referred to as a *draft*, although sometimes members of a professional team are chosen through a competition. Usually, the draft occurs between the college and professional levels of the sport. The National Basketball Association (NBA), for example, has its NBA College Draft. During the draft, the owners and managers of professional basketball teams choose players in an order based on the team's performance in the previous season. This means that the team with the worst record in the previous season has a greater chance of getting to choose first from the list of available players.

Furthermore, professional athletes must meet the requirements established by the organizing bodies of their respective sport. Sometimes this means meeting a physical requirement, such as age, height, and weight; and sometimes this means fulfilling a number of required stunts, or participating in a certain number of competitions. Professional organizations usually arrange it so that athletes can build up their skills and level of play by participating in lower-level competitions. College sports, as mentioned before, are an excellent way to improve one's skills while pursuing an education.

■ Advancement

Professional athletes in team sports advance in three ways—when their team advances, when they are traded to better teams, and when they negotiate better contracts. In all three instances, this is achieved by the individual team member who works and practices hard, and who gives his or her best performance in game after game. Winning teams also receive a deluge of media attention that often creates celebrities out of individual players which in turn provides these top players with opportunities for financially rewarding commercial endorsements.

Professional athletes are usually represented by *sports agents* in the behind-the-scenes deals that determine for which teams they will be playing and what they will be paid. These agents may also be involved with other key decisions involving commercial endorsements, personal income taxes, and financial investments of the athlete's revenues.

In the moves from high school athletics to collegiate athletics and from collegiate athletics to the pros, coaches and scouts are continually scouring the ranks of high school and college teams for new talent; they're most interested in the athletes who consistently deliver points or prevent the opposition from scoring. There is simply no substitute for success.

A college education, however, can prepare all athletes for the day when their bodies can no longer compete at the top level, whether because of age or an unforeseen injury. Every athlete should be prepared to move into another career, related to the world of sports or not.

Professional athletes do have other options, especially those who have graduated from a four-year college or university. Many go into some area of coaching, sports administration, management, or broadcasting. The professional athlete's unique insight and perspective can be a real asset in careers in these areas. Other athletes have been simultaneously pursuing other interests, some completely unrelated to their sport, such as education, business, social welfare, or the arts. Many continue to stay involved with the sport they have loved since childhood, coaching young children or volunteering with local school teams.

■ Earnings

Today, professional athletes who are members of top-level teams earn hundreds of thousands of dollars in prize money at professional competitions; the top players or athletes in each sport earn as much or more in endorsements and advertising, usually for sports-related products and services, but increasingly for products or services completely unrelated to their sport. Michael Jordan, for example, earned an incredible $78 million in 1997, counting salary and endorsement revenue. Such salaries and other incomes are not representative of the whole field of professional athletes, but are only indicative of the fantastic revenues a few rare athletes with extraordinary talent can hope to earn. Others earn as little as $20,000.

Perhaps the only caveat to the financial success of an elite athlete is the individual's character or personality. An athlete with a bad temper or prone to unsportsmanlike behavior may still be able to participate in team play, helping to win games and garner trophies, but he or she won't necessarily be able to cash in on the commercial endorsements. Advertisers are notoriously fickle about the spokespeople they choose to endorse products; some athletes have lost million-dollar accounts because of their bad behavior on and off the court.

■ Work Environment

Athletes compete in many different conditions, according to the setting of the sport (indoors or outdoors) and the rules of the organizing or governing bodies. Athletes who participate in football or soccer, for example, often compete in hot, rainy, or freezing conditions, but at any point, organizing officials can call off the match, or postpone competition until better weather.

Indoor events are less subject to cancellation. However, since it is in the best interests of an organization not to risk the athletes' health, any condition which might adversely affect the outcome of a competition is usually reason to cancel or postpone it. The coach or team physician, on the other hand, may withdraw an athlete from a game if he or she is injured or ill. Nerves and fear are not good reasons to default on a competition, and part of ascending into the ranks of professional athletes means learning to cope with the anxiety that comes with competition. Some athletes, however, actually thrive on the nervous tension.

In order to reach the elite level of any sport, athletes must begin their careers early. Most professional athletes have been honing their skills since they were quite young. Athletes fit hours of practice time into an already full day; many famous players practiced on their own in the hours before school, as well as for several hours after school during team practice. Competitions are often far from the young athlete's home, which means they must travel on a bus or in a van with the team and coaching staff. Sometimes young athletes are placed in special training programs far from their homes and parents. They live with other athletes training for the same sport or on the same team and only see their parents for holidays and vacations. The separation from a child's parents and family can be difficult; often an athlete's family decides to move to be closer to the child's training facility.

The expenses of a sport can be overwhelming, as is the time an athlete must devote to practice and travel to and from competitions. Although most high school athletic programs pay for many expenses, if the athlete wants additional training or private coaching, the child's parents must come up with the extra money. Sometimes, young athletes can get official sponsors or they might qualify for an athletic scholarship from the training program. In addition to specialized equipment and clothing, the athlete must sometimes pay for a coach, travel expenses, competition fees and, depending on the sport, time at the facility or gym where he or she practices. Gymnasts, for example, train for years as individuals, and then compete for positions on national or international teams. Up until the time they are accepted (and usually during their participation in the team), these gymnasts must pay for their expenses—from coach to travel to uniforms to room and board away from home.

Even with the years of hard work, practice, and financial sacrifice that most athletes and their families must endure, there is no guarantee that an athlete will achieve the rarest of the rare in the sports world—financial reward. An athlete needs to truly love the sport at which he or she excels, and also have a nearly insatiable ambition and work ethic.

■ Outlook

Again, the outlook will vary depending on the sport, its popularity, and the number of positions open with professional teams. On the whole, the outlook for the field of professional sports is healthy, but the number of jobs will not increase dramatically. Some sports, however, may experience a rise in popularity, which will translate into greater opportunities for higher salaries, prize monies, and commercial endorsements.

■ For More Information

Individuals interested in pursuing a career in a professional team sport should speak to their coach and contact the professional organization for that sport to receive further information. For other ideas on how to pursue a career in a professional team sport, contact:

American Alliance for Health, Physical Education, Recreation, and Dance
1900 Association Drive
Reston, VA 20191
Tel: 703-476-3400
Web: http://www.aahperd.org/

■ Related Articles

Recreation
Sports
Jockeys
Professional Athletes—Individual Sports
Sports Executives
Sports Instructors and Coaches
Sports Scouts

Professors

■ See College Professors

Programmers

■ See Computer Programmers, Data Processing Technicians

Proofreaders

■ See Book Editors, Editors, Magazine Editors, Newspaper Editors

Prop Designers

■ See Cartoonists and Animators

Property and Casualty Insurance Agents and Brokers

■ Overview

Property and casualty insurance agents and brokers sell policies that help individuals and companies cover expenses and losses from such disasters as fires, burglaries, traffic accidents, and other emergencies. These salespeople also may be known as *fire, casualty, and marine insurance agents or brokers*. There are over 400,000 insurance agents and brokers employed in the United States.

■ History

The development of the property and casualty insurance industry parallels the history of human economic development. This type of insurance was first established in the maritime field. A single shipwreck could put a ship owner out of business, so it became essential for trade financiers to share this risk. Organized maritime insurance began in the late 17th century at Lloyd's coffeehouse in London, where descriptions of individual ships, their cargoes, and their destinations were posted. Persons willing to share the possible loss, in return for a fee, signed their names below these descriptions indicating what percentage of the financial responsibility they were willing to assume. Those who signed were known as "underwriters," a term still used in the insurance business.

As people became more experienced in this procedure, predictions of loss became more accurate and rates were standardized. To provide protection for larger risks, individuals organized companies. The first marine insurance company in the United States—the Insurance Company of North America—was founded in Philadelphia in 1792, and still does business today.

Other types of insurance developed in response to people's need for protection. Insurance against loss by fire became available after the disastrous lesson of the London Fire of 1666. The first accident insurance policy in the United States was sold in 1863. Burglary insurance—protection against property taken by forced entry—was offered soon thereafter. Theft insurance, which covers any form of stealing, was first written in 1899.

Around the turn of the century, the development of the "horseless carriage" led to the automobile insurance industry. The first automobile policy was sold in 1898. This area of the insurance field grew rapidly. In the mid-1990s premiums written for automobile insurance (including liability and collision and comprehensive policies) totaled more than $102 billion.

Growth of business and industrial organizations required companies to offer protection for employees injured on the job. The first workers' compensation insurance was sold in 1910.

Insurance companies have always been alert to new marketing possibilities. In the past few decades, increasing emphasis has been placed upon "package" policies offering comprehensive coverage. A typical package policy is the homeowner's policy which, in addition to fire protection for the insured's home and property, also covers losses for liability, medical payments, and additional living expenses. In the mid-1950s, a group of private firms provided the first insurance on the multimillion-dollar reactors used in atomic energy plants.

Over the course of the past decade, costs associated with the property and casualty insurance industry (including underwriting losses) have outstripped the annual rate of inflation. This has generally led to an increase in the premium rates charged to customers. The largest increases have occurred in the automobile insurance sector of the industry. The overall trend reflects some basic changes in American society, including a substantial rise in crime and litigation and the development of expensive new medical technologies. The main challenge of the property and casualty insurance industry in the coming years is to stabilize premium rates to remain competitive with alternative forms of risk financing.

■ The Job

Property and casualty insurance salespeople work under one of two types of relationships with insurers and clients. An agent serves as an authorized representative of the insurance company or companies with which the agent has a contract. A broker, on the other hand, serves as the representative for the client and has no contracts with insurance companies.

Agents can be *independent agents*, *exclusive agents*, or *direct writers*. Independent agents may represent one or more insurance companies, are paid by commission, are responsible for their own expenses, and own the rights to the policies they sell. Exclusive agents represent only one insurance company, are generally paid by commission, are generally responsible for all of their own expenses, and usually own the rights to the policies that they sell. Direct writers represent only one insurance company, are employees of that company (and therefore are often paid a salary and are not responsible for their own expenses), and do not own the rights to the policies that are owned by the company.

Regardless of the system that is used, salespeople operate in a similar fashion. Each one orders or issues policies, collects premiums, renews and changes existing coverage, and assists clients with reports of losses and claims settlement. Backed by the resources of the companies that they represent, individual agents may issue policies insuring against loss or damage for everything from furs and automobiles to ocean liners and factories.

Agents are authorized to issue a "binder" to provide temporary protection for customers between the time they

PROPERTY AND CASUALTY INSURANCE AGENTS AND BROKERS	
SCHOOL SUBJECTS	Business Speech
PERSONAL SKILLS	Leadership/management
WORK ENVIRONMENT	Primarily indoors Primarily one location
MINIMUM EDUCATION LEVEL	High school diploma
SALARY RANGE	$21,100 to $31,500 to $76,900+
CERTIFICATION OR LICENSING	Required by all states
OUTLOOK	About as fast as the average
DOT	250
GOE	08.01.02
NOC	6231
O*NET	43002

sign the policy application and the policy is issued by the insurance company. Naturally, the agent must be selective in the risks accepted under a binder. Sometimes a risk will be refused by a company, which might cause the agent to lose goodwill with the customer. Since brokers do not directly represent or have contracts with insurance companies, they can not issue binders.

Some agents or brokers specialize in one type of insurance such as automobile insurance. All agents or brokers, however, must have a knowledge of the kind of protection required by their clients and the exact coverage offered by each company that they represent.

One of the most significant aspects of the property and casualty agent's work is the variety encountered on the job. An agent's day may begin with an important conference with a group of executives seeking protection for a new industrial plant and its related business activities. Following this meeting, the agent may proceed to the office and spend several hours studying the needs of the customer and drafting an insurance plan. This proposal must be thorough and competitively priced because several other local agents will likely be competing for the account. While working at the office, the agent usually receives several calls and visits from prospective or current clients asking questions about protection, policy conditions, changes, or new developments.

At noon, the agent may attend a meeting of a service club or have lunch with a policyholder. After lunch, the agent may visit a garage with a customer to discuss the car repairs needed as the result of a client's automobile accident. Back at the office, the agent may talk on the telephone with an adjuster from the insurance company involved.

In the late afternoon, the agent may call on the superintendent of schools to discuss insurance protection for participants and spectators at athletic events and other public meetings. If the school has no protection, the agent may evaluate its insurance needs and draft a proposed policy.

Upon returning to the office, the agent may telephone several customers, dictate responses to the day's mail, and handle other matters that have developed during the day. In the evening, the agent may call on a family to discuss insurance protection for a new home.

■ Requirements

High School

Most insurance companies insist that their agents have at least a high school education, although many strongly prefer college training. High school courses that will be useful for work in this field include English, computer science, economics, finance, business law, sociology, and psychology.

Postsecondary Training

Although college training is not a prerequisite, an increasing number of agents and brokers hold a college degree. Many have taken insurance courses, which are offered in hundreds of colleges and universities in the United States as well as by many professional insurance associations. Others find a general background in business administration, accounting, economics, or business law helpful. For some specialized areas of property insurance, such as fire protection for commercial establishments, an engineering background may prove helpful.

Certification or Licensing

All agents and brokers must obtain licenses from the states in which they sell insurance. Most states require that the agent pass a written examination dealing with state insurance laws and the fundamentals of property and casualty insurance. Often, candidates for licenses must show evidence of some formal study in the field of insurance.

Those agents who wish to seek the highest professional status may pursue the designation of Chartered Property Casualty Underwriter (CPCU). The CPCU requires the agent to complete at least 3 years in the field successfully, demonstrate high ethical practices in all work, and pass a series of 10 examinations offered by the American Institute for Chartered Property and Casualty Underwriters. Agents and brokers may prepare for these examinations through home study or by taking courses offered by colleges, insurance associations, or individual companies. As an intermediate step, many agents complete a study and examination program conducted by the Insurance Institute of America. One such program is the Accredited Adviser in Insurance (AAI). To earn the AAI designation an agent must pass 3 national exams. Although independent study for the AAI is possible, most agents complete a series of 3 courses given at a state independent agents' association prior to taking the exams.

Other Requirements

An agent or broker must thoroughly understand insurance fundamentals and recognize the differences between the many options provided by various policies. This knowledge is essential for the salesperson to gain the respect and confidence of clients. To provide greater service to customers and increase sales volume, beginning agents must study many areas of insurance protection. This requires an analytical mind, the ability to teach oneself how to use standard manuals and computer information systems, as well as the capacity for hard work.

Agents or brokers must be able to interact with strangers easily and talk readily with a wide range of people. They may need to talk with teenagers about their first cars, business executives faced with heavy responsibilities, or widows confronted for the first time with financial management of a home. Agents must be resourceful, self-confident, conscientious, and cheerful. As in other types of sales occupations, a strong belief in the service being sold helps agents to be more successful in their presentations.

Because they spend so much of their time with others, agents must have a genuine liking for people. Equally important is the desire to serve others by providing financial security. To be successful, agents must be able to present insurance information in a clear, nontechnical fashion. They must be able to develop a logical sales sequence and presentation style that is comfortable for prospects and clients.

Successful agents usually participate in a number of social activities, such as church groups, community organizations, and service organizations. They must stay visible within their communities to keep their volume of business up. It is essential that people respond positively to them. They often have an unusual facility for recalling people's names and past conversations they've had with them.

Because they work in small organizations, agents must possess both personal sales and management abilities. Many insurance offices consist of the agent and a single secretary. The freedom enjoyed by the agent necessitates discipline and careful self-planning.

■ Exploring

Because of state licensing requirements, it is sometimes difficult for young people to obtain part-time experience in this field. Summer employment of any sort in a property and casualty insurance office may provide helpful insights into the field. Since many offices are small and must have someone on premises during business hours, you may find summer positions with individual agencies or brokerage firms. Colleges with work-study programs may offer opportunities for practical experience in an insurance agency.

■ Employers

Insurance companies are the principal employers of property and casualty insurance agents and brokers. Other agents and brokers—approximately 30 percent—are self-employed.

■ Starting Out

College graduates are frequently hired through campus interviews for salaried sales positions with major companies. Other graduates secure positions directly with local agencies or brokerages through placement services, employment offices, or classified advertisements in newspapers. Many high school and college graduates apply directly to insurance companies. Sometimes persons employed in other fields take evening or home-study courses in insurance to prepare for employment in this field.

Once hired, the new agent or salesperson uses training materials prepared by the company or by industry trade groups. In smaller agencies, newcomers may be expected to assume most of the responsibility for their own training by using the agency's written resources and working directly with experienced agents. In larger organizations, initial training may include formal classroom instruction and enrollment in education programs such as those offered by the Insurance Institute of America. Sometimes insurance societies sponsor courses designed to help the beginning agent. Almost all agents receive directed, on-the-job sales supervision.

■ Advancement

Sales agents may advance in one of several ways. They may decide to establish their own agency or brokerage firm, join or buy out an established agency, or advance into branch or home office management with an insurance company.

Self-employed agents or brokers often remain with the organization that they have developed for the length of their careers. They may grow professionally by expanding the scope of their insurance activities. Many agents expand their responsibilities and their office's sales volume by hiring additional salespeople. Occasionally an established agent may enter related areas of activity. Many property insurance agents, for example, branch out into real estate sales. Many agents and brokers devote an increasing amount of their time to worthwhile community projects, which helps to build goodwill and probable future clients.

■ Earnings

Recently hired sales agents are usually paid a moderate salary while learning the business. After becoming established, however, most agents are paid on the basis of a commission on sales. Agents who work directly for an insurance company often receive a base salary in addition to some commission on sales production. Salespeople employed by companies often receive fringe benefits (such as retirement income, sick leave, and paid vacations), whereas self-employed agents or brokers receive no such benefits.

According to the U.S. Department of Labor, the median annual salary for all types of insurance agents and brokers was $31,500 in 1996. Agents and brokers with little experience or small client-base earned as little as $21,100 per year, while the most experienced agents and brokers with a large clientele earned over $76,900 annually.

Unlike life insurance agents, who receive a high first-year commission, the property and casualty agent usually receives the same percentage each time the premium is paid.

■ Work Environment

Property and casualty insurance agents must be in constant contact with people—clients, prospective clients, and the workers in the home office of the insurance companies. This can be very time-consuming, and occasionally frustrating, but it is an essential element of the work.

Two of the biggest drawbacks to this type of work are the long hours and irregular schedule. Agents often are required to work their schedules around their clients' availability. Especially in their first years in the business, agents may find that they have to work three or four nights a week and one or two days on the weekend.

■ Outlook

Approximately 409,000 people work as insurance agents and brokers in the United States. About 12 percent of these work primarily in the property and casualty insurance field.

The overall demand for insurance should increase as the general population grows and the amount of personal and corporate possessions rises. Most homeowners and business executives budget insurance as a necessary expense. Their dependence on insurance coverage is reflected in the fact that insurance premium rates have gone up about 100 percent in the past 10 years.

Laws that require businesses to provide workers' compensation insurance and car owners to obtain automobile liability protection help to maintain an insurance market.

Despite increasing sales, however, the U.S. Department of Labor predicts that the employment of insurance agents will probably grow only as fast as the average for all occupations through the year 2006. Computers enable agents to perform routine clerical tasks more efficiently, and more policies are being sold by mail and phone. Also, as insurance becomes more and more crucial to their financial health, many large businesses are hiring their own risk managers, who analyze their insurance needs and select the policies that are best for them.

There is a high turnover in this field. Many beginning agents and brokers find it hard to establish a large, profitable client-base, and eventually move on to other areas in the insurance industry. Most openings will occur as a result of this turnover and as workers retire or leave their positions for other reasons.

■ For More Information

For information regarding the CPCU designation, contact:

American Institute for Chartered Property and Casualty Underwriters
720 Providence Road
PO Box 3016
Malvern, PA 19355-0716
Tel: 610-644-2101

For general information on the insurance industry, contact the following organizations:

Association of Professional Insurance Women
285 Hunting Ridge Road
Stamford, CT 06903
Tel: 203-329-0854
Web: http://www.apiw.org

Independent Insurance Agents of America
127 South Peyton Street
Alexandria, VA 22314
Tel: 800-221-7917
Email: info@iiaa.org
Web: http://www.independentagent.com/

For information on the AAI designation and other educational programs, contact:

Insurance Institute of America
720 Providence Road
PO Box 3016
Malvern, PA 19355-0716
Tel: 610-644-2101

■ Related Articles

Insurance
Insurance Claims Representatives
Insurance Policy Processing Occupations
Insurance Underwriters
Life Insurance Agents and Brokers
Risk Managers

Property and Real Estate Managers

■ Overview

Property and real estate managers plan and supervise the activities that affect land and buildings. Most of them manage rental properties, such as apartment buildings, office buildings, and shopping centers. Others manage the services and commonly owned areas of condominiums and community associations.

■ History

The first property managers, in the early 1900s, were real estate agents who earned additional income by collecting rent and negotiating leases. During the 1920s, the job became a menial position that was necessary in a real estate brokerage firm but was not considered a full-fledged part of the business. After the collapse of the financial market in 1929, banks, insurance companies, and other mortgage holders found themselves owners of multiple properties because of foreclosures. These new owners had neither the skills nor the inclination to manage the properties. Suddenly, the position of "rent man," which had been despised in the 1920s, became more respected and more in demand.

The new importance of the property manager, plus a corresponding increase in industry abuses, led to the formation of a professional association for property managers, the Institute of Real Estate Management. The new members quickly set out to establish industry ethics and standards, professional designations, and industry education and seminars.

■ The Job

Most property and real estate managers are responsible for day-to-day management of residential and commercial real estate and usually manage several properties at one time. Acting as the owners' agents and advisers, they supervise the marketing of space, negotiate lease agreements, direct bookkeeping activities, and report to owners on the status of the property. They also negotiate contracts for trash removal and other services and hire the maintenance and on-site management personnel employed at the properties.

Some managers buy and develop real estate for companies that have widespread retail operations, such as franchise restaurants and hotel chains, or for companies that build such projects as shopping malls and industrial parks.

On-site managers are based at the properties they manage and may even live on the property. Most of them are responsible for apartment buildings and work under the direction of property managers. They train, supervise, and assign duties to maintenance staffs; inspect the properties to determine what maintenance and repairs are needed; schedule routine service of heating and air-conditioning systems; keep records of operating costs; and submit cost reports to the property managers or owners. They deal with residents on a daily basis and are responsible for handling their requests for service and repairs, resolving complaints concerning other tenants, and enforcing rules and lease restrictions.

Apartment house managers work for property owners or property management firms and are usually on-site managers. They show apartments to prospective tenants, negotiate leases, collect rents, handle tenants' requests, and direct the activities of maintenance staffs and outside *contractors*.

Building superintendents are responsible for operating and maintaining the facilities and equipment of such properties as apartment houses and office buildings. At small properties, the superintendent may be the only on-site manager and report directly to property managers; at larger properties, superintendents may report to on-site managers and supervise maintenance staffs.

Housing project managers direct the operation of housing projects provided for such groups as military families,

low-income families, and welfare recipients. The housing is usually subsidized by the government and may consist of single-family homes, multiunit dwellings, or house trailers.

Condominium managers are responsible to unit-owner associations and manage the services and commonly owned areas of condominium properties. They submit reports to the association members, supervise collection of owner assessments, resolve owners' complaints, and direct the activities of maintenance staffs and outside contractors. In some communities, such as planned unit developments (PUDs), homeowners belong to associations that employ managers to oversee the homeowners' jointly used properties and facilities.

Real estate asset managers work for institutional owners such as banks and insurance companies. Their responsibilities are larger in scope. Rather than manage day-to-day property operations, asset managers usually have an advisory role regarding the acquisition, rehabilitation, refinancing, and disposition of properties in a particular portfolio, and they may act "as the owner" in making specific business decisions, such as selecting and supervising site managers, authorizing operating expenditures, review-

PROPERTY AND REAL ESTATE MANAGERS	
SCHOOL SUBJECTS	**Business** **English** **Mathematics**
PERSONAL SKILLS	**Communication/ideas** **Leadership/management**
WORK ENVIRONMENT	**Primarily indoors** **Primarily multiple locations**
MINIMUM EDUCATION LEVEL	**Bachelor's degree**
SALARY RANGE	**$12,000 to $28,500 to $60,700**
CERTIFICATION OR LICENSING	**Required for certain positions**
OUTLOOK	**About as fast as the average**
DOT	**186**
GOE	**11.05.01**
NOC	**0121**
O*NET	**15011B**

ing and approving leases, and monitoring local market conditions.

Specialized property and real estate managers perform a variety of other types of functions. *Market managers* direct the activities of municipal, regional, or state markets where wholesale fruit, vegetables, or meat are sold. They rent space to buyers and sellers and direct the supervisors who are responsible for collecting fees, maintaining and cleaning the buildings and grounds, and enforcing sanitation and security rules. *Public events facilities rental managers* negotiate contracts with organizations that wish to lease arenas, auditoriums, stadia, or other facilities that are used for public events. They solicit new business and renewals of established contracts, maintain schedules to determine the availability of the facilities for bookings, and oversee operation and maintenance activities.

Real estate firm managers direct the activities of the *sales agents* who work for real estate firms. They screen and hire sales agents and conduct training sessions. They confer with agents and clients to resolve such problems as adjusting selling prices and determining who is responsible for repairs and closing costs. *Business opportunity-and-property-investment brokers* buy and sell business enterprises and investment properties on a commission or speculative basis. They investigate such factors as the financial ratings of businesses that are for sale, the desirability of a property's location for various types of businesses, and the condition of investment properties.

Businesses employ real estate managers to find, acquire, and develop the properties they need for their operations and to dispose of properties they no longer need. Real estate agents often work for companies that operate retail merchandising chains, such as fast food restaurants, gasoline stations, and apparel shops. They locate sites that are desirable for their companies' operations and arrange to purchase or lease them. They also review their companies' holdings to identify properties that are no longer desirable and then negotiate to dispose of them. (*Real estate sales agents* also may be called real estate agents, but they are not involved in property management.) *Land development managers* are responsible for acquiring land for such projects as shopping centers and industrial parks. They negotiate with local governments, property owners, and public interest groups to eliminate obstacles to their companies' developments, and they arrange for architects to draw up plans and construction firms to build the projects.

■ Requirements

High School
High school students interested in this field should enroll in college preparatory programs.

Postsecondary Training
Most employers prefer college graduates for property and real estate management positions. They prefer degrees in real estate, business management, finance, and related fields, but they also consider liberal arts graduates. In some cases, inexperienced college graduates with bachelor's or master's degrees enter the field as assistant property managers.

Many property and real estate managers attend training programs offered by various professional and trade associations. Employers often send their managers to these programs to improve their management skills and expand their knowledge of such subjects as operation and maintenance of building mechanical systems, insurance and risk management, business and real estate law, and accounting and financial concepts. Many managers attend these programs voluntarily to prepare for advancement to positions with more responsibility.

Certification or Licensing
Certification or licensing is not required for most property managers. Managers who have appropriate experience, complete required training programs, and achieve satisfactory scores on written exams, however, can earn certification and such professional designations as *certified property manager* (CPM), *accredited residential manager* (ARM), *real property administrator* (RPA), and *certified shopping center manager* (CSM). (Note that CPM and ARM are registered trademarks of the Institute of Real Estate Management.) Such designations are usually looked upon favorably by employers as a sign of a person's competence and dedication.

The federal government requires certification for managers of public housing that is subsidized by federal funds. Business opportunity-and-property-investment brokers must hold state licenses, and some states require real estate managers to hold licenses.

Other Requirements
Property and real estate managers must be skilled in both oral and written communications and be adept at dealing with people. They need to be good administrators and negotiators, and those who specialize in land development must be especially resourceful and creative to arrange financing for their projects. Managers for small rental or condominium complexes may be required to have building repair and maintenance skills as well as business management skills.

■ Exploring

If you are interested in property and real estate management, you should seek activities that help you to develop management skills, such as serving as an officer in an organization or participating in Junior Achievement projects. You also should seek part-time or summer jobs in sales or volunteer for work that involves public contact.

You may be able to tour apartment complexes, shopping centers, and other real estate developments and should take advantage of any opportunities to talk with property and real estate managers.

■ Employers

Property and real estate managers can find employment in many different aspects of the real estate business, depending upon their qualifications and interests. Managers may oversee condominiums and apartment buildings in the employ of owners' associations or building owners, for example. Institutions such as banks employ asset managers. Many managers work for residential and commercial real estate owners, property management firms, or developers.

■ Starting Out

Students who are about to graduate from college can obtain assistance from their school placement offices in finding their first job. You can also apply directly to property management firms and check ads in the help wanted sections of local newspapers. Property and real estate managers often begin as on-site managers for small apartment house complexes, condominiums, or community associations.

■ Advancement

With experience, entry-level property and site managers may transfer to larger properties or they may become assistant property managers, working closely with property managers and acquiring experience in a variety of management tasks. Assistant managers may advance to property manager positions, in which they most likely will be responsible for several properties. As they advance in their careers, property managers may be responsible for larger or more complex operations, may specialize in managing specific types of property, or may eventually establish their own companies.

To be considered for advancement, property managers must demonstrate the ability to deal effectively with tenants, contractors, and maintenance staff. They must be capable administrators and possess business skills, initiative, good organization, and excellent communication skills. Companies may offer management service to property owners, or experienced managers may choose to invest in properties to lease or rent.

■ Earnings

Managers of residential and commercial rental real estate are usually compensated by a fee based on the gross rental income of the properties. Managers of condominiums and other homeowner-occupied properties also are usually paid on a fee basis. Site managers and others employed by a management company are typically salaried.

According to the 1998-99 *Occupational Outlook Handbook,* annual earnings for all property managers in 1996 ranged from a low of $12,000 or less to a high of more than $60,700. The median annual average for property managers in 1996 was $28,500.

Property and real estate managers usually receive such benefits as medical and health insurance. On-site apartment building managers may have rent-free apartments, and many managers have the use of company automobiles. In addition, managers involved in land development may receive a small percentage of ownership in their projects.

■ Work Environment

Property and real estate managers usually work in offices but may spend much of their time at the properties they manage. On-site apartment building managers often leave their offices to inspect other areas, check maintenance or repair work, or resolve problems reported by tenants.

Many apartment managers must live in the buildings they manage so they can be available in emergencies, and they may be required to show apartments to prospective tenants at night or on weekends. Property and real estate managers may attend evening meetings with property owners, association boards of directors, or civic groups interested in property planned for development. Real estate managers who work for large companies frequently travel to inspect their companies' property holdings or locate properties their companies might acquire.

■ Outlook

About 271,000 people in the United States were employed as property and real estate managers in 1996. Most worked for real estate operators and property management firms. Others worked for real estate developers, government agencies that manage public buildings, corporations with large property holdings used for their retail operations, real estate investors, and mining and oil companies. Many are self-employed as developers, apartment building owners, property management firm owners, or owners of full-service real estate businesses.

Employment of property and real estate managers is expected to increase as fast as the average for all occupations in the United States through 2006. Job openings are expected to occur as older, experienced managers transfer to other occupations or leave the labor force. The best opportunities will be for college graduates with degrees in real estate, business administration, and related fields.

In the next decade, many of the economy's new jobs are expected to be in wholesale and retail trade, finance, insurance, real estate, and other service industries. Growth in these industries will bring a need for more office and retail properties and for people to manage them.

In housing, there will be a greater demand for apartments because of the high cost of owning a home. New home developments also are increasingly organized with community or homeowner associations that require managers. In addition, more owners of commercial and multi-unit residential properties are expected to use professional managers to help make their properties more profitable.

■ For More Information

Apartment Owners and Managers Association of America
65 Cherry Plaza
Watertown, CT 06795
Tel: 860-274-2589

For information on education programs, contact:

Building Owners and Managers Association International
1201 New York Avenue, NW, Suite 300
Washington, DC 20005
Tel: 202-408-2662
Web: http://www.boma.org

For information on property management in Canada, contact:

Canadian Real Estate Association
344 Slater Street, Suite 1600
Canada Building
Ottawa, ON K1R 7Y3 Canada
Tel: 613-237-7111
Web: http://realtors.mls.ca/crea

The following organization represents condominium, cooperative, and homeowners' associations. For a publications catalog, contact:

Community Associations Institute
1630 Duke Street
Alexandria, VA 22314
Tel: 703-548-8600
Web: http://www.caionline.org

For information on training programs, certification, and industry research, contact:

Institute of Real Estate Management
430 North Michigan Avenue, Suite 700
Chicago, IL 60611
Tel: 312-329-6000
Web: http://www.irem.org

This organization is devoted to the multihousing industry and represents developers, owners, managers, and suppliers.

National Apartment Association
201 North Union Street, Suite 200
Alexandria, VA 22314
Tel: 703-518-6141
Web: http://www.naahq.org

■ Related Articles

Business
Insurance
Law
Real Estate
Real Estate Agents and Brokers
Real Estate Developers
Title Searchers and Examiners

Property Custodians

■ **See Stock Clerks**

Property Developers

■ **See Real Estate Developers**

Prosthodontists

■ **See Dental Care, Dentists**

Protestant Ministers

■ Overview

Protestant ministers provide for the spiritual, educational, and social needs of Protestant congregations and other people of the community. They lead services, perform religious rites, and provide moral and spiritual guidance to their members. Ministers also help the sick and needy and supervise the religious educational programs of their church. Protestant ministers also have administrative duties in their congregations and may take on further responsibilities in their denomination at the regional or national level, or in community or ecumenical groups. Some Protestant ministers may also be involved in missionary work; this may include establishing or continuing religious education in foreign or remote posts.

History

The Protestant tradition arose from discontent and disagreement with the Roman Catholic Church. The seminal figure in its history is Martin Luther, a Catholic priest who came to lead the Protestant Reformation of 1517. At that time, Luther posted 95 theses, or articles of debate, on a church door in Wittenberg, Germany. He questioned various Catholic practices and doctrines and strongly condemned abuses by the clergy. Through public appearances and especially through the new medium of print, Luther gathered support for his ideas.

As a result, growing numbers of people began to break away from the Roman Catholic Church, forming their own congregations and establishing their own doctrines and practices. Those who followed Martin Luther's interpretation of the Christian faith became known as Lutherans, but there were also many people who developed or followed other interpretations, giving rise over time to such Protestant denominations as Methodism and Presbyterianism.

Today, the six largest Protestant groups in the United States are the Assemblies of God, Baptists, Episcopalians, Lutherans, Presbyterians, and United Methodists. Many other Protestant congregations are not formally associated with any particular denomination and therefore may be called nondenominational churches. The leaders of all Protestant congregations are Protestant ministers.

The Job

Protestant ministers are the spiritual leaders of their congregations. Their primary responsibility is leading their congregations in worship and preparing for those worship services. Some Protestant denominations or congregations within a denomination have a traditional order of service. Others require that the minister adapt the service to the specific needs of the congregation. Most Protestant services include Bible readings, hymn singing, prayers, and a sermon written and delivered by the minister.

Protestant clergy also administer specific church rites, such as baptism, holy communion, and confirmation. They conduct weddings and funerals. Ministers advise couples concerning the vows and responsibilities of marriage. They may also act as marriage counselors for couples who are having marital difficulties. They visit the sick and comfort the bereaved.

Protestant ministers usually play an important part in the religious education of their congregations. They supervise Sunday School and similar Bible study programs and usually teach confirmation and adult education courses. The extent of their involvement in religious education programs and other church activities is often determined by the size of their congregations. In small churches, ministers may know most of the members personally and take an active role in everything that goes on. In larger churches, ministers may have to devote more time to administrative duties and delegate some of their other responsibilities.

Some ministers teach in seminaries and other schools. Others write for publications and give speeches within the Protestant community and to those in the community at large. A growing number of ministers are employed only part-time and may serve more than one congregation or have a secular part-time job.

Requirements

High School

In high school, prospective Protestant ministers should study history and religion, plus English and speech to improve their teaching and oration skills. Music and fine arts classes will help strengthen their understanding and appreciation of the liturgy. Knowledge of a foreign language may help ministers better serve the needs of their congregations.

Postsecondary Training

While some denominations require little more than a high school education or Bible study, the majority of Protestant groups demand a bachelor's degree plus several years of specialized theological training. Professional study in these theological schools, of which there are about 150 in the United States and Canada, generally lasts about three years and leads to the degree of Master of Divinity.

An undergraduate degree in the liberal arts is the typical college program for prospective clergy, although entrants come from a range of academic backgrounds. Course work should include English, foreign languages, philosophy, the natural sciences, psychology, history, social sciences, comparative religions as well as fine arts and music.

Seminary curriculum generally covers four

PROTESTANT MINISTERS	
SCHOOL SUBJECTS	Religion Speech
PERSONAL SKILLS	Communication/ideas Helping/teaching
WORK ENVIRONMENT	Primarily indoors Primarily one location
MINIMUM EDUCATION LEVEL	Master's degree
SALARY RANGE	$18,000 to $27,000 to $50,000
CERTIFICATION OR LICENSING	None available
OUTLOOK	Little change or more slowly than the average
DOT	120
GOE	10.01.01
NOC	4154
O*NET	27502

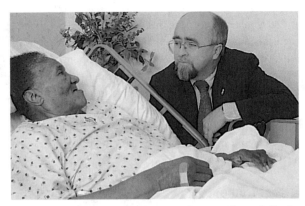

Many ministers routinely spend a portion of their time in hospitals comforting sick members of their congregation.

areas: history, theology, the Bible, and practical ministry techniques. Practical ministry techniques include counseling, preaching, church administration, and religious education. In addition to classroom study and examinations, the seminary student serves at least one year as an intern to gain practical experience in leading services and other ministerial duties.

In general, the major Protestant denominations have their own schools of theological training, but many of these schools admit students of other denominations. There are also several interdenominational colleges and theological schools that give training for the ministry. This may be augmented by training in the denomination in which the student will be ordained. Nearly 200 Protestant schools in the United States and Canada are accredited by the Association of Theological Schools. Accredited schools require a bachelor's degree, or its equivalent, for admission. After three years of study and an internship, students earn a Master of Divinity degree.

Other Requirements

Protestant ministers must meet the requirements of their individual denominations. Both men and women can become ordained ministers in most denominations today. Beyond formal ordination requirements, Protestant ministers must possess a religious vocation—a strong feeling that God is calling them to the service of others through religious ministry. For most, this means giving material success a lower priority than spiritual matters.

Ministers need to be outgoing and friendly and have a strong desire to help others. They need to be able to get along with people from a wide variety of backgrounds. They need patience, sympathy, and open-mindedness to be able to listen to the problems of others, while maintaining a discreet and sincere respect. They need leadership abilities, including self-confidence, decisiveness, and

the ability to supervise others. Ministers need to be aware that they will be relied on heavily by their congregation in times of trouble and stress, therefore making it more important they keep the needs of their own families balanced with that of their congregations.

■ Exploring

The first step in exploring this career is to speak with your own minister about it. He or she can tell you more about it, help you discern your own calling, and put you in touch with other people and resources. It also makes sense to become as involved with your church as possible: teaching Sunday School, attending weekly services and Bible study, helping at congregational events. You might also want to volunteer with the sick or the elderly, particularly in institutions affiliated with your church.

■ Employers

Protestant ministers are usually employed by the congregations they serve. Most, but not all, congregations play a decisive role in selecting someone to serve as their pastor. Other ministers may choose to work in seminaries, hospitals, or other church-run institutions. Other employment opportunities for clergy include social service work, such as counseling, youth work, family relations guidance, and teaching. Ministers may also find opportunities as chaplains in the armed forces, hospitals, mental health centers, prisons, and social agencies such as the YMCA.

■ Starting Out

Students should consult with their minister or contact the appropriate theological seminary to learn how to best meet entrance requirements. Some denominations do not require seminary training to become ordained. Smaller denominations may train part-time leaders, who eventually may seek ordination. Seminary graduates who cannot find ready employment may become directors of homes for the aged or mentally handicapped, or of orphanages. Others may find employment in the social services, as missionaries, or in church-sponsored summer camps. Some ministers may take an unpaid position with a financially disadvantaged church in order to gain valuable experience.

■ Advancement

Newly ordained ministers generally begin their careers as pastors of small congregations or as *assistant pastors* (*curates*) in larger congregations. Advancement may take the form of getting a new or larger congregation of one's own. Protestant ministers may also advance into the hierarchy or controlling bodies of their denominations. Many, though, do not seek advancement in the material sense, but find satisfaction in serving wherever they are most needed.

▪ Earnings

Salaries vary substantially for Protestant clergy depending on the individual's experience, as well as the size of the congregation, its denominational branch, location, and financial status. The estimated average income of ministers is about $27,000 per year. Additional benefits usually include a housing stipend, which includes utilities, a monthly transportation allowance, health insurance, and other fringe benefits, which raise the average compensation for senior pastors in large congregations to over $50,000. Pension plans, travel stipends for research and rest, and grants for the education of their children are also frequently included in many compensation packages. Clergy often are given a monetary gift when they officiate at weddings and funerals. This is sometimes donated to the church or a charity by the minister. Some ministers of smaller congregations may add to their earnings by working at part-time secular jobs.

▪ Work Environment

Ministers spend long hours working under a variety of conditions. There is no such thing as a standard work-week. They are very likely to have a set schedule of services, classes, and meetings, but ministers are on call at all times. They are called upon to visit the sick and the dying and to minister to the grieving at all hours. Protestant ministers may also be needed to fill in for colleagues who are away or otherwise unavailable—conducting services and meeting the pastoral needs of their colleagues' congregations.

Ministers in the mainstream Protestant denominations are well provided for—they usually have an office in the church building and a residence nearby. Such centrally located facilities make it easier to discharge their duties. It is the ministers' personal responsibility, however, to ensure that they strike the proper balance between work and family life.

▪ Outlook

Currently, nearly 300,000 Protestant ministers serve a variety of congregations. While overall membership in Protestant churches is growing, most of the mainline denominations, such as the Baptist, Lutheran, Methodist, and Presbyterian churches, are not. Aging membership has caused church budgets and membership to shrink, lessening the demand for full-time ministers. There has been a significant increase in nondenominational congregations. Overall, the increased cost of church operations is expected to limit the demand for ministers. The closing or combining of smaller parishes, and the reduced availability of funds, has lessened the need for full-time ministers. And, although the number of ministry graduates is also declining, ministers should expect competition for some parish jobs, especially the more desirable, urban ones.

MARTIN LUTHER

Born in Germany in 1483, Martin Luther began his post-college career as an Augustinian monk. He was ordained to the Roman Catholic priesthood in 1507 and shortly thereafter became a lecturer in philosophy and the Scriptures at the University of Wittenberg. Luther became increasingly uneasy about the Catholic faith, finding many of its doctrines and practices to be unnecessary or just plain wrong. He ultimately determined that faith alone was needed for salvation, as in the Bible verse "The just shall live by faith" (Romans 1:17).

In 1517, Martin Luther posted 95 theses protesting the Church's most grievous error—the selling of indulgences (pardons from punishment for sin). He continued to oppose more aspects of Catholic faith and practice via debate and publications. In 1521, Luther was excommunicated from the Catholic Church. His beliefs and leadership qualities put him at the head of the Protestant Reformation, and gave rise to Lutheranism. Martin Luther apparently never sought this complete break with the church, just reform. The Catholic Council of Trent (held from 1545 to 1563) did indeed institute some of the reforms that Luther demanded.

Demand for ministers will vary depending on affiliation, with nondenominational churches needing the most ministers. Graduates of theological schools have the best prospects for employment, as do ministers willing to work in rural churches with smaller congregations, salary, and benefits. They may also have to minister to two or more smaller congregations to earn a sufficient salary. Employment opportunities may depend on ministers retiring, passing away, or leaving the profession.

▪ For More Information

Besides your own pastor, you can consult the headquarters of your denomination for information about becoming a Protestant minister. Through the Web sites listed below, you can gather information and link to affiliated seminaries:

Evangelical Lutheran Church in America (ELCA)
8765 West Higgins Road
Chicago, IL 60631
Tel: 800-638-3522
Web: http://www.elca.org

Presbyterian Church (USA)
100 Witherspoon Street
Louisville, KY 40202
Tel: 800-872-3283
Web: http://www.pcusa.org/

Southern Baptist Convention
901 Commerce
Nashville, TN 37203
Tel: 615-244-2355
Web: http://www.sbc.net

United Methodist Church
Board of Higher Education and Ministry
PO Box 871
Nashville, TN 37202
Tel: 615-340-7356
Web: http://www.umc.org or http://www.gbhem.org/

■ **Related Articles**

Education

Religious Ministries

Social Services

College Professors

Guidance Counselors

Social Workers

Psychiatric Technicians

■ **Overview**

Psychiatric technicians work with mentally ill, emotionally disturbed, or developmentally disabled people. Their duties vary considerably depending on place of work but may include helping patients with hygiene and housekeeping and recording patients' pulse, temperature, and respiration rate. Psychiatric technicians participate in treatment programs by having one-on-one sessions with patients, under a *nurse*'s or *counselor*'s direction.

Another prime aspect of the psychiatric technician's work is reporting observations of patients' behavior to medical and psychiatric staff. Psychiatric technicians may also fill out admitting forms for new patients, contact patients' families to arrange conferences, issue medications from the dispensary, and maintain records.

PSYCHIATRIC TECHNICIANS	
SCHOOL SUBJECTS	Health Psychology
PERSONAL SKILLS	Communication/ideas Helping/teaching
WORK ENVIRONMENT	Primarily indoors Primarily one location
MINIMUM EDUCATION LEVEL	Some postsecondary training
SALARY RANGE	$10,000 to $27,000 to $40,000
CERTIFICATION OR LICENSING	Required by certain states
OUTLOOK	Faster than the average
DOT	354
GOE	10.03.02
NOC	3413
O*NET	66014

■ **History**

Although some mentally ill people were treated as early as the 15th century in institutions like the Hospital of Saint Mary of Bethlehem in London (whose name was often shortened to Bedlam, hence the modern word "bedlam"), the practice of institutionalizing people with mental disorders did not become common until the 17th century.

During the 17th, 18th, and even into the 19th centuries, treatment of mentally ill patients was quite crude and often simply barbarous. This state of affairs started to change as medical practitioners began to see mental illness as a medical problem. During the late 18th and early 19th centuries, hospitals began concentrating on keeping patients clean and comfortable, building their self-respect, and treating them with friendliness and encouragement. This conception of mental illness treatment resulted in the establishment of specially designed institutions for the care of mental patients.

Beginning in the 1940s, mental health institutions sought more effective therapeutic services for their patients, including more social activities and innovative treatment programs. Treatment shifted from a sole reliance on state mental hospitals to provision of more services in general hospitals and community mental health centers.

The object was to shorten periods of institutionalization and to decrease the stigma and dislocation associated with treatment in mental hospitals. However, these changes also sharply increased personnel needs. One strategy for dealing with this has been to train more professionals—psychiatrists, psychologists, social workers, nurses, and others. Another strategy has focused on training more nonprofessionals—aides, attendants, orderlies, and others.

The drive to develop new therapies and the trend toward deinstitutionalizing patients have led to the creation of a new category of mental health worker with a training level between that of the professional and the nonprofessional. Workers at this level are usually referred to as paraprofessionals or technicians, and in the mental health field they are known as psychiatric technicians or mental health technicians.

■ **The Job**

Psychiatric technicians not only take over for or assist professionals in traditional treatment activities but also provide new services in innovative ways.

They may work with alcohol and drug abusers, psychotic or emotionally disturbed children and adults, developmentally disabled people, or the aged. They must be skilled and specially trained.

Psychiatric technicians are supervised by health professionals, such as *registered nurses, counselors, therapists,* or, more and more frequently, *senior psychiatric technicians.* Psychiatric technicians work as part of a team of mental health care workers and provide physical and mental rehabilitation for patients through recreational, occupational, and psychological readjustment programs.

In general, psychiatric technicians help plan and implement individual treatment programs. Specific activities vary according to work setting, but they may include the following: interviewing and information gathering; working in a hospital unit admitting, screening, evaluating, or discharging patients; record keeping; making referrals to community agencies; working for patients' needs and rights; visiting patients at home after their release from a hospital; and participating in individual and group counseling and therapy.

Psychiatric technicians endeavor to work with patients in a broad, comprehensive manner and to see each patient as a person whose peculiar or abnormal behavior stems from an illness or disability. They strive to help each patient achieve a maximum level of functioning. This means helping patients strengthen social and mental skills, accept greater responsibility, and develop confidence to enter into social, educational, or vocational activities.

In addition, psychiatric technicians working in hospitals handle a certain number of nursing responsibilities. They may take temperatures, pulses and respiration rates; measure blood pressures; and help administer medications and physical treatments. In many cases, technicians working in hospitals will find themselves concerned with all aspects of their patients' lives—from eating, sleeping, and personal hygiene to developing social skills and improving self-image.

Technicians working in clinics, community mental health centers, halfway houses, day hospitals, or other non-institutional settings also perform some activities special to their situation. They interview newly registered patients and their relatives and visit patients and their families at home. They also administer psychological tests, participate in group activities, and write reports about their observations to supervising psychiatrists or other mental health professionals. They try to ease the transition of patients leaving hospitals and returning to their communities. They may refer patients to and arrange for consultations with mental health specialists. They may also help patients resolve problems with employment, housing, and personal finance.

Most psychiatric technicians are trained as generalists in providing mental health services. But some opportunities exist for technicians to specialize in a particular aspect of mental health care. For example, some psychiatric technicians specialize in the problems of mentally disturbed children. Others work as counselors in drug and alcohol abuse programs or as members of psychiatric emergency or crisis-intervention teams.

Another area of emphasis is working in community mental health. Technicians employed in this area are sometimes known as *human-services technicians*. They use rehabilitation techniques for nonhospitalized patients who have problems adjusting to their social environment. These technicians may be primarily concerned with drug and alcohol abuse, parental effectiveness, the elderly, or problems in interpersonal relationships. Human-services technicians work in social welfare departments, child care centers, preschools, vocational rehabilitation workshops, and schools for the learning disabled, emotionally disturbed, and mentally handicapped. This concentration is particularly popular in college curriculums, according to the American Association of Psychiatric Technicians (AAPT), although it has yet to find wide acceptance in the job market.

With slightly different training, psychiatric technicians may specialize in the treatment of developmentally disabled people. *Developmentally disabled psychiatric technicians* work with patients by doing such things as teaching recreational activities. They generally work in halfway houses, state hospitals, training centers, or state and local service agencies. Jobs as a "DD" tech are among the easiest psychiatric technician jobs to get, and many techs start out in this area. On average, however, the pay of the DD tech is considerably less than that of other psychiatric technicians.

■ Requirements

High School

A high school diploma is the minimum education requirement to find work as a psychiatric technician, although in many cases psychiatric technicians are expected to have two years of training beyond high school. In general, high school students should take courses in English, biology, psychology, and sociology.

Postsecondary Training

The two-year postsecondary training programs usually lead to an associate of arts or associate of science degree. It is important to note that many hospitals prefer to hire applicants with bachelor's degrees.

In general, study programs include human development, personality structure, the nature of mental illness, and to a limited extent, anatomy, physiology, basic nursing, and medical science. Other subjects usually include some introduction to basic social sciences so that technicians can better understand relevant family and community structures; an overview of structure and functions of institutions that treat patients; and most important, practical instruction.

GLOSSARY

Neurosis: A mental and emotional disorder that affects only part of the personality. A neurosis does not disturb the use of language, and it is accompanied by various physical, physiological, and mental disturbances, the most usual being anxieties or phobias.

Obsessive-compulsive: A neurosis that results in the patient's compulsion to carry out certain acts, no matter how odd or illogical or repetitive they are. This sort of neurosis is evident once the obsession or compulsive act interferes with normal life. For example, a person obsessed with cleanliness might take a dozen or more showers a day.

Paranoid schizophrenic: The most common and destructive of the psychotic disorders, characterized by departure from reality, inability to think clearly, difficulty feeling and expressing emotions, and a retreat into a fantasy life

Phobias: Irrational or overblown fears that prevent a person from living a normal life

Psychosis: A more complete disintegration of personality and loss of contact with the outside world than with neurosis

Certification and Licensing

Psychiatric technicians must be licensed in California, Colorado, Kansas, and Arkansas. Certification is voluntary in most other states. Prospective technicians and technicians-in-training should consult their guidance or placement counselors for more information about requirements in their states. Certification is available through the American Association of Psychiatric Technicians. Level 1 techs must have a high school diploma and pass a written test. Level 2 techs must have 30 semester credits and one year of experience and pass a written test. Level 3 techs must have an associate's degree and two years of experience and pass a written test. Level 4 techs must have a bachelor's degree and three years of experience and pass a written test.

Most mental health technology programs emphasize interviewing skills. Such training guides technicians to correctly describe a patient's tone of voice and body language so that they are well equipped to observe and record behavior that will be interpreted by the treatment team, and sometimes even a court of law. Some programs also teach administration of selected psychological tests. You may also gain knowledge and training in crisis intervention techniques, child guidance, group counseling, family therapy, behavior modification, and consultation skills.

Other Requirements

Because psychiatric technicians interact with people, you must be sensitive to others' needs and feelings. Some aspects of sensitivity can be learned, but this requires a willingness to listen, being extremely observant, and risking involvement in situations that at first may seem ambiguous and confusing. In addition, you need to be willing to look at your own attitudes and behavior and to be flexible and open about effecting changes in them. The more you know of yourself, the more effective you will be in helping others.

Patience, understanding, and a "thick skin" are required in working with people who may be disagreeable and unpleasant because of their illnesses. Patients can be particularly adept at finding a person's weaknesses and exploiting them. This is not a job for the tender hearted. A sense of responsibility and the ability to remain calm in emergencies are also essential characteristics.

■ Exploring

Prospective psychiatric technicians can gather personal experience in this field in a number of ways. You can apply for a job as a nurse's aide at a local general hospital or volunteer at a hospital part-time or during the summer. Volunteering is an excellent way to become acquainted with the field, and many techs' full-time jobs evolve from volunteer positions. Most volunteers must be 21 years of age to work in the mental health unit. Younger students who are interested in volunteering can often find places in the medical records department or other areas to get their feet in the door.

You might also consider volunteering at a local mental health association or a local social welfare agency. In some cases, the mental health association can arrange opportunities for volunteer work inside a mental hospital or mental health clinic. Finally, either on your own or with your teachers, you can arrange a visit to a mental health clinic. You may be able to talk with staff members and observe first-hand how psychiatric technicians do their jobs.

■ Employers

Psychiatric technicians work in a variety of settings: the military, hospitals, mental hospitals, community mental health centers, psychiatric clinics, schools and day centers for the developmentally disabled, and social service agencies. They also work at residential and nonresidential centers, such as geriatric nursing homes, child or adolescent development centers, and halfway houses.

Other potential places of employment for psychiatric technicians include correctional programs and juvenile courts, schools for the blind and deaf, community action programs, family service centers, and public housing programs.

■ Starting Out

Graduates from mental health and human services technology programs can usually choose from a variety of job possibilities. College placement officers can be extremely helpful in locating employment. Students can follow want ads or apply directly to clinics, agencies, or hospitals of their choice. Job information can also be obtained from the department of mental health in each state.

■ Advancement

Working as a psychiatric technician is still a relatively new occupation, and sequences of promotions have not yet been clearly defined. Seeking national certification through the AAPT is one way to help to set up a career path in this field. Advancement normally takes the form of being given greater responsibilities with less supervision. It usually results from gaining experience, developing competence and leadership abilities, and continuing formal and practical education. In cases where promotions are governed by civil service regulations, advancement is based on experience and test scores on promotion examinations.

In large part, advancement is linked to gaining further education. Thus, after working a few years, technicians may decide to obtain a bachelor's degree in psychology. Advanced education, coupled with previous training and work experience, greatly enhance advancement potential. For instance, with a bachelor's degree, experienced technicians may be able to find rewarding positions as instructors in programs to train future mental health workers.

■ Earnings

Salaries for psychiatric technicians vary according to geographical area and work setting: technicians in California generally receive substantially higher wages than those in other areas of the country, and technicians in community settings generally receive higher salaries than those in institutional settings. On average, psychiatric technicians receive starting salaries ranging anywhere from minimum wage, or less than $10,000 a year, to as much as $20,000 a year or more. Most technicians are hourly employees, receiving $7 to $12 an hour, some even as high as $15 an hour. With increased experience, technicians can expect at least modest increases in their salaries each year. Some senior psychiatric technicians earn as much as $27,000 a year or more (those in California can earn as much as $35,000 to $40,000 a year or more with 10 to 15 years of experience).

Most psychiatric technicians receive fringe benefits, including hospitalization insurance, sick leave, and paid vacations. Technicians working for state institutions or agencies will probably also be eligible for financial assistance for further education.

■ Work Environment

Psychiatric technicians work in a variety of settings and their working conditions vary accordingly. Typically they work 40 hours a week, five days a week, although one may be a weekend day. Some psychiatric technicians work evening or night shifts, and all technicians may sometimes be asked to work holidays.

For the most part, the physical surroundings are pleasant. Most institutions, clinics, mental health centers, and agency offices are kept clean and comfortably furnished. Technicians who work with the mentally ill must nonetheless adjust to an environment that is normally chaotic and sometimes upsetting. Some patients are acutely depressed and withdrawn or excessively agitated and excited. Some patients may become unexpectedly violent and verbally abusive. However, institutions treating these kinds of patients maintain enough staff to keep the patients safe and to protect workers from physical harm. Psychiatric technicians who make home visits also may sometimes confront unpleasant conditions.

Finally, psychiatric technicians work not only with individuals but often with the community. In that role, technicians can be called upon to advocate for their patients by motivating community agencies to provide services or obtaining exceptions to rules when needed for individuals or groups of patients. Successful psychiatric technicians become competent in working and dealing with various decision-making processes of community and neighborhood groups.

■ Outlook

The number of psychiatric technicians in the United States is estimated at about one million. This number is expected to rise because of, in large part, a well-established trend of returning hospitalized patients to their communities after shorter and shorter periods of hospitalization. The trend has encouraged development of comprehensive community mental health centers and has led to an increased need for psychiatric technicians to staff these facilities.

Concerns over rising health care costs should increase employment levels for technicians, because they and other paraprofessionals can take over some functions of higher-paid professionals. This kind of substitution has been demonstrated to be an effective way of reducing costs without reducing quality of care.

■ For More Information

For a two-page flyer on psychiatric technician careers or for information on becoming a nationally certified psychiatric technician, contact:

American Association of Psychiatric Technicians, Inc.
1879 North Neltnor Boulevard, Suite 260
West Chicago, IL 60185-2997
Tel: 800-391-7589
Web: http://www.aapt.com

Psychiatrists

■ Overview

Psychiatrists are physicians who attend to patients' mental, emotional, and behavioral symptoms. They try to help people function better in their daily lives. Different kinds of psychiatrists use different treatment methods depending on their fields. They may explore a patient's beliefs and history. They may prescribe medicine, including tranquilizers, antipsychotics, and antidepressants. If they specialize in treating children, they may use play therapy.

PSYCHIATRISTS	
SCHOOL SUBJECTS	Health Psychology Sociology
PERSONAL SKILLS	Helping/teaching Technical/scientific
WORK ENVIRONMENT	Primarily indoors Primarily one location
MINIMUM EDUCATION LEVEL	Medical degree
SALARY RANGE	$137,200 to $150,900 to $207,500
CERTIFICATION OR LICENSING	Required by all states
OUTLOOK	Faster than the average
DOT	070
GOE	02.03.01
NOC	3111

■ History

The greatest advances in psychiatric treatment came in the latter part of the 19th century. Emil Kraepelin, a German psychiatrist, made an important contribution when he developed a classification system for mental illnesses that is still used for diagnosis. Sigmund Freud (1856-1939), the famous Viennese psychiatrist, developed techniques for analyzing human behavior that have strongly influenced the practice of modern psychiatry. Freud first lectured in the United States in 1909. Swiss psychiatrist Carl Jung (1875-1961), a former associate of Freud's, revolutionized the field with his theory of a collective unconscious.

Another great change in treatment began in the 1950s with the development of medication that could be used in treating psychiatric problems, such as depression and anxiety.

■ The Job

Psychiatrists treat patients who suffer from mental and emotional illnesses that make it hard for them to cope with everyday living or to behave in socially acceptable ways. Problems treated range from being irritable and feeling frustrated to losing touch with reality. Some patients may abuse alcohol or drugs or commit crimes. Others may have physical symptoms that spring from mental or emotional disorders. Such disorders no longer are viewed with such shame as they were in the past. The more enlightened view of today is that emotional or mental problems need to be diagnosed and treated just like any other medical problem.

Some psychiatrists run general practices, treating patients with a variety of mental disorders. Others may specialize in certain types of therapy or kinds of patients, for example, the chronically ill.

Treatment varies according to patient needs. Psychiatrists may prescribe medication that affects the patient's mood or behavior, such as tranquilizers or antidepressants. Medication, an important part of treatment nowadays, may be used alone or with other treatment. Sometimes a psychiatrist may refer a patient to another psychiatrist well-versed in a particular treatment.

Psychiatrists must deal compassionately with patients who may be in bad shape physically as well as mentally. They may be homeless or suicidal, for example, and have neglected to take care of themselves. "I treat anything that a family practitioner would treat," says ward supervisor Dr. Jenny Kane. "If it's necessary, I call in a specialist."

Dr. Kane is one of a growing number of women joining the ranks of psychiatrists. The number of women psychiatrists has grown from 14.5 percent in 1982 to 25 percent in 1996, according to the American Psychiatric Association's 1996 National Survey of Psychiatric Practice.

The survey said that female psychiatrists see, on average, about 32 patients a week and male psychiatrists, about 37. Psychiatrists treat the largest number of their patients—36 percent—for mood disorders. The remainder of their caseloads is made up of patients with anxiety disorders (about 14 percent); schizophrenia, a condition where thoughts are disconnected and hallucinations may be seen and voices heard, and other psychoses, such as when a person is out of touch with reality (13 percent); infant, child, or adolescent disorders (10 percent); personality disorders (also 10 percent); other mental problems (7 percent); alcohol use problems (6 percent) and substance use disorders (4 percent), according to the survey.

Different kinds of psychiatrists use different methods to treat their patients.

Behavior therapists use a carrot-and-stick method to change patients' behavior. They may also use meditation, relaxation, and other treatment methods, such as biofeedback, a process where patients use electronic monitors to measure the effects that their thoughts and feelings have on bodily functions like muscle tension, heart rate, or brain waves so that they can consciously control them through stress reduction.

Psychotherapists use what is often called "talking therapy." The therapist helps overcome emotional pain by helping the patient uncover and understand the feelings and ideas that form the root of the problem. Therapy is given to individuals, groups, couples, or families.

Psychoanalysts encourage the patient to talk freely or "free associate" in a form of psychotherapy to uncover troubling subconscious beliefs or conflicts and their causes. Dreams may also be examined for hints about the unconscious mind. Subconscious conflicts are believed to cause neurosis, which is an emotional disorder in which the patient commonly exhibits anxious behavior.

Child psychiatrists work with youth and usually their parents as well. At the opposite end of the age scale, other psychiatrists prefer to work with geriatric patients.

Industrial psychiatrists are employed by companies to deal with problems that affect employee performance, such as alcoholism or absenteeism.

Forensic psychiatrists work in the field of law. They evaluate defendants and testify on their mental state. They may help determine whether or not defendants understand the charges against them and if they can contribute to their own defense.

Psychologists also work with mentally or emotionally disturbed clients. They are not physicians, however, and cannot prescribe medication. In some cases, disturbed behavior results from disorders of the nervous system. These conditions are diagnosed and treated by *neurologists*, who are physicians specializing in problems of the nervous system.

■ Requirements

High School

High school students should enroll in college-preparatory programs, taking courses in English, languages, the humanities, social studies, mathematics, biology, chemistry, and physics.

Postsecondary Training

College freshmen should plan their undergraduate programs so they meet the admission requirements that are explained in the annual publication of the Association of American Medical Colleges, "Admission Requirements of American Medical Colleges Including Canada." During

---

GLOSSARY

Neurosis: An emotional disorder that arises due to unresolved conflicts, with anxiety often being the main characteristic

Phobia: An obsessive, persistent, unrealistic fear of an object or situation

Psychoanalysis: A method of treating mental disorders by bringing unconscious fears and conflicts into the conscious mind

Psychosis: A major mental disorder, in which the personality is seriously disorganized and contact with reality is impaired

Psychosomatic: A physical illness caused or aggravated by a mental condition

Psychotherapy: The treatment of mental disorders by psychological, rather than physical, means

---

their second or third year in college, students should take the Medical College Admission Test, which most medical schools require.

In medical school, students must complete a four-year program of medical studies and supervised clinical work leading to their M.D. degrees.

New physicians who plan to specialize in psychiatry must complete a residency. In the first year, they work in several specialties, such as internal medicine and pediatrics. Then they work for three years in a psychiatric hospital or a general hospital's psychiatric ward. To become a child psychiatrist, for example, a doctor must train for at least three years in general residency and two years in child psychiatry residency. Psychiatrists who wish to become psychoanalysts spend six years in part-time training, either during or after residency. Part of their training involves undergoing psychoanalysis themselves.

After they complete their resident training in psychiatry, candidates take an intensive examination given by the Board of Psychiatry and Neurology, and if they pass, they become Diplomates in Psychiatry.

Certification or Licensing

Upon completion of the M.D., students must pass a test to be licensed to practice medicine in their states. Depending on the requirements of the state in which they plan to practice, they may be required to pass the National Board of Medical Examiners test, the Federal Licensing Examination, or an individual state licensing test.

Other Requirements

To complete the required studies and training, students need outstanding mental ability and perseverance. Psychiatrists must be emotionally stable so they can deal with their patients objectively. They must be able to listen well.

Exploring

Students who wish to find out more about the field of psychiatry should read all they can about it to get a feel for what the job entails. A recent book, *Career Planning for Psychiatrists* (1995), edited by Kathleen M. Mogul, M.D. and Leah J. Dickstein, M.D. provides a comprehensive guide to the various career opportunities available in psychiatry. Students also should talk with their high school counselors and take advantage of any chance to interview psychiatrists or other physicians.

It would also be helpful to volunteer or work part-time at hospitals, clinics, or nursing homes. College students may be able to find summer jobs as hospital orderlies, nurse's aides, or ward clerks.

Employers

According to the American Psychiatric Association's 1996 survey, about 40.5 percent of psychiatrists work mainly in solo office practice; 10 percent work in a group office practice. About 25 percent work at various kinds of hospitals, while about 12 percent work in a public clinic or outpatient facility. Smaller percentages work in private clinics and outpatient facilities, nursing homes, correctional facilities, health maintenance organizations, or other work settings. A majority of psychiatrists are connected in some way with a medical school, as volunteer or paid faculty members.

Starting Out

Psychiatrists in residency can find job leads in professional journals and through professional organizations such as the American Psychiatric Association. Many are offered permanent positions with the same institution where they complete their residency.

Advancement

Most psychiatrists advance in their careers by enlarging their knowledge and skills, clientele, and earnings. Those who work in hospitals, clinics, and mental health centers may become administrators. Those who teach or concentrate on research may become department heads.

Earnings

Psychiatrists' earnings are determined by the kind of practice they have and its location, their experience, and the number of patients they treat. Like other physicians, their average income is among the highest of any occupation.

Average income for psychiatrists is $137,200 a year, according to the American Medical Association. Psychiatrists in private practice earn about $148,800 a year, making higher average incomes than salaried employees working for hire, who earn an average of $127,500 a year.

Psychiatrists on staff at psychiatric facilities earn an average salary of $126,585, according to a 1997 salary survey by The National Association of Psychiatric Health Systems. Psychiatric medical directors at such facilities earn an average of $150,890 a year, according to the survey. Psychiatrists who serve soley as chief executive officers of psychiatric facilities and who are not medical directors earn an average of $197,834 a year. Those who are CEOs and also medical directors make the highest average salaries, $207,498 a year.

Work Environment

Psychiatrists in private practice set their own schedules and usually work regular hours. They may work some evenings or weekends to see patients who cannot take time off during business hours. Most psychiatrists, however, put in long workdays, averaging 52 hours a week, according to American Medical Association statistics. Like other physicians, psychiatrists are always on call. Dr. Kane likens the obligations of her job to parenting. "Whatever and whenever a patient needs me, it's my job to be there—or at least to make arrangements to have them taken care of," she says.

Psychiatrists in private practice typically work in comfortable office settings. Some private psychiatrists also work as hospital staff members, consultants, lecturers, or teachers.

Salaried psychiatrists work in private hospitals, state hospitals, and community mental health centers. They also work for government agencies, such as the U.S. Department of Health and Human Services, the Department of Defense, and the Veterans Administration.

Psychiatrists who work in public facilities often bear heavy workloads. Changes in treatment have reduced the number of patients in hospitals and have increased the number of patients in community health centers.

Outlook

Opportunities for private practice and salaried positions are excellent. Demand is great for child psychiatrists, and other types as well are in short supply, especially in rural areas and public facilities.

A number of factors contribute to this shortage. Growing population and increasing life span add up to more people who need psychiatric care; rising incomes enable more people to afford treatment; and higher educational levels make more people aware of the importance of mental health care. Medical insurance, although it usually limits the amount of mental health care, at least provides some coverage. However, the amount of benefits being paid out has been more than cut in half over the past 10 years.

Psychiatrists are also needed as researchers to explore the causes of mental illness and develop new ways to treat it.

■ For More Information

For information on choosing a medical specialty, as well as a description of psychiatry, please contact:

American Medical Association
515 North State Street
Chicago, IL 60610
Tel: 312-464-5000

For brochures with general information, please contact:

American Psychiatric Association
1400 K Street, NW
Washington, DC 20005
Tel: 202-682-6000

For a brochure on careers in medicine, please contact:

Association of American Medical Colleges
2450 N Street, NW
Washington, DC 20037
Tel: 202-828-0400

For information on mental illness, please contact:

National Mental Health Association
1021 Prince Street
Alexandria, VA 22314-2971
Tel: 703-684-5968
Web: http://www.com/pfalzgraf/nmha.html

■ Related Articles

Health Care
Social Services
Physicians
Psychiatric Technicians
Psychologists

Psychoanalysts
■ See Psychiatrists

Psychologists

■ Overview

Psychologists teach, counsel, conduct research, or administer programs to understand people and help people understand themselves. Psychologists examine individual and group behavior through testing, experimenting, and studying personal histories.

Psychologists normally hold doctorates in psychology. Unlike psychiatrists, they are not medical doctors and cannot prescribe medication.

■ History

The first syllable in psychology derives from "psyche," a Greek word meaning soul. The second half of psychology contains the root of the word "logic." Thus "psychology" translates as "the science of the soul."

Early philosophers emphasized differences between body and soul. Plato, for example, believed they were two entirely different parts. Modern scholars tend to emphasize the unity between mind and body rather than their dissimilarity.

The founder of experimental psychology, Wilhelm Wundt (1832-1920), held both an M.D. and a Ph.D. A physician, he taught at the University of Leipzig, where his title was Professor of Philosophy. Like Wundt, German scholars of the 19th century were committed to the scientific method. Discovery by experiment was considered the only respectable way for learned thinkers to work. Thus it was not thought strange that in 1879, Dr. Wundt set up an experimental laboratory to conduct research upon human behavior. Many people who later became famous U.S. psychologists received their training under Dr. Wundt.

At the turn of the 20th century, Russian physiologist Dr. Ivan Pavlov (1849-1936) discovered a key aspect of behaviorist theory while studying the process of digestion. While experimenting on dogs, he found that they began to salivate in anticipation of their food. He discovered that if he rang a bell before presenting their meat, the dogs associated the sound of a bell with mealtime. He then would ring the bell but withhold the food. The dogs' saliva flowed anyway, whether or not they saw or smelled food. Dr. Pavlov called this substitute stimulus a "conditioned response." Many psychologists began to incorporate the theory of conditioned response into theories of learning.

One of the most famous pioneers in psychology was Dr. Sigmund Freud (1856-1939), whose work led to many of the modern theories of behavior. Dr. Freud lived

PSYCHOLOGISTS	
SCHOOL SUBJECTS	Health Psychology Sociology
PERSONAL SKILLS	Helping/teaching Technical/scientific
WORK ENVIRONMENT	Primarily indoors Primarily one location
MINIMUM EDUCATION LEVEL	Master's degree
SALARY RANGE	$20,000 to $64,000 to $255,000
CERTIFICATION OR LICENSING	Required by all states
OUTLOOK	Faster than the average
DOT	045
GOE	11.03.01
NOC	4151
O*NET	27108A, B, C, D

Austrian psychologist Alfred Adler was founder of the school of individual psychology. He believed that humans strive throughout their lives to achieve contentment and fulfillment, in an attempt to compensate for strong feelings of inferiority developed in childhood. Most persons are able to compensate satisfactorily; those who are unsuccessful develop neuroses. Adler explained his theories in *The Theory and Practice of Individual Psychology* (1918), *Understanding Human Nature* (1927), and *Pattern of Life* (1930).

Adler was born in Vienna. He received a degree in medicine from the University of Vienna in 1895. In 1902, Adler became associated with Sigmund Freud, founder of psychoanalysis. Rejecting Freud's emphases upon sex as a significant motive behind human behavior, Adler broke with Freud in 1911. Adler spent much of his time after 1925 lecturing in the United States.

and practiced in Vienna, Austria, until Hitler's forces caused him to flee to England. His work on the meaning of dreams, the unconscious, and the nature of various emotional disturbances has had a profound effect upon the profession and practice of psychology for more than 60 years, although many psychologists now disagree with some of his theories.

Many Americans have contributed greatly to the science that seeks to understand human behavior: William James, Robert Woodworth, E. L. Thorndike, Clark Hull, B. F. Skinner, and others.

■ The Job

Psychology is both a science and a profession. As a science, it is a systematic approach to the understanding of people and their behavior; as a profession, it is the application of that understanding to help solve human problems. Psychology is a rapidly growing field, and psychologists work on a great variety of problems.

The field of psychology is so vast that no one person can become an expert in all phases of it. The psychologist usually concentrates on one specialty. Many of the specialties overlap in subject matter and methodology.

Many psychologists teach some area of basic psychology in colleges and universities. They are also likely to conduct research and supervise graduate student work in an area of special interest.

Clinical psychologists concern themselves with people's mental and emotional disorders. They assess and treat problems ranging from normal psychological crises, such as adolescent rebellion or middle-age loss of self-esteem, to extreme conditions, such as severe depression and schizophrenia.

Some clinical psychologists work almost exclusively with children. They may be staff members at a child guidance clinic or a treatment center for children at a large general hospital. Child psychologists and other clinical psychologists may engage in private practice, seeing clients at offices. Clinical psychologists comprise the largest group of specialists.

Developmental psychologists study development of people from birth through old age. They describe, measure, and explain age-related changes in behavior, stages of emotional development, universal traits and individual differences, and abnormal changes in development. Many developmental psychologists teach and research in colleges and universities. Some specialize in programs for children in day care centers, preschools, hospitals, or clinics. Others specialize in programs for the elderly.

Social psychologists study how people interact with each other and how they are affected by their environment. Social psychology has developed from four sources: sociology, cultural anthropology, psychiatry, and psychology. Social psychologists are interested in individual and group behavior. They study the ways groups influence individuals and vice versa. They study different kinds of groups: ethnic, religious, political, educational, family, and many others. The social psychologist has devised ways to research group nature, attitudes, leadership patterns, and structure.

Counseling psychologists work with people who have problems they find difficult to face alone. These clients are not usually mentally or emotionally ill, but they are emotionally upset, anxious, or struggling with some conflict within themselves or their environment. By helping people solve their problems, make decisions, and cope with everyday stresses, the counseling psychologist actually is working in preventive mental health.

School psychologists frequently do diagnosis and remediation. They may engage primarily in preventive and developmental psychology. Many school psychologists are assigned the duty of testing pupils surmised to be exceptional. Other school psychologists work almost entirely with children who have proven to be a problem to themselves or to others and who have been referred for help by teachers or other members of the school system. Many school psychologists are concerned with pupils who reveal various kinds of learning disabilities. School psychologists may also be called upon to work with relationship problems between parents and children.

Industrial-organizational psychologists are concerned with the relation between people and work. They deal with organizational structure, worker productivity, job satisfaction, consumer behavior, personnel training and development, and the interaction between humans and machines. Industrial-organizational psychologists may work with a sales department to help salespeople become more effective. Some study assembly line procedures and suggest changes to reduce monotony and increase worker responsibility. Others plan various kinds of tests to help screen applicants for employment. Industrial-organizational psychologists conduct research to determine qualities that seem to produce the most efficient employees or help management develop programs to identify staff with management potential. They may be asked to investigate and report on certain differences of opinion between a supervisor and one of the workers. Some may design training courses to indoctrinate new employees or counsel older employees on career development or retirement preparation.

Other industrial psychologists, referred to as *engineering psychologists,* help engineers and technicians design systems that require workers or consumers and machines to interact. They also develop training aids for those systems.

Consumer psychologists are interested in consumer reactions to products or services. These psychologists may be asked to determine the kinds of products the public will buy. They may study, for instance, whether people prefer big cars or little cars. They might be asked to make decisions about the most appealing ways to present a product through advertising. Many of today's most established advertising, promotion, and packaging practices have been influenced by the opinions and advice of consumer psychologists. Consumer psychologists also try to improve product acceptability and safety in addition to helping the consumer make better decisions.

Psychometrists work with intelligence, personality, and aptitude tests used in clinics, counseling centers, schools, and businesses. They administer tests, score them, and interpret results as related to standard norms. Psychometrists also study methods and techniques used to acquire and evaluate psychological data. They may devise new, more reliable tests. These specialists are usually well trained in mathematics, statistics, and computer programming and technology.

The *educational psychologist* is concerned primarily with how people teach, learn, and evaluate learning. Many educational psychologists are employed on college or university faculties, and they also conduct research into learning theory. Some, however, are interested in evaluating learning.

Experimental psychologists conduct scientific experiments on particular aspects of behavior, either animal or human. Much experimental study is done in learning, in physiological psychology (the relationship of behavior to physiological processes), and in comparative psychology (sometimes called animal psychology). Many experimental psychological studies are carried out with animals, partly because their environments can be carefully controlled.

Many psychologists of all kinds find that writing skills are helpful. They may write up the results of research efforts for a scholarly journal. Some prepare papers for presentation at professional association meetings or sometimes write books or articles. As consultants or industrial psychologists, they may write instruction manuals. Educational psychologists may prepare test manuals.

Some psychologists become administrators who direct college or university psychology departments or personnel services programs in a school system or industry. Some become agency or department directors of research in scientific laboratories. They may be promoted to department head in a state or federal government agency. *Chief psychologists* in hospitals or psychiatric centers plan psychological treatment programs, direct professional and nonprofessional personnel, and oversee psychological services provided by the institution.

■ Requirements

High School
High school students interested in becoming psychologists should enroll in college preparatory courses. They should concentrate on English courses, mathematics, and sciences. They should also take modern foreign languages, especially French and German, because reading comprehension of these languages is one of the usual requirements for obtaining the doctoral degree.

Postsecondary Training
A doctorate in psychology (Ph.D. or Psy.D.) is recommended. While most new doctorates in the psychology field received a Ph.D., the number of Psy.D. recipients has more than doubled—to 16 percent—over the past decade. Some positions are available to people with a master's degree, but they are jobs of lesser responsibility and lower salaries than those open to people with a doctorate.

In clinical or counseling psychology, requirements for a Ph.D. or Psy.D. usually include one year of internship or supervised experience. The American Board of Examiners in Professional Psychology offers diplomas in clinical, counseling, industrial-organizational, and school psychology to doctorate recipients with outstanding educational records and experience who pass required psychology examinations. In many research fields, psychologists are required to complete a postdoctoral fellowship. Unlike psychiatrists, psychologists do not need to attend medical school.

Certification or Licensing
Psychologists who wish to enter private practice and school psychologists employed in the public school system must meet state certification or licensing requirements.

■ Exploring

Students interested in exploring the profession of psychology should read all they can about it, including biographies of and works by noted psychologists. In addition, they may seek an appointment to talk with a psychologist who may work at a nearby school, college, hospital, or clinic. Those with access to the Internet may wish to check out the web site of the National Mental Health Association at http://www.nmha.org or the American Psychological Association at http://www.apa.org/students.

■ Employers

A clinical psychologist may teach in a college or university. Or clinical psychologists may work with patients in a hospital, where they provide therapy after evaluation through special tests.

Many developmental psychologists teach and research in colleges and universities. Some specialize in programs for children in day care centers, preschools, hospitals, or clinics.

Social psychologists teach and conduct research in colleges or universities. They also work for agencies of the federal or state government or in private research firms. Some work as consultants. An increasing number of social psychologists work as researchers and personnel managers in such nontraditional settings as advertising agencies, corporations, and architectural and engineering firms.

Counseling psychologists work in college or university counseling centers; they also teach in psychology departments. They may be in private practice. Or they may work at a community health center, a marriage counseling agency, or a federal agency such as the Department of Veterans Affairs.

Consumer psychologists study consumer reactions to products or services. They are hired by advertising, promotion, and packaging companies..

Psychometrists may be employed in colleges and universities, testing companies, private research firms, or government agencies.

Educational psychologists may work for test publishing firms devising and standardizing tests of ability, aptitude, personal preferences, attitudes, or characteristics.

■ Starting Out

A university placement office will be able to help a college graduate find a position. The student's major professor, colleagues, or friends also may know of vacancies in professional positions. The American Psychological Association lists job vacancies in a monthly employment bulletin for its members. Other job search methods include searching newspaper ads or meeting an employer through a former job.

■ Advancement

A psychologist at a college or university may advance through the academic ranks from instructor to professor. Some college teachers who enjoy administrative work become department heads.

Psychologists who work for state or federal government agencies may, after considerable experience, be promoted to head a section or department. School psychologists might become directors of pupil personnel services. Industrial psychologists can rise to managerial or administrative positions.

After several years of experience, many psychologists enter private practice or set up their own research or consulting firms.

■ Earnings

Average salaries for psychologists with master's degrees range from $40,500 for faculty positions to $67,500 for research administration positions. Starting salaries for psychologists with master's degrees are about $20,000 or perhaps less, depending on the region and position.

The median salary for all psychologists with doctoral degrees is about $64,000. Average starting salaries range from slightly more than $29,200 for counseling at a university or college counseling center over the nine- to ten-month academic year to $61,000 for an applied psychologist working in business or industry.

Psychologists in private practice and in applied specialties generally have higher earnings than other psychologists. Many psychologists are able to supplement their basic earnings with fees from consulting, writing, or lecturing. Psychologists with doctorates who work in administration of education, research, or human services in general earn comparatively higher salaries than other psychologists who work in those same fields in other psychology positions. Average salaries for psychologists with doctorates who work in faculty positions range from near $35,000 for a lecturer/instructor to $72,000 for a full professor. Psychologists who administer educational programs earn an average of from $53,000 after 2 to 4 years experience to $104,000 after 30 or more years. Psychologists in research positions start out making an average of $38,500 and can progress to an average salary of $85,800 after 30 or more years. Those in research administration have average salaries ranging from about $48,000 with 2 to 4 years experience up to $102,000 after 30 or more years. Licensed clinical psychologists, who work primarily in private practice, hospitals, or health centers, start out making an average of $48,000. Those with 25 or more years experience make an average of $86,000. Licensed counseling psychologists make an average of about $49,000 within the first 2 to 4 years up to an average of about $98,000 after 30 or more years. Licensed school psychologists earn an average of about $52,000 after 2 to 4 years and up to about $85,000 after 30 or more years. Psychologists who administrate human services, whose duties include personnel supervision, start out making an average of $42,333 and can make up to about $85,000 after 30 or more years.

Psychologists employed in business or industry earn higher average salaries than psychologists in any other setting. They start out higher, earning an average of about $63,000 a year with 2 to 4 years experience and end up higher, averaging about $145,000 a year after 30 or more years. At the highest end, an industrial/organizational psychologist who has worked in a consulting firm for 30 or more years can earn up to $255,000 a year.

■ Work Environment

Psychologists work under many different conditions. Those who work as college or university teachers usually have offices in a building on campus and access to a laboratory in which they carry out experiments.

Offices of school psychologists may be located in the school system headquarters. They may see students and their parents at those offices, or they might work in space set aside for them in several schools within the school district that they may visit regularly.

Psychologists in military service serve in this country or overseas. They may be stationed in Washington and assigned to an office job, or they may be stationed with other military personnel at a post or, more likely, in a military hospital.

Psychologists employed in government work in such diverse places as public health or vocational rehabilitation agencies, the Department of Veterans Affairs, the Peace Corps, the U.S. Office of Education, or a state department of education. Their working conditions depend largely on the kind of jobs they have. They may be required to travel a lot or to produce publications. They may work mainly with people or be assigned entirely to research.

Some psychologists are self-employed. Most work as clinical psychologists and have offices where they see clients. Others work as consultants to business firms. Self-employed psychologists rent or own their office spaces and arrange their own work schedules.

To be a psychologist, one must have a desire to help people understand themselves and others. A basic curiosity is required as well as a fascination with the way the human mind works.

■ Outlook

The career of psychologist has been named by the Bureau of Labor Statistics as being one of the 10 fastest growing jobs for college graduates through the first decade of the next century, as long as the student carries an advanced degree such as a master's or doctorate. The Bureau of Labor Statistics projects that the number of employed psychologists will grow 8 percent over the 10-year period from 1996 to 2006, with the biggest increase in industrial/organizational jobs and the biggest decrease in hospital jobs. Increased emphasis on health maintenance and illness prevention as well as growing interest in psychological services for special groups, such as children or the elderly, will create a greater demand for psychologists. Many of these areas depend on government funding, however, and could be adversely affected in an economic downswing when spending is likely to be curtailed. Many openings should be available in business and industry, and the outlook is very good for psychologists who are in full-time independent practice.

Universities have remained one of the top arenas for full-time employment over the past decade. Outstanding psychologists with doctorates from leading universities will have no problem obtaining employment in top academic institutions.

Prospects look best for doctorate holders in applied areas, such as clinical, counseling, health, and industrial-organizational psychology, and for those with extensive technical training in quantitative research methods and computer applications. Post-doctorates are becoming increasingly crucial in the fields of research psychology that deal with behavior based on biology.

Fewer opportunities will be available for people with only a bachelor's degree. They may find openings as assistants in rehabilitation centers, or if they meet state certification requirements, as high school psychology teachers.

■ For More Information

For a publication or video on careers in psychology, please contact:

American Psychological Association
750 1st Street, NE
Washington, DC 20002-4242
Tel: 202-336-5707
Web: http://www.apa.org

For brochures on careers in school psychology, please contact:

National Association of School Psychologists
4340 East-West Highway, Suite 402
Bethesda, MD 20814
Tel: 301-657-0270

■ Related Articles

Health Care

Social Services

Psychiatric Technicians

Psychiatrists

Sports Psychologists

Psychometrists

■ **See Psychologists**

Psychotherapists

■ See Psychiatrists

Public Opinion Researchers

■ Overview

Public opinion researchers help measure public sentiment about various products, services, or social issues by gathering information from a sample of the population through questionnaires and interviews. They collect, analyze, and interpret data and opinions to explore issues and forecast trends. Their poll results help business people, politicians, and other decision makers determine what's on the public's mind. It is estimated that there are fewer than 100,000 full-time employees currently in the field, primarily working for the government or private industry in large cities.

■ History

Public opinion research was started in a rudimentary way in the 1830s and 1840s when local newspapers asked their readers to fill out unofficial ballots indicating for whom they had voted in a particular election. Since that time, research on political issues has been conducted with increasing frequency—especially during presidential election years. However, public opinion research is most widely used by businesses to determine what products or services consumers like or dislike.

As questionnaires and interviewing techniques have become more refined, the field of public opinion research has become more accurate at reflecting the individual attitudes and opinions of the sample groups. Companies like the Gallup Poll and the Harris Survey conduct surveys for a wide range of political and economic purposes. While some people continue to question the accuracy and importance of polls, they have become an integral part of our social fabric.

PUBLIC OPINION RESEARCHERS	
SCHOOL SUBJECTS	Business Mathematics Psychology
PERSONAL SKILLS	Communication/ideas Technical/scientific
WORK ENVIRONMENT	Indoors and outdoors Primarily multiple locations
MINIMUM EDUCATION LEVEL	Bachelor's degree
SALARY RANGE	$28,000 to $75,000 to $100,000
CERTIFICATION OR LICENSING	None available
OUTLOOK	About as fast as the average
DOT	205
GOE	07.04.01
NOC	1454

■ The Job

It is the role of public opinion researchers to conduct interviews and gather data that accurately reflect public opinions so decision makers in the business and political worlds have a better idea of what people want on a wide range of issues. Public opinion is sometimes gauged by interviewing a small percentage of the population containing a variety of people who closely parallel the larger population in terms of age, race, income, and other factors. At other times, researchers interview people who represent a certain demographic group. Public opinion researchers may help a company implement a new marketing strategy or help a political candidate decide which campaign issues the public considers important.

Researchers use a variety of methods to collect and analyze public opinion. The particular method depends on the target audience and the type of information desired. For example, if the owner of a shopping mall is interested in gauging the opinions of shoppers, the research company will most likely station interviewers in selected areas around the mall so they can question the shoppers. On the other hand, an advertising firm may be interested in the opinions of a particular demographic group, such as working mothers or teenagers. In this case, the research firm would plan a procedure (such as a telephone survey) providing access to that group. Other field collection methods include interviews in the home and at work as well as questionnaires that are filled out by respondents and then returned through the mail.

Planning is an important ingredient in developing an effective survey method. After they receive an assignment, researchers decide what portion of the population they will survey and develop questions that will result in an accurate gauging of opinion. Researchers investigate whether previous surveys have been done on a particular topic, and if so, what the results were.

It is important that exactly the same procedures be used throughout the entire data collection process so that the survey is not influenced by the individual styles of the interviewers. For this reason, the process is closely monitored by supervisory personnel. *Research assistants* help train survey interviewers, prepare survey questionnaires and related materials, and tabulate and code survey results.

Other specialists within the field include *market research analysts,* who collect, analyze, and interpret survey results to determine what they mean. They prepare reports and make recommendations on subjects ranging from preferences of prospective customers to future sales trends. They use mathematical and statistical models to analyze research. Research analysts are careful to screen out unimportant or invalid information that could skew their survey results. Some research analysts specialize in one industry or area. For example, *agricultural marketing research analysts* prepare sales forecasts for food businesses, which use the information in their advertising and sales programs. *Survey workers* conduct public opinion interviews to determine people's buying habits or opinions on public issues. Survey workers contact people in their homes, at work, at random in public places, or via the telephone, questioning the person in a specified manner, usually following a questionnaire format.

At times public opinion researchers are mistaken for *telemarketers*. According to the Council for Marketing and Opinion Research, public opinion researchers are conducting serious research, collecting opinions whereas telemarketers ultimately are in the business of sales.

■ Requirements

High School

Prospective public opinion researchers should be interested in dealing with problem-solving situations involving data collection and analysis. Because the ability to communicate in both spoken and written form is crucial, high school students interested in becoming public opinion researchers should take courses in English, speech arts, and social studies. In addition, students should take mathematics (especially statistics) and any courses in journalism or psychology that are available. Knowledge of a foreign language is also helpful.

Postsecondary Training

A college degree in economics or business administration provides a good background for public opinion researchers. A degree in sociology or psychology is very helpful for those interested in studying consumer demand or opinion research, while work in statistics or engineering might be helpful for those interested in certain types of industrial or analytical research.

Because of the increasingly sophisticated techniques used in public opinion research, most employers expect researchers to be familiar with computer applications, and many require a master's degree in business administration, sociology, educational psychology, or political science. While a doctorate is not necessary for most researchers, it is highly desirable for those who plan to become involved with complex research studies or work in an academic environment.

A public opinion researcher conducts a marketing survey at a shopping mall using a hand-held computer.

Other Requirements

Public opinion researchers who conduct interviews must be outgoing and enjoy interacting with a wide variety of people. Because much of the work involves getting people to reveal their personal opinions and beliefs, public opinion researchers must be good listeners and as nonjudgmental as possible. Researchers must be patient and be able to handle rejection because some people may be uncooperative during the interviewing process.

Those who work in data analysis should be able to pay close attention to detail and spend long hours analyzing complex data. They may experience some pressure when forced to collect data or solve a problem within a specified period of time. Those who plan questionnaires should have good analytical skills and a strong command of the English language.

■ Exploring

It is often possible for high school students to work as survey workers for a telemarketing firm or other consumer research company. Work opportunities may also be available where one can learn about the coding and tabulation of survey data. Actual participation in a consumer survey may also offer insight into the type of work involved in the field. People interested in pursuing a career as a public opinion researcher are encouraged to talk with professionals already working in the field to learn more about the profession.

■ Employers

Public opinion workers are primarily employed by private companies, such as public and private research firms and advertising agencies. They also work for the government and for various colleges and universities, often in research and teaching capacities. As is usually the case, those with the most experience and education should find the greatest number of job opportunities. Sue Bath, director of human resources for the Gallup Organization, adds that gaining experience in a specific area (such as food products) can give prospective researchers an edge.

■ Starting Out

Many people enter the field in a support position such as a *survey worker, research assistant* or a *coder and tabulator,* and with experience become *interviewers* or work as *data analysts*. Those with applicable education, training, and experience may begin as interviewers or data analysts. College placement counselors can often help qualified students find an appropriate position in public opinion research. Contacts can also be made through summer employment or by locating public and private research companies in the phone book.

■ Advancement

Advancement opportunities are numerous in the public opinion research field. Often a research assistant will be promoted to a position as an interviewer or data analyst and, after sufficient experience in these or other aspects of research project development, become involved in a supervisory or planning capacity.

With a master's degree or doctorate, a person can become a manager of a large private research organization or marketing research director for an industrial or business firm. Those with extended work experience in public opinion research and with sufficient credentials may choose to start their own companies. Opportunities also exist in university teaching or research and development.

■ Earnings

Starting salaries vary according to the skill and experience of the applicant, the nature of the position, and the size of the company. According to a 1997 survey by the National Association of Colleges and Employers, college graduates with degrees in marketing receive starting offers averaging nearly $28,000, depending on the geographical location of the firm. Those working as consultants tend to earn much more, as much as $100,000 per year. Those in academic positions may earn somewhat less than their counterparts in the business community, but federal government salaries are competitive with those in the private sector.

Most full-time public opinion researchers receive the usual medical, pension, vacation, and other benefits that other professional workers do. Managers may also receive bonuses based on the company's performance.

■ Work Environment

Public opinion researchers usually work a standard 40-hour week, although they may have to work overtime occasionally if a project has a tight deadline. Those in supervisory positions may work especially long hours overseeing the collection and interpretation of information.

When conducting telephone interviews or organizing or analyzing data, researchers work in comfortable offices, with typewriters, calculators, and data processing equipment close at hand. When collecting information via personal interviews or questionnaires, it is not unusual to spend time outside in shopping malls, on the street, or in private homes. Some evening and weekend work may be involved because people are most readily available to be interviewed at those times. Some research positions may include assignments that involve travel, but these are generally short assignments.

■ Outlook

According to the U.S. Department of Labor, employment of market research analysts, one type of public opinion researcher, is expected to grow about as fast as the average through 2006. Due to an increasingly competitive economy, employment opportunities in this field are expected to be strong. Job opportunities should be ample for those trained in public opinion research, particularly those with graduate degrees. Specialties in marketing, mathematics, and statistics improve your chances, as does related work experience. Marketing research firms, financial services organizations, health care institutions, advertising firms, and insurance firms are potential employers.

■ For More Information

This nonprofit corporate membership association for advertising, marketing, and media research provides research projects and industry studies.

Advertising Research Foundation
641 Lexington Avenue
New York, NY 10022
Tel: 212-751-5656
Email: arfsite.org
Web: http://www.arfsite.org

The following is an association of 1,500 members who are producers and users of survey research, including those with academic and commercial organizations, foundations, and voluntary groups.

American Association for Public Opinion Research
PO Box 17
47 Hulfich Street
Princeton, NJ 08540
Tel: 609-924-9600
Email: aapor@umich.edu
Web: http://www.aapor.org
Web: http://www.gallup.com

The following professional nonprofit organization for marketing practitioners, educators, and students assists with professional career development and promotes education. It has 45,000 members in 92 countries and 500 chapters in North America.

American Marketing Association
250 South Wacker Drive, Suite 200
Chicago, IL 60606
Tel: 312-648-0536
Email: info@ama.org
Web: http://www.ama.org

This organization is dedicated to the ongoing development, advertising, and promotion of quality concepts, principles, and techniques.

American Society for Quality
611 East Wisconsin
Milwaukee, WI 53202
Tel: 800-248-1946
Email: asqc@asqc.org
Web: http://www.asqc.org

This trade association of 170 commercial, full-service survey research companies in the United States offers networking, a national conference, and legal and financial information.

Council of American Survey Research Organizations
3 Upper Devon
Port Jefferson, NY 11777
Tel: 516-928-6954
Email: casro@casro.org
Web: http://www.casro.org

MRA provides members with opportunities for expanding and developing market research and business skills, and offers assistance and training.

Marketing Research Association
1344 Silas Deane Highway, Suite 306
PO Box 230
Rocky Hill, CT 06067-0230
Tel: 860-257-4008
Web: http://www.mra-net.org

This nonprofit trade association protects the interests of the marketing and opinion research industry. It is involved in consumer awareness campaigns, investigations into abuses of the survey research process, and government lobbying efforts.

Council for Marketing and Opinion Research
170 North Country Road, Suite 1
Port Jefferson, NY 11777
Tel: 800-887-CMOR
Email: info@cmor.org
Web: http://www.cmor.org

■ Related Articles
Advertising and Marketing
Public Relations
Demographers
Marketing Research Analysts

Public Relations Specialists

■ Overview
Public relations specialists develop and maintain programs that present a favorable public image for an individual or organization. They provide information to the target audience (generally, the public at large) about the client, its goals and accomplishments, and any further plans or projects that may be of public interest.

According to the Public Relations Society of America (PRSA), there are approximately 110,000 public relations professionals in the United States. PR specialists may be employed by corporations, government agencies, nonprofit organizations—almost any type of organization. Many PR specialists hold positions in public relations consulting firms or work for advertising agencies. PRSA reports that there are between 7,200 and 12,000 public relations providers, including firms and sole practitioners, in the United States. Most public relations firms are located in large cities, such as New York, Chicago, Los Angeles, and Washington, DC.

■ History
The first public relations counsel was a reporter named Ivy Ledbetter Lee, who in 1906 was named press representative for coal-mine operators. Labor disputes were becoming a large concern of the operators, and they had run into problems because of their continual refusal to talk to the press and the hired miners. Lee convinced the mine operators to start responding to press questions and supply the press with information on the mine activities.

During and after World War II, the rapid advancement of communications techniques prompted firms to realize the need for professional

PUBLIC RELATIONS SPECIALISTS	
SCHOOL SUBJECTS	Business English Journalism
PERSONAL SKILLS	Leadership/management Communication/ideas
WORK ENVIRONMENT	Primarily indoors One location with some travel
MINIMUM EDUCATION LEVEL	Bachelor's degree
SALARY RANGE	$15,000 to $50,000 to $150,000
CERTIFICATION OR LICENSING	None available
OUTLOOK	Faster than the average
DOT	165
GOE	11.09.03
NOC	5124
O*NET	34008

help to ensure their messages were given proper public attention. Manufacturing firms who had turned their productive facilities over to the war effort returned to the manufacture of peacetime products and enlisted the aid of public relations professionals to bring products and the company name forcefully before the buying public.

Large business firms, labor unions, and service organizations, such as the American Red Cross, Boy Scouts of America, and the YMCA, began to recognize the value of establishing positive, healthy relationships with the public that they served and depended on for support. The need for effective public relations was often emphasized when circumstances beyond a company's or institution's control created unfavorable reaction from the public.

Public relations specialists must be experts at representing their clients before the media. The rapid growth of the public relations field since 1945 is testimony to the increased awareness in all industries of the need for professional attention to the proper use of media and the proper public relations approach to the many publics of a firm or an organization—customers, employees, stockholders, contributors, and competitors.

■ **The Job**

Public relations specialists are concerned with one or more of the following types of work: writing reports, news releases, booklet texts, speeches, copy for radio, TV, and film sequences; editing employee publications, newsletters, shareholder reports, and other management communications; contacting the press, radio, and TV as well as magazines on behalf of the employer; handling special events, such as press parties, convention exhibits, open houses, new facility, or anniversary celebrations; making appearances before groups and selecting appropriate platforms for company officers; using a background knowledge of art and layout for developing brochures, booklets, and photographic communications; programming and determining the public relations needs of the employer, defining the goals of the public relations effort, and recommending steps to carry out the program; and supervising the advertising of a company's or an institution's name and reputation as opposed to advertising a company's wares.

The public relations executive consults with management on company behavior to ensure that the company or institution conducts itself in a way that merits public confidence. Public relations workers are alert to any and all company or institutional events that are newsworthy. They prepare news releases and direct them toward the proper media. Public relations specialists working for manufacturers and retailers are concerned with efforts that will promote sales and create goodwill for the firm's products. They work closely with the marketing and sales departments in announcing new products, preparing displays, and attending occasional dealers' conventions.

A large firm may have a *director of public relations* who is a vice president of the company and in charge of a staff that includes writers, artists, researchers, and other specialists. Publicity for an individual or a small organization may involve many of the same areas of expertise but be carried out by only a few people or possibly one person.

Many public relations people work as consultants, rather than as members of the staff of a corporation, college, or hospital. As staff members of a consulting firm, they have the advantage of being able to operate independently, state opinions objectively, and work with more than one type of business or association.

Public relations people are called upon to work with the public opinion aspects of almost every corporate or institutional problem. These can range from a plant opening to a dormitory dedication, from a merger or sale of a subsidiary to the condemnation of land for campus expansion.

Public relations professionals may specialize. *Lobbyists* try to persuade legislators and other office holders to pass laws favoring the interests of the firms or people they represent. *Fund-raising directors* develop and direct programs designed to raise funds for social welfare agencies and other nonprofit organizations.

Early in their careers, public relations specialists become accustomed to having others receive credit for their behind-the-scenes work. The speeches they draft will be delivered by company officers, the magazine articles they prepare may be credited to the president of the company, and they may be consulted to prepare the message to stockholders from the chairman of the board that appears in the annual report.

■ **Requirements**

High School

High school students should take courses in English, journalism, public speaking, humanities, and languages because public relations is based on effective communication with others. Courses such as these will help to develop skills in written and oral communication as well as provide an understanding of different fields and industries to be publicized.

Postsecondary Training

Most people employed in public relations service have a college degree. Major fields of study most beneficial to developing the proper skills are public relations, English, and journalism. Some employers feel that majoring in the area in which the public relations person will eventually work (for example, a science degree) is the best training. A knowledge of business administration is most helpful as is a native talent for selling. A graduate degree may be required for managerial positions, while people with a bachelor's degree in public relations find staff positions with either an organization or a public relations firm.

In 1996, more than 200 colleges and about 100 graduate schools offered degree programs or special courses in public relations. In addition, many other colleges offered at least one course in the field. Public relations programs are sometimes administered by the journalism or communication departments of schools. In addition to courses in theory and techniques of public relations, interested individuals may study organization, management and administration, and practical applications and often specialize in areas such as business, government, and nonprofit organizations. Other preparation includes courses in creative writing, psychology, communications, advertising, and journalism.

Certification or Licensing

The Public Relations Society of America and the International Association of Business Communicators accredit public relations workers who have passed a comprehensive examination. Such accreditation is a sign of competence in this field, although it is not a requirement for employment.

Other Requirements

Today's public relations specialist must be a businessperson first, both to understand how to perform successfully in business and to comprehend the needs and goals of the organization or client. Additionally, the public relations specialist needs to be a strong writer and speaker, with good interpersonal, leadership, and organizational skills.

■ Exploring

Almost any experience in working successfully with other people will help students seeking opportunities in the field of public relations to develop strong interpersonal skills, which are crucial in public relations. Summer work on a newspaper or a PR trade paper or a job with a radio or television station may give insight into communications media. Work as a volunteer on a political campaign can help stu-

dents understand the ways in which people can be persuaded. Being selected as a page for the U.S. Congress or a state legislature may help students grasp the fundamentals of government processes. A job in retail will help them understand some of the principles of product presentation; a teaching job will help them organize their presentation in a logical way.

■ Employers

Public relations workers may be paid employees of the organization they represent or they may be part of a public relations firm that works for organizations on a contract basis. Others are involved in fund-raising or political campaigning. Public relations may be done for a corporation, retail business, service company, utility, association, nonprofit organization, or educational institution.

Most PR firms are located in large cities that are centers of communications. The main offices of most large industries or associations are also in these same large cities, and it is from these offices that the public relations department functions. New York, Chicago, Los Angeles, and Washington, DC, are good places to start a search for a public relations job. Nevertheless, there are many good opportunities in cities across the United States.

According to "Corporate Communications Benchmark-1997," a major research initiative sponsored by Edelman Public Relations Worldwide, Opinion Research Corporation, and the Integrated Marketing Communications Department of Northwestern University's Medill School of Journalism, nearly 90 percent of the 100 major companies surveyed used external communications agencies at corporate headquarters, while only 5 percent reported that their companies did not use any outside agency. Results of this study were reported in IABC's *Communication World Online* in July 1997.

■ Starting Out

There is no clear-cut formula for getting a job in public relations. A person often enters the field after gaining preliminary experience in another occupation closely allied to the field, usually some segment of communications, and frequently, in journalism. Coming into public relations from newspaper work is still a recommended route. Another good method is to gain initial employment as a public relations trainee or intern, or as a clerk, secretary, or research assistant in a public relations department or a counseling firm.

■ Advancement

In some large companies, an entry-level public relations specialist may start as a trainee in a formal training program for new employees. In others, new employees may expect to be assigned to work that has a minimum of responsibility.

They may assemble clippings or do rewrites on material that has already been accepted. They may make posters or assist in conducting polls or surveys, or compile reports from data submitted by others.

As workers acquire experience, they are given more responsibility. They write news releases, direct polls or surveys, or advance to writing speeches for company officials. Progress may seem to be slow, because some skills take a long time to master.

Some advance in responsibility and salary in the same firm in which they started. Others find that the path to advancement is to accept a more attractive position in another firm.

The goal of many public relations specialists is to open an independent office or to join an established consulting firm. To start an independent office requires a large outlay of capital and an established reputation in the field. However, those who are successful in operating their own consulting firms probably attain the greatest financial success in the public relations field.

■ Earnings

A beginning public relations salary might be about $15,000 a year, but within a few years it can increase to $21,000 or more, according to the Public Relations Society of America. Public relations specialists have median annual earnings of about $50,000. Top salaries generally approach $150,000.

According to a 1997 salary survey conducted by the International Association of Business Communicators, account executives in the United States had median salaries of $36,000 and averaged $38,549; specialists had median salaries of $38,300 and averaged $39,287; and independent or self-employed public relations professionals had median salaries of $40,000 and averaged $46,124. Public affairs specialists in the federal government averaged about $52,240 in 1996.

According to a 1996 study by executive search firm Marshall Consultants, as reported in IABC's *Communication World Online*, overall compensation for communications professionals rose 5 to 8 percent. The study also found that investor relations professionals earn higher-than-average incomes, as do media relations specialists, and communicators in the fields of high technology and health care also earn higher incomes. Geographically, compensation was found to be higher in the northeastern United States, especially the New York metropolitan area and other urban areas.

Many PR workers receive a range of fringe benefits from corporations and agencies employing them, including bonus/incentive compensation, stock options, profit sharing/pension plans/401(k) programs, medical benefits, life insurance, financial planning, maternity/paternity leave, paid vacations, and family college tuition. Bonuses can range from 5 to 100 percent of base compensation and often are based on individual and/or company performance.

■ Work Environment

Public relations specialists generally work in offices with adequate secretarial help, regular salary increases, and expense accounts. They are expected to make a good appearance in tasteful, conservative clothing. They must have social poise, and their conduct in their personal life is important to their firms or their clients. The public relations specialist may have to entertain business associates.

The public relations person seldom works the conventional office hours for many weeks at a time; although the workweek may consist of 35 to 40 hours, these hours may be supplemented by evenings and even weekends when meetings must be attended and other special events covered. Time behind the desk may represent only a small part of the total working schedule. Travel is often an important and necessary part of the job.

The life of the public relations executive is so greatly determined by the job that many consider this a disadvantage. Because public relations is concerned with public opinion, it is often difficult to measure the results of performance and to sell the worth of a public relations program to an employer or client. Competition in the consulting field is keen, and if a firm loses an account, some of its personnel may be affected. The demands it makes for anonymity will be considered by some as one of the profession's less inviting aspects. Public relations involves much more hard work and a great deal less glamour than is popularly supposed.

■ Outlook

According to PRSA, employment of public relations professionals is expected to grow faster than average for all other occupations through the year 2006, according to the U.S. Department of Labor Statistics. Competition will be keen for beginning jobs in public relations because so many job seekers are enticed by the perceived glamour and appeal of the field; those with both education and experience will have an advantage.

Most large companies have some sort of public relations resource, either through their own staff or through the use of a firm of consultants. They are expected to expand their public relations activities and create many new jobs. More of the smaller companies are hiring public relations specialists, adding to the demand for these workers.

According to the study by Marshall Consultants (published in IABC's *Communication World Online* in July 1997), the 1996 surge in hiring and today's low unemployment in the corporate communications and public relations fields indicates that compensation levels will continue to increase, even outpacing inflation. The hottest industry appears to be high technology, followed closely by health care. The consumer product or industrial-based business-to-business trade fields seem to be slowing down, and those recruiting PR professionals show less interest in those whose experience is in the nonprofit sector, unless the position is one with a nonprofit organization.

■ For More Information

IABC provides products, services, and activities for professionals in the public relations, employee communications, marketing communications, and public affairs industries. It publishes Communications Worldmagazine, *holds an annual conference, and provides other resource materials.*

International Association of Business Communicators
One Halladie Plaza, Suite 600
San Francisco, CA 94102
Tel: 800-776-4222
Web: http://www.iabc.com

To subscribe to this weekly newsletter for PR professionals, contact:

PR Reporter
PR Publishing Company, Inc.
PO Box 600
Exeter, NH 03833
Tel: 603-778-0514
Web: http://www.prpublishing.com

The world's largest organization for PR professionals provides a forum for addressing relevant issues, plus opportunities for professional development, including seminars, publications, and a national conference.

Public Relations Society of America
Career Information
33 Irving Place
New York, NY 10003
Tel: 212-995-2230
Email: hq@prsa.org
Web: http://www.prsa.org

■ Related Articles

Advertising and Marketing
Public Relations
Advertising Workers
Reporters
Writers

Public Service Directors

■ **See Radio and Television Program Directors**

Public Stenographers

■ **See Stenographers**

Public Transportation Operators

■ Overview

Public transportation operators include drivers of intercity buses, local commuter buses, and local transit railway systems, such as subways and streetcars. Drivers of local bus and railway systems run a predetermined route within a city or metropolitan area, transporting passengers from one designated place to another. Intercity bus drivers travel between cities and states, transporting passengers and luggage on more lengthy trips.

PUBLIC TRANSPORTATION OPERATORS	
SCHOOL SUBJECTS	Mathematics Speech
PERSONAL SKILLS	Following instructions Mechanical/manipulative
WORK ENVIRONMENT	Primarily indoors Multiple locations
MINIMUM EDUCATION LEVEL	High school diploma
SALARY RANGE	$24,044 to $32,094 to $44,595+
CERTIFICATION OR LICENSING	Required by all states
OUTLOOK	About as fast as the average
DOT	913
GOE	09.03.01
NOC	7412
O*NET	97199

Bus drivers must be able to concentrate on the task of maneuvering a large bus through busy city streets without being distracted by the noise from passengers and other traffic.

■ History

In both the United States and Europe, public transportation systems were first developed in the 19th century. As early as 1819, there was a successful horse-drawn bus service in Paris. The idea was subsequently adopted by other major cities, such as New York and London.

The first subway system, initially four miles long, was opened in London in the 1860s. The railcars were powered by steam until 1890, when the system was converted to electricity. New York, Chicago, Paris, Budapest, and many other cities followed with their own subway systems. Streetcar, or trolley, lines and elevated tracks were also built around this time. The first electric-powered elevated train system opened in Chicago in 1895.

The 20th century began with a new vehicle for public transportation—the gasoline-powered bus. Various cities throughout the United States established bus services in the first decade of the century. Trucks fitted with seats and automobiles lengthened for increased seating capacity were among the first buses. As roads improved and better equipment became available, bus systems expanded.

Toward the middle of the 20th century, some transit systems came under the ownership of automotive- or oil-

related businesses that had little interest in maintaining trolley lines. Around the same time, bus systems began to receive government assistance because of greater routing flexibility and other advantages. By the 1950s, buses had largely replaced the country's trolley lines. Subways and elevated tracks, however, stayed in service, as did a few of the trolley systems, notably in San Francisco. In the latter half of the 20th century, some American cities, such as Washington, DC, and San Francisco, built new subway systems, while others expanded their existing underground lines.

■ The Job

The work of an *intercity bus driver* commonly begins at the terminal, where he or she prepares a trip report form, and inspects the bus. Safety equipment, such as a fire extinguisher and a first-aid kit, as well as the vehicle's brakes, lights, steering, oil, gas, water, and tires are checked. The driver then supervises the loading of baggage, picks up the passengers, collects fares or tickets, and answers questions about schedules and routes.

At the final destination, the intercity driver oversees the unloading of passengers and baggage and then prepares a report on the trip's mileage, fares, and time, as required by the Interstate Commerce Commission (ICC). Another report must be completed if an accident or unusual delay occurs.

Intercity bus drivers may make only a single one-way trip to a distant city or a round trip each day, stopping at towns and cities along the route. Drivers who operate chartered buses typically pick up groups, drive them to their destination, and remain with them until it is time for the return trip.

Within a town, city, or extended urban area, *local commuter bus drivers* usually make scheduled stops every block or two. As passengers board the bus, the driver notes passes and discount cards; collects fares, transfers, tokens, or tickets; and issues transfers. Drivers in many cities check student or senior citizen identification cards to be certain that individuals qualify for discount fares. At the end of the day, drivers of local transit buses turn in trip sheets, which might include records of fares received, the trips made, and any delays or accidents during their shift.

In order to reduce the threat of armed robbery, local bus drivers in most major cities do not give change. Passengers instead deposit their exact fare or token in a tamper-resistant box, and the driver looks at the fare through a viewing window to make sure that the correct amount was paid. Some buses have electronic boxes that count the bills and coins and then display the total of the transaction.

Drivers of both intercity buses and local commuter buses must operate their vehicles carefully during trips.

They are required to follow established schedules, but they must do so within the legal speed limits. Bus drivers are also responsible for regulating the interior lights and the heating and air-conditioning systems.

Drivers of subway, streetcar, and other local railway systems have many of the same duties as bus drivers. Subway/elevated train drivers control trains that transport passengers throughout cities and suburbs. They usually sit in special compartments at the front of the train from which they start, slow, and stop the train. Subway drivers obey the signals along their routes, which run underground, at surface levels, or elevated above ground.

Some operators announce stops over the loudspeaker, open and close doors, and make sure passengers do not get caught in the closing doors. Some drivers are assisted by other operators, who collect fares and transfers, open and close doors, and announce stops. In order to remain on schedule, drivers control train speed and the amount of time they spend at each train station. When train malfunctions or emergencies occur, drivers contact dispatchers and may have to evacuate passengers from the train cars.

In general, all public transportation operators must answer questions from passengers concerning schedules, routes, transfer points, and addresses. They are also required to enforce safety regulations, such as a ban on smoking, established by the transit company or the government.

■ Requirements

High School

While still in high school, prospective drivers should take English and speech classes to make them more effective communicators. Math classes might also be helpful in calculating fares and making change. Finally, a driver's education class would be a great start.

Postsecondary Training

Qualifications and standards for bus drivers are established by state and federal regulations. Federal regulations require drivers who operate vehicles designed to transport 16 or more passengers to obtain a commercial or chauffeur's license. In order to receive this license, applicants must pass a knowledge test and a driving test in the type of vehicle they will be operating.

Federal regulations state that intercity bus drivers must be at least 21 years old and in good general health. They must have good hearing and vision; be able to speak, read, and write English well enough to fill out reports, read signs, and talk to passengers; and pass both a written and driving test in the type of bus they wish to drive. A high school diploma is also required. Some companies require bus drivers to be 24 years of age and prefer previous truck or bus driving experience.

Most intercity bus companies and local transit systems give their driver trainees two to eight weeks of classroom and "behind-the-wheel" instruction. In the classroom, trainees learn U.S. Department of Transportation and company work rules, state and municipal driving regulations, and general safe driving practices. They also learn how to read schedules, determine fares, and keep records.

For subway operator jobs, local transit companies prefer that applicants be high school graduates and that they be at least 21 years old. Good vision and hearing and a clean driving record are necessary. For some subway systems, previous experience driving a bus is required. New operators are generally placed in training programs, including classroom and on-the-job training, that range from a few weeks to six months. At the end of the training program, operators must pass qualifying exams covering the operating system, troubleshooting, and emergency procedures.

Other Requirements

Good hand, foot, and eye coordination is important in this career. Because drivers are required to deal regularly with passengers, it is important that they be courteous. An even temperament and a cool head are also very important in driving in heavy or fast-moving traffic or bad weather conditions. Drivers should be able to stay alert and attentive to the task at hand. They must be dependable and responsible, since the lives of their passengers are literally in their hands.

■ Exploring

Any job that requires driving all day can provide important experience for the prospective public transportation operator. Possibilities include a part-time, summer, or full-time position as a truck or taxi driver. Some companies and stores hire pickup and delivery drivers.

It might also be possible to arrange to talk personally with a bus driver or subway operator. Persons already employed in this capacity can give a good, detailed description of the duties, pros, and cons of the position.

■ Employers

The majority of jobs for bus drivers exist in school systems; approximately three out of every four drivers are employed by a school system or a company that provides contract school bus service. The second largest group of drivers work for local transit systems, with the smallest portion working as intercity drivers. According to a 1996 Bureau of Labor Statistics report, there are about 12,000 subway and streetcar operators—located almost exclusively in major urban areas.

■ Starting Out

Those high school students interested in the field should directly contact public transportation companies as well as government and private employment agencies. Labor unions, such as the Amalgamated Transit Union, might know about available jobs. Positions for drivers are sometimes listed in the classified section of the newspaper.

After completing the training program, new drivers may be placed on probation for 30 to 90 days. During this time, they perform their jobs under careful supervision. Many new drivers are initially given only special or temporary assignments—for example, substituting for a sick employee or driving a charter bus to a sporting event. These new drivers may work for several years in these part-time, substitute positions.

■ Advancement

Advancement is usually measured by greater pay and better assignments or routes. For example, senior drivers may have routes with lighter traffic, weekends off, or higher pay rates. Although opportunities for promotion are limited, some drivers may be moved to supervisory or training positions. It is also possible to become a dispatcher—the person who assigns each driver a bus or train, determines whether the buses or trains are running on time, and sends out help when there is a breakdown or accident. A small number of managerial positions also exist. Experienced subway or streetcar operators, for example, may become station managers.

■ Earnings

Earnings for public local transportation operators vary by location and experience. According to the American Public Transit Association, in 1997 local transit bus drivers in cities with more than 2 million inhabitants were paid $17 per hour on average by companies with over 1,000 employees. Companies with fewer than 1,000 employees paid on average $15 per hour. In smaller cities, bus drivers made an average of $14 per hour where populations ranged from 250,000 to 500,000. They made on average $12 per hour where populations were below 50,000. According to American Public Transit Association data, subway train drivers earned an average of $21 per hour.

Almost all public transportation operators belong to a union, such as the Amalgamated Transit Union or the Transport Workers Union. Wages and benefits packages are usually determined through bargaining agreements between these unions and the management of the transit system. Often, benefits include paid health and life insurance, sick leave, free transportation on their line or system, and as much as four weeks of vacation per year.

■ Work Environment

Most public transportation operators work about 35 to 40 hours per week. New drivers, however, often work part-time, though they may be guaranteed a minimum number of hours.

Driving schedules for intercity bus drivers may require working nights, weekends, and holidays. Drivers may also have to spend nights away from home, staying in hotels at company expense. Senior drivers who have regular routes typically have regular working hours and set schedules; however, others do not have regular schedules and must be prepared to work on short notice. The hours can range from six to ten hours a day and from three and a half to six days per week. The Department of Transportation restricts intercity bus drivers from working more than ten hours per day and more than 60 hours per week.

Local transit drivers and subway operators usually have a five-day workweek, with Saturdays and Sundays being considered regular workdays. Some of these employees work evenings and night shifts. Also, to accommodate commuters, some work "split shifts," such as four hours in the morning and four hours in the afternoon and evening, with time off in between.

The lack of direct supervision is one of the advantages of being a bus driver or subway operator. Intercity bus drivers may also find the travel to be a benefit. Disadvantages might include weekend, holiday, or night shifts, and, in some cases, being called to work on short notice. Drivers with little seniority may be laid off when business declines.

Although driving a bus is usually not physically exhausting, drivers are exposed to tension that comes from driving a large vehicle on heavily congested streets and from dealing with many types of passengers.

■ Outlook

The employment outlook for intercity bus and local transit operators is expected to grow as fast as the average for all occupations through the year 2006. As the population increases and local and intercity travel increases, ridership on local and intercity buses should likewise increase. Future government efforts to reduce traffic and pollution through greater funding of public transportation could also greatly improve job opportunities. In addition, thousands of job openings are expected to occur each year because of the need to replace workers who retire or leave the occupation. Because many of these positions offer relatively high wages and attractive benefits, however, job seekers may face heavy competition. Those who have good driving records and are willing to work in rapidly growing metropolitan areas will have the best opportunities.

The outlook for subway operators is expected to be very good. As more cities build new subway systems and add new lines onto existing systems, the need for subway operators will increase. Again, however, because of the attractive features of the job, competition may be intense.

■ For More Information

For salary information on public transit operators, contact:

American Public Transit Association
1201 New York Avenue, NW, Suite 400
Washington, DC 20005
Tel: 202-898-4000

For information on careers in public transportation, contact:

Transport Workers Union
80 West End Avenue
New York, NY 10023
Tel: 212-873-6000

■ Related Articles

Railroads
Transportation
Travel and Tourism
Trucking
Locomotive Engineers
Railroad Clerks
Reservation and Ticket Agents
Route Drivers
Truck Drivers

Publicists
■ See Sports Publicists

Pulp Plant Supervisors
■ See Paper Processing Occupations

Pulp-and-Paper Lab Testers
■ See Paper Processing Occupations

Pumpers
■ See Petroleum Technicians

Purchasing Agents

■ Overview

Purchasing agents work for businesses and other large organizations, such as hospitals, universities, and government agencies. They buy raw materials, machinery, supplies, and services required for the organization. They must consider cost, quality, quantity, and time of delivery.

■ History

Careers in the field of purchasing are relatively new and have come into real importance only in the last half of the 20th century. The first purchasing jobs emerged during the Industrial Revolution, when manufacturing plants and businesses became bigger. This led to the division of management jobs into various specialties, one of which was buying.

By the late 1800s buying was considered a separate job in large businesses. Purchasing jobs were especially important in such industries as railroads, automobiles, and steel. The trend toward creating specialized buying jobs was reflected in the founding of professional organizations, such as the National Association of Purchasing Agents (now the National Association of Purchasing Management) and the American Purchasing Society. It was not until after World War II, however, with the expansion of the U.S. government and the increased complexity of business practices, that the job of purchasing agent became firmly established.

■ The Job

Purchasing agents generally work for organizations that buy at least $100,000 worth of goods a year. Their primary goal is to purchase the best quality materials for the best price. To do this, the agent must consider the exact specifications for the required items, cost, quantity discounts, freight han-

PURCHASING AGENTS	
SCHOOL SUBJECTS	Business Economics Mathematics
PERSONAL SKILLS	Helping/teaching Technical/scientific
WORK ENVIRONMENT	Primarily indoors Primarily one location
MINIMUM EDUCATION LEVEL	High school diploma
SALARY RANGE	$18,400 to $35,000 to $63,000
CERTIFICATION OR LICENSING	Voluntary
OUTLOOK	Little change or more slowly than the average
DOT	162
GOE	11.05.04
NOC	1225
O*NET	13008

LEARN MORE ABOUT IT

Following are some books related to purchasing.

Banning, Kent. *Opportunities in Purchasing Careers.* Lincolnwood, IL: VGM Career Horizons, 1998.

National Learning Corporation. *Assistant Purchasing Agent.* Syosset, NY: National Learning Corp., 1986.

Ritterskamp, James J. *Purchasing Manager's Desk Book of Purchasing Law.* Englewood Cliff, NJ: Prentice-Hall, 1987.

dling or other transportation costs, and delivery time. In the past, much of this information was obtained by comparing listings in catalogs and trade journals, interviewing suppliers' representatives, keeping up with current market trends, examining sample goods, and observing demonstrations of equipment. Increasingly, information can be found through computer databases. Sometimes agents visit plants of company suppliers. The agent is responsible for following up on orders and ensuring that goods meet the order specifications.

Most purchasing agents work in firms that have fewer than five employees in the purchasing department. In some small organizations, there is only one person responsible for making purchases. Very large firms, however, may employ as many as a hundred purchasing agents, each responsible for specific types of goods. In such organizations there is usually a *purchasing director* or *purchasing manager.*

Some purchasing agents seek the advice of *purchase-price analysts,* who compile and analyze statistical data about the manufacture and cost of products. Based on this information, they can make recommendations to purchasing personnel regarding the feasibility of producing or buying certain products and suggest ways to reduce costs.

Purchasing agents often specialize in a particular product or field. For example, *procurement engineers* specialize in aircraft equipment. They establish specifications and requirements for construction, performance, and testing of equipment.

Field contractors negotiate with farmers to grow or purchase fruits, vegetables, or other crops. These agents may advise growers on methods, acreage, and supplies and arrange for financing, transportation, or labor recruitment.

Head tobacco buyers are engaged in the purchase of tobacco on the auction warehouse floor. They advise other buyers about grades and quantities of tobacco and suggest prices.

Grain buyers manage grain elevators. They are responsible for evaluating and buying grain for resale and milling. They are concerned with the quality, market value, shipping, and storing of grain.

Grain broker-and-market operators buy and sell grain for investors through the commodities exchange. Like other brokers, they work on a commission basis.

■ Requirements

High School

Most purchasing and buying positions require at least a bachelor's degree. Helpful high school subjects are English, mathematics, social science, and economics.

Postsecondary Training

Although it is possible to obtain an entry-level purchasing job with only a high school degree, many employers prefer to hire college graduates, and some require college degrees. College work should include courses in general economics, purchasing, accounting, statistics, and business management. A familiarity with computers also is desirable. Some colleges and universities offer majors in purchasing.

Purchasing agents with a master's degree in business administration, engineering, technology, or finance tend to have the best jobs and highest salaries. Companies that manufacture machinery or chemicals may require a degree in engineering or a related field. A civil service examination is required for employment in government purchasing positions.

Certification or Licensing

There are no specific licenses or certification requirements imposed by law for purchasing agents. There are, however, several professional organizations to which many purchasing agents belong, including the National Association of Purchasing Management, the National Institute of Government Purchasing, and the American Purchasing Society. These organizations confer certification on applicants who meet their educational and other requirements and who pass the necessary examinations. The American Purchasing Society, for example, offers two types of certification, the certified purchasing professional (CPP) and certified purchasing executive (CPE). Although such certification is not essential, it is a recognized mark of professional competence that enhances a purchasing agent's opportunities for promotion to top management positions.

Other Requirements

Purchasing agents should have calm temperaments and the self-confidence to be firm in decision making. Because they work with other people, they need to be diplomatic, tactful, and cooperative. A thorough knowledge of business practices and understanding of the needs and activities of the employer are essential. It also is helpful to be familiar with social and economic changes in order to predict the amounts or types of products to buy.

Exploring

If you are interested in becoming a purchasing agent, you can learn more about the field through a summer job in the purchasing department of a business. Even working as a stock clerk can offer some insight into the job of purchasing agent or buyer. You may also talk with experienced purchasing agents about the job and read periodicals, such as *Purchasing Magazine* (http://www.manufacturing.net/magazine/purchasing/), that publish articles on the field. Keeping abreast of economic trends, fashion styles, or other indicators may help you to predict the market for particular products, and making educated and informed predictions is a basic part of any buying job.

Employers

Purchasing agents and buyers work for a wide variety of businesses, both wholesale and retail, as well as for government agencies. Employers range from small stores, where buying may be only one function of a manager's job, to multinational corporations, where a buyer may specialize in one type of item and buy in enormous quantity. Nearly every business that sells products requires someone to purchase the goods to be sold. These businesses are located nearly everywhere there is a community of people, from small towns to large cities. Of course, the larger the town, the more businesses and thus more buying positions. Larger cities provide the best opportunities for higher salaries and advancement.

Starting Out

Students without a college degree may be able to enter the field as clerical workers and then receive on-the-job training in purchasing. A college degree, though, is required for most higher positions. College and university placement services offer assistance to graduating students in locating jobs.

Entry into the purchasing department of a private business can be made by direct application to the company. Some purchasing agents start in another department, such as accounting, shipping, or receiving, and transfer to purchasing when an opportunity arises. Many large companies send newly hired agents through orientation programs, where they learn about goods and services, suppliers, and purchasing methods.

Another means of entering the field is through the military. Service in the Quartermaster Corps of the Army or the procurement divisions of the Navy or Air Force can provide excellent preparation either for a civilian job or a career position in the service.

Advancement

In general, purchasing agents begin by becoming familiar with departmental procedures, such as keeping inventory records, filling out forms to initiate new purchases, checking purchase orders, and dealing with vendors. With more experience, they gain responsibility for selecting vendors and purchasing products. Agents may become *junior buyers* of standard catalog items, *assistant buyers,* or managers, perhaps with overall responsibility for purchasing, warehousing, traffic, and related functions. The top positions are *head of purchasing, purchasing director, materials manager,* and *vice-president of purchasing.* These positions include responsibilities concerning production, planning, and marketing.

Many agents advance by changing employers. Frequently an assistant purchasing agent for one firm will be hired as a purchasing agent or head of the purchasing department by another company.

Earnings

How much a buyer earns depends on various factors, including the employer's sales volume. Mass merchandisers, such as discount or chain department stores, pay among the highest salaries.

In the late 1990s earnings for buyers ranged from about $18,000 for the lowest 10 percent to a high of $63,000 for the top 10 percent. Average salaries ranged from $23,300 to $45,900. In addition to their salaries, buyers often receive cash bonuses based on performance and may be offered incentive plans, such as profit sharing and stock options. Most buyers receive the usual company benefits, such as vacation, sick leave, life and health insurance and pension plans. They generally also receive an employee's discount of 10 to 20 percent on merchandise purchased for personal use.

According to *Purchasing* magazine's 1998 salary survey, the average annual salary for purchasing agents was $54,700. The lowest paid purchasing professional made $15,000 while the highest paid earned $530,000. Nearly half of the survey respondents said they received bonuses as part of their compensation. The survey also found that bigger companies pay more, service buyers earn the most, and the chemical industry pays best. In addition, according to the survey, college graduates fill the highest ranking positions, have the greatest purchasing responsibilities, work for the largest companies, and generally earn the highest average annual compensation.

Work Environment

Working conditions for a purchasing agent are similar to those of other office employees. They usually work in rooms that are pleasant, well lighted, and clean. Work is year-round and generally steady because it is not particularly influenced by seasonal factors. Most have 40-hour workweeks, although overtime is not uncommon. In addition to regular hours, agents may have to attend meetings, read, prepare reports, visit suppliers' plants, or travel. While most work is done indoors, some agents occasionally need to inspect goods outdoors or in warehouses.

It is important for purchasing agents to have good working relations with others. They must interact closely with suppliers as well as with personnel in other departments of the company. Because of the importance of their decisions, purchasing agents sometimes work under great pressure.

■ Outlook

The number of purchasing agents is likely to grow at the average rate for all occupations through the year 2006. Computerized purchasing methods and the increased reliance on a select number of suppliers boost the productivity of purchasing personnel and reduce the number of new job openings. But as more and more hospitals, schools, state and local governments, and other service-related organizations turn to professional purchasing agents to help reduce costs, they will become good sources of employment. Nevertheless, most job openings will be to replace workers who retire or otherwise leave their jobs.

Demand will be strongest for those with a master's degree in business administration or an undergraduate degree in purchasing. Among firms manufacturing complex machinery, chemicals, and other technical products, the demand will be for graduates with a master's degree in engineering, another field of science, or business administration. Graduates of two-year programs in purchasing or materials management should continue to find good opportunities, especially in smaller companies.

■ For More Information

For materials on educational programs in the retail industry, contact:

National Retail Federation
325 7th Street, NW, Suite 1000
Washington, DC 20004
Attn: Vice President of Research, Education and Community Affairs
Tel: 202-783-7971
Web: http://www.nrf.com

For career information, send request marked "Careers" to:

American Purchasing Society
30 West Downer Place
Aurora, IL 60506
Tel: 630-859-0250
Web: http://www.american-purchasing.com

For information about Your Future Purchasing Career *magazine, lists of colleges with purchasing programs, and bios of people in the field, contact:*

National Association of Purchasing Management
Customer Service
2055 East Centennial Circle
PO Box 22160
Tempe, AZ 85285
Tel: 800-888-6276, Ext. 401
Web: http://www.napm.org

For an information packet on purchasing careers in government, contact:

National Institute of Government Purchasing, Inc.
11800 Sunrise Valley Drive, Suite 1050
Reston, VA 20191-5302
Tel: 703-715-9400
Web: http://www.nigp.org

■ Related Articles

Business

Sales

Auctioneers

Buyers

Cashiers

Counter and Retail Clerks

Merchandise Displayers

Retail Business Owners

Retail Managers

Retail Sales Workers

Sales Representatives

Services Sales Representatives

Stock Clerks

Pyrotechnic Effects Specialists

■ **See Special Effects Technicians**

Quality Assurance Analysts

■ See Quality Assurance Testers

Quality Assurance Inspectors

■ See Health and Regulatory Inspectors

Quality Assurance Managers

■ See Quality Assurance Testers

Quality Assurance Testers

■ Overview

Quality assurance testers examine new or modified computer software applications to evaluate whether or not they perform at the desired level. Testers might also verify that computer-automated quality assurance programs function properly. Their work entails trying to crash computer programs by punching in certain characters very quickly, for example, or by clicking the mouse on the border of an icon. They keep very close track of the combinations they enter so that they can replicate the situation if the program does crash. They also offer opinions on the user-friendliness of the program. Any problems they find or suggestions they have are reported in detail both verbally and in writing to supervisors.

■ History

The first major advances in modern computer technology were made during World War II. After the war, it was thought that the enormous size of computers, which easily took up the space of entire warehouses, would limit their use to huge government projects. Accordingly, the 1950 census was computer-processed.

The introduction of semiconductors to computer technology made possible smaller and less expensive comput-

ers. Businesses began adapting computers to their operations as early as 1954. Within 30 years, computers had revolutionized the way people work, play, and shop. Today, computers are everywhere, from businesses of all kinds, to government agencies, charitable organizations, and private homes. Over the years, the technology has continued to shrink computer size and increase speed at an unprecedented rate.

Engineers have been able to significantly increase the memory capacity and processing speed of computer hardware. These technological advances enable computers to work effectively processing more information than ever before. Consequently, more sophisticated software applications have been created. These programs offer extremely user-friendly and sophisticated working environments that would not have been possible on older, slower computers. In addition, the introduction of CD-ROMs to the mass computer market enabled the production of complex programs stored on compact discs.

As software applications became more complicated, the probability and sheer number of errors increased. Quality assurance departments were expanded to develop methods for testing software applications for errors, or "bugs." Quality assurance is now a branch of science and engineering in its own right. "Testing is finally being recognized as an important phase of the product cycle," says Steve Devinney, vice president and managing director of the Quality Assurance Institute in Orlando, Florida. The importance of good testing procedures came to the forefront of the computer industry in the late 1990s with the emergence of the Year 2000 (Y2K) problems. "Testers were second-class citizens," says Steve. "The thought was that if the project was running late, you could just skip the testing. Now, because of the Y2K situation, testing is becoming more important."

The field has changed with the advent of automated testing tools. As technology continues to advance, many quality assurance tests are auto-

QUALITY ASSURANCE TESTERS	
SCHOOL SUBJECTS	Computer science Mathematics
PERSONAL SKILLS	Mechanical/manipulative Technical/scientific
WORK ENVIRONMENT	Primarily indoors Primarily one location
MINIMUM EDUCATION LEVEL	High school diploma
SALARY RANGE	$25,000 to $49,000 to $60,000+
CERTIFICATION OR LICENSING	None available
OUTLOOK	Faster than the average
DOT	033
GOE	11.01.01
NOC	2233

mated. Quality assurance testers also "test the tests," that is, look for errors in the programs that test the software. There will always be a need for quality assurance testers, however, since they, not another computer, are best suited to judge a program from a user's point of view. "The use of tools will increase, but they can never replace humans," notes Steve.

■ The Job

Before manufacturers can introduce a product on the consumer market, they must run extensive tests on its safety and quality. Failing to do so thoroughly can be very expensive, resulting in liability lawsuits when unsafe products harm people or in poor sales when products do not perform well. The nature and scope of quality assurance testing varies greatly. High-tech products, such as computers and other electronics, require extremely detailed technical testing.

Computer software applications undergo a specific series of tests designed to anticipate and help solve problems that users might encounter. Quality assurance testers examine new or modified computer software applications to evaluate whether or not they function at the desired level. They also verify that computer automated quality assurance programs perform in accordance with designer specifications and user requirements. This includes checking the product's functionality (how it will work), network performance (how it will work with other products), installation (how to put it in), and configuration (how it is set up).

Some quality assurance testers spend most of their time working on software programs or playing computer games, just as an average consumer might. If it is a game, for example, they play it over and over again for hours, trying to make moves quickly or slowly to "crash" it. A program crashes if it completely stops functioning due to, among other things, an inability to process incoming commands. For other types of programs, like word processors, quality assurance testers might type very quickly or click the mouse on inappropriate areas of the screen to see if the program can correctly handle such usage.

Quality assurance testers keep detailed records of the hours logged working on individual programs. They write reports based on their observations about how well the program performed in different situations, always imagining how typical, nontechnical users would judge it. The goal is to make the programs more efficient, user-friendly, fun, and visually exciting. Lastly, they keep track of the precise combinations of keystrokes and mouse clicks that made the program crash. This type of record is very important because it enables supervisors and programmers to replicate the problem. Then they can better isolate its source and begin to design a solution.

Programs to be tested arrive in the quality assurance department after programmers and software engineers have finished the initial version. Each program is assigned a specific number of tests, and the quality assurance testers go to work. They make sure that the correct tests are run, write reports, and send the program back to the programmers for revisions and correction. Some testers have direct contact with the programmers. After evaluating a product, they might meet with programmers to describe the problems they encountered and suggest ways for solving glitches. Others report solely to a quality assurance supervisor.

When automated tests are to be run, quality assurance testers tell the computer which tests to administer and then make sure they run smoothly by watching a computer screen for interruption codes and breakdown signals. They also interpret test results, verifying their credibility by running them through special programs that check for accuracy and reliability. Then, they write reports explaining their conclusions.

Some quality assurance testers have direct contact with users experiencing problems with their software. They listen closely to customer complaints to determine the precise order of keystrokes that led to the problem. Then, they attempt to duplicate the problem on their own computers and run in-depth tests to figure out the cause. Eventually, if the problem is not simply a result of user error, they inform programmers and software engineers of the problems and suggest certain paths to take in resolving them.

Some quality assurance testers with solid work experience and bachelor's degrees in a computer-related field might go on to work as *quality assurance analysts*. Analysts write and revise the quality standards for each software program that passes through the department. They also use computer programming skills to create the tests and programs the quality assurance testers use to test the programs. They might evaluate proposals for new software applications, advising management about whether or not the program will be able to achieve its goals. Since they know many software applications inside and out, they might also train users on how to work with various programs.

■ Requirements

High School

Interested in becoming a quality assurance tester? If so, then take as many computer classes as possible to become familiar with how to effectively operate computer software and hardware. Math and science courses are very helpful for teaching the necessary analytical skills. English and speech classes will help you improve your verbal and written communication skills, which are also essential to the success of quality assurance testers.

Postsecondary Training

It is debatable whether or not a bachelor's degree is necessary to become a quality assurance tester. Some companies require a bachelor's degree in computer science, while others prefer people who come from the business sector who have a small amount of computer experience because they best match the technical level of the software's typical users. If testers are interested in advancement, however, a bachelor's degree is almost a mandate.

Most companies offer in-house training on how to test their particular products, since few universities or colleges offer courses on quality assurance testing. "Because no 'state-of-the-art' exists for software testing, especially in packaged software, many companies must scrape together their own ideas of testing competence, or hire outside consultants who can provide useful training," writes James Bach in *The Challenge of Training Testers.*

Certification or Licensing

As the Information Technology industry becomes more competitive, the necessity for management to be able to distinguish professional and skilled individuals in the field becomes mandatory, according to the Quality Assurance Institute. Certification demonstrates a level of understanding in carrying out relevant principles and practices, as well as providing a common ground for communication among professionals in the field of software quality. The organization offers certification programs in certified quality analyst, certified software test engineer, and certified SPICE assessor.

Other Requirements

Quality assurance testers need superior verbal and written communication skills, according to information supplied by ST Labs/Data Dimensions, Inc. They also must show a proficiency in critical and analytical thinking and be able to critique something diplomatically. Quality assurance testers should have an eye for detail, be focused, and have a lot of enthusiasm because sometimes the work is monotonous and repetitive, notes ST Labs/Data Dimensions, Inc. Testers should definitely enjoy the challenge of breaking the system.

Some companies recommend testers have some programming skills in languages such as C, C++, SQL, or Visual Basic. Others prefer testers with no programming ability. "The most important thing is that testers understand the business and the testing tools with which they are working," says Steve. "You have to be a good problem-solver and detective. Testing is a difficult job."

■ Exploring

Students interested in quality assurance and other computer jobs should gain wide exposure to computer systems and programs of all kinds. ST Labs/Data Dimensions, Inc. offers the following advice. Become a power user. Get a computer at home, borrow a friend's, or check out the computer lab at your school. Work on becoming comfortable using the Windows programs and learn how to operate all of the computer, including the hardware, thoroughly. Look for bugs in your software at home and practice writing them up. Keep up with emerging technologies. If you cannot get hands-on experience, read about them. Join a computer group or society. Read books on testing and familiarize yourself with methodology, terminology, the development cycle, and where testing fits in. Subscribe to newsletters or magazines that are related to testing or quality assurance. Get involved with online newsgroups that deal with the subject. Check out sites on the World Wide Web that deal with quality assurance.

If you live in an area where numerous computer software companies are located, like the Silicon Valley in northern California, for example, you might be able to secure a part-time or summer job as a quality assurance tester. In addition, investigate the possibility of spending an afternoon with an employed quality assurance tester to find out what a typical day is like for him or her.

■ Employers

Quality assurance testers are employed throughout the United States. Opportunities are best in large cities and suburbs where business and industry are active. Many work for software manufacturers, a cluster of which are located in Silicon Valley, in northern California. There is also a concentration of software manufacturers in Boston, Chicago, and Atlanta.

■ Starting Out

Positions in the field of quality assurance can be obtained several different ways. Many universities and colleges host computer job fairs on campus throughout the year that include representatives from several hardware and software companies. Internships and summer jobs with such corporations are always beneficial and provide experience that will give you the edge over your competition. General computer job fairs are also held throughout the year in larger cities. Some job openings are advertised in newspapers. There are many online career sites listed on the World Wide Web that post job openings, salary surveys, and current employment trends. The Web also has online publications that deal specifically with quality assurance. You can also obtain information from associations for quality professionals, such as the Quality Assurance Institute, and from computer organizations, including the IEEE Computer Society.

■ Advancement

Quality assurance testers are considered entry-level positions in some companies. After acquiring more experience and technical knowledge, testers might become quality assurance analysts, who write and revise the quality assurance standards or specifications for new programs. They also create the quality assurance examinations that testers use to evaluate programs. This usually involves using computer programming. Some analysts also evaluate proposals for new software products to decide whether the proposed product is capable of doing what it is supposed to do. Analysts are sometimes promoted to *quality assurance manager* positions, which requires some knowledge of software coding, the entire software production process, and test automation. They manage quality assurance teams for specific software products before and beyond their release.

Some testers also go on to become programmers or software engineers.

■ Earnings

Full-time, entry-level quality assurance testers initially earn $25,000 to $43,000 or more per year, depending on the location and size of the company. Testers with degrees who have worked in the industry for less than 10 years usually make approximately $49,000 to $53,000 per year. High-end salaries for those with many years of technical and management experience can reach $60,000 or higher. Testers also generally receive a full benefits package as well, including health insurance, paid vacation, and sick leave. As in many industries, people with advanced degrees have the potential to make the most money.

■ Work Environment

Quality assurance testers work in computer labs or offices. The work is generally repetitive and even monotonous. If a game is being tested, for example, a tester may have to play it for hours until it finally crashes, if at all. This might seem like great fun, but most testers agree that even the newest, most exciting game loses its appeal after several hours. This aspect of the job proves to be very frustrating and boring for some individuals.

Since quality assurance work involves keeping very detailed records, the job can also be stressful. For example, if a tester works on a word processing program for several hours, he or she must be able to recall at any moment the last few keystrokes entered in case the program crashes. This requires long periods of concentration, which can be tiring. Monitoring computer screens to make sure automated quality assurance tests are running properly often has the same effect.

Meeting with supervisors, programmers, and engineers to discuss ideas for the software projects can be intellectually stimulating. At these times, testers should feel at ease communicating with superiors. On the other end, testers who field customer complaints on the telephone may be forced to bear the brunt of customer dissatisfaction, an almost certain source of stress.

Quality assurance testers generally work regular, 40-hour weeks. During the final stages before a program goes into mass production and packaging, however, testers are frequently called on to work overtime.

■ Outlook

The number of positions in the field of quality assurance is expected to grow faster than the average through 2006, according to the U.S. Department of Labor. This trend is predicted despite an increasing level of quality assurance automation. Before, software companies were able to make big profits by being the first to introduce a specific kind of product, such as a word processor or presentation kit, to the marketplace. Now, with so many versions of similar software on the market, competition is forcing firms to focus their energies on customer service. Many companies, therefore, aim to perfect their software applications before they hit the shelves. Searching for every small program glitch in this way requires the effort of a lot of quality assurance testers.

This same push toward premarket perfection helps explain the development of more accurate and efficient quality assurance automation. To stay competitive, companies must refine their quality assurance procedures to ever-higher levels. "In the next few years, testing will begin on Day One of the project," says Steve. "This means that testers will be involved in the process from the beginning because they are the ones who know what the product's functionality should be. Without testing requirements, you cannot do anything."

■ For More Information

For information on the certified quality analyst, certified software test engineer, and certified SPICE assessor certifications, contact:

Quality Assurance Institute
7575 Dr. Phillips Boulevard, Suite 350
Orlando, FL 32819
Tel: 407-363-1111
Web: http://www.qaiusa.com

For information on scholarships, student memberships, and the student newsletter, looking.forward, *contact:*

IEEE Computer Society
1730 Massachusetts Avenue, NW
Washington, DC 20036-1992
Tel: 202-371-0101
Web: http://www.computer.org

Quality Control Engineers and Technicians

■ Overview

Quality control engineers plan and direct procedures and activities involved in the processing and production of materials and goods in order to ensure specified standards of quality. They select the best techniques for a specific process or method, determine the level of quality needed, and take the necessary action to maintain or improve quality performance. *Quality control technicians* assist quality control engineers in devising quality control procedures and methods, implement quality control techniques, test and inspect products during different phases of production, and compile and evaluate statistical data to monitor quality levels.

■ History

Quality control technology is an outgrowth of the Industrial Revolution. As it began in England in the 18th century, each person involved in the manufacturing process was responsible for a particular part of the process. The worker's responsibility was further specialized by the introduction of the concept of interchangeable parts in the late 18th and early 19th centuries. In a manufacturing process using this concept, a worker could concentrate on making just one component, while other workers concentrated on creating other components. Such specialization led to increased production efficiency, especially as manufacturing processes became mechanized during the early part of the 20th century. It also meant, however, that no one worker was responsible for the overall quality of the product. This led to the need for another kind of specialized production worker whose primary responsibility was not one aspect of the product but rather its overall quality.

This responsibility initially belonged to the mechanical engineers and technicians who developed the manufacturing systems, equipment, and procedures. After World War II, however, a new field emerged that was dedicated solely to quality control. Along with specially trained persons to test and inspect products coming off assembly lines, new instruments, equipment, and techniques were developed to measure and monitor specified standards.

At first, quality control engineers and technicians were primarily responsible for random checks of products to ensure they met all specifications. This usually entailed testing and inspecting either finished products or products at various stages of production.

During the 1980s, a quality movement spread across the United States. Faced with increased global competition, especially from Japanese manufacturers, many U.S. companies sought to improve quality and productivity. Quality improvement concepts, such as total quality management, continuous improvement, quality circles, and zero defects gained popularity and changed the way companies viewed quality and quality control practices. A new philosophy emerged, emphasizing quality as the concern of all individuals involved in producing goods and directing that quality be monitored at all stages of manufacturing—not just at the end of production or at random stages of manufacturing.

Today, most companies focus on improving quality during all stages of production, with an emphasis on preventing defects rather than merely identifying defective

QUALITY CONTROL ENGINEERS AND TECHNICIANS	
SCHOOL SUBJECTS	**Mathematics** **Physics**
PERSONAL SKILLS	**Mechanical/manipulative** **Technical/scientific**
WORK ENVIRONMENT	**Primarily indoors** **Primarily one location**
MINIMUM EDUCATION LEVEL	**Associate's degree**
SALARY RANGE	**$17,000 to $40,000 to $70,000**
CERTIFICATION OR LICENSING	**Voluntary**
OUTLOOK	**About as fast as the average**
DOT	**012**
O*NET	**22128**

parts. There is an increased use of sophisticated automated equipment that can test and inspect products as they are manufactured. Automated equipment includes cameras, X rays, lasers, scanners, metal detectors, video inspection systems, electronic sensors, and machine vision systems that can detect the slightest flaw or variance from accepted tolerances. Many companies use statistical process control to record levels of quality and determine the best manufacturing and quality procedures. Quality control engineers and technicians work with employees from all departments of a company to train them in the best quality methods and to seek improvements to manufacturing processes to further improve quality levels.

Many companies today are seeking to conform to international standards for quality, such as ISO 9000, in order to compete with foreign companies and to sell products to companies in countries around the world. These standards are based on concepts of quality regarding industrial goods and services and include documenting quality methods and procedures.

■ The Job

Quality control engineers are responsible for developing, implementing, and directing processes and practices that result in the desired level of quality for manufactured parts. They identify standards to measure the quality of a part or product, analyze factors that affect quality, and determine the best practices to ensure quality.

Quality control engineers set up procedures to monitor and control quality, devise methods to improve quality, and analyze quality control methods for effectiveness, productivity, and cost factors. They are involved in all aspects of quality during a product's life cycle. Not only do they focus on ensuring quality during production operations, they also get involved in product design and product evaluation. Quality control engineers may be specialists who work with engineers and industrial designers during the design phase of a product, or they may work with sales and marketing professionals to evaluate reports from consumers on how well a product is performing. Quality control engineers are responsible for ensuring that all incoming materials used in a finished product meet required standards and that all instruments and automated equipment used to test and monitor parts during production perform properly. They supervise and direct workers involved in assuring quality, including quality control technicians, inspectors, and related production personnel.

Quality control technicians work with quality control engineers in designing, implementing, and maintaining quality systems. They test and inspect materials and products during all phases of production in order to ensure they meet specified levels of quality. They may test random samples of products or monitor production workers and automated equipment that inspect products during manufacturing. Using engineering blueprints, drawings, and specifications, they measure and inspect parts for dimensions, performance, and mechanical, electrical, and chemical properties. They establish *tolerances,* or acceptable deviations from engineering specifications, and direct manufacturing personnel in identifying rejects and items that need to be reworked. They monitor production processes to be sure that machinery and equipment are working properly and set to established specifications.

Quality control technicians also record and evaluate test data. Using statistical quality control procedures, technicians prepare charts and write summaries about how well a product conforms to existing standards. Most important, they offer suggestions to quality control engineers on how to modify existing quality standards and manufacturing procedures. This helps to achieve the optimum product quality from existing or proposed new equipment.

Quality control technicians may specialize in any of the following areas: product design, incoming materials, process control, product evaluation, inventory control, product reliability, research and development, and administrative applications. Nearly all industries employ quality control technicians.

■ Requirements

High School

In high school, prospective engineers and technicians should take classes in English, mathematics (including algebra and geometry), physical sciences, physics, and chemistry. They should also take shop, mechanical drawing, and computer courses. Students should especially seek English courses that will develop their reading skills, the ability to write short reports with good organization and logical development of ideas, and the ability to speak comfortably and effectively in front of a group.

Postsecondary Training

Quality control engineers must have a bachelor's degree in engineering. Many quality control engineers receive degrees in industrial or manufacturing engineering. Some receive degrees in metallurgical, mechanical, electrical, or chemical engineering depending on where they plan to work. College engineering programs vary based on the type of engineering program. Most programs take four to five years to complete and include courses in mathematics, physics, and chemistry. Other useful courses include statistics, logistics, business management, and technical writing.

Educational requirements for quality control technicians vary by industry. Most employers of quality control technicians prefer to hire applicants who have received some specialized training. A small number of positions for technicians require a bachelor of arts or science degree. In most cases, though, completion of a two-year technical program is sufficient. Students enrolled in such a program at a community college or technical school take courses in the physical sciences, mathematics, materials control, materials testing, and engineering-related subjects.

Certification or Licensing

Although there are no licensing or certification requirements designed specifically for quality control engineers or technicians, some may need to meet special requirements that apply only within the industry employing them. Many quality control engineers and technicians pursue voluntary certification to indicate that they have achieved a certain level of competency, either through education or work experience. Such certification is offered through professional associations, such as the American Society for Quality Control (ASQC), and requires passing an examination. Many employers value this certification and regard it as a demonstration of professionalism.

Other Requirements

Quality control engineers need scientific and mathematical aptitudes, strong interpersonal skills, and leadership abilities. Good judgment is also needed, as quality control engineers must weigh all the factors influencing quality and determine procedures that incorporate price, performance, and cost factors.

Quality control technicians should enjoy and do well in mathematics, science, and other technical subjects and should feel comfortable using the language and symbols of mathematics and science. They should have good eyesight and good manual skills, including the ability to use hand tools. They should be able to follow technical instructions and to make sound judgments about technical matters. Finally, they should have orderly minds and be able to maintain records, conduct inventories, and estimate quantities.

■ Exploring

Because quality control engineers and technicians work in a wide variety of settings, prospective engineers and technicians who want to learn more about quality control technology can consider a range of possibilities for experiencing or further exploring such work. Quality control activities are often directly involved with manufacturing processes. Students may be able to get part-time or summer jobs in manufacturing settings, even if not specifically in the quality control area. Although this type of work may consist of menial tasks, it does offer firsthand experience and demonstrates interest to future employers.

Quality control engineers and technicians work with scientific instruments; therefore, academic or industrial arts courses that introduce different kinds of scientific or technical equipment will be helpful, along with electrical and machine shop courses, mechanical drawing courses, and chemistry courses with lab sections. Joining a radio, computer, or science club is also a good way to gain experience and to engage in team-building and problem-solving activities. Active participation in clubs is a good way to learn skills that will benefit you when working with other professionals in manufacturing and industrial settings.

■ Employers

The majority of quality control engineers and technicians are employed in the manufacturing sector of the economy. Because engineers and technicians work in all areas of industry, their employers vary widely in size, product, location, and prestige.

■ Starting Out

Students enrolled in two-year technical schools may learn of openings for quality control technicians through their schools' job placement services. Recruiters often visit these schools and interview graduating students for technical positions. Quality control engineers also may learn of job openings through their schools' job placement services, recruiters, and job fairs. In many cases, employers prefer to hire engineers who have some work experience in their particular industry. For this reason, applicants who have had summer or part-time employment or participated in a work-study or internship program have greater job opportunities.

Students may also learn about openings through help wanted ads or by using the services of state and private employment services. They also may apply directly to companies that employ quality control engineers and technicians. Students can identify and research such companies by using job resource guides and other reference materials available at most public libraries.

■ Advancement

Quality control technicians usually begin their work under the direct and constant supervision of an experienced technician or engineer. As they gain experience or additional education, they are given more responsible assignments. They can also become quality control engineers with additional education. Promotion usually depends upon additional training as well as job performance. Technicians who obtain additional training have greater chances for advancement opportunities.

Quality control engineers may have limited opportunities to advance within their companies. However, because quality control engineers work in all areas of industry, they have the opportunity to change jobs or companies to pursue more challenging or higher-paying positions. Quality control engineers who work in companies with large staffs of quality personnel can become quality control directors or advance to operations management positions.

■ Earnings

Earnings vary according to the type of work, the industry, and the geographical location. Quality control engineers earn salaries comparable to other engineers. Beginning engineers with a bachelor's degree generally earn between $31,000 and $35,000 a year. Those with master's degrees earn salaries of about $41,322 in their first jobs upon graduation. Experienced quality control engineers earn salaries ranging from $35,000 to $70,000.

Most beginning quality control technicians who are graduates of two-year technical programs earn salaries ranging from $17,000 to $21,000 a year. Experienced technicians with two-year degrees earn salaries that range from $21,000 to $36,000 a year; some senior technicians with special skills or experience may earn much more.

Most companies offer benefits that include paid vacations, paid holidays, and health insurance. Actual benefits depend upon the company, but may also include pension plans, profit sharing, 401(k) plans, and tuition assistance programs.

■ Work Environment

Quality control engineers and technicians work in a variety of settings, and their conditions of work vary accordingly. Most work in manufacturing plants, though the type of industry determines the actual environment. For example, quality control engineers in the metals industry usually work in foundries or iron and steel plants. Conditions are hot, dirty, and noisy. Other factories, such as for the electronics or pharmaceutical industries, are generally quiet and clean. Most engineers and technicians have offices separate from the production floor, but they still need to spend a fair amount of time there. Engineers and technicians involved with testing and product analysis work in comfortable surroundings, such as a laboratory or workshop. Even in these settings, however, they may be exposed to unpleasant fumes and toxic chemicals. In general, quality control engineers and technicians work inside and are expected to do some light lifting and carrying (usually not more than 20 pounds). Because many manufacturing plants operate 24 hours a day, some quality control technicians may need to work second or third shifts.

As with most engineering and technical positions, the work can be both challenging and routine. Engineers and technicians can expect to find some tasks repetitive and tedious. In most cases, though, the work provides variety and satisfaction from using highly developed skills and technical expertise.

■ Outlook

The employment outlook depends, to some degree, on general economic conditions. Although many economists forecast low to moderate growth in manufacturing operations through the year 2007, employment opportunities for quality control personnel should remain steady or slightly increase as many companies place increased emphasis on quality control activities.

Many companies are making vigorous efforts to make their manufacturing processes more efficient, lower costs, and improve productivity and quality. Opportunities for quality control engineers and technicians should be good in the food and beverage industries, pharmaceutical firms, electronics companies, and chemical companies. Quality control engineers and technicians also may find employment in industries using robotics equipment or in the aerospace, biomedical, bioengineering, environmental controls, and transportation industries. Lowered rates of manufacturing in the automotive and defense industries will decrease the number of quality control personnel needed for these areas. Declines in employment in some industries may occur because of the increased use of automated equipment that tests and inspects parts during production operations.

■ For More Information

American Society for Quality Control
PO Box 3005
Milwaukee, WI 53201-3005
Tel: 800-248-1946

■ Related Articles

Manufacturing

Construction Inspectors

Industrial Safety and Health Technicians

Manufacturing Supervisors

Paper Processing Occupations

Quality Assurance Testers

Quality Control Inspectors, Coordinators, and Supervisors

■ **See Health and Regulatory Inspectors**

Rabbis

■ Overview

Rabbis are the spiritual leaders of Jewish religious congregations. They interpret Jewish law and tradition and conduct religious services on the sabbath and holy days. Rabbis perform wedding ceremonies and funeral services, counsel members of the congregation, visit the sick, and often take part in community and interfaith affairs.

■ History

The term *rabbi* comes from a Hebrew word meaning "master," and has been used to describe Jewish leaders and scholars for the last 2,000 years. During the Talmudic period (from the 1st to the 5th century AD), the term was used to refer to preachers and scholars.

Over the centuries, rabbis became the leading religious authorities in Jewish communities. It has only been in the last 150 years that rabbis have become salaried officials in religious congregations.

■ The Job

Rabbis serve congregations affiliated with the four separate movements of American Judaism: Conservative, Orthodox, Reconstructionist, and Reform. Regardless of their affiliation, all rabbis have similar responsibilities. Their primary duty is conducting religious services on the sabbath and on holy days. They also officiate at weddings, funerals, and other rites of passage in the Jewish tradition. Rabbis further serve their congregations by counseling members and visiting the sick, as well as supervising and even teaching some religious education courses.

Within Judaism, the rabbi has an elevated status in spiritual matters, but most Jewish synagogues and temples have a relatively democratic form of decision making in which all members participate. Rabbis of large congregations spend much of their time working with their staffs and various committees. They often receive assistance from an associate or assistant rabbi.

Naturally, the Jewish traditions differ among themselves in their view of God and of history. These differences also extend to such variations in worship as the wearing of head coverings, the amount of Hebrew used during prayer, the use of music, the level of congregational participation, and the status of women. Whatever their particular point of view, all rabbis help their congregations learn and understand their traditions and the role of their faith in everyday life.

Many rabbis take on additional responsibilities in the community at large. They may become involved with such social concerns as poverty and drug abuse, or they may take part in interfaith activities with ministers of other religions.

A small but significant number of rabbis do not serve as congregational leaders. They instead serve as educators at Jewish schools and seminaries, as writers and scholars, or as chaplains at hospitals or in the armed forces.

■ Requirements

High School

Many aspiring rabbis informally begin their training early in life in Jewish grade schools and high schools. Aspiring rabbis should take all religious and Hebrew language courses available to them. It is also important to study English and communications to become an effective leader. Business and mathematics courses are a good foundation for administrative work as the leader of a congregation.

Postsecondary Training

Completion of a course of study in a seminary is a prerequisite for ordination as a rabbi. Entrance requirements, curriculum, and length of the seminary program vary depending on the particular branch of Judaism. Prospective rabbis normally need to complete a bachelor's degree before entering the seminary. Degrees in Jewish studies, philosophy, and even English and history can fulfill seminary entrance requirements. It is advisable to study Hebrew at the undergraduate level if at all possible. Seminarians without a solid background in Jewish studies and the Hebrew language may have to take remedial courses.

While seminary studies differ between the four movements of Judaism, there are many similarities between them. Most seminary programs lead to the Master of Arts in Hebrew Letters degree and ordination as a rabbi. Most programs last about five years, and many of them include a period of study in Jerusalem. It is becoming more common for seminarians to complete internships—usually as assistants to experienced rabbis in the area—as part of their educational requirements.

RABBIS	
SCHOOL SUBJECTS	**Foreign language** **Religion**
PERSONAL SKILLS	**Helping/teaching** **Leadership/ management**
WORK ENVIRONMENT	**Primarily indoors** **Primarily one location**
MINIMUM EDUCATION LEVEL	**Master's degree**
SALARY RANGE	**$30,000 to $50,000 to $80,000+**
CERTIFICATION OR LICENSING	**None available**
OUTLOOK	**About as fast as the average**
DOT	**120**
GOE	**10.01.01**
NOC	**4154**
O*NET	**27502**

A rabbi at a Bat Mitzvah

The general curriculum of ordination for all branches of Judaism includes courses in the Torah, the Talmud (post-biblical writings), rabbinic literature, Hebrew philosophy, Jewish history, and theology. Students should expect to study Hebrew for both verbal and written skills. Courses are also offered in education, public speaking, and pastoral psychology. Practical courses in conducting religious services are usually required. Training for leadership in community service and religious education may be available to those who wish to serve outside the traditional synagogue situation.

Other Requirements

In addition to the ordination requirements, a primary consideration in choosing a career in the clergy is a strong religious faith coupled with the desire to help others. Rabbis should be able to communicate effectively and supervise others. They must have self-confidence, initiative, and the ability to deal with pressure. They need to be impartial and attentive when listening to the troubles and worries of congregants. They must be tactful and compassionate in order to deal with people of many backgrounds. They must set a high moral and ethical standard for the members of their congregation. Orthodox seminaries only accept men, but all other denominations accept men and women into the rabbinate.

■ Exploring

Those interested in becoming a rabbi should talk with their own rabbi and others involved in the work of the synagogue or temple to get a clearer idea of the rewards and responsibilities of this profession. Choosing a career as a rabbi requires a good deal of level-headed self-assessment of your suitability for the rabbinate. Prospective rabbis should also spend time in prayer to determine whether they are called to this ministry.

Aspiring rabbis may volunteer at a temple or synagogue in order to get better acquainted with the work of rabbis. Most Jewish seminaries are also eager to speak and work with young people to help them learn about the rabbinate before making a firm decision about it.

■ Employers

Most rabbis are employed by their congregations. Others work for schools, colleges, seminaries, and publications. Some serve as chaplains in hospitals or in the various branches of the armed forces.

■ Starting Out

Only ordained rabbis can work in this profession. Many newly ordained rabbis find jobs through the seminary from which they graduated or through professional rabbinical organizations within their particular Jewish movement. With the growing popularity of internships for seminaries, it is possible that these will lead to permanent positions after ordination. Rabbis generally begin their careers as leaders of small congregations, assistants to experienced rabbis, directors of Hillel foundations on college campuses, or chaplains in the armed forces.

■ Advancement

With experience, rabbis may acquire their own or larger congregations or choose to remain in their original position. The pulpits of large, well-established synagogues and temples are usually filled by rabbis of considerable experience. They may also choose to open new synagogues in growing communities that require more religious facilities. Others may discover that their talents and abilities are most useful in teaching, fund-raising, or leadership positions within their particular movement.

■ Earnings

Salaries for rabbis vary according to the size, branch, location, and financial status of their congregations. Information is limited, but the earnings of rabbis tend to range from $30,000 to $80,000. Smaller congregations offer salaries on the lower end of the scale, usually between $30,000 and $50,000 a year. Other benefits include health insurance, paid vacations, pensions, and car and housing allowance. Rabbis usually receive gifts or fees for officiating at weddings and other ceremonies. Some congregations may allow their rabbi to teach at local universities or other settings to earn additional income.

■ Work Environment

Rabbis work long hours. Like all clergy, rabbis are on call at any hour of the day or night. This can make a rabbi's private life difficult at times, particularly if he or she is married and has a family. As far as accommodations and professional offices are concerned, rabbis are usually well provided for by their congregations.

There is no such thing as a standard workweek. Rabbis have to divide their time between religious services, administrative duties, and pastoral care of their congregations as they see fit. They must also take time for personal prayer and the continuing study of Jewish faith and traditions. Rabbis are generally independent in their positions, responsible only to the board of directors of their congregation rather than to any formal hierarchy.

■ Outlook

Job opportunities for rabbis are generally good but the availability of positions varies with the branch of Judaism to which a rabbi belongs. Orthodox rabbis should have fairly good job prospects as older rabbis retire and smaller communities become large enough to hire their own rabbi. Conservative and Reform rabbis should also have good employment opportunities, especially because of retirement and new Jewish communities. Reconstructionist rabbis should find very good opportunities because this branch of Judaism is growing rapidly.

Opportunities exist in Jewish communities throughout the country. Small communities in the South, Midwest, and Northwest offer the best opportunities for those rabbis who do not mind receiving less compensation and working away from big metropolitan areas.

■ For More Information

The following organizations serve ordained rabbis but can be of some help to those considering the ministry:

Central Conference of American Rabbis (Reform)
355 Lexington Avenue
New York, NY 10017
Tel: 212-972-3636
Web: http://ccarnet.org/

Jewish Reconstructionist Federation
7804 Montgomery Avenue, Suite 9
Elkins Park, PA 19027
Tel: 215-782-8500
Web: http://shamash.org/jrf/

Rabbinical Assembly (Conservative)
3080 Broadway
New York, NY 10027
Tel: 212-280-6000
Web: http://www.rabbinicalassembly.org/

Rabbinical Council of America (Orthodox)
305 Seventh Avenue
New York, NY 10001
Tel: 212-807-7888
Web: http://rabbis.org/

CANTORS

If you are considering a ministry in the Jewish faith and have a good singing voice, you might think about becoming a cantor. *Cantors* are singers who lead the liturgies in synagogues. They are professionals who have almost as much training as rabbis. They generally need to earn a Master of Arts in Sacred Music degree before undergoing investiture as a cantor. While working on the M.A., cantors study the Hebrew language, Jewish history, and the chants used for daily services as well as high holy days. Many also take part in internships at local synagogues to gain practical experience. For someone with a love of music and the Jewish faith, this can be a very rewarding career. The American Conference of Cantors (http://rj.org/acc/) can provide more information.

The following educational institutions can provide information on the training required to become a rabbi; their Web sites are a good place to start:

Hebrew Union College-Jewish Institute of Religion (Reform)
National Office of Admissions
3101 Clifton Avenue
Cincinnati, OH 45220
Tel: 513-221-1875
Web: http://www.huc.edu/

Jewish Theological Seminary of America (Conservative)
3080 Broadway
New York, NY 10027
Tel: 212-678-8000
Web: http://www.jtsa.edu/

Reconstructionist Rabbinical College
1299 Church Road
Wyncote, PA 19095
Tel: 215-576-0800
Web: http://www.rrc.edu/

■ Related Articles

Education

Religious Ministries

Social Services

College Administrators

College Professors

Social Workers

Writers

Radiation Protection Technicians

■ Overview

Radiation protection technicians monitor radiation levels, protect workers, and decontaminate radioactive areas. They work under the supervision of *nuclear scientists, engineers,* or *power plant managers* and are trained in the applications of nuclear and radiation physics to detect, measure, and identify different kinds of nuclear radiation. They know federal regulations and permissible levels of radiation.

■ History

All forms of energy have the potential to endanger life and property if allowed to get out of control. This potential existed with the most primitive uses of fire, and it exists in the applications of nuclear power. Special care must be taken to prevent uncontrolled radiation in and around nuclear power plants. Skilled nuclear power plant technicians are among the workers who monitor and control radiation levels.

RADIATION PROTECTION TCHNICIANS	
SCHOOL SUBJECTS	Mathematics Physics
PERSONAL SKILLS	Mechanical/manipulative Technical/scientific
WORK ENVIRONMENT	Indoors and outdoors Primarily one location
MINIMUM EDUCATION LEVEL	Associate's degree
SALARY RANGE	$25,000 to $33,000 to $42,000
CERTIFICATION OR LICENSING	None available
OUTLOOK	About as fast as the average
DOT	199
GOE	05.03.08
NOC	2263
O*NET	21911T

Around 1900, scientists discovered that certain elements give off invisible rays of energy. These elements are said to be radioactive, which means that they emit radiation. Antoine-Henri Becquerel (1852-1908), Marie Curie (1867-1934), and Pierre Curie (1859-1906) discovered and described chemical radiation before the turn of the century. In 1910, Marie Curie isolated pure radium, the most radioactive natural element, and in 1911 she was awarded the Nobel Prize for Chemistry for her work related to radiation.

Scientists eventually came to understand that radiation has existed in nature since the beginning of time, not only in specific elements on earth, such as uranium, but also in the form of cosmic rays from outer space. All parts of the earth are constantly bombarded by a certain background level of radiation, which is considered normal or tolerable.

During the 20th century, research into the nature of radiation led to many controlled applications of radioactivity, ranging from X rays to nuclear weapons. One of the most significant of these applications, which has impacted our everyday life, is the use of nuclear fuel to produce energy. Nuclear power reactors produce heat that is used to generate electricity.

The biological effects of radiation exposure continue to be studied, but we know that short-term effects include nausea, hemorrhaging, and fatigue; long-range and more dangerous effects include cancer, lowered fertility, and possible birth defects. These factors have made it absolutely clear that if radiation energy is to be used for any purpose, the entire process must be controlled. Thus, appropriate methods of radiation protection and monitoring have been developed; it is the radiation protection technician's job to insure that these methods are accurately and consistently employed.

■ The Job

The work of radiation protection technicians is to protect workers, the general public, and the environment from overexposure to radiation. Many of their activities are highly technical in nature: they measure radiation and radioactivity levels in work areas and in the environment by collecting samples of air, water, soil, plants, and other materials; record test results and inform the appropriate personnel when tests reveal deviations from acceptable levels; help power plant workers set up equipment that automatically monitors processes within the plant and records deviations from established radiation limits; and calibrate and maintain such equipment using hand tools.

Radiation protection technicians work efficiently with people of different technical backgrounds. They instruct operations personnel in making the necessary adjustments to correct problems such as excessive radiation levels, discharges of radionuclide materials above acceptable levels, or improper chemical levels. They also prepare reports for supervisory and regulatory agencies.

Radiation protection technicians are concerned with "ionizing radiation," particularly three types known by the Greek letters alpha, beta, and gamma. Ionization occurs when atoms split and produce charged particles. If these particles strike the cells in the body, they cause damage by upsetting well-ordered chemical processes.

In addition to understanding the nature and effects of radiation, technicians working in nuclear power plants also know the principles of nuclear power plant systems. They have a thorough knowledge of the instrumentation that is used to monitor radiation in every part of the plant and its immediate surroundings. They also play an important role in educating other workers about radiation monitoring and control.

Radiation protection technicians deal with three basic radiation concepts: time, distance from the radiation source, and shielding. When considering time, technicians know that certain radioactive materials break down into stable elements in a matter of days or even minutes. Other materials, however, continue to emit radioactive particles for thousands of years. Radiation becomes less intense in proportion to its distance from the source, so distance is an important concept in controlling radiation exposure. Shielding is used to protect people from radiation exposure and appropriate materials with a specific thickness need to be used to block emission of radioactive particles.

Because radiation generally cannot be seen, heard, or felt, radiation protection technicians use special instruments to detect and measure it and to determine the extent of radiation exposure. Technicians use devices that measure the ionizing effect of radiation on matter to determine the presence of radiation and, depending on the instrument used, the degree of radiation danger in a given situation.

Two such devices are Geiger counters and dosimeters, which measure received radiation doses. Dosimeters are often in the form of photographic badges worn by personnel and visitors. These badges are able to detect radioactivity because it shows up on photographic film. Radiation protection technicians calculate the amount of time that personnel may safely work in contaminated areas, considering maximum radiation exposure limits and the radiation level in the particular area. They also use specialized equipment to detect and analyze radiation levels and chemical imbalances.

Finally, although the radiation that is released into the environment surrounding a nuclear facility is generally far less than that released through background radiation sources, radiation protection technicians must be prepared to monitor people and environments during abnormal situations and emergencies.

A radiation protection technician monitors the mechanical removal of hazardous waste from electrical transfomers and capacitors.

Under normal working conditions, technicians monitor the work force, the plant, and the nearby environment for radioactive contamination; test plant workers for radiation exposure, both internally and externally; train personnel in the proper use of monitoring and safety equipment; help *nuclear materials handling technicians* prepare and monitor radioactive waste shipments; perform basic radiation orientation training; take radiation contamination and control surveys, air sample surveys, and radiation level surveys; maintain and calibrate radiation detection instruments using standard samples to determine accuracy; ensure that radiation protection regulations, standards, and procedures are followed and records kept of all regular measurements and radioactivity tests; and carry out decontamination procedures that ensure the safety of plant workers and the continued operation of the plant.

■ Requirements

High School

Prospective technicians should have a solid background in basic high school mathematics and science. Other courses include four years of English, two years of mathematics including algebra, and one year of physical science, preferably physics. Computer courses, vocational machine shop operations, and blueprint reading also provide a good foundation for further studies.

Postsecondary Training

After high school, the prospective technician should study at a two-year technical school or community college. Several public or private technical colleges offer programs designed to prepare nuclear power plant radiation protection technicians. Other programs, called nuclear technology or nuclear materials handling technology, also provide a good foundation. You should be prepared to spend from one to two years in postsecondary technical training taking courses in chemistry, physics, laboratory procedures, and technical writing. Because the job entails accurately recording important data and writing clear, concise technical reports, technicians need excellent writing skills.

A typical first year of study for radiation protection technicians includes introduction to nuclear technology, radiation physics, mathematics, electricity and electronics, technical communications, radiation detection and measurement, inorganic chemistry, radiation protection, blueprint reading, quality assurance/quality control, nuclear systems, computer applications, radiation biology, as well as industrial organizations and institutions.

Coursework in the second year includes technical writing, advanced radiation protection, applied nuclear chemistry, radiological emergencies, advanced chemistry, radiation shielding, radiation monitoring techniques, advanced radionuclide analysis, occupational safety and health, nuclear systems and safety, radioactive materials disposal and management, and industrial economics.

Students who graduate from nuclear technician programs are usually hired by nuclear power plants or other companies and institutions involved in nuclear-related activities. These employers provide a general orientation to their operations and further training specific to their procedures.

Certification or Licensing

At present, there are no special requirements for licensing or certification of nuclear power plant radiation protection technicians. Some graduates of radiation control technology programs, however, may want to become *nuclear materials handling technicians*. For this job, licensing may be required, but the employer usually will arrange for the special study needed to pass the licensing test.

Other Requirements

Federal security clearances are required for workers in jobs that involve national security. Nuclear Regulatory Commission (NRC) clearance is required for both government and private industry employees in securing related positions. Certain projects may necessitate military clearance with or without NRC clearance. Employers usually help arrange such clearances.

■ Exploring

The school's vocational guidance counselor is a valuable resource for high school students interested in this occupation. Students also can obtain information from the occupational information centers and their staff at community and technical colleges.

High school science classes may be the best places to gain familiarity with the nature of this career. Science teachers may be able to arrange field trips and invite speakers to describe various careers. Nuclear reactor facilities are unlikely to provide tours, but they may be able to furnish literature on radiation physics and radiation control. Radiation protection technicians employed at nuclear-related facilities may be invited to speak about their chosen field.

Radiation is used for medical diagnosis and treatment in hospitals all over the country. Radiology departments of local hospitals often provide speakers for science or career classes.

In addition, a utilities company with a nuclear-fired plant may be able to offer a tour of the visitor's center at the plant, where much interesting and valuable information about nuclear power plant operation is available. Small reactors used for experiments, usually affiliated with universities and research centers, also may give tours.

■ Employers

Radiation protection technicians are employed by government agencies, such as the Department of Energy and the Department of Defense as well as electric power utilities that operate nuclear plants. Other than utilities, technicians are employed by nuclear materials handling and processing facilities, regulatory agencies, nondestructive testing firms, radiopharmaceutical industries, nuclear waste handling facilities, nuclear service firms, and national research laboratories.

■ Starting Out

The best way to enter this career is to graduate from a radiation control technology program. Another excellent way to enter the career is to join the United States Navy and enter its technical training program for various nuclear specialties.

Graduates of radiation control technology programs are usually interviewed and recruited while in school by representatives of companies with nuclear facilities. At that time, they may be hired with arrangements made to begin work soon after graduation. Graduates from strong programs may receive several attractive job offers.

Entry-level jobs for graduate radiation protection technicians include the position of *radiation monitor*. This position involves working in personnel monitoring, decontamination, and area monitoring and reporting. Another entry-level job is *instrument calibration technician*. These technicians test instrument reliability, maintain standard sources, and adjust and calibrate instruments. *Accelerator safety technicians* evaluate nuclear accelerator operating procedures and shielding to ensure personnel safety. *Radiobiology technicians* test the external and internal effects of radiation in plants and animals, collect data on facilities where potential human exposure to radiation exists, and recommend improvements in techniques or facilities.

Hot-cell operators conduct experimental design and performance tests involving materials of very high radioactivity. *Environmental survey technicians* gather and prepare radioactive samples from air, water, and food specimens. They may handle nonradioactive test specimens for test comparisons with National Environmental Policy Act standards. *Reactor safety technicians* study personnel safety through the analysis of reactor procedures and shielding and through analysis of radioactivity tests.

■ Advancement

A variety of positions is available for experienced and well-trained radiation protection technicians. *Research technicians* develop new ideas and techniques in the radiation and nuclear field. *Instrument design technicians* design and prepare specifications and tests for use in advanced radiation instrumentation. *Customer service specialists* work in sales, installation, modification, and maintenance of customers' radiation control equipment. *Radiochemistry technicians* prepare and analyze new and old compounds, utilizing the latest equipment and techniques. *Health physics technicians* train new radiation monitors, analyze existing procedures, and conduct tests of experimental design and radiation safety. *Soils evaluation technicians* assess soil density, radioactivity, and moisture content to determine sources of unusually high levels of radioactivity. *Radioactive waste analysts* develop waste disposal techniques, inventory stored waste, and prepare waste for disposal.

Some of the most attractive opportunities for experienced radiation protection technicians include working as radiation experts for a company or laboratory, or as acting as consultants. Consultants may work for nuclear engineering or nuclear industry consulting firms or manage their own consulting businesses.

■ Earnings

The earnings of radiation protection technicians who are beginning their careers depend on what radiation safety program they work in (nuclear power, federal or state agencies, research laboratories, medical facilities, etc.). They may begin as salaried staff or be paid hourly wages. Technicians who receive hourly wages usually work in shifts and receive premium pay for overtime.

Trained technicians earn annual salaries of up to $25,000 a year. After three to five years of experience, they can expect to earn as much as $33,000 a year. Consultants may earn as much as $42,000 a year. Earnings are also affected by whether technicians remain in their entry-level jobs or become supervisors and whether they are able to

pass a national competency test that makes them a Nationally Registered Radiation Protection Technologist.

Technicians usually receive benefits, such as paid holidays and vacations, insurance plans, and retirement plans. Because of the rapid changes that occur in the radiation safety industry, many employers pay for job-related study and participation in workshops, seminars, and conferences.

■ Work Environment

Depending on the employer, work environments vary from offices and control rooms to relatively cramped and cold areas of power plants.

Radiation protection technicians wear film badges or carry pocket monitors to measure their exposure to radiation. Like all other nuclear power plant employees, technicians wear safety clothing, and radiation-resistant clothing may be required in some areas. This type of clothing contains materials that reduce the level of radiation before it reaches the human body.

In some of the work done by radiation protection technicians, radiation shielding materials, such as lead and concrete, are used to enclose radioactive materials while the technician manipulates these materials from outside the contaminated area. These procedures are called hot-cell operations. In some areas, automatic alarm systems are used to warn of radiation hazards so that proper protection can be maintained.

■ Outlook

At the end of the 1990s, there were 110 nuclear power plants licensed to operate in 32 of the United States. However, there are no orders for new nuclear power plants to be built, and several have begun plans to permanently shut down and become decommissioned. Consequently, the total number of plants in the United States will begin to decrease in the foreseeable future.

Even if the nuclear power industry experiences a decline, the employment outlook for radiation protection technicians should remain strong. Technicians are needed to support radiation safety programs in Department of Energy facilities, Department of Defense facilities, hospitals, universities, state regulatory programs, federal regulatory agencies, and many industrial activities. New technicians will be needed to replace retiring technicians or technicians who leave the field for other reasons. Increased efforts to enforce and improve safety standards may also result in new jobs for technicians. Because radiation programs have been in development for half a century, most of the radiation safety programs are well-established and rely primarily on technicians to keep them running.

■ For More Information

This nonprofit, international, scientific, educational organization provides career information, publications, scholarships, and seminars and cooperates in educational efforts.

American Nuclear Society
555 North Kensington Avenue
La Grange Park, IL 60525
Tel: 708-352-6611
Web: http://www.ans.org

This professional organization of more than 6,000 members promotes the practice of radiation safety. Society activities include encouraging research and radiation science, developing standards, and disseminating radiation safety information.

Health Physics Society
1313 Dolly Madison Boulevard, Suite 402
McLean, VA 22101
Tel: 703-790-1745
Email: HPS@BurkInc.com
Web: http://www.hps.org

This organization is dedicated to the peaceful use of nuclear technologies. Its 300 members provide a strong voice in matters of national energy policy.

Nuclear Energy Institute
1776 I Street, NW, Suite 400
Washington, DC 20006
Tel: 202-739-8000
Web: http://www.nei.org/intro store.html

■ Related Articles

Energy
The Environment
Nuclear Power
Health and Regulatory Inspectors
Industrial Radiographers
Industrial Safety and Health Technicians
Nuclear Engineers
Nuclear Reactor Operators and Technicians
Occupational Safety and Health Workers
Physicists
Power Plant Occupations

Radio and Television Broadcast News Analysts

■ See Radio and Television Newscasters, Reporters, and Announcers

Radio and Television Newscasters, Reporters, and Announcers

■ Overview

Radio and television announcers present news and commercial messages from a script. They identify the station, announce station breaks, and introduce and close shows. Interviewing guests, making public service announcements, and conducting panel discussions may also be part of the announcer's work. In small stations the local announcer may keep the program log, run the transmitter, and cue the changeover to network broadcasting as well as write scripts or rewrite news releases. About 52,000 people are employed as radio and television announcers and newscasters in the United States.

■ History

Guglielmo Marconi, a young Italian engineer, first transmitted a radio signal in his home in 1895. Radio developed rapidly as people began to comprehend the tremendous possibilities. The stations KDKA in Pittsburgh and WWWJ in Detroit began broadcasting in 1920. Within 10 years, there were radio stations in all the major cities in the United States and broadcasting had become big business. The National Broadcasting Company became the first network in 1926 when it linked together 25 stations across the country. The Columbia Broadcasting System was organized in the following year. In 1934, the Mutual Broadcasting Company was founded. The years between 1930 and 1950 may be considered the zenith years of the radio industry. With the coming of television, radio broadcasting took second place in importance as entertainment for the home—but radio's commercial and communications value should not be underestimated.

Discoveries that led to the development of television can be traced as far back as 1878, when William Crookes invented a tube that produced the cathode ray. Other inventors who contributed to the development of television were Vladimir Zworykin, a Russian-born scientist who came to this country at the age of 20 and is credited with inventing the iconoscope before he was 30; Charles Jenkins, who invented a scanning disk, using certain vacuum tubes and photoelectric cells; and Philo Farnsworth, who invented an image dissector. WNBT and WCBW, the first commercially licensed television stations, went on the air in 1941 in New York. Both suspended operations during World War II but resumed them in 1946 when television sets began to be manufactured on a commercial scale.

As radio broadcasting was growing across the country in its early days, the need for announcers grew. They identified the station and brought continuity to broadcast time by linking one program with the next as well as participating in many programs. In the early days (and even today in smaller stations) announcers performed a variety of jobs around the station. When television began, many radio announcers and newscasters started to work in the new medium. The need for men and women in radio and television broadcasting has continued to grow. Television news broadcasting requires specialized "on-camera" personnel—anchors, television news reporters, broadcast news analysts, consumer reporters, and sports reporters (sportscasters).

■ The Job

Some announcers merely announce; others do a multitude of other jobs, depending on the size of the station. But the nature of their announcing work remains the same.

An announcer is engaged in an exacting career. The necessity for finishing a sentence or a program at a precisely planned moment makes this a demanding and often tense career. It is absolutely essential that announcers project a sense of calm to their audiences, regardless of the activity and tension behind the scenes.

The announcer who plays recorded music interspersed with a variety of advertising material and informal commentary is called a *disc jockey*. This title arose when most music was recorded on conventional flat records or discs. Today much of the recorded music used in commercial radio stations is on magnetic tape or compact discs. Disc jockeys serve as a bridge between the music itself and the listener. They may perform such public services as announcing the time, the weather forecast, or important news. It can be a lonely job, since many disc jockeys are the only person in the studio. But because their job is to maintain the good spirits of their audience and to attract new listeners, disc jockeys must possess the ability be relaxed and cheerful. (For more information on this career, see the article, *Disc Jockeys*.)

Unlike the more conventional radio or television announcer, the disc jockey is not bound by a written script. Except for the commercial announcements, which must be read as written, the disc jockey's statements are usually spontaneous. Disc jockeys usually are not required to play a musical selection to the end; they may fade out a record when it interferes with a predetermined schedule for commercials, news, time checks, or weather reports.

Announcers who cover sports events for the benefit of the listening or viewing audience are known as *sportscast-*

ers. This is a highly specialized form of announcing as sportscasters must have extensive knowledge of the sports that they are covering, plus the ability to describe events quickly and accurately.

Often the sportscaster will spend several days with team members, observing practice sessions, interviewing people, and researching the history of an event or of the teams to be covered. The more information that a sportscaster can acquire about individual team members, company they represent, tradition of the contest, ratings of the team, and community in which the event takes place, the more interesting the coverage is to the audience.

The announcer who specializes in reporting the news to the listening or viewing public is called a *newscaster.* This job may require simply reporting facts, or it may include editorial commentary. Newscasters may be given the authority by their employers to express their opinions on news items or the philosophies of others. They must make judgments about which news is important and which is not. In some instances, they write their own scripts, based on facts that are furnished by international news bureaus. In other instances, they read text exactly as it comes in over a teletype machine. They may make as few as one or two reports each day if they work on a major news program, or they may broadcast news for five minutes every hour or half-hour. Their delivery is usually dignified, measured, and impersonal.

RADIO AND TELEVISION NEWSCASTERS, REPORTERS, AND ANNOUNCERS	
SCHOOL SUBJECTS	English Speech
PERSONAL SKILLS	Communication/ideas
WORK ENVIRONMENT	Primarily indoors Primarily one location
MINIMUM EDUCATION LEVEL	Some postsecondary training
SALARY RANGE	$8,000 to $23,000 to $85,000+
CERTIFICATION OR LICENSING	None available
OUTLOOK	Decline
DOT	131
GOE	11.08.03
NOC	5231
O*NET	34017

A newscaster delivers the nightly news.

The *anchor* generally summarizes and comments on one aspect of the news at the end of the scheduled broadcast. This kind of announcing differs noticeably from that practiced by the sportscaster, whose manner may be breezy and interspersed with slang, or from the disc jockey, who may project a humorous, casual, or intimate image.

The newscaster may specialize in certain aspects of the news, such as economics, politics, or military activity. Newscasters also introduce films and interviews prepared by *news reporters* that provide in-depth coverage and information on the event being reported. *Radio and television broadcasting news analysts* are often called *commentators,* and they interpret specific events and discuss how these may affect individuals or the nation. They may have a specified daily slot for which material must be written, recorded, or presented live. They gather information that is analyzed and interpreted through research and interviews and cover public functions such as political conventions, press conferences, and social events.

Smaller television stations may have an announcer who performs all the functions of reporting, presenting, and commenting on the news as well as introducing network and news service reports.

Many television and radio announcers have become well-known public personalities in broadcasting. They may participate in community activities as master of ceremonies at banquets and other public events.

■ Requirements

Although there are no formal educational requirements for entering the field of radio and television announcing, many large stations prefer college-educated applicants. The general reason given for this preference is that announcers with broad educational and cultural backgrounds are better prepared to successfully meet a variety of unexpected or emergency situations. The greater the knowledge of geography, history, literature, the arts, political science, music, science, and of the sound and structure of the English language, the greater the announcer's value.

High School

In high school, you should focus on a college preparatory curriculum, according to Steve Bell, a professor of telecommunications at Ball State University. A former network anchor who now teaches broadcast journalism, he says, "One trend that concerns me is that some high schools are developing elaborate radio and television journalism programs that take up large chunks of academic time, and I think that is getting the cart before the horse. There's nothing wrong with one broadcast journalism course or extracurricular activities, but not at the expense of academic hours."

In that college preparatory curriculum, you should learn how to write and use the English language in literature and communication classes. Subjects such as history, government, economics, and a foreign language are also important.

Postsecondary Training

When it comes to college, having your focus in the right place is essential, according to Professor Bell. "You want to be sure you're going to a college or university that has a strong program in broadcast journalism, where they also put a strong emphasis on the liberal arts core."

Some advocate a more vocational type of training in preparation for broadcast journalism, but Bell cautions against strictly vocational training. "The ultimate purpose of college is to have more of an education than you have from a trade school. It is important to obtain a broad-based understanding of the world we live in, especially if your career goal is to become an anchor."

A strong liberal arts background with emphasis in journalism, English, political science, or economics is advised, as well as a telecommunications or communications major.

Other Requirements

A pleasing voice and personality are of great importance to prospective announcers. They must be levelheaded and able to react calmly in the face of a major crisis. People's lives may depend on an announcer's ability to remain calm during a disaster. There are also many unexpected circumstances that demand the skill of quick thinking. For example, if guests who are to appear on a program do not arrive or become too nervous to go on the air, the announcer must compensate immediately and fill the airtime. He or she must smooth over an awkward phrase, breakdown in equipment, or other technical difficulty.

Good diction and English usage, thorough knowledge of correct pronunciation, and freedom from regional dialects are very important. A factual error, grammatical error, or mispronounced word can bring letters of criticism to station managers.

Those who aspire to careers as television announcers must present a good appearance and have no nervous mannerisms. Neatness, cleanliness, and careful attention to the details of proper dress are important. The successful television announcer must have the combination of sincerity and showmanship that attracts and captures an audience.

Broadcast announcing is a highly competitive field. Although there may not be any specific training program required by prospective employers, station officials pay particular attention to taped auditions of an applicant's delivery or, in the case of television, to videotaped demos of sample presentations.

A Federal Communications Commission license or permit is no longer required for broadcasting positions. Union membership may be required for employment with large stations in major cities and is a necessity with the networks. The largest talent union is the American Federation of Television and Radio Artists (AFTRA). Most small stations, however, are nonunion.

■ Exploring

If a career as an announcer sounds interesting, try to get a summer job at a radio or television station. Although you will probably not have the opportunity to broadcast, you may be able to judge whether or not the type of work appeals to you as a career.

Any chance to speak or perform before an audience should be welcomed. Appearing as a speaker or performer can show whether or not you have the stage presence necessary for a career in front of a microphone or camera.

Many colleges and universities have their own radio and television stations and offer courses in radio and television. You can gain valuable experience working at college-owned stations. Some radio stations, cable systems, and TV stations offer financial assistance, internships, and co-op work programs, as well as scholarships and fellowships.

■ Employers

Almost all radio and television announcers are on staff at one of the 12,199 radio stations or 1,580 television stations around the country. Some, however, work on a freelance basis on individual assignments for networks, stations, advertising agencies, and other producers of commercials.

Some companies own several television or radio stations; some belong to networks such as ABC, CBS, NBC, or FOX, while others are independent. While radio and television stations are located throughout the United States,

GLOSSARY

Audition tape: Sent by applicants to stations where they would like to work

FCC: The Federal Communications Commission is an independent federal agency that regulates television, cable, and radio.

Newscast: The program that airs the news on television or radio.

Ratings: Determined by Nielsen (television) or Arbitron (radio), ratings help rank the stations and attract advertising dollars.

Script: The written copy read by the reporters.

TelePrompTer: For television broadcasts, this machine projects the script for on-air reporters to read.

major markets where better paying jobs are found, are generally near large metropolitan areas.

■ Starting Out

One way to enter this field is to apply for an entry-level job rather than an announcer position. It is also advisable to start at a small station. Most announcers start in jobs such as production secretary, production assistant, researcher, or reporter in small stations. As opportunities arise, they move from one job to another. Work as a disc jockey, sportscaster, or news reporter may become available. Network jobs are few, and the competition for them is great. An announcer must have several years of experience as well as a college education to be considered for these positions.

An announcer is employed only after an audition. Applicants should carefully select audition material to show a prospective employer the full range of one's abilities. In addition to presenting prepared materials, applicants may be asked to read material that they have not seen previously, such as a commercial, news release, dramatic selection, or poem.

■ Advancement

Most successful announcers advance from small stations to large ones. Experienced announcers usually have held several jobs. The most successful announcers may be those who work for the networks. Usually, because of network locations, announcers must live in or near the country's largest cities.

Some careers lead from announcing to other aspects of radio or television work. More people are employed in sales, promotion, and planning than in performing; often they are paid more than announcers. Because the networks employ relatively few announcers in proportion to the rest of the broadcasting professionals, a candidate must have several years of experience and specific background in several news areas before being considered for an audition. These top announcers generally are college graduates.

■ Earnings

According to a 1998 Salary Survey by the Radio and Television News Directors Association (RTNDA), there is a wide range of salaries for announcers. For radio reporters and announcers, the median salary was $20,000 with a low of $10,000 and a high of $75,000. For television reporters and announcers, the median salary was $23,000 with a low of $8,000 and a high of $85,000.

For both radio and television, salaries are higher in the larger markets. Nationally known announcers and newscasters who appear regularly on network television programs receive salaries that may be quite impressive. For those who become top television personalities in large metropolitan areas, salaries also are quite rewarding.

Most radio or television stations broadcast 24 hours a day. Although much of the material may be prerecorded, announcing staff must often be available and as a result may work considerable overtime or split shifts, especially in smaller stations. Evening, night, weekend, and holiday duty may provide additional compensation.

■ Work Environment

Work in radio and television stations is usually very pleasant. Almost all stations are housed in modern facilities. The maintenance of technical electronic equipment requires temperature and dust control, and people who work around such equipment benefit from the precautions taken to preserve it.

Announcers' jobs may provide opportunities to meet well-known or celebrity persons. Being at the center of an important communications medium can make the broadcaster more keenly aware of current issues and divergent points of view than the average person.

Announcers and newscasters usually work a 40-hour week, but they may work irregular hours. They may report for work at a very early hour in the morning or work late into the night. Some radio stations operate on a 24-hour basis. All-night announcers may be alone in the station during their working hours.

■ Outlook

About 52,000 people are employed as radio and television announcers and newscasters in the United States. Competition for entry-level employment in announcing during the coming years is expected to be keen as the broadcasting industry always attracts more applicants than are needed to fill available openings. There is a better chance of working in radio than in television because there are more radio stations. Local television stations usually carry a high percentage of network programs and need only a very small staff to carry out local operations.

The U.S. Department of Labor predicts that opportunities for experienced broadcasting personnel will decrease through the year 2006 due to the lack of growth in the number of new radio and television stations. Openings will result mainly from those who leave the industry or the labor force. The trend among major networks, and to some extent among many smaller radio and TV stations, is toward specialization in such fields as sportscasting or weather forecasting. Newscasters who specialize in such areas as business, consumer, and health news should have an advantage over other job applicants.

■ For More Information

For information on its summer internship program, please contact:

The Association of Local Television Stations
1320 19th Street, NW, Suite 300
Washington, DC 20036
Tel: 202-887-1970
Email: info@altv.com
Web: http://www.altv.com

For a list of schools offering degrees in broadcasting, write to:

Broadcast Education Association
1771 N Street, NW
Washington, DC 20036-2891
Tel: 202-429-5354
Email: fweaber@nab.org
Web: http://www.beaweb.org

For broadcast education, support, and scholarship information, contact:

National Association of Broadcasters
1771 N Street, NW
Washington, DC 20036-2891
Tel: 202-429-5300
Web: http://www.nab.org

For college programs and union information, contact:

National Association of Broadcast Employees and Technicians
501 3rd Street, NW, 8th Floor
Washington, DC 20001
Tel: 202-434-1254
Email: nabet@nabetcwa.org
Web: http://nabetcwa.org

For general information, contact:

National Association of Farm Broadcasters
26 East Exchange Street, Suite 307
St. Paul, MN 55101
Tel: 612-224-0508
Email: nafboffice@aol.com
Web: http://nafb.com

For a booklet on careers in cable, contact:

National Cable Television Association
1724 Massachusetts Avenue, NW
Washington, DC 20036
Tel: 202-775-3550
Web: http://www.ncta.com

For scholarship and internship information, contact:

Radio-Television News Directors Association
Radio-Television News Directors Foundation
1000 Connecticut Avenue, NW, Suite 615
Washington, DC 20036-5302
Tel: 202-659-6510
Web: http://www.rtnda.org

■ Related Articles
Broadcasting
Radio
Television
Broadcast Engineers
Disc Jockeys
Radio and Television Program Directors
Radio Producers
Sports Broadcasters and Announcers
Writers

Radio and Television Program Directors

■ Overview
Program directors plan and schedule program material for radio and television stations and networks. They determine the entertainment programs, news broadcasts, and other program material their organizations offer to the public. At a large network the program director may supervise a large programming staff. At a small station one person may manage the station and also handle all programming duties.

■ History
Radio broadcasting in the United States began after World War I. The first commercial radio station, KDKA in Pittsburgh, came on the air in 1920 with a broadcast of presidential election returns. About a dozen radio stations were broadcasting by 1921. In 1926 the first national network linked stations across the country. Today there are 12,199 commercial and public radio stations in the United States.

The first public demonstration of television in the United States came in 1939 at the opening of the New York World's Fair. Further development was limited during World War II, but by 1953 there were about 120 stations. In the late 1990s, the United States had over 1,580 commercial and public television stations and more than 164 national cable networks.

■ The Job
Program directors plan and schedule program material for radio and television stations and networks. They work in both commercial and public broadcasting and may be employed by individual radio or television stations, regional or national networks, or cable television systems.

The material program directors work with includes entertainment programs, public service programs, newscasts, sportscasts, and commercial announcements. Program directors decide what material is broadcast and when it is scheduled; they work with other staff members to develop programs and buy programs from independent producers. They are guided by such factors as the budget available for program material, the audience their station or network seeks to attract, their organization's policies on content and other matters, and the kinds of products advertised in the various commercial announcements.

In addition, program directors may set up schedules for the program staff, audition and hire announcers and other on-the-air personnel, and assist the sales department in negotiating contracts with sponsors of commercial announcements. The duties of individual program directors are determined by such factors as whether they work in radio or television, for a small or large organization, for

RADIO AND TELEVISION PROGRAM DIRECTORS	
SCHOOL SUBJECTS	Business Journalism
PERSONAL SKILLS	Communication/ideas Leadership/management
WORK ENVIRONMENT	Primarily indoors Primarily one location
MINIMUM EDUCATION LEVEL	Bachelor's degree
SALARY RANGE	$14,315 to $78,851 to $550,000
CERTIFICATION OR LICENSING	None available
OUTLOOK	Little change or more slowly than the average
DOT	962
GOE	05.03.08
NOC	2263
O*NET	34056H

A television program director at work in the control room with his crew.

one station or a network, or in a commercial or public operation.

At small radio stations the owner or manager may be responsible for programming, but at larger radio stations and at television stations the staff usually includes a program director. At medium to large radio and television stations the program director usually has a staff that includes such personnel as music librarians, music directors, editors for tape or film segments, and writers. Some stations and networks employ *public service directors*. It is the responsibility of these individuals to plan and schedule radio or television public service programs and announcements in such fields as education, religion, and civic and government affairs. Networks often employ *broadcast operations directors,* who coordinate the activities of the personnel who prepare network program schedules, review program schedules, issue daily corrections, and advise affiliated stations on their schedules.

Program directors must carefully coordinate the various elements for a station while keeping in tune with the listeners, viewers, advertisers, and sponsors.

Other managers in radio and television broadcasting include *production managers, operations directors, news directors, and sports directors.* The work of program directors usually does not include the duties of *radio directors* or *television directors,* who direct rehearsals and integrate all the elements of a performance.

■ Requirements

High School
High school students who are interested in radio and television programming should take courses that develop their communication skills, such as English, writing, and public speaking. They also should take business courses to develop

their management skills; current events and history courses to develop their understanding of the news and the trends that affect the public's interests; and such courses as dance, drama, music, and painting to expand their understanding of the creative arts.

Postsecondary Training
College students should work toward four-year degrees in radio and television production and broadcasting, communications, liberal arts, or business administration. Students also may wish to acquire some technical training that will help them understand the engineering aspects of broadcasting.

Other Requirements
Program directors must be creative, alert, and adaptable people who stay up-to-date on the public's interests and attitudes and are able to recognize the potential in new ideas. They must be able to work under pressure and be willing to work long hours, and they must be able to work with all kinds of people. Program directors also must be good managers who can make decisions, oversee costs and deadlines, and attend to details.

■ Exploring
Students whose high schools or colleges have radio or television stations should volunteer to work on their staffs. You also should look for part-time or summer jobs at nearby stations. In addition, you can visit radio and television stations and talk with their personnel.

■ Employers
Program director jobs are not entry-level positions. A degree and extensive experience in the field is required. Most program directors have technical and on-air experience in either radio or television.

According to the National Association of Broadcasters (NAB), there are 1,580 broadcast television stations and 12,199 radio stations in the United States. Cable television stations add another option for employment.

Large conglomerates own some stations while others are owned individually. While radio and television stations are located all over the country, the largest stations with the highest paid positions are located in large metropolitan areas.

■ Starting Out
College students should investigate the availability of internships since internships are almost essential for prospective job candidates. New graduates should register with their college placement offices and with private and state employment agencies. They also can send resumes to radio and television stations or apply in person.

Beginners should be willing to relocate as they are unlikely to find employment in large cities. They usually start at small stations with fewer employees; allowing them a chance to learn a variety of skills.

■ Advancement

Most beginners start in entry-level jobs and work several years before they have enough experience to become program directors. Experienced program directors usually advance by moving from small stations to larger stations and networks or by becoming station managers.

■ Earnings

Television stations usually pay higher salaries than radio stations, and large stations and networks usually offer more compensation than small stations. According to a National Association of Broadcasters survey, radio program directors averaged $78,851 a year in 1998; the lowest reported salary was $14,315, the highest was $550,000. Television program directors averaged $47,828 a year in 1997. Program directors usually receive health and life coverage benefits and sometimes receive yearly bonuses as well.

■ Work Environment

Program directors at small stations often work 44 to 48 hours a week and frequently work evenings, late at night, and weekends. At larger stations, which have more personnel, program directors usually work 40-hour weeks.

Program directors frequently work under pressure because of the need to maintain precise timing and meet the needs of sponsors, performers, and other staff members.

Although the work is sometimes stressful and demanding, program directors usually work in pleasant environments with creative staffs. They also interact with the community to arrange programming and deal with a variety of people.

■ Outlook

In the 1990s more than 13,000 radio and television stations, cable television systems, and regional and national networks employ program directors or have other employees whose duties include programming. Competition for jobs, however, is expected to remain strong. There are more opportunities for beginners in radio than there are in television. Most radio and television stations in large cities only hire experienced workers.

New radio and television stations and new cable television systems are expected to create additional openings for program directors, but some radio stations are eliminating program director positions by installing automatic programming equipment or combining those responsibilities with other positions.

GLOSSARY

Adjacency: A commercial announcement positioned immediately before or after a specific program.

Coverage: The percentage of households in a signal area

Dayparts: Segments of the television or radio broadcast day

Fixed position: An advertisement that must run at a specific time.

Frequency: The number of times an advertisement or promotion will run.

O & O Station: A station owned and operated by a network.

PSA: A public service announcement, provided free by a radio or television station for an organization.

Preemption: The interruption of regularly scheduled programming.

Rating: Estimated size of audience

Simulcast: Simultaneous broadcast of the same program on two different stations.

Spot: Purchased broadcast time

Storyboard: Layout for advertisement or sequence

Sweep: Television and radio survey periods when audience listening habits are measured.

Syndicated program: A program offered by an independent organization for sale to stations.

■ For More Information

For information on its summer internship program, contact:

Association of Local Television Stations
1320 19th Street, NW, Suite 300
Washington, DC 20036
Tel: 202-887-1970
Web: http://www.altv.com

For a list of schools offering degrees in broadcasting, contact:

Broadcast Education Association
1771 N Street, NW
Washington, DC 20036-2891
Tel: 202-429-5354
Web: http://www.beaweb.org

For broadcast education, support, and scholarship information, contact:

National Association of Broadcasters
1771 N Street, NW
Washington, DC 20036-2891
Tel: 202-429-5300
Web: http://www.nab.org

For college programs and union information, contact:

National Association of Broadcast Employees and Technicians
501 3rd Street, NW, 8th Floor
Washington, DC 20001
Tel: 202-434-1254
Web: http://nabetcwa.org

For information on student membership, contact:

National Association of Farm Broadcasters
26 East Exchange Street, Suite 307
St. Paul, MN 55101
Tel: 612-224-0508
Web: http://nafb.com

For a booklet on careers in cable, contact:

National Cable Television Association
1724 Massachusetts Avenue, NW
Washington, DC 20036
Tel: 202-775-3550
Web: http://www.ncta.com

For scholarship and internship information, contact:

Radio-Television News Directors Association
Radio-Television News Directors Foundation
1000 Connecticut Avenue, NW, Suite 615
Washington, DC 20036-5302
Tel: 202-659-6510
Web: http://www.rtnda.org

■ Related Articles

Broadcasting

Radio

Television

Disc Jockeys

Media Planners and Buyers

Media Relations Specialists

Radio and Television Newscasters, Reporters, and Announcers

Radio Producers

Reporters

Sports Broadcasters and Announcers

Radio Interference Investigators

■ **See Line Installers and Cable Splicers**

Radio Producers

■ Overview

Radio producers plan, rehearse, and produce live or recorded programs. They work with the music, on-air personalities, sound effects, and technology to put together an entire radio show. They schedule interviews and arrange for promotional events.

According to 1999 figures from the National Association of Broadcasters (NAB), the United States alone has 12,199 radio stations. Larger stations employ radio producers while smaller stations may combine those duties with those of the program director or disc jockey. While most radio producers work at radio stations, some work to produce a particular show and then sell that show to various stations.

■ History

As long as radio has existed people have been behind the scenes to make sure that what the audience hears is what the station wants them to hear. A wide variety of administrative, programming, and technical people work to behind the scenes of radio shows to create a professional broadcast.

Scheduled broadcasting began with a program broadcast by radio station KDKA in Pittsburgh, and by 1923, 2.5 million radios had been purchased. In the 1930s, radio personalities were household names, and even then, numerous people worked behind the scenes, arranging interviews and coordinating production.

Before television, radio producers would direct the on-air soap operas as well as the news, weather, and music. With the added technology of today's radio broadcast, radio producers are even more important in mixing the special effects, locations, personalities, and formats in a way that creates a good radio show.

The Internet has made the radio producer's job easier in some ways and more challenging in others. Web sites specifically for producers provide a community where ideas can be exchanged for shows, news, jokes, and more. However, with the new frontier of broadcasting on the Internet, radio producers have one more duty to add to their long list of responsibilities.

■ The Job

The identity and style of a radio program is a result of the collaborations of on-air and off-air professionals. Radio disc jockeys talk the talk during a broadcast, and producers walk the walk behind the scenes. But in many situations, particularly with smaller radio stations, the disc jockey and the show's producer are the same person.

Also, many show producers have disc jockey experience. This experience, combined with technical expertise, helps producers effectively plan their shows.

Brent Lee, a radio producer for WFMS, a country radio station in in Indianapolis, began his career while still in high school at the small radio station in his home town. This early on-air experience, combined with his degree in telecommunications and political science from Ball State University, helped to give Brent the necessary background for his current position.

Radio producers rely on the public's very particular tastes—differences in taste allow for many different kinds of radio to exist, to serve many different segments of a community. In developing radio programs, producers take into consideration the marketplace—they listen to other area radio stations and determine what's needed and appreciated in the community, and what there may already be too much of. They conduct surveys and interviews to find out what the public wants to hear. They decide which age groups they want to pursue, and develop a format based on what appeals to these listeners. This all results in a station's "identity," which is very important. Listeners associate a station with the kind of music it plays, how much music it plays, the type of news and conversation presented, and the station's on-air personalities.

Based on this feedback, and on market research, radio disc jockeys/producers devise music playlists and music libraries. They each develop an individual on-air identity, or personality. And they invite guests who will interest their listeners. Keeping a show running on time is also the responsibility of a producer. This involves carefully weaving many different elements into a show, including music, news reports, traffic reports, and interviews.

As the producer of the "Jim, Kevin, and Bill Show," Brent arrives at the station at about 4:15 AM each morning to prep for the morning show. The show broadcasts from 5 AM to 9 AM each morning and considers its main audience to be the "morning drivers" on their way to work or school.

The time of the broadcast is one key to planning a radio show. Because of the typical listeners of the morning show, traffic reports are given every 10 minutes. These reports are mixed with weather, news, and music. While the rest of the day, WFMS listeners will hear 13 songs each hour, the morning show typically plays between 6 and 8 songs per hour. Those songs are interspersed with 6 traffic reports, 4 weather forecasts, a variety of national, local, and entertainment news, and the typical morning disc jockey banter.

The audience of the country music radio station is mostly female, and the morning show is billed as "good, clean fun" by the station promoting the family nature of the program.

In addition to keeping in touch with the listening public, producers also keep track of current events. They consult newspapers and other radio programs to determine what subjects to discuss on their morning shows. One of the newest tools that Brent uses is a Web site designed specifically for morning shows. The site provides a forum to share ideas and ask questions.

"There are a couple of things each day that can be used," says Brent. "Since we're a family show, we have to throw some of it out, but it's a really good resource."

Radio producers write copy for and coordinate on-air commercials, which are usually recorded in advance. They also devise contests, from large public events to small, on-air trivia competitions.

Though a majority of radio stations have music formats, radio producers also work for 24-hour news stations,

public broadcasting, and talk radio. Producing news programs and radio documentaries involves a great deal of research, booking guests, writing scripts, and interviewing.

"One of the most attractive qualities about this job, is it's fun," says Brent. "Each day, I spend half of my first five hours laughing."

■ Requirements

High School

Writing skills are valuable in any profession, but especially in radio. Take composition and literature courses, and other courses that require essays and term papers. Journalism courses will not only help you develop your writing skills, but will teach you about the nature and history of media. You'll learn about deadlines and how to put a complete project (such as a newspaper or yearbook) together.

If your school has a radio station, get involved with it in any way you can. Check with your local radio stations; some may offer part-time jobs to high school students interested in becoming producers and disc jockeys.

Business courses and clubs frequently require students to put together projects; starting any business is similar to producing your own radio show. Use such a project as an opportunity to become familiar with the market research, interviewing, and writing that are all part of a radio producer's job. For both the future radio producer and the future disc jockey, a theater department offers great learning opportunities. Theater productions require funding, advertising, and other fundamentals similar to a radio production.

Postsecondary Training

Most journalism and communications schools at universities offer programs in broadcasting. Radio producers and announcers often start their training in journalism schools, and receive hands-on instruction at campus radio stations. These broadcasting programs are generally news-

RADIO PRODUCERS	
SCHOOL SUBJECTS	English Journalism Speech
PERSONAL SKILLS	Communication/ideas Leadership/management
WORK ENVIRONMENT	Primarily indoors Primarily one location
MINIMUM EDUCATION LEVEL	Bachelor's degree
SALARY RANGE	$14,000 to $27,400 to $45,000
CERTIFICATION OR LICENSING	None available
OUTLOOK	Little change or more slowly than the average
DOT	159
GOE	01.03.01
O*NET	34056F

centered, providing great opportunities for students interested in producing news programs, daily newscasts, and documentaries. News directors and program managers of radio stations generally want to hire people who have a good, well-rounded education with a grounding of history, geography, political science, and literature.

Other Requirements

Radio producers should be well versed in the English language (or the language they broadcast in), and be creative thinkers who can combine several elements into one project. The ability to understand technical equipment and coordinate it with on-air events is necessary.

A healthy curiosity about people and the world will help radio producers find new topics for news shows, new guests for call-ins, and new ideas for music formats. There are no physical requirements to be a radio producer, although those starting as disc jockeys need a strong, clear voice to be heard over the airwaves.

■ Exploring

Small radio stations are often willing to let young, inexperienced people work either behind-the-scenes or on-air. Getting a job or an internship at one of the small stations in your area may be as simple as asking for one.

Many high schools and universities have on-site radio stations where students can get hands-on experience at all different levels. You also might want to talk with a radio producer about his or her job. Since most people don't start out as a producer, experience in any area of radio is helpful, so talk to local disc jockeys or program directors as well.

■ Employers

There has been a steady growth in the number of radio stations in the United States. According the National Association of Broadcasters (NAB), there are 10,300 commercial stations and 1,899 public radio stations in the United States.

However, many stations combine the position of radio producer with that of the disc jockey or program director, so depending on the size of the station and market, producers may or may not be able to find a suitable employer.

Due to the Telecommunications Act of 1996, companies can own an unlimited number of radio stations nationwide with an eight-station limit within one market area, depending on the size of the market. When this legislation took effect, mergers and acquisitions changed the face of the radio industry. So, while the pool of employers is smaller, the number of stations continues to rise.

■ Starting Out

Radio producers usually start work at radio stations in any capacity possible. After working for a while in a part-time position gaining experience and making connections, a young, dedicated producer will find opportunities to work in production or on-air.

Both experience and a college education are generally needed to become a radio producer. It is best if both the experience and the education are well rounded with exposure to on-air and off-air positions as well as a good working knowledge of the world in which we live.

Although some future producers begin their first radio jobs in paid positions, many serve unpaid internships or volunteer to help run their college or high school station. Even if this entry-level work is unpaid, the experience gained is one of the key necessities to furthering a career in any type of radio work.

With experience as a disc jockey or behind-the-scenes person, an aspiring radio producer might try to land a position at another station, but more likely within a station and format they are used to.

■ Advancement

Radio producers are a key link in putting together a radio show. Once they have the experience coordinating all the elements that go into a radio production, it is possible to move into a program director position or, possibly in the future, to general manager.

Another way to advance is to move from being the producer of a small show to a larger one, or move from a small station to a larger one. Some producers move into the freelance arena, producing their own shows which they sell to several radio stations.

■ Earnings

According to the Radio and Television News Directors Association (RTNDA) 1997 Salary Survey, radio producers can expect to earn from $14,000 to $45,000 per year with an average of $27,400. Like many radio jobs, there is a wide range resulting from differences in market size and station size of each radio station. Salaries for radio producers are relatively flat, according to the RTNDA survey, with no growth over the previous year.

Most large stations offer employees typical fringe benefits, although part-time employees may not be eligible for those.

■ Work Environment

Radio producers generally work indoors in a busy environment although some location and outdoor work might be required. The atmosphere at a radio station is generally very pleasant; however, smaller stations may not be modern with much of the investment going into high-tech equipment for the broadcasts.

Full-time radio producers usually work over 40 hours per week planning, scheduling, and producing radio shows. Also, according to the schedule of their show, early morning, late night, or weekend work might be required. Radio is a 24-hour a day, 7-day a week production, requiring constant staffing.

Producers work with disc jockeys and program directors in planning radio shows, and also with advertising personnel to produce radio commercials. In addition to this collaboration, they may also work alone doing research for the show. Working with the public is another aspect of the radio producer's job. Promotions and events may require contact with the people in the business and listeners.

■ Outlook

In the past, radio station ownership was highly regulated by the government, limiting the number of stations a person or company could own. Recent deregulation has made multiple station ownership possible. Radio stations now are bought and sold at a more rapid pace. This may result in a radio station changing formats, as well as entire staffs. Though some radio producers are able to stay at a station over a period of several years, people going into radio should be prepared to change employers at some point in their careers.

You should also be prepared for heavier competition for radio jobs. Graduates of college broadcasting programs are finding a scarcity of work in media. Paid internships will also be difficult to find—many students of radio will have to work for free for a while to gain experience. Radio producers may find more opportunities as freelancers, developing their own programs independently and selling them to stations.

■ For More Information

For a list of schools offering degrees in broadcasting as well as scholarship information, contact:

Broadcast Education Association
1771 N Street, NW
Washington, DC 20036-2891
Tel: 202-429-5354
Email: fweaber@nab.org
Web: http://www.beaweb.org

For broadcast education, support, and scholarship information, contact:

National Association of Broadcasters
1771 N Street, NW
Washington, DC 20036-2891
Tel: 202-429-5300
Web: http://www.nab.org

For college programs and union information, contact:

National Association of Broadcast Employees and Technicians
501 3rd Street, NW, 8th Floor
Washington, DC 20001
Tel: 202-434-1254
Web: http://nabetcwa.org

For scholarship and internship information, contact:

Radio-Television News Directors Association
Radio-Television News Directors Foundation
1000 Connecticut Avenue, NW, Suite 615
Washington, DC 20036
Tel: 202-659-6510
Web: http://www.rtnda.org

■ Related Articles

Broadcasting

Radio

Disc Jockeys

Radio and Television Newscasters, Reporters, and Announcers

Sports Broadcasters and Announcers

Radio Repairers and Mechanics

■ **See Communications Equipment Technicians**

Radiologic Technologists

■ Overview

Radiologic technologists operate equipment that creates images of the body's tissues, organs, and bones for medical diagnoses and therapy. These images allow physicians to know the exact nature of a patient's injury or disease, such as the location of a broken bone or the confirmation of an ulcer.

Before an X-ray examination, radiologic technologists may administer drugs or chemical mixtures to the patient to better highlight internal organs. They place the patient in the correct position between the X-ray source and film and protect body areas that are not to be exposed to radiation. After determining the proper duration and intensity of the exposure, they operate the controls to beam X rays through the patient and expose the photographic film.

They may operate computer-aided imaging equipment that does not involve X rays and may help to treat diseased or affected areas of the body by exposing the patient to specified concentrations of radiation for prescribed times.

■ History

Radiography uses a form of electromagnetic radiation to create an image on a photographic film. Unlike photography, where the film is exposed to ordinary light rays (the most familiar kind of electromagnetic radiation), in radiography, the film is exposed to X rays, which have shorter wavelengths and different energy levels.

X rays were discovered by Wilhelm Conrad Roentgen in 1895. X rays, or roentgen rays, are generated in a glass vacuum tube (an X-ray tube) that contains two differently charged electrodes, one of which gives off electrons. When the electrons travel from one electrode to the other, some of the energy they emit is X-radiation. X rays are able to pass through skin and muscle and other soft body tissue, while bones and denser objects show up as white images on the photographic emulsion when film is exposed to X rays. A picture of the inside of the body can thus be developed.

All forms of radiation are potentially harmful. Exposure to ultraviolet radiation may tan the skin, but it can also result in burning and other damage to tissue, including the development of cancer cells. Low-level infrared radiation can warm tissues, but at higher levels it cooks them like microwaves do; the process can destroy cells. Protective measures to avoid all unnecessary exposure to radiation must be taken whenever X rays are used, because they can have both short- and long-term harmful effects.

There are other forms of diagnostic imaging that do not expose patients to any potentially harmful radiation. Sound waves are used in ultrasound technology, or sonography, to obtain a picture of internal organs. High-frequency sound waves beamed into the patient's body bounce back and create echoes which can be recorded on a paper strip or photograph. Ultrasound is very frequently employed to determine the size and development of a human fetus. Magnetic resonance imaging (MRI) uses magnetic fields, radio waves, and computers to create images of the patient's body.

The use of imaging techniques that do not involve radiation has grown rapidly during the 1980s and 1990s because of their safety and because of great improvements in computer technology. Computers can now handle a vast quantity of data much more rapidly, making it possible to enhance images to great clarity and sharpness.

■ The Job

All radiological work is done at the request of and under the supervision of a *physician*. Just as a prescription is required for certain of drugs to be dispensed or administered, so also must a physician's request be issued before a patient can receive any kind of imaging procedure.

There are four primary disciplines in which radiologic technologists may work: radiography, which is taking X-ray pictures or radiographs; nuclear medicine; radiation therapy; and sonography. In each of these, the technologist works under the direction of a physician who specializes in interpreting the pictures produced by X rays, other imaging techniques, or radiation therapy. Technologists can work in more than one of these areas. Some technologists specialize in working with a particular part of the body or a specific condition.

X-ray pictures, or radiographs, are the most familiar use of radiologic technology. They are used to diagnose and determine treatment for a wide variety of afflictions, including ulcers, tumors, and bone fractures. Chest X-ray pictures can determine whether a person has a lung disease. Radiologic technologists who operate X-ray equipment first help the patient prepare for the radiologic examination. After explaining the procedure, they may administer a substance that makes the part of the body being imaged more clearly visible on the film. They make sure that the patient is not wearing jewelry or other metal that would obstruct the X rays. They position the person sitting, standing, or lying down so that the correct view of the body can be radiographed, and then they cover adjacent areas with lead shielding to prevent unnecessary exposure to radiation.

The technologist positions the X-ray equipment at the proper angle and distance from the part to be radiographed and determines exposure time based on the location of the particular organ or bone and thickness of the body in that area. The controls of the X-ray machine are set to produce pictures of the correct density, contrast, and detail. Placing the photographic film closest to the body part being X rayed, the technologist takes the requested images, repositioning the patient as needed. Typically, there are standards regarding the number of views to be taken of a given body part. The film is then developed for the radiologist or other physician to interpret.

RADIOLOGIC TECHNOLOGISTS	
SCHOOL SUBJECTS	Biology Health
PERSONAL SKILLS	Helping/teaching Technical/scientific
WORK ENVIRONMENT	Primarily indoors Primarily one location
MINIMUM EDUCATION LEVEL	Some postsecondary training
SALARY RANGE	$23,400 to $27,700 to $33,300
CERTIFICATION OR LICENSING	Required by certain states
OUTLOOK	About as fast as the average
DOT	078
O*NET	32919

In a fluoroscopic examination, a more complex imaging procedure that examines the gastrointestinal area, a beam of X rays passes through the body and onto a fluorescent screen, enabling the physician to see the internal organs in motion. For these, the technologist first prepares a solution of barium sulfate to be administered to the patient, either rectally or orally, depending on the exam. The barium sulfate increases the contrast between the digestive tract and surrounding organs, making the image clearer. The technologist follows the physician's guidance in positioning the patient, monitors the machine's controls, and takes any follow-up radiographs as needed.

Radiologic technologists may learn other imaging procedures such as computed tomography (CT) scanning, which uses X rays to get detailed cross-sectional images of the body's internal structures, and magnetic resonance imaging (MRI), which uses radio waves, powerful magnets, and computers to obtain images of body parts. These diagnostic procedures are becoming more common and usually require radiologic technologists to undergo additional on-the-job training.

Other specialties within the radiography discipline include mammography and cardiovascular interventional technology. In addition, some technologists may focus on radiography of joints and bones, or they may be involved in such areas as angiocardiography (visualization of the heart and large blood vessels) or neuroradiology (the use of radiation to diagnose diseases of the nervous system).

Radiologic technologists perform a wide range of duties, from greeting patients and putting them at ease by explaining the procedures to developing the finished film. Their administrative tasks include maintaining patients' records, recording equipment usage and maintenance, organizing work schedules, and managing a radiologist's private practice or hospital's radiology department. Some radiologic technologists teach in programs to educate other technologists.

■ Requirements

High School

High school courses in mathematics, physics, chemistry, biology, and photography are useful background preparation.

Postsecondary Training

Students who wish to become radiologic technologists must complete an education program in radiography. Programs range in length from two to four years. Depending on length, the programs award a certificate, associate's degree, or bachelor's degree.

Educational programs are available in hospitals, medical centers, colleges and universities, and vocational and

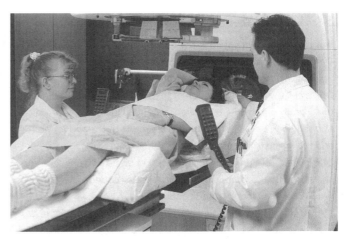

A radiologic technologist prepares a patient for a test.

technical institutes. It is also possible to get radiologic technology training in the armed forces.

To enter an accredited program, you must be a high school graduate; some programs require one or two years of higher education. Courses in radiologic technology education programs include anatomy, physiology, patient care, physics, radiation protection, medical ethics, principles of imaging, medical terminology, radiobiology, and pathology. For some supervisory or administrative jobs in this field, a bachelor's or master's degree may be required.

Certification or Licensing

Radiologic technologists may register with the American Registry of Radiologic Technologists after graduating from an accredited program in radiography, radiation therapy, or nuclear medicine. Sonographers may register with the American Registry of Diagnostic Medical Sonographers. Although registration and certification are voluntary, many jobs are open only to technologists who have acquired these credentials.

In addition to being registered in the various imaging disciplines, radiologic technologists can receive advanced qualifications in each of the four radiography specializations: mammography, computed tomography (CT), magnetic resonance imaging (MRI), and cardiovascular interventional technology. As the work of radiologic technologists grows increasingly complex and employment opportunities become more competitive, the desirability of registration and certification will also grow. An increasing number of states have licensing requirements. In 1995, licenses were needed by radiologic technologists in 30 states.

Other Requirements

Radiologic technologists should be responsible individuals with a mature and caring nature. They should be personable and enjoy interacting with all types of people, includ-

GLOSSARY

Bucky: The tray in which X-ray film is loaded

Columnator: A dial on the X-ray machinery that controls and adjusts the area of radiation exposure

Contrast medium: A solution of barium sulfate that is administered orally or rectally to highlight organs in the abdomen, which normally can't be distinguished. This medium is used for upper and lower gastrointestinal examinations (GIs).

Diagnostic imaging: Preliminary testing of the body tissues and skeletal structures through the use of X rays, sound waves, tomographic scans, and magnetic scans

Fluoroscopy: A procedure that examines the upper or lower gastrointestinal areas

Pigastat: A device used for children that immobilizes them during an examination, lifting arms and holding them in place

Radiographs: X-ray films

ing those who are very ill. A compassionate attitude is essential.

■ Exploring

There is no way to gain direct experience in this profession without the appropriate qualifications. However, it is possible to learn about the duties of radiologic technologists by talking with them and observing the facilities and equipment they use. It is also possible to have interviews with teachers of radiologic technology. Guidance counselors and teachers can contact local hospitals or schools with radiography programs to locate technologists who are willing to talk to interested students.

As with any career in health care, volunteering at a local hospital, clinic, or nursing home provides an excellent opportunity to test one's real interest in the field. Most hospitals are eager for volunteers, and working in such a setting gives a chance to see health care professionals in action as well as to have some patient contact.

■ Employers

Radiologic technologists may find employment in hospitals, clinics, X-ray labs, or nursing homes.

■ Starting Out

With more states regulating the practice of radiologic technology, certification by the appropriate accreditation body for a given specialty is quickly becoming a necessity for employment. Persons who acquire training in schools that have not been accredited, or who learn on the job, may have difficulty in qualifying for many positions, especially those with a wide range of assignments. Students enrolled in hospital educational programs often work for the hospital upon completion of the program. Those who attend

degree programs can get help finding jobs through their schools' placement offices.

■ Advancement

About three-quarters of all radiologic technologists are employed in hospitals where there are opportunities for advancement to administrative and supervisory positions such as chief technologist or technical administrator. Other technologists develop special clinical skills in advanced imaging procedures, such as computed tomography scanning or magnetic resonance imaging. Some radiologic technologists qualify as instructors. There are more chances for advancement if you hold a bachelor's degree. If you wish to become a teacher or administrator, a master's degree and considerable experience are necessary.

■ Earnings

Salaries for radiologic technologists compare favorably with those of similar health care professions. The starting salary in a hospital or medical center averages about $23,400 a year for radiologic technologists. With experience, technologists earn average salaries of about $29,100 a year.

Technologists with specialized skills may have larger incomes. Radiation therapists earn about $30,700 to start, and the average salary for experienced employees is about $34,300. In ultrasound technology, the average pay for graduates of an accredited program is $27,700 for beginning technologists and about $33,300 for those with experience. Most technologists are covered by the same vacation and sick leave provisions as other employees in the organizations that employ them, and some receive free medical care and pension benefits.

■ Work Environment

Full-time technologists generally work eight hours a day, 40 hours a week; and may be on call for some night emergency duty or weekend hours, which pays in equal time off or additional compensation.

In diagnostic radiologic work, technologists perform most of their tasks while on their feet. They move around a lot and often are called upon to lift patients who need help in moving.

Great care is exercised to protect technologists from radiation exposure. Each technologist wears a badge that measures radiation exposure, and records are kept of total exposure accumulated over time. Other routine precautions include the use of safety devices, such as lead aprons, lead gloves, and other shielding and the use of disposable gowns, gloves, and masks. Careful attention to safety procedures has greatly reduced or eliminated radiation hazards for the technologist.

Radiologic technology is dedicated to conserving life and health. Technologists derive satisfaction from their work, which helps promote health and alleviate human suffering. Those who specialize in radiation therapy need to be able to handle the close relationships they inevitably develop while working with very sick or dying people over a period of time.

■ Outlook

The number of people working in the field of radiologic technology has stabilized. Although enrollments in accredited schools have equalized in recent years, the demand for qualified people in some areas of the country far exceeds the supply. This shortage is particularly acute in rural areas and small towns.

In the years to come, increasing numbers of radiologic technologists will be employed in nonhospital settings, such as physicians' offices, clinics, health maintenance organizations, laboratories, government agencies, and diagnostic imaging centers. This pattern will be part of the overall trend toward holding down health care costs by delivering more care outside of hospitals. Nevertheless, hospitals will remain the major employers of radiologic technologists for the near future. Because of the increasing importance of radiologic technology in the diagnosis and treatment of disease, it is unlikely that hospitals will do fewer radiologic procedures than in the past. Instead, they try to do more on an outpatient basis and on weekends and evenings. This should increase the demand for part-time technologists and thus open more opportunities for flexible work schedules.

■ For More Information

The following organization has information about radiologic technologists, a catalog of educational products, and a job bank.

American Society of Radiologic Technologists
15000 Central Avenue, SE
Albuquerque, NM 87123
Tel: 505-298-4500
Web: http://www.asrt.org

For an educational resource guide, contact:

Society of Diagnostic Medical Sonographers
12770 Coit Road, Suite 508
Dallas, TX 75251
Tel: 214-239-7367
Web: http://www.sdms.org

For information on accreditation, contact:

American Cancer Society
1599 Clifton Road
Atlanta, GA 30329
Tel: 404-320-3333
Web: http://www.cancer.org

■ Related Articles

Health Care
Biomedical Equipment Technicians
Cardiovascular Technologists
Cytotechnologists
Diagnostic Medical Sonographers
Dialysis Technicians
Dietetic Technicians
Electroneurodiagnostic Technologists
Histologic Technicians
Medical Assistants
Medical Laboratory Technicians
Medical Technologists
Nuclear Medicine Technologists
Ophthalmic Laboratory Technicians
Optics Technicians
Orthotic and Prosthetic Technicians
Perfusionists
Phlebotomy Technicians
Physical Therapy Assistants
Psychiatric Technicians
Respiratory Therapists and Technicians
Surgical Technologists

Radiology and Surgical Recorders

■ See Medical Secretaries

Railroad Clerks

■ Overview

Railroad clerks perform the clerical duties involved in transacting business and keeping records for railroad companies. Their jobs may involve many different kinds of clerical work or only one or two specialized duties, depending on the size and type of their railroad company or location.

■ History

The modern era of railroading began in the early 1800s, when two Englishmen—Richard Trevithick and George Stephenson—perfected their versions of the steam locomotive. In the early days, railroads were largely short lines, and a few clerks could keep track of the trains' cargo and destinations. But as railroads expanded, both geographically and in the types of freight they could carry, clerks became essential to keep track of what was being hauled where, when it was needed, and who would pay for it. The railroad industry reached an historic climax on May 10, 1869, with the completion of the first transcontinental railway. The Union Pacific Railroad, building west from Nebraska, and the Central Pacific Railroad, building east from California, met at Promontory Point, Utah, where a golden spike was driven to set the merging rails.

Passenger and freight business on the nation's rail lines peaked in the 1920s and 1930s, then went into decline. Still, rail is an important method of transportation. For example, automobile manufacturers use the railroad more than any other means of transportation to ship completed automobiles. Other commodities, such as coal and farm products, still rely heavily on rail. The railroad system is now a complex, interconnecting network of some 200,000 miles of lines that serve all parts of the country. While computers have eliminated some clerical jobs, clerks are still needed to keep accurate records, compile statistics, and transact railroad business for the complex systems of freight, express, and passenger rail service.

■ The Job

Volumes of paperwork are necessary to keep accurate records and provide information on the business transactions of railroad companies. Railroad clerks are responsible for completing and maintaining this paperwork. They interact with customers of the railroad and railroad employees at all levels.

Traditionally, railroad clerks have been employed in railroad yards, terminals, freight houses, railroad stations, and company offices. However, as railroad companies have merged, and as computerization has increasingly been used, railroads have tended to consolidate much of their operation into a centralized location. As a result, most railroad clerks no longer work on-site in the terminals; instead, they work at the railroad's central office. The information they need from the various terminals, yards, and stations is transmitted to them via computer and TV camera.

Clerks may perform a variety of duties, depending upon the size of the company they work for and the level of seniority they have achieved. Railroad clerks employed on Class I "line-haul" railroads perform such clerical duties as selling tickets, bookkeeping, compiling statistics, collecting bills, investigating complaints and adjusting claims, and tracing lost or misdirected shipments. *Yard clerks* use information from records or other personnel to prepare orders for railroad yard switching crews. They also keep records of cars moving into or out of the yard.

Pullman car clerks assign and dispatch sleeping cars to railroad companies requesting them and assign Pullman conductors to trains. *Dispatcher clerks* schedule train crews for work, notify them of their assignments, and record the time and distance they work.

Train clerks record the exact time each train arrives at or leaves the station, compare those times with schedules, and inquire about reasons for delays. They also process other data about train movements. *Railroad-maintenance clerks* keep records about repairs being made to tracks or rights-of-way, including the location and type of repair and the materials and time involved.

A great deal of railroad business and income involves moving freight. *Documentation-billing clerks* prepare the billing documents that list a freight shipper's name, the type and weight of cargo, destination, charges, and so on. They total the charges, check for accuracy, and resolve discrepancies. *Demurrage clerks* compute charges for delays in loading or unloading freight, prepare bills for these charges, and send the bills to the shippers or receivers responsible for the delays. They also communicate with shippers and receivers about the time and place of shipment arrival and the time allowed for unloading freight before they levy any charges.

Revising clerks verify and revise freight and tariff charges on shipment bills. *Interline clerks* examine waybills and ticket sales records to compute the charges payable to the various carriers involved in interline business. Accounts adjustable clerks compute corrected freight charges from waybill data. *Voucher clerks* receive claims for lost or damaged goods and prorate the cost of the goods to the various carriers involved in an interline shipment. *Express clerks* receive packages from customers, compute charges, write bills, receive payments, issue receipts, and release packages to the proper recipients.

Secretaries, typists, stenographers, bookkeepers, and operators of business and computing machines constitute a second group of railroad clerical workers. All of these employees perform clerical duties that are similar to those performed in other types of business and industry.

Thousands of railroad clerks are employed in higher-level jobs that require technical skills and knowledge. Such workers might include collectors, who pursue uncollected bills; accountants, who are concerned with company financial transactions; and *records and statistical clerks,* responsible for statistical compilations on railroad traffic, employees, and other business details. In addition, these employees are also frequently responsible for compiling periodic reports for the federal government on railroad business, transactions, and operational traffic.

■ Requirements

High School
A high school education is the minimum educational requirement for most railroad clerk positions. Business, computer, and communications courses will be helpful to prospective railroad clerks. Typing class is a must.

Postsecondary Training
Students who have postsecondary training in accounting, office management, or computer applications may be in a better position to get hired as a railroad clerk than students with high school diplomas only. In many instances, companies also require that potential employees successfully pass clerical aptitude tests and be able to type 35 to 40 words per minute. Finally, because computers are now commonplace in the railroad industry, potential clerks will find that they need a certain degree of computer literacy.

Other Requirements
Patience and attention to detail are important for clerical workers, especially those whose work may be repetitive. For those clerks who must deal regularly with the public, a congenial disposition, a pleasant phone voice, and the ability to get along well with others are valued assets. For example, one major railroad—Norfolk Southern—outlines the following standards for successful candidates for clerk positions: "be responsible and reliable, able to make quick decisions and prioritize work; be energetic and able to handle inquiries with strong interpersonal skills and a customer focus."

■ Exploring
One way to observe the work performed by railroad clerks is to obtain a part-time or summer job with a railroad company as a messenger or office assistant. If a railroad job is not available, working in any sort of office setting might give the prospective clerk experience with clerical work such as typing, stenography, bookkeeping, and the operation of common office equipment.

■ Employers
Railroad clerks may be employed by passenger lines or freight lines. They may work for one of the major railroads, such as Burlington Northern Santa Fe, Norfolk Southern,

CSX, or Atchison-Topeka-Santa Fe, or they may work for one of the 500 smaller short line railroads across the country. Clerks who work for a major railroad generally work in a large centralized office with many other workers. Railroad clerks may work in any part of the country, urban or rural. Clerks who are employed by commuter passenger lines work in large metropolitan areas.

■ Starting Out
Railroad companies frequently fill railroad clerical positions by promoting current office assistants, janitors, or messengers. Therefore, the job seeker is most likely to find entrance into the field via a lower-level job. Once accepted for employment with a railroad company, a person may be given a temporary appointment as an "extra" and listed for "extra board" work until such time as a regular job appointment becomes available.

Individuals interested in railroad clerical jobs may apply directly to the railroad companies or inquire about job application procedures through the union representing this group of employees. Newspaper advertisements may sometimes list openings for clerical employees.

■ Advancement
Seniority plays a key role in advancement within the railroad industry. Jobs with higher pay, better hours, and more responsibility almost always go to those workers who have put in many years with the company. Most clerks are designated trainees for a period of 14 to 90 days when they first begin working before they advance to full-fledged clerks.

Railroad clerks who have achieved a high level of seniority and who have proven their abilities are sometimes promoted to assistant chief clerks or to positions of higher administrative status. Clerks who continue their formal education and training in some field of specialization, such as accounting or statistics, may have opportunities for promotions into jobs as auditors or statisticians. Other advancement opportunities may include advancement to traffic agent, buyer, storekeeper, or ticket and station agent.

■ Earnings
Salaries for railroad clerks vary depending on union agreements, training, experience, job responsibilities, and the type of operation in which the employee works. In most cases, hourly wages are set by the agreement between the railroad and the union. In 1998, clerks represented by the Transportation Communications Union who worked for a major railroad started at around $28,500 a year. Those workers on the low end of the pay scale make between $19,500 and $20,800 annually, while those at the top end can make between $41,600 and $44,200.

Railroad employees are usually paid time and a half for any time worked over eight hours a day. Most railroad employees are given paid vacation, sick days, and holidays. Retired railroad workers receive pensions and retirement insurance from the federal Railroad Retirement Administration, which they pay into while they are working.

■ Work Environment

A 40-hour workweek is the typical schedule for railroad clerical employees in nonsupervisory positions. Individuals who have temporary appointments may have an irregular work schedule, depending on the type of railroad setting in which they are employed. Clerks are sometimes expected to be available to work in a three-shift operation. Many clerks work strictly during the day, though. The majority of these workers perform their duties in comfortable, well-lit offices or stations. Large company offices may be more elaborately furnished and equipped than those of smaller stations.

The work of railroad clerks is not considered hazardous or physically strenuous; much of it is done while sitting down. Some types of clerical work can be tedious and unexciting, however, and in some cases, can result in eyestrain. Some clerks have to interact with the public, either by phone or in person. These workers are exposed to various sorts of people, some of whom may be difficult to deal with.

■ Outlook

Railroad clerks have been hit hard by the overall decline in railroad business; in the last 15 years, the total number of clerks employed has decreased by 50 to 60 percent. The increasing use of electronic data processing and computers have also played a large part in the employment decline for these workers, as machines have come to do more and more of the freight bill processing and recording of information on freight movements and yard operations.

Although this decline in employment is expected to continue, some job opportunities are expected to become available each year for these workers. Job turnover in this occupational group is relatively high as a result of retirements and employees transferring to other fields.

■ For More Information

For general information on the railroad industry, contact:

Association of American Railroads
50 F Street, NW
Washington, DC 20001
Tel: 202-639-2555
Web: http://www.aar.org/

For information on the career of railroad clerk, contact:

Transportation Communications International Union
Three Research Place
Rockville, MD 20850
Tel: 301-948-4910

■ Related Articles

Accounting

Business

Railroads

Accountants and Auditors

Billing Clerks

Bookkeeping and Accounting Clerks

Data Entry Clerks

Financial Institution Clerks and Related Workers

Office Clerks

Railroad Conductors

Reservation and Ticket Agents

Secretaries

Shipping and Receiving Managers and Clerks

Statistical Clerks

Stenographers

Railroad Conductors

■ Overview

Railroad conductors supervise trains and train crews on passenger trains, on freight trains, or in the rail yards. They are responsible for keeping track of the train's operating instructions and of its makeup and cargo.

■ History

The word "conductor" is likely to conjure up an image of the man who calls "All aboard!" before a train leaves the station. In the early days of the railroad, this association was accurate. Today, however, railroad conductors are more than a passenger liaison. With today's smaller crews, conductors and engineers often make up the entire crew aboard a train.

On many early passenger trains, the railroad conductor's most important task was to see to the comfort and safety of the passengers. For the first conductors, this was no simple task. The earliest trains had seats bolted to platforms that looked much like today's flat cars. There were no roofs over those cars, and consequently passengers were exposed to the elements, such as rain and wind, and to flying sparks from the tender boxes of locomotives. More often than not, the conductor had to extinguish fires started by flying sparks on the train and in passengers' clothing.

By the late 1830s, as trains crossed the unsettled western areas of the United States, the conductor's job became even more difficult and dangerous. Outlaws frequently attacked trains or tore up tracks and damaged bridges. Once rail came to be a popular method of both passenger and freight transportation in the latter half of the 1800s and early 1900s, railroad companies had the means to improve the quality of their locomotives and trains.

As locomotives and trains became more complex machines, conductors became well-versed in all areas of train operation. They were required to know a lot about all aspects of a train, from the engines, cars, and cargo to the track and signal systems. Today's conductors are responsible for the proper functioning of the entire train.

■ The Job

Railroad conductors fall into two basic categories: road conductors and yard conductors. Within the category of road conductors are included conductors of both freight and passenger trains, although their duties vary somewhat. The conductor is in charge of the train in its entirety, including all equipment and the crew.

Before a freight or passenger train departs from the terminal, the *road conductor* receives orders from the dispatcher regarding the train's route, timetable, and cargo. He or she then confers with the engineer and other members of the train crew, if necessary. During the run, conductors may receive additional communication by radio, such as information on track conditions or the instruction to pull off at the next available stop. They then relay this information to the engineer via a two-way radio. Conductors also receive information about any operating problems while underway and may make arrangements for repairs or removal of defective cars. They use a radio or wayside phone to keep dispatchers informed about the status of the trip.

Conductors on freight trains are responsible for getting bills of loading, lists of cars in their train, and written orders from the station agent and dispatcher. They keep records of each car's content and eventual destination, and see to it that cars are dropped off and picked up along the route as specified. Both before and during the run, they inspect the cars to make sure everything is as it should be.

On passenger trains, conductors see to it that passenger cars are clean and that passengers are seated and comfortable. They collect tickets and cash and attend to the passengers' needs. At stops, they supervise the disembarking of the passengers and tell the engineer when it is safe to pull out of the station. If an accident occurs, conductors take charge and direct passengers and other crew members.

Yard conductors are usually stationed at a switching point or terminal where they signal the engineer and direct the work of switching crews who assemble and disassemble the trains. Based on a knowledge of train schedules, the yard conductor or yard foreman is responsible for seeing that cars destined to arrive at various points along one of many routes are put together and ready to leave on time. He or she sends cars to special tracks for unloading and sends other cars to tracks to await being made into trains. Conductors tell switching crews which cars to couple and uncouple and which switches to throw to divert the locomotive or cars to the proper tracks. Today, many yards are mechanized. In this case, yard conductors supervise the movement of cars through electronic devices.

All conductors perform strenuous, outside work in all weather conditions and travel extensively. Usually, conductors are required to work on-call, on an as-needed basis. Railroads expect conductors, as well as most of their other employees, to be available to work 24 hours a day, seven days a week in all weather conditions. A certain time period is allotted, usually 12 hours, from the time of call to report to work.

■ Requirements

High School

The high school student interested in becoming a conductor will benefit from taking as many shop classes as possible. Any course that teaches electrical principles is particularly helpful. Because on-board computers are increasingly used in this profession, computer training would be a plus. Finally, academic subjects such as English and speech are also important because conductors are required to write some reports and speak to fellow workers and passengers.

Postsecondary Training

Many conductors acquire the knowledge to assume their positions through years of practical experience in other positions on the railroad. Railroads prefer that applicants for these jobs have high school diplomas, but further education, outside of the railroad's training school, is not typically required. To be eligible for a conductor's position, applicants must have passed examinations testing their knowledge of signals, timetables, air brakes, operating rules, and related subjects.

RAILROAD CONDUCTORS	
SCHOOL SUBJECTS	Computer science Technical/Shop
PERSONAL SKILLS	Leadership/management Mechanical/manipulative
WORK ENVIRONMENT	Indoors and Outdoors Multiple locations
MINIMUM EDUCATION LEVEL	Apprenticeship
SALARY RANGE	$16,000 to $28,496 to $62,169
CERTIFICATION OR LICENSING	None available
OUTLOOK	Decline
DOT	910
GOE	09.05.08
NOC	7362
O*NET	97302

A railroad conductor signals to the engineer that all passengers have boarded.

Other Requirements

Conductors must pass an entrance-to-service medical examination and must pass further physicals at regular intervals. They are also required to take tests that screen for drug use. Conductors must be able to lift 80 pounds, as required when replacing knuckles that connect rail cars. Because conductors are responsible for overseeing the activities of the other crew members and for dealing with the public, they must be capable of assuming responsibility, directing the work activities of others, and acting as the railroad's representatives to passengers. A conductor must have a good working knowledge of the operation of the train and of its mechanical details. In addition, he or she must be self-sufficient and capable of occupying free hours because much of the time is spent away from home. Finally, it is important that conductors have good judgment skills, be dependable, and be able to make quick, responsible decisions.

■ Exploring

A visit to a rail yard might give the interested person some insight into the work of a yard conductor and into the operations of railroads in general. It might be possible to arrange to talk with a conductor who works on a freight train or a passenger train for further insight. It might even be possible to obtain summer or part-time work for a railroad company.

Many conductors have an engineering or mechanical background, so students may find it helpful to explore such areas in high school through vocational clubs or classes. The Junior Engineering Technical Society is a nationwide organization that provides training and competition for students in engineering and technical subject areas. Visit the JETS Web site at http://www.asee.org/jets

for more information or talk to a guidance counselor or vocational coordinator to see if your school or a school in your area has a chapter that you can participate in.

■ Employers

Railroad conductors may be employed by passenger lines or freight lines. They may work for one of the major railroads, such as Burlington Northern Santa Fe, Norfolk Southern, CSX, or Atchison-Topeka-Santa Fe, or they may work for one of the 500 smaller short line railroads across the country. Many of the passenger lines today are commuter lines located near large metropolitan areas. Railroad conductors who work for freight lines may work in a rural or an urban area and will travel more extensively than the shorter, daily commuter routes passenger railroad conductors make. There were 83,000 rail transportation workers in 1996, according to the Bureau of Labor Statistics, 25,000 of whom were conductors.

■ Starting Out

The method of becoming a conductor varies and is usually determined by a particular railroad company. Most often, applicants must start at entry-level jobs—such as messengers or janitors—and work their way up to foreman or conductor positions. After acquiring experience, they may be considered for the position of conductor. Some companies promote experienced personnel to conductor positions. At other companies, there is a specific sequence of jobs and training required before one becomes a conductor.

For example, one of the major railroads, Norfolk Southern, requires class and field training for freight service trainees to become conductor trainees. Field experience includes training with yard, local, and through freight crews. Completion of written exams is also required. Conductor trainees for Norfolk Southern undergo locomotive engineer training, including four weeks at a training facility and eight to twelve months of field training. The railroad lists the following duties for its conductor trainees: operate track switches, couple cars, and work on freight trains in yard operations and on the road.

Thus, the person interested in becoming a conductor must first seek employment at a lower-level job with a railroad company. Direct contact with unions and railroad companies is recommended for those interested in obtaining more information about an entry-level job. Such jobs serve as training for future conductors as they will be required to know all aspects of train operation.

■ Advancement

When conductors first begin their careers, they are seldom assigned regular full-time positions. Instead, they are put on a list called an "extra board" and are called in only when the railroad needs a substitute for a regular employee. On most railroads, conductors who are assigned to the extra board may work as brakers if there are not enough conductor runs available that month. The first form of promotion, then, is receiving a regular assignment as a conductor. Conductors who show promise and ability may eventually be promoted to managerial positions.

■ Earnings

As is the case with most rail occupations, the daily wage or hourly rate varies with the size of the railroad. Other factors that affect wages are the type of service, number of cars on the train, and the location of the train's run. For example, conductors receive extra pay on trains passing through mountainous regions. Usually, basic wages, as well as fringe benefits, for conductors are guaranteed by union contract.

The average annual wage for yard-freight conductors is $48,991, according to 1997 National Railroad Labor Conference figures. Local-freight conductors averaged $62,169 annually. Conductors generally belong to a union, so their rates of pay follow a specific schedule. In 1998, one major railroad paid conductor trainees $300 to $400 a week before taxes, or about $16,000 a year. Once they became full-fledged conductors, they earned $28,496 annually for the first year. After the fifth year of being a conductor, earnings increased to $35,672.

Conductors, like other railroad workers, receive a generous benefits package including health and life insurance, paid holidays and vacations, sick leave, and a pension plan. In addition to retirement plans sponsored by unions and railroads, conductors are eligible for Social Security and other government benefits.

■ Work Environment

Road conductors spend much of their time traveling and must be away from home on a constant basis. While assigned to the extra board, they usually have irregular hours. Once they receive a regular assignment, however, they may maintain a regular schedule and remain on a run for years. Although the basic workweek is eight hours for five days a week, days and nights are not considered different, and Sunday is treated as a workday. Along with other members of the train's crew, conductors work extra hours—including nights, weekends, and holidays—when travel is especially heavy. Mandatory rest periods are required for safety purposes. If a conductor is required to "lay over" while awaiting a train to return to the home terminal, he or she must pay for meals and other living expenses.

In addition to being a leader among other members of the train crew, the conductor also has the most direct and frequent contact with the public. The position can carry heavy responsibilities; it can also be very rewarding.

■ Outlook

Job opportunities are not promising for railroad conductors. Rail passenger services to many points have been discontinued. Although the volume of railroad freight business is expected to increase in the coming years, the use of mechanization, automation, and larger, faster trains is expected to cause a continued decline in the employment of rail transportation workers. Computers are now used to keep track of empty freight cars, match empty cars with the closest load, and dispatch trains. Also, new work rules that allow two- and three-person crews instead of the traditional five-person crews are becoming more widely used, and these factors combine to lessen the need for conductors and other crew workers.

Most job openings that arise in the future will be from a need to replace conductors who transfer to other kinds of work or who retire.

■ For More Information

For general information on the railroad industry, contact:

Association of American Railroads
50 F Street, NW
Washington, DC 20001
Tel: 202-639-2555
Web: http://www.aar.org

For information on the career of conductor, contact:

United Transportation Union
14600 Detroit Avenue
Cleveland, OH 44107-4250
Tel: 216-228-9400
Web: http://www.utu.org

■ Related Articles

Railroads

Shipping

Flight Attendants

Locomotive Engineers

Merchant Mariners

Public Transportation Operators

Railroad Clerks

Shipping and Receiving Managers and Clerks

Railroad Inspectors

■ See Health and Regulatory Inspectors

Range Conservationists

■ See Soil Conservationists and Technicians

Range Managers

■ Overview

Range managers work to maintain and improve grazing lands on public and private property. They research, develop, and carry out methods to improve and increase the production of forage plants, livestock, and wildlife without damaging the environment; develop and carry out plans for water facilities, erosion control, and soil treatments; restore rangelands that have been damaged by fire, pests, and undesirable plants; and manage the upkeep of range improvements, such as fences, corrals, and reservoirs.

RANGE MANAGERS	
SCHOOL SUBJECTS	Biology
	Earth science
PERSONAL SKILLS	Leadership/management
	Technical/scientific
WORK ENVIRONMENT	Indoors and outdoors
	Primarily multiple locations
MINIMUM EDUCATION LEVEL	Bachelor's degree
SALARY RANGE	$17,200 to $25,000 to $34,000
CERTIFICATION OR LICENSING	None available
OUTLOOK	About as fast as the average
DOT	040
GOE	02.02.02
NOC	2223
O*NET	24302D

■ History

Early in the history of the world, primitive peoples grazed their livestock wherever forage was plentiful. As the supply of grass and shrubs became depleted, they simply moved on, leaving the stripped land to suffer the effects of soil erosion. When civilization grew and the nomadic tribes began to establish settlements, people began to recognize the need for conservation and developed simple methods of land terracing, irrigation, and the rotation of grazing lands.

Much the same thing happened in the United States. The rapid expansion across the continent in the 19th century was accompanied by the destruction of plant and animal life and the abuse of the soil. Because the country's natural resources appeared inexhaustible, the cries of alarm that came from a few concerned conservationists went unheeded. It was not until after 1890 that conservation became a national policy. Today several state and federal agencies are actively involved in protecting the nation's soil, water, forests, and wildlife.

Rangelands cover more than a billion acres of the United States, mostly in the western states and Alaska. Many natural resources are found there: grass and shrubs for animal grazing, wildlife habitats, water from vast watersheds, recreation facilities, and valuable mineral and energy resources. In addition, rangelands are used by scientists who conduct studies of the environment.

■ The Job

Range managers are sometimes known as *range scientists, range ecologists,* or *range conservationists.* Their goal is to maximize range resources without damaging the environment. They accomplish this in a number of ways.

To help ranchers attain optimum livestock production, range managers study the rangelands to determine the number and kind of livestock that can be most profitably grazed, the grazing system to use, and the best seasons for grazing. The system they recommend must be designed to conserve the soil and vegetation for other uses, such as wildlife habitats, outdoor recreation, and timber.

Grazing lands must continually be restored and improved. Range managers study plants to determine which varieties are best suited to a particular range and to develop improved methods for reseeding. They devise biological, chemical, or mechanical ways of controlling undesirable and poisonous plants, and they design methods of protecting the range from grazing damage.

Range managers also develop and help carry out plans for water facilities, structures for erosion control, and soil treatments. They are responsible for the construction and maintenance of such improvements as fencing, corrals, and reservoirs for stock watering.

Although a great deal of range managers' time is spent outdoors, they also spend some time in offices, consulting with other conservation specialists, preparing written reports, and doing administrative work.

Rangelands have more than one use, so range managers often work in such closely related fields as wildlife and watershed management, forest management, and recreation. *Soil conservationists* and *naturalists* are concerned with maintaining ecological balance both on the range and in the forest preserves.

■ Requirements

High School

High school students who are interested in pursuing a career in range management should begin planning their education early. Courses in science, mathematics, English, economics, and computer science are good preparation for college studies.

Postsecondary Training

The minimum educational requirement for range managers is usually a bachelor's degree in range management or range science. To be hired by the federal government, graduates need at least 42 credit hours in plant, animal, or soil sciences and natural resources management courses, including at least 18 hours in range management. For teaching and research positions, graduate degrees in range management are generally mandatory. Advanced degrees may also prove helpful for advancement in other jobs.

To receive a degree in range management, students must have acquired a basic knowledge of biology, chemistry, physics, mathematics, and communication skills. Specialized courses in range management combine plant, animal, and soil sciences with the principles of ecology and resource management. Students in degree programs are also encouraged to take electives, such as economics, forestry, hydrology, agronomy, wildlife, and computer science.

While a number of schools offer some courses related to range management, only about 18 colleges and universities have degree programs in range management or range science.

Other Requirements

Along with their technical skills, range managers must be able to speak and write effectively and to work well with others. Range managers need to be self-motivated and flexible. They are generally persons who do not want the restrictions of an office setting and a rigid schedule. They should have a love for the outdoors as well as good health and physical stamina for the strenuous activity that this occupation requires.

■ Exploring

High school students considering a career in range management may test their appetite for outdoor work by applying for summer jobs on ranches or farms. Other ways of exploring this occupation include a field trip to a ranch or interviews with or lectures by range managers, ranchers, or conservationists. Any volunteer work with conservation organizations—large or small—will give you an idea of what range managers do and will help you when you apply to colleges and for employment.

College students can get more direct experience by applying for summer jobs in range management with such federal agencies as the Forest Service, the Soil Conservation Service, and the Bureau of Land Management. This experience may better qualify them for jobs when they graduate.

Roundup time at the Fort Keogh Livestock and Range Research Station in Montana. At this station, researchers help to ensure a plentiful supply of meat while protecting the rangeland environment.

■ Employers

Between 8,000 and 10,000 range managers are currently employed. The federal government employs most of them in the agencies mentioned above, while state governments employ range managers in game and fish departments, state land agencies, and extension services.

In private industry, the number of range managers is increasing. They work for coal and oil companies to help reclaim mined areas, for banks and real estate firms to help increase the revenue from landholdings, and for private consulting firms and large ranches. Some range managers with advanced degrees teach and do research at colleges and universities. Others work overseas with the U.S. and U.N. agencies and with foreign governments.

■ Starting Out

The usual way to enter this occupation is to apply directly to the appropriate government agencies. People interested in working for the federal government may contact the Department of Agriculture's Forest Service or Soil Conservation Service, or the Department of the Interior's Bureau of Indian Affairs or Bureau of Land Management. Others may apply to local state employment offices for jobs in state land agencies, game and fish departments, or agricultural extension services. College placement offices have listings of available jobs.

■ Advancement

Range managers may advance to administrative positions in which they plan and supervise the work of others and write reports. Others may go into teaching or research. It should be remembered that an advanced degree is often necessary for the higher-level jobs in this occupational field. Another way for range managers to advance is to enter business for themselves as *range management consultants* or *ranchers*.

■ Earnings

Experienced range managers with the federal government earn an average of about $34,000 a year. Those with bachelor's degrees can expect starting salaries in the range of $17,200 to $21,300 a year. State governments and private companies pay their range managers salaries that are about the same as those paid by the federal government. Range managers are also eligible for paid vacations and sick days, health and life insurance, and other benefits.

■ Work Environment

Range managers, particularly those just beginning their careers, spend a great deal of time on the range. That means they must work outdoors in all kinds of weather. They usually travel by car or small plane, but in rough country they use four-wheel-drive vehicles or get around on horseback or on foot. When riding the range, managers may spend a considerable amount of time away from home, and the work is often quite strenuous.

As range managers advance to administrative jobs, they spend more time working in offices, writing reports, and planning and supervising the work of others. Range managers may work alone or under direct supervision; often they work as part of a team. In any case, they must deal constantly with people—not only their superiors and co-workers but with the general public, ranchers, government officials, and other conservation specialists.

■ Outlook

This is a small occupation, and most of the openings will arise when older, experienced range managers retire or leave the occupation. Job growth will be about the same as the average for all occupations in the next decade. The need for range managers should be stimulated by a growing demand for wildlife habitats, recreation, and water as well as by an increasing concern for the environment. A greater number of large ranches will employ range managers to improve range management practices and increase output and profitability. Range specialists will also be employed in larger numbers by private industry to reclaim lands damaged by oil and coal exploration.

An additional demand for range managers could be created by the conversion of rangelands to other purposes, such as wildlife habitats and recreation. Federal employment for these activities, however, depends upon the passage of legislation concerning the management of range resources, an area that is always controversial. Smaller budgets may also limit employment growth in this area.

■ For More Information

Career information and a list of schools offering range management training may be obtained from:

National Recreation and Park Association
22377 Belmont Ridge Road
Ashburn, VA 20148-4510
Tel: 703-858-0784
Web: http://www.nrpa.org/nrpa

To obtain career and educational information concerning range management, contact:

Society for Range Management
1839 York Street
Denver, CO 80206
Tel: 303-355-7070

For information about career opportunities in the federal government, write to:

U.S. Forest Service
U.S. Department of Agriculture
14th Street and Independence Avenue, SW
Washington, DC 20250
Tel: 202-205-8333

Soil Conservation Service
U.S. Department of Agriculture
PO Box 2890
Washington, DC 20013
Tel: 202-205-0026

Bureau of Land Management
U.S. Department of the Interior
1849 C Street, NW
Washington, DC 20240
Tel: 202-452-5120

National Park Service
U.S. Department of the Interior
1849 C Street, NW
Washington, DC 20240
Tel: 202-208-4648
Web: http://www.nps.gov/nps

■ Related Articles

The Environment

Parks and Public Lands

Agribusiness Technicians

Agricultural Consultants

Ecologists

Land Trust or Preserve Managers

Park Rangers

Range Technicians

■ **See Soil Conservationists and Technicians**

Rate Reviewers

■ **See Billing Clerks**

Raters

■ **See Billing Clerks**

Real Estate Agents and Brokers

■ Overview

Real estate brokers execute instructions from buyers or sellers for the sale or rental of property. Brokers employ agents to rent or sell property for clients on a commission basis. Both of these workers are sometimes called *real estate agents.*

■ History

Three factors contributed to the rise of the modern real estate business: first, the general increase in the total population and in the number of pieces of real estate for sale; second, the growing percentage of people owning property; and third, the complexity of laws regarding the transfer of real estate. These factors led to the need for experienced agents, on whom both sellers and buyers increasingly rely.

Professionalization of the real estate field developed rapidly in the 20th century. In 1908, the National Association of Real Estate Boards (NAREB), now called the National Association of Realtors (NAR), was founded. This huge trade group has encouraged the highest ethical standards for the field and has lobbied hard in Congress for many of the tax advantages that homeowners and property owners now enjoy.

■ The Job

The primary responsibility of real estate brokers and agents is to help clients buy, sell, rent, or lease a piece of real estate. *Real estate* is a piece of land or property and all improvements attached to it. The property may be residential, commercial, or agricultural. When people wish to put property up for sale or rent, they contract with real estate brokers to arrange the sale and to represent them in the transaction. This contract with a broker is called a *listing.*

One of the main duties of brokers is to actively solicit listings for the agency. They develop leads for potential listings by distributing promotional items, by advertising in local publications, and by showing other available properties in open houses. They also spend a great deal of time on the phone exploring leads gathered from various sources, including personal contacts.

Once the listing is obtained, real estate brokers must analyze the property to best present it to prospective buyers. They have to recognize and promote the property's strong selling points while also being aware of its weaknesses. Agents usually develop descriptions of properties to be used in ads and promotions, and they have properties photographed. They may also advise owners on ways to make their properties more attractive to prospective buyers.

Frequently, the broker counsels the owner about the asking price for the property. This is done by comparing it with similar properties in the area that have recently been sold to determine the property's fair market value. The owners usually sign a contract agreeing that if they sell the property, they will pay the broker a percentage of the selling price. Unless stated in the contract, the broker and any agents of the brokerage are working to obtain the best selling price for the seller. Home buyers in some states are allowed to engage a broker as a buyer's broker, which means the broker is committed to work for the buyer's best interests.

When the property is ready to be shown, agents in the office review their files to identify prospective buyers. Frequently, after a week or two of exclusive marketing by one broker, the property for sale is entered into a computerized multiple-listing service so that other local real estate firms may show the property. To stimulate interest in the property, the broker advertises the house in local newspapers.

As potential buyers are contacted, the agent arranges a convenient time for them to see the property. If the property is vacant, the broker usually retains the key. To

REAL ESTATE AGENTS AND BROKERS	
SCHOOL SUBJECTS	Business English Mathematics
PERSONAL SKILLS	Communication/ideas Helping/teaching
WORK ENVIRONMENT	Primarily indoors Primarily multiple locations
MINIMUM EDUCATION LEVEL	High school diploma
SALARY RANGE	$25,000 to $45,000 to $100,000
CERTIFICATION OR LICENSING	Required by all states
OUTLOOK	More slowly than the average
DOT	250
GOE	08.02.04
NOC	6232
O*NET	43008

A real estate agent congratulates a couple on the purchase of their new home.

adjust to the schedules of potential buyers, agents frequently show properties in the late afternoon or evening and on weekends. In many areas, Sunday-afternoon open houses are used to provide easy access to available properties. Because a representative of the broker's firm is usually on the premises in each house, open houses are a good way to put part-time or beginning agents to work.

An agent may have to meet several times with a prospective buyer to discuss and view available properties. The successful real estate agent has to determine the style and size of property the buyer is looking for and the price the buyer will be able to pay. The agent will often emphasize points that might be of particular interest to the buyer. To people with young families, for example, the agent may emphasize the convenient floor plan or the proximity of schools and shopping centers. To people looking for investment rental properties, the agent may stress available financing arrangements, the ease of finding a tenant, and factors that may contribute to the long-range value of the property. In addition to this, the agent points out features that the buyer should weigh when considering alternative purchases. The agent must also be familiar with tax rates, zoning regulations, home construction methods, and insurance needs.

When the buyer finds an affordable and desirable property, the agent must bring the buyer and seller together at terms agreeable to both. In many cases, different brokers or agents will represent the seller and buyer. Very often, the parties must bargain over the price of the property. In such situations, good negotiating skills become very important. Both agents may have to present counteroffers to get the best possible price for the seller and buyer.

Once both parties have signed the contract, the broker or agent must see to it that all special terms of the contract are carried out before the closing date. For example, if the seller has agreed to a home inspection or a termite inspection, the agent must make sure that the inspection is carried out. If the seller has agreed to make any repairs, again the broker or agent must make sure that they have been made; otherwise, the sale cannot be completed.

Brokers often provide buyers with information on loans to finance their purchase. They also arrange for title searches and title insurance. A broker's knowledge, resourcefulness, and creativity in arranging financing that is favorable to the buyer can mean the difference between success and failure in closing a sale. In some cases, agents assume the responsibilities of closing the sale, but in many areas this is accomplished by *lawyers* or *loan officers*.

Specialists in commercial or agricultural real estate operate in much the same fashion. Their clients usually have well-established priorities about what an acceptable property must have. For example, any property that would be of interest to a trucking firm must be located near major highways. These real estate specialists often conduct extensive searches for property that meets clients' specifications, so they must study the properties more carefully. They usually make fewer sales but receive higher commissions.

In addition to selling real estate, some brokers rent and manage properties for a fee. Some brokers combine other types of work, such as selling insurance or practicing law, with their real estate businesses.

■ Requirements

High School

There are no standard educational requirements for the real estate field. However, most employers require at least a high school diploma.

Postsecondary Training

An increasing percentage of real estate agents and brokers have some college education. A good general education provides background helpful in working with the many different types of people that an agent encounters. College courses in psychology, economics, sociology, marketing, finance, business administration, architecture, and engineering are helpful. Many agents and brokers have taken formal college courses in real estate. A complete list of the hundreds of colleges and universities offering courses in real estate is available from the National Association of Realtors (NAR).

Certification or Licensing

Every state and the District of Columbia require that real estate agents and brokers be licensed. Most states ask prospective agents to complete at least 30 hours of classroom training and to pass written examinations on real estate fundamentals and state laws. Brokers must pass more extensive examinations and must usually complete at least 90 hours of classroom training. They are also often required to have sales experience of one to three years.

State licenses are usually renewed annually without examination. Agents who move to another state must qualify under the licensing laws of that state. To supplement minimum state requirements, many agents take courses in real estate principles, laws, financing, appraisal, and property development and management. These courses are often sponsored by local real estate boards that are members of the NAR or its affiliates.

Qualified agents and brokers are usually affiliated with the NAR through membership in one of the more than 1,300 local boards or its affiliated associations. Only those active members who subscribe to the NAR Code of Ethics may legally use the term "realtor." Qualified specialists may join such NAR affiliates such as the Institute of Real Estate Management, the Society of Industrial and Office Realtors, or the REALTORS(r) Land Institute.

Other Requirements

Successful brokers and agents must be willing to study the industry and improve their skills constantly. For example, those who sell or rent business property must stay abreast of the latest business and economic trends as well as the prices being charged for competing properties in the market. *Residential real estate brokers* have to keep up with the latest trends in mortgage financing, construction, and community development. Real estate agents and brokers must have a thorough knowledge of the housing market in their communities. They must know which neighborhoods will best fit their clients' needs and budgets. They must be familiar with local zoning and tax laws and know where buyers can obtain reasonable financing. Agents and brokers must also act as go-betweens in the price negotiations between buyers and sellers. Many real estate firms, especially the larger ones, offer formal training programs for both beginners and experienced agents.

In most cases, educational experience is less important than the right personality. Brokers want agents who possess a pleasant personality, exude honesty, and maintain a neat appearance. To be successful as an agent requires a general liking for people. Agents must work with many different types of people and inspire their trust and confidence. They must be able to express themselves well and show enthusiasm to motivate customers.

Agents must have good judgment to combine knowledge of current real estate market values with informed predictions of future developments in the communities they serve. They should also be well organized and detail oriented, as well as having a good memory for names, faces,

and business details, such as taxes, zoning regulations, and local land-use laws.

Maturity is an asset in this profession. In fact, many successful agents enter the field in middle age. A thorough knowledge of the general geographic area will help those entering the field. To drum up new listings and prospective buyers, agents must be willing to participate in local civic and social organizations.

Agents must be tactful. Frequently, an agent receives a listing that exactly meets the specifications established by a customer. Unfortunately, after seeing the property, the customer may be indecisive about what he or she really wants. In such cases, the agent must be patient and allow customers to make their own decisions. An agent may show one customer through dozens of properties before closing a sale.

■ Exploring

Calling on local real estate brokers and agents should provide useful information on the field. Information on licensing requirements may be obtained from local real estate boards or from the real estate departments of each state. State licensing requirements prohibit inexperienced workers from gaining sales experience. Part-time and summer employment in a real estate office, however, may provide a clearer picture of the field.

■ Employers

Real estate agents and brokers may work in small offices or larger organizations, or they may work for themselves. Opportunities exist at large real estate firms specializing in commercial real estate, at smaller, local offices that sell residential properties, and everything in between. Agents work semiautonomously, developing their own client bases and setting their own schedules, often under the aegis of a firm or office.

■ Starting Out

The typical entry position in this field is as an agent working for a broker with an established office. Another opportunity may be in inside sales with a construction firm that is building a new housing development. Beginners usually apply directly to local real estate firms or may be referred through public and private employment services. Brokers looking to hire agents may run newspaper advertisements. Local real estate boards may be able to steer applicants toward offices that are hiring. People often contact firms in their own communities, where their knowledge of local neighborhoods is an advantage.

The beginning agent must choose between the advantages of joining a small or a large organization. In a small office, the newcomer will train informally under an experienced agent. The newcomer's duties will be broad and varied, and if the new agent is the junior member of a small organization, the duties may often be menial. However, this is a good chance to learn all the basics of the business, including the use of computers to locate available properties or identify available sources of financing. In larger firms, the new agent may proceed through a more standardized training process and may specialize in one phase of the real estate field, such as commercial real estate, mortgage financing, or property management.

The first months are usually difficult for beginning agents. They need to develop a reputation for service and a clientele of satisfied customers. People who have successfully purchased or sold a home through an agent are inclined to turn to that person for help with future real estate transactions and to recommend that agent to their relatives and friends. The beginner spends a great deal of time on the telephone seeking listings of properties to sell and answering calls in response to advertisements.

■ Advancement

While many successful agents develop professionally by expanding the quality and quantity of their services, others seek advancement by entering management or by specializing in residential or commercial real estate. The agent may enter management by becoming the head of a major division of a large real estate firm. Other agents purchase an established real estate business, join one as a partner, or set up their own offices. Self-employed agents must meet the state requirements for a broker's license.

Agents who wish to specialize have a number of available options. They may have to decide between residential and commercial sales. Real estate brokers may develop property management businesses. In return for approximately 5 percent of the gross receipts, *property managers* operate apartment houses or multiple-tenant business properties for their owners. Property managers are in charge of renting (including advertising, tenant relations, and collecting rents), building maintenance (heating, lighting, cleaning, and decorating), and accounting (financial recording and filing tax returns).

There are a number of professional designations available to both residential and commercial real estate agents. These designations demonstrate an advanced level of experience and knowledge and focus on various specialty areas.

A limited number of agents may qualify for the complex role of the *appraiser*, who estimates the current market value of land and buildings. Highly experienced agents may serve as *real estate counselors*, advising clients on the suitability of available property. Other agents may enter mortgage financing, placing real estate loans with interested financial institutions or private lenders.

Real estate brokers sometimes play a key role in land development through their cooperation in long-range plans for cities, subdivisions, housing tracts, shopping centers, and industrial sites. Some brokers engage in the business of buying and selling homes for their own account. Anticipating metropolitan expansion, they buy up lands that may appreciate in value, thus facilitating development. Occasionally, experienced brokers may join the real estate departments of major corporations or large government agencies.

■ Earnings

Compensation in the real estate field is based almost entirely upon commissions. Commissions range from 5 to 10 percent of the selling price, averaging about 7 percent. Agents usually split commissions with the brokers who employ them. The broker may take half the commission in return for providing the agent with the office space, advertising support, sales supervision, and the use of the broker's good name. When two or more agents are involved in a transaction (for example, one agent listing the property for sale and another selling it), the commission is usually divided between the two on the basis of an established formula. Agents can earn more if they both list and sell the property.

Full-time residential real estate agents earn an average of about $31,500 per year. Commercial agents usually earn $50,000 or more annually. Brokers may advance their agents (especially those new to the business) a stated amount each month against future commissions on sales. Brokers earn a median gross personal annual income (after expenses) of about $50,000 in residential real estate and about $100,000 in commercial real estate. The most successful people in the field earn much more. Brokers have a much higher gross salary, out of which they have to pay staff and office expenses, advertising costs, travel and entertainment expenses, and other costs of doing business. Agents may have to pay their own travel expenses.

Because most agents work on a commission basis and as such are considered independent from the firms they work with, they do not usually receive standard benefits like paid vacations, health insurance, or sick leave.

Agents and brokers may supplement their income by appraising property, placing mortgages with private lenders, or selling insurance. Since earnings are irregular and economic conditions unpredictable, agents and brokers should maintain sufficient cash reserves for slack periods.

■ Work Environment

It is relatively simple to enter the real estate field. Anyone who qualifies for a license needs only a telephone number to be in business. However, a glance at the real estate advertisements in any newspaper will offer a picture of a highly competitive field. In addition to full-time workers, the existence of many part-time agents increases competition for those making their entire living from the field.

Beginning agents must accept the frustration inherent in the early months in the business. All agents must begin by accepting modest listings, which they work hard to get. Building a client base and developing sales skills can take some time.

After agents become established, they can expect to work many evenings and weekends. Agents work on their own schedule and are free to take a day off when they choose. However, this also means they may be missing out on an important lead or may not be available to serve their clients. Unlike in some other areas of sales, real estate agents do little overnight travel. Some real estate brokers do much of their work out of their own homes. Successful agents will spend little time in an office, instead being out showing properties to potential buyers or meeting with sellers to set up a listing.

Most real estate agents and brokers work in small business establishments. Only in metropolitan areas do agents have the option of joining larger organizations. Real estate positions are found in every part of the country but are concentrated in large urban areas and in smaller, rapidly growing communities. Regardless of the size of the community in which they work, good agents should know its economic life, the personal preferences of its citizens, and the demand for real estate.

■ Outlook

About 408,000 people worked as real estate agents and brokers in 1996, many of them part-time. Employment of these workers is expected to grow more slowly than the average through 2006. However, as the average age of real estate agents and brokers is considerably higher than for workers in many other occupations, many opportunities for new agents will be made available because of agents retiring or transferring to other types of work. Because of this high job turnover, tens of thousands of real estate openings are expected yearly.

The country's expanding population will create additional demand for real estate services, and growing affluence suggests that the percentage of Americans owning their own homes will increase. Continuing mobility among Americans also indicates a continued high volume of real estate transactions. People are buying their first homes later in life, but as the general age of the population increases, the overall number of property owners should continue to rise.

Increased use of technology, such as computers, faxes, and databases, will help improve an agent's productivity. Computer-generated images now allow agents and customers to view multiple property listings without leaving the office. Well-trained, ambitious people who enjoy selling should have the best chance for success in this field.

Employment of real estate agents and brokers is sensitive to economic swings. A downturn in the general economy usually results in a diminishing of mortgage financing and slows construction of new homes. During these periods, the earnings of agents and brokers decline, and many people work fewer hours or leave the profession.

■ For More Information

For information on professional designations, real estate courses, and publications, contact:

National Association of Realtors
430 North Michigan Avenue
Chicago, IL 60611
Tel: 312-329-8200
Web: http://nar.realtor.com

For information on land real estate, contact:

REALTORS(r) Land Institute
430 North Michigan Avenue
Chicago, IL 60611
Tel: 312-329-8440

For information on industrial and office real estate, contact:

Society of Industrial and Office Realtors
700 11th Street, NW, Suite 510
Washington, DC 20001
Tel: 202-737-1150
Web: http://www.sior.com

■ Related Articles

Business

Insurance

Law

Real Estate

Property and Real Estate Managers

Real Estate Developers

Title Searchers and Examiners

Real Estate Developers

■ Overview

Real estate developers envision, organize, and execute construction or renovation projects for commercial or private use. This process involves negotiation with *property owners, real estate agents, investors*, lending institutions such as banks and insurance companies, *architects, lawyers, general contractors, government officials*, and other interested parties. Developers may work independently as consultants or in partnership with other professionals involved in real estate development.

■ History

The United States is a comparatively young country without a long history of densely populated cities. But in Europe, there is evidence of city-dwelling patterns as far back as 3,000 years ago. In areas of early Roman settlement, archaeologists have discovered the remnants of street grids, sewage lines, and uniform construction indicating some level of formal planning. Since the Middle Ages, Paris has had municipal regulations governing the placement and use of buildings.

Such planning and regulations emerge when many people try to live harmoniously in a limited space. In these situations, land has value and, therefore, is expensive. Construction of homes, roads for travel, or public buildings for commerce and government requires a substantial investment of money. The developer is the entrepreneur who sees an opportunity to make money by providing services, in the form of buildings or infrastructure, to the community. The developer's role throughout history has been to envision development, organize investors to fund land purchase and construction, and oversee the project.

Individuals have played this role in much the same way as long as people have lived in settled communities. What has changed, and what continues to change, are the zoning laws and building codes regulating development and the tax laws affecting the organization of the development entity.

■ The Job

A developer may be involved in purchasing 500 suburban acres and developing 1,000 condominiums, a couple of parks, a golf course, and a small shopping center with a grocery store, full-service dry cleaner, video rental store, and health club. Or a developer may renovate and remodel an existing structure, such as a warehouse, for use as a restaurant and office space. The developer's actual day-to-day activities vary depending upon the type and size of the project and the structure of the development entity.

Whether a group of investors approaches the developer or the developer searches out investors, the first step is to structure the development entity, a group

made up of the owner of the project (the person or group who will receive the profits or suffer the losses from the proposed development), the investors who put up the initial equity funds, and the developer. In many cases, the developer is the owner. These individuals may establish a development entity with only one owner, a partnership with a lead owner, a limited partnership, or a corporation that sells stock to stockholders.

The legal definitions of each type of entity vary according to locale, and the benefits and risks of each are quite different. The developer, who facilitates the process of structuring the contract, is concerned with three main issues—managing risk, gathering equity to facilitate borrowing money, and creating a functioning structure with a limited number of people involved in decision-making.

The developer's job at the beginning of a project has been compared to pitching a tent in high wind. The toughest thing is getting the first corner nailed down. In negotiating with potential investors, the developer brings all interested parties to the table to secure an initial commitment of equity funds. Without equity, the developer is unable to approach banks or insurance companies for loans to complete the project.

The developer may come to the table with $100,000 of personal money to invest—or none. With an excellent track record and a solid proposal, the developer's involvement in the project may be enough to secure the confidence of potential investors. But the developer must show a willingness to protect these investors by creating a development entity that exposes them only to reasonable risk.

Most investors want to risk only the equity money they contribute. If the project fails, they do not want to be held liable for all the money lost. The contract needs to protect their other assets, such as their homes, savings accounts, and other investments, in case of a default on the loans. So the contract must be written in such a way that the investors are willing to accept the risk involved.

After securing the equity necessary to convince financial institutions to participate in the project, the developer approaches these institutions, primarily banks and insurance companies, to secure financing.

Most development projects require both short-term and long-term financing. Banks often provide the money to buy land and complete construction. However, to receive this short-term financing, sometimes called a *construction loan*, the developer must already have equity funds from the investors. The equity money might equal from 10 to 40 percent of the total amount of the loan.

Insurance companies are the most common providers of long-term financing, which is used to pay off the construction loan. Long-term financing commitments are based on the economic projections of the completed development and usually must be obtained before securing short-

REAL ESTATE DEVELOPERS	
SCHOOL SUBJECTS	Business Mathematics
PERSONAL SKILLS	Communication/ideas Leadership/management
WORK ENVIRONMENT	Indoors and outdoors Primarily multiple locations
MINIMUM EDUCATION LEVEL	High school diploma
SALARY RANGE	$20,000 to $100,000 to $1,000,000
CERTIFICATION OR LICENSING	None available
OUTLOOK	Little change or more slowly than the average
NOC	0121

term financing. Occasionally one institution will provide both the short-term and long-term financing, but this is less likely to happen with larger projects.

Another participant in real estate financing is the government. Sometimes a municipal government will issue a bond to raise money from taxes. These funds may provide long-term financing to a private developer for the construction of a stadium, for example, or for some infrastructure improvement, such as widening the streets. Municipal governments frequently participate in projects to develop run-down areas of the city. In exchange for shouldering some of the financial risk, the city stands to benefit from the increased productivity of the renovated neighborhood.

Before receiving a building permit, the developer may have to complete impact studies to assess how the proposed project will affect the community and the environment. He or she may also have to meet with the zoning board if there are regulations that the new building will be unable to meet.

At this stage, the project needs an architect. The architect's first job usually is to hire a *structural engineer* and a *mechanical engineer*. Together they create the building plans, which the developer submits to the building department.

This process of creating the plans involves consideration of economics, aesthetic architectural concerns, building codes, and other legal constraints imposed by the community. This is one of the most exciting and important times in the development process. Through the competition of the interests of all the involved parties, the best use for the site evolves, and the project is born.

While waiting for the building permit to be issued, the developer also puts the building plans out for bids from general contractors. The general contractor selected for the job hires subcontractors, such as carpenters, plumbers, roofers, and drywallers.

In applying for the building permit and preparing to break ground on the construction site, developers spend a lot of time dealing with government regulations. They must make sure that they understand and meet building codes designed to ensure the safety of future occupants. Windows in a residential building, for example, must have a certain number of square feet for light and a certain number for ventilation.

Developers must be aware not only of building codes but also of laws affecting construction. New buildings, for example, must meet handicap access codes to comply with the Americans with Disabilities Act.

On large projects, such as the development of a skyscraper in downtown Chicago, the developer will contract out much of the work, such as public relations and advertising, the completion of impact studies, and the general contractor's job. On smaller projects, however, the developer may perform some or all of these functions.

As general contractor, the developer is involved on a daily basis with work at the construction site. If someone else is hired as general contractor, the developer may only be involved at weekly construction meetings, where the architect, engineers, and various subcontractors discuss progress and changes necessary in the plans.

In either case, the developer, who is ultimately responsible for the success or failure of the project, must be knowledgeable about all aspects of the development process and capable of hiring a group of people who can work successfully as a team. Though the developer may or may not be an investor who stands to lose money, the developer's career is on the line with every project.

If a developer secures city approval and necessary funds to construct a new office building in a highly visible spot, the whole city may be watching. The local government officials may have used their influence to change zoning laws in favor of the project. Therefore, their reputations also may be riding on the building's success. If, for example, the construction costs exceed the initial estimates, and the developer is unable to raise the additional money to cover the costs, construction on the building may be halted at any stage, and the empty shell may stand for years as an eyesore in the community.

Failure to successfully complete such projects inhibits the developer's ability to secure investors and government cooperation in the future. Depending on the terms of the developer's contract, it may also mean that the developer is never compensated for the time and work spent on the project.

Once the project is complete, the developer's role depends upon the specifications set forth in the development entity. With a high-rise residential building, for example, the developer may be involved in selling or renting the apartments. As an owner in the project, the developer may be involved in the management of rental property for many years.

■ Requirements

High School

There are no specific educational requirements or certifications for becoming a real estate developer, but many developers have college degrees, and some have advanced degrees. High school students can prepare for careers in real estate development by pursuing a broad-based liberal arts curriculum that will prepare them for a college education. In addition, courses in economics, finance, mathematics, business, speech communications, drafting, and shop will be helpful.

Postsecondary Training

Schools generally do not offer a specific curriculum that leads to a career as a real estate developer. And because the position requires a broad base of knowledge as well as some experience in the business community, most people become real estate developers after leaving an earlier career.

Graduate degrees in law, business, and architecture are among the most beneficial to the real estate developer. For students interested in pursuing an advanced degree in one of these areas, the necessary preparatory work should be completed as an undergraduate.

To pursue a law degree, one needs a strong background in the liberal arts, including English, philosophy, history, and government. Good preparation for a master's degree in business includes course work in finance, marketing, accounting, business communications, and higher-level mathematics. An advanced degree in architecture requires an emphasis on drafting, mathematics, engineering, and physics.

Other Requirements

Real estate development is regarded as one of the most challenging careers in the real estate industry. A developer must have the ability to speculate about the economy and envision profitable ventures as well as a broad knowledge of the legal, financial, political, and construction issues related to development. Consequently, a background as a lawyer, architect, or general contractor can be highly beneficial to a real estate developer.

It is useful for a developer to have a working knowledge of both zoning laws and building codes. While it is the architect's primary responsibility to ensure that the plans ultimately submitted to the building department will be approved, the knowledgeable developer may decide it is appropriate to seek a variance in zoning or code. This is most common in nonsafety areas, such as the number of parking spaces required. A municipality might grant a variance if the developer presents a convincing case that the project will create a significant number of jobs for the community.

A real estate developer also must understand the marketplace. For this reason, experience in appraising, leasing, or selling real estate can prove very helpful. Real estate brokers who lease office space often have excellent contacts and knowledge for entering the development business. They know where the potential tenants are, and they understand the issues involved in developing large buildings for commercial use. Developers also must grasp the basics of finance to structure the development entity effectively.

■ Exploring

Reading the real estate section of the local newspaper and following the building and development activities in the community are good ways to gain exposure to this industry. A local librarian should also be able to refer interested students to books and magazines about real estate development. Sometimes a teacher will be able to arrange for a developer or other real estate professional to visit and talk about his or her work.

Aspiring developers can also prepare for their careers by working in the offices of the following professionals: real estate developers, lawyers practicing within the real estate industry, architects, and general contractors. Spending time in any of these offices will introduce individuals to the general milieu of the real estate developer's world. The early exposure can also help prospective real estate developers decide in which of these areas they most want to develop expertise.

Students can gain good experience in certain aspects of real estate development by doing public relations, publicity, or advertising work and participating in fund-raising campaigns for school and community organizations. Volunteering with a housing advocacy organization, such as Habitat for Humanity, may provide opportunities to learn about home construction, bank financing, and legal contracts.

■ Employers

Real estate developers often work independently or open offices in communities that have property with the potential for development. The activity of the real estate marketplace will dictate the number of opportunities in a given community.

■ Starting Out

There is no specific way to become a real estate developer. Successful real estate developers are always the heart of the project, facilitating communication among the various participants. This often requires finely tuned diplomatic skills. Their proven track record, professional manner, and influence in the real estate world are their biggest assets. They have the ability to sell ideas and secure large sums of money from investors and lending institutions.

Most developers do not begin their careers in this field. They frequently have backgrounds as lawyers, architects, real estate brokers, or general contractors, positions which allow them to gain the expertise and contacts necessary for success in real estate development.

Many real estate developers secure work because they have established a reputation. Their contacts and knowledge in a particular community or type of real estate allow them to work more effectively than others. But developers also are successful because of their abilities in analyzing the marketplace, structuring solid investment proposals, facilitating the creation of the development entity, and overseeing projects.

■ Advancement

The real estate developer is really at the top of the profession. Advancement involves larger, more prestigious projects and earning more money. Such achievement may take several years. It is important to keep in mind that even the most successful developers suffer setbacks when projects fail. For those not-so-successful developers, such setbacks can end a career.

■ Earnings

There is no set pay scale for real estate developers. How much developers make depends upon their skill and experience, the size of the projects they work on, the structure established for their payment in the development entity contract, and the successful completion of the project.

Sometimes, developers are contracted by a group of individual investors or a company to manage a project. In this case they may work out a consulting agreement with a certain secured fee up front, preset fees paid throughout the duration of the project, and some percentage of the profits once the project is complete. Or the agreement may contain some combination of these payment options.

A less experienced developer will often shoulder more risk on a project to gain expertise and complete work that will improve the developer's reputation. In these instances, developers may be undercompensated or not paid at all for their time and effort if the project fails.

■ Work Environment

Real estate developers are often highly visible individuals in the community. It is important that they have excellent communication skills, be able to work with all kinds of people, and enjoy the speculative nature of the business.

They spend a great deal of time negotiating with executives in banks and insurance companies, government officials, and private or corporate business investors. A certain professionalism and comfort in executive situations is necessary for success.

However, some developers will report to the job site every day, don a hard hat, and oversee the work of roofers, plumbers, and electricians. The developer must be flexible enough to adjust to the job's varying demands.

In addition to staying in touch with investors and overseeing the project, developers sometimes may need to respond to the public and the media. Controversial, high-profile projects often put the developer under a spotlight, requiring excellent public relations skills.

Real estate developers, because of the complexity of their job and the often large sums of money at stake, work under a great deal of pressure and stress. While the level of risk and the potential profit depend upon the developer's role in the development entity, those who like a steady schedule with a dependable paycheck may not be well-suited to this career.

Hours can be long and frequently vary with the type of project and stage of development. Developers may have to attend city council meetings or neighborhood meetings in the evening if they are seeking changes in zoning laws before applying for a building permit. In addition to having the potential to earn a large sum of money, developers enjoy the satisfaction of seeing a project evolve from idea inception through various stages of planning and finally into a finished usable structure.

Though their work depends upon the cooperation of other individuals and organizations, developers also enjoy a certain level of independence and flexibility in their lifestyles. As entrepreneurs, they shoulder a lot of personal risk for their businesses, but this brings with it great opportunities to do creative work and positively influence their communities while potentially earning a handsome profit.

■ Outlook

The outlook for real estate developers is subject to the fluctuations of the general economy. In the late 1990s, economic conditions were excellent for real estate developers. Record-low interest rates roused many formerly depressed areas of the country to renewed economic vigor. However, according to *Jobs '97*, industry experts predict a decline in the number of real estate developers and emergence of two tiers: larger, well-financed firms able to withstand the market's changes and smaller developers who are more flexible and in touch with local markets. The Bureau of Labor Statistics indicates that growth in the industry will be slower than the average through 2006.

But economic conditions are never fixed. In the early 1990s, the country experienced a recession, which halted growth in many industries and dampened the prospects for real estate developers. In addition, the real estate market can be quite strong in some parts of the country and weak in others.

■ For More Information

For information on the real estate industry and career opportunities, contact:

National Association of Realtors
430 North Michigan Avenue
Chicago, IL 60611
Tel: 312-329-8292
Web: http://www.realtor.com

■ Related Articles

Banking and Financial Services
Construction
Law
Real Estate

Real-Time Captioners

■ Overview

Real-time captioners operate a computer-aided transcription (CAT) stenotype system to create closed captions for use in live television broadcasts, in classroom instruction, or in other scenarios requiring live translating or interpreting on the computer. Computer-Aided Real-time Translation, or CART, refers to use of machine steno shorthand skills to produce real-time text on a computer.

Generally, captioning systems use a modified stenotype machine connected to a computer. The real-time captioner inputs the captions phonetically (transcription or speech sounds) on the steno machine, and the sounds are then translated into English words by the computer using a special dictionary created by the captioner. During a live broadcast, the captions are entered as the program progresses, much as a court reporter transcribes a trial as it progresses. The input data is sent along telephone lines to the broadcast point, where the caption codes become part of the television signal.

REAL-TIME CAPTIONERS	
SCHOOL SUBJECTS	English Government
PERSONAL SKILLS	Communication/ideas Following instructions
WORK ENVIRONMENT	Primarily indoors Primarily one location
MINIMUM EDUCATION LEVEL	Bachelor's degree
SALARY RANGE	$28,000 to $50,000 to $65,000
CERTIFICATION OR LICENSING	Recommended
OUTLOOK	Faster than the average
DOT	203
GOE	07.05.03
O*NET	34002J

■ History

Real-time captioning technology arose from a need to make live broadcasts accessible to deaf and hard-of-hearing people. To meet this need, the National Captioning Institute (NCI), founded in 1979, became the chief architect of the computer-based technology needed to bring captions to real-time audiences nationwide. At first, NCI, headquartered in Vienna, Virginia, provided captions only for pre-recorded programs. Captions were prepared in advance by people who were not court reporters. It soon became apparent, however, that captions were needed for live television, so NCI went to work developing a system that could prepare captions for live broadcast.

NCI first introduced real-time captioning to eager audiences in April 1982 when it captioned the Academy Awards. Today, real-time captioners create captions for a wide range of live broadcasts on network, cable, syndication, and pay-per-view services. All programs on prime-time schedules of the three major commercial networks are now captioned, many by real-time captioners.

Real-time captions are generated within seconds after a word is spoken. They are made possible by highly skilled court reporters who receive months of specialized retraining to become first-class real-time captioners.

■ The Job

The refined skills of real-time captioners are called upon every day to bring the latest news, sports, and entertainment to a diverse group consisting not only of the deaf and hard-of-hearing, but young children learning to read and those learning English as a second language. While captioning a live program, meeting, or other event may seem rather straightforward on the surface, there is a great deal of work, anxiety, and preparation that goes into ensuring that the words appearing on screen come out as smoothly and effortlessly as possible. Real-time captioning requires much dexterity and discipline to be able to reach the higher speeds required—240 words a minute—and good brain-to-hand coordination to get it all down quickly *and* accurately.

There is also much preparation work that must be done by real-time captioners before they can caption a live television broadcast. It takes about one and a half to two hours to prepare for an average news broadcast, using preparation materials obtained from the broadcaster and the captioner's own research. (Special broadcasts like holiday parades, the Super Bowl, or the Olympics can take days or even weeks of preparation.) Captioners call this pre-show preparation "dictionary-building."

Captioners working for established captioning houses will usually have access to all types of reference materials-everything from *Star Stats Who's Who in Hollywood* to the *Congressional Staff Directory*. Captioners working on their own will want to think about what kinds of materials to include in their own libraries.

As a real-time captioner, you'll dig through resource materials to find words that might come up during a broadcast, then develop "briefs" or steno codes that you will use to "write" these words when you hear them during the broadcast. It is important that you test all the briefs developed for complicated names to make sure you are translating properly. Because you'll hear names and words you have not prepared dictionary entries for, you must learn to "write around" the actual words and listen for titles. In this way you can write "The former Secretary of State" instead of "Henry Kissinger," for example.

While striving to keep them to a minimum, you will occasionally make mistakes that go out over the air. For example, in real-time captioning, the phrase "Olympic try-outs," which would require the captioner to type five key strokes on a stenotype machine, might come out (and actually did) as "old limp pig tryouts" if strokes are entered that the computer cannot match correctly.

CART reporters also work in classroom settings, where they might be seen with a notebook computer and steno keyboard, sitting next to a deaf person. As a CART reporter, you'll write everything that happens, making sure the notebook computer screen is turned so the deaf person can see it. To help the client better understand what is going on, you may paraphrase or interpret the proceedings, not just create a verbatim record, as in a courtroom. Real-time reporters can also cover meetings, with captions shown on large projection screens. Additionally, computer technology allows highly skilled court reporters to provide real-time captioning in the courtroom, which has great value for large numbers of deaf or hard-of-hearing judges, attorneys, and litigants, or those who have difficulty understanding English. Also, judges and attorneys can scroll back to earlier statements during the trial and mark text for later reference.

One major difference between real-time captioning for television broadcast and other live-display settings and verbatim reporting, as is frequently done in courtrooms and lawyer's offices, is that captioning's main purpose is to let the viewer who is deaf or hard-of-hearing understand the story being told on the screen. It is not enough to listen only for the phonetic strokes; the real-time captioner must also listen for context.

Sheri Smargon works for a captioning company in Tampa, Florida. "I caption the news for about 12 different stations around the country," she says. "My company has more, but I have regular cities that I'm usually responsible for. The news consists of anything from a half-hour program to two hours of straight news. I also caption NBA and MLB games." While captioning, Sheri doesn't receive a TV picture. "I get an audio feed only, so I just write what I hear," she says. "Hockey games were the hardest...everyone's name sounds alike!"

Before beginning even limited on-air captioning, you will have spent at least three to six months in training, eight hours a day, five days a week, and up to one year of real-time captioning before doing certain specialized programming. A vital part of the production team, you must also become intimately familiar with the programs you are captioning to know what to expect and to anticipate the unexpected.

A typical day for a captioner trainee would include preparing for a practice broadcast by creating a job dictionary, then writing that practice broadcast for supervisors, who would make suggestions as to conflict resolution, editing, brief form, style, and format. Later, the trainee would review the broadcast and make the necessary dictionary entries. Trainees would sit in on a variety of broadcasts with more experienced captioners.

Real-time captioning for television is generally performed in a production control room, equipped with several television sets and networked computer systems, giving the environment a high-tech look and feel. Sometimes, one captioner will write a show alone; sometimes two captioners will share a show, depending on whether there are commercials or not. No captioner can maintain a high accuracy level without taking regular breaks. On a show with no commercials, two captioners would typically switch back and forth about every ten minutes.

As a show gets closer to air, the environment in the control room becomes tense, as the real-time captioner scrambles to get last-minute information in the computer. Then a deep breath, and the countdown begins . . . "Good evening, I'm Peter Jennings."

The captioner strokes the steno keys while listening to the live broadcast, transcribing the broadcast accurately while inserting correct punctuation and other symbols. (Double arrows at the beginning of a sentence indicate that a new speaker is speaking.) Those strokes are converted to electronic impulses, which travel through a cable to the computer. The steno strokes are matched with the correct entries on the captioner's personal dictionary. That data is then sent by modem to the broadcast site, where it gets added to the broadcaster's video signal. Within two to three seconds, people across the country can see those captions— if they have televisions with a built—in decoder chip or a set with a decoder connected to it.

Some kinds of captioning can be done from home, mainly broadcasts for local television stations. The equipment needed (which may be provided by the employer) includes a computer, modem, steno machine, and the appropriate software. Captioners may even choose to work for companies that specialize in producing captions remotely, with just an audio feed, thereby allowing more home-based operations. Getting started in the business, however, usually requires an on-site presence, until confidence and trust is established. Obviously, live events that are not broadcast will require a real-time captioner on site.

■ Requirements

High School

You should take typing and computer courses to increase keyboard speed and accuracy and to develop an understanding of word processing programs. Because you'll be working with a variety of news, sports, and entertainment programs, you should keep up on current events by taking journalism and government courses. English composition and speech classes can help you develop your vocabulary and grammar skills.

Postsecondary Training

You should first complete training to become a court and conference reporter (stenographer), which takes anywhere from two to four years. An associate's or bachelor's degree in court and conference reporting, or satisfactory completion of other two-year equivalent programs, is usually required. Because of the additional training needed to learn computer and English grammar skills, some of the formerly two-year programs have gone to three. In fact, many real-time reporters and their employers believe that additional formal education in the arts and sciences is needed to perform the work properly and to adapt to the swift technological changes taking place. They are urging the National Court Reporters Association (NCRA), to which most captioners and other reporters belong, to require a bachelor's degree for entry into the court reporting profession, which would extend to captioning as well. A few four-year college programs already exist, to allow students a well-rounded background. A degree in English (or the primary language in which captioning will be done) or linguistics would be helpful. Others argue, however, that while a formal education is beneficial, many court reporters who never earned a four-year degree are working successfully with high skill levels.

Even after graduating from court reporting school, you will have to undergo more specialized training, during which you'll hone your reporting skills to achieve the proficiency needed to create broadcast-quality captions.

Certification or Licensing

Typically, the reporter considering real-time captioning work has passed the Registered Professional Reporter (RPR) exam given by the NCRA, or a comparable state certification exam. Potential employers may even require it. The skills and knowledge needed to pass this exam are similar to those required for captioning, though not as stringent. Anyone capable of doing broadcast-quality captioning work can easily get RPR certification.

Other Requirements

You should have extreme proficiency in machine shorthand skills, and an ability to perform under pressure. Familiarity with CAT systems is usually preferred, as is previous court or field reporting experience. It generally takes several years of court reporting experience to be able to take and transcribe complex testimony with the high levels of speed and accuracy that real-time captioning demands.

Real-time captioners must also possess an incredible amount of concentration. Besides typing accurately at speeds of 190 to 240 words a minute to keep up with the fastest natural speakers, they must also anticipate commercial breaks so as not to cut off captions in mid-sentence, insert appropriate punctuation marks and symbols, and watch their own translation closely to correct any problems on the spot.

"I try to stay informed about what's going on in the world," Sheri says, "not just in the news. It helps to know that 'Eminem' has a new record, as well as to know that Kosovo is a province, not a city."

■ Exploring

Although some core classes on captioning technology are being injected into court reporting and other stenographic curricula around the country, it is still a "hit or miss" situation, with many schools simply intimidated by the new technology. Good programs exist, however, that are providing beneficial exposure and actually working with local TV stations and area colleges to provide both news captioning and real-timing or steno interpreting in the classroom for deaf students and those with disabilities.

A smart way to prepare for real-time captioning, according to a real-time captioner who hires new graduates for a captioning company, is to practice by transcribing or writing newspaper articles or those from news magazines. Along with helping to build vocabulary skills, this exercise enables you to focus on conflict resolution by seeing the word in print, helps to familiarize you with difficult foreign names and words, and increases awareness of current events, both national and international.

While honing your skills, you may also get good exposure by working with local organizations, such as the Association of Late Deafened Adults, Self-Help for Hard of Hearing Persons, the National Association for the Deaf, the Alexander Graham Bell Society, and other nonprofit groups that might eventually need captioning services. Although the pay will not be as high as it would at a captioning house, the job satisfaction level will be high. It is good to keep in mind that while the major captioning companies do sometimes hire people with little or no training for internships or on-the-job training, there is no substitute for experience.

■ Employers

Captioners are employed primarily by captioning companies such as NCI and VITAC. These companies contract with broadcasters and production companies to caption live and recorded events. You'll either work as a full-time employee for a captioning company, or you'll work freelance, as an independent contractor.

■ Starting Out

You should seek employment at one of the few large captioning companies in the country or contact station managers at your local television stations to inquire about real-time captioning positions. As with many other businesses, the best approach may be simply to start calling the leading companies in the field and the local companies and see who is hiring. Gallaudet University (http://www.gallaudet.edu/) in Washington, DC, puts out a list of captioning companies.

Before securing a real-time captioning position, you may have to "audition" as part of a pre-interview screening process that involves preparing raw steno notes from a sample tape-recorded program. The notes are then analyzed, with employment consideration based on the results of the evaluation and job experience. A good way to prepare for employment evaluation is to practice on the kind of material you wish to caption and to offer to demonstrate your skills.

■ Advancement

Advancement for a real-time captioner is dependent upon performance, with salary increases and promotions to more responsible positions awarded with greater proficiency and tenure. Skilled real-time captioners may advance to supervisory positions.

■ Earnings

It is difficult to show anything but a broad range for the earning potential of a real-time captioner. Earning power is dependent upon many variables and is often region-specific and a product of "what the market will bear." In large captioning organizations, real-time captioners can make anywhere from $28,000 for a recent graduate in training to $65,000 or even higher for those experienced and tireless workers who always volunteer for extra hours, overflow work, etc., and who are capable of captioning all kinds of programming. Trainee salaries increase once the captioner goes on the air.

Salaries for real-time captioners are often in line with salaries for court reporters. According to the NCRA, the 1997 salary for an official court reporter was $43,366 a year. For a freelance reporter, the salary was $51,524 a year.

A fringe benefit of working for a captioning agency for most reporters (particularly students just out of school) is that such agencies generally provide all the equipment, which would cost individuals approximately $15,000, were they to do captioning on their own. Large captioning organizations also offer benefits, such as vacation and health insurance, likely to be provided at a courthouse for court reporters but not at a freelance firm of deposition reporters, for instance.

■ Work Environment

Real-time captioning for television broadcast is not a nine-to-five job. While many reporting jobs require erratic hours, broadcast captioning is done seven days a week, around the clock. Real-time captioners producing captions for television broadcast will likely work nights, weekends, or holidays, as directed. Shows can air at 5:30 in the morning, at midnight on a Saturday night, or during Thanksgiving dinner.

Given the irregularity of TV schedules, several shifts are needed to cover programming hours scheduled throughout the day. It is imperative that captioners be flexible and dependable and that they not get fatigued, so they can maintain high accuracy levels. How many hours a day a captioner is on the air depends on the level of experience. If new to the air, captioners may do only one or two shows a day, as it takes longer to prepare for a broadcast and review the result in the beginning. An experienced captioner may be on the air three to five hours a day, writing short programs or a news broadcast or sporting event. At least, in the broadcast setting, real-time captioners do not have to produce transcripts, which eliminates the long hours that go along with that aspect of reporting.

Real-time captioning work can be physically demanding. Along with suffering the mental stress of performing in a live environment, real-time captioners may also be subject to repetitive stress injury, a prevalent industrial hazard for those who perform repeated motions in their daily work. Carpal tunnel, a type of repetitive stress injury, sometimes afflicts real-time captioners after several years. It can cause prickling sensation or numbness in the hand, and sometimes a partial loss of function.

"Captioning and real-timing are totally different from regular court reporting," Sheri says. "You have to be a certain kind of person to real-time. I find captioning challenging and rewarding and fun, usually."

■ Outlook

The NCRA reports a decline in enrollment in court reporting schools. This may be because of the development of voice and speech systems—the computer programs that automatically convert speech to written text. However, there are no current systems that can accurately handle multiple speakers, and it's unlikely that such technology will exist in the near future. Therefore, captioners and court reporters will be in high demand for years to come. New requirements by the FCC are also increasing demands for captioners—since 1997, the FCC has required captioning on nearly all TV programming in the United States. All new programs must be captioned by 2006.

Digital TV (DTV) will also make captioning more desirable and useful to more people, thereby increasing demand for captioners. DTV enhancements will allow viewers with poor vision to adjust text-size, styles, and fonts. DTV will also allow for more non-English letters, as well as more information transmitted per minute.

You should focus first on the area where you want to live and work. To caption area news or city council meetings in a local area, or do conventions in a large hotel, you must first obtain some costly supplies. These include a laptop or notebook computer, a compatible steno writer, cables, modem, and captioning software. You may also need a character generator to project onto a large convention screen.

To position yourself as advantageously as possible, you should learn the basic real-time skills that will enable you to do any live translating or interpreting on the computer. As such, you will be eligible for a variety of positions, including working in a computer-integrated courtroom; taking real-time depositions for attorneys; providing accompanying litigation support, such as key word indexing; real-timing or captioning in the classroom or doing broadcast captioning. The future looks great for those who qualify themselves to perform real-time translation.

Other opportunities for the real-time captioner include working with hospitals that specialize in cochlear implants. For late-deafened adults who learned English before sign language, if they learned to sign at all, captions provide a far greater comprehension level. Additionally, some local news stations across the country are working to expand and improve the quality of their local captioning capabilities, providing yet another source of potential employment for the real-time captioner.

■ For More Information

Visit the NCRA Web site for extensive career and certification information, as well as information about technology, education programs, and access to the NCRA monthly magazine:

National Court Reporters Association
8224 Old Courthouse Road
Vienna, VA 22182-3808
Tel: 800-272-6272
Email: msic@ncrahq.org
Web: http://www.verbatimreporters.com

The NCI Web site features historical information, a list of captioning terms, and employment information:

National Captioning Institute
1900 Gallows Road, Suite 3000
Vienna, VA 22182
Tel: 703-917-7600
Web: http://www.us.net/nci

■ Related Articles

Broadcasting

Law

Television

Court Reporters

Stenographers

Receptionists

■ Overview

Receptionists greet a business's clients and visitors, answer their questions, and direct them to the people they wish to see. Receptionists also answer telephones, take and distribute messages for other employees, and make sure no one enters the office unescorted or unauthorized. Many receptionists perform additional clerical duties. *Switchboard operators* perform similar tasks but primarily handle equipment that receives an organization's telephone calls. There are over one million receptionists employed throughout the United States.

■ History

In the 18th and 19th centuries, as businesses began to compete with each other for customers, merchants and other business people began to recognize the importance of giving customers the immediate impression that the business was friendly, efficient, and trustworthy. These businesses began to employ hosts and hostesses—workers who would greet customers, make them comfortable, and often serve them refreshments while they waited or did business with the owner. As businesses grew larger and more diverse, these hosts and hostesses—only recently renamed receptionists—took on the additional duties of answering phones, keeping track of workers, and directing visitors to the employee they needed to see. Receptionists also began to work as information dispensers, answering growing numbers of inquiries from the public. In the medical field, as services expanded, more receptionists were needed to direct patients to physicians and clinical services and to keep track of appointments and payment information.

Soon receptionists became indispensable to business and service establishments. Today, it is hard to imagine most medium-sized or large businesses functioning without a receptionist.

■ The Job

The receptionist is a specialist in human contact: the most important part of a receptionist's job is dealing with people in a courteous and effective manner. Receptionists greet customers, clients, patients, and salespeople, take their names, and determine the nature or their business and the person they wish to see. The receptionist then pages the requested person, directs the visitor to that person's office or location, or makes an appointment for a later visit. Receptionists often keep records of all visits by writing down the visitor's name, purpose of visit, person visited, and date and time.

Most receptionists answer the telephone at their place of employment; many operate switchboards or paging systems. These workers usually take and distribute messages for other employees and may receive and distribute mail. Receptionists may perform a variety of other clerical duties, including keying in and filing correspondence and other paperwork, proofreading, preparing travel vouchers, and preparing outgoing mail. In some businesses, receptionists are responsible for monitoring the attendance of other employees. In businesses where employees are frequently out of the office on assignments, receptionists may keep track of their whereabouts to ensure they receive important phone calls and messages. Many receptionists use computers and word processors in performing their clerical duties.

Receptionists are partially responsible for maintaining office security, especially in large firms. They may require all visitors to sign in and out and carry visitors' passes during their stay. Since visitors may not enter most offices unescorted, receptionists usually accept and sign for packages and other deliveries.

Receptionists are frequently responsible for answering inquiries from the public about a business's nature and operations. To answer these questions efficiently and in a manner that conveys a favorable impression, a receptionist must be as knowledgeable as possible about the business's products, services, policies, and practices and familiar with the names and responsibilities of all other employees. They must be careful, however, not to divulge classified information such as business procedures or employee activities that a competing company might be able to use. This part of a receptionist's job is so important that some businesses call their receptionists *information clerks.*

A large number of receptionists work in physicians' and dentists' offices, hospitals, clinics, and other health care establishments. Workers in medical offices receive patients, take their names, and escort them to examination rooms. They make future appointments for patients and may prepare statements and collect bill payments. In hospitals, receptionists obtain patient information, assign patients to rooms, and keep records on the dates they are admitted and discharged.

In other types of industries, the duties of these workers vary. Receptionists in hair salons arrange appointments for clients and may escort them to stylists' stations. Workers in bus or train companies answer inquiries about departures, arrivals, and routes. *In-file operators* collect and distribute credit information to clients for credit purposes. *Registrars*, *park aides*, and *tourist-information assistants* may be employed as receptionists at public or private facilities. Their duties may include keeping a record of the visitors entering and leaving the facility, as well as providing information on services that the facility provides. Information clerks, *automobile club information clerks,* and *referral-and-information aides* provide answers to questions by telephone or in person from both clients and potential clients and keep a record of all inquiries.

Switchboard operators may perform specialized work, such as operating switchboards at police district offices to take calls for assistance from citizens. Or, they may handle airport communication systems, which includes public address paging systems and courtesy telephones, or serve as *answering-service opera-*

RECEPTIONISTS	
SCHOOL SUBJECTS	Business English
PERSONAL SKILLS	Communication/ideas Helping/teaching
WORK ENVIRONMENT	Primarily indoors Primarily one location
MINIMUM EDUCATION LEVEL	High school diploma
SALARY RANGE	$11,900 to $18,600 to $24,250
CERTIFICATION OR LICENSING	None available
OUTLOOK	Faster than the average
DOT	237
GOE	07.04.04
NOC	1414
O*NET	55305

A receptionist greets a caller on a busy switchboard.

tors, who record and deliver messages for clients who cannot be reached by telephone.

■ Requirements

Most employees require receptionists to have a high school diploma. Some businesses prefer to hire workers who have completed post–high school courses at a junior college or business school. Many employers require typing, switchboard, computer, and other clerical skills, but may provide on-the-job training as the work is typically entry level.

High School

High school students may prepare for receptionist or switchboard operator positions by taking courses in business procedures, office machine operation, keyboarding, computers, business math, English, and public speaking.

Postsecondary Training

Students interested in post–high school education may find courses in basic bookkeeping and principles of accounting helpful in finding higher-paying receptionist jobs with better chances for advancement.

Other Requirements

Good receptionists need to be well-groomed, have pleasant voices, and be able to clearly express themselves. Because receptionists sometimes deal with demanding people, a smooth, patient disposition and good judgment are important. All receptionists need to be courteous and tactful. A good memory for faces and names also proves very valuable. Most important are good listening and communications skills and an understanding of human nature.

■ Exploring

A good way to obtain experience in working as a receptionist is through a high school work-study program. Students participating in such programs spend part of their school day in classes and the rest working for local businesses. This arrangement will help you gain valuable practical experience before you look for your first job. High school guidance counselors can provide information about work-study opportunities.

■ Employers

Almost all types of companies hire receptionists. They work in manufacturing, wholesale, retail, real estate, insurance, medicine, advertising, government, banking, church administration, and law.

■ Starting Out

High school students may be able to learn of openings with local businesses through their school guidance counselors or newspaper want ads. Local state employment offices frequently have information about receptionist work. Students should also contact area businesses for whom they would like to work; many available positions are not advertised in the paper because they are filled so quickly. Temporary-work agencies are a valuable resource for finding jobs, too, some of which may lead to permanent employment. Friends and relatives may also know of job openings.

■ Advancement

Advancement opportunities are limited for receptionists, especially in small offices. The more clerical skills and education workers have, the greater their chances for promotion to such better-paying jobs as secretary, administrative assistant, or bookkeeper. College or business school training can help receptionists advance to higher-level positions. Many companies provide training for their receptionists and other employees, helping workers gain skills for job advancement.

■ Earnings

Earnings for receptionists vary widely with the education and experience of the worker and type, size, and geographic location of the business. According to the U.S. Department of Labor, receptionists earned starting salaries of over $11,900 in 1996. Those with experience earned $24,250 or more.

In 1997, the federal government paid beginning receptionists salaries ranging from $18,900 to $19,200 a year; the average annual salary for experienced receptionists in the federal government was $21,240.

Receptionists are usually eligible for paid holidays and vacations, sick leave, medical and life insurance coverage, and a retirement plan of some kind.

Most receptionists work 5 days, 35 to 40 hours a week. Some may work weekend and evening hours, especially those in medical offices. Switchboard operators may have to work any shift of the day if their employers require 24-hour phone service, such as hotels and hospitals. These workers usually work holidays and weekend hours.

■ Work Environment

Because receptionists usually work near or at the main entrance to the business, their work area is one of the first places a caller sees. Therefore, these areas are usually pleasant and clean and are carefully furnished and decorated to create a favorable, businesslike impression. Work areas are almost always air-conditioned, well lit, and relatively quiet, although a receptionist's phone rings frequently. Receptionists work behind a desk or counter and spend most of their workday sitting, although some standing and walking is required when filing or escorting visitors to their destinations. The job may be stressful at times, especially when a worker must be polite to rude callers.

■ Outlook

According to the U.S. Department of Labor, over one million people were employed as receptionists in 1996, accounting for about a third of all information clerks. Factories, wholesale and retail stores, and service providers employ a large percentage of these workers. Nearly one-third of the receptionists in the United States work in health care settings, including offices, hospitals, nursing homes, urgent care centers, and clinics. Almost one-third work part time.

This field is expected to grow faster than the average through the year 2006. Many openings will occur due to the occupation's high turnover rate. Opportunities will be best for those with wide clerical skills and work experience. Growth in jobs for receptionists are expected to be greater than for other clerical positions because automation will have little effect on the receptionist's largely interpersonal duties and because of an anticipated growth in the number of businesses providing services. In addition, more and more businesses are learning how valuable a receptionist can be in furthering their public relations efforts and helping them convey a positive image.

■ For More Information

For industry information, contact:

International Association of Administrative Professionals
PO Box 20404
10502 NW Ambassador Drive
Kansas City, MO 64195-0404
Tel: 816-891-6600
Web: http://www.iaap-hq.org

■ Related Articles

Business

Office Clerks

Recreation Aides, Leaders, Specialists, and Supervisors

■ **See Recreation Workers, Divers and Diving Technicians**

Recreation Center Directors

■ **See Recreation Workers**

Recreation Workers

■ Overview

Recreation workers help people, as groups and as individuals, enjoy and use their leisure time constructively. They organize and administer physical, social, and cultural programs. They also operate recreational facilities and study recreation needs. There are over 230,000 recreation workers employed in the United States.

■ History

Americans enjoy more leisure time today than at any other period in history. The introduction of new technology, along with changing labor laws, has shrunk the work day and week. Workers receive increased vacation time, often setting their own, flexible hours and, in many cases, retiring at an earlier age. The use of

RECREATION WORKERS	
SCHOOL SUBJECTS	Physical education Theater/Dance
PERSONAL SKILLS	Following instructions Helping/teaching
WORK ENVIRONMENT	Indoors and outdoors Primarily one location
MINIMUM EDUCATION LEVEL	Bachelor's degree
SALARY RANGE	$16,000 to $18,700 to $37,500+
CERTIFICATION OR LICENSING	Required in certain positions
OUTLOOK	Faster than the average
DOT	195
GOE	09.01.01
NOC	4167
O*NET	27311

labor-saving devices and convenience foods in the home adds more free hours to a family's time, while increased income provides extra money for recreational activities.

During the last generation, leisure has become a time for planned activity. New services and revolutionized old ones have been developed to help Americans find beneficial ways in which to use their spare time.

Organized recreation has been of great value to those in nursing homes and other extended-care facilities. The occupations in recreation work grew out of the awareness that people were happier when they had an activity to participate in or look forward to. Today's recreation professionals are specialists in motivating people. They are trained, responsible leaders who understand and are sensitive to human needs and who are dedicated to helping people help themselves through recreation.

■ The Job

Recreation workers plan, organize, and direct recreation activities for people of all ages, social and economic levels, and degrees of physical and emotional health. The exact nature of their work varies and depends on their individual level of responsibility.

Recreation workers employed by local governments and voluntary agencies include *recreation supervisors* who coordinate recreation center directors, who in turn supervise recreation leaders and aides. With the help of volunteer workers, they plan and carry out programs at community centers, neighborhood playgrounds, recreational and rehabilitation centers, prisons, hospitals, and homes for children and the elderly, often working in cooperation with social workers and sponsors of the various centers.

Recreation supervisors plan programs to meet the needs of the people they serve. Well-rounded programs may include arts and crafts, dramatics, music, dancing, swimming, games, camping, nature study, and other pastimes. Special events may include festivals, contests, pet and hobby shows, and various outings. Recreation supervisors also create programs for people with special needs, such as the elderly or people in hospitals. Supervisors have overall responsibility for coordinating the work of the recreation workers who carry out the programs and supervise several recreation centers or an entire region.

Recreation center directors run the programs at their respective recreation buildings, indoor centers, playgrounds, or day camps. In addition to directing the staff of the facility, they oversee the safety of the buildings and equipment, handle financial matters, and prepare reports.

Recreation leaders, with the help of *recreation aides*, work directly with assigned groups and are responsible for the daily operations of a recreation program. They organize and lead activities such as drama, dancing, sports and games, camping trips, and other recreations. They give instruction in crafts, games, and sports, and work with other staff on special projects and events. Leaders help train and direct volunteers and perform other tasks, as required by the director.

In industry, recreation leaders plan social and athletic programs for employees and their families. Bowling leagues, softball teams, picnics, and dances are examples of company-sponsored activities. In addition, an increasing number of companies are providing exercise and fitness programs for their employees.

Camp counselors lead and instruct children and adults in nature-oriented forms of recreation at camps or resorts. Activities usually include swimming, hiking, horseback riding, and other outdoor sports and games, as well as instruction in nature and folklore. Camp counselors teach skills such as wood crafting, leather working, and basket weaving. Some camps offer specialized instruction in subjects such as music, drama, gymnastics, and computers. In carrying out the programs, camp counselors are concerned with the safety, health, and comfort of the campers. Counselors are supervised by a *camp director*.

Another type of recreation worker is the *social director*, who plans and organizes recreational activities for guests in hotels and resorts or for passengers aboard a ship. Social directors usually greet new arrivals and introduce them to other guests, explain the recreational facilities, and encourage guests to participate in planned activities. These activities may include card parties, games, contests, dances, musicals, or field trips and may require setting up equipment, arranging for transportation, or planning decorations, refreshments, or entertainment. In general, social directors try to create a friendly atmosphere, paying particular attention to lonely guests and trying to ensure that everyone has a good time.

■ Requirements

For some recreation positions, a high school diploma or an associate degree in parks and recreation, social work, or other human service discipline is sufficient preparation. However, most full-time career positions require a bachelor's degree, and a graduate degree is often a necessity for high-level administrative posts.

High School

High school students interested in recreation work should get a broad liberal arts and cultural education and acquire at least a working knowledge of arts and crafts, music, dance, drama, athletics, and nature study.

Postsecondary Training

Acceptable college majors include parks and recreation management, leisure studies, fitness management, and related disciplines. A degree in any liberal arts field may be sufficient if the person's education includes courses relevant to recreation work.

In industrial recreation, employers usually prefer applicants with a bachelor's degree in recreation and a strong background in business administration. Some jobs require specialized training in a particular field, such as art, music, drama, or athletics. Others need special certifications, such as a lifesaving certificate to teach swimming.

Over 200 community and junior colleges offer associate degrees in parks and recreation programs, and about 300 colleges and universities have similar, but more extensive programs leading to a bachelor's, master's, or doctoral degree. In 1997, there were 93 parks and recreation curriculums at the bachelor's degree level accredited by the National Recreation and Park Association (NRPA).

Certification or Licensing
Many recreation professionals apply for certification as evidence of their professional competence. The National Recreation and Park Association, the American Camping Association, and the National Employee Services and Recreation Association award certificates to individuals who meet their standards. More than 40 states have adopted NRPA standards for park/recreation professionals.

The federal government employs many recreation leaders in national parks, the armed forces, the Department of Veterans Affairs, and correctional institutions. It may be necessary to pass a civil service examination to qualify for these positions.

Other Requirements
Personal qualifications for recreation work include a desire to work with people, outgoing personality, even temperament, and ability to lead and influence others. Recreation workers should have good health and stamina and should be able to stay calm and think clearly and quickly in emergencies.

■ Exploring
Young people interested in this field should obtain related work experience as part-time or summer workers or volunteers in recreation departments, neighborhood centers, camps, and other organizations.

■ Employers
There were about 233,000 recreation workers, not counting summer workers or volunteers, in the late 1990s. More than 50 percent worked for government agencies, mostly at the municipal or county level. Nearly 20 percent were employed by civic, social, fraternal, or religious membership organizations such as the Boy Scouts, YWCA, or Red Cross. The rest worked in social service organizations such as centers for seniors and adult day care, and residential-care facilities, such as halfway houses, institutions for delinquent youths, and group homes or commercial recreation establishments and private industry.

■ Starting Out
College placement offices are useful in helping graduates find employment. Most college graduates begin as either recreation leaders or specialists and, after several years of experience, may become recreation directors. A few enter trainee programs leading directly to recreation administration within a year or so. Those with graduate training may start as recreation directors.

■ Advancement
Recreation leaders without graduate training will find advancement limited, but it is possible to obtain better-paying positions through a combination of education and experience. With experience it is possible to become a recreation director. With further experience, directors may become supervisors and eventually head of all recreation departments or divisions in a city. Some recreation professionals become consultants.

■ Earnings
Full-time recreation workers earned an average of $18,700 a year in 1996, according to the *Occupational Outlook Handbook*. Some earned up to $37,500 or more, depending on job responsibilities and experience. Some top level managers can make considerably more.

Salaries in industrial recreation are higher. Newly hired recreation workers in industry have starting salaries of about $18,000 to $24,000 a year. Camp directors average about $1,600 per month in municipally operated camps; in private camps, earnings are higher. Camp counselors employed seasonally are paid anywhere from $200 to $800 a month. Recreation workers in the federal government start at about $16,000 a year.

■ Work Environment
Physical conditions vary greatly from outdoor parks to nursing homes for the elderly. A recreation worker can choose the conditions under which he or she would like to work. Recreation workers with an interest in the outdoors may become camp counselors. Those who have an interest in travel may seek a job as a social director on a cruise ship. There are opportunities for people who want to help the elderly or mentally handicapped, as well as for people with an interest in drama or music.

Generally, recreation workers must work while others engage in leisure activities. Most recreation workers work 44-hour weeks. But they should expect, especially those just entering the field, some night and weekend work. A compensating factor is the pleasure of helping people enjoy themselves.

Many of the positions are part time or seasonal, and many full-time recreation workers spend more time performing management duties than in leading hands-on activities.

■ Outlook

The U.S. Bureau of Labor Statistics predicts that employment opportunities for recreation workers will increase faster than the average through the end of 2006. The expected expansion in the recreation field will result from increased leisure time and income for the population as a whole combined with a continuing interest in fitness and health and a growing elderly population in nursing homes, senior centers, and retirement communities. There also is a demand for recreation workers to conduct activity programs for special needs groups.

Two areas promising the most favorable opportunities for recreation workers are the commercial recreation and social service industries. Commercial recreation establishments include amusement parks, sports and entertainment centers, wilderness and survival enterprises, tourist attractions, vacation excursions, hotels and other resorts, camps, health spas, athletic clubs, and apartment complexes. New employment opportunities will arise in social service agencies such as senior centers, halfway houses, children's homes, and day-care programs for the mentally or developmentally disabled.

Recreation programs that depend on government funding are most likely to be affected in times of economic downturns when budgets are reduced. During such times, competition will increase significantly for jobs in the private sector. In any case, competition is expected to be keen because the field is open to college graduates regardless of major; as a result, there are more applicants than there are job openings. Opportunities will be best for individuals who have formal training in recreation and for those with previous experience.

■ For More Information

For information regarding industry trends, education, and scholarships, or for a copy of Leisure Today, *contact:*

American Association for Leisure and Recreation
1900 Association Drive
Reston, VA 20191
Tel: 703-476-3472
Web: http://www.aahperd.org

For information on the recreation industry, career opportunities, and certification qualifications, contact:

National Recreation and Park Association
22377 Belmont Ridge Road
Ashburn, VA 20148
Web: http://www.nrpa.org

For information on certification qualifications, contact:

American Camping Association
5000 State Road, 67 North
Martinsville, IN 46151-7902
Tel: 765-342-8456
Web: http://www.acacamps.org/

For information on certification qualifications, contact:

National Employee Services and Recreation Association
2211 York Road, Suite 207
Oak Brook, IL 60523-2371
Tel: 630-368-1280
Web: http://www.nesra.org/

■ Related Articles

Recreation

Sports

Amusement Park Workers

Cruise Ship Workers

Lifeguards

Recreational Therapists

Resort Workers

Ski Resort Workers

Recreational Therapists

■ Overview

Recreational therapists plan, organize, direct, and monitor medically approved recreation programs for patients in hospitals, clinics, and various community settings. These therapists use recreational activities to assist patients with mental, physical, or emotional disabilities to achieve the maximum possible functional independence.

■ History

The field of therapy has expanded in the past few decades to include recreational therapy as a form of medical treatment. Its use grew out of the realization that soldiers suffering from battle fatigue, shock, and emotional trauma respond positively to organized recreation and activity programs.

As a result, people in nursing homes, hospitals, mental institutions, and adult-care facilities are no longer limited to physical therapy. Experiments have shown that recovery is aided by recreational activities such as sports, music, art, gardening, dance, drama, field trips, and other pastimes. Elderly people are more healthy and alert when their days are filled with activities, field trips, and social get-togethers. People with disabilities can gain greater self-confidence and awareness of their own abilities when they get involved with sports, crafts, and other activities. People recovering from drug or alcohol addiction can reaffirm their self-worth through directed, enjoyable hobbies, clubs, and sports. The recreational therapist is a health professional who organizes these types of activities and helps patients take an active role in their own recovery.

■ The Job

Recreational therapists work with people who are mentally, physically, or emotionally disabled. They are professionals who employ leisure activities as a form of treatment, much as other health practitioners use surgery, drugs, nutrition, exercise, or psychotherapy. Recreational therapists strive to minimize patients' symptoms, restore function, and improve their physical, mental, and emotional well-being. Enhancing the patient's ability to take part in everyday life is the primary goal of recreational therapy; interesting and rewarding activities are the means for working toward that goal.

Recreational therapists work in a number of different settings, including mental hospitals, psychiatric day hospitals, community mental health centers, nursing homes, adult day care programs, residential facilities for the mentally disabled, school systems, and prisons. They can work as individual staff members, as independent consultants, or as part of a larger therapeutic team. They may get personally involved with patients, or direct the work of assistants and support staff.

The recreational therapist first confers with the doctors, psychiatrists, social workers, physical therapists, and other professionals on staff to coordinate their efforts in treatment. The recreational therapist needs to understand the nature of the patient's ailment, current physical and mental capacities, emotional state, and prospects for recovery. The patient's family and friends are also consulted to find out the patient's interests and hobbies. With this information, the recreational therapist then plans an agenda of activities for that person.

To enrich the lives of people in hospitals and other institutions, recreational therapists use imagination and skill in organizing beneficial activities. Sports, games, arts and crafts, movie screenings, field trips, hobby clubs, and dramatics are only a few examples of activities that can enrich the lives of patients. Some therapists specialize in certain areas. *Dance therapists* plan and conduct dance and body movement exercises to improve patients' physical and mental well-being. *Art therapists* work with patients in various art methods, such as drawing, painting, and ceramics, as part of their therapeutic and recovery programs. Therapists may also work with pets and other animals, such as horses. *Music therapists* design programs for patients that can involve solo or group singing, playing in bands, rhythmic and other creative activities, listening to music,

or attending concerts. Even flowers and gardening can prove beneficial to patients, as is proved by the work of *horticultural therapists.* When the treatment team feels that regular employment would help certain patients, the *industrial therapist* arranges a productive job for the patient in an actual work environment, one that will have the greatest therapeutic value based on the patient's needs and abilities. *Orientation therapists* for the blind work with people who have recently lost their sight, helping them to readjust to daily living and independence through training and exercise. All of these professional therapists plan their programs to meet the needs and capabilities of patients. They also carefully monitor and record each patient's progress and report it to the other members of the medical team.

As part of their jobs, recreational therapists need to understand their patients and set goals for their progress accordingly. A patient having trouble socializing, for example, may have an interest in playing chess, but be overwhelmed by the prospect of actually playing, since that involves interaction with another person. A therapist would proceed slowly, first letting the patient observe a number of games and then assigning a therapeutic assistant to serve as a chess partner for weeks or even months, as long as it takes for the patient to gain enough confidence to seek out other patients for chess partners. The therapist makes a note of the patient's response, modifies the therapy program accordingly, and lets other professionals know of the results. If a patient is responding more enthusiastically to the program, working more cooperatively with others, or is becoming more disruptive, the therapist must note these reactions and periodically reevaluate the patient's activity program.

Responsibilities and elements of the job can vary, depending on the setting in which the recreational therapist works. In nursing homes, the therapist often groups residents according to common or shared interests and ability levels and then plans field trips, parties, entertainment, and other group

RECREATIONAL THERAPISTS	
SCHOOL SUBJECTS	**Biology** **Psychology**
PERSONAL SKILLS	**Helping/teaching** **Technical/scientific**
WORK ENVIRONMENT	**Indoors and outdoors** **Primarily one location**
MINIMUM EDUCATION LEVEL	**Bachelor's degree**
SALARY RANGE	**$23,936 to $30,116 to $65,000**
CERTIFICATION OR LICENSING	**Required by certain states**
OUTLOOK	**Much faster than the average**
DOT	**076**
GOE	**10.02.02**
NOC	**3144**
O*NET	**32317**

A recreational therapist leads a game of bingo at a rehabilitation hospital.

activities. The therapist documents residents' responses to the activities and continually searches for ways of heightening residents' enjoyment of recreational and leisure activities, not just in the facility but in the surrounding community as well. Because nursing home residents are likely to remain in the facility for months or even years, the activities program makes a big difference in the quality of their lives. Without the stimulation of interesting events to look forward to and participate in, the daily routine of a nursing home can become monotonous and depressing, and some residents are apt to deteriorate both mentally and physically. In some nursing homes, recreational therapists direct the activities program. In others, *activities coordinators* plan and carry out the program under the part-time supervision of a consultant who is either a recreational or occupational therapist.

The therapist in a community center might work in a day-care program for the elderly or in a program for mentally disabled adults operated by a county recreation department. No matter what the disability, recreational therapists in community settings face the added logistical challenge of arranging transportation and escort services, if necessary, for prospective participants. Coordinating transportation is less of a problem in hospitals and nursing homes, where the patients all live under one roof. Developing therapeutic recreation programs in community settings requires a large measure of organizational ability, flexibility, and ingenuity.

Recreational therapy is a relatively new field, but it is already a respected, integral part of the treatment of many elderly and disabled people. Clients often need extra encouragement and support to stay active and build on the things they can, rather than can't, do. The activity programs that recreational therapists design and operate can add immeasurable enjoyment to the lives of patients. Beyond this, the activities provide opportunities for exercise and social interaction and may also help relieve anxiety and loneliness, build confidence, and promote each patient's independence.

■ Requirements

High School

Interested high school students should follow a college preparatory program. Recommended courses include biology and other sciences, English, speech, mathematics, psychology, physical education, art, music, and drama. Verbal and written communication skills are essential because of the interaction with people and the report writing that the job requires.

Postsecondary Training

A bachelor's degree is required for employment as a recreational therapist. More than 170 academic programs in this field are offered at colleges and universities in the United States. Four-year programs include courses in both natural science, such as biology, behavioral science, and human anatomy, and social science, such as psychology and sociology. Courses more specific to the profession include programming for special populations; rehabilitative techniques including self-help skills, mobility, signing for the deaf, and orientation for the blind; medical equipment; current treatment approaches; legal issues; and professional ethics. Students also take recreation courses and are required to serve 360 hours of internship under the supervision of a certified therapeutic recreation specialist.

Continuing education is increasingly becoming a requirement for professionals in this field. Many therapists attend conferences and seminars and take additional university courses. Those with degrees in related fields can enter the profession by earning master's degrees in therapeutic recreation. Advanced degrees are advisable for those seeking advancement to supervisory, administrative, and teaching positions. These requirements will become more strict as more professionals enter the field.

Certification or Licensing

A number of states regulate the profession of therapeutic recreation. Licensing is required in some states; professional certification (or eligibility for certification) is required in in others; while titling is regulated in some states and facilities. In other states, many hospitals and other employers require recreational therapists to be certified. Certification for recreational therapists is available through the National Council for Therapeutic Recreation, which awards credentials for therapeutic recreation specialists and assistants. Recreation therapists must check requirements for the states in which they want to work as well as requirements for different types of facilities.

Several other professional organizations offer continuing education classes and additional benefits to professional members. These include the National Therapeutic Recreation Society; the American Therapeutic Recreation Association; and the American Alliance for Health, Physical Education, Recreation, and Dance. These groups also work to improve the salaries and working conditions of the people in the profession.

■ Exploring

Students interested in recreational therapy can find part-time work as a sports coach or referee, park supervisor, or camp counselor. Volunteer work in a nursing home, hospital, or care facility for disabled adults is also a good way to learn about the daily realities of institutional living. These types of facilities are always looking for volunteers to work with and visit patients. Working with people with physical, mental, or emotional disabilities can be stressful, and volunteer work is a good way for a prospective therapist to test whether they can handle this kind of stress.

■ Employers

Hospitals employ 42 percent of recreational therapists; nursing homes employ 38 percent; other employers include residential facilities and substance abuse centers, and some therapists are self-employed. Employment opportunities also exist in long-term rehabilitation, home health care, psychiatric facilities, and transitional programs.

■ Starting Out

There are many methods for finding out about available jobs in recreational therapy. A good place to start is the job notices and want ads printed in the local newspapers, bulletins from state park and recreation societies, and publications of the professional associations previously mentioned. State employment agencies and human service departments will know of job openings in state hospitals.

GLOSSARY

Geriatrics and gerontology: The medical study of the physical processes and problems of old age. Either of these terms may be used in hospital departments with elderly patients.

Leisure education: The use of sports, hobbies, and other activities to acquire skills and abilities to lead an independent lifestyle

Orient: To acquaint with an existing situation or environment; for example, to indicate obstacles for a blind person in a place he or she frequents so that they may make a mental "map" of the area and be able to guide themselves

Recreation: The opportunity to participate in leisure activities that improve health and well-being

Special Olympics: A program of physical fitness, sports training, and athletic competition for children and adults with disabilities

College placement offices might also be able to put new recreational therapy graduates in touch with prospective employers. Internship programs are sometimes available, offering good opportunities to find potential full-time jobs.

Recent graduates should also make appointments to meet potential employers personally. Most colleges and universities offer career counseling services. Most employers will make themselves available to discuss their programs and the possibility of hiring extra staff. They may also guide new graduates to other institutions currently hiring therapists. Joining professional associations, both state and national, and attending conferences are good ways to meet potential employers and colleagues.

■ Advancement

Newly graduated recreational therapists generally begin as staff therapists. Advancement is chiefly to supervisory or administrative positions, usually after some years of experience and continuing education. Some therapists teach, conduct research, or do consulting work on a contract basis; a graduate degree is essential for moving into these areas.

Many therapists continue their education but prefer to continue working with patients. For variety, they may choose to work with new groups of people or get a job in a new setting, such as moving from a retirement home to a facility for the disabled. Some may also move to a related field, such as special education, or sales positions involving products and services related to recreational therapy.

■ Earnings

Salaries of recreational therapists vary according to employment setting, educational background, experience, and region of the country. According to a survey published by the American Therapeutic Recreation Association in 1995, salaries for beginning therapists ranged from $16,500 to

$38,750, with an average salary of $23,963 for those with up to two years' experience. The average for all therapists with six to ten years' experience was $30,116. The mean for all therapists with a bachelor's degree was $28,963; for a master's degree, the average salary was $38,031; and therapists holding a doctorate earned an average of $46,326. Supervisors earned top salaries of $50,000 per year; administrators reported maximum earnings of $65,000 per year; and some consultants and educators reported even higher earnings.

Therapists employed at hospitals, clinics, and other facilities generally enjoy a full benefit package, including health insurance and vacation, holiday, and sick pay. Consultants and self-employed therapists must provide their own benefits.

■ Work Environment

Working conditions vary, but recreational therapists generally work in a ward, a specially equipped activity room, or at a nursing home, a communal room or hall. In a community setting, recreational therapists may interview subjects and plan activities in an office, but they might be in a gymnasium, swimming pool, playground, or outdoors on a nature walk when leading activities. Therapists may also work on horse ranches, farms, and other outdoor facilities catering to people with disabilities.

The job may be physically tiring because therapists are often on their feet all day and may have to lift and carry equipment. Recreational therapists generally work a standard 40-hour week, although weekend and evening hours may be required. Supervisors may have to work overtime, depending on their workload.

■ Outlook

Recreational therapists held more than 38,000 jobs in 1996, according to the U.S. Department of Labor. About 42 percent of these people work in nursing homes. Hospitals, chiefly psychiatric, rehabilitation, and other specialty hospitals, are the second leading employer. Other employers include community mental health centers, adult day care programs, residential facilities for the mentally disabled, and community programs for people with disabilities. A small number of therapists work as independent consultants.

Recreational therapy is one of the fastest-growing of all occupations, and employment for recreational therapists is expected to continue to grow much faster than the average, chiefly because of anticipated expansion of long-term care facilities and services. By 2006, the number of recreational therapists employed in the United States is expected to grow to more than 45,000. Reasons for this include the increased life expectancies of the elderly and people with developmental disabilities, such as Down's syndrome. Significant growth is also projected for the mentally ill, in part because of the large number of young adults who have reached the age of peak risk for schizophrenia and other chronic mental illnesses. The incidence of alcohol and drug dependency problems is also growing.

Most openings for recreational therapists will be in nursing homes because of the increasing numbers and greater longevity of the elderly. There is also greater public pressure to regulate and improve the quality of life in retirement centers, which may mean more jobs and increased scrutiny of recreational therapists.

Growth in hospital jobs is not expected to be great. Many of the new jobs created will be in hospital-based adult day care programs or in units offering short-term mental health services. Because of economic and social factors, no growth is expected in public mental hospitals. Many of the programs and services formerly offered there are being shifted to community residential facilities for the disabled. Community programs for special populations are expected to expand significantly through the year 2006.

■ For More Information

For career information and resources, contact:

American Therapeutic Recreation Association
PO Box 15215
Hattiesburg, MS 39404-5215
Tel: 601-262-3413
Web: http://www.atra.org

This organization is for professionals in the leisure and recreation industry. It has several books and a video on therapeutic recreation.

American Association for Leisure and Recreation
1900 Association Drive
Reston, VA 22091
Tel: 703-476-3472
Web: http://www.aahperd.org/aalr/aalr-main.html

For information on certification, contact:

National Council for Therapeutic Recreation
7 Elmwood Drive
New City, NY 10956
Tel: 914-639-1439

The following organization has career information, a journal, and other resources.

National Therapeutic Recreation Society
National Recreation and Park Association
22377 Belmont Ridge Road
Ashbrun, VA 20148-9901
Tel: 703-858-0784
Web: http://www.nrpa.org/branches/ntrs.htm

■ Related Articles

Health Care

Social Services

Creative Arts Therapists

Human Services Workers

Kinesiologists

Occupational Therapists

Physical Therapists

Recreation Workers

Rehabilitation Counselors

Sports Instructors and Coaches

Recruitment Scouts

■ See Sports Scouts

Recycling Coordinators

■ Overview

Recycling coordinators manage recycling programs for city, county, or state governments or large organizations, such as colleges or military bases. They work with waste haulers and material recovery facilities (MRFs), to arrange for collecting, sorting, and processing recyclables from households and businesses. They are also often responsible for educating the public about the value of recycling as well as instructing residents on how to properly separate recyclables in their homes. Recycling coordinators keep records of recycling rates in their municipality and help set goals for diversion of recyclables from the waste stream.

■ History

Recycling coordinators have a brief history in the job as it is known today. Only in the 1980s and early 1990s did many states begin setting recycling goals, creating the need for recycling coordinators at the local level. Before then, there was little need for municipal recycling coordinators. Most recycling efforts were made by private citizen groups or industry. While much of today's recycling is driven by a desire to improve the environment, earlier recycling was often driven by economic forces. During the Great Depression, individual citizens or groups, such as the Boy Scouts, held newspaper drives and turned the newspaper in to a recycler. During World War II, shortages in raw materials to support the war prompted citizens to hold drives for aluminum, rubber, paper and scrap metal; this time the spirit of recycling was patriotic, as well as economic.

Other than times of shortage, governments had little concern with how people disposed of waste, simply because there was relatively little waste. Municipalities had been dumping, burning, burying, or otherwise disposing of residents' waste for years with little consequence. In 1898, New York City opened the first garbage-sorting plant in the United States, recycling some of the trash. The first aluminum recycling plants were built in the early 1900s in Chicago and Cleveland. By the 1920s, about 70 percent of U.S. cities had limited recycling programs, according to the League of Women Voters.

Can buybacks began in the 1950s; newspaper was first recycled in 1961 by a mill in New Jersey. By 1960, the U.S. recycled about 7 percent of its municipal waste. In the mid-1960s, the federal government began to take greater interest in municipal waste-handling methods. Part of the Solid Waste Disposal Act of 1965 granted money for states to develop waste-handling programs. The Resource Conservation and Recovery Act (RCRA) of 1970 and 1976 amendments defined types of municipal solid waste (MSW) and spelled out minimum standards for waste handling.

State and federal governments, such as branches of the Environmental Protection Agency were the earliest to hire people who specialized in recycling. These recycling experts usually acted in an advisory capacity to local governments that were trying to develop their own programs.

In the 1990s, more states began to set recycling goals, driving the increase in need for recycling coordinators. By 1998, all but six states had set formal recycling goals. These goals are generally stated in terms of the percentage of waste to be diverted from ending up in a landfill. Most states set goals between 20 and 50 percent. To encourage counties to make the effort at a local level, many state governments offered grants to counties to fund new recycling programs, hence many counties found they needed a full-time person to coordinate the new effort. Initially, only the most populous counties qualified for the grants to afford a recycling program, because they could divert the highest volume from landfills.

■ The Job

As recycling becomes more widespread, fewer recycling coordinators are faced with the task of

RECYCLING COORDINATORS	
SCHOOL SUBJECTS	Business Earth science
PERSONAL SKILLS	Communication/ideas Leadership/management
WORK ENVIRONMENT	Primarily indoors Multiple locations
MINIMUM EDUCATION LEVEL	Bachelor's degree
SALARY RANGE	$22,000 to $40,000 to $50,000+
CERTIFICATION OR LICENSING	None available
OUTLOOK	Much faster than the average
NOC	4161

Recycling coordinators can direct and assist consumers in recycling at home and at work, but it is up to the consumer to find ways to support the other side of the recyclables market—buying recycled content products. Some products, such as aluminum and glass containers, egg cartons and steel products from cans to bicycle frames, always contain a significant amount of recycled material, though they may not be labeled as "recycled." The average automobile has 44 percent recycled steel content. Consumers may be surprised at other items that are labeled as "postconsumer recycled products." For example, plastic soda bottles can be turned into carpet fibers or park benches; the rubber from old tires can be used as floor mats or as an additive in asphalt. Some playgrounds use shredded tires as a cushiony base for children to play in instead of gravel or wood chips. In some cities, the streets are even paved with asphalt containing broken glass chips (they are embedded in the asphalt, so no one gets a flat tire, and less asphalt is used because the glass acts as a filler). Those who make an effort to learn about the products they use can reward their recycling efforts at home by helping make sure there is a market for the recyclables they have contributed. Perhaps one day you'll drive on a street paved with glass from a mayonnaise jar you cleaned and recycled, or you'll buy a car made of steel from the tuna can you recycled a few years ago!

organizing a municipal program from scratch. Instead, recycling coordinators work to improve current recycling rates in several ways. While recycling coordinators spend some time on administrative tasks, such as meeting with waste haulers and government officials and writing reports, a considerable amount of time is often needed for public education purposes. One recycling coordinator in North Dakota notes that only a small portion of the average recycling coordinator's job is spent sitting behind a desk.

Educating the public on proper separation of recyclables as well as explaining the need for recycling are a large part of a recycling coordinator's job. Good oral communication skills are essential for a recycling coordinator to succeed in this role. Getting people who haven't recycled before to start can take some convincing. Recycling coordinators spread their message by speaking to community groups, businesses, and schools. Persuasive speaking skills are useful here, because as a recycling coordinator, you are asking people to do extra work—peeling labels from and washing bottles and jars instead of just throwing them out, separating newspapers, magazines, cardboard, and other types of paper. Even as recycling increases in this country, many people are accustomed to disposing of trash as quickly as possible without giving it a second thought. It is the task of a recycling coordinator to get people to change such habits, and how well a recycling coordinator is able

to do this can make the difference in the success of the entire program.

In some communities, recycling coordinators have economics on their side when it comes to getting people to change their habits. In so-called "pay-as-you-throw" programs, residents pay for garbage disposal based on how much waste their household produces. So recycling, although it may mean extra work, makes sense because it saves the homeowner money. For example, residents may be charged extra for any waste they set out at the curb beyond one garbage can per week. In communities with these programs, recycling rates tend to be higher and recycling coordinators have an easier task of convincing people to recycle. Another part of a recycling coordinator's role as educator is answering questions about how recyclables are to be separated. Especially with new programs, residents often have questions about separating recyclables, such as what type of paper can be set out with newspaper, whether labels should be peeled from jars, and even keeping track of which week of the month or day of the week they should set their recyclables out with the trash. Fielding these types of calls always demands some portion of a recycling coordinator's time.

Most recycling coordinators spend a minimal amount of time on record keeping, perhaps 5 percent, one coordinator estimates. The coordinator is responsible for making monthly, or sometimes quarterly, reports to state and federal government agencies. Recycling coordinators also fill out grant applications for state and federal funding to improve their programs.

Some recycling coordinators work on military bases or college campuses. The goal of a recycling coordinator who works in one of these settings is the same as a municipal recycling coordinator—getting people to recycle; how they go about it may differ. The recycling coordinator on a college campus, for example, has a new set of residents every year to educate about the college's recycling program.

Recycling coordinators who come up with creative uses for waste may find opportunities in other fields as well. For example, recycling of computers and computer parts is a growing area. Some with knowledge in this area have founded their own companies or work for computer manufacturers.

■ Requirements

High School

Recycling coordinators need a variety of skills and doing well in a variety of classes in high school is a good start. Classes in business, economics, and civics are a good idea to help build an understanding of the public sector in which most recycling coordinators work. Knowledge of how local governments and markets for recycled materials function are things a recycling coordinator will need to know later, and civics and economics courses provide this framework. English and speech classes are vital to developing good oral and written communication skills that recycling coordinators use to spread the word about the importance of recycling. Mathematics and science will prove useful in setting recycling goals and understanding how recycling helps the environment.

Postsecondary Training

Until recently, people with all different types of backgrounds and experience were becoming recycling coordinators. Enthusiasm, an understanding of recycling issues, and business acumen were more important than any specific degree or professional background. This is still true to some extent, as colleges generally don't offer degrees in recycling coordination. Instead, a bachelor's degree in environmental studies or a related area and strong communication skills are desirable. Some schools offer minors in integrated waste management. Classes may include public policy, source reduction, transformation technology (composting/waste energy) and landfills, according to the Environmental Careers Organization (ECO).

Other Requirements

Useful personal skills include good communication and people skills for interacting with staff, contractors, government officials, and the public. Leadership, persuasiveness, and creativity (ability to think of new ways to use collected materials, for example) also will serve the future recycling coordinator well.

■ Exploring

Those interested in exploring a career as a recycling coordinator should start by getting familiar with the issues. Why is sorting garbage so costly? Why are some materials recycled and not others? Where are the markets? What are some creative uses for recyclable materials? You can explore what's going on both nationally and in your area. Some states have more extensive recycling programs than others; for example, some have bottle deposit laws or other innovative programs to boost recycling efforts. Get to know who's doing what and what remains to be done. Read industry related magazines; two informative publications are *Recycling Today* and *Resource Recycling*. A useful book that focuses on environmental career possibilities is *The Complete Guide to Environmental Careers in the 21st Century*, by the Environmental Careers Organization.

Next, someone considering this field could tour a local material recovery facility and talk with the staff there. You might even volunteer to work for a recycling organization. Large and small communities often have groups that support recycling with fund drives and information campaigns.

STATE RECYCLING GOALS

Each state sets its own goal for recycling. Because the federal government has not mandated a nationwide goal, state goals vary from 20 to 50 percent. One number many states agree on is their target year, 2000, to reach their recycling goals. Other than that common denominator, methods and expectations of recycling vary widely. Eight states—California, Colorado, Georgia, Indiana, Iowa, Missouri, North Carolina, and North Dakota—have specified waste reduction or diversion goals instead of a strict recycling goal. As of mid-1998, six states had not set recycling goals—Arizona, Delaware, Idaho, Kansas, Utah, and Wisconsin. Of these, only Wisconsin's recycling rate, 36 percent, surpassed 20 percent. The states reporting the highest rates as of the summer of 1998 were Minnesota, with a 46 percent recycling rate, and New Jersey, with a 60 percent recycling rate. Fifteen states have goals above 50 percent; most of those have set their goal deadlines for later than 2000. Rhode Island has the highest goal: 70 percent of the municipal and commercial waste stream. To find out what your state's goal is, contact your city or county health or solid waste department, or ask a teacher to help you find which state agency is responsible for overseeing recycling.

Also, most municipal public meetings and workshops are good places to learn about how you can help with recycling in your community.

■ Employers

Recycling coordinators are almost exclusively employed by some level of government; they oversee recycling programs at the city, county, or state level. A limited number of recycling coordinators may find work with waste haulers that offer recycling coordination as part of their contracts to municipalities. Recycling coordinators work in communities of all sizes—from rural countywide programs to urban ones. When states first mandated recycling, larger counties that generated more waste generally were the first to hire recycling coordinators. However as more states set and achieve higher recycling goals, smaller cities and even rural areas need someone to coordinate their growing programs. At the state level, state environmental protection agencies or community development agencies may employ coordinators to administer state grants to and advise local recycling programs all over the state. Large organizations, such as colleges or military bases, are other employers of recycling coordinators.

■ Starting Out

A first job as a recycling coordinator is most likely to be with a smaller municipal program. Most colleges have a network of career referral services for their graduates and city or county governments with openings for recycling coordinators often use these services to advertise positions to qualified graduates. Positions at the state level also may be available. Someone with previous experience with waste management projects, issues, and operations in addition to the right educational background, is likely to get the more sought-after positions in larger cities and state governments. Hands-on experience can be obtained via internships, volunteering, cooperative education, summer employment, or research projects, says ECO.

Students can gain experience during summers off from college, or if necessary, after college by volunteering or serving an internship with a recycling program in their area. If internships aren't available, paid work at a waste facility is a way for students interested in recycling to earn money over the summer and learn the very basics of recycling. Volunteering for a waste management consulting firm or nonprofit environmental organization is another way to get practical experience with recyclables. Some students may benefit by looking no further than their own college. Most colleges have their own recycling programs and students may find part-time work during the school year in their own college's recycling program. Contact the physical plant operations department or student employment services at your school.

■ Advancement

In most cases, "recycling coordinator" is the top spot in the recycling program. Advancement isn't really an option, unless the coordinator moves to another, perhaps larger municipal program, to a private employer, or in some cases, to a different field. There is a fair amount of turnover in the field because recycling coordinator positions, in many cases, are training ground for college graduates who eventually move on to other fields where they use skills they developed as recycling coordinators. Because recycling coordinators develop so many useful skills, they often find work in related fields, such as for small business administrations and nonprofit organizations or as government administrators.

Since many states have waste-handling projects, someone with good experience at the local level might move into a state-level job—"recycling expert" is a position in some states' waste-handling departments. Opportunities with private businesses with in-house recycling needs or with solid waste management consultants or businesses might also constitute advancement. Finally, recycling coordinators also have the opportunity to expand their own programs. Through their efforts, a modest program with a limited staff and budget could blossom into a full-scale, profitable venture for the community. The coordinator could conceivably extend the scope of the program; improve links with state or local government officials, the public, and private business and industry; receive more funding; add staff; and otherwise increase the extent and prominence of the program.

■ Earnings

Salaries vary widely for recycling coordinators. Starting salaries range from $22,000 per year in smaller counties or cities to $40,000 and higher for coordinators in larger municipalities, according to the 1998 book by ECO, *The Complete Guide to Environmental Careers in the 21st Century.* Another salary survey, conducted by the National Association of Counties in 1997, puts the average starting wage in counties with populations under 25,000 at $19,568. The average starting wage in counties with populations of 100,000 to 249,999 was $41,968. Some of the highest salaries reported were in counties with populations over 1 million, such as Maricopa County, Ariz., where the starting wage was $60,507 in 1997. Salaries vary in different regions of the country. Positions in areas with a higher cost of living, such as California, Arizona, New York, and Washington, DC, for example, tend to pay more. Benefits vary too, but most local governments offer full-time employees a good, though basic, benefit program that generally includes paid health insurance; a retirement plan; and holiday, vacation, and sick pay.

■ Work Environment

Recycling coordinators are essentially administrators. As such, they primarily work indoors, either in their offices, or in meetings or giving speeches. Recycling coordinators need to watch costs, understand markets, and work within budgets. They should be able to be firm with contractors when necessary. They need to demonstrate good judgment and leadership, and they may need to justify their decisions and actions to city council members or others. Stresses are part of the job, including dealing with government bureaucracy, dips in community participation, services that fall short of expectation, fluctuating markets for recyclables, and other less-than-ideal situations.

Generally, recycling coordinators work 40 hours per week if they are full-time. Some positions may be part-time, but for both work arrangements, working hours are generally during the day with weekends off. Occasionally, recycling coordinators may need to attend meetings in the evening, such as a county or city board meeting, or speak before a community group that meets at night. Sometimes facility or landfill tours that a recycling coordinator may arrange or participate in to generate publicity for the program may be offered on weekends. Also occasionally, recycling coordinators may leave the office setting to visit the material recovery facility, which can be noisy and dirty if compacting equipment and conveyers are running.

■ Outlook

The outlook for municipal recycling coordinators is excellent. According to ECO, thousands of these professionals will be needed into the early part of the 21st century, as more and more municipalities commit to full recycling programs. ECO says the job of municipal recycling coordinator is not only one of the fastest growing jobs in the environmental industry but also in any industry. As states strive to meet their increasingly ambitious waste-reduction and recycling goals, people who can make it happen on the local level are going to be crucial. Although the recycling industry is subject to business fluctuations, demand and new technologies have created a viable market for the recycled materials. Consumers generally respond favorably to buying products made from recycled goods, as long as they are quality products. With new uses and improved production of such goods, demand is expected to be steady into the next century.

Nationwide, the waste management and recycling industries will be needing more people to run recovery facilities, design new recycling technologies, come up with new ways to use recyclables, and do related work. Private businesses are also expected to hire recycling coordinators to manage in-house programs.

■ For More Information

For information on education and training:

Environmental Careers Organization
179 South Street
Boston, MA 02111
Tel: 617-426-4375
Web: http://www.eco.org

These trade groups promote recycling:

Environmental Industries Associations/National Solid Wastes Management Association
4301 Connecticut Avenue, NW
Washington, DC 20008
Tel: 202-244-4700
Web: http://www.envasns.org/nswma

National Recycling Coalition
1727 King Street, Suite 105
Alexandria, VA 22314
Tel: 703-683-9025
Web: http://www.earthsystems.org

■ Related Articles

Waste Management
Hazardous Waste Management Specialists
Hazardous Waste Management Technicians
Pollution Control Technicians

Reference Librarians

■ **See Librarians**

Refinery Laborers

■ **See Petroleum Refining Workers**

Reflexologists

■ Overview

Reflexologists base their work on the theory that "reflexes," specific points on the hands and feet, correspond to specific points on other parts of the body. They apply pressure to the feet or hands of their clients in order to affect the areas of the body that correspond to the areas that they are manipulating. Reflexologists believe that their work promotes overall good health, helps clients relax, and speeds the healing process.

■ History

Reflexology—or something similar to it—was practiced thousands of years ago. More than 2,000 years before the common era, the Chinese learned that foot massage was a useful adjunct to the practice of acupuncture. Many modern practitioners of reflexology believe that reflexology utilizes the principles on which acupuncture and traditional Chinese medicine (TCM) are based. A 4,000-year-old fresco that appears in the tomb of Ankhmahor, physician to a pharaoh, in the Egyptian city of Saqqara depicts the practice of foot massage. In North America, the Cherokee people have emphasized the importance of the feet in health, partly because it is through the feet that human beings connect

REFLEXOLOGISTS	
SCHOOL SUBJECTS	**Biology** **Health** **Psychology**
PERSONAL SKILLS	**Communication/ideas** **Helping/teaching**
WORK ENVIRONMENT	**Primarily indoors** **Primarily one location**
MINIMUM EDUCATION LEVEL	**High school diploma**
SALARY RANGE	**$7,000 to $35,000 to $100,000+**
CERTIFICATION OR LICENSING	**Recommended**
OUTLOOK	**Much faster than the average**

with the earth. Zone theory, which provides the theoretical basis for reflexology, existed in Europe as early as the 1500s.

Although reflexology is an ancient practice, its modern form originated in the early 20th century. William Fitzgerald, a Connecticut-based physician who was an ear, nose, and throat specialist, revived the practice of reflexology in the West in 1913, when he found that applying pressure to a patient's hands or feet just before surgery decreased the level of pain experienced by the patient. In 1917, Fitzgerald wrote *Zone Therapy, or Relieving Pain at Home,* which described his work. Fitzgerald believed that "bioelectrical energy" flows from points in the feet or hands to specific points elsewhere in the body, and he thought that applying tourniquets and various instruments to the feet or hands enhanced the flow of energy. He set out to map the flow of that energy, and in the process he set up correspondences between areas on the feet or hands and areas throughout the body.

The next important figure in modern reflexology, Eunice Ingham, was a physiotherapist who had worked with Joseph Shelby Riley, a follower of William Fitzgerald. Riley had decided against using instruments to manipulate the feet and hands, opting to use his hands instead. Ingham practiced and taught extensively, mapped the correspondences between the reflexes and the parts of the body, and wrote books chronicling her work with her patients, which helped to promote the field of reflexology. She went on to found the organization now known as the International Institute of Reflexology (IIR), which continues to promote the Original Ingham Method of Reflexology. Ultimately, Ingham became known as the mother of modern reflexology. Her students have played major roles in spreading reflexology throughout the world.

■ The Job

Reflexologists believe that the standing human body is divided vertically into ten zones, five zones on each side of the imaginary vertical line that divides the body in two. On both sides, the zone closest to the middle is zone one, while the zone farthest from the middle is zone five. These zones also appear on the hands and feet. Reflexologists believe that by massaging a spot in a zone on the foot, they can stimulate a particular area in the corresponding zone of the body. By massaging the reflex in the middle of the big toe, for example, a reflexologist attempts to affect the pituitary gland, which is the corresponding body part.

Reflexologists also believe that their ministrations help their clients in two other ways. First, they believe that their treatments reduce the amount of lactic acid in the feet. Lactic acid is a natural waste product of the metabolic process, and its presence in large quantities is unhealthful. Second, they believe that their treatments break up calcium crystals that have built up in the nerve endings of the feet. It is their theory that the presence of these crystals inhibits the flow of energy, which is increased when the crystals are removed. Reflexologists also emphasize that their techniques improve circulation and promote relaxation.

It is worth noting that modern science has not validated the theoretical basis of reflexology, which is even less well accepted in the scientific world than are some other alternative therapies. Yet it is also worth noting that some therapies whose underlying theories have not been validated by science have been shown to be effective. Relatively few scientific studies of reflexology have been completed, but much research is underway at present, and it is likely that reflexology will be better understood in the near future.

An initial visit to a reflexologist generally begins with the practitioner asking the client questions about his or her overall health, medical problems, and the reason for the visit. The reflexologist makes the client comfortable and begins the examination and treatment.

Although most reflexologists, such as the followers of Eunice Ingham, work on their clients' feet or hands with their hands, some prefer to use instruments. In either case, the reflexologist works on the feet and looks for sore spots, which are thought to indicate illness or other problems in the corresponding part of the body. On occasion, the problem will not be manifested in the corresponding organ or part of the body, but will instead be manifested elsewhere within the zone. Usually, the reflexologist will spend more time on the sore spots than on other parts of the foot. On the basis of information provided by the client and information obtained by the reflexologist during the examination, the reflexologist will recommend a course of treatment that is appropriate for the client's physical condition. In some cases, such as those of extreme illness, the reflexologist may ask the client to check with his or her physician to determine whether the treatment may be in conflict with the physician's course of treatment. Most reflexologists will not treat a client who has a fever. In addition, because reflexology treatments tend to enhance circulation, it is sometimes necessary for a client who is taking medication to decrease the dosage, on the advice of a doctor, to compensate for the increased circulation and the resulting increased effectiveness of the medication.

One of the most important aspects of the reflexologist's skill is knowing exactly how much pressure to apply to a person's feet. The pressure required for a large, healthy adult, for example, would be too much for a young child or a baby. Different foot shapes and weights may also require different levels of pressure. The practitioner must also know how long to work on the foot, since the benefits of the treatment may be offset if the treatment lasts too long. In her book *Reflexology Today,* Doreen E. Bayly, one of Eunice Ingham's students, recalled that Ingham once told her: "If you work on the reflex too long, you are undoing the good you have done." Ingham recommended 30-minute sessions, but most modern reflexologists conduct 45-minute or 60-minute sessions unless the client's condition dictates otherwise.

Most reflexologists work primarily on feet, but some work on the hands or even the ears. If a foot has been injured or amputated, it is acceptable to work on the hands. For the most part, reflexologists work on the feet because the feet are so sensitive. In addition, feet that are encased in shoes during most of the day typically require more attention than hands do. Furthermore, the feet, because of their size, are easier to manipulate. It is somewhat more difficult to find the reflexes on the hands.

■ Requirements

High School

Those interested in reflexology should study biology, chemistry, and health. Since reflexologists must make their clients comfortable and gain their trust, some study of psychology may be useful. You would also do well to investigate areas of bodywork and alternative medicine that are not taught in school. Having some knowledge of or practical skill in some area of massage (shiatsu, Swedish massage, and so forth) will give you a head start, especially since some states require reflexologists to be licensed massage therapists.

Postsecondary Training

The single most important part of a reflexologist's training is the completion of a rigorous course of study and practice, such as that provided by the International Institute of Reflexology. Many courses are available, and they range from one-day sessions to comprehensive courses that require a commitment of nine months or longer. Naturally, a student who wishes to practice professionally should select a comprehensive course. Correspondence courses are available, but any reputable correspondence course will require that the student complete a required number of hours of supervised, hands-on work. Some aspects of the technique must be demonstrated, not simply read, especially concerning the amount of pressure that the reflexologist should apply to different kinds of feet. Many reflexologists offer services other than reflexology, and the student may wish to be trained in aromatherapy or in various kinds of bodywork. Such training may also increase the likelihood that the practitioner, especially at the beginning of his or her career, will make a decent living.

Certification or Licensing

In some states, such as North Dakota, a reflexologist who has completed a course given by a reputable school of reflexology can be licensed specifically as a reflexologist. In most states, however, reflexologists are subject to the laws that govern massage therapists. That often means that a reflexologist must complete a state-certified course in massage before being licensed to practice reflexology. In many cases, reflexologists are subject to laws that are designed to regulate "massage parlors" that are fronts for prostitution. In some places, these laws require that practitioners be subjected to disease testing and walk-in inspections by police. It is common for those who are medical doctors or licensed cosmetologists to be exempt from massage-licensing regulations. Because there is such wide variation in the law, anyone who wishes to practice reflexology should carefully study state and local regulations before setting up shop.

Reflexologists-to-be should enroll in a course that requires a substantial number of hours of training and certifies the student upon graduation. Those who are at least 18 years old, have a high school diploma or its equivalent, have completed a course that requires at least 110 hours of training, and have at least 90 documented postgraduate reflexology sessions under their belts can apply to be tested by the American Reflexology Certification Board (ARCB), which was created in 1991. The organization is designed to promote reflexology by recognizing competent practitioners. Testing is purely voluntary, but a high score from the ARCB is certainly a good sign that a practitioner is competent.

Other Requirements

Reflexologists work closely with their clients, so it is essential that they be friendly, open, and sensitive to the feelings of others. They must be able to gain their clients' trust, make them comfortable and relaxed, and communicate well enough with them to gather the information that they need in order to treat them effectively. It is highly unlikely that an uncommunicative person who is uncomfortable with people will be able to build a reflexology practice. A reflexologist who practices in a state that has licensing regulations that require training in a field such as massage must also be able to complete that training. In addition, a reflexologist must be comfortable making decisions and working alone. Most reflexologists have their own practices, and anyone who sets up shop will need to deal with the basic tasks and problems that all business owners face: advertising, accounting, taxes, legal requirements, and so forth.

■ Exploring

The best way to learn about the field of reflexology is to speak with reflexologists. Call practitioners and ask to interview them. Find reflexologists in your area if you can, but do not hesitate to contact people in other areas. There is no substitute for learning from those who actually do the work. Although most reflexologists run one-person

LEARN MORE ABOUT IT

Byers, Dwight C. *Better Health with Foot Reflexology: The Original Ingham Method.* St. Petersburg, FL: Ingham Publishing, 1991.

Dougans, Inge, with Suzanne Ellis. *Reflexology: Foot Massage for Total Health.* Rockport, MA: Element Books, 1991.

Ingham, Eunice D. *The Original Works of Eunice D. Ingham: Stories the Feet Can Tell and Stories the Feet Have Told Through Reflexology.* St. Petersburg, FL: Ingham Publishing, 1984.

Kunz, Kevin, and Barbara Kunz. *The Complete Guide to Foot Reflexology.* Thorsons, 1983.

Norman, Laura, with Thomas Cowan. *Feet First: A Guide to Foot Reflexology.* New York, NY: Simon & Schuster, 1988.

practices, it may be possible to find clerical work of some kind with a successful practitioner in your area, especially if you live in a large city.

You should also do as much reading as you can on the subject. Many books are currently available, and many more will be available in the near future, since the field is growing rapidly. Look for information on reflexology in magazines that deal with alternative medicine and bodywork. Learn as much as you can about alternative therapies. You may find that you wish to practice a number of techniques in addition to reflexology.

■ Employers

For the most part, reflexologists work for themselves, although they may work at businesses that include reflexology as one of a number of services that they provide. It is probably wise to assume that you are going to run your own business, even if you do end up working for another organization. In most cases, organizations that use reflexologists bring them in as independent contractors rather than employees.

■ Starting Out

You should begin by taking the best, most comprehensive course of study you can find from a school that will certify you as a practitioner. After that, if you have not found an organization that you can work for, you should begin to practice on your own. You may rent an office or set up shop at home in order to save money. You may begin by working part-time, so that you can earn money by other means while you are getting your business underway. Be sure to investigate the state and local laws that may affect you.

A reflexologist who runs his or her own business needs to be well versed in basic business skills. You may want to take courses in business or seek advice from the local office of the Small Business Administration. Seek advice from people you know who run their own businesses. Your financial survival will depend on your business skills, so be sure that you know what you are doing.

■ Advancement

Because most reflexologists work for themselves, advancement in the field is directly related to the quality of treatment they provide and their business skills. The best way to get ahead as a reflexologist is to prove to the members of your community that you are skilled, honest, professional, and effective. Only when there is a strong demand for your services can you expect to thrive financially. When you have attained a high level of skill and your clients are urging their friends to take their business to you, financial success is probable.

■ Earnings

There are no reliable figures to indicate what reflexologists earn per year. In most cases, however, reflexologists charge between $30 and $60 per hour. Some practitioners may charge as little as $15 per hour, while a small number of well-respected reflexologists in large cities may earn $100 or even substantially more per hour. Many reflexologists do not work 40 hours per week doing reflexology exclusively. It is likely that most reflexologists earn between $7,000 and $35,000 per year, while some may earn more than $100,000 per year. Typically, it takes quite some time for new practitioners to build up a practice, so many of them rely on other sources of income in the beginning. Many reflexologists offer other holistic treatments and therapies, which means that they do not rely on reflexology to provide all their income.

■ Work Environment

Reflexologists almost always work in their homes or in their own offices. Although some reflexologists may have office help, most work alone. For this reason, practitioners must be independent enough to work effectively on schedules of their own devising. Because they must make their clients comfortable in order to provide effective treatment, they generally try to make their workplaces as pleasant and relaxing as possible. Many practitioners play soothing music while they work. Some—especially those who practice aromatherapy as well as reflexology—use scents to create an attractive atmosphere.

■ Outlook

Although no official government analysis of the future of reflexology has yet been conducted, it seems safe to say that the field is expanding much more rapidly than the average for all fields. Although science still views it with skepticism, reflexology has become relatively popular in a short period of time. It has certainly benefited from the popular acceptance of alternative medicine and therapies in recent years, particularly because it is a holistic practice that aims to treat the whole person rather than the symptoms of disease or discomfort. Because reflexology treatments entail little risk to the client in most cases, they provide a safe and convenient way to improve health.

■ For More Information

The IIR promotes the Original Ingham Method of Reflexology, providing seminars worldwide as well as a thorough certification program. The Institute also sells books and charts.

The International Institute of Reflexology
PO Box 12642
St. Petersburg, FL 33733-2642
Tel: 727-343-4811
Web: http://ourworld.compuserve.com/ homepages/Mike Levick/

The ARCB was created in order to promote reflexology by recognizing competent practitioners. It provides voluntary testing for working reflexologists and maintains lists of certified practitioners.

American Reflexology Certification Board
PO Box 620607
Littleton, CO 80162
Tel: 303-933-6921

Laura Norman's organization provides training and certification in reflexology. It also sells books, reflexology products, and aromatherapy supplies.

Laura Norman and Associates
41 Park Avenue, Suite 8A
New York, NY 10016
Tel: 212-532-4404
Web: http://lauranormanrefl.oxology.com

■ Related Articles

Alternative Health Care

Aromatherapists

Chiropractors

Kinesiologists

Massage Therapists

Oriental Medicine Practitioners

Refuge Rangers
■ **See Fish and Game Wardens**

Refuse Collectors

■ Overview

Refuse collectors gather garbage and other discarded materials set out by customers along designated routes in urban and rural communities and transport the materials to sanitary landfills or incinerator plants for disposal. Refuse collectors may specialize in collecting certain types of material, such as recyclable glass, newsprint, or aluminum.

■ History

Refuse, or the solid waste generated by a community, has presented problems for just about every society throughout history; previously, the accepted method for disposal of refuse was burning at home or haphazard dumping into open pits or waterways. In the past couple of centuries, heavier population concentrations and industrial growth have vastly increased the quantity of refuse produced, making unregulated dumping impractical as well as unhealthy. As waste disposal has become more regulated, the job of the waste hauler has changed as well.

The first sanitary landfill was opened in 1912. In a sanitary landfill, refuse gathered from a community is deposited in a large pit in shallow layers, compacted, and covered daily with earth. Sealed in, the refuse undergoes slow, natural decomposition. When the pit is full, the top is sealed over and the land is available for reuse, often as a public park or other recreational area. Landfills are increasingly regulated in regards to their location, operation, and closure. The number of landfills, which peaked nationwide in the mid-1980s, is now dropping as communities fight against having landfills in their midst. The result is fewer, larger landfills that are sited in communities that favor the jobs that the landfill offers. As a result, refuse collectors who transport waste

REFUSE COLLECTORS	
SCHOOL SUBJECTS	Physical education Technical/Shop
PERSONAL SKILLS	Following instructions Mechanical/manipulative
WORK ENVIRONMENT	Primarily outdoors One location with some travel
MINIMUM EDUCATION LEVEL	High school diploma
SALARY RANGE	$13,104 to $17,160 to $24,856
CERTIFICATION OR LICENSING	Required for certain positions
OUTLOOK	Little change or more slowly than the average
DOT	955
GOE	05.12.03
NOC	7621
O*NET	98705

Refuse collectors work in all kinds of weather and must take care to wear protective clothing.

to landfills may spend greater parts of their workday driving longer distances to the landfill.

Increases in recycling have also changed the job of the refuse collector. In more and more communities around the United States, people separate out materials such as glass bottles, metal cans, newspapers, certain plastics, and other designated refuse for recycling, thus limiting the flow of refuse into landfills and incinerators. The sale of recyclable materials can help to reduce the cost of the refuse disposal operation. Refuse collectors are the ones who pick up recyclables in most communities, sometimes on the same day, and even in the same truck, as the garbage is collected. Some trucks are equipped with separate bins for refuse and recyclables. Other refuse collectors may pick up only recyclables, usually in larger communities. The trend toward recycling requires refuse collectors who deal with these items to be familiar with how they are to be properly separated.

Another form of reclaiming materials is the composting of plant wastes, such as grass clippings, brush, and leaves, in community compost heaps. *Composting* is a way to decompose this material into mulch, which is rich in minerals and can be reclaimed for fertilizer. This mulch, or compost, may be used by the municipality or made avail-

able to its citizens. Refuse collectors sometimes pick up yard wastes and are therefore required to know when the resident has used the proper container for grass clippings.

■ The Job

In general, refuse collection teams of two or three workers drive along established routes and empty household trash containers into garbage trucks. The refuse, which is often mechanically compacted in the truck, is taken to a landfill or other appropriate disposal facility.

Refuse workers may collect all kinds of solid wastes, including food scraps, paper products, and plastics. Depending on local requirements, the refuse may be loose in containers, in packaging such as plastic bags, in preapproved containers that indicate recyclable materials, or, for newspapers and magazines, tied in bundles. When the truck is full, the workers drive with the load to the disposal site and empty the truck. Workers also may pick up cast-off furniture, old appliances, or other large, bulky items, although usually such items are collected only on certain days.

An average day for refuse collectors often begins before dawn, according to *Waste Age* magazine, which featured an article in February 1998 that followed a refuse collector along his daily duties. The day begins with an inspection of the truck that includes checking lights, tires, testing air and oil pressure gauges, and making sure a spill kit is on board. Refuse collectors who work on commercial routes or pick up dumpsters stay in contact with dispatchers via radio or cellular phone to learn where they are needed to pick up. Refuse collectors gas up their trucks as needed and recheck the truck's vital equipment at the end of the day.

As they move along their routes, refuse collectors are constantly getting on and off the truck to lift trash containers onto the truck. The containers are often heavy. Sometimes the different work duties are divided among the workers, with the driver doing only the driving all day long. In other cases, the workers alternate between driving and loading and unloading throughout the day.

Some employers send refuse collectors on routes alone and they are responsible for driving the truck and loading the refuse. Usually, however, refuse collectors working alone have special routes, such as driving a truck that can lift and empty dumpsters. The refuse collector operates the levers and buttons that lift and dump the dumpster's contents into the truck. This kind of system is particularly useful for apartment buildings, construction sites, and other locations that need containers so large they are too heavy to empty by hand. The use of mechanical hoists on trucks makes refuse pickup much faster and more efficient.

Some trucks are built with different bins, so that recyclable items that customers have set out separately, such as aluminum or newspaper, can be kept separate in the truck and later taken to buyers. In some communities, the pickup days and the company responsible for disposal are different for recyclable materials than for other mixed general refuse.

Garbage-collection supervisors direct and coordinate the tasks of the various workers involved in the collecting and transporting of refuse. They make work assignments and monitor and evaluate job performance.

■ Requirements

High School

Employers prefer applicants who are high school graduates. Workers who hope to advance to a supervisory position ought to have at least a high school diploma. High school classes that may be helpful include any shop classes that provide hands-on learning opportunities and physical education classes that teach students how to develop strength and endurance. A good understanding of basic math and English is also necessary to read instructions and operate equipment in the job.

Postsecondary Training

Generally, employers will hire people without work experience or specific training. Most employers, however, do require workers to be at least 18 years old and physically able to perform the work.

Refuse workers need to be physically fit and able to lift heavy objects. Sometimes a health examination is required for employment. Employers look for workers who are reliable and hardworking.

Experience in driving a truck and in loading and unloading heavy material is helpful. Many refuse workers, especially those in metropolitan areas, are members of a union such as the International Brotherhood of Teamsters, Chauffeurs, Warehousemen and Helpers of America. Those who work for private firms might not be unionized.

Certification or Licensing

Workers who drive collection trucks need a commercial driver's license (CDL). In some areas, where the workers alternate jobs, a CDL is required even of those who are generally loaders. A clean driving record is often a necessity. Refuse collectors may have to pass a civil service test in order to work for a city or town.

■ Exploring

People who are thinking about getting into this kind of work may find it helpful to talk with experienced workers in similar jobs. In some areas, there may be opportunities for summer or part-time work, although workers in these positions generally have to meet the same requirements as

WHERE DOES THE GARBAGE GO?

Talk to anyone in the solid waste management industry today and it's unlikely you'll hear them use the word "dump." Yesterday's dumps are today's landfills—highly regulated and carefully engineered. Open land dumps have been banned in the United States. When refuse collectors pick up garbage at the curbside, the garbage is usually crushed once it's deposited into the truck. When the collector takes the waste to the landfill, the garbage is compacted even further to reduce volume and conserve landfill space. Landfills are expensive to build and maintain, so every effort is made to make the best use of them. Once the garbage is dumped at the landfill, it is covered with a layer of earth. The earth reduces odors and keeps away disease-carrying pests, such as rats and flies. Building today's landfills requires extensive planning, engineering, monitoring, and supervision. Many landfills are made with liners of compacted clay (as thick as 10 feet) or impermeable materials such as plastic to prevent contamination of soil and water outside the landfill. Another method of preventing contamination is a drainage system in which rainwater and runoff are pumped to the surface, where they are treated and discharged. When landfills reach their capacity, they are sealed and covered with a layer of clay and dirt, where grass is planted, and the large hill that is left can be used for recreational purposes.

full-time employees. Contact local recycling centers to check on availability of volunteer or part-time work. A job as a furniture mover or truck driver is another way to learn about some of the responsibilities of refuse collectors. Any experience you can gain in a related job that requires physical strength and reliability is useful to test your work endurance. Work as a material handler, equipment cleaner, helper, or laborer would be useful.

■ Employers

In the past, refuse collectors were employed almost exclusively by municipalities. Today, refuse collectors may work for private waste haulers that contract with local governments or even specialized firms, such as recycling haulers. Some local governments still operate their own waste hauling programs, and in these communities, refuse collectors are city employees. But many have found it more cost-effective to contract with private waste haulers who employ their own refuse collectors. Similar jobs may be found at landfills, where workers are needed to assist drivers in dumping collected refuse, or at material recovery facilities (MRFs) where recyclables are taken. MRFs need workers to separate materials, load and unload trucks, and operate equipment, such as balers that condense the recyclables into large, dense bales.

■ Starting Out

Prospective applicants for refuse collector jobs can contact the local city government's personnel department or department of sanitation. Employees in these offices may be able to supply information on job openings and local requirements. People interested in working for a private disposal firm should contact the firm directly. Listings for specific job opportunities can sometimes also be found through the state employment service or newspaper classified ads. Contacting a waste disposal union's local branch and becoming a member may help workers land a job when one becomes available in their area.

■ Advancement

Opportunities for advancement are usually limited for refuse collectors. Those who work for municipal governments may be able to transfer to better-paying jobs in another department of city government, such as public works. Sometimes advancement means becoming the driver of a refuse truck, rather than a worker who loads and unloads the truck. In larger organizations, refuse collectors who prove to be reliable employees may be promoted to supervisory positions, where they coordinate and direct the activities of other workers. Others may develop a knowledge of recyclables, for example, and help coordinate a waste hauler's recycling business.

■ Earnings

Earnings of these workers vary widely depending on their employer, union status, and other factors. Beginning refuse collectors who work for small, private firms and are not union members are sometimes paid at hourly wages not far above the federal minimum wage. On the low end, refuse collectors average an annual salary of $13,104. On the upper end of the scale, workers can average as much as $24,856 a year, with most making closer to the national average of $17,160 in 1996, according to the Bureau of Labor Statistics' *Occupational Outlook Handbook*. In general, workers employed by large cities under union contracts make more money, and those working for small companies without union contracts make less.

Refuse collectors get overtime pay for working extra hours, during the evenings, or on weekends. They may receive paid time during each shift to shower and change clothes. Union workers receive benefits such as health insurance and paid sick leave and vacation days. Most full-time workers with private companies also receive benefits, although they may not receive as desirable a benefits package.

■ Work Environment

Refuse workers must work outdoors in all kinds of weather, including cold, snow, rain, and heat, and they must handle dirty, smelly objects. The work is active and often strenuous, requiring the lifting of heavy refuse containers, hopping on and off the truck constantly, and operating hoists and other equipment. Workers often encounter garbage that is not packed correctly. Because there is a danger of infection from raw garbage, they must wear protective gloves and are sometimes provided with uniforms. Workers must always be aware of the dangers of working around traffic and mechanical compactors. Most workers wear heavy steel-toe boots to help avoid foot injuries from accidentally dropping containers or large objects. New employees receive instruction on safety precautions they will need to take as well as instructions about their responsibilities.

Most refuse collectors work during weekday daylight hours, with regular shifts totaling 35 to 40 hours per week. Many workers put in slightly longer hours. Many workers begin their shifts in the predawn hours, while other workers routinely work in the evenings. In emergencies (for removal of storm-downed tree branches, for instance), weekend hours may be necessary. Workers who drive the trucks must have a CDL, and federal law prohibits CDL drivers from working more than 60 hours per week.

■ Outlook

There were over 116,000 refuse collectors employed in 1996, up from about 111,000 in the early 1990s. Municipal waste is expected to increase at a rate of 1 to 2 percent annually until at least 2000, creating up to 225 million tons of waste a year. The government predicts jobs for refuse collectors will grow more slowly than the average through 2006. The number employed is expected to increase to 123,000 by 2006. However, job turnover is high in this field. Every year, many positions will become available as workers transfer to other jobs or leave the workforce.

Opportunities will be best in heavily populated regions in and near big cities, where the most waste is generated. In cities, increasing use of mechanized equipment for lifting and emptying large refuse containers may decrease the need for these workers. However, as communities encourage more recycling and more resource recovery technologies, job availability may change somewhat for refuse collectors. More varied pickup services may tend to require more workers, expanding the employment opportunities in both the public and private sector.

A trend that favors use of large, nationally based waste management corporations is eliminating smaller competitors in some areas. This suggests that job security may depend on the size of the employer. As recycling becomes more lucrative, large companies may concentrate on this aspect of waste disposal.

■ For More Information

The Environmental Industry Association is an umbrella organization that includes organizations of interest to the solid waste management industry. It publishes two magazines that follow trends and news of the waste industry; call 800-424-2869 for Waste Age *magazine or* Recycling Times *magazine.*

Environmental Industry Association
4301 Connecticut Avenue, NW, Suite 300
Washington, DC 20008
Web: http://www.wasteage.com

A national union whose members include refuse collectors:

International Brotherhood of Teamsters, Chauffeurs, Warehousemen and Helpers of America
25 Louisiana Avenue, NW
Washington, DC 20001
Tel: 202-624-6800
Web: http://www.teamster.org

The NSWMA is an industry organization that is also part of EIA:

National Solid Wastes Management Association
4301 Connecticut Avenue, NW, Suite 300
Washington, DC 20008
Tel: 202-624-6800
Web: http://www.envasns.org/nswma

■ Related Articles

Waste Management

Hazardous Waste Management Technicians

Pollution Control Technicians

Regional and Local Officials

■ Overview

Regional and local officials hold positions in the legislative, executive, and judicial branches of government at the local level. They include mayors, commissioners, and city and county council members. These officials direct regional legal services, public health departments, and police protection. They serve on housing, budget, and employment committees and develop special programs to improve communities.

■ History

The first U.S. colonies adopted the English "shire" form of government. This form was 1,000 years old and served as the administrative arm of both the national and local governments; a county in medieval England was overseen by a sheriff (originally a "shire reeve") appointed by the crown and was represented by two members in Parliament.

When America's founding fathers composed the Constitution, they didn't make any specific provisions for the governing of cities and counties. This allowed state governments to compose their own definitions; when drawing up their own constitutions, the states essentially considered county governments to be extensions of the state government.

City governments, necessary for dealing with increased industry and trade, evolved during the 19th century. Population growth and suburban development helped to strengthen local governments after World War I. The county governments grew even stronger after World War II, due to rising revenues and increased independence from the states.

■ The Job

There are a variety of different forms of local government across the country, but they all share similar concerns. County and city governments make sure that the local streets are free of crime as well as free of pot holes. They create and improve regional parks and organize music festivals and outdoor theater events to be staged in these parks. They identify community problems and help to solve them in original ways: King County in Washington state, in an effort to solve the problem of unemployment among those recently released from jail, developed a baking training program for county inmates. The inmates' new talents with danishes and bread loaves have opened up good-paying job opportunities in grocery store bakeries all across the county. King County also has many youth programs, including the Paul Robeson Scholar-Athlete Award recognizing students who excel in both academics and athletics.

Consumer protection, water quality, affordable housing: the needs of cities and counties increase every year. As a regional or local official, you're elected to deal with issues such as public health, legal services, housing, and budget and fiscal management. You'll attend meetings and serve on committees. Aware of the industry and agriculture of the area, as well as the specific problems facing your constituents, you'll offer educated solu-

REGIONAL AND LOCAL OFFICIALS	
SCHOOL SUBJECTS	English Government History
PERSONAL SKILLS	Communication/ideas Leadership/management
WORK ENVIRONMENT	Primarily indoors One location with some travel
MINIMUM EDUCATION LEVEL	Bachelor's degree
SALARY RANGE	$0 to $38,000 to $56,000
CERTIFICATION OR LICENSING	None available
OUTLOOK	Little change or more slowly than the

COUNTY MODEL PROGRAMS

The National Association of Counties (NACO) sponsors achievement awards that recognize innovative government programs and projects in such areas as arts and historic preservation, children and youth, and employment and training. Here are a few of NACO's "County Model Programs":

Students in the local schools of Jane City, Virginia, were invited to draw an ideal playground. Volunteers and donations were then sought by the Parks and Recreation Department, and "Kidsburg" was built from these student designs.

Johnson County, Kansas, introduced a program to bring more older volunteers into public schools for tutoring and for speaking to students in the Living History Program, which features stories of the past.

After Hurricane Andrew, many lost pets could not be returned to their owners because of loss of identification and lack of communication among humane organizations. In response, Orange County, Florida, has developed disaster planning kits and new animal shelters in the event of future natural disasters.

tions, vote on laws, and generally represent the people in your district within the county. In addition to the programs mentioned above, counties across the country have initiated a number of creative programs: The Innovative Farmer Program in Huron County, Michigan, was developed to introduce new methods of farming to keep agriculture part of the county's economy. The program is studying new cover-crops, tillage systems, and herbicides. In Onondaga County, New York, the public library started a program of basic reading instruction for deaf adults. In Broward County, Florida, a new program provides a homelike setting for supervised visitation and parenting training for parents who are separated from their children due to abuse or domestic violence.

There are two forms county government: the commissioner/administrator form, in which the county board of commissioners appoints an administrator who serves the board; and the council-executive form, in which a county executive is the chief administrative officer of the district and has the power to veto ordinances enacted by the county board. A county government may include a chief executive, who directs regional services; *council members*, who are the county legislators; a *county clerk*, who keeps records of property titles, licenses, etc.; and a *county treasurer* who is in charge of the receipt and disbursement of money.

A county government doesn't tax its citizens, so its money comes from state aid, fees, and grants. A city government funds its projects and programs with money from sales and other local taxes, block grants, and state aid. Directing these funds and services are executives. *Mayors* serve as the heads of city governments who are elected by the general populace. Their specific functions vary depend-

ing on the structure of their government. In mayor-council governments, both the mayor and the city council are popularly elected. The council is responsible for formulating city ordinances, but the mayor exercises control over the actions of the council. In such governments, the mayor usually plays a dual role, serving not only as chief executive officer but also as an agent of the city government responsible for such functions as maintaining public order, security, and health. In a commission government, the people elect a number of *commissioners*, each of whom serves as head of a city department. The presiding commissioner is usually the mayor. The final type of municipal government is the council-manager structure. Here, the council members are elected by the people, and one of their functions is to hire a *city manager* to administer the city departments. A mayor is elected by the council to chair the council and officiate at important municipal functions.

■ Requirements

High School

You should take courses in government, civics, and history to gain an understanding of the structure of government. English courses are important because you'll need good writing skills to communicate with your constituents and other government officials. Math and accounting will help you to develop the analytical skills needed for examining statistics and demographics. Journalism classes will help you develop the research and interview skills you'll need for identifying problems and developing programs.

Postsecondary Training

To serve on a local government, your experience and understanding of the city or county are generally more important than your educational background. Some mayors and council members are elected into their positions because they've long lived in the region and have had experience with local industry and other concerns. For example, someone with years of experience with farming in the region may be the best candidate to serve for a small agricultural community. Voters in local elections may be more impressed by a candidate's previous occupations and roles in the community than they are by a candidate's postsecondary degrees.

But to serve as an executive or council member for a large city or county, you are likely to need an undergraduate degree. Officials have undergraduate or graduate degrees in such areas as public administration, law, economics, political science, history, and English. Regardless of your major as an undergraduate, you are likely to be required to take classes in English literature, statistics, foreign language, western civilization, and economics.

Other Requirements

You have to deeply understand the city and region you're serving. You should have a lot of knowledge about the local industry, private businesses, and social problems. You'll have gained this knowledge and understanding by having lived for some time in the region. In some cases, you'll be making less money than you could in the private sector, or you'll be volunteering your time; therefore you'll need a personal connection to the region and personal investment in the region's improvement.

You should have good people skills to be capable of listening to the concerns of constituents and other officials and exchanging ideas with them. Problem-solving skills and creativity will help you develop innovative programs.

■ Exploring

Depending on the size of your city or county, you can probably become involved with your local government at a young age. Your council members and other government officials should be more accessible to you than state and federal officials, so take advantage of that. Visit the county court house and volunteer in whatever capacity you can with county-organized programs—you could tutor in a literacy program or lead children's reading groups at the public library. Become involved with local elections. Many candidates for local and state offices welcome young people to assist with campaigns. You'll make calls, post signs, and get to see a candidate at work. You'll also meet others with an interest in government, and the experience will help you to gain a more prominent role in later campaigns. Another great way to learn about government is to become involved in an issue of interest to you. Maybe there's an old building in your neighborhood you'd like to save from destruction, or maybe you have some ideas for youth programs or programs for senior citizens. Research what's being done about your concerns and come up with solutions to offer local officials.

■ Employers

Every city in the United States requires the services of local officials; in some cases, the services of a small town or suburb may be overseen by the government of a larger city or by the county government. Forty-eight states have operational county governments—a total of over 3,000 counties. (Connecticut and Rhode Island are the only two states without counties.) The counties with the largest populations are: Los Angeles County, California; Cook County, Illinois; and Harris County, Texas. There are also 31 governments that are consolidations of city and county governments; New York, Denver, and San Francisco are among them.

■ Starting Out

There is no direct career path for gaining public office. The way you pursue a local office will be greatly effected by the size and population of the region in which you live. When running for mayor or council of a small town, you may have no competition at all; but to become mayor of a large city, you'll need extensive experience in the city's politics. If you're interested in pursuing a local position, research the backgrounds of your city mayor, county commissioner, and council members to get an idea of how they approached their political careers.

Some stumble into government offices after some success with political activism on the grassroots level. Others have had success in other areas, such as agriculture, nursing, and law enforcement; they use their particular understanding of an area to help improve the community. Many local politicians get their starts assisting someone else's campaign or advocating for an issue, or they assist elected officials in developing programs for the community.

■ Advancement

Some successful local and regional officials maintain their positions for many years, gaining reelection over and over again. Others only hold local office for one or two terms, then return full-time to their businesses and other careers. You might also choose to use a local position as a stepping stone to a position of greater power within the region or to a state office. Many mayors of a state's largest cities run for governor or state legislature and may eventually move into federal office.

■ Earnings

In general, salaries for government officials tend to be lower than what the official could make working in the private sector. In many local offices, you'll be volunteering your time or working only part-time. According to a salary survey published in 1998 by the International City/County Management Association (ICMA), the chief elected official of a city makes an average salary of $12,870 a year. City clerks, treasurers, and chief law enforcement officials fare better: clerks earn about $37,000 a year; treasurers $38,000; and chief law enforcement officials $54,000.

The ICMA survey also compiled figures for county officials. A county's chief elected official averages $26,420 a year. County clerks make about $38,000, while treasurers make $36,000, and chief law enforcement officials make $48,000.

A job with a local or regional government may or may not provide benefits. Some positions may include accounts for official travel and other expenses.

■ Work Environment

Most government officials work in a typical office setting. Some may work a regular 40-hour week, while others work long hours and weekends. Though some positions may only be considered part-time, they may take up nearly as many hours as full-time work. You'll have the opportunity to meet with the people of your region, but you will also devote a lot of your time to clerical duties. If serving a large community, you may have some assistants to help with phones, filing, and preparing documents, but most of these responsibilities will be your own.

Because officials must be appointed or elected in order to keep their jobs, determining long-range career plans can be difficult. There may be extended periods of unemployment, where living off of savings or other jobs may be necessary. And because of the low pay of some positions, you may have to work another job even while you serve in office. This can result in little personal time and the need to juggle many different responsibilities at once.

■ Outlook

Though the form and structure of state and federal government are not likely to change, the form of your local and county government can be altered by popular vote. Every election, voters somewhere in the country are deciding whether to keep their current forms of government or to introduce new forms. But these changes don't greatly effect the number of officials needed to run your local government. Your chances of holding office will be greater in a smaller community. The races for part-time and nonpaying offices will also be less competitive.

The issues facing your community will have the most effect on your experience as a local official. In a city with older neighborhoods, you'll be dealing with historic preservation, improvements in utilities, and water quality. With a growing city of many suburbs, you'll have to make decisions regarding development, roads, and expanded routes for public transportation.

The federal government has made efforts to shift costs to the states; if this continues, states may offer less aid to counties. A county government's funds are also affected by changes in property taxes.

■ For More Information

For information about the forms of city and county governments around the country, and to learn about programs sponsored by local and regional governments, contact these organizations:

National Association of Counties
440 First Street, NW
Washington, DC 20001
Tel: 202-393-6226
Web: http://www.naco.org

International City/County Management Association
777 North Capitol Street, NE, Suite 500
Washington, DC 20002
Tel: 202-289-4262
Web: http://www.icma.org

■ Related Articles

Government
Campaign Workers
City Managers
Congressional Aides
Federal and State Officials
Political Scientists
Press Secretaries

Registered Nurses

■ Overview

Registered nurses (RNs) help individuals, families, and groups to achieve health and prevent disease. They care for the sick and injured in hospitals and other health care facilities, physicians' offices, private homes, public health agencies, schools, camps, and industry. Some registered nurses are employed in private practice.

■ History

Modern ideas about hospitals and nursing as a profession did not develop until the 19th century. The life and work of Florence Nightingale (1820-1910) were a strong influence on the profession's development. Nightingale, who came from a wealthy, upper-class British family, dedicated her life to improving conditions in hospitals, beginning in an army hospital during the Crimean War. In this country, many of Nightingale's ideas were put into practice for the care of the wounded during the Civil War. The care, however, was provided by concerned individuals who nursed rather than by trained nurses. They had not received the kind of training that is required for nurses today.

The first school of nursing in the United States was founded in Boston in 1873. In 1938, New York State passed the first state law to require that practical nurses be licensed. Even though the first school for the training of practical nurses was started almost 74 years ago, and the establishment of other schools followed, the training programs lacked uniformity.

After the 1938 law was passed, a movement began to have organized training programs that would assure new standards in the field. The role and training of the nurse have undergone radical changes since the first schools were opened.

Education standards for nurses have been improving constantly since that time. Today's nurse is a highly educated, licensed health care professional. Now extended programs of training are offered throughout the country, and all states have enacted laws to assure training standards are maintained and to assure qualification for licensure. The field of nursing serves an important role as a part of the health care system.

■ The Job

Registered nurses work under the direct supervision of nursing departments and in collaboration with physicians. Two-thirds of all nurses work in hospitals, where they may be assigned to general, operating room, or maternity room duty. They may also care for sick children or be assigned to other hospital units, such as emergency rooms, intensive care units, or outpatient clinics. There are many different kinds of RNs.

General duty nurses work together with other members of the health care team to assess the patient's condition and to develop and implement a plan of health care. These nurses may perform such tasks as taking patients' vital signs, administering medication and injections, recording the symptoms and progress of patients, changing dressings, assisting patients with personal care, conferring with members of the medical staff, helping prepare a patient for surgery, and completing any number of duties that require skill and understanding of patients' needs.

Surgical nurses oversee the preparation of the operating room and the sterilization of instruments. They assist surgeons during operations and coordinate the flow of patient cases in operating rooms.

Maternity nurses help in the delivery room, take care of newborns in the nursery, and teach mothers how to feed and care for their babies.

The activities of staff nurses are directed and coordinated by *head nurses and supervisors.* Heading up the entire nursing program in the hospital is the nursing service director, who administers the nursing program to maintain standards of patient care. The *nursing service director* advises the medical staff, department heads, and the hospital administrator in matters relating to nursing services and helps prepare the department budget.

Private duty nurses may work in hospitals or in a patient's home. They are employed by the patient they are caring for or by the patient's family. Their service is designed for the individual care of one person and is carried out in cooperation with the patient's physician.

Office nurses usually work in the office of a dentist, physician, or health maintenance organization (HMO). They may be one of several nurses on the staff or the only staff nurse. If a nurse is the only staff member, this person may have to combine some clerical duties with those of nursing, such as serving as receptionist, making appointments for the doctor, helping maintain patient records,

sending out monthly statements, and attending to routine correspondence. If the physician's staff is a large one that includes secretaries and clerks, the office nurse will concentrate on screening patients, assisting with examinations, supervising the examining rooms, sterilizing equipment, providing patient education, and performing other nursing duties.

Occupational health nurses, or *industrial nurses,* are an important part of many large firms. They maintain a clinic at a plant or factory and are usually occupied in rendering preventive, remedial, and educational nursing services. They work under the direction of an industrial physician, nursing director, or nursing supervisor. They may advise on accident prevention, visit employees on the job to check the conditions under which they work, and advise management about the safety of such conditions. At the plant, they render treatment in emergencies.

School nurses may work in one school or in several, visiting each for a part of the day or week. They may supervise the student clinic, treat minor cuts or injuries, or give advice on good health practices. They may examine students to detect conditions of the eyes or teeth that require attention. They also assist the school physician.

Community health nurses, also called *public health nurses,* require specialized training for their duties. Their job usually requires them to spend part of the time traveling from one assignment to another. Their duties may differ greatly from one case to another. For instance, in one day they may have to instruct a class of expectant mothers, visit new parents to help them plan proper care for the baby, visit an aged patient requiring special care, and conduct a class in nutrition. They usually possess many and varied nursing skills and often are called upon to meet unexpected or unusual situations.

Administrators in the community health field include nursing directors, educational directors, and nursing supervisors. Some

REGISTERED NURSES	
SCHOOL SUBJECTS	Biology Chemistry
PERSONAL SKILLS	Helping/teaching Technical/scientific
WORK ENVIRONMENT	Primarily indoors Primarily multiple locations
MINIMUM EDUCATION LEVEL	Some postsecondary training
SALARY RANGE	$22,000 to $28,000 to $75,000
CERTIFICATION OR LICENSING	Required by all states
OUTLOOK	Faster than the average
DOT	075
GOE	10.02.01
NOC	3152
O*NET	32502

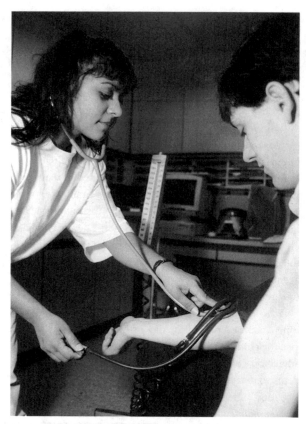

A registered nurse takes a patient's blood pressure.

nurses go into nursing education and work with nursing students to instruct them on theories and skills they will need to enter the profession. Nursing instructors may give classroom instruction and demonstrations or supervise nursing students on hospital units. Some instructors eventually become nursing school directors, university faculty, or deans of a university degree program. Nurses also have the opportunity to direct staff development and continuing education programs for nursing personnel in hospitals.

Advanced practice nurses are nurses with training beyond that required to have the RN designation. There are four primary categories of nurses included in this category: certified nurse midwives, clinical nurse specialists, nurse anesthetists, and nurse practitioners.

Some nurses are consultants to hospitals, nursing schools, industrial organizations, and public health agencies. They advise clients on such administrative matters as staff organization, nursing techniques, curricula, and education programs. Other administrative specialists include educational directors for the state board of nursing, who are concerned with maintaining well-defined educational standards, and executive directors of professional nurses' asso-

ciations, who administer programs developed by the board of directors and the members of the association.

Some nurses choose to enter the armed forces. All types of nurses, except private duty nurses, are represented in the military services. They provide skilled nursing care to active-duty and retired members of the armed forces and their families. In addition to basic nursing skills, military nurses are trained to provide care in various environments, including field hospitals, on-air evacuation flights, and onboard ships. Military nurses actively influence the development of health care through nursing research. Advances influenced by military nurses include the development of the artificial kidney (dialysis unit) and the concept of the intensive care unit.

■ Requirements

High School

High school students interested in becoming a registered nurse should take mathematics and science courses, including biology, chemistry, and physics. English and speech courses should not be neglected because the nurse must be able to communicate well with patients.

Postsecondary Training

There are three basic kinds of training programs that prospective nurses may choose to become registered nurses: associate's degree programs, diploma programs, and bachelor's degree programs. Which of the three training programs to choose depends on one's career goals. A bachelor's degree in nursing is required for most supervisory or administrative positions, for jobs in public health agencies, and for admission to graduate nursing programs. A master's degree is usually necessary to prepare for a nursing specialty or to teach. For some specialties, such as nursing research, a Ph.D. is essential.

The bachelor's degree program is offered by colleges or universities. It requires four (in some cases, five) years to complete. The graduate of this program receives a Bachelor of Science in Nursing degree. The Associate in Arts in Nursing is awarded after completion of a two-year study program that is usually offered in a junior or community college. The student receives hospital training at cooperating hospitals in the general vicinity of the community college. The diploma program, which usually lasts three years, is conducted by hospitals and independent schools. At the conclusion of each of these programs, the student becomes a graduate nurse, but not, however, a registered nurse. To obtain the RN designation the graduate nurse must take and pass a licensing examination required in all states.

In 1996, there were over 1,500 entry-level nursing programs offered in the United States. In addition, there were

198 master's degree and 33 doctoral degree programs. Nurses can pursue postgraduate training that allows them to specialize in certain areas, such as emergency room, operating room, premature nursery, or psychiatric nursing. This training is sometimes offered through hospital on-the-job training programs.

Certification or Licensing

All states and the District of Columbia require a license to practice nursing. To obtain a license, graduates of approved nursing schools must pass a national examination. Nurses may be licensed by more than one state. In some states, continuing education is a condition for license renewal. Different titles require different education and training levels.

■ Exploring

High school students can explore their interest in the nursing field in a number of ways. They may read books on careers in nursing and talk with high school guidance counselors, school nurses, and local public health nurses. Visits to hospitals to observe the work and to talk with hospital personnel are also valuable.

Some hospitals now have extensive volunteer service programs in which high school students may work after school, on weekends, or during vacations in order to both render a valuable service and to explore their interests. Other volunteer work experiences may be found with the Red Cross or community health services. Camp counseling jobs sometimes offer related experiences. Some schools offer participation in Future Nurses programs.

■ Employers

Nurses are employed by hospitals, managed-care facilities, long-term-care facilities, clinics, industry, private homes, schools, camps, and government agencies.

■ Starting Out

The only way to become a registered nurse is through completion of one of the three kinds of educational programs, plus passing the licensing examination. Registered nurses may apply for employment directly to hospitals, nursing homes, companies, and government agencies that hire nurses. Jobs can also be obtained through school placement offices, by signing up with employment agencies specializing in placement of nursing personnel, or through the state employment office. Other sources of jobs include nurses' associations, professional journals, and newspaper want ads.

■ Advancement

Increasingly, administrative and supervisory positions in the nursing field go to nurses who have earned at least the bachelor of science degree in nursing. Nurses with many years of experience who are graduates of the diploma program may achieve supervisory positions, but requirements for such promotions have become more difficult in recent years and in many cases require at least the bachelor of science in nursing degree.

Nurses with bachelor's degrees are usually those who are hired as public health nurses. Nurses with master's degrees are often employed as clinical nurse specialists, faculty, instructors, supervisors, or administrators.

RNs can pursue further education to become advanced practice nurses, who have greater responsibilities and command higher salaries.

■ Earnings

According to the 1998-99 *Occupation Outlook Handbook*, registered nurses earned an average of $36,244 annually in 1996. Fifty percent earned between $29,692 and $45,136. The top 10 percent made over $54,028 a year.

A Buck Survey found that staff RNs working in a nursing home setting earned an average of about $32,968 a year. Entry-level positions with the Department of Veterans Affairs started at approximately $16,500 for nurses who were graduates of the diploma program or the associate's of arts program. The average annual salary for all nurses in federal government agencies was about $26,100.

Salary is determined by several factors: setting, education, and work experience. Most full-time nurses are given flexible work schedules as well as health and life insurance; some are offered education reimbursement and year-end bonuses. A staff nurse's salary is limited only by the amount of work one is willing to take on. Many nurses take advantage of overtime work and shift differentials. About 10 percent of all nurses hold more than one job.

■ Work Environment

Most nurses work in facilities that are clean and well lighted and where the temperature is controlled, although some work in rundown inner city hospitals in less than ideal conditions. Usually, nurses work eight-hour shifts. Those in hospitals generally work any of three shifts: 7:00 AM to 3:00 PM; 3:00 PM to 11:00 PM; or 11:00 PM to 7:00 AM.

Nurses spend much of the day on their feet, either walking or standing. Handling patients who are ill or infirm can also be very exhausting. Nurses who come in contact with patients with infectious diseases must be especially careful about cleanliness and sterility. Although many nursing duties are routine, many responsibilities are unpredictable. Sick persons are often very demanding, or they may be depressed or irritable. Despite this, the nurse must retain her or his composure and should be cheerful to help the patient achieve emotional balance.

Community health nurses may be required to visit homes that are in poor condition or very dirty. They may

Nurses who specialize in lactation consultation were recently included in *U.S. News & World Report* 's 1998 article "Best Jobs for the Future." The article says the rise in breast feeding rates is creating the need. Lactation specialists earn $25,000+.

also come in contact with social problems, such as family violence. The nurse is an important health care provider, and in many communities the sole provider.

Both the office nurse and the industrial nurse work regular business hours and are seldom required to work overtime. In some jobs, such as where nurses are on duty in private homes, they may frequently travel from home to home and work with various cases.

■ Outlook

In 1996, there were almost 2 million nurses employed in the United States—making this field the largest of all health care occupations. Employment prospects for nurses look good. The U.S. Department of Labor projects registered nurses to be one of the top 25 occupations with fastest growth, high pay, and low unemployment. In fact, it is predicted that there will be about 425,000 additional jobs available through the year 2006.

Increasing numbers of nurses who have been attracted to the profession in recent years have, however, lessened the demand for nurses in some areas. Even so, there are still many employment opportunities for nurses, especially in the inner cities and in rural areas. Employment opportunities for nurses will be best in home health situations. The increased number of older people and better medical technology have spurred the demand for nurses to bring complicated treatments to the patients' homes.

Employment in nursing homes is expected to grow much faster than the average. Though more people are living well into their 80s and 90s, many need the kind of long term care available at a nursing home. Also, because of financial reasons, patients are being released from hospitals sooner and admitted into nursing homes. Many nursing homes have facilities and staff capable of caring for long term rehabilitation patients, as well as those afflicted with Alzheimer's. Many nurses will also be needed to help staff the growing number of outpatient facilities, such as HMOs, group medical practices, and ambulatory surgery centers.

Two-thirds of all nursing jobs are found in hospitals. However, because of administrative cost cutting, increased nurse's work load, and rapid growth of outpatient services, hospital nursing jobs will experience slower than average growth.

Nursing specialties will be in great demand. There are, in addition, many part-time employment possibilities—approximately 30 percent of all nurses work on a part-time basis.

■ For More Information

American Association of Colleges of Nursing
1 Dupont Circle, Suite 530
Washington, DC 20036
Tel: 202-463-6930
Web: http://www.aacn.nche.edu

For information about opportunities as an RN, contact:

American Nurses' Association
600 Maryland Avenue, SW, Suite 100W
Washington, DC 20024-2571
Tel: 800-274-4ANA
Web: http://www.nursingworld.org

For information about state-approved programs and information on nursing, contact:

National Association for Practical Nurse Education and Service, Inc.
1400 Spring Street, Suite 310
Silver Spring, MD 20910
Tel: 301-588-2491
Email: napnes@aol.com
Web: http://www.aoa.dhhs.gov/aoa

National League for Nursing
Communications Department
350 Hudson Street
New York, NY 10014
Tel: 212-989-9393
Email: nlnweb@nln.org
Web: http://www.nln.org

■ Related Articles

Alternative Health Care

Health Care

Advanced Practice Nurses

Certified Nurse-Midwives

Clinical Nurse Specialists

Home Health Care Aides

Licensed Practical Nurses

Nurse Anesthetists

Nurse Practitioners

Physician Assistants

Physicians

Registered Representatives

■ **See Financial Services Brokers**

Rehabilitation Counselors

■ Overview

The *rehabilitation counselor* provides counseling and guidance services to people with disabilities to help them resolve life problems and to train for and locate work that is suitable to their physical and mental abilities, interests, and aptitudes.

■ History

Today it is generally accepted that people with disabilities can and should have the opportunity to become as fully independent as possible in all aspects of life, from school to work to social activities. In response to the needs of disabled war veterans, Congress passed the first Vocational Rehabilitation Act in 1920. The act set in place the Vocational Rehabilitation Program, a federal-state program that provides for the delivery of rehabilitation services, including counseling, to eligible people with disabilities.

The profession of rehabilitation counseling has its roots in the Rehabilitation Act, which allowed for funds to train personnel. What was at first a job title developed into a fully recognized profession as it became evident that the delivery of effective rehabilitation services required highly trained specialists. Early efforts for providing rehabilitation counseling and other services were often directed especially toward the nation's veterans. In 1930, the Veterans Administration was created to supply support services to veterans and their families, and in 1989, the U.S. Department of Veterans Affairs was created as the 14th cabinet department in the U.S. government.

The passage of the Americans with Disabilities Act in 1990 recognized the rights and needs of people with disabilities and developed federal regulations and guidelines aimed at eliminating discrimination and other barriers preventing people with disabilities from participating fully in school, workplace, and public life. Many state and federal programs have since been created to aid people with disabilities.

■ The Job

The rehabilitation counselor works with people with disabilities to identify barriers to medical, psychological, personal, social, and vocational adjustment and to develop a plan of action to remove or reduce those barriers.

Clients are referred to rehabilitation programs from many sources. Sometimes they seek help on their own initiative; sometimes their families bring them in. They may be referred by a physician, hospital, or social worker, or they may be sent by employment agencies, schools, or accident commissions. A former employer may seek help for the individual.

The counselor's first step is to determine the nature and extent of the disability and evaluate how that disability interferes with work and other life functions. This determination is made from medical and psychological reports as well as from family history, educational background, work experience, and other evaluative information.

The next step is to determine a vocational direction and plan of services to overcome the handicaps to employment or independent living.

The rehabilitation counselor coordinates a comprehensive evaluation of a client's physical functioning abilities and vocational interests, aptitudes, and skills. This information is used to develop for the client a vocational or independent-living goal and the services necessary to reach that goal. Services that the rehabilitation counselor may coordinate or provide include physical and mental restoration, academic or vocational training, vocational counseling, job analysis, job modification or reasonable accommodation, and job placement. Limited financial assistance in the form of maintenance or transportation assistance may also be provided.

The counselor's relationship with the client may be as brief as a week or as long as several years, depending on the nature of the problem and the needs of the client.

■ Requirements

High School

High school students interested in rehabilitation counseling should enroll in a college preparatory course, including sociology, biology, English, speech, mathematics, psychology, and social studies.

Postsecondary Training

Although there are some positions available for people with a bachelor's degree in rehabilitation counseling, a master's degree in rehabilitation counseling, counseling and guidance, or counseling psychology is pre-

REHABILITATION COUNSELORS	
SCHOOL SUBJECTS	Psychology Sociology
PERSONAL SKILLS	Helping/teaching Technical/scientific
WORK ENVIRONMENT	Primarily indoors Primarily one location
MINIMUM EDUCATION LEVEL	Bachelor's degree
SALARY RANGE	$21,500 to $40,000 to $50,000
CERTIFICATION OR LICENSING	Recommended
OUTLOOK	Faster than the average
DOT	045
GOE	10.01.02
NOC	4153
O*NET	31517B

Caseload management: The ratio of clients to counselors, takes into account characteristics of each case

Disability management: The process of returning a person with a disability to work

Peer counseling: Guidance and support given to a person by a person who has had similar experiences

Prevocational services: The evaluation, training, and assessment that a rehabilitation counselor uses prior to training a person with a disability for a specific vocation

Rehabilitation engineering: Encompasses many disciplines including engineering and medicine, with the aim of improving the quality of life for persons with disabilities

Supported employment: competitive employment for persons with severe disabilities who require ongoing support

Work adjustment: Training designed to help persons with disabilities form work habits that will increase their productivity; seeks to promote self-confidence, tolerance, and interpersonal communications

ferred for those entering the field. Preparation for a master's degree program requires an undergraduate major in behavioral sciences, social sciences, or a related field or the completion of an undergraduate degree program in rehabilitation counseling. This degree is offered at more than 30 colleges and universities in the United States. Students preparing for this career should take courses in sociology, psychology, physiology, history, and statistics as well as courses in English and communications. Several universities now offer courses in various aspects of physical therapy and special education training. Students also should consider courses in sign language and speech therapy. Foreign language skills are also helpful in this field.

The master's degree program in rehabilitation counseling is usually a two-year program. There are graduate programs in rehabilitation counseling in many large universities. The program includes courses in medical aspects of disability, psychosocial aspects of disability, testing techniques, statistics, personality theory, personality development, abnormal psychology, techniques of counseling, occupational information, and vocational training and job placement. More than 75 graduate programs in rehabilitation counseling have been accredited by the Council on Rehabilitation Education.

Certification or Licensing

Most state government rehabilitation agencies, which employ about 40 percent of all rehabilitation counselors, require future counselors to meet state civil service and merit system rules. The applicant must take a competitive written examination and may also have an individual interview and evaluation by a special board.

Many employers now require their rehabilitation counselors to be certified by the Commission on Rehabilitation Counselor Certification (CRCC). The purpose of certification is to provide assurance that professionals engaged in rehabilitation counseling meet acceptable standards and maintain those standards through continuing education. To become certified, counselors must pass an extensive written examination to demonstrate their knowledge of rehabilitation counseling. The CRCC requires the master's degree as the minimum educational level for certification.

In about 35 states, counselors in private practice must be licensed by the state. Licensing requirements vary by state; however, not all states include rehabilitation counselors under state regulatory boards.

Other Requirements

The most important personal attribute required for rehabilitation counseling is the ability to get along well with other people. Rehabilitation counselors work with many different kinds of clients and must be able to see situations and problems from the client's point of view. They must be both patient and persistent. Rehabilitation may be a slow process with many delays and setbacks. The counselor must maintain a calm, positive manner even when no progress is made.

■ Exploring

Students considering a career with disabled people should seek opportunities to work in this field. They may volunteer to work as a counselor at a disabled children's camp. They also may volunteer with a local vocational rehabilitation agency or a facility such as the Easter Seal Society or Goodwill. Students may be able to read to the blind or teach a hobby to someone who has been disabled by accident or illness.

■ Employers

Rehabilitation counselors work in a variety of settings. About three-quarters of rehabilitation counselors work for state agencies; some also work for local and federal agencies. Employment opportunities are available in rehabilitation centers, mental health agencies, developmental disability agencies, sheltered workshops, training institutions, and special schools.

■ Starting Out

School placement offices are the best places for the new graduate to begin the career search. In addition, the National Rehabilitation Counseling Association and the American Rehabilitation Counseling Association (a division of the American Counseling Association) are sources for employment information. The new counselor may also apply directly to agencies for available positions. State and local vocational rehabilitation agencies employ about ten thousand rehabilitation counselors. The Department of Veterans Affairs employs several hundred people to assist with the rehabilitation of disabled veterans. Many rehabilitation counselors are employed by private for-profit or nonprofit rehabilitation programs and facilities. Others are employed in industry, schools, hospitals, and other settings, while others are self-employed.

■ Advancement

The rehabilitation counselor will usually receive regular salary increases after gaining experience in the job. He or she may move from relatively easy cases to increasingly challenging ones. Counselors may advance into such positions as administrator or supervisor after several years of counseling experience. It is also possible to find related counseling and teaching positions, which may represent an advancement in other fields.

■ Earnings

Information about salaries for rehabilitation counselors is limited. Salaries vary widely according to each state and community. Starting salaries tend to average around $20,000 per year, and rehabilitation counselors with many years of experience can earn up to $50,000 per year. Those in supervisory and administrative positions can earn up to $65,000 per year. Self-employed counselors with established practices generally earn the highest salaries.

Rehabilitation counselors employed by the federal government generally start at the GS-9 or GS-11 level. In 1995, the GS-9 level salary was between $23,345 and $36,850. Those with master's degrees generally began at the GS-11 level, with a starting salary of $34,295 in 1995. Salaries for federal government workers vary according to the region of the country in which they work. Those working in areas with a higher cost of living receive additional locality pay.

Counselors employed by government and private agencies and institutions generally receive health insurance, pension plans, and other benefits, including vacation, sick, and holiday pay. Self-employed counselors must provide their own benefits.

■ Work Environment

Rehabilitation counselors work approximately 40 hours each week and do not usually have to work during evenings or weekends. They work both in the office and in the field. Depending on the type of training required, lab space and workout or therapy rooms may be available. Rehabilitation counselors must usually keep detailed accounts of their progress with clients and write reports. They may spend many hours traveling about the community to visit employed clients, prospective employers, trainees, or training programs.

■ Outlook

The passage of the Americans with Disabilities Act of 1990 has increased the demand for rehabilitation counselors through the year 2006, as more local, state, and federal programs are initiated that are designed to assist people with disabilities, and as private institutions and companies seek to comply with this new legislation. Budget pressures may serve to limit the numbers of new rehabilitation counselors to be hired by government agencies, however, the overall outlook remains excellent.

■ For More Information

The following is a professional organization for rehabilitation counselors, interested professionals, and students, and is a division of the American Counseling Association:

American Rehabilitation Counseling Association
c/o American Counseling Association
5999 Stevenson Avenue
Alexandria, VA 22304
Tel: 703-823-9800
Web: http://www.counseling.org

For information on credentialing and education, contact:

National Rehabilitation Counseling Association
8807 Sudley Road, Suite 102
Manassas, VA 22110-4719
Tel: 703-361-2077
Web: http://www.nchrtm.okstate.edu/ARCA/

For certification information, contact:

Commission on Rehabilitation Counselor Certification
1835 Rohlwing Road, Suite E
Rolling Meadows, IL 60008
Tel: 847-394-2104

■ Related Articles

Health Care
Creative Arts Therapists
Ergonomists
Interpreters and Translators
Occupational Therapists
Parole Officers
Psychologists
Recreational Therapists
Social Workers

Rehabilitation Engineers

■ **See Biomedical Engineers**

Renal Dialysis Technicians

■ **See Dialysis Technicians**

Reporters

■ **Overview**

Reporters are the foot soldiers for newspapers, magazines, and television and radio broadcast companies. They gather and analyze information about current events and write stories for publication or for broadcasting.

■ **History**

Newspapers are primary disseminators of news in the United States. People read newspapers to learn about the current events that are shaping their society and societies around the world. Newspapers give public expression to opinion and criticism of government and societal issues, and of course, provide the public with entertaining, informative reading.

Newspapers are able to fulfill these functions because of the freedom given to the press. However, this was not always the case. The first American newspaper, published in 1690, was suppressed four days after it was published. And it was not until 1704 that the first continuous newspaper appeared.

One early newspaperman who later became a famous writer was Benjamin Franklin. Franklin worked for his brother at a Boston newspaper before publishing his own two years later in 1723 in Philadelphia.

A number of developments in the printing industry made it possible for newspapers to be printed more cheaply. In the late 19th century, new types of presses were developed to increase production, and more important, the linotype machine was invented. The linotype mechanically set the letters so that handset type was no longer necessary. This dramatically decreased the amount of prepress time needed to get a page into print. Newspapers could respond to breaking stories more quickly; late editions with breaking stories became part of the news world.

These technological advances, along with an increasing population, factored in the rapid growth of the newspaper industry in the United States. In 1776, there were only 37 newspapers in the United States. Today there are more than 1,500 daily and nearly 7,500 weekly newspapers in the country.

As newspapers grew in size and widened the scope of their coverage, it became necessary to increase the number of employees and to assign them specialized jobs. Reporters have always been the heart of newspaper staffs. However, in today's complex world, with the public hungry for news as it occurs, reporters and correspondents are involved in all media—not only newspapers, but magazines, radio, and television as well. Today, with the advent of the Internet, many newspapers are going online, causing many reporters to become active participants on the information superhighway.

■ **The Job**

Reporters collect information on newsworthy events and prepare stories for newspaper or magazine publication or for radio or television broadcast. The stories may simply provide information about local, state, or national events, or they may present opposing points of view on issues of current interest. In this latter capacity, the press plays an important role in monitoring the actions of public officials and others in positions of power.

Stories may originate as an assignment from an editor or as the result of a lead or news tip. Good reporters are always on the lookout for good story ideas. To cover a story, they gather and verify facts by interviewing people involved in or related to the event, examining documents and public records, observing events as they happen, and researching relevant background information. Reporters generally take notes or use a tape recorder as they collect information and write their stories once they return to their offices. In order to meet a deadline, they may have to telephone the stories to *rewriters,* who write or transcribe the stories for them. After the facts have been gathered and verified, the reporters transcribe their notes, organize their material, and determine what emphasis, or angle, to give the news. The story is then written to meet prescribed standards of editorial style and format.

The basic functions of reporters are to observe events objectively and impartially, record them accurately, and

REPORTERS	
SCHOOL SUBJECTS	English Journalism
PERSONAL SKILLS	Communication/ideas Helping/teaching
WORK ENVIRONMENT	Indoors and outdoors Primarily multiple locations
MINIMUM EDUCATION LEVEL	Bachelor's degree
SALARY RANGE	$25,000 to $50,000 to $100,000+
CERTIFICATION OR LICENSING	None available
OUTLOOK	Little change or more slowly than the average
DOT	131
GOE	11.08.02
NOC	5123
O*NET	34011

explain what the news means in a larger, societal context. Within this framework, there are several types of reporters.

The most basic is the news reporter. This job sometimes involves covering a beat, such as the police station, courthouse, or school system. It may involve receiving general assignments, such as a story about an unusual occurrence or an obituary of a community leader. Large daily papers may assign teams of reporters to investigate social, economic, or political events and conditions.

Many newspaper, wire service, and magazine reporters specialize in one type of story, either because they have a particular interest in the subject or because they have acquired the expertise to analyze and interpret news in that particular area. Topical reporters cover stories for a specific department, such as medicine, politics, foreign affairs, sports, consumer affairs, finance, science, business, education, labor, or religion. They sometimes write features explaining the history that has led up to certain events in the field they cover. Feature writers generally write longer, broader stories than news reporters, usually on more upbeat subjects, such as fashion, art, theater, travel, and social events. They may write about trends, for example, or profile local celebrities. Editorial writers and syndicated news columnists present viewpoints that, although based on a thorough knowledge, are opinions on topics of popular interest. Columnists write under a byline and usually specialize in a particular subject, such as politics or government activities. Critics review restaurants, books, works of art, movies, plays, musical performances, and other cultural events.

Specializing allows reporters to focus their efforts, talent, and knowledge on one area of expertise. It also allows them more opportunities to develop deeper relationships with contacts and sources necessary to gain access to the news.

Correspondents report events in locations distant from their home offices. They may report news by mail, telephone, fax, or computer from rural areas, large cities throughout the United States, or countries. Many large newspapers, magazines and broadcast companies have one correspondent who is responsible for covering all the news for the foreign city or country where they are based.

Reporters on small or weekly newspapers not only cover all aspects of the news in their communities, but they also may take photographs, write editorials and headlines, lay out pages, edit wire-service copy, and help with general office work. Television reporters may have to be photogenic as well as talented and resourceful: they may at times present live reports, filmed by a mobile camera unit at the scene where the news originates, or they may tape interviews and narration for later broadcast.

A reporter goes over his notes aboard an election campaign bus.

■ Requirements

High School

High school courses that provide a firm foundation for a career as reporter include English, journalism, social studies, speech, typing, and computer science.

Postsecondary Training

A bachelor's degree is essential for aspiring reporters. Graduate degrees give students a great advantage over those entering the field with lesser degrees. Most editors prefer applicants with degrees in journalism because their studies include liberal arts courses as well as professional training in journalism. Some editors consider it sufficient for a reporter to have a good general education from a liberal arts college. Others prefer applicants with an undergraduate degree in liberal arts and a master's degree in journalism. The great majority of journalism graduates hired today by newspapers, wire services, and magazines have majored specifically in news-editorial journalism.

More than 400 colleges offer programs in journalism leading to a bachelor's degree. In these schools, around three-fourths of a student's time is devoted to a liberal education and one-fourth to the professional study of journalism, with required courses such as introductory mass media, basic reporting and copy editing, history of journalism, and press law and ethics. Students are encouraged to select other journalism courses according to their specific interests.

Journalism courses and programs are also offered by more than 350 community and junior colleges. Graduates of these programs are prepared to go to work directly as general assignment reporters, but they may encounter difficulty when competing with graduates of four-year pro-

Nellie Bly was the first woman to achieve fame as a reporter and was one of the most adventurous journalists of the nineteenth century. She became world-renowned as a result of a 72-day trip around the world undertaken to best the fictional record set by Phineas Fogg in Jules Verne's *Around the World in 80 Days.*

Bly was born Elizabeth Cochran in Cochran Mills, Pennsylvania. She received most of her education at home, spending only one year in school. In 1885, she began her career in journalism as a reporter for the Pittsburgh *Dispatch,* at which time she adopted the pseudonym Nellie Bly. In 1887, she joined Joseph Pulitzer's New York *World.* She wrote about social issues, and many of her articles were exposes growing out of undercover investigations she conducted. In 1895, Bly married Robert L. Seaman and retired to private life, but in 1919, she returned to reporting with the New York *Journal,* remaining there until her death.

grams. Credit earned in community and junior colleges may be transferable to four-year programs in journalism at other colleges and universities. Journalism training may also be obtained in the armed forces. Names and addresses of newspapers and a list of journalism schools and departments are published in the *Editor and Publisher International Year Book,* which is available for reference in most public libraries and newspaper offices.

A master's degree in journalism may be earned at more than 100 schools, and a doctorate at about 20 schools. Graduate degrees may prepare students specifically for careers in news or as journalism teachers, researchers, and theorists or for jobs in advertising or public relations.

A reporter's liberal arts training should include courses in English, sociology, political science, economics, history, psychology, business, speech, and computer science. Knowledge of foreign languages is also useful. To be a reporter in a specialized field, such as science or finance, requires concentrated course work in that area.

Other Requirements

A crucial requirement for reporters is typing skill. Reporters type their stories using word processing programs. Although not essential, a knowledge of shorthand or speed-writing makes note taking easier, and an acquaintance with news photography is an asset.

Reporters must be inquisitive, aggressive, persistent, and detail-oriented. They must enjoy interaction with people of various races, cultures, religions, economic levels, and social statuses.

■ Exploring

You can explore a career as a reporter in a number of ways. You can talk to reporters and editors at local newspapers and radio and TV stations. You can interview the admis-

sions counselor at the school of journalism closest to your home.

In addition to taking courses in English, journalism, social studies, speech, computer science, and typing, high school students can acquire practical experience by working on school newspapers or on a church, synagogue, or mosque newsletter. Part-time and summer jobs on newspapers provide invaluable experience to the aspiring reporter.

College students can develop their reporting skills in the laboratory courses or workshops that are part of the journalism curriculum. College students might also accept jobs as campus correspondents for selected newspapers. People who work as part-time reporters covering news in a particular area of a community are known as *stringers* and are paid only for those stories that are printed.

More than 3,000 journalism scholarships, fellowships, and assistantships are offered by universities, newspapers, foundations, and professional organizations to college students. Many newspapers and magazines offer summer internships to journalism students to provide them with practical experience in a variety of basic reporting and editing duties. Students who successfully complete internships are usually placed in jobs more quickly upon graduation than those without such experience.

■ Employers

Of the approximately 60,000 reporters and correspondents employed in the late 1990s, about 63 percent worked for newspapers of all sizes. The rest were employed by wire services, magazines, and radio and television broadcasting companies.

■ Starting Out

Jobs in this field may be obtained through college placement offices or by applying directly to the personnel departments of individual employers. Applicants with some practical experience will have an advantage; they should be prepared to present a portfolio of material they wrote as volunteer or part-time reporters or other writing samples.

Most journalism school graduates start out as general assignment reporters or copy editors for small publications. A few outstanding journalism graduates may be hired by large city newspapers or national magazines. They are trained on the job. But they are the exception, as large employers usually require several years' experience. As a rule, novice reporters cover routine assignments, such as reporting on civic and club meetings, writing obituaries, or summarizing speeches. As reporters become more skilled, they are assigned to more important events or to a regular beat, or they may specialize in a particular field.

■ Advancement

Reporters may advance by moving to larger newspapers or press services, but competition for such positions is unusually keen. Many highly qualified reporters apply for these jobs every year.

A select number of reporters eventually become columnists, correspondents, editorial writers, editors, or top executives. These important and influential positions represent the top of the field, and competition is strong for them.

Many reporters transfer the contacts and knowledge developed in newspaper reporting to related fields, such as public relations, advertising, or preparing copy for radio and television news programs.

■ Earnings

There are great variations in the earnings of reporters. Salaries are related to experience, kind of employer for which the reporter works, geographical location, and whether the reporter is covered by a contract negotiated by the Newspaper Guild.

In the late 1990s, reporters on daily newspapers having Newspaper Guild contracts receive starting salaries that ranged from about $10,000 in Battle Creek, Michigan, to $68,000 in New York City. The average starting salary was about $25,000. Reporters with between two and six years of experience earned salaries that ranged from $18,000 to $70,000. Some top reporters on big city dailies earned even more, on the basis of merit or seniority.

Reporters who worked for radio earned an average salary of $15,000 a year. Some who worked for stations in large cities earned up to $36,000. Reporters who worked in television earned between $17,000 and $75,000, depending on the size of the station. High-profile columnists and newscasters working for prestigious papers or network television stations earned over $100,000 a year.

■ Work Environment

Reporters work under a great deal of pressure in settings that differ from the typical business office. Their jobs generally require a five-day, 35- to 40-hour week, but overtime and irregular schedules are very common. Reporters employed by morning papers start work in the late afternoon and finish around midnight, while those on afternoon or evening papers start early in the morning and work until early or midafternoon. Foreign correspondents often work late at night to send the news to their papers in time to meet printing deadlines.

The day of the smoky, ink-stained newsroom has passed, but newspaper offices are still hectic places. Reporters have to work amid the clatter of computer keyboards and other machines, loud voices engaged in telephone conversations, and the bustle created by people hurrying about. An atmosphere of excitement and bustle prevails, especially as press deadlines approach.

Travel is often required in this occupation, and some assignments may be dangerous, such as covering wars, political uprisings, fires, floods, and other events of a volatile nature.

■ Outlook

The employment outlook for reporters and correspondents through 2006 is expected to grow somewhat slower than the average for all occupations. According to the Bureau of Labor Statistics projections, the number of employed reporters and correspondents is projected to decline by about 3 percent within the next several years. While the number of self-employed reporters and correspondents is expected to grow about 9 percent by 2006, and magazine workers by about 7 percent, newpaper jobs are expected to decrease by about 9 percent, and jobs in other communications settings also are projected to decline slightly.

Because of an increase in the number of small community and suburban daily and weekly newspapers, opportunities will be best for journalism graduates who are willing to relocate and accept relatively low starting salaries. With experience, reporters on these small papers can move up to editing positions or may choose to transfer to reporting jobs on larger newspapers or magazines.

Openings will be limited on big city dailies. While individual papers may enlarge their reporting staffs, little or no change is expected in the total number of these newspapers. Applicants will face strong competition for jobs on large metropolitan newspapers. Experience is a definite requirement, which rules out most new graduates unless they possess credentials in an area for which the publication has a pressing need. Occasionally, a beginner can use contacts and experience gained through internship programs and summer jobs to obtain a reporting job immediately after graduation.

A significant number of jobs will be provided by magazines and in radio and television broadcasting, but the major news magazines and larger broadcasting stations generally prefer experienced reporters. For beginning correspondents, small stations with local news broadcasts will continue to replace staff who move on to larger stations or leave the business. Network hiring has been cut drastically in the past few years and will probably continue to decline.

Overall, the prospects are best for graduates who have majored in news-editorial journalism and completed an internship while in school. The top graduates in an accredited program will have a great advantage, as will talented *technical* or *scientific writers*. Small newspapers prefer to hire beginning reporters who are acquainted with the community and are willing to help with photography and other aspects of production. Without at least a bachelor's degree in journalism, applicants will find it increasingly difficult to obtain even an entry-level position.

Those with doctorates and practical reporting experience may find teaching positions at four-year colleges and universities, while highly qualified reporters with master's degrees may obtain employment in journalism departments of community and junior colleges.

Poor economic conditions do not drastically affect the employment of reporters and correspondents. Their numbers are not severely cut back even during a downturn; instead, employers forced to reduce expenditures will suspend new hiring.

■ For More Information

AEJMC provides general educational information on all areas of journalism. A Look at Careers in Journalism and Mass Communications, *12 pages, describes the various career opportunities in the field.*

Association for Education in Journalism and Mass Communications
University of South Carolina
1621 College Street
Columbia, SC 29208
Tel: 803-777-2006

To receive a copy of The Journalist's Road to Success, *which lists schools offering degrees in news-editorial and financial aid to those interested in print journalism, contact:*

Dow Jones Newspaper Fund
PO Box 300
Princeton, NJ 08543-0300
Tel: 609-452-2820
Web: http://www.dj.com/newsfund

To receive a free copy of Newspaper: What's in It for Me? *write:*

Newspaper Careers Project
Fulfillment Department NAA Foundation
11600 Sunrise Valley Drive
Reston, VA 22091

■ Related Articles

Broadcasting

Newspapers and Magazines

Radio

Television

Foreign Correspondents

Photographers

Radio and Television Newscasters, Reporters, and Announcers

Writers

Repossessors

■ See Collection Workers

Research and Development Technicians

■ See Plastics Technicians

Research Assistants

■ Overview

Research assistants work to help writers, scientists, radio, film and television producers, marketing and advertising executives, attorneys, professors, publishers, politicians, museum curators, and a wide variety of other professionals get their jobs done. They are information specialists who find the facts, data, and statistics that their employers need, leaving the employers free to pursue the larger task at hand.

■ History

The sun is just emerging from between the mountain peaks to the east. There is a chill in the air. The promise of a long, cold winter blows in with the morning wind, whipping across the valley. A solitary man stands at the edge of a plateau, looking down at the herd of animals below. He is dressed in animal skins, and the combination of hair on his body and the long, tangled masses of hair on his head and face make him seem fierce, brutal, even beastly. The elders of the clan have sent this scout to trace the movements of the animals. The information he gathers will be used to help the group hunt the animals they use for food, shelter, clothing, and other supplies. This prehistoric man is...a research assistant.

Sound preposterous? Perhaps that example is a little outlandish, but it is hard to pinpoint the exact origins of the research assistant profession. Assistants have been around for as long as people have worked, and the first time a worker sent an assistant out to gather information, a research assistant was born.

Although the job of the research assistant has changed little since the early days, the tools used to gather information have changed dramatically. An assistant to a doctor a hundred years ago would have had to travel to libraries and other information centers to gather data on a disease from books and then laboriously take down notes to take back to the doctor. Nowadays, that same research assistant could do an Internet search and print up the findings in only a few minutes. As technology becomes more advanced, research assistants will have the convenience of using new methods to complete their research, but they will also bear the burden of having to master the techniques to get the information they need.

■ The Job

Although the fields in which they work may differ greatly, all research assistants work to help their employers complete a job more easily and more thoroughly. A research assistant may work for one person, such as a university professor, or for a team of people, such as the writers of brochures, newsletters, and press releases at a large non-profit organization. If the research assistant works for more than one person, a system must be developed to determine whose work will be done when. Sometimes the team assigning the work determines the order in which jobs should be done; other times, research assistants keep sign-up sheets and perform the research requests in the order they are listed. Often, an urgent job will make it necessary for the research assistant to disregard the sheet and jump to the new task quickly. Sometimes research assistants help with clerical duties, such as transcription, word processing, and reception, or, in the case of scientific research assistants, with cleaning and maintaining laboratories and equipment.

After receiving a research assignment from the person or people they assist, research assistants must first determine how to locate the desired information. Sometimes this will be as simple as making a single phone call and requesting a brochure. At other times, it may involve hours, days, or even weeks of research in libraries, archives, museums, or laboratories—to name just a few places—going from book to book, source to source, or experiment to experiment until all of the necessary information has been compiled and consolidated. Research assistants must then prepare the material for presentation to the person who requested it. If specific brochures or catalogs are requested, the research assistant need only hand them over when they arrive. More often than not, however, the research assistant has to write up notes or even a report outlining the research efforts and presenting the information they were asked to locate. These reports may include graphs, charts, statistics, and even drawings or photographs. They include a listing of sources and the exact specifications of any interviews conducted, surveys taken, or experiments performed. Sometimes research assistants are asked to present this information verbally as well.

Because research assistants work in almost every field imaginable, it is impossible to list all the possible research assistant positions in this chapter. Following are some of the most common areas or situations in which research assistants work.

Research assistants work for writers in a wide variety of circumstances. They may work for commercial magazines and newspapers where they might locate possible interview candidates, conduct surveys, scan other periodicals for relevant articles and features, or help a writer gather information for an article. For example, a writer doing an article on the history of rap music might send a research assistant to compile statistics on rap music sales from over the years or create a comprehensive list of artists signed by a specific record label. Some research assistants working for periodicals and other publications do nothing but confirm facts, such as dates, ages, and statistics. These researchers are called *fact checkers*. Research assistants who work in radio, film, or television often help locate and organize historical facts, find experts to be interviewed, or help follow up on ideas for future programs.

Many large companies, agencies, and organizations hire research assistants to help their in-house writing staff produce brochures, newsletters, and press releases. Research assistants may gather facts and statistics, retrieve applicable quotes, and conduct preliminary phone interviews.

Advertising and marketing agencies hire research assistants to help them discover consumer desires and the best ways to advertise and market products. Imagine that a small toy company is considering marketing a new toy. Research assistants for the company might be assigned to help find out how much it would cost to make the toy, whether or not there is already a similar toy on the market, who might buy the toy, and who might sell the toy. This would help the marketing department decide in what ways the toy should be marketed. In advertising, research assistants may be asked to provide executives with statistics and quotes so that the executives may determine whether a product is appealing to a certain portion of the population.

University professors hire research assistants to help them in their research in all fields. For example, a history profes-

RESEARCH ASSISTANTS	
SCHOOL SUBJECTS	English History
PERSONAL SKILLS	Communication/ideas Following instructions
WORK ENVIRONMENT	Primarily indoors Primarily multiple locations
MINIMUM EDUCATION LEVEL	Bachelor's degree
SALARY RANGE	$12,500 to $22,800 to $52,000+
CERTIFICATION OR LICENSING	None available
OUTLOOK	About as fast as the average
DOT	109
GOE	11.03.03
NOC	4122
O*NET	31511C

sor working on a paper about the Italian military might send a research assistant to the library to uncover everything possible about the Italian military presence in Greece during World War II. A research assistant in microbiology will help a biologist prepare and perform experiments and record data. Often, professors hire graduate students from their departments as research assistants, either during the summer or in addition to the student's regular course load. Sometimes a research assistantship is part of a financial aid package; this ensures that the professor has help with research and gives the students an opportunity to earn money while learning more about their chosen field outside of class.

Politicians hire research assistants to help find out how a campaign is succeeding or failing, to find statistics on outcomes of past elections, and to determine the issues that are especially important to the constituents, among other things. Research assistants who work for politicians may also follow the opponent's campaign, trying to find ways to win over new supporters.

Some research assistants work for museums where they try to determine ways to add to a collection, develop signs and explanations for public education, and keep an inventory of all collection pieces. Research assistants may also do research to help curators learn more about the pieces in the museum's collection.

Again, these are only a few of the areas in which research assistants may work, and their duties may be as varied as the many fields and organizations that employ them.

■ Requirements

High School

Requirements for becoming a research assistant vary depending upon the field in which you hope to work. In high school, you should keep your options open by taking a wide variety of college preparatory courses, including English, history, mathematics, and the sciences. Knowledge of at least one foreign language can be extremely helpful in gaining employment as a research assistant, especially in the fields of marketing, publishing, and the arts. Since writing and presenting research are important aspects of the research assistant's work, you should take classes that strengthen these skills, such as public speaking, journalism, and statistics. Knowledge of computers and excellent library skills are absolutely vital to this profession. If you will be working in the hard sciences or engineering, laboratory skills are essential.

Postsecondary Training

By college, potential research assistants should begin thinking about a specific field in which they are interested in working and take courses in that field. If you are inter-

ested in advertising research but your college does not offer an advertising degree, you should plan to major in English or psychology but take a large concentration of communications, business, and economics courses. Often, English and journalism are good majors for the research assistant career as the work requires so much reading and writing.

Some fields will require degrees beyond a bachelor's degree for research assistants. This is often true in the hard sciences, engineering, medicine, and law. Depending on the field, some employers require a master's degree, or some advanced study in the area. For instance, an insurance company that hires a research assistant may require the employee to take insurance courses in order to become more knowledgeable about the industry.

Other Requirements

Aspiring research assistants should be curious and enjoy doing research, finding and organizing facts, working with other people, and handling a variety of tasks. They should be self-motivated, take instruction well, and be able to think on their feet. For example, a research assistant assigned by an attorney to research marriage records at the county clerk's office should not be calling the law firm every few minutes to ask for further direction. A good research assistant must be able to take an assignment, immediately ask any questions necessary to clarify the task, and then set to retrieving the requested information.

■ Exploring

Students can begin exploring this career while working on their own school assignments. Experimenting with different types of research using newspapers, magazines, library catalogs, computers, the Internet, and official records and documents can provide a good sample of what many research assistants work with each day. If you are interested in becoming a research assistant in the sciences or medicine, be sure to pay close attention to procedures and methods in your laboratory classes.

Consider joining groups in your school devoted to research or fieldwork. Take a position as a reporter for your school newspaper, or volunteer to write feature articles for your yearbook. You can also create your own research opportunities. If you are a member of the marching band, for instance, you could research the history of the clarinet and write an article for the band newsletter.

Occasionally, small newspapers, nonprofit groups, political campaigns, and other organizations will accept student interns, volunteers, or even summer employees to help out with special projects. If you obtain such a position, you may have the opportunity to help with research, or at least, to see professionals in action, learn valuable work skills, and help support a good cause.

There are many books available describing the techniques of basic research skills. Ask a librarian or bookstore worker to help you locate them, or better yet, begin developing your research skills by tracking down materials yourself.

■ Employers

All types of companies, organizations, and private individuals employ research assistants. Most college and university professors have a research assistant on staff to help them with articles and books they are writing. Newspapers and magazines need research assistants to find information for articles and verify facts. Companies in all fields need people to help find information on products, ingredients, production techniques, and even on competitors.

The government is a major employer of research assistants as well. Local, state, and federal government offices often hire research assistants to conduct interviews, gather statistics, compile information, and synthesize data. Research assistants for the government can work for the U.S. Census Bureau, the Bureau for Labor Statistics, and the Library of Congress, among other divisions.

■ Starting Out

How you begin a career as a research assistant depends largely upon the field in which you are interested in working. In college, you may wish to pursue an assistantship with a professor. He or she can act as a mentor while you are earning your degree and offer valuable advice and feedback on your research techniques.

After receiving a bachelor's degree, you might begin by contacting agencies, firms, or companies where you are interested in working. For example, a student interested in doing research to support writers might apply to newspapers, magazines, and large companies that produce their own publications. Also, some college and university career offices have listings of job openings in the research fields; occasionally these jobs are advertised in newspapers and magazines.

There may also be freelance opportunities for the beginning research assistant. Try marketing your services in the school newspaper or bulletin boards of your alma mater. Perhaps you could set up a Web page that lists your qualifications and the services you offer. Ask for referrals from professors with whom you have studied or worked. If you do a thorough, competent job on assignments, you may be able to use positive word-of-mouth to get more work.

■ Advancement

A research assistant who gains a high skill level and demonstrates dedication to the employer and the field may earn the opportunity to lead other assistants on a special project. Some research assistants who work for writers and prove to have excellent writing skills themselves may get hired to write newsletter articles or brochures for publications. Depending on departmental needs, research assistants who work for a university while earning a degree may be offered a full-time position upon completion of their studies. Research assistants who work for clients on a freelance basis may find that they get more assignments and can command higher fees as they gain experience and a good reputation.

Advancement in this field is usually up to the individual. You will need to seek out opportunities. If you are interested in getting better assignments, you will probably need to ask for them. If you would like to supervise a newsletter or brochure project within your company, try making a proposal to your manager. With a proven track record and a solid idea of how a project can be accomplished, increased responsibility (and pay!) is there for the asking.

■ Earnings

Earnings vary widely, depending on field, level of education, and employer. Generally, large companies pay their research assistants more than smaller businesses and nonprofit organizations do. Research assistants with advanced degrees make more than those with only a bachelor's degree. Research assistants who work for large pharmaceutical companies or engineering laboratories (and have advanced science degrees) make among the highest wages in the field

Research assistants working part-time while in graduate school generally earn $12,500 per academic year. They may earn more after subsequent years working with the same professor, but the increase is often negligible because of inadequate departmental funding.

Self-employed research assistants get paid by the hour or by assignment. Depending their experience, the complexity of the assignment, and the location of the job, pay rates may be anywhere from $7 to $25 per hour.

Benefits, such as health insurance, vacation, and sick leave vary by field and employer. Universities generally provide health care coverage, paid vacations, sick time, and a pension plan for full-time employees. Research assistants employed full-time by a private company are also eligible for similar benefits; some companies may provide benefits to part-time or contract workers. Freelancers must provide their own benefits.

Research assistants who work in some fields may receive additional bonuses. A person working on a research project about movies, for instance, may receive free passes to a local theater. A woman's magazine may send research assistants cosmetics samples so they can test different lipsticks for staying power. Research assistants charged with finding information about another country's economy may even be sent abroad. All of these perks, of course, vary depending on the needs of the employer and the experience of the researcher.

■ Work Environment

Most research assistants work indoors in clean, climate-controlled, pleasant facilities. Many spend most of their time at the business that employs them, checking facts over the phone, finding data on a computer, searching the company's records, writing up reports, or conducting laboratory research. Others spend a great deal of time in libraries, government offices, courthouses, museums, archives, and even in such unlikely places as shopping malls and supermarkets. In short, research assistants go wherever they can obtain the information requested.

Most assignments require that research assistants do their work on their own, with little direct supervision. Research assistants need to be very self-motivated in order to get the work done since they often do not have someone readily available to support them. It is important for research assistants who leave their offices for work to remember that they are representatives of their company or employer and to act and dress according to the employer's standards.

Full-time research assistants work 35 to 40 hours a week. They may have to work overtime or on weekends right before deadlines or when involved in special projects. Some research assistants, especially those who work for smaller organizations or for professors or private employers, work only part-time. They may work as little as 10 hours a week. These research assistants are usually graduate students or freelancers who have a second job in a related field.

■ Outlook

The outlook for the research assistant career generally depends upon the outlook for the field in which the researcher works. That is, a field that is growing quickly will usually need many new researchers, whereas a field with little growth will not. A researcher with good background in many fields will be in higher demand, as will a researcher with specialized knowledge and research techniques specific to a field.

Although definite statistical data as to the present and future of all researchers is sketchy at best, as technology becomes more advanced and the amount of information available through newer media like the Internet increases, knowledgeable research assistants will be essential to find, sort, compile, present, and analyze this information. Also, as the standard of living increases in the United States, individuals will have more disposable income to employ researchers to assist with projects in the private sector.

Since many people take research assistant positions as stepping-stones to positions with more responsibility or stability, positions are often available to beginning researchers. Research assistants with good experience, excellent work ethics, and the drive to succeed will rarely find themselves out of work. The jobs will be available, but it may take some creative fact-finding for research assistants to locate positions that best meet their needs and interests.

■ For More Information

To find out about health care research projects and opportunities with the U.S. Department of Health and Human Services, contact:

Agency for Health Care Policy and Research
Executive Office Center, Suite 600
2101 East Jefferson Street
Rockville, MD 20852
Tel: 301-594-6662
Web: http://www.ahcpr.gov/

For information on research assistant positions with the U.S. Census Bureau, contact:

U.S. Census Bureau
Washington, DC 20005
Tel: 301-457-4100
Web: http://www.census.gov/

For a list of research opportunities and student internships with National Institutes of Health, contact:

National Institutes of Health
Office of Human Resources Management
6100 Executive Boulevard, Room 3E-01
Washington, DC 20005
Web: http://ohrm.cc.nih.gov/

For a national list of research opportunities in physics, contact:

The University of Pennsylvania School for Arts and Sciences
Web: http://dept.physics.upenn.edu/undergraduate/lablist.html

For information on issues that may concern you as a research assistant, consult:

Research and Technology Management Office
University of Illinois at Urbana-Champaign
601 East John Street, 4th Floor Swanlund
Champaign, IL 61820
Tel: 217-333-7862
Web: http://www.oc.uiuc.edu/rtmo/

■ Related Articles

Book Publishing

Information Services

Literary Arts

Newspapers and Magazines

Publishing

Congressional Aides

Demographers

Historians

Public Opinion Researchers

Reporters

Research Ceramists

■ See Ceramics Engineers

Research Specialists

■ See Plastics Engineers

Researchers

■ See Indexers

Reservation and Ticket Agents

■ Overview

Reservation and ticket agents are employed by airlines, bus companies, railroads, and cruise lines to help customers in several ways. *Reservation agents* make and confirm reservations for passengers and use computers and manuals containing timetables, tariffs, and other information to plan the reservations and itinerary of travelers.

Ticket agents sell tickets at ticket counters in terminals or in ticket offices. They use computers and manuals containing scheduling, boarding, and rate information to plan routes and calculate ticket costs; make sure that seating is available; answer inquiries; check baggage and direct passengers to proper places for boarding; announce arrivals and departures; and assist passengers in boarding.

■ History

Since the earliest days of commercial passenger transportation by boat and overland stagecoach, someone has been responsible for making sure that space is available for all passengers and that everyone on board pays the fare. As transportation grew into a major industry over the years, the job of making reservations and selling tickets became a specialized occupation.

The airline industry experienced its first boom in the early 1930s. By the end of that decade, millions of people were flying each year. Since the introduction of passenger-carrying jet planes in 1958, the number of people traveling by air has multiplied many times over. Today the airlines handle more than 85 percent of all public travel within the United States and an even larger percentage of travel to cities overseas. These companies employ about three-fourths of all reservation and ticket agents.

A number of innovations have helped make the work of reservations and ticket agents easier and more efficient. The introduction of automated telephone services allows customers to be quickly transferred to a waiting agent. Computers have both simplified the agents' work and put more resources within their reach. Since the 1950s, many airlines have operated computerized scheduling and reservations systems, either individually or in partnership with other airlines. Until recently, these systems were not available to the general consumer. In the 1990s, however, the growth of the Internet and online services has permitted travelers to access scheduling and rate information, make reservations, and to purchase tickets without contacting an agent. The airlines have also begun to experiment with the so-called "electronic ticket," which they expect will eventually replace the traditional paper ticket. With these innovations, it is conceivable that one day there will be less need for reservation and ticketing agents. For the near future, however, these employees will still fill a vital role in the transportation industry.

■ The Job

Airline reservation agents are telephone-sales agents who work in large central offices run by the airline companies. Their primary job is to book and confirm reservations for passengers on scheduled airline flights. At the request of the customer or a ticket agent, they plan the itinerary and other arrangements. While many agents still use timetables, airline manuals, reference guides, and a tariff book, most of this work is performed using specialized computer programs.

After asking for the passenger's destination, desired travel time, and airport of departure, reser-

RESERVATION AND TICKET AGENTS	
SCHOOL SUBJECTS	**Business** **English**
PERSONAL SKILLS	**Communication/ideas** **Helping/teaching**
WORK ENVIRONMENT	**Primarily indoors** **Primarily one location**
MINIMUM EDUCATION LEVEL	**High school diploma**
SALARY RANGE	**$11,000 to $25,000 to $39,000**
CERTIFICATION OR LICENSING	**None available**
OUTLOOK	**Decline**
DOT	**238**
GOE	**07.03.01**
NOC	**6433**
O*NET	**53805**

vation agents type instructions into a computer and quickly obtain information on all flight schedules and seating availability. If the plane is full, the agent may suggest an alternate flight or check to see if space is available on another airline that flies to the same destination. Agents may even book seats on the competing airline, especially if their own airline can provide service on the return trip. Computers are used to make, confirm, change, and cancel reservations.

Reservation agents also answer telephone inquiries about such things as schedules, fares, arrival and departure times, and cities serviced by their airline. They may maintain an inventory of passenger space available so they can notify other personnel and ticket stations of changes and try to book all flights to capacity. Some reservation agents work in more specialized areas, handling calls from travel agents, or, with the airlines, bookings from members of the company's frequent flyer program. Agents working with international airlines must also be informed of any changes in visa regulations and other travel developments. This information is usually supplied by the *senior reservation agent,* who supervises and coordinates the activities of the other agents.

In the railroad industry, *reservation clerks* perform similar tasks. They receive requests for and assign seats or compartments to passengers, keep station agents and information clerks advised about available space, and communicate with reservation clerks in other towns.

Ticket agents for any transportation service—air, bus, rail, or ship—sell tickets to customers at terminals or at separate ticket offices. Like reservation agents, they book space for customers. In addition, they use computers to prepare and print tickets, calculate fares, and collect payment. At the terminals they check and tag luggage, direct passengers to the proper areas for boarding, keep records of passengers on each departure, and help with customer problems, such as lost baggage or missed connections. Airline ticket agents may have additional duties, such as paging arriving and departing passengers and finding hotel accommodations or new travel arrangements for passengers in the event of flight cancellations.

In airports, *gate agents* assign seats, issue boarding passes, make public address announcements of departures and arrivals, and help elderly or disabled passengers board the planes. They also make sure that the flight attendants have all the equipment they will need for their flight. They sometimes provide information to disembarking passengers about ground transportation, connecting flights, and local hotels.

The work of airline ticket agents is supervised by *ticket sales supervisors,* who may also perform the same duties as ticket agents. In airline central offices, *ticketing clerks*

compile and record the information needed to assemble tickets that are mailed or otherwise sent to customers.

Regardless of where they work, reservation and transportation ticket agents must be knowledgeable about their companies' policies and procedures, as well as the standard procedures of their industry. They must be aware of the availability of special promotions and services and be able to answer any questions their customers may have.

■ Requirements

High School
Reservation and ticket agents are generally required to have at least a high school diploma. Job applicants should be able to type and have good communication and problem-solving skills. Because computers are being used more and more in this field, students should have at least a basic knowledge of computers and computer software. Previous experience working with the public is also helpful. Knowledge of foreign languages is also useful, especially for agents of companies providing international service.

Postsecondary Training
Some college is preferred, although it is not considered essential. (Some junior colleges offer courses specifically designed for students wanting to become ticket agents.) New reservation agents are given about a month of classroom instruction. They are taught to read schedules, calculate fares, and plan itineraries. They learn how to use the computer to get information and reserve space. They also learn about company policies and government regulations that apply to the industry.

Ticket agents receive about one week of classroom instruction. They learn how to read tickets and schedules, assign seats, and tag baggage. This is followed by one week of on-the-job training, working alongside an experienced agent. After mastering the simpler tasks, the new ticket agents are trained to reserve space, make out tickets, and handle the boarding gate.

Other Requirements
Because reservation and ticket agents are in constant contact with the public, a well-groomed, professional appearance, a clear and pleasant speaking voice, and a friendly personality are important qualities. Agents need to be tactful in keeping telephone time to a minimum without alienating their customers. In addition, agents must enjoy working with people, have a good memory, and be able to maintain their composure when working with harried or unhappy travelers. Reservation and ticket agents form a large part of the public image of their company.

Many agents belong to such labor unions as the Air Line Employees Association; the Transport Workers Union of America; the Transportation Communications International Union; and the International Brotherhood of Teamsters, Chauffeurs, Warehousemen and Helpers of America.

Exploring

High school students may wish to apply for part-time or summer work with transportation companies in their central offices or at terminals. A school counselor can try to arrange an informational interview with an experienced reservation and transportation ticket agent. This interview may provide more information on the daily activities of such individuals. Even if the duties are only vaguely related, the students will at least have the opportunity to become familiar with transportation operations.

Employers

The commercial airlines are the main employers of reservation and ticket agents. However, other transportation companies—rail, ship, and bus, primarily—also require their services.

Starting Out

College placement services may be able to provide information or job listings for those students entering this field. High school students can find part-time or summer work in these or related jobs. Job applicants may also apply directly to the personnel or employment offices of the transportation companies for current information about job openings, requirements, and possible training programs. Many unions also provide lists of job openings.

Advancement

With experience and a good work record, some reservation and ticket agents can be promoted to supervisory positions. A few may become city and district sales managers for ticket offices. Beyond this, opportunities for advancement are limited. However, achieving seniority with a company may give the agent the first choice of shifts and available overtime.

Earnings

Starting salaries for airline reservation agents vary widely depending on the airline, although most fall between $11,000 and $19,000 per year. Ticket agents and reservation agents overall earn between $12,000 and $40,000 per year, with supervisors earning the top salaries. In 1995, the average weekly wage for reservation agents was $467, while ticket agents averaged $511 per week. In the railroad industry, Amtrak agents earned between $22,000 and $30,000. Bus companies tended to pay lower wages to their agents. Most agents can earn overtime pay; many employers also pay extra for night work. Benefits vary according

to the place of work, the number of years worked, and union membership, although most agents receive vacation and sick pay, health insurance, and retirement plans. Agents, especially when employed by the airlines, often receive free or reduced-fare transportation for themselves and their families.

Work Environment

Reservation agents typically work in cubicles with their own computer terminals and telephone headsets. Reservation and ticket agents generally work 40 hours a week. These agents speak all day on the telephone, while using their computers. Their telephone conversations and computer activity may be monitored and recorded by their supervisors. They might also be required to achieve sales or reservations quotas. The work is very hectic during holidays and other busy periods or when special promotions and discounts are being offered. At these and other times, such as periods of severe weather, passengers may become difficult. Such situations can make the job stressful. Nevertheless, agents must maintain their composure and a pleasant manner when speaking with customers.

Ticket agents work in airports and train and bus stations, which can be busy and noisy. These agents stand most of the day and often lift heavy objects such as luggage and packages. During holidays and busy times, their work can become extremely hectic as they process long lines of waiting customers. Storms and other factors may delay or even cancel flights, trains, and bus services, and at these times the agent may be confronted with upset passengers. The agent must be able to maintain his or her composure at all times.

Outlook

Three out of four of the more than 100,000 reservation and transportation ticket agents work for the airlines. However, the position is likely to decline through the year 2006. Technology is changing the way consumers purchase tickets. "Ticketless" travel, or automated reservations ticketing, is reducing the need for ticket agents. Most airports have kiosks that allow passengers to reserve and purchase tickets themselves. Passengers can also access information about fares and flight times on the Internet, where they can make reservations and purchase tickets. For security reasons, all of these services cannot be fully automated, so reservation and transportation ticket agents will not be phased out.

Most openings will occur as experienced agents transfer to other occupations or retire. Competition, however, is heavy because of the glamour of working for an airline and because of the attractive travel benefits. Competition is also keen because of the relatively low turnover rate among these workers and the fact that the supply of applicants greatly exceeds the demand. Overall, the transportation industry will remain heavily dependent on the state of the economy.

■ For More Information

For information on education, internship, scholarship, or certification in travel and tourism, contact:

National Tourism Foundation
546 East Main Street
PO Box 3071
Lexington, KY 40596-3071
Tel: 800-682-8886 or 606-226-4251
Web: http://www.ntaonline.com

■ Related Articles

Airlines
Travel and Tourism
Customer Service Representatives
Flight Attendants
Office Clerks
Receptionists
Secretaries
Travel Agents

Residential Designers

■ See Interior Designers and Decorators

Resort Workers

■ Overview

Resort workers assist the public at spas, luxury hotels, casinos, theme parks, and lodges. Employment opportunities range from entry-level housekeepers and retail clerks, to highly specialized game attendants and ski instructors. Each worker, however, is necessary to ensure the smooth daily operation of the business and comfort of the resort patron. Club Med, the largest resort chain in the world, employs about 11,000 workers every season.

■ History

The travel and tourism industry is currently enjoying tremendous growth. Factors such the rising number of two-income families, a healthy economy, easier, affordable means of travel, and the public's love for fun and relaxation, have triggered an explosion of travel destinations in the United States and abroad. There are different kinds of resorts each catered to meet specific tastes, expectations, and budgets. Here are some of the more popular types of resorts:

Beach Resorts. Great locations and warm, temperate climates make beach resorts popular vacation destinations. The same factors create tough competition when it comes to employment at such resorts. Does the idea of working in the Florida Keys or Hawaiian Islands sound attractive to you? Here's the downside: the high cost of living in such regions may really eat into your paycheck. Beach resorts offer outdoor activities such as snorkeling, surfing, sailing, and swimming.

Alpine Resorts. Sun and surf doesn't appeal to everyone, believe it or not. Alpine resorts are popular winter vacation destinations—offering downhill skiing, sledding, and snowboarding. Many alpine resorts market warm weather activities such as hiking and biking in the off season. However, some resorts areas, especially those located in Colorado, have a high cost of living.

Adventure Resorts. Dude ranches and rafting companies are some examples of adventure travel destinations. Traditionally, they are smaller operations and employ fewer workers, though many applicants are attracted to the family-like atmosphere. Most adventure resorts are found in out-of-the-way locations. If you crave big city night life during your off hours, think again.

Hotels, Spas, and Casinos. They are the biggest employers in the industry, offering many entry-level positions, as well as openings for specially trained dealers, concierges, golf instructors, and masseurs. Busy seasons vary, though you can expect to have a job year-round. These resorts tend to cater to an upscale clientele, so service standards are quite high and the work atmosphere is more structured. Luxury hotels and spas are located throughout the United States; the larger casino/resorts are located in the gambling meccas of Las Vegas and Atlantic City.

Theme Parks. Theme and amusement parks, located throughout the country, employ thousands of workers every year. Many job opportunities, such as ride attendants, food service, and retail, are entry-level positions; most are seasonal. Some of the larger theme resorts do offer internships, or work/study programs.

■ The Job

Resort employment opportunities are endless. Many different positions, all as important as the next, are required for the successful operation of a resort business. Here are some types of jobs typically found in the industry:

Business department. Accountants, human resource specialists, managers, departmental supervisors, and general managers, are just some positions found in the business department of a resort. While industry jobs are seasonal, expect to work year round if you're employed in the business department. The off season can be quite busy—budgets for the next year are set, marketing and advertising strategies are made, new hires and interns are interviewed. The number of workers employed in the business department is dependent on the size of the resort. A large casino/resort may employ hundreds of business professionals, while a dude ranch may have a single individual responsible for bookkeeping, advertising, and managerial duties. Traditionally, such positions are not considered entry-level, but rather require a college degree or prior work experience. Many interns are assigned to a resort's business department.

Food service. This is one of the largest departments in the industry. Every resort offers food and beverage service, whether simple buffets, or elaborate gourmet dinners. *Waiters and waitresses* are needed to serve food to resort patrons in dining rooms and restaurants. *Bussers,* or *buspersons,* help set and clear tables, and assist the waitstaff serve food, especially when dealing with large parties. They may also be asked to fill water glasses and bread baskets. *Dishwashers* clean plates, glasses, utensils, and other cooking or serving implements. *Hosts and hostesses* show diners to their tables, and may take dinner reservations over the phone. They are careful to rotate table occupation so all waiters and waitresses get an equal share of customers. *Prep cooks, sous chefs,* and *executive chefs* prepare all meals served at a resort. Some resorts are known for their food service, so the best trained chefs are often recruited. *Bartenders* mix and serve alcoholic drinks.

Front desk. *Desk clerks* and *reservation clerks* assign guests to their hotel room, or guest quarters. They are also in charge of giving guests their mail or packages, taking reservations over the phone, collecting payment, and answering any questions regarding the resort. *PBX operators* work the resort switchboard, field calls, and sometimes take reservations.

Guest services. *Concierges* assist resort guests with travel arrangements, reservations, or provide information. The bell staff, supervised by the *bell captain,* bring guests' luggage to their room, run short errands, or make deliveries. They may also be asked to drive resort vehicles. *Doormen* open doors for guests and help with the luggage. They may also be asked to hail taxis or provide information or directions.

Housekeeping and maintenance. A resort's reputation rests largely on its appearance. *Housekeepers* and *cleaners* tidy guest rooms and common areas such as the lobby, dining rooms, and the pool and spa. Most housekeeping positions are entry-level and need little or no experience. *Maintenance workers* make repairs throughout the resort ranging from mending broken chairs to fixing electrical circuits.

Security. *Guards* are often employed to provide safety and security for all guests. While most guards are uni-

A resort worker gives a couple a scuba lesson.

formed, some wear plain-clothes and act as undercover security. Casino resorts employ a large number of security personnel to deter would-be thieves and dishonest gamblers. Security personnel, especially if they are armed, must receive some sort of formal training.

Retail. *Retail clerks* and *retail managers* work at the shopping galleries and gift shops found at many resorts, selling everything from exclusive clothing labels and cosmetics to souvenirs to candy and snacks. Most retail positions are entry-level.

Childcare and healthcare. Many resorts cater to growing families, and therefore provide childcare and baby-sitting services for their patrons. Many resorts, especially those that are island-based, keep a formal medical or first aid department on the premises.

Specialty workers. Specialty workers fill the industry niche or provide services advertised by the particular resort. Most occupations in this category are highly specialized or require particular training, or in some cases, certification and licensure. *Lifeguards* are employed by resorts to supervise beaches and swimming pools. *Ski instructors* provide group or individual lessons for alpine resort patrons. Many beach resorts employ *attendants* to manage water activities such as water skiing, snorkeling, scuba diving, sailing, and deep sea fishing. Dude ranches need wranglers, trail guides, and horse groomers. Theme resorts employ many *entertainers* for parades, musicals, and shows. *Guides* work for adventure resorts leading tours of wilderness areas. Casinos hire many people to work as table dealers, pit bosses, and change clerks. Golf resorts need golf professionals to give instruction.

■ Requirements

Most resort jobs are on a seasonal calendar and attract many students. Area high school students are often recruited to work at theme and amusement parks. Many

At Club Med, the world's largest resort chain, you are not called an employee, but a *Gentils Organisateur* (French for Congenial Host, and G.O. for short), and you don't work at a resort, but rather a village. Club Med, in business since the 1940s, innovated the idea of all-inclusive vacations: for one price, you get room and board, entertainment, activities, and all the sun and surf you want.

Club Meds are located all over the world and actively recruit young and energetic men and women to staff their villages. The typical G.O. is about 28 years old and works for the company about 2 years. Different employment opportunities are available, such as hospitality administration, culinary arts, resort maintenance, childcare and healthcare, sports instruction (both land and water), and entertainment. On off days G.O.s are encouraged to mingle—share meals, play sports, and plan activities—with the village guests. New hires are assigned to a North American village for at least 6 months. After that G.O.s can apply to transfer to different villages as demand allows. Besides room and board, a G.O. receives round trip transportation to their assigned village, health and accident insurance, and a monthly stipend of approximately $530 for an entry-level position, but more for skilled positions. Most G.O.s do not work at Club Med to make money, but rather for the experience of working with a diverse group of people and a chance to travel to many exotic ports of call. Interested? Here are some G.O requirements.

You must:

- Be at least 20 years old; 21 if hired for a childcare position
- Hold a valid passport
- Commit for at least 6 months at a time, to any assigned location.
- Speak a foreign language, besides your own. German, French, and Italian are encouraged.

resorts actively recruit at college campuses and job fairs and offer internships or programs to earn college credit.

Postsecondary Training

If you are interested in something other than an entry-level job, or wish to make this industry a lifelong career, then a college education will be helpful. Many companies look for college graduates with degrees in hospitality, communications, or business management.

Certification and Licensing

Most entry level resort jobs do not require certification or a license. This, however, is not the case with specialty workers. Ski instructors, scuba instructors, child care workers, and lifeguards, just to name a few, must be certified.

Other Requirements

Your place of residence is an important factor when applying for a resort job, especially with some of the larger Alpine resorts, and almost all resorts in Hawaii. Blame it on the high cost of living at such places. Since employer-provided housing in Hawaii, for example, is scarce, and rental properties and apartments are so expensive, most resorts will not consider applicants without a local address. So, unless your grandparents live in Hawaii, another island, or a mountain paradise, it would be best to look for employment elsewhere.

Also, some resorts insist that applicants be trained in CPR and first aid. Check with the human resource department of your potential employer to learn what their requirements are.

■ Exploring

Convince your parents that a family vacation at a Hawaiian resort is really for education's sake. While there you can get an idea at how many hard working employees it takes to keep a resort running smoothly. Take it up a notch and contact the human resources or public relations department for a tour of the facilities.

You can get work related experience right now—without leaving your hometown! Get a job working at a nearby golf course, hotel, or restaurant. These types of jobs offer a great introduction to the industry, help you hone your people skills, and give your resume substance!

So you're thinking of becoming a ski instructor . . . why not join your high school's ski club? (Or start one!) This suggestion goes for whatever activity piques your interest—swimming, horseback riding, surfing, sailing, etc. Excelling, as well as enjoying, a particular activity, is a good stepping stone for a career in the resort industry.

Subscribe to a travel magazine. They often feature unique and out of the way destinations and attractions.

Check the Internet for resort related Web sites and employment opportunities.

■ Employers

Resorts are located all over the country, from multimillion dollar hotels to smaller, family owned adventure companies. Jobs are plentiful. The hard part, especially if relocation is not a problem, is deciding which type of resort to work for. There are several important factors to consider before starting your job search—location, size of company, cost of living, and work availability. Here are profiles of three popular resort regions.

Aspen, Colorado. There are many jobs available in Aspen—waiting on tables, housekeeping, or bellhopping. Most pay minimum wage or higher, but tips can greatly increase your weekly salary. Besides world class venues for skiing, biking, and hiking, spectacular views, and clean mountain air, Aspen attracts a diverse group of people from different backgrounds and interests. Be forewarned. Aspen, as with many other Colorado resort towns, is very expensive. You may have to share the rent with a roommate(s), or consider finding more affordable housing outside of town. Most resort jobs are seasonal, from mid-October to mid-April. Unless you are fortunate enough to land a job year-round, save up for the off season. The big employer in Aspen is The Aspen Skiing Company—which has seasonal and some year-round work at their four ski areas and three hotel resorts.

Las Vegas, Nevada. Not only is this town a gambler's haven, but a place to go for entertainment, culture, sightseeing, and outdoor activities. The growth of mega-resorts catering to a diverse crowd of tourists, from wealthy gamblers to families, has turned Vegas into a hot travel destination. The good news: Most resort jobs in Vegas are year-round. This town is host to the largest business conventions and trade shows, so in addition to entry level jobs, conference planners, chefs, hotel managers, and entertainers are needed to take care of the millions of conventioneers that come to Vegas each year. Housing in Las Vegas is very affordable. Many apartments advertise one month free as an incentive to potential renters. The bad news: It gets really hot in the summer. With temperatures rising over 100 degrees Fahrenheit, be sure to find out whether your resort job is primarily indoors during the months of June, July, and August. Check out the Mirage Resorts, Inc., which owns the Mirage Hotel as well as the Bellagio.

Martha's Vineyard, Massachusetts. You can find a job as a waitress/waiter, bartender, beach lifeguard, or as a guide for fishing tours. Most jobs are seasonal, lasting from mid-April to the end of October. Because of the location, a ferry ride away from the mainland, and the relatively small size of the island, expect housing to be as costly as it is in Colorado. You may want to consider working at some of the larger hotels; the hourly pay may be low, minimum wage or little better, but at least they offer free or subsidized housing. The Harbor View and Kelley House Hotel often have positions available for front office workers, housekeeping staff, food service workers, and lifeguards. Applicants with hotel or restaurant experience are desired.

■ Starting Out

This is a popular industry, so it's important to apply early in order to get a choice position. A good rule of thumb is to submit your application at least two seasons in advance. That means no later than early spring for warm weather resorts, and the end of summer for Alpine resorts. Since many resorts recruit heavily at college campuses, and some high schools, your career guidance center would be a good place to start your job search. See if they post job opportunities, or have information on resort companies. The Internet offers a wealth of information on resort employment. Visit http://www.resortjobs.com for industry information, tips on how to land the right jobs, and a listing of available positions. You may also want to check the chamber of commerce in a particular town of interest, or check

your local bookstore for a copy of the local paper. If an East Coast island job looks appealing, look at the job ads in the *Nantucket Beacon,* or the *Nantucket Inquirer and Mirror.*

Good work skills and a friendly disposition are important qualities in this industry. But guess what else recruiters look for when interviewing applicants? The commitment to stay the length of the season. When new hires leave mid-season, resort managers find themselves scrambling to find a replacement, or the entire department ends up pulling the slack.

■ Advancement

Many employees return to resort jobs year after year. If you spend your first summer in an entry-level position, chances are you can advance to a job with more responsibility the next season. Bussers can advance to a waitstaff position, PBX operators to a job as a front desk clerk, and housekeepers can become floor managers.

■ Earnings

Most entry-level jobs in this industry pay an hourly wage anywhere from minimum wage on up. Waiters and waitresses, bussers, dishwashers, cleaning workers, the bell staff, and doormen earn low hourly salaries which are offset by tips. Specialty workers who need certification or special training, such as instructors, bartenders, entertainers, lifeguards, wranglers, or blackjack dealers, may be paid a higher hourly wage. Some resorts supply free room and board for their employees, and offer only a small monthly stipend. According to the ResortJobs Web site, the average entry-level resort worker in Aspen, Colorado, earns about $7.50 an hour.

Since most jobs are seasonal, very few employee benefits are given apart from free use of resort facilities on off days, and some subsidized or free room and board. Some larger companies provide transportation to and from the resort. Full-time, year-round employees receive a standard benefits package including health insurance and paid sick and vacation time.

■ Work Environment

Just because you work at a vacation resort doesn't mean you are on holiday. All employees, regardless of their position, are expected to work hard. Hours will vary depending on the job and season. Most resort workers work eight hours a day, five or six days a week. Some employers, such as hotels, casinos and spas, require their employees to wear company uniforms. Many places allow their employees to use the resort facilities on off days. Ski resorts give their employees free lift passes for the season. Employees of beach resorts enjoy swimming and sailing during their free time.

Resorts are service oriented so employees are required to be courteous, helpful, and friendly at all times. You will be expected to dress and behave properly whether or not on call. Many places, especially spas that cater to an upscale clientele or family resorts, look for wholesome types. No, you don't have to look like you hail from "Leave It To Beaver," but maybe it would be wise to leave the nose ring at home. Some resorts such as Disney World, for example, consider their employees as "the cast," and expect them to be on their best behavior when "on stage" (working hours).

Not only will you be expected to mix well with the resort patrons, but your co-workers, as well. Only team players are needed in this industry. Many resorts offer housing options for their employees, with assignments grouping two or more employees to an apartment or room. Oftentimes, especially if the resort is in a remote location, seasonal workers have no choice but to "hang out" with each other during their free time.

■ Outlook

Until the public has enough of rest and relaxation, or tires of adventure travel and exotic locales, employment prospects in the resort industry will continue to be good. Mega-resorts in Las Vegas, the popularity of all-inclusive vacation packages, and alternative vacation destinations will supply endless employment opportunities where you can really mix work with pleasure. Understand, however, that most jobs are seasonal. Some resorts will offer year-round employment—Las Vegas locations, larger theme parks, or hotels—but at other places you'll probably end up with two or three job descriptions if you desire 12 months of work.

Many positions require little experience, but if you want something with more responsibility (and better pay), hone your skills and find your niche. Management and hospitality graduates, entertainers, activity instructors, and chefs fare better in this respect. Also, applicants with industry exposure, or the ability to speak a foreign language, will be in high demand.

■ For More Information

For industry information, resort backgrounds, and job postings, check:

Resort Jobs
Web: http://www.resortjobs.com

Cool Jobs
Web: http://www.cooljobs.com

The Aspen Skiing Company
Web: http://www.aspen-snowmass.com/opportunities

Club Med
Web: http://www.clubmed.com

■ Related Articles

Hospitality
Recreation
Travel and Tourism
Adventure Travel Specialists
Amusement Park Workers
Baggage Porters and Bellhops
Bartenders
Caterers
Cooks, Chefs, and Bakers
Cruise Ship Workers
Food Service Workers
Gaming Occupations
Hotel and Motel Industry Workers
Hotel and Motel Managers
Hotel Concierges
Hotel Desk Clerks
Hotel Executive Housekeepers
Hotel Restaurant Managers
Lifeguards
Recreation Workers
Reservation and Ticket Agents
Restaurant and Food Service Managers
Security Consultants and Technicians
Ski Resort Workers
Tour Guides

Respiratory Therapists and Technicians

■ Overview

Respiratory therapists, or *respiratory care practitioners,* evaluate, treat, and care for patients with deficiencies or abnormalities of the cardiopulmonary (heart/lung) system, either providing temporary relief from chronic ailments or administering emergency care where life is threatened.

Working under a physician's direction, these workers set up and operate respirators, mechanical ventilators, and other devices. They monitor the functioning of the equipment and the patients' response to the therapy and maintain the patients' charts. They also assist patients with breathing exercises, and inspect, test, and order repairs for respiratory therapy equipment. They may demonstrate procedures to trainees and other health care personnel.

History

In normal respiration, the chest muscles and the diaphragm (a muscular disk that separates the chest and abdominal cavities) draw in air by expanding the chest volume. When this automatic response is impaired because of illness or injury, artificial means must be applied to keep the patient breathing and to prevent brain damage or death. Respiratory problems can result from many conditions. For example, with bronchial asthma, the bronchial tubes are narrowed by spasmodic contractions, and they produce an excessive amount of mucus. Emphysema is a disease in which the lungs lose their elasticity. Diseases of the central nervous system and drug poisoning may result in paralysis, which could lead to suffocation. Emergency conditions such as heart failure, stroke, drowning, or shock also interfere with the normal breathing process.

Respirators, or ventilators, are mechanical devices that enable patients with cardiorespiratory problems to breathe. The original "iron lung" was designed in 1937 by Philip Drinker and Louise A. Shaw, of the Harvard School of Public Health in Boston, primarily to treat people with polio. It was a cylindrical machine that enclosed the patient's entire body, except the head. This type of respirator is still in use today. The newer ventilators, however, are much smaller, dome-shaped breast plates that wrap around the patient's chest and allow more freedom of motion. Other sophisticated, complex equipment to aid patients with breathing difficulties includes mechanical ventilators, apparatuses that administer therapeutic gas, environmental control systems, and aerosol generators.

Respiratory therapists and technicians and their assistants are the workers who operate this equipment and administer care and life support to patients suffering from respiratory problems.

The Job

Respiratory therapists treat patients with various cardiorespiratory problems. They may provide care that affords temporary relief from chronic illnesses such as asthma or emphysema, or they may administer life-support treatment to victims of heart failure, stroke, drowning, or shock. These specialists often mean the difference between life and death in cases involving acute respiratory conditions, as may result from head injuries or drug poisoning. Adults who stop breathing for longer than three to five minutes rarely survive without serious brain damage, and an absence of respiratory activity for more than nine minutes almost always results in death. Respiratory therapists carry out their duties under a *physician*'s direction and supervision. They set up and operate special devices to treat patients who need temporary or emergency relief from breathing difficulties. The equipment may include respirators, positive-pressure breathing machines, or environmental control systems. Aerosol inhalants are administered to confine medication to the lungs. Patients who have undergone surgery are often treated by these workers because anesthesia depresses normal respiration, and the patients need some support to restore their full breathing capability and to prevent respiratory illnesses.

In evaluating patients, therapists test the capacity of the lungs and analyze the oxygen and carbon dioxide concentration and potential of hydrogen (pH), a measure of the acidity or alkalinity level of the blood. To measure lung capacity, therapists have patients breathe into an instrument that measures the volume and flow of air during inhalation and exhalation. By comparing the reading with the norm for the patient's age, height, weight, and sex, respiratory therapists can determine whether lung deficiencies exist. To analyze oxygen, carbon dioxide, and pH levels, therapists draw an arterial blood sample, place it in a blood gas analyzer, and relay the results to a physician.

Respiratory therapists watch equipment gauges and maintain prescribed volumes of oxygen or other inhalants. Besides monitoring the equipment to be sure it is operating properly, they observe the patient's physiological response to the therapy and consult with physicians in case of any adverse reactions. They also record pertinent identification and therapy information on each patient's chart

RESPIRATORY THERAPISTS AND TECHNICIANS	
SCHOOL SUBJECTS	Health Mathematics
PERSONAL SKILLS	Helping/teaching Technical/scientific
WORK ENVIRONMENT	Primarily indoors Primarily one location
MINIMUM EDUCATION LEVEL	Some postsecondary training
SALARY RANGE	$25,000 to $30,000 to $37,000
CERTIFICATION OR LICENSING	Recommended
OUTLOOK	Faster than the average
DOT	079
GOE	10.02.02
NOC	3214
O*NET	32302

and keep records of the cost of materials and the charges to the patients.

Therapists instruct patients and their families on how to use respiratory equipment at home, and they may demonstrate respiratory therapy procedures to trainees and other health care personnel. Their responsibilities include inspecting and testing equipment. If it is faulty, they either make minor repairs themselves or order major repairs.

Respiratory therapy workers include therapists, technicians, and assistants. The duties of therapists and technicians are essentially the same, although therapists are expected to have a higher level of expertise, and their responsibilities often include teaching and supervising other workers. Assistants clean, sterilize, store, and generally take care of the equipment but have very little contact with patients.

■ Requirements

High School

High school courses that will best prepare a student for further education in this field include health, biology, mathematics, chemistry, and physics.

Postsecondary Training

Formal training is necessary for entry to this field. Training is offered at the postsecondary level by hospitals, medical schools, colleges and universities, trade schools, vocational-technical institutes, and the armed forces. Some programs prepare graduates for jobs as respiratory therapists; other, shorter programs lead to jobs as respiratory therapy technicians. In 1994, 275 programs for respiratory therapists were accredited by the Commission on Accreditation of Allied Health Education Programs (CAAHEP). Another 174 programs offered CAAHEP-accredited preparation for respiratory therapy technicians. To be eligible for these programs, you must have graduated from high school.

Accredited programs in respiratory therapy combine both theory and clinical work and last from 21 months to four years. A bachelor's degree is awarded to students who successfully complete the four-year program. Students who complete shorter programs may earn an associate's degree. The program for technicians runs approximately one year

and results in a certificate. The areas of study for both therapists and technicians cover human anatomy and physiology, chemistry, physics, microbiology, and mathematics. Technical courses cover procedures, equipment, and clinical tests.

There are no standard hiring requirements for assistants. The individual department head who is doing the hiring sets the standards and may require only a high school diploma.

Certification and Licensing

Thirty-seven states license respiratory care personnel. The National Board for Respiratory Care (NBRC) offers voluntary certification and registration to graduates of CAAHEP-accredited programs. Two credentials are awarded to respiratory care practitioners who satisfy the requirements: Certified Respiratory Therapy Technician (CRRT) and Registered Respiratory Therapist (RRT). All graduates—those from two- and four-year programs in respiratory therapy as well as those from one-year technician programs—take the CRTT examination first. CRTTs who meet education and experience requirements can take a separate examination, leading to the award of the RRT.

Most employers require that applicants for entry-level or generalist positions hold the CRTT or are eligible to take the certification examination. Supervisory positions and those in intensive care specialties usually require the RRT (or RRT eligibility).

Other Requirements

Respiratory therapists must enjoy working with people. You must be sensitive to your patients' physical and psychological needs because you will be dealing with people who may be in pain or who may be frightened. The work of this occupational group is of great significance. Respiratory therapists are often responsible for the life and well-being of people already in critical condition. You must pay strict attention to detail, be able to follow instructions and work as part of a team, and remain cool in emergencies. Mechanical ability and manual dexterity are necessary to operate much of the respiratory equipment.

■ Exploring

Those considering advanced study may obtain a list of accredited educational programs in respiratory therapy by writing to the American Association for Respiratory Care (AARC) at the address listed at the end of this article. Formal training in this field is available in hospitals, vocational-technical institutes, private trade schools, and other noncollegiate settings as well. Local hospitals can provide information on training opportunities. School vocational counselors may be sources of additional information about educational matters and may be able to set up interviews with or lectures by a respiratory therapy practitioner from a local hospital.

Hospitals are excellent places to obtain part-time and summer employment. They have a continuing need for helpers in many departments. Even though the work may not be directly related to respiratory therapy, you will gain knowledge of the operation of a hospital and may be in a position to get acquainted with respiratory therapists and observe them as they carry out their duties. If part-time or temporary work is not available, you may wish to volunteer your services.

■ Employers

Most respiratory therapy technicians work in hospitals in the respiratory therapy, anesthesiology, or pulmonary medicine departments. The rest are employed by oxygen equipment rental companies, ambulance services, nursing homes, and home health agencies.

■ Starting Out

Graduates of CAAHEP-accredited respiratory therapy training programs may have the school's placement service to aid them in finding a job. Otherwise, they may apply directly to the individual local health care facilities.

High school graduates may apply directly to local hospitals for jobs as respiratory therapy assistants. If your goal is to become a therapist or technician, however, you would do better to enroll in a formal respiratory therapy educational program.

■ Advancement

Many respiratory therapists start out as assistants or technicians. With appropriate training courses and experience, they advance to the therapist level. Respiratory therapists with sufficient experience may be promoted to assistant chief or chief therapist. With graduate education, they may be qualified to teach respiratory therapy at the college level.

■ Earnings

In the 1990s, the average minimum annual salary for respiratory therapists was $24,770. The overall median salary was $29,228, and the average maximum was $36,553. Part-time therapists earned an average of $14.55 per hour.

Hospital workers receive benefits that include health insurance, paid vacations and sick leave, and pension plans. Some institutions provide additional benefits, such as uniforms and parking, and offer free courses or tuition reimbursement for job-related courses.

■ Work Environment

Respiratory therapists generally work in extremely clean, quiet surroundings. They usually work 40 hours a week, which may include nights and weekends because hospitals are in operation 24 hours a day, seven days a week. The work requires long hours of standing and may be very stressful during emergencies.

A possible hazard is that the inhalants these employees work with are highly flammable. The danger of fire is minimized, however, if the workers test equipment regularly and are strict about taking safety precautions. As do workers in many other health occupations, respiratory therapists run a risk of catching infectious diseases. Careful adherence to proper procedures minimizes the risk.

■ Outlook

There were approximately 100,000 respiratory therapists in the United States in the 1990s. Employment growth is expected to be more rapid than the average for all occupations through the year 2006, despite the fact that efforts to control rising health care costs has reduced the number of job opportunities in hospitals.

The increasing demand for therapists is the result of several factors. The fields of neonatal care and gerontology are growing. Also, there is a greater incidence of cardiopulmonary and AIDS-related diseases, coupled with more advanced methods of diagnosing and treating them.

Employment opportunities for therapists should be very favorable in the rapidly growing field of home health care, although this area accounts for only a small number of respiratory therapy jobs. There should also be numerous openings for respiratory therapists in equipment rental companies and in firms that provide respiratory care on a contract basis.

■ For More Information

For information on scholarships, continuing education, job listings, and other resources, contact:

American Association for Respiratory Care (AARC)
11030 Ables Lane
Dallas, TX 75229
Tel: 214-243-2272
Email: info@aarc.org
Web: http://www.aarc.org

For information on licensing and certification, contact:

National Board for Respiratory Care (NBRC)
8310 Nieman Road
Lenexa, KS 66214
Tel: 913-599-4200
Web: http://www.nbrc.org

For information on accreditation, contact:

Commission on Accreditation of Allied Health Education Programs (CAAHEP)
American Medical Association
515 North State Street, Suite 7530
Chicago, IL 60610
Tel: 312-464-4625
Web: http://www.caahep.org

Joint Review Committee for Respiratory Therapy Education (JRCRTE)
1701 West Euless Boulevard, Suite 300
Euless, TX 76040
Tel: 817-283-2835

■ **Related Articles**

Restaurant and Food Service Managers

■ **Overview**

Restaurant and food service managers are responsible for the overall operation of businesses that serve food. This includes the purchasing of a variety of food, selection of the menu, preparation of the food, and, most importantly, maintenance of health and sanitation levels. Managers oversee staffing for each task in addition to performing the business and accounting functions of restaurant operations.

■ **History**

The word "restaurant" comes from the French word *restaurer,* "to restore." It is believed that "restaurant" was first used in its present sense in the 18th century by a soup vendor in Paris, who offered his customers a choice of soups, or restoratives (*restaurants*). The first restaurants in the United States were patterned after European restaurants and coffeehouses. During the 20th century, many innovations in the restaurant industry led to the development of new kinds of eating establishments, including the cafeteria, automat, counter-service restaurant, drive-in, and fast food chain.

■ **The Job**

Restaurant and food service managers work in restaurants ranging from elegant hotel dining rooms to fast food restaurants. They also may work in food service facilities ranging from school cafeterias to hospital food services. Whatever the setting, these managers coordinate and direct the work of the employees who prepare and serve food and perform other related functions. Restaurant managers set work schedules for wait staff and host staff. Food service managers are responsible for buying the food and equipment necessary for the operation of the restaurant or facility, and they may help with menu planning. They inspect the premises periodically to ensure compliance with health and sanitation regulations. Restaurant and food service managers perform many clerical and financial duties, such as keeping records, directing payroll operations, handling large sums of money, and taking inventories. Their work usually involves much contact with customers and vendors, such as taking suggestions, handling complaints, and creating a friendly atmosphere. Restaurant managers generally supervise any advertising or sales promotions for their operations.

In some very large restaurants and institutional food service facilities, one or more *assistant managers* and an *executive chef* or *food manager* assist the manager. These specially trained assistants oversee service in the dining room and other areas of the operation and supervise the kitchen staff and preparation of all foods served.

Restaurant and food service managers are responsible for the success of their establishments. They continually analyze every aspect of its operation and make whatever changes are needed to guarantee its profitability.

These duties are common, in varying degrees, to both *owner-managers* of relatively small restaurants and to nonowner-managers who may be salaried employees in large restaurants or institutional food service facilities. The owner-manager of a restaurant is more likely to be involved in service functions, sometimes operating the cash register, waiting on tables, and performing a wide variety of tasks.

■ **Requirements**

Educational requirements for restaurant and food service managers vary greatly. In many cases, no specific requirements exist and managerial positions are filled by promoting experienced food and beverage preparation and service workers. However, as more colleges offer programs in restaurant and institutional food service management—programs that combine academic work with on-the-job experience—more restaurant and food service chains are seeking individuals with this training.

Postsecondary Training

In the 1990s, more than 160 colleges and universities offered four-year programs leading to a bachelor's degree in restaurant and hotel management or institutional food service management. Some individuals qualify for management training by earning an associate's degree or other formal award below the bachelor's degree level from one of the more than 800 community and junior colleges, technical institutes, or other institutions that offer programs in these fields. Students hired as management trainees by restaurant chains and food service management companies undergo vigorous training programs.

Other Requirements

Experience in all areas of restaurant and food service work is an important requirement for successful managers. Managers must be familiar with the various operations of the establishment: food preparation, service operations, sanitary regulations, and financial functions.

One of the most important requirements for restaurant and food service managers is to have good business knowledge. They must possess a high degree of technical knowledge in handling business details, such as buying large items of machinery and equipment and large quantities of food. Desirable personality characteristics include poise, self-confidence, and an ability to get along with people. Managers may be on their feet for long periods, and the hours of work may be both long and irregular.

■ Exploring

Practical restaurant and food service experience is usually easy to get. In colleges with curriculum offerings in these areas, summer jobs in all phases of the work are available and, in some cases, required. Some restaurant and food service chains provide on-the-job training in management.

■ Employers

Restaurants and food service make up one of the largest and most active sectors of the nation's economy. Employers include restaurants of various sizes, hotel dining rooms, ships, trains, institutional food service facilities, and many other establishments where food is served. No matter the size or style of the establishment, managers are needed to oversee the operation and to ensure that records are kept, goals are met, and things run smoothly.

■ Starting Out

Many restaurants and food service facilities provide self-sponsored, on-the-job training for prospective managers. There are still cases in which people work hard and move up the ladder within the organization's workforce, finally arriving at the managerial position. More and more, people with advanced education and specialized training move directly into manager-trainee positions and then on to managerial positions.

■ Advancement

In large restaurants and food service organizations, promotion opportunities frequently arise for employees with knowledge of the overall operation. Experience in all aspects of the work is an important consideration for the food service employee who desires advancement. The employee with a knowledge of kitchen operations may advance from *pantry supervisor* to food manager, assistant manager, and finally restaurant or food service manager. Similar advancement is possible for dining room workers with knowledge of kitchen operations.

Advancement to top executive positions is possible for managers employed by large restaurant and institutional food service chains. A good educational background and some specialized training are increasingly valuable assets to employees who hope to advance.

RESTAURANT AND FOOD SERVICE MANAGERS	
SCHOOL SUBJECTS	**Business** **Health**
PERSONAL SKILLS	**Communication/ideas** **Leadership/management**
WORK ENVIRONMENT	**Primarily indoors** **Primarily one location**
MINIMUM EDUCATION LEVEL	**High school diploma**
SALARY RANGE	**$18,600 to $29,000 to $45,000+**
CERTIFICATION OR LICENSING	**None available**
OUTLOOK	**Faster than the average**
DOT	**157**
GOE	**09.05.02**
NOC	**0631**
O*NET	**15026B**

A restaurant manager discusses the day's menu with her chef.

■ Earnings

The earnings of salaried restaurant and food service managers vary a great deal, depending on the type and size of the establishment. According to a 1995 salary survey conducted by the National Restaurant Association, manager-trainees earned an average salary of $21,000 a year. Those working in larger restaurants and food service facilities received about $30,000. In addition, most trainees earn annual bonuses or incentive payments ranging from $1,000 to $3,000. Experienced managers receive an average of approximately $30,000 a year. Those in charge of the largest restaurants and institutional food service facilities often earn over $50,000. Managers of fast-food restaurants average about $25,000 per year. In addition to a base salary, most managers receive bonuses based on profits, which can range from $2,000 to $7,500 a year.

■ Work Environment

Work environments are usually pleasant. There is usually a great deal of activity involved in preparing and serving food to large numbers of people, and managers usually work 40 to 48 hours per week. In some cafeterias, especially those located within an industry or business establishment, hours are regular, and little evening work is required. Many restaurants serve late dinners, however, necessitating the manager to remain on duty during a late-evening work period.

Many restaurants furnish meals to employees during their work hours. Annual bonuses, group plan pensions, hospitalization, medical, and other benefits may be offered to restaurant managers.

■ Outlook

The industry is rapidly growing and employs about 493,000 professional managers. Opportunities for well-qualified restaurant and food service managers appear to be excellent through 2006, especially for those with bachelor's or associate's degrees. New restaurants are always opening to meet increasing demand. It has been estimated that at least 25 percent of all of the food consumed in the United States is eaten in restaurants and hotels.

Many job openings will arise from the need to replace managers retiring from the workforce. Also, population growth will result in an increased demand for eating establishments and, in turn, a need for managers to oversee them. As the elderly population increases, managers will be needed to staff dining rooms located in hospitals and nursing homes.

Economic downswings have a great effect on eating and drinking establishments. During a recession, people have less money to spend on luxuries such as dining out, thus hurting the restaurant business. However, greater numbers of working parents and their families are finding it convenient to eat out or purchase carryout food from a restaurant.

■ For More Information

For information on careers and education, contact the following organizations:

Canadian Restaurant and Foodservices Association
316 Bloor Street West
Toronto, ON M5S 1W5
Canada
Tel: 800-387-5649

Council on Hotel, Restaurant, and Institutional Education
1200 17th Street, NW
Washington, DC 20036-3097
Tel: 202-331-5990
Email: alliance@access.digex.net
Web: http://chrie.org/

National Restaurant Association Educational Foundation
250 South Wacker Drive, Suite 1400
Chicago, IL 60606
Tel: 800-765-2122
Web: http://www.edfound.org

■ Related Articles

Food Processing
Hospitality
Restaurants and Food Service
Bartenders
Caterers
Cooks, Chefs, and Bakers
Fast Food Workers
Food Service Workers
Hotel Restaurant Managers

Retail Business Owners

■ Overview

Retail business owners are entrepreneurs who start or buy their own businesses or franchise operations. They are responsible for all aspects of a business operation, from planning and ordering merchandise to overseeing day-to-day operations. Retail business owners sell such items as clothing, household appliances, groceries, jewelry, and furniture.

■ History

Retailing is a vital commercial activity, providing customers with an opportunity to purchase goods and services from various types of merchants. The first retail outlets in America were trading posts and general stores. At trading posts, goods obtained from Native Americans were exchanged for items imported from Europe or manufactured in other parts of the country. As villages and towns grew, trading posts developed into general stores and began to sell food, farm necessities, and clothing. Typically run by a single person, these stores sometimes served as the post office and became the social and economic center of their communities.

Since World War II, giant supermarkets, discount houses, chain stores, and shopping malls have grown popular. Even so, individually owned businesses still thrive, often giving customers more personal and better informed service. Moreover, despite the large growth in retail outlets and the increased competition that has accompanied it, retailing still provides the same basic, important function it did in early years of the United States.

■ The Job

Although retail business owners sell a wide variety of products, from apples to automobiles, the basic job responsibilities remain the same. Simply stated, the retail business owner must do everything necessary to ensure the successful operation of a business.

There are five major categories of job responsibilities within a retail establishment: merchandising and buying, store operations, sales promotion and advertising, bookkeeping and accounting, and personnel supervision. Merchandising and buying determine the type and amount of actual goods to be sold. Store operations involve maintaining the building and providing for the movement of goods and personnel within the building. Sales promotion and advertising are the marketing methods used to inform customers and potential customers about the goods and services that are available. In bookkeeping and account-

ing, records are kept of payroll, taxes, and money spent and received. Personnel involves staffing the store with people who are trained and qualified to handle all the work that needs to be done.

The owner must be aware of all aspects of the business operation so that informed decisions can be made. Specific duties of an individual owner depend on the size of the store and the number of employees. In a store with more than 10 employees, many of the operational, promotional, and personnel activities may be supervised by a manager. The owner may plan the overall purpose and function of the store and hire a manager to oversee the day-to-day operations. In a smaller store, the owner may also do much of the operational activities, including sweeping the floor, greeting customers, and balancing the accounting books.

In both large and small operations, an owner must keep up to date on product information, as well as on economic and technological conditions that may have an impact on business. This entails reading catalogs about product availability, checking current inventories and prices, and researching and implementing any technological advances that may make the operation more efficient. For example, an owner may decide to purchase data processing equipment to help with accounting functions, as well as to generate a mailing list to inform customers of special sales.

Because of the risks involved in opening a business and the many economic and managerial demands put on individual owners, a desire to open a retail business should be combined with proper management skills, sufficient economic backing, and a good sense of what the public wants. The large majority of retail businesses fail because of a lack of managerial experience on the part of owners.

Franchise ownership, whereby an individual owner obtains a license to sell an existing company's goods or services, grew phenomenally during the 1980s. Franchise agreements enable the person who wants to open a business to have expert advice from the sponsoring company about location, hiring and training of employees, arrangement of merchandise, display of goods, and record keeping. Some entrepreneurs, however, do not want to be limited to the product lines and other restrictions that accompany run-

RETAIL BUSINESS OWNERS	
SCHOOL SUBJECTS	**Business** **Mathematics**
PERSONAL SKILLS	**Helping/teaching** **Technical/scientific**
WORK ENVIRONMENT	**Primarily indoors** **Primarily one location**
MINIMUM EDUCATION LEVEL	**High school diploma**
SALARY RANGE	**$15,000 to $35,000 to $100,000+**
CERTIFICATION OR LICENSING	**None available**
OUTLOOK	**About as fast as the average**

Owners of small businesses often have to do everything from ordering merchandise to keeping accounting records and helping customers.

ning a franchise store. Franchise operations also may fail, but their likelihood of success is greater than that of a totally independent retail store.

■ Requirements

High School

A high school diploma is important in order to understand the basics of business ownership, though there are no specific educational or experiential requirements for this position. Course work in business administration is helpful, though, as is previous experience in the retail trade. Hard work, constant analysis and evaluation, and sufficient capital are important elements of a successful business venture.

High school students interested in owning a business should take courses in mathematics, business management, and any of a variety of business-related subjects, such as accounting, typing, and computer science. In addition, English and other courses enhancing communications skills should be pursued. Specific skill areas also should be developed. A person who wants to open an electronics repair shop, for example, should study as much about electronics as possible.

Owners of small retail businesses often manage the store and work behind the counter. In such case, the owner of a meat market is the butcher as well.

Postsecondary Training

As the business environment gets more and more competitive, many people are opting for an academic degree as a way of getting more training. An undergraduate college program emphasizing business communications, marketing, business law, business management, and accounting should be pursued. Some people choose to get a master's

in business administration (MBA) or other related graduate degree. There are also special business schools that offer a one- or two-year program in business management. Some correspondence schools also offer courses on how to plan and run a business.

Other Requirements

Whatever the experience and training, a retail business owner needs a lot of energy, patience, and fortitude to overcome the slow times and other difficulties involved in running a business. Other important personal characteristics include maturity, creativity, and good business judgment. Retail business owners also should be able to motivate employees and delegate authority.

Although there are no special licenses or certificates needed to open a business, individual states or communities may have zoning codes or other regulations specifying what type of business can be located in a particular area. Owners should contact the appropriate city or municipality to determine any relevant regulations.

■ Exploring

Working full or part-time as a sales clerk or in some other capacity within a retail business is a good way to learn about the responsibilities of operating a business. Talking with owners of small shops also is helpful, as is reading periodicals that publish articles on self-employment, such as *Entrepreneur* magazine (http://www.entrepreneurmag.com).

Most communities have a chamber of commerce whose members usually will be glad to share their insights into the career of a retail business owner. The Small Business Administration, an agency of the U.S. government, is another possible source of information.

■ Starting Out

Few people start their career as an owner. Many start as a manager or in some other position within a retail business. While developing managerial skills or while pursuing a college degree or other relevant training, you should decide what type of business you would like to own. Many people decide to buy an existing business because it already has a proven track record and because banks and other lending institutions often are more likely to loan money to an existing facility. A retail business owner should anticipate having at least 50 percent of the money needed to start or buy a business. Some people find it helpful to have one or more partners in a business venture.

Owning a franchise is another way of starting a business without a large capital investment, as franchise agreements often involve some assistance in planning and start-up costs. Franchise operations, however, are not necessarily less expensive to run than a totally independent business.

■ Advancement

Because an owner is by definition the boss, there are limited opportunities for advancement. Advancement often takes the form of expansion of an existing business, leading to increased earnings and prestige. Expanding a business also can entail added risk, as it involves increasing operational costs. A successful franchise owner may be offered an additional franchise location or an executive position at the corporate headquarters.

A small number of successful independent business owners choose to franchise their business operations in different areas. Some owners become part-time consultants, while others teach a course at a college or university or in an adult education program. This teaching often is done not only for the financial rewards but as a way of helping others investigate the option of retail ownership.

■ Earnings

Earnings vary widely and are greatly influenced by the ability of the individual owner, the type of product or service being sold, and existing economic conditions Some retail business owners may earn only about $15,000 a year, while the most successful earn $100,000 or more.

■ Work Environment

Retail business owners generally work in pleasant surroundings. Even so, ownership is a demanding occupation, with owners often working six or seven days a week. Working more than 60 hours a week is not unusual, especially during the Christmas season and other busy times. An owner of a large establishment may be able to leave a manager in charge of many parts of the business, but the owner still must be available to solve any pressing concerns. Owners of small businesses often stay in the store throughout the day, spending much of the time on their feet.

A retail business owner may occasionally travel out of town to attend conferences or to solicit new customers and product information. An owner of a small business, especially, should develop a close relationship with steady customers.

■ Outlook

There are more than 175,000 retail business owners in the United States. This number is expected to grow about as fast as the average for all occupations through the year 2006.

The retail field is extremely competitive, and many businesses fail each year. The most common reason for failure is poor management. Thus people with some managerial experience or training will likely have the best chance at running a successful business.

■ For More Information

For a business starter packet with information about their loan program and services, and basic facts about starting a business, contact:

U.S. Small Business Administration
409 Third Street, SW
Washington, DC 20416
Tel: 800-827-5722

The following foundation conducts research and analysis of women-owned businesses.

National Foundation for Women Business Owners (NFWBO)
100 Wayne Avenue, Suite 830
Silver Springs, MD 20910-5602
Tel: 301-495-4979

For materials on educational programs in the retail industry, contact:

National Retail Federation
325 7th Street, NW, Suite 1000
Washington, DC 20004
Tel: 202-783-7971
Web: http://www.nrf.com

■ Related Articles

Business

Entrepreneurs

Sales

Counter and Retail Clerks

Retail Managers

Retail Sales Workers

Sales Representatives

Services Sales Representatives

Retail Managers

■ Overview

Retail managers are responsible for the profitable operation of retail trade establishments. They oversee the selling of food, clothing, furniture, sporting goods, novelties, and many other items. Their duties include hiring, training, and supervising other employees, maintaining the physical facilities, managing inventory, monitoring expenditures and receipts, and maintaining good public relations.

■ History

In the United States, small, family-owned stores have been around for centuries. The first large chain store began to operate in the late 19th century. One of the aims of early chain stores was to provide staples for the pioneers of the newly settled West. Because chain store corporations were able to buy goods in large quantities and store them in warehouses, they were able to undersell private merchants.

The number of retail stores, especially supermarkets, began to grow rapidly during the 1930s. Stores often were owned and operated by chain corporations, which were able to benefit from bulk buying and more sophisticated storage practices. Cheaper transportation also contributed to the growth of retail stores because goods could be shipped and sold more economically.

Unlike the early family-owned stores, giant retail outlets employed large numbers of people, requiring various levels of management to oversee the business. Retail managers were hired to oversee particular areas within department stores, for example, but higher-level managers also were needed to make more general decisions about a company's goals and policies. Today, retailing is one of the nation's largest industries, employing more than five million people.

■ The Job

Retail managers are responsible for every phase of a store's operation. They often are one of the first employees to arrive in the morning and the last to leave at night. Their duties include hiring, training, and supervising other employees, maintaining the physical facilities, managing inventory, monitoring expenditures and receipts, and maintaining good public relations.

Perhaps the most important responsibility is hiring and training qualified employees. Managers then assign duties to employees, monitor their progress, promote employees, and increase salaries when appropriate. When an employee is not performing satisfactorily, a manager must find a way to improve the performance or, if necessary, fire him or her.

Managers should be good at working with people. Differences of opinion and personality clashes among employees are inevitable, and the manager must be able to restore good feelings among the staff. Managers often have to deal with customers' grievances and must attempt to restore goodwill toward the store when customers are dissatisfied.

Retail managers keep accurate and up-to-date records of store inventory. When new merchandise arrives, the manager ensures items are recorded, priced, and displayed or shelved. They must know when stock is getting low and order new items in a timely manner.

Some managers are responsible for advertising and merchandise promotions. The manager may confer with an advertising agency representative to determine appropriate advertising for the store. The manager also may decide what products to put on sale for advertising purposes.

The duties of store managers vary according to the type of merchandise sold, size of store, and number of employees. In small, owner-operated stores, managers often are involved in accounting, data processing, marketing, research, sales, and shipping. In large retail corporations, however, managers may be involved in only one or two activities.

■ Requirements

High School

A minimum high school education generally is required for this position. Helpful courses include English, mathematics, marketing, and economics.

Postsecondary Training

Most retail stores prefer applicants with a college degree, and many hire only college graduates. Liberal arts, social sciences, and business are the most common degrees held by retail managers.

To prepare for a career as a retail store manager, students should take courses in accounting, business, marketing, English, advertising, and computer science. If you are unable to attend college as a full-time student, you should consider obtaining a job in a store to gain experience and attend college part time. All managers, regardless of their education, must have good marketing, analytical, communications, and people skills.

Many large retail stores and national chains have established formal training programs, including classroom instruction, for their new employees. The training period may last a week or as long as one year. Training for a department store manager, for example, may include working as a salesperson in several departments in order to learn about the store's operations.

Other Requirements

A retail manager may put in very long hours. He or she should have good communication skills and enjoy working with and supervising people. Diplomacy often is necessary when creating schedules for workers and in

RETAIL MANAGERS	
SCHOOL SUBJECTS	Business Mathematics
PERSONAL SKILLS	Helping/teaching Leadership/management
WORK ENVIRONMENT	Primarily indoors Primarily one location
MINIMUM EDUCATION LEVEL	High school diploma
SALARY RANGE	$18,000 to $40,000 to $100,000+
CERTIFICATION OR LICENSING	None available
OUTLOOK	About as fast as the average
DOT	185
GOE	11.11.05
NOC	6211
O*NET	19005B

disciplinary matters. There is a great deal of responsibility in retail management and such positions often are stressful. A calm disposition and ability to handle stress will serve the manager well.

■ Exploring

People interested in becoming retail managers may be able to find part-time, weekend, or summer jobs in a clothing store, supermarket, or other retail trade establishment. Students can gain valuable work experience through such jobs and will have the opportunity to observe the retail industry to determine whether they are interested in pursuing a career in it. It also is useful to read periodicals that publish articles on the retail field, such as *Stores* (http://www.stores.org), published by the National Retail Federation.

■ Employers

Nearly every type of retail business requires management, though small businesses may be run by their owners. Wherever retail sales are made there is an opportunity for a management position, though you may have to begin in a much lower job. The food industry employs more workers than nearly any other and retail food businesses always need managers, though smaller ones may not pay very well. In general, the larger the business and the bigger the city, the more you can earn.

■ Starting Out

Many new college graduates are able to find managerial positions through their schools' placement service. Some of the large retail chains engage in campus recruitment.

Not all store managers, however, are college graduates. Many store managers are promoted to their positions from jobs of less responsibility within the organization. Some may be in the retail industry for more than a dozen years before being promoted. Those with more education often receive promotions faster.

Regardless of educational background, people who are interested in the retail industry should consider working in a retail store at least part time or during the summer. Although there may not be an opening when the application is made, there often is a high turnover of employees in retail management, and vacancies occur from time to time.

■ Advancement

Advancement opportunities in retailing vary according to the size of the store, where the store is located, and the type of merchandise sold. Advancement also depends on the individual's work experience and educational background.

A store manager who works for a large retail chain, for example, may be given responsibility for a number of stores

LEARN MORE ABOUT IT

Farber, Barry J. *Superstar Sales Managers' Secrets.* Franklin Lakes, NJ: Career Press, 1995.

Garofalo, Gene. *Sales Manager's Desk Book.* Englewood Cliffs, NJ: Prentice-Hall, 1996.

Henry, Porter. *Secrets of the Master Sales Managers.* New York: AMACOM, 1993.

in a given area or region or transferred to a larger store in another city. Willingness to relocate to a new city may increase an employee's promotional opportunities.

Some managers decide to open their own stores after they have acquired enough experience in the retail industry. After working as a retail manager for a large chain of clothing stores, for example, a person may decide to open a small boutique.

Sometimes becoming a retail manager involves a series of promotions. A person who works in a supermarket, for example, may advance from clerk, checker, or bagger, to a regular assignment in one of several departments in the store. After a period of time, he or she may become an assistant manager and eventually, a manager.

■ Earnings

Salaries depend on the size of the store, the responsibilities of the job, and the number of customers served. Some managers earn as little as $12,900 but median earnings are about $24,400. Experienced managers average about $40,000 and the top 10 percent earn more than $50,400. Salaries in smaller stores are lower. Those who oversee and entire region for a retail chain can earn more than $100,000.

In addition to a salary, some stores offer their managers special bonuses, or commissions, which are typically connected to the store's performance. Many stores also offer employee discounts on store merchandise.

■ Work Environment

Most retail stores are pleasant places to work, and managers often are given comfortable offices. Many, however, work long hours. Managers often work six days a week and as many as 60 hours a week, especially during busy times of the year such as the Christmas season. Because holiday seasons are peak shopping periods, it is extremely rare that managers can take holidays off or schedule vacations around a holiday, even if the store is not open on that day.

Although managers usually can get away from the store during slack times, often they must be present if the store is open at night. It is important that the manager be available to handle the store's daily receipts, which usually are put in a safe or taken to a bank's night depository at the close of the business day.

■ Outlook

Although some retailers have reduced their management staff to cut costs and make operations more efficient, there still are good opportunities in retailing. In fact, despite these cuts, the number of retail managers is expected to increase as fast as the average for all occupations through the year 2006. However, competition for jobs probably will continue to increase, and computerized systems for inventory control may reduce the need for some managers. Applicants with the best educational backgrounds and work experience will have the best chances of finding jobs.

■ For More Information

For materials on educational programs in the retail industry, contact:

National Retail Federation
325 7th Street, NW, Suite 1000
Washington, DC 20004
Attn: Vice President of Research, Education and Community Affairs
Tel: 202-783-7971
Web: http://www.nrf.com

For a copy of "How Many People Does It Take to Sell a Lightbulb?" which describes jobs in retail, contact:

International Mass Retail Association
1700 N. Moore Street, Suite 2250
Arlington, VA 22209
Tel: 703-841-2300
Web: http://www.imra.org
Web: http://www.massretailcareers.com

■ Related Articles

Business
Entrepreneurs
Auctioneers
Buyers
Cashiers
Counter and Retail Clerks
Merchandise Displayers
Purchasing Agents
Retail Business Owners
Retail Managers
Retail Sales Workers
Sales Representatives
Services Sales Representatives
Stock Clerks

Retail Sales Workers

■ Overview

Retail sales workers assist customers with purchases by identifying their needs, showing or demonstrating merchandise, receiving payment, recording sales, and wrapping their purchases or arranging for their delivery. They are sometimes called *sales clerks, retail clerks,* or *salespeople.*

■ History

The development of retailing has paralleled the growth of civilization. When planning their cities, the Greeks and Romans established large marketplaces where individual merchants could display and sell their wares. As Europe emerged from the Middle Ages, organized trade began again with the development of medieval fairs. During the 13th century, more than three thousand fairs were held on a regular basis. By the 15th century, weekly markets in various cities began to replace the fairs.

As specialization in manufacture developed, the medieval artisan appeared. The artisans were craft workers, such as weavers and metalsmiths, who sold the products they made. Most of the goods they produced were made after they received a specific order from a customer.

The Industrial Revolution and its techniques of mass production encouraged the development of specialized retail establishments. The first retail outlets in the United States were trading posts and general stores. At trading posts, goods obtained from Naative Americans were exchanged for items imported from Europe or manufactured in the eastern United States. Trading posts had to be located on the fringes of settlements and relocated to follow the westward movement of the frontier. As villages and towns grew, what had been trading posts frequently developed into general stores. General stores sold food staples, farm necessities, and clothing. They often served as the local post office and became the social and economic centers of their communities. They were sometimes known as dry goods stores.

A number of changes occurred in the retail field during the second half of the 19th century. The growth of specialized retail stores (such as hardware, feed, grocery, and drug stores) reflected the growing sophistication of available products and customer tastes. The first grocery chain store, which started in New York City in 1859, led to a new concept in retailing. Later, merchants such as Marshall Field developed huge department stores, so named because of their large number of separate departments. Their variety of merchandise, ability to advertise their products, and low selling prices contributed to the rapid growth and success of these stores. Retail sales workers staffed the departments, and for the public they became the stores' primary representatives.

The 20th century witnessed the birth of supermarkets and suburban shopping centers, the emergence of discount houses, and the expansion of credit buying. Today, retailing is the second largest industry in the United States. Grocery stores and chains have the highest annual sales in the retail field—followed, in order of size, by automobile dealers, department stores, restaurants and cafeterias, lumber and building suppliers, drug and proprietary stores, furniture stores, variety stores, liquor stores, hardware stores, and jewelry stores. All of these retailers hire sales workers.

■ The Job

Salespeople work in more than a hundred different types of retail establishments in a variety of roles. Some, for example, work in small specialty shops where, in addition to waiting on customers, they might check inventory, order stock from sales representatives (or by telephone or mail), place newspaper display advertisements, prepare window displays, and rearrange merchandise for sale.

Other salespeople may work in specific departments, such as the furniture department, of a large department store. The employees in a department work in shifts to provide service to customers six or seven days a week. To improve their sales effectiveness and knowledge of merchandise, they attend regular staff meetings. The work of retail salespeople is supported by advertising, window decorating, sales promotion, buying, and market research specialists.

Whatever they are selling, the primary responsibility of retail sales workers is to interest customers in the merchandise. This might be done by describing the product's features, demonstrating its use, or showing various models and colors. Some retail sales workers must have specialized knowledge, particularly those who sell such expensive, complicated products as stereos, appliances, and personal computers.

In addition to selling, most retail sales workers make out sales checks; receive cash, check, and charge payments; bag or package purchases; and give change and receipts. Depending on the hours they work, retail sales workers might have to open or close the cash register. This might include counting the money in the cash register; separating charge slips, coupons, and exchange vouchers; and making deposits at the cash office. The sales records they keep are normally used in inventory control. Sales workers are often held responsible for the contents of their registers, and repeated shortages are cause for dismissal in many organizations.

Sales workers must be aware of any promotions the store is sponsoring and know the store's policies and procedures, especially on returns and exchanges. Also, they often must recognize possible security risks and know how to handle such situations.

Consumers often form their impressions of a store by its sales force. To stay ahead in the fiercely competitive retail industry, employers are increasingly stressing the importance of providing courteous and efficient service. When a customer wants an item that is not on the sales floor, for example, the sales worker might be expected to check the stockroom and, if necessary, place a special order or call another store to locate the item.

■ Requirements

High School

Employers generally prefer to hire high school graduates for most sales positions. Such subjects as English, speech, and mathematics provide a good background for these jobs. Many high schools and two-year colleges have special programs that include courses in merchandising, principles of retailing, and retail selling.

Postsecondary Training

In retail sales, as in other fields, the level of opportunity tends to coincide with the level of a person's education. In many stores, college graduates enter immediately into on-the-job training programs to prepare them for management assignments. Successful and experienced workers who do not have a degree might also qualify for these programs. Useful college courses include economics, business administration, and marketing. Many colleges offer majors in retailing. Executives in many companies express a strong preference for liberal arts graduates, especially those with some business courses or a master's degree in business administration.

RETAIL SALES WORKERS	
SCHOOL SUBJECTS	English Mathematics Speech
PERSONAL SKILLS	Helping/teaching Communication/ideas
WORK ENVIRONMENT	Primarily indoors Primarily one location
MINIMUM EDUCATION LEVEL	High school diploma
SALARY RANGE	$8,840 to $18,096 to $31,800
CERTIFICATION OR LICENSING	None available
OUTLOOK	About as fast as the average
DOT	290
GOE	09.04.02
NOC	6421
O*NET	49011

A retail sales worker discusses a custom furniture contract with his customers

Other Requirements

The retail sales worker must be in good health. Many selling positions require standing most of the day. The sales worker must have stamina to face the grueling pace of busy times, such as weekends and the Christmas season, while at the same time remaining pleasant and effective. Personal appearance is important. Salespeople should be neat and well groomed and have an outgoing personality.

A pleasant speaking voice, natural friendliness, tact, and patience are all helpful personal characteristics. The sales worker must be able to converse easily with strangers of all ages. In addition to interpersonal skills, sales workers must be equally good with figures. They should be able to add and subtract accurately and quickly and operate cash registers and other types of business machines.

Most states have established minimum standards that govern retail employment. Some states set a minimum age of 14, require at least a high school diploma, or prohibit more than 8 hours of work a day or 48 hours in any 6 days. These requirements are often relaxed for those people employed during the Christmas season.

■ Exploring

Because of its seasonal nature, retailing offers numerous opportunities for temporary or part-time sales experience. Most stores add extra personnel for the Christmas season. Vacation areas may hire sales employees, usually high school or college students. Fewer sales positions are available in metropolitan areas during the summer, as this is frequently the slowest time of the year.

Many high schools and junior colleges have developed "distributive education" programs that combine courses in retailing with part-time work in the field. The distributive education student may receive academic credit for this

work experience in addition to regular wages. Store owners cooperating in these programs often hire students as full-time personnel upon completion of the program.

■ Employers

There are more than a hundred different types of retail establishments. Among these are small specialty shops, large department stores, retail chains, and drug, variety, and grocery stores. Sales workers are needed in all of these.

■ Starting Out

If they have openings, retail stores usually hire beginning salespeople who come in and fill out an application. Major department stores maintain extensive personnel departments, while in smaller stores the manager might do the hiring. Occasionally, sales applicants are given an aptitude test.

Young people might be hired immediately for sales positions. Often, however, they begin by working in the stockroom as clerks, helping to set up merchandise displays, or assisting in the receiving or shipping departments. After a while they might be moved up to a sales assignment.

Training varies with the type and size of the store. In large stores, the beginner might benefit from formal training courses that discuss sales techniques, store policies, the mechanics of recording sales, and an overview of the entire store. Programs of this type are usually followed by on-the-job sales supervision. The beginner in a small store might receive personal instruction from the manager or a senior sales worker, followed by supervised sales experience.

College graduates and people with successful sales experience often enter executive training programs (sometimes referred to as "flying squads" because they move rapidly through different parts of the store). As they rotate through various departments, the trainees are exposed to merchandising methods, stock and inventory control, advertising, buying, credit, and personnel. By spending time in each of these areas, trainees receive a broad retailing background designed to help them as they advance into the ranks of management.

■ Advancement

Large stores have the most opportunities for promotion. Retailing, however, is a mobile field, and successful and experienced people can readily change employment. This is one of the few fields where, if the salesperson has the necessary initiative and ability, advancement to executive positions is possible regardless of education.

When first on the job, sales workers develop their career potential by specializing in a particular line of merchandise. They become authorities on a certain product line, such as sporting equipment, women's suits, or building materials. Many good sales workers prefer the role of the senior sales worker and remain at this level. Others might be asked to become supervisor of a section. Eventually they might develop into a department manager, floor manager, division or branch manager, or general manager.

People with sales experience often enter related areas, such as buying. Other retail store workers advance into support areas, such as personnel, accounting, public relations, and credit.

Young people with ability find that retailing offers the opportunity for unusually rapid advancement. One study revealed that half of all retail executives are under 35 years of age. It is not uncommon for a person under 35 to be in charge of a retail store or department with an annual sales volume of over $1,000,000. Conversely, the retail executive who makes bad merchandising judgments might quickly be out of a job.

■ Earnings

Most beginning sales workers start at the federal minimum wage, which is currently $5.15 an hour. Wages vary greatly, depending primarily on the type of store and the degree of skill required. Businesses might offer higher wages to attract and retain workers. Some sales workers make as much as $12 an hour or more.

Department stores or retail chains might pay more than smaller stores. Higher wages are paid for positions requiring a greater degree of skill. Many sales workers also receive a commission (often 4 to 8 percent) on their sales or are paid solely on commission. According to the 1998-99 *Occupational Outlook Handbook,* sales workers earned the following average annual salaries: motor vehicles and boats, $30,836; apparel, $13,780; furniture and home furnishings, $20,956; and various door-to-door sales, $19,344.

Salespeople in many retail stores are allowed a discount on their own purchases, ranging from 10 to 25 percent. This privilege is sometimes extended to the worker's family. Meals in the employee cafeterias maintained by large stores might be served at a price that is below cost. Many stores provide sick leave, medical and life insurance, and retirement benefits. Most stores give paid vacations.

■ Work Environment

Retail sales workers generally work in clean, comfortable, well-lighted areas. Those with seniority have reasonably good job security. When business is slow, stores might curtail hiring and not fill vacancies that occur. Most stores, however, are able to weather mild business recessions without having to release experienced sales workers. During periods of economic recession, competition among salespeople for job openings can become intense.

With nearly two million retail stores across the country, sales positions are found in every region. An experienced salesperson can find employment in almost any state. The vast majority of positions, however, are located in large cities or suburban areas.

The 5-day, 40-hour workweek is the exception rather than the rule in retailing. Most salespeople can expect to work some evening and weekend hours, and longer than normal hours might be scheduled during Christmas and other peak periods. In addition, most retailers restrict the use of vacation time between Thanksgiving and early January. Most sales workers receive overtime pay during Christmas and other rush seasons. Part-time salespeople generally work at peak hours of business, supplementing the full-time staff. Because competition in the retailing business is keen, many retailers work under pressure. The sales worker might not be directly involved but will feel the pressures of the industry in subtle ways. The sales worker must be able to adjust to alternating periods of high activity and dull monotony. No two days—or even customers— are alike. Because some customers are hostile and rude, salespeople must learn to exercise tact and patience at all times.

■ Outlook

In 1996, about 4,522,000 people were employed as sales workers in retail stores of all types and sizes. The employment of sales personnel should grow about as fast as the average for all occupations through 2006. Turnover among sales workers is much higher than average. Many of the expected employment opportunities will stem from the need to replace workers. Other positions will result from existing stores' staffing for longer business hours or reducing the length of the average employee workweek.

Several factors—the full effects of which have yet to be measured—might reduce the long-range demand for sales personnel. As drug, variety, grocery, and other stores rapidly convert to self-service operations, they will need fewer sales workers. In contrast, many other stores are trying to stay competitive by offering better customer service and more sales staff attention.

At the same time, many products (such as stereo components, electrical appliances, computers, and sporting goods) do not lend themselves to self-service operations. These products require extremely skilled sales workers to assist customers and explain the benefits of various makes and models. On balance, as easy-to-sell goods will be increasingly marketed in self-service stores, the demand in the future will be strongest for sales workers who are knowledgeable about particular types of products.

During economic recessions, sales volume and the resulting demand for sales workers generally decline. Purchases of costly items, such as cars, appliances, and furniture, tend to be postponed during difficult economic times. In areas of high unemployment, sales of all types of goods might decline. Since turnover of sales workers is usually very high, however, employers often can cut payrolls simply by not replacing all those who leave.

There should continue to be good opportunities for temporary and part-time workers, especially during the holidays. Stores are particularly interested in people who, by returning year after year, develop good sales backgrounds.

■ For More Information

For materials on educational programs in the retail industry, contact:

National Retail Federation
325 7th Street, NW, Suite 1000
Washington, DC 20004
Tel: 202-783-7971
Web: http://www.nrf.com

■ Related Articles

Business
Sales
Auctioneers
Buyers
Cashiers
Counter and Retail Clerks
Merchandise Displayers
Purchasing Agents
Retail Business Owners
Retail Managers
Sales Representatives
Services Sales Representatives
Stock Clerks

Retailers

■ **See Sales**

Retainer Recruiters

■ **See Executive Recruiters**

Retirement Planners

■ Overview

Financial planners help people invest for the future. *Retirement planners* are financial planners who specialize in the financial needs and concerns of people planning for retirement. Some retirement planners work for corporations of all sizes; many others are self-employed. In 1999, the American Association of Retired Persons (AARP), estimated that approximately 250,000 to 400,000 people worked as financial planners in some capacity. Retirement planners have diverse backgrounds in fields such as banking, accounting, law, and life insurance.

■ History

In the 20th century, several factors, including population growth, technological advances, and work efficiency, greatly affected employment for older employees. As the pool of young workers grew, employers began to set work age restrictions that were altered by several laws through the years. (However, in 1986, a federal law was passed that prohibited mandatory retirement for most workers.) The Social Security Act of 1935 gave workers and their families, among other social welfare programs, retirement benefits. Depending on the age of retirement, insured workers receive monthly benefits—full benefits are allowed after age 65; early retirement after age 62 allows for 80 percent of benefits. Workers who choose to work beyond age 65 receive increased benefits.

However, most people have found Social Security insufficient, especially to maintain their previous standard of living during their retirement years. To supplement retirement income, people have increasingly relied on pension plans; company profit-sharing; individual retirement accounts, (IRA); and other forms of investments. Today, new workers, as well as those quite familiar to the employment grind, are aware of the importance of saving and planning for retirement. They often turn to knowledgeable professionals for financial advice and strategies. Retirement planners grew as a specialty from traditional financial planning services. Such planners and counselors are in demand to create and administer financial retirement plans. They also address other important retirement issues such as relocation, medical insurance needs, income tax, wills, and estate planning.

■ The Job

Jan Perogstat knows the importance of saving for the future. Having been a financial planner for Mayster & Hambourger for the past four years, and in the banking and mutual fund industries before that, she has considerable experience in financial planning, and advocates the idea of managing and investing money wisely for the future. Financial planners like Jan, especially those specializing in retirement issues, tailor saving strategies to ensure that a client can live a comfortable lifestyle during their retirement years.

"The first part of the task," says Jan, "is gathering the information." She must ascertain a client's net worth by collecting tax forms, insurance papers, and data regarding income, assets and debts, and trusts, among other information. Jan then determines what the client's needs and goals will be for their retirement years. There is a big difference between simple living and first class travel to exotic locales. Relocation and medical insurance are also major concerns to address. Once the data is compiled Jan researches, and presents the best means to achieve the client's retirement objectives.

A good retirement planner will assess a client's financial history—pointing out relevant areas such as tax returns, insurance policies, company savings plans, and investments. Planners also identify what areas, if any, a client needs to strengthen, such as improving investment returns or consolidating debts. They will discuss investment preferences and risk levels comfortable to the client. Traditional sources of retirement funds include Social Security, personal savings (IRAs, stocks and bonds, real estate, and other investments), employer-sponsored plans, post retirement employment, and inheritance.

Retirement planners also help prepare clients for the possibility of incapacity, disability, and the need for chronic illness care during retirement. Disability income insurance, long-term care insurance, or a medical savings account may be suggested as precautions for such situations. Many companies, in an attempt to restructure or downsize, offer their employees the option for early retirement, complete with incentives. Retirement planners are consulted on the benefits or downfalls of early retirement.

Jan keeps in touch with her clients quarterly. The economy and stock market are often volatile, and clients' needs and situations change, so it is imperative to make reassessments. A yearly reevaluation is the minimum. "I like to help people with their financial future," says Jan. She educates her clients by bringing a level of specialized knowledge to them. When asked if it is ever too late to save for retirement, Jan asserts, "Never!"

■ Requirements

High School

Take as many business and mathematics courses in high school as possible. Speech classes will help you hone your oral communication skills, while English classes will give you the basics necessary to write reports for your clients.

Postsecondary Training

Earning a bachelor's degree starts financial planners on the right track, but it will help if your degree indicates a skill with numbers, be it in science or business. A business administration degree with a specialization in financial planning or a liberal arts degree with courses in accounting, business administration, economics, finance, marketing, human behavior, counseling, and public speaking is excellent preparation for this sort of job.

Certification or Licensing

Because of their diverse backgrounds, financial planners have many different educational degrees and licenses. Planners who seek specialized training can earn credentials such as Chartered Financial Consultant (ChFC) or Certified Financial Planner (CFP). Professionals who wish to specialize in retirement issues, may opt to become a Chartered Retirement Plans Specialist (CRPS), or a Chartered Retirement Planning Counselor (CRPC). What's the difference between the two? CRPSs advise businesses on employee retirement plans, while CRPCs work with individuals who are retired or nearing retirement age.

Certification requirements vary depending on the specialty, though all programs demand continuing education credits for yearly recertification.

Other Requirements

This job will require you to be in constant contact with your customers. You will need excellent communication skills, as well as be comfortable dealing with all kinds of people. "Gaining a customer's trust," says Jan, "is all important in this industry." The most successful planner is able to express and deliver a sense of expertise and professionalism to his or her clients.

■ Exploring

Are you wondering if this is the job for you? Start by checking out the financial planning information available on the Internet to familiarize yourself with the industry. Jan suggests interning with a financial planner or brokerage house to get work experience, as well as an insider's peak at the industry.

RETIREMENT PLANNERS	
SCHOOL SUBJECTS	Business Mathematics
PERSONAL SKILLS	Helping/teaching Leadership/management
WORK ENVIRONMENT	Primarily indoors One location with some travel
MINIMUM EDUCATION LEVEL	Bachelor's degree
SALARY RANGE	$25,000 to $50,000 to $100,000+
CERTIFICATION OR LICENSING	Recommended
OUTLOOK	Faster than the average

Employers

Retirement planners are employed by businesses such as consulting firms, brokerage houses, accounting firms, and banks. Some retirement planners are self-employed. Numerous planners have careers in related fields such as accounting, insurance, real estate, and do consulting on a part-time basis.

Starting Out

Retirement planning is a specialty that takes special training and education. Many, like Jan, transfer to financial planning after working in related fields. Most college graduates interested in this career would probably start at a brokerage house like Charles Schwab or Merrill Lynch earning a base salary plus commission.

Does your school have a job placement program or career center? If so, take advantage of the information and services they offer. Also, consider job fairs, newspaper wants ads—look under finance or employment recruiters. Do you know any financial planners? Pick their brains on the best ways to enter the business.

Advancement

Advancement in this occupation can take several forms. For some, this may mean working towards having a larger, more diverse client base. Others may consider starting their own financial consulting business.

Self-employed retirement planners need to be responsible for numerous details of running a business—accounting, insurance, overhead costs—as well as finding your customer leads and referrals. Being your own boss may sound appealing, but it carries much responsibility, not to mention risk. You may first want to speak with others in the industry to weigh the pros and cons of self-employment.

Earnings

Many retirement planners earn part of their annual salaries from commissions on the products they sell; some work strictly on commission. Starting annual earning for this industry is about $25,000 to $30,000 base plus commissions. With work experience, planners can build their roster of clients, thus raising their income.

Work Environment

Most retirement planners work 40 hours or more a week, depending on the number of clients and businesses they represent. The majority of their work day is spent in the office doing research or meeting with clients. However, financial planners may also travel to their client's business, home, or other designated place.

Outlook

In 1997, according to the *Profile of Older Americans*, conducted by the Administration On Aging (AOA), there were 34.1 million people living in the United States aged 65 years or older. This number is expected to dramatically increase through the year 2030, as the "baby boom" generation reaches retirement age. The AOA estimates there will be about 70 million people 65 or older by the year 2030, more than double the current figure.

The government's Social Security system is often not enough to meet the financial needs of seniors as they continue to live longer and more productively. People are increasingly dependent on pension plans, savings plans, and investments to help maintain a comfortable standard of living through their retirement years. Financial planners, especially those that specialize in retirement plans, will be in high demand for their advice and recommendations on the best way to build and manage retirement funds. Job opportunities for certified retirement planners, whether affiliated with a company or self-employed, will be plentiful.

For More Information

For information on financial planning and certification, contact:

Certified Financial Planner Board of Standards
1700 Broadway, Suite 2100
Denver, CO 80290-2101
Tel: 303-830-7500
Web: http://www.cfp-board.org

For information on educational opportunities, contact:

College of Financial Planning
6161 South Syracuse Way
Greenwood Village, CO 80111-4707
Tel: 303-220-1200
Web: http://www.fp.edu

For information on the Certified Financial Planner designation, contact:

Institute of Certified Financial Planners
3801 East Florida Avenue, Suite 708
Denver, CO 80210-2544
Tel: 303-759-4900
Web: http://www.icfp.org

Related Articles

Banking and Financial Services

Accountants and Auditors

Commodities Brokers

Economists

Financial Planners

Financial Services Brokers

Tax Preparers

Retouchers

■ **See Prepress Workers**

Revenue Officers

■ **See Health and Regulatory Inspectors**

Ride Attendants and Operators

■ **See Amusement Park Workers**

Rig Builders

■ **See Petroleum**

Risk Managers

■ Overview

Risk managers help businesses control risks and losses while maintaining the highest production levels possible. They work in industrial, service, nonprofit, and public-sector organizations. By protecting a company against loss, the risk manager helps it to improve operating efficiency and meet strategic goals.

■ History

Entrepreneurs have always taken steps to prevent losses or damage to their businesses. Only since the mid-1950s, however, has risk management developed into a specialized field. During the Industrial Revolution, business owners recognized that as production levels increased, risks increased at the same rate. The risks were often managed at the expense of worker health and safety.

With the rapid growth of technology came greater and more varied risks. Risk management changed from simply buying insurance against risks, to planning a wide variety of programs to prevent, minimize, and finance losses.

■ The Job

Risk management protects people, property, and inventory. For example, factories that use hazardous chemicals require employees to wear protective clothing; department stores use closed-circuit surveillance to minimize shoplifting and vandalism; and manufacturers have a plan of action to follow should their products injure consumers. The five general categories of risks are damage to property, loss of income from property damage, injury to others, fraud or criminal acts, and death or injury of employees.

Risk managers first identify and analyze potential losses. They examine the various risk management techniques and select the best ones, including how to pay for losses that may occur. After the chosen techniques are implemented, they closely monitor the results.

Risk management has two basic elements: risk control and risk finance. Risk control involves loss prevention techniques to reduce the frequency and lower the severity of losses. Risk managers make sure operations are safe. They see that employees are properly trained and that workers have and use safety equipment. This often involves conducting safety and loss prevention programs for employees. They make recommendations on the safe design of the workplace, and make plans in case of machinery breakdowns. They examine company contracts with suppliers to ensure a steady supply of raw materials.

Risk finance programs set aside funds to pay for losses not anticipated by risk control. Some losses can be covered by the company itself; others are covered by outside sources, such as insurance firms. Risk finance programs try to reduce costs of damage or loss, and include insurance programs to pay for losses.

Large organizations often have a risk management department with several employees who each specialize in one area, such as employee-related injuries, losses to plant property, automobile losses, and insurance coverage. Small organizations have risk managers who may serve as safety and training officers in

RISK MANAGERS	
SCHOOL SUBJECTS	Economics Mathematics
PERSONAL SKILLS	Communication/ideas Helping/teaching
WORK ENVIRONMENT	Primarily indoors One location with some travel
MINIMUM EDUCATION LEVEL	Bachelor's degree
SALARY RANGE	$21,800 to $40,700 to $81,100+
CERTIFICATION OR LICENSING	Recommended
OUTLOOK	About as fast as the average
DOT	186
GOE	11.06.03
NOC	0111

Two risk managers discuss the plans for a new building.

addition to handling workers' compensation and employee benefits.

■ Requirements

High School

Those interested in a risk management career should take high school courses in business, history, public administration, mathematics, accounting, and economics. Other helpful courses include physics, chemistry, engineering, law, management, and accounting.

Postsecondary Training

Risk managers generally need a college degree with a broad business background. A major in risk management or insurance is best, but other management or finance programs are appropriate, such as accounting, economics, engineering, finance, law, management, and political science. There are about 100 schools that offer courses or degrees in insurance and risk management.

Certification or Licensing

Many organizations require an MBA and an Associate in Risk Management (ARM) or the Canadian Risk Management (CRM) designation, offered by the Risk and Insurance Management Society (RIMS). Requirements for this designation include the completion of 3 graduate-level courses and 3 examinations. More than 15,000 people have completed the ARM and CRM educational programs to date.

The Risk and Insurance Management Society also offers an advanced designation in risk management. The Fellow in Risk Management (FRM) consists of 10 courses—the first 3 from ARM or CRM, with the additional 7 courses focusing on advanced issues in business, insurance, and risk management. Candidates must also pass an examination, sign off on a Code of Ethics, and complete continuing education requirements.

Other Requirements

Communications skills are important for risk managers. They must regularly interact with other departments, such as accounting, engineering, finance, human resources, environmental, legal, research and development, safety, and security. They must also be able to communicate with outside sources, such as attorneys, brokers, union officials, consultants, and insurance agents.

Risk managers must have analytical and problem-solving skills in order to foresee potential problem situations and recommend appropriate solutions. They must be able to examine and prepare reports on risk costs, loss statistics, cost-versus-benefit data, insurance costs, and depreciation of assets.

A knowledge of insurance fundamentals and risk financing is necessary. Risk managers must know loss-control issues such as employee health, worker and product safety, property safeguards, fire prevention, and environmental protection.

Management skills help risk managers set goals, plan strategies, delegate tasks, and measure and forecast results. Computer skills and familiarity with business law are also very helpful.

■ Exploring

You may wish to ask your family's insurance agent to help you contact a colleague who has commercial accounts and might introduce you to a risk manager for one of their larger clients.

The Risk and Insurance Management Society, Inc. (RIMS), is the largest organization for risk managers, with more than 9,000 members in 100 chapters in the United States and Canada. It offers books, monographs, a bimonthly newsletter, education programs, and an annual conference. Students may be able to attend local chapter meetings. The Spencer Educational Foundation, affiliated with RIMS, provides annual scholarships to academically outstanding full-time students of risk management and insurance. (See the "For More Information" for contact information.)

■ Employers

Airlines, banks, insurance companies, manufacturers, government agencies, municipalities, hospitals, retailers, school districts, and universities employ risk managers.

■ Starting Out

Most risk managers start with a bachelor's degree in risk management. College placement offices can put students in touch with recruiting officers from industries that employ risk managers. Recent graduates can also send resumes to employers of risk managers, such as corporations, service providers, government agencies, and other public and private organizations. Some risk managers join insurance companies, insurance brokerage firms, or consulting firms that provide risk management services to clients.

Some individuals gain experience and education while working in accounting or personnel departments and later move into risk management positions.

■ Advancement

There is good potential for advancement in the risk management field. Many risk managers work in a related field, such as in a human resources department handling employee benefits.

Risk managers may eventually head a personnel or finance department, become a human resources director, or join the insurance industry. Some become independent consultants. Membership in professional associations that offer networking opportunities can lead to better positions in the field.

Risk managers usually hold mid-level management positions, and often report to a financial officer. Some, however, become vice presidents or presidents of their organizations.

■ Earnings

Risk managers' salaries vary depending on level of responsibility and authority, type of industry, organization size, and geographic region. According to the *Occupational Outlook Handbook,* earnings for financial managers (which includes risk managers) range from $21,800 to $80,100 or more a year. The median annual salary for financial managers was $40,700 in 1996. Risk managers who work for the federal government generally earn less—$37,000 to $48,000 on the average.

Risk managers usually receive benefits, bonuses, paid vacation, health and life insurance, pensions, and stock options.

■ Work Environment

Risk managers work in a variety of settings from schools, stores, and government agencies to manufacturers and airlines. Most work in offices, not on the production line, but they may be required to spend some time in production departments. They may have to travel to study risks in other companies or to attend seminars.

Risk managers usually work a 40-hour week, Monday through Friday. They may have to spend much of their time at a computer, analyzing statistics and preparing reports.

■ Outlook

Since advanced technology continues to increase productivity as well as the potential for disaster, the need for risk management will continue to grow. Organizations now recognize risk management as an integral and effective tool for cost-containment. The profession will continue to gain recognition in the next decade, so salaries and career opportunities are expected to continue to escalate.

■ For More Information

The American Risk and Insurance Association has about 1,800 members whose goal is to further the science of risk and insurance through education, research, literature, and communications. The Association also offers student membership.

American Risk and Insurance Association
716 Providence Road
PO Box 3028
Malvern, PA 19355-0728
Tel: 610-640-1997
Web: http://www.aria.org/

The Public Risk Management Association has 2,200 risk managers employed in municipal and state governments.

Public Risk Management Association
1815 North Fort Myer Drive, Suite 1020
Arlington, VA 22209
Tel: 703-528-7701
Web: http://www.primacentral.org

For information on continuing education, internships, the ARM, CRM, and FRM designations, and student membership, contact:

Risk and Insurance Management Society, Inc.
655 Third Avenue
New York, NY 10017
Tel: 212-286-9292
Web: http://www.rims.org/

■ Related Articles

Accounting
Business
Insurance
Accountants and Auditors
Actuaries
Cost Estimators
Insurance Claims Representatives
Insurance Policy Processing Occupations
Insurance Underwriters
Life Insurance Agents and Brokers
Management Analysts and Consultants
Property and Casualty Insurance Agents and Brokers

Robot Assemblers, Field Technicians, and Operators

■ See Robotics Engineers and Technicians

Robotics Engineers and Technicians

■ Overview

Robotics engineers design, develop, build, and program robots and robotic devices, including peripheral equipment and computer software used to control robots. *Robotics technicians* assist robotics engineers in a wide variety of tasks relating to the design, development, production, testing, operation, repair, and maintenance of robots and robotic devices.

■ History

Robots are devices that perform tasks ordinarily performed by humans; they seem to operate with an almost-human intelligence. The idea of robots can be traced back to the ancient Greek and Egyptian civilizations. An inventor from

ROBOTICS ENGINEERS AND TECHNICIANS	
SCHOOL SUBJECTS	Computer science Mathematics
PERSONAL SKILLS	Mechanical/manipulative Technical/scientific
WORK ENVIRONMENT	Primarily indoors Primarily one location
MINIMUM EDUCATION LEVEL	Bachelor's degree
SALARY RANGE	$20,000 to $35,000 to $60,000
CERTIFICATION OR LICENSING	None available
OUTLOOK	About as fast as the average
DOT	019
O*NET	22197

the first century AD, Hero of Alexandria, invented a machine that would automatically open the doors of a temple when the priest lit a fire in the altar. During the later periods of the Middle Ages, the Renaissance, and the 17th and 18th centuries, interest in robot-like mechanisms turned mostly to automatons, devices that imitate human and animal appearance and activity but perform no useful task.

The Industrial Revolution inspired the invention of many different kinds of automatic machinery. One of the most important robotics inventions occurred in 1804: Joseph-Marie Jacquard's method for controlling machinery by means of a programmed set of instructions recorded on a punched paper tape that was fed into a machine to direct its movements.

The word *robot* and the concepts associated with it were first introduced in the early 1920s. They made their appearance in a play titled *R.U.R.,* which stands for Rossum's Universal Robots, written by Czechoslovakian dramatist Karel Capek. The play involves human-like robotic machines created to perform manual tasks for their human masters.

During the 1950s and 1960s, advances in the fields of automation and computer science led to the development of experimental robots that could imitate a wide range of human activity, including self-regulated and self-propelled movement (either on wheels or on legs), the ability to sense and manipulate objects, and the ability to select a course of action on the basis of conditions around them.

In 1954, George Devol designed the first programmable robot in the United States. He named it the Universal Automation, which was later shortened to Unimation, which also became the name of the first robot company. Hydraulic robots, controlled by numerical control programming, were developed in the 1960s and were used initially by the automobile industry in assembly line operations. By 1973, robots were being built with electric power and electronic controls, which allowed greater flexibility and increased uses.

Robotic technology has evolved significantly in the past few decades. Early robotic equipment, often referred to as first-generation robots, were simple mechanical arms or devices that could perform precise, repetitive motions at high speeds. They contained no artificial intelligence capabilities. Second-generation robots, which came into use in the 1980s, are controlled by minicomputers and programmed by computer language. They contain sensors, such as vision systems and pressure, proximity, and tactile sensors, which provide information about the outside environment. Third-generation robots, also controlled by minicomputers and equipped with sensory devices, are currently being developed. Referred to as "smart" robots, they can work on their own without supervision by an external computer or human being.

The evolution of robots is closely tied to the study of human anatomy and movement of the human body. The early robots were modeled after arms, then wrists. Second-generation robots include features that model human hands. Third-generation robots are being developed with legs and complex joint technology. They also incorporate multisensory input controls, such as ultrasonic sensors or sensors that can "sniff" and "taste."

■ The Job

The majority of robotics engineers and technicians work within the field of computer-integrated manufacturing or programmable automation. Using computer science technology, engineers design and develop robots and other automated equipment, including computer software used to program robots.

The title *robotics engineer* may be used to refer to any engineer who works primarily with robots. In many cases, these engineers may have been trained as mechanical, electronic, computer, or manufacturing engineers. A small, but growing, number of engineers trained specially in robotics are graduating from colleges and universities with robotics engineering or closely related degrees.

Robotics engineers have a thorough understanding of robotic systems and equipment and know the different technologies available to create robots for specific applications. They have a strong foundation in computer systems and how computers are linked to robots. They also have an understanding of manufacturing production requirements and how robots can best be used in automated systems to achieve cost efficiency, productivity, and quality. Robotics engineers may analyze and evaluate a manufacturer's operating system to determine whether robots can be used efficiently instead of other automated equipment or humans.

Many other types of engineers are also involved in the design, development, fabrication, programming, and operation of robots. Following are brief descriptions of these types of engineers and how they relate to robotics.

Electrical and electronics engineers research, design, and develop the electrical systems used in robots and the power supply, if it is electrical. These engineers may specialize in areas such as integrated circuit theory, lasers, electronic sensors, optical components, and energy power systems.

Mechanical engineers are involved in the design, fabrication, and operation of the mechanical systems of a robot. These engineers need a strong working knowledge of mechanical components such as gripper mechanisms, bearings, gears, chains, belts, and actuators. Some robots are controlled by pneumatic or mechanical power supplies and these engineers need to be specialists in designing these systems. Mechanical engineers also select the material used to make robots. They test robots once they are constructed.

This robotics technician operates a robot with a master unit in a control room. He uses video screens to observe the movements of the robot.

Computer engineers design the computer systems that are used to program robots. Sometimes these systems are built into a robot and other times they are a part of separate equipment that is used to control robots. Some computer engineers also write computer programs.

Industrial engineers are specialists in manufacturing operations. They determine the physical layout of a factory to best utilize production equipment. They may determine the placement of robotic equipment. They also are responsible for safety rules and practices and for ensuring that robotic equipment is used properly.

CAD/CAM engineers (computer-aided design/computer-aided manufacturing) are experts in automated production processes. They design and supervise manufacturing systems that utilize robots and other automated equipment.

Manufacturing engineers manage the entire production process. They may evaluate production operations to determine whether robots can be used in an assembly line and make recommendations on purchasing robotic equipment. Some manufacturing engineers design robots. Other engineers specialize in a specific area of robotics, such as artificial intelligence, vision systems, and sensor systems. These specialists are developing robots with "brains" that are similar to those of humans.

Robotics technicians assist in all phases of robotics engineering. They install, repair, and maintain finished robots. Others help design and develop new kinds of robotics equipment. Technicians who install, repair, and maintain robots and robotic equipment need knowledge of electronics, electrical circuitry, mechanics, pneumatics, hydraulics, and computer programming. They use hand and power tools, testing instruments, manuals, schematic diagrams, and blueprints.

Before installing new equipment, technicians review the work order and instructional information; verify that the intended site in the factory is correctly supplied with the necessary electrical wires, switches, circuit breakers, and other parts; position and secure the robot in place, sometimes using a crane or other large tools and equipment; and attach various cables and hoses, such as those that connect a hydraulic power unit with the robot. After making sure that the equipment is operational, technicians program the robot for specified tasks, using their knowledge of its programming language. They may write the detailed instructions that program robots or reprogram a robot when changes are needed.

Once robots are in place and functioning, they may develop problems. Technicians then test components and locate faulty parts. When the problem is found, they may replace or recalibrate parts. Sometimes they suggest changes in circuitry or programming, or may install different end-of-arm tools on robots to allow machines to perform new functions. They may train robotics operators in how to operate robots and related equipment and help establish in-house basic maintenance and repair programs at new installations.

Companies that only have a few robots don't always hire their own robotics technicians. Instead they use *robot field technicians* who work for a robotic manufacturer. These technicians travel to manufacturing sites and other locations where robots are used to repair and service robots and robotic equipment.

Technicians involved with the design and development of new robotic devices are sometimes referred to as *robotics design technicians*. As part of a design team, they work closely with robotics engineers. The robotics design job starts as the engineers analyze the tasks and settings to be assigned and decide what kind of robotics system will best serve the necessary functions. Technicians involved with robot assembly, sometimes referred to as *robot assemblers,* commonly specialize in one aspect of robot assembly. *Materials handling technicians* receive requests for components or materials, then locate and deliver them to the technicians doing the actual assembly or those performing tests on these materials or components. *Mechanical assembly technicians* put together components and subsystems and install them in the robot. *Electrical assembly technicians* do the same work as mechanical assembly technicians but specialize in electrical components such as circuit boards and automatic switching devices. Finally, some technicians test the finished assemblies to make sure the robot conforms to the original specifications.

Other kinds of robotics technicians include *robot operators,* who operate robots in specialized settings, and *robotics trainers,* who train other employees in the installation, use, and maintenance of robots.

Robotics technicians may also be referred to as *electromechanical technicians, manufacturing technicians, robot mechanics, robotics repairmen, robot service technicians,* and *installation robotics technicians.*

■ Requirements

High School

In high school, students should take as many science, math, and computer classes as possible. Recommended courses are biology, chemistry, physics, algebra, trigonometry, geometry, calculus, graphics, computer science, English, speech, composition, social studies, and drafting. In addition, students should take shop and vocational classes that teach blueprint and electrical schematic reading, the use of hand tools, drafting, and the basics of electricity and electronics.

Postsecondary Training

Because changes occur so rapidly within this field, it is often recommended that engineers and technicians get a broad-based education that encompasses robotics but does not focus solely on robotics. Programs that provide the widest career base are those in automated manufacturing, which includes robotics, electronics, and computer science.

In order to become an engineer it is necessary to earn a bachelor of science degree. These programs generally take four or five years to complete. More than 400 colleges and universities offer courses in robotics or related technology. Many different types of programs are available. Some colleges and universities offer robotics engineering degrees and others offer engineering degrees with concentrations or options in robotics and manufacturing engineering. For some higher-level jobs, such as robotics designer, a master of science or doctoral degree is required.

Although the minimum educational requirement for a robotics technician is a high school diploma, many employers prefer to hire technicians who have received formal training beyond high school. Two-year programs are available in community colleges and technical institutes that grant an associate's degree upon completion. The armed forces also offer technical programs that result in associate's degrees in electronics, biomedical equipment, and computer science. The military uses robotics and other advanced equipment and offers excellent training opportunities to members of the armed forces. This training is highly regarded by many employers and can be an advantage in obtaining a civilian job in robotics.

Other Requirements

Because the field of robotics is rapidly changing, one of the most important requirements for a person interested in a career in robotics is the willingness to pursue additional training on an ongoing basis during his or her career. After completing their formal education, engineers and technicians may need to take additional classes in a college or university or take advantage of training offered through their employers and professional associations.

People planning on becoming robotics technicians need manual dexterity, good hand-eye coordination, and mechanical and electrical aptitudes.

■ Exploring

People interested in robotics can explore this field in many different ways. Because it is such a new field, it is important to learn as much as possible about current trends and recent technologies. Reading books and articles in trade magazines provides an excellent way to learn about what is happening in robotics technologies and expected future trends. Trade magazines with informative articles include *Robotics Engineering, Robotics Quarterly, Personal Robotics Magazine,* and *Robotics Today.*

Students can become robot hobbyists and build their own robots or buy toy robots and experiment with them. Complete robot kits are available through a number of companies and range from simple, inexpensive robots to highly complex robots with advanced features and accessories. A number of books that give instructions and helpful hints on building robots can be found at most public libraries and bookstores. In addition, relatively inexpensive and simple toy robots are available from electronics shops, department stores, and mail order companies.

Students can also participate in competitions. The Robotics International of the Society of Manufacturing Engineers sponsors a contest called the Student Robotics Automation Contest. Held every year, it is open to middle school through university-level students. Eight different categories challenge students in areas such as problem-solving skills, robot construction, and teamwork ability. Another annual competition, the International Aerial Robotics Competition, is sponsored by the Association for Unmanned Vehicle Systems. This competition, which requires teams of students to build complex robots, is open to college students. (Addresses for both associations are listed at the end of this article.)

Another great way to learn about robotics is to attend trade shows. Many robotics and automated machinery manufacturers exhibit their products at shows and conventions. Numerous such trade shows are held every year in different parts of the country. Information about these trade shows is available through association trade magazines and periodicals such as *Managing Automation.*

Other activities that foster knowledge and skills relevant to a career in robotics include membership in high school science clubs, participation in science fairs, and pursuing hobbies that involve electronics, mechanical equipment, and model building.

■ Employers

Robotics engineers and technicians are employed in virtually every manufacturing industry. Within the trend toward automation continuing—often via the use of robots—people trained in robotics can expect to find employment with almost all types of manufacturing companies in the future.

■ Starting Out

Many people entered robotics technician positions in the 1980s and early 1990s who were formerly employed as automotive workers, machinists, millwrights, computer repair technicians, and computer operators. In the mid-1990s, some companies began retraining current employees to troubleshoot and repair robots rather than hiring new workers. Because of these trends, entry-level applicants without any work experience may have difficulty finding their first jobs. Students who have participated in a cooperative work program or internship have the advantage of some work experience.

Graduates of two- and four-year programs may learn about available openings through their schools' job placement services. It also may be possible to learn about job openings through want ads in newspapers and trade magazines.

In many cases, it will be necessary to research companies that manufacture or use robots and apply directly to them. A number of directories are available that list such companies. One such directory is *Robotics and Vision Supplier Directory.* It is available for purchase from the Robotic Industries Association. Other directories that may be available at public or college libraries include *The CAD/CAM Industry Directory* and *Robotics, CAD/CAM Marketplace.*

Job opportunities may be good at small start-up companies or a start-up robotics unit of a large company. Many times these employers are willing to hire inexperienced workers as apprentices or assistants. Then, when their sales and production grow, these workers have the best chances for advancement.

Robotics engineers also may have difficulty finding their first jobs as many companies have retrained existing engineers in robotics. Job hunters may learn about job openings through their colleges' job placement services, advertisements in professional magazines and newspapers, or job fairs. In addition, recruiters may come to colleges to interview graduating students for prospective positions. In many cases, though, applicants will need to research a company using robotics engineers and apply directly to it.

■ Advancement

Engineers may start as part of an engineering team and do relatively simple tasks under the supervision of a project manager or more experienced engineer. With experience and demonstrated competency, they can move into higher engineering positions. Engineers who demonstrate good interpersonal skills, leadership abilities, and technical expertise may become team leaders, project managers, or chief engineers. Engineers can also move into supervisory or management positions. Some engineers pursue an MBA (master of business administration) degree. These engineers are able to move into top management positions. Some engineers also develop specialties, such as artificial intelligence, and move into highly specialized engineering positions.

After several years on the job, robotics technicians who have demonstrated their ability to handle more responsibility may be assigned some supervisory work or, more likely, will train new technicians. Experienced technicians and engineers may teach courses at their workplace or find teaching opportunities at a local school or community college.

Other routes for advancement include becoming a sales representative for a robotics manufacturing or design firm or working as an independent contractor for companies that use or manufacture robots.

With additional training and education, such as a bachelor's degree, technicians can become eligible for positions as robotics engineers.

■ Earnings

Earnings and benefits in manufacturing companies vary widely based on the size of the company, geographic location, nature of the production process, and complexity of the robots. In general, engineers with a bachelor of science degree earn annual salaries between $32,000 and $35,000 in their first job after graduation. Engineers with several years of experience earn salaries ranging from $35,000 to $60,000 a year.

Robotics technicians who are graduates of a two-year technical program earn between $22,000 and $26,000 a year. With increased training and experience, technicians can earn much more. Technicians with special skills, extensive experience, or added responsibilities can earn $36,000 or more. Technicians involved in design and training generally earn the highest salaries, with experienced workers earning $45,000 or more a year; those involved with maintenance and repair earn relatively less, with some beginning at salaries around $20,000 a year.

Employers offer a variety of benefits that can include the following: paid holidays, vacations, personal days, and sick leave; medical, dental, disability, and life insurance; 401-K plans, pension and retirement plans; profit sharing; and educational assistance programs.

■ Work Environment

Robotics engineers and technicians may work either for a company that manufactures robots or a company that uses robots. Most companies that manufacture robots are relatively clean, quiet, and comfortable environments. Engineers and technicians may work in an office or on the production floor. A large number of robotics manufacturers are found in California, Michigan, Illinois, Indiana, Pennsylvania, Ohio, Connecticut, Texas, British Columbia, and Ontario, although companies exist in many other states and parts of Canada.

Engineers and technicians who work in a company that uses robots may work in noisy, hot, and dirty surroundings. Conditions vary based on the type of industry within which one works. Automobile manufacturers use a significant number of robots, as well as manufacturers of electronics components and consumer goods and the metalworking industry. Workers in a foundry work around heavy equipment and in hot and dirty environments. Workers in the electronics industry generally work in very clean and quiet environments. Some robotics personnel are required to work in clean room environments, which keep electronic components free of dirt and other contaminants. Workers in these environments wear face masks, hair coverings, and special protective clothing.

Some engineers and technicians may confront potentially hazardous conditions in the workplace. Robots, after all, are often designed and used precisely because the task they perform involves some risk to humans: handling laser beams, arc-welding equipment, radioactive substances, or hazardous chemicals. When they design, test, build, install, and repair robots, it is inevitable that some engineers and technicians will be exposed to these same risks. Plant safety procedures protect the attentive and cautious worker, but carelessness in such settings can be especially dangerous.

In general, most technicians and engineers work 40-hour workweeks, although overtime may be required for special projects or to repair equipment that is shutting down a production line. Some technicians, particularly those involved in maintenance and repairs, may work shifts that include evening, late night, or weekend work.

Field service technicians travel to manufacturing sites to repair robots. Their work may involve extensive travel and overnight stays. They may work at several sites in one day or stay at one location for an extended period for more difficult repairs.

■ Outlook

Employment opportunities for robotics engineers and technicians are closely tied to economic conditions in the United States and in the global marketplace. During the late 1980s and early 1990s, the robotics market suffered because of a lack of orders for robots and robotic equipment and intense foreign competition, especially from Japanese manufacturers.

In addition, many manufacturers reduced their number of employees significantly. Some companies cut their staffs by as many as 70,000 employees. Many companies that use large numbers of robotics personnel, such as those in the automobile industry, are represented by unions. These unions have agreements with companies that humans will not lose their jobs because of automation. When companies do downsize, existing workers are given priority and are retrained to work in positions such as robotics technicians. This makes it more difficult for inexperienced workers to enter the field.

However, in 1995, U.S. robot manufacturers shipped record numbers of robots and robotic equipment. In addition, some Japanese robot builders shifted production to U.S. facilities. After a slump of several years, it is expected that the robotics industry will once again pick up. Some robotics industry experts are predicting that during the next decade there will be a robotics boom and robotics sales will double.

The use of industrial robots is expected to grow as robots become more programmable and flexible and as manufacturing processes become more automated. Growth is also expected in nontraditional applications, such as education, health care, security, and nonindustrial purposes.

It is difficult to predict whether recent sales and the rising production of robots will increase employment opportunities, but trends for automated manufacturing equipment and a willingness by manufacturers to invest in capital expenditures are promising signs of growth. For prospective robotics engineers and technicians, this expansion suggests that more workers will be needed to design, build, install, maintain, repair, and operate robots.

■ For More Information

To purchase a copy of Robotics and Vision Supplier Directory *and for information on educational programs and student membership in the International Service Robot Association and Global Automation Information Network, contact:*

Robotic Industries Association
PO Box 3724
Ann Arbor, MI 48106
Tel: 313-994-6088
Web: http://www.robotics.org

For information on educational programs, competitions, and student membership in SME, Robotics International, or Machine Vision Association, contact:

Society of Manufacturing Engineers (SME)
Education Department
PO Box 930
Dearborn, MI 48121-0930
Tel: 313-271-1500
Web: http://www.sme.org

For information on careers and educational programs, contact:

Robotics and Automation Council
Institute of Electrical and Electronics Engineers (IEEE)
Education Information
345 East 47th Street
New York, NY 10017
Tel: 212-705-7900
Web: http://www.ieee.org

For information on competitions and student membership, contact:

Association for Unmanned Vehicle Systems
1735 North Lynn Street, Suite 950
Arlington, VA 22209
Tel: 703-524-6646

■ Related Articles

Computer Hardware

Electronics

Engineering

Manufacturing

Computer-Aided Design Drafters and Technicians

Electrical and Electronics Engineers

Electronics Engineering Technicians

Hardware Engineers

Industrial Engineering Technicians

Industrial Engineers

Mechanical Engineering Technicians

Mechanical Engineers

Robotics Trainers

■ **See Robotics Engineers and Technicians**

Roman Catholic Priests

■ Overview

Roman Catholic priests serve as either *diocesan priests* (sometimes called *secular priests*), leading individual parishes within a certain diocese, or as *religious priests*, living and working with other members of their religious order. The primary function of all priests is administering the church's seven sacraments: baptism, confirmation, confession, holy communion, marriage, holy orders, and last rites. Diocesan priests also visit the sick, oversee religious education programs, and generally provide pastoral care to their parishioners. Religious priests often serve as educators and missionaries, or they may be cloistered in a monastery.

■ History

Priests and other clergy are part of the hierarchical structure of the Roman Catholic Church. This hierarchy began historically with Jesus Christ, who is believed by Catholics and other Christians to have been both God and man. Peter, the leader of the twelve apostles, is considered the priestly human successor to Jesus Christ. The spiritual successor of Peter is the pope, who is the leader of the worldwide Roman Catholic Church. The pope appoints bishops who oversee a diocese, a territorial district of the church. The bishops appoint the priests, who are spiritual leaders of individual parishes. Religious priests work under the direction of the superiors of their community and their order.

■ The Job

All priests have the same powers bestowed on them through ordination by a bishop, but their way of life, the type of work they do, and the authority to whom they report depends on whether they are members of a religious order or working in a diocese. Diocesan priests generally work in parishes to which they are assigned by their bishop. Religious priests—such as Dominicans, Jesuits, or Franciscans—work as members of a religious community, teaching, doing missionary work, or engaging in other specialized activities as assigned by their superiors. Both categories of priests teach and hold administrative positions in Catholic seminaries and educational institutions.

Diocesan priests are the spiritual leaders of their congregations. They are responsible for leading liturgical celebrations—especially the Mass. They also provide pastoral care for their parishioners in times of sickness, death, or personal crisis. Diocesan priests oversee the religious education of everyone in their congregation and take care of administrative duties. Some work in parochial schools attached to parish churches or in diocesan high schools. Religious priests perform similar duties but usually in monastic or missionary settings, or in such institutions as boarding schools, medical facilities, and residential homes.

All priests take time each day to nurture their own spiritual lives through Mass, private prayer, and recitation of the Liturgy of the Hours (the offices of Morning Prayer, Evening Prayer, etc.). They also devote time to studying the Bible, church history, and the doctrines and practices of the faith. All of this gives them the spiritual strength necessary to carry out their ministries.

Catholic clergy do not choose their own work assignments; this is done in collaboration with their religious superiors. Work assignments, however, are always made with the interests and abilities of the individual priest in mind. Every effort is made to place a priest in the type of ministry he prepares for. Priests may serve in a wide range of ministries, from counseling full-time and working in social services to being chaplains in the armed forces, prisons, or hospitals.

■ Requirements

High School

Some high schools offer preparation for the priesthood that is similar to that of a college preparatory high school. High school seminary studies focus on English, speech, literature, and social studies. Latin may or may not be required; the study of other foreign languages, such as Spanish, is encouraged. Other recommended high school courses include typing, debating, and music.

Postsecondary Training

Eight years of post-high school study are usually required to become an ordained priest. Candidates for the priesthood often choose to enter at the college level or begin their studies in theological seminaries after college graduation. The liberal arts program offered by seminary colleges stresses philosophy, religion, the behavioral sciences, history, the natural sciences, and mathematics. Some priestly formation programs may insist on seminarians majoring in philosophy.

The additional four years of preparation for ordination are given over entirely to the study of theology, including studies in moral (ethics) and pastoral and dogmatic (doctrine) theology. Other areas of study include church history, scripture, homiletics (the art of preaching), liturgy (worship), and canon (church) law. In the third year of advanced training, candidates undertake fieldwork in parishes and the wider community. Because the work expected of secular and religious priests differs, they are trained in different major seminaries offering slightly varied programs.

Postgraduate work in theology and other fields is available and encouraged for priests, who may study in

ROMAN CATHOLIC PRIESTS	
SCHOOL SUBJECTS	English Religion
PERSONAL SKILLS	Communication/ideas Helping/teaching
WORK ENVIRONMENT	Primarily indoors Primarily one location
MINIMUM EDUCATION LEVEL	Bachelor's degree
SALARY RANGE	$0 to $9,000 to $15,000
CERTIFICATION OR LICENSING	None available
OUTLOOK	Faster than the average
DOT	120
GOE	10.01.01
NOC	4154
O*NET	27502

American Catholic universities, ecclesiastical universities in Rome, or other places around the world. Continuing education for ordained priests in the last several years has stressed sociology, psychology, and the natural sciences.

All Catholic seminaries offer scholarships and grants to qualified students; no one is denied the chance to study for the priesthood because he cannot afford it.

Other Requirements

Those interested in the priesthood should possess a strong religious faith, coupled with the belief that they have received a special call from God to serve and help others. All other interests and potential vocations should be considered secondary to this call. In addition to a strong desire for helping others, priests need to be able to communicate effectively and supervise others. They must have common sense, initiative, and self-confidence in order to be able to effectively oversee a parish or mission. They must also have compassion, humility, and integrity so as to be able to set an example for others. They must be open-minded and good listeners in order to successfully interact with and help those who seek their counsel.

In the Roman Catholic Church, only men are called to the priesthood. A vow of celibacy is required, along with vows of poverty and obedience. Some orders take a special fourth vow, often related to the charism of their community; for example, a vow of stability to stay in one place or a vow of silence.

■ Exploring

If you are interested in the priesthood, talk with your parish priest and others involved in the pastoral work of the church to get a clearer idea of the rewards and responsibilities. Your priest or diocesan vocations office can put you in touch with a religious order if that is where you would like to serve. Aspiring priests may wish to volunteer at a church or other religious institution to become better acquainted with the type of responsibilities a priest has. Those interested in becoming a religious priest may choose to spend time in a monastery; many monasteries are open to the public for weekend or even week-long retreats.

In exploring the priesthood, you should be conscientious about living the Catholic faith as fully as you can— that is the essence of the vocation. Attend Mass and other services frequently; read about church history and doctrine; take part in parish activities. Finally, those with experience in religious ministries will tell you that the very best way to prepare for a vocation and to discern it is to pray.

■ Employers

While some priests serve in dioceses and others serve in religious orders, all priests ultimately serve the church. Most priests can count on a pretty conventional life in the

A priest elevates the Chalice during a Roman Catholic mass.

settings they have chosen: the hustle and bustle of an urban mission, the steady work of a suburban parish or school, the serenity of a monastery. Still, it is important to be ready and willing to serve wherever the church needs you. A good example is Great Britain's Cardinal Basil Hume, who was a content priest in a quiet Benedictine monastery until called by the pope to become Archbishop of Westminster (London) and Primate of All England. Priests believe that by following the church's call to wherever they are needed, they are accomplishing God's will.

■ Starting Out

Newly ordained diocesan priests generally begin their ministry as *associate pastors*, while new priests of religious orders are assigned duties for which they are specially trained, such as missionary work. Both diocesan and religious priests work under the supervision of experienced colleagues until they are deemed ready for more responsibility.

■ Advancement

Because serving God and other people through the church is a priest's main concern, advancing to positions of power or prestige is not an important goal. Most priests do, however, advance to positions of some responsibility or move into altogether different positions. Some may become teachers in seminaries and other educational institutions, or chaplains in the armed forces. The pulpits of large, well-established churches are usually filled by priests of considerable experience. A small number of priests become bishops, archbishops, and cardinals.

■ Earnings

Religious priests take a vow of poverty and are supported by their orders. Any salary that they may receive for writing or other activities is usually turned over to their reli-

CELIBACY AND CHASTITY

Although priests take a vow of celibacy while sisters and brothers take vows of chastity, they amount to essentially the same thing: they will never form romantic relationships with other people. Some people shy away from religious vocations because of this requirement—but it is actually a blessing to those pursuing full-time ministries within the church. These vows allow priests and religious sisters and brothers to devote all of their time and attention to living out their vocations; if they had spouses and children, they would naturally want and need to give much of their time and attention to them. Vows of celibacy or chastity help men and women to concentrate on spiritual things.

Perhaps more importantly, when priests, sisters, and brothers are living out the call to give themselves to God through the church, they don't *want* to give themselves to other people through dating or marriage. This doesn't mean that they are cold or distant with others, and it doesn't mean that they don't experience human desires—it means that they seek the spiritual dimensions of love and sacrifice the physical dimensions to God.

gious orders. Diocesan priests receive small salaries calculated to cover their basic needs. These salaries vary according to the size of the parish, as well as its location and financial status, and average approximately $9,000 per year. Additional benefits usually include a monthly travel allowance, room and board in the parish rectory, car allowance, health insurance, retirement benefits, and educational allowance. Priests who teach or do specialized work usually receive a small stipend that is less than that paid to lay persons in similar positions. Occasionally, priests who do special work are compensated at the same level as a lay person. Priests who serve in the armed forces receive the same amount of pay as other officers of equal rank.

■ Work Environment

There is no such thing as a standard workweek for diocesan priests. Like all clergy, priests who function as pastors are on call at any hour of the day or night. They may be called to visit the sick or administer last rites at any time of the day or night. They may be asked to counsel families or individuals in times of crisis. Priests also must prepare sermons and keep up with religious and secular events. They may also have a great deal of administrative duties working with staff and various committees. As a result, priests encounter a significant amount of daily stress. A deep prayer life, plus the support of other priests, is necessary to reduce this stress. Parish priests usually live in quiet, simply furnished rectories with other priests. They may have a housekeeper to cook and perform cleaning duties.

Religious priests who live in monasteries devote themselves to liturgical celebration, mental prayer, and manual labor on the monastery grounds. While they do not experience the stresses of parish life, religious priests do face the challenges of the contemplative life and of living in a small, close community. Those who pursue missionary work must adapt to difficult working conditions, usually in poorer countries and often in uncomfortable climates.

■ Outlook

There is a shortage of priests in the Catholic Church. In the last 30 years, the number of priests has declined by about 25 percent because of retirement and those leaving the profession for other reasons. Opportunities for positions in the priesthood are increasing and will probably continue to do so for the foreseeable future. Currently, there are about 32,000 diocesan priests and 16,000 religious priests serving America's 62 million Catholics. Priests are needed in all areas of the country, but the greatest need is in metropolitan areas that have large Catholic populations and in communities near Catholic educational institutions.

As a result of the continuing shortage of priests, over 10,000 deacons have been ordained to preach and administer all the sacraments except Mass and confession. While they are now playing an important part in parish life, deacons cannot actually take the place of priests in the Roman Catholic Church.

■ For More Information

Your diocese has a vocations office that will be happy to provide you with information on the priesthood. You are also welcome to contact individual religious orders.

The NRVC can provide information about all kinds of Catholic vocations; it also publishes Vision, *a vocation discernment guide available in print and online.*

National Religious Vocation Conference
5420 South Cornell Avenue, Suite 105
Chicago, IL 60615
Tel: 773-363-5454
Web: http://www.visionguide.org

■ Related Articles

Religious Ministries
Social Services
Active Religious Sisters and Brothers
College Administrators
College Professors
Contemplative Religious Sisters and Brothers
Elementary School Teachers
Guidance Counselors
School Administrators
Secondary School Teachers
Social Workers

Roofers

■ Overview

Roofers install and repair roofs of buildings using a variety of materials and methods, including built-up roofing, single-ply roofing systems, asphalt shingles, tile, and slate. They may also waterproof and damp-proof walls, swimming pools, and other building surfaces.

■ History

Roofs have always been needed to cover buildings to protect their interiors against snow, rain, wind, temperature extremes, and strong sunlight. The earliest roofs were probably thatched with plant materials such as leaves, branches, or straw. With clay or a similar substance pressed into any open spaces, such a roof can provide good protection from the weather. Roofs constructed on frameworks of thick branches or timbers allowed different roof designs to develop, including the flat and pitched, or sloping, forms that are in use today. When brick and stone began to be used in building, it became possible to construct domes and vaults, roof forms based on arches.

Throughout most of history, flat roofs have been associated with dry climates, where drainage of water off the roof is seldom a concern. In the 19th century, new roofing and building materials made flat roofs an economical alternative to pitched roofs in somewhat wetter conditions, such as those in much of the United States. Today, flat or very slightly sloped roofs are common on commercial buildings and are also used on some residential buildings. Pitched roofs in various forms have been used for many centuries, largely in climates where drainage is a concern. Most houses have pitched roofs.

All roofs must keep out water. There are two basic types of roof covering that do this: separate shingles, or flat pieces of a waterproof material that are placed so that water cannot get through at the joints; and a continuous layer or sheet membrane of a material that is impermeable to water. Different kinds of roofing materials are appropriate for different kinds of roofs, and each material has its own method of application.

The occupation of roofer has developed along with the various kinds of modern roofing materials. Roofers today must know about how the elements in each roofing system are used, and how water, temperature, and humidity affect the roof. While asphalt shingle roofs on homes may require only relatively simple materials and application procedures, large commercial building roofs can involve complex preparation and layering of materials to produce the necessary protective covering.

■ The Job

Although roofers usually are trained to apply most kinds of roofing, they often specialize in either sheet membrane roofing or prepared roofings such as asphalt shingles, slate, or tile.

One kind of sheet membrane roofing is called "built-up roofing." Built-up roofing, used on flat roofs, consists of roofing felt (fabric saturated in bitumen, a tar-like material) laid into hot bitumen. To prepare for putting on a built-up roof, roofers may apply a layer of insulation to the bare roof deck. Then they spread molten bitumen over the roof surface, lay down overlapping layers of roofing felt, and spread more hot bitumen over the felt, sealing the seams and making the roof watertight. They repeat this process several times to build up as many layers as desired. They then give the top a smooth finish or embed gravel in the top for a rough surface.

Single-ply roofing, a relatively new method, uses a waterproof sheet membrane and employs any of several different types of chemical products. Some roofing consists of polymeria-modified bituminous compounds that are rolled out in sheets on the building's insulation. The compound may be remelted on the roof by torch or hot anvil to fuse it to or embed it in hot bitumen in a manner similar to built-up roofing. Other single-ply roofing is made of rubber or plastic materials that can be sealed with contact adhesive cements, solvent welding, hot-air welding, or other methods. Still another type of single-ply roofing consists of spray-in-place polyurethane foam with a polymeric coating. Roofers who apply these roofing systems must be trained in the application methods for each system. Many manufacturers of these systems require that roofers take special courses and receive certification before they are authorized to use the products.

To apply asphalt shingles, a very common roofing on houses, roofers begin by cutting strips of roofing felt and

ROOFERS	
SCHOOL SUBJECTS	Mathematics Technical/Shop
PERSONAL SKILLS	Following instructions Mechanical/manipulative
WORK ENVIRONMENT	Primarily outdoors Primarily multiple locations
MINIMUM EDUCATION LEVEL	Apprenticeship
SALARY RANGE	$18,000 to $28,000 to $40,000
CERTIFICATION OR LICENSING	Required for certain positions
OUTLOOK	About as fast as the average
DOT	866
GOE	04.10.01
NOC	7291
O*NET	87808

This roofer wears a protective mask while working with noxious roofing materials.

tacking them down over the entire roof. They nail on horizontal rows of shingles, beginning at the low edge of the roof and working up. Sometimes they must cut shingles to fit around corners, vent pipes, and chimneys. Where two sections of roof meet, they nail or cement flashing, which is strips of metal or shingle that make the joints watertight.

Tile and slate shingles, which are more expensive types of residential roofing, are installed slightly differently. First, roofing felt is applied over the wood base. Next, the roofers punch holes in the slate or tile pieces so that nails can be inserted, or they embed the tiles in mortar. Each row of shingles overlaps the preceding row.

Metal roofing is applied by specially trained roofers or by *sheet metal workers*. One type of metal roof uses metal sections shaped like flat pans, soldered together for weatherproofing and attached by metal clips to the wood below. Another kind of metal roofing, called "standing seam roofing," has raised seams where the sections of sheet metal interlock.

Some roofers waterproof and damp-proof walls, swimming pools, tanks, and structures other than roofs. To prepare surfaces for waterproofing, workers smooth rough surfaces and roughen glazed surfaces. They then brush or spray waterproofing material on the surface. Damp-proofing is done by spraying a coating of tar or asphalt onto interior or exterior surfaces to prevent the penetration of moisture.

Roofers use various hand tools in their work, including hammers, roofing knives, mops, pincers, caulking guns, rollers, welders, chalk lines, and cutters.

■ Requirements

High School

Most employers prefer to hire applicants at least 18 years of age who are in good physical condition and have a good sense of balance. Although a high school education or its equivalent is not required, it is generally preferred. Students can also take courses that familiarize them with some of the skills that are a regular part of roofing work. Beneficial courses include shop, basic mathematics, and mechanical drawing.

Postsecondary Training

Roofers learn the skills they need through on-the-job training or by completing an apprenticeship. Most roofers learn informally on the job while they work under the supervision of experienced roofers. Beginners start as helpers, doing simple tasks like carrying equipment and putting up scaffolding. They gradually gain the skills and knowledge they need for more difficult tasks. Roofers may need four or more years of on-the-job training to become familiar with all the materials and techniques they need to know.

Apprenticeship programs generally provide more thorough, balanced training. Apprenticeships are three years in length and combine a planned program of work experience with formal classroom instruction in related subjects. The work portion of the apprenticeship includes a minimum of 1,400 hours each year under the guidance of experienced roofers. The classroom instruction, at least 144 hours per year, covers such topics as safety practices, how to use and care for tools, and arithmetic.

■ Exploring

High school or vocational school students may be able to get firsthand experience of this occupation through a part-time or summer job as a roofer's helper. It may be possible to visit a construction site to observe roofers at work, but a close look is unlikely as roofers do most of their work at heights.

■ Employers

There are approximately 140,000 people employed as roofers in the United States. Most work for established roofing contractors, while some go into business for themselves.

■ Starting Out

People who are planning to start out as helpers and learn on the job can directly contact roofing contractors to inquire about possible openings. Job leads may also be located through the local office of the state employment service or newspaper classified ads. Graduates of vocational schools may get useful information from their schools' placement offices.

People who want to become apprentices can learn about apprenticeships in their area by contacting local roofing contractors, the state employment service, or the local office of the United Union of Roofers, Waterproofers and Allied Workers.

■ Advancement

Experienced roofers who work for roofing contractors may be promoted to supervisory positions in which they are responsible for coordinating the activities of other roofers. Roofers also may become estimators, calculating the costs of roofing jobs before the work is done. Roofers who have the right combination of personal characteristics, including the ability to deal with people and good judgment and planning skills may be able to go into business for themselves as independent roofing contractors.

■ Earnings

The earnings of roofers vary widely depending on how much time they work, geographical location, skills and experience, and other factors. Roofers work an average of 33 hours a week. Sometimes bad weather prevents them from working, and some weeks they work fewer than 20 hours. They make up for lost time in other weeks, and if they work longer hours than the standard workweek (usually 40 hours), they receive extra pay for the overtime. While roofers in northern states may not work in the winter, most roofers work year round.

The average hourly wage for roofers is $13, with weekly earnings at about $430 and annual earnings at about $20,000. Some workers make less, and a few make nearly twice as much. Skilled and experienced roofers may earn $600 or more per week (about $28,000 annually). Annual earnings may not reflect hourly figures because layoffs in bad weather limit the number of hours roofers work.

Hourly rates for apprentices usually start at about 55 percent of the skilled worker's rate and increase periodically until the pay reaches 90 percent of the full rate during the final six months.

■ Work Environment

Roofers work outdoors most of the time they are on the job. They work in the heat and cold, but not in wet weather. Roofs can get extremely hot during the summer. The work is physically strenuous, involving lifting heavy weights, prolonged standing, climbing, bending, and squatting. Roofers must work while standing on surfaces that may be steep and quite high; they must use caution to avoid injuries from falls while working on ladders, scaffolding, or roofs.

■ Outlook

Over the next 10 years, employment in this field is expected to increase at about the same rate as the average for all occupations. There are several reasons for this outlook. Roofers will continue to be in demand for the construction of new buildings. Furthermore, roofs tend to need more maintenance and repair work than other parts of buildings. The majority of roofing work is on existing structures. Roofers will always be needed for roof repairs and replacement, even during economic downturns when construction activity generally decreases. Also, damp-proofing and waterproofing are expected to provide an increasing proportion of the work done by roofers.

Every year, many openings will become available as people in the field transfer to other work or retire. Because most roofing work is done during the warmer part of the year, job opportunities will probably be best during spring and summer.

■ For More Information

This organization offers plenty of information and membership benefits to professional roofers, including a magazine.

National Roofing Contractors Association
10255 West Higgins Road, Suite 600
Rosemont, IL 60018-5607
Tel: 847-299-9070
Web: http://nrca.net/

This union's Web site has information on careers in roofing.

United Union of Roofers, Waterproofers and Allied Workers
1660 L Street, NW, Suite 800
Washington, DC 20036
Web: http://www.unionroofers.com/

■ Related Articles

Construction

Carpenters

Floor Covering Installers

Room Stewards

■ **See Cruise Ship Workers**

Roughnecks

■ **See Petroleum and Petroleum Technicians**

Roustabouts

■ Overview

Roustabouts do the routine physical labor and maintenance around oil wells, pipelines, and natural gas facilities. Sample tasks include clearing trees and brush, mixing concrete, manually loading and unloading pipe and other materials onto or from trucks or boats, and assembling pumps, boilers, valves, and steam engines and performing minor repairs on such equipment. Roustabouts find work in about 30 states nationwide, especially Texas, California, Oklahoma, New Mexico, Kansas, Illinois, Kentucky, Wyoming, Colorado, Pennsylvania, and West Virginia.

■ History

In the 19th century, people began to search for oil and extract it from deposits inside the earth. The first exploratory oil well was drilled in 1859 in Titusville, Pennsylvania. After much hard work with crude equipment, the drilling crew struck oil, and within a short time the first oil boom was on.

From the earliest days of drilling for oil, roustabouts have performed the necessary manual labor tasks of clearing the land and preparing the site for drilling. Nowadays, with increasing automation and mechanization in the oil industry, roustabouts routinely operate motorized lifts, power tools, electronic testers, and hand-held computers. Although roustabouts still perform such chores as digging trenches or cutting down trees and brush, the advent of labor-saving equipment has enabled roustabouts to assume more maintenance and troubleshooting responsibilities.

■ The Job

Roustabouts perform a wide range of labor tasks, from picking up trash at well sites to running heavy equipment. Part of their work involves clearing sites that have been selected for drilling and building a solid base for drilling equipment. Roustabouts cut down trees to make way for roads or to reduce fire hazards. They dig trenches for foundations, fill excavated areas, mix up batches of wet concrete, and pour concrete into building forms. Other jobs include loading and unloading pipe and other materials onto or from trucks and boats.

Roustabouts also dig drainage ditches around wells, storage tanks, and other installations. They walk flow lines to locate leaks and clean up spilled oil by bailing it into barrels or other containers. They also paint equipment such as storage tanks and pumping units and clean and repair oil field machinery and equipment.

The tools roustabouts use range from simple hand tools like hammers and shovels to heavy equipment such as backhoes or trackhoes. Roustabouts use heavy wrenches and other hand tools to help break out and replace pipe, valves, and other components for repairs or modifications and truck winches for moving or lifting heavy items. Roustabouts also operate motorized lifts, power tools, and electronic sensors and testers. They also may operate tractors with shredders, forklifts, or ditching machines.

■ Requirements

High School

Little or no formal training or experience is required to get a job as a roustabout. However, there are more applicants than there are jobs, which allows employers to be selective, choosing people who have previous experience as a roustabout or formal training in a related area. While in high school, classes in mathematics, shop, and technical training will be helpful preparation.

Postsecondary Training

More and more applicants have earned an associate's degree in petroleum technology, which demonstrates their familiarity with oil field operations and equipment. In general, any technical training, specialized courses, or pertinent experience can be a definite advantage in securing a job and later in getting promotions to more responsible positions.

Certification or Licensing

Most roustabouts are not union members. Those who are, however, may be represented by the International Union of Petroleum and Industrial Workers, the International Federation of Petroleum and Chemical Workers, or the Oil, Chemical and Atomic Workers International Union.

Other Requirements

Roustabouts must be physically fit, with good coordination, agility, and eyesight. They need a current valid vehicle operator's license and a good driving record. Depending

ROUSTABOUTS	
SCHOOL SUBJECTS	Mathematics Technical/Shop
PERSONAL SKILLS	Mechanical/manipulative Technical/scientific
WORK ENVIRONMENT	Primarily outdoors Primarily multiple locations
MINIMUM EDUCATION LEVEL	High school diploma
SALARY RANGE	$10,400 to $26,000 to $37,400
CERTIFICATION OR LICENSING	Required for certain positions
OUTLOOK	Decline
DOT	869
GOE	05.10.01
NOC	8615
O*NET	87921

on the equipment they operate, roustabouts also may need a commercial driver's license as well as crane and forklift licenses. They must enjoy working out of doors, be willing to work in extreme weather, and often are required to work more than 40 hours a week. In addition, employers may require that job applicants pass a physical examination and a screening test for drug use before hiring them. Applicants also might have to take aptitude tests to determine their mechanical ability.

People who become roustabouts often have some unique personal characteristics. In general, they should be ready to pitch in with extra work when the situation requires it. They should work well both on their own and as part of a crew. Those on offshore platforms must be able to get along with the same people for extended periods of time.

Roustabouts need to be comfortable with an unpredictable field; at times they do not have steady work, and at other times they work several weeks straight with only a few days off. Many roustabouts have a taste for challenge, travel, and adventure rather than a settled home life. Others look at the job as a short-term way to gain experience, earn money for college or some other specific expense, or to prepare for a better-paying job in the oil industry.

■ Exploring

Talking with someone who has worked as a roustabout or in another oil field operations job would be a very helpful and inexpensive way of exploring this field. You can find industry-related information and commercial sites, including a specific energy section that includes oil and gas sites, at http://www.industrylink.com.

Those who live near an oil field may be able to arrange a tour by contacting the public relations department of oil companies or drilling contractors. Another option is to drive by oil fields that lie along public roads and public lands and take an unofficial tour by car.

Some summer and other temporary jobs as roustabouts are available, and they provide a good way to find out about this field. Temporary workers can learn first-hand the basics of oil field operations, equipment maintenance, safety, and other aspects of the work. Those individuals who are thinking about this kind of work should also consider entering a two-year training program in petroleum technology to learn about the field.

■ Employers

Most roustabouts are employed by oil companies, working with production crews around existing oil wells. Others work for drilling contractors, which are companies that specialize in drilling new wells. Roustabouts usually work under the supervision of a maintenance superintendent and frequently assist skilled workers such as *welders, electricians,* and *mechanics.*

A roustabout on an oil rig

■ Starting Out

Potential roustabouts can contact drilling contractors or oil companies directly about possible job openings. Directories to consult for the names and addresses of oil companies are *U.S.A. Oil Industry* or the *Time Oil and Gas Directory.* Information may also be available through the local office of the state employment service. Graduates of technical training programs may find assistance in locating employment through the placement office at their schools.

Roustabouts usually are hired in the field by the maintenance superintendent or by a local company representative. Many roustabouts learn their skills on the job by working under the supervision of experienced workers. Roustabouts with no previous experience are considered "hands" who learn by helping the lead roustabout and crew. They begin with simple labor jobs, like unloading trucks, and gradually take on more complicated work. As they progress, they learn about oil field operations and equipment, safety practices, and maintenance procedures for the machinery.

To learn the skills they need, some newly hired roustabouts take courses at junior colleges or self-study courses such as those offered by the University of Texas at Austin. Some employers, particularly the major oil companies, help pay for job-related courses that employees take during their own time. Because the turnover rate among roustabouts is fairly high, however, employers are usually reluctant to invest a great deal in specialized training for beginning workers.

■ Advancement

A job as a roustabout is usually an entry-level position. To advance, roustabouts will need to prove that they can do the work; advancement to a variety of other jobs comes with experience. Roustabouts who are part of maintenance and operation crews may advance to such positions as *switcher, gauger, pumper,* or *lease operator.* Those with proven leadership abilities may eventually become chief operators or maintenance superintendents. Roustabouts who are on drilling crews may advance to become *roughnecks, floor hands,* or *rotary helpers,* and, later, *derrick operators, drillers,* and *tool pushers,* who are in charge of one or more drilling rigs; they also might become engineering technicians. All of these positions represent a special set of responsibilities in a complex operation. (See *Petroleum Technicians*)

Some companies run their own training programs offering employees the opportunity to take courses in welding, electricity, and other craft areas; roustabouts who participate in such courses may be prepared to advance into jobs as welders, electricians, *pipefitters,* and other *craftworkers.*

■ Earnings

The earnings of roustabouts vary depending on the branch of the industry they work in, the region of the country, the hours they work, and other factors. Offshore workers generally earn more than on-shore, and roustabouts who work for oil companies generally earn more than those who work for drilling contractors.

Some beginning salaries are on a par with minimum wage, according to the Association of Energy Service Companies. The average salary of all workers is $12.50. The most experienced roustabouts earn up to $18 an hour. Generally, roustabouts receive time and a half for overtime; conversely, employers do not pay them if they finish early during a slow time. Those who work away from home receive additional "sub pay" plus reimbursement for their hotel and other expenses. Benefits and medical coverage are comparable to other manual laborers.

■ Work Environment

Roustabouts work in and around oil fields, on drilling platforms in oceans, on pipelines that transport oil or gas long distances, and at facilities that capture and distribute nat-

ural gas. In on-shore oil fields or on ocean platforms, roustabouts work outside in all types of weather. On offshore rigs and platforms, they can experience strong ocean currents, violent storms, and bitterly cold winds. Workers in oil fields on shore may have to contend with extremely hot or cold weather, dust, or insects.

Roustabouts on offshore drilling rigs generally work 12-hour days, seven days a week. After seven days on, they usually get seven days off, although some crews may have to work two to four weeks at a stretch, followed by an equal amount of time off. Workers generally stay on the ocean platform during their whole work shift and return to shore via helicopter or crew boat. It is not unusual for offshore roustabouts to live hundreds of miles from the ocean platform where they work.

In on-shore oil fields, roustabouts are more likely to work five-day, 40-hour weeks, although this is not always the case, especially during a "boom." Some roustabouts average between 120 and 130 hours in a two-week pay period. Roustabouts may travel anywhere from a half-mile away to 100 or more miles away to a work site. They take short lunch and other breaks depending on how busy the crew is. The end of the day might come early in the afternoon or in the middle of the night. Many drilling operations work around the clock until discovering oil or abandoning the location as a dry hole. This requires shifts of workers every day of the week.

Being a roustabout can be stressful due to the long hours and time away from home, family, and friends. Some roustabouts work away from home one to three weeks at a time with only a few days off.

Roustabouts' work is strenuous and potentially dangerous, especially on open-sea drilling platforms. They lift heavy materials and equipment and frequently must bend, stoop, and climb. They have to use caution to avoid falling off derricks and other high places, as well as injuries from being hit by falling objects. They are subject to cuts, scrapes, and sore or strained muscles. Because fire is a hazard around oil operations, roustabouts and other workers must be trained in firefighting and be ready to respond to emergencies.

Roustabouts who work on drilling crews can expect to move from place to place, since drilling at a site may be completed in a few weeks or months. If they are working at a site that is producing oil, they usually remain there for longer periods of time.

■ Outlook

The number of roustabout jobs is expected to decline slightly due to continuing advances in oil field automation, changes in production methods, and the overall decline in manufacturing employment. This projection also assumes continued stagnation in the oil and gas industries.

In the decade 1985-95, a worldwide surplus of oil and resultant reduced price of oil, coupled with rising environmental regulations and dwindling reserves at home, forced U.S. companies into a costly overseas hunt for crude. In an effort to cut costs, the oil industry slashed its workforce, eliminating about 500,000 jobs in the past 10 years.

Companies are likely to continue to restructure and look for cost-effective technology that permits new drilling abroad and offshore in the Gulf of Mexico, which experts predict will be one of the most significant exploration hot spots in the world for the next decade.

Continued low oil prices, the worldwide surplus, and anticipated low global demand (partly due to the growing use of more energy-efficient cars and other equipment) mean conditions will continue to be tough for the oil industry for the next several years. But it is always possible that the anticipated pattern could change. According to an Energy Department study, as legislation and international agreements open up more markets, there is the potential for producing thousands of jobs. Economic recoveries abroad also could help brighten the picture.

Despite its difficulties, the oil industry still plays an important role in the economy and employment. Oil and gas will continue to be primary energy sources well into the next century. According to the Association of Energy Service Companies, the field is in such a state of decline as to be considered in crisis. While few new jobs for roustabouts are expected to develop, they always will be needed, and there will be some openings, as turnover is high among roustabouts, especially in offshore drilling. The work is difficult and dirty enough that many people stay in the job only a short time. The need to replace workers who leave will account for nearly all job openings. Workers who have experience or formal training in the field will have the best chance of being hired.

■ For More Information

For facts and statistics about the petroleum industry, contact:

American Petroleum Institute
1220 L Street, NW
Washington, DC 20005
Tel: 202-682-8000
Email: info@api.org
Web: http://www.api.org

For information on well-servicing careers, write:

Association of Energy Service Companies
6060 North Central Expressway, Suite 428
Dallas, TX 75206
Tel: 214-692-0771
Email: info@aesc.net
Web: http://www.aesc.net

For a copy of Oil, *a booklet describing all phases of the oil industry, contact:*

Shell Oil Company
PO Box 2463, Suite 4124
Houston, TX 77252-2463
Attn: Corporate Relations
Tel: 713-241-4552
Web: http://www.countonshel.com

For a list of petroleum technology schools, contact:

Society of Petroleum Engineers
PO Box 833836
Richardson, TX 75083
Tel: 214-952-9393

For a training catalog listing publications, audiovisuals, and short courses, including correspondence courses, contact:

The University of Texas at Austin
Petroleum Extension Service
J. J. Pickle Research Campus
Austin, TX 78712-1100
Tel: 512-471-5940
Email: rbpetex@mail.utexas.edu
Web: http://www.utexas.edu/dce/petex

■ Related Articles

Construction

Energy

Mining

Petroleum

Coal Miners

Construction Laborers

Petroleum Engineers

Petroleum Refining Workers

Petroleum Technicians

Route Drivers

■ Overview

Route drivers, also known as *route-sales drivers* or *driver-sales workers,* drive trucks over established routes and deliver products such as milk, baked goods, soft drinks, laundry, dry cleaning, and ice cream to regular customers. What a driver delivers depends on his or her employer's products. Customers may be retail establishments, the general public, or both. Drivers usually collect payments from customers and attempt to interest them in new products or services offered by the company.

Route drivers may use their own trucks and operate as independent businesspersons. Otherwise, drivers work for businesses that provide the vehicles. Most route drivers work for companies based in large urban areas. Over 500,000 route drivers are employed in the United States.

■ History

In the United States, there have always been individuals who earned their livelihoods by selling materials and merchandise from door to door. The peddler is probably the oldest sales worker in the United States. By going from door to door, with their goods loaded in a horse-drawn cart, peddlers established wide commercial networks and were able to provide a supply of goods to remote areas of the United States.

To some extent, the Yankee peddler of colonial times has been replaced by the route-sales drivers. Industries have delegated the responsibilities of merchandising and marketing to their own sales departments and other employees. Route drivers not only deliver the company's products, but must also be skilled in the art of sales, which the peddler first developed.

Over the years, the products sold by route drivers and the manner in which they are delivered have been influenced by important developments in society. For example, in the early 20th century, automobiles and trucks replaced horse-drawn carts as transportation for sales workers. Also, construction of new and better roads made it possible for one driver to cover more territory and serve more people.

A route driver interacted with people all day as he or she stopped at several businesses and residences to pick up and deliver parcels. As industry advanced, new products and new merchandising methods continued to change the demands placed on route drivers. For example, as convenience stores became more numerous and people increasingly relied on them for everyday items, fewer people had milk and baked goods delivered to their homes. The growth of mail-order catalog houses as well as the trend of stores buying directly from suppliers, further decreased the number of positions open for route drivers.

Today, route drivers are more specialized than their predecessors. Instead of selling many things to a small number of people,

ROUTE DRIVERS	
SCHOOL SUBJECTS	Business Computer science Technical/Shop
PERSONAL SKILLS	Following instructions
WORK ENVIRONMENT	Indoors and outdoors Primarily multiple locations
MINIMUM EDUCATION LEVEL	High school diploma Apprenticeship
SALARY RANGE	$12,000 to $20,000 to $25,000+
CERTIFICATION OR LICENSING	Required by all states
OUTLOOK	Little change or more slowly than the average
DOT	292
GOE	08.02.07
NOC	7414

as did the all-purpose peddler, they sell fewer products and services to a larger number of people.

The items sold and customer base aren't the only things that have changed. For many sales route drivers, the route map, sales slips, and paper receipts have all been automated. Although many route drivers still use the paper-based forms, many route drivers have electronic maps, computerized inventory takers, and electronic hand-held receipt/signature machines.

■ The Job

Route drivers usually drive panel or light trucks. They not only deliver, but also sell products that range from dry-cleaning services to pastries. Drivers' duties vary with the kinds of items or services they sell, the size of the company they work for, and the kind of route they service.

Route drivers who sell, collect, or deliver to retail establishments, are known as *wholesale route drivers*, and those who provide similar services directly to the public, are known as *retail route drivers*. Retail route drivers make 5 to 10 times more deliveries per day than wholesale route drivers.

The majority of route drivers are employed by dairies, bakeries, and laundry and dry-cleaning plants located in large cities. These men and women provide bakery, milk, dry cleaning, laundry, newspapers, and other goods and services that people use everyday.

The particular duties of route drivers vary according to the industry in which they are employed, the policies of their particular company, and how strongly their sales responsibilities are emphasized. Route drivers may load or supervise the loading of their delivery truck, deliver previously ordered material to stops on assigned routes, obtain new orders, collect payments, and keep records of the transactions. From time to time, drivers solicit the business of new stores on their route.

After completing the day's deliveries, route drivers turn in the payments they have collected. Then route drivers order items for the next day that they think customers are likely to buy, based primarily on what products have been selling well, the weather, time of year, and any discussions they may have had with customers.

Wholesale bakery route drivers, for example, deliver and arrange bread, cakes, rolls, and other baked goods on display racks in grocery stores. By paying close attention to the items that are selling well and those that are just sitting on the shelves, they estimate the amount and variety of baked goods that will be sold. A driver may recommend changes in a store's order or may encourage the manager to stock new bakery products.

Newspaper-delivery drivers deliver newspapers and magazines to dealers and vending machines; *newspaper carriers* deliver them directly to subscribers. Both types of workers collect money and keep records. *Lunch-truck drivers* sell sandwiches, box lunches, drinks, and similar items to factory and office workers, students, and people attending outdoor events. *Coin collectors* collect and distribute coins to vending machines.

■ Requirements

High School
Employers prefer that potential route drivers be high school graduates. Interested high school students should take courses in sales, public speaking, driver training, mechanics, bookkeeping, and business arithmetic. Courses in merchandising and retailing are also helpful.

Postsecondary Training
College and university level training is not necessary for route sales drivers, although classes in sales and business may give you the advantage over others applying for these positions.

Certification or Licensing
In most states, drivers must qualify for a commercial driver's license. State motor vehicle departments can provide information on how to qualify for this license. An attractive candidate will also know the location of streets in certain sections of an urban area and be able to use maps. Route drivers must also be excellent drivers. For insurance reasons, employers generally prefer to hire drivers who are at least 25 years of age and have an impeccable driving record.

Other Requirements
Drivers work without direct supervision and must be extremely responsible individuals. Drivers must have orderly work habits because they prepare instructions for other workers who are to fill orders. Bookkeeping skills and an eye for detail helps a driver keep accurate records of the payments his or her customers must make.

Bruce Lane, a delivery route driver from California, comments on the importance of being a responsible worker, "Generally, you are working alone, with little or no supervision or guidance. You must assume the responsibility for making sure the job gets done every day."

The success of route drivers depends on how well they keep their present customers happy and the number of new customers they enlist. To fulfill these requirements, route drivers must have self-confidence, initiative, and tact. Above all, they must be honest and have personal integrity. Route drivers should enjoy meeting a wide variety of people and be able to interact with them comfortably, especially those route drivers who work directly with the public. They must also help customers who have complaints about the products or services they receive. Handling customer

A route driver interacts with people all day as he stops at several businesses and residences to pick up and deliver parcels.

complaints well can mean the difference between keeping and losing a client. In addition, a driver's effectiveness as a salesperson is increased if he or she is neat in appearance and pleasant in manner. Most route drivers wear uniforms. In some cases, companies pay for these uniforms and for their cleaning.

■ Exploring

If you are a high school student and interested in this career, you may want to obtain a part-time or summer job as a route driver's helper, in order to see if a career as a route driver is right for you. You can also visit laundries, bakeries, dry-cleaning plants, and other establishments to observe route drivers preparing their trucks for deliveries. Professional route drivers can also answer questions about job responsibilities.

Newspaper delivery jobs are a good first step to learning the daily routine of a route driver. Although sales isn't usually a part of this type of delivery work, customer service, responsibility for cargo, and timeliness are paramount. The Internet also provides a forum for discussing a career as a route driver. The site for the trucking news group is news.misc.transport.trucking. The American Trucking Associations has a Web site at http://www.truckline.com.

■ Employers

Route drivers are employed by companies of all kinds. Any business that needs to get their product from the warehouse, plant, or store and into the hands of their customers uses delivery drivers to make that happen. Some employers simply need the product delivered, such as newspaper publishers, package delivery services, and florists; other employers need the product delivered and new sales generated, such as restaurant equipment companies, cleaning supply companies, and so on. Route driver positions are available across the country, although more positions are usually found in the larger cities.

■ Starting Out

Route drivers can attain their positions in several ways. Some begin in a job as a retail sales worker or other type of salesperson. Others start out as a route driver's helper upon graduation from high school or during summer vacations and accept positions as route drivers when openings develop. *Sales route-driver helpers* assist the route driver in various ways, such as loading and unloading the truck; carrying goods from the truck to the customer's office, store, or house; and driving. Still others wait for the proper opportunity and look for jobs, as dockworkers or other positions, in plants that employ route drivers.

If you are interested in being an independent route driver, Bruce suggests preparing yourself with the correct tools, "When you take a delivery job, you are basically going into business for yourself. You need to prepare by getting the right vehicle and insurance. Access to a second vehicle as backup is a necessity."

Many large companies have on-the-job training programs. Employees who look like good candidates for route driver jobs are trained to ensure that they are knowledgeable of the products they will sell. A company may also assign new drivers to work a route with an experienced driver or supervisor for a brief period of time.

■ Advancement

Many route drivers look forward to moving into positions as sales supervisors and route supervisors, but these positions are relatively scarce. *Route sales-delivery driver supervisors* supervise and coordinate the work of route drivers. They plan routes and schedules, collect cash receipts, handle customer complaints, keep records, and solicit new business.

Most retail route drivers advance by taking positions as wholesale route drivers because higher salaries usually come with wholesale routes. Other route drivers use the experience they have gained on their routes to take sales positions in other fields in which earnings are higher. Also, route drivers that have gained driving experience may aspire to become long-distance truck drivers.

■ Earnings

Most route drivers work for a salary plus a commission on their sales. Wholesale route drivers generally make more money than retail route drivers because they sell items in large quantities and therefore get larger commissions. The earnings of route drivers are related to their effectiveness

as persuasive salespeople. Wages also differ depending on the region in which a route driver works and the kind of product they deliver. On average, route drivers earn between $12,000 and $25,000 annually. Some route drivers may contract with an organization, such as a newspaper publisher, and then be paid by the customers on a monthly basis.

Route drivers are a highly unionized group within the trucking industry. The largest number of route drivers belong to the International Brotherhood of Teamsters, Chauffeurs, Warehousemen, and Helpers of America. Other route drivers are members of the unions representing plant workers or their employers. Generally, union drivers receive higher wages than nonunion drivers.

Route drivers enjoy various fringe benefits. Some have paid vacations ranging from one to four weeks, and some have paid holidays. Some route drivers are provided medical benefits and are covered by pension plans.

■ Work Environment

There are great differences in the number of hours route drivers work. Some route drivers work more than 60 hours a week; others work only 30 hours. The number of hours that route drivers work is determined by a number of factors, including the season of the year, the ambition of the individual route driver, union regulations, and the nature of the route. Some route drivers, such as those delivering milk or newspapers, have to work unusual hours, typically beginning their routes at 4:00 or 5:00 AM. Bruce knows that scenario well, "In most cases you are working at night, so the traffic and parking hassles are minimum, but some people are afraid to be out alone in the dark. Also, most routes are 2 to 4 hours per day, and because of the hours involved it is difficult to work the route around another full-time job."

Retail route drivers have to make deliveries in all kinds of weather and do a good deal of lifting, carrying, and climbing. Working indoors and outdoors is an attractive benefit of being a route driver. This means that route drivers get to enjoy beautiful weather, as well as suffer through extreme heat and cold. Improvements in technology have made the cabs of trucks much more comfortable, but on the hottest of summer days this is of little solace.

Traffic conditions can also make driving a truck in a major urban center rather stressful. Excellent driving skills and the ability to keep calm is essential when navigating congested streets and narrow alleys. Route drivers should also be aware of road restrictions. Some roads have size and weight limitations, while others have commercial vehicle restrictions. Some communities have barred vehicles such as ice cream trucks because of the potential danger of a child running into the road.

Despite these conditions, many drivers find the opportunity to work independently and the challenge of selling essential products and services very satisfying.

■ Outlook

According to the U.S. Bureau of Labor Statistics, more than 500,000 sales route drivers are employed in the United States. The country has experienced a decline in the number of retail route drivers since 1940, due to a number of factors. During World War II, the shortage of workers and gasoline made it necessary to cut sharply the number of home deliveries of products. Delivery was never fully resumed after the war. Also, many people now have large refrigerators and home freezers, which reduces the need for fresh bakery and dairy products to be delivered at homes daily.

A number of large companies have developed so many products that one route driver cannot handle all of them. As a result, many wholesale route drivers have been replaced by sales workers. These sales workers take orders, which are later delivered by truck drivers. This is especially true in areas where large supermarkets have replaced small grocery stores. The development of new products, however, has increased the need for wholesale route drivers to introduce these products in food stores throughout the country.

These changes may have run their course, and the number of route drivers is expected to change little in the foreseeable future. Because of retirements, deaths, and transfers, there will continue to be a need for retail route drivers each year. In addition, the population of the nation continues to move toward the suburbs, where there is expected to be an increased need for these services.

■ For More Information

To learn more about the union most sales route drivers join, contact:

International Brotherhood of Teamsters, Chauffeurs, Warehousemen, and Helpers of America
25 Louisiana Avenue, NW
Washington, DC 20001
Tel: 202-624-6800
Web: http://www.teamster.org/

For general information about route driving, contact:

American Trucking Associations
Office of Public Affairs
2200 Mill Road
Alexandria, VA 22314-4677
Tel: 703-838-1700
Web: http://www.truckline.com

■ Related Articles

Letter and Package Delivery

Sales

Transportation

Trucking

Mail Carriers

Public Transportation Operators

Refuse Collectors

Retail Sales Workers

Sales Representatives

Services Sales Representatives

Taxi Drivers

Truck Drivers

Rubber Cutters

■ **See Rubber**

Rubber Goods Production Workers

■ Overview

Workers in the rubber goods industry make items out of natural and synthetic rubber materials. They soften, shape, cure, cut, mold, and otherwise treat rubber to make thousands of different products from household products to spacecraft parts.

■ History

Natural rubber is a pliable, stretchy material made from the milky juice of various tropical plants. Rubber was given its name in 1770 when a chemist observed it could be used to rub away, or erase, pencil marks. The earliest commercial use for rubber was in the 1840s, when Charles Goodyear (1800-60), an American, invented the

RUBBER GOODS PRODUCTION WORKERS	
SCHOOL SUBJECTS	Chemistry Technical/Shop
PERSONAL SKILLS	Following instructions Mechanical/manipulative
WORK ENVIRONMENT	Primarily indoors Primarily one location
MINIMUM EDUCATION LEVEL	High school diploma
SALARY RANGE	$19,500 to $23,300 to $34,500
CERTIFICATION OR LICENSING	None available
OUTLOOK	About as fast as the average
DOT	690
GOE	06.01.03
NOC	9214

vulcanization process. Vulcanization improves the properties of rubber, making it more elastic, stronger, and more durable. Beginning as early as 1845, long before bicycles and motor vehicles became common, vulcanized rubber was occasionally used in wheels. Rubber tire-making became an industry in 1888, when John Dunlop, a British surgeon, developed pneumatic tires for bicycles. Not long after that, rubber found an important new market in automobile tires. By the early 20th century, a useful kind of synthetic rubber was being produced to supplement natural rubber supplies for a growing list of purposes, although vehicles depended on tires made of natural rubber all the way until World War II.

Before World War I, most rubber used in the United States was imported from South America. From then until World War II, most rubber came from Southeast Asia. When the supply was cut off by war, the industry entered a crash program and quickly developed new and better kinds of synthetic rubber. Since that time, both natural and synthetic rubber have continued to be important commodities. Today, both are found in countless products, from shoes to conveyor belts, baby bottles to mammoth storage containers, rubber balls to gaskets on spacecraft. Well over half of the rubber used in the United States is made into tires for automobiles, trucks, and other vehicles.

■ The Job

Rubber goods are formed from natural or synthetic materials. Different products go through different processes, but generally all rubber is heated, shaped, and finished. Most of this work is done by machine.

The first step in rubber goods production is breaking up and mixing the crude rubber. *Rubber cutters* operate machines to cut bales of crude rubber into pieces. *Rubber-mill tenders* tend milling machines that mix, blend, knead, or refine scrap, crude, or synthetic rubber. The machines have corrugated rolls that break the rubber apart and soften it. Rubber is then mixed with chemicals to give it various desirable properties. *Formula weighers* operate tram cars on monorails beneath storage bins to collect and weigh ingredients. Rubber is mixed with ingredients such as zinc oxide, sulfur, stearic acid, or fillers in mixing machines such as banbury mixers. *Chemists* and others decide which chemicals to use, and they test samples of the mix before further processing. *Foam rubber mixers, frothing-machine operators,* and *cement mixers* tend special machines that mix air and chemicals into rubber to produce foam rubber and rubber cement.

Mixed and heated rubber is then shaped in one of several ways. It may be squeezed into sheets, molded in shapes, or extruded into tubing or other forms. *Calender operators* run machines that form rubber sheets of specified thickness. *Sponge-press operators* run machines that form and cure

sponge rubber into sheeting for gaskets, insulation, and carpet padding. *Dusting-and-brushing-machine operators* may dust the sheets with talc to keep them from sticking together before further processing. Other workers shape rubber into products using various processes, including building up thin layers (plies) of rubber sheeting. Among these workers and products are *self-sealing-fuel-tank builders,* who make airplane fuel tanks; *belt builders, sectional-belt-mold assemblers, v-belt builders,* and *belt-builder helpers,* who make rubber belts; and *expansion-joint builders,* who make expansion joints for ends of rubber hoses.

Some rubber is formed by molding. *Pourers* fill curing molds with latex using a hose or a machine lever on a conveyor-belt machine. Some rubber products are formed by injection. *Injection-molding-machine tenders* inject hot rubber into molds to form molded products. Products such as balloons and rubber gloves are formed by *dippers,* who dip forms into liquid compounded latex rubber to coat them. Most other molded rubber products, including tires, are pressed and heated in molds. *Foam-rubber molders* make foam cushions and mattresses this way. *Press tenders* make hard objects such as golf and bowling balls. *Arch-cushion press operators* heat-press sponge rubber into arch cushions for rubber shoes and boots. Other molding is done by spraying. *Foam dispensers* spray liquid foam rubber into shaped plastic sheets to make padded dashboards and door panels for vehicles. *Skin formers* shape the plastic sheeting for these products. *Mold strippers* remove molded items from molds and prepare molds for further use. *Mold cleaners* clean, store, and distribute these molds.

The final method of forming rubber is extrusion. In this method, rubber is forced through dies to form continuous shaped rubber products such as tubes and strips. *Extruder operators* and *extruder helpers* set up and run extrusion machines. They select the proper die and install it on the machine, feed rubber stock into the machine, and set the speed at which the rubber is to be forced through the die. *Extruder tenders* regulate and run machines that extrude rubber into strands for elastic yarn. In shoe and boot making, *wink-cutter operators* extrude and cut rubber strips for rubber soles.

Rugs and other fabric goods are often given a rubber backing using calenders, which are machines that press materials between rollers to give a particular finish. Among the workers who operate these machines are *four-roll calender operators,* who use calenders to coat fabric with rubber to a specified thickness. *Calender-let-off operators* use machines to cure and dry fabrics after they are coated. *Calender-wind-up tenders* accumulate the coated fabric into rolls of specified size. *Fabric normalizers* shrink rubberized fabric to increase its strength.

Rubber is cured after it assumes its final shape. In curing, rubber is subjected to heat and pressure to increase its hardness, durability, stability, and elasticity. One such curing process is vulcanization. Foam-rubber sheeting is cured by *foam-rubber curers*, who roll a latex mixture into curing ovens. *Belt-press operators* and *v-belt curers* cure rubber transmission and conveyor belting. *Weather-strip machine operators* mold and vulcanize sponge-rubber beading to make weather-stripping for automobiles.

Rubber sheets, strips, and tubing must be cut into lengths and shapes to form products of specified types and sizes. *Rubber-goods cutter-finishers* use machines to cut, drill, and grind rubber goods, and they verify the sizes of goods using rulers, calipers, gauges, and templates. *Extruder cutters* cut extruded rubber into lengths. *Automatic-die-cutting-machine operators* stamp out rubber shapes using machines with sharp dies. *Roll cutters* use a lathe to cut rolls of rubber or rubberized fabric. *Rubber-cutting-machine tenders* use a guillotine-type machine to cut rubber slabs. *Molded-rubber-goods cutters* use cutting dies to trim molded articles.

Other workers cut rubber for specific products or purposes. Examples of these workers include *strap-cutting-machine operators*, who cut leg straps for hip boots; *band machine operators*, who cut rubber bands from special tubing; and *hose cutters*, who cut rubber hose into specified lengths. *Mat punchers* punch automobile floor mats from sheeting. *Splitting-machine operators* cut scrap tires or rubber sheets into pieces for reclamation.

Rubber items made of a single piece of rubber often need to go through a finishing process. *Buffers* may buff items to smooth and polish them; *dippers* may coat them with vinyl. Workers called *openers* pull weather-stripping through a machine to force apart sides stuck together during curing. *Machine skivers* bevel edges of shoe parts to prepare them for cementing or stitching. *Padded-products finishers* repair defects in padded automobile parts by injecting wrinkles and gaps with liquid rubber foam. Other workers do many other specialized finishing tasks, such as splicing tubing, rolling rings on the mouths of balloons, pressing seams on shoes together to make them watertight, and crimping the edges of articles to reinforce them.

The final processing of rubber items may involve assembling several pieces, decorating surfaces, and quality inspections. Workers who assemble items position and cement or stitch pieces together to make such goods as footwear, shock absorbers for airplane gas tanks, pneumatic airplane deicers, inflatable animals and figures for parades, and many other types of rubber goods. Among the specialized workers who decorate rubber goods are those who print designs or lettering on balloons, brand names on rubber hoses, and designs on rubber sheeting that will be made into footwear. Once goods are finished, *inspectors* make sure company standards are met—they may repair defects they find.

■ Requirements

High School

Because most rubber goods production workers learn their skills on the job, a high school diploma is often the only necessary qualification.

Postsecondary Training

Workers may need college degrees, however, if they plan to pursue chemistry, engineering, or research jobs in the rubber goods industry.

Other Requirements

Production workers need to be in good health and they must have some aptitude for working with machines and other tools. Those who work as inspectors must have good eyesight and be able to make quick decisions.

■ Exploring

Students in college or technical school training programs may be able to obtain summer jobs in rubber goods plants. The experience can help them decide whether they like the work and also may be an advantage if they want full-time employment in the field when they graduate. Another useful experience would be to visit a local rubber goods plant. Some companies allow group tours of their facilities to educate the public about their operations.

■ Employers

Many of the rubber goods plants in the United States are located in Ohio and Indiana, although new plants are springing up in the South. There are rubber plants around the world, especially in Europe, North America, and Japan.

■ Starting Out

The best way to look for work in this industry is to apply directly to rubber goods plants that may be hiring new employees. Jobs may also be located through the local offices of the state employment service, newspaper classified ads, or offices of the unions that organize workers in local plants.

■ Advancement

Most beginning workers enter the industry with few, if any, specialized skills, and they learn what they need to know on the job. After they have gained experience and shown that they are reliable employees, they may be promoted to positions in which they are responsible for supervising other workers or for performing tasks that require higher skill levels. Taking courses in technical schools or colleges can speed advancement for many workers.

■ Earnings

The earnings of workers in rubber goods production vary widely according to the workers' skills, seniority, the hours they work, and other factors. Many workers are members of unions, and their pay is determined by agreements between the union and company management. In general, earnings compare favorably to those of workers in other production jobs in industry. Tire production workers average $33,600 to $34,500 a year. Workers making hoses and belts average $22,100 to $23,300 per year. Miscellaneous and fabricated rubber product workers average $19,500 to $20,300 annually. Workers on night shifts are usually paid more than those who work day shifts.

In addition to their regular earnings, rubber goods workers generally receive benefits such as paid vacation days and holidays, sick leave, and employer contributions to pension plans, and life and health insurance.

■ Work Environment

Most employees in rubber goods production plants work 40 to 46 hours per week. Conditions on the job are generally quite safe. Plants are equipped with special ventilation systems to remove heat, fumes, and dust, and safety features on machinery protect workers from most injuries. Most plants are well lighted and have comfortable heating and cooling systems.

Like most production work, rubber goods jobs often involve repetitive tasks. Working with hot presses, sharp tools, and heavy machinery requires steady nerves and mechanical aptitude.

■ Outlook

In coming years, growth of employment in rubber goods production jobs will probably be limited by increasing automation in manufacturing processes and technological advances that make some rubber goods better and longer-lasting.

Because an important part of the rubber industry is devoted to tires for vehicles, rubber goods production will always be related to the state of the automobile industry. When fewer cars are being manufactured and sold, there is less need for workers who make tires. The 1980s saw a slump in auto sales, and some tire plants were forced to close. The automobile industry began recovering in the early 1990s, which has lead to greater job opportunities.

As new uses for synthetic rubber are developed, probably a smaller portion of the rubber industry will depend on making rubber tires. Instead, new products such as rubber-like paints, waterproofings, and noise-control pads for use in building construction may make up a larger part of the industry's production. Use of synthetic rubber in North American grew by 3.1 percent in 1998 and consumption is expected to increase by an average of 1.5 percent per year by 2003, according to the International Institute of Synthetic Rubber Producers. Natural rubber grew by 3.4 percent in 1998 and is predicted to increase at an annual average rate of 1.3 percent through 2003.

Normal employee turnover in this industry will mean that every year, many new openings will become available as experienced workers move into new jobs or leave the workforce altogether.

■ For More Information

For information on the rubber industry in North America and worldwide, contact:

International Institute of Synthetic Rubber Producers
2077 South Gessner Road, Suite 133
Houston, TX 77063
Tel: 713-783-7511
Web: http://www.iisrp.com

The following is an association for manufacturers of tires, tubes, roofing, sporting goods, mechanical, and industrial products.

Rubber Manufacturers Association
1400 K Street, NW, Ninth Floor
Washington, DC 20005
Tel: 202-682-4800
Web: http://www.rma.org

This union represents workers in the rubber industry.

United Rubber, Cork, Linoleum and Plastics Workers of America
570 White Pond Drive
Akron, OH 44320
Tel: 216-869-0320

■ Related Articles

Rubber

Plastics Products Manufacturing Workers

Textile Manufacturing Occupations

Tire Technicians

Rubber-Mill Operators

■ See Rubber

Safety Coordinators and Safety Engineers

■ See Occupational Safety and Health Workers

Safety Inspectors

■ See Industrial Safety and Health Technicians, Occupational Safety and Health Workers

Safety Officers and Safety Technicians

■ See Industrial Safety and Health Technicians

Sales Clerks

■ See Retail Sales Workers

Sales Managers

■ See Printing Sales Representatives

Sales Representatives

■ Overview

Sales representatives, also called *sales reps,* sell the products and services of manufacturers and wholesalers. They look for potential customers or clients such as retail stores, other manufacturers or wholesalers, government agencies, hospitals, and other institutions; explain or demonstrate their products to these clients; and attempt to make a sale. The job may include follow-up calls and visits to ensure the customer is satisfied.

Sales representatives work under a variety of titles. Those employed by manufacturers are typically called *manufacturers' sales workers* or *manufacturers' representatives.*

Those who work for wholesalers are sometimes called *wholesale trade sales workers* or *wholesale sales representatives. A manufacturers' agent* is a self-employed salesperson who agrees to represent the products of various companies. A *door-to-door sales worker* usually represents just one company and sells products directly to consumers, typically in their homes.

■ History

Sales representatives for manufacturers and wholesalers have long played an important role in the U.S. economy. By representing products and seeking out potential customers, they have helped in the efficient distribution of large amounts of merchandise.

The earliest wholesalers were probably the ship "chandlers," or suppliers, of colonial New England, who assembled in large quantities the food and equipment required by merchant ships and military vessels. Ship owners found that a centralized supply source enabled them to equip their vessels quickly.

Various changes in the 19th century made wholesalers more prominent. Factories were becoming larger, thus allowing for huge amounts of merchandise to be manufactured or assembled in a single location. New forms of transportation, especially the railroad, made it more practical for manufacturers to sell their products over great distances. Although some manufacturers would sell their goods directly to retail outlets and elsewhere, many found it easier and more profitable to let wholesalers do this job. Retail stores, moreover, liked working with wholesalers, who were able to sell them a wide range of merchandise from different manufacturers and from different areas of the country and the world.

The sales representatives hired by manufacturers and wholesalers were typically given a specific territory in which to

SALES REPRESENTATIVES	
SCHOOL SUBJECTS	Business Mathematics
PERSONAL SKILLS	Helping/teaching Communication/ideas
WORK ENVIRONMENT	Indoors and outdoors Primarily multiple locations
MINIMUM EDUCATION LEVEL	High school diploma
SALARY RANGE	$12,000 to $32,000 to $100,000+
CERTIFICATION OR LICENSING	None available
OUTLOOK	Little change or more slowly than the average
DOT	250
GOE	08.02.06
NOC	6421
O*NET	49005D

sell their goods. Armed with illustrated product catalogs, special promotional deals, and financial support for advertising, they traveled to prospective customers and tried to explain the important qualities of their products. Competition between sales representatives sometimes was fierce, leading some to be less than scrupulous. Product claims were exaggerated, and retail stores were sometimes supplied with shoddy merchandise. Eventually more fact-based sales pitches were emphasized by manufacturers and wholesalers, who in the long run benefited from having responsible, honest, well-informed representatives. Products also began to be backed by written guarantees of quality.

Meanwhile, some manufacturers were employing door-to-door sales workers to sell their products directly to consumers. Direct selling in the United States goes back to the famous "Yankee Peddler" who, during colonial times, traveled by wagon, on horseback, and sometimes on foot, bringing to isolated settlers many products that were not easily available otherwise. A forerunner of the modern door-to-door sales worker, peddlers also tried to anticipate the settlers' needs and wants. They frequently represented new or unknown products with the hope of creating a demand for them.

Changes in the 20th century, once again including improvements in transportation, brought still more possibilities for sales representatives. Automobiles allowed representatives to travel to many more communities and to carry more product samples and descriptive catalogs. Trucks provided a new means of transporting merchandise. The growth of commercial aviation further expanded the opportunities for salespeople. Sales representatives would eventually be able to travel to customers in New York, Atlanta, Los Angeles, and Minneapolis, for example, all during a single week.

By the late 20th century, the food products industry was one of the largest employers of sales representatives. Other important fields included printing, publishing, fabricated metal products, chemicals and dyes, electrical and other machinery, and transportation equipment. Among the many establishments helped by sales representatives were retail outlets, who needed a constant supply of clothing, housewares, and other consumer goods, and hospitals, who purchased specialized surgical instruments, drugs, rubber gloves, and thousands of other products from representatives.

■ The Job

Manufacturers' representatives and wholesale sales representatives sell goods to retail stores, other manufacturers and wholesalers, government agencies, and various institutions. They usually do so within a specific geographical area. Some representatives concentrate on just a few products. An electrical appliance salesperson, for example, may

sell 10 to 30 items ranging from food freezers and air-conditioners to waffle irons and portable heaters. Representatives of drug wholesalers, however, may sell as many as 50,000 items.

The duties of sales representatives usually include locating and contacting potential new clients, keeping a regular correspondence with existing customers, determining their clients' needs and informing them of pertinent products and prices. They also travel to meet with clients, show them samples or catalogs, take orders, arrange for delivery, and possibly provide installation. A sales representative also must handle customer complaints, keep up to date on new products, and prepare reports. Many salespeople attend trade conferences, where they learn about products and make sales contacts.

Finding new customers is one of the most important tasks. Sales representatives often follow leads suggested by other clients, from advertisements in trade journals, and from participants in trade shows and conferences. They may make "cold calls" to potential clients. Sales representatives frequently meet with and entertain prospective clients during evenings and weekends.

Representatives who sell highly technical machinery or complex office equipment often are referred to as *sales engineers* or *industrial sales workers*. Because their products tend to be more specialized and their clients' needs more complex, the sales process for these workers tends to be longer and more involved. Before recommending a product, they may, for example, carefully analyze a customer's production processes, distribution methods, or office procedures. They usually prepare extensive sales presentations that include information on how their products will improve the quality and efficiency of the customer's operations.

Some sales engineers, often with the help of their company's research and development department, adapt products to a customer's specialized needs. They may provide the customer with instructions on how to use the new equipment or work with installation experts who provide this service. Some companies maintain a sales assistance staff to train customers and provide specific information. This permits sales representatives to devote a greater percentage of their time to direct sales contact.

Other sales workers, called *detail people,* do not engage in direct selling activities but strive instead to create a better general market for their companies' products. A detail person for a drug company, for example, may call on physicians and hospitals to inform them of new products and distribute samples.

The particular products sold by the sales representative directly affect the nature of the work. Salespeople who represent sporting goods manufacturers may spend most of their time driving from town to town calling on retail stores that carry sporting equipment. They may visit with coaches and athletic directors of high schools and colleges. A representative in this line may be a former athlete or coach who knows intimately the concerns of his or her customers.

Food manufacturers and wholesalers employ large numbers of sales representatives. Because these salespeople usually know the grocery stores and major chains that carry their products, their main focus is to ensure the maximum sales volume. Representatives negotiate with retail merchants to obtain the most advantageous store and shelf position for displaying their products. They encourage the store or chain to advertise their products, sometimes by offering to pay part of the advertising costs or by reducing the selling price to the merchant so that a special sale price can be offered to customers. Representatives check to make sure that shelf items are neatly arranged and that the store has sufficient stock of their products.

Sales transactions can involve huge amounts of merchandise, sometimes worth millions of dollars. For example, in a single transaction, a washing-machine manufacturer, construction company, or automobile manufacturer may purchase all the steel products it needs for an extended period of time. Salespeople in this field may do much of their business by telephone because the product they sell is standardized and, to the usual customer, requires no particular description or demonstration.

Direct, or door-to-door, selling has been an effective way of marketing various products, such as appliances and housewares, cookware, china, tableware and linens, foods, drugs, cosmetics and toiletries, costume jewelry, clothing, and greeting cards. Like other sales representatives, door-to-door sales workers find prospective buyers, explain and demonstrate their products, and take orders. Door-to-door selling has waned in popularity, and Internet selling has taken over much of the door-to-door market.

Several different arrangements are common between companies and their door-to-door sales workers. Under the "direct company plan," for example, a sales representative is authorized to take orders for a product, and the company pays the representative a commission for each completed order. Such workers may be employees of the company and may receive a salary in addition to a commission, or they may be independent contractors. They usually are very well trained. Sales workers who sell magazine subscriptions may be hired, trained, and supervised by a *subscription crew leader,* who assigns representatives to specific areas, reviews the orders they take, and compiles sales records.

Under the "exhibit plan" a salesperson sets up an exhibit booth at a place where large numbers of people are expected to pass, such as a state fair, trade show, or product exposition. Customers approach the booth and schedule appointments with the salespersons for later demonstrations at home.

The "dealer plan" allows a salesperson to function as the proprietor of a small business. The salesperson, or *dealer,* purchases the product wholesale from the company and then resells it to consumers at the retail price, mainly through door-to-door sales.

Under various "group plans," a customer is contacted by a salesperson and given the opportunity to sponsor a sales event. In the "party plan," for example, the sales representative arranges to demonstrate products at the home of a customer, who then invites a group of friends for the "party." The customer who hosts the party receives free or discounted merchandise in return for the use of the home and for assembling other potential customers for the salesperson.

Finally, the "COD plan" allows representatives to sell products on a cash-on-delivery (COD) basis. In this method, the salesperson makes a sale, perhaps collecting an advance deposit, and sends the order to the company. The company, in turn, ships the merchandise directly to the customer, who in this case makes payment to the delivery person, or to the salesperson, who then delivers the product to the customer and collects the balance owed.

Whatever the sales plan, door-to-door sales workers have some advantages over their counterparts in retail stores. Direct sellers, for example, do not have to wait for the customer to come to them; they go out and find the buyers for their products. The direct seller often carries only one product or a limited line of products and thus is much more familiar with the features and benefits of the merchandise. In general, direct sellers get the chance to demonstrate their products where they will most likely be used—in the home.

There are drawbacks to this type of selling. Many customers grow impatient or hostile when salespeople come to their house unannounced and uninvited. It may take several visits to persuade someone to buy the product. In a brief visit, the direct seller must win the confidence of the customer, develop the customer's interest in a product or service, and close the sale.

■ Requirements

High School

A high school diploma is required for most sales positions, although an increasing number of salespeople are graduates of two- or four-year colleges.

Postsecondary Training

The more complex a product, the greater the likelihood that it will be sold by a college-trained person. About 30 percent of all door-to-door sales workers have a college degree.

Some areas of sales work require specialized college work. Those in engineering sales, for example, usually have

LEARN MORE ABOUT IT

Kuswa, Webster. *The Sales Rep's Letter Book.* New York: American Management Association, 1984.

Novick, Harold J. *Selling Through Independent Reps.* New York: American Management Association, 1994.

Spears, Timothy. *100 Years on the Road: The Traveling Salesman in American Culture.* 1995.

a college degree in a relevant engineering field. Other fields that demand specific college degrees include chemical sales (chemistry or chemical engineering), office systems (accounting or business administration), and pharmaceuticals and drugs (biology, chemistry, or pharmacy). Those in less technical sales positions usually benefit from course work in English, speech, psychology, marketing, public relations, economics, advertising, finance, accounting, and business law.

Other Requirements

Sales representatives should enjoy working with people. Other important personal traits include self-confidence, enthusiasm, and self-discipline.

■ Exploring

A student interested in becoming a sales representative may benefit from part-time or summer work in a retail store. Working as a telemarketer also is useful. Some high schools and junior colleges offer programs that combine classroom study with work experience in sales.

Various opportunities exist that provide experience in direct selling. Students can take part in sales drives for school or community groups.

Occasionally manufacturers hire college students for summer assignments. These temporary positions provide an opportunity for the employer and employee to appraise each other. A high percentage of students hired for these specialized summer programs become career employees after graduation. Some wholesale warehouses also offer temporary or summer positions.

■ Employers

In the United States, more than two million people work as manufacturers' and wholesale sales representatives. About 70 percent work in wholesale, many as sellers of machinery. Food, drugs, electrical goods, hardware, and clothing are among the most common products sold by sales representatives.

■ Starting Out

Firms looking for sales representatives sometimes list openings with high school and college placement offices, as well as with public and private employment agencies. In many areas, professional sales associations refer people to suitable openings. Contacting companies directly also is recommended. A list of manufacturers and wholesalers can be found in telephone books and industry directories, which are available at public libraries.

Although some high school graduates are hired for manufacturers' or wholesale sales jobs, many join a company in a nonselling position, such as office, stock, or shipping clerk. This experience allows an employee to learn about the company and its products. From there, he or she eventually may be promoted to a sales position.

Most new representatives complete a training period before receiving a sales assignment. In some cases new salespeople rotate through several departments of an organization to gain a broad exposure to the company's products. Large companies often use formal training programs lasting two years or more, while small organizations frequently rely on supervised sales experience.

Direct selling usually is an easy field to enter. Direct sale companies advertise for available positions in newspapers, in sales workers' specialty magazines, and on television and radio. Many people enter direct selling through contacts they have had with other door-to-door sales workers. Most firms have district or area representatives who interview applicants and arrange the necessary training. Part-time positions in direct selling are common.

■ Advancement

New representatives usually spend their early years improving their sales ability, developing product knowledge, and finding new clients. As sales workers gain experience they may be shifted to increasingly large territories or more difficult types of customers. In some organizations, experienced sales workers narrow their focus. For example, an office equipment sales representative may work solely on government contracts.

Advancement to management positions, such as regional or district manager, also is possible. Some representatives, however, choose to remain in basic sales. Because of commissions, they often earn more money than their managers do, and many enjoy being in the field and working directly with their customers.

A small number of representatives decide to become manufacturers' agents, or self-employed salespeople who handle products for various organizations. Agents perform many of the same functions as sales representatives but usually on a more modest scale.

Door-to-door sales workers also have advancement possibilities. Some are promoted to supervisory roles and recruit, train, and manage new members of the sales force. Others become area, branch, or district managers. Many managers of direct selling firms began as door-to-door sales workers.

■ Earnings

Many beginning sales representatives are paid a salary while receiving their training. After assuming direct responsibility for a sales territory, they may receive only a commission (a fixed percentage of each dollar sold). Also common is a modified commission plan (a lower rate of commission on sales plus a low base salary). Some companies provide bonuses to successful representatives.

Because manufacturers' and wholesale sales representatives typically work on commission, salaries vary widely. Some make as little as $16,000 a year. More successful representatives earn more than $100,000. Most, however, earn between $23,000 and $47,000. The average salary is about $32,000.

Earnings can be affected by changes in the economy or industry cycles, and great fluctuations in salary from year to year or month to month are common. Employees who travel usually are reimbursed for transportation, hotels, meals, and client entertainment expenses.

Door-to-door sales workers usually earn a straight commission on their sales, ranging from 10 to 40 percent of an item's suggested retail price. A typical or average income for this occupation is hard to estimate. It is not uncommon, however, for an experienced, full-time door-to-door salesperson to make between $12,000 and $20,000 a year.

Sales representatives typically receive vacation days, medical and life insurance, and retirement benefits. However, manufacturers' agents and some door-to-door sales workers do not receive benefits.

■ Work Environment

Salespeople generally work long and irregular hours. Those with large territories may spend all day calling and meeting customers in one city and much of the night traveling to the place where they will make the next day's calls and visits. Sales workers with a small territory may do little overnight travel but, like most sales workers, may spend many evenings preparing reports, writing up orders, and entertaining customers. Several times a year, sales workers may travel to company meetings and participate in trade conventions and conferences. Irregular working hours, travel, and the competitive demands of the job can be disruptive to ordinary family life.

Sales work is physically demanding. Representatives often spend most of the day on their feet. Many carry heavy sample cases or catalogs. Occasionally, sales workers assist a customer in arranging a display of the company's products or moving stock items. Many door-to-door sellers work in their own community or nearby areas, although some cover more extensive and distant territories. They often are outdoors in all kinds of weather. Direct sellers must treat customers, even those who are rude or impatient, with tact and courtesy.

■ Outlook

The number of manufacturers' and wholesale sales representatives is expected to grow more slowly than the average for all occupations through the year 2006. In part this is because of technological advances. Electronic data interchange (EDI), a system that improves communication between computers, for example, allows customers to order goods from suppliers more easily.

Future opportunities will vary greatly depending upon the specific product and industry. For example, as giant food chains replace independent grocers, fewer salespeople will be needed to sell groceries to individual stores. By contrast, greater opportunities will probably exist in the air-conditioning field, and advances in consumer electronics and computer technology also may provide many new opportunities.

■ For More Information

For career information, including career brochures, a list of colleges that teach marketing, and a list of job titles, sources and salaries, contact:

Direct Marketing Association
Direct Marketing Educational Foundation
1120 Avenue of the Americas
New York, NY 10036
Tel: 212-768-7277

For referrals to industry trade associations, contact:

Manufacturers' Agents National Association
PO Box 247
Geneva, IL 60134
Tel: 630-208-1466

■ Related Articles

Business

Sales

Auctioneers

Buyers

Cashiers

Counter and Retail Clerks

Merchandise Displayers

Plastics Technicians

Purchasing Agents

Retail Business Owners

Retail Managers

Retail Sales Workers

Services Sales Representatives

Stock Clerks

Salespeople

■ **See Retail Sales Workers**

Sales Technicians

■ **See Plastics Technicians**

Salon Managers

Salon managers are responsible for many important functions of a beauty salon, including overseeing the finances, hiring employees and ensuring that their licenses are current, enforcing health codes, and maintaining records. They should be familiar with insurance policies for fire, theft, and health. Salon managers must maintain communication with the salon's accountants and lawyers and ensure that the salon and its operators remain in compliance with state regulations. Salon managers oversee the staff of the shop, from stylists to receptionists, to ensure that customers feel welcome and are pleased with the services they receive. Salon managers must always look their best, be personable and professional, and represent the salon in a positive light. Their communication skills are key because they must be able to handle complaints from customers and build good will. Other managerial concerns include the décor and cleanliness of the salon. The main function of salon managers is to ensure that the shop runs smoothly and the customers are happy. This can be a high-pressure job with long hours, so a salon manager must be energetic, upbeat, and a genuine people-person.

Most salon managers are former stylists who have been promoted into management. A few states have separate requirements and licenses for cosmeticians who are also managers (called *manager-operators*). Unlike managers who are not operators, manager-operators are allowed to style hair and are paid a percentage of the shop's profits.

The outlook for salon managers is good. The beauty industry is recession-proof and continues to expand rapidly. The aging population's desire to remain youthful and attractive is contributing significantly to the demand for beauty professionals, including salon managers.

■ **Related Articles**
    Cosmetology
    Barbers
    Cosmetologists/Hair Stylists
    Nail Technicians

Sand Molders

■ **See Molders**

Sanitarians

■ **See Health and Regulatory Inspectors**

Sawyers

■ **See Plastics Products Manufacturing Workers**

Scanner Operators

■ **See Prepress Workers**

Schactos

■ **See Meatcutters**

School Administrators

■ **Overview**

School administrators are leaders who plan and set goals related to the educational, administrative, and counseling programs of schools. They coordinate and evaluate the activities of teachers and other school personnel to ensure that they adhere to deadlines and budget requirements and meet established objectives.

■ **History**

The history of school administrators is almost as old as the history of education itself. The first American colonists of the 17th century set up schools in their homes. In the 18th century, groups of prosperous parents established separate schools and employed schoolmasters. In these small early schools, the teachers were also the administrators, charged with the operation of the school as well as with the instruction of the pupils.

In the early 1800s, the importance of education gained recognition among people from all classes of society and the government became involved in providing schooling without cost to all children. Schools grew larger, a more complex system of education evolved, and there developed a demand for educators specializing in the area of administration.

In the United States, each state has its own school system, headed by a state superintendent or commissioner of education who works in conjunction with the state board of education. The states are divided into local school districts, which may vary in size from a large urban area to a sparsely populated area containing a single classroom of children. The board of education in each district elects a professionally trained superintendent or supervising principal to administer the local schools. In most school districts the superintendent has one or more assistants, and in a very large district the superintendent may also be assisted by business managers, directors of curriculum, or research and testing personnel. Individual schools within a district are usually headed by a school principal, with one or more assistant principals. The administrative staff of a very large secondary school may also include deans, registrars, department heads, counselors, and others.

The problems of school administrators today are much more complex than in the past and require political as well as administrative skills. School leaders are confronted by such volatile issues as desegregation, school closings and reduced enrollments, contract negotiations with teachers, student and staff safety, and greatly increased costs coupled with public resistance to higher taxes.

■ The Job

Teachers have long threatened to send unruly students to the principal's office; perhaps you've even taken a few trips down the hall yourself. The next time you have to sit in detention, don't look at it as discipline—use the opportunity to get to know how school administration works. The occupation of school administrator includes school district superintendents, assistant superintendents, school principals, and assistant principals. Private schools also have administrators—often known as school directors or headmasters. As an administrator in either a public or private school, you are responsible for the smooth, efficient operation of an individual school or an entire school system. The nature of your job will depend on the size and type of your school or the size of the district. You'll make plans, set goals, and supervise and coordinate the activities of teachers and other school personnel in carrying out those plans within the established time framework and budget allowance. The general job descriptions that follow refer to administrators in the public school system.

School principals far outnumber the other school administrators and are the most familiar to the students, who often think of them as disciplinarians. As a principal, you will spend a great deal of your time resolving conflicts that students and teachers may have with one another, with parents, or with school board policies, but your authority extends to many other matters. You're responsible for the performance of an individual school, directing and coor-

dinating educational, administrative, and counseling activities according to standards set by the superintendent and the board of education. You hire and assign teachers and other staff, help them improve their skills, and evaluate their performance. You plan and evaluate the instructional programs jointly with teachers. Periodically, you'll visit classrooms to observe the effectiveness of the teachers and teaching methods, review educational objectives, and examine learning materials—always seeking ways to improve the quality of instruction.

You're responsible for the registration, schedules, and attendance of pupils. In cases of severe educational or behavioral problems, you may confer with teachers, students, and parents and recommend corrective measures. You cooperate with community organizations, colleges, and other schools to coordinate educational services. You oversee the day-to-day operations of the school building and requisition and allocate equipment, supplies, and instructional materials.

Your numerous duties as a school principal necessitate a great deal of paperwork: filling out forms, preparing administrative reports, and keeping records. Nevertheless, you also spend much of each day meeting with people: teachers and other school personnel, colleagues, students, parents, and other members of the community.

In larger schools, usually secondary schools, principals may have one or more assistants. *Assistant principals,* who may be known as *deans of students,* provide counseling for individuals or student groups related to personal problems, educational or vocational objectives, and social and recreational activities. They often handle discipline, interviewing students, and taking whatever action is necessary in matters such as truancy and delinquency. Assistant principals generally plan and supervise social and recreational programs and coordinate other school activities.

Superintendents are responsible for managing the affairs of an entire school district, which may range in size from

SCHOOL ADMINISTRATORS	
SCHOOL SUBJECTS	Business English
PERSONAL SKILLS	Helping/teaching Leadership/management
WORK ENVIRONMENT	Primarily indoors Primarily one location
MINIMUM EDUCATION LEVEL	Master's degree
SALARY RANGE	$52,000 to $82,000 to $120,000
CERTIFICATION OR LICENSING	Required by all states
OUTLOOK	About as fast as the average
DOT	099
GOE	11.07.03
NOC	0313
O*NET	15005B

A high school principal searches the locker of a student caught stealing.

a small town with a handful of schools to a city with a population of millions. To work as a superintendent, you must be elected by the board of education to oversee and coordinate the activities of all the schools in the district in accordance with board of education standards. As a superintendent, you select and employ staff and negotiate contracts. You're responsible for the development and administration of a budget, the acquisition and maintenance of school buildings, and the purchase and distribution of school supplies and equipment. You coordinate related activities with other school districts and agencies. You speak before community and civic groups and try to enlist their support. In addition, you'll collect statistics, prepare reports, enforce compulsory attendance, and oversee the operation of the school transportation system and provision of health services.

School district superintendents usually have one or more assistants or deputies, whose duties vary depending on the size and nature of the school system. Assistant superintendents may have charge of a particular geographic area

or may specialize in activities pertaining, for example, to budget, personnel, or curriculum development.

Boards of education vary in their level of authority and their method of appointment or election to the post of board member. Normally, board members are elected from leaders in the community in business and education. It is not uncommon to have the board selected by the mayor or other city administrator.

■ Requirements

School administration calls for a high level of education and experience. Principals and assistant principals are generally required to have a master's degree in educational administration in addition to several years' experience as a classroom teacher.

High School

You should begin preparing by taking a wide range of college-preparatory courses, including English, mathematics, science, music, art, history, and computers.

Postsecondary Training

School superintendents usually must have had graduate training in educational administration, preferably at the doctoral level. Some larger districts require a law degree or a business degree in addition to a graduate degree in education. Candidates for the position of school superintendent generally must have accumulated previous experience as an administrator.

Around 250 universities offer graduate programs in educational administration accredited by the National Council for Accreditation of Teacher Education. Programs are designed specifically for elementary school principals, secondary school principals, or school district superintendents and include such courses as school management, school law, curriculum development and evaluation, and personnel administration. A semester of internship and field experience are extremely valuable.

Certification or Licensing

Licensure of school administrators is mandatory in all 50 states and the District of Columbia. Requirements to become licensed may include U.S. citizenship or state residency, graduate training in educational administration, experience, and good health and character. In some states, candidates must pass a qualifying examination. You can obtain information on specific requirements from the department of education in your state.

Other Requirements

You should have leadership skills necessary for keeping the school operating smoothly. You also need good communication skills and the ability to get along with many different types and ages of people. Strong self-motivation and self-confidence are important for putting your plans into action, and for withstanding criticism.

■ Exploring

If you've been attending a private or public school, you're already very familiar with the nature of education, and already know many great resources of information—your own teachers and school administrators. Because you'll first work as a teacher before moving into administration, make sure teaching is of interest to you. Talk to your teachers about their work, and offer to assist them with some projects before or after school. School counselors can offer vocational guidance, provide occupational materials, and help students plan appropriate programs of study.

You can gain experience in the education field by teaching Sunday school classes, getting summer jobs as camp counselors or day care center aides, working with a scouting group, volunteering to coach a youth athletic team, or tutoring younger students.

■ Employers

As a principal, you'll be working in either a public or private school, at the elementary or secondary level. Superintendents work for a school district, which may include many elementary and secondary schools. School administrators are also needed for large preschools and job training programs. See the chapter on *College Administrators* to learn about opportunities with colleges and universities.

■ Starting Out

Most school administrators enter the field as teachers. College and university placement offices may help place you in your first teaching job, or you may apply directly to a local school system. Teachers, of course, must meet the requirements for state licensure. Many school districts and state departments of education maintain job listings that notify potential teachers and administrators of openings. Qualified candidates may also come from other administrative jobs, such as curriculum specialist, financial advisor, or director of audiovisual aids, libraries, arts, or special education. The important thing is that you be experienced in organizing and supervising school programs and activities.

■ Advancement

A teacher may be promoted directly to principal, but more often teachers begin as assistant principals and in time are promoted. Experienced administrators may advance to assistant superintendent and then superintendent. In fact, many school superintendents are former principals who worked their way up the administrative ladder. Each

WOMEN IN SCHOOL ADMINISTRATION

According to the American Association of School Administrators, 88 percent of the nation's superintendents were male, and just 12 percent female, in 1998. Though the percentages are very unbalanced, they are cause for celebration. They demonstrate a great improvement over previous years: in 1993, only 7 percent of superintendents were women; only 1.2 percent in 1982.

increase in responsibility usually carries a corresponding salary increase.

■ Earnings

The income of school administrators depends on the position, the level of responsibility, and the size and geographic location of the school or school district. The highest salaries are paid in the far western and mid-Atlantic states; the lowest, in the Southeast.

The Educational Research Service conducted a survey of the salaries of public school administrators for the 1996-97 school year. Assistant principals earned an average of $52,300 a year in elementary schools, and $59,700 a year in high schools. Elementary school principals made about $62,900 a year, while high school principals made $72,400. The average annual salary for a deputy superintendent was $94,400. Superintendents earned annual salaries of $98,100. Superintendents of large school districts (25,000 or more pupils) can make over $120,000 a year.

School administrators also receive a variety of other benefits including health insurance, retirement plans, and vacation and sick leave.

■ Work Environment

Your standard workweek as a school administrator will be 40 hours, though you may work longer if there are meetings to attend or urgent matters to handle in the evenings or on weekends. Also, your job requires year-round attention, even during school vacations.

You'll work in a pleasant office environment, usually at a desk. At times, however, you'll attend meetings elsewhere with PTA members, the school board, and civic groups. Principals and their assistants periodically sit in on classes, attend school assemblies and sporting events, and conduct inspections of the school's physical facilities.

■ Outlook

The number of school administrators employed is determined to a large extent by state and local expenditures for education. Budget cuts not only affect the number of available positions in administration, but also affect how an administrator can perform his or her job. Administrators in the coming years will have to remain creative in finding funds for their schools. School administrators are also faced with developing additional programs for children as more parents work outside the home. Schools may be expected to help care for children before and after regular school hours.

Administrators may also be overseeing smaller learning environments in the coming years. Research has proven that smaller classrooms and more individual attention not only improve education, but help educators identify students with personal and emotional problems. In order to keep students safe from violence, drug abuse, and street gangs, administrators may be called upon to develop more individualized education.

■ For More Information

For articles and news reports about the career of school administrator, visit the Web sites of these organizations.

American Association of School Administrators
1801 North Moore Street
Arlington, VA 22209
Tel: 703-528-0700
Web: http://www.aasa.org

National Association of Elementary School Principals
1615 Duke Street
Alexandria, VA 22314
Tel: 703-684-3345
Web: http://www.naesp.org

National Association of Secondary School Principals
1904 Association Drive
Reston, VA 20191
Tel: 703-860-0200
Web: http://www.nassp.org

■ Related Articles

Education
Adult and Vocational Education Teachers
College Administrators
College Professors
Guidance Counselors
Special Education Teachers

School Media Center Directors

■ See Library Media Specialists

School Psychologists

■ See Psychologists

Scientific Programmers

■ See Computer Programmers

Scopists

■ See Court Reporters

Screenwriters

■ Overview

Screenwriters write scripts for entertainment, education, training, sales, and films. They may choose themes themselves, or they may write on a theme assigned by a producer or director, sometimes adapting plays or novels into screenplays. Screenwriting is an art, a craft, and a business. It is a career that requires imagination and creativity, the ability to tell a story using both dialogue and pictures, and the ability to negotiate with producers and studio executives.

■ History

In 1894, Thomas Edison invented the kinetograph to take a series of pictures of actions staged specifically for the camera. In October of the same year, the first film opened at Hoyt's Theatre in New York. It was a series of acts performed by such characters as a strongman, a contortionist, and trained animals. Even in these earliest motion pictures, the plot or sequence of actions the film would portray was written down before filming began.

Newspaperman Roy McCardell was the first person to be hired for the specific job of writing for motion pictures. He wrote captions for photographs in an entertainment weekly. When he was employed by Biograph to write 10 scenarios, or stories, at $10 apiece, it caused a flood of newspapermen to try their hand at screenwriting.

The early films, which ran only about a minute and were photographs of interesting movement, grew into story films, which ran between 9 and 15 minutes. The demand for original plots led to the development of story departments at each of the motion picture companies in the period from 1910 to 1915. The story departments were responsible for writing the stories and also for reading and evaluating material that came from outside sources. Stories usually came from writers, but some were purchased from actors on the lot. The actor Genevieve (Gene) Gauntier, was paid $20 per reel of film for her first scenarios.

There was a continuing need for scripts because usually a studio bought a story one month, filmed the next, and released the film the month after. Some of the most popular stories in these early films were Wild West tales and comedies.

Longer story films began to use titles, and as motion pictures became longer and more sophisticated, so did the titles. In 1909-10, there was an average of 80 feet of title per 1,000 feet of film. By 1926, the average increased to 250 feet of title per 1,000 feet. The titles included dialogue, description, and historical background.

In 1920, the first Screen Writers Guild was established to ensure fair treatment of writers, and in 1927 the Academy of Motion Picture Arts and Sciences was formed, including a branch for writers. The first sound film, *The Jazz Singer*, was also produced in 1927. Screenwriting changed dramatically to adapt to the new technology.

From the 1950s to the 1980s, the studios gradually declined and more independent film companies and individuals were able to break into the motion picture industry. The television industry began to thrive in the 1950s, further increasing the number of opportunities for screenwriters. During the 1960s, people began to graduate from the first education programs developed specifically for screenwriting.

Today, most Americans have spent countless hours viewing programs on television and movie screens. Familiarity with these mediums has led many writers to attempt writing screenplays. This has created an intensely fierce marketplace with many more screenplays being rejected than accepted each year.

■ The Job

Screenwriters write dramas, comedies, soap operas, adventures, westerns, documentaries, newscasts, and training films. They may write original stories, or get inspiration from newspapers, magazines, or books. They may also write scripts for continuing television series. *Continuity writers* in broadcasting create station announcements, previews of coming shows, and advertising copy for local sponsors. *Broadcasting scriptwriters* usually work in a team, writing for a certain audience, to fill a certain time slot. *Motion picture writers* submit an original screenplay or adaptation of a book to a motion picture producer or studio. *Playwrights* submit their plays to drama companies for performance or try to get their work published in book form.

Screenwriters may work on a staff of writers and producers for a large company. Or they may work independently for smaller companies which hire only freelance production teams. Advertising agencies also hire writers, sometimes as staff, sometimes as freelancers.

Scripts are written in a 2-column format, 1 column for dialogue and sound, the other for video instructions. One page of script equals about 1 minute of running time, though it varies. Each page has about 150 words and takes about 20 seconds to read. Screenwriters send a query letter outlining their idea before they submit a script to a production company. Then they send a standard release form and wait at least a month for a response. Studios buy many more scripts than are actually produced, and studios often will buy a script only with provisions that the original writer or another writer, will rewrite it to their specifications.

■ Requirements

High School

You can develop your writing skills in English, theater, speech, and journalism classes. Belonging to a debate team can also help you learn how to express your ideas within a specific time allotment and framework. History, government, and foreign language can contribute to a well-rounded education, necessary for creating intelligent scripts. A business course can be useful in understanding the complex nature of the film industry.

Postsecondary Training

There are no set educational requirements for screenwriters. A college degree is desirable, especially a liberal arts education which exposes you to a wide range of subjects. An undergraduate or graduate film program will likely include courses in screenwriting, film theory, and other subjects that will teach you about the film industry and its history. A creative writing program will involve you with workshops and seminars that will help you develop fiction writing skills.

Other Requirements

As a screenwriter, you must be able to create believable characters and develop a story. You must have technical skills, such as dialogue writing, creating plots, and doing research. In addition to creativity and originality,

SCREENWRITERS	
SCHOOL SUBJECTS	English Theater/Dance
PERSONAL SKILLS	Artistic Communication/ideas
WORK ENVIRONMENT	Primarily indoors Primarily one location
MINIMUM EDUCATION LEVEL	High school diploma
SALARY RANGE	$15,000 to $83,542 to $500,000+
CERTIFICATION OR LICENSING	None available
OUTLOOK	Faster than the average
DOT	131
GOE	01.01.02
NOC	5121
O*NET	34002C

you also need an understanding of the marketplace for your work—you should be aware of what kinds of scripts are in demand by producers.

■ Exploring

One of the best ways to learn about screenwriting is to read and study scripts. It is advisable to watch a motion picture while simultaneously following the script. The scripts for such classic films as *Casablanca, Network,* and *Chinatown* are often taught in college screenwriting courses. You should read film-industry publications, such as *Daily Variety, Hollywood Reporter,* and *The Hollywood Scriptwriter.* There are a number of books about screenwriting, but they're often written by those outside of the industry. These books are best used primarily for learning about the format required for writing a screenplay. There are also computer software programs which assist with screenplay formatting.

The Sundance Institute, a Utah-based production company, accepts unsolicited scripts from those who have read the Institute's submission guidelines. Every January they choose a few scripts and invite the writers to a five-day program of one-on-one sessions with professionals. The process is repeated in June, and also includes a videotaping of sections of chosen scripts. The Institute doesn't produce features, but they can often introduce writers to those who do. (For guidelines, send a self-addressed, stamped envelope with your request to The Sundance Institute, 225 Santa Monica Boulevard, 8th Floor, Santa Monica, CA, 90401, or visit their Web site at http://www.sundance.org.)

Most states offer grants for emerging and established screenwriters and other artists. Contact your state's art council for guidelines and application materials. In addition, several arts groups and associations hold annual contests for screenwriters. To find out more about screenwriting contests, consult a reference work such as *The Writer's Market.*

Students may try to get their work performed locally. A teacher may be able to help you submit your work to a local radio or television station or to a publisher of plays.

■ Employers

Most screenwriters work on a freelance basis, contracting with production companies for individual projects. Those who work for television may contract with a TV production company for a certain number of episodes or seasons.

■ Starting Out

The first step to getting a screenplay produced is to write a letter to the script editor of a production company describing yourself, your training, and your work. Ask if the editors would be interested in reading one of your scripts. You should also pursue a manager or agent by sending along a brief letter describing a project you're working on.

(A list of agents is available from the Writers Guild of America (WGA).) If you receive an invitation to submit more, you'll then prepare a synopsis or treatment of the screenplay, which is usually from 1 to 10 pages. It should be in the form of a narrative short story, with little or no dialogue.

Whether you are a beginning or experienced screenwriter, it is best to have an agent, since studios, producers and stars often return unsolicited manuscripts unopened to protect themselves from plagiarism charges. Agents provide access to studios and producers, interpret contracts, and negotiate deals.

It is wise to register your script ($10 for members, $20 for nonmembers) with the WGA. Although registration offers no legal protection, it is proof that on a specific date you came up with a particular idea, treatment, or script. You should also keep a detailed journal that lists the contacts you've made, the people who have read your script, etc.

■ Advancement

Competition is stiff among screenwriters, and a beginner will find it difficult to break into the field. More opportunities become available as you gain experience and a reputation, but that is a process that can take many years. Rejection is a common occurrence in the field of screenwriting. Most successful screenwriters have had to send their screenplays to numerous production companies before they find one who likes their work.

Once you've sold some scripts, you may be able to join the WGA. Membership with the WGA guarantees you a minimum wage for a production and other benefits such as arbitration. Some screenwriters, however, writing for minor productions, can have regular work and successful careers without WGA membership.

Those screenwriters who manage to break into the business can benefit greatly from recognition in the industry. In addition to creating their own scripts, some writers are also hired to "doctor" the scripts of others, using their expertise to revise scripts for production. If a film proves very successful, a screenwriter will be able to command higher payment, and will be able to work on high-profile productions. Some of the most talented screenwriters receive awards from the industry, most notably the Academy Award for best original or adapted screenplay.

■ Earnings

Wages for screenwriters are nearly impossible to track. Some screenwriters make hundreds of thousands of dollars from their scripts, while others write and film their own scripts without any payment at all, relying on backers and loans. Screenwriter Joe Eszterhas made entertainment news in the early 1990s when he received $3 million for each of his treatments for *Basic Instinct, Jade,* and *Showgirls.* In

1999, many scripts by first-time screenwriters have been sold for between $500,000 and $1 million. Typically, a writer will earn a percentage (approximately 1 percent) of the film's budget. Obviously, a lower budget film pays considerably less than a big production. According to statistics compiled in 1998 by the WGA, the median income for WGA members was $83,542 a year. As a member of the WGA, you can receive health benefits.

■ Work Environment

Screenwriters who choose to freelance have the freedom to write when and where they choose. They must be persistent and patient—only 1 in 20 to 30 purchased or optioned screenplays is produced.

Screenwriters who work on the staff of a large company, for a television series, or under contract to a motion picture company, may share writing duties with others.

Screenwriters who do not live in Hollywood or New York will likely have to travel to attend script conferences. They may even have to relocate for several weeks while a project is in production. Busy periods before and during film production are followed by long periods of inactivity and solitude. This forces many screenwriters, especially those just getting started in the field, to work other jobs and pursue other careers while they develop their talent and craft.

■ Outlook

There is intense competition in the television and motion picture industries. There are currently over 9,300 members of the WGA. A 1998 report by the WGA found that only 4,164 of its members were actually employed the previous year. The report also focused on the opportunities for women and minority screenwriters throughout the 1990s. Despite employment for minority screenwriters substantially increasing, employment for women changed little in that decade. Eighty percent of those writing for feature films are white males. Though this domination in the industry will eventually change because of efforts by women and minority filmmakers, the change may be slow in coming. The success of independent cinema, which has introduced a number of women and minority filmmakers to the industry, will continue to contribute to this change.

As cable television expands and digital technology allows for more programming, new opportunities may emerge. Television networks continue to need new material and new episodes for long-running series. Studios are always looking for new angles on action, adventure, horror, and comedy, especially romantic comedy stories. The demand for new screenplays should increase slightly in the next decade, but the number of screenwriters is growing at a faster rate. Writers will continue to find opportunities in advertising agencies and educational and training video production houses.

OSCARS

Screenwriters who have won the Oscar for best original screenplay in the 1990s:

1998: Marc Norman and Tom Stoppard for *Shakespeare In Love*

1997: Matt Damon and Ben Affleck for *Good Will Hunting*

1996: Ethan Coen and Joel Coen for *Fargo*

1995: Christopher McQuarrie for *The Usual Suspects*

1994: Quentin Tarantino and Roger Avary for *Pulp Fiction*

1993: Jane Campion for *The Piano*

1992: Neil Jordan for *The Crying Game*

1991: Callie Khouri for *Thelma and Louise*

1990: Bruce Joel Rubin for *Ghost*

■ For More Information

To learn more about the film industry, to read interviews and articles by noted screenwriters, and to find links to many other screenwriting-related sites on the Internet, visit the Web sites of the WGA:

Writers Guild of America
West Chapter
7000 West Third Street
Los Angeles, CA 90048
Tel: 310-550-1000
Web: http://www.wga.org

Writers Guild of America
East Chapter
555 West 57th Street
New York, NY 10019
Tel: 212-767-7800
Web: http://www.wgaeast.org

Check out this site for a number of Web resources for screenwriters:

Screenwriters & Playwrights Home Page
Web: http://www.teleport.com/~cdeemer/scrwriter.html

■ Related Articles

Film

Television

Actors

Cinematographers and Directors of Photography

Film and Television Directors

Producers

Writers

Second Assistant Camera Operators

■ See Camera Operators, Cinematographers and Directors of Photography

Secondary School Teachers

■ Overview

Secondary school teachers teach students in grades seven through 12. Specializing in one subject area, such as English or math, these teachers work with five or more groups of students during the day. They lecture, direct discussions, and test students' knowledge with exams, essays, and homework assignments.

■ History

Early secondary education was typically based upon training students to enter the clergy. Benjamin Franklin pioneered the idea of a broader secondary education with the creation of the academy, which offered a flexible curriculum and a wide variety of academic subjects.

It was not until the 19th century, however, that children of different social classes commonly attended school into the secondary grades. The first English Classical School, which was to become the model for public high schools throughout the country, was established in 1821, in Boston. An adjunct to the high school, the junior high school, was conceived by Dr. Charles W. Eliot, president of Harvard. In a speech before the National Education Association in 1888, he recommended that secondary studies be started two years earlier than was then the custom. The first such school opened in 1908, in Columbus, Ohio. Another opened a year later in Berkeley, California. By the early 20th century, secondary school attendance was made mandatory in the United States.

SECONDARY SCHOOL TEACHERS	
SCHOOL SUBJECTS	English Psychology
PERSONAL SKILLS	Communication/ideas Helping/teaching
WORK ENVIRONMENT	Primarily indoors Primarily one location
MINIMUM EDUCATION LEVEL	Bachelor's degree
SALARY RANGE	$25,000 to $38,000 to $50,000
CERTIFICATION OR LICENSING	Required by all states
OUTLOOK	About as fast as the average
DOT	091
O*NET	31308

■ The Job

Many successful people credit secondary school teachers with helping guide them into college, careers, and other endeavors. When you are teaching in a middle or high school, your students may look to you for help in a number of areas. Your primary responsibility to your students in grades 7 through 12 will be to educate them in a specific subject. But you'll also inform students about colleges, occupations, and such varied subjects as the arts, health, and relationships. You may teach in a traditional area, such as science, English, history, and math, or you may teach more specialized classes, such as information technology, business, and theater. Many secondary schools are expanding their course offerings to better serve the individual interests of their students. "School-to-work" programs, which are vocational education programs designed for high school students and recent graduates, involve lab work and demonstrations to prepare students for highly technical jobs. Though you'll likely be assigned to one specific level in your subject area, you may be required to teach multiple levels. For example, a secondary school mathematics teacher may teach algebra to a class of ninth-graders one period and trigonometry to high school seniors the next.

In the classroom, you'll rely on a variety of teaching methods. You'll spend a great deal of time lecturing, but you'll also facilitate student discussion and develop projects and activities to interest the students in the subject. You'll show films and videos, use computers and the Internet, and bring in guest speakers. You'll assign essays, presentations, and other projects. Each individual subject calls upon particular approaches, and may involve laboratory experiments, role-playing exercises, shop work, and field trips.

Outside of the classroom, you'll prepare lectures, lesson plans, and exams. You'll evaluate student work and calculate grades. In the process of planning your class, you'll read textbooks, novels, and workbooks to determine reading assignments; you'll photocopy notes, articles, and other handouts; and you'll develop grading policies. You'll also continue to study alternative and traditional teaching methods to hone your skills. You'll prepare students for special events and conferences and submit student work to competitions. Many secondary school teachers also serve as sponsors to student organizations in their field. For example, a French teacher may sponsor the French club and a journalism teacher may advise the yearbook staff. Some secondary school teachers also have the opportunity for extracurricular work as athletic coaches or drama coaches. You'll also monitor students during lunch or break times, and sit in on study halls. You may also accompany student groups on field days, and to competitions and events. Some teachers also have the opportunity to escort students on educational vacations to foreign countries, and to Washington, DC, and other major U.S. cities. You'll attend faculty meetings, meetings with parents, and state and national teacher conferences.

Some teachers explore their subject area outside of the requirements of the job. English and writing teachers may publish in magazines and journals; business and technology teachers may have small businesses of their own; music teachers may perform and record their music; art teachers may show work in galleries; sign-language teachers may do freelance interpreting.

■ Requirements

High School
You should follow your guidance counselor's college preparatory program and take advanced classes in such subjects as English, science, math, and government. You should also explore an extracurricular activity, such as theater, sports, and debate, so that you can offer these additional skills to future employers. If you're already aware of which subject you'd like to teach, take all the courses in that area that are available. You should also take speech and composition courses to develop your communication skills.

Postsecondary Training
There are about 500 accredited teacher education programs in the United States. Most of these programs are designed to meet the certification requirements for the state in which they're located. Some states may require that you pass a test before being admitted to an education program. You may choose to major in your subject area while taking required education courses, or you may major in secondary education with a concentration in your subject area. You'll probably have advisors in both colleges to help you select courses. Practice teaching, also called student teaching, in an actual school situation is usually required. The student is placed in a school to work with a full-time teacher. During the period of practice teaching, the undergraduate student will observe the ways in which lessons are presented and the classroom is managed, learn how to keep records of such details as attendance and grades, and get actual experience in handling the class, both under supervision and alone. Besides licensure and courses in education, prospective high school teachers usually need 24 to 36 hours of college work in the subject they wish to teach. Some states require a master's degree; teachers with master's degrees can earn higher salaries. Private schools generally do not require an education degree.

Certification or Licensing
Public school teachers must be licensed under regulations established by the department of education of the state in which they are teaching. Not all states require licensure for teachers in private or parochial schools. When you've received your teaching degree, you may request that a transcript of your college record be sent to the licensure section of the state department of education. If you have met licensure requirements, you will receive a certificate and thus be eligible to teach in the public schools of the state.

In some states, you may have to take additional tests. If you move to another state, you will have to resubmit college transcripts, as well as comply with any other regulations in the new state to be able to teach there.

Other Requirements
You'll need respect for young people, and a genuine interest in their success in life. You'll also need patience—adolescence can be a troubling time for children, and these troubles often affect behavior and classroom performance. You'll also be working with students who are at very impressionable ages; you should serve as a good role model. You should also be well organized, as you'll have to keep track of the work and progress of a number of different students.

■ Exploring
By attending your high school classes, you've already gained a good sense of the daily work of a secondary school teacher. But the requirements of a teacher extend far beyond the classroom, so ask to spend some time with one of your teachers after school, and ask to look at lecture notes and record-keeping procedures. Interview your teachers about the amount of work that goes into preparing a class and directing an extracurricular activity. To get some firsthand teaching experience, volunteer for a peer tutoring program. Many other teaching opportunities may exist in your community—look into coaching an athletic team at the YMCA, counseling at a summer camp, teaching an art course at a community center, or assisting with a community theater production.

■ Employers
Secondary school teachers are needed at public and private schools, including parochial schools, juvenile detention centers, vocational schools, and schools of the arts. Some Montessori schools are also expanding to include high school courses. Secondary school teachers work in middle schools, junior high schools, and high schools. Though some rural areas maintain schools, most secondary schools are in towns and cities of all sizes. Teachers are also finding opportunities in "charter" schools, which are smaller, deregulated schools that receive public funding.

■ Starting Out
After completing the teacher certification process, including your months of student teaching, you'll work with your college's placement office to find a full-time position. The departments of education of some states maintain listings of job openings. Many schools advertise teaching positions in the classifieds of the state's major newspapers. You may also directly contact the principals and superintendents of the schools in which you'd like to work. While waiting for full-time work, you can work as a substitute teacher. In

A high school biology teacher during a lecture

urban areas with many schools, you may be able to substitute full-time.

■ Advancement

Most teachers advance in the sense that they become more expert in the job that they have chosen. There is usually an increase in salary as teachers acquire experience. Additional training or study can also bring an increase in salary.

A few teachers with administrative ability and interest in administrative work may advance to the position of principal. Others may work into supervisory positions, and some may become helping teachers who are charged with the responsibility of helping other teachers find appropriate instructional materials and develop certain phases of their courses of study. Others may go into teacher education at a college or university. For most of these positions, additional education is required. Some teachers also make lateral moves into other education-related positions such as guidance counselor or resource room teacher.

■ Earnings

Most teachers are contracted to work nine months out of the year, though some contracts are made for 10 or a full 12 months. (When regular school is not in session, teachers are expected to conduct summer teaching, planning, or other school-related work.) In most cases, teachers have the option of prorating their salary up to 52 weeks.

The National Education Association's (NEA) "Rankings of the States, 1997," reported the average annual teacher salary was $38,611. Average salaries ranged from $26,764 in South Dakota to $50,647 in Alaska. The American Federation of Teachers also released survey results in 1997. This report found that the average beginning salary for a teacher with only a bachelor's degree was $25,190. The average maximum salary for a teacher with a master's degree was $44,694.

Teachers can also supplement their earnings through teaching summer classes, coaching sports, sponsoring a club, or other extracurricular work.

On behalf of the teachers, unions bargain with schools over contract conditions such as wages, hours, and benefits. Most teachers join the American Federation of Teachers or the National Education Association. Depending on the state, teachers usually receive a retirement plan, sick leave, and health and life insurance. Some systems grant teachers sabbatical leave.

■ Work Environment

Although the job of the secondary school teacher is not overly strenuous, it can be tiring and trying. You must stand for many hours each day, do a lot of talking, show energy and enthusiasm, and have to handle discipline problems. But you'll also have the reward of guiding your students as they make decisions about their lives and futures.

You'll work under generally pleasant conditions, though some older schools may have poor heating and electrical systems. Though violence in schools has decreased in recent years, media coverage of the violence has increased, along with student fears. In most schools, your students are prepared to learn and to perform the work that's required of them. But in some schools, students may be dealing with gangs, drugs, poverty, and other problems, so the environment can be tense and emotional.

School hours are generally 8 AM to 3 PM, but you'll work more than 40 hours a week teaching, preparing for classes, grading papers, and directing extracurricular activities. As a coach, or as a music or drama director, you may have to work some evenings and weekends. Many teachers enroll in master's or doctoral programs and take evening and summer courses to continue their education.

■ Outlook

The U.S. Department of Education predicts 1 million new teachers will be needed by 2006 to meet rising enrollments and to replace the large number of retiring teachers. The NEA believes this will be a difficult challenge because of low teacher salaries that are in decline. Better salaries will be necessary to attract new teachers and retain experienced ones, along with other changes such as smaller classroom sizes and safer schools. Other challenges for the profession involve attracting more men into teaching. The percentage of male teachers continues to decline.

In order to improve education for all children, changes are being considered by some districts. Some private companies are managing public schools. Though it is believed that a private company can afford to provide better facilities, faculty, and equipment, this hasn't been proven. Teacher organizations are concerned about taking school management away from communities and turning it over to remote corporate headquarters. Charter schools and voucher programs are two other controversial alternatives to traditional public education. Charter schools, which are small schools that are publicly funded but not guided by the rules and regulations of traditional public schools, are viewed by some as places of innovation and improved educational methods; others see charter schools as ill-equipped and unfairly funded with money that could better benefit local school districts. Vouchers, which exist only in a few cities, allow students to attend private schools courtesy of tuition vouchers; these vouchers are paid for with public tax dollars. In theory, the vouchers allow for more choices in education for poor and minority students, but private schools still have the option of being highly selective in their admissions. Teacher organizations see some danger in giving public funds to unregulated private schools.

■ For More Information

For information about careers, and about the current issues affecting teachers, contact the following:

American Federation of Teachers
555 New Jersey Avenue, NW
Washington, DC 20001
Tel: 202-879-4400
Web: http://www.aft.org

National Education Association
1201 16th Street, NW
Washington, DC 20036
Tel: 202-833-4000
Web: http://www.nea.org

■ Related Articles

Education
Adult and Vocational Education Teachers
College Professors
Elementary School Teachers
Guidance Counselors
School Administrators
Special Education Teachers

Secret Service Special Agents

■ Overview

U.S. Secret Service special agents are employed by the U.S. Secret Service, part of the Department of the Treasury. They work to protect the president and other political leaders of the United States, as well as heads of foreign states or governments when they are visiting the United States. Special agents also investigate financial crimes and work to suppress the counterfeiting of U.S. currency.

■ History

The Secret Service was established in 1865 to suppress the counterfeiting of U.S. currency. After the assassination of President William McKinley in 1901, the Secret Service was directed by Congress to protect the president of the United States. Today it is the Secret Service's responsibility to protect the following people: the president and vice president (also president-elect and vice president-elect) and their immediate families; former presidents and their spouses for 10 years after the president leaves office (spouses lose protection if they remarry); children of former presidents until they are 16 years old; visiting heads of foreign states or governments and their spouses traveling with them, along with other distinguished foreign visitors to the United States and their spouses traveling with them; official representatives of the United States who are performing special missions abroad; major presidential and vice-presidential candidates and, within 120 days of the general presidential election, their spouses.

■ The Job

The U.S. Secret Service employs about 5,000 people, about 2,100 of whom are special agents. Secret Service special agents are charged with two missions: protecting U.S. leaders or visiting foreign dignitaries (likewise, U.S. leaders on missions to other countries), and investigating the counterfeiting of U.S. currency. Special agents are empowered to carry and use firearms, execute warrants, and make arrests.

When assigned to a permanent protection duty—for the president, for example—special agents are usually assigned to the Washington, DC, area. They are responsible for planning and executing protective operations for their protectees at all times. Agents can also be assigned to a temporary protective duty to provide protection for candidates or visiting foreign dignitaries. In either case, an advance team of special agents surveys each site that will be visited by the protectee. Based on their survey, the team determines how

SECRET SERVICE SPECIAL AGENTS	
SCHOOL SUBJECTS	English Foreign language Physical education
PERSONAL SKILLS	Communication/ideas Helping/teaching
WORK ENVIRONMENT	Indoors and outdoors One location with some travel
MINIMUM EDUCATION LEVEL	Bachelor's degree
SALARY RANGE	$25,735 to $67,241 to $151,800
CERTIFICATION OR LICENSING	None available
OUTLOOK	About as fast as the average
DOT	375
O*NET	63028A

much manpower and what types of equipment are needed to provide protection. They identify hospitals and evacuation routes and work closely with local police, fire, and rescue units to develop the protection plan and determine emergency routes and procedures, should the need arise. Then a command post is set up with secure communications to act as the communication center for protective activities. The post monitors emergencies and keeps participants in contact with each other.

Before the protectees arrive, the *lead advance agent* coordinates all law enforcement representatives participating in the visit. The assistance of military, federal, state, county, and local law enforcement organizations is a vital part of the entire security operation. Personnel are told where they will be posted and are alerted to specific problems associated with the visit. Intelligence information is discussed and emergency measures are outlined. Just prior to the arrival of the protectee, checkpoints are established and access to the secure area is limited. After the visit, special agents analyze every step of the protective operation, record unusual incidents, and suggest improvements for future operations.

Protective research is an important part of all security operations. *Protective research engineers* and *protective research technicians* develop, test, and maintain technical devices and equipment needed to provide a safe environment for the protectee.

When assigned to an investigative duty, special agents investigate threats against Secret Service protectees. They also work to detect and arrest people committing any offense relating to coins, currency, stamps, government bonds, checks, credit card fraud, computer fraud, false identification crimes, and other obligations or securities of the United States. Special agents also investigate violations of the Federal Deposit Insurance Act, the Federal Land Bank Act, and the Government Losses in Shipment Act. Special agents assigned to an investigative duty usually work in one of the Secret Service's 125 domestic and foreign field offices. Agents assigned to investigative duties in a field office are often called out to serve on a temporary protective operation.

Special agents assigned to investigate financial crimes may also be assigned to one of the Secret Service's three divisions in Washington, DC, or they may receive help from the divisions while conducting an investigation from a field office. The Counterfeit Division constantly reviews the latest reprographic and lithographic technologies to keep a step ahead of counterfeiters. The Financial Crimes Division aids special agents in their investigation of electronic crimes involving credit cards, computers, cellular and regular telephones, narcotics, illegal firearms trafficking, homicide, and other crimes. The Forensic Services Division coordinates forensic science activities within the

Secret Service. The division analyzes evidence such as documents, fingerprints, photographs, and video and audio recordings.

The Secret Service employs a number of specialist positions such as electronics engineers, communications technicians, research psychologists, computer experts, armorers, intelligence analysts, polygraph examiners, forensic experts, security specialists, and more.

For some 15 years, Norm Jarvis has been a special agent for the Secret Service. He has protected a variety of U.S. political leaders including President Bill Clinton and past presidents Nixon, Carter, and Ford. He has also protected foreign dignitaries including the president of Sudan and the prime minister of Israel. In addition, Norm has investigated criminal activity in a number of cities and served in the Secret Service's Montana and Utah field offices.

While his primary responsibility is to investigate crimes, Norm is called out regularly to protect a political or foreign leader. During those times, he serves as a member of a team of special agents who work to ensure there is always a "protective bubble"—a 360-degree virtual boundary of safety—surrounding the protectee, regardless of whether he or she is in a moving or stationary location. Protective operations can be complicated, with special agents working together around the clock, using intelligence and special technologies, and working in conjunction with local authorities to make sure the protectee is safe. "We don't believe anybody can do bodyguard work just by walking around with somebody," Norm says. "Scowls and large muscles don't mean a lot if somebody is bound and determined to kill you." While special agents don't change their protective techniques when they work overseas, they often work in conjunction with foreign security agencies. "Other security forces usually defer to the Secret Service, which is considered a premier security agency," Norm says.

When Norm is not on a protective assignment, he spends his time investigating a variety of crimes. Special agents assigned to smaller field offices typically handle a wide variety of criminal investigations. But special agents usually work for a specialized squad in a field office, handling specific investigations like counterfeit currency, forgery, and financial crimes. Special agents may receive case referrals from the Secret Service headquarters, from other law enforcement agencies, or through their own investigations. Investigating counterfeit money requires extensive undercover operations and surveillance. Special agents usually work with the U.S. Attorney's Office and local law enforcement for counterfeit cases. Through their work, special agents detect and seize millions of dollars of counterfeit money each year—some of which is produced overseas. Special agents working in a fraud squad often receive complaints or referrals from banking or financial institutions that have been defrauded. Fraud investigations involve painstaking and long-term investigations to reveal the criminals, who are usually organized groups or individuals hiding behind false identifications. Special agents working for forgery squads often have cases referred to them from banks or local police departments that have discovered incidents of forgery.

■ Requirements

High School

You can help prepare for a career as a special agent by doing well in high school. You may receive special consideration by the Secret Service if you have computer training, which is needed to investigate computer fraud, or if you can speak a foreign language, which is useful during investigations and while protecting visiting heads of state or U.S. officials who are working abroad. Highly regarded are specialized skills in electronics, forensics, and other investigative areas. Aside from school, doing something unique and positive for your city or neighborhood, or becoming involved in community organizations can improve your chances of being selected by the Secret Service.

Postsecondary Training

The Secret Service recruits special agents at the GS-5 and GS-7 grade levels. You can qualify at the GS-5 level in one of three ways: obtain a four-year degree from an accredited college or university; work for at least three years in a criminal investigative or law enforcement field and gain knowledge and experience in applying laws relating to criminal violations; or obtain an equivalent combination of education and experience. You can qualify at the GS-7 level by achieving superior academic scores (defined as a grade point average of at least 2.95 on a 4.0 scale), going to graduate school and studying a directly related field, or gaining an additional year of criminal investigative experience.

All newly hired special agents go through 9 weeks of training at the Federal Law Enforcement Training Center in Glynco, Georgia, and then 11 weeks of specialized training at the Secret Service's Training Academy in Beltsville, Maryland. During training, new agents take comprehensive courses in protective techniques, criminal and constitutional law, criminal investigative procedures, use of scientific investigative devices, first aid, the use of firearms, and defensive measures. Special agents also learn about collecting evidence, surveillance techniques, undercover operation, and courtroom demeanor. Specialized training includes skills such as fire fighting and protection aboard airplanes. The classroom study is supplemented by on-the-job training, and special agents go through advanced in-service training throughout their careers.

New special agents usually begin work at the field offices where they first applied. Their initial work is investigative

---

GLOSSARY

Choke point: A potential ambush site—like a bridge—where a protectee or motorcade may be more vulnerable to attack.

Protective bubble: A 360-degree virtual boundary of safety that the Secret Service maintains around each of its protectees. Special agents work to ensure that nothing dangerous penetrates the bubble.

Protectee: A person—usually a political leader of the United States or a foreign dignitary—that the Secret Service is responsible for protecting. Protectees may also include the spouse or family of the primary protectee.

---

in nature and is closely supervised. After about five years, agents are usually transferred to a protection assignment.

Other Requirements

In addition to the educational requirements, special agents must meet the following criteria: have U.S. citizenship; be at least 21 and less than 37 years of age at the time of appointment; have uncorrected vision no worse than 20/60 in each eye, correctable to 20/20 in each eye; be in excellent health and physical condition; pass the Treasury Enforcement Agent exam; and undergo a complete background investigation, including in-depth interviews, drug screening, medical examination, and polygraph examination.

The Secret Service is looking for smart, upstanding citizens who will give a favorable representation of the U.S. government. The agency looks for people with strong ethics, morals, and virtues—and then they teach them how to be special agents. "You can be a crackerjack lawyer, but have some ethical problems in your background, and we wouldn't hire you as an agent even though we would love to have your expertise," Norm says.

Special agents also need dedication, which can be demonstrated through a candidate's grade point average in high school and college. Applicants must have a drug-free background. Even experimental drug use can be a reason to dismiss an applicant from the hiring process. Special agents also need to be confident and honest—with no criminal background. "It's important as a representative of the President's Office that you conduct yourself well, that you look good, and that you're able to command some respect," Norm says. "Anything even as minor as shoplifting is an indicator of a personality problem."

Since special agents must travel for their jobs—Norm spends about 30 percent of his time on the road—interested applicants should be flexible and willing to be away from home. Norm says the traveling is one of the downfalls of the job, often requiring him to leave his wife and two children at a moment's notice.

■ Exploring

The Secret Service offers the Stay-In-School Program for high school students. The program allows students who meet financial eligibility guidelines to earn money and some benefits by working part time, usually in a clerical job, for the agency. There are many requirements and application guidelines for this program, so contact the Secret Service's Stay-In-School office.

The Secret Service also offers the Cooperative Education Program as a way for the agency to identify and train highly motivated students for careers as special agents. Participants in this paid program learn more about the Secret Service and gain on-the-job training, with the possibility of working full time for the Secret Service upon graduation. The two-year work-study program includes classroom training and hands-on training that will prepare students for the following Secret Service careers: accountant, budget analyst, computer specialist, computer research specialist, electronic engineer, intelligence research specialist, management specialist, personnel management specialist, telecommunications specialist, and visual information specialist. Students working toward a bachelor's degree must complete 1,040 hours of study-related work requirements.

There is also a Cooperative Education Program for criminal investigators (special agents). This two-year program, available only in the Washington, DC, area, provides rudimentary training for the special agent position, introducing participants to the investigative and protective techniques that agents use.

Students in the Cooperative Education Program work part time, between 16 and 32 hours a week. They may work full time during holidays and school breaks. They receive some federal benefits including a retirement plan, life and health insurance, annual and sick leave, holiday pay, awards, and promotions.

You must submit a variety of forms to apply for this program, so contact the Secret Service's Cooperative Education coordinator for more information. In addition, you may be able to apply for the program through your school.

■ Starting Out

Norm Jarvis didn't set out to become a special agent. As a teenager, he admired a neighbor who worked as a deputy sheriff. As Norm grew older and had to make decisions about college and work, he realized he wanted to go into law enforcement. At the age of 18, he volunteered to go into the U.S. Army to train with the military police. When Norm left the service, he used his veteran's benefits to help him get a bachelor's degree in psychology from Westminster College. "I have an innate interest in why people do the things they do," he says. Norm also earned a master's degree in public administration from Utah University. He spent 8 years working as a police officer before he decided to apply to the Secret Service. He wasn't satisfied with his police officer's salary and was tired of the "day-to-day emotional trauma of being an officer." Norm loved to travel and was impressed by some special agents he had met, so he decided that becoming a special agent would be a way for him to progress professionally and work in an exciting position. He applied for the job and began working as a special agent assigned to Salt Lake City in 1984.

The Secret Service warns that because they have many well-qualified applicants and few anticipated vacancies, the chance that you will be hired is limited. On top of that, the hiring process can take up to a year or more because of the thoroughness of the selection process.

If you are ready to apply for a special agent job, make sure you meet the requirements described above, then submit a typewritten Standard Form 171, Application for Federal Employment. If you have graduated from college, you will also need to submit an official transcript. Alternatively, you can submit an Optional Application for Federal Employment or a resume, but you will have to complete some accompanying forms, so be sure to check with the Secret Service field office nearest you before doing so to find out exactly what forms to fill out. The field office in your area should be listed in the government section of your telephone book.

The Secret Service only accepts applications for current job openings. To find out what vacancies currently exist, use the contact information at the end of this article.

■ Advancement

Norm began working in the Secret Service's Salt Lake City field office in 1984. He was transferred to the Organized Crime Task Force in the Washington, DC, field office in 1987. In 1990 Norm was promoted to the position of instructor at the Office of Training, and he was transferred to the Presidential Protective Division in 1994. Norm went to Montana in 1997 after being promoted to the position of resident agent of the Great Falls field office. Currently he is a special agent once again in the Salt Lake City office.

Generally, special agents begin their careers by spending 5 to 10 years performing primarily investigative duties at a field office. Then they are usually assigned to a protective assignment for 3 to 5 years. After 12 or 13 years, special agents become eligible to move into supervisory positions. A typical promotion path moves special agents to the position of senior agent, then resident agent in charge of a district, assistant to the special agent in charge, and finally special agent in charge of a field office or headquarters division. Promotion is awarded based upon performance, and since the Secret Service employs many highly skilled professionals, competition for promotion is strong.

Special agents can retire after 20 years and after they reach the age of 50. Special agents must retire before the age of 57. Norm plans to continue working with the Secret Service until retirement. When he does retire, Norm does not plan on pursuing law enforcement activities. Instead, he would like to earn a doctorate in psychology, sociology, or criminology and teach at the college level.

Some retired agents are hired by corporations to organize the logistics of getting either people or products from one place to another. Others work as bodyguards, private investigators, security consultants, and local law enforcement officials.

■ Earnings

Special agents generally receive Law Enforcement Availability Pay (LEAP) on top of their base pay. Agents usually start at the GS-5 or GS-7 grade levels, which in 1999 were $25,735 and $31,876, respectively, including LEAP. (Salaries may be slightly higher in some areas with high costs of living.) Agents automatically advance by two pay grades each year until they reach the GS-12 level, which in 1999 was $56,545, including LEAP. Agents must compete for positions above the GS-12 level; however, the majority of agents reach GS-13—$67,241 with LEAP in 1999—in the course of their careers. Top officials in the Secret Service are appointed to Senior Executive Service (SES) positions; they do not receive the availability pay. The top SES salary in 1999 was $151,800.

Benefits for special agents include health and life insurance, annual and sick leave, paid holidays, and a comprehensive retirement program. In addition, free financial protection is provided to agents and their families in the event of job-related injury or death.

■ Work Environment

A Secret Service special agent is assigned to a field office or 1 of 3 Washington, DC, divisions. Agents on investigative assignments may spend much time doing research with the office as base, or they may be out in the field, doing undercover or surveillance work. Protective and investigative assignments can keep a special agent away from home for long periods of time, depending on the situation. Preparations for the president's visits to cities in the United States generally take no more than a week. However, a large event attracting foreign dignitaries—such as the Asian Pacific Conference in the state of Washington—can take months to plan. Special agents are already working on providing a safe environment for the 2002 Winter Olympics to be held in Salt Lake City, Utah, because of the sheer size of the event and the large numbers of people who will attend. Special agents at field offices assigned to investigate crimes are called out regularly to serve temporary protective missions. During presidential campaign years, agents

typically serve 3-week protective assignments, work 3 weeks back at their field offices, and then start the process over again. Special agents always work at least 40 hours a week and often work a minimum of 50 hours each week.

One of the drawbacks of being a special agent is the potential danger involved. A special agent was shot in the stomach in 1981 during an assassination attempt on President Ronald Reagan. Other agents have been killed on the job in helicopter accidents, surveillance assignments, and protective operations, to name a few.

For most agents, however, the benefits outweigh the drawbacks. For Norm, the excitement and profound importance of his work give him great job satisfaction. "There are times when you are involved in world history and you witness history being made, or you are present when historical decisions are being made, and you feel privileged to be a part of making history, albeit you're behind the scenes and never recognized for it," he says. However, according to one of Norm's coworkers, the job is not always glamorous and can be "like going out in your backyard in your best suit and standing for three hours."

■ Outlook

Compared to other federal law enforcement agencies, the Secret Service is small. The agency focuses on its protective missions and is not interested in expanding its responsibilities. "We want to be the best at protection, and I think we are the best in the world and that suits us fine," Norm says. As a result, the Secret Service will likely not grow much, unless the president and Congress decide to expand the agency's duties.

Since the Secret Service employs a small number of people, their new hires each year are limited. The agency anticipated hiring about another 100 special agents in 1998. Officials anticipate that the job availability will remain about the same, although it could increase slightly over the next few years.

■ For More Information

Your local Secret Service field office or the Personnel Office, at the following address, can provide more information on becoming a special agent. If you are writing about the Stay-In-School program, mark the envelope "Attention: Stay-In-School Program"; for the Cooperative Education Program, mark it "Attention: CO-OP Coordinator."

U.S. Secret Service
Personnel Division
1800 G Street, NW, Room 912
Washington, DC 20223
Tel: 800-827-7783
Web: http://www.treas.gov/usss

Secretaries

■ Overview

Secretaries perform a wide range of jobs that vary greatly from business to business. However, most secretaries key in documents, manage records and information, answer telephones, handle correspondence, schedule appointments, make travel arrangements, and sort mail. The amount of time secretaries spend on these duties depends on the size and type of the office as well as on their own job training. There are approximately 3.4 million secretaries employed in the United States.

SECRETARIES	
SCHOOL SUBJECTS	Business English
PERSONAL SKILLS	Communication/ideas Following instructions
WORK ENVIRONMENT	Primarily indoors Primarily one location
MINIMUM EDUCATION LEVEL	High school diploma
SALARY RANGE	$17,400 to $27,900 to $40,600
CERTIFICATION OR LICENSING	Voluntary
OUTLOOK	About as fast as the average
DOT	201
GOE	07.01.03
NOC	1241
O*NET	55108

■ History

People have always needed to communicate with one another for societies to function efficiently. Today, as in the past, secretaries play an important role in keeping lines of communication open. Before there were telephones, messages were transmitted by hand, often from the secretary of one party to the secretary of the receiving party. Their trustworthiness was valued because the lives of many people often hung in the balance of certain communications.

Secretaries in the ancient world developed methods of taking abbreviated notes so that they could capture as much as possible of their employers' words. In 16th-century England, the modern precursors of the shorthand methods we know today were developed. In the 19th century, Isaac Pitman and John Robert Gregg developed the shorthand systems that are still used in offices and courtrooms in the United States.

The equipment secretaries use in their work has changed drastically in recent years. Almost every office, from the smallest to the largest, is automated in some way. Familiarity with machines including switchboards, dictaphones, photocopiers, fax machines, and personal computers has become an integral part of the secretary's day-to-day work.

■ The Job

Secretaries perform a variety of administrative and clerical duties. The goal of all their activities, however, is to assist their employers in the execution of their work and to help their companies conduct business in an efficient and professional manner.

Secretaries' work includes processing and transmitting information to the office staff and to other organizations. They operate office machines and arrange for their repair or servicing. These machines include computers, typewriters, dictating machines, photocopiers, switchboards, and fax machines. These secretaries also order office supplies and perform regular duties such as answering phones, sorting mail, managing files, taking dictation, and composing and keying in letters.

Some offices have word processing centers that handle all of the firm's typing. In such a situation, *administrative secretaries* take care of all secretarial duties except for typing and dictation. This arrangement leaves them free to respond to correspondence, prepare reports, do research and present the results to their employers, and otherwise assist the professional staff. Often these secretaries work in groups of three or four so that they can help each other if one secretary has a workload that is heavier than normal.

In many offices, secretaries make appointments for company executives and keep track of the office schedule. They make travel arrangements for the professional staff or for clients, and occasionally are asked to travel with staff members on business trips. Other secretaries might manage the office while their supervisors are away on vacation or business trips.

Secretaries take minutes at meetings, write up reports, and compose and type letters. They often will find their responsibilities growing as they learn the business. Some are responsible for finding speakers for conferences, planning receptions, and arranging public relations programs. Some write copy for brochures or articles before making the arrangements to have them printed or microfilmed. Or, they might use desktop publishing software to create the documents themselves. They greet clients and guide them to the proper offices, and often supervise and train other staff members and newer secretaries, especially in computer software programs.

Some secretaries perform very specialized work. *Legal secretaries* prepare legal papers including wills, mortgages, contracts, deeds, motions, complaints, and summonses. They work under the direct supervision of an attorney or paralegal. They assist with legal research by reviewing legal journals and organizing briefs for their employers. They must learn an entire specialized vocabulary that is used in legal papers and documents. For more information on this career, see the article, *Legal Secretaries*.

Medical secretaries take medical histories of patients, make appointments; prepare and send bills to patients, as well as track and collect them; process insurance billing, maintain medical files; and pursue correspondence with patients, hospitals, and associations. They assist physicians or medical scientists with articles, reports, speeches, and conference proceedings. Some medical secretaries are responsible for ordering medical supplies. They, too, need to learn an entire specialized vocabulary of medical terms and be familiar with laboratory or hospital procedures. For more information on this career, see the article, *Medical Secretaries*.

Technical secretaries work for engineers and scientists preparing reports and papers that often include graphics and mathematical equations that are difficult to format on paper. The secretaries maintain a technical library and help with scientific papers by gathering and editing materials.

Social secretaries, often called *personal secretaries*, arrange all of the social activities of their employers. They handle private as well as business social affairs, and may plan parties, send out invitations, or write speeches for their employers. Social secretaries are often hired by celebrities or high-level executives who have busy social calendars to maintain.

Many associations, clubs, and nonprofit organizations have *membership secretaries* who compile and send out newsletters or promotional materials while maintaining membership lists, dues records, and directories. Depending on the type of club, the secretary may be the one who gives out information to prospective members and who keeps current members and related organizations informed of upcoming events.

Education secretaries work in elementary or secondary schools or on college campuses. They take care of all clerical duties at the school. Their responsibilities may include preparing bulletins and reports for teachers, parents, or students, keeping track of budgets for school supplies or student activities, and maintaining the school's calendar of events. Depending on the position, they may work for school administrators, principals, or groups of teachers or professors. Other education secretaries work in administration offices, state education departments, or service departments.

■ Requirements

Secretaries need a high school diploma to enter this field. High school courses that will be helpful include business, communications, English, keyboarding, and computers.

Postsecondary Training

Secretaries need good office skills that include rapid and accurate keyboarding skills, good spelling and grammar, and they should enjoy handling details. Some positions require typing a minimum number of words per minute, as well as shorthand ability. Knowledge of word processing, spreadsheet, and database management is important, and many employers require it. Some of these skills can be learned in business education courses taught at vocational and business schools.

Certification or Licensing

Qualifying for the designation Certified Professional Secretary (CPS) rating is increasingly recognized in business and industry as a consideration for promotion as a senior level secretary. The examinations required for this certification are given by the International Association of Administrative Professionals. Secretaries with limited experience can become an Accredited Legal Secretary (ALS) by obtaining certification from the Certifying Board of the National Association of Legal Secretaries. Those with at least three years of experience in the legal field can be certified as a Professional Legal Secretary (PLS) from this same organization. Board Certified Civil Trial Legal Secretaries have five or more years of experience in litigation and probate and have passed an examination given by Legal Secretaries International.

Other Requirements

Personal qualities are important for secretaries. They often are the first employees of a company that clients meet, and therefore must be friendly, poised, and professionally dressed. Because they must work closely with others, they should be personable and tactful. Discretion, good judgment, organizational ability, and initiative are also important. These traits will not only get them hired, but will also help them advance in their careers.

Some employers encourage their secretaries to take advanced courses and to be trained to use any new piece of equipment in the office. Requirements vary widely from company to company.

A secretary shows her boss some letters he needs to look at.

■ Exploring

High school guidance counselors can give interest and aptitude tests to help you assess your suitability for a career as a secretary. Local business schools often welcome visitors, and sometimes offer courses that can be taken in conjunction with a high school business course. Work-study programs will also provide you with an opportunity to work in a business setting to get a sense of the work performed by secretaries.

Part-time or summer jobs as receptionists, file clerks, and office clerks are often available in various offices. These jobs are the best indicator of future satisfaction in the secretarial field. Students who are computer-literate may find part-time jobs. Cooperative education programs arranged through schools and "temping" through an agency also are valuable ways to acquire experience. In general, any job that teaches basic office skills is helpful.

■ Employers

Secretaries are employed in almost every type of industry. Approximately 60 percent of secretaries are employed by the legal, education, health, and business industries. Others work in banking, financial services, real estate, construction, manufacturing, transportation, communications, and retail and wholesale trade. A large number of secretaries are employed by federal, state, and local governments.

■ Starting Out

Most people looking for work as secretaries find jobs through the newspaper want ads or by applying directly to local businesses. Both private employment offices and state employment services place secretaries, and business schools help their graduates find suitable jobs. Temporary-help agencies also are an excellent way to find jobs, many of which may turn into permanent ones.

■ Advancement

Secretaries often begin by assisting executive secretaries and work their way up by learning the way their business operates. Initial promotions from a secretarial position are usually to jobs such as secretarial supervisor, office manager, or administrative assistant. Depending on other personal qualifications, college courses in business, accounting, or marketing can help the ambitious secretary enter middle and upper management. Training in computer skills can also lead to advancement. Secretaries who become proficient in word processing, for instance, can get jobs as instructors or as sales representatives for software manufacturers.

Many legal secretaries, with additional training and schooling, become paralegals. Secretaries in the medical field can advance into the fields of Radiological and Surgical Records or Medical Transcription.

■ Earnings

Salaries for secretaries vary widely by region; type of business; and the skill, experience, and level of responsibility of the secretary. Medical secretaries, according to Wageweb, earned salaries that ranged from $24,065 to $35,476 in 1999. As reported by Abbott, Langer & Associates, experienced legal secretaries averaged an annual salary of over $30,000. Ten percent earned a low average of $22,204; 10 percent averaged over $39,450. The Pacific states pay the highest, about $37,000 a year for legal secretaries with at least three year of experience; though states such as California and Hawaii have a higher cost of living. An attorney's rank in the firm will also affect the earnings of a legal secretary; secretaries who work for a partner will earn higher salaries than those who work for an associate.

In other industries, secretaries with limited experience earned an average of $19,700 annually, according to the *Occupational Outlook Handbook*. Those with experience averaged about $40,600 a year; some with executive titles earned considerably more. Secretaries employed by the federal government earned a starting salary of $17,400 a year; with experience, $27,900.

Secretaries, especially those working in the legal profession, earn considerably more if certified. Most secretaries receive paid holidays and two weeks vacation after a year of work, as well as sick leave. Many offices provide benefits including health and life insurance, pension plans, overtime pay, and tuition reimbursement.

■ Work Environment

Most secretaries work in pleasant offices with modern equipment. Office conditions vary widely, however. While some secretaries have their own offices and work for one or two executives, others share crowded workspace with other workers.

Most office workers work 35 to 40 hours a week. Very few secretaries work on the weekends on a regular basis, although some may be asked to work overtime if a particular project demands it.

The work is not physically strenuous or hazardous, although deadline pressure is a factor and sitting for long periods of time can be uncomfortable. Many hours spent in front of a computer can lead to eyestrain or repetitive-motion problems for secretaries. Most secretaries are not required to travel. Part-time and flexible schedules are easily adaptable to secretarial work.

■ Outlook

There were 3.4 million secretaries employed in 1996, making this profession one of the largest in the United States. Of this total, 284,000 specialized as legal secretaries and 239,000 worked as medical secretaries. Good job growth is expected for secretaries who specialize in legal (about as fast as the average employment growth) or medical (faster than the average growth) fields. Those secretaries who do not specialize can expect job opportunities to decline through the year 2006. Industries such as computer and data processing, public relations, and personnel supply may create some new jobs to offset this decline. As common with large occupations, the need to replace retiring workers will generate many openings.

Computers, fax machines, electronic mail, copy machines, and scanners are some technological advancements that have greatly improved the work productivity of secretaries. Company downsizing and restructuring, in some cases, have redistributed traditional secretarial duties to other employees. There has been a growing trend in assigning one secretary to assist two or more managers, adding to this field's decline. Though more professionals are using personal computers for their correspondence, some administrative duties will still need to be handled by secretaries. The personal aspects of the job and responsibilities such as making travel arrangements, scheduling conferences, and transmitting staff instructions have not changed.

Many employers currently complain of a shortage of capable secretaries. Those with skills and experience will have the best chances for employment. Specialized secretaries should attain certification in their field to stay competitive.

■ For More Information

For information about certification, contact:

Legal Secretaries International, Inc.
8902 Sunnywood Drive
Houston, TX 77088-3729
Tel: 281-847-9754
Web: http://www.compassnet.com/legalsec

For information on the Certified Professional Legal Secretary and the Accredited Legal Secretary designations, contact:

National Association of Legal Secretaries
314 East 3rd Street, Suite 210
Tulsa, OK 74120-2409
Tel: 918-582-5188
Web: http://www.nals.org

For general career information, contact:

Association of Business Support Services International
22875 Savi Ranch Parkway, Suite H
Yorba Linda, CA 92887-4619
Tel: 800-237-1462
Web: http://www.abssi.org/

For information regarding union representation, contact:

Office and Professional Employees International Union
265 West 14th Street, Sixth Floor
New York, NY 10011
Tel: 800-346-7348
Web: http://www.opeiu.org/

For information on the Certified Professional Secretary Designation, contact:

International Association of Administrative Professionals
PO Box 20404
10502 NW Ambassador Drive
Kansas City, MO 64195-0404
Tel: 816-891-6600
Web: http://www.iaap-hq.org

■ Related Articles

Business
Billing Clerks
Bookkeeping and Accounting Clerks
Customer Service Representatives
Legal Secretaries
Medical Secretaries
Office Clerks
Receptionists
Statistical Clerks
Stenographers
Typists and Word Processors

Section Line Maintainers

■ **See Line Installers and Cable Splicers**

Securities Compliance Examiners

■ **See Health and Regulatory Inspectors**

Securities Sales Representatives

■ **See Financial Services Brokers**

Securities Traders

■ **See Financial Services Brokers**

Security Consultants and Technicians

■ Overview

Security consultants and technicians are responsible for protecting public and private property against theft, fire, vandalism, illegal entry, and acts of violence. They may work for commercial or government organizations or private individuals.

■ History

People have been concerned with protecting valuable possessions since they began accumulating goods. At first, most security plans were rather simple. In earliest times, members of extended families or several families would band together to watch food, clothing, livestock, and other valuables. As personal wealth grew, the wealthier members of a society would often assign some of their servants to protect their property and families from theft and violence. Soldiers often filled this function as well. During the Middle Ages, many towns and villages hired guards to patrol the streets at night as protection against fire, theft, and hostile intrusion. Night watchmen continued to play an important role in the security of many towns and cities until well into the 19th century.

The first public police forces were organized in about the middle of the 19th century. These were largely limited to cities, however, and the need for protection and safety of goods and property led many to supplement police forces with private security forces. In the United States, ranchers and others hired armed guards to protect their property. Soon, people began to specialize in offering comprehensive security and detective services. Allan Pinkerton was one of the first such security agents. In 1861, Pinkerton was hired to guard President-elect Abraham Lincoln on his way to his inauguration.

As police forces at local, state, and federal levels were established across the country, night watchmen and other security personnel continued to play an important role in protecting the goods and property of private businesses. The growth of industry created a need for people to patrol factories and warehouses. Many companies hired private security forces to guard factories during strikes. Banks, department stores, and museums employed security guards to guard against theft and vandalism. Other security personnel began to specialize in designing security systems—with considerations including the types of safes and alarms to be used and the stationing of security guards—to protect both public and private facilities. Government and public facilities, such as ammunition dumps, nuclear power facilities, dams, and oil pipelines also needed security systems and guards to protect them.

Security systems have grown increasingly sophisticated with the introduction of technologies such as cameras, closed-circuit television, video, and computers. The security guard continues to play an important role in the protection of people and property. The increasing use of computers has aided the guard or security technician by protecting electronic data and transmissions. The increasing number of terrorist threats has also led to the more frequent use of personal security services. Today, commercial security services is one of the fastest growing fields of employment.

■ The Job

A security consultant is engaged in protective service work. Anywhere that valuable property or information is present or people are at risk, a security consultant may be called in to devise and implement security plans that offer protection. Security consultants may work for a variety of clients, including large stores, art museums, factories, laboratories, data processing centers, and political candidates. They are involved in preventing theft, vandalism, fraud, kidnapping, and other crimes. Specific job responsibilities depend on the type and size of the client's company and the scope of the security system required.

Security consultants always work closely with company officials or other appropriate individuals in the development of a comprehensive security program that will fit the needs of individual clients. After discussing goals and objectives with the relevant company executives, consultants study and analyze the physical conditions and internal operations of a client's operation. They learn much by simply observing day-to-day operations.

The size of the security budget also influences the type of equipment ordered and methods used. For example, a large factory that produces military hardware may fence off its property and place electric eyes around the perimeter of the fence. They may also install perimeter alarms and use passkeys to limit access to restricted areas. A smaller company may use only entry-control mechanisms in specified areas. The consultant may recommend sophisticated technology, such as closed circuit surveillance or ultrasonic motion detectors, alone or in addition to security personnel. Usually, a combination of electronic and human resources is used.

Security consultants not only devise plans to protect equipment but also recommend procedures on safeguarding and possibly destroying classified material. Increasingly, consultants are being called on to develop strategies to safeguard data processing equipment. They may have to develop measures to safeguard transmission lines against unwanted or unauthorized interceptions.

Once a security plan has been developed, the consultant oversees the installation of the equipment, ensures that it is working properly, and checks frequently with the client to ensure that the client is satisfied. In the case of a crime against the facility, a consultant investigates the nature of the crime (often in conjunction with police or other investigators) and then modifies the security system to safeguard against similar crimes in the future.

Many consultants work for security firms that have several types of clients, such as manufacturing and telecommunications plants and facilities. Consultants may handle a variety of clients or work exclusively in a particular area. For example, one security consultant may be assigned to handle the protection of nuclear power plants and another to handle data processing companies.

Security consultants may be called on to safeguard famous individuals or persons in certain positions from kidnapping or other type of harm. They provide security services to officers of large companies, media personalities, and others who want their safety and privacy pro-

tected. These consultants, like bodyguards, plan and review client travel itineraries and usually accompany the client on trips, checking accommodations and appointment locations along the way. They often check the backgrounds of people who will interact with the client, especially those who see the client infrequently.

Security consultants are sometimes called in for special events, such as sporting events and political rallies, when there is no specific fear of danger but rather a need for overall coordination of a large security operation. The consultants oversee security preparation—such as the stationing of appropriate personnel at all points of entry and exit—and then direct specific responses to any security problems.

Security officers develop and implement security plans for companies that manufacture or process material for the federal government. They ensure that their clients' security policies comply with federal regulations in such categories as the storing and handling of classified documents and restricting access to authorized personnel only.

Security guards have various titles, depending on the type of work they do and the setting in which they work. They may be referred to as patrollers, merchant patrollers, *bouncers* (people who eject unruly people from places of

SECURITY CONSULTANTS AND TECHNICIANS	
SCHOOL SUBJECTS	**Business** **Psychology**
PERSONAL SKILLS	**Communication/ideas** **Mechanical/manipulative**
WORK ENVIRONMENT	**Indoors and Outdoors** **One location with some travel**
MINIMUM EDUCATION LEVEL	**High school diploma (security technicians)** **Bachelor's degree (security consultants)**
SALARY RANGE	**$11,400 to $35,600 to $100,000+**
CERTIFICATION OR LICENSING	**Recommended**
OUTLOOK	**Faster than the average**
DOT	**199**
GOE	**11.05.02**
NOC	**6651**
O*NET	**19999F**

entertainment), *golf-course rangers* (who patrol golf courses), or *gate tenders* (who work at security checkpoints). They may work as airline security representatives in airports or as armored-car guards and drivers.

Many security guards are employed during normal working hours in public and commercial buildings and other areas with a good deal of pedestrian traffic and public contact. Others patrol buildings and grounds outside normal working hours, such as at night and on weekends. Guards usually wear uniforms and may carry a nightstick. Guards who work in situations where they may be called upon to apprehend criminal intruders are usually armed. They may also carry a flashlight, a whistle, a two-way radio, and a watch clock, which is used to record the time at which they reach various checkpoints.

Guards in public buildings may be assigned to a certain post or they may patrol an area. In museums, art galleries, and other public buildings, guards answer visitors' questions and give them directions; they also enforce rules against smoking, touching art objects, and so forth. In commercial buildings, guards may sign people in and out after hours and inspect packages being carried out of the building. *Bank guards* observe customers carefully for any sign of suspicious behavior that may signal a possible robbery attempt. In department stores, security guards often work with undercover detectives to watch for theft by customers or store employees. Guards at large public gatherings such as sporting events and conventions keep traffic moving, direct people to their seats, and eject unruly spectators. Guards employed at airports limit access to boarding areas to passengers only. They make sure people entering passenger areas have valid tickets and observe passengers and their baggage as they pass through X-ray machines and metal detection equipment.

After-hours guards are usually employed at industrial plants, defense installations, construction sites, and transport facilities such as docks and railroad yards. They make regular rounds on foot or, if the premises are very large, in motorized vehicles. They check to be sure that no unauthorized persons are on the premises, that doors and windows are secure, and that no property is missing. They may be equipped with walkie-talkies to report in at intervals to a central guard station. Sometimes guards perform custodial duties, such as turning on lights and setting thermostatic controls.

In a large organization, a security officer is often in charge of the guard force; in a small organization, a single worker may be responsible for all security measures. As more businesses purchase advanced electronic security systems to protect their properties, more guards are being assigned to stations where they monitor perimeter security, environmental functions, communications, and other systems. In many cases, these guards maintain radio contact with other guards patrolling on foot or in motor vehicles. Some guards use computers to store information on matters relevant to security such as visitors or suspicious occurrences during their time on duty.

Security technicians work for government agencies or for private companies hired by government agencies. Their task is usually to guard secret or restricted installations domestically or in foreign countries. They spend much of their time patrolling areas, which they may do on foot, on horseback, or in automobiles or aircraft. They may monitor activities in an area through the use of surveillance cameras and video screens. Their assignments usually include detecting and preventing unauthorized activities, searching for explosive devices, standing watch during secret and hazardous experiments, and performing other routine police duties within government installations.

Security technicians are usually armed and may be required to use their weapons or other kinds of physical force to prevent some kinds of activities. They are usually not, however, required to remove explosive devices from an installation. When they find such devices, they notify a bomb disposal unit, which is responsible for removing and then defusing or detonating the device.

■ Requirements

High School

A high school diploma is preferred for security guards and required for security consultants, who should also go on to obtain a college degree. Security technicians are required to be high school graduates. In addition, they should expect to receive from three to six months of specialized training in security procedures and technology. If you would like to be a security technician, while in high school you should take mathematics courses to ensure that you can perform basic arithmetic operations with different units of measure, compute ratios, rates, and percentages, and interpret charts and graphs.

You should take English courses to develop your reading and writing skills. You should be able to read manuals, memos, textbooks, and other instructional materials and write reports with correct spelling, grammar, and punctuation. You should also be able to speak to small groups with poise and confidence.

Postsecondary Training

Most companies prefer to hire security consultants who have at least a college degree. An undergraduate or associate's degree in criminal justice, business administration, or related field is best. Coursework should be broad and include business management, communications, computer courses, sociology, and statistics. As the security consulting field becomes more competitive, many consultants choose to get a master's in business administration (MBA) or other graduate degree.

Although there are no specific educational or professional requirements, many security consultants have had previous experience with police work or other forms of crime prevention. It is helpful if a person develops an expertise in a specific area. For example, if you want to work devising plans securing data processing equipment, it is helpful to have previous experience working with computers.

Certification or Licensing

Many security consultants are certified by the Certified Protection Professionals. To be eligible for certification, a consultant must pass a written test and have 10 years work and educational experience in the security profession. Information on certification is available from the American Society for Industrial Security, a professional organization to which many security consultants belong.

Virtually every state has licensing or registration requirements for security guards who work for contract security agencies. Registration generally requires that a person newly hired as a guard be reported to the licensing authorities, usually the state police department or special state licensing commission. To be granted a license, individuals generally must be 18 years of age, have no convictions for perjury or acts of violence, pass a background investigation, and complete classroom training on a variety of subjects, including property rights, emergency procedures, and capture of suspected criminals.

Other Requirements

For security guards, general good health (especially vision and hearing), alertness, emotional stability, and the ability to follow directions are important characteristics. Military service and experience in local or state police departments are assets. Prospective guards should have clean police records. Some employers require applicants to take a polygraph examination or a written test that indicates honesty, attitudes, and other personal qualities. Most employers require applicants and experienced workers to submit to drug screening tests as a condition of employment.

For some hazardous or physically demanding jobs, guards must be under a certain age and meet height and weight standards. For top-level security positions in facilities such as nuclear power plants or vulnerable information centers, guards may be required to complete a special training course. They may also need to fulfill certain relevant academic requirements.

Guards employed by the federal government must be U.S. armed forces veterans, have some previous experience as guards, and pass a written examination. Many positions require experience with firearms. In many situations, guards must be bonded.

Security technicians need good eyesight and should be in good physical shape, able to lift at least 50 pounds, climb ladders, stairs, poles, and ropes, and maintain their balance on narrow, slippery, or moving surfaces. They should be able to stoop, crawl, crouch, and kneel with ease.

■ Exploring

Part-time or summer employment as a clerk with a security firm is an excellent way to gain insight into the skills and temperament needed to become a security consultant. Discussions with professional security consultants are another way of exploring career opportunities in this field. You may find it helpful to join a safety patrol at school.

If you are interested in a particular area of security consulting, such as data processing, for example, you can join a club or association to learn more about the field. This is a good way to make professional contacts.

Opportunities for part-time or summer work as security guards are not generally available to high school students. You may, however, work as a lifeguard, on a safety patrol, and as a school hallway monitor, which can provide helpful experience.

■ Employers

Security services is one of the largest employment fields in the United States. About 995,000 persons are employed as security guards in the United States. Industrial security firms and guard agencies, also called contract security firms, employ over 50 percent of all guards, while the remainder are in-house guards employed by various establishments.

■ Starting Out

People interested in careers in security services generally apply directly to security companies. Some jobs may be available through state or private employment services. People interested in security technician positions should apply directly to government agencies.

Beginning security personnel receive varied amounts of training. Training requirements are generally increasing as modern, highly sophisticated security systems become more common. Many employers give newly hired security guards instruction before they start the job and also provide several weeks of on-the-job training. Guards receive training in protection, public relations, report writing, crisis deterrence, first aid, and drug control.

Those employed at establishments that place a heavy emphasis on security usually receive extensive formal training. For example, guards at nuclear power plants may undergo several months of training before being placed on duty under close supervision. Guards may be taught to use firearms, administer first aid, operate alarm systems and electronic security equipment, handle emergencies, and spot and deal with security problems.

Many of the less strenuous guard positions are filled by older people who are retired police officers or armed forces veterans. Because of the odd hours required for many positions, this occupation appeals to many people seeking part-time work or second jobs.

Most entry-level positions for security consultants are filled by those with a bachelor's or associate's degree in criminal justice, business administration, or a related field. Those with a high school diploma and some experience in the field may find work with a security consulting firm, although they usually begin as security guards and become consultants only after further training.

Because many consulting firms have their own techniques and procedures, most require entry-level personnel to complete an on-the-job training program, during the course of which company policy is introduced.

■ Advancement

In most cases, security guards receive periodic salary increases, and guards employed by larger security companies or as part of a military-style guard force may increase their responsibilities or move up in rank. A guard with outstanding ability, especially with some college education, may move up to the position of *chief guard*—gaining responsibility for the supervision and training of an entire guard force in an industrial plant or a department store— or become director of security services for a business or commercial building. A few guards with management skills open their own contract security guard agencies; other guards become licensed private detectives. Experienced guards may become bodyguards for political figures, executives, and celebrities or choose to enter a police department or other law enforcement agency. Additional training may lead to a career as a corrections officer.

Increased training and experience with a variety of security and surveillance systems may lead security guards into higher-paying security consultant careers. Security consultants with experience may advance to management positions or they may start their own private consulting firms. Instruction and training of security personnel is another advancement opportunity for security guards, consultants, and technicians.

■ Earnings

Earnings for security consultants vary greatly depending on the consultant's training and experience. Entry-level consultants with bachelor's degrees commonly start at $26,000 to $32,000 per year. Consultants with graduate degrees begin at $34,000 to $41,000 per year, and experienced consultants may earn $50,000 to $100,000 per year or more.

Many consultants work on a per-project basis, with rates of up to $75 per hour.

Average starting salaries for security guards and technicians vary according to their level of training and experience, and the location where they work. Starting salaries generally range between $5.50 and $11.73 per hour in 1996, according to the U.S. Department of Labor. Experienced security guards average as high as $35,600 per year, with those employed in manufacturing facilities receiving the highest wages.

Entry-level guards working for contract agencies may receive little more than the minimum wage, however. In-house guards generally earn higher wages and have greater job security and better advancement potential.

Security guards and technicians employed by federal government agencies earn starting salaries of $15,500 or $17,500 per year, and they average $22,900 per year with experience. The location of the work also affects earnings, with higher pay in locations with a higher cost of living. Government employees typically enjoy good job security and generous benefits. Benefits for positions with private companies vary significantly.

■ Work Environment

Consultants usually divide their time between their offices and a client's business. Much time is spent analyzing various security apparatuses and developing security proposals. The consultant talks with a variety of employees at a client's company, including the top officials, and discusses alternatives with other people at the consulting firm. A consultant makes a security proposal presentation to the client and then works with the client on any modifications. Consultants must be sensitive to budget issues and develop security systems that their clients can afford.

Consultants may specialize in one type of security work (nuclear power plants, for example) or work for a variety of large and small clients, such as museums, data processing companies, and banks. Although there may be a lot of travel and some work may require outdoor activity, there will most likely be no strenuous work. A consultant may oversee the implementation of a large security system but is not involved in the actual installation process. A consultant may have to confront suspicious people but is not expected to do the work of a police officer.

Security guards and technicians may work indoors or outdoors. In high-crime areas and industries vulnerable to theft and vandalism, there may be considerable physical danger. Guards who work in museums, department stores, and other buildings and facilities remain on their feet for long periods of time, either standing still or walking while on patrol. Guards assigned to reception areas or security control rooms may remain at their desks for the entire shift. Much of their work is routine and may be tedious at times, yet guards must remain constantly alert during their shift. Guards who work with the public, especially at sporting events and concerts, may have to confront unruly and sometimes hostile people. Bouncers often confront intoxicated people and are frequently called upon to intervene in physical altercations.

Many companies employ guards around the clock in three shifts, including weekends and holidays, and assign workers to these shifts on a rotating basis. The same is true for security technicians guarding government facilities and installations. Those with less seniority will likely have the most erratic schedules. Many guards work alone for an entire shift, usually lasting eight hours. Lunches and other meals are often taken on the job, so that constant vigilance is maintained.

■ Outlook

The demand for guards and other security personnel is expected to increase faster than the average through the year 2006, as crime rates rise with the overall population growth. The highest U.S. Department of Labor estimates call for more than 1.25 million guards to be employed by the year 2006. Many job openings will be created as a result of the high turnover of workers in this field.

A factor adding to this demand is the trend for private security firms to perform duties previously handled by police officers, such as courtroom security and crowd control in airports. Private security companies employ security technicians to guard many government sites, such as nuclear testing facilities. Private companies also operate many training facilities for government security technicians and guards, as well as providing police services for some communities.

■ For More Information

For information on union membership, contact the following:

International Security Officers' Police and Guard Union
321 86th Street
Brooklyn, NY 11209
Tel: 718-836-3508

International Union of Security Officers
2404 Merced Street
San Leandro, CA 94577
Tel: 510-895-9905

For information on certification procedures, please contact:

American Society for Industrial Security
1625 Prince Street
Alexandria, VA 22314
Tel: 703-522-5800

■ Related Articles

Public Safety
Bail Bondsmen
Bodyguards
Border Patrol Officers
Bounty Hunters
Corrections Officers
Deputy U.S. Marshals
Detectives
FBI Agents
Park Rangers
Parole Officers
Police Officers
Process Servers
Secret Service Special Agents

Security Officers
■ See Security Consultants and Technicians

Seismologists
■ See Geophysicists

Semiconductor Development Technicians
■ See Semiconductor Technicians

Semiconductor Process Technicians
■ See Semiconductor Technicians

Semiconductor Technicians

■ Overview

Semiconductor technicians are highly skilled workers who test new kinds of semiconductor devices being designed for use in many kinds of modern electronic equipment. They may also test samples of devices already in production to assess production techniques. Moreover, they help develop and evaluate the test equipment used to gather information about the semiconductor devices. Working under the direction provided by engineers in research laboratory settings, they assist in the design and planning for later production or help to improve production yields. There are close to 250,000 technicians employed in the United States in the semiconductor industry. Those identified as semiconductor technicians account for 58,000 of those jobs, according to the U.S. Bureau of Labor Statistics.

■ History

Semiconductors and devices utilizing them are found in nearly every electronic product made today, from complicated weapons systems and space technology, to personal computers, video cassette recorders, and programmable coffee makers. The manufacturing of semiconductors and microelectronics devices requires the efforts of a variety of people, from the engineers who design them, to the technicians who process, construct, and test them.

Although the word semiconductor is often used to refer to microchips or integrated circuits, a semiconductor is actually the basic material of these devices. Semiconductor materials are so titled because they can be treated to act with properties between that of an insulator, which does not conduct electrical current, and that of a true conductor of electrical current, such as metal.

Silicon is the most common material used as a semiconductor. Other semiconductor materials may be gallium arsenide, cadmium sulfide, and selenium sulfide. Doping, or treating, these materials with substances such as aluminum, arsenic, boron, and phosphorous gives them conducting properties. By applying these substances according to a specifically designed layout, engineers and technicians construct the tiny electronic devices—transistors, capacitors, and resistors—of an integrated circuit. A microchip no larger than a fingernail may contain many thousands of these devices.

■ The Job

There are many steps that occur in processing semiconductors into integrated circuits. The technicians involved in these processes are called semiconductor development technicians and semiconductor process technicians. They may be involved in several or many of the steps of semiconductor manufacturing, depending on where they work. Often, semiconductor technicians function as a link between the engineering staff and the production staff in the large-scale manufacturing of semiconductor products.

The making of semiconductors begins with silicon. To be used, the silicon must be extremely pure. The silicon used for semiconductors is heated in a furnace and formed into cylinder rods between one and six inches in diameter, and three or more feet in length. These rods are smoothed and polished until they are perfectly round, and then sliced into wafers of between one-quarter and one-half millimeter in thickness. Then the wafers are processed, by etching, polishing, heat-treating, and lapping, to produce the desired dimensions and surface finish. After the wafers are tested, measured, and inspected for any defects, they are coated with a photosensitive substance called a photoresist.

The engineering staff and the technicians assigned to assist them prepare designs for the layout of the microchip. This work is generally done using a computer-aided design (CAD) system. The large, completed design is then miniaturized as a photomask when it is applied to the wafer. The photomask is placed over the wafer and the photoresist is developed, much like film in a camera, with ultraviolet light, so that the layout of the microchip is reproduced many times on the same wafer. This work takes place in a specially equipped clean room, or laboratory, kept completely free of dust and other impurities. During the miniaturization process, the tiniest speck of dust will ruin the reproduction of the layout on the wafer.

Next, the wafer is doped with the substances that will give it the necessary conducting properties. Technicians follow the layout, like a road map, when adding these substances. The proper combinations of materials create the

SEMICONDUCTOR TECHNICIANS	
SCHOOL SUBJECTS	Chemistry Mathematics Physics
PERSONAL SKILLS	Communication/ideas Technical/scientific
WORK ENVIRONMENT	Primarily indoors Primarily one location
MINIMUM EDUCATION LEVEL	Associate's degree
SALARY RANGE	$25,000 to $43,750 to $62,000
CERTIFICATION OR LICENSING	Voluntary
OUTLOOK	About as fast as the average
DOT	003
GOE	05.01.01
NOC	9483
O*NET	92402A, B

various components of the integrated circuit. When this process is complete, the wafer is tested by computerized equipment that can test the many thousands of components in a matter of seconds. Many of the integrated circuits on the wafer will not function properly, and these are marked and discarded. After testing, the wafer is cut up into its individual chips.

The chips are then packaged by placing them in a casing usually made of plastic or ceramic, which also contains metal leads for connecting the microchip into the electronic circuitry of the device for which it will be used. It is this package that people usually refer to as a chip or semiconductor.

Semiconductor process technicians are generally responsible for the fabrication and processing of the semiconductor wafer. *Semiconductor development technicians* usually assist with the basic design and development of rough sketches of a prototype chip; they may be involved in transferring the layout to the wafer and in assembling and testing the semiconductor. Both types of technicians gather and evaluate data on the semiconductor, wafer, or chip. They are responsible for making certain that each step of the process precisely meets test specifications, and also for identifying flaws and problems in the material and design. Technicians may also assist in designing and building new test equipment, and in communicating test data and production instructions for large-scale manufacture. Technicians may also be responsible for maintaining the equipment and for training operators on their use.

■ Requirements

The nature of the microelectronics industry, where technological advances are continuous and rapid, means that some form of higher education, whether in a two-year or four-year program, is a must.

High School

Math and science courses, as well as classes in computers and computer science, are obvious requirements for students wishing to enter the semiconductor and microelectronics field. Physics and chemistry will be helpful for understanding many of the processes involved in developing and fabricating semiconductors and semiconductor components. Strong communications skills are also important.

Postsecondary Training

Technician jobs in microelectronics and semiconductor technology require at least an associate's degree in electronics or electrical engineering or technology. Students may attend a two-year program at a community college or vocational school. Students interested in a career at the engineering level should consider studying for a bachelor's degree. The trend toward greater specialization within the

GLOSSARY

Circuit: The complete path of an electric current.

Clean-room: The area where the semiconductors or microchips are manufactured.

Clean-room suit: The outfit worn by someone in a "clean room." The suit is kept in a changing area where workers must change each day before working in the clean room. Sometimes called a "bunny suit."

Semiconductors: Sometimes called microchips, these tiny devices are made from silicon and produced in high-tech manufacturing environments.

Silicon: A nonmetalic chemical element that is used to manufacture microchips.

Silicon Valley: The Silicon Valley is an area in California, named for the many semiconductor and other technical manufacturing located there.

Transistors: Printed on the wafers to allow the chips to interact with other parts of the machine which the microchip will become a part of, such as a toaster or a rocket.

Wafer: After the silicon is melted, a single, crystal cylinder is produced. This is then sliced into very thin wafers.

industry may make a bachelor's degree more desirable over an associate's degree in the future.

An electronics engineering program will include courses in electronics theory, as well as math, science, and English courses. Students can expect to study such subjects as the principle and models of semiconductor devices; physics for solid state electronics; solid state theory; introduction to VLSI systems; and basic courses in computer organization, electromagnetic fundamentals, digital and analog laboratories, and the design of circuits and active networks. Companies will also provide additional training on the specific equipment and software they use. Many companies also offer training programs and educational opportunities to employees to increase their skills and their responsibilities.

Courses are available at many community and junior colleges, which may be more flexible in their curriculum, and better able to keep up with technological advances than vocational training schools. The latter, however, will often have programs geared specifically to the needs of the employers in their area, and may have job placement programs and relationships with the different companies available as well. If you are interested in these schools, you should do some research to determine whether the training offered is thorough, and that the school has a good placement record. Training institutes should also be accredited by the National Association of Trade and Technical Schools.

Military service will also provide a strong background in electronics. In addition, the tuition credits available to military personnel will be helpful when continuing your education.

Certification or Licensing

Certification is not mandatory, but voluntary certification may prove useful in locating work, and in increasing your pay and responsibilities. The International Society of Certified Electronics Technicians (ISCET) offers certification testing at various levels and fields of electronics. The ISCET also offers a variety of study and training material to help prepare for the certification tests.

Other Requirements

A thorough understanding of semiconductors, electronics, and the production process is necessary for semiconductor technicians. Investigative and research skills, and a basic knowledge of computers and computer programs are also important skills for the prospective semiconductor technician. "You have to be very patient and not easily discouraged to work in this industry," says Jan Gilliam, a semiconductor technician at Advanced Micro Devices, located in Austin, Texas. "You have to really focus on the goal while paying close attention to details."

■ Exploring

You can develop your own interest in computers and microelectronics while in school. Because of the rapid advances in electronics technology, most high schools will be unable to keep up, and you will need to read and explore on your own. Joining extracurricular clubs in computers or electronics will give you an opportunity for hands-on learning experiences.

You should also begin to seek out the higher education appropriate for your future career interests. Your high school guidance counselor should be able to help you find a training program that will match your career goals.

■ Employers

Finding a job in the semiconductor industry may mean living in the right part of the country. Certain states, such as California, Texas, and Massachusetts, have many more opportunities than others do. Some of the big names in semiconductors are Intel, Motorola, Texas Instruments, and National Semiconductor. These companies are very large and employ many technicians, but there are smaller and mid-size companies in the industry as well.

■ Starting Out

Semiconductor technician positions can be located through the job placement office of a community college or vocational training school. Since an associate's degree is recommended, many of these degree programs provide students with job interviews and introductions to companies in the community who are looking for qualified workers.

Job listings in the newspaper or at local employment agencies are also good places for locating job opportunities. Aspiring semiconductor technicians can also find lower-skilled positions in the semiconductor industry and work hard for promotion to a technician position. The huge market for semiconductors and the devices related to them means that many job opportunities are available to qualified people.

■ Advancement

As with any manufacturing industry, the advancement possibilities available to semiconductor technicians will depend on their levels of skill, education, and experience. Technicians may advance to senior technicians or may find themselves in supervisory or management positions. Technicians with two-year associate's degrees may elect to continue their education. Often, their coursework will be transferable to a four-year engineering program, and many times their employer may help pay for their continuing education. Semiconductor technicians may ultimately choose to enter the engineering and design phases of the field. Also, a background in semiconductor processing and development may lead to a career in sales or purchasing of semiconductor components, materials, and equipment.

■ Earnings

Because of the stringent requirements, qualified semiconductor technicians command salaries which tend to be higher than many other professions. According to a 1998 salary survey by *Circuits Magazine*, the average technician with a two-year degree earned $43,750, with starting salaries at about $25,000 and upper salaries of $62,000. Technicians earning the higher salaries have more education and have worked in the industry for many years.

■ Work Environment

The work of semiconductor technicians is not physically strenuous and is usually done in an extremely clean environment. Technicians may work with hazardous chemicals, however, and proper safety precautions must be strictly followed. Because of the large demand for semiconductors and related devices, many facilities, like Advanced Micro Devices, where Jan works, operate with two 12-hour shifts, meaning that a technician may be assigned to the night or weekend shift, or on a rotating schedule. Jan works for 3 days and then is off for 4.

Because of the need for an extremely clean environment, technicians are required to wear clean-suits to keep dust, lint, and dirt out of the clean room where the production takes place.

An important component in most manufacturing processes is the speed with which products are produced. Workers may find themselves under a great deal of pressure to maintain a certain level of production volume. The ability to work well in a sometimes stressful environment is an important quality for any prospective semiconductor technician.

■ Outlook

The semiconductor industry is expected to remain a strong source of employment into the next century, but dramatic increases in technical positions are not expected. A variety of factors will affect employment levels. The increasing demand for semiconductors and related devices in most areas of industry, manufacturing, and consumer services will mean the steady need for personnel trained in their development and processing. New applications for semiconductor technology are continually being created, and these too will spur the demand for trained technical staff. Advancements in technology will require increased and continuing educational requirements for persons seeking and holding positions in this industry.

■ For More Information

For certification information, contact:

International Society of Certified Electronics Technicians
2708 West Berry Street
Fort Worth, TX 76109-2356
Tel: 817-921-9101
Web: http://www.iscet.org/

For industry information and educational programs, contact:

Semiconductor Equipment and Materials International
805 East Middlefield Road
Mountain View, CA 94043-4080
Tel: 605-964-5111
Web: http://www.semi.org/

For industry information, contact:

Semiconductor Industry Association
181 Metro Drive, Suite 450
San Jose, CA 95110
Tel: 408-436-6600
Web: http://www.semichips.org/

SEMATECH, a non-profit research and development consortium of U.S. semiconductor manufacturers, sponsors the Discover a New World of Opportunity Web site. Visit the site to get information on careers, associate's degree and certification programs, and profiles of workers in the field. Additionally, the site has a FAQ section and a Glossary of semiconductor industry terms:

Discover a New World of Opportunity
http://www.4chipjobs.com/index.html

■ Related Articles

Electronics
Computer-Aided Design Drafters and Technicians
Electrical and Electronics Engineers
Electronics Engineering Technicians
Microelectronics Technicians

Senators

■ **See Federal and State Officials**

Senior Programmers and Analysts

■ **See Data Processing Technicians**

Service Agents

■ **See Postal Clerks**

Service Observers

■ **See Telephone Operators**

Service Technicians

■ **See Cable Television Technicians**

Services Clerks

■ **See Billing Clerks**

Services Sales Representatives

■ Overview

Services sales representatives sell a variety of services, from furniture upholstery and graphic arts to pest control and telephone communications systems. In general, they try to find potential clients, describe or demonstrate the services to them, answer any questions they may have, and attempt to make sales. Services sales representatives usually telephone their customers or travel to their homes or places of business. Some, however, work out of an office and meet clients who come to them.

■ History

For many centuries, people who performed services for a living did not have to advertise. Blacksmiths, weavers, printers, and other workers relied on word of mouth from satisfied customers to get new business. As cities grew, however, competition among trades people increased. As a result, businesses selling services began to hire sales agents who could contact potential clients and interest those clients in their services.

The invention of the telephone and improvements in travel have greatly expanded the territory that services sales representatives can cover. Companies that offer very specialized services can approach clients all over the country or the world. The direct selling of services has developed along the same lines as the direct selling of products; the sales representative has become the key to the successful interaction between those who need services and those who provide them.

■ The Job

Although specific job responsibilities depend on the type of service being sold, all services sales representatives have a variety of duties in common. For

SERVICES SALES REPRESENTATIVES	
SCHOOL SUBJECTS	Business Mathematics
PERSONAL SKILLS	Helping/teaching Communication/ideas
WORK ENVIRONMENT	Primarily indoors Primarily multiple locations
MINIMUM EDUCATION LEVEL	High school diploma
SALARY RANGE	$20,000 to $30,000 to $100,000
CERTIFICATION OR LICENSING	None available
OUTLOOK	Much faster than the average
DOT	251
GOE	08.02.06
NOC	1453
O*NET	49999C

example, most contact prospective clients, try to determine the clients' needs, and describe or demonstrate the pertinent services. It is vital that sales representatives understand and be able to discuss the services provided by their company. For example, a services sales representative who works for a shipping company must be familiar with shipping rates, import and export regulations, industry standards, and a host of other factors involving packaging and handling.

The sales procedure usually begins with developing lists of prospective clients. A sales representative may be able to form a list from telephone and business directories, by asking existing customers and other business associates for leads, or by receiving inquiries from potential customers. The representative can then call the potential clients and either begin the sales pitch over the phone or set up a meeting. Sales pitches typically are made in person, as they often require the use of literature or a demonstration of the service. Sales representatives also try to analyze their clients' specific needs and answer any questions they may have.

Keeping in constant touch with customers and potential customers is another important component of the job. If he or she fails to make a sale to a potential customer, for example, the services sales representative may follow up with more visits, letters, and phone calls. Periodic contact with customers can encourage the continued use of the services and increases the likelihood that a customer will recommend the services to friends or business acquaintances.

Job responsibilities vary with the size of the company. Those working for large companies generally have more specialized responsibilities and are assigned to specific territorial boundaries. Those who work for small companies may have public relations and administrative tasks in addition to their sales responsibilities.

There are many specialized jobs within the services sales field. These include *sales-service promoters,* who create goodwill for companies by attending appropriate conventions and advising other sales representatives on ways to increase sales of a particular service. Sales representatives sell warehouse space and services to manufacturers and others who need it.

Data-processing services sales representatives sell various complex services, such as inventory control and payroll processing, to companies using computers in their business operations. *Travelers' checks sales representatives* visit banks, consumer groups, and travel agencies to explain the benefits of travelers' checks. *Business services sales agents* sell business services, such as linen supply and pest control services, usually within a specified territory.

Financial-report service sales agents sell such services as credit and insurance investigation reports to stores and other business establishments. *Communications consultants* discuss communications needs with residential and commercial customers and suggest services that would help clients meet those needs. *Telephone services sales representatives* visit commercial customers to review their telephone systems, analyze their communications needs and, if necessary, recommend additional telecommunication services.

Public utilities sales representatives visit commercial and residential customers to promote an increased or more economical use of gas, electricity, or telephone service. They quote rates for changes in service and installation charges.

Advertising sales representatives sell advertising space or broadcast time to advertising firms or to other companies that maintain their own advertising departments. *Hotel services sales representatives* contact business, government, and social groups to solicit conference and convention business for their hotel. *Group sales representatives* work for sports teams or other entertainment organizations and promote group ticket sales or season ticket sales. They also may arrange for group seating and special activities on the day of the event. Sales promotion representatives visit retail outlets and encourage the use of display items, such as posters, that can increase retail sales.

Education courses sales representatives recruit students for technical or commercial training schools. They inform prospective applicants of enrollment requirements and tuition fees. *Psychological test and industrial relations sales agents* sell programs of psychological, intelligence, and aptitude tests to businesses and schools. They aid in integrating the programs into the school or business operation and help in the administration, scoring, and interpretation of the tests.

Other services sales representatives sell pest control services, franchises, herbicide services, shipping services, graphic art services, signs and displays, printing, audiovisual program production, electroplating, elevators and escalators, dancing instruction, and television cable service.

■ Requirements

High School

For most positions, a college degree is required, though some companies of nontechnical services hire high school graduates. High school students should take college-preparatory courses, including English, speech arts, mathematics, and history.

Postsecondary Training

The more complex a service, the greater the likelihood of the need for a higher level of education. For example, a company that markets advertising services would likely seek a sales representative with an undergraduate degree in advertising or a master's degree in business administration.

LEARN MORE ABOUT IT

Camenson, Blythe. *Real People Working in the Service Businesses.* Lincolnwood, IL: VGM Career Horizons, 1997.

Macdonald, Cameron Lynn and Carmen Sirianni. *Working in the Service Society.* Philadelphia, PA: Temple University Press, 1996.

Rothery, Brian. *Standards in the Service Industry.* Brookfield, VT: Gower, 1997.

College programs will vary depending on the student's particular area of interest but may include course work in psychology, marketing, public relations, finance, and business law.

Other Requirements

It is important for salespeople to work well with other people. A successful salesperson should be sincere, tactful cheerful, optimistic, and sociable with both acquaintances and strangers. He or she must be able to make a good initial impression and maintain it while working repeatedly with the same customers.

Many services sales representatives work without direct supervision and create their own schedules. Thus, they must be efficient and well organized and have sufficient self-motivation to continue to go after potential customers even after a long day or a series of setbacks.

■ Exploring

Because many services require that salespeople have specialized knowledge, untrained workers have few opportunities to explore the field directly. Students, however, can measure their abilities and interest in sales work by finding a part-time sales job in a store. In addition, some school work-study programs offer opportunities with local businesses for part-time, practical on-the-job training. It may also be helpful to read periodicals, such as *SalesDoctors Magazine* (http://salesdoctors.com) and *Selling Power* (http://www.sellingpower.com), that publish articles on the sales field.

■ Employers

Services sales representatives currently hold more than 500,000 jobs. About half work for firms providing business services, including computer and data processing, advertising, personnel, equipment rental, mailing, printing, and stenographic services.

■ Starting Out

Because maturity and the ability to work independently are so important, many employers prefer to hire people who have achieved success in other jobs, either in sales or in a related field. Small companies in particular are reluctant to hire applicants without previous sales experience. In contrast, extremely large companies sometimes prefer applicants who are recent college graduates.

For those entering the job market just out of college, school placement offices may be helpful in supplying job leads. In addition, those interested in securing an entry-level position can contact appropriate companies directly. Jobs may also be located through help wanted advertisements.

Most new sales representatives must complete a training period before receiving their first sales assignment. Large companies may use formal training classes that last several months, while smaller organizations may emphasize supervised sales experience.

Selling highly technical services, such as communications or computer systems, usually involves more complex and lengthy sales training. In these situations, sales representatives usually work as part of a team and receive technical assistance from support personnel. For example, those who sell telecommunications equipment may work with a communications consultant.

■ Advancement

The primary form of advancement for services sales representatives is an increase in the number and size of accounts they handle and, possibly, an increase in their sales territory. Some experienced representatives with leadership ability become *branch office managers* and supervise other sales representatives. A few representatives advance to top management positions or become partners in their companies. Some go into business for themselves.

It is not unusual for someone to begin as a sales representative and then enter a related position with a company. For example, a successful sales representative may become a *purchasing agent* or a *marketing executive*.

■ Earnings

Earnings for sales service representatives depend on a number of variables, including sales skills, the quality of the services, geographic location, the number of potential customers and their need for the services, and the health of the economy. A beginning services sales representative can expect to earn between $20,000 and $25,000 a year; experienced sales representatives average more than $30,000. Those who work for large companies receive considerably better salaries. Extremely successful sales representatives (especially those who sell technical services) can earn more than $100,000. Experienced sales workers often earn more than their branch managers. It is important to realize, however, that the amount of sales in almost every industry is directly affected by the overall economy. Because sales can go up and down frequently, earnings can fluctuate widely.

Sales representatives work on different types of compensation plans. Some get a straight salary; others are paid commissions based on the total volume of sales. Most sales representatives are paid a combination of salary, commission, and bonuses. Bonuses may be based on the increase in number of new clients brought to the company or an increase in overall sales. Bonuses may amount to several thousand dollars at some companies.

■ Work Environment

Services sales representatives work long and irregular hours. Sales workers with large territories frequently spend all day calling on customers in one city and then travel to another city to make calls the next day. Many sales representatives spend at least several nights a month away from home. Those sales workers with limited territories may have less overnight travel, but, like all sales workers they may have to spend many evenings preparing reports, writing up orders, and entertaining customers and potential customers. Some representatives who sell primarily by phone spend the majority of their time in the office.

Although most services sales representatives work long hours and make appointments to fit the convenience of customers, they usually have a considerable amount of flexibility. They can set their own schedules as long as they meet their company's goals.

Sales work is physically demanding. Sales representatives may spend most of the day on their feet. Many travel constantly from one place to another. Sales workers also face competition from other representatives and the possibility that their customers may switch their business to another organization. This, coupled with the uncertainty of sales during tough economic times, can add greatly to the stress of the job.

■ Outlook

As a result of the continued demand for services in general, employment opportunities for services sales representatives are expected to much grow faster than average through the year 2006. Future opportunities, however, will vary greatly depending on the service involved. For example, the continued growth in office automation should lead to greatly increased opportunities for data-processing services sales representatives, while only average growth is expected in the number of advertising sales representatives. Employment growth for education course sales representatives will probably be slower than average.

As with other sales occupations, the high turnover among services sales representatives will lead to many new job openings each year, especially for those who sell non-technical services. Those with the most education, training, and sales experience will have the best job opportunities.

■ For More Information

For referrals to industry trade associations, contact:

Manufacturers' Representatives Educational Research Foundation
PO Box 247
Geneva, IL 60134
Tel: 630-208-1466

■ Related Articles

Business
Business and Consulting Services
Sales
Purchasing Agents
Retail Business Owners
Retail Managers
Retail Sales Workers
Sales Representatives
Stock Clerks

Settlement Clerks
■ See Billing Clerks

Setup Operators
■ See Job and Die Setters

Sewers
■ See Apparel Industry Workers

Sewing Machine Operators
■ See Fashion

Shaping-Machine Operators
■ See Plastics Products Manufacturing Workers

Sheet Metal Workers

■ Overview

Sheet metal workers fabricate, assemble, install, repair, and maintain ducts used for ventilating, air-conditioning, and heating systems. They also work with other articles of sheet metal, including roofing, siding, gutters, downspouts, partitions, chutes, and stainless steel kitchen and beverage equipment for restaurants. Not included in this group are employees in factories where sheet metal items are mass produced on assembly lines.

■ History

Not until the development of mills and processes that form various kinds of metal into thin, strong, flat sheets and strips did sheet metal became important in many products. The processes for making sheet metal have undergone a long series of improvements in the 20th century. As the methods were refined and made more economical, new uses for sheet metal were developed, and making sheet metal products became a well-established skilled craft field. Today, sheet metal workers are concerned with cutting, shaping, soldering, riveting, and other processes to fabricate, install, and maintain a wide range of articles. Heating, ventilating, and air-conditioning systems for all kinds of buildings—residential, commercial, industrial—provide the most important source of employment for sheet metal workers.

■ The Job

Most sheet metal workers handle a variety of tasks in fabricating, installing, and maintaining sheet metal products. Some workers concentrate on just one of these areas. Skilled workers must know about the whole range of activities involved in working with sheet metal.

Many sheet metal workers are employed by building

SHEET METAL WORKERS	
SCHOOL SUBJECTS	Mathematics Physics
PERSONAL SKILLS	Following instructions Mechanical/manipulative
WORK ENVIRONMENT	Primarily indoors Primarily multiple locations
MINIMUM EDUCATION LEVEL	Apprenticeship
SALARY RANGE	$20,000 to $39,000 to $50,000
CERTIFICATION OR LICENSING	None available
OUTLOOK	About as fast as the average
DOT	804
GOE	05.05.06
NOC	7261
O*NET	89132

A sheet metal worker measures the height of a duct that will be used in a ventilating system.

contracting firms that construct or renovate residential, commercial, and industrial buildings. Fabricating and installing air-conditioning, heating, and refrigeration equipment is often a big part of their job. Some workers specialize in adjusting and servicing equipment that has already been installed so that it can operate at peak efficiency. Roofing contractors, the federal government, and businesses that do their own alteration and construction work also employ sheet metal workers. Other sheet metal workers are employed in the shipbuilding, railroad, and aircraft industries or in shops that manufacture specialty products such as custom kitchen equipment or electrical generating and distributing machinery.

Fabricating is often done in a shop away from the site where the product is to be installed. In fabricating products, workers usually begin by studying blueprints or drawings. After determining the amounts and kinds of materials required for the job, they make measurements and lay out the pattern on the appropriate pieces of metal. They may use measuring tapes and rulers and figure dimensions with the aid of calculators. Then, following the pattern they have marked on the metal, they cut out the sections with hand or power shears or other machine tools. They may shape the pieces with a hand or machine brake, which is a type of equipment used for bending and forming sheet metal, and punch or drill holes in the parts. As a last step

before assembly, workers inspect the parts to verify that all of them are accurately shaped. Then they fasten the parts together by welding, soldering, bolting, riveting, cementing, or using special devices such as metal clips. After assembly, it may be necessary to smooth rough areas on the fabricated item with a file or grinding wheel.

Computers play an increasingly important role in several of these tasks. Computers help workers plan the layout efficiently, so that all the necessary sections can be cut from the metal stock while leaving the smallest possible amount of waste sheet metal. Computers also help guide saws, shears, and lasers that cut metal, as well as other machines that form the pieces into the desired shapes.

If the item has been fabricated in a shop, it is taken to the installation site. There, the sheet metal workers join together different sections of the final product. For example, they may connect sections of duct end to end. Some items, such as sections of duct, can be bought factory-made in standard sizes, and workers modify them at the installation site to meet the requirements of the situation. Once finished, duct work may be suspended with metal hangers from ceilings or attached to walls. Sometimes sheet metal workers weld, bolt, screw, or nail items into place. To complete the installation, they may need to make additional sheet metal parts or alter the items they have fabricated.

Some tasks in working with sheet metal, such as making metal roofing, are routinely done at the job site. Workers measure and cut sections of roof paneling, which interlock with grooving at the edges. They nail or weld the paneling to the roof deck to hold it in place and put metal molding over joints and around the edges, windows, and doors to finish off the roof.

■ Requirements

High School

Requirements vary slightly, but applicants for sheet metal training programs must be high school graduates. High school courses that provide a good background include shop classes, mechanical drawing, trigonometry, and geometry.

Postsecondary Training

The best way to learn the skills necessary for working in this field is to complete an apprenticeship. Apprenticeships generally consist of a planned series of on-the-job work experiences plus classroom instruction in related subjects. The on-the-job training portion of apprenticeships, which last at least four years, includes about 8,000 hours of work. The classroom instruction totals approximately 600 hours, spread over the years of the apprenticeship. The training covers all aspects of sheet metal fabrication and installation.

Apprentices get practical experience in layout work, cutting, shaping, and installing sheet metal. They also learn to work with materials that may be used instead of metal, such as fiberglass and plastics. Under the supervision of skilled workers, they begin with simple tasks and gradually work up to the most complex. In the classroom, they learn blueprint reading, drafting, mathematics, computer operations, job safety, welding, and the principles of heating, air-conditioning, and ventilating systems.

Apprenticeships may be run by joint committees representing locals of the Sheet Metal Workers' International Association, an important union in the field, and local chapters of the Sheet Metal and Air Conditioning Contractors' National Association. Other apprenticeships are run by local chapters of a contractor group, the Associated Builders and Contractors.

A few sheet metal workers learn informally on the job while they are employed as helpers to experienced workers. They gradually develop skills when opportunities arise for learning. Like apprentices, helpers start out with simple jobs and in time take on more complicated work. However, the training that helpers get may not be as balanced as that for apprentices, and it may take longer for them to learn all that they need to know. Helpers often take vocational school courses to supplement their work experience.

Even after they have become experienced and well qualified in their field, sheet metal workers may need to take further training to keep their skills up to date. Such training is often sponsored by union groups or paid for by their employers.

Other Requirements

Sheet metal workers need to be in good physical condition, with good manual dexterity, eye-hand coordination, and the ability to visualize and understand shapes and forms.

■ Exploring

High school students can gauge their aptitude for and interest in some of the common activities of sheet metal workers by taking courses such as metal shop, blueprint reading, and mechanical drawing. A summer or part-time job as a helper with a contracting firm that does sheet metal work could provide an excellent opportunity to observe workers on the job. If such a job cannot be arranged, it may be possible to visit a construction site and perhaps to talk with a sheet metal worker who can give an insider's view of this job.

■ Employers

Most workers in this field are employed by sheet metal contractors; some workers with a great deal of experience go into business for themselves. Many sheet metal workers are members of the Sheet Metal Workers' International Association.

■ Starting Out

People who would like to enter an apprentice program in this field can seek information about apprenticeships from local employers of sheet metal workers, such as sheet metal contractors or heating, air-conditioning, and refrigeration contractors; from the local office of the Sheet Metal Workers' International Association; or from the local Sheet Metal Apprentice Training office, the joint union-management apprenticeship committee. Information on apprenticeship programs also can be obtained from the local office of the state employment service or the state apprenticeship agency.

People who would rather enter this field as on-the-job trainees can contact contractors directly about possibilities for jobs as helpers. Leads for specific jobs may be located through the state employment service or newspaper classified ads. Graduates of vocational or technical training programs may get assistance from the placement office at their schools.

■ Advancement

Skilled and experienced sheet metal workers who work for contractors may be promoted to positions as supervisors and eventually job superintendents. Those who develop their skills through further training may move into related fields, such as welding. Some sheet metal workers become specialists in particular activities, such as design and layout work or estimating costs of installations. Some workers eventually go into business for themselves as independent sheet metal contractors.

■ Earnings

The median annual earnings for all sheet metal workers in the United States is roughly $39,000. Earnings vary in different parts of the country and tend to be highest in industrialized urban areas. Apprentices begin at about 40 percent of the rate paid to experienced workers and receive periodic pay increases throughout their training. Some workers who are union members are eligible for supplemental pay from their union during periods of unemployment or when they are working less than full-time.

■ Work Environment

Most sheet metal workers have a regular 40-hour workweek and receive extra pay for overtime. Most of their work is performed indoors, so they are less likely to lose wages due to bad weather than many other craftworkers involved in construction projects. Some work is done outdoors, occasionally in uncomfortably hot or cold conditions.

Workers sometimes have to work high above the ground, as when they install gutters and roofs, and sometimes in awkward, cramped positions, as when they install ventilation systems in buildings. Workers may have to be on their feet for long periods, and they may have to lift heavy objects. Possible hazards of the trade include cuts and burns from machinery and equipment, as well as falls from ladders and scaffolding. Workers must use good safety practices to avoid injuries and sometimes wear protective gear such as safety glasses. Sheet metal fabrication shops are usually well ventilated and properly heated and lighted, but at times they are quite noisy.

■ Outlook

Over the next 10 years, employment in this field is expected to grow at about the same rate as the average for other occupations. The growth in employment will be related to several factors. Many new residential, commercial, and industrial buildings will be constructed, requiring the skills of sheet metal workers, and many older buildings will need to have new energy-efficient heating, cooling, and ventilating systems installed in place of outdated systems. Existing equipment will need routine maintenance and repair. Decorative sheet metal products are becoming more popular for some uses, a trend that is expected to provide an increasing amount of employment for sheet metal workers. Still, most of the demand for new workers in this field will be to replace experienced people who are transferring to other jobs or leaving the workforce altogether.

Job prospects will vary somewhat with economic conditions. In general, the economy is closely tied to the level of new building construction activity. During economic downturns, workers may face periods of unemployment, while at other times there may be more jobs than skilled workers available to take them. But overall, sheet metal workers are less affected by economic ups and downs than some other craftworkers in the construction field. This is because activities related to maintenance, repair, and replacement of old equipment comprise a significant part of their job, and even during an economic slump, building owners are often inclined to go ahead with such work.

■ For More Information

National Training Fund for the Sheet Metal and Air Conditioning Industry
Edward F. Carlough Plaza
601 North Fairfax Street, Suite 240
Alexandria, VA 22314
Tel: 703-739-7200

The SMWIA offers a great deal of information to those already in the sheet metal business and those considering a career in it; you can access a lot of this information through the Web site:

Sheet Metal Workers' International Association
1750 New York Avenue, NW
Washington, DC 20006
Tel: 202-783-5880
Web: http://www.smwia.org/

■ Related Articles

Construction
Machining and Machinery
Heating and Cooling Technicians
Layout Workers
Roofers

Shoe Industry Workers

■ Overview

Shoe industry workers turn materials such as leather, rubber, fabrics, and plastic into finished shoes, boots, moccasins, sandals, slippers, and other footwear. Most of these workers operate machines. Shoe and leather repairers repair and re-style shoes and other products, such as saddles, harnesses, handbags, and luggage. More highly skilled custom shoemakers and *orthopedic boot and shoe designers* and makers may design, construct, or repair orthopedic shoes in accordance with foot specialists' prescriptions.

■ History

Shoemaking in North America began as a craft in 1629 when London shoemaker Thomas Beard settled in Salem, Massachusetts, to make shoes under contract for the Massachusetts Bay Colony. Later, itinerant colonial cobblers made crude, buckled shoes that could be worn on either foot. Shoemakers set up shops in villages and passed on their trade to apprentices. In 1760, a Welshman, John Adam Dagyr, the father of American shoemaking, began operating the first shoe factory in Lynn, Massachusetts. Under this system, workers specialized in one shoemaking operation.

Until the 18th century, good quality, shaped footwear was made by shoemakers who used essentially the same methods that had been used everywhere since ancient times. Shoemakers were skilled artisans who could take raw materials like leather, wood, thread, glue, and nails, and construct a pair of shoes from start to finish, to the size and specifications of each customer.

With the coming of the Industrial Revolution, handmade shoes gradually were replaced by factory-made footwear. Machines could produce more shoes faster with fewer workers than was possible with traditional methods.

Around the middle of the 19th century, several changes took place in shoe manufacturing. In 1845, the rolling machine, an important labor saving device for preparing leather, was invented. The following year, Elias Howe (1819-67) patented a sewing machine in the United States, which was adapted for use in stitching shoe uppers. In

1858, Lyman R. Blake patented a machine for sewing the parts of shoes together. In 1874, Charles Goodyear, Jr. (1800-60) invented the welt stitcher, which made possible machine production of high grade welt shoes.

With the application of power to these machines, shoe-making was revolutionized. Shoes now could be made very quickly and cheaply. Furthermore, manufacturers began to produce better fitting, more comfortable shoes. Factories began to produce many kinds of footwear in large quantities, and it became much easier for ordinary people to own comfortable shoes of the proper size.

Today, shoes are available in countless styles and designs, and Americans are buying more shoes than ever; an average of four to five pairs every year. However, about 90 percent of these shoes are made overseas, in Taiwan, China, Korea, Brazil, and other countries where the cost of labor is less than in the United States. Since 1968, the number of Americans employed in the manufacture of footwear has declined steadily. Some companies, notably those that make specialty footwear, such as cowboy boots, work shoes, and quality athletic shoes, have factories in the United States.

■ The Job

Even with competition from imports, shoe factories in America still produce 376 million pairs of shoes in thousands of styles every year. Most of this work is done on machines, although some work is performed by hand. A single pair of shoes may consist of as many as 280 different parts and require 150 different machine steps. Nearly all shoes are made in batches, not in individual pairs. These batches may consist of a dozen or more pairs of shoes, which are kept together through the entire manufacturing process to ensure that the shoes are consistent in color, texture, size, and pattern.

The leather on the top side of a pair of shoes starts out as tanned animal hides that the manufacturer purchases and keeps in storage. Keeping track of these hides is the job of *upper-leather sorters,* who sort, grade, and issue the hides that will be cut into shoe uppers. The leather is spread out under a cutting machine, which stamps down and cuts the leather into the various sections used for the shoe. This machine, tended by *cut-out-and-marking-machine operators,* also marks patterns for stitching, beveling, and punching holes and eyelets. The workers take care to avoid the imperfections that are in each hide and to cut the leather against the grain to minimize stretching when the shoes are worn.

Next, the lining, tongue, toe, and other parts of the shoe are sewn together on machines operated by *standard machine stitchers.* Shoe parts may be attached by machine using glue, nails, staples, and other fasteners. Other workers taper leather edges, trim linings, flatten seams, and attach buckles or eyelets. The throat of the shoe is then laced together by *lacers.*

At this point the shoe upper is still mostly flat and is missing its insole (the inside sole, on which the foot rests), outsole (the outside sole), and heel. Before these are added, the shoe needs to be shaped and made into the proper shoe size. This is done using individually sized molds called lasts, which may be made of wood or plastic and are shaped like feet. The shoe upper and lining are steamed to soften the leather, and then are secured to the lasts and stretched to conform to the last shape. This task is done by *lasters,* either by hand or with a lasting machine.

While this is being done, other workers prepare insoles, outsoles, and heels to be attached to the shoe uppers. They include *stock fitters,* who stamp rough forms for soles out of tanned hides, and *rounders,* who trim the rough soles to the proper size. Meanwhile, other workers may cut heel blanks out of wood, leather, or fiberboard and glue strips of leather trim to the heels.

The insole is the first piece that is attached to the shoe upper. It will be sewn or glued on by thread lasters. Next, bottom fillers may insert foam filling between the insole and outsole to provide a cushion for the ball of the foot and an even surface for attaching the outsole. The outsole is then stitched to the shoe by the welt, or lip of leather, that runs along the outside of the shoe. Now the shoe can be removed from the last and made ready for finishing. Heels are nailed on by *heel-nailing-machine operators,* and any excess leather or glue is removed by *machine trimmers. Inkers* apply ink, stain, color, glaze, or wax to the shoe parts and along the seams to color and protect the shoe, after which *brushers* hold and turn the shoe against revolving brushes to clean and polish it. After a final inspection, the shoes are ready to pack and ship to stores. If shoes have come out of the manufacturing process damaged or unfit for sale, they are sent

SHOE INDUSTRY WORKERS	
SCHOOL SUBJECTS	**Family and consumer science** **Technical/Shop**
PERSONAL SKILLS	**Following instructions** **Mechanical/manipulative**
WORK ENVIRONMENT	**Primarily indoors** **Primarily one location**
MINIMUM EDUCATION LEVEL	**High school diploma** **Apprenticeship**
SALARY RANGE	**$8,840 to $17,000 to $21,800+**
CERTIFICATION OR LICENSING	**None available**
OUTLOOK	**Decline**
DOT	**788**
GOE	**06.04.33**
NOC	**7343**

to *cobblers,* who may use hand tools and machines to fix defects.

For shoes made of rubber, plastic, fabric, or other material, the manufacturing process is approximately the same. However, the die that cuts out the basic shoe pieces usually is heated. Many layers of material can be cut at once because, unlike leather, the layers are uniform in color, texture, and thickness. Also, cementing and heating are used more often to join the pieces of nonleather shoes.

Custom shoemakers may assemble shoes by hand individually or they may modify manufactured shoes to meet the needs of individual customers.

Most shoe and leather repair work still is done by hand. However, the work of shoe repairers has been made easier by such technological innovations as power operated equipment and the introduction of mass produced replacement parts and decorative ornaments. The most frequently performed task of shoe repairers is replacing worn heels and soles. In small shops, a single worker may perform all the tasks necessary to repair an item, but in large shops, individual workers may be assigned specialized tasks. For example, sewing, trimming, buffing, and dying may be the duties of different workers called *pad hands.* However, most workers eventually move from one task to another to learn and master different skills.

When filling orders for customized products, workers first choose and check a piece of leather for texture, color, and strength. Then they place a pattern of the item being produced on the leather, trace the pattern onto the leather, cut the leather, and sew the pieces together.

Custom shoe workers also modify existing footwear for people with foot problems and special needs. They may prepare inserts, heel pads, and lifts based on plaster casts of customers' feet.

Shoe and leather workers use both hand tools and machines in their work. The most commonly used hand tools are knives, hammers, awls (used to punch holes in leather), and skivers (for splitting leather). Power-operated equipment includes sewing machines, heel nailing machines, hole punching machines, and sole stitchers.

Between 30 and 50 percent of shoe and leather repairers own their own shops. Shoe repairers who run their own establishments must be business-minded. In addition to actual repair work, they have managerial responsibility for estimating repair costs, preparing sales slips, keeping records, buying supplies, and receiving payments. They also may supervise their employees.

A few shoe repairers are employed in the shoe repair services of department stores, shoe stores, and cleaning plants. Other related types of workers include leather stampers, who imprint designs on leather goods, and *custom leather products makers* such as *harness makers, luggage makers,* and *saddle makers.*

■ Requirements

High School

Although a high school diploma may not be required of applicants for jobs in this field, as more people apply for a shrinking number of positions, employers are increasingly likely to prefer those who have completed high school and have some experience in operating machines. High school courses in shop and sewing are desirable for people seeking work in this field.

Postsecondary Training

Shoe production workers usually are trained on the job. Beginners may go through in-house training programs operated by their employer, or they may start out in helper positions and learn the skills they need as they assist experienced workers. The training period varies; for some kinds of tasks, training can last up to two years; other operations can be learned in much less time.

A few vocational schools offer courses in shoe and boot making. These courses, which last from six months to a year, can prepare workers to start out in positions with higher wages than those with no specialized training. Shoe and leather workers and repairers generally learn their craft on the job, either through in-house training programs or working as helpers to experienced craftspeople. Helpers generally begin by performing simple tasks and progress to more difficult projects such as cutting or sewing leather. Trainees generally become fully skilled in six months to two years, depending on their aptitude and dedication and the nature of the work.

Training programs for shoe repairers are offered under the provisions of the Manpower Development and Training Act. Many vocational and trade schools also provide courses in the area of shoe making and repair.

A limited number of schools offer vocational training in shoe repair and leather work. These programs may last from six months to one year and teach basic skills, including leather cutting, stitching, and dying. Students in these programs learn shoe construction, practice shoe repair, and study the fundamentals of running a small business. Graduates are encouraged to gain additional training by working with an experienced leather worker or repairer. National and regional associations also offer specialized training seminars and workshops in custom shoe making, shoe repair, and other leather work.

Other Requirements

Shoe repairers should have considerable manual dexterity, hand-eye coordination, and general physical stamina. They also must have self-discipline to in order to work alone with little supervision. Mechanical aptitude and manual dexterity are desirable for many jobs in the shoe industry.

For workers who do custom work, artistic ability is important. Approximately half of the workers in the shoe industry belong to a union, such as the United Food and Commercial Workers International Union or the Amalgamated Clothing and Textile Workers Union.

■ Exploring

Students may be able to find summer or part-time jobs in the shoe industry and thus gain valuable firsthand experience as maintenance workers or assistants to experienced shoe repairers or craftworkers. However, very few jobs are available for inexperienced people who want to work on a part-time or temporary basis. It may be possible to get an insider's view of this work by talking with someone employed in a production job in the shoe industry.

Shoe Trades Publishing Company in Arlington, Massachusetts, produces two magazines in the industry: *She World Footwear* and *American Shoemaking*, which may be helpful in learning about the field.

■ Employers

Shoe industry workers are employed in a variety of settings from multinational corporations to small businesses, though many companies now import shoes from other countries where wages are lower. In addition, workers may work in repair shops or open their own repair business. Those who prefer to leave the production field may work in buying or selling shoes for a retail establishment.

■ Starting Out

Job seekers should apply directly to shoe factories that employ entry-level workers. The usual method of entering the shoe repair field is to be hired as a helper in a shoe repair shop that offers on-the-job training or some sort of apprenticeship program. Leads to specific jobs may be located through the local offices of the state employment service or newspaper classified ads. Graduates of vocational training programs often can get assistance in finding jobs through the placement office of the school they attended. State employment services also may list job openings.

■ Advancement

In the shoe industry, advancement often involves learning new skills on more complex machines. It can take from six weeks to six months to become skilled at operating some processing machines. Skill in cutting shoe uppers may take up to two years to learn. Higher wages usually accompany a change to more complicated tasks.

Some people who begin as production workers move into positions as supervisors and managers in factories. Those with the right combination of skills may open their own shoe repair shops.

Shoe repair helpers begin doing such simple tasks as staining, brushing, and shining shoes. As they gain experience, they progress to more complex jobs. After approximately two years of apprenticeship, helpers who demonstrate ability and initiative can become qualified shoe repairers. Skilled craftsworkers employed in large shops may advance to become supervisors or managers. For those who open their own shops, hard work and friendly service usually translate into increased clientele and greater income.

■ Earnings

Limited information on earnings suggests that most new workers in the shoe industry start out at low wages, perhaps as low as the federal minimum wage level. The U.S. Bureau of Labor Statistics reports than in 1998, footwear industry workers (except rubber) earned an average of $9.07. For men's footwear (except athletic), the average hourly wage was $9.77. In women's footwear (except athletic), average pay was $7.92 per hour.

The highest paid shoe industry workers are cutters, who average about $17,000 per year. Often workers receive increases within a few months, after they have gained some experience and developed job skills. Many production workers with experience are paid piecework rates, meaning that their pay is related to how much work they produce. Their actual earnings vary greatly, depending on such factors as the company that employs them and the nature of the job they do.

According to the *Occupational Employment Handbook*, in 1997 there were 21,362 precision shoe and leather workers and repairers in the United States. They earned a mean annual wage of $17,310. Shoe sewing machine operators and tenders earned a mean annual wage of $16,320.

Shoe repairers on average earn about $300 a week. One in 10 earns $420 or more, and shop owners earn considerably more. Assuming a 40-hour workweek, these workers earn an average of $15,600 a year. Employees in large shops receive from one to four weeks' paid vacation and at least six paid holidays a year.

For many shoe industry workers who are union members, pay rates and benefits are set by agreements between the union and company management. Fringe benefits may include health and life insurance, employer contributions to pension plans, and paid vacation days.

■ Work Environment

In many shoe factories, production workers generally work 35 hours a week or less. In companies that produce custom goods, the standard workweek is about 40 hours.

The work is not strenuous, but it can require stamina. Many workers are on their feet much of the time and many jobs involve repetitive tasks. Workers who are paid according to how much they produce have an incentive to work accurately and at a brisk pace.

Conditions in plants vary. Many factories have modern, air-conditioned, well-lighted work areas, but some older plants are not as comfortable. For the most part, hazards are few if safety precautions are followed. Because so much machinery is used, plants can be very noisy. Some workers are exposed to unpleasant odors from dyes, stains, and other chemicals.

Although some repair shops are crowded, noisy, poorly lit, and characterized by unpleasant odors, working conditions in large repair shops, shoe repair departments, and in more modern shoe service stores generally tend to be good. Most shoe repairers work eight hours a day for a five- or six-day week. Self-employed individuals work considerably longer—often 10 hours a day.

■ Outlook

Employment in the shoe manufacturing industry is expected to continue declining in the coming years. By the year 2006, there may be a 20 percent reduction in workers. Foreign competition has resulted in many American shoe factories closing as the labor costs for the shoes they produced were too high compared to foreign-made shoes. In fact, the United States now exports raw materials for shoes to foreign countries where workers make shoes that are returned to be sold here. Ninety percent of shoes now are manufactured overseas.

Increased automation also is causing a decline in the number of workers needed in the shoe industry. Innovations in the shoe manufacturing process such as laser cutting of materials and computer aided design and manufacturing mean that far fewer workers are needed for many tasks, and few new jobs will open up in the future. Most job openings in this field will come about only as experienced workers retire, switch to other jobs, or otherwise leave.

Prospects are better for workers who make custom built shoes or modify shoes for special needs. As the average age of Americans increases, more people will need special footwear, and the demand for molded and orthopedic shoes may increase.

In the mid-1990s, approximately 22,000 shoe and leather workers and repairers are employed in the United States, a drop of 5,000 from the early 1990s. Self-employed individuals who own and operate small shoe repair shops or specialty leather manufacturing firms hold about 4,000 of these jobs. More than half of the remaining workers are employed in the manufacture of footwear products, and an additional one-fifth are employed in the production of leather goods, such as luggage, handbags, and apparel. Another fifth work in shoe repair and shoeshine shops.

According to the Bureau of Labor Statistics, in 1998 there were 57,000 production or nonsupervisory workers overall. About 42,000 women were employed in the leather and leather products industry. Factors that limit growth are the increasing popularity of footwear that cannot be repaired; more durable, longer-wearing materials that require less frequent repair; and inexpensive imports that have made the cost of replacing shoes and leather goods cheaper or more convenient than repairing them. Nevertheless, retirements and job changes of experienced repairers are expected to create numerous job openings each year.

■ For More Information

For statistical information on the footwear industry, contact:

Footwear Industries of America
Communications Director
1420 K Street, NW, Suite 600
Washington, DC 20005
Tel: 202-789-1420

For a brochure that describes the certification process, education courses, and general information on pedorthics, contact:

The Board for Certification in Pedorthics
9861 Broken Land Parkway, Suite 255
Columbia, MD 21046-1151
Tel: 800-560-2025
Web: http://www.cpeds.org

For a list of shoe repair schools and mentors, contact:

Shoe Service Institute of America
Manager of Meetings and Member Services
5024-R Campbell Boulevard
Baltimore, MD 21236
Tel: 410-931-8100
Web: http://www.shoeservice.com/shoesmarts

■ Related Articles

Fashion

Textiles

Apparel Industry Workers

Costume Designers

Leather Tanning and Finishing Workers

Orthotics and Prosthetic Technicians

Pedorthists

Rubber Goods Production Workers

Tailors and Dressmakers

Shop Tailors

■ **See Tailors and Dressmakers**

Short-Order Cooks

■ **See Cooks, Chefs, and Bakers**

Sign Language and Oral Interpreters

■ Overview

Sign language interpreters help people who use sign language communicate with people who can hear and speak. They translate a message from spoken words to signs, and from signs to spoken words. They are fluent in American Sign Language, and/or sign systems based on English (such as Seeing Essential English, Signing Exact English, and Linguistics of Visual English). *Oral interpreters* help deliver a spoken message from someone who hears to someone who is deaf. They also have the ability to understand the speech and mouth movements of someone who is deaf or hard of hearing, and to deliver the message to someone who is hearing.

■ History

Until the 1960s, sign language was considered by many educators to be inferior to spoken and written language. "Oralism," the tradition of teaching deaf children to speak and lip-read, was practiced exclusively in deaf schools, and sign language was forbidden.

A child born deaf can learn sign language as naturally as a hearing child learns English, but English does not come naturally to deaf children. Hearing children pick up many of their English words and language skills from listening to all the noise that surrounds them—a radio or TV on in the room; a phone conversation down the hall; older siblings playing in the front yard. Deaf children can only carefully, painstakingly study the English language and are limited to watching the movement of a person's mouth, and to touching a person's neck and throat to learn sounds. Lipreading is difficult at best, as many words require the same shaping of the lips. Even the best lip-readers can become lost quickly during a normal conversation.

Various forms of sign language were widely used in the 19th century. Laurent Clerc, a deaf Frenchman, and Thomas Gallaudet, a hearing minister, introduced French Sign Language to America in 1816. This, integrated with the signs Americans were already using, served as the foundation for American Sign Language (though the language did not come to be called ASL until the 1960s). It also led to the establishment of the first school for the deaf in Hartford, Connecticut. Many schools for the deaf followed and, by 1867, all of them used sign language in their lessons, resulting in the spread of ASL. But even educators who supported the use of sign language criticized ASL, favoring instead sign systems that followed English sentence structure and word order. (American Sign Language is considered a "natural sign language," a language completely separate from English.)

By the mid-1800s, some educators came to believe that by letting deaf children sign, they were preventing the children from developing speech and English language skills. This led to a conference on deaf education in Milan, Italy, in 1880. There, a resolution was passed to ban all sign language from deaf education. This ban was widely accepted in America, and all schools for the deaf had eliminated ASL from their lessons by 1907. In some classrooms, teachers even tied down the student's hands to prevent them from signing. American Sign Language survived despite this devastating resolution. The language was passed secretly from deaf parents to deaf children, from deaf teachers to deaf students. The resilience of the language, through nearly one hundred years of oralism, was finally acknowledged with a series of linguistic studies in the 1960s. In the 1970s, ASL was reintroduced to deaf education, and is now considered important in the teaching of English to deaf students.

SIGN LANGUAGE AND ORAL INTERPRETERS	
SCHOOL SUBJECTS	English Foreign language
PERSONAL SKILLS	Communication/ideas Helping/teaching
WORK ENVIRONMENT	Primarily indoors Primarily multiple locations
MINIMUM EDUCATION LEVEL	Bachelor's degree
SALARY RANGE	$25,000 to $50,000 to $90,000
CERTIFICATION OR LICENSING	Recommended
OUTLOOK	Faster than the average
DOT	137
GOE	01.03.02
NOC	5125
O*NET	39999A

A sign language interpreter interprets a speech. Interpreters normally stand several feet away from the speakers so as not to interfere with their delivery.

American Sign Language has enabled members of the deaf community to accurately express their cultural values, beliefs, and ideas, and interpreters help to communicate them to the English-speaking majority. The Registry of Interpreters for the Deaf (RID), established in 1964, introduced certification standards in 1972. The Rehabilitation Act of 1973 led the way for better opportunities for deaf people; by mandating interpreters, the legislation gave deaf people access to employment, education, health, and social services. The Americans with Disabilities Act, and the Individuals with Disabilities Education Act, were both passed in 1990, and guarantee, in some instances, interpreters for deaf students and even deaf workers.

■ The Job

In a classroom in New York City, a deaf teacher instructs hearing students in ASL. No speaking or writing is allowed. The teacher uses pictures, gestures, and pantomime to teach the meaning of a sign. He stands in front of the class, and without words, emphasizes not only the importance of finger and hand movement, but of a raised eyebrow, a nod, or a smile. The room is filled with people who spend their days speaking to co-workers and friends, talking on the phone, yelling for cabs, and ordering in restaurants. Tonight the classroom is silent but for the occasional clap of a hand, or the buzzing of the fluorescent lights, or laughter.

This class, taught at the American Sign Language Institute in Manhattan, is composed of people who want access to deaf communities. A social worker wants to be able to communicate with deaf clients; a history teacher wants to interact directly with her deaf students; a man plays Saturday morning basketball games with a deaf neighbor. There's even an anthropologist who wants to communicate with the apes in a study lab. With about a half

million Americans using ASL as their main language, ASL has come to be used in many different settings. Deaf actors perform plays using sign language. Deaf poets have developed a body of sign-language literature. Scientists, inventors, school administrators, and many others are making important contributions to society using ASL. Just as speakers of foreign languages sometimes need interpreters to help them express their ideas to English speakers, so do the users of ASL.

Interpreters are also increasingly in demand for doctors, social service workers, and others who work with elderly populations. People over the age of 65, a rapidly growing segment of society, are threatened with a number of disorders that can lead to hearing loss. Though many hearing-impaired elderly people may rely on a hearing aid, others may need to develop some sign language skills.

The Americans with Disabilities Act (ADA) guarantees the services of interpreters in some situations. Large private companies are required to accommodate employees who have physical limitations. In addition to working with deaf employees, interpreters work in schools helping deaf students learn from English-speaking teachers. They work in legal settings, such as law offices and court rooms. In hospitals, doctors and nurses need the aid of interpreters in communicating with deaf patients. Social service and religious agencies need interpreters to offer counseling and other services to deaf clients. Deaf audience members rely on interpreters for theatrical or televised performances. When an interpreter is needed, the client can check with the school or theater or social service agency to make sure interpreting is provided. If not, there are interpreter provider organizations that can direct the client to an interpreter. The Registry of Interpreters for the Deaf (RID) publishes state-by-state listings of these organizations, as well as a directory of individual interpreters.

Deaf interpreters translate spoken material into a language that can be understood by the deaf. This may be done in either of two ways. Sign language interpreters translate a speaker's words into American Sign Language (ASL), using their hands and fingers, and then repeat aloud the deaf person's signed response to the speaker. Oral interpreters carefully mouth words without voicing them aloud for deaf people who can speech-read. *Tactile interpreters* work with deaf individuals who also have a visual impairment and communicate only through touch.

Interpreters must be very visible; proper lighting and backgrounds should contribute to their visibility, not distract from it. Furthermore, they should obtain any written supplements to assist in accurate interpretation. The interpreter's role is only to interpret; they are not part of the conversation, and any personal asides or additions only cause confusion.

This professional distance is part of an established code of ethics for interpreters. Confidentiality is also part of the code, as is impartiality (strong biases toward a subject matter can affect the ability to interpret accurately). An interpreter also has the responsibility of educating the public about deaf issues. Before going to work as an interpreter, candidates should be aware of the complete code of ethics as established by RID.

■ Requirements

High School

In high school, interested students should take English and composition courses, as well as foreign language courses. ASL is taught in some high schools and some community learning centers.

Postsecondary Training

Many colleges offer sign language courses, courses in deaf culture, and some offer complete deaf studies programs. A college degree is not required for a qualified interpreter, but a solid education will help ensure better jobs and better pay. A postsecondary education will also provide the background and skills necessary for passing the certification exams.

Certification or Licensing

There are two classifications of interpreters: qualified and certified. Certification by RID is recommended, and required in some instances (such as in legal or recorded situations). But a qualified interpreter, with good skills and experience, can also find a lot of work due to a shortage of interpreters. It is important, however, than an uncertified interpreter use careful judgment in taking on assignments; interpreters should not accept work that is beyond their skill level.

RID certification is the only national certification system for sign language interpreters. Different certificates are available according to the candidate's talents or areas of service. An interpreter can hold a CI (Certificate of Interpretation) and a CT (Certificate of Transliteration) for a broad range of assignments. A CLIP (Conditional Legal Interpreting Permit) is necessary for assignments in legal settings. Oral interpreting requires an OIC (Oral Interpreting Certificate). A number of different certificates are also available for deaf or hard-of-hearing interpreters, such as the CDI (Certified Deaf Interpreter) and the RSC (Reverse Skills Certificate). To receive certification, a candidate is first evaluated for eligibility, then tested with a written exam and a performance exam. Most qualified sign language interpreters without certification are in the process of getting certified. Tests are expensive and are only offered at various times of the year, at random sites. As a result, interpreters don't take the tests until they are certain they can pass them.

Other Requirements

Interpreters should be interested in the ways people communicate. They should also be prepared to learn all about complex languages, and to take on the responsibility of conveying accurate messages from one person to another. Sign language and oral interpreting is difficult and demanding work. It requires a careful understanding of English and ASL. Interpreters must also be honest and trustworthy—people will be relying upon them to get their messages and meanings across.

Some experience with the deaf community is very important. Though interpreters may spend many hours studying ASL, they will need to see the language in use among deaf people to gain a more complete understanding of ASL. This will require a commitment to a continuing education in deaf culture. Interpreters should be aware of the issues that affect deaf people, such as the debate of ASL versus oralism, or special residential schooling versus mainstreaming into an English-based classroom. They also need to learn about the technological tools of the deaf: devices that assist in amplification, phone calls, and watching television and movies.

It is also important that interpreters remain on an equal level with the clientele they serve. The interpreter should remain cooperative and respect the client's self-esteem and independence. In working with the deaf community, theirs is not a parental or leadership, role; interpreters are providing a service.

■ Exploring

Many books about sign language and interpreting have been published and can give students a good idea of the demands of the job. To find publications on sign language and interpreting, visit the local library, or write to RID for their list of publications. *Train Go Sorry,* a book by Leah Hager Cohen, is a vivid and authentic account of life as a hearing person within the deaf community. Cohen also describes her experiences as an interpreter and the particular problems with which she was confronted.

Some exposure to American Sign Language will help candidates decide if interpreting is for them. They should learn some sign language, or visit someplace in their community where signing is used. If courses in ASL are not available, interested students should study Spanish, German, French, or any foreign language course, as learning another language will help gauge translating and comprehension skills.

An excellent way to get an insight into the career of an interpreter is to talk to an interpreter, a teacher of deaf students, or any other professional who works with deaf

Oral interpreters must:

• Be speech-readable

• Be naturally expressive when speaking

• Have excellent short-term memory

• Be able to concentrate for long periods of time in the middle of all kinds of distractions

• Have a high comfort level with the English language

• Have a degree of flexibility and open-mindedness

• Be comfortable in front of large groups of people

• Have knowledge of speech production and speechreading

• Be able to easily understand the speech of a wide variety of deaf speakers

• Be able to speak inaudibly when interpreting to the deaf

Source: Views, Vol. 15, Issue 6, June 1998, Registry of Interpreters for the Deaf

people. In some cases, students may be allowed to watch an interpreter at work in the court room, classroom, or at a presentation.

■ Employers

There is a demand for deaf interpreters in many fields. Possible employers include public health agencies, employment agencies, hearing and speech clinics, hospitals, rehabilitation centers, public schools, trade and technical schools, colleges and universities, business and industry, government agencies, theaters, television stations, churches and religious agencies, law enforcement agencies, and the courts.

■ Starting Out

Once sign language skills have sufficiently been developed, interpreting students may then tutor deaf students or volunteer in a social service agency that works with deaf clients. In either case, they should become familiar with the deaf community centers and any other deaf organizations in the area. The more experience with deaf people, the more the certification process will be aided. Also, to help prepare for certification, students should study the RID Code of Ethics and the other books and videotapes recommended by RID.

Once certified, interpreters can be listed in various directories, including directories published by RID. RID also publishes *Views,* which is a monthly newsletter listing employment opportunities and issues affecting interpreters.

■ Advancement

Because most interpreters work on a freelance basis, the best way to advance is to take on more clients and to remain active in the community. The key to becoming a successful interpreter is a continued study of language and deaf cul-

ture. By being part of a deaf community, interpreters can always learn something new about ASL. Just as the English language grows and changes, so does ASL. New developments need new signs, and some old signs become outdated. Also, by staying involved with the deaf community, interpreters can make their services readily available.

To retain certification, interpreters are required to earn continuing education units. This continuing education will allow them to maintain their skills and learn about new developments in interpreting. With a background of continuing education, interpreters can attract more clients and organizations, as well as charge higher fees.

■ Earnings

Freelance interpreters can charge by the hour or the day, providing services to a variety of organizations and institutions. Their fees will be determined primarily by their skills and experience. Other factors include the type of RID certification held, educational background, and previous employer. A beginning interpreter will charge about $15 to $25 per hour, and an experienced interpreter can charge from $50 to $60 per hour.

Interpreters living in large cities like New York, Los Angeles, or Chicago will have many opportunities to interpret and will be able to charge more. Living in a city with a deaf college or residential school, or a college where there is a lot of deaf research and cultural study, will also increase business opportunities. Some rural areas may offer good, varied work for an interpreter.

■ Work Environment

Working as an interpreter can be stressful. When interpreting from ASL to English, or from English to ASL, translators must make many quick decisions. The two languages are very different structurally, and an inexperienced interpreter can get lost in their complexities. In some situations, such as in a court case or in a public presentation or performance, many people are relying on the interpreter's ability to translate messages clearly, quickly, and accurately. But in other situations, such as one-on-one interviews or counseling sessions, things can be more relaxed. Interpreters should only accept the assignments they feel they can perform well and with confidence. This will help lower the stress level.

Generally, interpreters work inside, in a variety of settings, including offices, meeting halls, and classrooms. They may be interpreting for just one person, a small group, or a very large group. Though working directly with many different people, the interpreter's role is limited to that of a translator.

◾ Outlook

Deafness inhibits a child's ability to communicate and interact with English-speaking children and adults. This makes English a difficult language for deaf children to learn. And for several years, there has been a great deal of concern about the quality of education for deaf children. Only one out of four deaf people is able to read a newspaper upon graduating from school. Some deaf students even refuse to learn English, preferring to live and work entirely within an ASL-using community. Regardless of whether ASL becomes more widely accepted, or more efforts are made to teach deaf students English, interpreters will be in high demand. While the prospects for deaf interpreters in general are good, there is also a growing need for *relay interpreters,* deaf individuals who use visual and gestural means to help other deaf people communicate.

Legislature enacted over the last 20 years has increased demand for interpreters. More deaf students are getting a postsecondary education because of access to classroom interpreters. A survey conducted in 1994 by the U.S. Department of Education estimated 20,400 deaf and hard-of-hearing students were pursuing postsecondary education in 1992-93 (not including the 2,900 deaf students enrolled in two colleges specifically for deaf students: Gallaudet University and the National Technical Institute for the Deaf).

About a half-million Americans have chosen ASL as their language. But the 1990 U.S. Census estimates that there are more than 2 million deaf people and more than 16 million people with some kind of hearing impairment (including deafness). The elderly population is growing as well, a population threatened with a number of disorders that can lead to hearing impairment. Society recognizes the need to involve more deaf people in the larger community and to pay more attention to deaf culture.

The role of the sign language interpreter will change as the deaf community changes. An interpreter's job can be greatly affected by the politics of the deaf community. There is much controversy concerning how deaf children should be educated and how involved deaf children need be with the hearing population. Some members of the deaf community want to be classified as a minority group instead of as a disability group; however, this would prevent deaf people from receiving most of the benefits they now receive, including interpreters in the schools. It could also result in difficulty "mainstreaming" deaf students into public schools. Without the interpreters guaranteed by the Americans with Disabilities Act, the parents of deaf students would have to hire their own interpreters, or send their children to residential schools.

For the last few years, however, legislation has fully supported mainstreaming. The U.S. Department of Education estimated that 71 percent of deaf students were mainstreamed in 1991. Government has even been moving toward "full inclusion," or the mainstreaming of all deaf students. This causes concern among many members of the deaf community—full inclusion could mean deaf students would not be allowed the opportunity of a special education environment.

Many more deaf people are enrolling in postsecondary programs, and occupational opportunities have improved for highly educated deaf people. But the overall employment rates for deaf people have not improved much. Interpreters may become more involved in correcting this imbalance; employee assistance programs will need interpreters to help train and integrate deaf people in new jobs. Businesses may also provide special programs for their deaf employees to help them earn promotions. Social services need also to focus on helping young ethnic-minority deaf persons. A number of problems affect this group, including a lack of role models and cultural confusion. Programs need to be established to help them become prepared for postsecondary education.

Because of such legislation as the Americans with Disabilities Act, opportunities will be good for the sign language interpreter. In addition, the increased demand for interpreters in the schools and in the workplace has resulted in a shortage of qualified professionals.

◾ For More Information

This organization has programs, publications, and financial aid programs for the hearing-impaired.

Alexander Graham Bell Association for the Deaf
3417 Volta Place, NW
Washington, DC 20007-2778
Tel (voice and TTY): 202-337-5220
Web: http://www.agbell.org

For career information, and information on educational programs and employment, contact:

American Speech-Language-Hearing Association
10801 Rockville Pike
Rockville, MD 20852
Tel (voice): 301-897-5700 (TTY): 301-897-0157
Web: http://www.asha.org

This center offers career information for all jobs related to working with the deaf.

National Information Center on Deafness
Gallaudet University
800 Florida Avenue, NE
Washington, DC 20002
Tel: 202-651-5051
Web: http://www.gallaudet.edu/~nicd

For information about certification, contact:

The Registry of Interpreters for the Deaf, Inc.
8630 Fenton Street, Suite 324
Silver Spring, MD 20910
Tel (voice): 301-608-0050 (TTY): 202-651-5052

Signal Maintainers

■ **See Communications Equipment Technicians, Signal Mechanics**

Signal Mechanics

■ Overview

Signal mechanics or *signal maintainers* are railroad employees who install, repair, and maintain the signals, signal equipment, and gate crossings that are part of the traffic control and communications systems along railroad tracks. They keep both electrical and mechanical components of signaling devices in good operating order by routinely inspecting and testing lights, circuits and wiring, crossing gates, and detection devices.

■ History

Railroad signals were developed to let train crews know about conditions on the track ahead of them. Signaling systems became necessary in the 19th century when early steam-driven trains began to operate so fast that they presented the danger of collision with one another. Smooth rails and wheels allowed trains to carry heavy loads easily and efficiently, but as speeds and load weights increased, trains needed longer stopping distances. Train crews had to be sure that they were not headed toward another train coming in the opposite direction on the same track, and they had to maintain a safe distance between trains moving in the same direction.

The first attempt to avoid accidents was the adoption of a timetable system. This system was based on running

trains on timed schedules, so that there was always a space between them. However, if a train broke down, the next train's crew had to be informed somehow so that it could react appropriately. In 1837, on a rail line in England, a telegraph system was introduced in which signals were sent on telegraph wires between stations up and down the tracks. The track was divided into blocks, or sections, with a signalman responsible for each block. As trains passed through the blocks, one signalman telegraphed messages to the next block, allowing the next signalman to decide whether it was safe for the train to proceed through that block.

In 1841, a system was devised for communicating with train operators using a mechanical version of semaphore arm signals. At night, when the signal flags could not be seen, a light source was used, with different colored lenses that were rotated in front of it. In time, various codes and rules were developed so that train crews could be kept informed about track conditions ahead as they moved from block to block.

As rail traffic increased, many refinements in signaling systems reduced the chance of human error and helped make train traffic run more smoothly. In 1872, an automatic block system was introduced in which the track itself was part of an electrical circuit, and various signals were activated when the train passed over the track. A modern version of this invention is the moving block system, in which a kind of zone is electronically maintained around a train, and the speed of nearby trains is regulated automatically. Today, traffic control in rail systems is largely centralized and computerized. Many trains and cars can be monitored at one time, and signals and switches can be operated remotely to manage the system with maximum safety and efficiency.

In order for these sophisticated controls to be effective, railroad signals and signaling equipment must function properly. Signal mechanics are the workers who are responsible for making sure that this vital equipment is working as it is intended.

■ The Job

Signal mechanics install, maintain, and repair signal equipment. Today's signal equipment includes computerized and electronic equipment detection devices and electronic grade crossing protection. To install signals, workers travel with road crews to designated areas. They place electrical wires, create circuits, and construct railway-highway crossing signals, such as flashers and gates. When signal mechanics install new signals or signal equipment, they or other crew members may have to dig holes and pour concrete foundations for the new equipment, or they may install precast concrete foundations. Because railroad signal systems are sometimes installed in the same areas as underground fiber optic cables, signal mechanics must be familiar with marking systems and take great care in digging.

Signal mechanics who perform routine maintenance are generally responsible for a specified length of track. They are often part of a team of several signal mechanics, called a signal construction gang. They drive a truck along the track route, stopping to inspect and test crossings, signal lights, interlock equipment, and detection devices. When servicing battery-operated equipment, they check batteries, refilling them with water or replacing them with fresh ones if necessary. They use standard electrical testing devices to check signal circuits and wiring connections, and they replace any defective wiring, burned-out light bulbs, or broken colored lenses on light signals. They clean the lenses with a cloth and cleaning solution and lubricate moving parts on swinging signal arms and crossing gates. They tighten loose bolts, and open and close crossing gates to verify that the circuits and connections in the gates are working.

Signal mechanics are often required to travel long distances as repairs are needed. Many are assigned to a large region by their employer, such as the entire Midwest, or may even be on call to work anywhere in the nation. Generally, employees are responsible for providing their own transportation from their home to the work location. The railroad company pays the cost of hotel rooms and provides a meal allowance. When signal mechanics are required to travel, their work week may begin on Sunday, when they travel to the work site so they can start early Monday. The work week may then include four 10-hour days, or longer, depending on the urgency of completing the job.

Sometimes signal mechanics are dispatched to perform repairs at specific locations along the track in response to reports from other rail workers about damaged or malfunctioning equipment. In these cases, the worker analyzes the problem, repairs it, and checks to make sure that the equipment is functioning properly.

Signal mechanics also compile written reports that detail their inspection and repair activities, noting the mileage of the track that they have traveled and the locations where they have done work.

■ Requirements

High School

Proven mechanical aptitude is very desirable, and a firm knowledge of electricity is a must. Because of the change in technology in signaling in the railroad industry, railroads are requiring new job applicants to pass written tests that include AC/DC electronics. Therefore, high school courses in electrical shop and electronics would provide a

good background for signal mechanics. Technical training in computers is also very helpful.

Postsecondary Training

Signal mechanics must have at least a high school diploma, although some railroads have gone so far as to require applicants to have college degrees in electronics or electrical engineering. Other railroads will consider applicants who have military experience in electronics, or who possess a two-year degree in electronics from a technical school.

Workers are usually trained both on the job and in the classroom. Some of the biggest railroads have their own schools; the smaller ones often contract to send their employees to those schools. For example, Norfolk Southern sends its signal trainees to its training center in McDonough, Georgia, during which they are paid a training wage and lodging and meals are paid for during the one-week training course.

Subjects studied in the classroom include electrical and electronics theory; mathematics; signal apparatus, protection devices, and circuits; federal railroad administration policies; and procedures related to signaling.

On the job, beginners often start out in helper positions, doing simple tasks requiring little special skill. Helpers work under the supervision of experienced signal mechanics. Later, they may become assistants and signal maintainers, based on their seniority and how much they have learned.

Other Requirements

Skilled workers in signal departments usually do not need great strength or stamina, although they may have to be active throughout the day, perhaps climbing poles or hand digging with shovels and picks. Signal mechanics need to be able to climb, stoop, kneel, crouch, and reach, and they should also be agile, with a good sense of balance. Good vision, normal hearing, and depth perception are important. Finally, alertness and

SIGNAL MECHANICS	
SCHOOL SUBJECTS	Computer science Technical/Shop
PERSONAL SKILLS	Mechanical/manipulative Technical/scientific
WORK ENVIRONMENT	Primarily outdoors Primarily multiple locations
MINIMUM EDUCATION LEVEL	Apprenticeship
SALARY RANGE	$27,500 to $33,456 to $37,428
CERTIFICATION OR LICENSING	None available
OUTLOOK	Little change or more slowly than the average
DOT	822
GOE	05.05.05
NOC	7242
O*NET	85511

A Union Pacific Railroad signal mechanic checks timing circuits inside the relay cabinet for a grade crossing protection system.

quick reflexes are needed for working in potentially dangerous circumstances on ladders, near high-voltage lines, and on moving equipment.

Most signal mechanics who work for the larger railroads are required to belong to a union—usually the Brotherhood of Railroad Signalmen. Those who work for the smaller railroads are typically nonunionized.

■ Exploring

A field trip to a rail yard can give a student a firsthand idea of the work done in this occupation. For a closer view, it may be possible to talk with a railroad employee who is involved in maintaining communications or control equipment. Professional journals, such as the *Signalman's Journal,* published by the Brotherhood of Railroad Signalmen, can provide useful information about the career of signal mechanics.

■ Employers

Signal mechanics may be employed by passenger lines or freight lines. They may work for one of the major railroads, such as Burlington Northern Santa Fe, Norfolk Southern, CSX, or Atchison-Topeka-Santa Fe, or they may work for one of the 500 smaller short-line railroads across the country. Many of the passenger lines today are commuter lines located near large metropolitan areas. Signal mechanics who work for freight lines may work in a rural or an urban area and travel more extensively than the shorter, daily commuter routes passenger railroad conductors make.

■ Starting Out

Prospective signal mechanics can contact the personnel offices of railroad companies for information about job opportunities. Another possibility is to check with the local,

state, or national office of the Brotherhood of Railroad Signalmen. Because signal mechanic positions are often union positions, they follow structured hiring procedures, such as specific times of the year when applications are accepted. Norfolk Southern holds hiring/recruiting sessions. Applications are not sent out for union positions; rather recruiting sessions are advertised in local newspapers, state job services, and schools. At recruiting sessions, supervisors explain the positions open, answer questions and oversee the application process. Some applicants may be selected for evaluations, which will be used to help determine who is hired.

■ Advancement

Workers generally advance from helper positions to become *assistant signal mechanics,* and from there to positions as *signal maintainers.* Other advanced positions include *signal shop foremen* and *signal inspectors.* These promotions, which are related to workers' seniority, sometimes take a number of years to achieve. Experienced signal mechanics can advance to such supervisory positions as gang foremen or leaders of work crews, directing and coordinating the activities of other signal mechanics. At one railroad, Norfolk Southern, signal mechanics are designated as assistant signal persons after qualifying as trainees. After completing two phases of training and based on seniority, assistant signal persons can bid for promotion to a signal maintainer position with territorial maintenance responsibilities.

■ Earnings

Currently, signal mechanics and signal maintainers earn almost $37,000 annually. Signal helpers and signal maintainer helpers earn about $27,500. According to the agreement between the Brotherhood of Railroad Signalmen and one major railroad, signal shop foremen earn the highest salary, $37,428 per year, followed by signal gang foremen at $34,848 and assistant signal foremen, who earn $33,456. These rates are based on 213 hours of work per month, which generally means workers work six-day weeks, and do not include overtime.

Workers receive extra pay for overtime work. In addition to regular earnings, they receive fringe benefits such as employer contributions to health insurance and retirement plans, paid vacation days, and travel passes.

■ Work Environment

Signal department workers do their work outdoors in a variety of weather conditions, sometimes at night. Some workers are regularly scheduled to be on call for emergency repairs.

In some cases, signal mechanics must lift, carry, and push or pull somewhat heavy objects. They may also be required to stoop, squat, climb, and crawl into small spaces. Mechanics must use caution on the job to avoid hazards such as falling from ladders or signal towers, being hit by falling objects, and electric shock.

There is variety in the kinds of signals a mechanic works on, and variety in the location of the work, so the job is rarely boring. In addition, workers in this field can take pride in the importance of their responsibilities, since railroad travel is heavily dependent upon the proper functioning of signals.

■ Outlook

In the coming years, the number of signal mechanics who install signal equipment is not expected to grow; however, the number of signal maintainers, who test the signaling and communications equipment may increase, due to the more complex circuitry involved in the signaling systems. Relatively few additional job openings will develop, and they will mostly occur when experienced workers transfer to other fields or leave the workforce altogether.

■ For More Information

For general information on the railroad industry, contact:

Association of American Railroads
50 F Street, NW
Washington, DC 20001
Tel: 202-639-2100
Web: http://www.aar.org

For information on the career of railroad signal mechanic, contact:

Brotherhood of Railroad Signalmen
601 West Golf Road, Box U
Mount Prospect, IL 60056
Tel: 847-439-3732
Web: http://www.brs.org

■ Related Articles

Electronics

Railroads

Electrical and Electronics Engineers

Electricians

Line Installers and Cable Splicers

Locomotive Engineers

Railroad Clerks

Railroad Conductors

Silversmiths

■ **See Jewelers and Jewelry Repairers, Silverware Artisans and Workers**

Silverware Artisans and Workers

■ Overview

Silverware workers manufacture metal utensils used at the table for holding, serving, and handling food and drink, such as platters, pitchers, forks, and spoons. *Silverware artisans* include *designers* and *artists*, as well as *silversmiths*, who are skilled workers and repairers of silver and a variety of other metals, including gold and platinum.

Part of the home furnishings industry, the creation and manufacture of silverware fall under a number of other areas as well, such as industrial design, metalworking, commercial art and design, and machine operation. There are currently about 200 U.S. plants that make flatware and hollowware, most of which have fewer than 20 workers each. While only about 9,000 production workers were employed in the silverware and plated ware industry in the United States in 1996, there were approximately 19,300 silversmiths in the country in 1997.

SILVERWARE ARTISANS AND WORKERS	
SCHOOL SUBJECTS	**Mathematics** **Technical/Shop**
PERSONAL SKILLS	**Artistic** **Following instructions** **Mechanical/manipulative**
WORK ENVIRONMENT	**Primarily indoors** **Primarily one location**
MINIMUM EDUCATION LEVEL	**High school diploma** **Apprenticeship**
SALARY RANGE	**$13,000 to $31,200 to $75,000**
CERTIFICATION OR LICENSING	**None available**
OUTLOOK	**Decline**
DOT	**700**
GOE	**06.04.23**
NOC	**9227**
O*NET	**89123B**

■ History

People have used an interesting variety of eating utensils throughout the ages. Dishes, flatware, and cutlery of all kinds have been made of wood, bone, stone, volcanic glass, shell, and a number of metals, including silver, tin, gold, pewter, and stainless steel.

Shells were probably the first rudimentary spoons. Primitive forks were just sticks with sharpened ends. And the first knives, sharpened with bone, wood, or stone, were used not only for cutting food but for warfare as well. By the Middle Ages, eating utensils became ornately decorated and more developed, according to each of their required uses.

With the invention of electroplating in the mid-18th century, the silver plating industry experienced enormous growth in the United States. The process, which involves coating inexpensive metals with silver, became a common method for producing attractive tableware.

Silversmiths of the day were seen as sculptors of sorts. Able to shape materials into pieces both attractive and functional, these artisans created not only utensils but hollowware as well, including bowls, creamers, teapots, pitchers, cups, and trays. In addition to Paul Revere, perhaps the best known silversmith in the United States, a number of other craftspeople played key roles in the emerging silver industry in colonial America.

James Geddy, Jr., for example, sold a variety of items that both he and other artisans made from 1766 to 1777. These pieces included silver flatware and hollowware, such as teaspoons, tureen ladles, cans, and tongs. Geddy's brother-in-law William Waddill, another well-known colonial silversmith, provided engraving services as well.

Today, about 60 different kinds of craftspeople work in the industry, transforming silver, stainless steel, nickel, zinc, copper, and other metals into contemporary silverware. Regardless of the metals used, many of the steps in the silverware manufacturing process are basically the same.

■ The Job

The manufacture of silverware requires contributions from many different types of artisans and production workers. The process begins with *flatware designers,* who, after considering current market trends and the products offered by competitors, make sketches or computerized three-dimensional models of styles and patterns for new lines of tableware.

Once management approves proposed designs, they are given to *model makers,* who create handmade, full-size models of all pieces in the line, sculpting or carving them in plastic, clay, or plaster. Based on these models, the designs are often altered. Then the model makers prepare models of the final version of the tableware designs, which serve as patterns for the molds and dies that will be used in producing the actual silverware.

Tool makers and *die makers* construct the dies—tools that can stamp, shape, or cut metal. These dies are used to create forks, spoons, knives, and other utensils, which begin as flat sheets of stainless steel, sterling silver, nickel silver, brass, or other metal. *Flatware press operators* feed the sheets into presses, which die-cut the metal into flat blanks roughly the same size and shape as the finished utensils. The blanks are then put into a drop press, which shapes each blank into the desired piece. Next, *flatware makers,* or *annealers,* heat, or anneal, the metal, softening it to help reduce the possibility of warping. The annealed flatware is then immersed in a chemical solution to cool and clean it.

Once all pieces have been thoroughly cleaned, *trimmers* use bench grinding machines or hand files to remove any undesirable irregularities on the surface and to round off edges in accordance with the design. Finally, the flatware is buffed and polished to a smooth finish by *mirror-finishing-machine operators* or *polishing-machine operators.*

While the process just described is used for most flatware, some pieces require the skills of additional specialists as well. The handles of many kinds of knives, for example, are stamped out as two separate halves, which are then joined together by *solderers* or *hollow handle bench workers.* The handles can be left hollow, or they may be filled so that the knife has more weight. *Hollow-handle-knife assemblers* then cement the knife blades into the handles. They check the finished pieces for alignment and clean any excess cement from the blade using a metal pick and brush. Inspected knives are placed in a rack to dry, while those that are rejected are set aside on a separate tray.

The manufacturing process for hollowware items, such as teapots, trays, and sugar bowls, also calls for workers with specialized skills because these pieces can be quite ornate. Most hollowware is made of a base metal, such as brass. The brass comes in rolled sheets, which workers cut into usable sections. *Press operators* mold the brass sheeting into the desired shapes using large presses. Then *profile-saw operators* and *profile trimmers* trim away excess metal from the edges. Other parts of hollowware vessels, such as handles, legs, and border trim, are made separately and attached by *silverware assemblers* using screws, bolts, pins, or adhesives. These parts may be cast in molds using molten Britannia metal, an alloy similar to pewter. Objects like goblets and candlesticks are stretched and shaped by *spinners* who use hand tools and bench-lathes.

Silversmiths and *hammersmiths* also create hollowware. Silversmiths are skilled craftworkers who perform many kinds of tasks related to the fabrication of fine hollowware, such as annealing metal, shaping it with various tools, adding embossed designs, and soldering on parts. In addition, they repair damaged pieces, using hammers, tongs, pliers, dollies, anvils, tracing punches, and other tools. Hammersmiths also repair hollowware, using many of the same tools. Both silversmiths and hammersmiths work with not only silver but also a variety of other metals, including pewter, chromium, nickel, and brass.

A final step often used in manufacturing flatware and hollowware is electroplating, a process that uses electric current to coat a metal with one or more thin layers of another metal. Using the electroplating process, workers coat articles made of an inexpensive metal with a precious metal, such as gold, silver, or platinum.

Platers, or *electroplaters,* first clean unplated articles in vats of cleaning solutions. They may initially coat the items with nickel or copper, either of which allows the plating metal to attach to the base metal. Then electroplaters suspend an unplated item and a piece of the plating metal in a tank containing a chemical solution. When they run electricity through the apparatus, plating metal is deposited on the piece, creating an item that looks as attractive as one made entirely of the precious metal. At the end of the process, platers check the finished objects for thickness of metal deposit using such instruments as calipers and micrometers. They are also responsible for marking, measuring, and covering any areas that have failed to be plated.

■ Requirements

High School

Although there are no formal educational requirements for silverware manufacturing workers, most employers prefer high school graduates. Courses in mathematics, especially plane geometry, will prove to be invaluable once you begin working in the field. Classes in such subjects as drafting, sketching, computer science, and shop are important for aspiring toolmakers, die cutters, machinists, and bench workers.

If you're planning on a career as a silverware designer, art courses at the high school level are a must. In particular, classes in design, computer graphics, drawing, and drafting are essential. In addition, you should take a sampling of liberal arts and business courses, including English, marketing, psychology, and management.

Postsecondary Training

Silverware manufacturing workers can receive postsecondary training through technical or vocational schools, community colleges, art schools, or correspondence courses. Course work usually includes applied mathematics, manufacturing arts, casting, enameling, metalworking, silversmithing, plating, and toolmaking. Specialized courses are often offered as well, including tool designing and programming, blueprint reading, and mechanical drawing.

Silverware has been an important Rhode Island product for more than 200 years. Here a craftsman works on a die to be used in making forks.

Alternatively, employees who aim to become skilled in a specialized craft can complete an apprenticeship, which may last four to five years. Apprentices learn on the job as they work in a silverware plant under the supervision of experienced craftworkers. They also receive related classroom instruction. Apprenticeships are the usual method by which workers are trained in silversmithing, soft soldering, spinning, engraving, model making, drafting, machining, tool and die making, and a variety of other areas.

Silverware designers generally need to have a college degree in a field such as industrial or applied design, along with training in fine art and the properties of metals. More than one hundred schools offer a bachelor's degree in metalsmithing and industrial design. Some colleges also offer master's degrees in these disciplines. Many schools require a prospective designer to complete a year of basic design and art courses before they are allowed formal entry into a design program. Students enrolled in a design program spend many hours designing three-dimensional objects. They gain experience using metalworking and woodworking machines to construct their designs. Among the courses they should take are drafting, drawing, and computer-aided design.

Other Requirements

Silverware manufacturing workers must be precise in their work and have good concentration. They should also have good vision and manual dexterity. Some employees must be able to handle the repetitive tasks that are often part of the job. Die makers, in particular, should be extremely patient, since their work requires highly precise computation. They also need to have mechanical aptitude and physical strength.

Silverware designers must be artistic and creative and have an eye for color and beauty. To be successful, they should have a thorough knowledge of the flatware industry, specifically the manufacturing techniques that are used to produce the products they design. In addition, designers need to keep abreast of current trends and develop their work accordingly.

Freelance designers must be willing to work long hours. They also need to be organized, detail-minded, self-disciplined, and prepared for downtime.

■ Exploring

A part-time or summer job in a silverware factory can provide you with an excellent opportunity to learn about the silverware industry. However, with relatively few plants in the United States, most employing no more than 20 workers each, such jobs are difficult to obtain. For this reason, you may want to consider a position at a metal manufacturing or machining company. Such a position can offer you the experience you'll need when you're ready to look for a job in silverware manufacturing.

If you're interested in silverware design or silversmithing, sampling similar activities will allow you to get a taste of some of the skills you'll need. Classes in ornamental metalwork, jewelry making, woodworking, ceramics, sketching, and drafting, for example, are usually offered at local community colleges or art centers.

You can also read professional magazines about art, design, manufacturing, and industry-specific topics in order to become familiar with the field and keep abreast of new products, trends, and developments. *AmericanStyle Magazine* and *The Crafts Report*, for exam-

ple, are specifically aimed at craftworkers, while *Silver Magazine* focuses on the field of silver and the products made from this material. *MetalForming Magazine, American Jewelry Manufacturer*, and other trade publications may also be of interest. In addition, you might want to contact Brynmorgen Press, a company that offers books on metalsmithing.

■ Employers

Of the 200 plants that manufacture flatware and hollowware in the United States, most are located in New England, particularly in Massachusetts, Connecticut, and New York. The major companies in the industry include Gorham, Kirk Stieff, Oneida, Towle, Wallace International, Lunt, and Reed and Barton, with four of the biggest firms accounting for over half of the U.S. market.

Many smaller companies are located in Rhode Island, Maryland, and other parts of the country. Among them are Regent-Sheffield, Lifetime Cutlery Corporation, and World Tableware International. Foreign manufacturers in Japan, Brazil, and various European countries specialize in the production and design of silverware as well.

In addition to production workers, manufacturing companies employ both staff and freelance flatware designers. These creative professionals also work at independent companies that provide flatware designs to manufacturers, as well as at New York's Tiffany and Company, a retailer and manufacturer.

■ Starting Out

Silverware production job seekers should apply directly, either in person or in writing, to manufacturing firms that may be hiring new workers. Leads to specific jobs can sometimes be found through state employment service offices or help wanted ads in trade publications and local newspapers. Graduates of technical training programs may learn about openings through school or college placement offices.

Many newly hired manufacturing workers begin as buffers, trimmers, edgers, or assemblers. Others learn skilled crafts through apprenticeship programs. If you're interested in entering the field as a tool and die maker, keep in mind that these specialists frequently move up from other related jobs, such as machine operators or machinists. (Tool and die makers are frequently considered advanced machinists.)

For those considering the design side of the silverware industry, the newsletter of the Industrial Designers Society of America sometimes lists ads placed by companies seeking design professionals. In addition, available positions are frequently posted at the Web sites of industry-related associations, as well as on job bulletin boards at colleges and universities and through school placement offices.

Aspiring designers will find better job opportunities if they have some experience in the industry before applying for positions. A part-time or summer job at a flatware company or another related firm can provide such experience. In addition, design students should assemble a portfolio of their artwork and designs to show potential employers during interviews. Once hired, beginning designers are often given drafting tasks to familiarize them with the company's products.

■ Advancement

Silverware workers who can produce high-quality pieces quickly and consistently have the best chances for advancement. Unskilled workers can apply to become apprentices, learning such specialized skills as soft soldering, engraving, spinning, and toolmaking. Skilled workers may be promoted to supervisory positions.

Production workers with many years of on-the-job experience sometimes move up to positions as silversmiths or designers. Experienced die makers, in particular, may move into supervisory and managerial jobs. Others become tool designers or tool programmers in related industries.

In the design area, highly skilled professionals may advance to become lead designers or directors of design departments. At companies where the design department is very small, advancement opportunities are often limited. Instead of promotions, designers at these firms are frequently given more job responsibilities and higher salaries. Well-known, highly experienced designers with strong financial backing can start their own consulting firms or concentrate solely on freelance work.

Production workers and design professionals alike can also advance to other fields that require their skills, such as glass manufacturing, ceramics, and ornamental metalwork.

■ Earnings

Production workers in the silverware industry are often paid an hourly rate. Alternatively, they can earn piecework or incentive rates, which are based on the amount of work they complete. Earnings vary with the particular job and skill level of the worker.

Some unskilled workers start as low as $6 or $7 an hour. Within a short time, however, they may be able to increase their pay by earning piecework rates. Overall, the average wage for these employees is roughly $11 an hour, or about $22,000 a year, although some people can do much better. Earnings are generally higher for workers with special training and skills.

According to the *Occupational Outlook Handbook,* the average annual pay for metalworkers in general ranged from $13,000 to $40,000 in 1996, with the middle 50 percent earning $16,640 to $31,200 per year. Most die makers averaged $31,200 to $47,320 per year, with the highest earners making more than $60,000 annually, while silversmiths earned a mean hourly wage of $11.95, or $24,850 annually, in 1997.

In the design area, the Industrial Designers Society of America reports that entry-level designers with one to two years of experience earned about $27,000 annually in 1996. Those with five years of experience earned $35,000 per year, while designers on the job for eight years made about $45,000. Top industrial designers, consultants, and well-known freelancers earn significantly higher salaries in the range of $50,000 to $75,000, while those in managerial or executive positions make up to $140,000 a year.

In addition to their regular pay, production workers and designers usually receive such benefits as health insurance, pensions, paid vacation days and sick leave, employee assistance programs, and profit sharing plans. Workers may also be able to buy company products at a discount.

■ Work Environment

Silverware factories usually have open and pleasant work areas. Many of the machines that silverware production workers use are small but noisy. The work is not physically strenuous, but some jobs, such as operating punch presses, are monotonous. Some employees may be required to lift and carry heavy objects, but mechanical devices perform much of this work.

To avoid injury, workers usually wear protective gear, such as safety glasses, ear protectors, and heavy gloves. Although electroplaters, in particular, are often exposed to strong and hazardous chemicals, factories have ventilation systems installed to remove fumes generated in the electroplating process and workers receive saftey training, as well as special clothing, to reduce any possible risks or danger.

Silverware designers work in well-lit, quiet, modern offices or studios, at drafting tables or computer terminals. They often work alone but spend time consulting with other employees as well. Sometimes they visit production areas to get a feel for the manufacturing process or to check on the progress of their designs.

Designers may travel to attend meetings, seminars, or conventions or to conduct research on design trends in the market. Occasionally they feel frustrated or disappointed when their designs are rejected or criticized or when production problems require them to adjust their designs.

Workweeks for all silverware industry employees average about 35 to 40 hours. Flatware designers may have to work additional hours to meet specific deadlines. Similarly, production workers are often required to put in overtime when there are big orders to complete. At other times, companies have very few orders and must lay off manufacturing workers for short periods of time.

Outlook

Employment levels in the U.S. silverware industry have been declining for years, and the trend is expected to continue. Among the reasons for this decline are competition from silverware manufacturers in other countries, high prices for silver and steel, and a decreased demand for expensive gifts, such as flatware settings and tea services.

On the technology front, the implementation of labor-saving machinery is resulting in increased productivity. However, according to the *Occupational Outlook Handbook*, lower-skilled workers who manually operate machines are likely to find their positions eliminated because their jobs can be easily automated.

Despite the dreary prospects, some job openings will continue to be available in the field, but most will come about as workers move to other jobs or leave the workforce altogether. In addition, competition for these jobs will be fierce. Designers, silversmiths, tool and die makers, and others who have skills and talents applicable to related fields or industries have the best chances for continued employment in their specific specialty. Workers who are willing to participate in continuing education programs or relocate will also have a competitive edge.

For More Information

The IDSA serves its members by recognizing excellence, promoting the exchange of information, and fostering innovation.

Industrial Designers Society of America
1142 Walker Road, Suite E
Great Falls, VA 22066
Tel: 703-759-0100
Web: http://www.idsa.org

The MJSA is a national trade organization supporting the jewelry/metals industry.

Manufacturing Jewelers and Silversmiths of America
One State Street, 6th floor
Providence, RI 02908
Tel: 800-444-6572
Web: http://mjsa.polygon.net

The NTMA is the national representative of the custom precision manufacturing industry in the United States.

National Tooling & Machining Association
9300 Livingston Road
Fort Washington, MD 20744
Tel: 800-248-6862
Web: http://www.ntma.org

The Silver Institute serves as the industry's voice in increasing public understanding of the many uses of silver.

The Silver Institute
1112 16th Street, NW, Suite 240
Washington, DC 20036
Tel: 202-835-0185
Web: http://www.silverinstitute.org

The SAS is the nation's only professional organization solely devoted to the preservation and promotion of contemporary silversmithing, specifically in the areas of hollowware, flatware, and sculpture.

Society of American Silversmiths
PO Box 704
Chepachet, RI 02814
Tel: 401-567-7800
Web: http://www.silversmithing.com

Related Articles

Fashion

Metals

Stone, Concrete, Ceramics, and Glass

Electroplating Workers

Industrial Designers

Jewelers and Jewelry Repairers

Machine Tool Operators

Metallurgical Technicians

Tool, Tap, and Die Makers

Singers

Overview

Professional *singers* perform opera, gospel, blues, rock, jazz, folk, classical, country, and other musical genres, before an audience or in recordings. Singers are musicians who use their voices as their instruments, and may perform as part of a band, choir, or other musical ensembles, or solo, whether with or without musical accompaniment.

History

"Song is man's sweetest joy," said a poet in the eighth century BC. Singers are those who use their voices as instruments of sound and are capable of relating music that touches the soul. The verb to sing is related to the Greek term omphe, which means "voice." In general, singing is related to music and thus to the Muses, the goddesses of ancient Greek religion who are said to watch over the arts and are sources of inspiration.

Singing, or vocal performance, is considered the mother of all music, which is thought of as an international language. In human history, before musical instruments were ever devised, there was always the voice, which has had the longest and most significant influence on the development of all musical forms and materials that have followed.

A precise, formal history of the singing profession is not feasible, for singing evolved in different parts of the world and in diverse ways at various times. A 40,000-year-old cave painting in France suggests the earliest evidence of music; the painting shows a man playing a musical bow and dancing behind several reindeer. Most civilizations have had legends suggesting that gods created song, and many myths suggest that nymphs have passed the art of singing to us. The Chinese philosopher Confucius (551-478 BC) considered music to be a significant aspect of a moral society, with its ability to portray emotions as diverse as joy and sorrow, anger and love.

There are certain differences between Eastern and Western music. In general, music of Middle Eastern civilizations has tended to be more complex in its melodies (although music from the Far East is often simplistic). Western music has been greatly influenced by the organized systems of musical scales of ancient Greece and has evolved through various eras, which were rich and enduring but can be defined in general terms. The first Western musical era is considered to have been the medieval period (c. 850-1450), when the earliest surviving songs were written by 12th-century French troubadours and German minnesingers; these poet-musicians sang of love, nature, and religion. The next periods include the Renaissance (c. 1450-1600), during which the musical attitude was one of calm and self-restraint; the Baroque (c. 1600-1750), a time of extravagance, excitement, and splendor; the Classical (c. 1750-1820), a return to simplicity; and the Romantic (c. 1820-1950), which represents a time of strong emotional expression and fascination with nature.

In primitive societies of the past and present, music has played more of a ritualistic, sacred role. In any case, singing has been considered an art form for thousands of years, powerfully influencing the evolution of societies. It is a large part of our leisure environment, our ceremonies, and our religions; the power of song has even been said to heal illness and sorrow. In antiquity, musicians tended to have more than one role, serving as composer, singer, and instrumentalist at the same time. They also tended to be found in the highest levels of society and to take part in events such as royal ceremonies, funerals, and processions.

The function of singing as an interpretive, entertaining activity was established relatively recently. Opera had its beginnings in the late 16th century in Italy and matured during the following centuries in other European countries. The rise of the professional singer (also referred to as the vocal virtuoso because of the expert talent involved) occurred in the 17th and 18th centuries. At this time, musical composers began to sing to wider audiences, who called for further expression and passion in singing.

Throughout the periods of Western music, the various aspects of song have changed along with general musical developments. Such aspects include melody, harmony, rhythm, tempo, dynamics, texture, and other characteristics. The structures of song are seemingly unlimited and have evolved from plainsong and madrigal, chanson and chorale, opera and cantata, folk and motet, anthem and

drama, to today's expanse of pop, rock, country, rap, and so on. The development of radio, television, motion pictures, and various types of recordings (LP records, cassettes, and compact discs) has had a great effect on the singing profession, creating smaller audiences for live performances yet larger and larger audiences for recorded music.

■ The Job

Essentially, singers are employed to perform music with their voices by using their knowledge of vocal sound and delivery, harmony, melody, and rhythm. They put their individual vocal styles into the songs they sing, and they interpret music accordingly. The inherent sounds of the voices in a performance play a significant part in how a song will affect an audience; this essential aspect of a singer's voice is known as its tone.

Classical singers are usually categorized according to the range and quality of their voices, beginning with the highest singing voice, the soprano, and ending with the lowest, the bass; voices in between include mezzo soprano, contralto, tenor, and baritone. Singers perform either alone (in which case they are referred to as soloists) or as members of an ensemble, or group. They sing by either following a score, which is the printed musical text, or by memorizing the material. Also, they may sing either with or without instrumental accompaniment; singing without accompaniment is called a cappella. In opera—actually plays set to music—singers perform the various roles, much as actors, interpreting the drama with their voice to the accompaniment of a symphony orchestra.

Classical singers may perform a variety of musical styles, or specialize in a specific period; they may give recitals, or perform as members of an ensemble. Classical singers generally undergo years of voice training and instruction in musical theory. They develop their vocal technique, and learn how to project without

SINGERS	
SCHOOL SUBJECTS	Music Speech
PERSONAL SKILLS	Artistic Communication/ideas
WORK ENVIRONMENT	Primarily indoors Primarily multiple locations
MINIMUM EDUCATION LEVEL	High school diploma
SALARY RANGE	$6,900 to $26,000 to $70,000
CERTIFICATION OR LICENSING	None available
OUTLOOK	About as fast as the average
DOT	152
GOE	01.04.03
NOC	5133
O*NET	34047C

Celine Dion performs in Paris.

harming their voices. Classical singers rarely use a microphone when they sing; nonetheless, their voices must be heard above the orchestra. Because classical singers often perform music from many different languages, they learn how to pronounce these languages, and often how to speak them as well. Those who are involved in opera work for opera companies in major cities throughout the country and often travel extensively. Some classical singers also perform in other musical areas.

Professional singers tend to perform in a certain chosen style of music, such as jazz, rock, or blues, among many others. Many singers pursue careers that will lead them to perform for coveted recording contracts, on concert tours, and for television and motion pictures. Others perform in rock, pop, country, gospel, or folk groups, singing in concert halls, nightclubs, and churches and at social gatherings and for small studio recordings. Whereas virtuosos, classical artists who are expertly skilled in their singing style, tend to perform traditional pieces that have been handed down through hundreds of years, singers in other areas often perform popular, current pieces, and often songs that they themselves have composed.

Another style of music in which formal training is often helpful is jazz. Jazz singers learn phrasing, breathing, and vocal techniques; often, the goal of a jazz singer is to become as much a part of the instrumentation as the piano, saxophone, trumpet, or trombone. Many jazz singers perform "scat" singing, in which the voice is used in an improvisational way much like any other instrument.

Folk singers perform songs that may be many years old, or they may write their own songs. Folk singers generally perform songs that express a certain cultural tradition; while some folk singers specialize in their own or another culture, others may sing songs from a great variety of cultural and musical traditions. In the United States, folk singing is particularly linked to the acoustic guitar, and many singers accompany themselves while singing.

A cappella singing, which is singing without musical accompaniment, takes many forms. A cappella music may be a part of classical music; it may also be a part of folk music, as in the singing of barbershop quartets. Another form, called doo-wop, is closely linked to rock and rhythm and blues music.

Gospel music, which evolved in the United States, is a form of sacred music; gospel singers generally sing as part of a choir, accompanied by an organ, or other musical instruments, but may also be performed a cappella. Many popular singers began their careers as singers in church and gospel choirs before entering jazz, pop, blues, or rock.

Rock singers generally require no formal training whatsoever. Rock music is a very broad term encompassing many different styles of music, such as heavy metal, punk, rap, rhythm and blues, rockabilly, techno, and many others. Many popular rock singers cannot even sing. But rock singers learn to express themselves and their music, developing their own phrasing and vocal techniques. Rock singers usually sing as part of a band, or with a backing band to accompany them. Rock singers usually sing with microphones so that they can be heard above the amplified instruments around them.

All singers practice and rehearse their songs and music. Some singers read from music scores while performing; others perform from memory. Yet all must gain an intimate knowledge of their music, so that they can best convey its meanings and feelings to their audience. Singers must also exercise their voices even when not performing. Some singers perform as featured soloists and artists. Other perform as part of a choir, or as backup singers adding harmony to the lead singer's voice.

■ Requirements

High School

As noted above, many singers require no formal training in order to sing. However, those interested in becoming classical or jazz singers should begin learning and honing their talent when they are quite young. Vocal talent can be recognized in grade school students and even in younger children. In general, however, these early years are a time of vast development and growth in singing ability. Evident changes occur in boys' and girls' voices when they are around 12 to 14 years old, during which time their vocal cords go through a process of lengthening and thickening. Boys' voices tend to change much more so than girls' voices, although both genders should be provided with challenges that will help them achieve their talent goals. Young students should learn about breath control and why it is necessary; they should learn to follow a conductor, including the relationship between hand and baton motions and the dynamics of the music; and they should learn about musical concepts such as tone, melody, harmony, and rhythm.

During the last two years of high school, aspiring singers should have a good idea of what classification they are in, according to the range and quality of their voices: soprano, alto, contralto, tenor, baritone, or bass. These categories indicate the resonance of the voice; soprano being the highest and lightest, bass being the lowest and heaviest. Students should take part in voice classes, choirs, and ensembles. In addition, students should continue their studies in English, writing, social studies, foreign language, and other electives in music, theory, and performance.

There tend to be no formal educational requirements for those who wish to be singers. However, formal education is valuable, especially in younger years. Some students know early in their lives that they want to be singers and are ambitious enough to continue to practice and learn. These students are often advised to attend high schools that are specifically geared toward combined academic and intensive arts education in music, dance, and theater. Such schools can provide valuable preparation and guidance for those who plan to pursue professional careers in the arts. Admission is usually based on results from students' auditions as well as academic testing.

Postsecondary Training

Many find it worthwhile and fascinating to continue their study of music and voice in a liberal arts program at a college or university. Similarly, others attend schools of higher education that are focused specifically on music, such as the Juilliard School in New York. Such an intense program would include a multidisciplinary curriculum of composition and performance, as well as study and appreciation of the history, development, variety, and potential advances of music. In this type of program, a student would earn a bachelor of arts degree. To earn a bachelor of science degree in music, one would study musicology, which concerns the history, literature, and cultural background of music; the music industry, which will prepare one for not only singing but also marketing music and other business aspects; and professional performance. Specific music classes in a typical four-year liberal arts program would include such courses as introduction to music, music styles and structures, harmony, theory of music, elementary and advanced auditory training, music history, and individual instruction.

In addition to learning at schools, many singers are taught by private singing teachers and voice coaches, who help to develop and refine students' voices. Many aspiring singers take courses at continuing adult education centers, where they can take advantage of courses in beginning and advanced singing, basic vocal techniques, voice coaching, and vocal performance workshops. When one is involved in voice training, he or she must learn about good articulation and breath control, which are very important qualities for all singers. Performers must take care of their voices and keep their lungs in good condition. Voice training, whether as part of a college curriculum or in private study, is useful to many singers, not only for classical and opera singers, but also for jazz singers and for those interested in careers in musical theater. Many professional singers who have already "made it" continue to take voice lessons throughout their careers.

Other Requirements

In other areas of music, learning to sing and becoming a singer is often a matter of desire, practice, and an inborn love and talent for singing. Learning to play a musical instrument is often extremely helpful in learning to sing and to read and write music. Sometimes it is not even necessary to have a "good" singing voice. Many singers in rock music have less-than-perfect voices, and rap artists do not really sing at all. But these singers learn to use their voice in ways that nonetheless provides good expression to their songs, music, and ideas.

■ Exploring

Anyone who is interested in pursuing a career as a singer should obviously have a love for music. Listen to recordings as often as possible, and get an understanding of the types of music that you enjoy. Singing, alone or with family and friends, is one of the most natural ways to explore music and develop a sense of your own vocal style. Join music clubs at school, as well as the school band if it does vocal performances. In addition, take part in school drama productions that involve musical numbers.

Older students interested in classical music careers could contact trade associations such as the American Guild of Musical Artists, as well as read such trade journals such as Hot Line News, which covers news about singers (and other types of musicians) and their employment needs and opportunities. For information and news about very popular singers, read *Billboard* magazine, which can be purchased at many local bookshops and newsstands. Those who already know what type of music they wish to sing should audition for roles in community musical productions or contact trade groups that offer competitions. For example, the Central Opera Service can provide information on competitions, apprentice programs, and performances for young singers interested in opera.

There are many summer programs offered throughout the United States for high school students interested in singing and other performing arts. For example, Stanford University offers its Stanford Jazz Workshop each summer for students who are at least 12 years old. It offers activities in instrumental and vocal music, as well as recreation in swimming, tennis, and volleyball. For college students who are 18 years and older, the jazz workshop has a number of job positions available. For more information about the program, contact the university at Box 11291, Stanford, CA 94309.

Another educational institute that presents a summer program is Boston University's Tanglewood Institute, which is geared especially toward very talented and ambitious students between the ages of 15 and 18. It offers sessions in chorus, musical productions, chamber music, classical music, ensemble, instrumental, and vocal practice. Arts and culture field trips are also planned. College students who are at least 20 years old can apply for available jobs at the summer Tanglewood programs. For more information, contact Boston University, Lenox, MA 01240.

Students interested in other areas of singing can begin while still in high school, or even sooner. Many gospel singers, for example, start singing with their local church group at an early age. Many high school students form their own bands, playing rock, country, or jazz, and can gain experience performing before an audience, and even being paid to perform at school parties and other social functions.

■ Employers

There are many different environments in which singers can be employed, including local lounges, bars, cafes, radio and television, theater productions, cruise ships, resorts, hotels, casinos, large concert tours, and opera companies.

Many singers hire agents, who usually receive a percentage of the singer's earnings for finding them appropriate performance contracts. Others are employed primarily as studio singers, which means that they do not perform for live audiences but rather record their singing in studios for albums, radio, television, and motion pictures.

An important tactic for finding employment as a singer is to invest in a professional quality tape recording of your singing that you can send to prospective employers.

■ Starting Out

There is no single correct way of entering the singing profession. It is recommended that aspiring singers explore the avenues that interest them, continuing to apply and audition for whatever medium suits them. Singing is an extremely creative profession, and singers must learn to be creative and resourceful in the business matters of finding "gigs."

High school students should seek out any opportunities to perform, including choirs, school musical productions, and church functions. Singing teachers can arrange recitals and introduce students to their network of musician contacts.

■ Advancement

In the singing profession and the music industry in general, the nature of the business is such that you can consider yourself to have "made it" when you get steady, full-time work. A measure of advancement is how well known and respected the singer becomes in his or her field, which in turn influences their earnings. In most areas, particularly classical music, only the most talented and persistent singers make it to the top of their profession. In other areas, success may be largely a matter of luck and perseverance. A singer on Broadway, for example, may begin as a member of the chorus, and eventually become a featured singer. On the other hand, those who have a certain passion for their work and accept their career position tend to enjoy working in local performance centers, nightclubs, and other musical environments.

Also, many experienced singers who have had formal training will become voice teachers. Reputable schools such as Juilliard consider it a plus when a student can say that he or she has studied with a master.

■ Earnings

As with many occupations in the performing arts, earnings for singers are highly dependent on one's professional reputation and thus cover a wide range. To some degree, pay is also related to educational background (as it relates to how well one has been trained) and geographic location of performances. In certain situations, such as singing for phonograph recordings, pay is dependent on the number of minutes of finished music (for instance, an hour's pay will be given for each three and a half minutes of recorded song).

Singing is often considered a glamorous occupation. However, because it attracts so many professionals, competition for positions is very high. Only a small proportion of those who aspire to be singers achieve glamorous jobs and extremely lucrative contracts. Famous opera singers, for example earn $8,000 and more for each performance. Singers in an opera chorus earn between $600 and $800 per week. Classical soloists can receive between $2,000 and $3,000 per performance, while choristers may receive around $70 per performance. For rock singers, earnings can be far higher. Within the overall group of professional singers, studio and opera singers tend to earn salaries that are well respected in the industry; their opportunities for steady, long-term contracts tend to be better than for singers in other areas.

In general, starting salaries could be as low as $6,900 per year or even far less. Average salaries tend to be around $26,000; the top earners in studio and opera earn an average of $70,000 per year, though some earn much more. Rock singers may begin by playing for drinks and meals only; if successful, they may earn tens of thousands of dollars for a single performance. Singers on cruise ships generally earn between $750 and $2,000 per week, although these figures can vary considerably. Also, many singers supplement their performance earnings by working at other positions, such as teaching at schools or giving private lessons or even working at jobs unrelated to singing. Full-time teachers in high school earn an average of $26,000 per year, while those at colleges earn an average of $35,500 per year.

Because singers rarely work for a single employer, they generally receive no benefits, and must provide their own health insurance and retirement planning.

■ Work Environment

The environments in which singers work tend to vary greatly, depending on such factors as type of music involved and location of performance area. Professional singers often work in the evenings and during weekends, and many are frequently required to travel. Many singers who are involved in popular productions such as in opera, rock, and country music work in large cities such as New York, Las Vegas, Chicago, Los Angeles, and Nashville. Stamina and endurance are needed to keep up with the hours of rehearsals and performances, which can be long; work schedules are very often erratic, varying from job to job.

Many singers are members of trade unions, which represent them in matters such as wage scales and fair working conditions. Vocal performers who sing for studio recordings are represented by the American Federation of Television and Radio Artists; solo opera singers, solo concert singers, and choral singers are members of the American Guild of Musical Artists.

■ Outlook

Any employment forecast for singers will most probably emphasize one factor that plays an important role in the availability of jobs: competition. Because so many people pursue musical careers and because there tend to be no formal requirements for employment in this industry (the main qualification is talent), competition is most often very strong.

According to the U.S. Department of Labor, available jobs for singers, as for musicians in general, are expected to grow slowly into the next century. However, others foresee growth in the entertainment industry during the next decade, which will create jobs for singers and other performers. Because of the nature of this work, positions tend to be temporary and part-time; in fact, of all members of the American Federation of Musicians, fewer than 2 percent work full-time in their singing careers. Thus, it is often advised that those who are intent on pursuing a singing career keep in mind the varied fields other than performance in which their interest in music can be beneficial,

such as composition, education, broadcasting, therapy, and community arts management.

Those intent on pursuing singer careers in rock, jazz, and other popular forms should understand the keen competition they will face. There are thousands of singers all hoping to make it; only a very few actually succeed. However, there are many opportunities to perform in local cities and communities, and those with a genuine love of singing and performing should also possess a strong sense of commitment and dedication to their art.

■ For More Information

The following organizations have information on career opportunities, certification, and education resources.

American Federation of Musicians of the United States and Canada
Paramount Building
1501 Broadway, Suite 600
New York, NY 10036
Tel: 212-869-1330

American Federation of Television and Radio Artists
260 Madison Avenue
New York, NY 10016
Tel: 212-532-0800

Musicians National Hot Line Association
277 East 6100 South
Salt Lake City, UT 84107

National Association of Schools of Music
11250 Roger Bacon Drive, Suite 21
Reston, VA 22090
Tel: 703-437-0700

Opera America
1156 15th Street, Suite 810
Washington, DC 20005-1704
Tel: 202-293-4466

■ Related Articles

Music

Music and Recording Industry

Theater

Composers

Musical Directors and Conductors

Musicians

Pop/Rock Musicians

Songwriters

Sisters

■ **See Active Religious Sisters and Brothers, Contemplative Religious Sisters and Brothers**

Ski Lift Operators and Ski Patrol Workers

■ See Ski Resort Workers

Ski Resort Workers

■ Overview

Ski resorts offer many different types of employment opportunities. Qualified people are needed to supervise the activities on ski slopes, run operations at the lodge, provide instruction to skiers, and insure the safety of resort patrons. There are numerous ski resorts located throughout the United States and the world. Jobs are plentiful, though the majority of them are seasonal, lasting from November to April. One ski resort in Colorado, for example, employs over 3,200 workers every season, 500 of which are employed as ski lift operators.

■ History

Skiing developed primarily as a means to travel from one place to another. Northern Europeans were the first people to wear skis, which they fashioned from tree branches. Armies used skis to travel snowy mountain regions beginning in the Middle Ages through World War II.

Though people started skiing for pleasure in the 18th century, it was not until the invention of the motorized ski lift in the 1930s that skiing grew in popularity. After World War II, hundreds of resorts opened to accommodate this growing form of recreation. Resorts, offering skiing opportunities combined with comfortable accomodations and entertainment, provided people with a new vacation alternative. In the United States, large ski communities, such as Vail and Aspen in Colorado, developed as a result of the sport. Today, many of these cities' principle revenues stem from skiing and related activities.

There are three types of skiing—Alpine, or downhill; Nordic, or cross country; and Freestyle, which incorporates acrobatic movements, stunts, and dance elements. Most resorts cater to the Alpine type of skiing. Other popular snow activities are snowboarding and sledding.

■ The Job

Ski resort workers run the gamut from entry-level to highly skilled. Each is important for maintaining the order and operations of the resort community. One of the largest departments is ski lift operation. *Ski lift operators* make

sure skiers have safe transport. There are several steps taken daily before a ski lift is opened to the public. First, ice, snow, or tree branches are cleared from the machinery, as well as the loading and unloading platforms. Next, all machinery and parts are cleaned and safety checked. Finally, a trial run is conducted by an experienced member of the lift staff.

Workers help passengers on or off the lift safely. They collect and punch lift tickets, adjust seats or the speed of the lift, and spot check for loose or dangling items that may catch on the lift's machinery. They answer any inquiries passengers may have about the run, or address general questions. They give directions and make sure skiers stay on the slopes and trails designated for their level of expertise—beginner, intermediate, and expert. Workers must sometimes reprimand unruly passengers.

Skiers who monitor the runs and surrounding areas are called the *ski patrol*. Considered the police of the mountains, they are specially trained ski experts responsible for preventing accidents and maintaining the safety standards of the resort. They mark off trails and courses that are not safe for the public. Patrol members also help injured skiers off the slopes and to proper first aid stations, or in extreme cases, to an ambulance. Ski patrol members are versed in emergency medical techniques, such as CPR and first aid.

Basic maneuvers to more advanced techniques can be learned from a *certified ski instructor.* Ski instruction at a resort is offered complimentary, or for a small fee. They teach group classes and private lessons, teaching clients to avoid injury by skiing safely and responsibly.

Ski technicians assist skiers in getting the proper sized boots, skis, and poles. They may answer questions regarding equipment and how it works.

Most ski resorts have chalets or lodges that offer skiers a place to rest and take refreshments between runs. These lodges serve as gathering places in the evenings for drinks and socialization. Some jobs at lodges include wait staff, housekeeping staff, gift shop or ski shop employees, and resort managers.

■ Requirements

High School

Most resorts expect at least a high school diploma for their entry-level positions. High school courses that will be helpful include general business, mathematics, speech, and physical education. Learning a foreign language will also be helpful.

Postseconday Training

Many resorts prefer to hire college students as seasonal help. Management positions usually require a college degree. Some institutions, such as the University of Maine at Farmington, offer a combined program of a bachelor's degree with a certificate concentration in the ski industry. Qualified students can link their passion for the sport with a degree in business, economics, rehabilitation services, or general studies.

Certification and Licensing

You must be certified to qualify as a professional ski instructor. Certification consists of skill tests, further education, and on the job experience. Satisfactory completion of a national certification exam is also required. Ski instructors must be re-certified every one to two years, depending on the region in which they teach.

Other Requirements

All employees, especially those who deal with customers, are a reflection of the resort for which they work. Different jobs call for different qualities in a worker. Responsibility is key when working the ski lift, as well as tact when confronting troublesome skiers. Ski instructors need to be physically fit, as well as patient and understanding with their students. Ski Patrol members must be able to react quickly in emergencies and have the foresight to spot potential trouble situations. What does Jay D. Thomas, Director of Employment for the Aspen Ski Company look for in a prospective employee? "We want people who are energetic and ready to give service above and beyond the average."

If you can speak a second language, then you're already ahead of the pack. Many ski enthusiasts from South America travel to the United States for world class skiing, so brush up on your Spanish and Portuguese! Most positions can be altered to accommodate employees that are physically challenged. It's best to check with each resort to learn their policies and employee requirements.

■ Employers

Many of the United States' ski meccas are located in Vermont, Maine, New Hampshire, California, and the Midwest region. Colorado and Utah are also popular skiing states, where many communities such as Vail, Aspen, and Telluride, have grown around the industry.

If you want employment that will continue well after spring, look for resorts that cater to year round business. The Aspen Ski Company, for example, has four mountain ski areas in operation during the winter months and three hotels that are open year round. Many employees work the slopes from November to April and the golf courses the rest of the year.

■ Starting Out

Many resorts actively recruit at college campuses and job fairs. Phone interviews and online applications are becoming more prevalent in this field. There are also several good Web sites that work as an online employment service. Visit them to find job descriptions, salary expectations, and job benefits.

It would be wise to first compile a list of resorts or locations that interest you. Trade magazines, such as *Powder*, or *SKI*, as well as your local library are helpful resources. Don't forget the Internet. Here's a great tip: Apply for work at least two seasons ahead—that means start looking for winter work in the summer to be considered for choice positions.

■ Advancement

Advancement is determined by your experience, skill, level of education, and also your starting position. Ski lift operators can be promoted to department supervisors of that division, general supervisors, and finally management. Ski instructors may begin their careers by giving beginner's lessons or children's lessons, and advance to intermediate or expert level classes. Experienced instructors with good reputations may develop a following of students. They may also be promoted to department supervisor or management. Lodge employees may be promoted to positions with increased responsibilities such as shift supervisor or manager.

■ Earnings

According to Jay Thomas, entry level positions with the Aspen Ski Company pay between $9.00 to $10.00 an hour. Employees are also given a year end bonus based on the amount of hours worked during the season. Pay rates will vary depending on the resort and region located. Large, well established resorts, especially those located in the mountain states and northeast, tend to pay higher hourly rates.

Most ski resort employees are given complimentary full, or partial, season ski passes. Some companies also provide their employees with housing at or near the resort. Full time employees receive the standard benefits package including paid vacation and health insurance.

■ Work Environment

Ski slopes open at around 8:00 AM and close at dusk; many resorts light some courses, to allow for night skiing. Ski lift operators, ski patrol, ski instructors, and other employees assigned to outdoor work prepare for the often blustery weather by wearing layers of clothes, water proof coats, ski pants, and boots, as well as hats and gloves. Some resorts supply their employees with uniform coats and accessories.

If the threat of wind chapped lips scares you, then it may be best to find work indoors. Employees that enjoy a warm and comfortable workplace and still have great customer contact, include lodge workers, gift shop employees, and ski technicians. Most ski resort employees work about 40 hours a week; ski instructors' schedules will vary depending on their class load. Since ski resorts are open 7 days a week, employees with low seniority are expected to work weekends and holidays—the busiest times for most resorts.

■ Outlook

Emphasis on physical health, interest in sport related vacations, and growing household incomes, point to a bright future for ski resorts and their employees. Weather may not always hamper this industry. Many resorts, using snow-making devices to create a snow covered run, can extend the season well into April.

Note, however, that the majority of jobs in this industry are seasonal. Many students use this opportunity to supplement their income during school vacations, as well as fuel their interest in the sport. Some resorts offer year round employment by shifting their employees to other jobs off season. Golf course attendants, tour guides, and spa workers are some examples of summer jobs. If you are interested in working in the management side of the business, further education will be a definite plus. Consider degrees in business management, rehabilitation services, or physical education.

■ For More Information

For information on the ski industry and ski instructor certification, contact:

Professional Ski Instructors of America
133 South Van Gordon Street, Suite 101
Lakewood, CO 80228
Tel: 303-987-9350
Web: http://www.psia.org

The University of Maine at Farmington offers the Ski Industries Certificate Program. This specialized program combines a bachelor's degree with a certificate concentration in the ski industry. For more information, contact:

The University of Maine at Farmington
Ski Industries Program
86 Main Street
Farmington, ME 04938
Tel: 207-778-7386
Web: http://www.umf.maine.edu/~ski/

For online applications to the Aspen Ski Company, contact:

Aspen Ski Company
Web: http://www.aspen-snowmass.com/opportunities/index

For ski resort employment services, contact:

SkiResorts.com
Web: http://www.skiresorts.com

■ Related Articles

Hospitality

Recreation

Travel and Tourism

Adventure Travel Specialists
Amusement Park Workers
Baggage Porters and Bellhops
Bartenders
Caterers
Cooks, Chefs, and Bakers
Cruise Ship Workers
Food Service Workers
Gaming Occupations
Hotel and Motel Industry Workers
Hotel and Motel Managers
Hotel Concierges
Hotel Desk Clerks
Hotel Executive Housekeepers
Hotel Restaurant Managers
Recreation Workers
Reservation and Ticket Agents
Resort Workers
Restaurant and Food Service Managers
Security Consultants and Technicians
Tour Guides

Skin Care Specialists

■ Overview

Skin care specialists, or *estheticians,* cleanse and beautify the skin by giving facials, full-body massages and wraps, cellulite treatments, and head and neck massages; provide makeup analysis and application; conduct aroma therapy treatments; perform surface skin peelings, tint brows and eyelashes; offer hair removal through waxing; and recommend products and treatments for at-home use.

■ History

Skin care can be traced back 6,000 years to ancient Egypt. It was initially associated with the practice of medicine, and at that time, both priests and physicians had important roles. Cosmetic products included ingredients such as special soils, wax, honey, and oils, formulated into masks, makeup, and lipsticks.

In ancient Greece, Hippocrates, known as the father of medicine, contributed to the development of *esthetics* (scientific skin care). Through archeological clues, we know that Greek women eliminated freckles with potions of plant roots and yeast and prevented wrinkles with masks made with bread crumbs and milk.

Roman society, famous for luxurious baths, facials, and body massages, further developed the art of skin care.

Artifacts include recipes for creams made from fruit juices, honey, and olive oil.

Interest in skin care waned during the Middle Ages, although certain orders of nuns devoted themselves to producing beauty products to support their convents. Perfume oils began to be used and the fragrance market was launched.

Renaissance Europe brought skin care and cosmetics into use in most of the major cities. The manufacture of perfumes became a major industry. From writings of the 16th century, we find that many formulas and mixtures are very similar to modern cosmetic products.

In modern times, the emphasis has shifted from "cover-up," which used heavy cosmetics to camouflage imperfections and blemishes to a more natural look, which is only truly attractive with healthy, clean skin. This has expanded the desire for skin care treatments.

Much progress has been made in medicine, chemistry, and technology to produce today's effective skin care treatments and products.

■ The Job

As opposed to *dermatologists*—physicians who treat diseases and ailments of the skin—the focus of skin care specialists is to care for and maintain healthy skin. They help people look their best by maintaining their skin at its healthy best. Healthy skin has been at the center of attention since beauty took on a more natural look in the 1970s.

The word *esthetic* comes from the Greek word meaning harmony, beauty, and perfection. Esthetics is based on an understanding of the skin's anatomy and function. Skin care specialists work to improve the skin's condition and restore its functions. It is a specialized discipline that requires the specialist to get to know the client's skin and lifestyle and tailor treatments specifically for the client's needs.

Through skin care treatments and product recommendations, skin care specialists work to maintain the normal functions of their clients' skin. Through systematic skin care, they help clients protect their skin from the effects of pollution, lack of exercise, poor nutrition, and stress, and they help the skin maintain optimal health and vitality.

Skin care services provided by most skin care specialists include skin analysis and examination; lifestyle analysis; medical/health history as it affects the skin; skin cleansing, toning, and protection; steaming out impurities, application of masks, cleansing pores, treatment of wrinkles and age spots; balancing skin oiliness and dryness, massage, skin peeling, and moisturizing. Additional services can include hair removal using waxing, depilation, or bleaching; scalp treatments; brow and lash tinting; hand massage and treatments; and full body massage and treatments. Skin care treatments may also be followed by makeup application and instruction.

Most skin care specialists provide recommendations for at-home skin care and treatment. They also refer clients to dermatologists or other medical practitioners if they believe it is necessary. Many recommend and sell skin care products and makeup through their salons.

In addition to treating clients, skin care specialists are expected keep their work areas clean and implements sanitized. In smaller salons, many make appointments and assist with day-to-day business. In larger salons, skin care specialists must be aware of keeping to appointment schedules. They may be juggling two or more clients, at different stages of treatment, at the same time.

Salon owners also have managerial responsibilities— accounting and record keeping, hiring, firing, and motivating workers, advertising and public relations, and ordering and stocking supplies and products.

People skills are very important as a skin care specialist's clientele determines his or here ultimate earnings and success. A critical part of the job of skin care specialists is to cultivate and maintain a growing clientele for themselves and their salons. Skin care specialists should be sensitive to the client's comfort and have dexterity and a sense of form and artistry. If the specialist's style of skin care is not suited to the client, he or she should be willing to refer the client to another specialist in the salon. This builds goodwill toward the skin care specialist and the salon.

Although including more technology in treatments and products, skin care is still a profession of art and beauty. The skin care specialist is helping clients take care of themselves and present the best appearance possible.

■ Requirements

High School

Those interested in a career in skin care must complete high school, successfully graduate from an approved cosmetology program, and pass a state licensing examination. High school students can prepare for this career by taking courses in health, art, and science-particularly biology, chemisty, and anatomy.

Postsecondary Training

Every state requires skin care specialists to be licensed, but the require-

SKIN CARE SPECIALISTS	
SCHOOL SUBJECTS	Biology Health
PERSONAL SKILLS	Communication/ideas Helping/teaching
WORK ENVIRONMENT	Primarily indoors Primarily one location
MINIMUM EDUCATION LEVEL	Some postsecondary training
SALARY RANGE	$10,700 to $16,200 to $28,600
CERTIFICATION OR LICENSING	Required by all states
OUTLOOK	Faster than the average

ments for eligibility are different for each state. Before enrolling in a skin care training program, contact the state board of cosmetology in your state for details on licensing requirements and a list of approved cosmetology schools.

Once you know what is required for licensing, look for an approved training program that fits your needs. Both public and private vocational schools offer daytime and evening classes. Depending on your schedule and the number of requirements for completion, the training program can take from a few months to a year to complete.

Most training programs include classroom study, live skin care demonstrations, and practical work covering topics such as the use and care of instruments, sanitation and hygiene, basic anatomy, and the recognition of certain skin ailments.

Certification or Licensing

After graduation, students are eligible to take their state licensing examinations. Usually the exam consists of a written test, and in some cases, may include a practical test of cosmetology knowledge and skin care treatment skills.

Licensing allows the skin care specialist to practice in the licensing state. Few states have reciprocity agreements, which would allow licensed skin care specialists to practice in a different state without additional formal training.

Other Requirements

Most successful skin care specialists enjoy dealing with the public and are willing to listen to their clients' needs and instructions. Some cosmetology schools include course work to enhance their students' people skills.

■ Exploring

Students interested in a career in skin care can visit beauty salons that offer skin care services and specialty skin care salons. They can talk to working skin care specialists in the field. One way to experience the salon environment firsthand is to obtain a summer or part-time job in a skin care salon as a receptionist or shop assistant. Interested students can also contact local or national cosmetology associations for information and become familiar with skin care trends through fashion and professional publications.

■ Employers

Skin care specialists may be employed by hair salons, spas, cosmetology schools (as instructors), or department stores. One out of five is self-employed. Some become cosmetics sales representatives, either exclusively or to augment other income. The majority of skin care specialists start out in salons. Because the outlook for skin care specialists is particularly good, those who wish to work in a salon, store, or spa have very good prospects, especially in larger cities where the demand for services is more concentrated.

■ Starting Out

Many cosmetology schools help their students find their first jobs. Most skin care specialists begin their careers working for established salons. Most begin being assigned relatively simple tasks and procedures until they prove their expertise. Once they have demonstrated their skills, they are permitted to perform more complicated tasks and treatments. As they begin to build their own clientele, they become more established in the salon and continue to take on more responsibilities and decisions.

■ Advancement

Advancement is usually in the form of higher earnings as skin care specialists gain experience and build a steady clientele. Many go on to manage large salons or open their own after several years of experience.

For many skin care specialists, formal training and licensing are only the first steps in a career that requires continuous education and study of new products and techniques for skin care. This is a dynamic, expanding field, that merges art and science. New product ingredients, new techniques, new treatments—from lasers to all-natural products to "cosmeceuticals"—will keep cutting-edge skin care specialists continually learning more to keep their clients' skin healthy and beautiful.

Establishing a salon is an expensive and risky business. Many skin care specialists take years to build up enough of a client base and savings to go solo. Some join forces with other skin specialists (e.g., dermatologists, *cosmetic surgeons*) or other beauty specialists (e.g., *hair stylists, nail technicians*) to create a full-service business.

As an alternative to working in a salon, some skin care specialists decide to teach in cosmetology schools or use their knowledge to demonstrate cosmetics and skin care products in department stores. Others become *cosmetics sales representatives* or start businesses as *beauty consultants*. Some skin care specialists work as examiners for state cosmetology boards.

■ Earnings

Approximately half of all skin care specialists work part-time and nearly 20 percent of them are self-employed. Nearly every town has some sort of skin care salon, but most of the jobs—and higher salaries—are concentrated in the most populous cities and states.

Skin care specialists receive income from commissions or wages and tips. Their median weekly income in 1997 was $311. Earning for entry-level workers begins at minimum wage, but experienced skin care specialists with an established clientele at a busy salon can make $550 per week or more. Earnings for skin care specialists who own a prestigious salon and sell a line of products can be much higher.

■ Work Environment

Skin care specialists work in clean, pleasant salons with good lighting, comfortable temperatures, and ventilation. They are expected to maintain good health and a neat, clean appearance as they come in personal contact with their customers.

Many skin care specialists work part-time, which makes this an attractive career for those who want to combine a job with family, school, or other responsibilities. Full-time workers and salon owners can easily work more than 40 hours per week. Work schedules very often include evenings and weekends to accommodate customers' busy work and home schedules, with weekends and lunch-hour time slots being especially busy.

■ Outlook

Statistics indicate that skin care is the fastest growing segment of the beauty profession based on a number of factors: (1) affluent, aging population concerned with maintaining health and appearance; (2) growing environmental awareness of sun, pollution, stress, and lifestyle on skin appearance and health; (3) shifts in customer preferences for personalized services; and (4) increased use of skin care services by men.

According to industry experts, the greatest challenges for people in the future will be the struggle to find a balance between work and family, as well as the growing need for personal fulfillment. This will lead to a demand for more specialized skin care services.

Most openings will result from the need to replace the large number of workers who leave the occupation each year and the need to increase the number of skin care specialists due to an expanding population. Opportunities for part-time work will continue to be very good.

Spending for grooming care is considered to be discretionary for most people. Therefore, during hard economic times, they tend to visit skin care specialists less frequently, which reduces earnings. However, rarely are good skin care specialists laid off solely because of economic downturns.

■ For More Information

National Accrediting Commission of Cosmetology Arts and Sciences
901 North Stuart Street, Suite 900
Arlington, VA 22203-1816
Tel: 703-527-7600
Email: naccas@erols.com
Web: http://www.naccas.org

National Cosmetology Association
401 North Michigan Avenue
Chicago, IL 60611
Tel: 800-527-1683 or 312-527-6765
Web: http://www.nca-now.com

■ Related Articles

Cosmetology
Cosmetics Sales Representatives
Cosmetologists/Hair Stylists
Electrologists
Makeup Artists
Mortuary Cosmetologists
Salon Managers
Spa Attendants

Skip Tracers
■ **See Bounty Hunters, Collection Workers**

Smokejumpers
■ **See Firefighters**

Social Psychologists
■ **See Psychologists**

Social Workers

■ Overview

Social workers help people and communities solve problems. These problems include poverty, racism, discrimination, physical and mental illness, addiction, and abuse. They counsel individuals and families, they lead group sessions, they research social problems, and they develop policy and programs. Social workers are dedicated to empowering people and helping people to preserve their dignity and worth.

■ History

Even before the United States became a country, poverty and unemployment were among society's problems. Almshouses and shelters that provided the homeless with jobs and rooms were established as early as 1657. The social work profession as we know it today, however, has its origins in the "friendly visitor" of the early 1800s; these charity workers went from home to home offering guidance in how to move beyond the troubles of poverty.

At a time when not much financial assistance was available from local governments, the poor relied on friendly visitors for instruction on household budgeting and educating their children. Despite their good intentions, however, the friendly visitors could not provide the poor with all the necessary support. The middle-class women who served as friendly visitors were generally far removed from the experiences of the lower classes. Most of the friendly visitors served the community for only a very short time and therefore did not have the opportunity to gain much experience with the poor. The great difference between the life experiences of the friendly visitors and the experiences of their clients sometimes resulted in serious problems: the self-esteem and ambitions of the poor were sometimes damaged by the moral judgments of the friendly visitors. In some cases, friendly visitors served only to promote their middle-class values and practices. By the late 1800s, many charitable organizations developed in U.S. and Canadian cities. With the development of these organizations came a deeper insight into improving the conditions of the poor. Serving as a friendly visitor came to be considered an apprenticeship; it became necessary for friendly visitors to build better relationships with their clients. Friendly visitors were encouraged to take the time to learn about their clients and to develop an understanding of each client's individual needs. Nevertheless, some sense of moral superiority remained, as these charitable organizations refused assistance to alcoholics, beggars, and prostitutes.

The birth of the settlement house brought charity workers even closer to their clients. Settlement houses served as communities for the poor and were staffed by young, well-educated idealists anxious to solve society's problems. The staff people lived among their clients and learned from them. In 1889, Jane Addams established the best known of the settlement houses, a community in Chicago called Hull House. Addams wrote extensively of the problems of the poor, and her efforts to provide solutions led to the foundation of social work education. She emphasized the importance of an education specific to the concerns of the social worker. By the 1920s, social work master's degree programs were established in many universities.

Theories and methodologies of social work have changed over the years, but the basis of the profession has remained the same: helping people and addressing social problems. As society changes, so do its problems, calling for redefinition of the social work profession. The first three fields of formal social work were defined by setting: medical social work; psychiatric social work; and child welfare. Later, practice was classified by different methodologies: casework; group work; and community organization. Most recently, the social work profession has been divided into two areas—direct practice and indirect practice.

■ The Job

After months of physical abuse from her husband, a young woman has taken her children and moved out of her house. With no job and no home, and fearing for her safety, she looks for a temporary shelter for herself and her children. Once there, she can rely on the help of social workers who will provide her with a room, food, and security. The social workers will offer counseling and emotional support to help her address the problems in her life. They will involve her in group sessions with other victims of abuse. They will direct her to job training programs and other employment services. They will set up interviews with managers of low-income housing. As the woman makes efforts to improve her life, the shelter will provide day care for the children. All these resources exist because the social work profession has long been committed to empowering people and improving society.

The social worker's role extends even beyond the shelter. If the woman has trouble getting help from other agencies, the social worker will serve as an advocate, stepping in to ensure that she gets the aid to which she is entitled. The woman may also qualify for long-term assistance from the shelter, such as a second-step program in which a social worker offers counseling and other support over several months. The woman's individual experience will also help in the social worker's research of the problem of domestic violence; with that research, the social worker can help the community come to a better understanding of the problem and can direct society toward solutions. Some of these solutions may include the development of special police procedures for domestic disputes, or court-ordered therapy groups for abusive spouses.

Direct social work practice is also known as clinical practice. As the name suggests, direct practice involves working directly with the client by offering counseling,

SOCIAL WORKERS	
SCHOOL SUBJECTS	Health Psychology
PERSONAL SKILLS	Communication/ideas Helping/teaching
WORK ENVIRONMENT	Primarily indoors Primarily multiple locations
MINIMUM EDUCATION LEVEL	Bachelor's degree
SALARY RANGE	$20,000 to $40,000 to $60,000
CERTIFICATION OR LICENSING	Required by all states
OUTLOOK	Faster than the average
DOT	195
GOE	10.01.02
NOC	4152
O*NET	27305B

advocacy, information and referral, and education. Indirect practice concerns the structures through which the direct practice is offered. Indirect practice (a practice consisting mostly of social workers with Ph.D.s) involves program development and evaluation, administration, and policy analysis. Of the 134,200 members of the National Association of Social Workers (NASW), 69 percent work in direct service roles and 19 percent in indirect roles (according to a recent survey conducted by the NASW).

Because of the number of problems facing individuals, families and communities, social workers find jobs in a variety of settings and with a variety of client groups. Some of these areas are discussed in the following paragraphs:

Health/mental health care. Mental health care has become the lead area of social work employment. These jobs are competitive and typically go to more experienced social workers. Settings include community mental health centers, where social workers serve persistently mentally ill people and participate in outreach services; state and county mental hospitals, for long-term, inpatient care; facilities of the Department of Veterans Affairs, involving a variety of mental health care programs for veterans; and private psychiatric hospitals, for patients who can pay directly. Social workers also work with patients who have physical illnesses. They help individuals and their families adjust to the illness and the changes that illness may bring to their lives. They confer with physicians and with other members of the medical team to make plans about the best way to help the patient. They explain the treatment and its anticipated outcome to both the patient and the family. They help the patient adjust to the possible prospect of long hospitalization and isolation from the family.

Child care/family services. Efforts are being made to offer a more universal system of care that would incorporate child care, family services, and community service. Child care services include day care homes, child care centers, and Head Start centers. Social workers in this setting attempt to address all the problems children face from infancy to late adolescence. They work with families to detect problems early and intervene when necessary. They research the problems confronting children and families, and they establish new services or adapt existing services to address these problems. They provide parenting education to teenage parents, which can involve living with a teenage mother in a foster care situation, teaching parenting skills, and caring for the baby while the mother attends school. Social workers alert employers to employees' needs for daytime child care.

Social workers in this area of service are constantly required to address new issues; in recent years, for example, social workers have developed services for families composed of different cultural backgrounds, services for

children with congenital disabilities resulting from the mother's drug use, and disabilities related to HIV or AIDS.

Gerontological social work. Within this field, social workers provide individual and family counseling services in order to assess the older person's needs and strengths. Social workers help older people locate transportation and housing services. They also offer adult day care services, or adult foster care services that match older people with families. Adult protective services protect older people from abuse and neglect, and respite services allow family members time off from the care of an older person. A little-recognized problem is the rising incidence of AIDS among the elderly; 10 percent of all AIDS patients are aged 50 or over.

School social work. In schools, social workers serve students and their families, teachers, administrators, and other school staff members. Education, counseling, and advocacy are important aspects of school social work. With education, social workers attempt to prevent alcohol and drug abuse, teen pregnancy, and the spread of AIDS and other sexually transmitted diseases. They provide multicultural and family life education. They counsel students who are discriminated against because of their sexual orientation or racial, ethnic, or religious background. They also serve as advocates for these students, bringing issues of discrimination before administrators, school boards, and student councils.

Jane Addams and friends

A smaller number of social workers are employed in the areas of social work education (a field composed of the professors and instructors who teach and train students of social work); group practice (in which social workers facilitate treatment and support groups); and corrections (providing services to inmates in penal institutions). Social workers also offer counseling, occupational assistance, and advocacy to those with addictions and disabilities, to the homeless, and to women, children, and the elderly who have been in abusive situations.

Client groups expand and change as societal problems change. Social work professionals must remain aware of the problems affecting individuals and communities in order to offer assistance to as many people as possible.

Computers have become important tools for social workers. Client records are maintained on computers, allowing for easier collection and analysis of data. Interactive computer programs are used in training social workers, as well as to analyze case histories (such as for an individual's risk of HIV infection).

■ Requirements

High School

To prepare for social work, you should take courses in high school that will improve your communications skills, such as English, speech, and composition. On a debate team, you could further develop your skills in communication as well as research and analysis. History, social studies, and sociology courses are important in understanding the concerns and issues of society. Although some work is available for those with only a high school diploma or associate's degree (as a social work aide or social services technician), the most opportunities exist for people with degrees in social work.

Postsecondary Training

The Council on Social Work Education requires that five areas be covered in accredited bachelor's degree social work programs: human behavior and the social environment; social welfare policy and services; social work practice; research; and field practicum. Most programs require two years of liberal arts study followed by two years of study in the social work major. Also, students must complete a field practicum of at least 400 hours. Graduates of these programs can find work in public assistance or they can work with the elderly or with people with mental or developmental disabilities.

Although no clear lines of classification are drawn in the social work profession, most supervisory and administrative positions require at least an MSW. Master's programs are organized according to fields of practice (such as mental health care), problem areas (substance abuse), population groups (the elderly), and practice roles (practice with individuals, families, or communities). They are usually two-year programs, with at least nine hundred hours of field practice. Most positions in mental health care facilities require an MSW. Doctoral degrees are also available and prepare students for research and teaching. Most social workers with doctorates go to work in community organizations.

Certification or Licensing

Licensing, certification, or registration of social workers is required by all states. To receive the necessary licensing, a social worker will typically have to gain a certain amount of experience and also pass an exam. Five voluntary certification programs help to identify those social workers who have gained the knowledge and experience necessary to meet national standards.

Other Requirements

Social work requires great dedication. As a social worker, you have the responsibility of helping whole families, groups, and communities, as well as focusing on the needs of individuals. Your efforts will not always be supported by the society at large; sometimes you must work against a community's prejudice, disinterest, and denial. You must also remain sensitive to the problems of your clients, offering support, and not moral judgment or personal bias. The only way to effectively address new social problems and new client groups is to remain open to the thoughts and needs of all human beings. Assessing situations and solving problems requires clarity of vision and a genuine concern for the well-being of others.

With this clarity of vision, your work will be all the more rewarding. Social workers have the satisfaction of making a connection with other people and helping them through difficult times. Along with the rewards, however, the work can provide a great deal of stress. Hearing repeatedly about the deeply troubled lives of prison inmates, the mentally ill, abused women and children, and others can be depressing and defeating. Trying to convince society of the need for changes in laws and services can be a long, hard struggle. You must have perseverance to fight for your clients against all odds.

■ Exploring

As a high school student, you may find openings for summer or part-time work as a receptionist or file clerk with a local social service agency. If there is no opportunity for paid employment, you could work as a volunteer. Good experience is also provided by work as a counselor in a camp for children with physical, mental, or developmental disabilities. Your local YMCA, park district, or other recreational facility may need volunteers for group recreation programs, including programs designed for the prevention of delinquency. By reporting for your high school newspaper, you'll have the opportunity to interview people, conduct surveys, and research social change, all of which are important aspects of the social work profession.

You could also volunteer a few afternoons a week to read to people in retirement homes or to the blind. Work as a tutor in special education programs is sometimes available to high school students.

■ Employers

Social workers can be employed in direct, or clinical, practice, providing individual and family counseling services, or they may work as administrators for the organizations that provide direct practice. Social workers are employed by community health and mental health centers; hospitals and mental hospitals; child care, family services, and community service organizations, including day care and Head Start programs; elderly care programs, including adult protective services and adult day care and foster care; prisons; shelters and halfway houses; schools; courts; and nursing homes.

■ Starting Out

Most students of social work pursue a master's degree and in the process learn about the variety of jobs available. They also make valuable connections through faculty and other students. Through the university's job placement service or an internship program, a student will learn about job openings and potential employers.

A social work education in an accredited program will provide you with the most opportunities, and the best salaries and chances for promotion, but practical social work experience can also earn you full-time employment. A part-time job or volunteer work will introduce you to social work professionals who can provide you with career guidance and letters of reference. Agencies with limited funding may not be able to afford to hire social workers with MSWs and will therefore look for applicants with a great deal of experience and lower salary expectations.

■ Advancement

The attractive and better-paying jobs tend to go to those with more years of practical experience. Dedication to your job, an extensive resume, and good references will lead to advancement in the profession. Also, many social work programs offer continuing education workshops, courses, and seminars. These refresher courses help practicing social workers to refine their skills and to learn about new areas of practice and new methods and problems. These courses are intended to supplement your social work education, not substitute for a bachelor's or master's degree. These continuing education courses can lead to job promotions and salary increases.

■ Earnings

The higher your degree, the more money you can make in the social work profession. Your area of practice also determines earnings. The areas of mental health, group services, and community organization and planning provide higher salaries, while elderly and disabled care generally provide lower pay. Salaries also vary among regions; social workers on the east and west coasts earn higher salaries than those in the Midwest. Earnings in Canada vary from province to province as well. During the first five years of practice, your salary will increase faster than in later years.

The median salary range for social workers in the United States is approximately $35,000 for those with an MSW. Those who hold a bachelor's degree earn about $25,000 a year. Social workers employed by the U.S. government earn an average annual salary of about $46,900. Average salaries in Canada are higher, with a median range of $40,000 to $45,000.

Although women make up a large percentage of the profession, only 2.2 percent of female social workers in the United States receive more than $60,000, as opposed to 6.3 percent of male social workers.

■ Work Environment

Social workers do not always work at a desk. When they do, they may be interviewing clients, writing reports, or conferring with other staff members. Depending on the size of the agency, office duties such as typing letters, filing, and answering phones may be performed by an aide or volunteer. Social workers employed at shelters or halfway houses may spend most of their time with clients, tutoring, counseling, or leading groups.

Some social workers have to drive to remote areas to make a home visit. They may go into inner city neighborhoods, schools, courts, or jails. In larger cities, domestic violence and homeless shelters are sometimes located in run-down or dangerous areas. Most social workers are involved directly with the people they serve and must carefully examine the client's living conditions and family relations. Although some of these living conditions can be pleasant and demonstrate a good home situation, others can be squalid and depressing.

Advocacy involves work in a variety of different environments. Although much of this work may require making phone calls and sending faxes and letters, it also requires meetings with clients' employers, directors of agencies, local legislators, and others. It may sometimes require testifying in court as well.

■ Outlook

The field of social work is expected to grow faster than the average for all occupations through 2006. The greatest factor for this growth is the increased number of older people who are in need of social services. Social workers that specialize in gerontology will find many job opportunities in nursing homes, hospitals, and home health care agencies. The needs of the future elderly population are likely to be different from those of the present elderly. Currently, the elderly appreciate community living, while subsequent generations may demand more individual care.

Schools will also need more social workers to deal with issues such as teenage pregnancies, children from single-parent households, and any adjustment problems recent immigrants may have. The trend to integrate students with disabilities into the general school population will require the expertise of social workers to make the transition smoother. However, job availability in schools will depend on funding given by state and local sources.

To help control costs, hospitals are encouraging early discharge for some of their patients. Social workers will be needed by hospitals to help secure health services for patients in their homes. There is also a growing number of people with physical disabilities or impairments staying in their own homes, requiring home health care workers.

Increased availability of health insurance funding and the growing number of people able to pay for professional help will create opportunities for those in private practice. Many businesses hire social workers to help in employee assistance programs, often on a contractual basis.

Poverty is still a main issue addressed by social workers. Families are finding it increasingly challenging to make ends meet on wages that are just barely above the minimum. The problem of fathers who do not make their court-ordered child support payments forces single mothers to work more than one job or rely on welfare. An increased awareness of domestic violence has also pointed up the fact that many of the homeless and unemployed are women

who have left abusive situations. Besides all this, working with the poor is often considered unattractive, leaving many social work positions in this area unfilled.

Competition for jobs in urban areas will remain strong. However, there is still a shortage of social workers in rural areas; these areas usually cannot offer the high salaries or modern facilities that attract large numbers of applicants.

The social work profession is constantly changing. The survival of social service agencies, both private and public, depends on shifting political, economic, and workplace issues.

Social work professionals are worried about the threat of declassification. Because of budget constraints and a need for more workers, some agencies have lowered their job requirements. When unable to afford qualified professionals, they hire those with less education and experience. This downgrading raises questions about quality of care and professional standards. Just as in some situations low salaries push out the qualified social worker, so do high salaries. In the area of corrections, attractive salaries (up to $40,000 for someone with a two-year associate's degree) have resulted in more competition from other service workers.

Liability is another growing concern. If a social worker, for example, tries to prove that a child has been beaten or attempts to remove a child from his or her home, the worker can potentially be sued for libel. At the other extreme, a social worker can face criminal charges for failure to remove a child from an abusive home. More social workers are taking out malpractice insurance.

■ For More Information

For information on educational programs, contact:

Council on Social Work Education
1600 Duke Street, Suite 300
Alexandria, VA 22314
Tel: 703-683-8080
Web: http://www.cswe.org

For job listings and information about careers and education, contact:

National Association of Social Workers
Career Information
750 First Street, NE, Suite 700
Washington DC 20002-4241
Tel: 202-408-8600
Web: http://www.naswdc.org

■ Related Articles

Health Care

Social Services

Adult Day Care Coordinators

Alcohol and Drug Abuse Counselors

Geriatric Social Workers

HIV/AIDS Counselors

Home Health Care Aides

Human Services Workers

Licensed Practical Nurses

Occupational Therapists

Orientation and Mobility Specialists

Physical Therapists

Recreational Therapists

Registered Nurses

Rehabilitation Counselors

Sign Language and Oral Interpreters

Sociologists

■ Overview

Sociologists study the behavior and interaction of people in groups. They research the characteristics of families, communities, the workplace, religious and business organizations, and many other segments of society. By studying a group, sociologists can gain insight about the individual; they can develop ideas about the roles of gender, race, age, and other social traits in human interaction. This research helps the government, schools and other organizations address social problems and understand social patterns. In addition to research, a sociologist may teach, publish, consult, or counsel.

■ History

The social science known today as sociology has its origins in the 19th century. As a science, it was based on experiment and measurement rather than philosophical speculation. Until an experimental basis for the testing of theory and speculation was devised, the study of society remained in the area of philosophy and not in that of science. Auguste Comte, a French mathematician, is generally credited with being the originator of modern sociology. He coined the term, which is derived from the Latin *socius,* meaning "companion." His idea was that sociology should become the science that would draw knowledge from all sciences to produce fundamental understandings of human society. It was his feeling that once all sciences were blended together, human society could be viewed as a totality. Comte's theories are not now widely held among scientists; in fact, the development of sociology through the past century has been basically in the opposite direction. It was Emile Durkheim, a French sociologist, who initiated the use of scientific study and research methods to develop and support sociological theories in the early part of the 20th century.

The field has become more specialized as it has grown. The study of the nature of human groups has proved to be all-encompassing; only by specializing in one aspect of this science can scholars hope to make progress toward the formulating of fundamental principles. For example, such areas as criminology and penology, while still technically within the field of sociology, have become very specialized; working in these areas requires training that is different in emphasis and content from that which is required in other areas of sociology.

■ The Job

Curiosity is the main tool of a successful sociologist. Have you ever wondered about the way the members of different high school sports teams interact with each other? Or why certain people work better in teams, or about the opportunities for promotion for workers with disabilities? Do many questions come to mind when you read a newspaper or a magazine? Maybe you're curious about the effect of a state's death penalty on the crime level. Or maybe you wonder how a gambling casino on a Native American reservation affects the local residents. This curiosity would serve you well as a sociologist.

With thoughtful questions and desire for knowledge, sociologists investigate the origin, development, and functioning of groups of people. This can involve extensively interviewing people, or distributing a form questionnaire. It can involve conducting surveys, or researching historical records, both public and personal. As a sociologist, you may need to set up an experiment, a study composed of a cross section of people from a given society. You may choose to watch the interaction from a distance, or to participate as you observe.

The information you compile from this variety of research methods is then used by administrators, lawmakers, educators, and other officials engaged in solving social problems. By understanding the common needs, thoughts, patterns, and ideas of a group of people, an organization can better provide for the individuals within those groups.

SOCIOLOGISTS	
SCHOOL SUBJECTS	History Psychology
PERSONAL SKILLS	Communication/ideas Helping/teaching
WORK ENVIRONMENT	Primarily indoors Primarily one location
MINIMUM EDUCATION LEVEL	Master's degree
SALARY RANGE	$21,000 to $35,000 to $53,000
CERTIFICATION OR LICENSING	None available
OUTLOOK	Little change or more slowly than the average
DOT	054
GOE	11.03.02
NOC	4169
O*NET	27199B

With a sociologist's help, a business may be able to create a better training program for its employees; counselors in a domestic violence shelter may better assist clients with new home and job placement; teachers may better educate students with special needs.

Sociologists work closely with many other professionals. One of the closest working relationships is between sociologists and statisticians, to analyze the significance of data. Sociologists also work with psychologists. Psychologists attempt to understand individual human behavior, while sociologists try to discover basic truths about groups. Sociologists also work with cultural anthropologists. Anthropologists study whole societies and try to discover what cultural factors have produced certain kinds of patterns in given communities. Sociologists work with economists. The ways in which people buy and sell are basic to understanding the ways in which groups behave. They also work with political scientists to study systems of government.

Ethnology and ethnography, social sciences that treat the subdivision of humans and their description and classification, are other fields with which sociologists work closely. Problems in racial understanding and cooperation, in failures in communication, and in differences in belief and behavior are all concerns of the sociologist who tries to discover underlying reasons for group conduct.

Sociologists and psychiatrists have cooperated to try to discover community patterns of mental illness and mental health. They have attempted to compare such things as socioeconomic status, educational level, residence, and occupation to the incidence and kind of mental illness or health to determine in what ways society may be contributing to or preventing emotional disturbances.

Some sociologists choose to work in a specialized field. The *criminologist* specializes in investigations of causes of crime and methods of prevention, and the *penologist* investigates punishment for crime, management of penal institutions, and rehabilitation of criminal offenders. The *social pathologist* specializes in investigation of group behavior

that is considered detrimental to the proper functioning of society. The *demographer* is a population specialist who collects and analyzes vital statistics related to population changes, such as birth, marriages, and death. The *rural sociologist* investigates cultures and institutions of rural communities, while the *urban sociologist* investigates origin, growth, structure, composition, and population of cities. The *social welfare research worker* conducts research that is used as a tool for planning and carrying out social welfare programs.

■ Requirements

High School

Take English classes to develop composition skills; you'll be expected to present your research findings in reports, articles, and books. In addition to sociology classes, you should take other classes in the social sciences, such as psychology, history, and anthropology. Math and business will prepare you for the analysis of statistics and surveys. Government and history classes will help you to understand some of the basic principles of society, and journalism courses will bring you up to date on current issues.

Postsecondary Training

It is difficult to find a job as a sociologist with only a bachelor's degree. However, new graduates may be able to enter a job with a research organization as an interviewer, or may assist in other ways with the collection of data for social service agencies or marketing departments.

Those with a master's degree may find employment as sociologists with the federal government, industrial firms, or research organizations. Those with specific training in research methods have a better advantage. Universities won't offer many teaching opportunities, though many community or junior colleges will hire someone with a master's degree.

More than half of all sociologists hold doctorates. A large majority of the sociologists at the doctoral level teach in four-year colleges and universities throughout the country. Job candidates fare better if their graduate work includes research and field work. Specialized study is also helpful.

Other Requirements

In addition to the natural curiosity mentioned above, a good sociologist must also possess an open mind. You must be able to assess situations without bias or prejudice that could affect the results of your studies. Social awareness is also important; as a sociologist, you must pay close attention to the world around you, to the way the world progresses and changes. Because new social issues arise every day, you will be frequently reading newspapers, magazines, and reports to maintain an informed perspective on these issues.

CREAM OF THE CROP

The International Sociological Association conducted an opinion survey of its members to find the most important books about sociology published in the 20th century. Here are the top five:

Economy and Society by Max Weber

The Sociological Imagination by Charles Wright Mills

Social Theory and Social Structure by Robert K. Merton

The Protestant Ethic and the Spirit of Capitalism by Max Weber

The Social Construction of Reality by P. L. Berger and T. Luckmann

Good communication skills are valuable to the sociologist. In many cases, gathering information will involve interviewing people and interacting within their societies. The better your communication skills, the more information you can get from the people you interview.

■ Exploring

There are books about sociology, and possibly some journals of sociology, in your school and public libraries. With recent books and articles, you can develop an understanding of the focus and requirements of sociological study. If no specific sociology courses are offered in your high school, courses in psychology, history, or English literature can prepare you for the study of groups and human interaction; within these courses you may be able to write reports or conduct experiments with a sociological slant. A school newspaper, magazine, or journalism course can help you to develop important interview, research, and writing skills, while also heightening your awareness of your community and the communities of others.

■ Employers

More than two-thirds of the sociologists working in this country teach in colleges and universities. Some sociologists work for agencies of the federal government. In such agencies, their work lies largely in research, though they may also serve their agencies in an advisory capacity. Some sociologists are employed by private research organizations, and some work in management consultant firms. Sociologists also work with various medical groups and with physicians—public health is in great measure dependent upon the research efforts of sociologists for its effectiveness. Some sociologists are self-employed, providing counseling, research, or consulting services.

■ Starting Out

Many sociologists find their first jobs through the placement offices of their colleges and universities. Some are placed through the professional contacts of faculty members. A student in a doctoral program will make many connections and learn about fellowships, visiting professorships, grants, and other opportunities.

Those who wish to enter a research organization, industrial firm, or government agency should apply directly to the prospective employer. If you've been in a doctoral program, you should have research experience and publications to list on your resume, as well as assistantships and scholarships.

■ Advancement

Sociologists who enter college or university teaching may advance through the academic ranks from instructor to full professor. Those who like administrative work may become a head of a department. Publications of books, and articles in journals of sociology, will assist in a professor's advancement.

Those who enter research organizations, government agencies, or private business advance to positions of responsibility as they acquire experience. Salary increases usually follow promotions.

■ Earnings

Sociologists working as full professors in colleges and universities have average salaries of $69,924 a year at public universities, and $84,970 a year at private, according to a 1998 survey by the *Chronicle of Higher Education*. Associate professors at public universities made an annual average of $50,186; $56,517 at private universities. For assistant professors, the average annual salaries were $42,335 public and $47,387 private. Full-time, permanent faculty positions usually include health benefits and paid vacation.

■ Work Environment

An academic environment can be ideal for a sociologist intent on writing and conducting research. If required to teach only a few courses a semester, a sociologist can then devote a good deal of time to his or her own work. And having contact with students can create a balance with the research.

The work of a sociologist takes place mostly in the classroom or at the computer writing reports and analyzing data. Some research requires visiting the interview subjects, or setting up an experiment within the community of study.

■ Outlook

Employment opportunities for sociologists are expected to increase more slowly than the average. Opportunities are best for those with a doctorate and experience in fields such as demography, criminology, environmental sociology, and gerontology. Competition will be strong in all areas, however, as more sociology graduates continue to enter the job market than there are positions to fill.

As society grows older, more opportunities of study will develop for those working with the elderly. Sociologists who specialize in gerontology will have opportunities to study the aging population in a variety of environments. Sociologists will find more opportunities in marketing, as companies conduct research on specific populations, such as the children of baby boomers. The Internet is also opening up new areas of sociological research; sociologists, demographers, market researchers, and other professionals are studying online communities and their impact.

■ For More Information

ASA offers many free career publications, as well as job information.

American Sociological Association
1307 New York Avenue NW, Suite 700
Washington, DC 20005
Tel: 202-383-9005
Web: http://www.asanet.org

To learn about sociologists working outside academia, contact:

Society for Applied Sociology
Baylor University
Center for Community Research and Development
PO Box 97131
Waco, TX 76798
Tel: 254-710-3811
Web: http://www.appliedsoc.org

■ Related Articles

Education

Human Resources

Social Services

Anthropologists

College Professors

Demographers

Economists

Political Scientists

Psychologists

Parole Officers

Social Workers

Software Designers

■ Overview

Software designers are responsible for creating new ideas and designing prepackaged and customized computer software. Software designers devise applications, such as word processors, front-end database programs, and spreadsheets, that make it possible for computers to complete given tasks and to solve problems. Once a need in the market has been identified, software designers first conceive of the program on a global level by outlining what the program will do. Then they write the specifications from which programmers code computer commands to perform the given functions.

■ History

The first major advances in modern computer technology were made during World War II. After the war, it was thought that the enormous size of computers, which easily took up the space of entire warehouses, would limit their use to huge government projects, such as processing the U.S. census, for example.

The introduction of semiconductors to computer technology made possible smaller and less-expensive computers. Businesses began adapting computers to their operations as early as 1954. Within 30 years, computers had revolutionized the way people work, play, and shop. Today, computers are everywhere, from the business world, to government agencies, charitable organizations, and private homes. Over the years, technology has continued to shrink computer size and increase speed at an unprecedented rate.

"In 1983, software development exploded with the introduction of the personal computer. Standard applications included not only spreadsheets and word processors, but graphics packages and communications systems," according to "Events in the History of Computing," compiled by the IEEE Computer Society.

Advances in computer technology have enabled professionals to put computers to work in a range of activities once thought impossible. Computer software designers have been able to take advantage of computer hardware improvements in speed, memory capacity, reliability, and accuracy to create programs to do just about anything. With the extensive proliferation of computers in our society, there is a great market for user-friendly, imaginative, and high-performance software. Business and industry relies heavily on the power of computers and uses both prepackaged software and software that has been custom-designed for its own specific use. Also, with more people purchasing computer systems for home use, the retail market for prepackaged software has grown steadily. Given these conditions, computer software designing will be an important field in the industry for years to come.

The software industry is comprised of many facets, including personal computer packaged applications (known as "shrink-wrapped software"); operating systems for stand-alone and networked systems; management tools for networks; enterprise software that enables efficient management of large corporations' production, sales, and information systems; software applications and operating systems for mainframe computers; and customized software for specific industry management, according to the Software Publishers Association (SPA).

Packaged software is written for mass distribution, not for the specific needs of a particular user. Broad categories include operating systems, utilities, applications, and programming languages. Operating systems, according to the SPA, control the basic functions of a computer or network. Utilities perform support functions, such as backup or virus protection. Programming software is used to develop the sets of instructions that build all other types of software. The software that most computer users are familiar with is called application software. This category includes word-processing, spreadsheets, and email packages, commonly used in business, as well as games and reference software that is used in homes, and subject- or skill-based software that is used in schools.

■ The Job

Without software, computer hardware would have nothing to do. Computers need to be told exactly what to do. Software is the set of codes that gives the computer those instructions. It comes in the form of the familiar prepackaged software that you find in a computer store, such as games, word processing programs, spreadsheets, and desktop publishing programs, and in a customized application designed to fit the specific need of a particular business. Software designers are the initiators of these complex programs. *Computer programmers* then create the software by writing the code that carries out the directives of the designer.

Software designers must envision every detail of what an application will do, how it will do it, and how it will look (the user interface). A simple example is how a home accounting program is created. The software designer first lays out the overall functionality of the program, specifying what it should be able to do, such as balancing a checkbook, keeping track of incoming and outgoing bills, and maintaining records of expenses. For each of these tasks, the software designer will outline the design detail for the specific functions that he or she has mandated, such as what menus and icons will be used, what each screen will look like, and whether there will be help or dialog boxes to assist the user. For example, the designer may specify that the expense record part of the program produce a pie chart that shows the percentage of each household expense in the overall household budget. The designer can specify that the program automatically display the pie chart each time a budget assessment is completed or only after the user clicks on the appropriate icon on the toolbar.

Some software companies specialize in building custom-designed software. This software is highly specialized for specific needs or problems of particular businesses. Some businesses are large enough that they employ in-house software designers who create software applications for their computer systems. A related field is software engineering, which involves writing customized complex software to solve a specific engineering or technical problem of a business or industry.

Whether the designer is working on a mass-market or a custom application, the first step is to define the overall goals for the application. This is typically done in consultation with management if working at a software supply company, or with the client if working on a custom-designed project. Then, the software designer studies the goals and problems of the project. If working on custom-designed software, the designer must also take into consideration the existing computer system of the client. Next, the software designer works on the program strategy and specific design detail that he or she has envisioned. At this point, the designer may need to write a proposal outlining the design and estimating time and cost allocations. Based on this report, management or the client decides if the project should proceed.

Once approval is given, the software designer and the programmers begin working on writing the software program. Typically, the software designer writes the specifications for the program, and the *applications programmers* write the programming codes.

In addition to the design detail duties, a software designer may be responsible for writing a user's manual or at least writing a report for what should be included in the user's manual. After testing and de-bugging the program, the software designer will present it to management or to the client.

■ Requirements

High School

High school students interested in computer science should take as many computer, math, and science courses as possible since they provide fundamental math and computer knowledge and teach analytical thinking skills. Classes that rely on schematic drawing and flowcharts are also very valuable. English and speech courses help students improve their communications skills, which are very important to software designers who must make formal presentations to management and clients. Also, many technical/vocational schools offer programs in software programming and design. The qualities developed by these classes, plus imagination and an ability to work well under pressure, are key to success in software design.

SOFTWARE DESIGNERS	
SCHOOL SUBJECTS	**Computer science** **Mathematics**
PERSONAL SKILLS	**Technical/scientific**
WORK ENVIRONMENT	**Primarily indoors** **Primarily one location**
MINIMUM EDUCATION LEVEL	**Bachelor's degree**
SALARY RANGE	**$38,000 to $51,000 to $75,000+**
CERTIFICATION OR LICENSING	**None available**
OUTLOOK	**Much faster than the average**
DOT	**030**
GOE	**11.01.01**
NOC	**2163**
O*NET	**22127**

Postsecondary Training

A bachelor's degree in computer science plus one year's experience with a programming language is required for most software designers.

In the past, the computer industry has tended to be pretty flexible about official credentials; demonstrated computer proficiency and work experience have often been enough to obtain a good position. However, as more people enter the field, competition increases, and job requirements become more stringent. Technical knowledge alone does not suffice in the field of software design. The successful software designer should have at least peripheral knowledge of the field for which he or she intends to design software, such as business, education, or science. An individual with a bachelor's degree in computer science with a minor in business or accounting has an excellent chance for employment in designing business/accounting software, for example. " . . . [I]ncreasingly, computer professionals need to be very good in business," says David Weldon, senior editor in charge of *Computerworld*'s Information Technology careers coverage, in the article "Scoring the Best Tech Jobs," by Susan Gregory Thomas, on *U.S. News Online*. "I have a stack of resumes three feet high of rejects, and it's not because these candidates didn't have technical backgrounds," says Andrew Popell, cofounder of Harvest Technology, a software company that develops applications for portfolio managers in the financial industry, in the same article. Another example of this is that those with degrees in education and subsequent teaching experience are much sought after as designers for educational software.

Other Requirements

Software design is project- and detail-oriented, and therefore software designers must be patient and diligent. They must also enjoy problem-solving challenges and be able to work under a deadline with minimal supervision. Software designers should also possess good communications skills for consulting both with management and with clients who will have varying levels of technical expertise.

Software companies are looking for individuals with vision and imagination to help them create new and exciting programs to sell in the ever-competitive software market. Superior technical skills and knowledge combined with motivation, imagination, and exuberance makes an attractive candidate.

■ Exploring

Spending a day with a working software designer or applications programmer will allow you to experience firsthand what this work entails. School guidance counselors can often help you organize such a meeting.

If you are interested in computer industry careers in general, you should learn as much as possible about computers. You should keep up with new technology by reading computer magazines and by talking to other computer users. You should join computer clubs and use online services and the Internet for information about this field.

Advanced students can put their design/programming knowledge to work by designing and programming their own applications, such as simple games and utility programs.

■ Employers

Software designers are employed throughout the United States. Opportunities are best in large cities and suburbs where business and industry are active. Programmers who develop software systems work for software manufacturers, many of whom are in Silicon Valley, in northern California. There is also a concentration of software manufacturers in Boston, Chicago, and Atlanta, among other places. Designers who adapt and tailor the software to meet specific needs of end-users work for those end-user companies, many of which are scattered across the country.

■ Starting Out

Software design positions are regarded as some of the most interesting, and therefore the most competitive, in the computer industry. Some software designers are promoted from an entry-level programming position; most positions in software supply companies and large custom software companies are difficult to secure straight out of school.

Entry-level programming and design jobs may be listed in the help wanted sections of newspapers. Employment agencies and online job banks are other good sources.

Students in technical schools or universities should take advantage of the campus placement office. They should check regularly for internship postings, job listings, and notices of on-campus recruitment. Internships and summer jobs with such corporations are always beneficial and provide experience that will give you the edge over your competition. General computer job fairs are also held throughout the year in larger cities.

There are many online career sites listed on the World Wide Web that post job openings, salary surveys, and current employment trends. The Web also has online publications that deal specifically with computer jobs. Because this is such a competitive field, applicants will need to show initiative and creativity that will set themselves apart from other applicants.

■ Advancement

In general, programmers work between one and five years before being promoted to software designer. A programmer can move up by demonstrating an ability to create new software ideas that translate well into marketable applications. Individuals with a knack for spotting trends in the software market are also likely to advance.

Those software designers who demonstrate leadership may be promoted to *project team leader.* Project team leaders are responsible for developing new software projects and overseeing the work done by software designers and applications programmers. With experience as a project team leader, a motivated software designer may be promoted to a position as a *software manager* who runs projects from an even higher level.

The key to advancement in software design is keeping up-to-date with changing technology. A career in the computer industry means that education never stops. For advancement as a software designer, it means not only keeping up with advances in computer technology, it means making the changes happen.

■ Earnings

Salaries for software designers vary with the size of the company and with location. Salaries may be slightly higher in areas where there is a large concentration of computer companies, such as the Silicon Valley in northern California and parts of Washington, Oregon, and the East Coast.

Software designers' salaries range from $38,000 for a beginning designer to $51,000 for a senior designer or project team leader. At the managerial level, salaries are even higher and can reach $75,000+.

Most designers work for large companies, which offer a full benefits package that includes health insurance, vacation and sick time, and a profit sharing or retirement plan.

■ Work Environment

Software designers work in comfortable environments. Many computer companies are known for their casual work atmosphere; employees generally do not have to wear suits, except during client meetings. Overall, software designers work standard weeks. However, they may be required to work overtime near a deadline. It is common in software design to share office or cubical space with two or three coworkers, which is typical of the team approach to working. As a software designer or applications programmer, much of the day is spent in front of the computer, although a software designer will have occasional team meetings or meetings with clients.

Software design can be stressful work for several reasons. First, the market for software is very competitive and companies are pushing to develop more innovative software and to get it on the market before the competitors. For this same reason, software design is also very exciting and creative work. Second, software designers are given a project and a deadline. It is up to the designer and team members to budget their time to finish in the allocated time. Finally, working with programming languages and so many details can be very frustrating, especially when the tiniest glitch

means the program will not run. For this reason, software designers must be patient and diligent.

■ Outlook

Jobs in software design are expected to grow faster than the average through the year 2006, according to the *Occupational Outlook Handbook.* Employment of computing professionals is expected to increase much faster than average as technology becomes more sophisticated and organizations continue to adopt and integrate these technologies, making for plentiful job openings. Hardware designers and systems programmers are constantly developing faster, more powerful, and more user-friendly hardware and operating systems. As long as these advancements continue, the industry will need software designers to create software to use these improvements.

Growth rates for the packaged software industry have been extremely vigorous through the 1990s, with an average growth rate of 12 percent per year. Experts are projecting an approximate 10 percent annual growth for software.

Business may have less need to contract for custom software as more prepackaged software arrives on the market that allows users with minimal computer skills to "build" their own software using components that they customize themselves. However, the growth in the retail software market is expected to make up for this loss.

The expanding integration of Internet technologies by businesses has resulted in a rising demand for a variety of skilled professionals who can develop and support Internet applications.

■ For More Information

Contact ACM for information on internships, student membership, and the ACM student magazine, Crossroads.

Association for Computing Machinery
1515 Broadway
New York, NY 10036-5701
Tel: 212-869-7440
Web: http://www.acm.org
Web: http://www.acm.org/membership/student/

For information on scholarships, student membership, and the student newsletter, looking.forward, *contact:*

IEEE Computer Society
1730 Massachusetts Avenue, NW
Washington, DC 20036
Tel: 202-371-0101
Web: http://www.computer.org

■ Related Articles
Computer Hardware

Computer Software

Computers

Software Engineering Technicians

■ **See Software Engineers**

Software Engineers

■ Overview

Software engineers are responsible for customizing existing software programs to meet the needs and desires of a particular business or industry. First, they spend considerable time researching, defining, and analyzing the problem at hand. Then, they develop software programs to resolve the problem on the computer. There are over 216,000 computer engineers employed in the United States.

■ History

The first major advances in modern computer technology were made during World War II. After the war, it was thought that the enormous size of computers, which easily took up the space of entire warehouses, would limit their use to huge government projects. Accordingly, the 1950 census was computer-processed.

The introduction of semiconductors to computer technology made possible smaller and less expensive computers. Businesses began adapting computers to their operations as early as 1954. Within 30 years, computers had revolutionized the way people work, play, and go shopping. Today, computers are everywhere, from businesses of all kinds, to government agencies, charitable organizations, and private homes. Over the years, technology has continued to shrink computer size and increase speed at an unprecedented rate.

Advances in computer technology have enabled professionals to put computers to work in a range of activities

once thought impossible. In the past several years, computer software engineers have been able to take advantage of computer hardware improvements in speed, memory capacity, reliability, and accuracy to create programs that do just about anything. Computer engineering blossomed as a distinct subfield in the computer industry after the new performance levels were achieved. This relative lateness is explained by the fact that the programs written by software engineers to solve business and scientific problems are very intricate and complex, requiring a lot of computing power. Although many computer scientists will continue to focus research on further developing hardware, the emphasis in the field has moved more squarely to software. Given this, computer engineering will be an important field in the industry for years to come.

■ The Job

Every day, businesses, scientists, and government agencies encounter difficult problems that they cannot solve manually, either because the problem is just too complicated or because it would take too much time to calculate the appropriate solutions. For example, astronomers receive thousands of pieces of data every hour from probes and satellites in space as well as telescopes here on earth. If they had to process the information themselves, that is, compile careful comparisons with previous years' readings, look for patterns or cycles, and keep accurate records of the origin of the various data, it would be so cumbersome and lengthy a project as to make it next to impossible. They can, however, process the data, but only thanks to the extensive help of computers. Computer software engineers define and analyze specific problems in business or science and help develop computer software applications that effectively solve them. The software engineers that work in the field of astronomy are well versed in its concepts, but many other kinds of software engineers exist as well.

The basic structure of computer engineering is the same in any industry. First, software engineers research specific problems and investigate ways in which computers can be programmed to perform certain functions. Then, they develop software applications customized to the needs and desires of the business or organization. For example, many software engineers work with the federal government and insurance companies to develop new ways of reducing paperwork, such as income tax returns, claims forms, and applications. There are currently several independent but major form automation projects taking place throughout the United States. As software engineers find new ways to solve the problems associated with form automation, more and more forms are completed online and less on paper.

Software engineers specializing in a particular industry, such as a particular science, business, or medicine, are expected to demonstrate a certain level of proficiency in that industry. Consequently, the specific nature of their work varies from project to project and industry to industry. Software engineers also differ by the nature of their employer. Some work for consulting firms, who complete software projects for different clients on an individual basis. Others work for large companies that hire engineers full time to develop software customized to their needs. Software engineering professionals also differ by level of responsibility. *Software engineering technicians* assist engineers in completing projects. They are usually knowledgeable in analog, digital, and microprocessor electronics and programming techniques. Technicians know enough about program design and computer languages to fill in details left out by engineers or programmers, who conceive of the program from a large-scale perspective. Technicians might also test new software applications with special diagnostic equipment.

Software engineering is extremely detail-oriented work. Since computers do only what they are programmed to do, engineers have to account for every bit of information with a programming command. Software engineers are thus required to be very well organized and precise. In order to achieve this, they generally follow strict procedures in completing an assignment.

First, they interview clients and colleagues in order to determine exactly what they want the final program to be able to do. Defining the problem by outlining the goal can sometimes be difficult, especially when clients have little technical training. Then, they evaluate the software applications already in use by the client to understand how and why they are failing to fulfill the needs of the operation. After this period of fact-gathering, the engineers use methods of scientific analysis and mathematical models to develop possible solutions to the problems. These analytical methods allow them to predict and measure the outcomes of different proposed designs.

When they have developed a good notion of what type of program is required to fulfill the client's needs, they draw up a detailed proposal which includes estimates of time and cost allocations. Management must then decide if the project will meet their needs, is a good investment, and whether or not it will be undertaken.

Once a proposal is accepted, both software engineers and technicians begin work on the project. They verify with hardware engineers that the proposed software program is completed with existing hardware systems. Typically, the engineer writes program specifications and the technician uses his or her knowledge of computer languages to write preliminary programming. Engineers focus most of their effort on program strategies, testing procedures, and reviewing technicians' work.

Software engineers are usually responsible for a significant amount of technical writing, including projects proposals, progress reports, and user manuals. They are required to meet regularly with the clients in order to keep project goals clear and learn about any changes as quickly as possible.

When the program is completed, the software engineer organizes a demonstration of the final product to the client. Supervisors, management, and users are generally present. Some software engineers may offer to install the program, train users on it, and make arrangements for ongoing technical support.

■ Requirements

A high school diploma is the minimum requirement for software engineering technicians. A bachelor's or advanced degree in computer science or engineering is required for most software engineers.

High School

High school students interested in pursuing this career should take as many computer, math, and science courses as possible, since they provide fundamental math and computer knowledge and teach analytical thinking skills. Classes that rely on schematic drawing and flowcharts are also very valuable. English and speech courses help students improve their communications skills, which is very important for software engineers.

Postsecondary Training

There are several ways to enter the field of software engineering, although it is becoming increasingly necessary to pursue formal postsecondary education. Individuals without an associate's degree may first be hired in the quality assurance or technical support departments of a company. Many complete associate degrees while working and then are promoted into software engineering technician positions. As more and more well-educated professionals enter the industry, however, it is becoming more important for applicants to have at least an associate's degree in computer engineering or

SOFTWARE ENGINEERS	
SCHOOL SUBJECTS	Computer science Mathematics
PERSONAL SKILLS	Mechanical/manipulative Technical/scientific
WORK ENVIRONMENT	Primarily indoors Primarily one location
MINIMUM EDUCATION LEVEL	Bachelor's degree
SALARY RANGE	$39,722 to $50,000 to $80,000+
CERTIFICATION OR LICENSING	Recommended
OUTLOOK	Much faster than the average
DOT	030
GOE	11.01.01
NOC	2147
O*NET	22127

programming. Many technical and vocational schools offer a variety of programs that prepare students for jobs as software engineering technicians.

Interested students should consider carefully their long-range goals. Being promoted from a technician's job to that of software engineer often requires a bachelor's degree. In the past, the computer industry has tended to be fairly flexible about official credentials; demonstrated computer proficiency and work experience has often been enough to obtain a good position. This may hold true for some in the future. The majority of young computer professionals entering the field for the first time, however, will be college educated. Therefore, those with no formal education or work experience will have less chance of employment.

Obtaining a postsecondary degree in computer engineering is usually considered challenging and even difficult. In addition to natural ability, students should be hard working and determined to succeed. Software engineers planning to work in specific technical fields, such as medicine, law, or business, should receive some formal training in that particular discipline.

Certification or Licensing

Another option for individuals interested in software engineering is to pursue commercial certification. These programs are usually run by computer companies that wish to train professionals in working with their products. Classes are challenging and examinations can be rigorous. New programs are introduced every year.

Other Requirements

Software engineers need strong communications skills in order to be able to make formal business presentations and interact with people having different levels of computer expertise. They must also be detail oriented and work well under pressure.

■ Exploring

Interested high school students should try to spend a day with a working software engineer or technician in order to experience firsthand what a typical day is like. School guidance counselors can help you arrange such a visit. You may also talk to your high school computer teacher for more information.

In general, you should be intent on learning as much as possible about computers and computer software. You should learn about new developments by reading trade magazines and talking to other computer users. You also can join computer clubs and surf the Internet for information about working in this field.

■ Employers

Software engineering is done in many fields, including medical, industrial, military, communications, aerospace, scientific, and other commercial businesses. The majority of software engineers, though, are employed by computer and data processing companies and by consulting firms.

■ Starting Out

Individuals with work experience and perhaps even an associate's degree are sometimes promoted to software engineering technician positions from entry-level jobs in quality assurance or technical support. Those already employed by computer companies or large corporations should read company job postings to learn about promotion opportunities. Employees who would like to train in software engineering, either on the job or through formal education, can investigate future career possibilities within the same company and advise management of their wish to change career tracks. Some companies offer tuition reimbursement for employees who train in areas applicable to business operations.

Technical, vocational, and university students of software engineering should work closely with their schools' placement offices, as many professionals find their first position through on-campus recruiting. Placement office staff are well trained to provide tips on resume writing and interviewing techniques, and locating job leads.

Individuals not working with a school placement office can check the classified ads for job openings. They also can work with a local employment agency that places computer professionals in appropriate jobs. Many openings in the computer industry are publicized by word of mouth, so interested individuals should stay in touch with working computer professionals to learn who is hiring. In addition, these people may be willing to refer interested job seekers directly to the person in charge of recruiting.

■ Advancement

With additional education and work experience, software engineering technicians may be promoted to software engineer. Software engineers who demonstrate leadership qualities and thorough technical know-how may become *project team leaders* who are responsible for full-scale software development projects. Project team leaders oversee the work of technicians and engineers. They determine the overall parameters of a project, calculate time schedules and financial budgets, divide the project into smaller tasks, and assign these tasks to engineers. Overall, they do both managerial and technical work.

Software engineers with experience as project team leaders may be promoted to a position as *software manager,* running a large research and development department. Managers oversee software projects with a more encompassing perspective; they help choose projects to be undertaken, select project team leaders and engineering teams, and assign individual projects. In some cases, they may be required to travel, solicit new business, and contribute to the general marketing strategy of the company.

Many computer professionals find that their interests change over time. As long as individuals are well qualified and keep up-to-date with the latest technology, they are usually able to find positions in other areas within the computer industry.

■ Earnings

Software engineering technicians usually earn beginning salaries of $24,000. Computer engineers with a bachelor's degree in computer engineering earned starting salaries of $39,722 in 1997, according to the *Occupational Outlook Handbook*. New computer engineers with a master's degree averaged $44,734, and those with a Ph.D., $63,367. Software engineers generally earn more in geographical areas where there are clusters of computer companies, such as the Silicon Valley in northern California.

Experienced software engineers can earn over $80,000 a year. When they are promoted into management, as project team leaders or software managers, they earn even more.

Most software engineers work for companies who offer extensive benefits, including health insurance, sick leave, and paid vacation. In some smaller computer companies, however, benefits may be limited.

■ Work Environment

Software engineers usually work in comfortable office environments. Overall, they usually work 40-hour weeks, but this depends on the nature of the employer and expertise of the engineer. In consulting firms, for example, it is typical for engineers to work long hours and frequently travel to out-of-town assignments.

Software engineers generally receive an assignment and a time frame within which to accomplish it; daily work details are often left up to the individuals. Some engineers work relatively lightly at the beginning of a project, but work a lot of overtime at the end in order to catch up. Most engineers are not compensated for overtime. Software engineering can be stressful, especially when working to meet deadlines. Working with programming languages and intense details is often frustrating. Therefore, software engineers should be patient, enjoy problem-solving challenges, and work well under pressure.

■ Outlook

The field of software engineering is expected to be one of the fastest growing occupations through the year 2006, according to the U.S. Department of Labor. Demands made

on computers increase every day and from all industries. The development of one kind of software sparks ideas for many others. In addition, users rely on software programs that are increasingly user-friendly.

Since technology changes so rapidly, software engineers are advised to keep up on the latest developments. While the need for software engineers will remain high, computer languages will probably change every few years and software engineers will need to attend seminars and workshops to learn new computer languages and software design. They also should read trade magazines, surf the Internet, and talk with colleagues about the field. These kinds of continuing education techniques help ensure that software engineers are best equipped to meet the needs of the workplace.

■ For More Information

For more information on careers in computer software, contact:

Software & Information Industry Association
1730 M Street, NW, Suite 700
Washington, DC 20036-4510
Tel: 202-452-1600
Web: http://www.siia.net

For certification information, contact:

Institute for Certification of Computing Professionals
2200 East Devon Avenue, Suite 247
Des Plaines, IL 60018
Tel: 847-299-4227
Web: http://www.iccp.org

Contact ACM for information on internships, student membership, and the ACM student magazine, Crossroads.

Association for Computing Machinery
1515 Broadway
New York, NY 10036-5701
Tel: 212-869-7440
Web: http://www.acm.org
Web: http://www.acm.org/membership/student/

For information on scholarships, student membership, and the student newsletter, looking.forward, *contact:*

IEEE Computer Society
1730 Massachusetts Avenue, NW
Washington, DC 20036
Tel: 202-371-0101
Web: http://www.computer.org

■ Related Articles

Computer Hardware

Computer Software

Computers

Electronics

The Internet

Computer and Office Machine Service Technicians

Software Managers

■ **See Software Engineers**

Software Vendor Trainers

■ **See Computer Trainers**

Soil Conservationists and Technicians

■ Overview

Soil conservationists develop conservation plans to help land users, such as farmers and ranchers, developers, homeowners, and government officials, best meet their land use goals while adhering to government conservation regulations. They suggest plans to conserve and reclaim soil, preserve or restore wetlands and other rare ecological areas, rotate crops for increased yields and soil conservation, reduce water pollution, and restore or increase wildlife populations. They assess the land users' needs, costs, maintenance requirements, and the life expectancy of various conservation practices. They plan design specifications using survey and field information, technical guides, and engineering field manuals. Conservationists also give talks to various organizations to educate land users and the public in general about how to conserve and restore soil and water resources. Many of their recommendations are based on information provided to them by soil scientists.

Soil conservation technicians work more directly with land users by putting the ideas and plans of the conservationist into action. In their work they use basic engineering and surveying tools, instruments, and techniques. They perform engineering surveys and design and implement conservation practices like terraces and grassed waterways. Soil conservation technicians monitor projects during and after construction, and periodically revisit the site to evaluate the practices and plans.

■ History

In 1908, President Theodore Roosevelt appointed a National Conservation Commission to oversee the proper conservation of the country's natural resources. As a result, many state and local conservation organizations were formed, and Americans began to take a serious interest in preserving their land's natural resources.

During World War I, farmers—who wished to capitalize on the shortage of wheat—planted many thousands of acres of wheat, mostly in Middle Western states. The crop was repeated year after year, until the soil was depleted. This depletion of the soil and the destruction of the natural cover of the land by too much cultivation led to the disastrous dust storms of the mid-1930s.

As a result of what happened in the "Dust Bowl," in 1935, Congress established the Soil Conservation Service of the U.S. Department of Agriculture. Because more than 800 million tons of topsoil had already been blown away by the winds over the plains, the job of reclaiming the land through wise conservation practices was not an easy one. In addition to the large areas of the Middle West which had become desert land, there were other badly eroded lands throughout the country.

Fortunately, emergency planning came to the aid of the newly established Soil Conservation Service. The Civilian Conservation Corps (CCC) was created to help alleviate unemployment during the Great Depression of the 1930s. The CCC established camps in rural areas and assigned people to aid in many different kinds of conservation. Soil conservationists directed those portions of the CCC program designed to halt the loss of topsoil by wind and water action.

Much progress has been made in the years since the Soil Conservation Service was established. Wasted land has been reclaimed and further loss has been prevented. Land-grant colleges have initiated programs to help farmers understand the principles and procedures of soil conservation. The Cooperative Research, Education and Extension Service (within the Department of Agriculture) provides workers who are skilled in soil conservation to work with these programs.

Throughout the United States today there are several thousand federally appointed soil conservation districts.

A worker employed by the government works in a particular district to demonstrate soil conservation to farmers and agricultural businesses. There are usually one or more professional soil conservationists and one or more soil conservation technicians working in each district.

■ The Job

Soil conservationists and technicians with the federal Soil Conservation Service help scientists and engineers obtain preliminary data used to establish and maintain soil and water conservation plans. They may also work closely with landowners and operators to establish and maintain sound conservation practices in land management and use.

Conservationists oversee soil conservation technicians who assist with preliminary engineering surveys; lay out contours, terraces, tile drainage systems, and irrigation systems; plant grasses and trees; collect soil samples and gather information from field notes; improve woodlands; assist in farm pond design and management; make maps from aerial photographs; and inspect specific areas to determine conservation needs.

Some conservationists and technicians work for the Bureau of Land Management which oversees hundreds of millions of acres of public domain. Workers in this federal agency help survey publicly owned areas, and pinpoint land features to determine the best use of public lands. They may be called upon to supervise a four- to six-person surveying team in carrying out the actual survey.

Soil conservation technicians in the Bureau of Reclamation serve as assistants to civil, construction, materials, or general engineers. Their job is to oversee certain phases of such projects as the construction of dams, and irrigation planning. The Bureau's ultimate goal is the control of water and soil resources for the benefit of farm, home, and city.

The following short paragraphs describe some positions typically held by entry-level soil conservationists and technicians.

Range technicians work closely with range conservationists helping to manage rangeland, most of which is in the western part of the United States. They determine the value of rangeland, its grazing capabilities, erosion hazards, and livestock potential.

Physical science technician aides gather data in the field, studying the physical characteristics of the soil, mapping land, and producing aerial survey maps for use by soil conservationists.

Engineering technician aides conduct field tests and oversee some phases of construction on dams and irrigation projects. They manage water resources and perform soil-conservation services. They also measure acreage, place property boundaries, and define drainage areas on maps.

Cartographic survey technician aides work with cartographers (map makers) to survey the public domain, setting boundaries, pinpointing land features, and determining the most beneficial public use.

The following short paragraphs describe some of the positions held by more experienced soil conservationists and technicians.

Cartographic technicians perform technical work in mapping or charting the earth or graphically representing geographical information.

Geodetic technicians perform nonprofessional work in the analysis, evaluation, processing, computation, and selection of geodetic survey data. (Geodesy is the science of determining the size and shape of the earth, the intensity and direction of the force of gravity, and the elevation of points on or near the earth's surface.)

Physical science technicians help professional scientists calibrate and operate measuring instruments; mix solutions; make routine chemical analyses; and set up and operate test apparatus.

Surveying technicians perform surveys to conduct field measurement and mapping, to lay out construction, to check the accuracy of dredging operations, or to provide reference points and lines for related work. They gather

SOIL CONSERVATIONISTS AND TECHNICIANS	
SCHOOL SUBJECTS	Agriculture Biology
PERSONAL SKILLS	Communication/ideas Helping/teaching
WORK ENVIRONMENT	Indoors and outdoors Primarily multiple locations
MINIMUM EDUCATION LEVEL	Associate's degree (soil conservationists) High school diploma (soil conservation technicians)
SALARY RANGE	$15,500 to $45,200 to $70,000
CERTIFICATION OR LICENSING	Voluntary
OUTLOOK	About as fast as the average
DOT	040
GOE	02.02.02
NOC	2115
O*NET	24302B

A soil conservation technician and his assistant identify the various types of soils in a forest preserve. The data will be used in a report concerning soil conservation.

data for the design of highways and dams, or the construction of topographic maps or nautical and aeronautical charts.

Range conservationists administer and operate range conservation programs to properly conserve, develop, and utilize ranges and rangeland; to provide for the conservation management and utilization of related resources; and to stabilize the livestock industry, which depends upon the range for its existence.

■ Requirements

High School

While in high school, prospective conservationists and technicians should take at least one year of algebra, enough English to be articulate and convincing in speech and writing, and one year of biology. For technicians who anticipate that they may work in areas of soil conservation involving contact with farmers and ranchers, high school courses in vocational agriculture are strongly recommended.

Postsecondary Training

The federal government requires soil conservationists to earn at least 30 college credit hours and significant work experience in order to be considered for a position. A bachelor's degree in agronomy, agricultural education, range management, forestry, or agricultural engineering will be especially helpful to the aspiring soil conservationist. Some conservationists may consider earning a master's degree in a natural resources field. A college education is not required of soil conservation technicians.

Typical first year courses in a two-year postsecondary program include such courses as applied mathematics, communications skills, basic soils, botany, chemistry, zoology, and introduction to range management. Typical second-year courses include American government, surveying, forestry, game management, soil and water conservation, economics, fish management, and soil and water conservation engineering.

Conservationists and technicians must have some practical experience in the use of soil conservation techniques before they enter the field. Therefore, a good part of their postsecondary education includes on-the-job training.

Certification or Licensing

No certification or license is required of soil conservationists and technicians. Employment by government agencies is usually based on a competitive examination. The American Society of Agronomy and the Soil and Water Conservation Society offer certification in soil science.

Other Requirements

Soil conservationists and technicians must be able to apply practical as well as theoretical knowledge to their work. They need to have a working knowledge of soil and water characteristics; be skilled in management of woodlands, wildlife areas, and recreation areas; and have a knowledge of surveying instruments and practices, mapping, and the procedures used for interpreting aerial photographs.

Soil conservationists and technicians should also be able to write clear, concise reports to demonstrate and explain the results of their tests, studies, and recommendations. It goes without saying that a love for the outdoors and an appreciation for all natural resources are essential for success and personal fulfillment in this job.

■ Exploring

One of the best ways for you to become acquainted with soil conservation work and technology is through summer or part-time work on a farm. Other ways to explore this career include joining a 4-H Club or the Future Farmers of America (FFA). Science courses that include lab sections, and mathematics courses that focus on practical problem-solving will also help give you a feel for this kind of work.

■ Employers

Most soil conservationists and technicians work for the federal government, specifically for the Soil Conservation Service, the Bureau of Land Management, and the Bureau of Reclamation. Others work for agencies at the state and county level. Soil conservationists and technicians also work for private agencies and firms such as banks and loan agencies, mining or steel companies, and public utilities companies.

■ Starting Out

Most students in a two-year technical institute gain work experience by working a summer job in his or her area of interest. Students can get information on summer positions through their school's placement office. Often, contacts made on summer jobs lead to permanent employment after graduation. In addition, college placement officers and faculty members are often valuable sources of advice and information in finding employment.

Most soil conservationists and technicians find work with state, county, or federal agencies. Specific details of the application procedure for these jobs vary according to the level of government in which the technician is seeking work. In general, however, students begin the application procedure during the fourth semester of their program and should expect some form of competitive examination as part of the process. College placement personnel can help students find out about the details of application procedures. Often representatives of government agencies visit college campuses to explain employment possibilities to students and sometimes to recruit for their agencies.

■ Advancement

Soil conservationists and technicians may continue their education while working, by taking additional courses at night at a local college or technical institute. Federal agencies that employ conservationists and technicians have a policy of "promotion from within." Because of this policy, there is a continuing opportunity for such workers to advance through the ranks. The degree of advancement that all conservationists and technicians can expect in their working careers is determined by their aptitudes, abilities, and of course their desire to advance.

■ Earnings

The majority of soil conservationists and technicians work for the federal government, and their salaries are determined by their government service rating. In 1997, the average annual salary for soil conservationists employed by the federal government was $45,200, according to the *Occupational Outlook Handbook*. Those with bachelor's degrees started at $19,500 or $24,200 a year depending on academic achievement; with a master's degree, $24,200 or $29,600; and with a doctorate, $35,800. The salaries of workers employed by state and local governments vary widely depending on the state or county for which they work.

The salaries of conservationists and technicians working for private firms or agencies will be roughly comparable to the earnings of other similarly trained agricultural technicians employed by private firms. In general, conservationists in this area receive beginning salaries of $19,800 a year. Those with a grade point average of at least 3.0 or who have a master's degree with two years work experience may earn a starting salary of $22,000 per year. Those conservationists with considerable experience who have gained consistent promotion can earn from $40,000 to $49,500 or more a year. Conservationists who have man-

agement responsibilities may earn as much as $65,000 to $70,000 a year. Soil conservation technicians, who do not usually have a college degree, earn starting salaries of $15,500; with top pay for this position reaching $20,000 per year.

■ Work Environment

Soil conservationists and technicians usually work 40 hours per week, except in unusual or emergency situations. They have opportunities to travel, and in some positions with federal agencies, they may travel frequently.

Soil conservation is an outdoor job. Conservation workers travel to work sites by car, but must often walk great distances to the problem area. Although they sometimes work from aerial photographs and other on-site pictures, they cannot work from pictures alone. They must visit the spot that presents the problem in order to make appropriate recommendations.

Although soil conservationists and technicians spend much of their working time outdoors, office work is also necessary when generating detailed reports of their work to agency offices.

In their role as assistants to professionals, soil conservation technicians often assume the role of public relations representatives of the government to landowners and land managers. They must be able to explain the underlying principles of the structures that they design and the surveys that they perform.

To meet these and other requirements of the job, conservationists and technicians should be prepared to continue their education both formally and informally throughout their careers. They must stay aware of current periodicals and studies so that they can keep up-to-date in their area of specialization.

Soil conservationists and technicians gain satisfaction from knowing that theirs is a vitally important job to the economy of the nation. Without their work, large portions of land in the United States could become barren within a generation.

■ Outlook

Most soil conservationists and technicians are employed by the federal government; therefore, employment opportunities will depend in large part on levels of government spending. It is always difficult to predict future government policies; however, this is an area where the need for government involvement is apparent and pressing. The vast majority of America's cropland has suffered from some sort of erosion, and only continued efforts by soil conservation professionals can prevent a dangerous depletion of our most valuable resource—fertile soil.

Some soil conservationists and technicians are employed by public utility companies, banks and loan agencies, state and local governments, and mining or steel companies. At present, a relatively small number of soil conservation workers are employed by these firms or agencies. However, decreased levels of employment by the federal government could lead to increased employment in these areas.

■ For More Information

For information on soil conservation careers and certification, contact:

American Society of Agronomy
Career Development and Placement Service
677 South Segoe Road
Madison, WI 53711
Tel: 608-273-8080
Email: headquarters@Agronomy.org
Web: http://www.agronomy.org

For information on careers in soil conservation and certification, contact:

Soil and Water Conservation Society
7515 NE Ankeny Road
Ankeny, IA 50021
Tel: 515-289-2331
Web: http://www.swcs.org/

For information on government soil conservation careers, contact:

Natural Resources Conservation Service
U.S. Department of Agriculture
Attn: Conservation Communications Staff
PO Box 2890
Washington, DC 20013
Web: http://www.nrcs.usda.gov/

■ Related Articles

Agriculture
The Environment
Government
Agricultural Consultants
Agricultural Scientists
Civil Engineering Technicians
Civil Engineers
Farm Crop Production Technicians
Foresters
Forestry Technicians
Geological Technicians
Geologists
Groundwater Professionals
Meteorologists
Range Managers
Soil Scientists
Surveying and Mapping Technicians
Surveyors

Soil Scientists

■ Overview

Soil scientists study the physical, chemical, and biological characteristics and behaviors of soils. They determine the origin, distribution, composition, and classification of soils so that they may be put to the most productive and effective use.

■ History

As recently as 200 years ago, no one suspected soil could be depleted by constant use. When crops were poor, everything was blamed except the soil in which they were grown. In some parts of the world, mysterious or supernatural forces are still considered responsible for poor harvests.

Soil is one of our most important natural resources. Like air, however, soil is often taken for granted until its condition becomes too bad to ignore. An increasing population, moreover, has made the United States conscious of the fact that its welfare is dependent upon fertile soil capable of producing food for hundreds of millions of people.

Soil is formed by the breaking of rocks and the decay of trees, plants, and animals. It may take as long as 500 years to make just one inch of topsoil. Unwise and wasteful farming methods can destroy that inch of soil in just a few short years.

Each rainstorm may carry thousands of pounds of precious topsoil away. Rains also dissolve the chemicals in unprotected soils, making it more difficult to grow healthy crops. Erosion has been a problem of major proportions in the United States, but soil scientists and soil conservationists have made some progress at halting it.

It was not until approximately 130 years ago that agriculture was considered important enough to deserve the attention of the federal government. In May 1862, the U.S. Department of Agriculture was formed. Its primary purpose at the time was to give farmers information about new crops and new farming techniques. Although the Department of Agriculture started as a small undertaking, it has become one of the largest agencies of the federal government, despite the fact that there are only half as many farmers in this country as there were 100 years ago.

The 1933 Agricultural Adjustment Act inaugurated a policy of giving direct government aid to farmers. The Soil Conservation Service was established two years later. This service developed as a direct result of the disastrous dust storms of the mid-1930s, which blew away millions of tons of valuable topsoil and destroyed fertile cropland throughout the Midwestern states. Because of the efforts of the scientists employed by the Soil Conservation Service, much of this ruined land has been reclaimed.

Since 1937, all 50 states, in cooperation with the Department of Agriculture, have organized themselves into soil conservation districts. The department sends soil scientists and soil conservationists to help farmers within each district establish and maintain farming practices that will use land in the wisest possible ways.

■ The Job

Soil scientists do much of their work outdoors. They must tramp over fields, confer with farmers, give advice on crop rotation or fertilizers, assess the amount of field drainage, and take soil samples. They advise farmers about proper cover crops to protect bare earth from the ravages of the wind and weather.

Soil scientists may also specialize in one particular aspect of the work. For example, they may work as a *soil mapper* or *soil surveyor*. These specialists study soil structure, origin, and capabilities through field observations, laboratory examinations, and controlled experimentation. Their investigations are aimed at determining the most suitable uses for a particular soil.

Soil fertility experts develop practices that will increase or maintain productivity. They test the soils chemically and conduct field investigations to determine the relation of soil acidity to plant growth. They also relate the use of various fertilizers and other soil additives to local soil characteristics; tillage, crop rotation, and other farm practices; and to the requirements of particular crops.

All soil scientists work in the laboratory. They make chemical analyses of the soil and examine soil samples under the microscope to determine bacterial and plant-food components. They write reports that are drawn from their field notes and from the samples of soil that they have analyzed.

Soil science is part of the science of agronomy, which also encompasses crop science. Soil and crop scientists work together in agricultural experiment stations during all seasons, doing research on crop production, soil fertility, and various kinds of soil management.

Some soil and crop scientists travel to remote sections of the world in search of plants and grasses that may thrive in this country and contribute to our food supply, pasture land, or soil replenishing efforts. Some crop scientists go overseas to advise farmers in other countries on how to treat their soils. A number of soil scientists with advanced degrees teach in colleges of agriculture. Many who teach also conduct research projects.

■ Requirements

High School

If you're interested in pursuing a career in agronomy or soil science, you should follow your high school's college preparatory course. Mathematics and science, as well as English and public speaking, are essential courses. A person

needs to be able to speak persuasively and effectively to become a convincing soil scientist. Report writing is also an important part of the job.

Postsecondary Training

A bachelor's degree in agronomy or soil science is the minimum educational requirement to become a soil scientist. Such courses as physics, geology, bacteriology, botany, chemistry, soil and plant morphology, soil fertility, soil classification, and soil genesis are all requirements for the prospective soil scientist.

Most colleges of agriculture also offer masters' and doctoral degrees in agronomy or soil science. To direct and administer research programs, soil scientists usually need doctoral degrees. The same is true for those seeking teaching positions at the university level. Master's degrees are helpful for many research positions.

Certification or Licensing

Soil scientists may seek to be listed in the American Registry of Certified Professionals in Agronomy, Crops, and Soils. To qualify for this, they must earn a bachelor's degree and work five years in the field. Those with advanced degrees can qualify with less experience.

Other Requirements

It's good to have some farm experience or background before going into soil science. You should be able to work effectively alone and with others on projects. You must have good communication skills in order to explain your findings. Computer skills are becoming increasingly important; you'll need an understanding of word processing, the Internet, multimedia software, databases, and possibly even programming languages. You will have to spend many hours outdoors in all kinds of weather, so you must be able to endure difficult and uncomfortable physical conditions.

SOIL SCIENTISTS	
SCHOOL SUBJECTS	**Agriculture** **Earth science**
PERSONAL SKILLS	**Leadership/management** **Technical/scientific**
WORK ENVIRONMENT	**Indoors and outdoors** **Primarily multiple locations**
MINIMUM EDUCATION LEVEL	**Bachelor's degree**
SALARY RANGE	**$26,000 to $49,000 to $87,000+**
CERTIFICATION OR LICENSING	**Voluntary**
OUTLOOK	**About as fast as the average**
DOT	**040**
GOE	**02.02.02**
NOC	**2115**

Soil core samples are withdrawn from a field in Colorado by a technician and a soil scientist. The samples will yield information on soil horizons and their physical and chemical properties.

Exploring

If you live in an agricultural community, you should be able to find some opportunities for part-time or summer work on a farm or ranch. A Future Farmers of America (FFA) program will introduce you to the concerns of farmers and researchers. A local 4-H club can also give you valuable experience in agriculture. Contact your county's soil conservation department, and other government agencies, to learn about regional projects.

Employers

Most soil scientists work for state or federal departments of agriculture. However, soil scientists are also employed by such private business firms as fertilizer companies, where they may engage in research work to improve the product or engage in sales work to increase the use of the product. Soil scientists may be employed by private research laboratories, real estate firms, or land appraisal boards. They may work for state road departments to determine the quality and condition of the soil over which roads will be built. Other soil scientists may work as private consultants

for bankers and other clients who are engaged in making loans on property. Some soil consultants work for park departments or for farm management agencies.

Starting Out

College graduates with degrees in agronomy or soil science should apply directly to the Resources Conservation Service of the Department of Agriculture, the Department of the Interior, the Environmental Protection Agency, or the appropriate state government agency. University placement services generally have listings for specific openings.

Private employers of soil scientists include agricultural service companies, banks, insurance and real estate firms, food products companies, wholesale distributors, and environmental and engineering consulting companies. Some public employers of soil scientists, other than the federal, state, and local governments, are land appraisal boards, experimental stations, land-grant colleges and universities, conservation departments, and Cooperative Extension agencies. Soil scientists who work overseas may be employed by the U.S. Agency for International Development.

Advancement

Salary increases are the most common form of advancement for soil scientists. The nature of the job may not change appreciably even after many years of service. There is, of course, always the possibility of advancement into positions of greater responsibility. Administrative and supervisory positions, however, are few in comparison with the number of jobs that must be done in the field. Those who go on to obtain graduate degrees may anticipate moving into more responsible positions, especially in soil research.

For those soil scientists engaged in college teaching, an advanced degree may well mean an advancement in academic rank and responsibility. For soil scientists employed by private business firms, there may be the opportunity to advance into positions such as department head or research director. Advancement to supervisory positions or other positions of responsibility is also possible in such state agencies as road departments.

Earnings

According to the U.S. Department of Labor, the average pay for soil scientists in 1997 was $49,400 a year. Soil scientists working for the government can enter the field at GS-7 (regulated government pay scale) which is between $26,000 and $35,000 a year. But government grade level and starting salary depend on experience, education, and grade point average. Those with doctorates and a great deal of experience may be qualified for GS-14, which is between $67,000 and $87,000. Unless you're hired for just a short-term research project, you'll likely receive health and retirement benefits in addition to your annual salary.

■ Work Environment

Most soil scientists work 40 hours a week. Their work is varied, ranging from field work to the work of examining samples of soil and constructing detailed maps that must be done in the laboratory. Some jobs may involve travel—even to foreign countries—and some may include teaching responsibilities or the supervision of training programs in the field.

■ Outlook

The career of soil scientist will be affected by USDA and Environmental Protection Agency involvement in farming studies. Technological advances, such as computer programs and new methods of conservation, will allow scientists to better protect the environment, as well as improve farm production. One of the challenges facing future soil scientists will be convincing farmers to change their current methods of tilling and chemical treatment in favor of environmentally safer methods.

Soil scientists will be able to better evaluate soils and plants with new, more precise research methods. Combine-mounted yield monitors will produce data as the farmer crosses the field, and satellites will provide more detailed field information. With computer images, scientists will also be able to examine plant roots more carefully.

■ For More Information

For a career resources booklet, contact SSSA, or visit its Web site.

Soil Science Society of America
677 South Segoe Road
Madison, WI 53711
Tel: 608-273-8095
Web: http://www.soils.org

For information about membership, seminars, and issues affecting soil scientists, visit the NSCSS Web site, or contact:

National Society of Consulting Soil Scientists
325 Pennsylvania Avenue, SE, Suite 700
Washington DC 20003
Tel: 800-535-7148
Web: http://www.nscss.org

■ Related Articles

Agriculture
Agribusiness Technicians
Agricultural Consultants
Agricultural Equipment Technicians
Agricultural Scientists
Animal Breeders and Technicians
Aquaculturists

Farm Crop Production Technicians
Farm Equipment Mechanics
Farmers
Fishers
Grain Merchants
Horticultural Technicians

Songwriters

■ Overview

Songwriters write the words and music for songs, including songs for recordings, advertising jingles, and theatrical performances. We hear the work of songwriters every day, and yet most songwriters remain anonymous, even if a song's performer is famous. Many songwriters, of course, perform their own songs.

■ History

Songwriting played an important part in the growth of the United States. The early pioneers wrote songs as a way to relax. Some of the difficult experiences of traveling, fighting over land, farming, and hunting for food were put into words by early songwriters, and the words set to music, for the guitar, banjo, piano, and other instruments. Francis Scott Key (1780?-1843) became famous for writing the words to the "Star Spangled Banner," set to a popular drinking tune.

Toward the end of the 19th century, sheet music was sold by dozens and even hundreds of publishing companies, centered in New York City in what became known as Tin Pan Alley. This name was coined by a songwriter and journalist named Monroe Rosenfeld, referring to the sounds of many voices and pianos coming from the open windows of the street where many of the music publishers were located. By the 1880s, sheet music sold in the millions; most

SONGWRITERS	
SCHOOL SUBJECTS	English Music
PERSONAL SKILLS	Artistic Communication/ideas
WORK ENVIRONMENT	Primarily indoors Primarily one location
MINIMUM EDUCATION LEVEL	High school diploma
SALARY RANGE	$20,000 to $50,000 to $1,000,000+
CERTIFICATION OR LICENSING	None available
OUTLOOK	About as fast as the average
DOT	131
GOE	01.01.02
NOC	5132
O*NET	34047C

SONGWRITING WEB SITE

Check out the *Independent Songwriter Web-Magazine* at http://www.independentsongwriter.com, where you can read feature articles, interviews, and columns from professionals on such subjects as manufacturing your own CD and organizations that support songwriters. The site also features many valuable songwriting links, and an online collaboration room, which allows you to work directly with other songwriters.

songs were introduced on the stages of musical theater, vaudeville, and burlesque shows. Radio became an important medium for introducing new songs in the 1920s, followed by the introduction of sound movies in the 1930s. Sheet music became less important as musical recordings were introduced. This presented difficulties for the songwriter and publisher, because the sales of sheet music were easier to control. In the 1940s, the first associations for protecting the rights of the songwriters and publishers were formed; among the benefits songwriters received were royalties for each time a song they had written was recorded, performed, or played on the radio or in film.

By the 1950s, Tin Pan Alley no longer referred to a specific area in New York but was used nationwide to denote popular songs in general, and especially a type of simple melody and sentimental and often silly lyric that dominated the pop music industry. The rise of rock and roll music in the 1950s put an end to Tin Pan Alley's dominance. Many performers began to write their own songs, a trend that became particularly important in the 1960s. In the late 1970s, a new type of songwriting emerged. Rap music, featuring words chanted over a musical background, seemed to bring songwriting full circle, back to the oral traditions of its origins.

■ The Job

There are many different ways to write a song. A song may begin with a few words—the lyric—or with a few notes of a melody, or a song may be suggested by an idea, theme, or product. A song may come about in a flash of inspiration or may be developed slowly over a long period of time. Songwriters may work alone, or as part of a team, in which one person concentrates on the lyrics while another person concentrates on the music. Sometimes there may be several people working on the same song.

"One of the most important things," says songwriter Beth McBride, "is collecting your ideas, even if they're only fragments of ideas, and writing them down. Sometimes a song comes to me from beginning to end, but I can't always rely on inspiration." Beth performed with the band "B and the Hot Notes," for which she wrote and recorded original music. She currently fronts a musical duo called "Acoustisaurus Rex" and is involved in another recording project. "A lot of my writing has been personal,

derived from experience. Also from the observation of others' experiences."

Most popular songs require words, or lyrics, and some songwriters may concentrate on writing the words to a song. These songwriters are called *lyricists*. Events, experiences, or emotions may inspire a lyricist to write lyrics. A lyricist may also be contracted to write the words for a jingle, a musical, or adapt the words from an existing song for another project.

Some songwriters do no more than write the words to a potential song, and leave it to others to develop a melody and musical accompaniment for the words. They may sell the words to a music publisher, or work in a team to create a finished song from the lyric. Some lyricists specialize in writing the words for advertising jingles. They are usually employed by advertising agencies and may work on several different products at once, often under pressure of a deadline.

In songwriting teams, one member may be a lyricist, while the other member is a composer. The development of a song can be a highly collaborative process. The composer might suggest topics for the song to the lyricist; the lyricist might suggest a melody to the composer. Other times, the composer plays a musical piece for the lyricist, and the lyricist tries to create lyrics to fit with that piece.

Composers for popular music generally have a strong background in music, and often in performing music as well. They must have an understanding of many musical styles, so that they can develop the music that will fit a project's needs. Composers work with a variety of musical and electronic equipment, including computers, to produce and record their music. They develop the different parts for the different musical instruments needed to play the song. They also work with musicians who will play and record the song, and the composer conducts or otherwise directs the musicians as the song is played.

Songwriters, composers, and musicians often make use of MIDI (musical instrument digital interface) technology to produce sounds through synthesizers, drum machines, and samplers. These sounds are usually controlled by a computer, and the composer or songwriter can mix, alter, and refine the sounds using mixing boards and computer software. Like analog or acoustic instruments, which produce sounds as a string or reed or drum head vibrates with air, MIDI creates digital "vibrations" that can produce sounds similar to acoustic instruments or highly unusual sounds invented by the songwriter. Synthesizers and other sound-producing machines may each have their own keyboard or playing mechanism, or be linked through one or more keyboards. They may also be controlled through the computer, or with other types of controls, such as a guitar controller, which plays like a guitar, or foot controls. Songs can be stored in the computer, or transferred to tape or compact disc.

Many, if not most, songwriters combine both the work of a lyricist and the work of a composer. Often, a songwriter will perform his or her own songs as well, whether as a singer, a member of a band, or both. Playing guitar has helped Beth in the writing of lyrics and music. "My songwriting has become more sophisticated as my playing has become more sophisticated," she says.

For most songwriters, writing a song is only the first part of their job. After a song is written, songwriters usually produce a "demo" of the song, so that the client or potential purchaser of the song can hear how it sounds. Songwriters contract with recording studios, studio musicians, and recording engineers to produce a version of the song. The songwriter then submits the song to a publishing house, record company, recording artist, film studio, or others, who will then decide if the song is appropriate for their needs. Often, a songwriter will produce several versions of a song, or submit several different songs for a particular project. There is always a chance that one, some, or all of their songs will be rejected.

■ Requirements

High School

You should take courses in music that involve you with singing, playing instruments, and studying the history of music. Theater and speech classes will help you to understand the nature of performing, as well as involve you in writing dramatic pieces. You should study poetry in an English class, and try your hand at composing poetry in different forms. Language skills can also be honed in foreign-language classes and by working on student literary magazines. An understanding of how people act and think can influence you as a lyricist, so take courses in psychology and sociology.

Postsecondary Training

There are no real requirements for entering the field of songwriting. All songwriters, however, will benefit from musical training, including musical theory and musical notation. Learning to play one or more instruments, such as the piano or guitar, will be especially helpful in writing songs. Not all songwriters need to be able to sing, but this is helpful.

Songwriting is an extremely competitive field. Despite a lack of formal educational requirements, prospective songwriters are encouraged to continue their education through high school and preferably towards a college degree. Much of the musical training a songwriter needs, however, can also be learned informally. In general, you should have a background in music theory, and in arrangement and orchestration for multiple instruments. You should be able to read music, and be able to write it in the

---

LEARN MORE ABOUT IT

There are a number of books available to help you start writing songs; here are a few:

Davis, Sheila. *The Songwriter's Idea Book: 40 Strategies to Excite Your Imagination, Help You Design Distinctive Songs, and Keep Your Creative Flow.* Cincinnati, OH: Writer's Digest Books, 1996.

Leikin, Molly-Ann. *How to Make a Good Song a Hit Song: Rewriting and Marketing Your Lyrics and Music.* Milwaukee, WI: Hal Leonard Publishing, 1996.

Luboff, Pat. *88 Songwriting Wrongs and How to Right Them: Concrete Ways to Improve Your Songwriting and Make Your Songs More Marketable.* Cincinnati, OH: Writer's Digest Books, 1992.

Zollo, Paul. *Beginning Songwriters Answer Book.* Cincinnati, OH: Writer's Digest Books, 1993.

---

proper musical notation. You should have a good sense of the sounds each type of musical instrument produces, alone and in combination. Understanding harmony is important, as well as a proficiency in or understanding of a variety of styles of music. For example, you should know what makes rock different from reggae, blues, or jazz. Studies in music history will also help develop this understanding.

On the technical side, you should understand the various features, capabilities, and requirements of modern recording techniques. You should be familiar with MIDI and computer technology, as these play important roles in composing, playing, and recording music today.

There are several organizations that help lyricists, songwriters, and composers. The National Academy of Songwriters offers weekly song evaluation workshops in California. The Nashville Songwriters Association offers workshops, seminars, and other services, as well as giving annual awards to songwriters. The Songwriters and Lyricists Club in New York provides contacts for songwriters with music-business professionals. These, and other organizations, offer songwriting workshops and other training seminars.

Other Requirements

Many elements of songwriting cannot really be learned but are a matter of inborn talent. A creative imagination and the ability to invent melodies and combine melodies into a song are essential parts of a songwriting career. As you become more familiar with your own talents, and with songwriting, you'll learn to develop and enhance your creative skills.

"I enjoy observing," Beth says. "I also enjoy the challenge of finding the most succinct way of saying something and making it poetic. I enjoy the process of finding that perfect turn of phrase. I really love language and words."

A songwriter uses a MIDI keyboard and a computer.

■ Exploring

The simplest way to gain experience in songwriting is to learn to play a musical instrument, especially the piano or guitar, and to invent your own songs. Joining a rock group is a way to gain experience writing music for several musicians. Most schools and communities have orchestras, bands, and choruses that are open to performers. Working on a student-written musical show is ideal training for the future songwriter.

If you have your own computer, think about investing in software, a keyboard, and other devices that will allow you to experiment with sounds, recording, and writing and composing your own songs. While much of this equipment is highly expensive, there are plenty of affordable keyboards, drum machines, and software available today. Your school's music department may also have such equipment available.

■ Employers

Most songwriters work freelance, competing for contracts to write songs for a particular artist, television show, video program, or for contracts with musical publishers and advertising agencies. They will meet with clients to determine the nature of the project and to get an idea of what kind of music the client seeks, the budget for the project, the time in which the project is expected to be completed, and in what form the work is to be submitted. Many songwriters work under contract with one or more music publishing houses. Usually, they must fulfill a certain quota of new songs each year. These songwriters receive a salary, called an advance or draw, that is often paid by the week. Once a song has been published, the money earned by the song goes to pay back the songwriter's draw. A percentage of the money earned by the song over and above the

amount of the draw goes to the songwriter as a royalty. Other songwriters are employed by so-called "jingle houses," that is, companies that supply music for advertising commercials. Whereas most songwriters work in their own homes or offices, these songwriters work at the jingle house's offices. Film, television, and video production studios may also employ songwriters on their staff.

■ Starting Out

Songwriting is a very competitive career and difficult to break into for a beginner. The number of high-paying projects is limited. Often, beginning songwriters start their careers writing music for themselves or as part of a musical group. They may also offer their services to student films, student and local theater productions, church groups, and other religious and nonprofit organizations, often for free or for a low fee.

Many songwriters get their start while performing their own music in clubs and other places; they may be approached by a music publisher, who contracts them for a number of songs. Other songwriters record demos of their songs and try to interest record companies and music publishers. Some songwriters organize showcase performances, renting a local club or hall and inviting music industry people to hear their work. Songwriters may have to approach many companies and publishers before they find one willing to buy their songs. A great deal of making a success in songwriting is in developing contacts with people active in the music industry.

Some songwriters get their start in one of the few entry-level positions available. Songwriters aspiring to become composers for film and television can find work as orchestrators or copyists in film houses. Other songwriters may find work for music agents and publishers, which will give them an understanding of the industry and increase their contacts in the industry, as they develop their songwriting skills. Those interested in specializing in advertising jingles may find entry level work as music production assistants with a jingle house. At first, such jobs may involve making coffee, doing paperwork, and completing other clerical tasks. As you gain more exposure to the process of creating music, you may begin in basic areas of music production, or assist experienced songwriters.

■ Advancement

It is important for a songwriter to develop a strong portfolio of work and a reputation for professionalism. Songwriters who establish a reputation for the quality of their work will receive larger and higher-paying projects as their careers proceed. They may be contracted to score major motion pictures, or to write songs for major recording artists. Ultimately, they may be able to support themselves on their songwriting alone and also have the ability to pick and choose the projects they will work on.

In order to continue to grow with the music industry, songwriters must be tuned into new musical styles and trends. They must also keep up with developments in music technology. A great deal of time is spent making and maintaining contacts with others in the music industry.

Songwriters specializing in jingles and other commercial products may eventually start up their own jingle house. Other songwriters, especially those who have written a number of hit songs, may themselves become recording artists.

For many songwriters, however, success and advancement is a very personal process. A confidence in your own talent will help you to create better work. "I'm not as vulnerable about my work," Beth says. "And I want to open up my subject matter, to expand and experiment more."

■ Earnings

Songwriters' earnings vary widely, from next to nothing to many millions of dollars. A beginning songwriter may work for free, or for low pay, just to gain experience. A songwriter may sell a jingle to an advertising agency for $1,000 or may receive many thousands of dollars if their work is well-known. Royalties from a song may reach $20,000 per year or more per song, and a successful songwriter may earn $100,000 or more per year from the royalties of several songs. A songwriter's earnings may come from a combination of royalties earned on songs and fees earned from commercial projects.

Those starting as assistants in music production companies or jingle houses may earn as little as $20,000 per year. Experienced songwriters at these companies may earn $50,000 per year or more.

Because most songwriters are freelance, they will have to provide their own health insurance, life insurance, and pension plans. They are usually paid per project, and therefore receive no overtime pay. When facing a deadline, they may have to work many more hours than 8 hours a day or 40 hours a week. Also, songwriters are generally responsible for recording their own demos and must pay for recording studio time, studio musicians, and production expenses.

■ Work Environment

Songwriters generally possess a strong love for music, and regardless of the level of their success, usually find fulfillment in their careers because they are doing what they love to do. As a freelancer, you'll have control over how you spend your day. You'll work out of your own home or office. You will have your own instruments, and possibly your own recording equipment as well. You may also work in recording studios, where conditions can vary, from noisy and busy, to relaxed and quiet.

Writing music can be stressful. When facing a deadline, you may experience a great deal of pressure while trying to get your music just right and on time. You may face a great deal of rejection before you find someone willing to publish or record your songs. Rejection remains a part of the songwriter's life, even after success.

Many songwriters will work many years with limited or no success. On the other hand, songwriters experience the joys of creativity, which has its own rewards.

■ Outlook

Most songwriters are unable to support themselves from their songwriting alone and must hold other part-time or full-time jobs while writing songs in their spare time. The competition in this industry is extremely intense, and there are many more songwriters than paying projects. This situation is expected to continue into the next decade.

There are a few bright spots for songwriters. The recent rise of independent filmmaking has created more venues for songwriters to compose film scores. Cable television also provides more opportunities for song writing, both in the increased number of advertisements and in the growing trend for cable networks to develop their own original programs. Many computer games and software feature songs and music, and this area should grow rapidly in the next decade. Another potential boom area is the World Wide Web. As more and more companies, organizations, and individuals set up multimedia Web sites, there may be an increased demand for songwriters to create songs and music for these sites. Songwriters with MIDI capability will be in the strongest position to benefit from the growth created by computer uses of music. In another field, legalized gambling has spread to many states in the country, a large number of resorts and theme parks have opened, and as these venues produce their own musical theater and shows, they will require more songwriters.

Success in songwriting is a combination of hard work, industry connections, and good luck. The number of hit songs is very small compared to the number of songwriters trying to write them.

■ For More Information

For information about the professional associations that serve songwriters, contact the following:

American Society of Composers, Authors, and Publishers (ASCAP)
One Lincoln Plaza
New York, NY 10023
Tel: 212-621-6000
Web: http://www.ascap.org

Visit the Songwriter's section of the BMI Web site to learn more about performing rights, music publishing, copyright, and the business of songwriting.

Broadcast Music Inc. (BMI)
320 West 57th Street
New York, NY 10019-3790
Tel: 212-586-2000
Web: http://www.bmi.com

For information about educational seminars, and to read Musepaper, *an industry newsletter, visit the academy's Web site, or contact:*

National Academy of Songwriters
6255 Sunset Boulevard, Suite 1023
Hollywood, CA 90028
Tel: 800-826-7287
Web: http://www.nassong.org

To learn about the annual young composer's competition, and other contests, contact:

National Association of Composers USA
PO Box 49256, Barrington Station
Los Angeles, CA 90049
Tel: 310-541-8213
Web: http://www.thebook.com/nacusa/index.html

■ Related Articles

Advertising and Marketing
Film
Music and Recording Industry
Television
Advertising Workers
Composers
Literary Agents
Music Producers
Musicians
Screenwriters
Singers
Writers

Sound Editors
■ **See Film Editors**

Sound Mixers
■ **See Audio Recording Engineers**

Sous Chefs
■ **See Cooks, Chefs, and Bakers**

Spa Attendants

■ Overview

Spa attendants work in hotels, resorts, and salons. They are specially trained in facial, body, and water treatments. They assist *massage therapists* and *estheticians*, and prepare and clean the treatment rooms and tables. They provide spa customers with refreshments, towels, washcloths, and robes.

■ History

Fossils prove that even the mammoths of over 20,000 years ago enjoyed a good spa treatment. The town of Hot Springs, a small resort village nestled in the hills of South Dakota, features a fossil excavation site; this site serves as evidence that mammoths were attracted to the area's pools of warm water. Humans share this attraction. Native Americans considered natural hot springs to be sacred healing grounds. All through Europe, the ancient Romans built colossal spas, including the Baths of Caracalla, one of the seven wonders of the world. Only its ruins remain, but Caracalla once featured hot and cold baths, a swimming pool, a gymnasium, shops, art galleries, and acres of gardens.

By the late 1800s, there was hardly a well of natural spring water in the United States that a businessman hadn't capitalized upon. At the turn of the century, people flocked to resorts and spas (with or without natural hot springs) for exercise and relaxation. Though spas were all the rage back then, by the mid-20th century, they were considered only the domain of rich old women. In the last 20 years, spas have come back into vogue, attracting both men and women, along with their families.

■ The Job

From the ylang ylang plant to the lomilomi massage, spa attendants are teaching vacationers a new language of health and rejuvenation. Although there were only 30 spas in the United States in the late 1970s, the number now has grown past 300. Spas and resorts have cropped up around natural hot springs, the seaside, the desert, the mountains, and even the plains. Some spas are designed to meet very specific needs, such as weight management and holistic wellness. While most spas offer the usual facials, body wraps, and massages, many are expanding to include "mind/body awareness" as people flock to spas for both physical and spiritual needs. In some spas, you can schedule hypnosis, yoga, and dream therapy sessions right after your horseback riding, tennis game, and round of golf. So the duties of a spa attendant can vary greatly from location to location. Spa attendants are also finding work outside of the vacation industry, at salons and "day spas," as cosmetologists recognize the need to expand into other areas of beauty care. In addition to actually performing treatments, spa attendants devise special treatment plans for individual clients. They also schedule appointments, order and sell products, launder linens, and clean all spa areas. They offer advice on treatments and skin care products.

Craig Rabago works as a men's spa technician for the Ihilani Resort and Spa in Kapolei, Hawaii. *Ihilani* means "heavenly splendor" and it is part of Rabago's job to help guests realize this splendor. "I create an atmosphere that is heavenly for them," Rabago explains. "I'm of Hawaiian descent, and a local. I give people a warm welcome and make them feel at home." Rabago has been trained in a variety of services, including seaweed wraps, salt scrubs, and thalasso hydrotherapy (a fresh seawater massage). The Ihilani features a fitness center, and separate spas for men and women; each spa includes a sauna, steam room, needle shower, hot tub, and cold plunge. For the popular "cool ti leaf wrap," Rabago prepares a table in one of the spa's private rooms, spreading out the long, frond-like Hawaiian ti leaves and treating them with special oils. When the guest arrives for his wrap, Rabago gives him a robe and sandals, and shows him to the lockers, then the showers. When the guest is ready for the treatment, Rabago then brings him to the treatment room and directs him to lie back on the table. As he explains the treatment, Rabago rubs the guest's skin with oils and lotions, making sure to pay special attention to sunburn, dry skin, and other trouble areas. He then wraps the guest in a damp sheet. Rabago leaves him wrapped for 25 minutes, checking in occasionally to make sure the guest is comfortable. In between treatments, Rabago must take linen inventory and keep the spa areas clean. He also does a fair amount of work on the computer. "But taking care of the guests' needs—that's my priority," Rabago says.

The Ihilani capitalizes on its locale, providing treatments with fresh sea water, sea salt, seaweed, and Hawaiian plants. In a different kind of environment, a spa and resort may provide very different services. Mud baths, natural hot spring whirlpools, volcanic mineral treatment—resort owners around the world develop their spas with the natural surroundings in mind. This results in very specific training for spa attendants. "The training was time-consuming," Rabago recalls. "The spa techs train with each other. We put in lots of hours of practice before we actually go to work on a guest."

■ Requirements

Take high school courses in anatomy, physiology, and biology to learn about the human body and muscle systems. Chemistry will prepare you for the use and preparation of skin care products. Health courses will teach you about nutrition, fitness, and other issues of importance to the

health-conscious patrons of resorts and spas. Because so many spas offer treatment for both the body and the mind, take some psychology courses to learn about the history of treating depression, anxiety, and other mental and emotional problems.

Some summer or part-time jobs can give you insight into the work of a spa attendant. Hotels often hire high school students during peak summer months. A local beauty or tanning salon may need an assistant for cleanup and laundering towels. Nursing homes and hospitals often employ high school students, giving them experience in providing personal care services. Working at a retail store specializing in products for skin care and beauty, aromatherapy, and massage can teach you about various spa treatments.

Some background experience in health care or cosmetology is helpful in getting a job as a spa attendant, but it is not necessary. Many spa attendants receive their training on the job. Some spas, however, only hire licensed estheticians to perform treatments, leaving preparation, scheduling, and cleanup to the unlicensed spa attendants. Licensed estheticians have degrees (usually associate's degrees offered by special colleges) in cosmetology. These estheticians have taken courses in anatomy, chemistry, and physiology. In addition to facials and body wraps, estheticians offer massage, waxing, manicures, and pedicures. Because many spas have fitness facilities, spas also hire fitness specialists with associate's degrees from fitness programs. Courses for such programs include muscle conditioning, nutrition, and injury prevention.

Work experience is more important to the career path of a spa attendant than any internship. The closest thing to an internship for a spa attendant is a summer job at one of the many resorts across the country. During peak vacation season, spas hire extra help to deal with the increased number of guests. The long hours and variety of responsibilities can give you great experience and background in resort work.

Most spas require attendants to have CPR and first aid certification. Though there is no specific certification program for spa attendants, some spas require attendants to be certified estheticians or

SPA ATTENDANTS	
SCHOOL SUBJECTS	**Chemistry** **Health**
PERSONAL SKILLS	**Communication/ideas** **Helping/teaching**
WORK ENVIRONMENT	**Primarily indoors** **Primarily one location**
MINIMUM EDUCATION LEVEL	**High school diploma**
SALARY RANGE	**$12,000 to $16,000 to $21,000**
CERTIFICATION OR LICENSING	**None available**
OUTLOOK	**Faster than the average**

Public baths date back 4,500 years. They have been found in Pakistan, ancient Babylon, and Egypt. The medieval Turks created the five stages of the spa bath still practiced today: dry heat, moist heat, massage, cold, and rest. Some cultural contributions to the spa experience have gained popularity more than others: Asian and European massages and whirlpools are all the stuff of the modern-day spa; the Finnish sauna practice of beating one another with tree branches, however, has failed to take the world by storm.

massage therapists. In state exams, estheticians are tested on their knowledge of skin care, massage techniques, anatomy, and nutrition. Schools in cosmetology and esthetics design their programs to train students for the exam. Many spas, however, will continue to hire uncertified spa attendants and offer their own training.

Rabago of the Ihilani advises that a good spa attendant should "be happy, courageous, and ambitious." Guests of resorts and spas expect to be pampered and welcomed, and can only fully relax during a spa treatment if the attendant is calm and considerate. Be prepared to serve your clients, and to remain friendly and helpful. "But don't be timid and shy," Rabago says. "This is a good way to meet people from all around the world. You can broaden your horizons."

Any shyness and excessive modesty may also prevent you from performing your spa duties properly. You'll be applying lotions and oils to the naked skin of your guests— if you're uncomfortable, your clients will detect it, and become uncomfortable themselves. You must take a professional approach so that your clients feel safe and at ease. You should have a good "bedside manner"—the calm, comforting approach health care professionals use. Self-confidence is also important; you must convey to your client that you're knowledgeable about the treatment.

■ Exploring

You may be surprised by the number of spas in your area. There may even be a resort on the outskirts of your city. Look in the yellow pages under "Beauty Salons and Services" as well as "Health Clubs" and "Massage." (Many of the listings under "Spa" are only for hot tub dealerships.) Visit a salon or day spa and ask to interview someone who works as a spa attendant. Some attendants may allow you to shadow them for a day or two. Larger salons may have openings for part-time attendants, allowing you to gather firsthand experience.

Many resorts across the country advertise nationally for summer help. Check the classifieds of vacation and travel magazines, and visit http://www.resortjobs.com for a listing. You could also select a resort and spa from the pages

of a tourism publication, such as *Resorts and Great Hotels,* and call the hotel directly to request information about summer jobs. *Spa Finder* magazine also publishes a directory of spas.

■ Employers

The primary employers of spa attendants are hotels, resorts, and salons. Increasing numbers of salons are adding spas to their facilities to maintain a competitive edge; this will lead to increased opportunities for spa attendants throughout the country, mostly in larger cities and metropolitan areas. The same is true for hotel spas. Many spas, however, are clustered in resort areas with attractions like hot springs and consistently pleasant climates. Employees of spas are likely to receive better benefits than many of their counterparts in the cosmetology field.

■ Starting Out

A degree in esthetics, cosmetology, fitness, or massage therapy can be valuable when looking for a job in a spa. Many of these degree programs require field work, or hands-on experience and will put you in touch with salons and fitness centers. Without a degree, you may be limited in the spa treatments you're allowed to perform. But, as more and more individual hair stylists and beauty salons open day spas to accommodate all the needs of their clients, both licensed and unlicensed spa attendants will find more job opportunities.

Some people become spa attendants after gaining experience in salons, or in health care. Before going to work for the Ihilani, Rabago worked as a surgical aide. "The work is related," he said, " but it's a very different atmosphere." He learned about the spa job from a listing in the newspaper. If you're not particular about your geographic location, check travel publications for listings of resorts and spas, or visit http://www.spafinders.com on the Web, and contact the spas about job openings. *Spa Finder,* both on-line and in their print directory, lists spas according to their specialties and locations.

■ Advancement

The longer you work in a spa, the more you'll learn about the services, and the more treatments you'll be allowed to perform. Though you may start off with only an hourly wage, you can eventually receive commissions and tips; the more guests you work with, the better tips and commission you'll make. In a salon or day spa situation, you'll be working with regular customers. If they're happy with your work, they'll request your services specifically. If you have a long list of regular customers, you may choose to open your own spa. Some spa attendants advance to program directors. As program director of a spa, you can add new services, train spa attendants, determine what skin products to use, and control other details of the spa's daily practices.

■ Earnings

Salaries for spa attendants vary greatly across the country, so no significant salary survey has been conducted in recent years. Spa attendants make from minimum wage to around $10 per hour. Salaries vary according to work environment (a large resort will pay more than a small salon) and the spa attendant's responsibilities. Spa attendants are either paid by the hour or by commission (a percentage of the spa treatments performed). Spa attendants also receive tips of between 10 and 15 percent. Some spas automatically bill guests an additional percentage to cover the tip, so that the guest doesn't have to worry about having the money on hand to give to the attendant. Licensed estheticians and cosmetologists don't necessarily make more money than unlicensed spa attendants. With tips from a wealthy clientele and a commission on higher-priced services, a spa attendant at a fine hotel will make much more than an attendant in a small town day spa. Spa attendants working at hotels may also receive a variety of perks, such as discounted spa treatments, guest rooms, meals in the hotel restaurants, and travel packages.

■ Work Environment

Working among vacationers in a sunny, scenic part of the world can be very comforting. Most spa attendants work within well-decorated, temperature-controlled buildings, with soothing music piped through the speaker systems. Fresh fruit, tea, and other refreshments are often readily available. Spa attendants work directly with a public that has come to a resort to alleviate stress and other worries, making for very relaxed interactions. Some hotel spa attendants even live on the premises in special employee quarters, or in nearby housing, allowing them to live close to the beaches, mountains, or whatever natural beauty surrounds the resort.

Because spas usually open in the wee hours of the morning and close after dark, spa attendants may have to work long, irregular hours. Depending on the codes of the spa, they wear uniforms and jackets. They also wear gloves if their skin is sensitive to some of the products.

In a local beauty salon, a spa attendant tries to maintain a similarly relaxed environment in the few rooms dedicated to spa treatment. The rest of the salon, however, may be noisy with waiting customers, hair dryers, electric clippers, and music. The salon may also affect allergies with cigarette smoke and hair treatment chemicals.

■ Outlook

The number of spas is growing, and these spas are offering more services. People are becoming more health conscious, and are looking to spas for both enjoyable and educational vacations. Spas are offering more than just a respite from the stresses of daily life—they are also teaching guests new patterns of diet, exercise, and skin care. Some health care professionals are even predicting that spas will be covered by health insurance plans; doctors will write prescriptions to patients for spa treatments. To compete with other spas, and to satisfy returning guests, spas are likely to offer even more diverse lists of services and treatments. The spa attendant will have to keep ahead of health and beauty trends and be capable of adapting to new programs and methods.

Anticipating a future of "one-stop" beauty treatment, the owners of hair and beauty salons are dedicating rooms to spa treatments. For the cost of a little remodeling, hair salons can stay competitive with local day spas, as well as generate more business. Spa attendants may find their best job opportunities at these salons, where they can earn a good commission and establish a client base.

■ For More Information

For information about cosmetology schools, scholarships, and career opportunities, contact:

Cosmetology Advancement Foundation
208 East 51st Street, Suite 143
New York, NY 10022

■ Related Articles

Cosmetology

Cosmetic Sales Representatives

Cosmetologists/Hair Stylists

Electrologists

Nail Technicians

Salon Managers

Skin Care Specialists

Special Ability Extras

■ **See Film Extras**

Special Agents

■ **See Border Patrol Officers**

Special Education Teachers

■ Overview

Special education teachers teach students, aged three through 21, with a variety of disabilities. They design individualized education plans and work with students one-on-one to help them learn academic subjects and life skills.

■ The Job

Special education teachers instruct students who have a variety of disabilities. Their students may have physical disabilities, such as vision, hearing, or orthopedic impairment. They may also have learning disabilities or serious emotional disturbances. Although less common, special education teachers sometimes work with students who are gifted and talented, children who have limited proficiency in English, children who have communicable diseases, or children who are neglected and abused.

In order to teach special education students, these teachers design and modify instruction so that it is tailored to individual student needs. Teachers collaborate with school psychologists, social workers, parents, and occupational, physical, and speech-language therapists to develop a specially-designed program—called an Individualized Education Program (IEP)—for each one of their students. The IEP sets personalized goals for a student, based upon his or her learning style and ability, and outlines specific steps to prepare him or her for employment or postsecondary schooling.

Special education teachers teach at a pace that is dictated by the individual needs and abilities of their students. Unlike most regular classes, special education classes do not have an established curriculum that is taught to all students at the same time. Because student abilities vary widely, instruction is individualized and it is part of the teacher's responsibility to match specific techniques with a student's learning style and abilities. They may spend much time working with students one-on-one or in small groups.

Working with different types of students requires a variety of teaching methods. Some students may need to use special equipment or skills in the classroom in order to overcome their disabilities. For example, a teacher working with a student with a physical disability might use a computer that is operated by touching a screen or by voice commands. To work with hearing-impaired students, the teacher may need to use sign language. With visually impaired students, he or she may use teaching materials that have Braille characters or large, easy-to-see type. Gifted and talented students may need extra challenging assignments, a faster learning pace, or special attention in one curriculum area, such as art or music.

In addition to teaching academic subjects, special education teachers help students develop both emotionally and socially. They work to make students as independent as possible by teaching them functional skills for daily living. They may help young children learn basic grooming, hygiene, and table manners. Older students might be taught how to balance a checkbook, follow a recipe, or use the public transportation system.

Special education teachers meet regularly with their students' parents to inform them of their child's progress and offer suggestions of how to promote learning at home. They may also meet with school administrators, social workers, psychologists, various types of therapists, and students' general education teachers.

The current trend in education is to integrate students with disabilities into regular classrooms to the extent that it is possible and beneficial to them. This is often called "mainstreaming." As mainstreaming becomes increasingly common, special education teachers frequently work with general education teachers in general education classrooms. They may help adapt curriculum materials and teaching techniques to meet the needs of students with disabilities and offer guidance on dealing with students' emotional and behavioral problems.

In addition to working with students, special education teachers are responsible for a certain amount of paperwork. They document each student's progress and may fill out any forms that are required by the school system or the government.

■ Requirements

High School

High school students should focus on courses that will prepare them for college. These classes include natural and social sciences, mathematics, English, speech, and psychology.

SPECIAL EDUCATION TEACHERS	
SCHOOL SUBJECTS	English Speech
PERSONAL SKILLS	Communication/ideas Helping/teaching
WORK ENVIRONMENT	Primarily indoors Primarily one location
MINIMUM EDUCATION LEVEL	Bachelor's degree
SALARY RANGE	$25,000 to $38,000 to $50,000
CERTIFICATION OR LICENSING	Required by all states
OUTLOOK	Faster than the average
DOT	094
O*NET	31311

Postsecondary Training

All states require that teachers have at least a bachelor's degree and that they complete a prescribed number of subject and education credits. It is increasingly common for special education teachers to complete an additional fifth year of training after they receive their bachelor's degree. Many states require special education teachers to get a master's degree in special education.

There are approximately 700 colleges and universities in the United States that offer programs in special education, including undergraduate, master's and doctoral programs. These programs include general and specialized courses in special education, including educational psychology, legal issues of special education, child growth and development, and knowledge and skills needed for teaching students with disabilities. The student typically spends the last year of the program student-teaching in an actual classroom, under the supervision of a licensed teacher.

Certification or Licensing

All states also require that special education teachers be licensed, although the particulars of licensing vary by state. In some states, these teachers must first be certified as elementary or secondary school teachers, then meet specific requirements to teach special education. Some states offer general special education licensure; others license several different sub-specialties within special education. Some states allow special education teachers to transfer their license from one state to another, but many still require these teachers to pass licensing requirements for that state.

Other Requirements

Special education teachers need to have many of the same personal characteristics as regular classroom teachers—the ability to communicate, a broad knowledge of the arts, sciences, and history, and a love of children. In addition, these teachers need a great deal of patience and persistence. They need to be creative, flexible, cooperative, and accepting of differences in others. Finally, they need to be emotionally stable and consistent in their dealings with students.

■ Exploring

There are a number of ways for the interested high school student to explore the field of special education. One of the first and easiest might be to approach a special education teacher at his or her school and ask to talk about the job. Perhaps the teacher could provide a tour of the special education classroom, or allow the student to visit while a class is in session.

Students might also become acquainted with special-needs students at their school, or become involved in a school or community mentoring program for these stu-

A special education teacher uses sign language as she works with some deaf children.

dents. There may also be other opportunities for volunteer work or part-time jobs in the school, communities agencies, camps, or residential facilities that allow students to work with persons with disabilities.

■ Employers

The majority of special education teachers work in public school systems. The next largest group are employed by local education agencies, and a minority of others work in colleges and universities, private schools, and state education agencies.

■ Starting Out

Because public school systems are by far the largest employers of special education teachers, this is where the beginning teacher should focus his or her job search.

Since the special education teacher must have at least a bachelor's degree, he or she should have access to his or her college's career placement center. This may prove a very effective place to begin. The student may also write to the state department of education for information on placement and regulations, or contact state employment offices to enquire about job openings. Applying directly to local school systems can sometimes be effective. Even if a school system does not have an immediate opening, it will usually keep applicant resumes on file, should a vacancy occur.

■ Advancement

Advancement opportunities for special education teachers, as for regular classroom teachers, are fairly limited. It may take the form of higher wages, better facilities, or more prestige. In some cases, these teachers do advance to become supervisors or administrators, although this may require continued education on the teacher's part. Another option is for special education teachers to earn advanced degrees and become instructors at the college level.

Earnings

In some school districts, salaries for special education teachers follow the same scale as general education teachers. According to the National Education Association, the average salary for special education teachers in 1996 was $37,900. Public secondary schools paid an average of $38,600; elementary schools, $37,300. Private school teachers usually earn less as compared with their public school counterparts. Teachers can supplement their annual salaries by becoming an activity sponsor, or by summer work.

Other school districts pay their special education teachers on a separate scale, which is usually higher than that of general education teachers.

Regardless of the salary scale, special education teachers usually receive a complete benefits package, which includes health and life insurance, paid holidays and vacations, and a pension plan.

Work Environment

The special education teacher usually works from 7:30 or 8:00 AM to 3:00 or 3:30 PM. Like most teachers, however, he or she typically spends several hours in the evening grading papers, completing paperwork, or preparing lessons for the next day. Altogether, most special education teachers work more than the standard 40 hours per week.

Although some schools offer year-round classes for students, the majority of special education teachers work the traditional 10-month school year, with a two-month vacation in the summer. Many teachers find this work schedule very appealing, as it gives them the opportunity to pursue personal interests or additional education during the summer break. Teachers typically also get a week off at Christmas and for spring break.

Special education teachers work in a variety of settings in schools, including both ordinary and specially equipped classrooms, resource rooms, and therapy rooms. Some schools have newer and better facilities for special education than others. Although it is less common, some teachers work in residential facilities or tutor students who are homebound or hospitalized.

Working with special education students can be very demanding, due to their physical and emotional needs. Teachers may fight a constant battle to keep certain students, particularly those with behavior disorders, under control. Other students, such as those with mental impairments or learning disabilities, learn so slowly that it may seem as if they are making no progress. The special education teacher must deal daily with frustration, setbacks, and classroom disturbances.

These teachers must also contend with heavy workloads, including a great deal of paperwork to document each student's progress. In addition, they may sometimes be faced with irate parents who feel that their child is not receiving proper treatment or an adequate education.

The positive side of this job is in helping students overcome their disabilities and learn to be as functional as possible. For a special education teacher, knowing that he or she is making a difference in a child's life can be very rewarding and emotionally fulfilling.

Outlook

The field of special education is expected to grow much faster than the average. As projected by the U.S. Bureau of Labor Statistics, about 300,000 new jobs will be created by the year 2006. This demand is caused partly by the growth in the number of special education students needing services. Medical advances resulting in more survivors of illness and accidents, the rise in birth defects, especially in older pregnancies, as well as general population growth, are also significant factors for strong demand. Because of the rise in the number of youths with disabilities under the age of 21, the government has given approval for more federally funded programs. Growth of jobs in this field has also been influenced positively by legislation emphasizing training and employment for individuals with disabilities and a growing public awareness and interest in those with disabilities.

Finally, there is a fairly high turnover rate in this field, as special education teachers find the work too stressful and switch to mainstream teaching or change jobs altogether. Many job openings will arise out of a need to replace teachers who have left their positions. There is a shortage of qualified teachers in rural areas and in the inner city. Jobs will also be plentiful for teachers who specialize in speech and language impairments, learning disabilities, and early childhood intervention. Bilingual teachers with multicultural experience will be in high demand.

For More Information

Council of Administrators of Special Education
615 16th Street, NW
Albuquerque, NM 87104
Tel: 505-243-7622

National Clearinghouse for Professions in Special Education, Council for Exceptional Children
1920 Association Drive
Reston, VA 20191
Tel: 800-328-0272
Web: http://www.cec.sped.org

National Resource Center for Paraprofessionals in Education and Related Services
25 W. 43rd Street
New York, NY 10036
Tel: 212-642-2948

Special Effects Camera Operators

■ See Camera Operators

Special Effects Technicians

■ Overview

Special effects technicians work to make the illusion of movies, theater, and television seem real. When a director wants us to see a man turn into a wolf or a train explode in a fiery crash, it is the job of special effects technicians to make it happen. They work with a variety of materials and techniques to produce the fantastic visions and seemingly real illusions that add dimension to a film.

■ History

At the turn of the century a French magician turned filmmaker named Georges Melies invented motion picture special effects. To film futuristic space flight in *A Trip to the Moon,* he made a model of a rocket and fired it from a cannon in front of an illusionistic, painted backdrop. By the 1920s, special effects, or "tricks," had become a department of the major film studios, and technicians were steadily inventing new techniques and illusions. For a tornado scene in *The Wizard of Oz,* a miniature house was filmed falling from the studio ceiling, and when the film was reversed it became Dorothy's house flying into the air. Effects departments still make extensive use of miniature models, which are easy to work with and save money.

In 1950 the Supreme Court broke up the movie studio monopolies. Independent, low-budget films began to proliferate and to affect audience tastes. They helped to make realistic, on-site shoots fashionable, and studio special effects departments became virtually extinct. It wasn't until the 1970s, when George Lucas brought his imagination and effects to *Star Wars,* that special effects were revived in force. The crew that Lucas assembled for that project formed the company Industrial Light & Magic (ILM),

which still commands prestige in a field that now includes hundreds of large and small special effects companies. ILM is responsible for the effects in over 100 feature films, including 6 of the top 10 box office hits in movie history.

The industry toyed with computer generated imagery (CGI) in the 1980s, with such films as *Tron* and *Star Trek II.* By the 1990s, the movie-going public was ready for an effects revolution which began with James Cameron's *The Abyss* and *Terminator 2: Judgment Day,* and reached full-force with 1993's *Jurassic Park. Twister* in 1996, *Titanic* in 1997, and *The Matrix* in 1999 raised the stakes for movie effects, and *Star Wars: Episode I—The Phantom Menace* used 2,000 digital shots (compared to *Titanic's* 500). Digital inking and painting, along with a software program called Deep Canvas, gave Disney's *Tarzan* its great depth and dimension and detail unlike any other film in the history of animation.

■ The Job

Special effects technicians are craftsmen who work in a variety of areas to provide seamless, illusionistic effects for film, television, and stage productions. Their work is very creative; they read scripts and consult with the director to determine the kinds of effects that will be required. Often the director has only a general idea of what he or she wants; technicians come up with the artistic specifics and functional designs, and then create what they have designed.

There are several trades that make up special effects, and special effects companies, known as shops, may do business in one or several of these trades. The services they may offer include mechanical effects, computer animation, make-up effects, and pyrotechnics.

Mechanical effects specialists build the props, sets, and backdrops for film, television, and theater productions. They

SPECIAL EFFECTS TECHNICIANS	
SCHOOL SUBJECTS	Chemistry Computer science
PERSONAL SKILLS	Mechanical/manipulative Technical/scientific
WORK ENVIRONMENT	Indoors and Outdoors Primarily multiple locations
MINIMUM EDUCATION LEVEL	Some postsecondary training
SALARY RANGE	$100 per day to $200 per day to $300 per day
CERTIFICATION OR LICENSING	Required for certain positions
OUTLOOK	About as fast as the average
DOT	962
GOE	01.06.02
NOC	5226
O*NET	34026

build, install, and operate equipment, working with a variety of materials depending on the effects required. They are usually skilled in several areas, including carpentry, welding, electricity, and robotics.

Computer animation specialists use computer programs to create effects that would be impossible or too costly to build otherwise. Computer animation, or computer generated imagery (CGI), has made advances into television commercials as well as film. These effects make it possible for a human face to transform or "morph" into an animal's, or for a realistic looking bear to drink from a soda can. Computer animation specialists typically work in offices, not on location as other specialists do. They must be highly skilled with computers and keep abreast of new technology.

Make-up effects specialists create elaborate costumes and masks for actors to wear in movies or on stage. They also build prosthetic devices to simulate human or animal heads and limbs. They may be skilled at modeling, sewing, applying make-up, and mixing dyes.

Pyrotechnic effects specialists are experts with explosives and firearms. They create explosions for dramatic scenes. Their work can be very dangerous, and they are required to be licensed in most states in order to handle and set off explosives.

Specialists who are union members are contracted to provide a specific service and rarely work outside their area of expertise. Nonunion people may be required to help out with tasks that fall outside the union members' areas of expertise. This may involve constructing sets, moving heavy equipment, or helping with last-minute design changes.

■ Requirements

High School

As a special effects technician, you'll rely on a mix of science and art. Take all the art courses you can, including art history; many filmmakers look to classical art when composing shots and lighting effects. Photography courses will help you understand the use of light and shadow. Chemistry can give you some insight into the products you'll be using. To work with computer animation, you should have an understanding of many of the latest graphics programs.

Postsecondary Training

While there are no formal educational requirements for becoming a special effects technician, some universities have film and television programs that include courses in special effects. Some special effects technicians major in theater, art history, photography, and related subjects. The masters of fine arts degrees offered at colleges across the country are studio programs in which you'll be able to gain hands-on experience in theater production and filmmaking with a faculty composed of practicing artists.

Some of the CGI technicians working today have not had any special schooling or training, having mastered graphics programs on their own. Light Matters-Pixel Envy, the digital effects company that created the iceberg for *Titanic* and the UFO for *The X-Files*, is partly owned by brothers Greg and Colin Strause who are in their early 20s. Greg used money intended for college to invest in a processor and software.

Certification or Licensing

To work as a pyrotechnics specialist, you will need a license in most states in order to handle explosives and firearms.

Other Requirements

Special effects work is physically and mentally demanding. Technicians must be able to work as members of a team, following instructions carefully in order to avoid dangerous situations. They often work long days, so they must possess stamina. In addition, the work on a set can be uncomfortable; a mechanical effects specialist may have to work under adverse weather conditions or wait patiently in a small space for the cue to operate an effect. Freelance technicians will often have to provide their own tools and equipment, which they either own or rent, when hired for a job.

Computer animation specialists may sit for long hours in front of a computer, performing meticulous and sometimes repetitive work. Make-up effects specialists spend most of their time working in a trailer on the set or in a shop where they construct and adjust the items required by the actors. Special effects technicians must work both carefully and quickly; a mistake or a delay can become very expensive for the production company.

■ Exploring

Students who like to build things, or who tend to be curious about how things work, might be well suited to a career in special effects. To learn more about the profession, visit your school or public library and bookstores to read more about the field. Browse magazine racks to find Hollywood trade magazines and other related material on your area of interest; *Animation Journal, Cinefex, Daily Variety,* and *Hollywood Reporter* are good places to start. Some of these publications also maintain Web sites.

Since experience and jobs are difficult to get in the film and television industry, it is important to learn about the career to be sure it is right for you. Working on high-school drama productions as a stage hand, "techie," or make-up artist can be helpful for learning set and prop design, methods of handling equipment, and artistry. Community theaters and independent filmmakers can provide volunteer work experience; they rely on volunteers because they have limited operating funds.

Alternatively, if you find you are adept in computer classes and curious about advances in computer animation, you may wish to pursue this field by continuing your learning and exploration of computer techniques.

■ Employers

The top special effects technicians work for special effects houses. These companies contract with individual film productions; one film may have the effects created by more than one special effects company. ILM is the top company, having done the effects for such films as *Men in Black, Star Wars: Episode I,* and *Wild Wild West.* Other major companies include Digital Domain (*Titanic*), Blue Sky/VIFX (*Armageddon*), and Banned From the Ranch (*Starship Troopers*). The top effects houses, along with links to their Web sites, are listed at the Visual Effects Headquarters Archives Web site (http://www.vfxhq.com). Some special effects technicians own their own effects company or work on a freelance basis. Freelance technicians may work in several areas, doing theater work, film and television productions, and commercials.

■ Starting Out

Internships are a very good way to gain experience and make yourself a marketable job candidate. Film and theater companies are predominantly located in Los Angeles or New York City, but there are opportunities elsewhere. Again, since theater and lower-budget film productions operate with limited funds, you could find places to work for course credit or experience instead of a salary.

Special effects shops are excellent places to try for an internship. You may find them in books and trade magazines, or try the yellow pages under Theatrical Equipment, Theatrical Make-up, and Theatrical and Stage Lighting Equipment. Even if one shop has no opportunities, it may be able to provide the name of another that takes interns.

You should keep a photographic record of all the work you do for theater and film productions, including photos

OSCARS

Films of the 1990s that have been awarded Oscars in the category of Special Effects:

1998: *What Dreams May Come*
1997: *Titanic*
1996: *Independence Day*
1995: *Babe*
1994: *Forrest Gump*
1993: *Jurassic Park*
1992: *Death Becomes Her*
1991: *Terminator 2: Judgment Day*
1990: *Total Recall*

of any drawings or sculptures you've done for art classes. It's important to have a portfolio or demo reel (a reel of film demonstrating your work) to send along with your resume to effects shops, makeup departments, and producers.

Special effects technicians may choose to join a union; some film studios will only hire union members. The principal union for special effects technicians is the International Alliance of Theatrical Stage Employees and Moving Picture Machine Operators of the United States and Canada (IATSE). To get into the union, a technician must complete a training program which includes apprenticing in a prop-making shop and passing an examination. Union members work under a union contract that determines their work rules, pay, and benefits.

■ Advancement

Good special effects technicians will acquire skills in several areas, becoming versatile and therefore desirable employees. Since many work freelance, it is useful to develop a good reputation and maintain contacts from past jobs. Successful technicians may be chosen to work on increasingly prestigious and challenging productions. Once they have a strong background and diverse experience, technicians may start their own shops.

■ Earnings

Some technicians have steady, salaried employment, while others work freelance for an hourly rate and may have periods with no work. The average daily rate for beginning technicians is $100 to $200 per day, while more experienced technicians can earn $300 per day or more. A 1998 member salary survey conducted by IATSE shows that employment in digital effects can pay very well, even in assistant positions. When adjusted to show annual figures, the survey found that character animators, CGI effects animators, and art directors had median yearly earnings of around $100,000. On the low end of the scale, these professionals earned around $55,000, and on the high end,

$350,000. Effects assistants had beginning wages of around $45,000, and median wages of $60,000.

Those working freelance won't have the benefits of full-time work, having to provide their own health insurance. Those working for special effects houses have the usual benefit packages including health insurance, bonuses, and retirement.

■ Work Environment

Special effects is an excellent field for someone who likes to dream up fantastic monsters and machines and has the patience to create them. Special effects technicians must be willing to work long hours, and have the stamina to work under strenuous conditions. Twelve hour days are not uncommon, and to meet a deadline technicians may work for 15 hours a day. Many special effects technicians work freelance, so there can be long periods of no work (and no pay) between jobs.

Because motion picture scripts often call for filming at various locations, special effects technicians may travel a great deal. Work environments can vary considerably; a technician may remain in a shop or at a computer terminal, or may go on location for a film or television shoot and work outdoors.

■ Outlook

According to *Forbes* magazine, the film industry spent over $600 million in special effects in 1997 (twice as much as in 1993, the year *Jurassic Park* premiered). The competition for jobs in film special effects houses is fierce. For over 20 years now, films of all genres have incorporated computer graphics and high-tech effects, inspiring a whole generation of young people with computers and imaginations. Many of today's top effects professionals credit their love for *Star Wars* with directing them toward careers in the industry. As the cost of powerful computers continues to decrease, even more people will be able to experiment with computer graphics and develop their skills and talents.

Though some special effects companies, such as Light Matters-Pixel Envy mentioned above, are very profitable, others are struggling to make enough money to meet their expenses. Production companies are attempting to tighten their budgets and to turn out movies quickly. Therefore, a contract for special effects goes to the lowest bidding effects company. Despite *Titanic*'s $40 million effects budget, Digital Domain (the company that produced the effects) has yet to see a profit from the film. The cost of the effects, including salaries for top technicians, are increasing, while film producers decrease their special effects budgets. This will either be corrected by effects companies demanding more money, or only a few of the very top companies will be able to thrive.

Digital technology will continue to rapidly change the industry. Experts predict that within 10 years, film will be eliminated and movies will be shot and projected digitally, enhancing computer effects. Filmmakers will edit their movies over the Internet. And it may not be long before filmmakers are able to make entire movies with CGI, employing only digital actors. Virtual Celebrities, a division of a celebrity licensing company, is a computer studio experimenting with taking screen images of past and present film stars and digitally creating new films and performances.

■ For More Information

For information about colleges with film and television programs of study, and to read interviews with filmmakers, visit the AFI Web site:

American Film Institute
2021 North Western Avenue
Los Angeles, CA 90027
Tel: 323-856-7600
Web: http://www.afionline.org

For extensive information about the digital effects industry, visit the AWN Web site. The site includes feature articles, a guide to education-related resources, and a career section:

Animation World Network
6525 Sunset Boulevard, Garden Suite 10
Hollywood, CA 90028
Tel: 323-468-2554
Web: http://www.awn.com

For information about festivals and presentations, and news about the industry, contact:

The Visual Effects Society
15118 Valley Vista Boulevard
Sherman Oaks, CA 91403
Tel: 818-789-7083
Web: http://www.visual-effects-society.org

■ Related Articles

Computers
Film
Television
Visual Arts
Actors
Art Directors
Broadcast Engineers
Camera Operators
Cartoonists and Animators
Cinematographers and Directors of Photography
Film Editors
Graphic Designers
Graphics Programmers
Lighting Technicians
Photographers
Producers

Special Event Coordinators

■ **See Event Planners**

Special Procedures Technologists

■ Overview

Special procedures technologists are trained individuals who operate medical diagnostic imaging equipment such as computer tomography (CT) and magnetic resonance imaging (MRI) scanners, and assist in imaging procedures such as angiography and cardiac catheterization (CC). They are employed in various health care settings such as hospitals, clinics, and imaging centers. The need for their skills will continue to be in high demand as the population ages and cancer and heart disease continue to be major health concerns.

■ History

Advances in medical technology have resulted in more sophisticated patient testing using more complex equipment. As this technology has become more sophisticated, the need for trained personnel to assist physicians and specially trained technologists to operate this equipment became apparent. In addition, trained personnel became essential to perform and document the testing procedures, as well as to assist with the patients. The special procedures technologist career field evolved from this need. Technologists are trained to understand the operation of some of the testing equipment and to assist medical personnel as they perform these tests. They are also taught how to position patients during the testing and how to deal with any fears and anxieties they might have during the procedures.

■ The Job

Special procedures technologists' duties vary depending on the training they have with specific diagnostic equipment and testing procedures. Job requirements also vary with the degree of assistance required for certain testing and diagnostic procedures.

Special procedures technologists may assist *radiologic technologists* with positioning a patient for examination, immobilizing them, preparing the equipment, and monitoring the equipment and patient's progress during the procedure. An *angiographer* is a special procedures technologist who assists with a procedure called an angiogram, which shows any changes that may have occurred to the blood vessels of the patient's circulatory system. The special procedures technologist may assist with many aspects of this test. Similarly, some special procedures technologists may assist *cardiologists* with the invasive procedure called cardiac catheterization by positioning the patients and explaining to them the procedures performed. They may also monitor and document the patients' vital signs such as blood pressure and respiration and enter that information directly into a computer that controls testing procedures. Some special procedures technologists may assist with CT scanning (also known as CAT scanning), which combines X rays with computer technology to create clear, cross-section images that provide more details than standard X rays with minimal radiation exposure. The *CT technologist* might enter data into the scanner's computer control, which includes the type of scan to be performed, the time required, and the thickness of the cross section. The technologist might also observe and reassure the patient while the testing procedure is performed. Another imaging procedure called magnetic resonance imaging (MRI) produces the most detailed and flexible images among the various imaging techniques. A special procedures technologist often assists with this procedure by explaining the test to the patient and making certain that the patient is not carrying any metal objects that could be hazardous to the patient during the test and could also damage the equipment. The *MRI technologist* might enter the necessary data, such as

SPECIAL PROCEDURES TECHNOLOGISTS	
SCHOOL SUBJECTS	Biology Chemistry
PERSONAL SKILLS	Helping/teaching Technical/scientific
WORK ENVIRONMENT	Primarily indoors Primarily one location
MINIMUM EDUCATION LEVEL	Associate's degree
SALARY RANGE	$13,000 to $25,000 to $30,000
CERTIFICATION OR LICENSING	Required by all states
OUTLOOK	Faster than the average
DOT	078
GOE	10.02.02
O*NET	32919

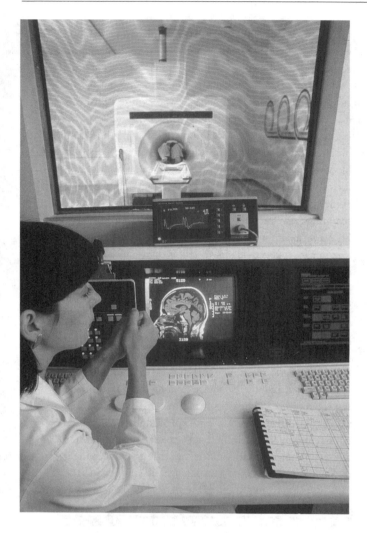

A special procedures technician operates a magnetic resonance imaging scanner.

patient information, the orientation of the scan, and the part of the body to be scanned into the computer. The technologist might initiate the scan and observe the patient through a window in the control room and on a closed-circuit video display, while maintaining voice contact and reassuring the patient.

■ Requirements

High School

High school classes that help you prepare for further education as a special procedures technologist include advanced courses in anatomy, physiology, math, and physics. Classes in communication such as speech and English, and classes that reinforce written and verbal skills are also helpful. Because most imaging specialties depend heavily on computer technology, you should gain a good understanding of the use of computers. Studies regarding various cultures will also help you deal with patients from various backgrounds.

Postsecondary Training

After receiving a high school diploma, you will have to attend a two-year program and earn an associate's degree in radiology before finding employment. These programs can be found at community colleges, vocational and technical training schools, or in the military. Most radiology technologists receive training through a program accredited by the American Medical Association's Committee on Allied Health Education and Accreditation (CAHEA). In all cases, special procedures technologists must complete additional training, usually offered through a hospital, medical center, college, or vocational or technical training school, in their specialty area.

Certification or Licensing

Graduates of accredited programs are eligible to take the four-hour certification examination offered by the American Registry of Radiologic Technologists (ARRT). In addition, federal legislation has made licensing for radiologic technologists a requirement. This requirement is usually satisfied by successfully receiving ARRT certification. Certification requirements vary by state for the individual special procedures. Where certification is available, technologists are strongly advised to complete those requirements, which will enhance employment opportunities.

Other Requirements

You should have an interest in medicine and compassion for patients to be a successful special procedures technologist. You should have an aptitude for science and math and have strong communication skills. In addition, you should be conscientious, responsible, efficient, and have the ability to work under stress and in emergency situations. You should also work well with people, both independently and as a part of a team. Manual dexterity and stamina are also required.

■ Employers

Special procedures technologists are employed in a variety of health care settings. Hospitals are the most likely source for employment, especially for techniques such as CT and MRI scanning, which require costly equipment. Health maintenance organizations and other health care clinics and centers also hire personnel trained to carry out the variety of testing procedures needed for medical care. Diagnostic imaging centers that are specifically dedicated to performing special imaging procedures are also likely employers. Also, the U.S. government employs radiologic and other imaging personnel, usually through the

Department of Veterans Affairs or as members of the armed forces.

■ Starting Out

If you are interested in entering the health care field, you can begin your involvement while still in high school. Most hospitals, nursing homes, mental health centers, and other treatment facilities have volunteer programs that allow you to explore the health care environment and gain insight into medicine and patient care. Students may also be able to find part-time work as a nurse's aide.

Most special procedures technologists begin their careers as radiology technologists and then receive additional training in their special procedure. Many technologists find employment through their school's placement service. Some trade journals and area newspapers also list job opportunities. Applying directly to health care and imaging facilities may also produce results.

■ Advancement

Advancement in special procedures fields is generally limited as these specialties already represent advanced areas of radiology. With experience, however, a special procedures technologist may advance to greater responsibilities and to supervisory positions. In addition, the field may be a valuable bridge to a more advanced medical career such as a doctor. Skills of a special procedures technologist are in demand in the United States and other countries as well, so there is a possibility of travel to, or employment in, other countries that recognize U.S. certification.

■ Earnings

Salaries for the different branches of special imaging procedures vary by type of procedure, geographic location, type of employer, and experience level. Salaries for special procedures technologists range from as little as $13,000 a year to as much as $30,000 a year. Radiologic technologists in general averaged $559 a week, or about $29,000 a year according to U.S. Department of Labor statistics for 1996.

Benefits vary widely. Most benefit packages, however, include paid vacation and holidays, as well as sick leave, and medical and dental insurance. Some employers may offer additional benefits such as on-site day care and tuition reimbursement.

■ Work Environment

Special procedures technologists usually work in one of several departments within a hospital or medical testing facility or clinic. These departments have rooms set up to perform specific tests, such as cardiac catheterization, MRIs, or CAT scans. The testing is usually done as part of a medical team; however, some of the setup may have to be done independently so technologists may be required to make critical decisions.

Daily schedules and shifts may vary according to the size of the hospital, the number of patients requiring testing, and the type of imaging techniques performed. Although a technologist may be scheduled to work an eight-hour shift, the health care environment is often unpredictable and longer hours may be required. Because technologists deal with sick and dying people, and medical personnel are often required to make life and death decisions, the job can be quite stressful.

■ Outlook

The outlook for employment in the special procedures technologist field is excellent. As the population ages and heart disease and cancer continue to be among the primary health concerns in the U.S., there will continue to be a high demand for skilled technologists to assist in the diagnosis, prevention, and treatment of these and other conditions. Also, as more and more sophisticated testing and imaging procedures are developed, and as new techniques become available, the demand for skilled technologists to operate, perform, and assist in these procedures will continue to grow.

■ For More Information

The following organizations provide information on special procedures technologists careers, accredited schools, and employment opportunities.

American Society of Nuclear Cardiology
911 Old Georgetown Road
Bethesda, MD 20814-1699
Tel: 301-493-2360
Web: http://www.asnc.org

Cardiovascular Credentialing International
4456 Corporation Lane, Suite 120
Virginia Beach, VA 23462
Tel: 804-497-3380

American Medical Technologists
710 Higgins Road
Park Ridge, IL 60068
Tel: 847-823-5169

American Registry of Radiologic Technologists
1255 Northland Drive
St. Paul, MN 55120
Tel: 612-687-0048

American Registry of Clinical Radiography Technologists
710 Higgins Road
Park Ridge, IL 60068
Tel: 847-318-9050

Committee on Allied Health and Accreditation
515 North State Street
Chicago, IL 60610
Tel: 312-464-4636

■ **Related Articles**

Health Care
Biomedical Equipment Technicians
Cardiovascular Technologists
Diagnostic Medical Sonographers
Dialysis Technicians
Electroneurodiagnostic Technologists
Nuclear Medicine Technologists
Radiologic Technologists

Speech-Language Pathologists and Audiologists

■ Overview

Speech-language pathologists and audiologists help people who have speech and hearing defects. They identify the problem, then use tests to further evaluate it. Speech-language pathologists and audiologists also try to improve the speech and hearing defect by treating the patient. Some speech-language pathologists and audiologists take their

SPEECH-LANGUAGE PATHOLOGISTS AND AUDIOLOGISTS	
SCHOOL SUBJECTS	Health Speech
PERSONAL SKILLS	Helping/teaching Technical/scientific
WORK ENVIRONMENT	Primarily indoors Primarily one location
MINIMUM EDUCATION LEVEL	Master's degree
SALARY RANGE	$32,000 to $44,000 to $55,000
CERTIFICATION OR LICENSING	Required by all states
OUTLOOK	Faster than the average
DOT	076
GOE	02.03.04
NOC	3141
O*NET	32314

expertise to the classroom to teach others, or they may investigate what causes certain speech and hearing defects through research.

Speech-language pathologists specialize in problems with speech disorders; audiologists work with hearing disorders. It's not uncommon for patients to require assistance in both areas, so the specialists may work together to help the patient.

■ History

The diagnosis and treatment of speech and hearing defects is a new part of medical science. In the past, physicians weren't able to help patients with these types of problems because there was usually nothing visibly wrong, and little was known about how speech and hearing were related. Until the middle of the 19th century, medical researchers didn't know whether speech defects were caused by lack of hearing, or whether the patient was the victim of two separate ailments. And even if they could figure out why something was wrong, doctors still couldn't communicate with the patient.

Alexander Graham Bell (1847-1922), the inventor of the telephone, provided some of the answers. His grandfather taught elocution (the art of public speaking), and Bell grew up interested in the problems of speech and hearing. It became his profession, and, by 1871, Bell was lecturing to a class of teachers of deaf people at Boston University. Soon afterward, Bell opened his own school, where he experimented with the idea of making speech visible to his pupils. If he could make them see the movements made by different human tones, they could speak by learning to produce similar vibrations. Bell's efforts not only helped deaf people of his day, but also led directly to the invention of the telephone in 1876. Probably the most famous deaf person was Helen Keller (1880-1968), whose teacher, Anne Sullivan (1866-1936), applied the discoveries of Bell to help Keller overcome her blindness and deafness.

■ The Job

Even though the two professions seem to blend together at times, speech-language pathology and audiology are very different from one another. However, because both speech and hearing are related to one another, a person competent in one must have familiarity with the other.

The duties performed by speech-language pathologists and audiologists differ depending on education and experience and place of employment. Most speech-language pathologists provide direct clinical services to individuals and independently develop and carry out treatment programs. In medical facilities, they may work with *physicians, social workers, psychologists,* and other therapists to develop and execute treatment plans. In a school environment, they develop individual or group programs, counsel parents, and sometimes help teachers with classroom activities.

Clients of speech-language pathologists include people who cannot make speech sounds, or cannot make them clearly; those with speech rhythm and fluency problems such as stuttering; people with voice quality problems, such as inappropriate pitch or harsh voice; those with problems understanding and producing language; and those with cognitive communication impairments, such as attention, memory, and problem solving disorders. Speech-language pathologists may also work with people who have oral motor problems causing eating and swallowing difficulties. Patients' problems may be congenital, developmental, or acquired and caused by hearing loss, brain injury or deterioration, cerebral palsy, stroke, cleft palate, voice pathology, mental retardation, or emotional problems.

Speech-language pathologists conduct written and oral tests and use special instruments to analyze and diagnose the nature and extent of impairment. They develop an individualized plan of care, which may include automated devices and sign language. They teach these individuals how to make sounds, improve their voices, or increase their language skills to communicate more effectively. Speech-language pathologists help patients develop, or recover, reliable communication skills.

People who have hearing, balance, and related problems consult audiologists, who use audiometers and other testing devices to discover the nature and extent of hearing loss. Audiologists interpret these results and may coordinate them with medical, educational, and psychological information to make a diagnosis and determine a course of treatment.

Hearing disorders can result from trauma at birth, viral infections, genetic disorders, or exposure to loud noise. Treatment may include examining and cleaning the ear canal, fitting and dispensing a hearing aid or other device, and audiologic rehabilitation (including auditory training or instruction in speech or lip reading). Audiologists provide fitting and tuning of cochlear implants and help implant patients adjust to their implant amplification systems. They also test noise levels in workplaces and conduct hearing protection programs in industry, as well as in schools and communities.

Audiologists provide direct clinical services to clients and sometimes develop and implement individual treatment programs. In some environments, however, they work as members of professional teams in planning and implementing treatment plans.

In a research environment, speech pathologists and audiologists investigate communicative disorders and their causes and ways to improve clinical services. Those teaching in colleges and universities instruct students on the principles

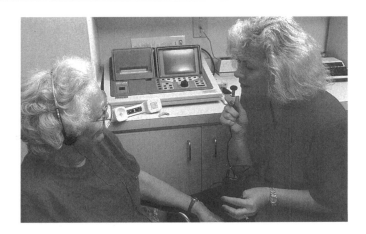

A speech-lanugage pathologist evaluates an elderly patient.

and bases of communication, communication disorders, and clinical techniques used in speech and hearing.

Speech-language pathologists and audiologists keep records on the initial evaluation, progress, and discharge of clients to identify problems and track progress. They counsel individuals and their families on how to cope with the stress and misunderstanding that often accompany communication disorders.

■ Requirements

Postsecondary Training

Most states require a master's degree in speech-language pathology or audiology for a beginning job in either profession. Undergraduate study in speech-language pathology and audiology should include courses in anatomy, biology, physiology, physics, and other related areas, such as linguistics, semantics, and phonetics. It's also helpful to have some exposure to child psychology.

There are many opportunities for graduate work in speech-language pathology and audiology. About 230 universities and colleges in the United States offer graduate programs in speech-language pathology; about 120 colleges and universities offer graduate programs in audiology. Course work involves extensive training in the fundamental areas of speech and hearing, such as acoustics, the psychological aspects of communication, the nature of hearing and speech disorders, and analysis of speech and auditory processes.

Certification or Licensing

Speech pathologists and audiologists working in the public schools are required to be certified teachers and must meet special state requirements if treating children with disabilities.

In most states, one must be licensed to offer speech-language pathology or audiology services in other than a school setting—in private practice or in a clinic, for example. The American Speech-Language-Hearing Association offers speech-language pathologists the Certificate of Clinical Competence in Speech-Language Pathology (CCC-SLP), and audiologists the Certificate of Clinical Competence in Audiology (CCC-A). To apply for certification, applicants must have earned a graduate degree in speech-language pathology or audiology and 375 hours of supervised clinical experience, and have completed a postgraduate clinical fellowship. An examination must also be passed. Some states may have additional requirements.

■ Exploring

Although the specialized nature of the work makes it difficult for those interested in speech-language pathology and audiology to get an informal introduction to either profession, there are opportunities to be found. Official training must begin at the college or university level, but it is possible for interested students to volunteer in clinics and hospitals. Prospective speech-language pathologists and audiologists also can learn sign language, or volunteer their time in speech, language, and hearing centers.

■ Employers

According to the *Occupational Outlook Handbook,* there were about 87,000 speech-language pathologists and audiologists employed in 1996, almost one-half of whom were employed in education, from elementary school to the university level. Others worked in speech, language, and hearing centers; hospitals; nursing homes; and physicians' offices. A small but growing number of speech-language pathologists and audiologists were in private practice, generally working with patients referred to them by physicians and other health practitioners.

Some speech-language pathologists and audiologists contract to provide services in schools, hospitals, or nursing homes, or work as consultants to industry. Audiologists are more likely to be employed in independent health care offices, while speech-language pathologists are more likely to work in school settings.

■ Starting Out

If you want to work in the public school systems, the college placement office can help you with interviewing skills. Professors sometimes know of job openings and may even post these openings on a centrally located bulletin board. It may be possible to find employment by contacting a hospital or rehabilitation center. To work in colleges and universities as a specialist in the classroom, clinic, or research center, it is almost mandatory to be working on a graduate degree. Many scholarships, fellowships, and grants for

assistants are available in colleges and universities giving courses in speech-language pathology and audiology. Most of these and other assistance programs are offered at the graduate level. The U.S. Rehabilitation Services Administration, the Children's Bureau, the U.S. Department of Education, and the National Institutes of Health allocate funds for teaching and training grants to colleges and universities with graduate study programs. In addition, the Department of Veterans Affairs provides stipends (a fixed allowance) for predoctoral work.

■ Advancement

Advancement in speech-language pathology and audiology is based chiefly on education. Individuals who have completed graduate study will have the best opportunities to enter research and administrative areas, supervising other speech-language pathologists or audiologists either in developmental work or in public school systems.

■ Earnings

According to a 1997 salary survey conducted by the American Speech-Language-Hearing Association, full-time, certified speech-language pathologists earned an average salary of $44,000; audiologists averaged $43,000. Pathologists, with one to three years experience, earned a median salary of $38,000, according to this survey. Beginning audiologists earned $32,000. Experienced pathologists, averaged $52,000 annually; audiologists earned $55,000. Geographic location and type of facility are important salary variables. Almost all employment situations provide fringe benefits such as paid vacations, sick leave, and retirement programs.

■ Work Environment

Most speech-language pathologists and audiologists work 40 hours a week at a desk or table in clean comfortable surroundings. Speech-language pathologists and audiologists who focus on research, however, may work longer hours. The job is not physically demanding but does require attention to detail and intense concentration. The emotional needs of clients and their families may be demanding.

■ Outlook

Population growth, lengthening life spans, and increased public awareness of the problems associated with communicative disorders indicate a highly favorable employment outlook for well-qualified personnel. This field is expected to grow much faster than the average through the year 2006. Much depends on economic factors, further budget cutbacks by health care providers and third-party payers, and legal mandates requiring services for people with disabilities.

Nearly half of the new jobs emerging through the end of the decade are expected to be in speech and hearing clinics, physicians' offices, and outpatient care facilities. Speech-language pathologists and audiologists will be needed in these places, for example, to carry out the increasing number of rehabilitation programs for stroke victims and patients with head injuries.

Substantial job growth has already occurred in elementary and secondary schools because of the Education for All Handicapped Children Act of 1975 and the Individuals with Disabilities Education Act in 1990. Such laws guarantee special education and related services to minors with disabilities.

Many new jobs will be created in hospitals, nursing homes, rehabilitation centers, and home health agencies; most of these openings will probably be filled by private practitioners employed on a contract basis. Opportunities for speech-language pathologists and audiologists in private practice should increase in the future. There should be a greater demand for consultant audiologists in the area of industrial and environmental noise as manufacturing and other companies develop and carry out noise-control programs.

■ For More Information

The American Auditory Society (AAS) is concerned with hearing disorders, how to prevent them, and the rehabilitation of individuals with hearing and balance dysfunction.

American Auditory Society
1966 Inwood Road
Dallas, TX 75235
Tel: 602-789-0755

This professional, scientific, and credentialing association offers information about communication disorders, and career and membership information.

American Speech-Language-Hearing Association
10801 Rockville Pike
Rockville, MD 20852
Tel: 301-897-5700
Web: http://www.asha.org

For information on campus chapters, contact:

National Student Speech, Language, and Hearing Association
10801 Rockville Pike
Rockville, MD 20852
Tel: 301-897-5700

■ Related Articles

Health Care

Social Services

Ear, Nose, and Throat Specialists

Psychologists

Sign Language and Oral Interpreters

Social Workers

Spin Doctors
■ **See Press Secretaries**

Sponge Buffers
■ **See Plastics Products Manufacturing Workers**

Sporting Goods Production Workers

■ Overview

Sporting goods production workers are involved in manufacturing, assembling, and finishing sporting goods equipment such as golf clubs, fishing tackle, basketballs, footballs, skis, and baseball equipment. Their tasks range from operating machines to fine hand-crafting of equipment.

SPORTING GOODS PRODUCTION WORKERS	
SCHOOL SUBJECTS	Physical education Technical/Shop
PERSONAL SKILLS	Following instructions Mechanical/manipulative
WORK ENVIRONMENT	Primarily indoors Primarily one location
MINIMUM EDUCATION LEVEL	High school diploma
SALARY RANGE	Minimum wage to $17,680 to $30,000
CERTIFICATION OR LICENSING	None available
OUTLOOK	Little change or more slowly than the average
DOT	732
GOE	06.04.34
NOC	9619
O*NET	93956

■ History

Throughout human history, every society and culture has developed games and sports for relaxation and competition. Modern technology has been applied to many aspects of sport and given us such things as better protective padding, livelier tennis rackets, and stronger golf balls. Computers are used to improve the design and composition of sports gear. The equipment used in each sport is unique in design and manufacture and is put together by skilled specialists.

■ The Job

Every sport involves its own equipment, and each kind of equipment is made somewhat differently. Basketballs and volleyballs are made by approximately the same process, which differs from the processes for making footballs and baseballs. But the manufacturing processes for sporting goods and for other products are also similar in many ways.

As in the manufacturing of other products, *machine operators* control large machine tools, such as presses, and smaller tools, such as saws and sewing machines. After they have done their tasks, they may pass the work on to different kinds of assemblers. *Floor assemblers* operate large machines and power tools; *bench assemblers* work with smaller machines to complete a product and perhaps to test it; *precision assemblers* perform highly skilled assembly work. They may work closely with engineers and technicians to develop and test new products and designs. These general categories can be applied to many of the occupations involved in sporting goods manufacturing, although the job titles vary with different kinds of products.

In the manufacturing of golf equipment, for example, the shaft of a golf club and the head, or club end, are made separately, then assembled, weighted, and balanced. *Golf-club assemblers* do much of the work. They use bench-mounted circular saws to cut the shaft for a club to a specified length, depending on the model of club being made. *Golf-club head formers* hammer precast metal club heads to the correct angle, then glue the proper club head onto a shaft and secure the head by drilling a small hole and inserting a pin. Wooden clubs are glued together the same way, except that once the assembly has dried, the weight of the club is checked and adjusted for the model type. Assemblers or *golf-club weighters* can adjust the weight by drilling a hole into the head and adding molten lead or threaded cylindrical metal weights.

Grip wrappers attach the handle of the golf club. They insert a club in a rotating machine, brush adhesive on the shaft, attach a leather strap, and then carefully spin the shaft to cover it tightly and evenly with the leather strap. When they are finished, they trim the excess leather and fasten the grip in place with tape or a sleeve. Finally, *golf-*

club head inspectors examine the head to verify that it conforms to specifications.

The manufacturing of fishing equipment is another instance of a production process involving a series of workers. It begins with *fishing-rod markers,* who mark the places on rod blanks where the line guides and decorative markings should be put. After this, *fishing-rod assemblers* use liquid cement to attach the hardware, such as reel seats, handles, and line guides, onto the rods. Line guides can also be attached with thread by guide winders, who decorate the rods by winding thread around them at intervals. Finally, *fishing-reel assemblers* assemble the parts of the intricate reel mechanisms, test the reels, and then attach them to rods.

Some processes used in manufacturing sporting goods, such as lathing (which is used in making baseball bats) and vulcanizing (which is used in making hockey pucks), are commonly used in making many other products too. But other processes are more specialized. To make basketballs, volleyballs, and soccer balls, for example, *ball assemblers* cement panels of rubberized fabric onto a hollow, spherical frame made of wax. A door opening is left in the ball carcass so that the wax frame can be broken and removed piece by piece. Once this is done, a bladder is inserted into the ball and inflated to a specific pressure. The flaps of the door opening are then aligned with the other seams of the ball and cemented onto the bladder, and the ball is complete.

Some baseball equipment is still made by hand, much the same way it was many years ago. Many wooden bats are hand-turned to the specifications of each player. Danny Luckett makes Louisville Slugger bats in Louisville, Kentucky, and has personally finished bats for many major league players. "We used to do everything by hand, but now a tracing machine helps make the bats," says Danny, who has worked for 30 years for the Hillerich & Bradsby Company, which is the manufacturer of Louisville Slugger bats. "The machine is similar to a key-making machine and uses a template. Before, we could make 32 to 35 in a day, and now we can make 250 to 260 in a day."

Baseballs themselves are assembled by *hand baseball sewers,* who cement the leather hide of the ball to the core and sew the sections of hide together using a harness needle and waxed linen thread. To make baseball gloves, *lacers* sew precut pieces of leather together, working with the glove inside out. Then *lining inserters* put a lining in place, and *reversers* turn the glove right-side out on a series of posts. Next, *baseball glove shapers* use a heated, hand-shaped form to open and stretch the finger linings. With various rubber mallets, they hammer the seams smooth and form the glove pocket. Finally, they try the glove on and pound the pocket to make sure it fits comfortably.

As these examples show, the manufacturing of sporting goods involves ordinary industrial processes, adapted to suit each product. Within the limits of sports safety and economical operation of their plants, sporting goods manufacturers are constantly trying to improve designs and manufacturing processes to make equipment that is reliable and durable and maximizes athletic performance.

■ Requirements

While most employers prefer that employees have a high school diploma, it is not a requirement for many jobs in this industry. Employers look for workers who can do accurate, high-quality work at a fast pace. Most employees in the industry learn their skills through on-the-job training. Training may take from a few days to several months, depending on the job.

High School

High school courses that can help prepare students for working in the sporting goods equipment industry include shop, basic mathematics, blueprint reading, sewing, and other classes that provide practice in following written instructions and diagrams or making items by hand. Speech classes will also be helpful.

Postsecondary Training

Electronic devices are used more and more in sports for purposes such as timing skiers and runners. As more applications are developed for electronic and electrical equipment, more manufacturing workers will be needed who have the kind of knowledge and training that is available at technical schools. Also, design, precision assembly, and production jobs increasingly rely on machinery that is controlled by computers. For these reasons, a background that includes training in electronics and computer applications is very important for many jobs in this industry.

Other Requirements

Sports equipment production workers generally need good eyesight and manual dexterity to work with small parts and operate machines. Interest in sports can be an advantage. For example, it helps for workers who shape baseball gloves to have experience playing baseball and using gloves, so they know the feel of a good fit.

Some sporting goods production workers belong to labor unions. Another union is the Amalgamated Clothing and Textile Workers Union, which represents workers who make shoes, caps, hats, uniforms, ski suits, golf gloves, leotards, and other apparel. Other unions include the United Garment Workers of America; the International Leather Goods, Plastic and Novelty Workers Union; the Leather Workers International Union; the Laborers' International Union of North America; the International Brotherhood of Electrical Workers; and the International Brotherhood of Boilermakers, Iron Ship Builders, Blacksmiths, Forgers and Helpers.

■ Exploring

To learn something about what the work is like in sporting goods production, you can try to get a summer job working in a nearby sports equipment factory. Such a job is likely to be in a warehouse or in custodial services, but it may still offer you a chance to observe the manufacturing processes firsthand and to talk with experienced employees about their jobs. Working part time can also be an opportunity to show dependability and good work habits to an employer, and it could lead to permanent employment in the future. Since an interest in sports is helpful, a knowledge of sports and sports equipment by actual participation would be beneficial.

■ Employers

There are more than 3,000 manufacturers of sporting goods equipment in the United States, according the Sporting Goods Manufacturers Association (SGMA). They are located throughout the United States and may be small companies or large conglomerates. The recent trend toward mergers has affected this industry; fewer companies are employing more workers. The largest merger was the acquisition of The Coleman Company by Sunbeam Corporation.

■ Starting Out

Job seekers in this field can contact sporting goods manufacturers directly to learn whether or not they have any job openings. Other possibilities for job leads include checking the listings at the local offices of the state employment service and in the classified ad sections of newspapers. Students may find that school counselors can provide information about local companies that are looking for workers.

■ Advancement

Newly hired employees in sporting goods factories usually are assigned simple tasks. Trainees may acquire their job skills informally as they work beside and watch more experienced workers. Others may enter into a formal training program. Workers who have completed training for their job category and have shown they can meet production requirements may be able move into higher-paying production jobs as they become available.

In companies that are large and diversified, workers may advance to jobs in other divisions. Qualified employees may also move to positions as product inspectors or supervisors of other production workers. Moving into management jobs usually requires further experience, technical training, and formal education in business subjects.

Some knowledgeable, experienced people with new product ideas or an urge for independence may decide to start their own sporting goods production company. Setting up a new business in any field is a risky venture, however, and anyone who is interested in taking this step needs first to take a hard and informed look at the high costs involved in addition to the potential benefits.

■ Earnings

According to the U.S. Bureau of Labor Statistics, the average yearly earnings of production workers is $17,680. Production worker's can earn up to $30,004 per year and as low as $11,180 per year. Assemblers may have earnings that range from close to the federal minimum wage level up to about $10 an hour or more. Beginning workers often start at between minimum wage and $8.50 per hour. Wages are generally higher for skilled, experienced machine operators. Most workers also get fringe benefits, such as health insurance, paid holidays and vacation days, and pension plans. Some firms offer stock purchase plans to employees.

■ Work Environment

Conditions in plants vary, with some factories having modern, well-equipped, well-lit work stations for employees. Other plants provide less comfortable working conditions. In some jobs, employees have to sit or stand in one place for the entire work shift, while other jobs require heavy lifting, hammering, or other physically strenuous activities. People who operate presses, molds, and other heavy machinery may have to load and remove heavy work pieces made of leather, metal, fiberglass, plastic, and other materials. Almost all workers have production quotas to meet, which can be stressful at times.

Heat, noise, dust, or strong odors are unavoidable in many production jobs. Workers may need to wear safety glasses, hard hats, ear plugs, or other protective clothing.

Sports equipment production workers average 40 hours of work per week. Many factories operate 2 or 3 shifts a day, so employees may be required to work days, evenings, nights, or weekends.

■ Outlook

As sports and fitness become more popular among health-conscious Americans, the market for sporting goods is expected to continue to grow. Exports of American-made goods may also increase in coming years.

This does not mean, however, that the number of jobs in sporting goods manufacturing will also increase. The manufacture of many kinds of sports gear is very labor-intensive, and to keep labor costs down, manufacturers have moved some of their operations to plants in other countries, where workers can be paid lower wages. In addition, advances in automation, robotics, and computer-aided manufacturing are allowing companies to phase out certain production jobs. In the future, the need will be for employees who can program machines, supervise production, and manage resources. Workers will also be needed to test product safety and quality.

The sporting goods manufacturing industry is generally a solid but not expanding business. Job turnover is fairly high among production and assembly workers, so most new workers will be hired to replace people who leave their jobs.

■ For More Information

For industry information and job listings, contact:

Sporting Goods Manufacturers Association
200 Castlewood Drive
North Palm Beach, FL 33418
Tel: 561-842-4100
Web: http://www.sportlink.com/

■ Related Articles

Machining and Machinery

Sports

Toys and Games

Gunsmiths

Machine Tool Operators

Plastics Products Manufacturing Workers

Rubber Goods Production Workers

Toy Industry Workers

Sports Agents

■ Overview

Sports agents act as representatives for professional athletes in many different types of negotiations, providing advice and representation concerning contracts, endorsement and advertisement deals, public appearances, and financial investments and taxes, among others. They may represent only one athlete or many, depending on the sport, the size of their agency, and the demands of the client or clients they represent. There are fewer than 10,000 agents employed in the United States.

■ History

People have been entertained by the spectacular feats and athletic skills of individuals and teams even before gladiators performed in front of thousands in the Colosseum in ancient Rome. In the 20th century the general public's passion for sports has grown to such an extent that sports consumes an increasingly larger and larger share of people's free time. Sports figures, like movie stars, have become internationally recognized figures, renowned not only for their athletic prowess, but for their charismatic personalities, as well. Instead of closing deals with a simple handshake, Hollywood and sports teams now "sign" new actors and athletes to contracts. Like movie stars, athletes began to realize the need to have talented representation—or agents—to protect and promote their interests during contract negotiations. The role of a sports agent has expanded to include many more duties than contract negotiation, although that area remains a crucial responsibility. Today, sports agents handle most, if not all, aspects of a professional athlete's career, from commercial endorsements to financial investments to postretirement career offers.

■ The Job

The sports agent's primary duties consist of negotiating contracts and finding endorsements for his or her clients. Contract negotiation requires great communication skills on the part of the sports agent. He or she not only needs to be able to clearly summarize the athlete's present demands in terms of salary and benefits, but the agent also needs to have a clear vision of the athlete's future and how any given contract might affect it. Agents usually represent their clients for the duration of their client's careers, which sometimes means finding work for athletes once their athletic careers are over. For example, an agent may be able to build into the contract a coaching position with a team, in the event that athlete is injured or otherwise unable to complete the contract. Having a good sense of timing helps the agent, as well. Part of understanding a bargaining situation means knowing when to stand your ground and when to cut a deal.

Endorsement and public appearance deals bring additional income to the athlete, but they also have the potential to create a great deal of media attention, or hype, around the athlete. It is the role of the sports agent to make certain this media attention is positive and works to the benefit of the athlete. Marketing the public image of an athlete is increasingly difficult in today's media-saturated world; in years past, all an athlete needed to do to be considered a winner was be successful at his or her sport. Today, the athlete who wants to attract top endorsements and public appearances must have incredible charisma and a blemish-free image in addition to being a top athletic performer. Generally speaking, agents must be extremely careful when choosing endorsements for their clients.

Often, a great deal of "schmoozing" is necessary to achieve the kind of contacts that will help clients. For example, an agent for a tennis player might court the attention of executives whose companies manufacture items related to tennis, like tennis racquets, balls, and clothing. By developing friendly business relationships with these individuals, the agent has a direct line to those in charge of dispersing product endorsements. If and when those companies decide to use an athlete to help promote their products, the agent's athlete hopefully will be the first considered. Networking like this is part of the sports agent's everyday work routine. In between reviewing contracts and financial arrangements, he or she might be on the phone, chatting to an advertiser, scheduling lunch with a sports scout to uncover fresh talent, or handling some other aspect of the athlete's life, such as renting the athlete an apartment for spring training.

Financial advising is a growing part of the agent's job. Successful athletes suddenly have a great deal of money and in order to manage those funds for the athlete, the agent needs to know a reliable financial advisor, or he or she needs to act as the athlete's financial advisor. Creating or finding tax shelters, investing money, and preparing for the athlete's retirement are all duties which agents routinely perform for their clients.

Still other duties, sometimes so small and trivial as to be deceptively insignificant, are many times what keeps a client happy and convinced that the agent has only the client's best interests in mind. This might mean making sure the athlete's mother always has a great seat at home games, or it might mean pestering a talk-show host for months to schedule the agent's client for a postgame interview on a popular sports radio program.

■ Requirements

High School

High school courses that will be helpful include business, mathematics, English, and speech.

Postsecondary Training

No educational requirements exist for sports agents, but it is increasingly difficult to enter the field without at least a bachelor's degree in business administration, marketing, or sports management. Dan Lewis, Director of Human Resources for International Management Group, stresses the necessity of a four-year degree when he says, "In this business you have to be smart, a cut above." Many who eventually become agents also went on

SPORTS AGENTS	
SCHOOL SUBJECTS	Business Speech
PERSONAL SKILLS	Leadership/management
WORK ENVIRONMENT	Primarily indoors One location with some travel
MINIMUM EDUCATION LEVEL	Bachelor's degree
SALARY RANGE	$20,000 to $40,000 to $60,000+
CERTIFICATION OR LICENSING	Recommended
OUTLOOK	Faster than the average
DOT	191
GOE	11.12.03
NOC	6411
O*NET	39999B

to pursue a graduate degree in law or business, two areas which increase but don't guarantee a sports agent's chances at success. Clearly, contract law and economics are courses that can help an agent better his clients chances, and thus, his or her own chances, at successful negotiation.

Certification or Licensing

Many sports agents obtain a license or professional registration as demonstration of their commitment and integrity. Although these are not yet mandatory, it is one way for athletes to determine who, among agents, is legitimate and therefore, a better person to hire. Agents working for clients who belong to unions, such as the National Football League Player's Association, however, are required to obtain a union franchise. Basically, the franchise is an agreement between the agent and the athlete's union in which the agent promises to abide by the standards which were created by the union to protect its members. All licenses, registrations, and franchises are easily obtained by paying a filing fee and do not represent a real challenge to the sports agent.

Other Requirements

Contacts and exposure to athletes are the unofficial requirements for sports agents. Simply put, without knowing or having access to athletes, it is next to impossible to represent them. Insiders say that often, a successful agent's first client is his or her college roommate-later hired when the college athlete turned professional.

An extroverted personality is more than helpful. As one insider put it, being just this side of annoying, obnoxious, or brash helps in this business. Often, the agent with the most name recognition is the one who ends up with the job. Those who hire for large management firms reiterate the importance of persistence, the ability to stay with a person through thick and thin. Other qualities essential to the work of a sports agent are top notch communication skills, which include small talk at cocktail parties and power lunches, and savvy politicking skills.

■ Exploring

Finding jobs in this field is as challenging for those just starting out as it is for those at the top. Even intern positions and entry-level jobs are hard to get, because so many people are struggling to enter the field. Insiders recommend starting as early as possible and taking any job that gives you exposure to athletes. High school students can start by shagging balls at tennis tournaments, golf caddying, or applying for coveted ballboy/girl and batboy/girl positions with major league ball teams.

College internships are probably the most valuable introduction to the field, especially when you consider that many of the top management firms that hire agents don't even accept younger applicants. These firms are looking for men and women who are eager and willing to learn about the field. Insiders believe the internship is crucial to getting a solid start because it's probably the last time when anyone will let you close enough to see how it is done; once someone passes the internship stage, they're viewed by other agents as competition and the avenues of communication close up. Which isn't to say that some informal training doesn't take place on the job for young recruits into an agency. The secrets of the trade, however, are highly individualized and developed by the truly successful among the agents.

■ Employers

Agents are employed by the professional athletes they represent. They are also employed by top management firms, such as International Management Group.

■ Starting Out

If you don't know an athlete, have no connections or access to athletes, and have had no experience prior to applying to agencies, chances are you'll find yourself changing fields pretty quickly. Just as there are no professional organizations and no formal training to do this job, there is no one way to do it, which only makes getting started more difficult. The best way of breaking into the field is to start early and obtain a good, solid internship—one that gives you some exposure to agents and athletes, as well as a chance to develop those contacts. Add to this any information or hot tips you might have on new, fresh talent, and you may have a chance.

Most people who become agents get involved with a sport, either because they once played it, or a sibling did, or they've followed it so closely as to have made important or solid contacts in the field. Coaches, scouts, and of course, the athletes themselves would all be considered good contacts. So, too, are newscasters, athletic trainers, even physicians; in short, anyone who can introduce you to athletes is a potential contact to cultivate.

■ Advancement

In the field of sports management, advancement comes with success, the formula for which is pretty straightforward; if an agent's athletes are successful (and the agent handles the careers of those athletes well), then the agent is successful, financially as well as in terms of reputation. A good, solid reputation will, in turn, garner that agent more successful clients.

■ Earnings

Sports agents can earn phenomenal amounts of money by representing a single star athlete like Michael Jordan, Steffi Graf, or Wayne Gretzky. Athletes of this stature earn 50 million dollars a year or more in salary and endorsements.

A 5 percent commission on such earnings would net the agent approximately 2.5 million a year. Agent commissions, or percentages, at top management firms run anywhere from 5 to 10 percent of the player's earnings, and up to 25 percent for endorsements the agency negotiates on behalf of the athlete.

Having said what you can earn, anyone interested in pursuing a career as a sports agent should understand that the typical sports agent represents athletes, most or all of whom are not of the rare starlike variety. The average yearly salary or income for an agent just starting out range from $20,000 to $25,000. As the agent acquires more athletes or the status (and thus, marketing appeal) of his or her stable of athletes increases, the agent's salary will increase to $35,000 to $40,000 per year. The high end for the typical agent is approximately $40,000 to $60,000 a year.

According to one insider, the sky's the limit; if an agent is extremely ambitious and the agent's contacts within the sports world are fruitful, he or she can earn well over a million dollars a year. People entering the field of sports management should know the realities of the job—the million dollar scenario is as likely for agents as it is for athletes. It takes ambition, talent, timing, and lots of luck to make it big in this field. Enjoyment of the work, then, is crucial to job satisfaction.

■ Work Environment

Sports agents work with athletes in various stages of their careers, often before those careers even take off. Agents may spend time with the athlete at practice, hours on the telephone in the office, a day or two scouting out new talent, and lunches and dinners with potential advertisers or employers of the athlete.

Sports agents arguably spend most of their time on the telephone, arranging meetings, discussing prospects, networking connections, keeping in touch with the industry trends and issues, and most of all, speaking with their client about strategies and whatever problems the client is dealing with, from negotiating a raise in salary to helping the player through a slump.

The sports industry generates revenue in the hundreds of billions of dollars, only a portion of which actually goes to the athlete, so everyone who comes to the bargaining table—from management to athlete to advertiser—has a lot at stake. Sports agents must be able to handle tension and stress well, arguing effectively for their client's interests whether the opponent is the head of an international shoe manufacturer or the local real estate agent trying to sell the athlete a new house.

Finally, many people are uncomfortable going up to people they don't know and starting a conversation. This type of interaction is the bread and butter of a sports agent's career. You need to be comfortable speaking with strangers, but more than that, you need to be comfortable asserting the demands of your clients with strangers. A large part of the sports agent's job is talking, making contacts, and then using those contacts to better a client's position.

■ Outlook

According to the U.S. Department of Labor, there are fewer than 10,000 agents gainfully employed in the United States. That figure, unfortunately, includes literary and talent agents, as well as sport agents. The unions for baseball, football, basketball, and hockey alone franchise approximately 1,500 agents; it is important to note, however, that the majority of sports do not require franchise agreements and that franchise agreements pertain only to professional athletes. The unfranchised agents who sign college athletes were not included in the survey.

The outlook, in general, looks strong. The sports industry is thriving and there is nothing to suggest that the public's interest in it will dwindle. In fact, as cable television brings greater choices to the viewer, it is possible that less publicized sports will gain in popularity through the increased exposure, thus breathing life and revenues into those sports and creating new demand.

■ For More Information

No professional organizations or associations exist for sports agents. Some sports management programs teach courses on the subject, but for the most part, an agent has to learn the ropes by observing the successes and mistakes of others, developing his or her own strategies, techniques, and contacts along the way. Insiders report that while established agents will often discuss their work with others, divulging contacts and secrets of the trade is simply not done. The following is one of the top management firms in the country, a good source for internships and jobs, as well as leads to other companies:

International Management Group
IMG Center, Suite 100
1360 East 9th Street
Cleveland, OH 44114
Tel: 216-522-1200

■ Related Articles

Sports
Literary Agents
Talent Agents and Scouts

Sports Broadcasters and Announcers

■ Overview

Sports broadcasters for radio and television stations select, write, and deliver footage of current sports news for the sports segment of radio and television news broadcasts or for specific sports events, channels, or shows. They may provide pre- and postgame coverage of sports events, including interviews with coaches and athletes, as well as play-by-play coverage during the game or event.

Sports announcers are the official voices of the teams. At home games it is the sports announcer who makes pregame announcements, introduces the players in the starting lineups, and keeps the spectators in the stadium or arena abreast of the details of the game by announcing such things as fouls, substitutions, and goals, and who is making them.

■ History

In the early days of radio broadcasts, anyone who operated the station would read, usually verbatim, news stories from the day's paper. Quickly, station managers realized

SPORTS BROADCASTERS AND ANNOUNCERS	
SCHOOL SUBJECTS	English Journalism Speech
PERSONAL SKILLS	Communication/ideas
WORK ENVIRONMENT	Indoors and outdoors Primarily multiple locations
MINIMUM EDUCATION LEVEL	Some postsecondary training
SALARY RANGE	$22,000 to $48,704 to $2,000,000
CERTIFICATION OR LICENSING	None available
OUTLOOK	About as fast as the average
DOT	159
NOC	5231
O*NET	34017

that the station's "voice" needed as much charisma and flair as possible. Announcers and journalists with good speaking voices were hired. With the arrival of television, many of those who worked in radio broadcasting moved to this new medium.

Corporate-sponsored radio stations weren't long in coming; Westinghouse Corporation and American Telephone and Telegraph (AT&T) raced to enter the market. Westinghouse engineer Frank Conrad received a license for what is viewed as the first modern radio station, KDKA, in Pittsburgh, Pennsylvania. KDKA broadcast music programs, the 1920 presidential election, and sports events. The next year, Westinghouse began to sell radio sets for as little as $25. By 1924, the radio-listening public numbered 20 million.

Meanwhile, as early as 1929 a Soviet immigrant employed by Westinghouse, Vladimir Kosma Zworykin, was experimenting with visual images to create an all-electronic television system. By 1939 the system was demonstrated at the New York's World Fair with none other than President Franklin D. Roosevelt speaking before the camera. World War II and battles over government regulation and AM and FM frequencies interrupted the introduction of television to the American public, but by 1944, the government had determined specific frequencies for both FM radio and television.

In 1946, the number of television sets in use was 6,000; by 1951, the number had risen to an astonishing 12 million sets. Unknowingly, the stage had been set for a battle between radio and television. In the ensuing years, expert after expert predicted the demise of radio. The popularity of television, its soap operas, family dramas, and game shows, was believed by nearly everyone to be too strong a competitor for the old-fashioned, sound-only aspect of radio. The experts proved wrong; radio flourished well into the 1990s, when the industry experienced some cutbacks in the number of stations and broadcast hours because of recession.

The national radio networks of the early days are gone, but satellites allow local stations to broadcast network shows anywhere with the equipment to receive the satellite link. The development of filmed and videotaped television, cable and satellite transmissions, broadcasting deregulation, and an international market through direct broadcast satellite systems has drastically changed the face and future of both radio and television. Today's sports broadcasters in radio and television have all these technological tools and more at their fingertips.

■ The Job

One of the primary jobs of most sportscasters for both radio and television stations is to determine what sports news to carry during a news segment. The sportscaster begins working on the first broadcast by reading the sports-related clippings that come in over the various news wire services, such as Associated Press (AP) and United Press International (UPI). To follow up on one of these stories, the sportscaster might telephone several contacts—a coach, a scout, an athlete—to see if he can get a comment or more information. The sportscaster also might want to prepare a list of upcoming games, matches, and other sports events. Athletes often make public appearances for charity events and the sportscaster might want to include a mention of the charity and the participating athlete or athletes.

After deciding which stories to cover and the lineup of the stories that will be featured in the first of the day's broadcasts, sportscasters then review any audio or video clips that will accompany the various stories. Sportscasters working for radio stations choose audio clips, usually interviews, that augment the piece of news they will read. Sportscasters working for television stations look for video footage—the best 10 seconds of this game or that play—to demonstrate why a certain team lost or won. Sometimes sportscasters choose footage that is humorous or poignant to illustrate the point of the news item.

After they decide which audio or video segments to use, sportscasters then work with sound or video editors to edit the data into a reel or video, or they edit the footage into a tape themselves. In either case, the finished product will be handed over to the news director or producer with a script detailing when it should play. The news producer or director will make certain that the reel or video comes in on cue during the broadcast.

Frequently, a sportscaster will make brief appearances at local sports events to interview coaches and players before and after the game, and sometimes during breaks in the action. These interviews, as well as any footage of the game that the station's camera crews obtain, are then added to the stock from which sportscasters choose for their segments.

Usually, the main broadcast for both radio and television sportscasters is the late evening broadcast following the evening's scheduled programming. This is when most of the major league sports events have concluded, the statistics for the game are released, and final, official scores are reported. Any changes that have occurred since the day's first sports broadcast are updated and new footage or sound bites are added. The final newscast for a television sportscaster will most likely include highlights from the day's sports events, especially dramatic shots of the most impressive or winning points scored.

Increasingly, in televised sports news the emphasis is on image. Often sportscasters—like other newscasters—are only on camera for several seconds at a time, but their voices continue over the videotape that highlights unique moments in different games.

Two sports announcers broadcasting a baseball game.

For many sportscasters who work in television, preparing the daily sportscasts is their main job and takes up most of their time. For others, especially sportscasters who work in radio, delivering a play-by-play broadcast of particular sports events is the main focus of their job. These men and women use their knowledge of the game or sport to create with words a visual picture of the game, as it is happening, for radio listeners. The most common sports for which sportscasters deliver play-by-play broadcasts are baseball, basketball, football, and hockey. A few sportscasters broadcast horse races from the race track and sometimes these broadcasts are carried by off-track betting facilities.

Sportscasters who give the play-by-play for a basketball game, for example, usually arrive an hour or so before the start of the game. Often, they have a pregame show that features interviews with, and a statistical review of, the competing teams and athletes. To broadcast a basketball game, sportscasters sit courtside in a special media section so that they can see the action up close. During football, baseball, and hockey games sportscasters usually sit in one of the nearby media boxes. Throughout the game sportscasters narrate each play for radio listeners using rapid, precise, and lively descriptions. During time-outs, half-times, or other breaks in play, sportscasters might deliver their own running commentaries of the game, the players' performances, and the coaching.

Although some skills are advantageous to both aspects of the job, the sportscaster who specializes in play-by-play broadcasts needs to have an excellent mastery of the rules, players, and statistics of a sport, as well as the hand signals used by officials to regulate the flow of a game. Some sportscasters provide play-by-play broadcasts for several different teams or sports, from college to professional levels, requiring them to know more than one sport or team well.

Some sportscasters—often former athletes or established sports personalities—combine the two aspects of the job. They act as anchors or co-anchors for sports shows and give some play-by-play commentary while also providing their television or radio audience with statistics and general updates.

In a related job, sports announcers provide spectators with public address announcements before and during a sports event. For this job, sportscasters must remain utterly neutral, simply delivering the facts—goals scored, numbers of fouls, or a time-out taken. Sports announcers may be sportscasters or they may be professional announcers or emcees who make their living recording voice-overs for radio and television commercials and for large corporations or department stores.

Sports announcers usually give the lineups for games, provide player names and numbers during specific times in a contest, make public announcements during time-outs and pauses in play, and generally keep the crowd involved in the event (especially in baseball). Baseball announcers may try to rally the crowd or start the crowd singing or doing the wave.

■ Requirements

High School

Graduating from high school is an important first step on the road to becoming a sports broadcaster or announcer. While in school, take classes that will allow you to work on your speaking and writing skills. Classes in speech, English, and foreign languages, such as Spanish and French, will be helpful.

Postsecondary Training

Educational requirements for sportscasting positions vary, depending on the position. Competition for radio and television sports broadcasting positions is especially fierce, so any added edge can make the difference.

Television sportscasters who deliver the news in sports usually have bachelor's degrees in communications or journalism, although personality, charisma, and overall on-camera appearance is so important to ratings that station executives often pay closer attention to the taped auditions they receive from prospective sportscasters than to the items on resumes. If you are interested in pursuing a career in sports broadcasting, keep in mind that the industry is finicky and subjective about looks and charisma, so you should continue to prepare yourself for the job by learning a sport inside and out, developing valuable contacts in the field through internships and part-time or volunteer jobs, and earning a degree in journalism or communications.

It isn't as crucial for sportscasters who deliver play-by-play broadcasts for radio stations to have the journalistic skills that a television sportscaster has, although good interviewing skills are essential. Instead, they need excellent verbal skills, a daunting command of the sport or sports which they will be broadcasting, and a familiarity with the competing players, coaches, and team histories. To draw a complete picture for their listeners, sportscasters often reach back into history for an interesting detail or statistic, so a good memory for statistics and trivia and a knowledge of sports history is helpful, too.

Other Requirements

A nice speaking voice, excellent verbal and interviewing skills, a pleasant appearance, a solid command of sports in general as well as in-depth knowledge of the most popular sports (football, hockey, basketball, and baseball), and an outgoing personality are all necessary for a successful career in sportscasting.

Sports announcers need to have strong voices, excellent grammar and English usage, a pleasant appearance, and the ability to ad-lib if and when it is necessary. A solid knowledge of the sport is essential.

■ Exploring

The most obvious way to gain experience for this career is to participate in a sport. By learning a sport inside and out, you can gain insight into the movements and techniques that, as a sportscaster, you will be describing. In addition, firsthand experience and a love of the sport itself makes it easier to remember interesting trivia related to the sport as well as the names and numbers of the pros who play it.

If you are not interested in playing, you can volunteer to help out with the team by shagging balls, running drills, or keeping statistics. The latter is perhaps the best way to learn the percentages and personal histories of athletes.

An excellent way to develop the necessary communications skills is to take a journalism course, join the school's speech or debate team, deliver the morning announcements, deejay on the school radio station, or volunteer at a local radio station or cable television station.

Finally, many aspiring sportscasters hone their skills on their own while watching their favorite sports event by turning down the sound on their televisions and tape-recording their own play-by-play deliveries.

■ Employers

Most sports broadcasters work for television networks or radio stations. The large sports networks also employ many broadcasters. Earnhardt says, "The main employers of sports broadcasters are sports networks that own the rights to broadcast sporting events and the broadcast stations themselves." Radio sportscasters are hired by radio stations that range from small stations to mega-stations.

Sports announcers work for professional sports arenas, sports teams, minor league and major league ball teams, colleges, universities, and high schools.

Because sports are popular all over the country, there are opportunities everywhere, although the smaller the town the fewer the opportunities. "Larger cities generally have more opportunities because of the number of stations and the number of spots teams that need to be covered," Earnhardt says.

■ Starting Out

Although an exceptional audition tape might land a beginner an on-camera or on-the-air job, most sportscasters get their start by writing copy, answering phones, operating cameras or equipment, or assisting the sportscaster with other jobs. Internships or part-time jobs that give the beginner the opportunity to grow comfortable in front of a camera or behind a microphone are invaluable experiences. Of course, contacts within the industry come in handy. In many cases, it is simply an individual's devotion to the sport and the job that makes the difference—that and being in the right place at the right time. Earnhardt adds that knowledge is key as well. "It obviously helps to know the sport you are reporting on—first, one needs to study the sport and know the sport's rules, history, and participants better than anyone," he advises.

Don't forget to put together an audio tape (if you are applying for a radio job or an announcer position) or a video tape (for television jobs) that showcases your abilities. On the tape give your real-live account of the sports events that took place on a certain day.

■ Advancement

In the early stages of their careers, sportscasters might advance from the position of "gofer" to a sports copywriter to actual broadcaster. Later in their careers, sportscasters advance by moving to larger and larger markets, beginning with local television stations and advancing to one of the major networks.

Sportscasters who work in radio may begin in a similar way; advancement for these individuals might come in the form of a better time slot for a sports show, or the chance to give more commentary.

Sports announcers advance by adding to the number of teams for whom they provide public address announcements. Some sports announcers also may start out working for colleges and minor leagues and then move up to major league work.

■ Earnings

Salaries in sportscasting vary, depending on the medium (radio or television), the market (large or small, commercial or public), and whether the sportscaster is a former athlete or recognized sports celebrity, as opposed to a newcomer trying to carve out a niche.

According to the *Occupational Outlook Handbook* (OOH), the average salaries of television sportscasters range from $22,000 at the smallest stations to $129,000 at the largest ones. For all stations, the median salary is $49,000.

Sportscasting jobs in radio tend to pay less than those in television. Beginners will find jobs more easily in smaller stations, but the pay will be correspondingly lower than it is in larger markets. The average salary for a sportscaster, according to a survey conducted recently by the National Association of Broadcasters and the Broadcast Cable Financial Management Association, is $48,704, ranging from $22,400 in the smallest markets to $128,877 in the largest markets.

Salaries are usually higher for former athletes and recognized sports personalities or celebrities, such as ex-coaches like John Madden. These individuals already have an established personality within the sports community and may thus have an easier time getting athletes and coaches to talk to them. Salaries for such recognizable personalities can be as high as $2,000,000 a year.

Radio announcers earn an average salary of $31,251 according to the *OOH,* with the low range at $23,000 and the high at $39,291.

Sports announcers are notoriously underpaid—some even are asked to accept free sporting event tickets and food as part of their compensation. Although salary ranges are difficult to determine, some sports announcers earn an average of $25,000, while most earn salaries in the low $20s.

■ Work Environment

Sportscasters usually work in clean, well-lighted, sound-proof booths or sets in radio or television studios, or in special sound-proof media rooms at the sports facility that hosts sports events. Depending on the sportscaster's scheduled broadcasts, he or she may work off hours, but no matter when the broadcasts are scheduled, it makes for a long day.

Time constraints and deadlines can create havoc and add stress to an already stressful job; often a sportscaster has to race back to the studio to make the final evening broadcast. Sportscasters who deliver play-by-play commentary for radio listeners have the very stressful job of describing everything going on in a game as it happens. They can't take their eyes off the ball and the players while the clock is running and this can be nerve-wracking and stressful.

On the other hand, sportscasters are usually on a first-name basis with some of the most famous people in the world, namely, professional athletes. They quickly lose the star-struck quality that usually afflicts most spectators and must learn to ask well-developed, concise, and sometimes difficult questions of coaches and athletes.

Sports announcers usually sit in press boxes near the action so they can have a clear view of players and their numbers when announcing. Depending on the type of sport, this may be an enclosed area or they may be out in the open air. Sports announcers start announcing before the event begins and close the event with more announcements, but then are able to end their work day. Because sporting events are scheduled at many different times of the day, announcers sometimes must be available at odd hours.

■ Outlook

Competition for jobs in sportscasting will continue to be fierce, with the better-paying, larger-market jobs going to experienced sportscasters who have proven they can keep ratings high. Sportscasters who can easily substitute for other on-camera newscasters or anchors may be more employable.

The projected outlook is one of average growth, as not that many new radio and television stations are expected to enter the market. Most of the job openings will come as sportscasters leave the market to retire, relocate, or enter other professions. In general, employment in this field is not affected by economic recessions or declines; in the event of cutbacks, the on-camera sports broadcasters and announcers are the last to go.

■ For More Information

To get general information about broadcasting, contact:

National Association of Broadcasters
1771 N Street, NW
Washington, DC 20036-2891
Tel: 202-429-5300
Web: http://www.nab.org

For more career information and helpful Internet links, contact:

Radio-Television News Directors Association
1000 Connecticut Avenue, NW, Suite 615
Washington, DC 20006-5302
Tel: 202-659-6510
Web: http://www.rtnda.org

For a list of schools that offer programs and courses in broadcasting, contact:

Broadcast Education Association
1771 N Street, NW
Washington, DC 20036-2891
Tel: 202-429-5354
Web: http://www.beaweb.org

For information on FCC licenses, contact:

Federal Communications Commission
1919 M Street, NW
Washington, DC 20554
Tel: 202-632-7000
Web: http://www.fcc.gov

The following networks employ sports broadcasters:

WABC
77 West 66th Street, 13th Floor
New York, NY 10023
Tel: 212-456-1000

ESPN International
ESPN Plaza
Bristol, CT 06010
Tel: 203-585-2000

ABC Sports
47 West 66th Street
New York, NY 10023
Tel: 212-456-7777

CBS Sports
51 West 52nd Street, 30th Floor
New York, NY 10019
Tel: 212-975-4321

Fox Sports
1211 Sixth Avenue, 2nd Floor
New York, NY 10036

NBC Sports
30 Rockefeller Plaza
New York, NY 10112
Tel: 212-664-4444

Turner Sports
Turner Broadcasting Inc.
One CNN Center
Atlanta, GA 30303
Tel: 404-827-1735

■ Related Articles

Broadcasting

Radio

Sports

Television

Disc Jockeys

Professional Athletes—Individual Sports

Professional Athletes—Team Sports

Radio and Television Newscasters, Reporters, and Announcers

Radio and Television Program Directors

Reporters

Sportswriters

Sports Equipment Managers

■ Overview

Sports equipment managers are responsible for maintaining, ordering, and inventorying athletic equipment and apparel. There are more than 800 equipment managers employed in the United States, with the majority working for collegiate and high school teams. They deal with everything from fitting football shoulder pads to sharpening hockey skates to doing the team's laundry.

■ History

Sports cannot be played without using some sort of equipment. Keeping that equipment in good working condition and safe for players to use is the job of equipment managers. One of the major reasons for the emergence of professional equipment managers was the need for qualified athletic personnel to fit football helmets, according to the Athletic Equipment Managers Association (AEMA). It was not until the advent of the plastic shell helmet, which contributed to a more intense-contact game, that the number of injuries in sports rose. The National Operating Committee on Standards in Athletic Equipment began developing standards for football helmets. This increased attention also focused on the need for properly fitted equipment and specially trained personnel to perform the sizing. The AEMA was formed in 1973 when "a handful of equipment managers got together to discuss how to promote our profession and enhance the protection of student athletes involved in football," says Terry Schlatter, AEMA president and head athletic equipment manager, University of Wisconsin-Madison.

■ The Job

The responsibilities of equipment managers vary greatly, depending on whether they work for high schools, colleges, universities, or professional teams. Duties are also different from sport to sport, because some have more participants than others. "My responsibilities include budgeting for all of the university's sports and requisitioning of equipment," says Terry. "Some equipment managers might not do anything with budgets and might just fit football equipment and do laundry." Other duties include purchasing, maintenance, administration and organization, management, professional relations and education, and keeping inventory of all the equipment.

Equipment managers order all of the equipment needed for teams or schools. They also fit this equipment, as well as uniforms, for each player. Properly fitted equipment is not only desirable for reducing injuries, but it also helps

foster confidence. With football helmets, for example, a proper fit helps maximize the athlete's visibility, comfort, and hearing. Impairment of any of these areas disrupts players' concentration, leading to poor judgment and mistakes that can result in injury. Equipment managers are also responsible for equipment control, which includes pre- and postseason inventory, use, and storage.

Contact sports are fast and violent. The only measure of defense for athletes is protective equipment. It is essential that this equipment is properly fitted, reconditioned, and maintained. Equipment managers check, clean, and inspect every piece of equipment weekly to ensure that each athlete receives the best possible protection available.

Not only do the responsibilities of equipment managers vary from place to place, but their relationship with athletic departments also does. Equipment managers need good communication and personnel management skills to work with their staffs, coaches, and athletic directors. They supervise staff members ranging from paid personnel to unpaid student volunteers.

"Duties also might include (but are not limited to) facility scheduling, maintaining relationships with vendors, keeping up-to-date on current trends and products available, compliance with NCAA and conference rule changes regarding uniforms and equipment, and game day management," says Sam Trusner, men's equipment manager, University of Illinois.

■ Requirements

High School

High school courses that will be helpful include computer science, mathematics, and business. Serving as the equipment manager of one of your high school athletic teams or clubs will give you a great introduction to work in this field.

Postsecondary Training

To become a professional equipment manager, the AEMA suggests one of the following paths: 1) high school/GED degree and 5 years of paid, nonstudent employment in athletic equipment management; 2) 4-year college degree

SPORTS EQUIPMENT MANAGERS	
SCHOOL SUBJECTS	Physical education Technical/Shop
PERSONAL SKILLS	Following instructions Leadership/management
WORK ENVIRONMENT	Indoors and Outdoors One location with some travel
MINIMUM EDUCATION LEVEL	High school diploma
SALARY RANGE	$20,000 to $35,000 to $60,000
CERTIFICATION OR LICENSING	Recommended
OUTLOOK	Faster than the average

MAKING FOOTBALL SAFER

During the 1960's, organized athletics enjoyed a popularity that was unmatched during previous times. Large crowds gathered to watch the games, and the media provided greater exposure. More young athletes were motivated to perform more aggressively to obtain athletic scholarships or lucrative professional contracts after college. Unfortunately, with the increased attention, came more serious injuries. This was particularly evident in football, where there were 32 fatalities in 1968 directly due to organized competitions and 4 in sandlot play. To counter this trend, the National Operating Committee on Standards in Athletic Equipment (NOCSAE) was formed in 1969 to begin research on injury reduction.

Several problems confronted the organization, one of which was the increased usage of the head as the initial point of contact in blocking and tackling. NOCSAE members were concerned that any improvements to the equipment might lead to more and harder hits in that area. Work on a helmet standard begun in 1970, and the findings were available in 1973. The certification testing equipment was installed in manufacturing plants, and eventually manufacturers assumed responsibility for certification. The National Collegiate Athletic Association rules began mandating use of certified helmets in 1978, and the National Federation of State High School Associations began requiring them in 1980. By 1985, a significant downward trend in head injury fatalities emerged. By 1990, no deaths occurred for the first time since the beginning of annual fatality reports in 1931.

During this period of progress, permanent quadriplegia from neck injuries was averaging 20 annually during 1971 to 1975. In 1976, rule-making committees initiated changes that prohibited initial head contact in blocking or tackling. These changes have helped to significantly reduce quadriplegic injuries.

and 2 years paid, nonstudent employment in athletic equipment management; or 3) 4-year college degree and 1,800 hours as a student equipment manager. Terry recommends taking some business classes to help prepare you for handling equipment budgets and negotiating contracts with manufacturers such as Nike, Reebok, and Adidas. The AEMA offers a scholarship program to help with college expenses.

Certification or Licensing

The AEMA began a professional certification program in 1991. There are more than 300 certified equipment managers in the United States and Canada. To obtain certification, equipment managers must be 21 years of age and be a member in good standing with the AEMA. They must fulfill 1 of the educational requirements stated above and pass a certification examination. The certification process also includes continuing education, such as annual conventions, workshops, seminars, and meetings. Candidates

must publish papers in the *AEMA Journal* and teach athletic equipment management classes. The process also involves student manager supervision and an independent study.

Other Requirements

"Equipment managers must have excellent organizational skills and the ability to get along with many people," Sam says. "They also must be able to take criticism, be creative and responsible, have basic computer skills, and, most of all, have patience." To that, Terry adds the willingness to work a lot of overtime. "Football people work between 70 and 80 hours a week during the season," he says.

■ Employers

High schools, colleges, universities, and professional sports teams throughout the country hire equipment managers, although the number of positions with professional teams is limited, and they are very difficult to obtain. Several sports need the help of equipment managers, including football, basketball, baseball, hockey, and lacrosse.

■ Starting Out

"I started out doing laundry, then went to fitting shoes and helmets," says Terry. "Then I was responsible for ordering all of the football equipment. From there, I became head equipment manager and was responsible for ordering equipment for all of the sports, as well as football. Now I handle budgeting for all of the sports, as well as Reebok contract operations."

Some equipment managers began exploring the field in high school, where they served as volunteers for their sports teams. Others worked in that position in college, which is helpful for developing contacts for potential employment after graduation.

■ Advancement

"Equipment managers can be promoted to administrative positions within the athletic department, such as athletic directors and administrative assistants. Some also obtain top positions with sporting goods companies," notes Sam. In this industry, it is important to work your way up through the system. "Not many people walk into head equipment jobs without working their way up through the system or knowing a head coach who promotes them to administration," says Terry.

■ Earnings

Sam says the salary range in 1998 was $20,000 to $60,000 for head equipment manager positions and $15,000 to $40,000 for assistants. Equipment managers' salaries depend a lot on if they work for a professional team or the local high school.

■ Work Environment

Equipment managers spend most of their time in schools or in professional team offices during the off-season. "Travel is generally limited to football," Terry adds. "Some schools might have the equipment manager travel with the basketball team. I would say 90 percent of the time is spent on campus."

Equipment managers who work for professional teams usually travel with those teams and coordinate shipping all of the gear to each game site. Some football equipment managers might also travel to training camp.

■ Outlook

"The profession is changing rapidly and growing by leaps and bounds for college and university equipment managers," says Sam. "With the current emphasis on adding more women's sports to comply with Title IX guidelines, there is a shortage of qualified women's equipment managers. AEMA certification has also brought about greater acceptance by administrators for the need to have qualified individuals in these positions. With the addition of computerized inventory programs, university-wide contracts with dealers, and the big-business atmosphere of athletics in general, equipment managers are being called upon to broaden their range of knowledge in many new areas."

■ For More Information

For information on scholarships and certification, contact:

Athletic Equipment Manufacturers Association
PO Box 2093
Ann Arbor, MI 48106-2093
Tel: 734-741-9447
Web: http://www.wisc.edu/ath/aema

For information on sports equipment standards, contact:

National Operating Committee on Standards for Athletic Equipment
PO Box 12290
Overland Park, KS 66282-2290
Tel: 913-888-1340
Web: http://www.nocsae.org

■ Related Articles

Recreation

Sports

Golf Course Superintendents

Groundsmanagers and Groundskeepers

Recreation Workers

Sports Executives

■ Overview

Sports executives, sometimes known as *team presidents, CEOs,* and *general managers,* manage professional, collegiate, and minor league teams. They are responsible for the teams' finances, as well as overseeing the other departments within the organization, such as marketing, public relations, accounting, ticket sales, advertising, sponsorship, and community relations. Sports executives also work on establishing long-term contacts and support within the communities where the teams play.

■ History

The sports industry has matured into the 11th largest industry in the United States, according to CBS Sportsline. Professional teams are the most widely recognized industry segment in sports. Professional teams include all of the various sports teams, leagues, and governing bodies for which individuals get paid for their performance. Some of the most notable areas include the National Football League, National Basketball Association, National Hockey League, and Major League Baseball. These are commonly known as the four majors. During recent decades, more professional leagues have started, such as the Women's National Basketball League, Arena Football, and Major League Soccer. There are also many minor league and collegiate organizations.

■ The Job

The two top positions in most sports organizations are team president and general manager. Depending on the size of the franchise, these two positions might be blended together and held by one person.

Team presidents are the chief executive officers of the club. They are responsible for the overall financial success of the team. Presidents oversee several departments within the organization: marketing, public relations, broadcasting, sales, advertising, ticket sales, community relations, and accounting. Since team

SPORTS EXECUTIVES	
SCHOOL SUBJECTS	**Business** **Physical education**
PERSONAL SKILLS	**Communication/ideas** **Leadership/management**
WORK ENVIRONMENT	**Primarily indoors** **Primarily one location**
MINIMUM EDUCATION LEVEL	**Bachelor's degree**
SALARY RANGE	**$20,000 to $100,00 to $1,000,000**
CERTIFICATION OR LICENSING	**None available**
OUTLOOK	**Little change or more slowly than the average**

presidents must develop strategies for encouraging fans to attend games, it is good if they have some background in public relations or marketing. Along with the public relations manager, team presidents create give-away programs, such as cap days or poster nights.

Another one of the team president's responsibilities is encouraging community relations by courting season ticket holders, as well as those who purchase luxury box seats, known as skyboxes. Usually, this involves selling these seats to corporations.

General managers handle the daily business activities of the teams, such as hiring or firing, promotions, supervising scouting, making trades, and negotiating player contracts. All sports teams have general managers, and usually the main functions of the job are the same no matter what level of team. However, some general managers that work with minor league teams might also deal with additional job duties, including managing the souvenir booths or organizing the ticket offices. The most important asset the general manager brings to an organization is knowledge of business practices. The sport can be learned later.

■ Requirements

High School
High school courses that will help you to become a sports executive include business, mathematics, English, and computer science. Managing a school club or other organization will give you a general idea of the responsibilities and demands that this career involves.

Postsecondary Training
At least a bachelor's degree is required to become a sports executive. Remember, even though this is a sport-related position, presidents and general managers are expected to have the same backgrounds as corporate executives. Most have master's degrees in sports administration, and some have master's in business administration.

Other Requirements
Sports executives must create a positive image for their teams. In this age of extensive media coverage, as well as the amount of public speaking engagements that sports executives engage in, excellent communications skills are a must. Sports executives need to be dynamic public speakers. They also need a keen business sense and an intimate knowledge of how to forge a good relationship with their communities. They also should have excellent organizational skills, be detail oriented, and be sound decision-makers.

■ Exploring

One way to start exploring this field is to volunteer to do something for your school's sports teams, whether it be charting statistics or being the equipment manager, for example. This is a way to begin learning how athletic departments work. Talk to the general manager of your local minor league baseball club, and try to get a part-time job with the team during the summer. When you are in college, try to get an internship within the athletic department to supplement your course of study. Any way you can gain experience in any area of sports administration will be valuable to you in your career as a sports executive.

■ Employers

Employers include professional, collegiate, and minor league football, hockey, baseball, basketball, soccer, and other sports teams. They are located across the United States and the world.

■ Starting Out

Seventy-two percent of all sports executives began their careers as interns, according to CareerSearch, Inc., a company that specializes in sports recruiting. Interning offers the opportunity to gain recognition in an otherwise extremely competitive industry. Internships vary in length and generally include college credits. They are available in hundreds of sports categories and are offered by more than 90 percent of existing sports organizations. If you are serious about working in the sports industry, an internship is the most effective method of achieving your goals.

Entry-level positions in the sports industry are generally reserved for individuals with intern or volunteer experience. One you have obtained this experience, you are eligible for thousands of entry-level positions in hundreds of fields. Qualified employees are hard to find in any industry, so the experience you have gained through internships will prove invaluable at this stage of your career.

■ Advancement

The experience prerequisite to qualify for a management-level position is generally three to five years in a specific field within the sports industry. At this level, you should have experience managing a small to medium-sized staff and possess specific skills, including marketing, public relations, broadcasting, sales, advertising, publications, sports medicine, licensing, and specific sport player development.

The minimum experience to qualify for an executive position is generally seven years. Executives with proven track records in the minors can be promoted to positions in the majors. Major league executives might receive promotions in the form of job offers from more prestigious teams.

■ Earnings

General managers, team presidents, and other sports executives earn salaries that range from $20,000 to $50,000 per year in the minor leagues to more than $1 million in the majors. Most sports executives are eligible for typical fringe benefits including medical and dental insurance, paid sick and vacation time, and access to retirement savings plans.

■ Work Environment

Sports team management is a fickle industry. When a team is winning, everyone loves the general manager or team president. When the team is losing, fans and the media often take out their frustrations on the team's executives. You have to be ready to handle that pressure. This industry is extremely competitive, and executives might find themselves without a job several times in their careers. Sports executives sleep, eat, and breathe their jobs, and definitely love the sports they manage.

■ Outlook

Although there are more sports executive positions available due to league expansion and the creation of new leagues, such as the Women's National Basketball Association, there still remain only a finite number of these jobs, and the competition for these is fierce.

■ For More Information

For information on educational programs, contact:

Sports Administration Specialization Coordinator
Department of Physical Education, Exercise, and Sport Science
Woollen Gymnasium, CB#8605
The University of North Carolina
Chapel Hill, NC 27599-8605
Tel: 919-962-3226
Web: http://www.unc.edu

CareerSearch, Inc. bills itself as a leader in personnel placement in the sports industry. They "locate interns, entry level, and management positions for sports organizations all over the country." Visit the Web site for links to tens of thousands of sports organizations.

CareerSearch, Inc. (Specializing in Sports Recruiting)
PO Box 328
Fairfax, VA 22030
Web: http://www.careersearchinc.com

■ Related Articles

Business

Sports

Business Managers

Office Administrators

Sports Facility Managers

Sports Publicists

Sports Facility Designers

■ Overview

Sports facility designers are architects and engineers who specialize in the planning, design, and construction of facilities used for sporting and other public events. The buildings that these professionals design may be anything from a community gymnasium to a retractable domed stadium accommodating nearly a 100,000 spectators.

■ History

Stadiums and arenas are structures that are specifically designed for sporting events, from football to figure skating to tennis. The name comes from the Greek word, *stade,* for a unit of measurement roughly equal to 606 feet—the length of the footrace in the ancient Olympics and the overall length of the ancient Greek stadia. The forum for the first Olympics, a stadium at Olympia, dates from the 4th century BC.

In addition to stadia, the Greeks built hippodromes for their chariot races. Wider than the horseshoe-shaped stadium used for all athletic events, the Greek hippodromes could accommodate several 4-horse chariots racing along side one another. Eventually, chariot racing became a featured part of athletic competitions, and the resulting structure was the Roman Circus. Rome's Circus Maximus was the finest example. Built in the 1st century BC, historians believe it held as many as 250,000 spectators who viewed the spectacular feats from 3 sides. The Romans also built amphitheaters, impressive less for the vast numbers of spectators who could view each event (only 50,000 Romans could squeeze inside these vast areas) than for the fact that nothing obstructed their views. While the most famous of these structures is the Col-

SPORTS FACILITY DESIGNERS	
SCHOOL SUBJECTS	**Art** **Mathematics**
PERSONAL SKILLS	**Communication/ideas** **Technical/scientific**
WORK ENVIRONMENT	**Primarily indoors** **One location with some travel**
MINIMUM EDUCATION LEVEL	**Bachelor's degree**
SALARY RANGE	**$27,000 to $66,300 to $100,000+**
CERTIFICATION OR LICENSING	**Required by all states**
OUTLOOK	**About as fast as the average**
DOT	**001**
GOE	**05.01.07**
NOC	**2151**

osseum in Rome, now in ruins, the best preserved amphitheater is located in Arles, France, and is still being used for events, including the renowned summer music series, Les Choregies.

From ancient Greece to the present, however, it is the requirements of different sports which have dictated the size, seating, and playing area of sports facilities. For example, a variety of shapes were originally used to construct stadia for American-style football, from Harvard's U-shaped stadium (Cambridge, Massachusetts, 1912) to the facing crescent stands featured at Northwestern University (Evanston, Illinois, 1926). Innovations to these basic shapes weren't long in coming; the original Yankee stadium in New York, built in 1923, added seats protected by a roof. Dodger Stadium in Los Angeles, built in 1962, was the first tiered stadium without columns, and offered every fan an unobstructed view.

As stadia and arenas began to be used for more than one sport or event, a trend toward multipurpose stadia developed. Movable seating, first introduced in New York's Shea Stadium in 1964, allowed seats to be moved or rearranged according to the sport or expected crowd capacity. Specialty flooring allowed a stadium to be used for both hockey and basketball games.

The domed stadium, featuring internal climate control and artificial turf, was the next innovation, and this changed the face of many sports. Where playing times and broadcasts had previously relied on good weather and daylight, domed stadiums meant that play could continue, in poor weather and at night. Houston's Astrodome can seat 65,000 fans under a plastic-paneled, steel-latticed dome that spans 643 feet.

The largest stadium in the world is Strahov Stadium in Prague; built in 1932, it can seat 240,000 spectators.

Today's stadium or arena provides more than a playing field and seats for the spectators, however. The modern sports facility usually has one or more of the following: practice areas; home and visiting team locker rooms; physical therapy areas; sports equipment storage; press rooms; press boxes; facility maintenance equipment storage; cafeterias; food vendor areas; and offices for those who run the various aspects of the facility and teams who play there, as well as promote and market both facility and team. The individuals who design these venues for sports events are responsible for making certain that the building functions to accommodate the varied events taking place there without sacrificing beauty or grace in structure. Today's stadiums are feats of engineering, combining structural integrity with space-age materials and engineering.

The field of modern sports facility design made a dramatic resurgence in the early 1980s. Prior to this time, no architectural firm existed that specialized in the design of sports facilities. Then, in 1983, 4 men created HOK Sports,

a division of Hellmuth, Obata, and Kassabaum, Inc., the largest architectural firm in the United States. The net earnings at HOK Sports grew from $1.7 million in 1985 to $16 million in 1996, proving that the need existed for a specialty firm devoted to facility design.

■ The Job

A sports facility designer normally has two responsibilities: to design a building that will satisfy the client (and the paying crowds) and protect the public's health, safety, and welfare. In order to accomplish these goals, facility designers must be licensed architects in the state in which they work. This means pursuing a difficult course of education, internships, apprenticeships, and examinations—all of which culminates in the architect receiving the proper credentials in the form of a license.

In order to create a design that is pleasing to the client and fan, alike, sports facility designers must wear many hats. The job begins with learning what the client wants; that is, for what purpose is the stadium or arena or other sports facility being constructed? Will the facility house one team? Will it be a multipurpose or multiuse facility? What is the budget? Are there any special requests or requirements, outside of those regulated by law? The answers to these questions inform the designer's approach to the project. Once these issues have been taken into consideration, the designer moves forward and begins to consider other, equally important issues, such as climate, water tables, zoning laws, fire regulation, local and state building regulations, the soil on which the building is to be constructed, the client's financial limitations, and many other requirements and regulations. The designer then prepares a set of plans that, upon the client's approval, will be developed into final design and construction documents. Many, many meetings take place in the interim, as the client's needs and requests are weighed against the legal issues involved. A certain amount of compromise generally occurs on the part of all the parties, involved, although much less leeway comes from those parties representing the legal requirements.

The final design shows the exact dimensions of every portion of the building, including the location and size of columns and beams, electrical outlets and fixtures, plumbing, heating and air-conditioning facilities, seats and seating arrangements, doors, and all other features of the building.

The sports facility designer works closely with consulting engineers to design the plumbing, air-conditioning, and electrical work to be done. If the facility is to be used for concerts, an acoustical expert might be brought into the project. *Lighting experts* are consulted to select and place lighting fixtures and elements for evening or indoor performances.

The sports facility designer then will assist the client in getting bids from general contractors, one of which will be selected to construct the building to the specifications. The sports facility designer will assist the client through the completion of the construction and occupancy phases, making certain the correct materials are used and that the drawings and specifications are faithfully followed.

Throughout the process the sports facility designer works closely with a design or project team. This team is usually made up of the following: *designers,* who specialize in design development; a *structural designer,* who designs the frame of the building in accordance with the work of the sports facility designer; the *project manager* or *job superintendent,* who sees that the full detail drawings are completed to the satisfaction of the sports facility designer; and the *specification writer* and *estimator,* who prepare a project manual that describes in more detail the materials to be used in the building, their quality and method of installation, and all details related to the construction of the building.

The sports facility designer's job is very complex. He or she is expected to know construction methods, engineering principles and practices, and materials. The sports facility designer must also be up-to-date on new design and construction techniques and procedures.

■ Requirements

High School

High school students hoping to enter the sports facility design profession should take a college-preparatory program that includes courses in English, mathematics, physics, art (especially freehand drawing), social studies, history, and foreign languages. Courses in business and computer science also will be useful.

Postsecondary Training

Most schools of architecture offer a five-year program leading to a bachelor of architecture degree or a six-year master of architecture program. In the six-year program, a pre-professional degree is awarded after four years, and the graduate degree after a two-year program. Many students prepare for an architectural career by first earning a liberal arts degree, then completing a three- to four-year master of architecture program.

A typical college architectural program includes courses in architectural history and theory, building design—including its technical and legal aspects—science, and liberal arts.

Certification or Licensing

All states and the District of Columbia require that individuals be licensed before calling themselves architects or contracting to provide sports facility design services in that particular state. The requirements for registration include graduation from an accredited school of architecture and three years of practical experience, or internship, in a licensed architect's office before the individual is eligible to take the rigorous four-day Architect Registration Examination. Because most state architecture boards require a professional degree, high school students are advised, early in their senior year, to apply for admission to a professional program that is accredited by the National Architecture Accrediting Board (NAAB). Competition to enter these programs is high. Grades, class rank, and aptitude and achievement scores play a very large part in determining who will be accepted.

Other Requirements

People interested in sports facility design should be well prepared academically and be intelligent, observant, responsible, and self-disciplined. They should have a concern for detail and accuracy, be able to communicate effectively both orally and in writing, and be able to accept criticism constructively.

Although great artistic ability is not necessary, future sports facility designers should be able to visualize spatial relationships and have the capacity to solve technical problems. Mathematical ability is also important. In addition, sports facility designers should possess organizational skills and leadership qualities and be able to work well with others.

■ Exploring

Most sports facility designers will welcome the opportunity to talk with you about entering the field and may be willing to let you visit their offices where you can gain a first hand knowledge of the type of work done by a sports facility designer.

Other opportunities may include visiting the design studios of a school of architecture or working for an architect or building contractor during summer vacations. Also, many architecture schools offer summer programs for high school students. Books and magazines on architecture and sports facility design provide a broad understanding of the nature of the work and the values of the profession.

■ Employers

While many design firms handle small community projects, the large stadiums, civic centers, arenas, ballparks, and other sports facilities are almost exclusively handled by one firm, the firm that practically created the field of facility design—Hellmuth, Obata, and Kassabaum, Inc., based in Kansas City, Missouri.

Most designers who work in this field work for HOK Sports because this division of the nation's largest architectural firm receives 95 percent of the major sports facility design commissions in the world. As the world's pre-eminent sports architecture design firm, HOK Sports has developed a diverse portfolio of arena and stadium projects worldwide for public sector clients, professional sports franchises, colleges and universities.

Starting Out

Those entering sports facility design following graduation start as interns in an architectural office which specializes in sports facility design. As interns, they assist in preparing architectural documents. They also handle related details, such as administering contracts, coordinating the work of other professionals on the project, researching building codes and construction materials, and writing specifications.

As an alternative to working for an architectural firm, some architecture graduates go into allied fields such as construction, engineering, interior design, landscape architecture, or real estate development. Others may develop graphic, interior design, or product specialties. Still others put their training to work in the theater, film, or television fields or in museums, display firms, and architectural product and materials manufacturing companies. No matter where the internship is served, it usually always adds to the individual's perception of space, materials, and techniques. However, those students who wish to enter the field of sports facility design should try and find internships with architectural or engineering firms that have worked on stadium, arena, or other facility projects in the past.

Advancement

Interns and architects alike are given progressively more complex jobs. Sports facility designers may advance to supervisory or managerial positions. Some sports facility designers become partners in established firms, but the eventual goal of many designers is to establish their own practice.

Earnings

The starting annual salary for graduates of schools of architecture working during their internship before licensing is $27,000, according to the *Occupational Outlook Handbook*. Newly registered architects and sports facility designers earn an average of $36,100, and those with several years of experience earn $66,300 or more.

Well-established sports facility designers who are partners in an architectural firm or who have their own businesses generally earn much more than do the salaried employees. Those who are partners in very large firms can earn more than $100,000 a year. Most employers offer such fringe benefits as health insurance, sick and vacation pay, and retirement plans.

Work Environment

Sports facility designers normally work a 40-hour week with their hours falling between 8:00 AM and 6:00 PM. There may be a number of times when they will have to work overtime, especially when under pressure to complete an assignment.

Sports facility designers usually work in comfortable offices, but they may spend a considerable amount of time outside of the office visiting clients or viewing the progress of a particular job in the field. Their routines usually vary considerably, which means they may go from the office to a hard-hat construction site to a materials plant to a swanky lunch and then back to the office until late that evening.

Outlook

As urban centers struggle to compete for tourism and convention business, the presence of a popular sports franchise becomes increasingly important. In order to lure large franchises within the major sports of baseball, basketball, football, and hockey, cities have gone to great lengths, the most successful of which has been the building of modern sports facilities. The boom in sports facility construction is far from over, but it might begin to show signs of slowing down around the year 2006.

There are approximately 94,000 registered architects employed in the United States. Certainly there are not nearly this number of sports facility designers, as this is a specialized discipline within the field of architecture. Most sports facility designers work in architectural firms. Others work in allied fields, such as construction, engineering, interior design, landscape architecture, or real estate development.

Job prospects are good since growth in the field is expected to be as fast as average through the rest of the decade. The number of sports facility designers needed will depend on the volume of construction but with more and more local municipalities constructing sports stadiums and convention centers in an effort to stimulate the local economy, the outlook is favorable. The construction industry is extremely sensitive to fluctuation in the overall economy, and a recession could result in layoffs.

On the positive side, employment of sports facility designers is not likely to be affected by the growing use of computer technologies. Rather than replacing sports facility designers, computers are being used to enhance the sports facility designer's work.

Competition for employment will continue to be strong, particularly for positions with HOK Sports. Openings will not be newly created positions but will become available as otherwise established architects transfer to other occupations or leave the field.

■ For More Information

HOK Sports Facilities Group is the main employer of sports facility designers. Contact them for employment information:

Hellmuth, Obata, and Kassabaum, Inc.
HOK Sports Facilities Group
323 West 8th Street, Suite 700
Kansas City, MO 64105
Tel: 816-221-1576
Web: http://www.hok.com/sport/

For career and scholarship information and a list of NAAB-Accredited Programs in Architecture, contact:

American Institute of Architects
1735 New York Avenue, NW
Washington, DC 20006
Tel: 202-626-7300
Web: http://www.e-architect.com/

For information on architectural schools, contact:

Association of Collegiate Schools of Architecture
1735 New York Avenue, NW
Washington, DC 20006
Tel: 202-785-2324
Web: http://www.acsa-arch.org/

For information on their Intern Development Program, the Architect Registration Examination, and certification and continuing education, contact:

National Council of Architectural Registration Boards
735 New York Avenue, NW, Suite 700
Washington, DC 20006
Tel: 202-783-6500
Web: http://www.ncarb.org/

■ Related Articles

Construction

Architects

Drafters

Engineers

Landscape Architects

Sports Facility Managers

■ Overview

Stadium, arena, and facility managers, sometimes called *general managers, sports facility managers,* or *stadium operations executives,* are responsible for the day-to-day operations involved in running a sports facility. They are involved in sports facility planning, including the buying, selling, or leasing of facilities; facility redesign and construction; and the supervision of sports facilities, including the structures and grounds, as well as the custodial crews.

■ History

Stadiums and arenas are structures that are specifically designed for sporting events, from football to figure skating to tennis. The name comes from the Greek word, *stade,* for a unit of measurement roughly equal to 606 feet—the length of the foot race in the ancient Olympics and the overall length of the ancient Greek stadia. The forum for the first Olympics, a stadium at Olympia, dates from the 4th century.

From ancient Greece to the present it is the requirements of different sports which have dictated the size, seating, and playing area of sports facilities. For example, a variety of shapes were originally used to construct stadia for American-style football, from Harvard's U-shaped stadium (Cambridge, Massachusetts, 1912) to the facing crescent stands featured at Northwestern University (Evanston, Illinois, 1926). Innovations to these basic shapes weren't long in coming; the original Yankee stadium in New York, built in 1923, added seats protected by a roof. Dodger Stadium in Los Angeles, built in 1962, was the first tiered stadium without columns, and offered every fan an unobstructed view.

As stadia and arenas began to be used for more than one sport or event, a trend toward multipurpose stadia developed. Movable seating, first introduced in New York's Shea Stadium in 1964, allowed seats to be moved or rearranged according to the sport or expected crowd capacity. Specialty flooring allowed a stadium to be used for both hockey and basketball games.

The domed stadium, featuring internal climate control and artificial turf, was the next innovation, and this changed the face of many sports. Where playing times and broadcasts had previously relied on good weather and daylight, domed stadiums meant that play could continue, in poor weather and at night. Houston's Astrodome can seat 65,000 fans under a plastic-paneled, steel-latticed dome that spans 643 feet.

Today's stadium or arena provides more than a playing field and seats for the spectators, however. The modern sports facility usually has one or more of the following: practice areas; home and visiting team locker rooms; physical therapy areas; sports equipment

SPORTS FACILITY MANAGERS	
SCHOOL SUBJECTS	Business English
PERSONAL SKILLS	Leadership/management
WORK ENVIRONMENT	Indoors and outdoors Primarily one location
MINIMUM EDUCATION LEVEL	Bachelor's degree
SALARY RANGE	$31,282 to $46,477 to $75,801
CERTIFICATION OR LICENSING	Recommended
OUTLOOK	About as fast as the average

storage; press rooms; press boxes; facility maintenance equipment storage; cafeterias; food vendor areas; and offices for those who run the various aspects of the facility and teams who play there, as well as promote and market both facility and team. Those who manage these venues for sports events are responsible for making certain that everything runs smoothly for the athlete, the fan, the advertiser, the media, and their own staff.

■ The Job

Stadium, arena, and facility managers are responsible for the day-to-day operations involved in running a sports facility. In simplest terms, the manager of a sports facility, like other facility managers, must coordinate the events which occur in the facility with the services and people who make those events possible.

Sports facility managers are involved in sports facility planning, including the buying, selling, or leasing of facilities; facility redesign and construction; and the supervision of sports facilities, including the structures and grounds, as well as the custodial crews. This may mean months, sometimes even years, of research and long-term planning. Crucial issues the manager might investigate include: sports facility design firms; prospective sites for the new facility and analyses of neighborhood support for a facility; and zoning laws or other federal, state, and local regulations concerning the construction of new buildings. Politics can play a key part in this process; the manager might be involved in these political meetings, as well. Once ground is broken on the new site, a sports facility manager may then divide his or her time between the construction site and the existing site, supervising both facilities until the new one is completed.

The manager of a sports facility, stadium, or arena who is not involved in the construction of a new facility, or the redesign of an existing one, spends most of his or her time in the office or somewhere in the facility itself, supervising the day-to-day management of the facility. The manager usually determines the organizational structure of the facility and establishes the personnel staffing requirements; setting up the manner in which things will be done and by whom. The facility manager is constantly analyzing how many different workers are needed to run the various areas of the facility efficiently, without sacrificing quality. As staffing needs arise, the manager addresses them, setting the education, experience, and performance standards for each position. Depending on the size of the facility and the nature of the manager's assigned responsibilities, this may mean hiring a *personnel director* to screen prospective employees, or it may mean the manager personally sifts through stacks of resumes whenever a position opens up. Usually, all policies and procedures having to do with the morale, safety, service, appearance, and performance of

facility employees (and which are not determined by the organization, itself) are determined by the manager.

The manager of a sports facility is also responsible for assisting with the development and coordination of the facility's annual operating calendar, including activity schedules, dates and hours of operation, and projections for attendance and revenue. Often, a manager for a sports facility directs and assists with the procurement of activities and events to take place at the facility; this, of course, depends on the size of the facility. A large, multipurpose stadium, for example, will probably have at least one individual devoted to event-planning and the acquisition of activities. Even in this case, however, the sports facility manager must be involved in order to coordinate the event with all the other aspects of the facility.

The sports facility manager handles the negotiations, contracts, and agreements with industry agents, suppliers, and vendors. These days, many jobs that used to be handled in-house by staff employees are now contracted out to private companies that specialize in that aspect of the event. Food service and security, for example, are two areas that are usually privately managed by outside vendors and firms. It is the responsibility of the sports facility manager to hire such contractors and to monitor the quality of their work.

Finally, it is the manager's duty to make certain that the facility, its workers, and the services which it offers are in accordance with federal, state, and local regulations.

Although certain responsibilities are shared, the job description for a sports facility manager will inevitably vary according to the type of sport played and the level of the organization that employs the manager. For example, the duties of a manager for a parks and recreation facility in a medium-sized town will differ considerably from those of the general manager of Churchill Downs in Louisville, Kentucky; the former will do many of the duties that the latter would most likely delegate to others.

The type of sports stadium, arena, or even auditorium, in which sports facility managers work also varies, from race tracks to natatoriums to large, multipurpose stadiums that host football games and rock concerts.

■ Requirements

High School

High school courses that will give you a general background for work in sports facility management include business, mathematics, government, and computer science. Speech and writing classes will help you to hone your communication skills. Managing a school club or other organization will give you an introduction to overseeing budgets and the work of others.

Postsecondary Training

These days, a bachelor's degree is pretty much required to enter the field of sports facility management. Although in the past it wasn't necessary, the competition for jobs in sports administration and facility management is so keen that a bachelor's degree is nearly mandatory. In fact, in many instances, a master's degree in sports administration or sports facility management is increasingly required of managers.

The oldest program in the country in sports administration and facility management is at Ohio University in Athens, Ohio. Administered by the School of Recreation and Sports Sciences within Ohio University's College of Health and Human Services, the program requires 55 credit hours (5 of which are completed during an internship) and leads to the Master of Sports Administration. The curriculum focuses on business, journalism, communications, management, marketing, sports administration and facility management. The required internship lasts anywhere from 3 months to a year and internship opportunities are provided by more than 400 different organizations worldwide.

Certification or Licensing

At the moment, certification in facility management is not mandatory, but it is becoming a distinguishing credential among the managers of the largest, most profitable venues. Put simply, a sports stadium or arena brings its owners a lot of revenue, and these owners aren't willing to trust the management of such lucrative venues to individuals who are not qualified to run them; certification is one way an administration can ensure that certain industry standards in facility management are met. The International Facility Management Association (IFMA), probably the industry leader in certification, offers the designation, Certified Facility Manager (CFM). For more information on the organization, see "For More Information."

Other Requirements

Most organizations want their facility managers to have, at a minimum, five years of experience in the field or industry. This may include related experiences, as well, such as participation in a sport at the professional level, marketing or promotions work, or related management experience that can be shown as relevant to the responsibilities and duties of a sports facility manager.

Leadership and communication skills are considered essential to a successful facility manager. In the course of an average day, he or she might review designs for a new stadium with top-level executives, release a statement to members of the press about the ground-breaking ceremony for the new stadium, and interview prospective foremen for maintenance work. The manager needs to be able to clearly and concisely state his or her ideas, information, and goals, regardless of who the audience is.

Finally, a sports facility manager should possess excellent strategic, budgetary, and operational planning skills; the day-to-day operations of the sports facility run on the decisions the manager makes, so he or she has to be capable of juggling many different balls.

■ Exploring

If you aren't actively involved with a sport as a participant, you can get involved with sports administration and management by volunteering for positions with your own high school teams. Any and all experience helps, beginning with organizing and managing the equipment for a football team, for example, all the way up to working as a team statistician. You can also work with their local Booster Club to sponsor events that promote athletics within the school district. These activities demonstrate your interest and devotion and may help in the future by providing you with an edge when searching for an internship.

Part-time or summer jobs as ushers, vendors, ball boys or girls, for example, not only provide firsthand experience for both high school and college students, but can lead to other contacts and opportunities.

College students interested in sports facility management can often locate valuable internships through contacts they have developed from part-time jobs, but the placement centers in undergraduate or graduate programs in business administration and facility management are also good places to consult for information on internships. The professional leagues and associations for specific sports, The National Hockey League, the National Football League, and the National Basketball Association, for example, all offer summer internships. Competition for positions with these organizations is extremely keen, so interested students should send for application materials well in advance, study them, and apply early.

Professional organizations within the field also sponsor opportunities to learn on-the-job. The International Association of Assembly Managers (IAAM) offers internships and scholarships to qualified students. Selected interns receive a $2,000 stipend, sometimes in addition to a salary, for a one-semester internship at a public assembly facility in North America. Internships are open to college students enrolled in a degree program including at least one course focusing on facility management. Typically, participating facilities that serve as sites for IAAM internships are responsible for the selection of their interns. Facilities that have hosted internships in the past include: Long Beach Entertainment & Convention Center, Long Beach, California; Delta Center, Salt Lake City, Utah; Pan American Center, Las Cruces, New Mexico; Yost Ice Arena, Ann Arbor, Michigan; and the AlamoDome, San Antonio, Texas.

While some of these facilities aren't specifically geared toward sporting events, much of the management skills and responsibilities are shared and will provide the intern with a wonderful opportunity to learn firsthand.

■ Employers

Sports facility managers may work for single team, a multisports arena or stadium, or they may work for a city or state organization, such as a parks and recreation department.

■ Starting Out

Graduates of programs in sports administration and sports facility management usually find jobs through internships they have had, personal contacts they developed in the field, or from job listings in their graduate programs' placement departments.

Entry-level jobs may be in facility management, or they may come in a related field. Most organizations like to promote from within, so it isn't uncommon for someone with a bachelor's or graduate degree in facility management who is working in say, public relations, to be considered first for an opening in the sports facility department. Associate or assistant level positions are the most likely entry point for graduates, but those with exceptional education and experience may qualify for managerial positions after graduation, although this is rare. In fact, as the field becomes more popular, it will be increasingly difficult to enter a sports facility management position without a bachelor's degree and a solid internship experience, at the very least.

Those who find jobs at the entry-level are helped by mentors. Mentoring is an industry-supported method in which an older, experienced member of a facility management team helps a younger, less-experienced individual to learn the ropes. This process helps the person learn and aids the organization by reducing problems caused by inexperienced beginners.

■ Advancement

Experience and certification are the best ways for someone to advance in this field. Years of successful, on-the-job experience count for a great deal in this industry; the owners and administrations of professional teams and sports venues look for someone who has demonstrated the ability to make things run smoothly. Certification is becoming another way in which success can be gauged; more and more frequently, certification garners salary increases and promotions for those who hold it. Increasingly, firms are asking for certified facility managers when they begin job searches. Since certification goes hand-in-hand with experience, it is assumed that those individuals who are certified are the best in their field.

Outside of experience and certification, a willingness and eagerness to learn and branch into new areas is a less objective manner for gauging which managers will land in top jobs. Those who are willing to embrace new technology and are open to new ideas and methods for improving efficiency, will very likely advance in their careers.

Advancement might also mean changing specialties, or developing one. Those who are interested in other areas of management may decide to leave the field of sports facility management and involve themselves with different venues, such as auditoriums, performing arts centers, or convention centers, to name just a few. Still others might advance to manage international venues.

■ Earnings

Earnings will vary considerably, depending upon experience and education levels, as well as certification, and the level of the facility. According to an IAAM industry profile survey conducted in 1996, the salaries of assistant or associate level managers ranged from $31,282 to $59,904 per year, while the salaries of general managers ranged from $46,447 to $75,801 per year. The salaries of sports facility managers fall roughly in the same range.

■ Work Environment

One of the perks of the profession is the glamorous atmosphere which the job promotes; sports facility managers work to provide a unique environment for amateur and professional athletes, sometimes even celebrities and other performers. Although their work most often is behind-the-scenes, they may have indirect or direct contact with the high-profile personalities who perform in large venues. Sports facility managers usually work in clean, comfortable offices. Since their work often involves other activities, such as construction, they also may spend a great deal of time on construction sites and in trailers, supervising the construction of a new facility.

The management of a sports arena or stadium naturally involves promotional events, both for the building and the teams or events which are staged there. To be successful in their work, facility managers must maintain regular contact with the members of other departments, such as marketing and public relations.

A sports facility manager's job can be stressful. Construction deadlines, renovation deadlines, cleaning and maintenance deadlines must all be met in order to ensure the efficient running of a sports facility, let alone one in which major sports events occur. Depending on the level of the facility and the nature of events which are staged there, the responsibilities of the manager often require more hours on the job than the typical nine-to-five day allows. Additional work may be necessary, but is often uncompensated.

■ Outlook

In general, the future for facilities managers is much brighter than it is for those in other administrative services. This relatively young field is growing quickly and, especially in the private sector, is not as subject to cost-cutting pressures or as vulnerable to government cutbacks. Demand for jobs in sports administration is great, and the newer field of sports facility management is quickly catching up.

■ For More Information

For industry information, job listings, and to participate in an online forum relating to issues in sports facility management, contact:

International Association of Assembly Managers
4425 West Airport Freeway, Suite 590
Irving, TX 75062-5835
Tel: 972-255-8020
Email: iaam.info@iaam.org
Web: http://www.iaam.org/

For information on certification, contact:

International Facility Management Association
1 East Greenway Plaza, Suite 1100
Houston, TX 77046-0194
Tel: 713-623-4362
Email: IFMAhq@ifma.org
Web: http://www.ifma.org/

For information on the Master of Sports Administration, contact:

Sports Administration/Facility Management Program
School of Recreation and Sport Sciences
Ohio University
Grover Center 6
Athens, OH 45701-2979
Tel: 614-593-4656
Email: ernce@ohio.edu
Web: http://www.ohio.edu/~rspsdept/

Visit the StadiaNet Web site (a service of the SMA), which provides links and contact information for major stadiums around the world:

Stadium Managers Association
19 Mantua Road
Mt. Royal, NJ 08061
Tel: 609-423-7222
Web: http://stadianet.vml.com/

■ Related Articles

Sports
Golf Course Superintendents
Groundsmanagers and Groundskeepers
Sports Executives
Stadium Ushers and Vendors

Sports Information Directors

■ **See Sports Publicists**

Sports Instructors and Coaches

■ Overview

Sports instructors demonstrate and explain the skills and rules of particular sports, like golf or tennis, to individuals or groups. They help beginners learn basic stances, grips, movements, and techniques of a game. Sports instructors often help experienced athletes to sharpen their skills.

Coaches work with a single, organized team or individual, teaching them the skills associated with that sport. A coach prepares her or his team for competition, and during the competition, continue to give instruction from a vantage point near the court or playing field. There are over 300,000 sports instructors and coaches employed in the United States.

■ History

Americans have more leisure time than ever and many have decided that they are going to put this time to good use by getting, or staying, in shape. This fitness boom has created employment opportunities for many sports related occupations.

Health clubs, community centers, parks and recreational facilities, and private business, now employ sports instructors who teach everything from tennis and golf to scuba diving.

SPORTS INSTRUCTORS AND COACHES	
SCHOOL SUBJECTS	English Physical education
PERSONAL SKILLS	Communication/ideas Helping/teaching
WORK ENVIRONMENT	Indoors and outdoors Primarily multiple locations
MINIMUM EDUCATION LEVEL	Some postsecondary training
SALARY RANGE	$6.00 an hour to $28,000 to $1,000,000+
CERTIFICATION OR LICENSING	Required in certain positions
OUTLOOK	Much faster than the average
DOT	153
GOE	12.01.01
NOC	5252
O*NET	34058B

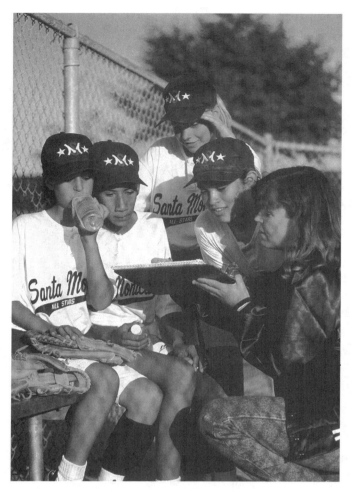

A baseball coach discusses strategy with her team.

As high school and college sports become even more organized, there continues to be a need for coaches, qualified to teach the intricate skills associated with athletics today.

■ The Job

The specific job requirements of sports instructors and coaches varies according to the type of sport and who they teach. For example, an instructor teaching advanced skiing at a resort in Utah will have different duties and responsibilities than an instructor teaching beginning swimming at a municipal pool. Nevertheless, all instructors and coaches are teachers. They must be very knowledgeable about rules and strategies for their respective sports, but without an effective teaching method that reinforces correct techniques and procedures, their students or players won't be able to share that valuable knowledge. Also, instructors and coaches need to be aware of and open to new procedures and techniques. Many attend clinics or seminars to learn more about their sport or even how to teach more effectively. Many are members of professional organizations that deal exclusively with their sport.

Safety is a primary concern for all coaches and instructors. Coaches and instructors make sure their students have the right equipment and know its correct use. A major component of safety is helping students feel comfortable and confident with their abilities. This entails teaching the proper stances, techniques, and movements of a game, instructing students on basic rules and answering any questions.

While instructors may tutor students individually, or in small groups, a coach works with all the members of a team. Both use lectures and demonstrations to show students the proper skills, and both point out the mistakes or deficiencies of individuals.

Motivation is another key element in sports instruction. Almost all sports require stamina, and most coaches will tell you that psychological preparation is every bit as important as physical training.

Coaches and instructors also have administrative responsibilities. College coaches actively recruit new players to join their team. Professional coaches attend team meetings with owners and general managers to determine which players they will draft the next season. Sports instructors at health and athletic clubs schedule classes, lessons and contests.

■ Requirements

Training and educational requirements vary, depending on the specific sport and the ability level of students being instructed. Most coaches who are associated with schools have bachelor's degrees. Many middle and high school coaches are also teachers within the school. Most instructors need to combine several years of successful experience in a sport with some educational background, preferably in teaching. A college degree is becoming more important as part of an instructor's background.

High School

To prepare for college courses, high school students should take courses that teach them human physiology; biology, health and exercise classes would all be helpful. Courses in English and speech are also important to improve or develop communication skills.

There is no substitute for developing an expertise in a sport. If you can play the sport well, and effectively explain to other people how they might play as well as you, you will most likely be able to get a job as a sports instructor. The most significant source of training for this occupation is gained while on the job.

Postsecondary Training

Postsecondary training in this field varies greatly. College and professional coaches often attended college as athletes, while others attended college and received their degrees without playing a sport. Certainly if you are interested in becoming a high school coach you will need a college degree because you will most likely be teaching as well as coaching. At the high school level, coaches spend their days teaching everything from physical education to English to mathematics, and so the college courses these coaches take vary greatly. Coaches of some youth league sports may not need a postsecondary degree, but they must have a solid understanding of their sport and of injury prevention.

Certification or Licensing

Many facilities require sports instructors to be certified. Information on certification is available from any organization that deals with the specific sport in which one might be interested.

Since most high school coaches also work as teachers, people interested in this job should plan to obtain teacher certification in their state.

Other Requirements

Coaches and have to be experts in their sport. They must have complete knowledge of the rules and strategies of the game, so that they can creatively design effective plays and techniques for their athletes. But the requirements for this job do not end here. Good coaches are able to communicate their extensive knowledge to the athletes in a way that not only instructs the athletes, but also inspires them to perform to their fullest potential. Therefore, coaches are also teachers.

"I think I'm good at my job because I love working with people and because I'm disciplined in everything I do," says Dawn Shannahan, assistant girls' basketball and track coach at Leyden High School in Franklin Park, Illinois. Discipline is important for athletes, as they must practice plays and techniques over and over again. Coaches who cannot demonstrate and encourage this type of discipline will have difficulty helping their athletes improve. Dawn adds, "I've seen coaches who are knowledgeable about their sport but who aren't patient enough to allow for mistakes or for learning." Patience can make all the difference between an effective coach and one who is unsuccessful.

Similarly, Dawn says, "A coach shouldn't be a pessimist. The team could be losing by a lot, but you have to stay optimistic and encourage the players." Coaches must be able to work under pressure, guiding teams through games and tournaments that carry great personal and possibly financial stakes for everyone involved.

■ Exploring

Try to gain as much experience as possible in all sports and a specific sport in particular. It is never too early to start. High school and college offer great opportunities to participate in sporting events either as a player, manager, trainer or in intramural leagues. Most communities have sports programs such as Little League baseball or track and field meets sponsored by the Recreation Commission. Get involved by volunteering as a coach, umpire, or starter. Talking with sports instructors already working in the field is also a good way of finding out about career opportunities.

■ Employers

Besides working in high schools, coaches are hired by colleges and universities, professional sports teams, individual athletes such as tennis players, and by youth leagues, summer camps, and recreation centers.

■ Starting Out

People with an expertise in a particular sport, who are interested in becoming an instructor, should apply directly to the appropriate facility. Sometimes a facility will provide training.

For those interested in coaching, many colleges offer positions to *graduate assistant coaches*. Graduate assistant coaches are recently graduated players who are interested in becoming coaches. They receive a stipend and gain valuable coaching experience.

■ Advancement

Advancement opportunities for both instructors and coaches depend on the individual's skills, willingness to learn, and work ethic. A sports instructor's success can be measured by caliber of play and number of students. Successful instructors may become well known enough to open their own schools or camps, and write books, or produce how-to videos.

A coach's success is often measured in the win/loss column. For professional coaches, that could, arguably, be their only criteria. However coaches in the scholastic ranks have other responsibilities and other factors that measure success. High school and college coaches must make sure their players are getting good grades, and middle school coaches can be successful if they produce a team who competes in a sportsmanlike fashion regardless of whether they win or lose.

Successful coaches are often hired by larger schools. High school coaches may advance to become college coaches and the most successful college coaches often are given the opportunity to coach professional teams. Former players sometimes land assistant or head coaching positions.

■ Earnings

Earnings for sports instructors vary considerably depending on the sport and to whom the lesson is being presented. The coach of a Wimbledon champion commands much more an hour than the swimming instructor for the tadpole class at the municipal pool.

Much of the work is part-time and part-time employees generally do not receive paid vacations, sick days, or health insurance. Instructors who teach group classes for beginners through park districts or at city recreation centers can expect to earn around $6.00 per hour. A hour-long individual lesson through a golf course or tennis club averages $75. Many times, coaches for children's teams work as volunteers.

Many sports instructors work in camps teaching swimming, archery, sailing and other activities. These instructors generally earn between $1,000 and $2,500, plus room and board, for a summer session.

Full time fitness instructors at gyms or health clubs can expect to earn between $13,000 and $28,000 per year. Instructors with many years of experience and college degree have the highest earning potential.

Most coaches who work at the high school level or below also teach within the school district. Besides their teaching salary and coaching fee—either a flat rate or a percentage of their annual salary—school coaches receive a benefits package that includes paid vacations and health insurance.

According to *American Almanac of Jobs and Salaries 1997,* college head football coaches generally earn an average of $50,000. Head coaches of men's college basketball teams average $69,400 annually, while coaches of women's teams average considerable less at $42,200 a year. Many larger universities pay more. Coaches for professional teams often earn between $125,000 and $500,000. Some top coaches can command million-dollar-salaries. Many popular coaches augment their salaries with personal appearances and endorsements.

■ Work Environment

An instructor or coach may work indoors, in a gym or health club, or outdoors, perhaps at a swimming pool. Much of the work is part time. Full time sports instructors generally work between 35 and 40 hours per week. During the season when their teams compete, coaches can work 16 hours each day, five or six days each week.

It's not unusual for coaches or instructors to work evenings or weekends. Instructors work then because that is when their adult students are available for instruction. Coaches work nights and weekends because those are the times their teams compete.

One significant drawback is the lack of job security. A club may hire a new instructor on very little notice, or may cancel a scheduled class for lack of interest. Athletic teams routinely fire coaches after losing seasons.

Sports instructors and coaches should enjoy working with a wide variety of people. They should be able to communicate clearly and possess good leadership skills to effec-

tively teach complex skills. They can take pride in the knowledge that they have helped their students or their players reach new heights of achievement and training.

■ Outlook

The fitness boom has created employment opportunities for many people employed in sports-related occupations. Health clubs, community centers, parks and recreational facilities, and private business, now employ sports instructors who teach everything from tennis and golf to scuba diving. According to the U.S. Department of Labor, this occupation will grow much faster than the average through the year 2006. There were 303,000 sports instructors and coaches employed in the United States in 1996. By the year 2006, a projected 125,000 additional jobs will be available.

Job opportunities will be greatest in urban areas, where population is the most dense. Those with the most training, education, and experience will have the best chance for employment.

Coaching jobs at the high school or amateur level will be plentiful as long as the public continues its quest for a healthier and more active lifestyle. The creation of the Women's National Basketball Association (WNBA) and the expansion of current professional leagues will open new employment opportunities for professional coaches. There will also be openings as other coaches retire, or are terminated. However, there is very little job security in coaching, unless you can consistently produce a winning team.

■ For More Information

For certification information, trade journals, and other publications, contact:

American Alliance for Health, Physical Education, Recreation and Dance
1900 Association Drive
Reston, VA 20191
Tel: 703-476-3400, ext 430
Web: http://www.aahperd.org/

For information on membership and baseball coaching education, contact:

American Baseball Coaches Association
108 South University Avenue, Suite 3
Mount Pleasant, MI 48858-2327
Tel: 517-775-3300

For a free position paper on the "Role of Teacher/Coaches in High School," contact:

National Association for Sport and Physical Education
1900 Association Drive
Reston, VA 20191
Tel: 800-213-7193, ext. 410
Web: http://www.aahperd.org/naspe/naspe-main.html

Sports Physicians

■ Overview

Sports physicians treat patients who have sustained injuries to their musculoskeletal systems during the play or practice of an individual or team sporting event. Sports physicians also do preparticipation tests and physical exams. Some sports physicians create educational programs to help athletes prevent injury. Sports physicians work for schools, universities, hospitals, and private offices; some also travel and treat members of professional sports teams.

■ History

The field of sports medicine, and nearly all the careers related to it, owes its foundation to the experiments and studies conducted by Aristotle (384-322 BC), Leonardo da Vinci (1452-1519), and Etienne Jules Marey (1830-1904). Aristotle's treatise on the gaits of humans and animals established the beginning of biomechanics. In one experiment, he used the sun as a transducer to illustrate how a person, when walking in a straight line, actually throws a shadow that produces not a correspondingly straight line, but a zigzag line. Leonardo da Vinci's forays into the range and type of human motion explored a number of questions, including grade locomotion, wind resistance on the body, the projection of the center of gravity onto a base of support, and stepping and standing studies.

It was Marey, however, a French physiologist, who created much more advanced devices to study human motion. In fact, sports medicine and modern cinematography claim him as the father of their respective fields. Marey built the first force platform, a device which was able to visualize the forces between the foot and the floor. His nonphotographic studies of the gait of a horse inspired Eadward Muybridge's (1830-1904) serial photographs of a horse in motion, which in turn inspired Marey's invention of the chronophotograph. In contrast to Muybridge's consecutive frames, taken by several cameras, Marey's pictures with the chronophotograph superimposed the stages of action onto a single photograph; in essence, giving form to motion. By 1892, Marey had made primitive motion pictures, but his efforts

were quickly eclipsed by those of Louis (1864-1948) and Auguste Lumiere (1862-1954).

Following both World War I and II, Marey's and others scientists' experiments with motion would combine with medicine's need to heal and/or completely replace the limbs of war veterans. To provide an amputee with a prosthetic device that would come as close as possible to replicating the movement and functional value of a real limb, scientists and doctors began to work together at understanding the range of motion peculiar to the human body.

Mechanically, sports can be categorized according to the kinds of movements used. Each individual sport uses a unique combination of basic motions, including walking, running, jumping, kicking, and throwing. These basic motions have all been rigidly defined for scientific study so that injuries related to these motions can be better understood and treated. For example, sports that place heavy demands on one part of an athlete's body may overload that part and produce an injury, such as "tennis elbow" and "swimmer's shoulder." Baseball, on the other hand, is a throwing sport and certain injuries from overuse of the shoulder and elbow are expected. Athletes who play volleyball or golf also use some variation of the throwing motion and therefore, also sustain injuries to their shoulders and elbows.

Today, sports medicine in particular deals with the treatment and prevention of injuries sustained while participating in sports and, as such, is not a single career but a group of careers that is concerned with the health of the athlete. For its specific purposes, the field of sports medicine defines "athlete" as both the amateur athlete who exercises for health and recreation, and the elite athlete who is involved in sports at the college, Olympic, or professional level. People of all ages and abilities are included, including those with disabilities.

Among the professions in the field of sports medicine are the trainer, physical therapist, physiologist, biomechanical engineer, nutritionist, psychologist, and physician.

SPORTS PHYSICIANS	
SCHOOL SUBJECTS	**Biology** **Health**
PERSONAL SKILLS	**Helping/teaching**
WORK ENVIRONMENT	**Indoors and outdoors** **One location with some travel**
MINIMUM EDUCATION LEVEL	**Medical degree**
SALARY RANGE	**$112,000 to $250,000 to $1,000,000+**
CERTIFICATION OR LICENSING	**Required by all states**
OUTLOOK	**Faster than the average**
DOT	**070**
GOE	**02.03.01**
O*NET	**32102A**

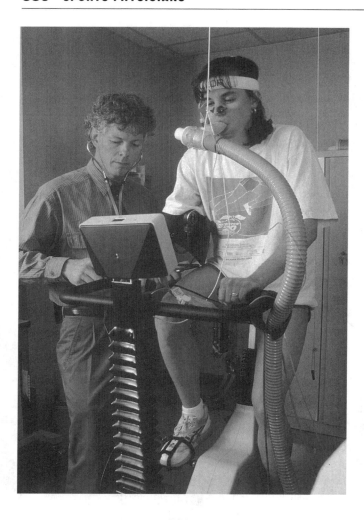

A sports physician tests an athlete's respiratory system.

In addition, the field of sports medicine also encompasses the work of those who conduct research to determine the causes of sports injuries. Discoveries made by researchers in sports medicine have spread from orthopedics to almost every branch of medicine.

Arthroscopic surgery falls into this category. It was developed by orthopedic surgeons to see and operate on skeletal joints without a large open incision. The arthroscope itself is a slender cylinder with a series of lenses that transmit the image from the joint to the eye. The lens system is surrounded by glass fibers designed to transfer light from an external source to the joint. Inserted into the joint through one small, dime- to quarter-sized incision, the arthroscope functions as the surgeon's "eyes" to allow pinpoint accuracy when operating. The surgical elements, themselves, are inserted through other small incisions nearby. In the 1970s the techniques of arthroscopy were used by only a few surgeons as an exploratory measure to determine whether or not traditional, open surgery had a

good chance of succeeding. Today, arthroscopy is the most commonly performed orthopedic surgery performed in the United States, and instead of being an exploratory procedure, 80 percent of all arthroscopic surgeries are performed to repair tissue damage.

■ The Job

Sports physicians treat the injuries and illnesses of both the amateur and elite athlete. They are often referred to as *team physicians*. Depending upon the level of athlete they are treating, sports physicians are usually either practitioners in family practice as medical doctors (M.D.s) or orthopedic surgeons. More often than not, the individual who works as the team physician for a professional sports team is too busy tending to the health needs of the team to have time for a private practice as well.

Brent Rich, M.D., Head Team Physician for Arizona State University and Team Physician for the Arizona Diamondbacks, agrees that there are some varieties of sports physicians: "Sports physicians come in two major varieties: primary care providers with training in non-surgical sports medicine and orthopedic surgeons. The majority of sports physicians are in private practice. Each area has its rewards and downfalls. As a board certified family physician, I deal with about 90 percent of what goes on in the sports medicine arena."

At the scholastic level, the team physician is usually the school physician and is appointed by the school board. Athletic programs at the collegiate level are usually capable of supporting a staff of one or more physicians who cater to the needs of the athletic teams. The size of the school and athletic program also determines the number of full-time physicians; for example, a state university basketball team might have one physician, even an orthopedic surgeon, dedicated wholly to that team's needs.

Professional teams, of course, have the necessary resources to employee both a full-time physician and an orthopedic surgeon. Generally, their presence is required at all practices and games. Often, professional teams have a sports medicine department to handle the various aspects of treatment, from training to nutrition to mental health. If they don't have their own department, they take advantage of the specialists at university hospitals and private care facilities in the area.

To fully understand the nature of a particular sports injury, sports physicians study the athlete as well as the sport. The musculoskeletal system is a complex organization of muscle segments, each related to the function of others through connecting bones and articulations. Pathological states of the musculoskeletal system are reflected in deficits (weaknesses in key muscle segments) that may actually be quite distant from the site of the injury or trauma. The risk factors for any given sport can be assessed by comparing the performance demands that regularly produce characteristic injuries with the risk factors that might predispose an athlete to injury.

Strength and flexibility, for example, are requirements for nearly every sport. Stronger muscles improve an athlete's performance, and deficits in strength can leave him or her prone to injury. Rehabilitation under the supervision of a sports physician focuses on rebuilding lost muscle strength. Likewise, an athlete who lacks flexibility may subject him or herself to strains or pulls on her muscles. For this athlete, rehabilitation would center on warming and stretching the isolated muscles, as well as muscle groups, to reduce or alleviate such muscle strains. In both cases, it is the responsibility of the sports physician to analyze the potential for injury and work with other sports health professionals to prevent it, as well as to treat the injury after it happens. The goal of every sports physician is to keep athletes performing to the best of their ability and to rehabilitate them safely and quickly after they are injured.

To prevent injuries, as well as treat them, sports physicians administer or supervise physical examinations of the athletes under their care to determine the fitness level of each athlete prior to that athlete actively pursuing the sport. During the exams, sports physicians note any physical traits, defects, previous injuries, or weaknesses. They also check the player's maturity, coordination, stamina, balance, strength, and emotional state. The physical examination accomplishes many different goals. To begin with, it quickly establishes the athlete's state of health and allows the sports physician to determine whether that athlete is physically capable of playing his or her sport. On the basis of the physical exam, the sports physician advises the coach on the fitness level of the athlete which, of course, determines a great deal about the athlete's position on the team. Furthermore, the exam alerts the sports physician to signs of injury, both old and new. Old or existing injuries can be noted and put under observation, and weaknesses can be detected early on so that proper conditioning and training patterns can be implemented by the coach and trainers.

Depending upon the results of their physical examinations, the sports physician may advise athletes to gain or lose weight, change their eating, drinking, and sleeping habits, or alter their training programs to include more strength or cardiovascular exercises. Routine physical checkups are also a common way of evaluating an athlete's performance level throughout a season, and many sports physicians will administer several exams to gauge the effect of their advice, as well as to ensure that the athlete is making the suggested changes in habits or training.

Preventing injuries is the sports physician's first goal and conditioning is probably the best way to accomplish that goal. Sports physicians are often responsible for developing and supervising the conditioning and training pro-

GLOSSARY

Arthroplasty: Procedures and artificial materials used to treat joint problems.

Clinical examination: Doctors determine the history of an injury by examining the patient.

Hard casts: Casts made of plaster or plastic that immobilize broken bones.

Immobilization: A common treatment that allows an injury to settle and healing to begin.

Magnetic Resonance Imaging (MRI): Computerized technique that uses magnetic fields to provide a picture of an injury.

Soft casts: Bandage wraps

grams that other sports health professionals will implement. The sports physician may work with the coaching staff and athletic trainers to help athletes develop strength, cardiovascular fitness, and flexibility, or the sports physician may advise the coaching and training staff members of the overall safety of a practice program. For example, the sports physician may evaluate the drills and practice exercises that a football coach is using on a given day to make certain that the exercises won't exacerbate old injuries or cause new ones. Sports physicians may even be involved in the selection of protective gear and equipment. The degree of their involvement, again, depends on the size of the team and the nature of the physicians' skills or expertise, as well as on the number of other people on the staff. Large, professional teams tend to have equally large staffs on which one person alone is responsible for ordering and maintaining the protective gear, for example.

Sports physicians are often in attendance at practices (or they are nearby, in case of an injury), but their presence at games is mandatory. If a player shows signs of undue fatigue, exhaustion, or injury, the sports physician needs to be there to remove the athlete from the competition. Dr. Rich says being at the games is one of the perks of his profession: "To see others accomplish what they desire gives me satisfaction. Another good part is covering sports events and feeling a part of the action on the sidelines, in the locker room, or in the heat of the battle."

After an athlete is injured, the sports physician must be capable of immediately administering first-aid or other procedures. He or she first examines the athlete to determine the gravity and extent of the injury. If the damage is extreme enough (or cannot be determined from a manual and visual exam), the sports physician may send the athlete to the hospital for X rays or other diagnostic examinations. Later, the team physician may perform surgery, or recommend that the athlete undergo treatment or surgery by a specialist. Some of the most common types of injuries are stress fractures, knee injuries, back injuries, shoulder injuries, and elbow injuries.

The sports physician oversees the athlete's recuperation and rehabilitation following an injury, including the nature and timing of physical therapy. The athlete's return to practice and competition is determined by the sports physician's analysis of the athlete's progress. Frequent physical examinations allow the physician to judge whether or not the athlete is fit enough to return to full activity. The decision to allow an athlete to compete again following an injury is a responsibility that sports physicians take seriously; whether the athlete is an amateur or an elite professional, the future health and well-being of the athlete is at stake and cannot be risked, even for an important championship game.

A developing area of the sports physician's responsibilities is the diagnosis and treatment of substance abuse problems. Unfortunately, even as research on the field of sports medicine has produced new methods and medications that mask pain and decrease inflammation—which shortens recovery time and lengthens athletic careers—some also produce unnatural performance enhancement. Most notable of these are anabolic steroids—synthetic modifications of the male hormone, testosterone—which have become widely abused by athletes who use them to better their performances. When taken while on a high protein diet and an intensive exercise regimen, these drugs can increase muscle bulk, which in turn can produce increased strength, speed, and stamina. The side effects of these drugs, however, include aggression, sterility, liver problems, premature closure of the growth plates of the long bones, and in women, male pattern baldness and facial hair. These side effects are usually irreversible and, as such, pose a significant health risk for young athletes.

Another method also banned from use in competition-level athletics is the withdrawal of an athlete's blood several weeks prior to competition. The blood is stored and then, just before the athlete competes, the blood is trans-fused back into his or her bloodstream. This process, blood doping, also has serious, even fatal, side effects, including heart failure and death.

Finally, professional athletes sometimes develop substance abuse problems, such as alcohol or drug use. Sports physicians are responsible for detecting all of these problems and helping the athlete return to a healthy lifestyle, which may include competition.

In addition to the responsibilities and duties outlined above, many sports physicians also perform clinical studies and work with researchers to determine ways of improving sports medicine practices. Often, the results of such studies and research are published in medical journals and even popular magazines.

■ Requirements

High School

During high school, take as many health and sports-related classes as possible. Biology, chemistry, health, computers, and English are important core courses. High grades in high school are important for anyone aspiring to join the medical profession, because competition for acceptance into medical programs at colleges and universities is always tough.

Postsecondary Training

Sports physicians have either an M.D. (medical doctor degree) or a D.O. (doctor of osteopathy degree). Each involves completing four years of college, followed by four years of medical school, study and internship at an accredited medical school, and up to six years of residency training in a medical specialty, such as surgery. Many physicians also complete a fellowship in sports medicine either during or after their residency.

During the first two years of medical school, medical students usually spend most of their time in classrooms learning anatomy, physiology, biology, and chemistry, among other subjects. In their last two years, they begin seeing patients in a clinic, observing and working with doctors to treat patients and develop their diagnostic skills. Some medical schools are beginning to alter this time-honored tradition by having the medical students begin to work with patients much sooner than two years into their schooling, but this method of combining classroom and clinical experiences is not yet fully accepted or integrated into the curriculum.

After medical school, the new doctors spend a year in an internship program, followed by several years in a residency training program in their area of specialty. Most sports physicians complete this stage of their training by working in orthopedics or general practice.

The fellowship portion of a doctor's training is essential if he or she has chosen to specialize. For example, the doctor specializing in general surgery and interested in sports medicine would probably seek an orthopedics fellowship providing further training in orthopedic surgery techniques.

Certification or Licensing

Finally, to become licensed, doctors must have completed the above training in accordance with the guidelines and rules of their chosen area or specialty. Beyond the formal requirements, this usually involves a qualifying written exam, followed by in-depth oral examinations designed to test the candidate's knowledge and expertise.

Other Requirements

Sports physicians must be able to learn and remember all the many parts and variations about the human body and how it functions. Knowledge of different sports and their demands on an athlete's body is also important. Like all medical doctors, sports physicians need to be able to communicate clearly to their patients with compassion and understanding.

■ Exploring

High school students interested in becoming sports physicians should look into the possibility of working with the physician, coach, or athletic trainer for one of their school's teams. Firsthand experience is the best way to gain fresh perspective into the role of the team physician. Later on, when applying for other paid or volunteer positions, it will help to have already had sports-related experience. Dr. Rich agrees, "Try to get experience with a physician who does what you think you want to do. Spending time in their offices, in surgery, or on the sidelines at high school games will give you exposure. As you learn more, you can do more."

■ Employers

Most sports physicians are in private practice, so they work for themselves or with other medical doctors. Some sports physicians, however, may work for sports clinics, rehabilitation centers, hospitals, and college/university teaching hospitals. Still other sports physicians travel with professional baseball, basketball, football, hockey, and soccer teams to attend to those specific athletes. Sports physicians are employed all over the country.

■ Starting Out

You won't become the team physician for a National Basketball Association team fresh out of medical school. Many sports physicians begin by joining an existing practice and volunteering with a local sports organization. After several years they may apply to the school board for consideration as a team physician for their local school district. Later, they may apply for a position with a college team until they ultimately seek a position with a national or international professional athletics team or organization. This gradual climb occurs while the individual also pursues a successful private practice and builds a strong, solid reputation. Often, the sports physician's established reputation in an area of specialty draws the attention of coaches and management looking to hire a physician for their team. Others take a more aggressive and ambitious route and immediately begin applying for positions with various professional sports teams as an assistant team physician. As in any other field, contacts can prove to be extremely useful, as are previous experiences in the field. For example, a summer volunteership or internship during high school or college with a professional hockey team might lead to a job possibility with that hockey team years later. Employment opportunities depend on the skill and ambitions of each job candidate.

■ Advancement

Depending on the nature of an aspiring sports physician's affiliation with athletic organizations (part time or full time), advancement paths will vary. For most sports physicians, advancement will accompany the successful development of their private practices. For those few sports physicians who are employed full time by professional athletic organizations, advancement from assistant to team physician is usually accompanied by increased responsibilities and a corresponding increase in salary.

■ Earnings

The earnings of a sports physician vary depending upon his or her responsibilities and the size and nature of the team. The private sports physician of a professional individual athlete, such as a figure skater or long distance runner, will most likely earn far less than the team physician for a professional football or basketball team, primarily because the earnings of the team are so much greater so the organization can afford to pay more for the physician's services. On the other hand, the team physician for the professional basketball team probably wouldn't have time for a private practice, although the sports physician for the figure skater or runner would, in all likelihood, also have a private practice or work for a sports health facility.

According to the American Medical Association, general practitioners and family practice physicians earn an annual net income of approximately $112,000, not including the fees and other income paid to them by the various athletic organizations for whom they work as team physicians. Again, these fees will vary according to the size of the team, the location, and the level of the athletic organization (high school, college, or professional, being the most common). The income generated from these fees is far less than what they earn in their private practices. On the other hand, those team physicians who are employed full time by a professional organization will likely make more than their nonprofessional sports counterparts, even as much as one million dollars or more.

■ Work Environment

Sports physicians must be ready for a variety of work conditions, from the sterile, well-lighted hospital operating room to the concrete bleachers at an outdoor municipal swimming pool. The work environment is as diverse as the sports in which athletes are involved. Although most of their day-to-day responsibilities will be carried out in clean, comfortable surroundings, on game day they are expected to be where the athletes are, and that might be a muddy field (football and soccer); a snow-covered forest (cross-country skiing); a hot, dusty track (track and field); or a steamy ring (boxing). Picture the playing field of any given sport and that is where you will find sports physicians. They are also expected to travel with the athletes whenever they go out of town. This means being away from their home and family, often for several days, depending on the nature, level, and location of the competition.

■ Outlook

After years of watching athletes like Babe Ruth close down the bars after a game, coaches and management now realize the benefits of good health and nutrition. Within the world of professional sports, the word is out: proper nutrition, conditioning, and training prevent injuries to athletes, and preventing injuries is the key when those athletes are making their owners revenues in the billions of dollars. A top sports physician, then, is a worthwhile investment for any professional team. Thus, the outlook for sports physicians remains strong.

Even outside the realm of professional sports, amateur athletes require the skills and expertise of talented sports physicians to handle the aches and pains that come from pulling muscles and overtaxing aging knees. Athletes of all ages and abilities take their competitions seriously, and are as prone to injury as any pro athlete, if not more, because amateur athletes in general spend less time conditioning their bodies.

■ For More Information

To obtain publications about sports medicine, contact:

American College of Sports Medicine
PO Box 1440
Indianapolis, IN 46206-1440
Tel: 317-637-9200, ext. 117
Web: http://www.a1.com/sportsmed/index.html

For a list of accredited athletic training programs, job listings, and information on certification, contact:

National Athletic Trainers Association (NATA)
2952 Stemmons Freeway
Dallas, TX 75247-6196
Tel: 214-637-6282
Web: http://www.nata.org

American Orthopaedic Society for Sports Medicine
6300 North River Road, Suite 200
Rosemont, IL 60018
Tel: 847-292-4900
Web: http://www.sportsmed.org

American Physical Therapy Association
1111 North Fairfax Street
Alexandria, VA 22314
Tel: 703-684-APTA (2782)
Web: http://www.apta.org

To join a forum on various medical issues, visit the AMA's Web site:

American Medical Association
515 North State Street
Chicago, IL 60610
Tel: 312-464-5000
Web: http://www.ama-assn.org

■ Related Articles

Health Care

Sports

General Practitioners

Physicians

Sports Trainers

Surgeons

Sports Psychologists

■ Overview

In general, *sports psychologists* work with amateur and professional athletes to improve their mental and physical health, as well as athletic performances, by using goal setting, imagery, attentional focus strategies, and relaxation techniques, among others. Sports psychologists also strive to help athletes to mentally prepare for competition. There are approximately 143,000 psychologists employed in the United States, but sports psychologists comprise only a small segment of this number.

Sports psychologists are divided into three categories: clinical, educational, and research. *Clinical sports psychologists* work mainly with individuals who are experiencing emotional problems that are usually, but not always, somehow connected to their sport. *Educational sports psychologists* have two roles, one as a classroom instructor and the other as a consultant. In the classroom, they teach students methods and techniques related to sports psychology. On the field, they usually function as members of the coaching staff. Just as the coach teaches physical skills, the sports psychologist teaches mental skills. *Research sports psychologists* conduct studies that provide the clinical and educational sports psychologists with scientific facts and statistics.

■ History

In the 17th century, René Descartes (1596-1650) described his belief that human behaviors could be classified in two ways—voluntary and involuntary. Those behaviors which were completely mechanical, instinctual, and similar to those of animals, he characterized as involuntary; those behaviors which required or submitted to reason were characterized as voluntary. Based on this early model, and the subsequent work of others, including John Locke (1632-1704), James Mill (1773-1836), and John Stuart Mill (1806-73), later philosophers and scientists experimented with sensation and perception, culminating with an introspective analysis of the many elements of an individual's experience.

William James (1842-1910) advanced modern psychology by asserting the theory of a stream of thought and G. Stanley Hall (1844-1924), a contemporary of James, established the first true laboratory of psychology at Clark University in 1883. Sigmund Freud (1856-1939) introduced the medical tradition to clinical psychology. A physician and neurologist, Freud's methods of psychoanalysis included word association techniques and later, inkblot techniques as developed by Hermann Rorschach (1844-1922).

After World War II, psychology as a profession became formally recognized, standards of training have been developed by the American Psychological Association (APA), and certification and licensing laws have been passed to regulate the practice of professional psychology.

Since psychology deals with human behavior, psychologists apply their knowledge and techniques to a wide range of endeavors including human services, management, law, and sports.

■ The Job

Sport and exercise psychology is the scientific study of the psychological factors that are associated with participation and performance in sport, exercise, and other types of physical activity. In general, sports psychologists work with amateur and professional athletes to improve their mental and physical health, as well as athletic performances, by using goal setting, imagery, attentional focus strategies, and relaxation techniques, among others. Sports psychologists also strive to help athletes to mentally prepare for competition.

Sport psychology professionals are interested in two main objectives: helping athletes use psychological principles to improve performance (performance enhancement) and understanding how participation in sport, exercise, and physical activity affects an individual's psychological development, health, and well-being throughout the life span.

Sports psychologists work with individual athletes and entire teams. They may concentrate on the problems the athlete is having with the sport, from a bad slump to the feelings of low self-esteem that come when the crowd jeers the athlete's performance. Sports psychologists also work to help the individual athlete to overcome feelings of depression, drug or substance abuse, and violence.

They work with teams in many ways, too, the most notable of which is creating a feeling of cohesion among the many different personalities which constitute a team. Team members are also counseled when they are traded to another team or released.

Sports psychologists also work with individual athletes and team members on improving their level of performance, concentration, and mental attitude. The phrase, "a winning attitude," derives its power from the fact that sports psychologists can help the athletes with whom they work to actually visualize a winning shot or a perfect golf swing and then execute that vision.

Sports psychologists don't work with only exceptional, elite athletes or teams; most sports psychologists, in fact, work with college athletes or amateur athletes, and many teach in academic settings or offer their own, motivational lecture series. Some sports psychologists have their own columns in specialized sports magazines and others work in athletic training facilities, hired full-time by the owners to work with the athletes who come to train there.

SPORTS PSYCHOLOGISTS	
SCHOOL SUBJECTS	**Biology** **Health** **Psychology**
PERSONAL SKILLS	**Communication/ideas** **Helping/teaching**
WORK ENVIRONMENT	**Primarily indoors** **Primarily one location**
MINIMUM EDUCATION LEVEL	**Master's degree**
SALARY RANGE	**$20,000 to $100,000 to $200,000**
CERTIFICATION OR LICENSING	**Required by all states**
OUTLOOK	**Little change or more slowly than the average**
DOT	**045**
GOE	**11.03.01**
NOC	**4151**
O*NET	**27108**

▪ Requirements

The requirements for entering the field of sports medicine as a sports psychologist are somewhat tricky to understand, so it helps to understand the various paths available in psychology in general, as determined by the American Psychological Association (APA). Students should expect to spend five to seven years in graduate work if they are interested in pursuing doctoral degrees.

High School

High school students should take a college-preparatory curriculum that concentrates on English, mathematics, and sciences. You should also take a foreign language, especially French and German, because reading comprehension of these languages is one of the usual requirements for obtaining a doctorate. Participation in sports will give you the background necessary to effectively understand the athletes you work with in your practice.

Postsecondary Training

A doctoral degree is generally required for employment as a psychologist, but there are two different degrees that psychologists can seek at the doctorate level. The first degree is called the Ph.D., and psychologists with this degree qualify for a wide range of teaching, research, clinical, and counseling positions in universities, elementary and secondary schools, and private industry. The second degree is called a Psy.D. (Doctor of Psychology) and psychologists with this degree qualify mainly for clinical positions. The Ph.D. degree culminates in a dissertation based on original research, while the Psy.D. is usually based on practical work and examinations rather than a dissertation. In clinical or counseling psychology, the requirements for a doctoral degree usually include a year or more of internship or supervised experience.

Individuals who have only a master's degree in psychology are allowed to administer tests as psychological assistants and, if they are under the supervision of doctoral level psychologists they can conduct research in laboratories, conduct psychological evaluations, counsel patients, and perform administrative duties. They are also allowed to teach in high schools and two-year colleges, and work as school psychologists or counselors.

Those individuals with only a bachelor's degree in psychology can assist psychologists and other professionals and work as research or administrative assistants, but without further academic training, they cannot advance further in psychology.

Having said all of this, it will perhaps come as a shock that there no APA-accredited sports psychology doctoral programs. One of the controversies behind this is whether professionals working with athletes in applied areas of sports psychology should be required to have doctoral training in clinical or counseling psychology—training which would qualify them to provide psychological treatment to athletes as well. The solution reached by the APA, along with the AAASP and NASPSPA, is that any practitioners of sports psychology who do not also have doctoral-level clinical or counseling training should refer athletes who need treatment to licensed professionals. Sports psychologists who work with Olympic athletes are required to have doctoral-level degrees.

Those students who are interested in academic teaching and research in sports psychology can earn doctoral degrees in sport sciences and take additional courses in psychology or counseling. Over 50 schools in the United States offer this type of program, including the University of North Carolina-Greensboro and the University of Florida. Typical subjects covered include sports psychology, performance enhancement, concentration skills, stress and attention management, and motivation.

Those students who want more emphasis on psychology in their training can pursue a psychology doctorate in areas such as group procedures, psychotherapy, learning, education, and human development or motivation, with a subspecialty in sports psychology. At most universities, students take courses like these in the sport sciences department, while at a few schools, such as the University of Washington and the University of Los Angeles, California, it is possible to take similar courses through the psychology department.

Students who wish to provide clinical services to athletes can pursue a doctoral degree in APA-accredited clinical or counseling psychology programs, with a concentration in sports psychology. This track offers students the widest range of job opportunities, from teaching and research in sports and psychology to counseling athletes as well as the general population. Institutions where this mode of study is typical include the University of Wisconsin-Madison and the University of North Texas.

For those students who are interested primarily in educating people about the health benefits of exercise or in helping student athletes, a master's degree is an option. More than a 100 sport sciences departments offer a master's degree in areas related to sports psychology.

For more detailed information on graduate programs in psychology and sports psychology, look for *The Directory of Graduate Programs in Applied Sport Psychology*, available from the APA.

Certification or Licensing

In addition to educational requirements, most states require that all practitioners of psychology meet certification or licensing requirements if they are in independent practice or involved in offering patient care of any kind (including clinical and counseling). Once the educational requirements are fulfilled, a sports psychologist should contact the APA for details about certification and licensing requirements, as they usually vary from state to state.

■ Exploring

You can gain experience in this field by volunteering to work for research programs at area universities or by working in the office of a psychologist. Another option is to learn more about sports by working as a gofer or intern with the sports medicine departments of college, university, or professional athletic teams. Even by participating in a sport in high school or college, you can gain valuable insight into the mental and emotional stresses and demands placed upon athletes.

In addition, students should begin their understanding of psychology by taking as many courses in the field as possible.

■ Employers

Sports psychologists are employed by athletes at the amateur, college, or professional level and by owners of professional, college, and private organizations. They may also be employed at colleges and universities as teachers and researchers.

■ Starting Out

Along the road toward a Ph.D. or Psy.D., students of all levels can get involved in the research or educational aspects of psychology, either as a volunteer subject or a paid helper. These positions will gradually increase in responsibility and scope as the student progresses in his or her studies. Eventually, the student will be eligible for internships that will, in turn, provide him or her with valuable contacts in the field.

Graduates can explore job opportunities with a wide variety of employers, from the university research branch of psychology or sport sciences to the world of elite athletes. Finding work with the latter, however, can prove extremely difficult.

■ Advancement

Sports psychologists advance in several ways, but primarily by increasing the scope and caliber of their reputations in the field. This is accomplished, of course, by consistently helping athletes to improve their athletic performance and to reduce the emotional and/or mental strain placed upon them. Advancement might come in the form of a new position (working for a professional team) or it might come in the form of a solid, private practice.

Sports psychologists who make their living largely in the academic world do so by successfully publishing the results of studies, research, or theories in specialized medical journals.

■ Earnings

Specific salary figures for sports psychologists are not readily available, but psychologists in general can earn anywhere from $20,000 to $200,000, depending the area of their expertise, the location of their practice, and whether or not they practice alone or in a partnership. Be forewarned, however, that with the higher salary comes long years of study in order to attain the educational background necessary to practice. In fact, in order to stay current with topics ranging from treatment to medication, psychologists must continue to learn and study their field for as long as they intend to practice.

■ Work Environment

Sports psychologists spend most of their time working in office and hospital environments, but some of their time is spent in the same environments as the athletes they counsel. This may mean spending several hours on a golf course, on a ski slope, or in the gymnasium. Much depends on the type of psychologist. For example, the clinical psychologist would probably spend most of his or her time with athletes in the relative comfort of an office setting and the psychologist would meet with athletes during a regular, nine-to-five day. Educational sports psychologists would be more likely to be in the gym or on the golf course, working side-by-side with the rest of the coaching staff. Finally, depending on the nature of the study, a research sports psychologist might spend some time with the athletes while they were practicing, but in general, the research psychologist would spend most of his or her time in an office or laboratory setting, reviewing or studying the data from his or her studies.

Sports psychologists, like other physicians, need to stay up-to-date with developing theories and research and to accomplish this, they may have to spend additional time reading journals, books, and papers; conducting research in the library; or attending conferences on relevant issues. They may need to take additional course work to stay abreast of new theories and techniques, as well as to maintain current certification or licensing. Although sports psychologists spend a lot of time with the athletes they're helping, they also spend large amounts of time alone.

■ Outlook

While employment in the field of psychology in general is likely to grow more slowly than the average for all occupations through the year 2006, it has yet to be determined how this prognosis affects the subspecialty of sports psychology. Largely due to the fact that so much time goes into the training, very few people leave the field entirely. Many stay in the general field of psychology and merely move around, switching specialties, but even this is rare.

While competition is incredibly tough for positions with elite athletes, most experts believe that other areas of sports psychology will continue to offer a substantial number of jobs to new graduates, especially in academe.

Sports psychology may, at first, seem lucrative, but it can lack the steady income of a private practice or academic teaching post because practitioners are frequently only on call, not steadily billing for their time. It can also be difficult to get work because while you might have a great, famous athlete for a client, chances are pretty good that the athlete doesn't want it known that he or she is getting counseling for a bad marriage, a slump, or a drug problem. This forces the sports psychologist to rely on referrals which, again, might not happen all that often when athletes and their agents are trying to keep the athlete's therapy a secret.

For More Information

The Student Information section of the APA Web site offers information on career options in psychology.

American Psychological Association (APA)
750 First Street, NE
Washington, DC 20002-4242
Tel: 202-336-5500
Web: http://www.apa.org

For certification info and an overview of the field, visit the "What is Sports Psychology?" section of the AAASP Web site:

Association for the Advancement of Applied Sports Psychology (AAASP)
Department of Psychology
The University of Memphis
Memphis, TN 38152-6400
Web: http://www.aaasponline.org/

The following organization brings together psychologists, as well as exercise and sport scientists, interested in research, teaching, and service in this area. The APA Running Psychologists is an affiliated group of Division 47. The Division currently has committees on diversity issues and education and training, sponsors preconvention workshops at the APA convention, and publishes, **The Exercise and Sport Psychology Newsletter** *three times a year, as well as other publications:*

Division 47 Administrative Office
750 First Street, NE
Washington, DC 20002-4242
Tel: 202-336-6013
Web: http://www.psyc.unt.edu/apadiv47

For subscription information, contact:

Journal of Applied Sport Psychology
c/o Allen Press
PO Box 1897
Lawrence, KS 66044-8897
Tel: 913-843-1235

Related Articles

Health Care
Social Services
Sports
Psychiatrists
Psychiatric Technicians

Sports Publicists

Overview

There are two types of *sports publicists:* those who work for professional and amateur teams and those who work for individual professional athletes. *Sports team publicists* handle the daily press operations for the organization. They handle the media relations, set up interviews with players, ensure that the correct information is distributed to the press, and write press releases. Sports publicists who work for individual players try to enhance their client's image by casting them in a positive light via newspaper, magazine, and television stories.

History

The sports industry has matured into the 11th largest industry in the United States, according to CBS Sportsline. Professional teams are the most widely recognized industry segment in sports. Professional teams include all of the various sports teams, leagues, and governing bodies for which individuals get paid for their performance.

Promoting sports has become a huge industry. There may be as many as 1.5 million marketing and 300,000 media front office personnel positions in professional and amateur sports, according to the article "Sports Information: The Most Coveted, Ignored Profession," by Nick Neupauer (*Public Relations Strategist*).

The Job

Sports publicists, sometimes called *sports information directors, press agents, PR directors, marketing directors,* or *directors of communication,* are responsible for all of the team's publications, including media guides, programs for all home games, schedule cards, mail order brochures, recruiting kits, annual reports, and booster club newsletters. They also handle all of the team's publicity, which includes news and feature releases, news conferences and background information, photography, media interviews, and media tours.

Publicity people also deal with game management, which includes PA announcers, scoreboard operations, telephone hook-ups, scorers, officiating facilities, press box seating and credentials, broadcast facilities, video facilities, and travel and lodging. They also are in charge of generating crowd participation by developing promotions, give-aways, half-time exhibitions, and music. Publicists also help design the uniform insignia and team banners.

Sports information directors might have other responsibilities, such as creating and placing advertising, attending league meetings, conventions, and workshops, coordinating booster club activities, fundraising, fan surveys, budgets, equipment negotiations, licensing, and merchandising.

Collegiate publicists might not be affiliated with the college or university's public relations department, but instead might be housed under the athletic department. Unlike other public relations practitioners, most sports information directors promote their competition as well as the team they work for. The better the opposition, the better the fan interest and ticket sales.

Publicists that work for athletes can be viewed as spin doctors, constantly creating angles and news events to get their clients into the spotlight. Many publicists try to show their clients in a positive light by having the athletes participate in goodwill appearances or work with organizations like the United Way. Maintaining that positive image increases the athletes' potential income and market value.

With the rising number of athletes getting into trouble with the law or showing generally bad behavior, another part of publicists' jobs is crisis management. In the article, "When the Sport Hits the Fan: Crisis PR in the Age of Athlete Scandals," by Ty Wenger, (*Tactics*), Marcia Robbins, founder of the Los Angeles-based Robbins Group and former publicist for Billie Jean King says, "Twenty years ago, when I started my career in sports PR, it never occurred to me that I would need to know anything about crisis PR. But over the years, I've practiced it more than I would really like to say."

■ Requirements

High School

You are the voice of the person or team that you represent, so it is very important that you are an effective communicator. Take classes in English and journalism to hone your writing skills, and speech to help you learn how to compose your ideas and thoughts and convey them to an audience.

Postsecondary Training

Most publicists working in the sports industry are college graduates with degrees in public relations, marketing, communications, journalism, or sports administration. A college degree is essential, according to the Public Relations Society of America.

■ Exploring

Ask your teacher or counselor to set up an information interview with a publicist. Volunteer to handle various public relations-type duties for your high school sports teams or clubs.

■ Employers

Sports publicists work in one of three areas. Some work for public relations firms that handle athletes or sports-oriented events. Others work directly for sports teams in their front offices. Some are self-employed, working directly with clients.

■ Starting Out

Neupauer's article features a quote from Melvin Helitzer, professor of journalism at Ohio State University and author of *The Dream Job: Sports Publicity, Promotion and Marketing*. Helizter says that the best way to enter the professional sports public relations level is by gaining experience at the collegiate ranks. "SID's [sports information directors] college staff averages 2.5 full-time employees and 15 to 20 interns. Getting 1 of those internships is the best way to get your feet wet in this business."

SIDs publish 118 publications, send out 5,000 individual releases, and work with 100 to 200 different media reporters and editors, according to Helitzer. This will give you a great opportunity not only to learn how to generate all of this material, but also to begin collecting samples of your writing and to develop your clip file. Every interviewer you will meet will ask you for your clip file, since they provide proof of your journalistic and PR writing skills.

There are also training programs within established PR companies. Such programs might be hard to obtain, but they are available.

■ Advancement

"Like baseball players, front office staff generally look to advance to higher levels, from single-A to double-A or triple-A onto the majors," says Gary Radke, marketing director of the Wisconsin Timber Rattlers minor league baseball team. "Within the given organizations,

SPORTS PUBLICISTS	
SCHOOL SUBJECTS	**English** **Journalism** **Speech**
PERSONAL SKILLS	**Communication/ideas** **Leadership/management**
WORK ENVIRONMENT	**Primarily indoors** **One location with some travel**
MINIMUM EDUCATION LEVEL	**Bachelor's degree**
SALARY RANGE	**$21,000 to $40,000 to $100,000+**
CERTIFICATION OR LICENSING	**None available**
OUTLOOK	**Faster than the average**

FOR THE LOVE OF THE GAME

Gary Radke, marketing director for the Wisconsin Timber Rattlers baseball team, discusses his position.

"The Wisconsin Timber Rattlers are the Class-A affiliate of the Seattle Mariners. As marketing director, I wear several hats. This is a year-round position. In the offseason, my duties include designing and printing all of the collateral materials for the upcoming season, such as sales and ticket brochures. During that time, I also set the advertising budget and meet with the media to purchase the time or space. We work with radio, newspaper, and television, as well as magazines.

"During the season, my position is a little more routine. It involves maintaining and updating all of the radio and newspaper advertising on a regular basis, as well as the Web site. I'm also responsible for all of the media relations and making sure that the statistics that appear in the programs are correct and updated. I also send out press releases and attend various speaking engagements and media appearances, not to mention pulling the tarp on rainy days.

"I think the most important thing in this position is the ability to improvise. There are crash deadlines to deal with, late roster additions, and media to call for interviews. An outgoing personality is a must.

"I got this job by applying to a classified ad. I had been working for an advertising agency and was looking for a change. This was the only thing I applied to and the rest is history.

"I love baseball, so working for a baseball team is great. I get to do a lot of different things, so the job stays interesting. I also have met a lot of interesting people and feel genuine satisfaction by providing fun for our fans. Sometimes, however, there are too many things going on, and it gets very hectic. The hours are probably the worst part. On game days, we are in here at 9 AM and get out of there about 10 PM. We are expected to attend all of the 70 home games during the season.

"This position requires a jack of all trades and a master of at least some of them. Desktop publishing, copywriting, and photography skills are desirable. Media buying, ad layout, and budget skills are necessary. Obviously, a knowledge of baseball helps, but is not necessary. The specific skills or knowledge you lack can be compensated for by using experts, but the more you bring to the job, the more successful you will be."

there really isn't much in the way of advancement because everyone is basically at the same level. Upper-management positions are the general manager and assistant general manager."

■ Earnings

Sports publicists can earn anywhere from $28,000 to more than $100,000 per year. People just starting out might make less, while those with proven track records command higher salaries. Publicist who work for individual athletes can earn more money.

"I think minor league marketing directors make anywhere from $21,000 up to $60,000," says Gary. "We receive health insurance, 10 sick days, 2 personal days, apparel discounts, health club memberships, and free soda at the games."

■ Work Environment

During the season, sports publicists may work 12- to 20-hour days, 7 days a week. Since most sporting events take place in the evening or on weekends, and half are played on the road, sports publicists spend a lot of time on the job. Some publicists travel with their teams, some do not. Either way, this job is very time-consuming.

■ Outlook

The field of sports publicity is very competitive, and even though it is expanding as more teams and leagues form, it is still difficult to land a job. The U.S. Department of Labor predicts that employment of public relations specialists in general is expected to increase faster than average for all occupations through the year 2006, but the number of applicants with degrees in the communications fields—journalism, public relations, and advertising—is expected to exceed the number of job openings.

■ For More Information

For information on careers in public relations, scholarships, and the Public Relations Student Society, contact:

The Public Relations Society of America
33 Irving Place
New York, NY 10003-2376
Tel: 212-995-2230
Web: http://www.prsa.org

■ Related Articles

Advertising and Marketing

Public Relations

Sports

Advertising Account Executives

Advertising Workers

Marketing Research Analysts

Media Planners and Buyers

Media Relations Specialists

Public Opinion Researchers

Public Relations Specialists

Sports Scouts

■ Overview

People who work as *sports scouts* observe athletic contests to gather information that will help the team that employs them. They may attend a game in the hopes of recruiting a player, or they may accumulate information about an opponent's players and strategies.

■ History

In the first part of the 20th century, baseball as a professional sport became popular. Large, eastern cities like New York and Boston were home to some of the best and most popular teams. While these teams were competing in baseball stadiums, their scouts were competing to find talented, young players.

Traveling by train through the South and Midwest, baseball scouts rushed from town to town in hopes of discovering the next Cy Young or Cap Anson.

Some scouts worked for professional teams while others signed players to personal contracts, hoping to sell those contracts to the owners of professional teams. As baseball became more organized, scouts worked almost exclusively for one professional team. Soon, young prospects no longer were sent directly to major league teams, but played in the minor leagues, or *farm teams*. These teams were set up to teach players, who already possessed excellent ability, the subtle nuances of the game.

This created a need for even more scouts. In addition to locating and signing talented young players, other scouts were assigned the task of watching these players develop and deciding when they were ready to advance to the next level.

■ The Job

Sports scouts attend sporting events and record their findings for pay. They may travel from city to city watching other teams from their league play, or they may attend games for the purpose of recruiting players for their own team.

Scouts are an extension of the coaching staff of a team, and in many cases, assistant coaches have scouting responsibilities.

There are two general tasks assigned to scouts. One is recruitment, the other is to gather information about an opposing team.

Scouts involved in recruitment attend high school and college games to look for talented young players. Coaches or general managers from professional teams may inform scouts about specific personnel needs. For example, a basketball coach may need a guard who can handle the ball well and shoot jump shots. A scout attends numerous college games and then returns to the coach with a list of players who meet the description. In most cases the list returned will rate the individual players and include some additional information, such as the players' ages, heights, and weights. Notes or impressions from an interview the scout conducted with the player would also be included. (The National Collegiate Athletic Association [NCAA] has set up many rules that regulate when scouts can speak with players.) *Recruitment scouts* may attend a game to see a particular individual play but will also make notes on other players. A scout may see 10 or more games a week, so it is very important to keep detailed notes. Scouts must also be comfortable with statistics, both compiling them and understanding them. Scouts examine statistics like earned run average, or yards per carry, and field goal percentage in order to assist them in their deliberations concerning players.

A scout may need to see a player more than once to determine if that player has the ability to play at the next level. Scouts report their findings back to the coach or general manager, and it is up to that person to act on the scout's recommendations.

Recruitment scouts need to see numerous games so that they acquire the ability to accurately assess talent. Scouts need to distinguish between players who have sound, fundamental skills and an understanding of the game and players who are natural athletes but have not yet acquired the finer skills.

Professional baseball is structured somewhat differently than basketball or football. Professional baseball has minor leagues, or a farm system, that is composed of players who have talent but are still maturing or learning skills. Many scouts are assigned to these leagues to keep a watchful eye on players as they develop. For example, the Cincinnati Reds baseball team employs 18 full-time scouts, and 15 part-time scouts, most of whom concentrate on players already playing in the minor leagues. They also receive a daily report compiled by the Major League Scouting Bureau.

SPORTS SCOUTS	
SCHOOL SUBJECTS	**Foreign language** **Psychology**
PERSONAL SKILLS	**Leadership/management**
WORK ENVIRONMENT	**Indoors and outdoors** **Primarily multiple locations**
MINIMUM EDUCATION LEVEL	**High school diploma**
SALARY RANGE	**$18,000 to $35,000 to $100,000**
CERTIFICATION OR LICENSING	**None available**
OUTLOOK	**Little change or more slowly than the average**
DOT	**153**
GOE	**12.01.01**
NOC	**5252**
O*NET	**34058A**

Assistant coaches and scouts often attend opponents' games to find out about players' abilities and team strategies. They watch the game, diagram set plays, and note the tendencies of players. During practice the following week, scouts share their findings and, when possible, detail plans to help offset an opponent's strength.

Requirements

There are no educational requirements for becoming a sports scout. Most scouts are former players or coaches in the particular sport they scout in.

High School

A general high school education will give you the basic skills you need to succeed in sports scouting. Speech and English courses will help you communicate easily with prospects as well as relay your findings to coaches, managers, and front office workers. Learn Spanish or Japanese; this will help you connect with foreign players, who are increasingly sought after by major league teams. Finally, take physical education classes and join sports teams—especially the sport you want to scout in.

Other Requirements

First and foremost, sports scouts should have vast knowledge of a particular sport. For them, an athletic contest is not only something to enjoy, but something to study. Sports scouts are detail-oriented, often methodical people who understand the rules, regulations, fundamentals, strategies, and personality types who are best suited to athletic competition.

Sports scouts need to have above-average organizational skills. More often than not, they will attend several games before reporting to a supervisor. They must be able to organize their thoughts and notes so that they can compare players from several games to come to conclusions about the ability of the athletes they have seen compete.

Sports scouts must also have above-average communication skills. They should be able to write and speak well. They will interact with other coaches and players daily. Recruitment scouts will be in contact with younger players, and so it is helpful to be able to work well with and understand younger people. A proficiency in a foreign language, especially Spanish or Japanese, is also of great help to modern scouts, who are increasingly sent to foreign countries to monitor the development of promising athletes.

Sports scouts are team players. They understand that each team member has a job to do, and only when each player does the job is the team successful.

Also, a sports scout needs to be a good judge of talent and to a certain degree, character. A sports scout knows what it takes to compete on a higher level, and must be able to spot that ability and mental toughness in others.

Exploring

It goes without saying that individuals interested in a career as a sports scout should participate in sporting events at the high school and college level. You can participate either as a player or as an assistant to players or coaches. You should also read a variety of books by coaches and athletes to learn fundamentals and strategies. You should also take part in community sports programs to interact with a variety of players and observe different styles of play.

Employers

Sports scouts are employed by major league organizations throughout North America. Others work for professional scouting organizations, such as the Major League Scouting Bureau.

Starting Out

Many sports scouts are former athletes who have retired from playing and apply their knowledge of the game to scouting for younger talent. Not only do athletes gain knowledge from years of playing, but they make valuable contacts in the sporting world.

An aspiring sports scout should become familiar with local sports activity and keep track of talented young players. Meeting people who are active in the sports community is a great help. Sports scouts are part of a vast network of people who gather, compile, and exchange information about sports. Coaches, broadcasters, and journalists are also members of this group.

Advancement

Sports scouts who provide accurate and concise reports often have the opportunity to observe more talented athletes. A professional baseball scout, for example, may begin scouting college players. As the scout gains experience, and if the scout's information proves reliable, the scout may be assigned to a minor league division, and eventually may become the director of scouting for a major league team.

Scouts who succeed and advance are organized, honest, and can effectively communicate both verbal and written ideas. Sports scouts build their reputations by identifying players who will be successful at the professional level. Advancement is often based on the success of the players the scout has selected.

Earnings

Beginning sports scouts can expect a starting salary of $18,000 or more. Sports scouts also are reimbursed for travel expenses and meals. Another fringe benefit is free admission to countless sporting events.

With three to five years' experience, a successful scout can expect to make between $30,000 and $35,000 a year.

A veteran scout with many success stories may earn up to $100,000 a year.

Many sports scouts also receive such fringe benefits as paid vacation and sick days, health insurance, and pension plans.

■ Work Environment

Sports scouts travel an average of three weeks out of every month, and they are away from home most nights and weekends. While on the road they stay in hotels and eat most of their meals in restaurants. They travel often by car or bus and also frequently by plane.

Workdays while on the road are quite long. A sports scout may be on the road by seven in the morning to drive four hours to meet with a player and watch an afternoon game. There may be another game to see that night in another location or the evening may be spent reviewing videotape of games attended over the last few days.

Long hours and near constant travel are typical of work as a sports scout, and more often than not, there is little reward for the effort. A scout may recommend several hundred players over the course of a career and only a handful of those players will ever make it to the professional level. Despite this, dedicated sports scouts continue to visit the isolated diamonds, the tiny high school and college gyms, or the cracked concrete of the urban ballcourt looking for the next superstar.

■ Outlook

There will be little change in the number of sports scouts employed in North America. There are approximately 1,000 professional sports scouts in the United States in the late 1990s. Most work for professional teams. Baseball is the sport that employs the greatest number of scouts.

A relatively new concept in the industry is *pool scouting.* The concept involves a group of scouts who collect data on a great many players and provide that information to several teams. The scouts are not employed by any one team, but by professional scouting organizations, such as the Major League Scouting Bureau.

As professional leagues add expansion teams and the talent pool diminishes, there will probably be more opportunities for sports scouts to travel and work in foreign countries.

■ For More Information

Contact the following organizations for information on careers:

American and National League of Baseball Clubs
350 Park Avenue
New York, NY 10022
Tel: 212-339-7600

National Basketball Association
645 Fifth Avenue
New York, NY 10022
Tel: 212-826-7000
Web: http://www.nba.com/

National Football League
410 Park Avenue
New York, NY 10022
Tel: 212-758-1500

■ Related Articles

Sports
Professional Athletes—Individual Sports
Professional Athletes—Team Sports
Sports Executives
Sports Instructors and Coaches
Talent Agents and Scouts

Sports Statisticians

■ Overview

Manually or by using computers, *sports statisticians* compute and record the statistics relating to a particular sports event, game, or competition, or the accomplishments of a team or single athlete during competition.

■ History

Statistics is a relatively new science relating to the collection and interpretation of data. Ancient record-keeping can be traced back to the Old Testament and to population records compiled by the Babylonians and the Romans. Formal population studies in a scientific sense, however, were only begun early in the 19th century in the United States and certain European countries. The motivation for such statistics was primarily to

SPORTS STATISTICIANS	
SCHOOL SUBJECTS	Computer science Mathematics
PERSONAL SKILLS	Leadership/management
WORK ENVIRONMENT	Indoors and outdoors Primarily multiple locations
MINIMUM EDUCATION LEVEL	High school diploma
SALARY RANGE	$5,000 to $35,000 to $100,000
CERTIFICATION OR LICENSING	None available
OUTLOOK	Faster than the average
DOT	020
GOE	11.01.02
NOC	2161
O*NET	25312

promote efficient bureaucracies, but statistical studies were being conducted to try and solve other problems, in fields as diverse as social science, biology, and physics.

In the late 19th century, British statistician Sir Ronald Aylmer Fisher began his investigations on experimental designs, randomization, and mathematical statistics. Fisher and others developed small-sample statistical techniques and methods, such as the analysis of variance and covariance. His contributions are regarded by many as the origin of modern statistics. Since then, the field of statistics has grown rapidly and statistics are used in nearly every area of study, from agriculture to health science to sports.

Sports fans, athletes, and coaches have been keeping informal records of the best and worst performances since before organized sports began. Early in the 19th century, as the rules and regulations of different sports began to be organized by official gaming associations, the importance of official record-keeping was recognized. Soon, statistics were not only a vital resource when deciding which records were set or broken, but they were being used to help determine the outcome of specific plays. For example, during a basketball game the referee asks the official scorer and sta-

---

GLOSSARY

Box score: The final, official game score

Charge: In basketball, when a player runs into another player while possessing the ball.

Double dribble: In basketball, dribbling again after having stopped

Error: In baseball, a misplay by a defensive player that gives the team that is batting an advantage.

Flash stats: The stats distributed during a basketball game at every 60-second time-out.

Foul: An infraction of the rules

Foul ball: In baseball, a ball hit outside of the first or third base line; not in fair territory

Free throw: In basketball, an unhindered shot at the basket

Fumble: In football, to accidentally lose physical possession of the ball, usually by dropping it

Hat trick: In a soccer or hockey game, three or more goals scored by a single player.

Rebound: In basketball, a retrieval of a missed shot after the ball bounces away from the basket rim or backboard

Roster: The official list of players on a team, usually including the positions played or events competed in

Stats: Short for "statistics"; numbers that denote an athlete's record in the sport. For example, a player's batting average in baseball is a stat.

Stat crew: Team of individuals who work to record and prepare statistics for the media and home and visiting team.

---

tistician how many time-outs the home team has already taken, or how many fouls a certain player has received.

Once, the statistician sat in the bleachers or on the bench, marking up a scoring book with slashes and checks to indicate runs, goals, fouls, etc. Later, the statistician would tally up the various totals, computing team averages, as well as individual play averages. Today, professional sports associations and leagues have highly sophisticated computers and programs that instantly tally the totals, averages, and percentages at the touch of a button.

■ The Job

Sports statisticians compute and record the statistics relating to a particular sports event, game, or competition, or the accomplishments of a team or single athlete during competition. They use their own knowledge of basic math and algebraic formulas, alone or in combination with calculators and computers to calculate the statistics related to a particular sport or athlete.

Most high school, college, and professional team sports have an *official scorer/statistician* who attends every home game and sits courtside, at what is called the scorer's table. The team scorer/statistician running stats at a basketball game, for example, keeps track of the score, the number of time-outs, and specific calls made by the referees, such as team and player fouls. The statistician is also referred to as the official scorer because if any item on the scoreboard is questioned—by a referee, one of the coaches, or another game official—the individual who ultimately has the power to determine the outcome is the statistician.

Many statisticians still work by hand with a special notebook for recording the game statistics. As each play and call occurs in the game, the statistician records the play or call in a particular column or row of the stat book. Later, the statistician will make a tally of the total number of player errors, rebounds, assists, goals, etc. He or she can determine such statistics as the average number of rebounds in a quarter or per game. The statistician uses the same, predetermined algebraic formulas to compute the statistics for a single athlete or an entire team. Usually, the statistician keeps the stats, for both the home team and the visiting team, by individual. At the end of the game, the statistician can then provide both coaches and teams with specific information on their respective play during the game.

Other statisticians use computers with specialized software programs that automatically compute the player and team statistics. Most professional athletic teams have both a manual scorer and one or more individuals keeping statistics with the league—or association—sponsored statistics program. For example, both the National Basketball Association (NBA) and the National Football League (NFL) have computerized statistics programs that are used throughout the league or association. These programs, created by independent, private companies, allow each team to choose the statisticians who will run the system, while ensuring that the statistics systems used will be universal. One such company, SuperStats, created the computerized system for the NFL. In many cases, the computer system that calculates the different statistics also controls the different scoreboards in the arena or stadium, and can quickly and efficiently produce flash and quarter stats for the teams, coaching staff, and various members of the media.

In professional team sports, the home team is responsible for making certain an official scorer/statistician is in attendance at all home games. The away or visiting team may have their own statistician or staff of statisticians, but the individual responsible for the official scores, etc., is hired by the home team and this is usually the same person throughout an entire season.

Statisticians begin work by arriving at the arena or stadium in plenty of time to set up, greet the officials, peruse any announcements or press releases from the public relations offices of the home or visiting team, and get the starting lineups from both the home and visiting team coaches. Statisticians who work with computer equipment may arrive even earlier to set up their equipment and make sure the system is up and running well in advance of game time.

Once the game begins, statisticians quite literally cannot take their eyes off of the game. They need to see every play as it happens in order to record it precisely in the stats book or computer. Often, the official team scorer/statistician keeps track of certain statistics, while other statisticians keep track of the remaining statistics. For example, Bob Rosenberg, the official team scorer for the Chicago Bulls, is responsible for tracking the field goals attempted and the field goals made, the three-point shots attempted and made, the free throws attempted and made, the number of personal fouls, and the number of time-outs taken. He may record other statistics, but if there is a discrepancy it is these stats for which he is responsible during the game. A team of statisticians who work the computers are responsible for taking down the number of rebounds, assists, steals, and so on. The most important aspect of the job is to remember that the statistician is doing more than compiling statistics; the statistician is recording the game, event by event.

Statisticians also work for television and radio stations and the sports information departments of colleges and universities. The jobs of these statisticians are nearly identical to that of the team scorer/statistician for a professional team, in that they might record statistics in a manner similar to the one described above, but they might also be asked to do a lot of research and writing. Television stations often have a statistics and research staff responsible for collecting and verifying the statistics of any given sport. If the sport is fairly popular, they might assign someone to cover the events in that area, but if the sport is relatively young or not as popular, they might be asked to research information and statistics for that sport. The statistics and information is usually passed along to the sportscasters who are covering a game or event in that sport. Often, the statisticians are asked to write up notes for the sportscasters to use. For example, if the sportscasters are covering a baseball game, the statistician might come up with trivia or examples throughout the history of baseball when someone pitched no-hitters back-to-back.

Statisticians who work for private companies might be asked to keep statistics, field calls from sportswriters the day after a game about the stats for that game, or write notes up for one of their company's clients—notes regarding stats or trivia, for example.

Statisticians work both part time and full time, depending on the level of athletics in which they are involved, their degree of computer literacy and education, and whether they pursue freelance or full-time employment opportunities. The vast majority of individuals work part time, simply because they enjoy keeping stats for a team in a sport they love. Competition is incredibly fierce for full-time positions, whether for a sports information department at a college or university, a radio or television station or network sports show, or a private statistics company. Most statisticians advise students interested in entering the field to be persistent in asking for volunteer or part-time positions, keep their schedules open in the event someone does call with a chance to score a game, and to be realistic about the chances of finding full-time work.

■ Requirements

Technically, there are no formal educational requirements for the job of sports statistician. Knowing how to manually score a game or event, and knowing as much as possible about the sport or sports for which you would like to keep statistics, are probably the only true requirements, but there are plenty of informal requirements that prospective sports statisticians should keep in mind.

First and foremost, although knowledge of manual scoring is essential, the future of sports statistics, like almost everything else, is tied to computers. The more you know about computers—from navigating your way around a keyboard, to programming and troubleshooting—the better. Since most of the computer systems for the professional teams are privately owned, created expressly for the league or association, there isn't any way to study the programs used by professional teams, per se. Becoming computer literate and having a working knowledge of common computer systems and programs, however, is the best way to ensure that, if necessary, you can pick up the intricacies of a new program.

Secondly, having a solid grasp of basic math skills is a necessity. In order to compute home run averages, you need to be able to figure averages. The formulas used to arrive at the different statistics are simple enough, but you must be good with math to figure them out yourself. On the job you will probably use a calculator or computer, but if the computer system goes out you need to be able to do the math yourself.

Good writing and communication skills are also vital to the statistician; you may find yourself trying to explain a statistic to a sportscaster or writer, or you may be asked to write notes concerning relevant statistics or trivia, even a press release. If you can't communicate information quickly and intelligently, you might find yourself out of a job.

Postsecondary Training

Private companies who employ sports statisticians will, however, most likely require candidates to have a bachelor's degree in a related field, such as marketing, accounting, communications, or sports administration.

■ Exploring

The best way to gain experience in this field is to learn as much as possible about how a sport is played and how to score it, especially those sports which you enjoy most. High school and college students can easily accomplish this by participating in sports or volunteering to act as statistician for one of the teams.

There are books available for nearly every sport which explain how to correctly score particular statistics, but there is a better, more expedient way. Look around you at the next high school baseball or basketball game. Chances are a seasoned veteran of statistics is no less than two yards away. During a break or—better yet—after the game introduce yourself and ask that person how to score a game; most statisticians learned how to score sports events in precisely this way—by asking the people who have been doing it for years.

■ Employers

Sports statisticians work for professional athletic teams, television and radio stations and networks, private companies, and colleges and university sports programs.

■ Starting Out

Many statisticians find part-time jobs when they are high school students and continue these jobs through college. Others go on to score stats for various teams at their college or university. The sports information departments at colleges and universities are also good places to look for part-time work. You might be assigned to the public rela-

tions office, in which case you would learn the related tasks—fielding calls from the media, writing press releases, and researching statistics for a specific team. Or, you might be assigned to work directly with a team as a statistician. In either case, many statisticians continue to volunteer or work part time at stats jobs, in order to maintain their scoring skills.

Television and radio stations are yet another way into the field of sports statistics. As mentioned, contacts are very helpful, but you can send your resume to the sports departments of various stations and channels, asking if they need another statistician. Be ready to volunteer if necessary or to work in the sometimes humbling position of a gofer. One longtime statistician advises prospective statisticians to be ready to score any game, anytime, anywhere, because one never knows which contact will eventually lead to something bigger and better. This also means being prepared to sacrifice personal time to a last-minute request from a statistician to cover a game in an emergency when the regular person can't be there.

Finally, there are three companies who work with sports statistics: Elias Sports Bureau; Stats, Inc.; and ESPN/Sportsticker. These companies employ statisticians and researchers to help provide clients (television, radio, and cable stations; magazines and newspapers) with sports statistics and research on a daily basis. These companies often offer internships and part-time jobs and are definitely one avenue to pursue for full-time jobs.

■ Advancement

Part-time jobs keeping statistics for high school and college and university athletic teams can often lead to stats jobs with other organizations, including radio and television stations and private organizations, like Elias Sports Bureau, ESPN/Sportsticker, and Stats, Inc. While not much of a hierarchy exists in these companies—most employees are either statisticians and researchers or executives—it is possible to advance to executive-level positions within these companies. While some people may leave these jobs to take others, most stay in these jobs for many years.

Statisticians who build solid reputations for themselves, who know the ins and outs of a particular sport, and who have excellent communication and math skills can often advance in the field to work for large radio and television networks.

■ Earnings

On the whole, competition will be keen for full-time jobs that offer competitive salaries in sports statistics. It is important to realize that many statisticians must work full-time jobs, often in totally unrelated fields, in order to support themselves. Only their love of the sport and statistics itself—and not the financial rewards of the jobs—keeps them involved with sports statistics.

Even for part timers, much depends on the level of athletics in which the statistician is involved. For example, a statistician working freelance for a radio station covering the Vancouver Grizzlies—an expansion professional basketball team—might receive $25 per game, whereas a statistician working freelance for one of the large, television networks, like Fox TV, might receive anywhere from $400 to $500 per game.

On the other hand, statisticians who work full-time for radio and television, or for companies like Elias Sports Bureau, receive salaries commensurate with jobs in other fields. An individual working with one of these companies for between 1 year and 5 years might earn $25,000 to $35,000 a year. If that person stayed with the company for another 5 to 10 years, he or she might earn between $35,000 and $50,000 a year. Statisticians who work for a company for many years can earn anywhere between $75,000 and $100,000 a year. Again, competition for these positions is extremely fierce.

In comparison to statisticians who work in the more traditional fields of statistical analysis, both in government and nongovernment jobs, sports statisticians with full-time positions have the opportunity to earn considerably higher salaries, although this may not always be the case. According to the *Occupational Outlook Handbook*, the average annual salary for statisticians in the federal government in nonsupervisory, supervisory, and managerial positions was $61,030 in 1997; mathematical statisticians averaged $65,600.

■ Work Environment

Statisticians routinely work in the same conditions as do others in professions related to sports coverage, such as sportscasters, sportswriters, and sports agents. That is, they may spend time outdoors, in pleasant and inclement weather, but they also spend a lot of time indoors, in the media and statistics areas of sports stadiums and arenas, and in their own offices.

Statisticians also work odd hours, including weekends and holidays. In short, whenever there is a sports event scheduled that requires score-keeping and statistics, one or more statisticians will be covering it. This can wreak havoc with the more nostalgic of holidays, such as Christmas and the Fourth of July; some football and many basketball games are scheduled on Christmas Eve and Christmas Day, while there are countless professional baseball games played on Independence Day.

■ Outlook

As the impact of cable television and satellite reception enhances the marketability of the top four sports—football, baseball, basketball, and hockey—it will also bring into viewers' living rooms many sports not previously carried by the major networks. All of this increased sports coverage, plus developing technologies and markets on the Internet, will only increase the demand for sports statistics and the individuals who record and catalogue them. More importantly, perhaps, is the effect this new technology will have on those seeking jobs in sports statistics, as computer skills will become just as valuable to those interested in a career in sports statistics as in-depth knowledge of a sport. Those individuals who do have computer skills will be all the more marketable in the years to come. People already in the field will probably want to develop some degree of computer literacy.

On another note, even as the field develops, those currently with full-time positions in sports statistics aren't likely to leave those jobs. Attrition rates due to retirement and advancement, combined with new jobs, should keep this field developing just slightly faster than the average.

■ For More Information

In addition to the following companies who do employ statisticians and researchers, students interested in internships, part-time jobs, and full-time jobs with sports statistics should also contact the sports information departments at colleges and universities in their area, local and major network television and radio, as well as the national and club offices of professional league/association sports, such as the National Basketball Association, the National Football League, the National Hockey League, and Major League Baseball.

Elias Sports Bureau
500 Fifth Avenue, 21st Floor
New York, NY 10110
Tel: 212-869-1530

ESPN/Sportsticker

Harborside Financial Center
600 Plaza Two
Jersey City, NJ 07311

Stats, Inc.
8130 Lehigh Avenue
Morton Grove, IL 60053
Tel: 847-677-3322
Email: support@stats.com
Web: http://www.stats.com

■ Related Articles

Sports

Statisticians

Statistical Clerks

Sports Team Publicists

■ See Sports Publicists

Sports Trainers

■ Overview

Sports trainers, also referred to as *athletic trainers, certified sports medicine trainers,* and *certified sports medicine therapists,* are concerned with preventing injuries to amateur and professional athletes through proper exercises and conditioning; providing immediate first-aid attention to injuries as they occur during a practice or event; and leading injured athletes safely through rehabilitation programs and routines.

Athletic trainers often consult with physicians during all stages of athletic training to ensure that athletes under their care are physically capable of participating in competition. In addition, they specialize in health care administration, education, and counseling.

SPORTS TRAINERS	
SCHOOL SUBJECTS	Health
	Physical education
PERSONAL SKILLS	Helping/teaching
	Leadership/management
WORK ENVIRONMENT	Indoors and outdoors
	Primarily multiple locations
MINIMUM EDUCATION LEVEL	Bachelor's degree
SALARY RANGE	$25,000 to $40,000 to $80,000+
CERTIFICATION OR LICENSING	Recommended
OUTLOOK	About as fast as the average
DOT	153
GOE	10.02.02
O*NET	34058B

■ History

Aristotle, Leonardo da Vinci, and Etienne Jules Marey all conducted experiments and studies involving motion and the human body, but it was the French physiologist Marey whose devices to study human motion really advanced the field of biomechanics and sports medicine. In fact, both modern cinematography and sports medicine claim him as the father of their respective fields. Marey's first contribution was the first force platform, a device which was able to visualize the forces between the foot and the floor. Later, his nonphotographic studies of the gait of a horse inspired Eadward Muybridge's serial photographs of a horse in motion in 1877 which, in turn, inspired Marey's invention of the chronophotograph. In contrast to Muybridge's consecutive frames, taken by several cameras, Marey's pictures with the chronophotograph superimposed the stages of action onto a single photograph; in essence, giving form to motion and allowing scientists to study it frame by frame, motion by motion. By 1892, Marey had even made primitive motion pictures, but his efforts were quickly eclipsed by those of Louis and Auguste Lumiere.

Following both World War I and II, Marey's and others scientists' experiments with motion would combine with medicine's need to heal and/or completely replace the limbs of war veterans. In order to provide an amputee with a prosthetic device that would come as close as possible to replicating the movement and functional value of a real limb, scientists and doctors began to work together at understanding the range of motion peculiar to the human body.

Mechanically, sports can be categorized according to the kinds of movements used. Each individual sport utilizes a unique combination of basic motions, including walking, running, jumping, kicking, and throwing. These basic motions have all been rigidly defined for scientific study so that injuries related to these motions can be better understood and treated. For example, sports that place heavy demands on one part of an athlete's body may overload that part and produce an injury, such as "tennis elbow" and "swimmer's shoulder." Baseball, on the other hand, is a throwing sport and certain injuries from overuse of the shoulder and elbow are expected. Athletes who play volleyball or golf also use some variation of the throwing motion and therefore, also sustain injuries to their shoulders and elbows.

Today, sports trainers are part of the team of sports medicine professionals that treat the injuries of both the amateur and elite athlete. Like sports physicians, certified sports medicine therapists are responsible for preventing injuries as well as treating them, and they use their knowledge of the human body and its wide range of motions to discover new ways of reducing stress and damage from athletic activities. They work in high schools, secondary schools, colleges and universities, and a smaller number work for professional teams. Many work in health clubs, sports medicine clinics, and other athletic health care settings. In 1990, the American Medical Association (AMA) recognized athletic training as an allied health profession.

■ The Job

Sports trainers are concerned with preventing injuries to amateur and professional athletes through proper exercises and conditioning; providing immediate first-aid attention to injuries as they occur during a practice or event; and leading injured athletes safely through rehabilitation programs and routines. For the most part, sports trainers are not medical doctors, and are not allowed to conduct certain procedures or provide advanced types of medical care, such as prescribing or administering drugs. Some trainers, however, are trained physicians. If an individual is also trained as an *osteopathic physician,* for example, he or she is licensed as a medical doctor and can conduct more advanced procedures and techniques, including diagnosis, surgery, and the prescription of drugs.

In order to prevent injuries, sports trainers organize team physicals, making certain that each player is examined and evaluated by a physician prior to that athlete's participation in the sport. Along with the team physician, they help to analyze each athlete's overall readiness to play, fitness level, and known or existing weaknesses or injuries. When necessary, they recommend stretching, conditioning, and strengthening exercises to aid the athlete in preventing or exacerbating an injury. This may involve developing specific routines for individual athletes. Finally, athletic trainers work with coaches, and sometimes team physicians, to choose protective athletic equipment. Before games and practice, they often inspect the playing field, surface, or area for any flagrant or subtle risks of injury to the athlete.

Prior to a practice or competition, the athletic trainer may help an athlete conduct special stretching exercises or, as a preventive measure, he or she might tape, wrap, bandage, or brace knees, ankles, or other joints, and areas of the athlete's body that might be at risk for injury. The trainer routinely treats cuts, scratches, and abrasions, among other minor injuries. He or she may tape, pad, or wrap injuries, and install face guards. When serious injuries do occur, whether in practice or during a competition, the athletic trainer's role is to provide prompt and accurate first-aid treatment to the athlete to ensure that athlete's full recovery. He or she is trained in emergency procedures and is prepared to provide emergency treatment for conditions such as shock, concussion, or bone fracture, stabilizing the athlete until they reach a hospital or trauma center. Often, the trainer will accompany the injured athlete to the hospital, making certain the team physician is still on hand to address the health concerns and needs of those athletes who are still competing.

Working in concert with the team physician and several other health professionals, athletic trainers often supervise the therapeutic rehabilitation of athletes under their care. They analyze the athlete's injury and create individualized therapy routines. Sometimes, the trainer may advise the athlete to wear a protective brace or guard to minimize damage while the athlete is recuperating from an injury. Athletic trainers in charge of every level of athlete should be licensed to perform specific medical functions and operate certain devices and equipment.

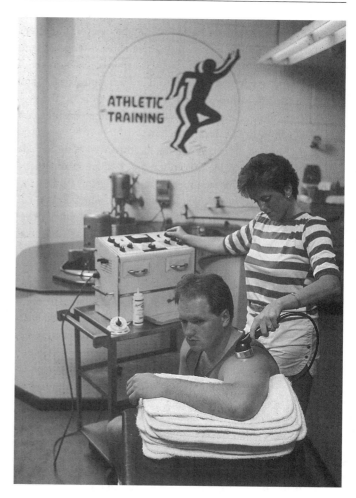

A sports trainer performs therapy on an athlete's shoulder.

■ Requirements

High School

If you're interested in this field, you should pay special attention to physical education classes and to high school subjects such as health and anatomy and physiology. Students with an interest in becoming athletic trainers will want to become certified in CPR and first aid. The American Sports Medicine Association offers support and courses for you to become a Student Trainer or Certified Student Trainer while you're still in high school. Contact the association for more information.

Postsecondary Training

The individual who is certain he or she wishes to become a sports trainer will usually earn a bachelor's degree from a college or university that offers a program in athletic training which is accredited by the Joint Review Committee on Educational Programs in Athletic Training. Later, the student interns with a certified athletic trainer. Another option is to earn a bachelor's degree or even a master's degree in a related health field, such as osteopathy, and then intern with a certified athletic trainer. The number of hours a student needs to spend in both clinical study and in the internship phase will vary, depending on the program the student selects and the professional organization which he or she decides to join.

Most accredited programs in athletic training include course work in the prevention and evaluation of athletic injuries and illnesses, first aid and emergency care, therapeutic exercises, therapeutic modalities, administration of athletic training programs, human anatomy, human physiology, exercise physiology, kinesiology, nutrition, psychology, and personal and community health.

Certification or Licensing

As mentioned above, athletic trainers in charge of every level of athlete should be licensed to perform specific medical functions and operate certain devices and equipment. Different membership organizations and their respective certifying bodies have different eligibility requirements; it is up to the individual to decide which organization best characterizes his or her ultimate goal.

For example, the National Athletic Trainer's Association (NATA) requires that each member have a bachelor's degree (in any field), be either a graduate of an accredited program in athletic training (with 800 clinical hours) or complete an internship (with 1,500 clinical hours), and pass a certification exam consisting of 3 sections—written, simulation, and oral practical. The American Sports Medicine Association and Certification Board, Inc., places its emphasis on medical preparation, believing that a strong medical background best qualifies an individual to help athletes prevent and evaluate injuries, as well as treat those injuries that do occur. To belong to the American Sports Medicine Association members must have completed either an Emergency Medical Technician course (EMT-1), or possess a current health profession medical license, such as licensed practical nurse, registered nurse, physical therapist assistant, doctor of chiropractic, registered physical therapist, doctor of osteopathy, or medical doctor.

Other Requirements

Workers in this field need an understanding of human anatomy and physiology, both in terms of physical capabilities and injury treatment and prevention. They should not be squeamish when it comes to blood, broken bones, or other wounds. Athletes do get hurt, and a trainer who is unable to cope well with this aspect of sports may have a difficult time succeeding in the career. The ability and knowledge to handle medical emergencies is especially important for certified athletic trainers, whose work focuses on injury prevention and treatment.

■ Exploring

Most trainers, like other professionals who work with athletes, were first drawn to sports as participants. High school and college students can gain valuable experience by actively participating in a sport. Such experience lends a prospective trainer added insight into the injuries typical of a given sport, as well as the compassion and empathy necessary to comfort an injured athlete who is forced to sit out a game. Most teams need help with everything from equipment to statistics, so plenty of opportunities exist to explore a variety of sports-related positions. If you are certain about becoming an athletic trainer, you can often work with a trainer or team physician, learning beside a professional. This type of experience will come in handy, later, when you are looking for an internship or a job; successful candidates are usually those with the most experience and on-the-job training.

■ Employers

Sports trainers are employed by professional and amateur sports teams, private sports organizations, sports facilities, educational institutions, and by individual athletes. Other possible athletic training employment opportunities include corporate health programs, health clubs, clinical and industrial health care programs, and athletic training curriculum programs.

■ Starting Out

Athletic trainers, regardless of the professional organization they join, are usually required to complete a period of training with a certified athletic trainer or sports medicine therapist. These internships provide students with the foundation for future networking possibilities. Many students find full-time jobs with the teams, organizations, or school districts with which they interned. At the very least, these internships offer students the chance to make valuable contacts and gain valuable on-the-job experience.

Most accredited programs in athletic training also have job placement departments that host recruitment seminars with major organizations, provide career counseling services, and put students in contact with prospective employers.

Finally, one of the benefits to belonging to a professional organization is that these associations publish newsletters and maintain Web sites, both of which feature job openings. Some organizations even offer job hotlines to their members. Through these media, as well as through meetings, seminars, and continuing education, students and trainers can make new contacts that will help them locate work and add to their base of knowledge. NATA, for example, boasts the most comprehensive job referral service in the United States for athletic trainers, listing job openings in all athletic training settings and locations.

■ Advancement

Acquiring additional training and education is the most common way of advancing in the field of sports training. Those trainers who have spent years working in the field and who update their skills each year by taking continuing education courses, sometimes even returning to school for an advanced degree, will be among the first to receive promotions.

Management responsibilities are the other way in which athletic trainers can advance in their field. Large universities often employ several trainers to serve the many different teams, with one trainer acting as the head trainer, sometimes also called the *director of sports medicine.* This individual coordinates the daily activities and responsibilities of the other trainers and works closely with the coaches of the school's various teams to ensure that all the demands are being met. Most often, trainers will advance by working for several years at one school, and then move on to another school when an opening is announced that will mean greater responsibilities and benefits.

■ Earnings

Earnings will vary depending on the level of athletics in which the trainer is involved, the trainer's education and credentials, and the number and type of his or her responsibilities. Those considering a career as an athletic trainer should keep all aspects of the job and salary in perspective; the slight increase in salary of a trainer working for a college team might be offset by the higher stress levels and longer hours away from home. Trainers who work with professional athletes are away from home a great deal, including evenings, weekends, and holidays.

In general, sports trainers who are just entering the field should expect to earn salaries in the mid-twenties. Trainers who work with college athletes may earn slightly more. Those athletic trainers with more experience earn anywhere between $40,000 and $80,000 annually. Only in a few, rare instances will a trainer with a professional athlete or team earn upwards of $80,000 a year.

■ Work Environment

Athletes train year round and so do the sports trainers who supervise their conditioning and rehabilitation programs. Depending upon the level and size of an athletic program, trainers may work with athletes in one or more sports. Sports trainers who work in high schools often act as the trainer for several, or all, of the athletic teams. A lot also depends on the school's budgetary restrictions. Generally speaking, though, most schools have a separate trainer for men's and women's sports. Trainers in professional sports work only in one sport and for one team.

Most of the trainer's time is spent in the school's athletic facility, either in preparation for work or in conditioning or rehab sessions. Athletic trainers are on a schedule similar to that of their athletes; they go to practices, schedule weight and rehab sessions, and attend games. They are expected to travel when and where the team travels.

■ Outlook

Depending on the level of athletics in which the trainer is involved, the outlook varies. Like most careers, competition for the more glamorous jobs is tough; positions with professional athletes and teams are extremely difficult to find and those working in them usually have years and years of experience. More opportunities exist for the certified athletic trainer who works with high school athletes, especially if the trainer has another skill that makes him or her more employable. For example, the athletic trainer wishing to work with high school athletes who also can teach biology, math, physical education, or other school subjects most likely will find a position sooner than the candidate with only a background in athletic training.

Positions at the college and university level offer the athletic trainer greater stability, with little turnover. Competition for these spots is also tough, however, and many schools are now requiring candidates to have a master's degree in order to be considered.

■ For More Information

For information on certification, contact:

American Athletic Trainers Association & Certification Board (AATA)
660 West Duarte Road, Suite 1
Arcadia, CA 91007
Tel: 818-445-1978

For information on the Student Trainer or Certified Student Trainer designations, contact:

American Sports Medicine Association
660 West Duarte Road, Suite 1
Arcadia, CA 91007
Tel: 818-445-1978

For a list of accredited athletic training programs, job listings, and information on certification, contact:

National Athletic Trainers Association (NATA)
2952 Stemmons Freeway
Dallas, TX 75247-6196
Tel: 214-637-6282
Web: http://www.nata.org

For information on certification, contact:

National Athletic Trainers Association Board of Certification (NATABOC)
1512 South 60th Street
Omaha, NE 68106
Tel: 402-559-0091
Web: http://www.nataboc.org/

■ **Related Articles**

Health Care

Sports

Aerobics Instructors and Fitness Trainers

Physical Therapist Assistants

Physical Therapists

Sports Physicians

Sportscasters

■ **See Radio and Television Newscasters, Reporters, and Announcers, Sports Broadcasters and Announcers**

Sportswriters

■ Overview

Sportswriters cover the news in sports for newspapers and magazines. They research original ideas or follow-up on breaking stories, contacting coaches, athletes, and team owners and managers for comments or more information. Sometimes a sportswriter is fortunate enough to get his or her own column, in which the sportswriter editorializes on current news or developments in sports.

■ History

Throughout the world there are some 7,200 daily newspapers and far more semiweeklies, biweeklies, and weeklies, circulating at least 500 million copies on a regular basis. In the international context the average newspaper is crude, poorly printed, heavy with sensational news, light on serious criticism, and burdened by all types of problems (especially economic). Outside Western Europe and North America there are very few "elite," or ultra serious, newspapers. Although most of the world's newspapers are privately owned, some degree of government control is evident in many countries.

Magazine journalism has been a potent force in the United States (and throughout the world), appealing mainly to the elite, the well-educated, and the opinion leaders. At least this is true in the sense of "journalistic" magazines. Generally more incisive, more articulate, more interpretive, and certainly more comprehensive than newspapers, magazines have supplied an important intellectual dimension to news-oriented journalism. Whereas the main function of newspaper journalism is to inform or summarize in brief fashion, the aim of most magazine journalism is to fill gaps—to explain, interpret, criticize, and comment. In short, magazine journalism in its many types and styles supplements newspapers and fleshes out the bare bones of newspaper journalism.

Most magazines and newspapers have sections that focus on sports; others, such as *Sports Illustrated,* focus entirely on sports reporting. In either case, sportswriters are needed to write articles about athletes, teams, and sports competitions. Sportswriters are employed by both newspapers and magazines throughout the United States.

■ The Job

The sportswriter's primary job is to report the outcomes of the sports events that occurred that day. Since one newspaper can't employ enough reporters to cover, in-person, every single high school, college, and professional sports event that happens on any given day, let alone sports events happening in other cities and countries, sportswriters use the wire news services to get the details. Major national and international wire services include Reuters, AP, UPI, Agence France-Presse, and ITAR-Tass. The entire body of statistics for tennis matches, hockey games, and track-and-field events, for example, can be sent over the wire service so that sportswriters can include the general story and the vital statistics in as condensed or lengthy a form as space allows.

A sportswriter begins work each day by reviewing the local, national, and international news that comes in over the wire news services for clips. He or she then begins researching the top or lead stories to try to flesh out the story, perhaps with a local perspective on it, or to come up with a new angle or spin, altogether. An example of a lead story might be the comeback of a professional tennis star; the underdog victory of a third-rate, much-maligned football team; the incredible pitching record of a high school athlete; or a running back who blew out his knee in a crucial last-minute play. The sportswriter then calls or interviews in person coaches, athletes, scouts, agents, promoters, and sometimes, in the case of an athletic injury, a physician or team of physicians.

Depending on the edition of the newspaper or magazine, the sportswriter might report events which happened any-

SPORTSWRITERS	
SCHOOL SUBJECTS	English Journalism Physical education
PERSONAL SKILLS	Communication/ideas
WORK ENVIRONMENT	Indoors and Outdoors Primarily multiple locations
MINIMUM EDUCATION LEVEL	Bachelor's degree
SALARY RANGE	$17,784 to $38,584 to $52,000+
CERTIFICATION OR LICENSING	None available
OUTLOOK	About as fast as the average
DOT	131
GOE	11.08.03
NOC	5231
O*NET	34011

where from the day before to events that took place within that week or month. For example, a sportswriter who writes for a magazine such as *Sports Illustrated* probably won't write articles with the same degree of detail per game. Instead, he or she writes articles, commonly called *features,* that explore an entire season for a team or an athlete. The magazine sportswriter might take the same story of the running back with the damaged knee ligaments and follow that athlete through his surgery and rehabilitation, interviewing not only the running back, but his wife, doctors, coach, and agent. This stage of gathering information is the same for both newspaper and magazine sportswriters, the only difference is the timeline; a newspaper sportswriter may have only a few hours to conduct research and call around for comments, while the sportswriter for a magazine may have anywhere from several weeks to several months to compose the story.

Regardless of whether the sportswriter works for a newspaper or magazine, the next step for the sportswriter is to write up the story. The method will vary, again, depending on the medium. Most sportswriters for newspapers are subject to the constraints of space, and these limits can change in a matter of minutes. On a dull day, up until the hour before the paper is published or, put to bed, the sportswriter might have a quarter of a page to fill with local sports news. At the last minute, however, an entire Super Bowl team could come down with food poisoning, in which case the sports page editor would probably want to cover this larger, breaking story. To accommodate the new articles about the poisoning, the effect on team morale, whether or not the Super Bowl might be postponed for the first time in history, the local sports news would either have to shrink considerably or be completely cut. To manage this, sportswriters, like other reporters who write for daily newspapers, compose their stories with the most crucial facts contained within the first 1 or 2 paragraphs of the story. They may write a 10-paragraph story, but if it had to be shortened, the pertinent information would be easily retained.

Sportswriters for magazines, on the other hand, seldom need to worry about their stories being cut down at the last minute. Rather, their stories are subject to more careful editing. Magazines usually have story meetings weeks or months in advance of the relevant issue, giving sportswriters ample time to plan, research and write their articles. As a result of the different timetable, the presentation of the story will change. The sportswriter will not cram all the essential facts into an opening paragraph or two. Instead, he or she is allowed much greater leeway with the introduction and the rest of the article. The sportswriter, in this case, will want to set a mood in the introduction, developing the character of the individuals being interviewed— literally, telling a story about the story. In short, details can hinder a newspaper sports story from accomplishing its goal of getting across the facts in a concise form, while in a magazine sports article those extraneous, revealing details actually become part of the story.

Even with the help of news services, sportswriters still couldn't have all the sports news at their fingertips without the help of other reporters and writers, known in the world of reporting as *stringers*. A stringer covers an event that, most likely, would not be covered by the wire services, events such as high school sports events, as well as games in professional sports that are occurring simultaneously with other major sports events. The stringer attends the sports event and phones in scores, or emails or faxes in a complete report.

While the sportswriters for magazines don't necessarily specialize in one area of sports, but instead, routinely write features on a wide variety of sports and athletes, sportswriters for newspapers do specialize. Many only cover a particular sport, such as baseball. Others are assigned a beat, or specific area, and like other reporters must cover all the events that fall into that beat. For example, a sportswriter assigned to the high school football beat for a newspaper in Los Angeles, California, would be expected to cover all the area high school football games. Since football is seasonal, he or she might be assigned to the high school basketball beat during the winter season. On the other hand, the sportswriter working in Lexington, Kentucky, might be assigned coverage of all the high school sports in the area, not simply one sport. Much of the way in which assignments are given depends on experience as well as budget and staffing constraints.

■ Requirements

High School

English, journalism, and speech are the most important high school classes for an aspiring sportswriter. You will need to master the art of writing in order to be able to convey your ideas concisely yet creatively to your readers. Speech classes will help you become comfortable interacting with others. Be sure to take physical education classes and participate in organized sports, be it as a competitor, a team manager, or an assistant. You also should join the staff of your school paper or yearbook. This will give you a chance to cover and write about your school's sports teams or other school activities.

Postsecondary Training

A bachelor's degree is usually the minimum level of education required of sportswriters, although many go on to study journalism at the graduate level. Most sportswriters concentrate on journalism while in college, either by attending a program in journalism or by taking whatever courses are available outside of a specialized program. This isn't to say that one can't become a sportswriter without a degree in journalism, but competition for sportswriting jobs is incredibly fierce. And why not? Sportswriters get great seats at sports events, and they have the credentials to get them into interviews with sports celebrities. Increasingly, a specialized education is becoming the means by which sports editors and managers sift through the stacks of resumes from prospective sportswriters.

Other Requirements

Clearly, the ability to write well and concisely is another requirement for the job of the sportswriter. In addition, sportswriters must have a solid understanding of the rules and play of many different sports. If they hope to specialize in the coverage of one particular sport, their knowledge of that sport has to be equal to that of anyone coaching or playing it at the professional level.

Finally, a sportswriter needs to be able to elicit information from a variety of sources, as well as to determine when information being leaked is closer to promotional spin than to fact. There will be more times when a coach or agent will not want to comment on a story than the times when they will want to make an on-the-record comment, so the sportswriter must be assertive in pressing the source for more information.

■ Exploring

You can learn on-the-job skills by working for your high school and college papers. The experience can be related to sports, of course, but any journalistic experience will help you develop the basic skills useful to any reporter, regardless of the area about which you are writing.

You can increase your chances and success in the field by applying to colleges or universities with renowned academic programs in journalism. Most accredited programs have a required period of training in which you will intern with a major newspaper somewhere in the United States; student-interns are responsible for covering a beat.

■ Employers

Sportswriters are employed by newspapers and magazines throughout the world. Sportswriters also work as freelance writers.

■ Starting Out

Some sportswriters began their careers by covering the games or matches that no else wanted to or could cover. As stringers, they didn't earn much money, probably had a second or even third job, but eventually the job lead to covering bigger and better games and teams. Some sportswriters make a living out of covering sports for very small towns, others only work at those jobs until they have gained the experience to move on.

Most journalists start their careers by working in small markets—little towns and cities with local papers. They may work for a newspaper for a year or two and then apply for positions with larger papers in bigger towns and cities. Sportswriters for newspapers follow the same routine, and more than a few end up pursuing areas other than sports because the job openings in sports simply weren't there. The lucky few who hang on to a small sports beat can often parlay that beat into a better position by sticking with the job and demonstrating a devotion to the sport, even cultivating a following of loyal fans. This could lead to a full-time column.

Most likely, a successful sportswriter will take advantage of opportunities to learn more about sports or a particular game. Becoming an expert on a little-known, but rapidly growing sport may be one way to do this. For example, a sportswriter who learns all he or she can about mountain biking might able to land a job with one of the magazines specializing in the sport of mountain biking.

Competition for full-time jobs with magazines as a sportswriter is just as keen as it is for major newspapers. Often, a sportswriter will write articles and try to sell them to one of the major magazines, hoping that when an opening comes, he or she will have first crack at it. Still, most sportswriters move into the world of sports magazines after they've proven themselves in newspaper sportswriting. It is possible, however, to get a job with a sports magazine straight from college or graduate school; chances are, you'll have to work your way up, though.

The placement centers of colleges or universities with accredited undergraduate and graduate programs in journalism can be extremely helpful in beginning a job search. In fact, many graduates of these programs are not only highly sought after by newspapers and magazines, but these graduates are often offered jobs by the newspapers and magazines with whom they had an internship during school.

■ Advancement

The constraints of budget, staffing, and time—which make a sportswriters' job difficult—are also often what can help a sportswriter rise through the ranks. For example, the writer asked to cover all the sports in a small area may have to hustle to cover the beat alone, but that writer also won't have any competition when covering the big events. Thus, he or she can gain valuable experience and bylines writing for a small paper, whereas in a larger market, the same sportswriter would have to wait much longer to be assigned an event that might result in a coveted byline.

Sportswriters advance by gaining the top assignments, covering the major sports in feature articles, as opposed to the bare bones summaries of events. They also advance by moving to larger and larger papers, by getting columns, and finally, by getting a syndicated column—that is, a column carried by many papers around the country or even around the world.

Sportswriters for magazines advance by moving up the publishing ladder, from editorial assistant to associate editor to writer. Often, an editorial assistant might be assigned to research a story for a sports brief—a quirky or short look at an element of the game. For example, *Sports Illustrated* might have a page devoted to new advances in sports equipment for the amateur athlete. The editorial assistant might be given the idea and asked to research it, or specific items. A writer might eventually write it up, using the editorial assistant's notes. Advancement, then, comes in being actually listed as the author of the piece.

In the publishing worlds of both newspapers and magazines, sportswriters can advance by becoming editors of a newspaper's sports page or of a sports magazine. There are also *sports publicists* and *sports information directors* who work for the publicity and promotions arms of colleges, universities, and professional sports teams. These individuals release statements, write and disseminate to the press articles on the organizations' teams and athletes, and arrange press opportunities for coaches and athletes. (See the article, *Sports Publicists*, for more information.)

■ Earnings

According the *Occupational Outlook Handbook*, the Newspaper Guild negotiates with individual newspapers on minimum salaries for both starting reporters and those still on the job after 3 to 6 years. The median minimum salary for new reporters was about $448 a week in 1996, or $23,036 annually. Ten percent of the contracts called for minimums of $342 or less; 10 percent, $698 or more. The median minimum weekly salary for reporters after 3 to 6 years on the job was about $742 a week. Ten percent of the contracts called for top minimums of $484 or less; 10 percent, $1,000 or more.

Sportswriters who cover the major sports events, who have their own column, or who have a syndicated column can expect to earn more than the salaries above. Sportswriters who write for major magazines can also expect to earn more, sometimes per article, depending on their reputations and the contracts worked out by themselves or their agents.

■ Work Environment

Like other journalists, sportswriters work in a variety of conditions, from the air-conditioned offices of a newsroom or magazine publisher to the sweaty, humid locker room of a professional basketball team, to the arid and dusty field where a baseball team's spring training is held. The sportswriter works irregular hours, putting in as much or as little time as the story requires, often traveling to small towns and out-of-the-way locales to cover a team's away games.

The benefits are obvious—for the individuals who love sports, the job offers the chance to cover sports events every day; to immerse themselves in the statistics and injury lists and bidding wars of professional and amateur sports; to speak, sometimes one-on-one, with the greatest athletes of yesterday, today, and tomorrow.

■ Outlook

The turnover rate for top sportswriters with major newspapers and magazines isn't very high, which means that job openings occur as sportswriters retire, die, are fired, or move into other markets. While the publishing industry may have room in it for yet another magazine devoted to a particular sports specialty, competition for sportswriting jobs will continue to be strong into the year 2006 and beyond.

■ For More Information

Career information, including a pamphlet called Facts about Newspapers, *is available from:*

Newspaper Association of America
1921 Gallows Road, Suite 600
Vienna, VA 22182
Tel: 703-902-1600
Web: http://www.naa.org/

For information on grants and awards, and to obtain the pamphlet, Newspaper: What's In It For Me?, *contact:*

Newspaper Association of America Foundation
1921 Gallows Road, Suite 600
Vienna, VA 22182
Tel: 703-902-1600
Email: levir@naa.org
Web: http://www.naa.org/foundation/index.html

■ Related Articles

Newspapers and Magazines
Sports
Columnists
Foreign Correspondents
Magazine Editors
Newspaper Editors
Reporters
Writers

Spreaders

■ See Fashion, Apparel Industry Workers

Sprinkler Fitters

Sprinkler fitters are specialized plumbers and pipefitters. Sprinkler fitters install and maintain indoor sprinkler systems designed to extinguish fires before any great damage is done. Accordingly, they usually work for companies specializing in fire protection. Sprinkler fitters must meet the same apprenticeship and training requirements as general plumbers. Those with a few years of experience earn an average of $22 per hour, amounting to more than $40,000 per year. Most sprinkler fitters are unionized. The job outlook for sprinkler fitters is good, as sprinkler systems are becoming more prevalent in private residences.

■ For More Information

The NFSA Web site provides some good information on the increasing importance of fire sprinklers and sprinkler fitters.

National Fire Sprinkler Association
Web: http://www.nfsa.org/

■ Related Articles

Construction

Plumbers and Pipefitters

Stadium Ushers and Vendors

■ Overview

Stadium ushers take tickets, escort spectators to their seats, and provide spectators with information and direction upon request. *Stadium vendors* sell a variety of food items and other wares either by walking around and calling out the name of the food or product they're selling, or by operating small booths or kiosks. Sometimes vendors are hired by the food service franchise that is licensed to sell food in a stadium or sports facility.

■ History

As long as people have been gathering in places such as theaters or sporting events, there has been a need for crowd control. In ancient times, it was customary among Roman dignitaries to have a servant called an *ustiarius,* from which the word usher is derived, standing at the door to announce the arrival of their guests. Vendors have an ancient tradition as well. The Latin word *vendre* means, literally, to sell. A stadium vendor is an independent, licensed operator selling to the stadium crowds.

■ The Job

The work of stadium ushers and vendors varies with the place, the event, and the audience, but their duties while working sports events are similar. The main job of the usher is to seat patrons. Other duties for the usher might include finding empty available seats for patrons, locating lost items, helping children find their parents, paging people, checking and recording thermometer readings, answering questions, giving directions, attempting to control unruly or ill-behaved people, and settling arguments about seat assignments. In the event that spectators grow unreasonably unruly or out-of-control, it is the responsibility of ushers to notify security of the disturbance. Ushers watch exits and show patrons to restrooms, drinking fountains, and telephones. They keep aisles clear of objects that might cause patrons to slip or fall.

Similarly, a vendor sells food and other items at a variety of sports events, although the amounts might vary depending on the event. For example, a vendor selling beer would probably sell more beers during a hockey or football game than during a figure-skating competition; in many cases, they might not even sell beer at such competitions. The vendor may be either an independent seller, licensed by the local government to sell his or her wares, or a vendor working as a freelance operator under license by the owner of the site. For example, the manager of the sports facility allows freelance operators to sell hot dogs, sodas, ice cream and all the other foods and services enjoyed during a ball game. Or, a vendor might be employed by the franchise licensed to sell T-shirts, caps, and other sports paraphernalia at sports events.

Food vendors are often responsible for preparing the food for sale (and sometimes this just means placing a hot dog inside a bun), as well as handling the sale, making change, and providing any additional items necessary to the consumption of the food, such as napkins, straws, and condiments.

■ Requirements

High School

High school students fill many of the usher and vendor positions in theaters and stadiums, although there is an age requirement for vendors who sell alcoholic beverages. Good standing in high school or a high school degree is usually required. Employers strongly consider an applicant's school attendance record, so regular and prompt attendance is advised.

Postsecondary Training
Vendors and ushers are not required to have college-level education or training. Most training is conducted on the job for a brief time and new employees are used to fill the less responsible jobs and quieter locations. While the trainees are learning, they are shifted to different parts of the stadium as the need arises.

Certification or Licensing
Although ushers and vendors are not required to be certified, those who sell alcohol or certain other items must have a license.

Other Requirements
Stadium ushers and vendors should be affable and friendly. They should have strong oral communication skills in order to interact successfully with the general public. Vendors need strong mathematical skills because they deal with the transfer of money. Both ushers and vendors should be physically fit because they must be on their feet during much of their shift. Finally, ushers and vendors should be willing to work outdoors in sometimes harsh weather conditions, such as extreme cold or heat, driving rain, sleet, or snow.

■ Exploring
Labor unions represent many ushers in stage production theaters, ball parks, and sports arenas and usually welcome the opportunity to talk with young people about working as an usher or vendor. Another option is to call the ball park or stadium directly to find out more about being an usher or vendor. When you learn of special events coming to your town, contact the coordinator and volunteer your services to get a taste for the job.

Although these jobs are not the most glamorous positions, they will give you a chance to learn about sport facility management and concessions, experience which may come in handy later if you are serious about exploring either career option.

■ Employers
Ushers are employed anywhere that a large group of people gather to watch some type of event or show. Movie theaters, sports stadiums, and colleges/universities are the largest employers of ushers.

Vendors are also employed wherever large groups of people gather to view an event or a show, but with one small difference. During these events, the people must have the time and the ability to spend money on food, drink, and souvenirs. For example, while a cotton candy vendor is

right at home at the circus or ball park, he might stick out like a sore thumb at the opera. You get the idea.

■ Starting Out
Check with all theaters, ball parks, convention centers, and colleges in your area and inquire about possible openings. There is a lot of turnover in this business, so openings are usually plentiful but are snatched up quickly.

Positions in stadiums are usually part time and seasonal; jobs as ushers or vendors in a stadium used only for baseball end in the fall; if the stadium is domed, there might be additional opportunities to usher or vend during concerts or conventions. Depending on whether or not the vendor is independent or employed by a food or clothing franchise, the vendor may have opportunities year-round. Also, the contacts one makes in these jobs can lead to better jobs in the future.

■ Advancement
Those stadium ushers or vendors with the most experience usually receive the positions with greater responsibilities, such as handling emergency evacuation procedures. Frequently, ushers and vendors work in crews of three or more, with one individual acting as the supervisor for that crew or team.

In addition to advancing within the categories of ushers and vendors, individuals who have interests in other areas of the game—from public relations to marketing—can make contacts with people who work full time in those areas and possibly arrange an internship or part-time job. Many people who now work for major sports franchises in a variety of front-office jobs once spent a summer working as a stadium usher or vendor.

■ Earnings
Three-fourths of all stadium ushers and vendors work part time or seasonally. The range of weekly hours is from 20 to 50 hours.

Hourly rates vary from job to job. Most ushers

STADIUM USHERS AND VENDORS	
SCHOOL SUBJECTS	**Business** **Speech**
PERSONAL SKILLS	**Following instructions** **Leadership/management**
WORK ENVIRONMENT	**Indoors and outdoors** **Primarily one location**
MINIMUM EDUCATION LEVEL	**High school diploma**
SALARY RANGE	**$5.15 per hour to $7.50 per hour to $9.50 per hour**
CERTIFICATION OR LICENSING	**None available**
OUTLOOK	**About as fast as the average**
DOT	**344**
GOE	**09.05.08**
O*NET	**68021**

A stadium vendor sells peanuts at a baseball game.

work at their job for such a short time that they seldom earn more than the starting wage. Hourly wages may range from the minimum wage to $9.50 an hour. The pay rate has increased somewhat due to the demand for this level of worker in most cities. Experienced ushers in metropolitan areas earn the highest wages. For vendors, the amount earned is usually on a commission basis and the competition can be fierce to get the most desired concessions in the park (hot dogs, ice cream, and so on).

For many ushers and vendors the real reward in working these jobs comes from the chance to be a part of a large-scale event, such as a baseball or football game, where they can be an integral part of the production of the event as well as enjoy the sport.

■ Work Environment

Stadium ushers and vendors working in domed stadiums or indoor arenas or other indoor sports facilities don't have to brave the elements, while ushers and vendors who work football games need to be dressed warmly, as they frequently work in cold, sometimes miserable conditions. Ushers spend most of their working time standing or walking up and down aisles. In stadiums, ushers and vendors may do considerable climbing up and down stairs or tiers to seat patrons. Work can be stressful when patrons complain or when a crowd gets out of hand.

■ Outlook

Stadium revenue rises and falls with the success and failure of the home team; if the team is doing well, crowds swell and fill the stands. Jobs will always exist for ushers and vendors in sports facilities, and these skills are applicable to other venues that use ushers and vendors, such as music halls and theaters.

Turnover in this work is high. Most openings arise as people leave the work for different reasons. Many leave to

take better paying jobs. Students working part time usually leave when they graduate from high school or college.

■ For More Information

In addition to the following organizations, individuals interested in pursuing a job as an usher or vendor should contact directly the sports facilities in their area, from colleges to universities to professional teams, to ask about job openings.

Stadium Managers Association
875 Kings Highway, Suite 200
Woodbury, NJ 08096-3172
Web: http://www.venue.org/sma.htm

For information about major convention and assembly management companies, contact:

International Association of Assembly Managers
4425 West Airport Freeway, Suite 590
Irving, TX 75062
Tel: 972-255-8020
Web: http://iaam.org

To learn about employment at concert venues, contact:

North American Concert Promoters Association
1622 North 41st Street
McLean, VA 22101
Tel: 703-534-4844

■ Related Articles

Business
Sales
Sports
Cashiers
Counter and Retail Clerks
Retail Sales Workers
Sales Representatives
Services Sales Representatives

Stage Production Workers

■ Overview

Stage production workers handle the behind-the-scenes tasks that are necessary for putting on theatrical performances and operating a theater. Their responsibilities include costume and set design; properties acquisition and arrangement; installing lights, rigging, sound equipment, and scenery; and sometimes building stages for special theatrical and musical events in parks, stadiums, arenas, and other places. During a performance they control the lighting, sound, and various other aspects of a production that add to its impact on an audience. These technicians work in close cooperation with the stage director, lighting director, actors, and various prop people. In addition, they work directly with theater shops in the construction of sets. Others are involved in the management of the theater or production.

■ History

Theatrical performance is among the most ancient of human art forms. Primitive societies most likely wore masks and costumes during ritual ceremonies designed to ward off evil spirits and to promote the welfare of the society.

Greek theater also included masks and costumes. As Greek theater developed, its costumes also became more elaborate and were used to emphasize characters' status within the world of the play. Greek theater was originally performed in a large circle, and the scenery was minimal; around 460 BC a wood *skene,* or stage structure, was added to the back of the circle through which the actors could enter or exit the circle. Painted scenery was attached to the skene; special effects included cranes for flying actors over the stage. As theater became more professional, people began to specialize in the different areas of theater, such as controlling the scenery, directing the action, and creating the costumes. An important development in early theater was the addition of the raised stage.

By the time of the Romans, theaters were freestanding structures that could be covered and hold large audiences. Scenery was often mounted on three-sided prismlike structures that could be rotated to change the scenery during a performance. Medieval performances were often extremely elaborate. Performances were generally held outdoors, and sometimes on wagon stages that moved through a town during the performance. Special effects were often spectacular, with flames and smoke, flood, realistic massacres complete with flowing blood, hangings, crucifixions, and the like.

Nonreligious theater rose into prominence during the 16th century. The first dedicated theater was build in 1576 in London, followed by many other theaters, including the famous Globe Theater where the work of William Shakespeare (1564-1616) was performed. Costumes, primarily representing contemporary dress, were often highly elaborate and quite costly.

The Renaissance and the rediscovery of Greek and Roman theater brought scenery back into prominence in the theater. The development of perspective techniques in painting and drawing led to more realistic settings as backdrops for the performance. More methods were developed for changing the scenery during the performance, although these scene changes continued to be made in front of the audience. Flying machines and other special effects were added; and as theater moved indoors stages were lighted by candles and oil lamps.

Many of the features of present-day theater evolved during the 17th and 18th centuries. A new profession emerged, that of stage designer. One of the most influential of these designers was Giacomo Torelli (1608-78), who invented a mechanical system for raising and lowering settings. Earlier settings, however, were not generally designed for a specific performance, and costumes were not often historically accurate. By the end of the 18th century, stage direction, which had generally been given by the playwright or by one of the leading actors, became a more recognized part of preparing a theatrical performance.

Lighting and scenery developed rapidly in the 19th century. Gas lamps replaced candles and oil lamps, and innovations such as the limelight (a stage light consisting of an oxyhydrogen flame directed on a cylinder of lime and usually equipped with a lens to concentrate the light in a beam) and the spotlight were introduced. Stages began to feature trap doors, and scenery could be raised from below the stage or lowered from above the stage. Many theaters incorporated hydraulic lifts to raise and lower scenery, props, and actors through the trap doors. The look of a theater production, in its costumes, settings, and props, became at once more realistic and more historically accurate. Settings became increasingly more elaborate, and the introduction of panoramas gave motion effects to the stage. Special effects could include the use of real animals on stage, volcanic eruptions, sinking ships, and storms complete with wind and rain. During this period, it became more common that a play would remain in the same theater through many performances. These elaborately planned and staged productions required dedicated directors to oversee the entire production. Another innovation of the 19th century was the use of a curtain to hide the stage during scene changes.

The art of stage production changed considerably with the introduction of electricity to theaters at the end of the 19th century. It became possible to use lighting effects as a major interpretive element in stage productions. Stage ma-

STAGE PRODUCTION WORKERS	
SCHOOL SUBJECTS	**Mathematics** **Theater/Dance**
PERSONAL SKILLS	**Artistic** **Technical/scientific**
WORK ENVIRONMENT	**Primarily indoors** **One location with some travel**
MINIMUM EDUCATION LEVEL	**High school diploma** **Apprenticeship**
SALARY RANGE	**$13,000 to $27,000 to $36,000**
CERTIFICATION OR LICENSING	**None available**
OUTLOOK	**About as fast as the average**
DOT	**962**
O*NET	**39999D**

This stage production worker paints "wallpaper" on a backdrop for an upcoming play.

chinery became more elaborate, even to the point of moving a whole stage, so that sets could be transformed in new ways. In the 20th century, recording and amplification techniques introduced a wider range of musical and sound effects than ever before. These changes added new dimensions to the tasks of stagehands and other workers.

Today, stage production workers are involved not only in theater performances, but also in some television performances, which utilize many of the same techniques. As they do on theater stages, workers in television do such tasks as building and changing sets and controlling lighting and sound effects.

■ The Job

For small productions, stage workers must be able to do a variety of tasks, while for larger productions (such as those on Broadway), responsibilities are divided among many different workers, each with a special area of expertise. The following paragraphs describe some of the areas of responsibility.

Stage technicians are known by a variety of titles, such as *carpenters, prop makers, lighting designers, lighting-equipment operators, sound technicians, electricians,* and *riggers.*

When installing stage equipment, stage technicians begin with blueprints, diagrams, and specifications concerning the stage area. They confer with the stage manager to establish what kinds of sets, scenery, props, lighting, and sound equipment are required for the event or show, and where each should be placed.

Then the technicians gather props provided by the production company and build other props or scenery using hammers, saws, and other hand tools and power tools. If they are working in a theater, they climb ladders or scaffolding to the gridwork at the ceiling and use cables to attach curtains, scenery, and other equipment that needs to be moved, raised, and lowered during performances. They may need to balance on and crawl along beams near the ceiling to connect the cables.

Stage technicians also position lights and sound equipment on or around the stage. They clamp light fixtures to supports and connect electrical wiring from the fixtures to power sources and control panels.

The sound equipment used on and around stages usually includes microphones, speakers, and amplifiers. Technicians position this equipment and attach the wires that connect it to power sources and to the sound-mixing equipment that controls the volume and quality of the sound.

During rehearsals and performances, stage technicians in some theaters may follow cues and pull cables that raise and lower curtains and other equipment. Sometimes they also operate the lighting and sound equipment.

Costume designers choose the costumes necessary for a production, including their style, fabric, color, and pattern. They may do research to design clothes that are historically and stylistically authentic. They discuss their ideas with the stage director and make sketches of costumes for the director's approval. They check stores and specialty clothing shops for garments that would meet their needs. If appropriate items are not found, designers may have the costumes made from scratch. They oversee the purchasing of fabric and supervise the workers who actually create the costumes. Costume designers also work with actors to make sure that costumes fit properly. In a large production, they may supervise several assistants who help in all aspects of the job, including locating hard-to-find items.

Other workers help to complete the desired appearance of the performers. *Hairstylists* and *makeup artists* use cosmetics, greasepaint, wigs, plastics, latex, and other materials to change the look of their hair and skin. Once costumes have been made for a show, *wardrobe supervisors* keep them in good condition for each performance by ironing, mending, and cleaning them and doing any necessary minor alterations. *Dressers* help performers to get dressed before a show and change quickly between scenes.

■ Requirements

High School

Requirements vary for the different kinds of stage production workers and technicians. In general, a high school diploma is likely to be necessary and a college degree is highly recommended. High school students interested in careers in theatrical production should take college-preparatory courses such as English, history, and mathematics. In addition, they should take drama courses and participate in school theatrical performances in a variety of capacities, from acting to working on sets to helping with promotion.

Postsecondary Training

People who want to work in technical fields such as lighting and sound design would benefit by taking courses in history and art, as well as subjects such as electricity, electronics, computers, mathematics, and physics. Craft workers such as carpenters and electricians do not need a college degree, and they may learn their skills through apprenticeships. Makeup artists need to study anatomy and art subjects like sculpture and portrait painting. Costume designers ought to have a graduate degree in design or fine arts, as well as a well-developed artistic sense.

Certification or Licensing

Many stage production workers belong to unions. Union membership may be required to get a job, although requirements vary in different areas and even in different theaters in the same city. For example, various workers, including costume designers, may belong to the United Scenic Artists; many other categories of workers may belong to the International Alliance of Theatrical Stage Employees and Moving Picture Machine Operators. Some unions require members to pass a competency test before they can begin work. Prospective stage production workers need to investigate the union requirements, if any, that apply in their field of interest in their local area.

Other Requirements

Passion for the work and theatre as an art form is essential, due to the long hours and often low pay associated with these professions. The ability to get along well with others is important, since stage technicians often work in teams. Patience and flexibility are also helpful, as directors and designers may change their minds from their original plans, or want to create a stage set, lighting effect or costume piece that might seem difficult or challenging creatively as well as financially.

■ Exploring

People who are interested in stage production careers can learn a great deal by becoming involved in high school theatrical performances, preferably in a variety of capacities, including acting, stage design, lighting, and special effects. Another way to get good experience is as a volunteer doing behind-the-scenes work for amateur community theater productions or special benefit events. Especially if they have such experience, students may be able to get a paid or volunteer summer job assisting in a professional theater.

Experiences gained in other fields may be helpful background for some stage production jobs. For example, aspir-

ing costume designers can learn by working for clothes designers in a fashion-oriented business.

■ Employers

Stage production workers and technicians may be employed by theatre, dance, music, opera, and other performing arts companies. They more often receive full-time employment from those companies that have their own facilities, although companies that tour year-round often need to keep technical workers on staff. In addition, those who manage performing arts facilities—theatres, opera houses, arenas, auditoriums—may hire full-time technicians. Often times, technical workers may find themselves employed by different companies and/or facility managers on a freelance basis.

■ Starting Out

Competition is very keen for nearly all positions associated with theatrical productions, so people who want a career in this field should get as much experience and become as versatile as possible. It is often necessary to begin as a volunteer or in a position unrelated to the desired field. Because of the great difficulty in securing satisfying jobs, many people who want to work in stage production end up in other professions.

Finding good jobs is often a matter of staying with the project. Job seekers need to keep up their confidence and keep searching out opportunities. In New York, Chicago, and Los Angeles, publications specifically about local activities in the theater and television industries are an excellent source of information that may lead to jobs. In many cities, local newspapers regularly list production plans for area community theater groups. Sometimes college internships in theater jobs or recommendations from drama teachers can lead to permanent employment.

■ Advancement

Advancement opportunities vary according to the type of work performed. Often, workers advance by moving to different theaters where they handle greater responsibilities associated with more complicated productions. Those who develop good reputations in the industry may be sought out by other employers to do similar jobs in new settings.

Costume designers can work on larger theatrical productions or for television production companies. Alternatively, they may establish independent consulting firms and work for a variety of clients.

It should be noted that competition for advancement is fierce enough that many theatrical workers have to be content with salary increases as the evidence of their success.

■ Earnings

Earnings vary widely according to the worker's experience, job responsibilities, the geographic location of the theater, and the budget of the performance. In addition, the International Alliance of Theatrical Stage Employees reports that different local chapters have different pay scales, although its members, who are mostly employed at the largest commercial houses and on Broadway, generally earn more than nonmembers.

According to a 1997 survey by Theatre Communications Group (TSG) of its nonprofit membership, a beginning carpenter might earn $13,000 annually. Scene shop supervisors average $27,000 per year, while production managers might average $36,000. Stage managers had a median salary of $31,000 per year. Set and lighting designers generally work on a freelance basis and are paid widely varying fees on a per-project basis.

The pay of costume designers is often based on the number of costumes designed. Experienced designers working in major markets such as New York and Chicago earn more than those in other markets. Local unions often determine salary scales. Some costume designers working in summer theaters earn around $500 or more a week, but others may earn substantially less. TCG reports that costume shop managers in fiscal year 1997 earned average salaries of $30,000 per year.

Most full-time workers receive health insurance and other benefits, as established by the local union contract. Because workers are hired for a particular time period, vacations are rarely provided.

■ Work Environment

Working conditions in theaters vary from the lavish in a few theaters to small, simply equipped facilities in many community theaters. Many theaters are hot and stuffy or drafty and cold when empty. Stage production workers can expect to work long hours and spend much time on their feet. Many work evenings and weekends. People who work behind the scenes in theaters must be concerned about safety. Those who work with lights and electric cables risk burns, while those who climb rigging or scaffolding need to use care to avoid falls.

Costume designers work in design shops sketching and designing costumes, in theaters fitting performers, and in libraries and other locations researching costume possibilities. They spend long hours preparing for a show, with most of their work done before and during the rehearsal period.

■ Outlook

Present employment patterns for workers in this field are probably a good guide to the situation for the foreseeable future. According to Theatre Communications Group, the industry is remaining steady; there are few new theaters appearing that can pay living wages for stage production workers and technicians, but those that have existed are healthy and surviving. Today, theaters tend to be concentrated in large metropolitan areas, so the number of job possibilities is greatest there, but so too is the competition for those jobs. Many people start out instead in small theatrical groups in out-of-the-way places. After they develop skills and a local reputation, they may be able to move to bigger, better-paying markets. They may have to work only part-time, do volunteer work in amateur theater, or support themselves in unrelated fields for extended periods while waiting for good theater jobs, and even good theater jobs may last only a short while.

In the late 1990s theater groups came under increasing financial pressures; public funding for the arts in general, which has never been very high in the United States, has been under attack. As a result, many smaller theaters are finding it difficult to survive. Productions, even among the larger theaters, are likely to become less elaborate to lower operating costs. These factors could limit the need for new stage production employees. However, theater remains a popular form of entertainment and an important cultural resource. People who can do a variety of tasks stand the best chance of employment. For example, someone who knows about both lighting and sound systems, or both set design and props, is more likely to get a desirable position.

■ For More Information

This labor union represents technicians, artisans and craftspersons in the entertainment industry, including live theater, film, and television production. It negotiates salaries and offers pension, insurance, and educational programs.

International Alliance of Theatrical Stage Employees (IATSE)
1515 Broadway, Suite 601
New York, NY 10036
Tel: 212-730-1770
Email: iatse@iatse.lm.com
Web: http://www.iatse.lm.com

The following organization for professional nonprofit theaters has educational programs, surveys, and publications. It also has career information and job listings.

Theater Communications Group
355 Lexington Avenue, 4th floor
New York, NY 10017
Tel: 212-697-5230
Email: tcg@tcg.org

■ Related Articles

Dance
Film
Television
Theater
Actors
Audio Recording Engineers
Carpenters
Construction Laborers
Costume Designers
Dancers and Choreographers
Electricians
Film and Television Directors
Lighting Technicians
Music Producers
Producers
Special Effects Technicians

Stand-Ins

■ See Film Extras

State Police Officers

■ See Police Officers

State Troopers

■ See Police Officers

Station Installers

■ See Telephone and PBX Installers and Repairers

Stationary Engineers

■ Overview

Stationary engineers operate and maintain boilers, engines, air compressors, generators, and other equipment used in providing utilities such as heat, ventilation, light, and power for large buildings, industrial plants, and other facilities. They are called stationary engineers because the equipment they work with is similar to equipment on ships or locomotives, except that it is stationary rather than located on a moving vehicle.

■ History

During the Industrial Revolution of the 18th and 19th centuries, many new inventions changed the way people lived and worked. Some of these inventions developed new energy sources, including steam engines, coal, electricity, and petroleum. When this power was applied to the new machines, many aspects of life began to alter dramatically.

As the Industrial Revolution spread, new, large factories were built. Sometimes working conditions for the construction and stationary workers was not good. Employees were required to work 60 to 90 hours per week, and their wages were low considering the number of hours they put in. So in 1896 a small group of stationary engineers met in Chicago to form the National Union of Steam Engineers of America. Each was from a small local union and all shared the skill of being able to operate the dangerous steam boilers of the day.

This ability also made the steam engineers vital to the construction industry, which used steam-driven equipment at the turn of the century. As more and more construction workers joined the early union, it changed its name to the International Union of Steam and

STATIONARY ENGINEERS	
SCHOOL SUBJECTS	Mathematics Physics Technical/Shop
PERSONAL SKILLS	Mechanical/manipulative Technical/scientific
WORK ENVIRONMENT	Primarily indoors Primarily one location
MINIMUM EDUCATION LEVEL	Apprenticeship
SALARY RANGE	$24,000 to $37,400 to $50,000+
CERTIFICATION OR LICENSING	Required by certain states
OUTLOOK	Decline
DOT	950
GOE	05.06.02
NOC	7351

Having finished his rounds, a stationary engineer checks off items on his status checklist.

Operating Engineers. As members began working with internal combustion engines, electric motors, hydraulic machinery and refrigerating systems as well as steam boilers and engines, the "steam" was dropped from the union's name in 1928. Nowadays, the IOE sponsors apprenticeship programs and is the primary union to which stationary engineers belong.

Wherever big equipment installations are located, stationary engineers are needed to operate and maintain the equipment. Once again, their jobs are changing. Equipment is becoming more automated and they have learned how to use computerized controls and operate the automated systems.

■ The Job

Stationary engineers are primarily concerned with the safe, efficient, economical operation of utilities equipment. To do their job, they must monitor meters, gauges, and other instruments attached to the equipment. They take regular readings of the instruments and keep a log of information about the operation of the equipment. This might include the amount of power produced; the amount of fuel consumed; the composition of gases given off in burning fuel; the temperature, pressure, and water levels inside equipment; and temperature and humidity of air that has been processed through air-conditioning equipment. When instrument readings show that the equipment is not operating in the proper ranges, they may control the operation of the equipment with levers, throttles, switches, and valves. They may override automatic controls on the equipment, switch to backup systems, or shut the equipment down.

Periodically, stationary engineers inspect the equipment and look for any parts that need adjustment, lubrication, or repair. They may tighten loose fittings, replace gaskets and filters, repack bearings, clean burners, oil moving parts, and perform similar maintenance tasks. They may test the water in boilers and add chemicals to the water to prevent scale from building up and clogging water lines. They keep records of all routine service and repair activities.

Stationary engineers try to prevent breakdowns before they occur. But if unexpected trouble develops in the system, they must identify and correct the problem as soon as possible. They may need only to make minor repairs, or they may have to completely overhaul the equipment, using a variety of hand and power tools.

In large plants, stationary engineers may be responsible for keeping several complex systems in operation. They may be assisted by other workers, such as boiler tenders, heating and cooling technicians, turbine operators, and assistant stationary engineers. In small buildings, one stationary engineer at a time may be in charge of operating and maintaining the equipment.

Often the instruments and equipment that stationary engineers work with are computer controlled. This means that stationary engineers can keep track of operations throughout a system by reading computer outputs at one central location, rather than checking each piece of equipment. Sensors connected to the computers may monitor factors such as temperature and humidity in the building, and this information can be processed to help stationary engineers make decisions about operating the equipment.

Boiler tenders on their own may be responsible for taking care of steam boilers in building or industrial facilities. In some cases, they tend boilers that produce power to run engines, turbines, or equipment used in industrial processes. Boiler tenders may feed solid fuel, such as coal or coke, into a firebox or conveyor hopper, or they may operate controls and valves. They may also be responsible for maintenance, minor repairs, and cleaning or the boiler and burners.

■ Requirements

High School

A high school diploma or its equivalent is required to become an apprentice stationary engineer. Courses in computers, mathematics, physics, chemistry, and mechanical drawing are good introductions to the field, along with vocational training in machinery operation.

Postsecondary Training

Stationary engineers learn the skills they need by completing an apprenticeship or through informal, on-the-job training, often in combination with course work at a vocational or technical school. Because of the similarities between marine and stationary power plants, training in marine engineering during service in the U.S. Navy or

Merchant Marines can be an excellent background for this field. However, even with such experience, additional training and study are necessary to become a stationary engineer.

Apprenticeships are administered by local committees that represent both company management and the union to which many stationary engineers belong, the International Union of Operating Engineers. Apprenticeships usually last four years. In the practical experience part of their training, apprentices learn how to operate, maintain, and repair stationary equipment such as blowers, generators, compressors, motors, and refrigeration machinery. They become familiar with precision measurement devices; hand and machine tools; and hoists, blocks, and other equipment used in lifting heavy machines. In the classroom, apprentices study subjects such as practical chemistry and physics, applied mathematics, computers, blueprint reading, electricity and electronics, and instrumentation.

People who learn their skills on the job work under the supervision of experienced stationary engineers. They may start as boiler tenders or helpers, doing simple tasks that require no special skills, and learn gradually through practical experience. The process may go more quickly if they take courses at a vocational or technical school in subjects such as computerized controls and instrumentation.

Even after they are well trained and experienced in their field, stationary engineers should take short courses to keep their knowledge current. Employers often pay for this kind of additional training. When new equipment is installed in a building, representatives of the equipment manufacturer may present special training programs.

Certification or Licensing

Most states and cities require licensing for stationary engineers to operate equipment. There are several classes of license, depending on the kind of equipment and its steam pressure or horsepower. A first-class license qualifies workers to operate any equipment, regardless of size or capacity. Stationary engineers in charge of large equipment complexes and those who supervise other workers need this kind of license. Other classes of licenses limit the capacities or types of equipment that the license holders may operate without supervision.

The requirements for obtaining these licenses vary from place to place. In general, applicants must meet certain training and experience requirements for the class of license, pass a written examination, and be at least 18 years old and a resident of the city or state for a specified period of time. When licensed stationary engineers move to another city or state, they may have to meet different licensing requirements and take an another examination.

Other Requirements

Stationary engineers possess mechanical aptitude, manual dexterity, and are in good physical condition. They like keeping track of details and understand the importance of following schedules and routines. A prospective stationary engineer should be able to work independently, without direct supervision.

■ Exploring

A good way to learn about this work is to get a part-time or summer job in an industrial plant or another large facility where utility equipment is run by a stationary engineer. Even an unskilled position, such as custodian in a boiler room, can provide an opportunity to observe the work and conditions in this occupation. A talk with a stationary engineer or a union representative may also prove helpful. Often, libraries have books on the technical aspects of the job.

■ Employers

Stationary engineers held about 29,000 jobs in the late 1990s. They work in a wide variety of places, including factories, hospitals, hotels, office and apartment buildings, schools, and shopping malls. Some are employed as contractors to a building or plant. They work throughout the country, generally in the more heavily populated areas where large industrial and commercial establishments are located.

■ Starting Out

Stationary engineers often start out working as a boiler tender or craftsworker in another field. Information about job openings, apprenticeships, and other training may be obtained through the local offices of the state employment service or the International Union of Operating Engineers. State and city licensing agencies can give details on local licensure requirements and perhaps possible job leads.

■ Advancement

Experienced stationary engineers may advance to jobs in which they are responsible for operating and maintaining larger or more complex equipment installations. Such job changes may become possible as stationary engineers obtain higher classes of licenses. Obtaining these licenses, however, does not guarantee advancement. Many first-class stationary engineers must work as assistants to other first-class stationary engineers until a position becomes available. Stationary engineers may also move into positions as boiler inspectors, chief plant engineers, building superintendents, building managers, or technical instructors. Additional training or formal education may be needed for some of these positions.

■ Earnings

Earnings of stationary engineers vary widely, usually falling between $27,000 and $50,000 a year. The median annual salary is $37,400, according to the U.S. Bureau of Labor Statistics. In metropolitan areas, where most jobs are located, earnings tend to be higher than other areas. Stationary engineers in metropolitan areas of the West have the highest average earnings; those in the South have the lowest; and workers in the Midwest and Northeast earn close to the national average for metropolitan areas.

Most stationary engineers receive fringe benefits in addition to their regular wages. Benefits may include life and health insurance, paid vacation and sick days, employer reimbursement for work-related courses, and retirement plans. Benefits for boiler tenders are similar.

■ Work Environment

Stationary engineers usually work eight-hour shifts, five days a week. Because the plants where they work may operate 24 hours a day, some stationary engineers regularly work afternoon or night shifts, weekends, or holidays. Some work rotating shifts. Occasionally, overtime hours are necessary, such as when equipment breaks down or new equipment is being installed.

Most boiler rooms, power plants, and engine rooms are clean and well lighted, but stationary engineers may still encounter some uncomfortable conditions in the course of their work. They may be exposed to high temperatures, dirt, grease, odors, and smoke. At times they may need to crouch, kneel, crawl inside equipment, or work in awkward positions. They may spend much of their time on their feet. There is some danger attached to working around boilers and electrical and mechanical equipment, but following good safety practices greatly reduces the possibility of injury. By staying constantly on the alert, stationary engineers can avoid burns, electrical shock, and injuries from moving parts.

■ Outlook

Employment opportunities for stationary engineers will be best for those with apprenticeship training or vocational school courses covering systems operations using computerized controls and instrumentation. Even with that training, workers will face competition for job openings. Employment is expected to decline through 2006, according to the Bureau of Labor Statistics.

Although industrial and commercial development will continue, and thus more equipment will be installed and need to be operated by stationary engineers, much of the new equipment will be automated and computerized. The greater efficiency of such controls and instrumentation will tend to reduce the demand for stationary engineers. Job openings will develop when workers transfer to other jobs

or leave the work force, but turnover in this field is low, due in part to its high wages.

■ For More Information

For information about apprenticeships and vocational training, contact:

International Union of Operating Engineers
1125 17th Street, NW
Washington, DC 20036
Tel: 202-429-9100
Web: http://www.iuoe.org

National Association of Power Engineers, Inc.
1 Springfield Street
Chicopee, MA 01013
Tel: 413-592-6273
Web: http://www.powerengineers.com

■ Related Articles

Energy

Machining and Machinery

General Maintenance Mechanics

Industrial Machinery Mechanics

Nuclear Reactor Operators and Technicians

Power Plant Occupations

Wastewater Treatment Plant Operators and Technicians

Statistical Clerks

■ Overview

Statistical clerks perform routine tasks associated with data collection, data file management, data entry, and data processing. They work in a number of different industries, including advertising, insurance, manufacturing, and the medical field to compile and manage information.

■ History

According to the earliest records, the study of mathematics was developed to meet the practical business needs of farmers and merchants between 3000 and 2000 BC in Egypt and Mesopotamia. One branch of applied mathematics—statistics—deals with the collection and classification of various data by certain numerical characteristics. These data are then used to make inferences and predictions in related situations. A relatively young discipline, statistics emerged in 1899 with the publication of the book, *The Grammar of Science*. Its author, Karl Pearson, a mathematics professor at the University of London, is generally regarded as the father of statistics.

Statistics is widely used by many types of businesses today. Insurance companies use statistics to determine the probability of accidents and deaths, thus enabling them to set reasonable premium rates for their policy holders. Statistics is used to determine the audience ratings of television shows and approval ratings of politicians. It can be used in disease prevention and economic projections. As business decisions increasingly depend on demographics and other information that can be tabulated, a limited number of statistical clerks will continue to play a role in the compilation of relevant data.

■ The Job

Statistical clerks are involved in record keeping and data retrieval. They perform data collection tasks, such as compiling numerical information (questionnaire results and production records, for example) and tabulating it according to statistical formulas so that it can be used for further study. They also perform data entry and data processing on computers, and are responsible for quality control of the collected data. With the advanced statistical software programs now available, almost all statistical clerks use computers in their work. They also perform other functions, such as filing and file management, which are mainly clerical.

Statistical clerks work in a number of fields in a variety of fields. *Compilers* analyze raw data gathered from surveys, census data, and the like, and organize and arrange this information into specified categories or groupings. These statistics are compiled into survey findings or census reports. Compilers may prepare graphs or charts to illustrate their findings.

Advertising statistical clerks tabulate statistical records for companies on the cost, volume, and effectiveness of their advertising. They often compare the amount of their customers' merchandise that is sold before an advertising campaign to that sold after the campaign to prove that it influenced consumer behavior.

Medical record clerks and technicians tabulate statistics to be used in reports and surveys to help medical researchers illustrate their findings. They also compile, verify, and file the medical records of hospital or clinic patients and make sure that these records are complete and up-to-date. Medical record technicians may assist in compiling the necessary information used in completing hospital insurance billing forms.

Chart calculators work for power companies. They compute the power factor and net amount of electric power used by the company's customers and determine the peak load demand to verify that the correct rates are being charged. They enter this information on record forms so that customers are billed at the appropriate rates. *Chart clerks* compile records measuring the quantity of natural or manufactured gas produced, transported, and sold to calculate the volume of gas and petroleum that flows through specific pipelines.

Planimeter operators use a special measuring tool to trace the boundaries of specified land areas. They usually use aerial photographs to help identify the boundary lines of individual plots of land.

Chart changers change the charts of and record data from instruments that measure industrial processes. They are also responsible for maintaining the recording instruments, such as pyrometers and flowmeters.

Actuarial clerks compile data on insurance policies, rates, and claims so that insurance commissioners and companies know how to set their rates.

■ Requirements

High School

A high school diploma is usually sufficient for beginning statistical clerks. High school students should take courses in English, mathematics, and science, and as many business-related courses, such as typing or keyboarding and bookkeeping, as possible. Because computers are so commonly used in this career, it is important to take as many basic computer courses as you can.

Postsecondary Training

Community colleges and vocational schools often offer business education courses that provide additional training for statistical clerks in the areas of data processing and office procedures. As in most career fields, those clerks who have obtained further education and have proven their capabilities typically have more advancement opportunities.

Other Requirements

Prospective clerks should have some mechanical aptitude in order to be able to operate business machines, especially computers. The ability to concentrate for long periods of time on repetitive tasks, and some mathematical acumen are also important. In addition, statistical clerks should have an

STATISTICAL CLERKS	
SCHOOL SUBJECTS	Business Computer science Mathematics
PERSONAL SKILLS	Following instructions Technical/scientific
WORK ENVIRONMENT	Primarily indoors Primarily one location
MINIMUM EDUCATION LEVEL	High school diploma
SALARY RANGE	$15,000 to $21,500 to $25,000
CERTIFICATION OR LICENSING	None available
OUTLOOK	Decline
DOT	050
GOE	11.06.03
NOC	1454
O*NET	55328A

even temperament and the ability to work well with others. They should find systematic and orderly work appealing and enjoy working on detailed tasks.

■ Exploring

If you are interested in a career as a statistical clerk, you might gain related experience by taking on clerical or book-keeping responsibilities with a school club or other organization. In addition, some school work-study programs may have opportunities with businesses for part-time, on-the-job training. You might also be able to get a part-time or summer job in a business office by contacting offices directly.

To learn how to operate business machinery and computer software programs, you might consider taking an evening course offered by a local business school or community college. Another way of gaining insight into the responsibilities of a statistical clerk is to talk to someone already working in the field.

■ Employers

In general, statistical clerks are employed by the same sorts of employers that hire statisticians. The Federal Government hires about one-fourth of statisticians in the United States, in such areas as the Departments of Commerce, Health and Human Services, and Agriculture. Various sectors of private industry also hire both statisticians and statistical clerks. Private industry employers include insurance companies, utility research and testing services, management and public relations firms, computer and data processing firms, manufacturing companies, and the financial services sector. Other statistical clerks may work for researchers in colleges or universities.

■ Starting Out

When looking for an entry-level statistical clerk's job, you might first scan the help wanted sections of area newspapers. Another avenue for job seekers is to contact the personnel or human resources offices of businesses or government agencies directly.

Most companies provide entry-level statistical clerks with on-the-job training, during which company policy and procedures are explained. Beginning clerks work with experienced personnel during this period.

■ Advancement

In many instances, statistical clerks begin their employment as general office clerks and with experience and further training, become statistical clerks. With experience, they may receive more complicated assignments and assume a greater responsibility for the total statistical work to be completed. Those with leadership skills may become group managers or supervisors. In order to become an

accountant or bookkeeper, it is usually necessary to get a degree or have other specialized training.

The high turnover rate in this profession increases opportunities for promotion. The number and kind of opportunities, however, may depend on the place of employment and the ability, training, and experience of the employee.

■ Earnings

Statistical clerks' earnings are similar to those of data entry keyers. Although salaries vary depending upon skill, experience, level of responsibility, and geographic location, a newly hired, inexperienced statistical clerk might expect to earn between $15,000 and $20,000 annually. With more experience and additional responsibilities, he or she might make between $21,000 and $25,000 or more. Fringe benefits for full-time workers include paid vacations, health insurance, and other benefits.

■ Work Environment

Statistical clerks work an average 37 to 40 hours per week. The work environment is usually well ventilated and lighted. Although statistical clerks perform a variety of tasks, the job itself can be fairly routine and repetitive. Statistical clerks who work at video display terminals for long periods of time may experience some eye and neck strain. Clerks often interact with accountants and other office personnel and may work under close supervision.

■ Outlook

According to the U.S. Bureau of Labor, job opportunities for statistical clerks are expected to decline through the year 2006. This is a result of new data processing equipment that can now do many of the record keeping and data retrieval functions previously performed by statistical clerks. Despite this decline, however, job openings in this career will arise, due to people retiring or otherwise leaving the field. Opportunities should be especially good for those trained in the use of computers and other types of automated office machinery.

■ For More Information

For information on careers in statistics or schools that offer degrees in statistics, contact:

American Statistical Association
1429 Duke Street
Alexandria, VA 22314-3402
Tel: 703-684-1221
Web: http://www.amstat.org

For information on schools and career opportunities in statistics in Canada, contact:

Statistical Society of Canada
582 Somerset Street West
Ottawa, ON K1R 5K2 Canada
Tel: 613-234-0171
Web: http://www.ssc.ca/

■ Related Articles

Statisticians

■ Overview

Statisticians use mathematical theories to collect and interpret information. This information is used to help various agencies, industries, and researchers determine the best ways to produce results in their work. There are approximately 14,000 statisticians in the United States, employed in a wide variety of work fields, including government, industry, and scientific research.

■ History

One of the first known uses of statistical technique was in England in the mid-1800s, when a disastrous epidemic of cholera broke out in a section of London. The usual medical practices of the day were unable to control it. A local physician named John Snow decided to conduct a survey to determine what sections of the city were affected by the disease. He then constructed a map showing how the infection was distributed and interviewed some people who had survived the illness to find out about their living habits. He discovered that everyone who had contracted the illness had drawn water from a certain pump in the area. Once the pump was sealed, the cholera epidemic subsided. This is how medical professionals first learned definitely that cholera was transmitted through an infected water supply. Knowing this, they were able to control cholera. Statistical methods uncovered a fact that has since saved countless lives.

In its simplest form, statistics is a science that organizes many facts into a systematized picture of the data. Modern statistics is based on the theory of probability, and the work of the statistician has been greatly enhanced by the invention of computers.

The need for statisticians has grown by leaps and bounds in modern times. Since 1945, the number of universities with programs leading to graduate degrees in statistics has jumped from a half dozen to more than 100. One reason for the increased demand is that one statistical method often has many important uses. For example, the same methods used to study waves from distant galaxies can also be used to analyze blood hormone levels, track financial market fluctuations, and find concentrations of atmospheric pollutants. Experts predict that the demand for such useful statistical methodology will continue to grow.

Statistics is now used in all areas of science, as well as in industry and business. Government officials are especially dependent on statistics—from politicians to education officials to traffic controllers.

■ The Job

Statisticians use their knowledge of mathematics and statistical theory to collect and interpret information. They determine whether data is reliable and useful, and search for facts that will help solve scientific questions.

Most statisticians work in one of three kinds of jobs: they may teach and do research at a large university; they may work in a government agency (such as the Bureau of Census); or they may work in a business or industry. A few statisticians work in private consulting agencies and sell their services to industrial or government organizations. Some statisticians work in well-known public opinion research organizations. Their studies help us understand what groups of people think about the major issues of the day.

There are two major areas of the science of statistics—mathematical statistics and applied statistics. *Mathematical statisticians* are primarily theoreticians. They develop and test new statistical methods and theories and devise new ways in which they can be applied. They also work on improving existing methods and formulas.

STATISTICIANS	
SCHOOL SUBJECTS	**Computer science** **Mathematics**
PERSONAL SKILLS	**Communication/ideas** **Technical/scientific**
WORK ENVIRONMENT	**Primarily indoors** **Primarily one location**
MINIMUM EDUCATION LEVEL	**Bachelor's degree**
SALARY RANGE	**$41,150 to $61,030 to $90,500**
CERTIFICATION OR LICENSING	**None available**
OUTLOOK	**Little change or more slowly than the average**
DOT	**020**
GOE	**11.01.02**
NOC	**2161**
O*NET	**25312**

Applied statisticians apply existing theories or known formulas to new questions. They may forecast population growth or economic conditions, estimate crop yield, predict and evaluate the result of a marketing program, or help engineers and scientists determine the best design for a jet airline.

In some cases, statisticians actually go out and gather the data to be analyzed. Usually, however, data are gathered by individuals who are trained especially in data-gathering techniques. In the Bureau of Census, for example, statisticians work with material that has been compiled by thousands of census takers. Once the census takers have gathered the data, it is turned over to the statistician for organization, analysis, and conclusions or recommendations.

Statisticians can be found in a wide variety of work fields, in both the private and the public sector. One of the largest employers of statisticians is the government, because many government operations depend on statisticians to provide estimates of activities. Their data on consumer prices, population trends, and employment patterns, for example, can affect public policy and social programs.

Statistical models and methods are necessary for all types of scientific research as well. For example, a geoscientist using radiocarbon dating to estimate the risk of earthquakes or ecologists using complex instruments to measure water quality both use statistical methods to determine the validity of their results. In business and industry, statistical theories are used to figure out how to streamline operations and optimize resources. For instance, statisticians may predict demand for a product, check the quality of manufactured items, or manage investments.

The insurance industry also uses statisticians to calculate fair and competitive insurance rates and to forecast the risk of underwriting activities. Ben Lamb is a statistician for Grain Dealers Mutual Insurance in Indianapolis, Indiana. When asked to sum up his job, he says, "I get data into the computers, get data back out, and send out reports." The data he puts into the computer includes the specific details of every policy signed, every insurance premium paid, and every insurance claim made. Once this information is in the computer, it is plugged into statistical formulas and used to generate reports. "We make detailed reports to our own management," Ben says. "We also file required reports with the National Insurance Services Office." This national office compiles insurance data from all over the nation and uses it to generate reports that are then sent to the insurance commissioners of the various states. Ben says that his office collects data and runs reports at the end of every day, as well as monthly. "We have a daily flow of work," he says. "The information comes in during the day, and we process it during the day to get it ready for that night." Processing the data may mean editing it to make sure it is correct or "coding" it—that is, assigning short number or letter codes to the information so that the computer can read it.

■ Requirements

According to Ben, his insurance company looks for candidates with a college degree, most often in computer science or programming, for their statistician positions.

High School

To become a statistician, you must have earned at least a bachelor's degree. This means, then, that in high school, you should take classes that prepare you for college. If you are interested in entering the field of statistics, you should focus especially on mathematics, computers, and science. Take as many of these classes as possible, but don't neglect other college preparatory courses—such as English and a foreign language.

Postsecondary Training

Statisticians usually graduate from college with strong mathematics and computer backgrounds. Some authorities advise college students to take an undergraduate major in mathematics or computer science. Bachelor's degrees in statistics are available at about 80 colleges and universities in the United States. Others believe the wisest course for students is to major in the field they hope to work in, such as chemistry, agriculture, or psychology.

Although a bachelor's degree is the minimum needed to become a statistician, your chances for success are better if you earn an advanced degree. Many positions are open only to those with a master's or doctorate. More than 100 universities offer a master's degree program in statistics, and about 60 have programs leading to a doctorate in statistics.

Other Requirements

Prospective statisticians should be able to think in terms of mathematical concepts. According to Ben, however, the ability to think logically is even more important for a good statistician. "Math skills are not as important as logic," he says. "You have to be able to use logic in the processing of those statistics.". Statisticians should also have a strong curiosity that will prompt them to explore any given subject. Finally a good statistician should be detail oriented and be able to handle stress well. "You have to be very attentive to details, but you can't be *too* much of a perfectionist," Ben says, "because there are too many things than can go wrong when you're dealing with a computer system. You have to be able to deal with it if there is something wrong with the system, because it does happen."

■ Exploring

High school students who are enrolled in mathematics courses might ask their teachers to give them some simple statistical problems, perhaps related to grades or student government, and let them practice the kinds of techniques that statisticians use. If you want to further explore the profession of statistician, you might visit a local insurance agency, the local office of the Internal Revenue Service, or a nearby college and talk to people who use statistical methods. You may also find part-time or summer employment in an industry related to the work of statisticians.

College students can frequently obtain jobs as student assistants in the offices of faculty members who are engaged in some kind of research. Although these jobs generally carry little responsibility, undergraduate students can at least gain some insights into the nature of the work.

■ Employers

There are approximately 14,000 statisticians employed in the United States. About one-quarter of these work for the Federal Government, especially in the Departments of Commerce, Health and Human Services, and Agriculture. Of the remaining statisticians, most work in private industry. Private industry employers include insurance companies, research and testing services, management and public relations firms, computer and data processing firms, manufacturing companies, and the financial services sector. Other statisticians work in colleges and universities.

Jobs for statisticians can be found throughout the United States, but are concentrated most heavily in large metropolitan areas such as New York, Chicago, Los Angeles, and Washington, DC.

■ Starting Out

Most new graduates find positions through their college placement offices. "We get most of our applicants through placement offices and agencies," Ben says. "We have very few walk-ins." For those students who are particularly interested in working for a government agency, jobs are listed with the Office of Personnel Management. Some government jobs may be obtained only after the successful passing of a civil service examination. Teaching at the college level is normally only open to candidates with doctorates. College teaching jobs are usually obtained by making a direct application to the dean of the school or college in which the statistics department is located.

■ Advancement

A statistician with only a bachelor's degree will probably begin in a position that is primarily routine or clerical work with little responsibility. He or she may spend many years in a routine job before being given greater responsibility, though the salary may be increased at regular intervals.

Statisticians who advance most rapidly to positions of responsibility are usually those with advanced degrees. Though it is possible to advance with a bachelor's degree, the person who does so must have unusual ability.

Most young statisticians enter a job with the rank of junior statistician; if they are in college teaching, they may enter a job with the rank of instructor. After having acquired experience on the job and value to the employer, the statistician may be promoted to a position as high as chief statistician, director of research, or full professor. Advancement usually takes many years, and may be dependent upon the statistician's returning to graduate school or a special technical school in order to achieve a higher level of competency.

■ Earnings

In 1997, the average annual salary for statisticians employed by the Federal Government was $61,030. Earnings for statisticians in private industry are generally somewhat higher than those paid by the federal government. The income for statisticians working in colleges and universities differs, depending upon what level of professor they are. According to the American Statistical Association, the median salary for assistant professors is between $41,150 and $52,250. Full professors might expect to earn anywhere between $60,000 and $90,500.

Most statisticians receive a benefits package from their employer that typically includes paid sick and vacation time, health insurance, and some sort of retirement plan.

■ Work Environment

Ben works Monday through Friday, from 8:00 AM to 4:15 PM. Other statisticians in his department, however, work different hours. "We have flex time, because we have to have someone here at all times to process the data and back up the system." While at work, Ben spends the majority of his time working on a computer. Because this field of work is so heavily computerized, most statistician's jobs will include a substantial amount of time on a computer.

Most statisticians work under pleasant circumstances. Government or industry employees usually have a desk job in a well-appointed office. Often, the statistician will have some responsibility for the supervision of other statisticians of a lower rank or grade, or clerical personnel.

■ Outlook

According to the U.S. Bureau of Labor Statistics, employment in this field is not expected to grow much through the year 2006. Even so, trained statisticians with advanced degrees or with a specialist's knowledge of one field should have good job opportunities. Although the Federal Government will continue to need statisticians for various uses, competition is predicted to be high for these jobs.

Private industry will also continue to use statisticians. Two areas of growth in the private sector are the pharmaceutical industry and automobile industry.

The opportunities for statisticians increase with each level of education. Graduates with a bachelor's degree, especially those with a strong background in mathematics and computer science, are most likely to find jobs related to their field of study in applied statistics in private industry or government. With the proper certification, they may teach statistics in high schools. In other cases, job seekers with bachelor's degrees may have to take entry-level jobs that are not actually considered statistician's jobs.

Statisticians with a master's degree and a knowledge of computer science should find openings in private industry in statistical computing and in research. These candidates can also teach in junior colleges and small four-year colleges. The employment outlook is best for those with doctorates in statistics. These individuals are eagerly sought by large corporations as consultants, and are also in demand by colleges and universities.

■ For More Information

For information on careers in statistics or schools that offer degrees in statistics, contact:

American Statistical Association
1429 Duke Street
Alexandria, VA 22314-3402
Tel: 703-684-1221
Web: http://www.amstat.org

For a brochure on careers in applied mathematics, contact or visit the Web site of:

Society for Industrial and Applied Mathematics
3600 University City Science Center
Philadelphia, PA 19104-2688
Tel: 215-382-9800
Web: http://www.siam.org

For information on educational and employment opportunities in statistics and related fields, contact:

Association for Women in Mathematics
4114 Computer and Space Sciences Building
University of Maryland
College Park, MD 10742-2461
Tel: 301-405-7892
Web: http://www.awm-math.org

■ Related Articles

Business

Computers

Insurance

Actuaries

Demographers

Economists

Geographic Information Systems Specialists

Operations Research Analysts

Sports Statisticians

Statistical Clerks

Steamfitters

■ **See Plumbers and Pipefitters**

Steel-Post Installers

■ **See Line Installers and Cable Splicers**

Stenographers

■ Overview

Stenographers take dictation using either shorthand notation or a stenotype machine, then later transcribe their notes into business documents. They may record people's remarks at meetings or other proceedings and later give a summary report or a word-for-word transcript of what was said. General stenographers may also perform other office tasks such as typing, filing, answering phones, and operating office machines.

■ History

Because of the need for accurate records of speeches, meetings, legal proceedings, and other events, people throughout history have experimented with methods and symbols for abbreviating spoken communications. Contemporary shorthand systems are based on the phonetic principle of using a symbol to represent a sound. Stenographers use a special keyboard called a steno keyboard or shorthand machine to "write" what they hear as they hear it.

Shorthand began to be applied to business communications with the invention of the typewriter. The stenotype, the first machine that could print shorthand characters, was invented by an American in 1910. Unlike a traditional typewriter keyboard, the steno keyboard allows more than one key to be pressed at a time. Although the basic concept behind machine shorthand is phonetic, where combinations of keys represent sounds, the actual theory used is much more complex than straight phonetics.

Today, stenographers, in addition to using stenotype machines, may use Dictaphones or computer-based systems to transcribe reports, letters, and official records of meetings or other events. Their careful and accurate work is essential to the proper functioning of various organizations of law, business, and government.

■ The Job

Stenographers take dictation and then transcribe their notes on a typewriter or word processor. They may be asked to record speeches, conversations, legal proceedings, meetings, or a person's business correspondence. They may either take shorthand manually or use a stenotype machine.

In addition to transcription tasks, general stenographers may also have a variety of other office duties, such as typing, operating photocopy and other office machines, answering telephones, and performing general receptionist duties. They may sit in on staff meetings and later transcribe a summary report of the proceedings for use by management. In some situations, stenographers may be responsible for answering routine office mail.

Experienced and highly skilled stenographers take on more difficult dictation assignments. They may take dictation in foreign languages or at very busy proceedings. Some work as *public stenographers,* who are hired out to serve traveling business people and unique meetings and events.

Steno pool supervisors supervise and coordinate the work of stenographers by assigning them to people who have documents to dictate or by giving stenographers manuscripts, spools of tape, or recordings to transcribe. They also check final typed copy for accuracy.

Skilled stenographers who receive additional training may learn to operate computer-aided transcription (CAT) systems—stenotype machines that are linked directly to a computer. Specialized computer software instantly translates stenographic symbols into words. This technology is most frequently used by real-time captioners or others doing computer-aided real-time translation in courtrooms, classrooms, or meetings, and requires a more sophisticated knowledge of computer systems and English grammar, along with enhanced technical skills. Other areas of specialization for stenographers include the following:

Print shop stenographers take dictation and operate a special typewriter that produces metal printing plates for use by addressing machines.

Transcribing-machine operators listen to recordings (often through earphones or earplugs) and use a typewriter or word processor to transcribe the material. They can control the speed of the tape so that they can type every word they hear at a comfortable speed. Transcribing-machine operators may also have various clerical duties, such as answering the telephones and filing correspondence.

Technical stenographers may specialize in medical, legal, engineering, or other technical areas. They should be familiar with the terminology and the practice of the appropriate subject. For example, a *medical transcriptionist* must be a medical language expert and be familiar with the processes of patient assessment, therapeutic procedures, diagnoses, and prognoses.

Court reporters specialize in taking notes for and transcribing legal and court proceedings. *Real-time captioners* operate CAT stenotype systems to create English closed captions for live television broadcasts. It should be noted that the body of knowledge required to perform the tasks of a court reporter or real-time captioner is greater than that which a stenographer needs to know. While a court reporter or captioner could readily perform the tasks of an office stenographer, the stenographer would be unable to perform either job without additional training.

■ Requirements

High School

Although there are no specific educational requirements, most stenographers should have a high school diploma. Some high school students follow a business education curriculum and take courses in typing, shorthand, and business procedures. These students may later enter a business school or college for more advanced technical training. Other students may follow a general education program and take courses in English, history, mathematics, and the sciences, intending to undergo all of their technical training after graduation.

Postsecondary Training

Although some students with a business curriculum background are able to obtain jobs immediately after graduation from high school, better job opportunities and higher salaries may be more readily available to those who have sought advanced technical training, a college degree, or some avenue of specialization. In many instances, training at a business school, vocational school, or college may be required. Those considering the more advanced career of court

STENOGRAPHERS	
SCHOOL SUBJECTS	Business English
PERSONAL SKILLS	Communication/ideas Following instructions
WORK ENVIRONMENT	Primarily indoors Primarily multiple locations
MINIMUM EDUCATION LEVEL	High school diploma
SALARY RANGE	$14,560 to $21,320 to $33,680
CERTIFICATION OR LICENSING	Voluntary
OUTLOOK	Decline
DOT	202
GOE	07.05.03
NOC	1244
O*NET	55302

Stenographers must be able to concentrate on what is being said without stopping to think about it.

reporter or real-time captioner should earn at least a two-year degree in court and conference reporting, although a four-year degree that includes courses in computers and English is preferable.

Numerous opportunities for advanced training exist. Hundreds of business schools and colleges throughout the country offer technical or degree programs with both day and evening classes. These schools can be located in the telephone directory or by contacting individual state employment services.

Certification or Licensing

Some stenographers, especially those who work for the federal government, may belong to a union such as the Office and Professional Employees' International Union. To work for the federal government, stenographers must pass a civil service test and be able to take dictation at the rate of 80 words per minute and type at least 40 words per minute. Tests of verbal and mathematical ability are also required. Employers in the private sector may require similar tests. The National Court Reporters Association (NCRA) confers the Registered Professional Reporter (RPR) designation on those who pass a two-part exam and participate in continuing education programs. The RPR is con-

sidered a good credential to have and may even be required for more demanding reporting jobs.

Other Requirements

Stenographers should have good reading comprehension and spelling skills, as well as good finger and hand dexterity. They should be even-tempered and be able to work well with others. They should also find systematic and orderly work appealing, and they should like to work on detailed tasks. Other personal qualifications include dependability, trustworthiness, and a neat personal appearance, given their high degree of visibility.

■ Exploring

You can get experience in the stenography field by assuming the clerical and typing responsibilities with a school club or other organization. In addition, some school work-study programs may have opportunities with businesses for part-time, on-the-job training. It may also be possible to get a part-time or summer job in a business office by contacting offices on your own. You may have the opportunity to get training in the operation of word processors and other office machinery through evening or continuing education courses offered by business schools and community colleges.

■ Employers

Stenographers, including those who have developed special skills through training, are employed in various organizations of law; business; and federal, state, and local government. Some specialist stenographers work in medical, legal, engineering, or other technical areas. Some stenographers develop their own freelance businesses.

■ Starting Out

High school guidance counselors and business education teachers may be helpful in locating job opportunities for would-be stenographers. Additionally, business schools and colleges frequently have placement programs to help their trainees and graduates find employment. Those interested in securing an entry-level position can also contact individual businesses or government agencies directly. Jobs may also be located through newspaper classified ads.

Many companies administer aptitude tests to potential employees before they are hired. Speed and accuracy are critical factors in making such evaluations. Individuals who are initially unable to meet the minimum requirements for a stenographer position may want to take jobs as typists or clerks and, as they gain experience and technical training, try for promotion to the position of stenographer.

■ Advancement

Skilled stenographers can advance to secretarial positions, especially if they develop their interpersonal communications skills. They may also become heads of stenographic departments or in some cases be promoted to office manager. In some instances, experienced stenographers may go into business for themselves as public stenographers serving traveling business people and others. Skilled freelance reporters may also find work in recording proceedings in the U. S. Congress, in state and local governing bodies, and in governing agencies at all levels.

■ Earnings

Salaries for stenographers vary widely, depending on their skill, experience, level of responsibility, and geographic location. New workers, according to the U.S. Department of Labor, may earn as little $14,560 a year, while the most experienced stenographers may earn $33,680 or more annually. Stenographers employed by private companies earned an average of about $21,320 per year in 1996. The median income for court reporters is about $56,000 annually.

■ Work Environment

As with most office workers, stenographers work an average of 37 to 40 hours per week. Relatively few office stenographers work in the evenings or on weekends. (This is not true of court reporters, real-time captioners, or those who freelance their services, as they often work long and irregular hours.) Full-time workers should also receive paid vacation, health insurance, and other benefits. Some stenographers take on part-time or temporary work during peak business periods.

The physical work environment is usually pleasant and comfortable, although stenographers may sometimes have to work under extreme deadline pressure. Stenographers may also be subject to repetitive stress injury, a prevalent industrial hazard for those who perform repeated motions in their daily work. Carpal tunnel syndrome is a type of repetitive stress injury that stenographers can sometimes develop, causing a prickling sensation or numbness in the hand and sometimes a partial loss of function. Stenographers generally perform their jobs while seated and so must be conscious of correct posture and proper seating.

The amount of supervision a stenographer receives will depend on the job level, such as junior or senior stenographer, and the nature of the work. Some firms offer more supervision than others. The majority of stenographers are not required to travel; however, some may accompany their employers on business trips to provide dictation services.

■ Outlook

Job opportunities for unspecialized stenographers have been declining and should continue to fall off sharply in the coming years. Audio recording equipment and the use of personal computers by managers and other professionals has greatly reduced the demand for these workers, while increasing demand for CAT system operators in real-time settings. The trend to provide instantaneous captions for the deaf and hearing-impaired and the growing use of CAT technology in courtroom trials should strengthen the demand for real-time reporters. Continued technological advances, such as computer-aided equipment that can print out what is being said by a spoken voice, will imperil this profession further.

Despite this decline, however, some jobs will become available as people retire or otherwise leave the profession. As always, those with the most skill and experience, or a particular area of expertise (such as legal or medical stenographers) will have the best employment possibilities.

■ For More Information

For information on union membership, contact:

Office and Professional Employees International Union
265 West 14th Street, 6th Floor
New York, NY 10011
Tel: 800-346-7348
Email: opeiu@opeiu.org
Web: http://www.opeiu.org

■ Related Articles

Business

Law

Bookkeeping and Accounting Clerks

Court Reporters

Data Entry Clerks

Indexers

Real-Time Captioners

Receptionists

Secretaries

Typists and Word Processors

Step-on Operators
■ **See Adventure Travel Specialists**

Stevedores

■ Overview

Stevedores, commonly known as *longshore workers* or *dockworkers,* handle cargo at ports, often using materials-handling machinery and gear. They load and unload ships at docks and transfer cargo to and from storage areas or other transports, such as trucks and barges. Members of the water transportation industry, stevedores are employed at ports all over the United States. The concentration of jobs is at the large ports on the coasts, and most of the positions are held by experienced, skilled workers.

■ History

There have been stevedoring workers in North America since colonial times. Long ago, when a sailing vessel arrived at the docks of a settlement, criers would go up and down the nearby streets summoning workers with a call like "Men along the shore!" Stevedores, or longshore workers, came quickly in hopes of a chance to make some extra cash by helping to unload the ship's cargo. Often, these longshore workers lived in town near the port and worked other occupations. Ships arrived too infrequently for them to make a living at the docks. But as the volume of shipping increased, a group of workers developed who were always available at the docks for loading and unloading activities.

STEVEDORES	
SCHOOL SUBJECTS	Mathematics Physical education
PERSONAL SKILLS	Following instructions Mechanical/manipulative
WORK ENVIRONMENT	Primarily outdoors Primarily multiple locations
MINIMUM EDUCATION LEVEL	High school diploma
SALARY RANGE	$45,000 to $60,000 to $100,000
CERTIFICATION OR LICENSING	None available
OUTLOOK	Little change or more slowly than the average
O*NET	98702

Ship owners usually wanted to have cargos moved through ports as soon as possible. They preferred to pick temporary workers from a large labor pool at the time there was work to be done. However, this practice produced unfavorable wages, hours, and working conditions for many workers. In the 19th century, longshore workers were among the first groups of American workers to organize labor unions to force improvements in working conditions.

In ancient times, a ship's cargo was handled in single "man-loads." Grain, a common item of cargo, was packed in sacks that could be carried on and off the ship on a man's shoulders. As methods progressed, the ship's rigging became used for hoisting cargo. The first cargo to need a special type of handling was fuel, which used to be transported in barrels. As the volume of fuel increased, barrels became inadequate. Since the late 19th century, oil products have been shipped in bulk, with no packaging, pumped directly into the hull cells of tankers.

Cargo handling has thus depended on the type of cargo shipped. Vehicles are simply rolled on and off; dry bulk like coal and grain is often poured into cargo holds. In the first part of the 20th century, longshore work slowly became mechanized, relying less on human labor and more on machines. Since the 1960s, containerization of cargos has been a major factor in ocean shipping. This method of transporting goods involves putting freight into large sealed boxes of standard sizes, sometimes fitted as truck trailers. The containers, which can be carried on ships that are specially built to hold them, are easily and quickly moved on and off ships at ports, thus keeping the cost of transport well below that for uncontainerized cargo. Such changes have greatly reduced the demand for stevedoring workers to do manual loading and unloading.

This can be considered a historic time for women's opportunities in these occupations. In the late 20th century, more longshore workers than ever before were women. Sexual discrimination lawsuits are forcing companies to hire more females. In California, for example, where there are many docks because of the state's long coastline, there were no women dockworkers until 1974. Now hundreds of women hold longshore positions at ports along the California coast.

■ The Job

Stevedores perform tasks involved in transferring cargo to and from the holds of ships and around the dock area. They may operate power winches or cranes to move items such as automobiles, crates, scrap metal, and steel beams, using hooks, magnets, or slings. They may operate grain trimmers (equipment that moves bulk grain through a spout and into the hatch of receiving containers). Stevedores may drive trucks along the dock or aboard ships to transfer items such as lumber and crates to within reach of winches. They may drive tractors to move loaded trailers from storage areas to dockside. They may load and unload liquid cargos—such as vegetable oils, molasses, or chemicals—by fastening hose lines to cargo tanks. Stevedores also do other manual tasks such as lashing cargo in place aboard ships, attaching lifting devices to winches, and signaling to other workers to raise or lower cargo. They may direct other dockworkers in moving cargo by hand or with handtrucks or in securing cargo inside the holds of ships.

Some stevedoring workers perform just one category of specialized tasks. For example, *boat loaders* may load liquid chemical and fuel cargos such as petroleum, gasoline, heating oil, and sulfuric acid by connecting and disconnecting hose couplings. At each stage in the process, they make sure various conditions are safe. Other boat loaders tend winches and loading chutes to load iron ore onto boats and barges. *Winch drivers* operate steam or electric winches to move various kinds of cargo in and out of a ship's hold. They may alternate jobs with *hatch tenders,* who signal to winch drivers when the cargo is secured and ready for transfer. *Gear repairers* fix gear that is used in lifting cargo and install appropriate equipment depending on the current cargo-handling needs on a particular vessel. Among the many other workers in the dock area are *drivers,* who drive rolling stock (including forklifts, trucks, and mobile cranes), and *carpenters,* who repair pallets and construct braces and other structures to protect cargo in holds or on deck.

Headers or *gang bosses* supervise stevedores. They assign specific duties and explain how the cargo should be handled and secured and how the hoisting equipment should be set up. They may estimate the amount of extra materials that will be needed to brace and protect the cargo, such as paper or lumber.

Stevedoring superintendents are responsible for coordinating and directing the loading and unloading of cargo. Before loading begins, they study the layout of the ship and the bill of lading to determine where to stow cargo and in what order. Freight that must come out first is usually the last to be loaded. Stevedoring superintendents estimate the time and number of workers they need for the job and give orders for hiring. They make sure that the available equipment is appropriate for the cargo load, and they may direct workers who are handling special materials, such as explosives. Stevedoring superintendents prepare reports on their operations and may make up bills, all while keeping in touch with the company representatives from whom they get their directions.

Pier superintendents manage business operations at freight terminals. They determine what cargo various vessels will be carrying and notify stevedoring superintendents to plan to have workers and dock space available for loading and unloading activities. They compute costs; oversee purchasing of cargo handling equipment and hiring of trucks, tractors, and railroad cars; and make sure that the terminal facilities and the company's equipment are properly maintained.

Shipping operations require individuals who have good recordkeeping and accounting skills as well. Workers who do these tasks include *shipping clerks,* who maintain information on all incoming and outgoing cargo, such as its quantity and condition, identification marks, and container

This stevedore is loading a ship with bags of grain.

size. *Location workers* keep track of where cargo is located on piers. *Delivery clerks* and *receiving clerks* keep records on the loading and discharging of vessels and on transferring cargo to and from truckers. *Timekeepers* record the work time of all workers on the pier for billing and payroll purposes.

■ Requirements

High School

If you think you might be interested in becoming a stevedore, you should take classes in mathematics and English as well as shop and physical education to help prepare you for the different aspects of the workload.

Postsecondary Training

Often, no special preparation is needed for this kind of work because many stevedores learn what they need to know, such as equipment operations, on the job. However, experience operating similar equipment is likely to be an advantage to any applicant and may result in more rapid advancement.

Workers in some positions need clerical or technical skills that can be learned in high school or vocational school. For administrative occupations, college-level training or experience as a ship's officer is often desirable. Supervisory personnel generally need an understanding of the whole process of loading and unloading a vessel. They must be able to deal with a labor force that may include inexperienced workers and that changes in number from day to day.

Many stevedoring jobs are open only to union workers. Unions to which stevedores belong are the International Longshoremen's Association and the International Longshoremen's and Warehousemen's Union. In some ports, jobs are allocated based on seniority, so newcomers may be left with the least desirable jobs.

Other Requirements

Stevedores who work on the docks need to be agile and physically fit. Their work may be strenuous, sometimes requiring lifting weights of up to 50 pounds. Good eyesight and dexterity are essential. Some jobs can be adapted to some extent for workers with disabilities. Stevedores may work in situations that are potentially dangerous, so they must be able to think clearly and quickly and be able to follow orders. Because longshore work is a team effort, stevedores must work well with others.

■ Exploring

To find out more about stevedoring occupations, contact the offices of the longshore workers' union in your area. Union representatives can provide you with information about the likely conditions and prospects for local jobs, as well as answer questions and provide an insider's view of the field. Students in coastal areas have an advantage over others because they can visit ports and ask questions about what is involved in being a dockworker.

■ Employers

Stevedores are employed at all U.S. ports. The bulk of jobs are concentrated on the coasts, and larger companies employ greater numbers of longshore workers. Usually, you must be a union member to secure a position with one of the larger companies.

■ Starting Out

To find a job as a stevedore, you should contact the local union offices or shipping companies to find out whether workers are being hired. Those who would like eventually to work in an administrative position, such as *pier superintendent,* should consider entering one of the maritime academies (schools that train officers and crew for merchant vessels). Another possibility for people interested in administrative work is to enter a training program conducted by a port authority, which is an organization at a port that controls harbor activities.

■ Advancement

Dockworkers may start out doing basic labor, such as loading trucks or following instructions to load cargo in holds. Later, if they prove to be responsible and reliable, they may learn how to operate equipment such as winches or forklifts. In general, this kind of advancement depends on the need for workers to do particular tasks as well as the individual's abilities. Those who demonstrate strong abilities, leadership, and judgment may have an opportunity to become gang bosses and supervise a crew of other work-

ers. Advancement into administrative positions may require additional formal education.

■ Earnings

Wages for stevedores on the east coast average around $60,000 per year, with supervisory and administrative workers averaging more. Experienced workers on the west coast can earn $85,000 to $100,000 per year. Minimum wages can be negotiated by unions; in 1994, the International Longshoremen's Association's union contract called for a minimum wage of $22 per hour. Stevedores receive extra pay for handling certain difficult or dangerous cargoes and for working overtime, nights, or holidays. In addition to earnings, full-time workers usually receive good benefits packages that may include pension plans, paid holiday and vacation days, and health insurance.

One type of benefit plan, Guaranteed Annual Income (GAI), a program that pays dockworkers even when they are not working, is being eliminated by many ports. When work is scarce, the GAI plan can be expensive for companies. Thus, one local union in Baltimore instead offered to pay cash to members who agreed to leave the industry. The Port of New York and New Jersey has offered early retirement programs in an effort to reduce its GAI programs.

■ Work Environment

Although parts of piers are covered by sheds, many stevedores must be outdoors much of the time, including in bad weather. Working around materials-handling machinery can be noisy. At times, hours may be very long, such as when it is important that a lot of cargo be moved on and off piers quickly. Stevedores work under stress to meet deadlines. Some work is strenuous, involving lifting heavy material. Stevedores must use care to avoid injury from falls, falling objects, and machines. Some workers, such as those in certain supervisory positions, move about fairly constantly.

■ Outlook

A number of factors are contributing to a lack of growth for longshore occupations, including increased automation, containerization, and the combining of jobs in the industry. Although certain large ports will experience growth and require larger numbers of stevedores, data from the U.S. Department of Transportation reflects a stabilization—and in some cases decline—throughout the 1990s in such areas as revenues and the number of people employed in the water transportation industry. Of course, increasing retirement among members of the Pacific Maritime Association and the International Longshoremen's Union will assure a certain number of new jobs each year. Also, to remedy labor disagreement problems at smaller ports, union officials have devised a travel plan for longshore workers in smaller ports who have decided to work at bigger ports whenever positions are available.

The trends toward automated materials-handling processes and containerizing cargo are well established. In the future, fewer people may be hired for manual loading and unloading tasks and the stevedoring work force will probably be highly skilled, well trained, and will consist mostly of full-time workers.

■ For More Information

For further information on stevedoring occupations, contact the following unions:

International Longshoremen's and Warehousemen's Union
1188 Franklin Street
San Francisco, CA 94109
Tel: 415-775-0533

International Longshoremen's Association
17 Battery Place, Room 1530
New York, NY 10004
Tel: 212-425-1200

■ Related Articles

Airlines

Construction

Shipping

Trucking

Construction Laborers

Industrial Machinery Mechanics

Merchant Mariners

Shipping and Receiving Managers and Clerks

Stewardesses
■ **See Flight Attendants**

Stitcher Operators
■ **See Bindery Workers**

Stockbrokers
■ **See Financial Services Brokers**

Stock Clerks

■ Overview

Stock clerks receive, unpack, store, distribute, and record the inventory for materials or products used by a company, plant, or store.

■ History

Almost every type of business establishment imaginable—shoe store, restaurant, hotel, auto repair shop, hospital, supermarket, or steel mill—buys materials or products from outside distributors and uses these materials in its operations. A large part of the company's money is tied up in these inventory stocks, but without them operations would come to a standstill. Stores would run out of merchandise to sell, mechanics would be unable to repair cars until new parts were shipped in, and factories would be unable to operate once their basic supply of raw materials ran out.

To avoid these problems, businesses have developed their own inventory-control systems to store enough goods and raw materials for uninterrupted operations, move these materials to the places they are needed, and know when it is time to order more. These systems are the responsibility of stock clerks.

■ The Job

Stock clerks work in just about every type of industry, and no matter what kind of storage or stock room they staff—food, clothing, merchandise, medicine, or raw materials—the work of stock clerks is essentially the same. They receive, sort, put away, distribute, and keep track of the items a business sells or uses. Their titles sometimes vary based on their responsibilities.

When goods are received in a stockroom, stock clerks unpack the shipment and check the contents against documents such as the invoice, purchase order, and bill of

STOCK CLERKS	
SCHOOL SUBJECTS	English Mathematics
PERSONAL SKILLS	Following instructions Helping/teaching
WORK ENVIRONMENT	Primarily indoors Primarily one location
MINIMUM EDUCATION LEVEL	High school diploma
SALARY RANGE	$8,840 to $15,000 to $20,000
CERTIFICATION OR LICENSING	None available
OUTLOOK	Little change or more slowly than the average
DOT	222
GOE	05.09.01
NOC	1474
O*NET	49021

Stock clerks must be well organized so that they can find things quickly, especially in a large stock room such as this.

lading, which lists the contents of the shipment. The shipment is inspected, and any damaged goods are set aside. Stock clerks may reject or send back damaged items or call vendors to complain about the condition of the shipment. In large companies this work may be done by a shipping and receiving clerk.

Once the goods are received, stock clerks organize them and sometimes mark them with identifying codes or prices so they can be placed in stock according to the existing inventory system. In this way the materials or goods can be found readily when needed, and inventory control is much easier. In many firms stock clerks use hand-held scanners and computers to keep inventory records up to date.

In retail stores and supermarkets stock clerks may bring merchandise to the sales floor and stock shelves and racks. In stockrooms and warehouses they store materials in bins, on the floor, or on shelves. In other settings, such as restaurants, hotels, and factories, stock clerks deliver goods when they are needed. They may do this on a regular schedule or at the request of other employees or supervisors. Although many stock clerks use mechanical equipment, such as forklifts, to move heavy items, some perform strenuous and laborious work. In general, the work of a stock clerk involves much standing, bending, walking, stretching, lifting, and carrying.

When items are removed from the inventory, stock clerks adjust records to reflect the products' use. These records are kept as current as possible, and inventories are periodically checked against these records. Every item is counted, and the totals are compared with the records on hand or the records from the sales, shipping, production, or purchasing departments. This helps identify how fast items are being used, when items must be ordered from outside suppliers, or even whether items are disappearing from the stockroom. Many retail establishments use computerized cash registers that maintain an inventory count automatically as they record the sale of each item.

The duties of stock clerks vary depending on their place of employment. Stock clerks working in small firms perform many different tasks, including shipping and receiving, inventory control, and purchasing. In large firms, responsibilities may be more narrow. More specific job categories include *inventory clerks, stock control clerks, material clerks, order fillers, merchandise distributors,* and *shipping and receiving clerks.*

At a construction site or factory that uses a variety of raw and finished materials, there are many different types of specialized work for stock clerks. *Tool crib attendants* issue, receive, and store the various hand tools, machine tools, dies, and other equipment used in an industrial establishment. They make sure the tools come back in reasonably good shape and keep track of those that need replacing. *Parts order and stock clerks* purchase, store, and distribute the spare parts needed for motor vehicles and other industrial equipment. *Metal control coordinators* oversee the movement of metal stock and supplies used in producing nonferrous metal sheets, bars, tubing, and alloys. In mining and other industries that regularly use explosives, *magazine keepers* store explosive materials and components safely and distribute them to authorized personnel. In the military, *space and storage clerks* keep track of the weights and amounts of ammunition and explosive components stored in the magazines of an arsenal and check their storage condition.

Many types of stock clerks can be found in other industries. At printing companies, *cut-file clerks* collect, store, and hand out the layout cuts, ads, mats, and electrotypes used in the printing process. *Parts clerks* handle and distribute spare and replacement parts in repair and maintenance shops. In eyeglass centers, *prescription clerks* select the lens blanks and frames for making eyeglasses and keep inventory stocked at a specified level. In motion picture companies, *property custodians* receive, store, and distribute the props needed for shooting. In hotels and hospitals, *linen room attendants* issue and keep track of inventories of bed linen, table cloths, and uniforms, while *kitchen clerks* verify the quantity and quality of food products being taken from the storeroom to the kitchen. Aboard ships, the clerk in charge of receiving and issuing supplies and keeping track of inventory is known as the *storekeeper.*

■ Requirements

High School

Although there are no specific educational requirements for beginning stock clerks, employers prefer to hire high school graduates. Reading and writing skills and a basic knowledge of mathematics are necessary; typing and filing skills are also useful. In the future, as more companies install computerized inventory systems, a knowledge of computer operations will be important.

Other Requirements

Good health and good eyesight is important. A willingness to take orders from supervisors and others is necessary for this work, as is the ability to follow directions. Organizational skills also are important, as is neatness. Depending on where they work, some stock clerks may be required to join a union. This is especially true of stock clerks who are employed by industry and who work in large cities with a high percentage of union-affiliated companies.

When a stock clerk handles certain types of materials, extra training or certification may be required. Generally those who handle jewelry, liquor, or drugs must be bonded.

■ Exploring

The best way to learn about the responsibilities of a stock clerk is to get a part-time or summer job as a sales clerk, stockroom helper, stockroom clerk, or, in some factories, stock chaser. These jobs are relatively easy to get and can help students learn about stock work, as well as about the duties of workers in related positions. This sort of part-time work can also lead to a full-time job.

■ Employers

More than two million people work as stock clerks. Of these, 60 percent work as stockroom, warehouse, or yard clerks, while 40 percent work as sales-floor stock clerks. Many sales floor clerks work part-time. Almost 60 percent of stockroom, warehouse, and yard clerks work in retail and wholesale firms, about 20 percent are in factories, and the remainder work in hospitals, government agencies, schools, and other organizations. Nearly all sales floor stock clerks are employed in retail establishments, with about two-thirds working in supermarkets.

■ Starting Out

Job openings for stock clerks often are listed in newspaper classified ads. Job seekers should contact the personnel office of the firm looking for stock clerks and fill out an application for employment. School counselors, parents, relatives, and friends also can be good sources for job leads and may be able to give personal references if an employer requires them.

Stock clerks usually receive on-the-job training. New workers start with simple tasks, such as counting and marking stock. The basic responsibilities of the job are usually learned within the first few weeks. As they progress, stock clerks learn to keep records of incoming and outgoing

materials, take inventories, and place orders. As wholesale and warehousing establishments convert to automated inventory systems, stock clerks need to be trained to use the new equipment. Stock clerks who bring merchandise to the sales floor and stock shelves and sales racks need little training.

■ Advancement

Stock clerks with ability and determination have a good chance of being promoted to jobs with greater responsibility. In small firms, stock clerks may advance to sales positions or become assistant buyers or purchasing agents. In large firms, stock clerks can advance to more responsible stock handling jobs, such as *invoice clerk, stock control clerk,* and *procurement clerk.*

Furthering one's education can lead to more opportunities for advancement. By studying at a technical or business school or taking home-study courses, stock clerks can prove to their employer that they have the intelligence and ambition to take on more important tasks. More advanced positions, such as *warehouse manager* and *purchasing agent,* are usually given to experienced people who have post-high school education.

■ Earnings

Beginning stock clerks usually earn the minimum wage or slightly more. Experienced stock clerks can earn anywhere from $5 to $10 per hour, with time-and-a-half pay for overtime. Average earnings vary depending on the type of industry and geographic location. Stock clerks working in the retail trade generally earn wages in the middle range. In transportation, utilities, and wholesale businesses, earnings usually are higher; in finance, insurance, real estate, and other types of office services, earnings generally are lower. Those working for large companies or national chains may receive excellent benefits. After one year of employment, some stock clerks are offered one to two weeks of paid vacation each year, as well as health and medical insurance and a retirement plan.

■ Work Environment

Stock clerks usually work in relatively clean, comfortable areas. Working conditions vary considerably, however, depending on the industry and type of merchandise being handled. For example, stock clerks who handle refrigerated goods must spend some time in cold storage rooms, while those who handle construction materials, such as bricks and lumber, occasionally work outside in harsh weather. Most stock clerk jobs involve much standing, bending, walking, stretching, lifting, and carrying. Some workers may be required to operate machinery to lift and move stock.

Because stock clerks are employed in so many different types of industries, the amount of hours worked every week depends on the type of employer. Usually stock clerks in retail stores work a five-day, 40-hour week, while those in industry work 44 hours, or five and one half day, a week. Many others are able to find part-time work. Overtime is common, especially when large shipments arrive or during peak times such as holiday seasons.

■ Outlook

Although the volume of inventory transactions is expected to increase significantly, employment for stock clerks is expected to grow more slowly than the average for all occupations through 2006. This is a result of increased automation and other productivity improvements that enable clerks to handle more stock. Manufacturing and wholesale trade industries are making the greatest use of automation. In addition to computerized inventory control systems, firms in these industries are expected to rely more on sophisticated conveyor belts, automatic high stackers to store and retrieve goods, and automatic guided vehicles that are battery-powered and driverless. Sales floor stock clerks probably will be less affected by automation as most of their work is done on the sales floor, where it is difficult to locate or operate complicated machinery.

Because this occupation employs a large number of people, many job openings occur each year to replace stock clerks who transfer to other jobs and leave the labor force. Stock clerk jobs tend to be entry-level positions, so many vacancies will be created by normal career progression to other occupations.

■ For More Information

For materials on educational programs in the retail industry, contact:

National Retail Federation
325 7th Street, NW, Suite 1000
Washington, DC 20004
Attn: Vice President of Research, Education, and Community Affairs
Tel: 202-783-7971
Web: http://www.nrf.com

■ Related Articles

Business

Sales

Auctioneers

Buyers

Cashiers

Counter and Retail Clerks

Merchandise Displayers

Purchasing Agents

Retail Business Owners

Retail Managers

Sales Representatives

Services Sales Representatives

Storekeepers
■ See Stock Clerks

Storyboard Artists
■ See Cartoonists and Animators

Strategic Intelligence Agents
■ See Intelligence Officers

Stratigraphers
■ See Geologists

Stress Test Technologists
■ See Cardiovascular Technologists

Stretch-Machine Operators
■ See Plastics Products Manufacturing Workers

Stringers
■ See Sportswriters

Structural Designers

■ **See Sports Facility Designers**

Studio Technicians

■ **See Audio Recording Engineers**

Stunt Coordinators

■ **See Stunt Performers**

Stunt Performers

■ Overview

Stunt performers, also called *stuntmen* and *stuntwomen,* are actors who perform dangerous scenes in motion pictures. They may fall off tall buildings, get knocked from horses and motorcycles, imitate fist fights, and drive in high-speed car chases. They must know how to set up "stunts" that are both safe to perform and believable to audiences. In these dangerous scenes, stunt performers are often asked to double, or take the place, of a star actor.

■ History

There have been stunt performers since the early years of motion pictures. Frank Hanaway, believed to be the first stunt performer, began his career in the 1903 film *The Great Train Robbery.* A former U.S. cavalryman, Hanaway had developed the skill of falling off a horse unharmed. Until the introduction of sound films in the 1920s, stunt performers were used mostly in slapstick comedy films, which relied on "sight-gags" to entertain the audience.

The first stuntwoman in motion pictures was Helen Gibson, who began her stunt career in the 1914 film series *The Hazards of Helen.* Chosen for the job because of her experience performing tricks on horseback, Gibson went from doubling for Helen Holmes, the star actress, to eventually playing the lead role herself. Among her stunts was jumping from a fast-moving motorcycle onto an adjacent moving locomotive.

Despite the success of Helen Gibson, most stunt performers were men. For dangerous scenes, actresses were usually doubled by a stuntman wearing a wig and the char-

acter's costume. Because films usually showed stunts at a distance, audiences could not tell the switch had been made.

Discrimination in the film industry also resulted in few minorities working as stunt performers. White men doubled for American Indians, Asians, Mexicans, and African-Americans by applying makeup or other material to their skin. This practice was called painting down.

As the motion picture industry grew, so did the importance of stunt performers. Because injury to a star actor could end a film project and incur a considerable financial loss for the studio, producers would allow only stunt performers to handle dangerous scenes. Even so, star actors would commonly brag that they had performed their own stunts. Only a few, such as Helen Gibson and Richard Talmadge, actually did.

Beginning in the 1950s the growth in the number of independent, or self-employed, producers brought new opportunities for stunt performers. In general, independent producers were not familiar with stunt work and came to rely on experienced stunt performers to set up stunt scenes and to find qualified individuals to perform them. Stunt performers who did this kind of organizational work came to be called stunt coordinators.

The Stuntmen's Association, the first professional organization in the field, was founded in 1960. Its goal was to share knowledge of stunt techniques and safety practices, to work out special problems concerning stunt performers, and to help producers find qualified stunt performers. Other organizations followed, including the International Stunt Association, the Stuntwomen's Association, the United Stuntwomen's Association, Stunts Unlimited, and Drivers Inc. As a result of these organizations, stunt performers are now better educated and trained in stunt techniques.

An increasing number of women and minorities have become stunt per-

STUNT PERFORMERS	
SCHOOL SUBJECTS	Physical education Theater/Dance
PERSONAL SKILLS	Following instructions Mechanical/manipulative
WORK ENVIRONMENT	Indoors and outdoors Primarily multiple locations
MINIMUM EDUCATION LEVEL	High school diploma
SALARY RANGE	$5,000 to $50,000 to $100,000+
CERTIFICATION OR LICENSING	None available
OUTLOOK	About as fast as the average
DOT	159
GOE	12.02.01
NOC	5135
O*NET	34056A

formers since the 1970s. The Screen Actors Guild (SAG), the union that represents stunt performers, has been at the vanguard of this change. In the 1970s SAG banned the practice of painting down, thus forcing producers to find, for example, an African-American stuntman to double for an African-American actor. SAG also began to require that producers make an effort to find female stunt performers to double for actresses. Only after showing that a number of qualified stuntwomen have declined the role can a producer hire a stuntman to do the job.

Over the years, new technology has changed the field of stunt work. Air bags, for example, make stunts safer, and faster cars and better brakes have given stunt performers more control. Stunt performers, however, still rely on their athletic ability and sense of timing when doing a dangerous stunt.

■ The Job

Stunt performers work on a wide variety of scenes which have the potential for causing serious injury, including car crashes and chases; fist and sword fights; falls from cars, motorcycles, horses, and buildings; airplane and helicopter gags; rides through river rapids; and confrontations with animals, such as in a buffalo stampede. Although they are hired as actors, they rarely perform a speaking role. Some stunt performers specialize in one type of stunt.

There are two general types of stunt roles: double and nondescript. The first requires a stunt performer to "double"—to the place of—of a star actor in a dangerous scene. As a double, the stunt performer must portray the character in the same way as the star actor. A nondescript role does not involve replacing another person and is usually an incidental character in a dangerous scene. An example of a nondescript role is a driver in a freeway chase scene.

The idea for a stunt usually begins with the screenwriter. Stunts can make a movie not only exciting but also profitable. Action films, in fact, make up the majority of box-office hits. The stunts, however, must make sense within the context of the film's story.

Once the stunts are written into the script, it is the job of the director to decide how they will appear on the screen. Directors, especially of large, action-filled movies, often seek the help of a stunt coordinator. *Stunt coordinators* are individuals who have years of experience performing or coordinating stunts and who know the stunt performer community well. A stunt coordinator can quickly determine if a stunt is feasible and, if so, what is the best and safest way to perform it. The stunt coordinator plans the stunt, oversees the setup and construction of special sets and materials, and either hires or recommends the most qualified stunt performer. Some stunt coordinators also take over the direction of action scenes. Because of this responsibility, many stunt coordinators are members not

only of the Screen Actors Guild but of the Directors Guild of America.

Although a stunt may last only a few seconds on film, preparations for the stunt can take several hours or even days. Stunt performers work with such departments as props, makeup, wardrobe, and set design. They also work closely with the special effects team to resolve technical problems and ensure safety. The director and the stunt performer must agree on a camera angle that will maximize the effect of the stunt. These preparations can save a considerable amount of production time and money. A carefully planned stunt can often be completed in just one take. More typically, the stunt person will have to perform the stunt several times until the director is satisfied with the performance.

Stunt performers do not have a death wish. They are dedicated professionals who take great precautions to ensure their safety. Air bags, body pads, or cables might be used in a stunt involving a fall or a crash. If a stunt performer must enter a burning building, special fire-proof clothing is worn and protective cream is applied to the skin. Stunt performers commonly design and build their own protective equipment.

Stunt performers are not only actors but also athletes. Thus, they spend much of their time keeping their bodies in top physical shape and practicing their stunts.

■ Requirements

High School

Take physical education, dance, and other courses that will involve you in exercise, weight-lifting, and coordination. Sports teams can help you develop the athletic skills needed. In a theater class, you'll learn to take direction, and you may have the opportunity to perform for an audience.

Postsecondary Training

There is no minimum educational requirement for becoming a stunt performer. Most learn their skills by working for years under an experienced stunt performer. A number of stunt schools, however, do exist, including the United Stuntmen's Association National Stunt Training School. You can also benefit from enrolling in theater classes.

Among the skills that must be learned are specific stunt techniques, such as how to throw a punch; the design and building of safety equipment; and production techniques, such as camera angles and film editing. The more a stunt performer knows about all aspects of filmmaking, the better that person can design effective and safe stunts.

Certification or Licensing

There's no certification available, but, like all actors, stunt performers working in film and TV must belong to the Screen Actors Guild (SAG). Many stunt performers also belong to the American Federation of Television and Radio Artists (AFTRA). As a member of a union, you'll receive special benefits, such as better pay and compensation for overtime and holidays.

Other Requirements

Stunt work requires excellent athletic ability. Many stunt performers were high school and college athletes, and some were Olympic or world champions. Qualities developed through sports such as self-discipline, coordination, common sense, and coolness under stress are essential to becoming a successful stunt performer. As a stunt performer, you must exercise regularly to stay in shape and maintain good health. You should also have some understanding of the mechanics of the stunts you'll be performing—you may be working with ropes, cables, and other equipment.

Because much of the work involves being a stunt double for a star actor, it is helpful to have a common body type. Exceptionally tall or short people, for example, may have difficulty finding roles.

■ Exploring

There are few means of gaining experience as a stunt performer prior to actual employment. Involvement in high school or college athletics is helpful, as is acting experience in a school or local theater. As an intern or extra for a film production, you may have the opportunity to see stunt people at work. Theme parks and circuses also make much use of stunt performers; some of these places allow visitors to meet the performers after shows.

■ Employers

Most stunt performers work on a freelance basis, contracting with individual productions on a project-by-project basis. Stunt performers working on TV projects may have long-term commitments if serving as a stand-in for a regular character. Some stunt performers also work in other aspects of the entertainment industry, taking jobs with theme parks, and live stage shows and events.

■ Starting Out

Most stunt performers enter the field by contacting stunt coordinators and asking for work. Coordinators and stunt associations can be located in trade publications. To be of interest to coordinators, you'll need to promote any special skills you have, such as stunt driving, skiing, and diving. Many stunt performers also have agents who locate work for them, but an agent can be very difficult to get if you've

---

FAMOUS DAREDEVILS

Stunt performers have been around much longer than the film industry—throughout the 19th century, circus performers leapt from buildings, hung from the neck, walked tight-ropes, swallowed swords, and contorted themselves into tiny boxes. Harry Houdini is one of the most famous showmen in entertainment history. Other "daredevils," as they were known, included Samuel Gilbert Scott who demonstrated "extraordinary and surpassing powers in the art of leaping and diving"—after swinging about a ship's riggings or jumping from a 240-foot cliff, he'd pass around a hat for contributions. He would receive nearly double the usual amount whenever he most closely skirted death. His final stunt took place at Waterloo Bridge—while performing predive acrobatics with a rope about his neck, he slipped and strangled to death. "A surgeon was immediately sent for," a printed broadside announced, "and an attempt was made to bleed the unfortunate man, but without success . . . as life was quite extinct."

The stunts of women daredevils in the 19th century drew as many spectators as those of the men. Signora Josephine Girardelli was promoted as the "Fire-Proof Lady," a title she earned by holding boiling oil in her mouth and hands, and performing other feats of stamina. Bess Houdini assisted her husband Harry in many famous tricks, including one which ended with her bound and sealed in a trunk. May Wirth was a talented equestrian credited as "The Wonder Rider of the World" for her somersaults and other stunts while atop a rushing horse. Even amateurs got into the act—Annie Taylor, a 63-year-old, Michigan schoolteacher, became the first person to go over the Niagara Falls in a barrel.

---

had no stunt experience. If you live in New York or Los Angeles, you should volunteer to work as an intern for an action film; you may have the chance to meet some of the stunt performers, and make connections with crew members and other industry professionals. You can also submit a resume to the various online services, such as StuntNET (http://www.stuntnet.com), that are used by coordinators and casting directors. If you attend a stunt school, you may develop important contacts in the field.

■ Advancement

New stunt performers generally start with simple roles, such as being one of 40 people in a brawl scene. With greater experience and training, stunt performers can get more complicated roles. Some stunt associations have facilities where stunt performers work out and practice their skills. After a great deal of experience, you may be invited to join a professional association such as the Stuntmen's Association of Motion Pictures, which will allow you to network with others in the industry.

About five to 10 years of experience are usually necessary to become a stunt coordinator. Some stunt coordinators eventually work as a director of action scenes.

■ Earnings

The earnings of stunt performers vary considerably by their experience and the difficulty of the stunts they perform. In 1998, the minimum daily salary of any member of the Screen Actors Guild, including stunt performers, was over $550. A stunt coordinator has a daily minimum wage of $950, and a weekly minimum of $3,750. Though this may seem like a lot of money, few stunt performers work every day. According to the SAG, more than 80 percent of its 90,000 members made less than $5,000 in 1996. But those who are in high demand can receive salaries of well over $100,000 a year.

Stunt performers usually negotiate their salaries with the stunt coordinator. In general, they are paid per stunt; if they have to repeat the stunt three times before the director likes the scene, the stunt performer gets paid three times. If footage of a stunt is used in another film, the performer is paid again. The more elaborate and dangerous the stunt, the more money the stunt performer receives. Stunt performers are also compensated for overtime and travel expenses. Stunt coordinators negotiate their salaries with the producer.

■ Work Environment

The working conditions of a stunt performer change from project to project. It could be a studio set, a river, or an airplane thousands of feet above the ground. Like all actors, they are given their own dressing rooms.

Careers in stunt work tend to be short. The small number of jobs is one reason, as are age and injury. Even with the emphasis on safety, injuries commonly occur, often because of mechanical failure, problems with animals, or human error. The possibility of death is always present. Despite these drawbacks, a large number of people are attracted to the work because of the thrill, the competitive challenge, and the chance to work in motion pictures.

■ Outlook

There are over 2,500 stunt performers who belong to the SAG, but only a fraction of those can afford to devote themselves to film work full time. Stunt coordinators will continue to hire only very experienced professionals, making it difficult to break into the business.

The future of the profession may be affected by computer technology. In more cases, filmmakers may choose to use special effects and computer-generated imagery for action sequences. Not only can computer effects allow for more ambitious images, but they're also safer. Safety on film sets has always been a serious concern; despite innovations in filming techniques, stunts remain very dangerous. However, using live stunt performers can give a scene more authenticity, so talented stunt performers will always be in demand.

■ For More Information

Visit the SAG Web site to read the online stunt performer's guide:

Screen Actors Guild
5757 Wilshire Boulevard
Los Angeles, CA 90036
Tel: 323-954-1600
Web: http://www.sag.com

For information about the USA training program, contact:

United Stuntmen's Association
2723 Saratoga Lane
Everett, WA 98203
Tel: 425-290-9957
Web: http://www.stuntschool.com

■ Related Articles

Film

Sports

Television

Actors

Circus Performers

Professional Athletes—Individual Sports

Professional Athletes—Team Sports

Submarine Cable Equipment Technicians

■ **See Communications Equipment Technicians**

Substation Operators

■ **See Energy Transmission and Distribution Workers**

Supermarket Managers

■ Overview

Supermarket managers work in grocery stores. They manage budgets, arrange schedules, oversee human resources, lead customer service, and manage each aspect of the day-to-day business of bringing the nation's food supply to the people. According to the Food Marketing Institute, there are 126,000 stores that sell groceries across the country and often several managers at each location.

Managers include store managers, assistant store managers, courtesy booth/service desk managers, customer service managers, receiving managers, and managers of such departments as bakery, deli/food service, food court, front end, grocery, meat/seafood, frozen foods, pharmacy, and produce/floral. The size and location of the store determines how many of these management levels exist in each store. In a small, family-owned grocery, the manager and owner may be the same person.

■ History

The supermarket industry, in the early 1900s, was really a group of small "mom and pop" grocery stores. At most of these stores, the owners or someone in their family managed the daily operations. The typical city street of that time resembled the supermarket departments of today with each store handling its own specialty. For example, the fish market and the bakery each had an individual owner and operator.

By 1902, the Kroger company, now the country's largest grocer, already had 40 stores and a factory as well as a management staff to keep the growing business efficient. As Americans began purchasing more of their food and relying less on their gardens and farms, the supermarket industry grew along with the need for professionals to manage the stores.

Technological innovations have increased the duties and responsibilities of supermarket managers. Bar codes, inventory systems, and complex delivery systems have increased the need for professionals who can use these tools to run an efficient store while still remembering that customer service is of utmost importance. With profit margins low and competition high in this $323 billion industry, careful business planning is imperative for each store's success.

At the beginning of the century, locally owned groceries were the norm, although some chains were already growing. However, that has changed with the rapid growth of chain supermarkets. While chains have purchased some local stores and companies, other small stores have simply gone out of business. The total number of grocery stores dropped from 150,000 in 1987 to 126,000 in 1997, according to the Food Marketing Institute.

Advances in technology will continue to alter the duties of the supermarket manager. Online grocery shopping, though in its infancy, is predicted to grow rapidly over the next few years. Qualified managers trained in the newest technology and management practices will be needed in this evolving industry.

■ The Job

Supermarket managers oversee a wide range of resources, both personal and professional, to do their jobs effectively. Their days are fast-paced and interesting; routine duties are often interspersed with the need to solve problems quickly and effectively.

Steve Edens is the associate manager of a Kroger supermarket in Columbus, Indiana. Like most supermarket managers, Steve works a variety of shifts and handles a range of responsibilities. Working as the liaison between the corporate office and his staff, Steve spends time each day handling correspondence, email, and verbal and written reports.

Supermarket managers often work on more than one task at once. Steve carries a note pad and a scan gun, and pushes a cart, as he checks the floor, inventory, and departments each day. While checking the inventory, Steve uses the scan gun to check on an item that is low in stock. The scan gun lets him know if the item has been ordered. "The technology keeps getting better and better," says Steve. The average supermarket carries 30,000 different items so the technology of today helps managers to keep those items on the shelves.

You may think that managers rarely get their hands dirty, but this is not the case for Steve and other managers. Steve carries a feather duster with him as he makes his daily rounds of the store. Appearance is key for a supermarket's image as well as customer comfort, so Steve occasionally straightens and dusts as he surveys the placement

SUPERMARKET MANAGERS	
SCHOOL SUBJECTS	**Business** **English** **Mathematics**
PERSONAL SKILLS	**Communication/ideas** **Leadership/management**
WORK ENVIRONMENT	**Primarily indoors** **Primarily one location**
MINIMUM EDUCATION LEVEL	**High school diploma**
SALARY RANGE	**$30,000 to $50,000 to $100,000+**
CERTIFICATION OR LICENSING	**None available**
OUTLOOK	**Faster than the average**
DOT	**185**
GOE	**11.11.05**

of advertising material, merchandise, and other store features. The typical supermarket covers 39,260 feet, so managers must be prepared to spend a lot of time each day walking.

Planning is key for supermarket managers. They must prepare weekly schedules, which are carefully coordinated with the wage budget. The managers work with the head cashier to check and coordinate schedules. The manager and associate manager oversee an immediate staff of department heads that vary with the size and location of the store.

These department and subdepartment managers are in charge of specific areas of the store, such as the bakery and deli, frozen foods, or produce. The department managers, along with the store managers, interview prospective employees while the store managers do the actual hiring and firing of personnel. Large supermarkets may employ more than 250 people, so supermarket managers need to have good human resources training.

Department heads also handle specific promotions within their areas as well as customer service within those areas. Many store managers have previously worked as a department manager.

Promotion and advertising are also on the managers' list of responsibilities. "We always plan a week ahead on displays and sales," says Steve, noting that seasonal displays are important in the grocery industry as in any other retail industry.

One of the major responsibilities of each of the managers is customer service. Managers need to courteously and competently address the requests and complaints of store customers. "I like working with people," says Steve. "It's very satisfying to me when I can help a customer out."

Though Steve acknowledges that the compensation—both monetarily and personally—is high, he has worked many 60- to 70-hour weeks and most holidays. Many stores are open 24 hours a day, 7 days a week, 365 days a year. With at least 2 managers required to be on duty at a time, supermarket managers can expect to work late nights, weekends, and holidays. "I don't think I've ever had a 3-day weekend off," says Steve. "You work most holidays."

At larger stores, like the Columbus Kroger, scheduling is often easier and requires less hours from each manager since the load can be split up between a larger management staff. Managers at smaller stores should expect to work more hours, weekends, and holidays.

Frequent transfers are also common. Steve has worked at over 10 stores during his 24-year career. Though his transfers have not involved household moves, larger companies do pay moving expenses for management transfers.

Problem solving and quick thinking are key skills to being a successful supermarket manager. Delayed deliveries, snowstorms, or holidays can throw a wrench into schedules, inventory, and effective customer service.

Managers need to deal with these problems as they happen while still preparing for the next day, week, and month.

■ Requirements

High School

Speech classes will help you build your communication skills, while business and mathematics courses will give you a good background for preparing budgets. Because reading is integral in evaluating reports and communicating with others, English classes are a must for workers in this field. Any classes in marketing, advertising, or statistics will also be helpful. Learning how to work well with others is important, so any classes that involve group projects or participation will help you to develop team skills.

Postsecondary Training

While a college degree is not required for a career in supermarket management, there is a trend toward hiring new managers straight out of college. Even for college-educated managers, stores have their own specific training programs, which may involve classes, on-site learning, and rotational training in different departments.

Some colleges offer degrees in retail management, but many people choose to major in business management to prepare for a management career. Even an associate's degree in retail or business management will give you an advantage over other applicants who only have a high school diploma.

Other Requirements

Interacting with people and handling customer service is the biggest requirement of the job. According to the Food Marketing Institute, the average consumer makes 2.2 trips per week to the grocery store. With this many people in each store, serving those people with professionalism and courtesy should be the number one goal of supermarket managers. "You have to be a people person to do this job," says Steve.

Supermarket managers should be able to handle a fast-paced and challenging work environment, and have the ability to calmly solve unexpected and frequent problems. Besides being able to "think on their feet," supermarket managers should be able to evaluate analytical problems with budgets, schedules, and promotions.

■ Exploring

If you are interested in becoming a supermarket manager, get a job at a supermarket. Any job, from bagger to cashier, will help you understand the industry better. Supermarket jobs are readily available to students, and the opportunity for on-the-job experience is great.

Interview managers to discuss the things they like and do not like about their jobs. Ask them how they got started and what influenced them to choose this career. When you set up your interview be sensitive to seasonal and weather concerns. Supermarket managers are extremely busy during holidays or other times when people flock to the stores in droves.

Look ahead. Online shopping is just one of the new trends in supermarkets. Be aware of new changes, and evaluate how your skills might fit into this changing industry.

Take some business classes. If you love people, but can't create a budget, this is not the career for you.

Hang out at your local store. Go on a busy day and a slow one. Study what activities are taking place and how management's role changes from day to day. Get a feel for the pace to decide if you would want to spend a lot of hours in a retail atmosphere.

■ Employers

The Kroger Company is the largest supermarket chain and employer, operating over 1,260 food stores and over 900 convenience stores in the United States. Albertson's and Safeway round out the top 3 chains.

There are 126,000 stores that sell groceries in the United States. Over the past 10 years, the number of chain supermarkets has grown while the number of small, independent grocers has decreased. While this makes the number of stores and employers smaller, the larger stores need a variety of management professionals for a diverse number of positions, from department managers to store managers.

Grocery stores are located in nearly every city. Though smaller cities and towns may have only one or two supermarkets to choose from, in larger cities, consumers and prospective employees have a wide selection of chains and smaller stores.

■ Starting Out

You won't be able to start out as a supermarket manager; some experience is usually necessary before assuming a management role. You can start as a bagger or cashier or as a management trainee. There are two basic career paths—either working through the ranks or being hired after completing a college program. Steve started in the stock room and has worked in a variety of positions from cashier to department manager and now as an associate manager. Working in many areas of the store is an important part of becoming an effective manager.

"This is one of the few companies where you can start as a bag boy and become the president," says Steve. Hard work and dedication are rewarded so paying your dues is important in this career.

To be considered for a management position, grocery experience is necessary. Even other retail experience is not enough to be hired as a manager because the grocery industry has so many specific challenges that are unique to the field.

Cold call applications are readily accepted at customer service counters in most grocery stores, and larger grocers do on-campus recruiting to attract future managers. Newspaper advertisements are also used to recruit new workers for this field.

■ Advancement

Department managers can advance up the management ladder to store manager or associate store manager. After reaching that level, the next step in advancement is to the corporate level—becoming a unit, district, or regional manager, responsible for a number of stores. The next step at the corporate level is to vice president or director of store operations. Managers at the store level can advance and receive higher salaries by transferring to larger and higher-earning stores. Some relocations may require a move to another city, state, or region, while others simply require a bit longer or shorter commute.

■ Earnings

Supermarket managers are well compensated. According to the 1998 Food Marketing Institute survey, starting managers can expect to make $30,000 a year. Department managers at large stores average $50,000 annually. Store managers average $75,000, while district managers earn average salaries of $100,000 annually. These salary numbers may include bonuses which are standard in the industry. Pay is affected by management level, the size of the store, and the location.

Benefits are also good, with most major employers offering health insurance, vacation pay, and sick pay. While some supermarket workers are covered by a union, managers are not required to pay union dues and do not receive overtime pay.

■ Work Environment

Supermarkets are clean and brightly lit. Depending on the time of day, they may be noisy or quiet, crowded or empty. Nearly all supermarket work takes place indoors, and most managers will spend several hours on their feet walking through the store while also spending time at an office desk.

A team environment pervades the supermarket, and managers are the head of that team. They must work well independently while supervising and communicating with others.

Supermarket managers are expected to work more than 40-hour weeks and also work holidays, weekends, and late hours. Because many supermarkets are open 24-hours a day, rotating schedules are usually required. Also, calls at home and last-minute schedule changes are to be expected.

■ Outlook

Though the outlook for all retail managers is expected to be slower than average, managers in the supermarket industry should expect growth that is faster than average. The number of stores is decreasing, but specialization and demand are growing in the industry.

"There is a big demand for qualified people," says Steve. "Supermarkets need people with experience, good records, and good people skills."

The growth in grocery management is due to an expanding line of inventory and specialization. Because there is strong competition in the supermarket industry, stores are creating new departments, such as restaurants, coffee shops, and video departments, to meet consumer's needs.

With total supermarket sales of $334.5 billion, the industry is huge and continues to grow as consumers spend more money on greater varieties of food and other merchandise. There will be a strong demand for people who can manage others while mastering the latest technology. Grocery stores are often at the forefront in exploring new technologies to improve efficiency, so computer literacy and business acumen will be increasingly important.

■ For More Information

For industry and employment information, contact:

Food Marketing Institute
800 Connecticut Avenue, NW
Washington, DC 20006-2701
Tel: 202-452-8444
Web: http://www.fmi.org

For information on all retail fields, contact:

National Retail Federation
325 7th Street, NW, Suite 1000
Washington, DC 20004
Tel: 202-783-7971
Web: http://www.nrf.com

For information on mass retail careers and a list of colleges with retail programs, contact:

International Mass Retail Association
1700 North Moore Street, Suite 2250
Arlington, VA 22209
Tel: 703-841-2300
Web: http://www.imra.org/

■ Related Articles

Supermarket Workers

■ Overview

Supermarket workers are a diverse group. Each supermarket worker is employed in one or more areas of a grocery store, from the checkout lane to the deli counter to the back stock room. There are 3.43 million people who work as employees of food stores, according to the U.S. Bureau of Labor Statistics. Supermarkets are located in cities and towns across the nation and include large chains and locally owned stores.

■ History

Grocery stores have existed in the United States since the 1800s. Those early stores did not carry a wide variety of merchandise and brands. Many specialized in one area such as bread, fish, or meat. Even these early stores needed workers to help run their businesses. At the time, the workers were less specialized; often, the same person who helped wrap the meat at a butcher shop might be found later in the day sweeping out the store.

In the early 1900s, small "mom and pop" stores opened. These stores were the beginning of the modern grocery industry. Soon, some of the stores expanded into chains and the role of the supermarket worker became even more important. With bigger stores, more merchandise, and more customers, more people were needed to work in the stores.

While technology has eliminated positions in other industries, the grocery industry has wisely utilized technology (like the bar code system) but has not seen a need to reduce staff. While the technology has made efficiency and customer service better, people are still needed to do most of the jobs in a grocery store. One technological change on the horizon is online grocery stores. This is a very new trend, but even this online ordering will involve order takers, delivery personnel, stock room personnel, inventory control, and more.

■ The Job

What is it like to be a supermarket worker? It really depends on who you ask. There are so many different types of work to do in a grocery that each job can be very different from the next.

One of the first positions most people think of in a grocery is the *cashier.* Cashiers are on the front lines for the store's customer service and order accuracy. Cashiers greet customers, scan merchandise, record coupons, present totals, take payments, and help to bag groceries. It is each cashier's responsibility to keep his or her work area clean and to ensure that their cash drawers balance at the end of their shift. If merchandise is incorrectly marked or damaged, the cashier calls the appropriate department to assist the customer.

Along with the cashiers, *clerks* help to bag the groceries, and, if necessary, help the customer transport the grocery bags to their vehicles. *Courtesy clerks,* sometimes called *bag boys* or *baggers,* also collect carts from the parking lots and help provide maintenance for those carts.

Stock personnel play an important behind-the-scenes role in supermarkets. They help unload trucks, inspect merchandise, stock shelves, and track inventory. If you visit a grocery late at night, you can see these workers busily preparing for the next day's customers.

One of the trends in the grocery industry is specialization. The supermarket industry is very competitive, so stores are adding more services and conveniences to attract and keep customers. Some of the specialized departments have historically been a part of grocery stores, such as bakeries and meat markets, while others, such as restaurants and baby-sitting services, are new.

Each area requires workers with specialized knowledge and training as well as experience in the grocery industry. Butchers, bakers, and deli workers are generally dedicated to their individual department in the store while other workers may "float" to the areas where they are needed.

Other supermarket workers are responsible for certain areas such as produce or dairy. While there is no preparation work involved such as there is in the bakery or deli departments, these workers regularly inspect merchandise, check expiration dates, and maintain displays.

Many supermarkets now include a restaurant or food court which require food preparers, servers, wait staff, and chefs.

Many larger chain supermarkets have a pharmacy onsite. *Pharmacists* fill prescriptions for customers, as well as offer counseling on both prescription and over-the-counter medications. *Pharmacy technicians* assist the pharmacist by filling prescriptions, taking inventory, and handling the cash register.

There are also many specialized support positions in supermarkets. *Store detectives* assist with security measures and loss prevention. *Human resource workers* handle personnel-related issues, such as recruiting and training, benefits administration, labor relations, and salary administration. These are very important members of the supermarket team since the average large grocery store employs 250 people. Supermarkets also require qualified accounting and finance workers, advertising workers, mar-

keting workers, information technology professionals, and community and public relations professionals.

Supermarket workers report to either a department or store manager. They may have to attend weekly departmental meetings and must communicate well with their management. Because many supermarket workers deal directly with the customers, their managers depends on them to relay information about customers needs, wants, and dissatisfactions.

Many supermarket workers work part time. For workers with school, family, or other employment, hours are scheduled at the time workers are available, such as evenings and weekends. Since many grocery stores are open 24-hours a day, employees may work during the day or evening hours. Weekend hours are also important, and most grocery stores are open on holidays as well.

All of the different jobs of a supermarket worker have one very important thing in common—they are customer-driven. Grocery sales nationwide continue to climb, and customer service is highly important in the grocery business as in all retail businesses.

With that in mind, the primary responsibility of all supermarket workers is to serve the customer. Many secondary duties such as keeping work areas clean, collecting carts from the parking lot, and checking produce for freshness are also driven by this main priority.

■ Requirements

High School

Many workers in the supermarket industry are recent high school graduates or present high school students. There is a large turnover in the field as many workers move on to other career fields. A high school diploma is not required, but enrollment in a high school program is encouraged if you do not have your degree. In high school, you should take English, mathematics, business, and computer science classes to learn the basic skills to do most supermarket jobs.

SUPERMARKET WORKERS	
SCHOOL SUBJECTS	Business English Mathematics
PERSONAL SKILLS	Communication/ideas Following instructions
WORK ENVIRONMENT	Primarily indoors Primarily one location
MINIMUM EDUCATION LEVEL	High school diploma (or enrolled in a high school program)
SALARY RANGE	$5.15 per hour to $8.40 per hour to $11.00 per hour
CERTIFICATION OR LICENSING	Required for certain positions
OUTLOOK	About as fast as the average
DOT	299
GOE	05.09.01

Postsecondary Training

Postsecondary training is not required in the supermarket industry but may be encouraged for specific areas such as the bakery, or for management positions. Stores offer on-the-job training and value employees who are able to learn quickly while they work.

Certification or Licensing

To protect the public's health, bakers, deli workers, and butchers are required by law in most states to possess a health certificate and to be examined periodically. These examinations, usually given by the state board of health, make certain that the individual is free from communicable diseases and skin infections.

Other Requirements

The most important requirement for a supermarket worker is the ability to work with people. "With every job I've done here, I've had to help people out," says Nick Williams, who works as a stock boy, bag boy, and cashier at Foods Plus supermarket in Columbus, Indiana. Because workers are required to work with both the public and their own management, communication and customer service skills are important. Following directions as well as accuracy and honesty are also important qualities that supermarket workers should have to be successful.

■ Exploring

The best way to find out about what it's like to be a supermarket worker is to become one. Openings for high school students are usually available, and it's a great way to find out about the industry.

Take a class in a supermarket specialty you find interesting. If you think the bakery looks like fun, take a cake-decorating class and find out.

Help out with inventory. Many grocery and retail stores offer limited short-term employment (a day or two a week) for people who can help with inventory during key times of the year. This is a good opportunity to get your foot in the store without making a greater commitment.

■ Employers

There are 126,000 grocery stores in the United States, according to the Food Marketing Institute. This number has dropped from 10 years ago when the total number was 150,000. These grocery stores are located across the nation, in towns and cities. Some are part of a large chain such as Kroger Company. Kroger is the nation's largest grocer with over 2,100 stores in 31 states. Albertson's and Safeway round out the top 3 chains. Other stores are a part of smaller chains or are independently owned.

Workers will have more employment opportunities in cities and large towns where several stores are located. In smaller towns, only one or two stores may serve the area.

■ Starting Out

Nick got his first job in the supermarket in the same way as many others. He applied at the customer service office at the front of the store. Nick was looking for a part-time job with flexible hours and applied at several retail stores in his area.

Besides walk-in applications, groceries use newspaper ads and job drives to attract new employees. Because some of the jobs a supermarket worker may do require little education and pay a modest hourly rate, there are often openings as workers move on to other positions or career fields.

If you apply in person, you should be ready to fill out application materials at the office. Neat dress and good manners are important when applying in person.

Many of today's grocery managers started out as high school clerks or cashiers. It is possible to turn a part-time job into a full-time career. "There are a lot of opportunities to learn different jobs, if you want to," says Nick.

■ Advancement

The opportunities to advance within a supermarket are good if you are dedicated and hard-working. It is possible, with a lot of hard work and dedication, to advance to a more specialized and better-paying position.

Supermarkets rely heavily on experienced workers, so while a college education might be helpful, it is certainly not required to advance in the field. Relevant experience and hard work are just as beneficial to advancement.

Steve Edens, an associate manager at a Kroger Company store, started out in the stock room and says that the supermarket industry is one of the few fields where you can start as a bagger and end up being the company president.

■ Earnings

According to the U.S. Bureau of Labor Statistics, the average nonsupervisory food store employee makes $8.40 per hour. Some employees may make less per hour down to the current minimum wage of $5.15 per hour, while more specialized workers in departments may earn more. In areas such as the bakery, workers may make more per hour while stock clerks make less.

Many supermarket workers are part-time employees and do not receive fringe benefits; full-time employees often receive medical benefits and vacation time. Supermarket workers often are eligible for discounts at the stores in which they work, depending on their company policy. The United Food & Commercial Workers International Union represents many supermarket workers concerning pay, benefits, and working condition issues.

■ Work Environment

Grocery stores are open 24-hours a day, so workers are required for a variety of shifts. Many supermarket workers are part-time employees and work a varied schedule that changes each week. Depending on the time of day they work, the store may be bustling or quiet. Most of the work is indoors although some outdoor work may be required to delivery groceries, collect carts, and maintain outside displays. Schedules are usually prepared weekly and most will include weekend work.

Supermarket workers work in shifts and must work with the managers and other workers in a supervisory environment. These managers may be within their department or within the entire store. They must follow directions and report to those managers when required.

■ Outlook

Though the number of grocery stores has declined in recent years, the employment outlook for supermarket workers is good. The field has a large turnover with workers leaving to pursue other careers. Many part-time employees are seasonal and must be replaced often.

As supermarkets add more conveniences for customers, workers will be needed to staff those areas. For example, adding restaurants to supermarkets creates a need for a whole new set of food service workers.

Also, although there are fewer grocery stores, consumers are spending more on groceries. According to a study by the Progressive Grocer, as reported by the Food Marketing Institute, consumers spent $436.3 billion on groceries in 1997. Ten years earlier, that figure was $313 billion.

One reason for the decline in the actual number of grocery stores is the trend toward supermarket chains. Many small chains and local groceries have been purchased by larger chains, and others have gone out of business in the face of the competition.

■ For More Information

For information about the food industry, contact:

Food Marketing Institute
800 Connecticut Avenue, NW
Washington, DC 20006-2701
Tel: 202-452-8444
Web: http://www.fmi.org

For information about the retail industry, contact:

National Retail Federation
325 7th Street, NW, Suite 1000
Washington, DC 20004
Tel: 202-783-7971
Web: http://www.nrf.com

For information about working in retail, contact:

International Mass Retail Association
1700 North Moore Street, Suite 2250
Arlington, VA 22209
Tel: 703-841-2300
Web: http://www.imra.org/

For information about union membership in the food industry, contact:

United Food & Commercial Workers International Union AFL-CIO/CLC
1775 K Street, NW
Washington, DC 20006
Tel: 202-223-3111
Web: http://www.ufcw.org

■ Related Articles

Business
Grocery Stores
Bakery Products Workers
Cashiers
Cooks, Chefs, and Bakers
Counter and Retail Clerks
Food Service Workers
Meatcutters
Pharmacists
Pharmacy Technicians
Retail Business Owners
Retail Sales Workers
Security Consultants and Technicians
Stock Clerks
Supermarket Managers

Surgeons

■ Overview

Surgeons are physicians who make diagnoses and provide preoperative, operative, and postoperative care in surgery affecting almost any part of the body. These doctors also work with trauma victims and the critically ill.

■ History

Surgery is perhaps the oldest of all medical specialties. Evidence from Egypt, Greece, China, and India suggests that humans have always performed and worked on developing surgical procedures.

The field of surgery advanced during the 18th century when knowledge of anatomy increased through developments in pathology. At this time, common procedures included amputations as well as tumor and bladder stone removal. Surgery patients were usually tied down or sedated with alcoholic beverages or opium during the procedures.

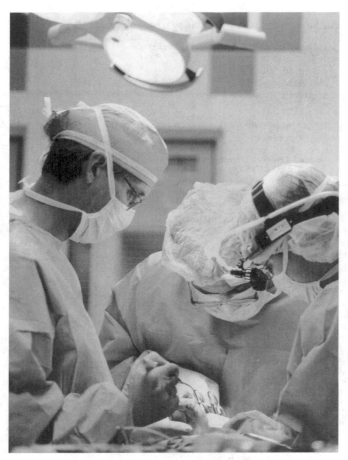

Three surgeons perform an operation.

The late 19th century brought major developments that advanced surgical procedures. Anesthesia was introduced in 1846. Also, Louis Pasteur's understanding of bacteria later resulted in the development of antiseptic by Joseph Lister in 1867. The introduction of anesthesia coupled with the use of antiseptic methods resulted in the new phase of modern surgery.

Surgical advances during the 20th century include the separation of surgical specialties, the development of surgical tools and X rays, as well as continued technological advances that create alternatives to traditional procedures, such as laproscopic surgery with lasers.

■ The Job

The work of a surgeon will vary according to the work environment. For example, a general surgeon who specializes in trauma care would most likely work in a large, urban hospital where he or she would spend a great deal of time in the operating room performing emergency surgical procedures at a moment's notice. On the other hand, a general surgeon who specializes in hernia repair would probably have a more predictable work schedule and would

spend most of the time in an ambulatory (also called outpatient) surgery center.

The surgeon is responsible for the diagnosis of the patient, for performing operations, and for providing patients with postoperative surgical care and treatment. In emergency room situations, the patient typically comes in complaining of some type of severe pain. If the patient needs surgery, the on-duty general surgeon will schedule the surgery. Depending on the urgency of the case, surgery may be scheduled for the following day or the patient will be operated on immediately.

A surgeon sees such cases as gunshot, stabbing, and accident victims. Other cases that often involve emergency surgery include appendectomies (removal of the spleen) and removal of kidney stones. When certain problems, such as a kidney stone or inflamed appendix, are diagnosed at an early stage, the surgeon can perform non-emergency surgery.

There are several specialties of surgery and four areas of subspecialization of general surgery. For these areas, the surgeon can receive further education and training leading to certification. A few of these specializations are neurosurgery (care for disorders of the nervous system), plastic and reconstructive surgery (care for defects of the skin and underlying musculoskeleton), orthopaedic surgery (care for musculoskeletal disorders that are present at birth or develop later), and thoracic surgery (care for diseases and conditions of the chest). The subspecializations for general surgery are: general vascular surgery, pediatric surgery, hand surgery, and surgical critical care.

■ Requirements

Postsecondary Training

To become a surgeon you must first earn an M.D. degree and become licensed to practice medicine (See *Physicians*). Physicians wishing to pursue general surgery must complete a five-year residency in surgery according to the requirements set down by the Accreditation Council for Graduate Medical Education (ACGME) and the Royal College of Physicians and Surgeons of Canada.

Throughout the surgery residency, residents are supervised at all levels of training by assisting on and then performing basic operations, such as the removal of an appendix. As the residency years continue, residents gain responsibility through teaching and supervisory duties. Eventually the residents are allowed to perform complex operations independently.

Subspecialties require from one to three years of additional training.

Certification and Licensing

Board certification in surgery is administered by the American Board of Surgery, Inc. While certification is a voluntary procedure, it is highly recommended. Most hospitals will not grant privileges to a surgeon without board certification. HMOs and other insurance groups will not make referrals or payments to a surgeon without board certification. Also, insurance companies are not likely to insure a surgeon for malpractice if he or she is not board certified.

To be eligible to apply for certification in surgery, a candidate must have successfully completed medical school and the requisite residency in surgery. Once a candidate's application has been approved, the candidate may take the written examination. After passing the written exam, the candidate may then take the oral exam.

Certification in surgery is valid for 10 years. To obtain recertification, surgeons must apply to the American Board of Surgery, Inc. with documentation of their continuing medical education activities and of the operations and procedures they have performed since being certified and submit to a review by their peers. They must also pass a written exam.

Other Requirements

To be a successful surgeon, you should be able to think quickly and act decisively in stressful situations, enjoy helping and working with people, have strong organizational skills, be able to give clear instructions, have good hand-eye coordination, and be able to listen and communicate well.

■ Earnings

According to a 1998 survey conducted by the American Medical Association, the average net pay for surgeons is about $275,200, but salaries may begin at roughly $137,700. Incomes may vary from specialty to specialty. Other factors influencing individual incomes include the type and size of practice, the hours worked per week, the geographic location, and the reputation a surgeon has among both patients and fellow professionals.

■ Outlook

The wide-ranging skills and knowledge of the surgeon will always be in demand, whether or not the surgeon has a subspecialty. According to the *Occupational Outlook Handbook,* physician jobs are expected to grow faster than the average through the year 2006. The job outlook for surgeons is expected to match this trend, and positions are projected to grow at a faster than average rate.

■ For More Information

Following are organizations that provide information on the position of surgeon. In particular, the Association of Women Surgeons publishes a guide for women in the surgical specialties, A Manual for Surgical Interns and Residents.

American Board of Surgery, Inc.
1617 John F. Kennedy Boulevard, Suite 860
Philadelphia, PA 19103
Tel: 215-568-4000
Web: http://www.absurgery.org

Association of Women Surgeons
414 Plaza Drive, Suite 209
Westmont, IL 60559
Tel: 630-655-0392

Society of Thoracic Surgeons
401 North Michigan Avenue
Chicago, IL 60611
Tel: 312-644-6610
Web: http://www.sba.com

American Academy of Orthopaedic Surgeons
6300 North River Road
Rosemont, IL 60018-4262
Tel: 847-823-7186
Web: http://www.aaos.org

American Board of Plastic Surgery
1635 Market Street, Suite 400
Philadelphia, PA 19103-2204
Tel: 215-587-9322
Web: http://www.abplsurg.org

American Association of Neurological Surgeons
22 South Washington Street
Park Ridge, IL 60068
Tel: 847-692-9500
Web: http://www.neurosurgery.org

■ Related Articles

Alternative Health Care

Health Care

Allergists/Immunologists

Anesthesiologists

Cardiologists

Dermatologists

Ear, Nose, and Throat Specialists

Epidemiologists

Gastroenterologists

General Practitioners

Geriatricians

Holistic Physicians

Neurologists

Obstetricians/Gynecologists

Oncologists

Ophthalmologists

Osteopaths

Pathologists

Pediatricians

Physicians

Podiatrists

Surgeons' Assistants

■ See Physician Assistants

Surgical Technologists

■ Overview

Surgical technologists, also called *surgical technicians* or *operating room technicians,* are members of the surgical team who work in the operating room with *surgeons, nurses, anesthesiologists,* and other personnel before, during, and after surgery. They perform functions that ensure a safe and sterile environment. To prepare a patient for surgery, they may wash, shave, and disinfect the area where the incision will be made. They arrange the equipment, instruments, and supplies in the operating room according to the preference of the surgeons and nurses. During the operation, they adjust lights and other equipment as needed. They count sponges, needles, and instruments used during the operation, hand instruments and supplies to the surgeon, and hold retractors and cut sutures as directed. They maintain specified supplies of fluids such as saline, plasma, blood, and glucose and may assist in administering these fluids. Following the operation, they may clean and restock the operating room and wash and sterilize the used equipment using germicides, autoclaves, and sterilizers, although in most larger hospitals these tasks are done by other central service personnel.

SURGICAL TECHNOLOGISTS	
SCHOOL SUBJECTS	Biology Health
PERSONAL SKILLS	Helping/teaching Technical/scientific
WORK ENVIRONMENT	Primarily indoors Primarily one location
MINIMUM EDUCATION LEVEL	Some postsecondary training
SALARY RANGE	$19,760 to $22,200 to $29,100
CERTIFICATION OR LICENSING	Recommended
OUTLOOK	Much faster than the average
DOT	079
GOE	10.03.02
NOC	3219
O*NET	32925

■ History

While the origins of surgery go back to prehistoric times, two scientific developments made modern surgery possible. The first was the discovery of anesthesia in the mid-19th century. Because the anesthesia eliminated the patient's pain, surgeons were able to take their time during operations, enabling them to try more complex procedures.

The second important discovery was that of the causes of infection. Until Louis Pasteur's discovery of germs and Joseph Lister's development of aseptic surgery in the 19th century, so many people died of infection after operations that the value of surgery was extremely limited.

During World War II, the profession of surgical technology grew when there was a critical need for assistance in performing surgical procedures and a shortage of qualified personnel. Shortly after, formal educational programs were started to teach these medical professionals.

Throughout the 20th century, the nature of most surgical procedures, with all of their sophisticated techniques for monitoring and safeguarding the patient's condition, has become so complex that more and more people are required to assist the surgeon or surgeons. While many of the tasks that are performed during the operation require highly trained professionals with many years of education, there are also simpler, more standardized tasks that require people with less complex training and skills. Over the years, such tasks have been taken care of by people referred to as orderlies, scrub nurses, and surgical orderlies.

Today, such people are referred to as surgical technologists, operating room technicians, or surgical technicians. For the most part, these medical professionals have received specialized training in a community college, vocational or technical school, or a hospital-sponsored program. They are eligible to earn certificates of competence, and, in general, enjoy a higher degree of professional status and recognition than did their predecessors.

■ The Job

Surgical technologists are health professionals who work in the surgical suite with surgeons, anesthesiologists, registered nurses, and other surgical personnel delivering surgical patient care.

In general, the work responsibilities of surgical technologists may be divided into three phases: preoperative (before surgery), intraoperative (during surgery), and postoperative (after surgery). Surgical technologists may work as the *scrub person, circulator,* or *surgical first assistant.*

In the preoperative phase, surgical technologists prepare the operating room by selecting and opening sterile supplies such as drapes, sutures, sponges, electrosurgical devices, suction tubing, and surgical instruments. They assemble, adjust, and check nonsterile equipment to ensure that it is in proper working order. Surgical technologists also operate sterilizers, lights, suction machines, electrosurgical units, and diagnostic equipment.

When patients arrive in the surgical suite, surgical technologists may assist in preparing them for surgery by providing physical and emotional support, checking charts, and observing vital signs. They properly position the patient on the operating table, assist in connecting and applying surgical equipment and monitoring devices, and prepare the incision site by cleansing the skin with an antiseptic solution.

During surgery, surgical technologists have primary responsibility for maintaining the sterile field. They constantly watch that all members of the team adhere to aseptic technique so the patient does not develop a postoperative infection. As the scrub person, they most often function as the sterile member of the surgical team who passes instruments, sutures, and sponges during surgery. After "scrubbing," which involves the thorough cleansing of the hands and forearms, they put on a sterile gown and gloves and prepare the sterile instruments and supplies that will be needed. After other members of the sterile team have scrubbed, they assist them with gowning and gloving and applying sterile drapes around the operative site.

Surgical technologists must anticipate the needs of surgeons during the procedure, passing instruments and providing sterile items in an efficient manner. Checking, mixing, and dispensing appropriate fluids and drugs in the sterile field are other common tasks. They share with the circulator the responsibility for accounting for sponges, needles, and instruments before, during, and after surgery. They may hold retractors or instruments, sponge or suction the operative site, or cut suture material as directed by the surgeon. They connect drains and tubing and receive and prepare specimens for subsequent pathologic analysis.

Surgical technologists most often function as the scrub person, but may function in the nonsterile role of circulator. The circulator does not wear a sterile gown and gloves, but is available to assist the surgical team. As a circulator, the surgical technologist obtains additional supplies or equipment, assists the anesthesiologist, keeps a written account of the surgical procedure, and assists the scrub person.

Surgical first assistants, those technologists with additional education or training, provide aid in retracting tissue, controlling bleeding, and other technical functions that help surgeons during the procedure.

After surgery, surgical technologists are responsible for preparing and applying dressings, including plaster or synthetic casting materials, and for preparing the operating room for the next patient. They may provide staffing in postoperative recovery rooms where patients' responses are carefully monitored in the critical phases following general anesthesia.

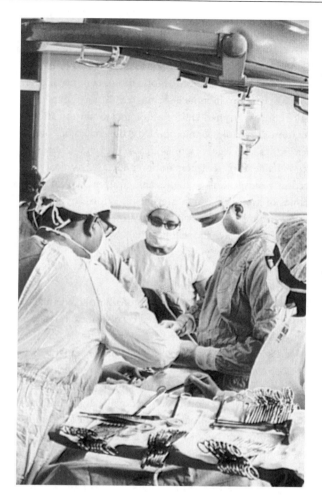

Surgical technologists are a vital part of the operating team.

Some of these responsibilities vary, depending on the size of the hospital and department in which the surgical technologist works; they also vary based on geographic location and health care needs of the local community.

■ Requirements

High School

During your high school years, you should take courses that develop your basic skills in mathematics, science, and English. You also should take all available courses in health and biology.

Postsecondary Training

Surgical technology education is available through postsecondary programs offered by community and junior colleges, vocational and technical schools, the military, universities, and structured hospital programs in surgical technology. A high school diploma is required for entry into any of these programs.

More than 150 of these programs are accredited by the Commission on Accreditation of Allied Health Education Programs (CAAHEP). The accredited programs vary from nine to 12 months for a diploma or certificate, to two years for an associate's degree. You can expect to take courses in medical terminology, communications, anatomy, physiology, microbiology, pharmacology, medical ethics, and legal responsibilities. You gain a thorough knowledge of patient preparation and care, surgical procedures, surgical instruments and equipment, and principles of asepsis (how to prevent infection). In addition to classroom learning, you receive intensive supervised clinical experience in local hospitals, which is an important component of your education.

Certification or Licensing

Surgical technologists may earn a professional credential by passing a nationally administered certifying examination. Those who become certified are granted the designation of certified surgical technologist (CST). Increasing numbers of hospitals are requiring certification as a condition of employment. To take the examination, an individual must be currently or previously certified or be a graduate of a formal educational program or its equivalent (starting in 2000, only graduates of CAAHEP-accredited programs will be eligible to take the test). The Liaison Council on Certification for the Surgical Technologist (LCC-ST), an independent affiliate of the Association of Surgical Technologists, is the certifying agency for the profession. Those who become certified demonstrate a commitment to maximum performance and quality patient care. To renew the six-year certificate, the CST must earn continuing education credits or retake the certifying examination. The LCC-ST also offers an advanced credential for surgical first assistants; this exam awards the designation of CST certified first assistant (CST/CFA).

Other Requirements

Surgical technologists must possess an educational background in the medical sciences, a strong sense of responsibility, a concern for order, and an ability to integrate a number of tasks at the same time. You need good manual dexterity to handle awkward surgical instruments with speed and agility. In addition, you need physical stamina to stand through long surgical procedures.

■ Exploring

It is difficult to gain any direct experience on a part-time basis in surgical technology. The first opportunities for direct experience generally come in the clinical and laboratory phases of your educational programs. However, interested students can explore some aspects of this career in several ways. You or your teachers can arrange a visit to a hospital, clinic, or other surgical setting in order to learn about the work. You also can visit a school with a CAAHEP-accredited program. During such a visit, you can discuss career plans with the admissions counselor. In addition, volunteering at a local hospital or nursing home can give you insight into the health care environment and help you evaluate your aptitude to work in such a setting.

■ Employers

Most surgical technologists are employed in hospital operating rooms, clinics, and surgicenters. They also work in delivery rooms, cast rooms, emergency departments, ambulatory care areas, and central supply departments. Surgical technologists may also be employed directly by surgeons as private scrubs or as surgical first assistants.

■ Starting Out

Graduates of programs are often offered jobs in the same hospital in which they received their clinical training. Programs usually cooperate closely with hospitals in the area, which are usually eager to employ technologists educated in local programs. Available positions are also advertised in newspaper want ads.

■ Advancement

With increased experience, surgical technologists can serve in management roles in surgical services departments and may work as central service managers, surgery schedulers, and materials managers. The role of surgical first assistant on the surgical team requires additional training and experience and is considered an advanced role.

Surgical technologists function well in a number of diverse areas. Their multicompetency is demonstrated by their employment in organ and tissue procurement/preservation, cardiac catheterization laboratories, medical sales and research, and medical-legal auditing for insurance companies. A number are instructors and directors of surgical technology programs.

■ Earnings

Salaries vary greatly in different institutions and localities. The average salary for surgical technologists is $22,200, but ranges from $19,760 to $29,100 a year (excluding overtime). Some technologists with experience earn much more. Most surgical technologists are required to be periodically on call—available to work on short notice in cases of emergency—and can earn overtime from such work. Graduates of educational programs usually receive salaries higher than technologists without formal education. In general, technologists working on the East and West coasts earn more than surgical technologists in other parts of the country. Surgical first assistants and private scrubs employed directly by surgeons tend to earn more than surgical technologists employed by hospitals.

■ Work Environment

Surgical technologists naturally spend most of their time in the operating room. Operating rooms are cool, well lighted, orderly, and extremely clean. Technologists are often required to be on their feet for long intervals during which their attention must be closely focused on the operation.

Members of the surgical team, including surgical technologists, wear sterile gowns, gloves, caps, masks, and eye protection. This surgical attire is meant not only to protect the patient from infection but also to protect the surgical team from any infection or bloodborne diseases that the patient may have. Surgery is usually performed during the day; however, hospitals, clinics, and other facilities require 24-hour-a-day coverage. Most surgical technologists work regular 40-hour weeks, although many are required to be periodically on call.

Surgical technologists must be able to work under great pressure in stressful situations. The need for surgery is often a matter of life and death, and one can never assume that procedures will go as planned. If operations do not go well, nerves may fray and tempers flare. Technologists must understand that this is the result of stressful conditions and should not take this anger personally.

In addition, surgical technologists should have a strong desire to help others. Surgery is performed on people, not machines. Patients literally entrust their lives to the surgical team, and they rely on them to treat them in a dignified and professional manner. Individuals with these characteristics find surgical technology a rewarding career in which they can make an important contribution to the health and well-being of their community.

■ Outlook

Job opportunities for competent surgical technologists far exceed the supply. According to the *Occupational Outlook Handbook,* the field of surgical technology is projected to experience rapid job growth through 2006. Population growth, longevity, and improvement in medical and surgical procedures have all contributed to a growing demand for surgical services and hence for surgical technologists. As long as the rate at which people undergo surgery continues to increase, there will continue to be a need for this profession. Also, as surgical methods become increasingly complex, more surgical technologists will likely be needed.

Other factors may weigh against the general trend. The need to contain health care costs has caused many surgical procedures to be done on an ambulatory or outpatient basis. If this trend continues, the demand for surgical technologists will remain strong. But if a significant amount of surgery is done in nonhospital settings, such as in clinics and surgeons' offices, the total demand for surgical technologists could drop, because fewer technologists are used in such settings.

Staffing patterns are also changing in response to the need to control costs. Hospitals are changing their staffing ratios of registered nurses to other health care workers and are employing more allied health professionals, such as surgical technologists, who can provide cost-effective care. On the other hand, hospitals are also increasing their use of multiskilled workers who can handle a wide variety of tasks in different areas of the hospital. A number of health care workers, including surgical technologists, are being asked by their employers to participate in training programs to become multiskilled.

■ For More Information

For information on education programs and certification, contact:

Association of Surgical Technologists (AST)
7108-C South Alton Way, Suite 100
Englewood, CO 80112-2106
Tel: 303-694-9130
Web: http://www.ast.org

■ Related Articles

Health Care
Biomedical Equipment Technicians
Cardiovascular Technologists
Cytotechnologists
Dental Assistants
Diagnostic Medical Sonographers
Dialysis Technicians
Electroneurodiagnostic Technologists
Emergency Medical Technicians
Histologic Technicians
Medical Assistants
Medical Laboratory Technicians
Medical Technologists
Nuclear Medicine Technologists
Ophthalmic Laboratory Technicians
Optics Technicians
Orthotic and Prosthetic Technicians
Perfusionists
Phlebotomy Technicians
Radiologic Technologists
Respiratory Therapists and Technicians

Surveying and Mapping Technicians

■ Overview

Surveying and mapping technicians help determine, describe, and record geographic areas or features. They are usually the leading helper to the professional surveyor, civil engineer, and mapmaker. In their work they use modern surveying and mapping instruments and are prepared to participate in photogrammetric surveying and mapping operations. Surveying and mapping technicians also have a basic knowledge of the current practices and legal implications of surveys to establish and record property size, shape, topography, and boundaries. They often supervise assistants during routine surveying conducted within bounds established by a professional surveyor.

■ History

From ancient times, people have needed to define their property boundaries. Marking established areas of individual or group ownership was a basis for the develop-

SURVEYING AND MAPPING TECHNICIANS	
SCHOOL SUBJECTS	Geography Mathematics
PERSONAL SKILLS	Following instructions Technical/scientific
WORK ENVIRONMENT	Primarily outdoors Primarily multiple locations
MINIMUM EDUCATION LEVEL	High school diploma
SALARY RANGE	$17,400 to $28,000 to $44,000
CERTIFICATION OR LICENSING	Voluntary
OUTLOOK	Little change or more slowly than the average
DOT	018
GOE	05.01.06
NOC	2254
O*NET	22521A

ment of early civilizations. Landholding became important in ancient Egypt, and with the development of hieroglyphics people were able to keep a record of their holdings. Eventually, nations found it necessary not only to mark property boundaries but also to lay out and record principal routes of commerce and transportation. For example, records of the Babylonians tell of their canals and irrigation ditches. The Romans surveyed and mapped their empire's principal roads.

The surveying process using instruments traditionally required at least two people. A scientist who had mastered the technology of the times was the leader, or professional surveyor. Helpers made measurements with chains, tapes, and wheel rotations, where each rotation accounted for a known length of distance. The helpers held rods with measured marks for location and drove stakes or placed other markers to define important points. As the measuring instruments became more complex, the speed, scope, and accuracy of the surveying process increased. As a result, the surveyor's assistants needed to know more about the equipment and the process to be able to work on the surveying team. For most modern surveying operations of any size, a surveying technician is the leading helper to the professional surveyor. Therefore, the technician's tasks are usually closely associated with those of the professional surveyor.

As the United States expanded, surveyors and their technical helpers were among the first and most needed workers: they established new land ownership by surveying and filing claims. Since then, precise and accurate geographical measurements have always been needed, whether to determine the location of a highway; the site of a building; the right-of-way for drainage ditches, telephone, or power lines; or for the charting of unexplored land, bodies of water, or underground mines. Through the years, the science of measurement has improved our ability to establish exact locations and determine distances. In these processes, most of the actual measuring work is done by surveying technicians and other helpers under the direction of professional surveyors.

Developments in surveying and mapping technology have made great changes in the planning and construction of highway systems, and in the design and building of stationary structures of all kinds. In surveying for roadway route selection and design, technicians increasingly use photogrammetry, which uses automatic plotting machines to scribe routes from aerial photographs of rural or urban areas. Route data obtained by photogrammetry may then be processed through computers to calculate land acquisition, grading, and construction costs. Photogrammetry is faster and far more accurate than former methods. New electronic distance-measuring devices have brought surveying to a higher level of technology. Technicians can measure distance more quickly, accurately, and economically than possible with tapes or rod and chain. This requires better educated technicians to serve as chief assistants in complex surveying operations.

The new technological advances and the use of computers in data processing have made surveying and mapping technical careers more complex and challenging than just a few decades ago. These changes have further increased surveying and mapping's accuracy, and extended its use to include making detailed maps of ocean floors and the moon. Surveying and mapping technicians must be able to use specialized techniques as they assist surveyors or scientists in charge of surveys. For example, every missile fired from the Kennedy Space Center is tracked electronically to determine if it is on course. Mapmakers have recently used photogrammetry to map the moon. The technological complexity of such undertakings allows professional surveyors to delegate more tasks to technicians than ever.

■ The Job

As essential assistants to civil engineers, surveyors, and mapmakers, surveying and mapping technicians are usually the first to be involved in any job that requires precise plotting. This includes highways, airports, housing developments, mines, dams, bridges, and buildings of all kinds.

The surveying and mapping technician is a key worker in field parties or major surveying projects and is often assigned the position of *chief instrument worker* under the surveyor's supervision. In this capacity, technicians use a variety of surveying instruments, including the theodolite, transit, level, and different types of electronic equipment, to measure distance or locate a position. As a transit worker, the technician uses many of these instruments—assembling, adjusting, sighting, and reading them. A rod worker, using a level rod or range pole, helps make elevation and distance measurements. A chain worker measures shorter distances and uses the surveyor's chain or a metal tape. In the course of a survey, it is important to accurately record all readings and keep orderly field notes so that the survey can be checked for accuracy.

Surveying and mapping technicians may specialize if they join a surveying firm that focuses on one or more particular types of surveying. In a firm that specializes in land surveying, technicians are highly skilled in technical measuring and tasks related to establishing township, property, and other tract-of-land boundary lines. They help the professional surveyor with maps, notes, or actual land title deeds. They help survey the land, check the accuracy of existing records, and prepare legal documents such as deeds and leases.

Similarly, technicians who work for highway, pipeline, railway, or power line surveying firms help to establish points, grades, lines, and other points of reference for construction projects. This survey information provides the exact locations for engineering design and construction work.

Technicians who work for geodetic surveyors help take measurements of large masses of land, sea, or space. These measurements must take into account the curvature of Earth and its geophysical characteristics. This information sets major points of reference for smaller land surveys, determining national boundaries, and preparing maps.

Technicians also specialize in measurements for hydrographic surveyors. Hydrographic surveyors make surveys of harbors, rivers, and other bodies of water. These surveys are needed to design navigation systems; plan and build breakwaters, levees, dams, locks, piers, and bridges; prepare nautical maps and charts; and establish property boundaries. Technicians are key workers in making these surveys; they often supervise other workers as they make measurements and record data.

In mining companies, the technician is usually a member of the engineering, scientific, or management team. Working from the survey or engineering office, technicians take part in regular mine surveying. They set up the instructions and limits of the work team. In the office, technicians make survey calculations, develop maps, and calculate the tonnage of ore and broken rock.

In recent years, costly new surveying instruments have changed the way *mining survey technicians* do their jobs. These technicians work on the geological staffs of either mining companies or exploration companies. At operating mines, technicians may map underground geology, take samples, locate diamond drill holes, log drill cores, and map geological data derived from boreholes. They may map data on mine plans and diagrams, and help the geologist determine ore reserves.

In the search for new mines, mining survey technicians operate delicate instruments to obtain data on variations in Earth's magnetic field, its conductivity, or gravity. They use the data to map the boundaries of potential areas for further exploration.

Surveying and mapping technicians may find topographical surveys to be interesting and challenging work. These determine the contours of the land, and indicate such features as mountains, lakes, rivers, forests, roads, farms, buildings, and other distinguishable landmarks. In topographical surveying, technicians often help take aerial or land photographs with photogrammetric equipment installed in an airplane or ground station that permits pictures of large areas to be made. The method is widely used to measure farmland planted with certain crops and to verify crop average allotments under government production planning quotas.

Entry-level technicians work in various positions, such as these:

Survey helpers or drafters operate surveying instruments to gather numerical data. They calculate tonnage broken and incentive pay, map mine development, and provide precise directions and locations to the workforce. Under direction, they conduct studies on operations and equipment to improve methods and reduce costs.

Assistant field or exploration geologists operate a variety of geophysical instruments on a grid pattern to obtain data on variations in Earth's magnetism, conductivity, and gravity. They map the data and analyze stream waters, soils, and rocks from known locations to search for ore occurrences. Such technicians often work in remote areas.

Highway technicians, under the direction of a surveyor, make surveys and estimate costs. They also help plan, lay out, and supervise the construction and maintenance of highways.

Photogrammetric technicians use aerial photographs to prepare maps, mosaics, plans, and profiles.

By far the largest number of survey technicians are employed in construction work. Technicians are needed from start to finish on any construction job. They keep the structure's progress within engineering specifications for size, height, depth, level, and geometric form. Surveying technicians locate the critical construction points on the job site as specified on design plans within the bounds of the property. They locate corners of buildings, foundation detail points, center points for columns, walls, and other features, height of floor or ceiling levels, and other points which require precise measurements and location.

■ Requirements

High School

Future surveying and mapping technicians should follow the school's college preparatory program. Mathematics courses should include at least two years of algebra, and plane and solid geometry and trigonometry, as well as mechanical drawing. Physics, including laboratory experience, as well as chemistry and biology are also valuable. High school students should take as many computer courses as possible. Reading, writing, and comprehension skills are vital in surveying and mapping, so four years of high school English and language skills courses are highly recommended.

Postsecondary Training

Graduates of accredited postsecondary training programs who have a strong background in surveying, photogrammetry, and mapping are in the best position to enter the field

as beginning surveying and mapping technicians. Opportunities for this kind of training are available at junior colleges, technical institutes, and specialized schools. These are demanding technical programs, usually two academic years long and sometimes with field study in the summer.

Such a program can form a base for employment; later, with additional part-time study, the technician can specialize in geodesy, topography, hydrography, or photogrammetry. Many graduates of two-year programs later pursue a bachelor's degree in surveying, engineering, or geomatics.

Certification or Licensing

Unlike professional land surveyors, there are no special requirements for registration or licensing for surveying and mapping technicians. However, technicians who seek government employment must pass a civil service examination.

To advance their professional standing and become more attractive to a wider variety of employers, surveying and mapping technicians should seek to become certified engineering technicians. This certification is similar to the licensing of engineers, but the requirements are based on and consistent with the tasks, skills, and responsibilities that are expected of these technicians.

Other Requirements

Surveying and mapping technicians must be patient, orderly, systematic, accurate, and objective in their work. They must be able to work in a subordinate role as an assistant to the surveyor or cartographer. They must be willing to work cooperatively and have the ability to think and plan ahead. One of the most important qualities is a willingness to work long hours for extended periods, as is sometimes required in the work of all technicians.

■ Exploring

One of the best opportunities for experience is a summer job with a construction firm or a company involved in survey work. Even if the job does not involve direct contact with survey crews, it will provide an opportunity to observe them and discover more about their activities.

■ Employers

Surveying and mapping technicians usually find work with construction companies and surveying firms. The government also employs a number of technicians as well.

■ Starting Out

Graduates of a technical institute or a four-year college will find their school's placement service helpful in arranging examinations or interviews. Regular employers of surveying technicians often send recruiters to schools before graduation and arrange to employ promising graduates. In many cities, there are employment agencies that specialize in placing technical workers in positions in surveying, mapping, construction, mining, and related fields.

Some community or technical colleges have work-study programs that provide cooperative part-time or summer work for pay. Employers involved with these programs often hire students full-time after graduation.

■ Advancement

Possibilities for advancement are linked to the level of formal education and experience. As they gain experience and technical knowledge, technicians can advance to positions of greater responsibility and eventually to surveyor or chief of a surveying party.

Steps are being taken by some of the professional engineering and surveying associations to increase the requirements needed to become a registered or licensed land surveyor. One requirement being considered is a bachelor's degree in engineering. Accordingly, advancement will be more difficult for the technicians who graduated from formal two-year technical programs in surveying technology. Graduates of two- and three-year programs can usually transfer at least a part of their college-level credits to degree-granting engineering programs if they decide they want to obtain a professional degree and become a registered professional surveyor.

The surveying technician must continue studying to keep up with the technological developments in surveying, measuring, and mapping. Computers, lasers, and microcomputers will continue to change the job requirements. Studying to keep up with changes, combined with experience gained on the job, increases the technicians' value to their employers.

■ Earnings

Most surveying and mapping technicians earn between $17,400 and $40,000 a year, and the average is around $28,000. The average is the same for technicians in the private sector and those employed by the government. In private industry, some senior technicians may earn $44,000 per year or more.

■ Work Environment

Surveying and mapping technicians usually work about 40 hours a week except when overtime is necessary. The peak work period for many kinds of surveying work is during the summer months when weather conditions are most favorable. However, it is not uncommon for surveying crews to be exposed to all types of weather conditions. Surveying technicians on construction jobs who, with their helpers, take daily point-to-point and step-by-step measurements on construction jobs must work in all kinds of weather.

Some survey projects involve certain hazards depending upon the region and the climate as well as local plant and animal life. Field survey crews encounter snakes and poison ivy. They are subject to heat exhaustion, sunburn, and frostbite. Some survey projects, particularly those being conducted near construction projects or busy highways, impose the dangers of injury from cars and flying debris. Unless survey technicians are employed for office assignments, where working conditions are similar to those of other office workers, their work location quite likely will change from survey to survey. Some assignments may require technicians to be away from home for varying periods of time.

While on the job, surveying crews and especially technicians who often supervise other workers must take special care to observe good safety practices. Construction and mining workplaces are usually "hard-hat" areas where special clothing and protective hats and shoes are required.

■ Outlook

The employment outlook in the surveying and mapping field is expected to be good through 2006, although the projected growth is slower than the average. This outlook applies to those students who have attained at least two years of junior college or technical institute preparation as surveying technicians.

One of the factors that is expected to increase the demand for surveying services—and therefore surveying technicians—is growth in urban and suburban areas. New streets, homes, shopping centers, schools, and gas and water lines will require property and boundary line surveys. Other factors are the continuing state and federal highway improvement programs and the increasing number of urban redevelopment programs. The expansion of industrial and business firms and the relocation of some firms in large undeveloped tracts are also expected to create a need for surveying services.

■ For More Information

Accreditation Board for Engineering and Technology, Inc.
111 Market Place
Baltimore, MD 21202
Tel: 410-347-7700

American Congress on Surveying and Mapping
5410 Grosvenor Lane, Suite 100
Bethesda, MD 20814
Tel: 301-493-0200
Web: http://www.acsm-hqtrs.org/acsm/

■ Related Articles

Construction

Mining

Cartographers

Surveyors

Surveyors

■ Overview

Surveyors mark exact measurements and locations of elevations, points, lines, and contours on or near Earth's surface. They measure the distances between points to determine property boundaries and to provide data for mapmaking, construction projects, and other engineering purposes.

■ History

As the United States expanded from the Atlantic to the Pacific, people moved over the mountains and plains into the uncharted regions of the West. They found it necessary to mark their routes and to mark property lines and borderlines by surveying and filing claims. The need for precise and accurate geographical measurements and precise records of those measurements has increased over the years: for the location of a trail, highway, or road; the site of a log cabin, frame house, or skyscraper; the right-of-way for water pipes, drainage ditches, or telephone lines; or for the charting of unexplored regions, bodies of water, land, or underground mines. As the establishment of exact locations and the need to measure points on the surface of Earth became more specialized, it created a demand for the professional surveyor.

■ The Job

On proposed construction projects—superhighways, airstrips, housing developments, and bridges—it is the surveyor's responsibility to make the necessary measurements by conducting an accurate and detailed survey of the area. The surveyor usually works with a field party consisting of several people. Instrument assistants handle a variety of surveying instruments including the theodolite, transit, level, surveyor's chain, rod, and different types of electronic equipment used to measure distance or locate a position. In the course of the survey, it is important that all readings be accurately recorded and field notes maintained so that the survey can be checked for accuracy by the surveyor.

Surveyors may become expert in one or more particular types of surveying:

Land surveyors establish township, property, and other tract-of-land boundary lines. Using maps, notes, or actual land title deeds, they survey the land, checking the accuracy of existing records. This information is used to prepare legal documents such as deeds and leases. Land surveying managers coordinate the work of land surveyors and their survey parties with that of legal, engineering, architectural, and other staff involved with the project. In addition, these managers develop policy, prepare budgets, certify work upon completion, and handle numerous other administrative duties.

Highway surveyors establish points, grades, lines, and other points of reference for highway construction projects. This survey information is essential to the work of the numerous engineers and the construction crews who actually plan and build the new highway.

Geodetic surveyors measure such large masses of land, sea, or space that the measurements must take into account the curvature of Earth and its geophysical characteristics. Their work is helpful in establishing points of reference for smaller land surveys, for determining national boundaries, and in preparing maps. Geodetic computers calculate latitude, longitude, angles, areas, and other information needed for mapmaking. They work from field notes made by an engineering survey party using reference tables and a calculating machine or computer.

Marine surveyors make surveys of harbors, rivers, and other bodies of water. They determine the depth of the water, usually by taking soundings or sound measurements, in relation to land masses. These surveys are essential in planning navigation projects, in developing plans for and constructing breakwaters, dams, piers, marinas, and bridges, and or in constructing nautical charts and maps.

Mine surveyors make surface and underground surveys, preparing maps of mines and mining operations. Such maps are helpful in examining underground passages on and between levels of a mine and in assessing the strata and volume of raw material available.

Geophysical prospecting surveyors locate and mark sites considered likely to contain petroleum deposits. *Oil-well directional surveyors* use sonic, electronic, or nuclear measuring instruments to gauge the characteristics of Earth formations in boreholes from which they evaluate the productivity of oil- or gas-bearing reservoirs. *Pipeline surveyors* determine rights-of-way for oil pipeline construction projects. They establish the right-of-way and property lines

SURVEYORS	
SCHOOL SUBJECTS	Geography Mathematics
PERSONAL SKILLS	Communication/ideas Technical/scientific
WORK ENVIRONMENT	Primarily outdoors Primarily multiple locations
MINIMUM EDUCATION LEVEL	Bachelor's degree
SALARY RANGE	$19,600 to $29,500 to $62,700
CERTIFICATION OR LICENSING	Required by all states
OUTLOOK	Little change or more slowly than the average
DOT	018
GOE	05.01.06
NOC	2154
O*NET	22311B

and assemble the information essential to the preparation for and laying of the lines.

Photogrammetric engineers determine the contour of an area to show elevations and depressions and indicate such features as mountains, lakes, rivers, forests, roads, farms, buildings, and other landmarks. Aerial, land, or water photographs used in this work are taken with special photographic equipment installed in the airplane or ground station that permits pictures of large areas to be made. From these pictures, accurate measurements of the terrain and surface features can be made. These surveys are helpful in highway and engineering planning and the preparation of topographical maps. Photogrammetry, as photo surveying is termed, is particularly helpful in charting areas that are inaccessible or difficult to travel.

■ Requirements

High School

If you are interested in a career as a surveyor, you should take algebra, geometry, trigonometry, physics, mechanical drawing, and other related science or drafting courses in high school. You should also take any available geography courses.

Postsecondary Training

After high school, you should take a four-year college program in surveying or engineering. Civil engineering, with a surveying emphasis, is a common major selected by students wishing to become surveyors because the two fields are so closely allied. Graduate study is necessary for advancement in the highly technical areas.

Certification or Licensing

All 50 states require that surveyors making property and boundary surveys be licensed or registered. The requirements for licensure vary, but in general they include one of the following: be a college graduate with two to four years of experience, have at least six years' experience and be able to pass an examination in land surveying, or have at least 10 years' experience. Information on specific requirements can be obtained by contacting the appropriate state agency in the capital of the state in which one plans to work. Those seeking employment in the federal government must take a civil service examination and meet the educational, experience, and other specified requirements for the position in which they are interested.

Other Requirements

The ability to work with numbers and perform mathematical computations accurately and quickly is very important. Other helpful abilities are the ability to visualize and understand objects in two and three dimensions (spatial

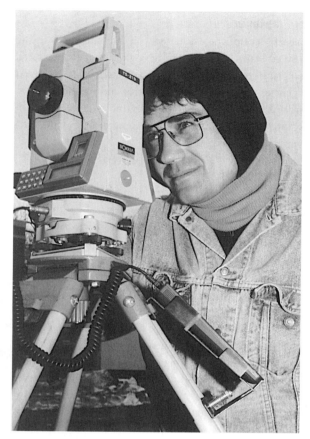

Surveyors must have good eyesight to measure accurately.

relationships) and the ability to discriminate between and compare shapes, sizes, lines, shadings, and other forms (form perception).

Surveyors walk a great deal and carry equipment over all types of terrain. Endurance, coordination, and the ability to compensate for physical impairment are important physical assets in the surveyor. Surveying involves working with other people and often requires directing or supervising the work of others. Therefore, a surveyor must have leadership qualities for supervisory positions.

■ Exploring

One of the best opportunities for experience is a summer job with a construction outfit or company that is planning survey work. This may be private or government work. Even if the job does not involve direct contact with survey crews, it will offer an opportunity to observe surveyors and talk with them about their work. Some colleges have work-study programs that offer periodic on-the-job experiences. These opportunities, like summer or part-time jobs, can be helpful to someone considering this field as a career.

■ Employers

Nearly half of the estimated 108,000 surveyors in the United States are employed in engineering, architectural, and surveying firms. Federal, state, and local government agencies employ about one-fourth, and most of the rest work for construction companies, oil and gas extraction companies, and public utilities. Approximately 6,000 surveyors are self-employed.

■ Starting Out

Some people get jobs as instrument assistants with a surveying firm. College graduates can learn about job openings through their schools' placement services. In many cities, employment agencies specialize in positions in surveying and related fields.

■ Advancement

Surveyors with the highest level of education and initiative in keeping up with technological developments in the field can become party chiefs. There are many who believe that surveying has been too long isolated from engineering, and that land surveying is engineering. With the increasing requirement of an engineering degree for entrance to surveying in several states, it will be easier to transfer to a larger number of related positions. Although a surveying or civil engineering program is recommended for a prospective surveyor, one could major in electrical, mechanical, or chemical engineering. Drafting is another related field to which a surveyor might move.

■ Earnings

The median annual earnings for surveyors are about $36,000. The federal government hires high school graduates as surveyor helpers at about $14,240 per year and as instrument assistants at about $15,100 per year. The federal government hires land surveyors at about $19,600 to $24,000 to $29,500 per year, depending on their qualifications. The average salary for all land surveyors in the federal government is $47,800. Highly skilled geodetic surveyors can earn up to $62,700. In private industry, beginning salaries are comparable to those offered by the federal government, according to the limited information available.

Most positions with the federal, state, and local governments and with private firms provide the usual medical, pension, insurance, vacation, and holiday benefits.

■ Work Environment

The surveyor works the usual 40-hour week except when overtime is necessary to complete a survey so that a project can be started immediately. The peak work period for the surveyor comes during the summer months when weather conditions are most favorable. However, it is not uncommon for the surveyor to be exposed to all types of weather conditions.

Some survey projects involve a certain amount of hazard, depending upon the region and climate as well as the plant and animal life. Field survey crews encounter snakes, poison ivy, and other plant and animal life; they are subject to heat exhaustion, sunburn, and frostbite. Some survey projects, particularly those being conducted near construction projects or busy highways, impose the danger of injury from heavy traffic, flying objects, and other accidental hazards. Much of the surveying of vast lands and large mountain formations is beginning to be done with satellite technology. Thus, remote area studies may become less frequent.

Unless the surveyor is employed for office assignments, where the working conditions are similar to those of other office workers, the work location most likely will change from survey to survey. Some assignments may necessitate being away from home for periods of time.

■ Outlook

The employment outlook in surveying in the near future is expected to be good, although the U.S. Department of Labor predicts the field will grow more slowly than the average. In view of the pressure for preparation in engineering as a prerequisite for professional status and licensure, opportunities will be better for those who have college degrees.

Some of the factors that are expected to increase the demand for surveyors include growth in urban and suburban areas, with new streets, homes, shopping centers, schools, gas and water lines requiring property and boundary line surveys, expanding state and federal highway improvement programs, increasing numbers of urban redevelopment programs, expansion of industrial and business firms and the relocation of some firms in large undeveloped tracts, and increasing demand for land and nautical maps and charts. However, many such projects can be canceled or postponed during times of economic stress; therefore, openings for surveyors depend in part on the state of the national and local economies.

■ For More Information

American Congress on Surveying and Mapping
5410 Grosvenor Lane, Suite 100
Bethesda, MD 20814
Tel: 301-493-0200
Web: http://www.acsm-hqtrs.org/acsm/

American Society for Photogrammetry and Remote Sensing
5410 Grosvenor Lane, Suite 210
Bethesda, MD 20814
Tel: 301-493-0290

Sweeps

■ **See Chimney Sweeps**

Swimming Pool Servicers

■ Overview

Swimming pool servicers clean, adjust, and perform minor repairs on swimming pools, hot tubs, and their auxiliary equipment. There are millions of swimming pools across the country in hotels, parks, apartment complexes, health clubs, and other public areas; these public pools are required by law to be regularly serviced by trained technicians. The number of homes with private pools is also increasing every year. The owner of a swimming pool service will also hire and train technicians, schedule and bill clients, and market the business.

■ History

Swimming is as old as walking and running, and swimming pools date back to the bathhouses in the palaces of ancient Greece. These bathhouses were elaborate spas, complete with steam rooms, saunas, and large pools. But swimming was a popular pastime even among those who didn't have access to bathhouses; many swam in the rivers, oceans, and the lakes of the world. The plagues of medieval Europe made people cautious about swimming in unclean waters, but swimming regained popularity in the 1880s in England. Swimmers swam with their heads above water in a style developed when people were still afraid of the water's contamination. This style changed in the mid-1800s when American Indians introduced an early version of the modern "crawl" to Europe. Swimming in natural spring waters was even recommended as a health benefit, inspiring hospitals and spas to develop around hot springs.

The first modern Olympics held in Athens featured swimming as one of the nine competitions, and swimming as both a sport and a pastime has continued to develop along with the technology of pool maintenance. By the 1960s, the National Swimming Pool Foundation had evolved to support research in pool safety and the education of pool operators.

■ The Job

With your swimming pool service, you'll travel a regularly scheduled route, visiting several pools a day. You'll be responsible for keeping pools clean and pool equipment operating properly. A pool that routinely receives adequate maintenance develops relatively few expensive problems. Mark Randall owns a pool service business in Malibu, California. "My tools range from a tile brush to a state of the art computer and printer," he says. Mark has two employees, so his day usually starts with phone calls to his crew and customers. "Then I go out and clean a few of the more difficult accounts," he says.

Cleaning is one of the regular duties of pool servicers. Leaves and other debris need to be scooped off the surface of the water with a net on a long pole. To clean beneath the surface, you use a special vacuum cleaner on the pool floor and walls. With stainless steel or nylon brushes, you scrub pool walls and the tiles and gutters around the pool's edge to remove the layer of grit and scum that collects at the water line. You also hose down the pool deck and unclog the strainers that cover the drains.

After the cleaning procedures, you test the bacterial content and pH balance (a measure of acidity and alkalinity) of the water. While the tests are simple and take only a few minutes, they are very important. You take a sample of the pool water in a jar and add a few drops of a testing chemical. This causes the water to change colors, indicating the water's chemical balance. You can then determine the amount of chlorine and other chemicals you should add to make the water safe. The chemicals often used, which include potassium iodide, hydrochloric acid, sodium carbonate, chlorine, and others, can be poured directly into the pool or added through a feeder device in the circulation system. These

SWIMMING POOL SERVICERS	
SCHOOL SUBJECTS	**Chemistry** **Technical/Shop**
PERSONAL SKILLS	**Following instructions** **Technical/scientific**
WORK ENVIRONMENT	**Indoors and outdoors** **Primarily multiple locations**
MINIMUM EDUCATION LEVEL	**High school diploma**
SALARY RANGE	**$18,000 to $32,000 to $50,000**
CERTIFICATION OR LICENSING	**Voluntary**
OUTLOOK	**About as fast as the average**
DOT	**891**
GOE	**05.10.04**
NOC	**7441**
O*NET	**87899C**

A swimming pool servicer does routine cleaning on a client's pool.

chemicals, when properly regulated, kill bacteria and algae that grow in water. However, too much of them can cause eye or skin irritation. You must wear gloves and be careful when adding the chemicals since they are dangerous in high concentrations. You must follow the correct procedures for applying these chemicals each time, and keep accurate records of what is added to the pool. The chemical makeup of every pool is different and can change daily or even hourly. Home pools usually have their water tested a few times a week, but large public pools are tested hourly.

You'll also inspect and perform routine maintenance on pool equipment, such as circulation pumps, filters, and heaters. In order to clean a filter, you force water backwards through it to dislodge any dirt and debris that have accumulated. You'll make sure there are no leaks in pipes, gaskets, connections, or other parts. If a drain or pipe is clogged, you use a steel snake, plunger, or other plumber's tools to clear it. You will adjust thermostats, pressure gauges, and other controls to make the pool water comfortable. You may make minor repairs to machinery, fixing or replacing small components. When you think major repairs are necessary, you'll inform the pool owner before beginning to make the repairs.

"An accomplished pool tech," Mark says, "can do a pool in about 20 minutes. Most pool techs would do this from 10 to 20 times a day."

Closing outdoor pools for the winter is a major task for swimming pool servicers in most regions of the country. In the fall, you'll drain the water out of the pool and its auxiliary equipment. Openings into the pool are plugged, and all the pool gear, such as diving boards, ladders, and pumps, is removed, inspected, and stored. The pool is covered with a tarpaulin lashed or weighted in place. In climates where water does not freeze, pools are usually kept full and treated with special chemicals through the winter.

Extra work is also required when a pool is opened in the spring. After the pool is uncovered and the tank and pool deck are swept clean, you inspect the pool for cracks, leaks, loose tiles, and broken lamps. You then repair minor items and make recommendations to the owner about any major work that is necessary, such as painting the interior of the pool. You then clean and install the equipment removed in the fall, such as ladders and diving boards. You test water circulation and heating systems to make sure they are operating properly, and then you fill the pool with water. Once the pool is filled, you test the water and add the proper chemicals to make it safe. Pool servicers keep careful records of the maintenance work they have done so they can inform the company and the customer.

■ Requirements

High School

Take science courses such as chemistry and biology so you can gain understanding of the chemicals you'll be using. Voc-tech courses with lessons in electrical wiring and motors will help you develop skills for repairing the pool servicing machines and equipment. Bookkeeping and accounting courses can teach you how to keep financial and tax records. You should also learn about spreadsheet and database software programs, as you'll be using computers to maintain files on profits and expenses, customers, equipment, and employees. Join a business club to meet small business owners in your area. Serving as an assistant on a swim team can teach you first-hand about the requirements of maintaining a regulation pool.

Postsecondary Training

You can gain the technical training on the job; by hiring on with a pool service business, you'll learn the basics of pool maintenance within a few months. To prepare yourself for the demands of running your own business, enroll in a small business program at your local community college, or take college courses in sales, math, and accounting. Mark has had college and technical training in various fields, and has worked as a mechanic, data analyst, and has built props for a movie studio. "I had no idea I would end up in the pool business," he says. "Luckily, my background was actually very good training for my current business." He recommends that people interested in pool maintenance take courses in electrical applications, electronics, plumbing, and hydraulics.

Certification and Licensing

Mark believes that certification and licensing are very important to running a professional outfit. He is certified by the health department, has a business license, and belongs to the Independent Pool and Spa Service Organization. Certification is also available from the National Swimming Pool Foundation, and by service franchisers. These programs consist of a set number of classroom hours and a written exam. While certification is not necessarily a requirement, it does indicate that you've reached a certain level of expertise and skill, and can help you promote your business.

Other Requirements

Because you'll often work alone, with minimum supervision, it is important that you have self-discipline and a responsible attitude. Your drive and ambition will determine the success of your business. "Persistence is probably the most important quality," Mark says, in listing necessary personal attributes. He also emphasizes a strong work ethic and good communication skills. You'll also need to keep up with the technology of swimming pool maintenance, staying knowledgeable about new equipment and services available to your clients.

■ Exploring

A summer or part-time job on the staff of a school, park district, community center, or local health club will provide you with a good opportunity to learn more about servicing swimming pools. Hotels, motels, apartment buildings, and condominium complexes also frequently have pools and may hire summer or part-time workers to service them. Such a job could offer firsthand insight into the duties of swimming pool servicers, as well as help in obtaining full-time employment with a pool maintenance company later. *Aqua Magazine* is a good source of technical information concerning pool service. Contact *Aqua Magazine* for a sample issue, or visit Aqua's Web site (http://www.aquamagazine.com) to read some of the articles it publishes.

■ Employers

The rate of new pool construction is growing 3 to 4 percent every year. With well over 6 million residential swimming pools in the country, pool service owners can find clients in practically every suburban neighborhood. In addition to servicing residential pools, you'll service the pools of motels, apartment complexes, and public parks. Some franchise opportunities, with companies such as PFS Swimming Pool Services, also exist. These franchisers often offer training, and have an initial investment of under $20,000.

■ Starting Out

Once you have the training, and the money to invest in equipment, you'll pursue a clientele. This may involve promoting your business through advertising, fliers, and word of mouth. You may be able to get referrals from local pool and spa construction companies. "I started out riding with a friend who worked for a large pool service company," Mark says, "and I learned as much as I could. After that, I found a small route for sale." Mark borrowed money from the bank to buy the established route of customers, then used his training to start servicing pools. "It was sink or swim, pardon the pun," he says. "But I worked very hard the first couple of years and got lucky and have been fairly successful."

■ Advancement

You'll advance as your business grows. More area pool construction, good word of mouth, and some years in the business will attract more clients and more routes to service. If your business does really well, you may be able to take on employees, allowing you to assign staff members to the service work while you focus on office work and administrative details. You could also expand your business to include the sale of pools, spas, and maintenance equipment. "I'm toying with the idea of getting a contractor's license," Mark says, "and building pools."

■ Earnings

The amount of money you'll make from your service depends upon the region of the country in which you work, and the length of the swimming season. Though no recent national survey has been conducted, experts in the business estimate that an experienced pool service owner can average $40,000 to $50,000 a year. However, when you're just starting in your business and building a clientele, or if you're working in an area of the country that allows for only a few summer months of swimming season, you may make less than $20,000.

■ Work Environment

You'll generally work alone and will probably have little client contact. Regular swimming pool servicing is not particularly strenuous, though you will be kneeling and bending, and also carrying your own equipment from your van to the pool. While you may work both indoors and outdoors, you'll usually work in pleasant weather. You'll be handling some chemicals, which may require wearing protective gloves, and possibly a mask if you're sensitive to fumes.

Pool servicing can be an excellent job for those who enjoy spending time outside. "I find cleaning pools to be kind of relaxing," Mark says, "and a good time to enjoy my surroundings. Some people find it boring and monotonous. I guess you just need a good perspective."

■ Outlook

Over 200,000 new pools are built every year, and this number will likely increase. With the growing number of pools, there's also growing concern for pool safety. New pool laws will be beneficial to your pool service, as you'll be hired to help pool owners meet regulations. New kinds of equipment such as solar heaters, automatic timers, pool covers, and chemical dispensers, will keep pool services in demand. Health organizations and publications will also keep pool owners aware of the necessity of pool and hot tub cleaning to prevent infection.

■ For More Information

To learn more about certification, contact:

Independent Pool and Spa Service Association
17715 Chatsworth Street, Suite 203
Granada Hills, CA 91344
Tel: 818-360-9505
Web: http://www.ipssa.com

To read about issues effecting the swimming pool industry, visit the Aqua Magazine Web page, or contact them for subscription information:

Aqua Magazine
2062 Business Center Drive
Irvine, CA 92612
Tel: 714-253-8725
Web: http://www.aquamagazine.com

■ Related Articles

Entreprenuers

Cruise Ship Workers

Resort Workers

Switch Technicians

■ **See Wireless Service Technicians**

Switchboard Operators

■ **See Receptionists**

Switching Equipment Technicians

■ **See Communications Equipment Technicians**

System Performance Workers

■ **See Wireless Service Technicians**

Systems Programmers

■ **See Computer Programmers**

Systems Set Up Specialists

■ Overview

Systems set up specialists are responsible for installing new computer systems and upgrading existing ones to meet the specifications of the client. They install hardware, such as memory, sound cards, fax/modems, fans, microprocessors, and systems boards. They also load software and configure the hard drive appropriately. Some systems set up specialists install computer systems at the client's location. Installation might include normal hard drive or network server configurations as well as connecting peripherals like printers, phones, fax machines, modems, and numerous terminals. They might also be involved with technical support in providing initial training to users. Systems set up specialists are employed by computer manufacturing companies or computer service companies nationwide, or may be employed as part of the technical support department of many businesses. Systems set up specialists are sometimes called *technical support technicians, desk top analyst/specialists,* and *PC set up specialists.*

■ History

The first major advances in modern computer technology were made during World War II. After the war, it was thought that the enormous size of computers, which easily took up the space of entire warehouses, would limit their use to huge government projects. Accordingly, the 1950 census was computer processed.

The introduction of semiconductors to computer technology made smaller and less expensive computers possible. Businesses began adapting computers to their operations as early as 1954. Within 30 years, computers had revolutionized the way people work, play, and shop. Today, computers are everywhere, from businesses of all kinds, to government agencies, charitable organizations, and private homes. Over the years, technology has continued to shrink computer size and increase speed at an unprecedented rate.

Several big companies like IBM, Apple, Microsoft, and Intel have been the driving force behind various stages of the computer revolution. As technology advances, however, increasingly new companies spring up to compete with them. For example, IBM's first competitive challenge came when other companies decided to produce IBM-compatible PC clones. Today, the market for computers is saturated with different brands offering similar features. As a result, many companies are attempting to distinguish themselves from the competition by providing extra service to clients. Offering customized hardware and software is one way for them to do this. Systems set up specialists, therefore, are a very important part of the selling process. They make sure that clients receive exactly what they need and want. If the computer system is not set up correctly to begin with, clients might take their business elsewhere in the future. As competition in the computer industry grows even fiercer, the customer service roles of systems set up specialists will become even more important.

■ The Job

Most businesses and organizations use computers on a daily basis. In fact, it is very difficult to find an office or store that does not use computer technology to help them with at least one business task. One thing is for sure—there are so many different ways in which a business or individual can use computer technology that it would be impossible to count them. The wide variety could translate into big problems for computer companies if they tried to sell identical computer systems to every client. For example, a freelance writer would probably not be interested in a math card used for advanced mathematical calculations on personal computers. Likewise, a bank or insurance company has different database needs than a law firm.

In order to meet the various needs of clients, many computer manufacturers, retailers, and service centers offer to customize commercial hardware and software for each client. Systems might differ by quantity of RAM (random access memory), speed and type of fax/modem, networking capabilities, and software packages. Systems set up specialists are responsible for installing new computer systems and upgrading existing ones to meet the specifications of the client. The main differences among set up specialists are their clients (individuals or businesses) and the level of systems they are qualified to work on.

Some specialists work in-house for large computer manufactures, retailers, or service centers. Their clients are typically individuals buying for home use as well as small- to medium-sized businesses with minimal computing needs.

In the set up lab, specialists receive orders that list system specifications. Then, they follow instructions on how to set up the computer properly. They install hardware, like memory chips, sound cards, fax/modems, fans, microprocessors, and system boards. They also install any software packages requested by the client. Next, they configure the hard drive so it knows exactly what hardware and software is connected to it. Finally, they run diagnostic tests on the system to make sure everything is running well.

The main goal is to eliminate the need for clients to do any set up work on the computer once they receive it. Clients should be able to plug it in, turn it on, and get it to work right away. In some cases, specialists even at this level will be sent to a client's location to install the system and provide some initial training on how to use it.

Other systems set up specialists work for companies that sell predominately to medium- and large-sized businesses. These specialists split their time between the employer's set up lab and the client's location. In the lab, they make initial preparations for installation. Some of the computer equipment might come from other manufacturers or suppliers, and so they have to verify that it is free of defects. They also check that they have all the necessary hardware parts, software packages, etc. before going to the client's location.

Depending on the size and complexity of the

SYSTEMS SET UP SPECIALISTS	
SCHOOL SUBJECTS	**Business** **Computer science**
PERSONAL SKILLS	**Mechanical/manipulative** **Technical/scientific**
WORK ENVIRONMENT	**Primarily indoors** **Primarily one location**
MINIMUM EDUCATION LEVEL	**High school diploma**
SALARY RANGE	**$26,130 to $32,300 to $40,000**
CERTIFICATION OR LICENSING	**None available**
OUTLOOK	**Faster than the average**
O*NET	**22127**

system to be installed, they might travel to the client's location one or more times before installation in order to map out the required wiring, communications lines, and space. It is very important to plan these details carefully. If wires are hard to reach, for example, future repairs and upgrade will be difficult. If the system is really big, set up specialists might recommend and build a raised floor in the client's computer center. The paneled floor allows easy access to the complex electrical and communications wiring.

Once thorough preparations have been made, set up specialists move the equipment to the clients' location to begin installation. Their on-site work might include configuring hard drives or network servers. They also connect peripherals like printers, phones, fax machines, modems, and numerous networked terminals. When everything is in place, they run extensive diagnostic tests in order to ensure that the system is running well. Invariably, they encounter problems. One terminal may not be able to send files to another, for example. Another might be unable to establish fax communications outside the company. Solving problems requires consulting flow charts, other computer professionals, and technical manuals. The next round of testing occurs when the users begin working on the system. Some clients might prefer to simulate normal use while set up specialists stand by to correct problems. Large business installations can take days or even weeks to complete.

Sometimes, set up specialists are involved with technical support in training client users on the new system. They have to be well-versed in the details of how to use the system properly and be able to explain it to individuals who might not know a lot about computers.

■ Requirements

High School

If this industry interests you, try to take any mechanics and electronics classes that focus on understanding how complex machinery works. These classes will introduce you to the basics of reading flow charts and schematic drawings and understanding technical documents. The ability to read these documents efficiently and accurately is a prerequisite for computer set up work. Don't forget to take computer classes, especially those that explain the basic functioning of computer technology. English and speech classes will also help you build your communications skills—another important quality since set up specialists often work closely with many different people.

Postsecondary Training

A high school diploma is a minimum educational requirement for most systems set up specialist positions. However, the competitive nature of this industry is increasing the importance of postsecondary education, such as an associate's degree. Computer technology is advancing so rapidly that without a solid understanding of the basics, set up specialists cannot keep up with the changes. Also, many aspiring computer professionals use system set up positions as a springboard to higher-level jobs in the company. Formal computer education, along with work experience, gives them a better chance for advancement.

Other Requirements

Do you work well with your hands? Manual work is performed on large and small scales—sometimes thick cables and communications lines must be installed; other times tiny memory chips or microprocessors are needed. Therefore, you'll need to demonstrate good manual dexterity.

You should also be curious about how things work. Systems set up specialists are typically the kind of people who tinker around the house on VCRs, televisions, small appliances, and computers. Genuine curiosity of this type is important because you'll constantly be challenged to learn about new equipment and technologies. When things go wrong during installation, you will be called on to become electronic and computer problem-solvers and so you must be prepared with a solid understanding of the basics.

■ Exploring

There are several ways to obtain a better understanding of what it is like to be a set up specialist. One way is to try to organize a career day through school or friends and relatives. In this way, you could spend a day on the job with set up specialists and experience firsthand what the work entails.

You might also want to work part time for a computer repair shop. Repair shops usually do many upgrades that involve the installation of new hardware, like faster modems and microprocessors and more memory. Working in such a shop after school or on weekends will give you the opportunity to observe or practice the precision work of a set up specialist.

Depending on your level of computer knowledge, you may want to volunteer to set up new personal computers for friends or charitable organizations in your neighborhood. What about installing software or customizing some features of the operating system to better meet the needs of the user?

■ Employers

In the early days of the computer industry, many jobs were clustered around northern California, where many of the big computer companies were headquartered. This is no longer true. Many top computer companies are located throughout the United States, and with them come a number of employment opportunities. Some computer hardware powerhouses include Dell, Hewlett-Packard, and IBM. Many mid- to small-sized companies may not have the need for a specific department devoted to computer setup. In such situations, other computer professionals may be assigned setup duties besides their regular job descriptions.

A number of jobs may also be found with smaller companies that contract their services to retail stores or offer them directly to the public. Services may include hardware and software installation, upgrading, and repair.

■ Starting Out

Most positions in systems set up are considered entry level. If you plan to enter this field without a postsecondary education but with computer skills and experience, you will need to network with working computer professionals for potential employment opportunities. Jobs are advertised in the newspaper every week; in fact, many papers devote entire sections to computer-related positions. Also, don't forget the benefits of working with employment agencies. Another job-hunting technique is to conduct online searches on the World Wide Web. Many computer companies post employment opportunities and accept resumes and applications online.

If you plan to enter the field by completing an advanced degree, say an associate's degree in computer technology, for example, work closely with your school's placement office. Many firms looking for computer professionals inform schools first, since they are assured of meeting candidates with a certain level of proficiency in the field.

■ Advancement

Within systems set up, there are several ways specialists can be promoted. One is by working on increasingly complex systems installations. Another is by having supervisory or managerial responsibility for the set up department. Other specialists choose to pursue promotion in different functional areas, like technical support, computer engineering, or systems analysis.

When set up specialists demonstrate strong ability and drive, they are often assigned to larger and more complex installations. Instead of installing commercial software, for example, the specialist might now be responsible for constructing flow charts or other drawings as part of the overall installation plan. Also, a specialist who at first works on relatively small departmental networks might be asked to work on company-wide networks.

Computer professionals who use systems set up as a springboard to other positions usually have formal education in a certain field, like software or hardware engineering, for example. They seek promotion by keeping an eye on job openings within their respective fields.

If specialists show leadership ability, they might be promoted to supervisory and then managerial positions. These positions require more administrative duties and less hands-on work. For example, supervisors are usually in charge of scheduling installation jobs and assigning different jobs to various individuals, taking into account their level of expertise and experience. With more formal education, managers might be involved with the strategic planning of a computer company, deciding what level of service the company is willing to offer to clients.

Specialists may also decide to start their own computer business. Many office supply and electronic stores contract with area computer companies to provide customers with services such as set up and installation, upgrading, and technical support. If this career path is appealing, educate yourself in the basics of operating a small business, such as accounting, marketing, and inventory.

■ Earnings

According to a 1997 Technical Support Salary Survey, systems set up specialists with entry-level customer service responsibilities earned an annual average of $26,130; those with experience earned an averaged annual salary of about $32,300. Senior level set up specialists with superior technical skills and work experience earned an average salary of about $40,000. Computer professionals typically earn more in areas where there are clusters of computer companies, like northern California and parts of the East Coast. However the high cost of living in these areas may offset the benefits of a higher salary.

Most full-time set up specialists work for companies that provide a full range of benefits, including health insurance, sick leave, and paid vacation. In addition, many employers offer tuition reimbursement programs to employees who successfully complete course work in the field. Set up specialists who operate their own businesses are responsible for providing their own benefits.

■ Work Environment

Systems set up specialists work primarily indoors, in a comfortable environment. This is not a desk job; specialists move around a lot either in the lab or at the client site. Travel to client locations is required for many set up specialists. The work also requires some lifting of heavy machinery, which can be avoided if an individual physically cannot perform this task. Given the nature of the work, dress is casual, although those who install systems at the client's site must be dressed in presentable business attire.

Set up specialists usually work a regular 40-hour week. However, they might be asked to work overtime when big installations are reaching final phases. They might have to work during off-hours if the client requires installation to be done then.

Installation work can be tedious. There are many details involving wiring, communications, and configurations. Set up specialists must therefore be patient and thorough, which can be frustrating at times. When problems arise, they must work well under stress and be able to think clearly about how to resolve the issues. If set up specialists are also involved in user training, they must communicate clearly and be understanding of others' problems.

■ Outlook

The demand for systems set up specialists is expected to grow faster than the average through 2006, according to the *Occupational Outlook Handbook*. Most jobs in the computer industry, especially those that provide a special or unique service to computer customers, will enjoy increased demand.

The ability to network and share information within the company allows businesses to be productive and work more efficiently. As new technology is developed, companies may upgrade, or replace their systems altogether. Skilled workers will be in demand by companies to staff their technical support departments and provide services ranging from set up and installation to diagnostics.

Also, because of falling hardware and software prices, it has become more affordable for consumers to purchase home computer setups. Although advances in software technology have made program installation easy, computer companies will continue to offer installation services as a way to win customers from competitors. In addition, fierce competition will push companies to provide increasingly specialized service in terms of customization of computer systems. As computers become more sophisticated, highly trained set up specialists will be needed to install them correctly. It will therefore be very important for set up specialists to stay up to date with technological advances through continuing education, seminars, or work training.

■ For More Information

For information regarding industry salary expectations or employment opportunities nationwide, contact:

Association of Support Professionals
17 Main Street
Watertown, MA 02172-4491
Tel: 617-924-3944, ext. 14
Web: http://www.asponline.com/

For information regarding the industry, career opportunities, or membership requirements, contact:

Association of Computing Machinery (ACM)
1515 Broadway, 17th Floor
New York, NY 10036-5701
Web: http://www.acm.org

For information on technical careers, scholarships, or a copy of Computer Magazine, *contact:*

The Computer Society
1730 Massachusetts Avenue, NW
Washington, DC 20036-1992
Tel: 202-371-0101
Web: http://www.computer.org

For employment information and online career sites for computer professionals, contact:

Institute of Electronic and Electrical Engineers
3 Park Avenue, 17th Floor
New York, NY 10016-5997
Tel: 212-419-7900
Web: http://www.ieee.org

For a history of computers, career descriptions, educational resources, or computer related interactive exhibits, contact:

The Computer Museum
Web: http://www.tcm.org

■ Related Articles

Computer Hardware
Computer Software
Computers
Electronics
Computer and Office Machine Service Technicians
Computer Support Service Owners
Computer Trainers
Hardware Engineers
Microelectronics Technicians
Quality Assurance Technicians
Technical Support Specialists

Systems Technicians

■ **See Telephone and PBX Installers and Repairers**

Systems Testing Laboratory Technicians

■ **See Electronics Engineering Technicians**

Tactical Agents

■ See Intelligence Officers

Tactile Interpreters

■ See Interpreters and Translators, Sign Language and Oral Interpreters

Tailors and Dressmakers

■ Overview

Tailors and dressmakers cut, sew, mend, and alter clothing. Typically, tailors work only with menswear, such as suits, jackets, and coats, while dressmakers work with women's clothing, including dresses, blouses, suits, evening wear, wedding and bridesmaids' gowns, and sportswear. Tailors and dressmakers are employed in dressmaking and custom tailor shops, department stores, and garment factories; others are self employed. According the *Occupational Outlook Handbook,* of the 87,000 custom tailors employed in the United States in 1996, over 50 percent worked in a retail clothing establishment.

■ History

The practice of making and wearing clothing evolved from the need for warmth and protection from injury. For example, in prehistoric times, people wrapped themselves in the warm skins of animals they killed for food. Throughout history, the making of clothing has been practiced by both men and women, in all cultures and every economic and social class.

Early clothing styles developed according to the climate of the geographical area: skirts and loose blouses of thin fabrics in warmer climates, pants and coats of heavier fabrics in cold climates. Religious customs and occupations also affected clothing styles. But as civilizations grew more and more advanced, clothing as necessity evolved into clothing as fashion.

The invention of the spinning wheel, in use in the 12th century, sped the process of making threads and yarns. With the invention of the two-bar loom, fabric making increased, styles became more detailed, and clothing became more widely available. Fabric production further increased with other inventions, such as the spinning jenny that could spin more than one thread at a time, power looms that ran on steam, and the cotton gin. The invention

of the sewing machine tremendously sped the production of garments, although tailors and dressmakers were never completely replaced by machines.

During the Industrial Revolution, factories replaced craft shops. High-production apparel companies employed hundreds of workers. Employees worked 12- to 14-hour workdays for a low hourly pay in crowded rooms with poor ventilation and lighting. The poor working conditions of these factories, known as "sweatshops," led to the founding of The International Ladies Garment Workers Union in 1900 and the Amalgamated Clothing Workers of America in 1914; these unions protected workers' rights, ensured their safety, and led to greatly improved working conditions.

Today, the precise skills of tailors and dressmakers are still in demand at factories, stores, and small shops. The limited investment required to cut and sew garments, the wide availability of fabrics, and the demand for one-of-a-kind, tailor-made garments are factors which continue to provide opportunities for self-employed tailors and dressmakers.

■ The Job

Some tailors and dressmakers make garments from start to completion. In larger shops, however, each employee usually works on a specific task, such as measuring, pattern-making, cutting, fitting, or stitching. One worker, for example, may only sew in sleeves or pad lapels. Smaller shops may only measure and fit the garment, then send piecework to outside contractors. Some tailors and dressmakers specialize in one type of garment, such as suits or wedding gowns. Many also do alterations on factory-made clothing.

Tailors and dressmakers may run their own businesses, work in small shops, or work in custom tailoring sections of large department stores. Some work out of their homes. Retail clothing stores, specialty stores, bridal shops, and dry cleaners also employ tailors and dressmakers to do alterations.

Tailors and dressmakers first help customers choose the gar-

TAILORS AND DRESSMAKERS	
SCHOOL SUBJECTS	Art Family and consumer science
PERSONAL SKILLS	Artistic Following instructions
WORK ENVIRONMENT	Primarily indoors Primarily one location
MINIMUM EDUCATION LEVEL	High school diploma
SALARY RANGE	$15,870 to $26,000 to $32,290+
CERTIFICATION OR LICENSING	None available
OUTLOOK	Decline
DOT	785
GOE	05.05.15
NOC	7342
O*NET	89505B

A tailor carefully takes a customer's measurements for proper fit of a new suit.

ment style and fabric, using their knowledge of the various types of fabrics. They take the customer's measurements, such as height, shoulder width, arm length, and waist, and note any special figure problems. They may use ready-made paper patterns or make one of their own. The patterns are then placed on the fabric and the fabric pieces are carefully cut. When the garment design is complex, or if there are special fitting problems, the tailor or dressmaker may cut the pattern from inexpensive muslin and fit it to the customer; any adjustments are then marked and transferred to the paper pattern before it is used to cut the actual garment fabric. The pieces are basted together first and then sewn by hand or machine. After one or two fittings, which confirm that the garment fits the customer properly, the tailor or dressmaker finishes the garment with hems, buttons, trim, and a final pressing.

Some tailors or dressmakers specialize in a certain aspect of the garment-making process. *Bushelers* work in factories to repair flaws and correct imperfect sewing in finished garments. *Shop tailors* have a detailed knowledge of special tailoring tasks. They use shears or a knife to trim and shape the edges of garments before sewing, attach shoulder pads, and sew linings in coats. *Skilled tailors* put fine stitching on lapels and pockets, make buttonholes, and sew on trim.

■ Requirements

High School

While in high school, the prospective garment worker should take any sewing, tailoring, and clothing classes offered by vocational or home economics departments. There are also a number of institutions that offer either on-site or home study courses in sewing and dressmaking. Art classes in sketching and design are also helpful.

Postsecondary Training

Tailors and dressmakers must have at least a high school education, although employers prefer college graduates with advanced training in sewing, tailoring, draping, patternmaking, and design. There are a limited number of schools and colleges in the United States that offer this type of training and include the Philadelphia College of Textiles and Science, the Fashion Institute of Technology in New York City, and the Parsons School of Design, also in New York. Students who are interested in furthering their career, and perhaps expanding from tailoring into design, may want to consider studying in one of these specialized institutions. It is, however, entirely possible to enter this field without a college degree.

Other Requirements

Workers in this field must obviously have the ability to sew very well, both by hand and machine, follow directions, and measure accurately. In addition to these skills, tailors and dressmakers must have a good eye for color and style. They need to know how to communicate with and satisfy customers. Strong interpersonal skills will help tailors and dressmakers get and keep clients.

■ Exploring

Take sewing classes at school. Also, check with your local park district or fabric and craft stores—they often offer lessons year-round. Find summer or part-time employment at a local tailor shop. This will give you valuable work experience. Contact schools regarding their programs in Fashion Design. If their course descriptions sound interesting, take a class or two. You can also create and sew your own designs or offer your mending and alteration services to your family and friends. Finally, visit department stores, clothing specialty stores, and tailor's shops to observe workers involved in this field.

■ Employers

If you like high fashion, then you should check the haute couture houses of Chanel or Yves Saint Laurent. These industry giants deal with expensive fabrics and innovative designs. They also cater to a high level of clientele. Be prepared—because such businesses will only consider the most experienced, highly skilled tailors and dressmakers.

Tailors and dressmakers employed at retail department stores make alterations on ready-to-wear clothing sold on the premises. They may perform a small task such as hemming pants or suit sleeves, or a major project such as custom fitting a wedding dress.

In some cases, it is possible for tailors or dressmakers to start their own businesses by making clothes and taking orders from those who like their work. Capital needed to start such a venture is minimum since the most important equipment, such as a sewing machine, iron and ironing board, scissors, and notions, are widely available and relatively inexpensive. Unless you plan to operate a home-based business, however, you will need to rent shop space. Careful planning is needed to prepare for your own tailoring or dressmaking business. You will need to learn bookkeeping, accounting, and how to keep and order supplies. Marketing is important too. You'll have to know how, when, and where to advertise your services to attract customers. Check the library or your local government to learn what is needed to set up your own small business. Don't forget to consult established tailors and dressmakers to learn the tricks of the trade.

■ Starting Out

Custom tailor shops or garment manufacturing centers sometimes offer apprenticeships to students or recent graduates, which gives them a start in the business. As a beginner you may also find work in related jobs, such as a sewer or alterer in a custom tailoring or dressmaking shop, garment factory, dry cleaning store, or department store. Apply directly to such companies and shops and monitor local newspaper ads for openings, as well. Check with your high school's career center to see if they have any industry information or leads for part-time jobs. Trade schools and colleges that have a programs in Textiles or Fashion often offer their students help with job placement.

■ Advancement

Workers in this field usually start by performing simple tasks. As they gain more experience and their skills improve, they may be assigned to more difficult and complicated tasks. However, advancement in the industry is typically somewhat limited. In factories, a production worker might be promoted to the position of line supervisor. Tailors and dressmakers can move to better shops, that offer higher pay or open their own businesses.

Some workers may find that they have an eye for color and style and an aptitude for design. With further training at an appropriate college, these workers may find a successful career in fashion design and merchandising.

■ Earnings

Salaries for tailors and dressmakers vary widely, depending on experience, skill, and location. According to the 1998 Apparel Plant Wages Survey, conducted by the American Apparel Manufacturers Association, the average hourly earnings were about $7.63. A bundle person earned an average of $6.94 an hour; a person assigned to the cutting room averaged $9.87 hourly; and an assembler earned an hourly average of $7.95. Experienced workers in supervisory sewing positions earned a weekly average of $477. Cutting room supervisors earned a weekly average of about $621.

THE SEWING MACHINE

It took more than one individual's ingenuity to develop the greatest sewing invention of all time—the sewing machine.

Thomas Saint designed a machine, in 1790, that could work with leather and canvas. However, he only built a patent model, and never mass produced his invention.

Barthelemy Thimonnier's invention, built in 1829, is considered the first practical sewing machine. Made entirely of wood, and using a barbed needle, this machine was able to sew a chain stitch. Thimonnier mass produced his machines and was under contract with the French government to sew army uniforms. Local tailors, afraid of the competition, raided his shop and destroyed his sewing machines. Thimonnier was able to save one machine and fled to America.

Elias Howe is commonly credited with inventing the first practical sewing machine in 1844, and patenting it in 1846. After marketing his machine abroad, Howe returned to America and found many other companies had infringed on his patent. He successfully sued.

Isaac Merrit Singer did much for the industry by mass producing the sewing machine. He also allowed the public to purchase machines on credit and implemented an aggressive sales campaign. Today, Singer company, the largest manufacturer and seller of consumer sewing machines, has merged with G. M. Pfaff AG, to become the largest industrial sewing machine manufacturer as well. Their New York Stock Exchange symbol is SEW.

Workers employed by large companies and retail stores receive benefits such as paid holidays and vacations, health insurance, and pension plans. They are often affiliated with one of the two labor unions of the industry—the International Ladies Garment Workers Union and the Amalgamated Clothing and Textile Workers of America—which may offer additional benefits. Self-employed tailors and dressmakers and small-shop workers usually provide their own benefits.

■ Work Environment

Tailors and dressmakers in large shops work 40 to 48 hours a week, sometimes including Saturdays. Union members usually work 35 to 40 hours a week. Those who run their own businesses often work longer hours. Spring and fall are usually the busiest times.

Since tailoring and dressmaking requires a minimal a investment, some tailors and dressmakers work out of their homes. Those who work in the larger apparel plants may find the conditions less pleasant. The noise of the machinery can be nerve-wracking, the dye from the fabric may be irritating to the eyes and the skin, and some factories are old and not well maintained.

Much of the work is done sitting down, in one location, and may include fine detail work that can be time consuming. The work may be tiring and tedious and occasionally can cause eye strain. In some cases, tailors and dressmakers deal directly with customers, who may be either pleasant to interact with, or difficult and demanding.

This type of work, however, can be very satisfying to people who enjoy using their hands and skills to create something. It can be gratifying to complete a project properly, and many workers in this field take great pride in their workmanship.

■ Outlook

According to the *Occupational Outlook Handbook,* employment prospects in this industry are expected to decline through the year 2006. Factors attributing to the decline include the low cost and ready availability of factory-made clothing and the invention of labor saving machinery such as computerized sewing and cutting machines. In fact, automated machines are expected to replace many sewing jobs in the next decade. The apparel industry has declined domestically as many businesses choose to produce their items abroad where labor is cheap and, many times, unregulated.

Tailors and dressmakers who do reliable and skillful work, particularly in the areas of mending and alterations, however, should be able to find employment. This industry is large, employing thousands of people. Many job openings will be created as current employees leave the work force due to retirement or other reasons.

■ For More Information

For information on careers in the apparel manufacturing industry, contact:

American Apparel Manufacturers Association
2500 Wilson Boulevard, Suite 301
Arlington, VA 22201
Tel: 703-524-1864
Web: http://www.americanapparel.org

For a listing of home study institutions offering sewing and dressmaking courses, contact:

Distance Education and Training Council
1601 18th Street, NW
Washington, DC 20009-2529
Tel: 202-234-5100
Web: http://www.detc.org

For information packets on college classes in garment design and sewing, contact the following schools:

Philadelphia College of Textiles and Science
School House Lane and Henry Avenue
Philadelphia, PA 19144
Tel: 215-951-2700
Web: http://www.philacol.edu

Parsons School of Design
66 Fifth Avenue
New York, NY 10011
Tel: 212-229-8910
Web: http://www.parsons.edu

Fashion Institute of Technology
7th Avenue at 27th Street
New York, NY 10001-5992
Tel: 212-217-7999
Web: http://www.fitnyc.suny.edu/

Fashion Institute of Design & Merchandising
919 South Grand Avenue
Los Angeles, CA 90015
Tel: 800-711-7175
Web: http://www.fidm.com

■ Related Articles

Fashion

Textiles

Apparel Industry Workers

Costume Designers

Fashion Designers

Textile Technicians

Talent Agents and Scouts

■ Overview

An agent is a salesperson who sells artistic talent. *Talent agents* act as the representatives for actors, directors, writers, and other people who work in film, television, and theater, promoting their talent and managing legal contractual business.

■ History

The wide variety of careers that exist in the film and television industries today evolved gradually. In the 19th century in England and America, leading actors and actresses developed a system, called the "actor-manager system," in which the actor both performed and handled business and financial arrangements. Over the course of the 20th century, responsibilities diversified. In the first decades of the century, major studios took charge of the actors' professional and financial management.

In the 1950s the major studio monopolies were broken, and control of actors and contracts came up for grabs.

Resourceful business-minded people became agents when they realized that there was money to be made by controlling access to the talent behind movie and television productions. They became middlemen between actors (and other creative people) and the production studios, charging commissions for use of their clients.

Currently, commissions range between 10 and 15 percent of the money an actor earns in a production. In more recent years, agents have formed revolutionary deals for their stars, making more money for agencies and actors alike. Powerful agencies such as Creative Artists Agency (CAA), International Creative Management (ICM), and The William Morris Agency are credited with (or, by some, accused of) heralding in the age of the multimillion dollar deal for film stars. This has proved controversial as some top actor fees have inflated to over $20 million per picture; some industry professionals worry that high actor salaries are cutting too deeply into film budgets, while others believe that actors are finally getting the fair share of the profits. Whichever the case, the film industry still thrives, and filmmakers still compete for the highest-priced talent. And the agent, always an active player in the industry, has become even more influential in how films are made.

■ The Job

As a talent agent, you'll act as the representative for actors, directors, writers, and/or others who work in film, television, and theater. You will look for clients who you believe to have potential for success and then work aggressively to promote the client to film and television directors and casting directors. You'll work carefully to shape your clients' careers rather than jump at every employment opportunity that presents itself. In addition, you will provide encouragement and support to actors and writers who are often between jobs.

You'll obtain a client in one of two ways. Either you'll scout out and bring the client to the agency, or you'll be assigned a client by the agency, based on experience or a compatible personality. The new client must sign a contract with the agency, which calls for you to represent the client in all areas for a specified time period. For example, if an actress wishes to find work in a film but is having difficulty, you may find her employment in commercials or voice roles. You'll work to develop a career, not just find as many parts as possible for the client; you may seek television roles for a young client who needs some exposure, and a movie role for another client who already has had television roles and is looking to round out her experience.

Talent agencies acquire movie scripts and "breakdowns," which are special versions of a script that break it down into the different acting parts available. Then the agents choose actors and actresses who would be appropriate for the roles

and begin their salesmanship. You'll spend a great deal of time calling directors and production companies to try to secure the best roles for your clients. You'll also work hard to get your hands on good scripts as early as possible in order to give your clients an advantage.

In addition to promoting individuals, agencies may also work to make package deals, combining a writer, director, and a star to make up a package, which then they market to production studios. The agency will charge a packaging commission to the customer in addition to the commissions agreed to in each package member's contract. A strong package can be very lucrative for the agency or agencies who represent the talent involved, since the package commission is often a percentage of the total budget of the production.

Agents may represent a variety of clients, or may specialize and represent one creative area. There are three basic types of agent: talent agents, who represent primarily actors and directors; *literary agents* who specialize in representing writers; and *packaging agents* who arrange packages. Within an agency there may be different levels of agents. *Senior agents* are the principle agents for clients; *covering agents* do not represent many clients of their own, but instead search for work opportunities for their agency's clients in general.

The film industry is dominated by three large agencies: Creative Artists Agency (CAA), International Creative Management (ICM), and The William Morris Agency. Because they are large and influential, they can offer good representation to talent; many of the most familiar movie stars working today are represented by these three agencies.

While these and many other agencies are located where the industry is most active, in Los Angeles and New York City, there are agencies in other cities as well that may offer prospective agents a different sort of work environment. And there are agencies that specialize in other areas: agencies for animators, composers, or comedians. Smaller agencies are known

TALENT AGENTS AND SCOUTS	
SCHOOL SUBJECTS	Business Theater/Dance
PERSONAL SKILLS	Communication/ideas Leadership/management
WORK ENVIRONMENT	Primarily indoors Primarily one location
MINIMUM EDUCATION LEVEL	Bachelor's degree
SALARY RANGE	$18,000 to $50,000 to $100,000+
CERTIFICATION OR LICENSING	None available
OUTLOOK	About as fast as the average
DOT	191
GOE	11.12.03
NOC	6411
O*NET	34056J

One of the most successful (and well-known) agents in the film industry is Michael Ovitz. Ovitz started as a tour guide at Universal Studios. He eventually got a job in the mail room of The William Morris Agency, where he worked himself up into an agent position. In 1975, Ovitz formed CAA with 4 partners. CAA came to great prominence in the 1980s, negotiating deals for not only film stars, but corporations such as Nike and Coca-Cola as well. Ovitz was hired as president of Walt Disney Co. in 1995, a position he lost in 14 months. Though many rumors suggested great failure in the following few years, he returned to the film industry by starting Artists Management Group (AMG) in 1998. AMG quickly rose in the industry, boasting a client list that included Robin Williams and Cameron Diaz.

as boutique agencies; many of these are owned by agents who formerly worked for the large agencies and decided to start their own businesses. Bigger is not necessarily better; small agencies have their share of well-known talent and may offer more individual attention to clients.

■ Requirements

High School

You should take courses in business, mathematics, and accounting to prepare for the management aspects of the job. Take English and speech courses to develop good communication skills—an agent must be gifted at negotiation. You'll also need a good eye for talent, so you should develop a sense of acting style and technique in theater and communication classes.

Postsecondary Training

There are no formal requirements for becoming an agent, but a bachelor's degree is strongly recommended. Advanced degrees in law and business are becoming increasingly prevalent; law and business training are useful because agents are responsible for writing contracts according to legal regulations. However, in some cases an agent may obtain this training on the job. Agents come from a variety of backgrounds; some of them have worked as actors and then shifted into agent careers because they enjoyed working in the industry. Agents who have degrees from law or business schools have an advantage when it comes to advancing their career or opening a new agency.

Other Requirements

It is most important to be willing to work hard and aggressively pursue opportunities for clients. You should be detail-oriented and have a good head for business; contract work requires meticulous attention to detail. You'll need a great deal of self-motivation and ambition—to be successful

you'll need to develop good contacts in an industry that is notoriously difficult to break into. If working in the film industry, you should have a sense of the industry's history, as well as current developments. You should be aware of what sorts of films, screenplays, and actors are in demand.

■ Exploring

You should first learn as much as you can about the industry by reading the publications agents read, such as *Daily Variety, The Hollywood Reporter, Premiere,* and *Entertainment Weekly.* Business magazines, such as *Fortune* and *Forbes,* will also give you insight into the film industry. You should also see all the current movies to get a sense of the established and up-and-coming talents in the film industry. If you live in Los Angeles or New York, you may be able to volunteer or intern at an agency to find out more about the career. Even to talk to an agent about volunteering your time with an unpaid internship could take a great deal of persistence—which could be a good introduction into the demands of the business. If you live outside Los Angeles and New York, check your phone book's Yellow Pages, or search the Web, for listings of local agencies. Most major cities have agents who represent local performing artists, actors, and models. If you contact them, they may be willing to offer you some insight into the nature of talent management in general. Experience with school theater projects can also help; since talent agents work with actors and directors, they often find it useful to have had some acting or directing experience themselves.

■ Employers

Talent agencies are located all across the United States, handling a variety of talents. Those agencies that represent artists and professionals in the film industry are located primarily in Los Angeles. Some film agencies, such as The William Morris Agency, are located in New York City. An agency may specialize in a particular type of talent, such as minority actors, extras, or TV commercial actors. The top three film agencies—CAA, ICM, and The William Morris Agency—employ approximately 1,500 agents.

■ Starting Out

The best way to enter this field is to seek an internship with an agency. If you live in or can spend a summer in Los Angeles or New York, you have an advantage in terms of numbers of opportunities. Libraries and bookstores will have resources for locating talent agencies. By searching the Web, you can find many free listings of reputable agents. The Screen Actors Guild (SAG) also maintains a list of franchised agents which is available on its Web site. The Yellow Pages will yield a list of local talent agencies; look under Theatrical Agencies. For those who live in Los Angeles, there are employment agencies that deal specifically with talent agent careers. Compile a list of agencies that may offer internship opportunities. Some internships will be paid, others may provide college course credit, but most importantly they will provide the student with experience and contacts in the industry. An intern who works hard and knows something about the business stands a good chance of securing an entry-level position at an agency. At the top agencies, this will be a coveted position in the mail room, where almost everyone starts. In smaller agencies, it may be an assistant position. Eventually persistence, hard work, and cultivated connections will lead to a job as an agent.

■ Advancement

Once you've got a job as an assistant, you'll be allowed to work closely with an agent to learn the ropes. You'll read scripts and contracts and listen in on phone calls and meetings. You'll also begin to take on some of your own clients as you gain experience. Agents who wish to advance must work aggressively on behalf of their clients, as well as seek out quality talent to bring into an agency. Those who are successful command more lucrative salaries and may choose to open their own agency. Some agents find that their work is a good stepping stone toward a different career in the industry. Working for a few years in a talent agency is excellent preparation for a career as a producer or studio executive.

■ Earnings

Earnings for agents vary greatly, depending upon the success of the agent and his or her clients. An agency will receive 10 to 15 percent of a client's fee for a project; an agent is then paid a commission by the agency, as well as a base salary. Assistants generally make low entry-level salaries of between $18,000 and $20,000 a year. In the first few years, an agent will make between $25,000 and $50,000 a year. However, those working for the top agencies can make much more. In 1999, *Forbes* magazine listed the top 40 money-making entertainers. Among the film stars listed were Harrison Ford, with an estimated film industry income of $58 million—a percentage of which his agency is entitled to.

Working for an agency, an experienced agent will receive health and retirement benefits, bonuses, and paid travel and accommodations.

■ Work Environment

Work in a talent agency can be lively and exciting. It is rewarding to watch a client attain success with your help. For those working in the film and TV industries, the work can seem very glamorous, allowing you to rub elbows with the rich and famous, and make contacts with the most powerful people in entertainment. Even if you're not representing the top talents, your work within the industry

LEARN MORE ABOUT IT

Here are some books offering insight into the movie business and the work of talent agencies:

McDougal, Dennis. *The Last Mogul: Lew Wasserman, MCA, and the Hidden History of Hollywood.* New York: Crown Publishing Group, 1998.

Resnik, Gail and Scott Trost. *All You Need to Know About the Movie and TV Business.* Fireside, 1996.

Taylor, Thom. *The Big Deal: Hollywood's Million-Dollar Spec Script Market.* New York: Quill, 1999.

will keep you informed about new film and TV projects. But the film industry is infamous for its complications, and for the lack of loyalty among professionals—work within the industry requires a great deal of stamina and determination in the face of setbacks. The work can be extremely stressful, even in small agencies—your clients rely upon you for work, and their futures depend on your deal-making. The work is more relaxing outside of the film industry—those booking performers and musicians for festivals, concerts, and other events typically deal with less intense schedules and budgets.

The work will demand much of your time, including evenings and weekends. To stay successful, agents at the top of the industry must constantly network. You'll spend a great deal of your time on the telephone, with both clients and others in the industry, and attending industry functions.

■ Outlook

The film industry is enjoying record box office receipts. With markets overseas expanding, even the films that don't do so well domestically can still turn a tidy profit. As a result, agents at all levels in the film industry will continue to thrive. Also, more original cable television programming will lead to more actors and performers seeking representation.

A major issue that agents will be dealing with in the early 21st century concerns the role of personal managers in handling talent. Only agents and lawyers are allowed to negotiate for clients and to solicit work, while managers advise their clients in their career choices. However, only managers are allowed to produce films, while agents have long been banned from owning any part of a client's work. The lines are blurring, and managers have become more active in their clients' film deals. (A few stars, like Leonardo DiCaprio, have managers but no agents.) Industry groups such as SAG and the Association of Talent Agents (a trade association representing talent agencies) will work to create more definite boundaries. In the meantime, look for managers to become more actively involved in linking clients with projects.

■ For More Information

Visit the SAG Web site for information about acting in films, and for a list of talent agencies:

Screen Actors Guild
5757 Wilshire Boulevard
Los Angeles, CA 90036-3600
Tel: 323-954-1600
Web: http://www.sag.com

Most NAPAMA members represent musicians, singers, and other live performers across the country; visit the Web site for insight into the career, and to read the newsletter:

National Association of Performing Arts Managers and Agents
459 Columbus Avenue, Suite 133
New York, NY 10024
Tel: 212-799-5308
Email: bcolton@napama.org
Web: http://www.napama.org

■ Related Articles

Film
Television
Visual Arts
Actors
Comedians
Producers
Screenwriters
Singers
Writers

Taproom Attendants

■ **See Bartenders**

Tax or Name Searchers

■ **See Title Searchers and Examiners**

Tax Preparers

■ Overview

Tax preparers prepare income tax returns for individuals and small businesses for a fee, either for quarterly or yearly filings. They help to establish and maintain business records to expedite tax preparations and may advise clients on how to save money on their tax payments.

■ History

President Franklin D. Roosevelt (1882-1945) once said, "Taxes are the dues that we pay for the privileges of membership in an organized society." Although most people grumble about paying income taxes and filling out tax forms, everyone carries a share of the burden, and it is still possible to keep a sense of humor about income taxes. As Benjamin Franklin (1706-90) succinctly said, "In this world nothing can be said to be certain, except death and taxes."

While the personal income tax may be the most familiar type of taxation, it is actually a relatively recent method for raising revenue. To raise funds for the Napoleonic Wars between 1799 and 1816, Britain became the first nation to collect income taxes, but a permanent income tax was not established there until 1874. In the same manner, the United States first initiated a temporary income tax during the Civil War. It wasn't until 1913, however, with the adoption of the 16th Amendment to the Constitution, that a tax on personal income became the law of the nation. In addition to the federal income tax, many states and cities have adopted income tax laws. Income taxes are an example of a "progressive tax," one that charges higher percentages of income as people earn more money.

Technology has recently made it possible to file taxes electronically. Electronic tax filing is a method by which a tax return is converted to computer readable form and sent via modem to the Internal Revenue Service. Electronically filed tax returns are more accurate than paper filed returns because of the extensive checking performed by the electronic filing software. Detecting and correcting errors early also allows the tax return to flow smoothly through the IRS, speeding up the refund process. New computer software is also available which gives individuals a framework in which to prepare and file their own taxes.

■ The Job

Tax preparers help individuals and small businesses keep the proper records to determine their legally required tax and file the proper forms. They must be well acquainted with federal, state, and local tax laws, and use their knowledge and skills to help taxpayers take the maximum number of legally allowable deductions.

The first step in preparing tax forms is to collect all the data and documents that are needed to calculate the client's tax liability. The client has to submit documents such as tax returns from previous years, wage and income statements, records of other sources of income, statements of interest and dividends earned, records of expenses, property tax records, and so on. The tax preparer then interviews the client to obtain further information that may have a bearing on the amount of taxes owed. If the client is an individual taxpayer, the tax preparer will ask about any important investments, extra expenses that may be deductible, contributions to charity, and insurance payments; events such as marriage, childbirth, and new employment are also important considerations. If the client is a business, the tax preparer may ask about capital gains and losses, taxes already paid, payroll expenses, miscellaneous business expenses, and tax credits.

Once the tax preparer has a complete picture of the client's income and expenses, the proper tax forms and schedules needed to file the tax return can be determined. While some taxpayers have very complex finances that take a long time to document and calculate, others have typical, straightforward returns that take less time. Often the tax preparer can calculate the amount a taxpayer owes, fill out the proper forms, and prepare the complete return in a single interview. When the tax return is more complicated, the tax preparer may have to collect all the data during the interview and perform the calculations later. If a client's taxes are unusual or very complex, the tax preparer may have to consult tax law handbooks and bulletins.

Computers are the main tools used to figure and prepare tax returns. The tax preparer inputs the data onto a spreadsheet, and the computer calculates and prints out the tax form. Computer software can be very versatile and may even print up data summary sheets that can serve as checklists and references for the next tax filing.

Tax preparers often have another tax expert or preparer check their work, especially if they work for a tax service firm. The second tax preparer will check to make sure the allowances and deductions taken were proper and that no others were overlooked. They also make certain that the tax laws are interpreted properly and that calculations are correct. It is very important that a tax preparer's work is accurate and error-free, and clients are given a guarantee covering additional taxes or fines if their work is found to be incorrect. Tax preparers are required by law to sign every return they complete for a client, along with providing their Social Security number or federal identification number. They must also provide the client with a copy of the tax return and keep a copy in their own files.

■ Requirements

There are no specific educational requirements for tax preparers, though a high school diploma is a necessity as is a thorough knowledge of tax laws. Proficiency in mathematics and computer applications is also a must.

High School

High school students interested in tax work should take courses in business, accounting, mathematics, communications, and computer software.

Postsecondary Training

For those students pursuing a college education, many universities offer individual courses and complete majors in the area of taxation. Students can elect to earn a bachelor's degree or a master's degree in business administration while earning a minor in taxation. Some universities offer master's degrees in taxation.

In addition to formal education, tax preparers must continue their professional education. Both federal and state tax laws are revised every year, and the tax preparer is obligated to understand these new laws thoroughly by January 1 of each year. Major tax reform legislation can increase this amount of study even further. One federal reform tax bill can take up thousands of pages, and this can mean up to 60 hours of extra study in a single month to fully understand all the intricacies and implications of the new laws. To help tax preparers keep up with new developments, the National Association of Tax Practitioners offers about 130 continuing education classes every year. Tax service firms also offer classes explaining tax preparation to both professionals and individual taxpayers.

Certification or Licensing

There are only a few licensing requirements for tax preparers in the United States. Since 1983, tax preparers in California have been required to register with the state Department of Consumers. Tax preparers who apply for registration in that state must be at least eighteen years old and have a high school diploma or the equivalent. In

TAX PREPARERS	
SCHOOL SUBJECTS	Business Mathematics
PERSONAL SKILLS	Helping/teaching
WORK ENVIRONMENT	Primarily indoors Primarily one location
MINIMUM EDUCATION LEVEL	High school diploma
SALARY RANGE	Minimum wage plus commission to $30 to $1,500 per tax return
CERTIFICATION OR LICENSING	Voluntary
OUTLOOK	Little change or more slowly than the average
DOT	219
GOE	07.02.02
NOC	1431

A tax preparer discusses deductions with his client.

addition, they need to have 60 hours of formal, approved instruction in basic income tax law, theory, and practice, or two years of professional experience in preparing personal income tax returns.

The Internal Revenue Service offers an examination for tax preparers. Those who complete the test successfully are called *enrolled agents* and are entitled to legally represent any taxpayer in any type of audit before the IRS or state tax boards. (Those with five years' experience working for the IRS as an auditor or in a higher position can become enrolled agents without taking the exam.) The four-part test is offered annually and takes two days to complete. There are no education or experience requirements for taking the examination, but the questions are roughly equivalent to those asked in a college course. Study materials and applications may be obtained from local IRS offices. The IRS does not oversee seasonal tax preparers, but local IRS offices may monitor some commercial tax offices.

To be eligible to process returns and transmit them directly to the Internal Revenue Service via modem, tax preparers must apply to the IRS to become an Electronic Return Originator (ERO). A background check and fingerprinting may be required.

The Institute of Tax Consultants offers an annual open book exam to obtain the title of Certified Tax Preparer. Certification also requires 30 hours of continuing education each year.

Other Requirements

Tax preparers should have an aptitude for math and an eye for detail. They should have strong organizational skills and the patience to sift through documents and financial statements. The ability to communicate effectively with clients is also key to be able to explain complex tax pro-

cedures and to make customers feel confident and comfortable. Tax preparers also need to work well under the stress and pressure of deadlines. They must also be honest, discreet, and trustworthy in dealing with the financial and business affairs of their clients.

■ Exploring

If a career in tax preparation sounds interesting, you should first gain some experience by completing income tax returns for yourself and for your family and friends. These returns should be double-checked by the actual taxpayers who will be liable for any fees and extra taxes if the return is prepared incorrectly. You can also look for internships or part-time jobs in tax service offices and tax preparation firms. Many of these firms operate nationwide, and extra office help might be needed as tax deadlines approach and work becomes hectic. The IRS also trains people to answer tax questions for its 800-number telephone advisory service; they are employed annually during early spring.

Try also to familiarize yourself with the tax preparation software available on the Internet and utilize Web sites to keep abreast of changing laws, regulations, and developments in the industry. The National Association of Tax Practitioners offers sample articles from its publication, *Tax Practitioners Journal,* online. (See the "For More Information" section for contact information.)

■ Employers

Tax preparers may work for tax service firms, such as H & R Block and other similar companies that conduct most of their business during tax season. Other tax preparers may be self-employed and work full or part time.

■ Starting Out

Because tax work is very seasonal, most tax firms begin hiring tax preparers in December for the upcoming tax season. Some tax service firms will hire tax preparers from among the graduates of their own training courses. Private and state employment agencies may also have information and job listings as will classified newspaper ads. Students should also consult their guidance offices to establish contacts in the field.

There are a large number of Internet sites for this industry, many of which offer job postings. Many large tax preparation firms, such as H & R Block also have their own Web pages.

■ Advancement

Some tax preparers may wish to continue their academic education and work toward becoming certified public accountants. Others may want to specialize in certain areas of taxation, such as real estate, corporate, or nonprofit work. Tax preparers who specialize in certain fields are able to charge higher fees for their services.

Establishing a private consulting business is also an option. Potential proprietors should consult with other self-employed practitioners to gain advice on how to start a private practice. Several Internet sites also give valuable advice on establishing a tax business.

■ Earnings

Tax preparers generally charge a fee per tax return, which may range from $30 to $1,500 or more, depending on the complexity of the return and the preparation time required. Seasonal or part-time employees usually earn minimum wage plus commission. Enrolled agents, certified public accountants and other professional preparers usually charge more. Fees vary widely in different parts of the country, however. Tax preparers in large cities and in the western United States generally charge more, as do those who offer year-round financial advice and services. Another factor in setting fees is the amount of time spent studying new tax laws and keeping up with new developments.

■ Work Environment

Tax preparers generally work in office settings which may be located in neighborhood business districts, shopping malls, or other high traffic areas. Employees of tax service firms may work at storefront desks or in cubicles during the three months preceding the April 15 tax-filing deadline. In addition, many tax preparers work at home to earn extra money while they hold a full-time job.

The hours and schedules that tax preparers work vary greatly, depending on the time of year and the manner in which they are employed. Because of the changes in tax laws that occur every year, tax preparers often advise their clients throughout the year about possible ways to reduce their tax obligations. The first quarter of the year is the busiest time, and even part-time tax preparers may find themselves working very long hours. Workweeks can range from as little as 12 hours to 40 or 50 or more, as tax preparers work late into the evening and on weekends. Tax service firms are usually open seven days a week and 12 hours a day during the first three months of the year. The work is demanding, requiring heavy concentration and long hours sitting at a desk and working on a computer.

■ Outlook

According to the IRS, 53 percent of U.S. taxpayers prepare their own returns, but because tax laws are constantly changing and growing more complex, demand for tax professionals will remain high. This demand, however, is expected to be met by the tax preparers already working because computers are increasingly expediting the process of tabulating and storing data. Recent surveys of employers in large metropolitan areas have found an adequate supply of tax preparers; prospects for employment may be better in smaller cities or rural areas.

Although tax laws are constantly evolving and people look to tax preparers to save time, money, and frustration, new tax programs and online resources are easing the process of preparing taxes, lessening the need for outside help. Information is available at the touch of a button on tax laws and regulations. Tax tips are readily available as are online seminars and workshops.

The IRS currently offers taxpayers and businesses the option to "e-file," or electronically file their tax returns on the Internet. While some people may choose to do their own electronic filing, the majority of taxpayers will still rely on tax preparers—licensed by the IRS as Electronic Return Originators—to handle their returns.

■ For More Information

For information on the Certified Tax Preparer designation, contact:

Institute of Tax Consultants
7500 212th SW, No. 205
Edmonds, WA 98026

For industry information, contact:

National Association of Tax Consultants
3829 SE 74th Street
Portland, OR 97206
Tel: 800-745-6282

For information on educational programs and online membership, contact:

National Association of Tax Practitioners
720 Association Drive
Appleton, WI 54914-1483
Tel: 800-558-3402
Web: http://www.natptax.com/

Check out the IRS Web site for information on becoming an enrolled agent or an Electronic Return Originator.

Internal Revenue Service
Department of Treasury
Web: http://www.irs.ustreas.gov/prod/cover.html

■ Related Articles

Accounting

Banking and Financial Services

Accountants and Auditors

Bookkeeping and Accounting Clerks

Financial Planners

Retirement Planners

Title Searchers and Examiners

Taxi Drivers

■ Overview

Taxi drivers, also known as *cab drivers,* operate automobiles to take passengers from one place to another for a fee. This fee is usually based on distance traveled or time as recorded on a taximeter. There are currently over 100,000 taxi drivers in the United States. As the population increases and traffic becomes more congested, the need for taxi drivers will increase, especially in metropolitan areas.

■ History

Today's taxis are the modern equivalent of vehicles for hire that were first introduced in England in the early 1600s. These vehicles were hackneys, four-wheeled carriages drawn by two horses that could carry up to six passengers. By 1654, there were already 300 privately owned hackneys licensed to operate in London. In the next century, hackneys were introduced in the United States. Around 1820, a smaller vehicle for hire, the cabriolet, became common in London. At first it had two wheels, with room only for a driver and one passenger, and one horse drew it. Some later cabriolets, or cabs, as they were soon called, were larger, and by mid-century, a two-passenger version, the hansom cab, became the most popular cab in London. Hansom cabs were successfully brought to New York and Boston in the 1870s.

Toward the end of the 19th century, motorized cabs began to appear in the streets of Europe and America. From then on, the development of cabs paralleled the development of the automobile. The earliest motorized cabs were powered by electricity, but cabs with internal combustion engines appeared by the early 20th century. Along with the introduction of these vehicles came the need for drivers, thus creating the cab driver profession. In 1891, a device called a "taximeter" (tax is from a Latin word meaning "charge") was invented to calculate the fare owed to the driver.

TAXI DRIVERS	
SCHOOL SUBJECTS	Business Mathematics
PERSONAL SKILLS	Following instructions Helping/teaching
WORK ENVIRONMENT	Primarily indoors Primarily multiple locations
MINIMUM EDUCATION LEVEL	High school diploma
SALARY RANGE	$10,000 to $20,500 to $45,000
CERTIFICATION OR LICENSING	Required by all states
OUTLOOK	Faster than the average
DOT	913
GOE	09.03.02
O*NET	97114

Taximeters found their first use in the new horseless carriages for hire, which were soon called "taxicabs" or just "taxis."

The use of taxis has increased especially in metropolitan areas where there is dense traffic, increasing population, and parking limitations. Modern taxis are often four-door passenger cars that have been specially modified. Depending on local regulations, the vehicles may have such modifications as reinforced frames or extra heavy-duty shock absorbers. Taxi drivers may be employees of taxi companies, driving cars owned by the company; they may be lease drivers, operating cars leased from a taxi company for a regular fee; or they may be completely independent, driving cars that they own themselves.

■ The Job

Taxicabs are an important part of the mass transportation system in many cities, so drivers need to be familiar with as much of the local geographical area as possible. But taxicab drivers are often required to do more than simply drive people from one place to another. They also help people with their luggage. Sometimes they pick up and deliver packages. Some provide sightseeing tours for visitors to a community.

Taxi drivers who are employed by, or lease from, a cab service or garage report to the garage before their shift begins and are assigned a cab. They receive a tripsheet and record their name, date of work, and identification number. They also perform a quick cursory check of the interior and exterior of the car to ensure its proper working condition. They check fuel and oil levels, brakes, lights, and windshield wipers, reporting any problems to the dispatcher or company mechanic.

Taxi drivers locate passengers in three ways. Customers requiring transportation may call the cab company with the approximate time and place they wish to be picked up. The dispatcher uses a two-way radio system to notify the driver of this pick-up information. Other drivers pick up passengers at cab stands and taxi lines at airports, theaters, hotels, and railroad stations, and then return to the stand after they deliver the passengers. Drivers may pick up passengers while returning to their stands or stations. The third manner of pick up for taxi drivers is by cruising busy streets to service passengers who hail or "wave them down."

When a destination is reached, the taxi driver determines the fare and informs the rider of the cost. Fares consist of many parts. The drop charge is an automatic charge for use of the cab. Other parts of the fare are determined by the time and distance traveled. A taximeter is a machine that measures the fare as it accrues. It is turned on and off when the passenger enters and leaves the cab. Additional portions of the fare may include charges for luggage handling and additional occupants. Commonly, a passenger will offer the taxi driver a tip, which is based on the customer's opinion of the quality and efficiency of the ride and the courtesy of the driver. The taxi driver also may supply a receipt if the passenger requests it.

Taxi drivers are generally required to keep accurate records of their activities. They record the time and place where they picked up and delivered the passengers on a trip sheet. They also have to keep records on the amount of fares they collect.

There are taxis and taxi drivers in almost every town and city in the country, but most are in large metropolitan areas.

■ Requirements

High School

Taxi drivers do not usually need to meet any particular educational requirements, but a high school education is desirable so that drivers can adequately handle the record-keeping part of their job. High school courses in driver education, business math, and English would also prove helpful to taxi drivers.

Certification or Licensing

In large cities, some taxi drivers belong to labor unions. The union to which most belong is the International Brotherhood of Teamsters, Chauffeurs, Warehousemen, and Helpers of America.

Those interested in becoming a taxi driver must have a regular driver's license. In most large cities, taxi drivers also must have a special taxicab operator's license—commonly called a hacker's license—in addition to a chauffeur's license. Police departments, safety departments, or public utilities commissions generally issue these special licenses. To secure the license, drivers must pass special examinations including questions on local geography, traffic regulations, accident reports, safe driving practices, and insurance regulations. Some companies help their job applicants prepare for these examinations by providing them with specially prepared booklets. The operator's license may need to be renewed annually. In some cities (New York, for example), new license applications can take several months to be processed because the applicant's background must be investigated. Increasingly, many cities and municipalities require a test on English usage. Those who do not pass must take a course in English sponsored by the municipality.

Other Requirements

People who want to be taxi drivers should be in reasonably good health and have a good driving record and no criminal record. In general, they need to be 21 years of age or older. While driving is not physically strenuous, sometimes drivers must lift heavy packages or luggage. In many places, drivers must have especially steady nerves because they spend considerable time driving in heavy traffic. They must also be courteous, patient, and able to get along with many different kinds of people.

Taxi drivers who own their own cab or lease one for a long period of time are generally expected to keep their cab clean. Large companies have workers who take care of this task for all the vehicles in the company fleet.

■ Employers

Taxi drivers are often employed by a cab service and drive cars owned by the company. Some drivers pay a fee and lease cabs owned by a taxi company while others own and operate their own cars.

■ Starting Out

Usually people who want to be a taxi driver apply directly to taxicab companies that may be hiring new drivers. Taxicab companies are usually listed in the Yellow Pages. It may take some time to obtain the necessary license to drive a cab, and some companies or municipalities may require additional training, so it may not be possible to begin work immediately. People who have sufficient funds may buy their own cab, but they usually must secure a municipal permit to operate it.

■ Earnings

Earnings for taxi drivers vary widely, depending on the number of hours they work, the method by which they are paid, the season, the weather, and other factors. In 1996, the median earnings for full-time taxi drivers was $20,124. The lowest 10 percent of full-time taxi drivers earned $9,984 annually, while the highest 10 percent averaged $44,200 a year.

Limited information suggests that independent owner-drivers can average anywhere between $20,000 to $30,000 annually, including tips. This assumes they work the industry average of eight to ten hours a day, five days a week.

Many taxi drivers are paid a percentage of the fares they collect, often 40 to 50 percent of total fares. Other drivers receive a base amount plus a commission related to the amount of business they do. A few drivers are guaranteed minimum daily or weekly wages. Drivers who lease their cabs may keep all the fare money above the amount of the leasing fee they pay the cab company. Tips are also an important part of the earnings of taxi drivers. They can equal 15 to 20 percent or more of total fares. Most taxi drivers do not enjoy company-provided fringe benefits, such as pension plans.

Earnings fluctuate with the season and the weather. Winter is generally the busiest season, and snow and rain almost always produce a busy day. There is also a relationship between general economic conditions and the earnings of taxi drivers, because there is more competition for less business when the economy is in a slump.

■ Work Environment

Many taxi drivers put in long hours, working up to nine or ten hours a day, five or six days a week. They do not receive overtime pay. Other drivers are part-time workers. Drivers may work Sundays, holidays, or evening hours.

Taxi drivers must be able to get along with their passengers, including those who try their patience or expect too much. Some people urge drivers to go very fast, for example, but drivers who comply may risk accidents or arrest for speeding. Drivers may have to work under other difficult conditions, such as heavy traffic and bad weather. Taxi drivers must be able to drive safely under pressure. In some places, drivers must be wary because there is a considerable chance of being robbed.

■ Outlook

There will always be a need for taxi drivers. Job opportunities for taxi drivers are expected to grow faster than the average through 2006. The high turnover rate in this occupation means that many of the new job openings that develop in the future will come when drivers leave their jobs to go into another kind of work. In addition, as the American population grows, the overall demand for taxi drivers will probably increase too; thus the total employment in this field will rise. At present many drivers work on a part-time basis, and that situation is likely to continue.

■ For More Information

The following association can provide additional information regarding the taxi driving profession.

International Taxicab and Livery Association
3849 Farragut Avenue
Kensington, MD 20895
Tel: 301-946-5701

■ Related Articles

Business, Personal, and Consulting Services
Transportation
Public Transportation Operators
Route Drivers
Truck Drivers

Taxidermists

■ Overview

Taxidermists preserve and prepare animal skins and parts to create lifelike animal replicas. The animals they mount or stuff may be for private or public display. Museums frequently use creations from taxidermists to display rare, exotic, or extinct animals. Hunters also use taxidermists' services to mount fishing and hunting trophies for display. The National Taxidermists Association estimates there are about 75,000 taxidermists in the United States working full or part time.

■ History

Animal tanning and skin preservation has been practiced over the millennia for clothing, decoration, and weapons. Native Americans used tanned hides to make their lodgings. Trophies from hunts of dangerous animals were often worn to display the bravery of the hunter. Tanning methods included stringing skins up to dry, scraping them, and perhaps soaking them in water with tannins from leaves. Animal skins were preserved for many different purposes, but not specifically from interest in the natural sciences until the 18th century. Tanning methods improved during this time. Displaying the skin on models stuffed with hay or straw became popular for museums and private collections. Animals were posed realistically and backgrounds were added to the display areas in museums to show the habitat of the animal.

By the 19th century, taxidermy was a recognized discipline for museum workers. In Paris, Maison Verreaux became the chief supplier of exhibit animals. Carl Akeley, who worked for Ward's Natural Science Establishment in New York, mastered a taxidermic technique that allowed for realistic modeling of large animals such as bears, lions, and elephants. His works are still on display in the Chicago Field Museum of Natural History and the New York Natural History Museum. In recent years, several taxidermy supply companies have developed lifelike mannequins to be used as the foundation for fish, birds, and fur-bearing animals. Such new techniques in the art and science of taxidermy continue to be developed and used.

■ The Job

Taxidermists use a variety of methods to create realistic, lifelike models of birds and animals. Although specific processes and techniques vary, most taxidermists follow a series of basic steps.

First, they must remove the skin from the carcass of the animal with special knives, scissors, and pliers. The skin must be removed very carefully to preserve the natural state of the fur or feathers. Once the skin is removed, it is preserved with a special solution.

Some taxidermists still make the body foundation, or skeleton, of the animal. These foundations are made with a variety of materials, including clay, plaster, burlap, papier-mâché, wire mesh, and glue. Other taxidermists, however, use ready-made forms, which are available in various sizes so taxidermists simply take measurements of the specimen to be mounted and order the proper size from the supplier. Metal rods are often used to achieve the desired mount of the animal.

The taxidermist uses special adhesives or modeling clay to attach the skin to the foundation or form. Then artificial eyes, teeth, and tongues are attached. Sometimes taxidermists use special techniques, such as airbrushing color or sculpting the eyelids, nose, and lips. They may need to attach antlers, horns, or claws. Finally they groom and dress the fur or feathers with styling gel, if necessary, to enhance the final appearance of the specimen.

Taxidermists work with a variety of animal types, including one-cell organisms, large game animals, birds, fish, and reptiles. They even make models of extinct animal species, based on detailed drawings or paintings. The specific work often depends on the area of the country where the taxidermist is employed, since the types of animals hunted vary by region.

■ Requirements

High School
Successful taxidermy requires many skills. Workers must have good manual dexterity, an eye for detail, knowledge of animal anatomy, and training in the taxidermy processes. High school classes in art, woodworking, and metal shop may help develop the skills necessary for this career. Also, a class or classes in biology might be helpful in teaching the student the bodily workings of certain animals.

Postsecondary Training
In the United States several schools offer programs or correspondence courses in taxidermy. Courses often last from four to six weeks, and subjects such as laws and legalities, bird mounting, fish mounting, deer, small mammals, diorama-making, air and brush painting, and form-making are covered. Taxidermists who hope to work in museums should expect to take further training and acquire additional skills in related subjects, which they can learn in museum classes.

Certification or Licensing
Taxidermists are required to be licensed in most states, with specific licensing requirements varying from state to state. Many taxidermists choose to become members of

national or local professional associations. The largest of these, the National Taxidermists Association (NTA), offers the designation of Certified Taxidermist to members who have met specific requirements. Members may be certified in one or all four categories of specialization—mammals, fish, birds, and reptiles. Certification indicates that they have reached a certain level of expertise and may allow them to charge a higher price for their work.

■ Exploring

Because taxidermy is a specialized occupation, there are few opportunities for part-time or summer work for students, though some larger companies will hire apprentices to help with the work load. However, you may learn more by ordering video tapes and beginning mounting kits to experience the mounting process. Other good learning opportunities include speaking to a museum taxidermist or writing to schools or associations that offer courses in taxidermy. Check with the NTA for upcoming conventions and seminars which are open to the public. Time spent at such an event would not only provide a solid learning experience, but a chance to meet and mingle with the pros.

■ Employers

Taxidermists can be found throughout the United States and abroad. Experienced and established taxidermists, especially those with a large client base, will often hire apprentices, or less experienced taxidermists, to assist with larger projects or undertake smaller jobs. Contact the NTA for a listing of such employers.

The majority of taxidermists, about 70 to 80 percent, are self-employed, according to Greg Crain, executive director of the NTA. His advice to aspiring entrepreneurs? Hone your skills in business, as well as your craft. Accounting, advertising, and marketing are good background courses to help any small business owner. Be prepared to attend to the

TAXIDERMISTS	
SCHOOL SUBJECTS	Art Biology Technical/Shop
PERSONAL SKILLS	Artistic Mechanical/manipulative
WORK ENVIRONMENT	Primarily indoors Primarily one location
MINIMUM EDUCATION LEVEL	Some postsecondary training
SALARY RANGE	$15,000 to $30,000 to $50,000+
CERTIFICATION OR LICENSING	Required
OUTLOOK	Faster than the average
DOT	199
GOE	01.06.02
NOC	5212
O*NET	39999E

A taxidermist adds the finishing touches to a fish replica.

many details of running a business such as maintaining an inventory of chemicals and supplies, advertising and promotion, and pricing your work.

▪ Starting Out

Taxidermy is a profession that requires experience. Most workers start out as hobbyists in their own homes, and eventually start doing taxidermy work part time professionally. Later, after they have built up a client base, they may enter the profession full time. Jobs in existing taxidermy shops or businesses are difficult to find, because most taxidermists are self-employed and prefer to do the work themselves. However, in some cases, it may be possible to become a journeyman or apprentice and work for an already established taxidermist on either an hourly basis or for a percentage of the selling price of the work they are doing.

Jobs in museums are often difficult to obtain: applicants should have a background in both taxidermy and general museum studies. Taxidermy schools primarily train their students to become self-employed but may sometimes offer job placement as well.

▪ Advancement

Advancement opportunities are good for those with the proper skills, education, and experience. Taxidermists who can work on a wide range of projects will have the best chances of advancing. Since larger game animals bring more money, one method of advancing would be to learn the skills necessary to work on these animals. Taxidermists who develop a large customer base may open their own shop. Workers employed in museums may advance to positions with more responsibilities and higher pay.

▪ Earnings

It is very difficult, if not impossible, to determine a nationwide earnings figure for taxidermists. The individual's level of experience, certification, speed, and quality of work are all factors that significantly affect income. Most taxidermists will charge by the inch or the weight of the animal. Difficult mounts, or unusual background accessories may add significantly to the final price. Here's an example: an open mouth on an animal, as opposed to a droopy mouth, or a closed mouth, can add about $100 to the price of a mounting. In addition, the region of the country and the type of game typically hunted and mounted are important variables. Most new taxidermists, however, might expect to earn about $15,000 annually. Those with 5 to 10 years of experience and a proven level of quality could earn $30,000 or more. Some exceptional taxidermists can earn upwards of $50,000 annually. Museum workers might also expect to average $20,000 yearly.

Because most are self-employed, or work for a very small operation, few taxidermists have any sort of benefits package. Those who work in museums may, however, be offered health insurance and paid vacation and sick leave.

▪ Work Environment

Most taxidermists work 40 hours a week, although overtime is not uncommon during certain times of the year. Taxidermists with their own shops may have to work long hours, especially when first starting out. They must often work with strong-smelling chemicals and sharp tools, and possibly diseased animals. If working on smaller animals and birds, they can sit or stand. However, creating larger mammal displays may require more physical work, such as climbing or squatting.

Workers in taxidermy will find it satisfying to see a project from beginning to completion. There is also the element of pride in good craftsmanship; it can be gratifying for workers to use their talents to recreate extremely realistic and lifelike animal forms.

▪ Outlook

The job outlook for taxidermists should be good over the next decade. Although jobs in museums may be scarce, the demand for hunting and fishing trophies continues to provide work for taxidermists. It is not unusual for qualified taxidermists to have a year's worth of work backlogged. In addition, many educational institutions actively seek models of animal and bird species that are nearing extinction. Talented taxidermists who can take on a variety of projects should be able to find steady employment. Those with an eye for unique poses and mounts, or unusual expressions will be in high demand.

■ For More Information

For information on the industry, certification, taxidermy schools, trade magazines, association membership, and career opportunities, contact:

National Taxidermists Association
108 Branch Drive
Slidell, LA 70461
Tel: 504-641-4682
Email: ntahq@aol.com
Web: http://www.taxidermy.net

The following schools offer training in taxidermy:

Rinehart School of Taxidermy
3032 McCormick Drive
Janesville, WI 53546
Tel: 608-755-5160
Web: http://www.taxidermyonline.com/school.html

Southland School of Taxidermy
2603 Osceola Street
Baton Rouge, LA 70805
Tel: 504-356-2903
Web: http://www.taxidermyschool.com/

Missoula Valley School of Taxidermy
PO Box 1169
Thompson Falls, MT 59873
Tel: 406-827-3170
Web: http://www.nwmontana.com/mvst.htm

Piedmont Community College
PO Box 1197
Roxboro, NC 27573
Tel: 910-599-1181, ext. 230
Web: http://bbs.roxboro.net/pcc/gen info/INDEX.HTM

■ Related Articles

Museums and Cultural Centers
Visual Arts
Leather Tanning and Finishing Workers
Museum Technicians
Painters and Sculptors

Teacher Aides

■ Overview

Teacher aides perform a wide variety of duties to help teachers run a classroom. Teacher aides prepare instructional materials, help students with classroom work, and supervise students in the library, on the playground, and at lunch. They perform administrative duties such as photocopying, keeping attendance records, and grading papers.

■ History

As formal education became more widely available in the 20th century, teachers' jobs became more complex. The size of classes increased, and a growing educational bureaucracy demanded that more records be kept of students'

achievements and classroom activities. Advancements in technology, changes in educational theory, and a great increase in the amount and variety of teaching materials available all contributed to the time required to prepare materials and assess student progress, leaving teachers less time for the teaching for which they had been trained.

To remedy this problem, teacher aides began to be employed to take care of the more routine aspects of running an instructional program. Today, many schools and school districts employ teacher aides, to the great benefit of hardworking teachers and students.

■ The Job

Teacher aides work in public, private, and parochial preschools and elementary and secondary schools. Your duties as a teacher aide will vary depending on the classroom teacher, school, and school district. Some teacher aides specialize in one subject and some work in a specific type of school setting. These settings include bilingual classrooms, gifted and talented programs, classes for learning disabled students and those with unique physical needs, and multiage classrooms. They conduct the same type of classroom work as other teacher aides, but may provide more individual assistance to students.

Fran Moker works as a teacher aide in a dropout prevention unit of a middle school. Her work involves enrolling students in the unit and explaining the program to parents. She maintains files on the students and attends to other administrative duties. "I work directly with the sixth, seventh, and eighth grade teachers," Moker says, "making all the copies, setting up conferences, and grading papers. I also cover their classes when necessary for short periods of time to give the teachers a break." She also works directly with students, tutoring and advising. "I listen to students when they have problems," she says. "We work with at-risk students, so it's necessary to be supportive. Many of our students come from broken

TEACHER AIDES	
SCHOOL SUBJECTS	Art English
PERSONAL SKILLS	Helping/teaching Leadership/management
WORK ENVIRONMENT	Primarily indoors Primarily one location
MINIMUM EDUCATION LEVEL	High school diploma
SALARY RANGE	$11,000 to $13,000 to $16,000
CERTIFICATION OR LICENSING	None available
OUTLOOK	Much faster than the average
DOT	099
GOE	11.02.01
NOC	4216
O*NET	31521

A teacher's aide works one-on-one with a student to help her improve her prereading skills.

homes and have parents with serious drug and alcohol problems. Consistent caring is a must."

No matter what kind of classroom you assist in, you'll likely be copying, compiling, and handing out class materials, setting up and operating audiovisual equipment, arranging field trips, and typing or word processing materials. You'll organize classroom files, including grade reports and attendance and health records. You may also obtain library materials and order classroom supplies.

You'll be in charge of keeping order in classrooms, school cafeterias, libraries, hallways, and playgrounds. Often, you'll wait with preschool and elementary students coming to or leaving school and make sure all students are accounted for. When a class leaves its room for such subjects as art, music, physical education, or computer lab, you may go with the students to help the teachers of these other subjects.

Another responsibility of teacher aides is correcting and grading homework and tests, usually for objective assignments and tests that require specific answers. You'll use answer sheets to mark students' papers and examinations and keep records of students' scores. In some large schools, an aide may be called a *grading clerk* and be responsible only for scoring objective tests and computing and recording test scores. Often using an electronic grading machine or computer, the grading clerk totals errors found and computes the percentage of questions answered correctly. The worker then records this score and averages students' test scores to determine their grade for the course.

Under the teacher's supervision, you may work directly with students in the classroom. You'll listen to a group of young students read aloud or involve the class in a special project such as a science fair, art project, or drama production. With older students, you'll provide review or study sessions prior to exams or give extra help with research projects or homework. Some teacher aides work with individual students in a tutorial setting, helping in areas of special need or concern. You may work with the teacher to prepare lesson plans, bibliographies, charts, or maps. You may help to decorate the classroom, design bulletin boards and displays, and arrange workstations. You may even participate in parent-teacher conferences to discuss students' progress.

■ Requirements

High School

Courses in English, history, social studies, mathematics, art, drama, physical education and the sciences will provide you with a broad base of knowledge. This knowledge will enable you to help students learn in these same subjects. Knowledge of a second language can be an asset, especially when working in schools with bilingual student, parent, or staff populations. Courses in child care, home economics, and psychology are also valuable for this career. You should try to gain some experience working with computers, as students at many elementary schools and even preschools now do a large amount of computer work, and computer skills are important in performing clerical duties.

Postsecondary Training

Postsecondary requirements for teacher aides depend on the school or school district and the kinds of responsibilities the aides have. In districts where aides perform mostly clerical duties, applicants may need only to have a high school diploma or the equivalent, Graduation Equivalency Degree (GED). Those who work in the classroom may be required to take some college courses and attend in-service training and special teacher conferences and seminars. Some schools and districts help teacher aides pay some of the costs involved in attending these programs. Often community and junior colleges have certificate and associate's programs that prepare teacher aides for classroom work, offering courses in child development, health and safety, and child guidance.

Newly hired aides participate in orientation sessions and formal training at the school. In these sessions, aides learn about the school's organization, operation, and philosophy. They learn how to keep school records, operate audiovisual equipment, check books out of the library, and administer first aid.

Many schools prefer to hire teacher aides who have some experience working with children and some schools prefer to hire workers who live within the school district. Some schools may require teacher aide applicants to pass written exams and health physicals. All teacher aides must be able to work effectively with both children and adults and should have good verbal and written communications skills.

Other Requirements

You must enjoy working with children and be able to handle their demands, problems, and questions with patience and fairness. You must be willing and able to follow instructions, but also should be able to take the initiative in projects. Flexibility, creativity, and a cheerful outlook are definite assets for anyone working with children. You should find out the specific job requirements from the school, school district, or state department of education in the area where you would like to work. Requirements vary from school to school and state to state. It is important to remember that an aide who is qualified to work in one state, or even one school, may not be qualified to work in another.

■ Exploring

You can gain experience working with children by volunteering to help with religious education classes at your place of worship. You may volunteer to help with scouting troops or work as a counselor at a summer camp. You may have the opportunity to volunteer to help coach a children's athletic team or work with children in after-school programs at community centers. Babysitting is a common way to gain experience in working with children and to learn about the different stages of child development.

■ Employers

With the national shortage of teachers, aides can find work in just about any preschool, elementary, or secondary school in the country. Teacher aides also assist in special education programs and in group home settings. Aides work in both public and private schools.

■ Starting Out

You'll apply directly to schools and school districts for teacher aide positions. Many school districts and state departments of education maintain job listings, bulletin boards, and hotlines that list available job openings. Teacher aide jobs are often advertised in the classified section of the newspaper. Once hired, you'll spend the first months in special training and will receive a beginning wage. After six months or so, you'll have regular responsibilities and possibly a wage increase.

■ Advancement

Teacher aides usually advance only in terms of increases in salary or responsibility, which come with experience. Aides in some districts may receive time off to take college courses. Some teacher aides choose to pursue bachelor's degrees and fulfill the licensing requirements of the state or school to become teachers. "I will probably always remain in the education field," Moker says, "maybe someday returning to school to get a degree in education."

LEARN MORE ABOUT IT

Here are some books used by teacher aides:

Paraprofessionals in Education by Kathryn Jane Skelton (Delmar, 1997)

The Paraprofessional's Guide to the Inclusive Classroom: Working as a Team by Mary Beth Doyle (Paul H. Brooks, 1997)

Handbook for Special Needs Assistants: Working in Partnership with Teachers by Glenys Fox (David Fulton, 1993)

Some aides, who find that they enjoy the administrative side of the job, may move into school or district office staff positions. Others choose to get more training and then work as resource teachers, tutors, guidance counselors, or reading, mathematics, or speech specialists. Some teacher aides go into school library work or become media specialists. While it is true that most of these jobs require additional training, the job of teacher aide is a good place to begin.

■ Earnings

Teacher aides are usually paid on an hourly basis and usually only during the nine or ten months of the school calendar. Salaries vary depending upon the school or district, region of the country, and the duties the aides perform. Some teacher aides may earn as little as minimum wage while others earn up to $15.00 an hour. A study by the Educational Research Service found that the average wage of an aide with teaching responsibilities was $9.04 an hour in 1996; those without teaching responsibilities earned $8.52 an hour.

Benefits such as health insurance and vacation or sick leave may also depend upon the school or district as well as the number of hours a teacher aide works. Many schools employ teacher aides only part time and do not offer such benefits. Other teacher aides may receive the same health and pension benefits as the teachers in their school and be covered under collective bargaining agreements.

■ Work Environment

You'll work in a well-lit, comfortable, wheelchair-accessible environment, although some older school buildings may be in disrepair with unpredictable heating or cooling systems. Most of your work will be indoors, but you will spend some time outside before and after school, and during recess and lunch hours, to watch over the students. You'll be on your feet a lot, monitoring the halls and lunch areas, and running errands for teachers. Although this work is not physically strenuous, working closely with children can be stressful and tiring.

If you love children, you'll find it rewarding to help students learn and develop. The pay, however, is not as rewarding. "As with all those in the entire education field," Moker says, "we are grossly underpaid. But that's the only nega-

PARA-TO-TEACHER

" Para-to-teacher" programs across the country are helping members of minority groups become teachers. With the field of teaching in desperate need of minority representatives, programs such as Urban Paraprofessional Teacher Preparation in Cambridge, Massachusetts, and the Latino Teacher Project in Los Angeles, California, are stepping in to offer stipends, mentors, and other assistance to teacher aides seeking teacher certification. There are about 150 para-to-teacher programs in the United States, enrolling more than 9,000 paraprofessionals. Over three-fourths of these paraprofessionals belong to minority groups.

tive. I truly enjoy my job." Because of her commitment to her work, Fran is allowed certain benefits, such as time off when needed.

■ Outlook

According to the American Federation of Teachers, approximately 500,000 paraprofessionals work in teacher aide or aide-related jobs. Growth in this field is expected to be much faster than the average into the next century because of an expected increase in the number of school-age children. As the number of students in schools increases, new schools and classrooms will be added and more teachers and teacher aides will be hired. A shortage of teachers will find administrators hiring more aides to help with larger classrooms. Because of increased responsibilities for aides, state departments of education will likely establish standards of training. The National Resource Center for Paraprofessionals in Education and Related Services is designing national standards for paraeducator training.

The field of special education-working with students with specific learning, emotional, or physical concerns or disabilities-is expected to grow rapidly, and more aides will be needed in these areas. The Individuals with Disabilities Education Act passed in 1997 will require a more specialized training for aides working with students with disabilities. Teacher aides who want to work with young children in day care or extended day programs will have a relatively easy time finding work because more children are attending these programs while their parents are at work.

■ For More Information

To learn about current issues affecting paraprofessionals in education, visit the AFT Web site or contact:

American Federation of Teachers, Paraprofessionals, and School-Related Personnel
555 New Jersey Avenue, NW
Washington, DC 20001
Tel: 202-879-4400
Web: http://www.aft.org

To order publications and to read current research and other information, visit the ACEI Web site or contact:

Association for Childhood Education International
17904 Georgia Avenue, Suite 215
Olney, MD 20832
Tel: 301-570-2111
Web: http://www.udel/bateman/acei

For information about training programs and other resources, contact:

National Resource Center for Paraprofessionals in Education and Related Services
CASE-SUNY
25 West 43rd Street, Room 620
New York, NY 10036
Tel: 212-642-2948

■ Related Articles

Education
Adult and Vocational Education Teachers
Child Care Workers
Elementary School Teachers
Preschool Teachers
Secondary School Teachers
Special Education Teachers

Team Physicians
■ See Sports Physicians

Technical Librarians
■ See Librarians

Technical Supervisors
■ See Cable Television Technicians

Technical Support Specialists

■ Overview

Technical support specialists investigate and resolve problems in computer functioning. They listen to customer complaints, walk customers through possible solutions, and write technical reports based on these events. Technical support specialists have different duties depending on whom they assist and what they fix. Regardless of specialty, all technical support specialists must be very knowledgeable about the products with which they work and be able to communicate effectively with users from different technical backgrounds. They must be patient with frustrated users and be able to perform well under stress. Technical support is basically like solving mysteries, so support specialists should enjoy the challenge of problem solving and have strong analytical thinking skills.

■ History

The first major advances in modern computer technology were made during World War II. After the war, it was thought that the enormous size of computers, which easily took up the space of entire warehouses, would limit their use to huge government projects. The 1950 census, for example, was computer-processed.

The introduction of semiconductors to computer technology made possible smaller and less expensive computers. Businesses began adapting computers to their operations as early as 1954. Within 30 years, computers had revolutionized the way people work, play, and go shopping. Today, computers are everywhere, from businesses of all kinds to government agencies, charitable organizations, and private homes. Over the years, technology has continued to shrink computer size and increase speed at an unprecedented rate.

Technical support has been around since the development of the first computers for the simple reason that, like all machines, computers always experience problems at one time or another. Several market phenomena explain the increase in demand for competent technical support specialists. First of all, as more and more companies enter the computer hardware, software, and peripheral market, the intense competition to win customers has resulted in many companies offering free or reasonably priced technical support as part of the purchase package. A company uses its reputation and the availability of technical support department to differentiate its products from those of other companies, even though the tangible products like a hard drive, for example, may actually be physically identical. Second, personal computers (PCs) have entered private homes in

large numbers, and the sheer quantity of users has risen so dramatically that more technical support specialists are needed to field their complaints. Third, technological advances hit the marketplace in the form of a new processor or software application so quickly that quality assurance departments cannot possibly identify all the glitches in programming beforehand. Finally, given the great variety of computer equipment and software on the market, it is often difficult for users to reach a high proficiency level with each individual program. When they experience problems, often due to their own errors, users call on technical support to help them. The goal of many computer companies is to release a product for sale that requires no technical support, so that the technical support department has nothing to do. Given the speed of development, however, this is not likely to occur anytime soon. Until it does, there will be a strong demand for technical support specialists.

■ The Job

It is relatively rare today to find a business that does not rely on computers for at least something. Some use them heavily and in many areas: daily operations, like employee time clocks; monthly projects, like payroll and sales accounting; and major reengineering of fundamental business procedures, like form automation in government agencies, insurance companies, and banks. Once employees get used to performing their work on computers, they soon can barely remember how they ever got along without them. As more companies become increasingly reliant on computers, it becomes increasingly critical that they function properly all the time. Any computer downtime can be extremely expensive, in terms of work left undone and sales not made, for example. When employees experience problems with their computer system, they call technical support for help. Technical support

TECHNICAL SUPPORT SPECIALISTS	
SCHOOL SUBJECTS	Computer science English Mathematics
PERSONAL SKILLS	Helping/teaching Technical/scientific
WORK ENVIRONMENT	Primarily indoors Primarily one location
MINIMUM EDUCATION LEVEL	High school diploma
SALARY RANGE	$25,000 to $36,500 to $50,000+
CERTIFICATION OR LICENSING	Voluntary
OUTLOOK	Much faster than the average
DOT	033
GOE	11.01.01
O*NET	25104

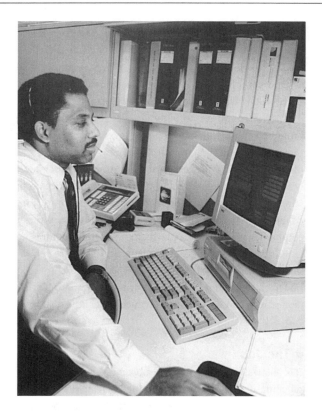

A technical support specialist listens to a customer's software problem while he tries to duplicate the error on his computer.

specialists investigate and resolve problems in computer functioning.

Technical support can generally be broken up into at least three distinct areas, although these distinctions vary greatly with the nature, size, and scope of the company. The three most prevalent areas are user support, technical support, and microcomputer support. Most technical support specialists perform some combination of the tasks explained below.

The jobs of technical support specialists vary according to whom they assist and what they fix. Some specialists help private users exclusively; others are on call to a major corporate buyer. Some work with computer hardware and software, while others help with printer, modem, and fax problems. *User support specialists,* also known as *help desk specialists,* work directly with users themselves, who call when they experience problems. The support specialist listens carefully to the user's explanation of the precise nature of the problem and the commands entered that seem to have caused it. Some companies have developed complex software that allows the support specialist to enter a description of the problem and wait for the computer to provide suggestions about what the user should do.

The initial goal is to isolate the source of the problem. If user error is the culprit, the technical support specialist explains procedures related to the program in question, whether it is a graphics, database, word processing, or printing program. If the problem seems to lie in the hardware or software, the specialist asks the user to enter certain commands in order to see if the computer makes the appropriate response. If it does not, the support specialist is closer to isolating the cause. The support specialist consults supervisors, programmers, and others in order to outline the cause and possible solutions.

Some technical support specialists who work for computer companies are mainly involved with solving problems whose cause has been determined to lie in the computer system's operating system, hardware, or software. They make exhaustive use of resources, such as colleagues or books, and try to solve the problem through a variety of methods, including program modifications and the replacement of certain hardware or software.

Technical support specialists employed in the information systems departments of large corporations do this kind of troubleshooting as well. They also oversee the daily operations of the various computer systems in the company. Sometimes they compare the system's work capacity to the actual daily workload in order to determine if upgrades are needed. In addition, they might help out other computer professionals in the company with modifying commercial software for their company's particular needs.

Microcomputer support specialists are responsible for preparing computers for delivery to a client, including installing the operating system and desired software. After the unit is installed at the customer's location, the support specialists might help train users on appropriate procedures and answer any questions they have. They help diagnose problems as they arise, transferring major concerns to other technical support specialists.

All technical support work must be well documented. Support specialists write detailed technical reports on every problem they work on. They try to tie together different problems on the same software, so programmers can make adjustments that address all of them. Record keeping is crucial because designers, programmers, and engineers use technical support reports to revise current products and improve future ones. Some support specialists help write training manuals. They are often required to read trade magazines and company newsletters in order to keep up-to-date on their products and the field in general.

■ Requirements

High School

A high school diploma is a minimum requirement for technical support specialists. Any technical courses you can take—like computer science, schematic drawing, or electronics—can help you develop the logical and analytical thinking skills necessary to be successful in this field. Courses in math and science are also valuable for this reason. Since technical support specialists have to deal with both computer programmers on the one hand and computer users who may not know anything about computers on the other, you should take English and speech classes to improve your communications skills, both verbal and written.

Postsecondary Training

Technical support is a field as old as computer technology itself, so it might seem odd that postsecondary programs in this field are not more common or standardized. The reason behind this situation is relatively simple—formal education curricula cannot keep up with the changes, nor can they provide specific training on individual products. Some large corporations might consider educational background, both as a way to weed out applicants and to insure a certain level of proficiency. Most major computer companies, however, look for energetic individuals who demonstrate a willingness and ability to learn new things quickly and who have general computer knowledge. These employers count on training new support specialists themselves.

Individuals interested in pursuing a job in this field should first determine what area of technical support appeals to them the most and then honestly assess their level of experience and knowledge. Large corporations often prefer to hire people with an associate's degree and some experience. They may also be impressed with commercial certification in a computer field, like networking. However, if they are hiring from within the company, they will probably weigh experience more heavily than education when making a final decision.

Employed individuals looking for a career change may want to commit themselves to a program of self-study in order to be qualified for technical support positions. Many computer professionals learn a lot of what they know by playing around on computers, reading trade magazines, and talking with computer professionals. Self-taught individuals should learn how to effectively demonstrate knowledge and proficiency on the job or during an interview. Besides self-training, employed individuals should investigate the tuition reimbursement programs offered by their company.

High school students with no experience should seriously consider earning an associate's degree in a computer-related technology. The degree shows the prospective employer that the applicant has attained a certain level of proficiency with computers and has the intellectual ability to learn technical processes, a promising sign for success on the job.

There are many computer technology programs that lead to an associate's degree. A specialization in PC support and administration is certainly applicable to technical support. Most computer professionals eventually need to go back to school to earn a bachelor's degree in order to keep themselves competitive in the job market and prepare themselves for promotion to other computer fields.

Other Requirements

Technical support specialists should be patient, enjoy challenges of problem solving, and think logically. They should work well under stress and demonstrate effective communication skills. Working in a field that changes rapidly, they should be naturally curious and enthusiastic about learning new technologies as they are developed.

■ Exploring

If you are interested in becoming a technical support specialist, you should try to organize a career day with an employed technical support specialist. Local computer repair shops that offer technical support service might be a good place to look. Otherwise, you should contact major corporations, computer companies, and even the central office of your school system.

If you are interested in any computer field, you should start working and playing on computers as much as possible; many working computer professionals became computer hobbyists at a very young age. You can surf the Internet, read computer magazines, and join school or community computer clubs.

You might also attend a computer technology course at a local technical/vocational school. This would give you hands-on exposure to typical technical support training. In addition, if you experience problems with your own hardware or software, you should call technical support, paying close attention to how the support specialist handles the call and asking as many questions as the specialist has time to answer.

■ Employers

Technical support specialists work for computer hardware and software companies, as well as in the information systems departments of large corporations and government agencies.

■ Starting Out

Most technical support positions are considered entry-level. They are found mainly in computer companies and large corporations. Individuals interested in obtaining a job in this field should scan the classified ads for openings in local businesses and may want to work with an employment agency for help finding out about opportunities. Since many job openings are publicized by word of mouth, it is also very important to speak with as many working computer professionals as possible. They tend to be aware of job openings before anyone else and may be able to offer a recommendation to the hiring committee.

If students of computer technology are seeking a position in technical support, they should work closely with their school's placement office. Many employers inform placement offices at nearby schools of openings before ads are run in the newspaper. In addition, placement office staffs are generally very helpful with resume and interviewing techniques.

If an employee wants to make a career change into technical support, he or she should contact the human resources department of the company or speak directly with appropriate management. In companies that are expanding their computing systems, it is often helpful for management to know that current employees would be interested in growing in a computer-related direction. They may even be willing to finance additional education.

■ Advancement

Technical support specialists who demonstrate leadership skills and a strong aptitude for the work may be promoted to supervisory positions within technical support departments. Supervisors are responsible for the more complicated problems that arise, as well as for some administrative duties like scheduling, interviewing, and job assignments.

Further promotion requires additional education. Some technical support specialists may become commercially certified in computer networking so that they can install, maintain, and repair computer networks. Others may prefer to pursue a bachelor's degree in computer science, either full time or part time. The range of careers available to college graduates is widely varied. *Software engineers* analyze industrial, business, and scientific problems and develop software programs to handle them effectively. *Quality assurance engineers* design automated quality assurance tests for new software applications. *Systems analysts* study the broad computing picture for a company or a group of companies in order to determine the best way to organize the computer systems.

There are limited opportunities for technical support specialists to be promoted into managerial positions. Doing so would require additional education in business but would probably also depend on the individual's advanced computer knowledge.

■ Earnings

Technical support specialist jobs are plentiful in areas where clusters of computer companies are located, such as northern California and Seattle, Washington. According to Robert Half International, Inc., the average technical support specialist earns between $25,000 to $36,500 a year. Those with more education, responsibility, and expertise have the potential to earn much more. Most technical support specialists work for companies that offer a full range of benefits, including health insurance, paid vacation, and sick leave. Smaller service or start-up companies may hire support specialists on a contractual basis.

■ Work Environment

Technical support specialists work in comfortable business environments. They generally work regular, 40-hour weeks. For certain products, however, they may be asked to work evenings or weekends or at least be on call during those times in case of emergencies. If they work for service companies, they may be required to travel to clients' sites and log overtime hours.

Technical support work can be stressful, since specialists often deal with frustrated users who may be difficult to work with. Communication problems with people less technically qualified may also be a source of frustration. Patience and understanding are essential to avoiding these problems.

Technical support specialists are expected to work quickly and efficiently and be able to perform under pressure. The ability to do this requires thorough technical expertise and keen analytical ability.

■ Outlook

The U.S. Department of Labor predicts that technical support specialists will be one of the fastest growing of all occupations through the year 2006. The U.S. Department of Labor forecasts huge growth—about 115 percent—of additional support jobs through the year 2006. Every time a new computer product is released on the market or another system is installed, there will unavoidably be problems, whether from user error or technical difficulty. Therefore, there will always be a need for technical support specialists to solve the problems. Since technology changes so rapidly, it is very important for these professionals to keep up-to-date on advances. They should read trade magazines, surf the Internet, and talk with colleagues in order to know what is happening on the cutting edge.

Since some companies stop offering technical support on old products or applications after a designated time, the key is to be technically flexible. This is important for another reason as well. While the industry as a whole will require more technical support specialists in the future, it may be the case that certain computer companies go out of business. It can be a volatile industry for start-ups or young companies dedicated to the development of one product. Technical support specialists interested in working for computer companies should therefore consider living in areas in which many such companies are clustered. In this way, it will be easier to find another job if necessary.

■ For More Information

For information about technical support careers, contact the following organizations:

The Association for Computing Machinery
One Astor Plaza
1515 Broadway
New York, NY 10036
Tel: 212-869-7440
Web: http://www.acm.org

IEEE Computer Society
1730 Massachusetts Avenue, NW
Washington, DC 20036-1992
Tel: 202-371-0101
Web: http://computer.org

■ Related Articles

Computer Hardware

Computer Software

Computers

Computer and Office Machine Service Technicians

Computer Network Administrators

Computer Programmers

Computer Support Service Owners

Computer Systems/Programmer Analysts

Computer Trainers

Quality Assurance Testers

Systems Set Up Specialists

Technical Writers and Editors

Technical Trainers

■ See Quality Assurance Testers

Technical Writers and Editors

■ Overview

Technical writers, sometimes called *technical communicators,* express technical and scientific ideas in easy-to-understand language. *Technical editors* revise written text to correct any errors and make it read smoothly and clearly. They also may coordinate the activities of technical writers, technical illustrators, and other staff in preparing material for publication and oversee the document development and production processes.

■ History

Humans have used writing as a means to communicate information for over 5,500 years. Technical writing, though, did not emerge as a specific profession in the United States until the early years of the 20th century. Before that time, engineers, scientists, and researchers did any necessary writing themselves.

During the early 1900s, technology rapidly expanded. The use of machines to manufacture and mass-produce a wide number of products paved the way for more complex and technical products. Scientists and researchers were discovering new technologies and applications for technology, particularly in electronics, medicine, and engineering. The need to record studies and research, and report them to others, grew. Also, as products became more complex, it was necessary to provide information that documented their components, showed how they were assembled, and explained how to install, use, and repair them. By the mid-1920s, writers were being used to help engineers and scientists document their work and prepare technical information for nontechnical audiences.

Editors had been used for many years to work with printers and authors. They often checked copies of a printed document to correct any errors made during printing, to rewrite unclear passages, and to correct errors in spelling, grammar, and punctuation. As the need for technical writers grew, so too did the need for technical editors. Editors became more involved in documents before the printing stage and worked closely with writers as they prepared

TECHNICAL WRITERS AND EDITORS	
SCHOOL SUBJECTS	**Business** **English**
PERSONAL SKILLS	**Communication/ideas** **Technical/scientific**
WORK ENVIRONMENT	**Primarily indoors** **Primarily one location**
MINIMUM EDUCATION LEVEL	**Bachelor's degree**
SALARY RANGE	**$28,600 to $44,800 to $72,000**
CERTIFICATION OR LICENSING	**None available**
OUTLOOK	**Faster than the average**
DOT	**131, 132**
O*NET	**34005**

their materials. Today, many editors coordinate the activities of all the people involved in preparing technical communications and manage the document development and production processes.

The need for technical writers grew still more with the growth of the computer industry beginning in the 1960s. Originally, many computer companies used computer programmers to write user manuals and other documentation. It was widely assumed that the material was so complex that only those who were involved with creating computer programs would be able to write about them. Although computer programmers had the technical knowledge, many were not able to write clear, easy-to-use manuals. Complaints about the difficulty using and understanding manuals were common. By the 1970s, computer companies began to hire technical writers to write computer manuals and documents. Today, this is one of the largest areas in which technical writers are employed.

The need for technical marketing writers also grew as a result of expanding computer technology. Many copywriters who worked for advertising agencies and marketing firms did not have the technical background to be able to describe the features of the technical products that were coming to market. Thus grew the need for writers who could combine the ability to promote products with the ability to communicate technical information.

The nature of technical writers' and technical editors' jobs continues to change with emerging technologies. Today, the ability to store, transmit, and receive information through computers and electronic means is changing the very nature of documents. Traditional books and paper documents are being replaced by floppy disks, CD-ROMs, interactive multimedia documents, and material accessed through bulletin board systems, faxes, the World Wide Web, and the Internet.

■ The Job

Technical writers and editors prepare a wide variety of documents and materials. The most common types of documents they produce are manuals, technical reports, specifications, and proposals. Some technical writers also write scripts for videos and audiovisual presentations and text for multimedia programs. Technical writers and editors prepare manuals that give instructions and detailed information on how to install, assemble, use, service, or repair a product or equipment. They may write and edit manuals as simple as a two-page leaflet that gives instructions on how to assemble a bicycle or as complex as a 500-page document that tells service technicians how to repair machinery, medical equipment, or a climate-control system. One of the most common types of manuals is the computer software manual, which informs users on how to

load software on their computers, explains how to use the program, and gives information on different features.

Technical writers and editors also prepare technical reports on a multitude of subjects. These reports include documents that give the results of research and laboratory tests and documents that describe the progress of a project. They also write and edit sales proposals, product specifications, quality standards, journal articles, in-house style manuals, and newsletters.

The work of a technical writer begins when he or she is assigned to prepare a document. The writer meets with members of an account or technical team to learn the requirements for the document, the intended purpose or objectives, and the audience. During the planning stage, the writer learns when the document needs to be completed, approximately how long it should be, whether artwork or illustrations are to be included, who the other team members are, and any other production or printing requirements. A schedule is created that defines the different stages of development and determines when the writer needs to have certain parts of the document ready.

The next step in document development is the research, or information gathering, phase. During this stage, technical writers gather all the available information about the product or subject, read and review it, and determine what other information is needed. They may research the topic by reading technical publications, but in most cases they will need to gather information directly from the people working on the product. Writers meet with and interview people who are sources of information, such as scientists, engineers, software developers, computer programmers, managers, and project managers. They ask questions, listen, and take notes or tape record interviews. They gather any available notes, drawings, or diagrams that may be useful.

After writers gather all the necessary information, they sort it out and organize it. They plan how they are going to present the information and prepare an outline for the document. They may decide how the document will look and prepare the design, format, and layout of the pages. In some cases, this may be done by an editor rather than the writer. If illustrations, diagrams, or photographs are going to be included, either the editor or writer makes arrangements for an illustrator, photographer, or art researcher to produce or obtain them.

Then, the writer starts writing and prepares a rough draft of the document. If the document is very large, a writer may prepare it in segments. Once the rough draft is completed, it is submitted to a designated person or group for technical review. Copies of the draft are distributed to managers, engineers, or subject matter experts who can easily determine if any technical information is inaccurate or missing. These reviewers read the document and suggest changes.

The rough draft is also given to technical editors for review of a variety of factors. The editors check that the material is organized well, that each section flows with the section before and after it, and that the language is appropriate for the intended audience. They also check for correct use of grammar, spelling, and punctuation. They ensure that names of parts or objects are consistent throughout the document and that references are accurate. They also check the labeling of graphs and captions for accuracy. Technical editors use special symbols, called proofreader's marks, to indicate the types of changes needed.

The editor and reviewers return their copies of the document to the technical writer. The writer incorporates the appropriate suggestions and revisions and prepares the final draft. The final draft is once again submitted to a designated reviewer or team of reviewers. In some cases, the technical reviewer may do a quick check to make sure that the requested changes were made. In other cases, the technical reviewer may examine the document in depth to ensure technical accuracy and correctness. A walkthrough, or test of the document, may be done for certain types of documents. For example, a walkthrough may be done for a document that explains how to assemble a product. A tester assembles the product by following the instructions given in the document. The tester makes a note of all sections that are unclear or inaccurate, and the document is returned to the writer for any necessary revisions.

For some types of documents, a legal review may also be done. For example, a pharmaceutical company that is preparing a training manual to teach its sales representatives about a newly released drug needs to ensure that all materials are in compliance with Food and Drug Administration (FDA) requirements. A member of the legal department who is familiar with these requirements will review the document to make sure that all information in the document conforms to FDA rules.

Once the final draft has been approved, the document is submitted to the technical editor who makes a comprehensive and detailed check of the document. In addition to checking that the language is clear and reads smoothly, the editor makes sure the table of contents matches the different sections or chapters of a document, all illustrations and diagrams are correctly placed, all captions are matched to the correct picture, consistent terminology is used, and correct references are used in the bibliography and text.

The editor returns the document to either the writer or a word processor who makes any necessary corrections. This copy is then checked by a *proofreader.* The proofreader compares the final copy against the editor's marked-up copy and makes sure that all changes were made. The document is then prepared for printing. In some cases, the writer is responsible for preparing camera-ready copy or electronic files for printing purposes, and in other cases, a print production coordinator prepares all material to submit to a printer.

Some technical writers specialize in a specific type of material. *Technical marketing writers* create promotional and marketing materials for technological products. They may write the copy for an advertisement for a technical product, such as a computer workstation or software, or write press releases about the product. They also write sales literature, product flyers, Web pages, and multimedia presentations.

Other technical writers prepare scripts for videotapes and films about technical subjects. These writers, called *scriptwriters,* need to have an understanding of film and video production techniques.

Some technical writers and editors prepare articles for scientific, medical, computer, or engineering trade journals. These articles may report the results of research conducted by doctors, scientists, or engineers or report on technological advances in a particular field. Some technical writers and editors also develop textbooks.They may receive articles written by engineers or scientists and edit and revise them to make them more suitable for the intended audience.

Technical writers and editors may create documents for a variety of media. Electronic media, such as compact discs and online services, are increasingly being used in place of books and paper documents. Technical writers may create materials that are accessed through bulletin board systems and the Internet or create computer-based resources, such as help menus on computer programs. They also create interactive, multimedia documents that are distributed on compact discs or floppy disks. Some of these media require knowledge of special computer programs that allow material to be hyperlinked, or electronically cross-referenced.

■ Requirements

High School

In high school, you should take composition, grammar, literature, creative writing, journalism, social studies, math, statistics, engineering, computer science, and as many science classes as possible. Business courses are also useful as they explain the organizational structure of companies and how they operate.

Postsecondary Training

Most employers prefer to hire technical writers and editors who have bachelor's or advanced degrees. Many technical editors graduate with degrees in the humanities, especially English or journalism. Technical writers typically need to have a strong foundation in engineering, computers, or science. Many technical writers graduate with degrees in engineering or science and take classes in technical writing.

Many different types of college programs are available that prepare people to become technical writers and editors. A growing number of colleges are offering degrees in technical writing. Schools without a technical writing program may offer degrees in journalism or English. Programs are offered through English, communications, and journalism departments. Classes vary based on the type of program. In general, classes for technical writers include a core curriculum in writing and classes in algebra, statistics, logic, science, engineering, and computer programming languages. Useful classes for editors include technical writing, project management, grammar, proofreading, copyediting, and print production.

Many technical writers and editors earn master's degrees. In these programs, they study technical writing in depth and may specialize in a certain area, such as scriptwriting, instructional design, or multimedia applications. In addition, many nondegree writing programs are offered to technical writers and editors to hone their skills. Offered as extension courses or continuing education courses, these programs include courses on indexing, editing medical materials, writing for trade journals, and other related subjects.

Technical writers, and occasionally technical editors, are often asked to present samples of their work. College students should build a portfolio during their college years in which they collect their best samples from work that they may have done for a literary magazine, newsletter, or yearbook.

Technical writers and editors should be willing to pursue learning throughout their careers. As technology changes, technical writers and editors may need to take classes to update their knowledge. Changes in electronic printing and computer technology will also change the way technical writers and editors do their jobs and they may need to take courses to learn new skills or new technologies.

Other Requirements

Technical writers need to have good communications skills, science and technical aptitudes, and the ability to think analytically. Technical editors also need to have good communications skills, and judgment, as well as the ability to identify and correct errors in written material. They need to be diplomatic, assertive, and able to explain tactfully what needs to be corrected to writers, engineers, and other people involved with a document. Technical editors should be able to understand technical information easily, but they need less scientific and technical backgrounds than writers. Both technical writers and editors need to be able to work as part of a team and collaborate with others on a project. They need to be highly self-motivated, well organized, and able to work under pressure.

■ Exploring

If you enjoy writing and are considering a career in technical writing or editing, you should make writing a daily activity. Writing is a skill that develops over time and through practice. Students can keep journals, join writing clubs, and practice different types of writing, such as scriptwriting and informative reports. Sharing writing with others and asking them to critique it is especially helpful. Comments from readers on what they enjoyed about a piece of writing or difficulty they had in understanding certain sections provides valuable feedback that helps to improve your writing style.

Reading a variety of materials is also helpful. Reading exposes you to both good and bad writing styles and techniques and helps you to identify why one approach works better than another.

You may also gain experience by working on a literary magazine, student newspaper, or yearbook (or starting one of your own if one is not available). Both writing and editing articles and managing production give you the opportunity to learn new skills and to see what is involved in preparing documents and other materials.

Students may also be able to get internships, cooperative education assignments, or summer or part-time jobs as proofreaders or editorial assistants that may include writing responsibilities.

■ Employers

Employment may be found in many different types of places, such as in the fields of aerospace, computers, engineering, pharmacy, and research and development, or with the nuclear industry, medical publishers, government agencies or contractors, and colleges and universities. The aerospace, engineering, medical, and computer industries hire significant numbers of technical writers and editors. So does the federal government, particularly in the departments of Defense and Agriculture, the National Aeronautics and Space Administration (NASA), and the Atomic Energy Commission.

■ Starting Out

Many technical writers start their careers as scientists, engineers, technicians, or research assistants and move into writing after several years of experience in those positions. Technical writers with a bachelor's degree in a technical subject such as engineering may be able to find work as a technical writer immediately upon graduating from college, but many employers prefer to hire writers with some work experience.

Technical editors who graduate with a bachelor's degree in English or journalism may find entry-level work as editorial assistants, copy editors, or proofreaders. From these positions they are able to move into technical editing positions. Or beginning workers may find jobs as technical editors in small companies or those with a small technical communications department.

If you plan to work for the federal government, you need to pass an examination. Information about examinations and job openings is available at federal employment centers.

You may learn about job openings through your college's job placement services and want ads in newspapers and professional magazines. You may also research companies that hire technical writers and editors and apply directly to them. Many libraries provide useful job resource guides and directories that provide information about companies that hire in specific areas.

■ Advancement

As technical writers and editors gain experience, they move into more challenging and responsible positions. At first, they may work on simple documents or be assigned to work on sections of a document. As they demonstrate their proficiency and skills, they are given more complex assignments and are responsible for more activities.

Technical writers and editors with several years of experience may move into project management positions. As project managers, they are responsible for the entire document development and production processes. They schedule and budget resources and assign writers, editors, illustrators, and other workers to a project. They monitor the schedule, supervise workers, and ensure that costs remain in budget.

Technical writers and editors who show good project management skills, leadership abilities, and good interpersonal skills may become supervisors or managers. Both technical writers and editors can move into senior writer and senior editor positions. These positions involve increased responsibilities and may include supervising other workers.

Many technical writers and editors seek to develop and perfect their skills rather than move into management or supervisory positions. As they gain a reputation for their quality of work, they may be able to select choice assignments. They may learn new skills as a means of being able to work in new areas. For example, a technical writer may learn a new desktop program in order to become more proficient in designing. Or, a technical writer may learn a hypermedia or hypertext computer program in order to be able to create a multimedia program. Technical writers and editors who broaden their skill base and capabilities can move to higher-paying positions within their own com-pany or at another company. They also may work as freelancers or set up their own communications companies.

■ Earnings

In the late 1990s, the average salary for technical writers and editors was $48,000. Salaries for entry-level technical writers and editors ranged from slightly less than $28,600 to more than $44,800. Writers and editors with more than 10 years of experience earned annual salaries between $45,000 and $67,000, with senior writers and editors with management responsibilities earning salaries as high as $72,000 a year. The average annual salary for technical writers and editors in the federal government was $47,440 in 1996. Writers and editors in the computer industry earn slightly higher salaries than in other industries. In general, writers and editors who work for firms with large writing staffs earn more than those who work at companies with less than ten writers and editors.

Most companies offer benefits that include paid holidays and vacations, medical insurance, and 401(k) plans. They may also offer profit sharing, pension plans, and tuition assistance programs.

■ Work Environment

Technical writers and editors usually work in an office environment, with well-lighted and quiet surroundings. They may have their own offices or share work space with other writers and editors. Most writers and editors have computers. They may be able to utilize the services of support staff who can word process revisions, run off copies, fax material, and perform other administrative functions or they may have to perform all of these tasks themselves.

Some technical writers and editors work out of home offices and use computer modems and networks to send and receive materials electronically. They may go in to the office only on occasion for meetings and gathering information. Freelancers and contract workers may work at a company's premises or at home.

Although the standard workweek is 40 hours, many technical writers and editors frequently work 50 or 60 hours a week. Job interruptions, meetings, and conferences can prevent writers from having long periods of time to write. Therefore, many writers work after hours or bring work home. Both writers and editors frequently work in the evening or on weekends in order to meet a deadline.

In many companies there is pressure to produce documents as quickly as possible. Both technical writers and editors may feel at times that they are compromising the quality of their work due to the need to conform to time and budget constraints. In some companies, technical writers and editors may have increased workloads due to company reorganizations or downsizing. They may need to do the work that was formerly done by more than one person.

Technical writers and editors also are increasingly assuming roles and responsibilities formerly performed by other people and this can increase work pressures and stress.

Despite these pressures, most technical writers and editors gain immense satisfaction from their work and the roles that they perform in producing technical communications.

■ Outlook

The writing and editing field is generally very competitive. Each year, there are more people trying to enter this field than there are available openings. The field of technical writing and editing, though, offers more opportunities than other areas of writing and editing, such as book publishing or journalism. Employment opportunities for technical writers and editors are expected to increase slightly in the coming years. Demand is growing for technical writers who can produce well-written computer manuals. In addition to the computer industry, the pharmaceutical industry is showing an increased need for technical writers. Currently, around 50,000 people are employed as technical writers and editors.

Writers may find positions that include duties in addition to writing. A growing trend is for companies to use writers to run a department, supervise other writers, and manage freelance writers and outside contractors. In addition, many writers are acquiring responsibilities that include desktop publishing and print production coordination.

The demand for technical writers and editors is significantly affected by the economy. During recessionary times, technical writers and editors are often among the first to be let go. Many companies today are continuing to downsize or reduce their number of employees and are reluctant to keep writers on staff. Such companies prefer to hire writers and editors on a temporary contract basis, using them only as long as it takes to complete an assigned document. Technical writers and editors who work on a temporary or freelance basis need to market their services and continually look for new assignments. They also do not have the security or benefits offered by full-time employment.

■ For More Information

For information on careers, please contact:

Society for Technical Communication
901 North Stuart Street, Suite 904
Arlington, VA 22203
Tel: 703-522-4114
Email: stc@stc-va.org
Web: http://www.stc-va.org

■ Related Articles

Advertising and Marketing
Book Publishing

Computers
Electronics
Newspapers and Magazines
Book Editors
Computer Programmers
Editors
Electrical and Electronics Engineers
Grant Coordinators and Writers
Indexers
Magazine Editors
Newspaper Editors
Research Assistants
Writers

Tectonophysicists
■ See Geophysicists

Telegraph-Service Raters
■ See Billing Clerks

Telemarketers

■ Overview

Telemarketers make and receive phone calls on behalf of a company in order to sell its goods, market its services, gather information, receive orders and complaints, and/or handle other miscellaneous business. According to the Direct Marketing Association, the activities most frequently performed by telemarketers are inputting mail orders and verifying names and addresses. A *Customer Service Newsletter* reader poll reports that the average telemarketer/customer service representative fields over 330 calls per week.

Telemarketing professionals might work directly for one company or for several companies that use the same service. In addition to selling, telemarketers place and receive calls in order to raise funds, conduct marketing research surveys, or raise public awareness. Accordingly, a wide variety of organizations in many industries employ telemarketers. There are currently about four million people who work part-time or full-time as telemarketers.

History

It is no exaggeration to say that the telephone has become an indispensable part of our daily lives. The speed of communicating by phone and the ability to reach the exact people with whom we want to speak have drastically changed the way business has been conducted over the past hundred years.

Since World War II, many companies have turned to marketing in order to expand business. Marketing involves finding the most likely customers for a product or service and then targeting those customers for sales, investment, or other business activity. An increasingly popular form of marketing is telemarketing, or the use of phone calls to sell a product or service, to find out about potential customers, to stay in touch with current customers, or to provide consumers with the most current information on new products and services. One of telemarketing's greatest strengths is that it allows callers direct contact with potential customers.

The Job

Telemarketers generally work for one of two types of businesses. Some telemarketers are part of the in-house staff of a company or corporation and make and receive calls on behalf of that company. Others work for a telemarketing service agency and make or receive calls for the clients of the agency. Telemarketing agencies are useful for companies that don't want to or can't keep a full-time telemarketing staff on the payroll or that need telemarketing services only occasionally. Both large corporations and small firms employ telemarketing agencies, which sometimes specialize in particular fields, such as fund-raising, product sales, and insurance.

Telemarketers are generally responsible for either handling incoming calls or placing calls to outside parties. Incoming calls may include requests for information or orders for an advertised product, such as clothing, magazines, appliances, or books. Telemarketers also staff the phones that handle toll-free, "800" numbers, which customers call to ask questions about the use of a product or to register complaints. Airline reservations, concert and sports tickets, and credit card problems are all transactions that can be handled by telemarketers. Newspapers often employ *classified ad clerks* to transcribe classified ads from callers. A person whose sole job is taking orders from callers over the phone is sometimes called an *order clerk*.

Telemarketers place outside calls for many purposes as well. One of the most important reasons to make such calls is to sell products and services to consumers. The phone numbers of the people that telemarkers call usually come from a prepared list of previous customers, the phone book, reply cards from magazines, or a list purchased from another source. Sometimes randomly dialed "cold calls"

are made. Once made, these calls often serve as a source of potential leads for the company's regular sales staff. A wide range of products—from newspaper subscriptions and credit cards to time-share resort condominiums and long-distance service—can be successfully sold in this way. Once a sale is made, the telemarketer records all necessary information, such as the buyer's name and address, product choices, and payment information, so that order fillers can prepare the product for shipment.

Cultural organizations, such as ballet and opera companies, public television stations, and theater troupes, use telemarketers to solicit subscriptions and donations. Charity fund-raising also relies heavily on telemarketing.

In addition to selling, telemarketers make calls for other reasons. They may conduct marketing surveys of consumers to discover the reasons for their buying decisions or what they like and dislike about a certain product. They may call to endorse a candidate in an upcoming election or tell citizens about an important vote in their city council. When making calls business-to-business, telemarketers may try to encourage attendance at important meetings, assist a company in recruitment and job placement, or collect demographic information for use in an advertising campaign.

When making outbound calls, telemarketers usually work from a prepared script that they must follow exactly. This is especially true of market-research surveys because people need to be asked the same questions in the same way if the survey data are to be valid. Often when a customer tries to resist a sales pitch, the telemarketer will read a standard response that has been prepared in anticipation of potential objections. At other times, the telemarketer must rely on persuasive sales skills and quick thinking to win over the customer and make the sale. Telemarketers have to be a little more skillful when selling business-to-business because these customers usually have a clear idea of the needs of their businesses and will ask specific questions.

TELEMARKETERS	
SCHOOL SUBJECTS	**Speech** **Business**
PERSONAL SKILLS	**Communication/ ideas** **Helping/teaching**
WORK ENVIRONMENT	**Primarily indoors** **Primarily one location**
MINIMUM EDUCATION LEVEL	**High school diploma**
SALARY RANGE	**$11,000 to $18,000 to $30,100**
CERTIFICATION OR LICENSING	**None available**
OUTLOOK	**Faster than the average**
DOT	**299**
GOE	**08.02.07**
NOC	**6623**
O*NET	**49026**

■ Requirements

High School

The type of skills and education you need to become a telemarketer depends in part on the firm for which you plan to work. A high school diploma is usually required for any type of position, while some employers hire only people who have earned college degrees.

Since they must be able to speak persuasively and listen to customers carefully, telemarketers will find classes in English, communications, speech, drama, and broadcasting particularly useful. Business and sales classes, as well as psychology and sociology, are also valuable. In addition, since many telemarketing positions require the use of computers for entering data, familiarity and experience with technology in general and word processing in particular are pluses.

Postsecondary Training

Although a college degree is not absolutely necessary for many telemarketing positions, some employers hire only college graduates. Since telemarketers sell and/or communicate over the telephone, college degrees in English, speech, drama, and communication are especially useful for those aspiring to the job of telemarketer. In addition, general business classes, such as marketing, advertising, and sales, are valuable. Also, courses in psychology and human behavior can help telemarketers gain insight to the wide variety of people that they often speak to during the course of a typical workday.

Other Requirements

If a telemarketer's phone calls will focus on a complex product or service, as is the case with many business-to-business calls, people trained in the specific field involved may be hired and then instructed in telephone and sales techniques.

Even though their work is done over the phone, telemarketers must be able to deal well with other people. This work requires the ability to sense how customers are reacting, to keep them interested in the sales pitch, to listen carefully to their responses and complaints, and to react tactfully to impatient and sometimes hostile people. In sum, telemarketers must be able to balance a sensitivity to their company's concerns with the needs of the customer.

Telemarketing workers must also have a warm, pleasant phone voice that conveys sincerity and confidence. They must be detail-oriented as well. While on the phone, they have to take orders, get other important information, and fill out complete sales records, all of which requires an accurate and alert mind.

Many federal, state, and local laws have been enacted governing the sort of language and sales tactics that can be used with phone solicitation. Such legislation is intended to protect consumers from unscrupulous telemarketers operating phone scams. Telemarketers must be aware of these laws and conduct their phone sales in an honest and unambiguous manner. To bolster the industry's image in the eyes of the public, several professional organizations exist to further the cause of ethical and effective telemarketing.

Some states have guidelines or legislation to further regulate the activities of telemarketers. In California, for example, certain types of telemarketing agencies must register each year with the state, although most business-to-business telemarketing is exempt because sales are usually not the main goal of such calls.

■ Exploring

There are many ways to gain practice and poise in telemarketing. Many organizations use volunteer phone workers during campaigns and fund drives. One of the most visible of these is public television stations, which conduct fund-raising drives several times a year and are always looking for volunteer help to staff the phone banks. Other groups that routinely need volunteer telemarketers include local political campaigns, theaters and other arts groups, churches, schools, and nonprofit social organizations, such as crisis centers and inner-city recreation programs.

■ Employers

Telemarketing work is available at a wide variety of establishments, from large multinational corporations, educational publishers, and government agencies to nonprofit organizations, retail catalog outlets, and service businesses. While jobs in telemarketing can be found nationwide, the cost of operating call centers varies, depending on their location. The most expensive cities in which to operate call centers, for example, are San Francisco, Washington, DC, and New York, while the least expensive cities include Columbia, South Carolina, and Mobile, Alabama. Large corporations often house their telemarketing centers in cities where both operating costs and salaries are low. According to the Direct Marketing Association, most telemarketing call centers are located in large cities, but a surprising 5 percent can be found in rural towns.

■ Starting Out

Agencies that hire telemarketers usually advertise for new employees in the classified section of newspapers, as well as on the Web. Another possible source of job leads is temporary employment agencies, many of which specialize in placing telemarketers with firms. A person who wishes to become an in-house telemarketer for a specific firm should call or write to the personnel office of that firm to find out if there are job openings. It is important to note that employers of telemarketers sometimes interview job applicants over the phone, judging a person's telephone voice, personality, demeanor, and assertiveness. Being prepared for such an interview before making that first call can make the difference between getting the job and having to continue to look.

Employees undergo a great deal of on-the-job training after they have been hired. Trainers instruct novice telemarketers on the use of equipment, characteristics of the product or service they will be selling, and proper sales techniques and listening skills. They rehearse the trainees on the script that has been prepared and guide them through some practice calls.

■ Advancement

Within telemarketing agencies, employees can advance to jobs as assistant managers, supervisors, managers, and directors. These professionals have a variety of responsibilities, including preparing reports, writing telephone scripts, setting goals and objectives, implementing new service programs, monitoring and analyzing inquiries and complaints, recruiting, scheduling, and training. Telemarketing managers sometimes enjoy rapidly increasing salaries because they can often earn commissions on the net sales achieved by the agency.

Some telemarketers move into telephone-sales training, either with agencies or as independent consultants. Experienced telemarketers can sometimes find new jobs with higher-paying firms, while still others start their own telemarketing agencies.

■ Earnings

Telemarketers' earnings vary with the type of work they do. For part-time phone solicitors making basic calls to consumers, the pay can range from the minimum wage to around $8.00 per hour. Pay may be higher for those who deliver more elaborate sales presentations, work weekends, or make business-to-business calls. As telemarketers gain experience and skills, their pay scales rise. According to the American Marketing Association, seasoned telemarketers can earn from $18,000 to $30,100 per year. Those telemarketers who start their own companies have the chance to earn even higher amounts. And those who rise through the management ranks can make even more. The Direct Marketing Association notes that corporate telemarketing directors can earn an average of $69,700 to $74,200; managers $47,400 to $49,700; and training managers $47,400.

Telemarketing workers also frequently enjoy such employee benefits as health and life insurance, paid vacation and sick days, and profit sharing. With such a wide range of organizations for which telemarketers can work, the benefits offered depend entirely on the employer.

TELEMARKETING—BY THE NUMBERS

- 5 percent of call centers are located in rural areas.
- 38 percent of call centers are located in large cities.
- Nearly half of call centers employ 10 or fewer telemarketing sales representatives.
- 41 percent of call centers are completely automated.
- 47 percent of call centers are partially automated (use office automation but not automated sales equipment).
- The most commonly performed activity of 48.8 percent of telemarketers is name and address verification.
- The most commonly performed activity of 61 percent of telemarketers is inputting of mail orders.
- An average of 330 calls are fielded by customer service representatives/telemarketers per week.
- 100 million adults ordered a product or service by telephone in 1996.

Source: Direct Marketing Association

■ Work Environment

The offices in which telemarketers work can range from the very basic, with standard phones and desks, to the highly advanced, with computer terminals, the latest in phone technology, and machines that automatically dial numbers from a database. There may be just four or five telemarketers in an office or more than a hundred. While the work is not strenuous, it can be very repetitive. The amount of supervision depends on the employer and the region of the country. California and a few other states, for example, have laws that prohibit call monitoring by supervisors unless both the telemarketer and the person being called are aware of it.

Telemarketing requires many hours of sitting and talking on the phone. Customer rejections, which range from polite to rude, can cause a great deal of stress. As a result, many telemarketers work only four- or five-hour shifts. Telemarketing is an ideal job for people looking for part-time work because workweeks generally run from 24 to 30 hours. Because many agencies need staff at unusual hours, telemarketers are often able to find positions offering schedules that match their lifestyles. Many agencies require staffing 24 hours a day to handle such calls as airline reservations and reports of stolen credit cards. Telemarketers who make business-to-business calls work during normal business hours, while those who call consumers make most of their calls in the evening and on weekends, when more people are at home.

■ Outlook

According to the Direct Marketing Association, more than 100 million people ordered a product or service by telephone in 1996. An estimated 275,000 firms are now using telemarketers. Because of the phenomenal growth of the telemarketing industry, the outlook for telemarketers is excellent. One trend supporting this growth is the advances in telephone technology. According to a recent poll conducted by the DMA, 41 percent of telemarketers work at firms that are completely automated, allowing them to use virtually paperless systems. In addition, many telemarketing agencies use automatic call distribution systems that distribute calls evenly among employees for the fast customer service. Through the use of database marketing and Internet registration services, firms can target markets even more accurately, thereby increasing the chances of successful calls.

Another trend that continues to advance the growth of telemarketing is the cost effectiveness of selling by phone. While a field sales representative makes an average of five in-person sales calls a day, typically at a cost of about $225 per visit, an experienced telemarketer can place 10 to 15 phone calls in an hour.

Many firms previously employing telemarketing agencies are now establishing their own telemarketing divisions. Other firms that cannot afford to keep telemarketers on staff use independent telemarketing agencies. Rapid growth combined with high turnover will result in many opportunities for new people entering the field.

■ For More Information

The AMA is an internal professional society of individual members with an interest in the practice, study, and teaching of marketing.

American Marketing Association
250 South Wacker Drive, Suite 200
Chicago, IL 60606
Tel: 312-648-0536
Web: http://ama.org

The DMA is the largest trade association for individuals interested in database marketing.

Direct Marketing Association
1120 Avenue of the Americas
New York, NY 10036-6700
Tel: 212-768-7277
Web: http://www.the-dma.org

■ Related Articles

Advertising and Marketing

Sales

Telecommunications

Collection Workers

Fund-Raisers

Marketing Research Analysts

Public Opinion Researchers

Reservation and Ticket Agents

Retail Sales Workers

Sales Representatives

Services Sales Representatives

Telephone Operators

Telephone and PBX Installers and Repairers

■ Overview

Telephone and private branch exchange (PBX) installers and repairers install, service, and repair telephone and PBX systems in customers' homes and places of business.

■ History

In 1876, the first practical device for transmitting speech over electric wires was patented by Alexander Graham Bell. The telephone device Bell invented worked on essentially the same principle as the telephones that are familiar to us today. Both transmit the vibrations of speech sounds by transferring them to solid bodies and converting them to electrical impulses, which can travel along wires. However, technological advances in telephone systems over the past century have turned telephones into powerful instruments for communication.

Within a few years after its introduction, many customers were having the new devices installed and were being connected into local telephone systems. Four years after Bell's patent, there were 30,000 subscribers to 138 local telephone exchanges. By 1887, there were 150,000 telephones in the United States. Long distance service developed slowly, because of problems with distortion and signal loss over longer transmission lines. Over time, advances such as amplifiers on transmission lines, microwave radio links, shortwave relays, undersea cables, and earth satellites that amplify and relay signals have so improved service that today's telephone customers expect that their telephone can be quickly linked to one of many millions of other telephones around the globe.

As telephones became a crucial part of 20th century life, a need arose for workers who specialized in installing, removing, and repairing telephone instruments and related devices. But today's technology has advanced to the point where fewer of these workers are needed than in the past. Once basic wiring is in place, customers can handle much of their own installation work, and telephones can be manufactured so cheaply that it is often simpler to replace instead of repair malfunctioning equipment.

■ The Job

When calls go from one telephone to another, they usually go through a telephone company facility that houses automatic switching equipment. For telephone calls to go through, an array of wires, cable, switches, transformers, and other equipment must be installed and in good operating order. Central office workers, cable splicers, and line repairers are among the workers who work on telephone equipment away from the customer's premises. Telephone and PBX installers and repairers are workers who service the systems on the customer's premises.

When customers request a new telephone line or equipment, telephone installers, also called *station installers,* do the necessary work. They often travel to the customer's home or business in a vehicle that contains a variety of tools and equipment. If they must make a new connection, they may have to work on roofs, ladders, or at the top of a telephone pole to attach an incoming wire to the service line. They install a terminal box and connect the appropriate wires. On some jobs, they may have to drill through walls or floors to run wiring. In large buildings, they may connect service wires or terminals in basements or wire closets. After installing equipment, they test it to make sure it functions as it should. Telephone installers may also install or remove telephone booths, coin collectors, and switching key equipment, in addition to private and business phones.

Wear and deterioration may cause telephones to function improperly. Telephone repairers can determine the cause of such problems, sometimes with the assistance of testboard workers or trouble locators in the central office, and then repair the problem and restore service.

Steve Markowsky installs and repairs residential telephones in upstate central New York for Alltel, a communications company. When a customer has a problem, Steve receives the service order via computer. He then attempts to contact the customer by phone. If unable to, he then goes to the customer's "telephone interface"—a box outside of the home. "With a 'telephone butt-in set'," Steve says, "I can clip into the line and listen for a dial tone, and even place a call." If the problem is not with the outside line, Steve can assist customers on a per hour basis to find the problem within the home. "The trouble might be as simple as a phone off the hook." To locate the problem, Steve uses a "bell meter" to test the phone and outlet. "If the trouble isn't in the phone or the outlet, it's in the wire." Steve must replace wire on a daily basis.

"I carry a small number of hand tools," Steve says. "Screwdrivers, needle-nose pliers, side-cutters, rechargeable drill, a stapler made for stapling wires."

Some larger users of telephone services, such as some businesses or hotels, have a single telephone number. Calls that come in may be routed to the proper telephone with PBX switching equipment located on the customer's premises. Outgoing calls also go through what is in effect a private telephone system within the building. In addition to handling regular phone calls, PBX equipment is often used for specialized services like electronic mail. PBX installers, also called *systems technicians,* set up the neces-

sary wiring, switches, and other equipment to make the system function, often creating customized switchboards. These workers often work as part of a crew, because the communications equipment they work with is heavy, bulky, and complex.

PBX repairers, with the assistance of testboard workers, locate malfunctions and repair PBX and other telephone systems. They may also maintain related equipment, such as power plants, batteries, and relays. Some PBX repairers service and repair mobile radiophones, microwave transmission equipment, and other sophisticated telecommunications devices and equipment.

Some experienced workers can handle a range of installation and repair work. They may put their skills to use handling special jobs, such as investigating unauthorized use of telephone equipment.

■ Requirements

High School

You'll need math courses to prepare for the technical nature of the career, along with voc-tech, electronics, and other courses that will involve you with hands-on experiments. Computer courses will also be valuable. You should take

TELEPHONE AND PBX INSTALLERS AND REPAIRERS	
SCHOOL SUBJECTS	**Mathematics** **Technical/Shop**
PERSONAL SKILLS	**Following instructions** **Mechanical/manipulative**
WORK ENVIRONMENT	**Indoors and Outdoors** **Primarily multiple locations**
MINIMUM EDUCATION LEVEL	**High school diploma**
SALARY RANGE	**$18,000 to $40,170 to $50,000+**
CERTIFICATION OR LICENSING	**None available**
OUTLOOK	**Decline**
DOT	**822**
GOE	**05.05.05**
NOC	**7246**
O*NET	**85702**

A telephone repairer checks a line.

English, speech, and other courses that will help you develop communications skills.

Postsecondary Training

Telephone companies usually prefer to hire applicants who have no previous experience with another telephone company and then train the beginners to work with the equipment used in their own system. Companies generally prefer applicants who are high school or vocational school graduates and who have mechanical ability and manual dexterity. Some employers may require an associate's or bachelor's degree in an area such as engineering. Because of the rapid advancements of telecommunications technology, installers may be required to take continuing education courses, either as part of in-house training or through a college program.

Other Requirements

Because installers and repairers deal with company customers, these workers should have a neat appearance and a pleasant manner. "I love to meet people," Steve says. "And I love problem solving. It's very gratifying work."

Good eyesight and color vision are needed for working with small parts and for distinguishing the color-coding of wires. Good hearing is necessary for detecting malfunctions revealed by sound.

Many telephone employees are members of unions, and union membership may be required. The Communications Workers of America and International Brotherhood of Electrical Workers are two unions representing many workers.

■ Exploring

High school courses in physics, mathematics, blueprint reading, and shop can help you gauge your aptitudes and interest in these occupations. Building electronic kits and assembling models also test manual dexterity and mechanical ability, as well as provide experience in following drawings and plans. Direct work experience in this field is probably unavailable on a part-time or summer job basis, but it may be possible to arrange a visit to a telephone company facility to get an overall view of the company's operations.

■ Employers

Telephone installers work for telecommunications companies. They also work for companies that provide phone equipment and services for hotels. Companies that install and service security systems for homes and businesses also employ installers.

■ Starting Out

Job seekers in this field should contact the employment offices of local telephone companies. Pre-employment tests may be given to determine the applicant's knowledge and aptitude for the work.

Newly hired workers learn their skills in programs that last several months. The programs may combine on-the-job work experience with formal classroom instruction and self-instruction using materials like videotapes and training manuals. Trainees practice such tasks as connecting telephones to service wires in classrooms that simulate real working conditions. They also accompany experienced workers to job sites and observe them as they work. After they have learned how to install telephone equipment, workers need additional training to become telephone repairers, PBX installers, or PBX repairers.

If there are no openings in the training program at the time they are hired, new workers are assigned instead to some other type of job until openings develop. It is common for openings for installer and repairer positions to be filled by workers who are already employed in other jobs with the same company. In the future, it probably will be even more difficult for workers coming in from outside to get these jobs.

■ Advancement

More experienced telephone installers may, with additional training, move into jobs as PBX installers or as telephone repairers. Similarly, additional training may allow telephone repairers to become PBX repairers. Some experienced workers become *installer-repairers,* combining installation and repair work on telephone company or PBX systems. Some workers may advance to supervisory positions, in which they coordinate and direct the activities of other installers or repairers.

■ Earnings

In comparison with workers in other craft fields, telephone and PBX installers and repairers are generally well paid. Their actual pay rates vary with their job responsibilities, geographical region, their length of service with the company, and other factors. According to the 1997 national employment and wage estimates of the U.S. Bureau of Labor Statistics, installers and repairers have a mean annual wage of $40,170. While some make less than $18,000 a year, others make more than $50,000. Workers in this occupation generally have a low turnover rate, therefore, many workers are in the higher wage categories. Fringe benefits for these workers usually include paid holidays and vacations, sick leave, health and disability insurance, and retirement plans.

■ Work Environment

Telephone installers and repairers often do their work independently, with a minimum of supervision. Especially during emergency situations they may need to work at night, on weekends, or on holidays to restore service. Most installers are on-call 24 hours a day. Most of the work is done in the field, in the homes and offices of clients.

Some installation work is done outside, including work on poles, ladders, and rooftops, and some work requires stooping, bending, reaching, and working in awkward or cramped positions. "I work outside in the elements every day," Steve says. "I'm exposed to all sorts of weather. Last year, I was involved with the unbelievable devastation of an ice storm in upstate New York. Thousands of phone lines came down. Those were long hours and long weeks."

PBX installers and repairers frequently work as part of crews. Most of their work is indoors, and it may involve crouching, crawling, and lifting.

■ Outlook

According to the U.S. Bureau of Labor Statistics, there are 41,000 central office and PBX installers and repairers in the country. This number is expected to decline significantly. Although some openings may become available due to workers retiring or leaving the field, the possibility of new workers filling these positions is slim. The reasons for

this drop in employment include sweeping technological changes that are making it possible to install and maintain phone systems with far fewer workers than in the past. Once the basic wiring is installed in a building, customers need only buy telephones and plug them into jacks wherever they want them. Customers can readily do some interior wiring and installation work without any help from the telephone company. These effects may be offset, however, by increased demand for a variety of services from phone and cable companies. The wide use of the Internet and fax machines has led to a number of homes with multiple lines. Because much business is now conducted through telephone lines, repairs during storms and other emergencies must be done quicker and more efficiently, requiring the skills of experienced installers and repairers.

Installers and repairers with additional training may be able to find work with the growing number of businesses that connect office computers and networks. Those with degrees in engineering can assist in the design for the cabling of business complexes, colleges, and other institutions requiring up-to-date communication services.

Employment of PBX installers and repairers will also continue to decline. New computerized systems are reliable and have self-diagnosing features that make it easier to locate problems and replace defective parts. As older equipment is taken out of service and new equipment is installed, the need for repairers and installers will decline even further.

■ For More Information

For information about unions and job opportunities, contact:

Communications Workers of America
501 Third Street, NW
Washington, DC 20001-2797
Tel: 202-434-1100
Web: http://www.cwa-union.org

For information about conferences, special programs, and membership, contact:

Women in Cable and Telecommunications
230 West Monroe, Suite 730
Chicago, IL 60606
Tel: 312-634-2330
Web: http://www.wict.org

■ Related Articles

Electronics

Telecommunications

Cable Television Technicians

Communications Equipment Technicians

Electronics Engineering Technicians

Electronics Service Technicians

Line Installers and Cable Splicers

Signal Mechanics

Wireless Service Technicians

Telephone Operators

■ Overview

Telephone operators help people using phone company services, as well as other telephone operators, to place calls and to make connections. In 1997 there were over 205,000 switchboard operators and over 22,000 directory assistance operators employed in the United States.

■ History

In the years since Alexander Graham Bell was granted a patent for his invention in 1876, the telephone has evolved from being a novelty gadget to an indispensable part of our daily lives. It is now possible to talk to someone in virtually any corner of the world on the telephone. Technological breakthroughs have allowed us to replace inefficient telephone cables with fiber optic lines and satellites for transmitting signals. Some phone features that we take for granted, such as conference calls, call waiting, and automatic call forwarding, have only been developed in the past few years.

Technology has also changed the job of the telephone operator. In the past, operators had to connect every phone call by hand, wrestling with hundreds of different cables and phone jacks and trying to match the person making the call to the number being dialed. Today, telephone switchboards are electronic, and the operator can connect many more calls by merely pushing buttons or dialing the proper code or number. Computers have replaced many of the old duties of telephone switchboard operators, such as directory assistance and the "automatic intercept" of nonoperating numbers. Still, telephone operators are needed to perform special duties and add a human touch to telecommunications.

TELEPHONE OPERATORS	
SCHOOL SUBJECTS	Business Speech
PERSONAL SKILLS	Following instructions Helping/teaching
WORK ENVIRONMENT	Primarily indoors Primarily one location
MINIMUM EDUCATION LEVEL	High school diploma
SALARY RANGE	$12,000 to $18,470 to $27,000+
CERTIFICATION OR LICENSING	None available
OUTLOOK	Decline
DOT	235
GOE	07.04.06
NOC	1424
O*NET	57199

■ The Job

If you've recently made a collect call, a fare request with an airline over the phone, or left a message for someone in a large company, you may have done so without the assistance of an operator. With automation, computers, and voice synthesizers, you can now place a call directly, and get all the information you need yourself, saving phone companies, and other businesses, time and money. The demand for telephone operators has dropped considerably from the days when operators were needed to physically connect and disconnect lines at a switchboard. AT&T has laid off thousands of operators in the last 20 years, but people can still find work with telecommunications companies and in corporations that handle a number of calls. Rynn Lemieux, an operator for the Hilton San Francisco, can remember the old "cord boards" from when she worked for an answering service over 15 years ago. "I have to say," she says, "when you disconnected a call from one of those boards, you really knew you disconnected a call. Pushing a button just does not have the oomph of yanking a cord." Though Rynn still works at a switchboard, she also uses a computer to find room numbers and in-house extensions. "I answer calls, connect to extensions and rooms, put in wake-up calls, as well as answer the TDD for the hearing impaired, page beepers, and answer questions concerning the city, the hotel, and pretty much anything else the caller can think of."

When a call comes into the phone company, a signal lights up on the switchboard, and the telephone operator makes the connection for it by pressing the proper buttons and dialing the proper numbers. If the person is calling from a pay phone, the operator may consult charts to determine the charges and ask the caller to deposit the correct amount to complete the call. If the customer requests a long-distance connection, the operator will calculate and quote the charges and then make the connection.

Directory assistance operators, also called *information operators,* answer customer inquiries for local telephone numbers by using computerized alphabetical and geographical directories. The directory assistance operator will type the spelling of the name requested and the possible location on a keyboard, then scan a directory to find the number. If the number can't be found, the operator may suggest alternate spellings of the name and look for those. When the name is located, the operator often doesn't need to read the number to the caller; instead, a computerized recording will provide the answer while the operator takes another call.

Telephone operators wear a headset that contains both an earphone and a microphone, leaving their hands free to operate the computer terminal or switchboard at which they are seated. They are supervised by central-office-operator supervisors.

Other types of switchboard supervisors perform advisory services for clients to show them how to get the most out of their phone systems. *Private branch exchange advisers* conduct training classes to demonstrate the operation of switchboard and teletype equipment, either at the telephone company's training school or on the customer's premises. They may analyze a company's telephone traffic loads and recommend the type of equipment and services that will best fit the company's needs. Service observers monitor the conversations between telephone operators and customers to observe the operators' behavior, technical skills, and adherence to phone company policies. Both of these types of workers may give advice on how operators can improve their handling of calls and their personal demeanor on the phone.

■ Requirements

High School

You should take speech, drama, and other classes that will help you with oral communication skills. Typing and computer fundamentals courses will prepare you for the demands of running a modern switchboard and for handling special services like TDD for the hearing impaired.

Postsecondary Training

Although a high school education is not a strict requirement for telephone operators, telephone companies prefer to hire people who are high school graduates. You'll likely receive most of your training from your employer, which may include classes in-house or telecommunications courses at a community college.

Certification or Licensing

Though a company may have its own training program leading to certification, there is no national certification. Many operators, however, do belong to local union chapters of such organizations as Communications Workers of America (CWA). CWA assists workers in obtaining fair wages, benefits, and working conditions.

Other Requirements

Manual dexterity is an asset to the telephone operator; however, the degree of dexterity needed is about the same as that required for the operation of any type of office equipment. Personal qualifications should include tact, patience, a desire to work with people and to be of service to others, a pleasing phone voice, an even-tempered disposition, and good judgment. Operators must also have legible handwriting and must be punctual and dependable in job attendance.

"A good memory for numbers helps," Rynn says. "It's also good to know the city where you work."

During training sessions, student operators practice using push-button consoles while they consult instruction booklets.

■ Exploring

You can explore this career by arranging a visit to a local or long-distance telephone company to observe operators at work. There you may also have the chance to talk with operators about the job. You can also learn about new developments in telephone technology and services by visiting the Web site of the United States Telephone Association (http://www.usta.org).

Part-time office jobs may give students experience in working in-company phone exchanges and switchboards, in addition to general office experience. While telephone company operations are more complex, applicants with previous experience in handling phone calls may be given preference in hiring.

■ Employers

Operators are still needed in telephone companies, but most find jobs handling the phone lines of hotels, retail stores, and other businesses with large numbers of employees. The customer service departments of companies and stores employ telephone operators to handle transactions, make courtesy calls, and answer customers' questions.

■ Starting Out

Individuals may enter this occupation by applying directly to telephone companies and long-distance carriers. In some cities, telephone offices maintain an employment office, while elsewhere employment interviews are conducted by a chief operator or personnel manager. Other job openings may be discovered through state or private employment

With call waiting, voice mail, cell phones, pagers, and all the other phone services available, it's hard to imagine a time when receiving a call wasn't so easy. Here are a few facts about the past:

• To make a long-distance call before 1910, a special operator assisted in conversation. You would tell the operator what you wanted to say to the other party, and the operator, known as a "repeater," would then repeat your message into the long-distance phone.

• The letters on your phone are frequently used for advertising purposes, but they were once used more regularly. Early "telephone exchanges" (or groups of service subscribers) were given the names of their towns, or locations within the city. To dial, you'd use the first two letters of the exchange name before dialing the subscriber's individual number.

• "Party lines" were used by more than one household—when one subscriber was making a call, another couldn't. Not only that, but subscribers could easily listen in on the phone conversations of other subscribers. (The Doris Day movie *Pillow Talk* illustrates this complication.)

agencies, newspaper advertisements, or school placement offices.

New telephone company employees are usually given a combination of classroom work and on-the-job practice. In the various telephone companies, classroom instruction usually lasts up to three weeks. The nation's time zones and geography are covered so that operators can understand how to calculate rates and know where major cities are located. Tapes are used to familiarize trainees with the various signals and tones of the phone system, as well as give them the chance to hear their own phone voices and improve their diction and courtesy. Close supervision continues after training is completed.

Telephone operators continue to receive on-the-job training throughout their careers as phone offices install more modern and automated equipment and as the methods of working with the equipment continue to change. Service assistants are responsible for instructing the new operators in various other types of special operating services.

■ Advancement

Telephone operators may have opportunities for advancement to positions as service assistant, and later to group or assistant chief operator. *Chief operators* are responsible for the planning and directing of the activities of a central office, as well as personnel functions and the performance of the employees. Service assistants may sometimes advance to become *PBX service advisors,* who go to individual businesses, assess their phone needs, and oversee equipment

installation and employee training. Some telephone operators take other positions within a telephone company, such as a clerical position, and advance within that position.

Opportunities for advancement usually depend upon the employee's personal initiative, ability, experience, length of employment, and job performance, as well as the size of the place of employment and the number of supervisors needed. Most telephone company operators are members of a union, and the union specifies the time and steps to advance from one position to another. However, many operators can become qualified for a higher-level position but then need to wait for years for an available opening. Some telephone operators become private branch exchange or switchboard operators in corporations and large businesses.

Rynn advises that you consider a job as a telephone operator as a stepping stone. "If the telecommunications industry is what interests you," she says, "aim towards installation and/or repair with a large company. That's where the real money is, and where you'll find the most respect."

■ Earnings

The wages paid to telephone operators vary from state to state, from one section of the country to another, and even from city to city. The types of duties performed by the employee also affect the salary earned.

According to the 1997 national wage estimates by the U.S. Bureau of Labor Statistics, switchboard operators had a mean annual wage of $18,470. Some made under $12,000 a year, while a small percentage made over $27,000 a year. Directory assistance operators had better wages: the mean annual wage was $27,660.

Operators are usually paid time-and-a-half for Sunday work and may receive an extra day's pay for working on legal holidays. Some additional remuneration is usually paid when employees work split shifts or shifts that end after 6:00 PM. Time-and-a-half pay is generally given if operators work more than a five-day week. Choice of work hours is usually determined on the basis of seniority. Pay increases in most instances are determined on the basis of periodic pay scales.

Fringe benefits for these employees usually include paid annual vacations of 1 week after 6 months' service, 2 weeks for 1 to 6 years, 3 weeks for 7 to 14 years, 4 weeks for 15 to 24 years, and 5 weeks for 25 or more years. The majority of companies give 9 or more paid holidays yearly. Most telephone company employees are covered by group insurance plans for sickness, accident, and death, and the majority have retirement and disability pension plans available to them.

■ Work Environment

The telephone industry operates around the clock giving the public 24-hour daily service. Operators may, therefore, be required to work evening hours, night shifts, and on Sundays and holidays. Some operators are asked to work split shifts to cover periods of heavy calling. Telephone company operators generally work 32 1/2 to 37 1/2 hours per week.

The telephone operator's job demands good physical health for punctual and regular job attendance; the work, however, is not physically strenuous or demanding. While working, operators are at the switchboard and are allowed to take periodic rest breaks. General working conditions are usually in pleasant surroundings with relatively little noise or confusion. Many telephone company operators work at video display terminals, which may cause eyestrain and muscle strain if not properly designed.

The work of a telephone operator can be very repetitive and is closely supervised. Calls are monitored by supervisors to check that operators are courteous and following company policies. Some operators find this stressful. In addition, telephone companies track the number of calls handled by each operator, and there is an increasing emphasis on operators handling a greater number of calls in order to improve cost-efficiencies. This need for higher productivity can also create stress for some workers. Many times the atmosphere becomes stressful and hectic during peak calling times, and operators need to manage a high volume of calls without becoming distressed.

■ Outlook

According to the 1997 national employment estimates by the U.S. Bureau of Labor Statistics, there were over 205,000 switchboard operators, and over 22,000 directory assistance operators. Employment of telephone operators is expected to decline significantly in the future. During the past 30 years, employment of operators in telephone companies has declined sharply due to automation which increases the productivity of these workers. Direct dialing and computerized billing have eliminated the need for many operators. Voice recognition technology, which gives computers the capacity to understand speech and to respond to callers, now offers directory assistance, and helps to place collect calls. Voice response equipment, which allows callers to communicate with computers through the use of touch tone signals, is used widely by a number of large companies. Using a combination of voice response equipment, voice mail and messaging systems, and automated call distribution, incoming phone calls can be routed to their destination without the use of an operator. The Internet is also expected to open up new avenues of phone service, allowing people to place calls at lower costs.

Operators will find most job opportunities outside the phone companies, with customer service departments, telemarketing firms, reservation ticket agencies, hotel switchboards, and other services that field a number of calls. TDD, phone services for the deaf, also requires operators, and the Americans with Disabilities Act is allowing people better access to such services. Unions have tried to make sure that companies reduce unemployment either through attrition or through retraining and reassigning workers. Many telephone companies, however, continue to make workforce reductions by eliminating telephone operator positions in an attempt to cut operating costs. There will be limited opportunities for employment as a telephone operator in the future.

■ For More Information

To learn about issues effecting jobs in telecommunications, visit the CWA Web site:

Communications Workers of America
501 Third Street, NW
Washington, DC 20001-2797
Tel: 202-434-1100
Web: http://www.cwa-union.org

■ Related Articles

Electronics

Telecommunications

Airplane Dispatchers

Receptionists

Telemarketers

Terminal Operators
■ **See Data Entry Clerks**

Test Desk Trouble Locators
■ **See Line Installers and Cable Splicers**

Test Pilots
■ **See Pilots**

Textile Conservators

■ See Textiles

Textile Manufacturing Occupations

■ Overview

Workers in textile manufacturing occupations are concerned with preparing natural and synthetic fibers for spinning into yarn and manufacturing yarn into textile products that are used in clothing, household goods, and for many industrial purposes. Among the processes that these workers perform are cleaning, carding, combing, and spinning fibers; weaving, knitting, or bonding yarns and threads into textiles; and dyeing and finishing fabrics.

TEXTILE MANUFACTURING OCCUPATIONS	
SCHOOL SUBJECTS	Computer science Voc-tech
PERSONAL SKILLS	Following instructions Mechanical/manipulative
WORK ENVIRONMENT	Primarily indoors Primarily one location
MINIMUM EDUCATION LEVEL	High school diploma
SALARY RANGE	$22,000 to $27,000 to $35,000
CERTIFICATION OR LICENSING	None available
OUTLOOK	Decline
DOT	68
GOE	06.04.10
NOC	9616
O*NET	92702

■ History

Archaeological evidence suggests that people have been weaving natural fibers into cloth for at least 7,000 years. Basketweaving probably preceded and inspired the weaving of cloth. By about 5,000 years ago, cotton, silk, linen, and wool fabrics were being produced in several areas of the world. While ancient weavers used procedures and equipment that seem simple by today's standards, some of the cloth they made was of fine quality and striking beauty.

Over time, the production of textiles grew into a highly developed craft industry with various regional centers that were renowned for different kinds of textile products. Yet, until the 18th century, the making of fabrics was largely a cottage industry in which no more than a few people, often family groups, worked in small shops with their own equipment to make products by hand. With the Industrial Revolution and the invention of machines such as the cotton gin and the power loom, a wide variety of textiles could be produced in factories at low cost and in large quantities. Improvements have continued into the 20th century, so that today many processes in making textiles are highly automated.

Other changes have revolutionized the production of fabrics. The first attempts to make artificial fibers date to the 17th century, but it was not until the late 19th and early 20th centuries that a reasonably successful synthetic, a kind of rayon, was developed from the plant substance cellulose. Since then, hundreds of synthetic fibers have been developed from such sources as coal, wood, ammonia, and proteins. Other applications of science and technology to the textile industry have resulted in cloth that has a wide variety of attractive or useful qualities. Many fabrics that resist creases, repel stains, or are fireproof, mothproof, antiseptic, nonshrinking, glazed, softened, or stiff are the product of modern mechanical or chemical finishing.

Of the textiles produced in the United States today, only about half are used for wearing apparel. The rest are used in household products (towels, sheets, upholstery) and industrial products (conveyor belts, tire cords, parachutes).

■ The Job

Most textile workers operate or tend machines. In the most modern plants, the machines are often quite sophisticated and include computerized controls.

Workers in textile manufacturing can be grouped in several categories. Some workers operate machines that clean and align fibers, draw and spin them into yarn, and knit, weave, or tuft the yarn into textile products. Other workers, usually employees of chemical companies, tend machines that produce synthetic fibers through chemical processes. Still other workers prepare machines before production runs. They set up the equipment, adjusting timing and control mechanisms, and often maintain the machines as well. Another category of workers specializes in finishing textile products before they are sent out to consumers. The following paragraphs describe just a few of the many kinds of specialized workers in textile manufacturing occupations.

In the transformation of raw fiber into cloth, one of the first steps may be performed by *staple cutters.* They place opened bales of raw stock or cans of sliver (combed, untwisted strands of fiber) at the feed end of a cutting machine. They guide the raw stock or sliver onto a conveyor belt or feed rolls, which pull it against the cutting blades. They examine the cut fibers as they fall from the blades and measure them to make sure they are the required length.

Spinneret operators oversee machinery that makes manufactured fibers from such nonfibrous materials as metal or plastic. Chemical compounds are dissolved or melted in a liquid, which is then extruded, or forced, through holes in a metal plate, called a spinneret. The size and shape of the holes determine the shape and uses of the fiber. Workers adjust the flow of fiber base through the spinneret, repair breaks in the fiber, and make minor adjustments to the machinery.

Frame spinners, also called *spinning-frame tenders,* tend machines that draw out and twist the sliver into yarn. These workers patrol the spinning-machine area to ensure that the machines have a continuous supply of sliver or roving (a soft, slightly twisted strand of fiber made from sliver). They replace nearly empty packages of roving or sliver with full ones. If they detect a break in the yarn being spun, or in the roving or sliver being fed into the spinning frame, they stop the machine and repair the break. They are responsible for keeping a continuous length of material threaded through the spinning frame while the machine is operating.

Spinning supervisors supervise and coordinate the activities of the various spinning workers. From the production schedule, they determine the quantity and texture of yarn to be spun and the type of fiber to be used. Then they compute such factors as the proper spacing of rollers and the correct size of twist gears, using mathematical formulas and tables and their knowledge of spinning machine processes. As the spun yarn leaves the spinning frame, they examine it to detect variations from standards.

A textile production worker adjusts the tension on one of the rapier weaving machines. Once the fiber is spun into yarn or thread, it is ready for weaving, knitting, or tufting. Woven fabrics are made on looms that interlace the threads. Knit products, such as socks or women's hosiery, are produced by intermeshing loops of yarn. The tufting process, used in making carpets, involves pushing loops of yarn through a material backing.

Beam-warper tenders work at high-speed warpers, which are machines that automatically wind yarn onto beams, or cylinders, preparatory to dyeing or weaving. A creel, or

A textile production worker adjusts the tension on one of the rapier weaving machines.

rack of yarn spools, is positioned at the feed end of the machine. The workers examine the creel to make sure that the size, color, number, and arrangement of the yarn spools correspond to specifications. They thread the machine with the yarn from the spools, pulling the yarn through several sensing devices, and fastening the yarn to the empty cylinder. After setting a counter to record the amount of yarn wound, they start the machine. If a strand of yarn breaks, the machine stops, and the tenders locate and tie the broken ends. When the specified amount of yarn has been wound, they stop the machine, cut the yarn strands, and tape the cut ends.

Weavers or *loom operators* operate a battery of automatic looms that weave yarn into cloth. They observe the cloth being woven carefully to detect any flaws, and they remove weaving defects by cutting out the filling (cross) threads in the area. If a loom stops, they locate the problem and either correct it or, in the case of mechanical breakdown, notify the appropriate repairer.

After the fabric is removed from the loom, it is ready for dyeing and finishing, which includes treating fabrics to make them fire-, shrink-, wrinkle-, or soil-resistant.

Dye-range operators control the feed end of a dye range, which is an arrangement of equipment that dyes and dries cloth. Operators position the cloth to be dyed and machine-sew its end to the end of the cloth already in the machine. They turn valves to admit dye from a mixing tank onto the dye pads, and they regulate the temperature of the dye and the air in the drying box. They start the machine, and when the process is complete, they record yardage dyed, lot numbers, and the machine running time. *Colorists, screen printing artists, screen makers,* and *screen printers* print designs on textiles.

Cloth testers perform tests on gray goods and finished cloth samples. They may count the number of threads in a sample, test its tensile strength in a tearing machine, and crease it to determine its resilience. They may also test for such characteristics as abrasion resistance, fastness of dye, flame retardance, and absorbency, depending on the type of cloth.

■ Requirements

High School

For some textile production jobs, a high school education is desirable but may not be necessary. Workers who operate machines are often hired as unskilled labor and trained on the job. However, with the increasingly complex machinery and manufacturing methods in this industry, more and more often a high school diploma plus some technical training is expected of job applicants. High school students interested in a textile career should take courses in physics, chemistry, mathematics, and English. Computer skills are necessary, since many machines are now operated by computer technology.

Postsecondary Training

Even those with postsecondary school education generally must go through a period of on-the-job training by experienced workers or representatives of equipment manufacturers where they learn the procedures and systems of their particular company. Some companies have coop programs with nearby schools. Participants in these programs work as interns during their academic training with the agreement that they will work for the sponsoring company upon graduation. A two-year associate degree in textile technology is required for technicians, laboratory testers, and supervisory personnel.

Other Requirements

Many machine operators need physical stamina, manual dexterity, and a mechanical aptitude to do their job. Changes are under way in the industry that make other kinds of personal characteristics increasingly important, such as the ability to assume responsibility, to take initiative, to communicate with others, and to work well as a part of a team.

About 15 percent of all textile production workers belong to a union, such as the Union of Needle Trades, Industrial, and Textile Employees (UNITE).

■ Exploring

High school courses in subjects such as shop, mechanical drawing, and chemistry and hobbies involving model-building and working with machinery can be good preparation for many jobs in the textile manufacturing field. Students may be able to find summer employment in a textile plant. If that cannot be arranged, a machine operator's job in another manufacturing industry may provide a similar enough experience that it is useful in understanding something about textile manufacturing work.

■ Employers

Most textile production workers are employed either in mills that spin and weave "gray goods," meaning raw, undyed, unfinished fabrics, or in finishing plants, where gray goods are treated with processes like dyeing and bleaching. Some textile companies combine these two stages of manufacturing under one roof.

Employment opportunities for textile manufacturing workers are concentrated in the South and the Northeast. Over half of the jobs in this industry are located in the states of North Carolina, Georgia, and South Carolina.

■ Starting Out

Most textile production workers obtain their jobs by answering newspaper advertisements or by applying directly to the personnel office of a textile plant. A new worker usually receives between a week and several months of on-the-job training, depending on the complexity of the job.

Graduates of textile technology programs in colleges and technical institutes may be informed about job openings through their school's placement office. They may be able to line up permanent positions before graduation. Sometimes students in technical programs are sponsored by a local textile company, and upon graduation, they go to work for the sponsoring company.

■ Advancement

Production workers in textile manufacturing who become skilled machine operators may be promoted to positions in which they train new employees. Other workers can qualify for better jobs by learning additional machine-operating skills. Usually the workers with the best knowledge of machine operations are those who set up and prepare machines before production runs. Skilled workers who show that they have good judgment and leadership abilities may be promoted to supervisory positions, in charge of a bank of machines or a stage in the production process. Some companies offer continuing education opportunities to dedicated workers.

Laboratory workers may advance to supervisory positions in the lab. If their educational background includes such courses as industrial engineering and quality control, they may move up to management jobs where they plan and control production.

■ Earnings

Earnings of textile industry workers vary depending on the type of plant where they are employed and the workers' job responsibilities, the shift they work, and seniority. Overall, the average annual wage for textile workers in 1998 was $425 a week or about $22,000 a year, according to the American Textile Manufacturers Institute. Workers at plants located in the North tend to be paid more than those in the South.

Beginning laboratory testers and technicians with associate degrees in textile technology can earn annual salaries ranging from $27,000 to about $35,000 after a few years of experience, according to the North Carolina Center for Applied Textile Technology. Salaries generally increase with more education and greater responsibility.

Most workers with a year or more of service receive paid vacations and insurance benefits. Many are able to participate in pension plans, profit sharing, or year-end bonuses. Some companies offer their employees discounts on the textiles or textile products they sell.

■ Work Environment

Work areas in modern textile plants are largely clean, well lighted, air-conditioned, and humidity-controlled. Older facilities may be less comfortable, with more fibers or fumes in the air, requiring some workers to wear protective glasses or masks. Some machines can be very noisy, and workers near them must wear ear protectors. Workers also must stay alert and use caution when working around high-speed machines that can catch clothing or jewelry. Those who work around chemicals must wear protective clothing and sometimes respirators. Increasing attention to worker safety and health has forced textile manufacturing companies to comply with tough federal, state, and local regulations.

Workweeks in this industry average 40 hours in length. Depending on business conditions, some plants may operate 24 hours a day, with three shifts a day. Production employees may work rotating shifts, so that they share night and weekend hours. Some companies have a four-shift continuous operating schedule, consisting of a 168-hour workweek made of up of four daily shifts totaling 42 hours a week. This system offers a rotating arrangement of days off. During production cutbacks, companies may go to a three- or four-day workweek, but they generally try to avoid layoffs during slow seasons.

Machine operators are often on their feet during much of their shift. Some jobs involve repetitive tasks that some people find boring.

■ Outlook

In 1997 more than 600,000 people were employed in the U.S. textile industry. About 500,000 were machine operators in textile mills. Over the next 10 to 15 years, employment in this field is expected to decline, even as the demand for textile products increases.

Changes in the textile industry will account for much of this decline. Factories are reorganizing production operations for greater efficiency and installing equipment that relies on more highly automated and computerized machines and processes. Such technology as shuttleless and air-jet looms and computer-controlled machinery allows several machines to be operated by one operator and still increase speed and productivity.

Another factor that will probably contribute to a reduced demand for U.S. textile workers is an increase in imports of textiles from other countries. There is a continuing trend toward freer world markets and looser trade restrictions.

While fewer workers will be needed to operate machines, there will continue to be many job openings each year as experienced people transfer to other jobs or leave the workforce. Workers who have good technical training and skills will have the best job opportunities. In fact, the demand for highly skilled workers, such as scientists, engineers, and computer specialists, will be even greater as companies strive to expand their markets globally.

■ For More Information

This union fights for workers' rights and represents workers in various industries, including basic apparel and textiles. It was recently formed from a merger of International Ladies' Garment Workers Union and the Amalgamated Clothing and Textile Workers Union.

UNITE (Union of Needle Trades, Industrial and Textile Employees)
1710 Broadway
New York, NY 10019
Tel: 212-265-7000
Web: http://www.uniteunion.org

This national trade association for the U.S. textile industry has member companies that operate in more than 30 states and process about 80 percent of all textile fibers consumed by plants in the United States. It works to encourage global competitiveness and increase foreign market access.

American Textile Manufacturers Institute
1130 Connecticut Avenue, NW, Suite 1200
Washington, DC 20006
Tel: 202-862-0500
Web: http://www.atmi.org

The following research and graduate education organization offers a master's degree in textile technology. It also offers fee-based library and information services.

Institute of Textile Technology
2551 Ivy Road
Charlottesville, VA 22903
Tel: 804-296-5511
Web: http://www.itt.edu

■ **Related Jobs**

Fashion

Machining and Machinery

Textiles

Apparel Industry Workers

Apparel Technicians

Chemical Technicians

Computer-Aided Manufacturing Technicians

Industrial Machinery Mechanics

Knit Goods Industry Workers

Laboratory Testing Technicians

Textile Technicians

Textile Technicians

■ Overview

Textile technicians help produce fibers, such as yarn and thread, textiles, and finished textile products, such as apparel, rugs, and canvas. Technicians may work in research, design, and development, creating new fibers and new ways to process them, or improving methods of converting fibers into textiles and textile products. Textile technicians may also work in the production of fibers, textiles, or textile products. They may be involved in such processes as combing, carding, spinning, weaving, knitting, extruding or casting film solutions, dyeing and finishing. They test fibers and textiles for tensile strength, heat resistance, crease resiliency, and laundering durability. Finally, textile technicians may work in sales and customer service, making sure textiles and fibers meet the specifications of customers.

■ History

The textile manufacturing industry has seen drastic changes since the Industrial Revolution, when textile mechanics and machinery operators were the predecessors of today's textile technicians. The development of the first synthetic fibers more than 75 years ago improved textiles' function and versatility, and changed how people lived. New fibers and finishes have made fabric care less time-consuming and costly. Stretch fabrics have kept pace with active sports and leisure interests. Durable, soil-resistant carpets cover the floors of U.S. homes, schools, offices, and hospitals. The car industry uses textiles in seat belts, upholstery, and carpeting and to reinforce tires, belts, and hoses.

New properties have been engineered into fibers and fabrics so that textiles now are used in medical dressings and bacteria-resistant hospital gowns, artificial veins and arteries, space suits, and flame-resistant coats for fire fighters. They are also used in cables for deep-sea oil-drilling rigs, reinforced boat hulls, road building, and industrial plant filters. The military uses textiles in a myriad of items, from rifle slings and body armor to parachutes and uniforms that resist infrared rays.

Production of this wide variety of goods creates employment for nearly two million people in the United States: 616,000 textile employees in more than 5,000 companies manufacture 22 billion square yards of textile products annually. There are 826,000 employees in the apparel industry. These two industries are among the largest employers of women and minorities and have served as an entry-level training ground for unskilled men and women entering industry. In addition, textile industry growth has created a demand for textile technicians who have more education and the skills to manage complex processes.

The textile and apparel industries operate in nearly every state. Fiber, either natural or manmade, is produced in 45 states, textile mill products are made in 48 states, and apparel is made in 49 states. The industries began in New England, where water power was abundant and workers were available. In the past five decades, however, these industries have grown rapidly in the southern states. Today, companies in three states—North Carolina, South Carolina, and Georgia—employ more than half of all U.S. textile and apparel workers.

During the past decade or so, the U.S. textile industry has been forced by intense foreign competition to improve its already highly developed technology and processing methods. Because the textile and apparel market in this country is so large, it has attracted imports from Japan, Hong Kong, Korea, Taiwan, China, and other countries. In response to this competition, the industry has undergone the most revolutionary changes in its history.

Open-end spinning, for instance, has boosted yarn production by four times the rate of the old spinning method. It has also reduced the steps in manufacturing yarn from as many as fifteen to as few as three.

Fabric used to be woven with a wooden shuttle moving back and forth across a loom. Now yarns are propelled by air or water jets that yield three times the speed and can produce seven to eight times the fabric, and are safer and quieter.

In the field of knitting, recent developments have been made in electronic knitting machines; perhaps the most important sweater production development in decades. With electronic machines, a sweater design is transferred to a computer tape that operates the machine automatically, producing a newly designed sweater in two to three hours. Previous knitting machines took as long as a week and were not nearly as accurate.

Other types of research and development have occurred. One leading textile company has developed a machine that applies complex colors and patterns to carpets and other fabrics through the use of thousands of tiny dye jets individually controlled by computer.

Better utilization of human effort in the industry through better management is also a part of the modernization of the industry. Quality circles, which are groups of workers, technicians, and managers, meet regularly to discuss and plan how to improve their departments' quality and efficiency. All of these improvements have produced a need for highly qualified technicians to assist scientists and engineers and act as links with production workers.

■ The Job

Textile technicians can work in three major areas: research, design, and development; quality control and production; and customer service and sales.

Those involved in research and development study natural, manufactured, and synthetic fibers and textiles to determine their nature, origin, use, improvement, and processing methods. Natural fibers include wool, mohair, cashmere, camel's hair, alpaca, bristles, feathers, similar animal and fowl fibers, and plant fibers, such as cotton, linen, and jute. Manufactured fibers include nylon, polyester, olefin, and acrylic.

Technicians involved in quality control and production are concerned with manufacturing methods for converting fibers into textiles and textile products, such as cloth, felts, rugs, mattresses, and brushes. Methods may include combing and carding, spinning, weaving, knitting, extruding, or casting film solutions. Some textile technicians work on the electronic controls of a knitting machine or a loom, and some oversee dyeing and finishing processes. Others test fibers, textiles, and apparel for tensile strength, stability and reactions to heat, light, and chemicals.

Technicians in customer service and sales act as liaisons between manufacturers and the buyers of their textiles and clothing. They make sure the textiles meet specifications and are delivered in the most timely, cost-effective way.

Research and development technicians, sometimes called *assistant research scientists* or *assistant engineers,* study polymer science, fiber chemistry, yarn production, fabrication

efficiency and flexibility, dyeing and finishing, development or modification of production machinery, and application of new technology to solve problems. Some research technicians develop new textiles to be used for a specific purpose, while others design new uses for existing textiles.

Product development technicians work with research and development staff to develop prototypes of products. Technicians conduct performance tests on samples and combine them with use, wear, or product tests. These may include tests for tensile strength, abrasion resistance, washability, flammability, elasticity, and comfort using standard test methods and specialized testing equipment. Depending on test results, technicians may then modify the product. *General laboratory technicians* test cloth samples and chemically analyze fiber blends. *Evenness tester technicians* operate electronic testers, analyze the results, and report needed changes in machine settings to the appropriate department, a critical quality-control task. *Dye-lab technicians* use sample dyeing equipment to dye sample cloth according to dye formulas in order to verify that products meet company specifications. Dye-lab technicians calculate the amount of dye required for machines of different capacities, and they weigh and mix dyes and other chemicals, using scales, graduated cylinders, and titration cylinders.

Quality control technicians make sure products meet or exceed standards and specifications, such as weight and count characteristics, colorfastness, and stability. These standards must be met in a safe, cost-effective, and efficient manner. Quality control technicians, engineers, and managers develop these standards and specifications, and conduct tests to be sure that both purchased and produced items meet them. Quality control technicians also develop procedures for troubleshooting and problem solving in purchasing, product specification, or production.

Production and quality control technicians need to understand the scientific principles behind textile products and must also know how to operate the

TEXTILE TECHNICIANS	
SCHOOL SUBJECTS	Chemistry Physics
PERSONAL SKILLS	Mechanical/manipulative Technical/scientific
WORK ENVIRONMENT	Primarily indoors Primarily one location
MINIMUM EDUCATION LEVEL	Associate's degree
SALARY RANGE	$27,000 to $40,000 to $60,000
CERTIFICATION OR LICENSING	None available
OUTLOOK	Little change or more slowly than the average
DOT	040
GOE	05.01.08
NOC	2233
O*NET	89599F

MILITARY BENEFITS FROM TEXTILE RESEARCH

Researchers are exploring the development of "intelligent" textiles primarily for military use. For example, adaptive camouflage would enable a soldier's uniform to change colors to blend in better with the surrounding environment.

Researchers are also looking into developing textiles that would enable medical teams to locate soldiers who are wounded in battle and determine the size and location of their wounds. The fabric, containing metallic fibers, would emit low-intensity signals when ripped. The signals would transmit information about the injury to a medical team. The textiles could also be interwoven with medication that would be released onto the skin in predetermined doses.

manufacturing and testing equipment; at times, they must operate the machinery or perform the tests themselves. They may also teach new operators the procedures.

Customer sales and service technicians have an intimate knowledge of production and quality control, as well as good communication skills. They have to understand customer needs and convey them to research and development or production personnel. They may be required to travel.

Textile technicians also work for the U.S. government, which is one of the world's largest consumers of textile products. *Purchasing officers* locate producers and suppliers of specific textile products and make sure they meet government requirements. *Textile testing engineers* test and evaluate a product or prototype using Federal Test Methods and Standards to verify that its performance meets the government's requirements. *Customs inspectors* examine all imported goods for correct quotas and labeling requirements, and to make sure they are free of insects and disease organisms. Many positions are also available for textile technicians in the military. Government research facilities employ technicians to develop textile products such as uniforms for adverse weather conditions, space suits, interiors for space vehicles and submarines, and suits to protect against biological and chemical warfare.

■ Requirements

High School

High school students can prepare for a textile technician career by taking four years of English and at least two years of mathematics, including algebra and geometry. Courses in physics, chemistry, and biology that include laboratory work are also very important preparation. High school courses in computer science and mechanical drafting and design are most valuable.

Postsecondary Training

In past years, technicians often began as machine operators and moved into their jobs after several years of experience. Although this may still happen occasionally, most companies today want to hire graduates of a two-year college or technical school with a degree in textile technology. Some companies even require a four-year degree.

Textile technicians must be broadly prepared and systems-oriented. They must be able to work with a wide variety of textile fibers and fabrics. Their work also involves equipment for producing textiles. Recent refinements and use of computers have made this equipment some of today's most technologically complex machinery. Textile technicians must have an understanding of the technical disciplines that support this kind of machinery.

The first year of a typical two-year associate degree program for textile manufacturing technicians includes courses in fabric manufacture, natural and synthetic fibers, yarn manufacturing, apparel and home furnishings, industrial safety, textile testing, textile cost analysis, industrial organization and management, public speaking, applied physics, algebra, trigonometry, and English composition. Second-year courses for textile manufacturing technicians might include textile quality control, general psychology, textile merchandising, engineering graphics, computer programming, fundamentals of supervision, economics, weaving and fabric analysis, managerial communications, finishing mill operations, and chemistry.

In some programs, the summer between the first and second years is devoted to an internship or cooperative education session that is spent working as a paid employee of a textile company.

Several schools, especially in the Southeast, have four-year degree programs in textile technology, textile engineering, textile management/production/service, textile design, textile chemistry, fiber/textiles/weaving, and textile marketing. A bachelor of science degree in physical sciences, chemistry, or science technologies can also provide the appropriate skills and knowledge for a career in the textile industry. Major centers for textile education include North Carolina State University in Raleigh; Center for Applied Textile Technology in Belmont, Georgia; Institute of Technology in Atlanta, Georgia; Clemson University in South Carolina; and Philadelphia College of Textiles and Science.

A bachelor of science degree in textile technology might require such courses as chemistry, geometry, calculus, yarn production systems, physics, textile form and structure, fiber science, knitting systems, technology of dyeing and finishing, weaving systems, textile yarn production and properties, textile measurement and quality control, physical properties of textile fibers, fiberweb and nonwoven production, and technical fabric design.

On-the-job training teaches technicians skills specific to a particular company, and retraining is necessary when companies acquire new, state-of-the-art equipment.

Other Requirements

In addition to educational requirements, certain personal qualifications are needed to be successful, including the ability to work with others and to accept supervision, to work independently and accept responsibility for one's work, and to work accurately and carefully. Technicians are often required to communicate with workers and customers from different cultures and educational backgrounds. Those in research and development must be able to communicate with scientists and engineers who supervise them. Those in product development must be creative, resourceful, and able to sell their ideas.

Physical requirements for this career are not especially demanding. Average or better hand-eye coordination and manual dexterity are required; color blindness can be a serious disadvantage for textile technicians.

There are no national or state certification requirements for textile technicians, although some companies have their own in-house testing procedures. About one-fifth of all textile workers belong to labor unions, but membership usually is not required for technicians.

■ **Exploring**

Interested students can obtain information from guidance centers in high schools, community colleges, or technical institutions. Occupational information centers and catalogs of schools that offer programs for textile and apparel technicians are also good sources of information.

Guidance counselors can obtain excellent descriptive materials and audiovisual presentations on the textile industry from the American Textile Manufacturer's Institute. Individual companies also produce informative brochures about their employment opportunities. A visit to a producing textile or clothing factory makes it possible to observe the machinery and work, and gives prospective technicians an opportunity to talk to workers and gain insight about the work. One of the best opportunities for experience is a summer job with a textile or apparel company, preferably in some activity closely related to the actual production operations.

■ **Employers**

There are both large and small companies whose primary concern is textiles and that offer employment opportunities for researchers, technicians, designers, production workers, managers, purchasers, and salespeople. There are opportunities available in other industries that are not textile-based, including automotive industries, chemical companies, and biomedical companies. Large firms, such as

A textile technician operates a machine that winds strands of yarn onto spools for weaving.

Allied-Signal, American Cyanamid, Hoechst Celanese, Amoco, and E. I. du Pont de Nemours, have a variety of concerns, including fiber and textile divisions, that employ large numbers of workers.

The Southeast, including North Carolina, South Carolina, and Georgia, has 60 percent of the textile jobs. The remaining jobs in the United States are found almost exclusively in the South and Northeast, particularly in New Jersey and Massachusetts. Technicians can find employment in research institutions, textile manufacturing plants, product design and development companies, raw materials manufacturers, testing facilities, apparel companies, and manufacturers of home furnishings. Companies need not necessarily be textile based, however, to have opportunities for textile technicians. There are also many jobs in industrial settings, such as the automotive industry, chemical companies that make binders for textiles, and biomedical companies that make textiles for a variety of uses in the health care field.

After accumulating a great deal of experience and knowledge in textiles, those involved in research, development of new products, or design of textiles and products can become independent consultants. They basically work for themselves and provide services to small- and medium-sized firms.

■ **Starting Out**

Graduate textile technicians are often hired by recruiters from the major employers in the field. Recruiters regularly visit schools with textile technician programs and arrange interviews with graduating students through the school's placement center.

Some students, however, attend school under the sponsorship of a textile or clothing company and usually go to work for their sponsor after graduation. Some are cooperative students who attend school with the understanding that they will return to their sponsor plant. Some sponsoring companies, however, do not place any restriction on their coop students and allow them to find the best job they can with any company. Students may also write to or visit potential employers that are of special interest.

The two-year college curriculum condenses the traditional four-year textile engineering program, yet includes the basics that industry needs. Many employers have a strong preference for graduates of the two-year program, and give such graduates a short, intensive in-plant orientation and training program so that they can be placed where their skills can be used immediately. Many graduate technicians who participated in a cooperative program are given responsible positions immediately upon graduation. Some in-plant training programs are designed to train new technicians to work as supervisors.

■ Advancement

Opportunities for advancement are excellent for textile technicians. They may become section supervisors, production superintendents, or plant managers. Not all technicians, however, are suited for the production floor. Those persons can advance to responsible positions in industrial engineering, quality control, production control, or specialized technical areas.

One advanced position is that of *fabric development specialist*. Technicians in this position help translate the designer's ideas into a new fabric. This work requires an expert knowledge of textile manufacturing processes and machinery. Fabric development specialists are employed by textile fiber producers and textile knitting and weaving firms. They may advance further to the position of *fabric development stylist* and finally to the management level.

Other advanced positions include *textile converter*, who decides how textile materials are to be dyed or printed, *textile dyeing and finishing specialist, quality-control analyst, textile purchasing agent,* and *technical service representative*.

Some technicians may become *plant training specialists* or *plant safety experts and directors*. Safety training on the job is important in textile manufacturing and is an attractive and satisfying career.

With the recent technological improvements in the textile industry, opportunities have increased for technical specialists to work as self-employed consultants or to start their own businesses.

■ Earnings

Graduates of two-year postsecondary textile manufacturing technician programs who have little or no previous textile experience start off making about $27,000 a year, according to the North Carolina Center for Applied Textile Technology.

After four to six years of experience, textile manufacturing technicians usually advance to annual salaries in the mid-thirties. A college graduate of a four-year textile program can start out as a management trainee earning on average $36,468 and can advance to an annual salary of $40,000 to $50,000, according to North Carolina State University College of Textiles.

After 10 to 20 years of advancement to top-level positions, persons who started as technicians can earn annual salaries up to and above $60,000.

Government positions generally pay less than those with private companies, and research and development technicians usually earn more than production technicians.

Textile technicians usually receive the benefits of salaried staff such as paid holidays, vacations, group insurance benefits, and employee retirement plans. In addition, they often have the benefit of company support for all or a part of educational programs. This is an important benefit because these technicians must continually study to keep up to date with technological changes in this rapidly developing field.

■ Work Environment

The textile industry of today is comparatively safe and grows more comfortable every year. Textile plants have temperature and humidity controls that outdo those in most homes and apartments. Heavy lifting is now handled by machines. Workers often are required to wear protective face masks, earplugs, and protective clothing. The new plant is typically a one-story building, clean, well-lighted, smaller than its counterpart of a few years ago, and much more efficient. The industry places great emphasis on safety, cleanliness, and orderliness.

The work of technicians involves handling a succession of highly technical problems in a wide variety of situations. Technicians must define each problem, gather pertinent information, use the appropriate measurements and methods to obtain accurate data, analyze the facts, and arrive at a solution to the problem through logic and sound judgment. This process may involve consultation with scientists, engineers, or managers. All of this requires patience, resourcefulness, and the ability to work calmly and systematically for extended periods of time. It also requires constant study of the new developments in the field.

Most technicians spend some time at a desk or at a computer screen, but much of their work takes place in the laboratory, which has very carefully controlled conditions, or on the plant floor, which can be noisy.

Research technicians usually report to a supervising engineer or scientist. Production technicians may be supervisors themselves or report to a production manager. Although they need to communicate well with other supervisors, workers, and customers, many technicians enjoy a certain amount of autonomy in their work.

■ Outlook

As automation increases and machinery replaces labor, the textile industry is changing from a labor-intensive to a technology-intensive operation. Technological advances have decreased the demand for many production occupations, and skill requirements for many jobs are changing.

The demand for textiles is likely to increase, but the number of new jobs will decrease, not only because of automation but because of competition from foreign imports and the increasing use of synthetic fibers. The demand for highly skilled workers such as dyers and knitting-machine mechanics should increase. Chemists, engineers, computer specialists, and textile technicians should also continue to be in demand.

For the foreseeable future, total textile employment is expected to grow more slowly than the industry's output. As older textile technicians retire, there will be a need to replace personnel, but cost-containment measures will curb the creation of new positions. Education is increasingly important to employers trying to fill the small number of positions. High school graduates will likely be passed over in favor of applicants with at least two years, and preferably four years, of technical training.

The textile industry in most developed countries has suffered in recent years because of the competition from third-world countries that hire 40 or more workers per hour at the cost of one American worker.

■ For More Information

This national trade association for the U.S. textile industry has member companies that operate in more than 30 states and process about 80 percent of all textile fibers consumed by plants in the United States. It works to encourage global competitiveness and increase foreign market access.

American Textile Manufacturers Institute
1130 Connecticut Avenue, NW, Suite 1200
Washington, DC 20006
Tel: 202-862-0500
Web: http://www.atmi.org

The following research and graduate education organization offers a master's degree in textile technology. It also offers fee-based library and information services.

Institute of Textile Technology
2551 Ivy Road
Charlottesville, VA 22903
Tel: 804-296-5511
Web: http://www.itt.edu

■ Related Articles

Chemicals

Fashion

Textiles

Apparel Industry Workers

Apparel Technicians

Chemical Engineers

Chemical Technicians

Computer-Aided Manufacturing Technicians

Industrial Engineering Technicians

Industrial Engineers

Knit Goods Industry Workers

Laboratory Testing Technicians

Quality Control Engineers and Technicians

Textile Manufacturing Occupations

Therapeutic Recreation Specialists
■ **See Child Life Specialists**

Ticket Attendants
■ **See Amusement Park Workers**

Ticketing Clerks
■ **See Reservation and Ticket Agents**

Tire Technicians

■ Overview

Tire technicians, employed by tire manufacturers, test tires to determine their strength, durability (how long they will last), and any defects in their construction.

■ History

Before tires came into use, wheels were banded by metal. Copper bands were used on chariot wheels in the Middle East as early as 2000 BC. Strips of metal were widely used on wheels in medieval and early modern times.

Robert Thomson patented the first pneumatic tire for carriages in 1845. Thirty-three years later, John Dunlop patented a pneumatic tire for automobiles and bicycles and created a company for the manufacture of such tires. Early automobiles used solid rubber tires or narrow pneumatic tires similar to inner-tube or single-tube bicycle tires. As automobiles grew heavier and as vehicle size and speed increased, tire manufacturers developed better and more durable tires. After World War II, synthetic rubber and synthetic fibers were used for most tire construction. In the following years, the tubeless automobile tire, puncture-sealing tires, and radial-ply tires were introduced for American trucks, cars, planes, and other vehicles. Throughout the last 150 years of tire innovation, tire technicians have been called upon to test and monitor the quality and durability of these tires.

■ The Job

Most tire technicians work either with experimental models of tires that are not yet ready for manufacturing or with production samples as they come out of the factory. Technicians who are involved mostly with testing tires from the factory are called *quality-control technicians.*

There are mainly two types of testing performed by tire technicians—dedicated and free flowing, or general, testing. Dedicated testing is a high-tech, electronically run procedure that measures rolling resistance. This is the resistance at which a tire meets force and momentum (the force acting against the tire). Dedicated testing requires the technician to be present at all times during the procedure, monitoring the machines, programming variables, and collecting data. Free flowing testing is a durability type testing. It may last for days or even weeks and covers many different operations that test the tire's durability. A tire technician might test 45 tires at once using different procedures.

To perform testing, tire technicians inflate the tires and mount them on testing machines. These machines recreate the stresses of actual road conditions, such as traveling at high speeds, carrying a heavy load, or going over bumpy roads. The technicians can adjust the machines to change the speed, the weight of the load, or the bumpiness of the road surface. Then they use pressure gauges and other devices to detect whether any parts of the tire are damaged and to evaluate tire uniformity, quality, and durability. This is done either while the tire is on the machine or after it is taken off. Technicians continue testing the tire until it fails or until it has lasted for some specified period of time.

Another test involves cutting cross-sections from brand new or road-tested tires. Technicians use power saws to cut up tires and then inspect the pieces to assess the condition of the cords, plies (which are rubbery sheets of material inside the tire), and the tread.

Throughout the testing, tire technicians keep careful records of all test results. Later, they prepare reports that may include charts, tables, and graphs to help describe and explain the test results. If a flaw is found, the technician records the data collected and reports it to the supervisor or the engineer in charge. The safety of all vehicles riding on all types of tires is dependent upon the role the tire technician plays in the tire manufacturing process.

■ Requirements

High School

Tire technicians need to be high school graduates. While in high school, take courses in science and mathematics, including algebra and geometry; English courses that improve reading and writing skills; and shop or laboratory science courses that introduce measuring devices, electrical machinery, and electronic testing equipment. Training in typing will also allow tire technicians to quickly input and deliver information.

Postsecondary Training

Increasingly, many employers prefer applicants with postsecondary training in a field related to manufacturing or product testing. Goodyear requires a two-year technical

TIRE TECHNICIANS	
SCHOOL SUBJECTS	Computer science Mathematics
PERSONAL SKILLS	Following instructions Mechanical/manip-ulative
WORK ENVIRONMENT	Primarily indoors Primarily one location
MINIMUM EDUCATION LEVEL	Some postsecondary training
SALARY RANGE	$26,400 to $37,000 to $40,000
CERTIFICATION OR LICENSING	None available
OUTLOOK	About as fast as the average
DOT	750
GOE	06.03.01
NOC	9423
O*NET	85953

certificate or an associate's degree in electronics for those seeking employment. This kind of training may be received at a vocational school or a community or junior college.

Other Requirements

Tire technicians must have good written and oral communications skills in order to relay results to other technicians engineers, managers, and supervisors. They need to be skillful in writing reports and adept at reading and producing charts and graphs. They must also be familiar with computers and able to collect and record data accurately and precisely.

■ Exploring

Students can get a general overview of the tire industry by reading *Tire & Rim Association Yearbook* or *Tire Review*. A high school science teacher or guidance counselor may also be able to arrange a presentation by an experienced tire technician. Students may gain indirect experience by working part-time or in the summer at a plant where tires are manufactured and tested.

■ Employers

Tire technicians are employed by tire manufacturers. The large manufacturing companies, such as Goodyear, Dunlop, and Michelin, all employ technicians to conduct testing on new tires.

■ Starting Out

A good way to find employment is to apply directly at personnel offices of tire manufacturers. Employment placement services at technical institutes and vocational schools also will be good sources of information. Employers looking for qualified technicians often contact these schools when there are job openings.

■ Advancement

Experienced tire technicians may also find opportunities in engineering. Those with advanced training in engineering may become tire test engineers or information processors. Those with considerable tenure with one company and proven organizational and communications skills may advance to management positions. Advanced tire technicians may become supervisors in the tire testing area or in other sections of the facility.

Experience as a tire technician may also provide a good background for work in quality control, which involves examining a product after it is produced. Quality control personnel can be found in many environments, from factories to offices.

A tire is assembled on a tire building machine.

■ Earnings

Starting salaries for tire technicians average $26,400 per year. The median salary for tire technicians is $37,000 per year. Technicians with advanced expertise and experience can make up to $40,000 a year. Those employed by large manufacturing facilities are usually eligible for paid vacations, holidays, sick days, and insurance. Many facilities operate around the clock, and opportunities to work off-shifts, Sundays, and holidays brings time-and-a-half and double-time compensation.

■ Work Environment

Many plants operate 24 hours a day. Newly hired technicians may have to work off-shifts, nights, and weekends. More experienced tire technicians usually get a choice of shifts.

Tire technicians are responsible for filling out reports, making charts and graphs, and relaying important information, both verbally and in writing. As a result, they are under considerable stress to provide accurate, detailed information in a timely manner. They also must frequently work on several projects simultaneously and be able to change projects midstream to address changing deadlines. Tire technicians can be proud that they are relied on to make decisions that affect both multimillion-dollar businesses and the driving public.

■ Outlook

Employment for tire technicians should grow about as fast as the average for all occupations through 2006. As long as tires are needed—not just for automobiles, but for trucks, buses, utility vehicles and airplanes—so too, will technicians. Manufacturers will likely continue to develop new and improved tires, and qualified tire technicians will be needed to test them.

■ For More Information

For information on technical standards and training programs, contact:

American Society for Testing and Materials
100 Barr Harbor Drive
West Conshohocken, PA 19428-2959
Tel: 610-832-9585
Web: http://www.astm.org

This organization offers training programs and publications.

International Tire and Rubber Association
3332 Gilmore Industrial Boulevard
Louisville, KY 40213-4113
Tel: 502-968-8900
Web: http://www.itra.com

For a list of U.S. tire manufacturers and consumer tire-safety information, contact:

Tire Industry Safety Council
1400 K Street, NW, Ninth Floor
Washington, DC 20005
Tel: 202-783-1022
Web: http://www.tmn.com/tisc

■ Related Articles

Plastics
Rubber
Industrial Designers
Plastics Products Manufacturing Workers
Plastics Technicians
Quality Control Engineers and Technicians
Rubber Goods Production Workers

Title Searchers and Examiners

■ Overview

Title searchers and *examiners* conduct searches of public records to determine the legal chain of ownership for a piece of real estate. Searchers compile lists of mortgages, deeds, contracts, judgments, and other items pertaining to a property title. Examiners determine a property title's legal status, abstract recorded documents (mortgages, deeds, contracts, etc.), and sometimes prepare and issue policy guaranteeing a title's legality. In 1996, 26,000 people worked as title searchers and examiners.

■ History

To mortgage, sell, build on, or even give away a piece of real estate, the ownership of the land must be first proven and documented. This ownership is known as a title. Establishing a clear title, however, is not an easy task. Land

may change hands frequently, and questions often arise as to the use and ownership of the property.

In the United States, most major real estate dealings are publicly recorded, usually with the county recorder, clerk, or registrar. This system began in colonial Virginia and has spread throughout the rest of the country, giving the nation a unique method for keeping track of real estate transactions. In some areas of the country, a title can be traced back 200 years or more.

Over that length of time, a parcel of land may change ownership many times. Owners divide large pieces of land into smaller parcels and may sell or lease certain rights, such as the right to mine beneath a property or run roads and irrigation ditches over it, separately from the land itself. Official records of ownership and interests in land might be contradictory or incomplete. Because of the profitability of the real estate business, the industry has devised methods of leasing and selling property, which makes the task of identifying interests in real property even more complicated and important.

■ The Job

Clients hire title searchers and examiners to determine the legal ownership of all parts and privileges of a piece of property. The client may need this information for many reasons: in addition to land sales and purchases, a lawyer may need a title search to fulfill the terms of someone's will; a bank may need it to repossess property used as collateral on a loan; a company may need it when acquiring or merging with another company; or an accountant may need it when preparing tax returns.

The work of the title searcher is the first step in the process. After receiving a request for a title search, the title searcher determines the type of title evidence to gather, its purpose, the people involved, and a legal description of the property. The searcher then compares this description with the legal description contained in public records to verify such facts as the deed of ownership, tax codes, tax parcel number, and description of property boundaries.

This task can take title searchers to a variety of places, including the offices of the county tax assessor, the recorder or registrar of deeds, the clerk of the city or state court, and other city, county, and state officials. Title searchers consult legal records, surveyors' maps, and tax rolls. Companies who employ title searchers also may keep records called indexes. These indexes are kept up-to-date to allow fast, accurate searching of titles and contain important information on mortgages, deeds, contracts, and judgments. For example, a law firm specializing in real estate and contract law keeps extensive indexes, using information gathered both in its own work and from outside sources.

While reviewing legal documents, the title searcher records important information on a standardized worksheet. This information can include judgments, deeds, mortgages (loans made using the property as collateral), liens (charges against the property for the satisfaction of a debt), taxes, special assessments for streets and sewers, and easements. The searcher must record carefully the sources of this information, the location of these records, the date on which any action took place, and the names and addresses of the people involved.

Using the data gathered by the title searcher, the title examiner then determines the status of the property title. Title examiners study all the relevant documents on a property, including records of marriages, births, divorces, adoptions, and other important legal proceedings, to determine the history of ownership. To verify certain facts, they may need to interview judges, clerks, lawyers, bankers, real estate brokers, and other professionals. They may summarize the legal documents they have found and use these abstracts as references in later work.

Title examiners use this information to prepare reports that describe the full extent of a person's title to a property; that person's right to sell, buy, use, or improve it; any restrictions that may exist; and actions required to clear the title. If employed in the office of a title insurance company, the title examiner provides information for the issuance of a policy that insures the title, subject to applicable exclusions and exceptions. The insured party then can proceed to use the property, having protection against any problems that might arise.

In larger offices, a *title supervisor* may direct and coordinate the activities of other searchers and examiners.

Requirements

High School

A high school diploma is necessary to begin a career as a title searcher. Helpful classes include business, business law, English, social studies, real estate, real estate law, computers, and typing. In addition, skills in reading, writing, and research methods are essential.

Postsecondary Training

Because their work is more complex, title examiners usually must have completed some college course work. Pertinent courses for title searchers and examiners include business administration, office management, real estate law, and other types of law. In some locales, attorneys typically perform title examinations.

Certification or Licensing

A few states require title searchers and examiners to be licensed or certified. Title firms may belong to the American Land Title Association, as well as to regional or state title associations. These groups maintain codes of ethics and standards of practice among their members and conduct educational programs. Title searchers and examiners who work for a state, county, or municipal government may belong to a union representing government workers.

Other Requirements

Title searchers must be methodical, analytical, and detail-oriented in their work. As they study the many hundreds of documents that may contain important data, they need to be thorough. Overlooking important points can damage the accuracy of the final report and may result in financial loss to the client or employer. It is important for title searchers not to lose sight of the reason for the title search, in addition to remembering the intricacies of real estate law.

In addition to detailed work, title examiners deal with clients, lawyers, judges, real estate brokers, and other people. This task requires good communications skills, poise, patience, and courtesy.

Exploring

There may be opportunities for temporary employment during the summer and school holidays at title companies, financial institutions, or law firms. Such employment may involve making copies or sorting and delivering mail, but it offers an excellent chance to see the work of a title

TITLE SEARCHERS AND EXAMINERS	
SCHOOL SUBJECTS	Computer science English
PERSONAL SKILLS	Communication/ideas Technical/scientific
WORK ENVIRONMENT	Primarily indoors Primarily one location
MINIMUM EDUCATION LEVEL	High school diploma
SALARY RANGE	$19,000 to $28,000 to $41,000
CERTIFICATION OR LICENSING	Required for certain positions
OUTLOOK	About as fast as the average
DOT	209
GOE	07.05.02
NOC	4211
O*NET	28308

searcher or examiner firsthand. Some law firms, real estate brokerages, and title companies provide internships for students who are interested in work as a title searcher or examiner. Information on the availability of such internships is usually available from the regional or local land title association or school guidance counselors.

■ Employers

Title searchers and examiners work in a variety of settings. Some work for law firms, title insurance companies, financial institutions, or companies that write title abstracts. Others work for various branches of government at the city, county, or state level. Title insurance companies, while frequently headquartered in large cities, may have branches throughout the United States.

■ Starting Out

Those workers interested in a career as a title searcher or examiner should send resumes and letters of application to firms in their area who employ these types of workers. Other leads for employment opportunities are local real estate agents or brokers, government employment offices, and local or state land title associations. Graduates from two- and four-year colleges usually have the added advantage of being able to consult their college placement offices for additional information on job openings.

■ Advancement

Title searchers and examiners learn most of their skills on the job. They may gain a basic understanding of the title search process in a few months, using public records and indexes maintained by their employers. Over time, employees must gain a broader understanding of the intricacies of land title evidence and record-keeping systems. This knowledge and several years of experience are the keys to advancement.

With experience, title searchers can move up to become *tax examiners, special assessment searchers,* or *abstractors.* With enough experience, a searcher or examiner may be promoted to title supervisor or head clerk. Other paths for ambitious title searchers and examiners include other types of paralegal work or, with further study, a law degree.

■ Earnings

According to the Economic Research Institute, beginning title searchers earned $19,400 annually in January 1998; those with at least 5 years of experience earned an average of $24,000, while those with 10 or more years of experience averaged $27,500. Experienced title searchers earned as much as $33,700. Title examiners generally earn more, with salaries ranging from $21,300 to $27,700 to $32,800. Experienced examiners in large cities might earn as much as $40,700. Title searchers and examiners may receive such fringe benefits as vacations, hospital and life insurance, profit sharing, and pensions, depending on their employers.

■ Work Environment

Title searchers and examiners generally work a 40-hour week. Because most public records offices are only open during regular business hours, title searchers and examiners usually will not put in much overtime work, except when using private indexes and preparing abstracts.

The offices in which title searchers and examiners work can be very different in terms of comfort, space, and equipment. Searchers and examiners spend much of their day poring over the fine print of legal documents and records, so they may be afflicted occasionally with eye strain and back fatigue. Generally, however, offices are pleasant and the work is not physically strenuous.

Because the work is conducted in a business environment, title searchers and examiners usually must dress in a businesslike manner. Dress codes, however, have become more casual recently and vary from office to office.

■ Outlook

According to the *Occupational Outlook Handbook,* employment of title searchers and examiners is expected to change about as fast as the average through 2006. The health of the title insurance business is directly tied to the strength of the real estate market. In prosperous times, more people buy and sell real estate, resulting in a greater need for title searches. While the real estate business in America continues to operate during periods of recession, activity does slow a little. In general, the outlook for title searchers and examiners is good.

■ For More Information

For information on the title insurance industry, please contact:

American Land Title Association
1828 L Street, NW, Suite 705
Washington, DC 20036
Tel: 202-296-3671
Web: http://www.alta.org

■ Related Articles

Insurance

Law

Real Estate

Assessors and Appraisers

Billing Clerks

Bookkeeping and Accounting Clerks

Insurance Claims Representatives

Insurance Policy Processing Occupations

Paralegals

Underwriters

Tobacco Products Industry Workers

■ Overview

Tobacco products industry workers manufacture cigars, cigarettes, chewing tobacco, smoking tobacco, and snuff from leaf tobacco. They dry, cure, age, cut, roll, form, and package tobacco in products used by millions of people in the United States and in other countries around the world.

■ History

The use of tobacco has been traced back to Mayan cultures of nearly 2,000 years ago. As the Mayas moved north, through Central America and into North America, tobacco use spread throughout the continent. When Christopher Columbus arrived in the Caribbean in 1492, he was introduced to tobacco smoking by the Arawak tribe, who smoked the leaves of the plant rolled into cigars. Tobacco seeds were brought back to Europe, where they were cultivated. The Europeans, believing tobacco had medicinal properties, quickly adopted the practice of smoking. Sir Walter Raleigh popularized pipe smoking around 1586, and soon the growing and use of tobacco spread around the world.

Tobacco growing became an important economic activity in America beginning in the colonial era, in part because of the ideal growing conditions found in many of the Southern and Southeastern colonies. Tobacco quickly became a vital part of the colonies' international trade.

Tobacco use remained largely limited to small per-person quantities until the development of cigarettes in the mid-1800s. The invention of the cigarette-making machine in 1881 made the mass production of cigarettes possible. Nevertheless, the average person smoked only 40 cigarettes per year. It was only in the early decades of the 20th century that cigarette consumption, spurred by advertising campaigns, became popular across the country. Soon, the average person smoked up to 40 cigarettes per day.

By the 1960s, it became increasingly apparent that tobacco use was detrimental to people's health. In 1969, laws were passed requiring warning labels to be placed on all tobacco products. During the 1970s, increasing agitation by the antismoking movement led to laws, taxes, and other regulations being placed on the sale and use of tobacco products. Many other countries followed with similar laws and regulations. The number of smokers dropped by as much as 30 percent, and those who still smoked, smoked less. In response, the tobacco industry introduced products such as light cigarettes and low tar and low nicotine cigarettes. In the late 1990s, the tobacco industry was at the center of debate, controversy, and subsequent state law-suits over addictive substances and cancer-causing agents contained in cigarettes. This controversy and the declining numbers of smokers in the United States and much of the West have had a strong impact on the employment levels in the tobacco industry.

■ The Job

Various kinds of tobacco plants are cultivated for use in tobacco products. After harvesting, the different types of tobacco are processed in different ways. Using one method or another, all tobacco is cured, or dried, for several days to a month or more in order to change its physical and chemical characteristics. Farmers sometimes air-cure tobacco by hanging it in barns to dry naturally. Other curing methods are fire-curing in barns with open fires and flue-curing in barns with flues that circulate heat. Some tobacco is sun-cured by drying it outdoors in the sun.

Cured tobacco is auctioned to tobacco product manufacturers or other dealers. The first step in the manufacturing process is separating out stems, midribs of leaves, and foreign matter. Usually this is done by workers who feed the tobacco into machines. Once stemmed, the tobacco is dried again by *redrying-machine operators*, who use machines with hot-air blowers and fans.

TOBACCO PRODUCTS INDUSTRY WORKERS	
SCHOOL SUBJECTS	Agriculture Biology
PERSONAL SKILLS	Following instructions Mechanical/manipulative
WORK ENVIRONMENT	Primarily indoors Primarily one location
MINIMUM EDUCATION LEVEL	High school diploma
SALARY RANGE	$25,000 to $39,600 to $50,700
CERTIFICATION OR LICENSING	None available
OUTLOOK	Decline
DOT	521
GOE	06.04.15
NOC	9617
O*NET	89899

The tobacco is then packed for aging. In preparation for packing, workers may adjust the moisture content of the dry tobacco by steaming the leaves or wetting them down with water. The tobacco is prized, or packed, into large barrels or cases that can hold about a thousand pounds of tobacco each. Workers, including *bulkers, prizers,* and *hydraulic-press operators*, pack the containers, which go to warehouses to be aged. The aging process, which may take up to two years, alters the aroma and flavor of the tobacco. After it is aged, workers take the tobacco to factories, where it is removed from the containers.

The tobacco is further conditioned by adding moisture. *Blenders* then select tobacco of various grades and kinds to produce blends with specific characteristics or for specific products, such as cigars or snuff. They place the tobacco on conveyors headed for processing. *Blending laborers* replenish supplies of the different tobaccos for the blending line. *Blending-line attendants* tend the conveyors and machines that mix the specified blends.

Some tobacco is flavored using casing fluids, which are water-soluble mixtures. *Casing-material weighers, casing-machine operators, wringer operators, casing cookers,* and *casing-fluid tenders* participate in this flavoring process by preparing the casing material, saturating the tobacco with it, and removing excess fluid before further processing.

The tobacco is ready to be cut into pieces of the correct size. Tobacco for cigars and cigarettes is shredded and cleaned in machines operated by *machine filler shredders* and *strip-cutting-machine operators. Snuff grinders* and *snuff screeners tend machines that pulverize chopped tobacco into snuff and sift it through screens to remove oversized particles. Riddler operators* tend screening devices that separate coarse pieces of tobacco from cut tobacco.

Once cut, the tobacco is made into salable products. Cigarettes are made by machines that wrap shredded tobacco and filters with papers. Workers feed these machines, make the filters, and run the machines, which also print the company's name and insignia on the rolling papers.

Cigar making is similar, except that the filler tobacco is wrapped in tobacco leaf instead of paper. The filler is held together and formed into a bunch in a binder leaf, and the bunch is rolled in a spiral in a wrapper leaf. Various workers sort and count appropriate wrapper leaves and binder leaves. They roll filler tobacco and binder leaves into bunches by hand or using machines. The bunches are pressed into cigar-shaped molds, and *bunch trimmers* trim excess tobacco from the molds before the bunches are wrapped.

Other workers operate machines that automatically form and wrap cigars. They include *auto rollers* and *wrapper layers,* who wrap bunches with sheet tobacco or wrapper leaves. Some workers wrap bunches by hand. *Cigar-head piercers* use machines to pierce draft holes in the cigar ends. Some cigars are pressed into a square shape by *tray fillers* and press-machine feeders before they are packaged in cigar bands and cellophane. *Patch workers* repair defective or damaged cigars by patching holes with pieces of wrapper leaf.

Some tobacco is made into other products, such as plugs, lumps, and twists. Some are made by hand and some are made by machine. The machines slice, mold, press, and wrap the tobacco, and various workers are responsible for feeding, regulating, and cleaning the machines.

Many workers are employed in packaging the manufactured tobacco products. *Cigar packers, hand banders, machine banders,* and *cellophaners* package cigars. *Cigar banders* stamp trademarks on cigar wrappers. *Cigarette-packing-machine operators* pack cigarette packs into cartons. *Case packers and sealers* pack the cartons into cases and seal them. Other workers pack snuff, chewing tobacco, and other products into cartons, tins, and other packaging. *Snuff-box finishers* glue covers and labels on boxes of snuff.

Finally, *tobacco inspectors* check that the products and their packaging meet quality standards, removing items that are defective. The industry also employs a variety of workers to maintain equipment; load, unload, and distribute materials; prepare tobacco for the different stages of processing; salvage defective items for reclamation; and maintain records of tobacco bought and sold.

■ Requirements

High School

The minimum requirement for all tobacco workers is a high school diploma. Maintenance and mechanical workers often need to be high school graduates with machine maintenance skills or experience.

Other Requirements

Tobacco buyers or graders, who must judge tobacco based on its smell, feel, and appearance need several years' experience working with tobacco to become familiar with its characteristics. Most tobacco workers are members of the Bakery, Confectionery and Tobacco Workers' International Union.

■ Exploring

Part-time or seasonal tobacco processing jobs may be available in your area. Some tobacco plants may allow visitors to observe their operations.

■ Employers

Most jobs in this industry are located in factories close to tobacco-growing regions, especially in the South and Southeast. Most cigarette factories are in North Carolina and Virginia. Many cigar factories are in Florida and Pennsylvania.

■ Starting Out

Job seekers should apply in person at local tobacco products factories that may be hiring new workers. Leads for specific job openings may be located through the local offices of the state employment service and through union locals. Newspaper classified ads may also carry listings of available jobs.

■ Advancement

In the tobacco products industry, advancement is related to increased skills. Machine operators may advance by learning how to run more complex equipment. Experienced workers may be promoted to supervisory positions. With sufficient knowledge and experience, some production workers may eventually become tobacco buyers for manufacturers or tobacco graders with the U.S. Department of Agriculture.

■ Earnings

Wages for tobacco production workers are generally higher than for most other producers of consumable goods. Earnings vary considerably with the plant and the workers' job skills and responsibilities. The average salary for all tobacco production workers in 1995 was around $39,600 per year. Cigarette workers have among the highest earnings of tobacco products workers, earning an average of around $50,700 a year in 1995. Cigar workers and other tobacco products workers tend to earn less. Starting salaries average around $25,000 per year. Tobacco products workers usually receive benefits that include health and life insurance, paid holiday and vacation days, profit-sharing plans, pension plans, and various disability benefits.

■ Work Environment

In most plants, worker comfort and efficiency are important concerns. Work areas are usually clean, well lighted, and pleasantly air-conditioned. Manufacturing processes are automated wherever possible, and the equipment is designed with safety and comfort in mind. On the downside, much of the work is highly repetitive, and people can find their work very monotonous. Also, tobacco has a strong smell that bothers some people. Some stages of processing produce large quantities of tobacco dust.

■ Outlook

Employment in the tobacco industry has decreased in recent decades, so that by 1995 there were only about 32,000 workers employed in tobacco production jobs in the United States. About 10,000 tobacco production jobs were lost between 1994 and 1995 alone. This decline is mainly the result of increased automation in manufacturing processes. While Americans are generally using less tobacco, exports of American-made tobacco products are increasing, especially to the former Soviet Union and Eastern Europe, the Middle East, and Asia. Further decline will result from the controversies and lawsuits in this country, which will cost tobacco companies millions of dollars. Most future demand for workers in this industry will probably be because of a need to replace workers who have moved to other jobs or left the workforce entirely.

■ For More Information

Tobacco Institute
1875 Eye Street, NW, Suite 800
Washington, DC 20006
Tel: 202-457-4800

■ Related Articles

Agriculture
Manufacturing
Manufacturing Supervisors

Toll Collectors

■ Overview

Toll collectors receive payments from private motorists and commercial drivers for the use of highways, tunnels, bridges, or ferries.

■ History

The upkeep and maintenance of roads around the world fell to the reigning powers. However, in 1663, three counties in England obtained authority to levy tolls on users to pay for the improvement of a major road linking York and London. By the 18th century, all major roads in Great Britain incorporated tolls, or turnpike trusts, to pay for maintenance.

In 1785, Virginia built a turnpike and other states quickly followed suit. The very first hard-surfaced road of any great length in the United States was the Lancaster Turnpike, com-

TOLL COLLECTORS	
SCHOOL SUBJECTS	Business Mathematics
PERSONAL SKILLS	Communication/ideas Helping/teaching
WORK ENVIRONMENT	Indoors and outdoors Primarily one location
MINIMUM EDUCATION LEVEL	High school diploma
SALARY RANGE	$15,900 to $21,900 to $28,000
CERTIFICATION OR LICENSING	None available
OUTLOOK	About as fast as the average
DOT	211
GOE	07.03.01
O*NET	49023A

A toll collector gives a driver her change.

pleted in 1794. Almost 150 years later, the first successful U.S. toll road for all types of motor vehicles was built in that same state.

The United States contains more than 3.9 million miles of paved and unpaved streets, roads, and highways. With the wear and tear brought on by harsh weather conditions and constant use, these road surfaces need to be repaired frequently. The building and repairing of streets and highways are funded primarily by state gasoline taxes, vehicle registrations, and other operating fees. However, some highway, bridge, and other transportation improvements are paid for by individual user fees known as tolls. The fees for using turnpikes and toll roads usually depend on the distance a motorist travels. Because their extra weight puts more strain on pavements and necessitates more frequent road repair, trucks, trailers, and other heavy vehicles pay more for using these roads than passenger cars.

■ The Job

Toll collectors have two main job responsibilities: accepting and dispensing money and providing personal service and information to motorists. Primarily, toll collectors act as cashiers, collecting revenue from motorists and truck drivers who use certain roads, tunnels, bridges, or auto ferries. They accept toll and fare tickets that drivers may have previously purchased or received. They check that the drivers have given them the proper amount and return correct change when necessary.

When handling money, toll collectors begin with a change bank containing bills and coins so they can make change for motorists who lack the exact change. Toll collectors organize this money by denomination, so they are able to make change quickly and accurately, especially

during rush-hour traffic. At the end of their shift, they calculate the amount of revenue received for the day by subtracting the original amount in the change bank from the total amount of money now in the till. Toll collectors also prepare cash reports, commuter ticket reports, and deposit slips that report the day's tallies. Many toll collectors have keen perception and are able to spot counterfeit currency immediately.

In addition to their cash-handling duties, toll collectors have a wide range of administrative duties that provide service to motorists and keep the toll plaza operating at peak efficiency. Drivers may ask for directions, maps, or an estimate of the distance to the nearest rest stop or service station. Toll collectors are sometimes the only human link on a particularly long stretch of highway, so they may need to lend assistance in certain emergencies or contact police or ambulance support. They may also notify their supervisors or the highway commission concerning hazardous roads, weather conditions, or vehicles in distress.

Toll collectors also may be responsible for filling out traffic reports and inspecting the toll plaza facility to make sure that the area is free of litter and that toll gates and automatic lanes are working properly. Sometimes toll collectors handle supervisory tasks such as monitoring automatic and nonrevenue lanes, relieving fellow employees for lunch or coffee breaks, or completing violation reports. They are often in contact with state police patrols to watch for drivers who have sped through the toll gate without paying.

In many situations, commercial trucks have to pay more when they are hauling larger loads. Toll collectors are able to classify these vehicles according to their size and calculate the proper toll rates. These workers also have to be aware of and enforce the safety regulations governing their area. Tanker trucks carrying flammable cargoes, for example, are usually barred from publicly used tunnels. Toll operators are responsible for the safety of everyone on the road and must enforce all regulations impartially. Toll collectors who operate ferries may direct the vehicles that are boarding and monitor the capacity of the ferry, as well as collect fares.

■ Requirements

High School

A high school diploma is required for people who want to work as toll collectors. Recommended high school courses include mathematics, speech, and English classes. These will help develop the communications skills—listening as well as speaking—that are so important in the job of toll collecting.

Postsecondary Training

Toll collectors may have to pass a civil service exam to test their skills and aptitude for the job. When hired, they receive on-the-job training; no formal postsecondary education is required.

Other Requirements

Toll collectors are usually required to be at least 18 years of age, with generally good health and reasonable stamina and endurance. Toll collectors must have good eyesight and hearing to determine a vehicle's class (and applicable toll), as well as to hear motorists' requests or supervisory instructions in the midst of heavy traffic noise. Manual dexterity in handling and organizing money and fare tickets, as well as giving change, is also important. Lost or confused motorists rely on the guidance of toll collectors, who should maintain a considerate and helpful attitude. They should also be perceptive and have professional work habits. Honesty in a toll collector is imperative.

■ Exploring

Students interested in careers as toll collectors should contact state and local departments of transportation, as well as state highway departments. School counselors may have additional information on such careers or related agencies to contact about the nature of the work and the applicable job requirements. They may also be able to arrange a talk by an experienced toll collector or supervisor. Many such professionals will be more than happy to share their experiences and detail the everyday duties of those involved in the profession.

■ Employers

Virtually all toll collectors work for a government transport agency, be it local, state, or federal. Simply because of their abundance, state departments of transportation employ the most toll collectors.

■ Starting Out

Those interested in becoming toll collectors should write to their state and local departments of transportation, highway agencies, or civil service organizations for information on education requirements, job prerequisites, and application materials. In those states that require qualification testing, potential applicants should also request information on test dates and preparation materials.

■ Advancement

Advancement for toll collectors may take the form of a promotion from part-time to full-time employment, or from the late evening shift to daytime work. These workers may also be promoted to supervisory or operations positions, with a corresponding increase in salary and benefits. Most promotions carry additional responsibilities that require further training. While some training may take place on the job, certain management topics are best learned from an accredited college or training program. Workers who aspire to higher positions may wish to take courses in advance so they will be ready when openings occur. It is important to note that there are few managerial positions compared to the vast number of toll collectors employed—competition for advanced jobs is intense.

■ Earnings

Wages for full-time toll collectors vary with the area and state where the collector is employed. Salaries begin at approximately $15,900 per year and increase to around $28,000 with additional experience and a good employment record. Managerial responsibilities also increase compensation. Part-time employees are usually paid by the hour and may begin at the minimum wage. Toll collectors who are members of a union generally earn more than those who are not. Collectors who work the later shifts may also earn more, and most employees earn time-and-a-half or double-time for overtime or holiday work.

Toll collectors receive vacation time calculated on the number of hours worked in conjunction with their years of employment. Those workers with up to five years of service may receive 80 hours of vacation. This scale can increase to 136 hours of vacation for seasoned workers with nine to 14 years of employment. Benefit packages usually include health and dental insurance coverage for employees and their families, as well as pension and retirement plans. Toll workers often enjoy the generous employee benefits of working in government service.

■ Work Environment

Toll collectors may either stand or sit on stools in the booths they occupy. Toll collectors are exposed to all types of weather, including hail, sleet, snow, or extreme heat or cold, but booths usually are equipped with space heaters and sliding doors to keep out dampness and cold. Collectors will also be exposed to exhaust and other potentially toxic fumes-those with respiratory difficulties need to be especially aware of this condition. Toll collectors will sometimes interact with stressed, impatient, or irate motorists and must be able to deflect potentially heated situations while maintaining a peak level of service and efficiency. While full-time toll collectors usually work an eight-hour shift, they may have to work at different times of the day, since many toll booths need to be staffed around the clock.

Most toll booth complexes have rest room and shower facilities for their employees. Some may have kitchens and break rooms as well. Some workers have assigned lockers or share lockers with workers on different shifts. Usually the employee facilities are better when no oasis or service stations are adjacent to the toll plaza. Toll stations have communications equipment so that they can notify state police or the state department of transportation of any emergencies, hazardous conditions, or violations of the law.

■ Outlook

Employment opportunities are relatively good. While many toll booths automatically accept and count drivers' tolls, automation cannot readily take the place of the personal service and human judgment that many positions require. Opportunities for toll collectors often hinge on economic factors such as automobile sales, gas prices, and trends in consumer spending for luxury items, such as travel. Although most segments of the federal highway system that was launched in the 1950s have been put in place, new roads and bridges will have to be built to augment existing highways. Much of this new construction is expected to be partially funded by toll revenues, which will increase opportunities for toll collectors.

Computerized toll-recording in the form of automatic vehicle identification (AVI) equipment or other similar technologies will eliminate some positions in the next decade, but AVI technology is not expected to make a significant impact on the employment of toll collectors until after 2001. Toll collectors will always be needed to monitor automatic gates, collect tolls, and supervise other collectors. Toll collectors may also be retrained to monitor and maintain this emerging AVI technology.

■ For More Information

Students interested in a career as a toll collector should contact their state department of transportation. Additional information may be obtained from:

American Association of State Highway and Transportation Officials
444 North Capitol Street, NW, Suite 225
Washington, DC 20001
Tel: 202-624-5800

International Bridge, Tunnel and Turnpike Association
2120 L Street, NW, Suite 305
Washington, DC 20037
Tel: 202-659-4620

■ Related Articles

Transportation
Cashiers
Counter and Retail Clerks
Customs Officials
Financial Institution Tellers
Public Transportation Operators
Retail Sales Workers
Route Drivers

Tool and Die Makers

■ **See Precision Metalworkers**

Tool Pushers

■ **See Petroleum Technicians**

Toolmakers

■ **See Silverware Artisans and Workers**

Tour Guides

■ Overview

Tour guides plan and oversee travel arrangements and accommodations for groups of tourists. They assist travelers with questions or problems and may provide travelers with itineraries of their proposed travel route and plans. Tour guides research their destinations thoroughly so that they can handle any unforeseen situation that may occur.

■ History

People have always had a certain fascination with the unknown. Curiosity about distant cities and foreign cultures was one of the main forces behind the spread of civilization. Traveling in the ancient world was an arduous and sometimes dangerous task. Today, however, travel is commonplace. People travel for business, recreation, and education. School children may take field trips to their state's capitol, and some college students now have the opportunity to study in foreign countries. Recreation and vacation travel account for much of people's spending of their disposable income.

Early travelers were often accompanied by guides who had become familiar with the routes on earlier trips. When leisure travel became more commonplace in the 19th century, women and young children were not expected to travel alone, so relatives or house servants often acted as companions. Today, tour guides act as escorts for people visiting foreign countries and provide them with additional information on interesting facets of life in another part of the world. In a way, tour guides have taken the place of the early scouts, acting as experts in settings and situations that other people find unfamiliar.

■ The Job

Acting as knowledgeable companions and chaperons, tour guides escort groups of tourists to different cities and countries. Their job is to make sure that the passengers in a group tour enjoy an interesting and safe trip. To do this, they have to know a great deal about their travel destination and about the interests, knowledge, and expectations of the people on the tour.

One basic responsibility of tour guides is handling all the details of a trip prior to departure. They may schedule airline flights, bus trips, or train trips, as well as book cruises, house boats, or car rentals. They also research area hotels and other lodgings for the group and make reservations in advance. If anyone in the group has unique requirements, such as a specialized diet or a need for wheelchair accessibility, the tour guide will work to meet these requests.

Tour guides plan itineraries and daily activities, keeping in mind the interests of the group. For example, a group of music lovers visiting Vienna may wish to see the many sites of musical history there, as well as attend a performance by that city's orchestra. In addition to sight-seeing tours, guides may make arrangements in advance for special exhibits, dining experiences, and side trips. Alternate outings are sometimes planned in case of inclement weather conditions.

The second major responsibility of tour guides is, of course, the tour itself. Here, they must make sure all aspects of transportation, lodging, and recreation meet the itinerary as it was planned. They must see to it that travelers' baggage and personal effects are loaded and handled properly. If the tour includes meals and trips to local establishments, the guide must make sure that each passenger is on time for the various arrivals and departures.

Tour guides provide the people in their groups with interesting information on the locale and alert them to special sights. Tour guides become familiar with the history and significance of places through research and previous visits and endeavor to make the visit as entertaining and informative as possible. They may speak the native language or hire an interpreter so as to get along well with the local people. They are also familiar with local customs so their group will not offend anyone unknowingly. They see that the group stays together so that they do not miss their transportation arrangements or get lost. Guides may also arrange free time for travelers to pursue their individual interests, although time frames and common meeting points for regrouping are established in advance.

Even with thorough preparation, unexpected occurrences can arise on any trip and threaten to ruin every-

one's good time. Tour guides must be resourceful to handle these surprises, such as when points of interest are closed or accommodations turn out to be unacceptable. They must be familiar with an area's resources so that they can help in emergencies such as an ill passenger or lost personal items. Tour guides often intercede on their travelers' behalf when any questions or problems arise regarding currency, restaurants, customs, or necessary identification.

■ Requirements

High School

Although tour guides do not need a college education, they should at least have a high school diploma. Courses such as speech, communications, art, sociology, anthropology, political science, and literature often prove beneficial. Some tour guides study foreign languages and cultures, as well as geography, history, and architecture.

Postsecondary Training

Some cities have professional schools that offer curricula in the travel industry. Such training may take 9 to 12 months and offer job placement services. Some 2- and 4- year colleges offer tour guide training that lasts from 6 to 8 weeks. Community colleges may offer programs in tour escort training. Programs such as these often may be taken on a part-time basis. Classes may include world geography, psychology, human relations, and communication courses. Sometimes students go on field trips themselves to gain experience. Some travel agencies and tour companies offer their own training so that their tour guides may receive instruction that complements the tour packages the company offers.

Other Requirements

Tour guides are outgoing, friendly, and confident people. They are aware of the typical travelers' needs and the kinds of questions and concerns they might have. Tour guides are comfortable being in charge of

TOUR GUIDES	
SCHOOL SUBJECTS	History / Foreign language
PERSONAL SKILLS	Helping/teaching / Leadership/management
WORK ENVIRONMENT	Indoors and outdoors / Primarily multiple locations
MINIMUM EDUCATION LEVEL	Some postsecondary training
SALARY RANGE	$9.75 per hour to $20.00 per hour to $65,000
CERTIFICATION OR LICENSING	Recommended
OUTLOOK	Faster than the average
DOT	353
GOE	07.05.01
NOC	6441
O*NET	68017B

A tour guide leads a group through a wilderness area.

large groups of people and have good time-management skills. They need to be resourceful and able to adapt to different environments. They are also fun-loving and know how to make others feel at ease in unfamiliar surroundings. Tour guides should enjoy working with people as much as they enjoy traveling.

Exploring

One way to become more familiar with the responsibilities of this job is to accompany local tours. Many cities have their own historical societies and museums that offer tours, as well as opportunities to volunteer. To appreciate what is involved with speaking in front of groups and the kind of research that may be necessary for leading tours, students may prepare speeches or presentations for class or local community groups.

Employers

The major employers of tour guides are, naturally, tour companies. Many tour guides work on a freelance basis, while others may own their own tour businesses.

Starting Out

Those wishing to be tour guides may begin as a guide for a museum or state park. This is a good introduction to handling groups of people, giving lectures on points of interest or exhibits, and developing confidence and leadership qualities. Zoos, theme parks, historical sites, or local walking tours need volunteers or part-time employees to work in their information centers, offer visitors directions, and answer inquiries. When openings occur, it is common for part-time workers to move into full-time positions.

Travel agencies, tour bus companies, and park districts need additional help during the summer when the travel season is in full swing. Architectural and natural history organizations, as well as other cultural groups, often train and employ guides. Students interested in working as tour guides for these groups should submit applications directly to the directors of personnel or managing directors.

Advancement

Tour guides gain experience by handling more complicated trips. Some workers may advance through specialization, such as tours to specific countries or to multiple destinations. Some tour guides choose to open their own travel agencies or work for wholesale tour companies, selling trip packages to individuals or retail tour companies.

Some tour guides become *travel writers* and report on exotic destinations for magazines and newspapers. Other guides may decide to work in the corporate world and plan travel arrangements for company executives. With the further development of the global economy, many different jobs have become available for people who know foreign languages and cultures.

Earnings

Tour guides may find that they have peak and slack periods of the year that correspond to vacation and travel seasons. Many tour guides, however, work eight months of the year. Salaries range from $9.75 to $20.00 an hour. Experienced guides with managerial responsibilities can earn up to $65,000 a year, including gratuities. According to *U.S. News & World Report,* the average salary for an entry-level *inbound tour guide* (tour guides who guide foreign visitors through famous American tourist sites) is $20,000, with average mid-level earnings approximately $35,000 per year. The most experienced guides can earn as much as $75,000 annually.

Guides receive their meals and accommodations free while conducting a tour, as well as a daily stipend to cover their personal expenses. Salaries and benefits vary depending upon the tour operators that employ guides and the location they are employed in. Generally, the Great Lakes, Mid-Atlantic, Southeast, and Southern regions of the country offer the highest compensation.

Tour guides very often receive paid vacations as part of their fringe benefits package; some may also receive sick pay and health insurance as well. Some companies may offer profit sharing and bonuses. They often receive discounts from hotels, airlines, and transportation companies in appreciation for repeat business.

■ Work Environment

The key word in the tour guide profession is variety. Most tour guides work in offices while they make travel arrangements and handle general business, but once on the road they experience a wide range of accommodations, conditions, and situations. Tours to distant cities involve maneuvering through busy and confusing airports. Side trips may involve bus rides, train transfers, or private car rentals, all with varying degrees of comfort and reliability. Package trips that encompass seeing a number of foreign countries may require the guide to speak a different language in each city.

The constant feeling of being on the go, plus the responsibility of leading a large group of people, can sometimes be stressful. Unexpected events and uncooperative people have the capacity to ruin part of a trip for everyone involved, including the guide. However, the thrill of travel, discovery, and meeting new people can be so rewarding that all the negatives can be forgotten (or eliminated by preplanning on the next trip).

■ Outlook

Because of the many different travel opportunities for business, recreation, and education, there will be a significant need for tour guides through the year 2006. This demand is due in part to the fact that when the economy is strong—which it is currently—people earn more and are able to spend more on travel.

Tours for special interests, such as to ecologically significant areas and wilderness destinations, continue to grow in popularity. Although certain seasons are more popular for travel than others, well-trained tour guides can keep busy all year long.

Another area of tourism that is on the upswing is inbound tourism. Many foreign travelers view the United States as a dream destination, with tourist spots such as Hollywood, Disney World, and Yellowstone National Park drawing millions of foreign visitors each year. Job opportunities in inbound tourism will likely be more plentiful than those guiding Americans in foreign locations. The best opportunities in inbound tourism are in large cities with international airports and in areas with a large amount of tourist traffic. Opportunities will also be better for those guides who speak foreign languages.

Aspiring tour guides should keep in mind that this field is highly competitive. Tour guide jobs, because of the obvious benefits, are highly sought after, and the beginning job seeker may find it difficult to break into the business. It is also important to remember that the travel and tourism industry is affected by the overall economy. When the economy is depressed, people have less money to spend and, therefore, travel less.

■ For More Information

For general information on the career of tour guide, as well as a listing of tour operators who are members of the association, contact:

National Tourism Foundation
546 East Main Street
PO Box 3071
Lexington, KY 40596-3071
Tel: 800-682-8886
Web: http://www.ntaonline.com

For information regarding its certification program and other general information concerning a career as a tour guide, contact:

The Professional Guides Association of America
2416 South Eads Street
Arlington, VA 22202-2532
Tel: 703-892-5757

For information on the travel industry and the related career of travel agent, contact:

American Society of Travel Agents
1101 King Street, Suite 200
Alexandria, VA 22314
Tel: 703-739-2782
Web: http://www.astanet.com

■ Related Articles

Airlines

Hospitality

Recreation

Travel and Tourism

Adventure Travel Specialists

Inbound Tour Guides

Travel Agents

Tower Erectors
■ **See Line Installers and Cable Splicers**

Tower Line Repairers
■ **See Line Installers and Cable Splicers**

Toxicologists

■ Overview

Toxicologists design and conduct studies to determine the potential toxicity of substances to humans, plants, and animals. They provide information on the hazards of these substances to the federal government, private businesses, and the public.

Toxicologists may suggest alternatives to using products that contain dangerous amounts of toxins, often by testifying at official hearings.

■ History

The study of the effects of poisons (toxins) began in the 1500s when doctors began to document changes in the body tissues of people who died after a long illness. Over the next 300 years, physicians and scientists continued to collect information on the causes and effects of various diseases, although the research was hampered by the lack of sophisticated research equipment.

As microscopes and other forms of scientific equipment improved, scientists were able to study in greater detail the impacts of chemicals on the human body and the causes of disease. In the mid-1800s, Rudolf Virchow, a German scientist who is considered the founder of pathology (the study of diseased body tissue), took a huge step toward unlocking the mystery of the nature of disease with his suggestion that body cells affected by disease should be studied. These studies helped pathologists pinpoint the paths diseases take in the body.

With the increasing use of chemicals and pharmaceutical and illegal drugs, the study of the impact of these potential toxins on public health and environmental quality has become more important. The toxicologist's role in determining the extent of the toxic problem, as well as suggest-ing possible alternatives or antidotes, will play an important part in any long-term solution to problems such as air and water pollution, the dumping of toxic waste into landfills, and the recognition of an unusual reaction to a pharmaceutical drug.

■ The Job

As scientists, toxicologists are concerned with the detection of toxins, the effects of toxins, and the treatment of intoxication (poisonings). A primary objective of a toxicologist is to reduce the hazards of accidental exposure to potential toxins and thereby increase consumer protection and industrial safety. This entails investigating the many areas in which our society uses chemicals or potential toxins, then documenting their impact. For example, a toxicologist may chemically analyze a fish to find the level of mercury that has accumulated in it. This information might be used by government or industry officials to assess the level of mercury that manufacturing companies, such as electronics companies, release during the manufacturing process.

On many projects, a toxicologist may be part of a research team, such as at a poison control center or a research laboratory. *Clinical toxicologists* may work to help save emergency drug overdose victims. *Industrial toxicologists* and *academic toxicologists* work on solving long-term issues, such as studying the toxic effects of cigarettes. They may work on developing research techniques that improve and speed up testing methods without sacrificing safety. They use the most modern equipment, such as electron microscopes, atomic absorption spectrometers, and mass spectrometers, and study new research instrumentation that may help with sophisticated research.

Industrial toxicologists test new products for private companies to determine the products' toxicity. For example, before a new cosmetic can be sold, it must be tested according to strict guidelines. Toxicologists oversee this testing, which is often done on laboratory animals. These toxicologists may apply the test article ingredients topically or orally, or they may inject them into the animals. They test the results through observation, blood analysis, and dissection and detailed pathologic examination. Results from the testing are used on labeling and packaging instructions to help physicians and customers to use the product safely. Toxicologists are required to use humane procedures when experimenting with animals, and although animal experimentation has created a great deal of controversy, humane procedures are stressed throughout.

Toxicologists carefully document research procedures and then write reports on their findings. They often interact with lawyers and legislators on writing legislation, and they may appear at official hearings designed to discuss policy decisions or to decide how to put them into effect.

TOXICOLOGISTS	
SCHOOL SUBJECTS	Chemistry Biology
PERSONAL SKILLS	Helping/teaching Technical/scientific
WORK ENVIRONMENT	Primarily indoors Primarily one location
MINIMUM EDUCATION LEVEL	Doctorate
SALARY RANGE	$45,000 to $75,000 to $200,000
CERTIFICATION OR LICENSING	Required by all states
OUTLOOK	Faster than the average
DOT	041
GOE	02.02.01
NOC	3111
O*NET	24308J

Because toxic materials are often handled during research and experimentation, a toxicologist must pay careful attention to safety procedures.

■ Requirements

High School

High school students can best prepare for a career as a toxicologist by taking courses in both the physical and biological sciences (chemistry and biology, for example), algebra and geometry, and physics. English and other courses that improve written and verbal communications skills should also be taken.

Postsecondary Training

Many years of training are needed in order to become a toxicologist. The successful applicant must have a doctorate in pharmacology, chemistry, or a related discipline. Some postdoctorate work in toxicology is also required. There are positions in toxicology for individuals with a master's degree, however, to be classified as a toxicologist, a doctorate is necessary. The undergraduate degree should be in a scientific field, such as pharmacology or chemistry. Course work should include mathematics (including courses on mathematical modeling), biology, chemistry, statistics, biochemistry, pathology, anatomy, and research methods. A toxicologist must also have a knowledge of computers.

Certification or Licensing

Two organizations are involved with the licensing and certification process. The Academy of Toxicological Sciences certifies a toxicologist after checking the references and work history of the applicants. The American Board of Toxicologists certifies a toxicologist after the applicant passes a comprehensive two-day examination and completes the necessary educational requirements. Further information on licensing and certification procedures is available from these organizations—the addresses are listed at the end of this article.

Other Requirements

Along with all the other medical professionals, toxicologists may belong to professional organizations that promote professional training and enrichment. These organizations include the College of American Pathologists, the American College of Toxicology, the Society of Toxicology, and the American Academy of Clinical Toxicology.

■ Exploring

High school students interested in pursuing a career as a toxicologist should join science clubs and use classes in biology and chemistry to learn laboratory skills. Discussions

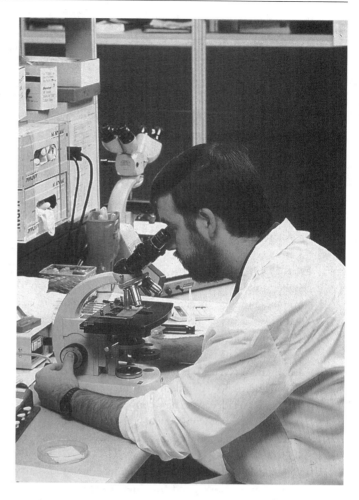

A toxicologist examines a slide.

with practicing toxicologists are also recommended as a way to explore career options. Some people may find a part-time job in a research laboratory or at a hospital helpful, although it is impossible to get any hands-on training without the required education and training.

■ Employers

Toxicologist are employed by chemical, pharmaceutical, and support industries. Employment opportunities for toxicologists also exist in academic and government settings. A small percentage of toxicologists work in the professional service area.

Academic institutions are the number one employer of toxicologists. Chemical, pharmaceutical, and support industries are the number two employers, while government is the third largest employer.

■ Starting Out

People with the necessary education and experience should contact the appropriate research departments in hospitals, colleges and universities, government agencies, or private

FYI

In 1984, one of the worst chemical industrial disasters in history occurred in Bhopal, India, when a pesticide factory leaked toxic gas, killing at least 4,000 people. In order to protect U.S. citizens from such a chemical disaster, in 1986 Congress passed the Emergency Planning and Community Right-to-Know Act requiring industries to immediately report the release of hazardous substances to local and state agencies.

businesses. Often, instructors at the school where a toxicologist trained can provide job leads and recommendations. University placement departments can also be of assistance.

■ Advancement

Skilled toxicologists will find many advancement opportunities, although specific promotions depend on the size and type of organization where the toxicologist is employed. Those toxicologists working for private companies may become heads of research departments. Because they often are often involved in developing company policy, highly skilled and respected toxicologists may become vice presidents or presidents of their companies. Obviously, this type of promotion would entail a change in job responsibilities, involving more administrative tasks than research activities.

Toxicologists working for educational institutions may become professors, heads of a department, and deans. Toxicologists who want to continue full-time research and teaching find advancement through higher pay and increased job responsibilities. Toxicologists working at universities usually write grant proposals, teach courses, and train graduate students. University positions often do not pay as well as industrial positions, but they offer more independence in pursuing research interests.

■ Earnings

As trained professionals, toxicologists have good earning potential. They can expect to make $40,000 to $50,000 a year to start, while mid-level toxicologists earn between $60,000 and $90,000 per year. Toxicologists with 20 or more years of experience can earn up to $200,000 per year, particularly if they work in the consumer product or pharmaceutical industries. Toxicologists working for the government usually make less than those working for industry.

■ Work Environment

Toxicologists usually work in well-equipped laboratories or offices, either as part of a team or alone. Research in libraries or in the field is a major part of the job. Some toxicologists work a standard 40-hour workweek, although many work longer hours. Overtime should be expected if an important research project is on deadline. Research and experimentation can be both physically and mentally tiring, with much of the laboratory work and analysis done while under time restrictions. Some travel may be required to testify at hearings, collect field samples, or to attend professional conferences.

The toxicologist's work demands patience and an eye for detail. A toxicologist may work on a research project for over a year with limited results—this requires perseverance and a good deal of self-confidence. The many years of training required to become a toxicologist also demand perseverance and a strong desire to enter this profession. A toxicologist must be able to work well with people, either as a leader of a group or as part of a team. The toxicologist must also be able to work alone, sometimes spending long periods poring over research material.

Because the work of a toxicologist involves studying the impact of toxic material, a toxicologist should be willing to handle contaminated material and adhere to the strict safety precautions required.

The toxicologist often works on research that has important health considerations. At a poison control center, for example, toxicologists may try to find information about the poisonous properties of a product while an overdose victim's life is in danger.

■ Outlook

Employment opportunities are expected to continue to be good, as the use of chemicals by our society creates the need for trained professionals to determine and limit the health risks of chemical usage. It is estimated that there will be a greater increase of toxicologists between 1996 and 2000 than there was between 1990 and 1995; however, some analysts say the market is soft overall. Job opportunities should be greatest in large urban areas, where most large hospitals, chemical manufacturers, and university research facilities are located. Those with the most training and experience should fare the best in finding employment.

■ For More Information

General career information is available from:

Society of Toxicology
1767 Business Center Drive, Suite 302
Reston, VA 20190
Tel: 703-438-3115

Certification and licensing information is available from:

American Board of Toxicology
PO Box 30054
Raleigh, NC 27622
Tel: 919-782-0036

■ **Related Articles**

Toy and Game Designers

■ Overview

Toy and game designers develop and create a variety of entertainment products, from stuffed animals and action figures to video games and virtual pets. While these creative specialists often determine the general design treatment to be used, they usually work with a team of developers—including editors, illustrators, production managers, and playtesters—in order to get a product to its intended audience.

Classified as *industrial designers,* toy and game specialists work primarily for publishers, development firms, and manufacturing companies. Most designers work on a self-employed basis, with probably no more than a few thousand full-time professionals employed in the United States.

■ History

children have always learned through play. As a result, toys and games have existed, in one form or another, since the dawn of civilization. In the Stone Age, rattles were made from gourds and musical instruments from bones. Wooden sleds, used by hunters to transport food, date back to 6500 BC. Toys and games have also been discovered in Roman, Greek, and Egyptian burial sites and among the remains of the Aztec and Mayan cultures.

Wooden toy carving has been done in many German towns since the Middle Ages, with each family member often developing a particular specialty. While these artisans and craftsworkers have been practicing their craft for centuries, they didn't receive any kind of formal recognition until the Renaissance. Although the toys and games of that period were relatively simple compared to those that we know today, automatic and mechanical toys made by skilled craftspeople created a sense of wonder among the people of the time.

The toymaking industry formally emerged in Germany, with the town of Nuremburg serving as a distribution center for local toymakers. By the end of the 1700s, toy sellers and designers were able to reach large numbers of customers through the use of price lists and catalogs.

In the United States, colonial period toys were made from scraps of cloth, wood, and even corncobs by people for their own use. Many of the designs for these folk toys were passed from one generation to the next. Throughout the 1700s, Americans continued to create homemade toys and games. In the late 1830s, William Tower organized a guild of toymakers in Massachusetts. And by the 1840s, the American toy and game industry was born.

A variety of toys and games was produced by designers and artists working in tool manufacturing or cabinetmaking, but these craftspeople developed these entertainment products on the side. It wasn't until after World War II that the toy and game industry grew big enough to support full-time professional designers.

Today, toy and game designers create everything from interactive dolls to role-playing video games. Advanced technologies, combined with the growing use of computers and the Internet, will give designers of the future unlimited opportunities to create unforgettable products for children and adults alike.

■ The Job

While most toy and game designers work on a freelance basis, full-time professionals are usually employed at publishing houses, manufacturing firms, or development companies. Whether they are self-employed or work on staff, however, most designers have similar duties and responsibilities.

In general, designers are charged with creating the primary design treatment for developing a new toy or game or for changing an existing product. In addition, designers must present ideas to management and/or clients, write up design documents describing every step required in creating a product, and work with either staff or outside sources in order to bring a given project to completion.

The first step in developing any design is to determine the needs of the client. In the toy and game industry, client needs focus not only on the physical product but also on safety issues (especially for items intended

TOY AND GAME DESIGNERS	
SCHOOL SUBJECTS	Art English
PERSONAL SKILLS	Artistic Communication/ideas
WORK ENVIRONMENT	Primarily indoors Primarily one location
MINIMUM EDUCATION LEVEL	Bachelor's degree
SALARY RANGE	$27,000 to $35,000 to $45,000
CERTIFICATION OR LICENSING	None available
OUTLOOK	Faster than the average

A toy designer uses a computer to design a space shuttle toy.

for children under the age of three), the cost of the design, the age-appropriateness of the product (given its target audience), and marketplace competition.

Once designers have clearly defined clients' needs, they usually conduct research on product use, materials, and production methods needed to create an appealing—and competitive—product. They also must make sure that the item, or a similar one, is not already in existence. In the toy industry, 5,000 to 6,000 new products are introduced every year, most developed by staff specialists at over 800 toy companies in the United States. With so many new products flooding the market each year, originality is essential in order for a new toy or game to catch the customer's eye.

With all research completed, the designer is ready to create a prototype-a mockup, a sketch, computer-aided control drawings, or plans drawn to scale-to present for client or management approval. Prototypes often are quite detailed so that clients can easily understand how the finished toy or game will actually look and/or operate. Indeed, much of a designer's work involves the communication of ideas—to clients, management, co-workers, and others.

After the general design treatment has been approved, designers work with other team members or with outside professionals in order to develop the actual product. In addition to *graphic designers, illustrators,* and *production personnel,* designers usually interact with or oversee the activities of *developers, editors, playtesters, marketing specialists,* and *engineers* as a toy or game goes through the various production stages.

Along with creative and artistic work, designers do a lot of writing. They are usually responsible, for example, for writing the first draft of game rules or product instructions. Explanations of complex design concepts are also written by designers, as are the goals of a toy or game.

In addition to all of the responsibilities just described, independent toy and game designers, also known as *independent inventors,* face a number of additional challenges. They must determine from the start, for example, whether they will sell their ideas to toy manufacturers (or have a broker sell the ideas for them) or manufacture and distribute their products themselves.

Self-employed designers who opt to sell their products or ideas must find a publisher or manufacturer, as well as a distributor, once the toy or game has been designed. Most companies seeking new products from outside sources purchase them from design firms and from independent inventors and agents with whom they already have an established business relationship. Milton Bradley and Parker Brothers, for example, prefer to work only with people they know.

For this reason, beginning independent designers may have a hard time penetrating the industry. Some major companies, however, having been forced to reduce their research and development departments because of economic pressures, are now turning to outside professionals more than ever. Games, in particular, are increasingly being designed by freelancers and then developed in-house by specialists at large firms. In addition, independent designers may find opportunities at small- and medium-sized firms, which often are more receptive to the ideas of freelancers than large companies are.

Those designers who decide to publish their own games or manufacture their own toys are, in effect, starting their own businesses. They, therefore, need to either sink a considerable sum of money into their start-ups or find investors. In addition, these designers must to be able to contract for production services at reasonable prices, track orders from retailers, ensure the timely delivery of all ordered products, and create promotional materials that stir customer interest.

As is true for all start-ups, proper planning is vital. Independent designers need to create a business plan, develop product ideas fully, project sales, and determine the most cost-effective ways to manufacture, distribute, and market their products. They also must attend trade shows, make sure that accounts are billed, and keep accurate records. In addition, these self-employed designers must obtain patent or trademark protection, especially if they hope to sell their products to a manufacturer or publisher once they have met with success in the marketplace.

Ultimately, designers who think that they want to start their own toy or game companies must realize that most of their time will be spent running their businesses, not designing products. If you're still set on traveling this route into the toy and game industry, you should also be aware that about 90 percent of all new businesses fail in the first two years. On the other hand, many hugely successful toys and games, such as Monopoly, Uno, and Scrabble, were designed and marketed by independent, inspired inventors.

■ Requirements

High School

In general, most toy and game designers must have a bachelor's degree, even for entry-level positions. Would-be designers can take a variety of classes at the high school level, however, to prepare for more advanced courses offered at colleges and universities. In the creative arena, you should take graphic art and design classes. You may also want to investigate such courses as animation, creative writing, photography, filmmaking, music, and theater.

While art-related offerings are important for aspiring toy and game designers, a solid liberal arts background is invaluable. Therefore, you should take a variety of courses, including math, anthropology, computer science, public speaking, history, and literature. Classes that emphasize writing are especially vital, since designers must be able to communicate complicated design ideas to coworkers and clients alike.

Postsecondary Training

By earning a bachelor's degree in either industrial design or fine arts at a four-year college or university, toy and game designers are exposed to a variety of courses that will help them both land entry-level jobs and rise up through the ranks as well. These classes include art and art history, designing and sketching, principles of design, and other specialized studies. In addition, liberal arts and business courses, such as merchandising, business administration, marketing, and psychology, will prove to be invaluable. Specialized courses in areas of particular interest to you are also recommended. For example, if you're thinking about becoming a video game designer, computer programming and computer-aided design (CAD) classes will be helpful.

While many colleges and universities across the nation and abroad offer excellent programs in industrial design and fine arts, some educational institutions provide specialized curricula geared especially to toy and game designers. The Fashion Institute of Technology in New York, for example, allows students to earn a bachelor of fine arts degree in toy design.

Other Requirements

In addition to being creative and imaginative, toy and game designers must be able to communicate their ideas, both visually and verbally. They should also work well both independently and as part of a development team. While motivation and perseverance are essential for success in the industry, it is equally important for designers to be able

GREAT IDEAS: THE AMERICAN GIRLS COLLECTION

How do toy and game designers come up with their ideas? In 1984, former teacher Pleasant Rowland felt inspired by the living history she found when visiting Colonial Williamsburg. Later that same year, she became disheartened by the scarcity of dolls available while looking for a Christmas present for her niece. From these two seemingly unrelated experiences, the American Girls Collection was born.

Today, Rowland's firm, Pleasant Company, offers beautiful dolls, as well as clothes, accessories, and accompanying books. In addition to the products themselves, the collection teaches girls about the traditions they share with girls from the past and aims to nurture a sense of community among girls all across the nation.

Source: The American Girl home page at http://www.americangirl.com/pr/pc.html

to solve problems, be open to the ideas of others, and see beyond their own personal preferences in order to create what customers want.

Self-discipline is vital, particularly for self-employed professionals. However, staff designers must also be able to initiate their own projects, budget their time wisely, and meet both deadlines and production schedules. In addition to having business sense and sales ability, both staff and freelance designers must keep abreast of new products and developments in the field.

■ Exploring

If you're thinking about becoming a toy or game designer, there are many ways that you can investigate the field. Attending an industry show allows you to keep abreast of the latest product offerings and to meet toy and game developers, publishers, and manufacturers at the same time. The American International Toy Fair, for example, the biggest toy trade show in the United States, attracts over 20,000 toy wholesale and retail buyers annually, as well as more than 1,600 exhibitors.

In addition to expositions, conferences, and trade shows, subscribing to industry-related publications can give you a sense of what is expected of toy and game designers, as well as where the market is heading. In addition to regular monthly issues, *Playthings Magazine,* for example, publishes a special *Buyers Guide,* which contains a section geared especially for designers and inventors.

For some hands-on experience, you may want to join a "virtual company" whose project team members design games at low or no cost in their spare time. You can also volunteer to help at a variety of Web sites that focus on toys and gaming. In addition, although toy and game firms usually hire professionals as playtesters, some seek in-house or off-site volunteers to test their products.

With thousands of would-be toy and game designers out there, the competition for jobs is fierce. Ultimately, the demand for design professionals depends to a large degree on consumers' desires for new and unique products. As you can see below, the toy and game industry experiences many "ups" and "downs." (All figures, except as noted, apply to 1998.)

- Size of the U.S. toy industry (1997): $22.58 billion
- Estimated amount spent per child per year: $350

UPS

- Plush toys up 19 percent (led by Beanie Babies, Furbies, Bounce-around Tiggers and Teletubbies)
- Nonpowered cars up 28 percent (primarily die-casts, such as Hot Wheels and Matchbox)
- Electronic hand-held/tabletop games up 20 percent
- Building sets up 7 percent

DOWNS

- Action figures down 13 percent (no new character to drive sales)
- Dolls down 3.2 percent (except for Spice Girls and Rugrats)
- Virtual pets down 78 percent

Finally, finding a mentor who is currently in the field will enable you to learn and grow in the industry once you find a job. Until then, such a person can serve as a resource and introduce you to others in the field.

■ Employers

Unlike many jobs in a variety of other industries, most toy and game designers are self-employed. Many create toys and games on a part-time basis in addition to working other jobs. Alternatively, some designers who opt to develop their own toys or publish their own games actually create their own businesses, handling all operational aspects required, from idea conception to marketing and production.

The small number of full-time toy and game designers is employed primarily by publishers, development firms, and manufacturing companies. While most industrial designers work for consulting firms or large corporations, toy and game designers can find job opportunities at every kind of toy company, from small start-ups to the industry giants, such as Parker Brothers, Milton Bradley, and Kenner.

■ Starting Out

Without experience, aspiring toy and game designers must begin as assistants to lead designers. Assistants are charged with working on the nuts and bolts of a developing product. At the same time, they're able to learn more about the toy and game market so that, in time, they can become lead designers. Large firms are more likely than smaller companies to hire assistants, who usually have little or no experience.

If a design opportunity is not available, you may want to consider a related position as a production assistant or playtester. Many designers actually get their jobs only after working in other positions in the industry.

Employers looking to hire designers often contact local universities or industry associations. In addition, many place ads in local newspapers in search of qualified candidates. However you make your initial contact with potential employers, most experts agree on the importance of developing a portfolio of design work, as well as familiarizing yourself with the products and future plans of various companies.

If you're interested in self-employment, it is relatively easy to enter the industry as a start-up, and toy and game companies frequently purchase ideas after they have been made successful. On the other hand, larger firms usually do not accept new product ideas from independent inventors. These companies find it more cost-effective to employ staff designers than to pay royalties to freelancers.

■ Advancement

Although it is virtually impossible to find an entry-level job as a toy or game designer, people with ambition and potential will find many opportunities to get into the industry and then rise through the ranks. A variety of junior positions, such as those in playtesting or customer service, can springboard qualified people into assistant designing jobs. After several years of experience, capable assistants at large companies, guided and nurtured by senior or lead designers, can then become full-fledged toy and game designers themselves.

Once you've penetrated the toy and game industry, you'll discover that there are various advancement paths possible. The current creative director at Parker Brothers, for example, began as a production assistant. From there she went on to become a graphic designer, a senior designer, the assistant art director, and, finally, the creative director.

While most people in the industry opt to work either for a company or for themselves, some staff designers decide to leave their salaried positions and start their own businesses. Others become department heads, industry executives, or brokers or agents, who negotiate the sale of ideas to various toy and game companies.

■ Earnings

In general, toy and game designers earn approximately as much as industrial designers in other specialty fields. According to the Industrial Designers Society of America, entry-level designers with one to two years of experience earn about $27,000 a year. Staff designers with five years of experience average $35,000 annually, and those with eight years in the industry make about $45,000 a year. Designers who climb the ladder to managerial or executive positions can earn up to $140,000 annually.

If you're interested in becoming an independent designer, the earnings picture is rather bleak. In the game designing arena, for example, even established professionals earn only about $2,000 for a typical game, although some can make upwards to $5,000 per game. Game designer Greg Costikyan suggests that independent inventors negotiate royalty arrangements rather than selling games for a flat fee. Unfortunately, even this type of arrangement provides designers with only 1 to 3 percent of the list price of a game, although computer game designers usually enjoy royalties that are considerably higher.

Unlike independent designers, professionals on staff often receive a variety of benefits in addition to their salaries, depending on the organization for which they work. These benefits may include health and life insurance, paid vacation and sick days, and pension plans.

■ Work Environment

The environment in which toy and game designers work varies, depending on the employer. Manufacturing firms and design companies usually provide designers with well-lit, comfortable offices or other work spaces. These design professionals generally work a regular 40-hour workweek, although overtime is occasionally required in order to complete projects by designated deadlines. Self-employed designers often work longer hours, especially when they are establishing themselves in the industry.

Both staff and freelance designers frequently schedule their days in order to accommodate clients. It is not unusual for a design specialist to meet with a client in the evenings or on weekends, for example. Such meetings may take place in the designer's office, at the client's home or place of business, or at other locations, such as manufacturing plants or showrooms.

With the exception of self-employed people who operate without any kind of assistance, toy and game designers work with other professionals, including editors, illustrators, graphic designers, playtesters, and production workers. The abilities to communicate and to get along with others are, therefore, imperative. In addition, many designers must work under pressure in order to please clients and finish projects on time. Finally, while most designers feel a sense of satisfaction and pride from developing creative ideas and products, some occasionally feel frustrated when their designs are rejected or substantially changed.

■ Outlook

According to the 1998-99 *Occupational Outlook Handbook* (OOH), employment opportunities for all designers are expected to grow faster than the average through 2006. Demand for toy and game designing professionals in particular will result from continued emphasis on the quality and safety of products, as well as on toys and games that are easy to understand and appropriate for their intended audiences. Increasing global competition will also play a role in the demand for toy and game designers.

Emerging technologies will continue to positively impact the employment outlook for design professionals as well. Those designers who have knowledge of and experience with high-tech toys, CD-ROM versions of board games, and interactive video games will definitely have a competitive edge in the job market. The Toy Manufacturers of America (TMA) predicts that the ultimate winners will be designers who are able to combine new technologies with familiar brands and products.

Demographic trends also support employment growth for toy and game designers into the next millennium. Since the 1970s, the number of births in the United States has been steadily increasing, resulting in a "baby boomlet" nearly as large as the baby boom of 1946-1964. Since children are the toy industry's primary consumers, the TMA predicts that their increasing numbers will continue to spur the demand for qualified toy and game designers.

Another significant demographic trend is that people are living longer. As baby boomers gray and grandparents and older adults become more involved in the daily activities of children than ever before, a substantial part of the population will be buying toys and games. In fact, the TMA estimates that 14 percent of all toys purchased today are bought by grandparents and older adults.

Although employment growth is expected, the OOH notes that designers will face intense competition for available job openings. Since many talented designers are attracted to the toy and game industry, those without formal design education, creativity, and perseverance will have trouble establishing careers in the field. Independent designers will also continue to have difficulty penetrating the industry, according to the TMA. On the upside, many job openings will be available for qualified designers as demand continues and as designers leave the field for a variety of reasons.

■ For More Information

ASTRA expands the business and professional knowledge of its members, gathers market data, identifies trends, and provides individual businesses with resources and information.

American Specialty Toy Retailing Association
900 Midland Building
Des Moines, IA 50309
Tel: 515-282-8192
Web: http://www.astratoy.org

ICTI is an association that serves as a center for discussion and the exchange of information in order to improve communication on important toy industry issues and trends.

International Council of Toy Industries
1115 Broadway, Suite 400
New York, NY 10010
Tel: 212-675-1141
Web: http://www.toy-icti.org/

IGDN is a nonprofit membership association for the game development community.

International Game Developers Network
1030 East El Camino Real, #210
Sunnyvale, CA 94087
Web: http://www.igdn.org/

Toy and Game Inventors of America evaluates members' products and provides them with lists of professional agents.

Toy and Game Inventors of America
5813 McCart Avenue
Fort Worth, TX 76333
Tel: 817-292-9021
Web: http://www.toyandgameinventors.com

The TMA fosters industry growth, represents the industry before U.S. and international governments, and supports the creative output of its members.

Toy Manufacturers of America
1115 Broadway, Suite 400
New York, NY 10010
Tel: 212-675-1141
Web: http://www.toy-tma.com

■ Related Jobs

Toys and Games
Visual Arts
Art Directors
Computer and Video Game Designers
Engineers
Graphic Designers
Illustrators
Painters and Sculptors
Photographers
Toy Industry Workers

Toy Industry Workers

■ Overview

Toy industry workers are the individuals who create, design, manufacture, and market toys and games to adults and children. Their jobs are similar to those of their counterparts in other industries. Some work on large machines, while others assemble toys by hand. According to the U.S. Bureau of Labor Statistics, 39,000 individuals were employed in the toy industry in 1997, approximately 67 percent working in production. Most toy companies are located in or near large metropolitan areas.

■ History

Toys and games probably have existed as long as there have been humans. Recreational games have roots in ancient cultures. For example, backgammon, one of the oldest known board games, dates back about 5,000 years to areas around the Mediterranean. Chess developed in about the sixth century in India or China and was based on other ancient games.

Dolls and figurines also have turned up among old artifacts. Some seem to have been used as playthings, while others apparently had religious or symbolic importance. More recently, European kings and noblemen gave elaborate dolls in fancy costumes as gifts. Fashion styles thus were spread through other regions and countries. Doll makers in cities such as Paris, France, and Nuremberg, Germany, became famous for crafting especially beautiful dolls. Over the years dolls have been made of wood, clay, china, papier-mâché, wax, and hard rubber, and they have been collected and admired by adults as well as children.

For centuries, most toys were made by hand at home. Mass production began in the 19th century during the Industrial Revolution. In the 20th century, one of the most enduringly popular toys was the teddy bear, named after President Theodore Roosevelt.

Toy companies generally devise their own products or adapt them from perennial favorites, but they occasionally buy ideas for new toys and games from outsiders. One famous example of this was a board game devised during the Depression by an out-of-work man in his kitchen. He drew a playing board on his tablecloth using the names of streets in his hometown of Atlantic City and devised a game that let him act out his fantasies of being a real estate and business tycoon. The game, which he called "Monopoly," became one of the most popular games of all time.

The popularity of certain toys rises and falls over time. Some toys maintain their popularity with successive generations of children or experience a comeback after a few years. Computer and video games have boomed during the past decade and will undoubtedly continue to become more complex and realistic as technology advances. Still, it is very difficult to predict which new toys will become popular. Introducing a new toy into the marketplace is a gamble, and that adds excitement and pressure to the industry.

■ The Job

Taking a toy from the idea stage to the store shelf is a long and complex operation, sometimes requiring a year or two or even longer. Ideas for new toys or games may come from a variety of sources. In large companies, the marketing department and the research and development department review the types of toys that are currently selling well, and they devise new toys to meet the perceived demand. Companies also get ideas from professional inventors, freelance designers, and ordinary people, including children, who write to them describing new toys they would like to see made.

Toy companies consider ideas for production that they sometimes end up scrapping. A toy company has two main considerations in deciding whether to produce a toy: the degree of interest children (or adults) might have in playing with the toy and whether the company can manufacture it profitably.

A toy must be fun to play with, but there are measures of a toy's worth other than amusement. Some toys are designed to be educational, develop motor skills, excite imagination and curiosity about the world, or help children learn ways of expressing themselves.

Often manufacturers test new ideas to determine their appeal to children. *Model makers* create prototypes of new toys. *Marketing researchers* in the company coordinate sessions during which groups of children play with the prototype toys. If the children in the test group enjoy a toy and return to play with it more than a few times, the toy has passed a major milestone.

The company also has to ask other important questions: Is the toy safe and durable? Is it similar to other toys on the market? Is there potential for a large number of buyers? Can the toy be mass-produced at a low enough cost per toy to ensure a profit? Such questions are usually the responsibility of *research and development workers,* who draw up detailed designs for new toys, determine materials to be used, and devise methods to manufacture the toy economically. After the research and development employees have completed their work, the project is passed on to engineers who start production.

Electronic toys, video games, and computer games have skyrocketed in popularity in the past decade. The people who develop them include *computer engineers, technicians,* and *software programmers. Technical development engineers* work on toys that involve advanced mechanical or acousti-

cal technology. *Plastics engineers* work on plans for plastic toys. They design tools and molds for making plastic toy parts, and they determine the type of molding process and plastic that are best for the job. Plastics engineers who work for large firms may design and build 150 or more new molds each year.

To determine the best way to manufacture a toy, *manufacturing engineers* study the blueprints for the new product and identify necessary machinery. They may decide that the company can modify equipment it already has, or they may recommend purchasing new machinery. Throughout the engineering process, it is important to find ways to minimize production costs while still maintaining quality.

After selecting the equipment for production, *industrial engineers* design the operations of manufacturing: the layout of the plant, the time each step in the process should take, the number of workers needed, the ways to measure performance, and other detailed factors. Next, the engineers teach supervisors and assembly workers how to operate the machinery and assemble the new toy. They inform shift supervisors the rate of production the company expects. Industrial engineers also might be responsible for designing the process of packaging and shipping the completed toys.

As toys are being built on the assembly line, *quality control engineers* inspect them for safety and durability. Most toy companies adhere to the quality standards outlined in ASTM F963-95, a set of voluntary guidelines the toy industry has developed for itself. The toy industry is also monitored by the Consumer Products Safety Commission and must adhere to various federal laws and standards that cover the safety of toys under normal use and any foreseeable misuse or abuse.

Finally, getting the toys from the factory to the store shelf is the responsibility of *sales and merchandising workers.* These employees stay in contact with toy stores and retail outlets and arrange for toy displays and in-store product promotions.

Factory workers on assembly lines mass-produce

TOY INDUSTRY WORKERS	
SCHOOL SUBJECTS	Mathematics
	Technical/Shop
PERSONAL SKILLS	Technical/scientific
	Mechanical/manipulative
WORK ENVIRONMENT	Primarily indoors
	Primarily one location
MINIMUM EDUCATION LEVEL	High school diploma
SALARY RANGE	$4.25 per hour to $25,000 to $150,000
CERTIFICATION OR LICENSING	None available
OUTLOOK	About as fast as the average
DOT	731
GOE	06.04.34
NOC	9619

A toy industry worker assembles a toy

practically all toys and games. The manufacturing processes can be as unique as the toys themselves. Workers first cast pieces of plastic toys in injection molds and then assemble them. They machine, assemble, and finish or paint wooden and metal toys. They make board games employing many of the same printing and binding processes used for books. They print the playing surface on a piece of paper, glue it to a piece of cardboard of the proper size, and tape the two halves of the board together with bookbinding equipment.

Toy assemblers put together various plastic, wood, metal, or fabric pieces to complete toys. They may sit at a conveyor belt or workbench, where they use small power tools or hand tools, such as pliers and hammers, to fasten the pieces together. Other toy assemblers operate larger machines such as drill presses, reamers, flanging presses, and punch presses. On toys like wagons that are made on assembly lines, assemblers may do only a single task, such as attaching axles or tires. Other toys may be assembled entirely by one person; for instance, one person at one station on an assembly line may attach the heads, arms, and legs of action figures.

The manufacture of dolls provides a good example of the various manual and mechanical operations that can go into the making of a single toy. *Plastic doll mold fillers* make the head, torso, arms, and legs of the doll in plastic-injection molds. Other workers cure and trim the molded parts and send them off on a conveyor belt. The doll's head may go to a *rooter operator,* who operates a large machine that roots or stitches a specific quantity of synthetic hair onto the head. After attaching the hair in the form of a wig, a *doll wigs hackler* combs and softens synthetic hair by pulling it

through a hackle, which is a combing tool with projecting bristles or teeth. Then, a *finisher* sets the hair in the specified style by combing, brushing, and cutting. A toy assembler puts together the doll's parts, and a *hand finisher* completes the doll by dressing it in clothes and shoes. An *inspector* examines the completed doll to make sure it meets the original specifications and then sends it on for packaging and shipment.

■ Requirements

High School
Employers usually prefer to hire high school graduates for production jobs in routine assembly of toys and games. Experience in working with machinery, even in high school shop classes, can be a plus. New employees learn most assembly skills on the job from experienced workers over a period of a few days to a few weeks.

Postsecondary Training
Workers need different skills for different types of positions. Engineers and management personnel usually need college degrees. Because of the wide range of activities in the toy business, people may be hired with training in various fields, including art, electronics, architecture, psychology, business, and the sciences.

Certification or Licensing
Many workers in toy factories join a labor union, the Amalgamated, Industrial and Toy and Novelty Workers of America.

Other Requirements
Some people succeed with skills other than those learned in college classrooms. Sales and inventing new toys are among the areas where a worker's success may depend more on creative, innovative approaches than on college training. Some of the production jobs involve repetitive work that must be completed quickly and accurately. Attention to detail is an important quality.

■ Exploring
To gain some experience working in the toy industry, students can apply for summer or part-time jobs with local manufacturers. The most likely areas to find jobs are in assembly work, sales, and marketing. A large portion of toys sell in the period before Christmas, so toy companies must have their products ready ahead of time. The months from July through September are usually the busiest in the year, and jobs may be most available during this time. Students with younger siblings can do some personal research right at home; determine which types of toys your brother or sister prefers and why. It might also prove worth-

while to spend some time at neighborhood day care centers to observe the habits of young children with their toys.

■ Employers

The most popular locations for toy companies in the United States are the largest cities and states, such as New York, Los Angeles, Chicago, and San Francisco, as well as Washington, Texas, Florida, New Jersey, Connecticut, and Pennsylvania.

In large toy firms, workers with many different titles may be involved in each of the activities described. Sometimes workers are grouped in teams, such as the research and development team, and as a team the members consider research and development aspects of every toy the company makes. In smaller firms, job distinctions may not be so precise and separate. A group of employees may work together on the entire process of developing and marketing a toy from the beginning to the end. The fewer employees in a firm, the more functions they can perform.

Some workers are employed on a temporary basis manufacturing toys during the busiest season—that is, before Christmas.

■ Starting Out

For entry-level positions in the toy industry, job seekers can contact the personnel offices of toy manufacturers. This is true for most factory jobs, whether applicants are looking for engineering, management, marketing, or factory production jobs. Some job listings and information may be available at the local offices of the state employment service, at local union offices, or in newspaper classified ads.

■ Advancement

In general, advancement to better jobs and higher pay depends on acquiring skills and gaining seniority. Some production workers advance by learning to operate more complex machinery. Reliable, experienced workers in production jobs might be promoted to supervisory positions. Professional and management staff can progress in various ways depending on their areas of expertise.

■ Earnings

Newly hired production workers may be paid at rates not much above the federal minimum wage. With experience, they may average as much as $9.50 an hour. Many workers are paid on a piecework basis—that is, according to the amount of work they complete or the number of items they assemble. Machine operators usually earn more than assemblers who work by hand. During the peak production season from July to September, factory workers may have to work long shifts, and they are paid overtime rates for the extra hours.

FACTS ABOUT CRAYONS

- Crayons were developed by cousins Edwin Binney and C. Harold Smith and their chemical company, Binney & Smith. They decided that the new wax crayon they had developed to mark crates would be a cheaper and better alternative for American schoolchildren than the charcoal and oil crayons imported from Europe.
- Edwin Binney's wife, Alice, chose the name "Crayola," from the French word for chalk, *craie*, and "ola," from oleaginous or oily.
- The first box of eight Crayola crayons appeared on the market in 1903 and sold for about five cents. The eight colors were red, orange, yellow, green, blue, violet, brown, and black.
- Today, Crayolas come in 120 different colors.
- Binney & Smith produce nearly three billion crayons each year, or about seven million a day.
- Crayons are sold in more than 80 countries and packaged in 12 languages.

Management and engineers are often paid a straight salary. Salary ranges vary from company to company and especially from job to job. For example, research and development employees can start at about $25,000 per year; some may eventually work their way up to $150,000 or more annually. Salary levels for these workers depend on their job responsibilities, experience, seniority, and quality of work. According to the *Occupational Outlook Handbook*, industrial designers overall had beginning salaries of about $27,000 in 1996, senior designers earned $45,000 and executives earned up to $140,000 annually. Beginning engineers averaged salaries around $38,000, growing to $59,000 at mid-level and $99,000 at senior level.

Wage scales and conditions for wage increases often are set according to agreements between the union and company management. In addition to wages, many workers receive other benefits, such as health and life insurance coverage, pension plans, and vacations.

■ Work Environment

The production floor of some toy factories is simply a large room in which workers perform routine tasks. A factory may employ as many as several hundred people to do production work. Some people work at machines, while others sit at tables or assembly lines. Some workers stand much of the day. Workers often have to meet production schedules and quotas, so they have to keep up a brisk work pace. Some people are bored by the repetition in many production jobs, because they must do the same few tasks over and over for long periods.

In smaller companies, the work may be highly seasonal. Getting the company's products ready for selling in the Christmas season, and to some extent, the Easter season, can mean that employees are asked to put in 10 or more hours of work a day. And if the company makes a product that becomes extremely popular, workers may have to scramble to make enough of the item to keep up with demand. But in the off-peak season, usually the winter months, and in average conditions, production workers may have reduced hours or they may be laid off. In many shops, some production workers are employed only five or six months a year. Management and other professional employees work year-round. They may need to put in over-time hours during peak seasons or before trade shows, but they do not earn overtime pay.

Outlook

According to the U.S. Industrial Outlook from the Department of Commerce, the toy industry experienced 3.4 percent growth in 1998. In the foreseeable future, employment in the U.S. toy industry probably will not undergo much net change. Sales of toys and games for both children and adults are increasing. On the other hand, some of these products, notably some electronic video games, are imports from abroad. If toy preferences change, employment patterns may shift in coming years but in ways that are hard to predict now.

There is a fairly high rate of job turnover among pro-duction workers, who make up a large part of the total workforce in the toy industry. Because of the low pay, repet-itive work, and seasonal fluctuations in workloads, pro-duction workers may quit after a time to find more stable employment. Consequently, manufacturers are often look-ing to hire new production workers.

For More Information

The following labor union represents toy industry workers.

Amalgamated, Industrial and Toy and Novelty Workers of America
147 East 26th Street
New York, NY 10010
Tel: 212-889-8180

This trade association is for U.S. producers and importers of toys and holiday decorations.

Toy Manufacturers of America
200 Fifth Avenue, Room 740
New York, NY 10010
Tel: 212-675-1141
Web: http://www.toy-tma.org

For information on a four-year program in toy design, contact:

Fashion Institute of Technology
227 W. 27th St.
New York, NY 10001
Tel: 212-217-7133
Web: http://www.toy-tma.org/ati/fit

Related Jobs
Toys and Games
Computer and Video Game Designers
Marketing Research Analysts
Plastics Products Manufacturing Workers
Sporting Goods Production Workers
Toy and Game Designers

Track Switch Maintainers

■ **See Communications Equipment Technicians**

Traditional Chinese Medicine Practitioners

■ **See Oriental Medicine Practitioners**

Traffic Engineers

Overview

Traffic engineers study factors that influence traffic condi-tions on roads and streets, including street lighting, visibility and location of signs and signals, entrances and exits, and the presence of factories or shopping malls. They use this information to design and implement plans and electronic systems that improve the flow of traffic.

History

During the early colonial days, dirt roads and Native American trails were the primary means of land travel. In 1806, the U.S. Congress provided for the construction of the first road, known as the Cumberland Road. More and more roads were built, connecting neighborhoods, towns, cities, and states. As the population increased and modes of travel began to advance, more roads were needed to facilitate commerce, tourism, and daily transportation. Electric traffic signals were introduced in the United States in 1928 to help control automobile traffic. Because land travel was becoming increasingly complex, traffic engi-neers were trained to ensure safe travel on roads and high-ways, in detours and construction work zones, and for special events such as sports competitions and presidential conventions, among others.

■ The Job

Traffic engineers study factors such as signal timing, traffic flow, high-accident zones, lighting, road capacity, and entrances and exits in order to increase traffic safety and to improve the flow of traffic. In planning and creating their designs, engineers may observe such general traffic influences as the proximity of shopping malls, railroads, airports, or factories, and other factors that affect how well traffic moves. They apply standardized mathematical formulas to certain measurements to compute traffic signal duration and speed limits, and they prepare drawings showing the location of new signals or other traffic control devices. They may perform statistical studies of traffic conditions, flow, and volume, and may—on the basis of such studies—recommend changes in traffic controls and regulations. Traffic engineers design improvement plans with the use of computers and through on-site investigation.

Traffic engineers address a variety of problems in their daily work. They may conduct studies and implement plans to reduce the number of accidents on a particularly dangerous section of highway. They might be asked to prepare traffic impact studies for new residential or industrial developments, implementing improvements to manage the increased flow of traffic. To do this, they may analyze and adjust the timing of traffic signals, suggest the widening of lanes, or recommend the introduction of bus or carpool lanes. In the performance of their duties, traffic engineers must be constantly aware of the effect their designs will have on nearby pedestrian traffic and on environmental concerns, such as air quality, noise pollution, and the presence of wetlands and other protected areas.

Traffic engineers use computers to monitor traffic flow onto highways and at intersections, to study frequent accident sites, to determine road and highway capacities, and to control and regulate the operation of traffic signals throughout entire cities. Computers allow traffic engineers to experiment with multiple design plans while monitoring cost, impact, and efficiency of a particular project.

Traffic engineers who work in government often design or oversee roads or entire public transportation systems. They might oversee the design, planning, and construction of new roads and highways or manage a system that controls the traffic signals by the use of a computer. Engineers frequently interact with a wide variety of people, from average citizens to business leaders and elected officials.

Traffic technicians assist traffic engineers. They collect data in the field by interviewing motorists at intersections where traffic is often congested or where an unusual number of accidents have occurred. They also use radar equipment or timing devices to determine the speed of passing vehicles at certain locations, and they use stopwatches to time traffic signals and other delays to traffic. Some traffic technicians may also have limited design duties.

■ Requirements

High School

High school students interested in a traffic engineering career should have mathematical skills through training in algebra, logic, and geometry and a good working knowledge of statistics. They should have language skills that will enable them to write extensive reports making use of statistical data, and they should be able to present such reports before groups of people. They should also be familiar with computers and electronics in general. Traffic engineers should have a basic understanding of the workings of government since they must frequently address regulations and zoning laws and meet and work with government officials. A high school diploma is the minimum educational requirement for traffic technicians.

Postsecondary Training

Traffic engineers must have a bachelor's degree in civil, electrical, mechanical, or chemical engineering. Because the field of transportation is so vast, many engineers have educational backgrounds in science, planning, computers, environmental planning, and other related fields. Educational courses for traffic engineers in transportation may include transportation planning, traffic engineering, highway design, and related courses such as computer science, urban planning, statistics, geography, business management, public administration, and economics.

Traffic engineers acquire some of their skills through on-the-job experience and training conferences and mini-courses offered by their employers, educational facilities, and professional engi-

TRAFFIC ENGINEERS	
SCHOOL SUBJECTS	Geography Mathematics
PERSONAL SKILLS	Communication/ ideas Technical/scientific
WORK ENVIRONMENT	Indoors and outdoors Primarily multiple locations
MINIMUM EDUCATION LEVEL	Bachelor's degree
SALARY RANGE	$34,800 to $51,600 to $86,400
CERTIFICATION OR LICENSING	None available
OUTLOOK	Faster than the average
DOT	199
GOE	05.03.06
NOC	2148
O*NET	39005

Two traffic engineers monitor traffic in a highway operations center.

neering societies. Traffic technicians receive much of their training on the job and through education courses offered by various engineering organizations.

Certification or Licensing

Currently, no certification exists in the field of traffic engineering. The Institute of Transportation Engineers (ITE) is working on a certification program, which it hopes to implement in the near future.

Other Requirements

Traffic engineers should enjoy the challenge of solving problems. They should have good oral and written communication skills since they frequently work with others. Engineers must also be creative and able to visualize the future workings of their designs; that is, how they will improve traffic flow, effects on the environment, and potential problems.

■ Exploring

Interested students can join a student chapter of the ITE to see if a career in transportation engineering is for them. An application for student membership in the ITE can be obtained by writing the association at the address listed in the "For More Information" section at the end of this article.

■ Employers

Traffic engineers are employed by federal, state, or local agencies or as private consultants by states, counties, towns, and even neighborhood groups. Many teach or engage in research in colleges and universities.

■ Starting Out

The ITE offers a resume service to students that are members of the organization. Student members can get their resumes published in the *ITE Journal*. The journal also lists available positions for traffic engineering positions throughout the country. Most colleges also offer job placement programs to help traffic engineering graduates locate their first jobs.

■ Advancement

Experienced traffic engineers may advance to become directors of transportation departments or directors of public works in civil service positions. A vast array of related employment in the transportation field is available for those engineers who pursue advanced or continuing education. Traffic engineers may specialize in transportation planning, public transportation (urban and intercity transit), airport engineering, highway engineering, harbor and port engineering, railway engineering, or urban and regional planning.

■ Earnings

Salaries for traffic engineers vary widely depending upon duties, qualifications, and experience. According to a salary survey by the ITE, professional entry-level junior traffic engineers (Level I) earn starting annual salaries of $34,772. Level II traffic engineers, with a minimum of two year's experience and who oversaw small projects, earned $41,318 per year. Level III engineers, who supervise others and organize small to mid-size projects, earn annual salaries of $51,563. Level IV engineers, who are responsible for the supervision of large projects, staffing, and scheduling, earn annual salaries of $61,908. Those traffic engineers who have titles such as director of traffic engineering, director of transportation planning, professor, or vice president (Level V) earn average salaries of $72,867 per year. Level VI engineers who have advanced to upper-level management positions, such as president, general manager, director of transportation or public workers, and who are responsible for major decision-making, earn the highest salaries: $86,375 per year. Traffic engineers are also eligible for paid vacation, sick, and personal days, health insurance, pension plans, and in some instances, profit sharing.

■ Work Environment

Traffic engineers perform their duties both indoors and outdoors, under a variety of conditions. They are subject to the noise of heavy traffic and various weather conditions while gathering data for some of their studies. They may speak to a wide variety of people as they check the success of their designs. Traffic engineers also spend a fair amount of time in the quiet of an office, making calculations and analyzing the data they have collected in the field. They also spend a considerable amount of time working with computers to optimize traffic signal timing, in general design, and to predict traffic flow.

Traffic engineers must be comfortable working with other professionals, such as traffic technicians, designers, planners, and developers, as they work to create a successful transportation system. At the completion of a project they can take pride in the knowledge that they have made the streets, roads, and highways safer and more efficient as a result of their designs.

■ Outlook

There were nearly 24,000 traffic engineers in the United States in the 1990s. Employment for traffic engineers is expected to increase faster than the average through 2006. More engineers will be needed to work with ITS (Intelligent Transportation System) technology such as electronic toll collection, cameras for traffic incidents/detection, and fiber optics for use in variable message signs. As the population increases and continues to move to suburban areas, qualified traffic engineers will be needed to analyze, assess, and implement traffic plans and designs to ensure safety and the steady, continuous flow of traffic. In cities, traffic engineers will continue to be needed to staff advanced transportation management centers that oversee vast stretches of road using computers, sensors, cameras, and other electrical devices.

■ For More Information

For information regarding fellowships, seminars, tours, and general information concerning the transportation engineering field, contact:

American Association of State Highway and Transportation Officials
444 North Capitol Street, NW
Washington, DC 20001
Tel: 202-624-5800

American Public Transportation Association
1201 New York Avenue, NW, Suite 400
Washington, DC 20005
Tel: 202-898-4000

Institute of Transportation Engineers
525 School Street, SW, Suite 410
Washington, DC 20024-2729
Tel: 202-554-8050
Web: http://www.ite.org

U.S. Department of Transportation
400 Seventh Street, SW
Washington, DC 20590
Tel: 202-366-4000

■ Related Articles

Automotives
Transportation
Civil Engineers
Civil Engineering Technicians
Industrial Engineering Technicians
Statistical Clerks
Statisticians
Urban and Regional Planners

Training Specialists

■ **See Personnel and Labor Relations Specialists**

Transfer Clerks

■ **See Postal Clerks**

Transplant Coordinators

■ Overview

Transplant coordinators are involved in practically every aspect of organ procurement (getting the organ from the donor) and transplantation. There are two types of transplant coordinators: *procurement coordinators* and *clinical coordinators*. Procurement coordinators help the families of organ donors deal with the death of a loved one as well as inform them of the organ donation process. Clinical coordinators educate recipients about how to prepare for an organ transplant and how to care for themselves after the transplant.

■ History

Scientists have been conducting research regarding human and animal organ transplantation since the 18th century. Greater research led to refinements in transplant technology and in 1954, the first successful human kidney transplant was performed in Boston. The 1960s brought many successes in the field of organ transplants including successful human liver and pancreas transplants. The first heart transplant was performed in 1967.

Despite these successes, many transplants

TRANSPLANT COORDINATORS	
SCHOOL SUBJECTS	Biology Chemistry
PERSONAL SKILLS	Helping/teaching Technical/scientific
WORK ENVIRONMENT	Primarily indoors Primarily one location
MINIMUM EDUCATION LEVEL	Associate's degree
SALARY RANGE	$24,500 to $59,000 to $75,000
CERTIFICATION OR LICENSING	Voluntary
OUTLOOK	Faster than the average
DOT	079
O*NET	32996B

eventually failed because of the body's immune system, which eventually rejected the new organ as a foreign object. Although drugs were designed in the 1960s to help the body accept transplanted organs, it wasn't until the early 1980s that a truly effective immunosuppressant drug, cyclosoporin, was available. This drug substantially improved the success rate of transplant surgeries. More precise tissue typing or matching of donor and recipient tissues also helped increase the success rate.

Though successful organ transplants have increased, some transplants still fail over time despite modern drug treatments and closer tissue matching. Research in this area continues with the hope of increasing the rate of successful transplants.

■ The Job

Transplant coordinators are involved in practically every aspect of organ procurement (getting the organ from the donor) and transplantation. This may involve working with medical records, scheduling surgeries, educating potential organ recipients, and counseling donor families.

There are two types of transplant coordinators: procurement coordinators and clinical coordinators. Although procurement and clinical coordinators are actively involved in evaluating, planning, and maintaining records, an important part of their job is helping individuals and families. Procurement coordinators help the families of organ donors deal with the death of their loved one and inform them of the organ donation process.

Clinical coordinators educate recipients in how to best prepare for organ transplant and how to care for the new organ. Many coordinators, especially clinical coordinators, are *registered nurses,* but it is not required to have a nursing degree to work as a coordinator. Some medical background is important, however. Many transplant coordinators have degrees in biology, physiology, accounting, psychology, business administration, or public health.

Once the donor patient has been declared brain dead and the patient is no longer breathing on his or her own, the procurement transplant coordinator approaches the donor's family about organ donation. If the family gives its consent, the coordinator then collects medical information and tissue samples for analysis. The coordinator also calls the United Network for Organ Sharing (UNOS), a member organization that includes every transplant program, organ procurement organization (OPO), and tissue typing laboratory in the United States. UNOS attempts to match organs with recipients within the OPO's region. If no local match can be made, the coordinator must make arrangements for the organs to be delivered to another state. In either case, the procurement coordinator schedules an operating room for the removal of the organs and coordinates the surgery.

Once the organs have been removed and transported, clinical transplant coordinators take over. Clinical transplant coordinators have been involved in preparing recipients for new organs. It is the clinical coordinators' job to see to the patients' needs before, during, and after organ transplants. This involves admitting patients, contacting surgeons, arranging for operating rooms, as well as contacting the anesthesiology department and the blood bank. After the transplants, coordinators help patients through their recovery and arrange for outpatient housing.

Another significant aspect of the job of all transplant coordinators is educating the public about the importance of organ donation. They speak to hospital and nursing school staffs and to the general public to encourage donations.

■ Requirements

High School

High school courses that will prepare you for a medical-based education will be the most valuable in this profession. Biology and chemistry are important, as are courses in psychology, sociology, math, and health.

If you live near a transplant center, there may be volunteer opportunities available at the center or in an outpatient care home for transplant recipients. Your local Red Cross also may need volunteers for promoting donor awareness.

Postsecondary Training

There is no specific educational track for transplant coordinators. One transplant coordinator may focus on financing and insurance, while another on education and awareness. Another coordinator may perform physical tests and evaluations, while another counsels grieving families. The more experience and education with health care and medicine you have, the better your job opportunities. Although a nursing degree isn't required of all coordinators, it does give you a good medical background. A bachelor's degree in one of the sciences, along with experience in a medical setting, will also open up job opportunities. Some people working as coordinators may have master's degrees in public health or in business administration. Other coordinators may hold doctorates in psychology or social work.

Certification or Licensing

Certification, though not required, is available through the American Board of Transplant Coordinators. To qualify for certification, an applicant must have completed a year of full-time work as a coordinator.

There are two separate tests given—one for clinical transplant coordinators and one for procurement transplant coordinators. Both tests cover all organs and ask questions about analysis, treatment, and education of patients.

Other Requirements

To be a successful transplant coordinator, you should have good organizational skills and be able to work quickly, accurately, and efficiently. You must be a detail-oriented person and have good record keeping and reporting skills. A transplant coordinator needs to be a compassionate person who is able to communicate well with doctors, patients, donors' families, and the public.

■ Employers

A number of different institutions and organizations require transplant coordinators. In addition to the 281 transplant centers across the country, there are 56 independent organ procurement organizations and 56 independent tissue-typing labs. There are also 12 organ procurement organizations and 100 tissue-typing labs within the transplant centers themselves. These organizations and centers may be hospital-based, independent, or university-based.

■ Starting Out

Positions for transplant coordinators are advertised nationally in medical publications and on the Internet. The North American Transplant Coordinators Organization (NATCO) also offers job referral information.

Many transplant coordinators begin their professional careers in other areas such as nursing, business, psychology, social work, or the sciences before they seek a career as a transplant coordinator.

■ Advancement

There may be internal advancement opportunities within a clinic such as senior coordinator or senior educator. Other managerial or supervisory positions may also be a way of advancing within the career. There are other aspects of transplantation, such as surgery or hospital administration, that may be available with additional education and experience.

■ Earnings

Your educational background, experience, and responsibilities as a coordinator will determine your salary. People who have a degree and work as directors or educators may earn a higher salary than those working at the clinical end.

Many transplant coordinators are registered nurses. Salaries are comparable to those of registered nurses in other fields and can range from $24,500 to $59,000 depending on geographical location and experience. Although transplant centers and organ procurement agencies are nonprofit organizations, transplant coordinators generally receive very good health and retirement benefits that are consistent with other medical professions.

■ Work Environment

Transplant coordinators can be found doing their jobs in various environments. They may be in an office completing paperwork, in a hospital visiting with patients, families, or other hospital staff, or at a school or business meeting promoting donor awareness. Sometimes coordinators must accompany the organ to the transplant center, and some may be required to be on call and to work long, irregular hours.

■ Outlook

The number of people waiting for organ donations is increasing, but there still is a need to find an increased number of donors. Therefore, a number of organizations have been developed to promote organ donations, particularly among minorities. These efforts require the skills of transplant coordinators. Because the stress level of the job is high, the burnout rate is also high. Also, because procurement coordinators' hours can be long and irregular, many procurement coordinators move on to other positions after only 18 months or less. This means continued job opportunities for those looking for work as coordinators.

■ For More Information

The following provide information on a career as a transplant coordinator and the certification process.

American Board of Transplant Coordinators
8310 Nieman Road
Lenexa, KS 66214
Tel: 913-599-0198

International Transplant Nurses Society
Foster Plaza 5, Suite 300
651 Holiday Drive
Pittsburgh, PA 15220
Tel: 412-928-3667
Web: http://www.transweb.org/itns

North American Transplant Coordinators Organization
8310 Nieman Road
Lenexa, KS 66214
Tel: 913-492-3600
Web: http://www.natco1.org

■ Related Articles

Health Care

Social Services

Advanced Practice Nurses

Grief Therapists

Nurse Practitioners

Physician Assistants

Physicians

Psychologists

Registered Nurses

Social Workers

Transportation Inspectors

■ See Health and Regulatory Inspectors

Travel Agents

■ Overview

Travel agents assist individuals or groups who will be traveling, by planning their itineraries, making transportation, hotel, and tour reservations, obtaining or preparing tickets, and performing related services. There are over 140,000 travel agents employed in the United States.

■ History

The first travel agency in the United States was established in 1872. Before this time, travel as an activity was not widespread, due to wars and international barriers, inadequate transportation and hotels, lack of leisure, the threat of contagious disease, and lower standards of living. Despite the glamour attached to such early travelers as Marco Polo (1254?-1324?), people of the Middle Ages and the 17th and 18th centuries were not accustomed to traveling for pleasure.

The manufacturing operations that started in the Industrial Revolution caused international trade to expand greatly. Commercial traffic between countries stimulated both business and personal travel. Yet until the 20th century, travel was arduous and most areas were unprepared for tourists.

The travel business began with Thomas Cook, an Englishman who first popularized the guided tour. In 1841, Cook arranged his first excursion—a special Midland Counties Railroad Company train to carry passengers from Leicester to a temperance meeting in Loughborough. His

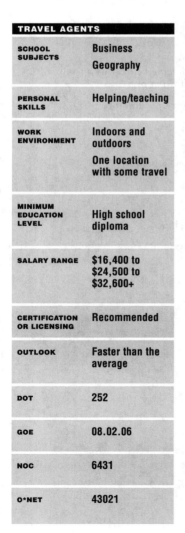

TRAVEL AGENTS	
SCHOOL SUBJECTS	Business Geography
PERSONAL SKILLS	Helping/teaching
WORK ENVIRONMENT	Indoors and outdoors One location with some travel
MINIMUM EDUCATION LEVEL	High school diploma
SALARY RANGE	$16,400 to $24,500 to $32,600+
CERTIFICATION OR LICENSING	Recommended
OUTLOOK	Faster than the average
DOT	252
GOE	08.02.06
NOC	6431
O*NET	43021

business grew rapidly. He made arrangements for 165,000 visitors to attend the Great Exhibition of 1851 in London. The following year, he organized the first "Cook's Tour." Earnest groups of English tourists were soon seen traveling by camel to view the Pyramids and the Sphinx, gliding past historic castles on the Rhine, and riding by carriage to view the wonders of Paris. The "Grand Tour" of Europe soon became an integral part of a young person's education among the privileged classes.

In the next hundred years, the development of the railroads, the replacement of sailing ships with faster steamships, the advent of the automobile and the bus, and the invention of the airplane provided an improved quality of transportation that encouraged people to travel for relaxation and personal enrichment. At the same time, cities, regions, and countries began to appreciate the economic aspects of travel. Promotional campaigns were organized to attract and accommodate tourists. Formal organization of the travel industry was reflected in the establishment in 1931 of the American Society of Travel Agents (ASTA).

In the past decade, travel agents have accommodated a great increase in family travel. This increase is in part a result of greater leisure time. As long as leisure time continues to grow and the nation's standard of living increases, there will be an even greater need for travel agents to help people in planning their vacations wisely.

■ The Job

The travel agent may work as a salesperson, travel consultant, tour organizer, travel guide, bookkeeper, or small business executive. If the agent operates a one-person office, he or she usually performs all of these functions. Other travel agents work in offices with dozens of employees, which allows them to specialize in certain areas. In such offices, one staff member may become an authority on sea cruises, another may work on trips to the Far East, and a third may develop an extensive knowledge of either low-budget or luxury trips. In some cases, travel agents are employed by national or international firms and can draw upon very extensive resources.

As salespeople, travel agents must be able to motivate people to take advantage of their services. Travel agents study their customers' interests, learn where they have traveled, appraise their financial resources and available time, and present a selection of travel options. Customers are then able to choose how and where they want to travel with a minimum of effort.

Travel agents consult a variety of published and computer-based sources for information on air transportation departure and arrival times, air fares, and hotel ratings and accommodations. They often base their recommendations on their own travel experiences or those of colleagues or clients. Travel agents may visit hotels, resorts, and restaurants to rate their comfort, cleanliness, and quality of food and service.

As travel consultants, agents give their clients suggestions regarding travel plans and itineraries, information on transportation alternatives, and advice on the available accommodations and rates of hotels and motels. They also explain and help with passport and visa regulations, foreign currency and exchange, climate and wardrobe, health requirements, customs regulations, baggage and accident insurance, traveler's checks or letters of credit, car rentals, tourist attractions, and welcome or escort services.

Many travel agents only sell tours that are developed by other organizations. The most skilled agents, however, often organize tours on a wholesale basis. This involves developing an itinerary, contracting a knowledgeable person to lead the tour, making tentative reservations for transportation, hotels, and side trips, publicizing the tour through descriptive brochures, advertisements, and other travel agents, scheduling reservations, and handling last-minute problems. Sometimes tours are arranged at the specific request of a group or to meet a client's particular needs.

In addition to other duties, travel agents may serve as *tour guides,* leading trips ranging from one week to six months to locations around the world. Agents often find tour leadership a useful way to gain personal travel experience. It also gives them the chance to become thoroughly acquainted with the people in the tour group, who may then use the agent to arrange future trips or recommend the agent to friends and relatives. Tour leaders are usually reimbursed for all their expenses or receive complimentary transportation and lodgings. Most travel agents, however, arrange for someone to cover for them at work during their absence, which may make tour leadership prohibitive for self-employed agents.

Agents serve as bookkeepers to handle the complex pattern of transportation and hotel reservations that each trip entails. They work directly with airline, steamship, railroad, bus, and car rental companies. They make direct contact with hotels and sight-seeing organizations or work indirectly through a receptive operator in the city involved. These arrangements require a great deal of accuracy, because mistakes could result in a client being left stranded in a foreign or remote area. After reservations are made, agents write up or obtain tickets, write out itineraries, and send out bills for the reservations involved. They also send out confirmations to airlines, hotels, and other companies.

Travel agents must promote their services. They present slides or movies to social and special interest groups, arrange advertising displays, and suggest company-sponsored trips to business managers.

A travel agent helps a couple book their vacation.

■ Requirements

High School

A high school diploma is the minimum requirement for becoming a travel agent. If you are interested in pursuing a career as an agent, be certain to include some computer courses, as well as typing or keyboarding courses, in your class schedule. Since much of your work as a travel agent will involve computerized reservation systems, it is important to have basic keyboarding skills and to be comfortable working with computers.

Because being able to communicate clearly with clients is central to this job, any high school course that enhances communication skills, such as English or speech, is a good choice. Proficiency in a foreign language, while not a requirement, might be helpful in many cases, such as when you are working with international travelers. Finally, geography, social studies, and business mathematics are classes that may also help prepare you for various aspects of the travel agent's work.

You can also begin learning about being a travel agent while still in high school by getting a summer or part-time job in travel and tourism. D. G. Elmore, president of Gant Travel—a national chain of corporate travel agencies—suggests that interested high school students find a job in a travel agency, doing whatever they can do. "I would advise them to get a job doing anything from tearing down tickets to delivering tickets. Anything that brings them in contact with the business will go a long way toward getting them a job," he says. "If they did that their senior year in high school in a major city, they'd have a job by the end of the summer, almost certainly." If finding a part-time or summer job in a travel agency proves impossible, you might consider looking for a job as a reservation agent for an airline, rental car agency, or hotel.

GLOSSARY

Airline Reporting Corporation (ARC): An autonomous corporation created by the domestic airlines that appoints travel agencies to sell airline tickets and oversees the financial details of tracking payments to airlines and commissions to agencies.

Booking: A reservation

Coach: The economy class on an airline

Computerized Reservation System (CRS): Any of several computer systems allowing immediate access to fares, schedules, and availability, and offering the capability of making reservations and generating tickets. The two most commonly used are Sabre and Apollo.

Confirmation number: An alphanumeric code used to identify and document the confirmation of a booking.

Fam: Abbreviation for "familiarization" trip or tour. A low-cost trip or tour offered to travel agents by a supplier or group of suppliers to familiarize the agents with their destination and services.

Layover: A stop on a trip, usually associated with a change of planes or other transportation

Luxury class: The most expensive accommodations or fare category

Satellite ticket printer: A ticket printer that generates airline tickets in an ARC-accredited travel agency

Postsecondary Training

Travel courses are available from certain colleges, private vocational schools, and adult education programs in public high schools. Some colleges and universities grant bachelor's and master's degrees in travel and tourism. Although college training is not required for work as a travel agent, it can be very helpful and is expected to become increasingly important for these workers in the future. It is predicted that in the future most agents will be college graduates. Travel schools provide basic reservation training and other training related to travel agents' functions, which is helpful but not required.

A liberal arts or business administration background is recommended for college students interested in this field. Useful liberal arts courses include foreign languages, geography, English, history, anthropology, political science, art and music appreciation, and literature. Pertinent business courses include transportation, business law, hotel management, marketing, office management, and accounting. As in many other fields, computer skills are increasingly important.

Certification or Licensing

To be able to sell passage on various types of transportation, a travel agent must be approved by the conferences of carriers involved. These are the Airlines Reporting Corporation, the International Air Transport Association, Cruise Lines International Association, and the Rail Travel Promotion Agency. To sell tickets for these individual conferences, the agent must be clearly established in the travel business and have a good personal and business background. Not all travel agents are authorized to sell passage by all of the above conferences. Naturally, those who wish to sell the widest range of services should seek affiliation with all four.

Currently, travel agents are not required to be federally licensed, except in the state of Rhode Island. However, Ohio, California, and Hawaii do require their travel agents to be registered. In California, agents not approved by a corporation must be licensed.

Travel agents may choose to become certified by the Institute of Certified Travel Agents (ICTA). ICTA offers certification programs leading to the designations of Certified Travel Associate (CTA) and Certified Travel Counselor (CTC). In order to become a Certified Travel Associate, agents must have 18 months of experience as a travel agent, complete a 12-course program, and pass a written test. In order to become a Certified Travel Counselor, agents must have 5 years of experience, must have attained their CTA status, must take a 12-course program, and take and pass a final exam. While not a requirement, certification by ICTA may help an agent progress in his or her career.

ICTA also offers travel agents a number of other programs such as sales skills development courses, and destination specialist courses, which provide a detailed knowledge of various geographic regions of the world.

Other Requirements

The primary requisite for success in the travel field is a sincere interest in travel. An agent's knowledge of and travel experiences with major tourist centers, various hotels, and local customs and points of interest make that person a more effective and convincing source of assistance. Yet the work of travel agents is not one long vacation. They operate in a highly competitive industry.

Travel agents must be able to make quick and accurate use of transportation schedules and tariffs. They must be able to handle addition and subtraction quickly. Almost all agents make use of computers to get the very latest information on rates and schedules and to make reservations.

Most travel agents work with a wide range of personalities, so their skills in psychology and diplomacy are always in use. They must also be able to generate enthusiasm among their customers and be resourceful in solving any problems that might arise. A knowledge of foreign languages is useful, because many customers come from other countries and agents are in frequent contact with foreign hotels and travel agencies.

Exploring

Any type of part-time experience with a travel agency would be helpful for those interested in this career. A small agency may welcome help during peak travel seasons or when an agent is away from the office. If your high school or junior college arranges career conferences, you may be able to invite a speaker from the travel industry. Visits to local travel agents will also provide you with helpful information.

Employers

Agents may work for commercial travel agents, in the corporate travel department of a large company, or be self-employed. Most agents work for travel agencies; approximately only 10 percent are self-employed.

In addition to the regular travel business, a number of travel jobs are available with oil companies, automobile clubs, and transportation companies. Some jobs in travel are on the staffs of state and local governments seeking to encourage tourism.

Starting Out

Young people seeking careers in the travel field usually begin by working for a company involved with transportation and tourism. Fortunately, a number of positions exist that are particularly appropriate for young people and those with limited work experience. Airlines, for example, hire flight attendants, reservation agents, and ticket clerks. Railroads and cruise line companies also have clerical positions; the rise in their popularity in recent years has resulted in more job opportunities. Those with travel experience may secure positions as tour guides. Organizations and companies with extensive travel operations may hire employees whose main responsibility is making travel arrangements.

Since travel agencies tend to have relatively small staffs, most openings are filled as a result of direct application and personal contact. In evaluating the merits of various travel agencies, job seekers may wish to note whether the agency's owner belongs to ASTA. This trade group may also help in several other ways. It sponsors adult night school courses in travel agency operation in some metropolitan areas. It also offers a 15-lesson travel agency correspondence course. Also available, for a modest charge, is a travel agency management kit containing information that is particularly helpful to people considering setting up their own agencies. ASTA's publication *Travel News* includes a classified advertising section listing available positions and agencies for sale.

Advancement

Advancement opportunities within the travel field are limited to growth in terms of business volume or extent of specialization. Successful agents, for example, may hire additional employees or set up branch offices. A travel agency worker who has held his or her position for a while may be promoted to become a *travel assistant*. Travel assistants are responsible for answering general questions about transportation, providing current cost of hotel accommodations, and providing other valid information.

Travel bureau employees may decide to go into business for themselves. Agents may show their professional status by belonging to ASTA, which requires its members to have three years of satisfactory travel agent experience and approval by at least two carrier conferences.

Earnings

Travel agency income comes from commissions paid by airlines, hotels, car rental companies, cruise lines, and tour operators. Although many suppliers pay a standard 8 percent—recently reduced from 10 percent—of the total cost to the customer, commissions do vary somewhat. Cruise lines, for example, pay commissions on a sliding scale depending upon the season.

Travel agents typically earn a straight salary. Although less common, some agents are paid a salary plus commission or entirely on a commission basis. Salaries of travel agents ranged from $16,400 to $32,600, with an average of $24,500 in 1996, according to the *Occupational Outlook Handbook*. Those with 5 years of experience earn an average of $22,300. Managers with 10 years of experience may earn from $26,300 to over $32,600 annually. In addition to experience level, the location of the firm is also a factor in how much travel agents earn. Agents working in larger metropolitan areas tend to earn more than their counterparts in smaller cities.

One of the benefits of working as a travel agent is the chance to travel at a discounted price. Major airlines offer special agent fares, which are often only 25 percent of regular cost. Hotels, car rental companies, cruise lines, and tour operators also offer reduced rates for travel agents. Agents also get the opportunity to take free or low-cost group tours sponsored by transportation carriers, tour operators, and cruise lines. These trips, called "fam" trips, are designed to familiarize agents with locations and accommodations so that they can better market them to their clients.

Work Environment

While this is an interesting and appealing occupation, the job of the travel agent is not as simple or glamorous as might be expected. Travel is a highly competitive field. Since almost every travel agent can offer the client the same service, agents must depend upon repeat customers for much of their business. Their reliability, courtesy, and effectiveness in past transactions will determine whether they will get repeat business.

Travel agents also work in an atmosphere of keen competition for referrals. They must resist direct pressure or indirect pressure from travel-related companies that have provided favors in the past (free trips, for example) and book all trips based only on the best interests of clients.

Most agents work a 40-hour week, although this frequently includes working a half-day on Saturday or an occasional evening. During busy seasons (typically from January through June) overtime may be necessary. Agents may receive additional salary for this work or be given compensatory time off.

As they gain experience, agents become more effective. One study revealed that 98 percent of all agents had more than 3 years' experience in some form of the travel field. Almost half had 20 years or more in this area.

Small travel agencies provide a smaller-than-average amount of fringe benefits such as retirement, medical, and life insurance plans. Self-employed agents tend to earn more than those who work for others, although the business risk is greater. Those who own their own businesses may experience large fluctuations in income because the travel business is extremely sensitive to swings in the economy.

■ Outlook

Although future prospects in the travel field will depend to some degree on the state of the economy, the travel industry is expected to expand rapidly as more Americans travel for pleasure and business. New travel agencies will open and existing ones will expand, causing employment of these workers to grow faster than the average for all occupations through the year 2006. The U.S. Department of Labor estimates that the number of travel agents will increase by at least 77,000 by the year 2006. Many of the expected job openings will result from workers leaving the field due to retirement or other reasons.

Certain factors may hinder growth for travel agents. Many airlines and other travel suppliers now offer consumers the option of making their own travel arrangements through on-line reservation services, readily accessible through the Internet. With this as an option, it is possible that travelers will become less dependent upon agents to make travel arrangements for them. In addition, airlines have placed a limit on the amount of commission they will pay travel agencies. This could potentially reduce an agency's income, thereby making it less profitable and less able to hire new travel agents. Since these innovations are recent, their full effect on travel agents has not yet been determined.

■ For More Information

For information on educational programs and the career of travel agent, contact:

American Society of Travel Agents
1101 King Street, Suite 200
Alexandria, VA 22314
Tel: 703-739-2782
Web: http://www.astanet.com

For information regarding certification, contact:

The Institute of Certified Travel Agents
PO Box 812059
148 Linden Street
Wellesley, MA 02482-0012
Tel: 800-542-4282
Web: http://www.icta.com/

For information on travel careers in the United States government, contact:

Society of Travel Agents in Government
6935 Wisconsin Avenue, NW, Suite 200
Bethesda, MD 20815
Tel: 301-654-8595
Web: http://www.government-travel.org/

■ Related Articles

Airlines
Hospitality
Recreation
Travel and Tourism
Adventure Travel Specialists
Hotel Concierges
Inbound Tour Guides
Reservation and Ticket Agents
Tour Guides

Tree Surgeons
■ See Arborists

Troubleshooters
■ See Energy Transmission and Distribution Workers, Line Installers and Cable Splicers

Truant Officers
■ See Health and Regulatory Inspectors

Truck Drivers

■ Overview

Truck drivers generally are distinguished by the distance they travel. *Over-the-road drivers,* also known as *long-distance drivers* or *tractor-trailer drivers,* haul freight over long distances in large trucks and tractor-trailer rigs that are usually diesel-powered. Depending on the specific operation, over-the-road drivers also load and unload the shipments and make minor repairs to vehicles. *Short-haul drivers* or *pickup and delivery drivers,* operate trucks that transport materials, merchandise, and equipment within a limited area, usually a single city or metropolitan area.

■ History

The first trucks were nothing more than converted automobiles. In 1904, there were only about 500 trucks in the United States. At that time, there was little need for goods to be transported across the country. Manufacturing was such that the same products were produced all over the nation, many in small "mom and pop" operations so that even small towns could supply all the food, clothing, tools and other materials that people needed. Today, manufacturing is centralized and "mom and pop" stores are all but gone, increasing the need for a way to move consumer goods to every corner of the country.

In World War I, the U.S. Army used trucks for the first time to haul equipment and supplies over terrain that was not accessible by train. After the war, the domestic use of trucks increased rapidly. In the 1920s, the nation became more mobile, as streets and highways improved. American businesses and industries were growing at an unprecedented rate, and trucks became established as a reliable way of transporting goods. In fact, trucking companies began to compete with railroads for the business of shipping freight long distances.

Since World War II, other innovations have shaped the trucking industry, including improvements in the design of the truck body and the mechanical systems in trucks. Tank trucks were built to carry fuel, and other trucks were designed specifically for transporting livestock, produce, milk, eggs, meat, and heavy machine parts. The efficiency of trucks was further increased by the development of the detachable trailer. Depending on what needed to be shipped, a different trailer could be hooked up to the tractor.

In addition to these technological advances, the establishment of the interstate highway system in 1956 allowed trucks to deliver shipments with increased efficiency. Along with the development of new trucks with better gas mileage, trucking companies now could offer their services to businesses at cheaper rates than railroads.

Trucking today is central to the nation's transportation system, moving dry freight, refrigerated materials, liquid bulk materials, construction materials, livestock, household goods, and other cargo. In fact, nearly all goods are transported by truck at some point after they are produced. Some drivers move manufactured goods from factories to distribution terminals, and after the goods arrive at destination terminals, other drivers deliver the goods to stores and homes. Certain carriers also provide shipping services directly from the supplier to the customer.

■ The Job

Truckers drive trucks of all sizes, from small straight trucks and vans to tanker trucks and tractors with multiple trailers. The average tractor-trailer rig is no more than 102 inches wide, excluding the mirrors, 13 feet and 6 inches tall, and just under 70 feet in length. The engines in these vehicles range from 250 to 600 horsepower.

Over-the-road drivers operate tractor-trailers and other large trucks that are often diesel-powered. These drivers generally haul goods and materials over long distances and frequently drive at night. Whereas many other truck drivers spend a considerable portion of their time loading and unloading materials, over-the-road drivers spend most of their working time driving.

At the terminal or warehouse where they receive their load, drivers get ready for long-distance runs by checking over the vehicle to make sure all the equipment and systems are functioning and that the truck is loaded properly and has on board the necessary fuel, oil, and safety equipment.

Some over-the-road drivers travel the same routes repeatedly and on a regular schedule. Other companies require drivers to do unscheduled runs and work when dispatchers call with an available job. Some long-distance runs are short enough that drivers can get to the destination, remove the load from the trailer, replace it

TRUCK DRIVERS	
SCHOOL SUBJECTS	**Business** **Technical/Shop**
PERSONAL SKILLS	**Following instructions** **Mechanical/manipulative**
WORK ENVIRONMENT	**Primarily outdoors** **Primarily multiple locations**
MINIMUM EDUCATION LEVEL	**Apprenticeship**
SALARY RANGE	**$20,000 to** **$40,000 to** **$53,000**
CERTIFICATION OR LICENSING	**Required by all states**
OUTLOOK	**Faster than the average**
DOT	**905**
GOE	**05.08.01**
NOC	**7411**
O*NET	**97117**

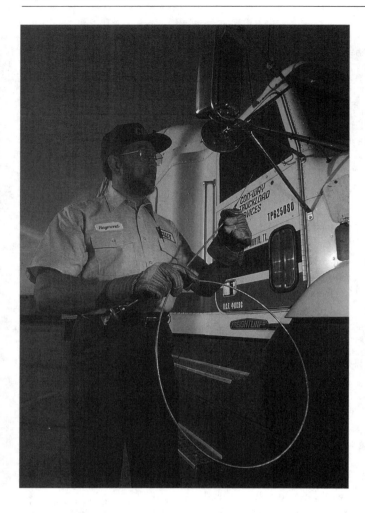

A truck driver checks his rig cable before his next run.

from swaying and rolling. After driving to the destination, the drivers remove the vehicles from the trailers.

Over-the-road drivers must develop a number of skills that differ from the skills needed for operating smaller trucks. Because trailer trucks vary in length and number of wheels, skilled operators of one type of trailer may need to undergo a short training period if they switch to a new type of trailer. Over-the-road drivers must be able to maneuver and judge the position of their trucks and must be able to back their huge trailers into precise positions.

Local truck drivers generally operate the smaller trucks and transport a variety of products. They may travel regular routes or routes that change as needed. Local drivers include delivery workers who supply fresh produce to grocery stores and drivers who deliver gasoline in tank trucks to gas stations. Other local truck drivers, such as those who keep stores stocked with baked goods, may sell their employers' products as well as deliver them to customers along a route. These drivers are known as *route drivers* or *route-sales drivers*.

Often local truck drivers receive their assignments and delivery forms from dispatchers at the company terminal each day. Some drivers load goods or materials on their trucks, but in many situations dockworkers have already loaded the trucks in such a way that the unloading can be accomplished along the route with maximum convenience and efficiency.

Local drivers must be skilled at maneuvering their vehicles through the worst driving conditions, including bad weather and traffic-congested areas. The ability to pull into tight parking spaces, negotiate narrow passageways, and back up to loading docks is essential.

Some drivers have helpers who travel with them and assist in unloading at delivery sites, especially if the loads are heavy or bulky or when there are many deliveries scheduled. Drivers of some heavy trucks, such as dump trucks and oil tank trucks, operate mechanical levers, pedals, and other devices that assist with loading and unloading cargo. Drivers of moving vans generally have a crew of helpers to aid in loading and unloading customers' household goods and office equipment.

Once a local driver reaches his or her destination, he or she sometimes obtains a signature acknowledging that the delivery has been made and may collect a payment from the customer. Some drivers serve as intermediaries between the company and its customers by responding to customer complaints and requests.

Each day, local drivers have to make sure that their deliveries have been made correctly. At the end of the day, they turn in their records and the money they collected. Local drivers may also be responsible for doing routine maintenance on their trucks to keep them in good work-

with another load, and return home all in one day. Many runs, however, take up to a week or longer, with various stops. Some companies assign two drivers to long runs, so that one can sleep while the other drives. This method ensures that the trip will take the shortest amount of time possible.

In addition to driving their trucks long distances, over-the-road drivers have other duties. They must inspect their vehicles before and after trips, prepare reports on accidents, and keep daily logs. They may load and unload some shipments or hire workers to help with these tasks at the destination. Drivers of long-distance moving vans, for example, do more loading and unloading work than most other long-haul drivers. Drivers of vehicle-transport trailer trucks move new automobiles or trucks from manufacturers to dealers and also have additional duties. At plants where the vehicles are made, transport drivers drive new vehicles onto the ramps of transport trailers. They secure the vehicles in place with chains and clamps to prevent them ing condition. Otherwise, any mechanical problems are reported to the maintenance department for repair.

■ Requirements

High School

High school students interested in working as truck drivers should take courses in driver training and automobile mechanics. In addition, some bookkeeping, mathematics, and business courses will teach methods that help in keeping accurate records of customer transactions.

Postsecondary Training

Drivers must know and meet the standards set by the state and federal governments for the particular work they do and they type of vehicle they drive. In some companies, new employees can informally learn the skills appropriate for the kind of driving they do from experienced drivers. They may ride with and watch other employees of the company or they may take a few hours of their own time to learn from an experienced driver. For jobs driving some kinds of trucks, companies require new employees to attend classes that range from a few days to several weeks.

One of the best ways to prepare for a job driving large trucks is to take a tractor-trailer driver training course. Programs vary in the amount of actual driving experience they provide. Programs that are certified by the Professional Truck Driver Institute of America meet established guidelines for training and generally provide good preparation for drivers. Another way to determine whether programs are adequate is to check with local companies that hire drivers and ask for their recommendations. Completing a certified training program helps potential truck drivers learn specific skills, but it does not guarantee a job. Vehicles and the freight inside trucks can represent a large investment to companies that employ truck drivers. Therefore, they seek to hire responsible and reliable drivers in order to protect their investment. For this reason, many employers set various requirements of their own that exceed state and federal standards.

Certification or Licensing

Truck drivers must meet federal requirements and any requirements established by the state where they are based. All drivers must obtain a state commercial driver's license. Truck drivers involved in interstate commerce must meet requirements of the U.S. Department of Transportation. They must be at least 21 years old and pass a physical examination that requires good vision and hearing, normal blood pressure, and normal use of arms and legs (unless the applicant qualifies for a waiver). Drivers must then pass physicals every two years and meet other requirements,

NO-ZONE CAMPAIGN

Safety is a major concern for truck drivers and should also be for the drivers they share the road with. That's why the Federal Highway Administration launched a campaign to educate other drivers about truck drivers' blind spots and how to avoid them. No-zones are the danger areas around commercial vehicles where crashes are more likely to occur. For example, a truck has a much larger blind spot on both of its sides than a car. When other drivers drive in these no-zones for any length of time, they can't be seen by truck drivers. Also, when cars cut in too soon after passing, then abruptly slow down, truck drivers are forced to compensate with little time or room to spare. Many trucks carry signs on the back that warn other drivers of wide right turns. Truck drivers sometimes need to swing wide to the left in order to safely negotiate a right turn. Rear blind spots are also a problem because trucks, unlike cars, have deep blind spots directly behind them. A truck driver can't see cars in this position and the car driver's view of traffic is also severely reduced. Generally speaking, the bigger the truck:

- The bigger its blindspots,
- The more room it needs to maneuver,
- The longer it takes to stop,
- The longer it takes to pass it,
- The more likely the car will be the loser in a collision.

including a minimum of 20/40 vision in each eye and no diagnosis of insulin-dependent diabetes or epilepsy.

Other Requirements

Many drivers work with little supervision, so they need to have a mature, responsible attitude toward their job. In jobs where drivers deal directly with company customers, it is especially important for the drivers to be pleasant, courteous, and able to communicate well with people. Helping a customer with a complaint can mean the difference between losing and keeping a client.

■ Exploring

High school students interested in becoming truck drivers may be able to gain experience by working as drivers' helpers during summer vacations or in part-time delivery jobs. Many people get useful experience in driving vehicles while they are serving in the armed forces. It may also be helpful to talk with employers of local or over-the-road truck drivers or with the drivers themselves.

The Internet provides a forum for prospective truck drivers to explore their career options. Two online magazines—*Overdrive* (http://www.overdriveonline.com) and *Landline* (http://www.landlinemag.com)—provide a look at issues in the trucking industry and a list of answers for frequently asked questions for people interested in trucking careers. There is also a truck driver's news group (http://www.misc.transport.trucking) where potential truck drivers can pose questions.

■ Employers

Over-the-road and local drivers may be employed by either private carriers or for-hire carriers. Food store chains and manufacturing plants that transport their own goods are examples of private carriers. There are two kinds of for-hire carriers: trucking companies serving the general public (common carriers) and trucking firms transporting goods under contract to certain companies (contract carriers).

Drivers who work independently are known as *owner-operators*. They own their own vehicles and often do their own maintenance and repair work. They must find customers who need goods transported, perhaps through personal references or by advertising their services. For example, many drivers find contract jobs through "Internet truck stops" where drivers can advertise their services and companies can post locations of loads they need transported. Some independent drivers establish long-term contracts with just one or two clients, such as trucking companies.

■ Starting Out

Prospective over-the-road drivers can gain commercial driving experience as local truck drivers and then attend a tractor-trailer driver training program. Driving an intercity bus or dump truck is also suitable experience for aspiring over-the-road truck drivers. Many newly hired long-distance drivers start by filling in for regular drivers or helping out when extra trips are necessary. They are assigned regular work when a job opens up.

Many truck drivers hold other jobs before they become truck drivers. Some local drivers start as drivers' helpers, loading and unloading trucks and gradually taking over some driving duties. When a better driving position opens up, helpers who have shown they are reliable and responsible may be promoted. Members of the armed forces who have gained appropriate experience may get driving jobs when they are discharged.

Job seekers may apply directly to firms that use drivers. Listings of specific job openings are often posted at local offices of the state employment service and in the classified ads in newspapers. Many jobs, however, are not posted. Looking in the yellow pages under trucking and moving and storage can provide names of specific companies to solicit. Also, large manufacturers and retailing companies sometimes have their own fleets. Many telephone calls and letters may be required, but they can lead to a potential employer. Personal visits, when appropriate, sometimes get the best results.

■ Advancement

Some over-the-road drivers who stay with their employers advance by becoming safety supervisors, driver supervisors, or dispatchers. Many over-the-road drivers look forward to going into business for themselves by acquiring their own tractor-trailer rigs. This step requires a significant initial investment and a continuing good income to cover expenses. Like many other small business owners, independent drivers sometimes have a hard time financially. Those who are their own mechanics and have formal business training are in the best position to do well.

Local truck drivers can advance by learning to drive specialized kinds of trucks or by acquiring better schedules or other job conditions. Some may move into positions as dispatchers and, with sufficient experience, eventually become supervisors or terminal managers. Other local drivers decide to become over-the-road drivers to receive higher wages.

■ Earnings

Wages of truck drivers vary according to their employer, size of the truck they drive, product being hauled, geographical region, and other factors. Drivers who are employed by for-hire carriers have higher earnings than those who work independently or for private carriers.

Pay rates for over-the-road truck drivers are often figured using a cents-per-mile rate. Most companies pay between 20 and 30 cents per mile, but large companies are advertising higher rates to attract good drivers. J. B. Hunt, for example, the nation's largest publicly held trucking company, advertised 37 to 40 cents per mile to start in early 1999. At that rate, based on a weekly average of 2,500 miles, a driver would earn $48,100 to $53,300 a year.

Tractor-trailer drivers usually have the highest earnings; average hourly pay generally increases with the size of the truck. Drivers in the South have lower earnings than those in the Northeast and West. The annual earnings of long-distance drivers can range from about $20,000 to well over twice that amount. Owner-operators have average earnings between $20,000 and $25,000 per year, after subtracting expenses. Although some local truck drivers are guaranteed minimum or weekly wages, most are paid an hourly wage and receive extra compensation for overtime work.

In addition to their wages, the majority of truck drivers receive benefits, many of which are determined by agreements between their unions and company management. The benefits may include health insurance coverage, pension plans, paid vacation days, and work uniforms.

■ Work Environment

Although there is work for truck drivers in even the smallest towns, most jobs are located in and around larger metropolitan areas. About a third of all drivers work for for-hire carriers, and another third work for private carriers. Less than 10 percent are self-employed.

Even with modern improvements in cab design, driving trucks is often a tiring job. Although some local drivers work 40-hour weeks, many work eight hours a day, six days a week, or more. Some drivers, such as those who bring food to grocery stores, often work at night or very early in the morning. Drivers who must load and unload their trucks may do a lot of lifting, stooping, and bending.

It is common for over-the-road truck drivers to work at least 50 hours a week. However, federal regulations require that drivers cannot be on duty for more than 60 hours in any seven-day period. Furthermore, after drivers have driven for 10 hours, they must be off duty for at least eight hours before they can drive again. Drivers often work the maximum allowed time to complete long runs in as little time as possible. In fact, most drivers drive 10 to 12 hours per day and make sure they have proper rest periods. A driver usually covers between 550 and 650 miles daily. The sustained driving, particularly at night, can be fatiguing, boring, and sometimes very stressful, as when traffic or weather conditions are bad.

Local drivers may operate on schedules that easily allow a social and family life, but long-distance drivers often find that difficult. They may spend a considerable amount of time away from their homes and families, including weekends and holidays. After they try it, many people find they do not want this way of life. On the other hand, some people love the lifestyle of the over-the-road driver. Many families are able to find ways to work around the schedule of a truck-driving spouse. In some cases, the two people assigned to a long-distance run are a husband and wife team.

■ Outlook

The employment of truck drivers is expected to increase well above the average rate for all other occupations. This increase will be related to overall growth in the nation's economy and in the volume of freight moved by trucks, both locally and over long distances. Currently, there is a shortage of both local and over-the-road drivers. The trucking industry expects to hire about 450,000 new drivers each year until 2000 with continued strong demand early in the 21st century.

The need for trucking services is directly linked to the growth of the nation's economy. During economic downturns, when the pace of business slows, some drivers may receive fewer assignments and thus have lower earnings or they may be laid off. Drivers employed in some vital industries, such as food distribution, are less affected by an economic recession. On the other hand, people who own and operate their own trucks usually suffer the most.

A large number of driver jobs become available each year. Most openings develop when experienced drivers transfer to other fields or leave the workforce entirely. There is a considerable amount of turnover in the field. Beginners are able to get many of these jobs. Competition is expected to remain strong for the more desirable jobs, such as those with large companies or the easiest routes.

■ For More Information

For further information and literature about a career as a truck driver, contact the following organizations:

American Trucking Associations
Office of Public Affairs
2200 Mill Road
Alexandria, VA 22314-4677
Tel: 703-838-1700
Web: http://www.trucking.org

Professional Truck Driver Institute of America
2200 Mill Road
Alexandria, VA 22314
Tel: 703-838-8842
Web: http://www.ptdia.org

■ Related Articles

Railroads

Shipping

Transportation

Trucking

Industrial Traffic Managers

Public Transportation Operators

Toll Collectors

Traffic Engineers

Trunk Technicians

■ **See Cable Television Technicians**

Typesetters

■ **See Prepress Workers**

Typists and Word Processors

■ Overview

Using typewriters, personal computers, and other office machines, *typists and word processors* convert handwritten or otherwise unfinished material into clean, readable, typewritten copies. Typists and word processors create reports, letters, forms, tables, charts, and other materials for all kinds of businesses and services. About 1.1 million people work as typists and word processors in the United States.

■ History

The invention of the typewriter in 1829 by W. A. Burt greatly increased business efficiency and productivity, and its benefits grew as typists became skilled at quickly transforming messy handwritten documents into neat, consistently typed copies.

More recently, the introduction of word processing into the workplace has revolutionized typing. This task may be done on a personal computer, a computer terminal hooked up to a network, or a computer that strictly handles word processing functions. As a person types, the words appear on a video display terminal (VDT) screen. Workers can correct errors and make any necessary changes right on the screen before a hard copy is printed on paper, thus eliminating the need for retyping whole pages to correct mistakes. The computer stores the information in its memory, so the worker can go back to it again and again for copies or changes.

The term "word processing" entered the English language in 1965, when International Business Machines (IBM) introduced a typewriter that put information onto magnetic tape instead of paper. Corrections could be made on this tape before running the tape through a machine that converted the signals on the tape into characters on a printed page. Today, word processing software and personal computers have virtually replaced typewriters in the office.

■ The Job

Some typists perform few duties other than typing. These workers spend approximately 75 percent of their time at the keyboard. They may input statistical data, medical reports, legal briefs, addresses, letters, and other documents from handwritten copies. They may work in pools, dividing the work of a large office among many workers under the supervision of a typing section chief. These typists may also be responsible for making photocopies of typewritten materials for distribution.

Beginning typists may start by typing address labels, headings on form letters, and documents from legible handwritten copy. More experienced typists may work from copy that is more difficult to read or needs to be printed in tabular form.

Clerk-typists spend up to 50 percent of their time typing. They also perform a variety of clerical tasks such as filing, answering the phone, acting as receptionists, and operating copy machines.

Many typists type from recorded audiotapes instead of written or printed copy. *Transcribing-machine operators* sit at keyboards and wear headsets, through which they hear the spoken contents of letters, reports, and meetings. Typists can control the speed of the tape so they can comfortably type every word they hear. They proofread their finished documents and may erase dictated tapes for future reuse.

Many typists work at computer terminals. *Magnetic-tape typewriter operators* enter information from written materials on computers to produce magnetic disks or tapes for storage and later retrieval. *In-file operators* use terminals to post or receive information about people's credit records for credit reporting agencies. When an agency subscriber calls with a question about a person's credit, the typist calls up that record on the VDT screen and reads the information.

Most common of the computer typists are *word processors*. These employees put documents into the proper format by entering codes into the word processing software, telling it which lines to center, which words to underline, where the margins should be set, and so forth, and how the document should be stored and printed. Word processors can edit, change, insert, and delete materials instantly just by pressing keys. Word processing is particularly efficient for form letters, in which only certain parts of a document change on each copy. When a word processor has finished formatting and keying in a document, it is electronically sent to a printer for a finished copy. The document is normally saved on a disk or the computer's hard drive so that any subsequent changes to it can be made easily and new copies produced immediately. Word

TYPISTS AND WORD PROCESSORS	
SCHOOL SUBJECTS	Computer science English
PERSONAL SKILLS	Following instructions Mechanical/manipulative
WORK ENVIRONMENT	Primarily indoors Primarily one location
MINIMUM EDUCATION LEVEL	High school diploma
SALARY RANGE	$14,500 to $21,500 to $30,750
CERTIFICATION OR LICENSING	None available
OUTLOOK	Decline
DOT	203
GOE	07.06.02
NOC	1412
O*NET	55307

processors also can send electronic files via email or modems to people in different locations.

Certain typists use special machines to create copy. *Perforator typists* type on machines that punch holes in a paper tape, which is used to create typewritten copy automatically. In publishing and printing, *photocomposing-perforator machine operators, photocomposing-keyboard operators, veritype operators,* and *typesetter-perforator operators* type on special machines that produce photographic negatives or paper prints of the copy. Some of these typists must also code copy to show what size and style of letters and characters should be used and how the layout of the page should look.

Braille typists and *Braille operators* use special typewriter-like machines to transcribe written or spoken English into Braille. By pressing one key or a combination of keys, they create the raised characters of the Braille alphabet. They may print either on special paper or on metal plates, which are later used to print books or other publications.

Cryptographic machine operators operate typewriter-like equipment that codes, transmits, and decodes secret messages for the armed forces, law enforcement agencies, and business organizations. These typists select a code card from a code book, insert the card into the machine, and type the message in English on the machine, which converts it to coded copy. A decoding card is used to follow the same process for decoding.

■ Requirements

High School
Most employers require that typists and word processors be high school graduates and able to type accurately at a rate of at least 40 or 50 words per minute. Typists need a good knowledge of spelling, grammar, and punctuation and may be required to be familiar with standard office equipment.

Postsecondary Training
In addition to high schools, there are colleges, business schools, and home-study courses that teach keyboarding skills. Some people learn keyboarding through self-teaching materials such as books, recordings, and computer programs. Business schools and community colleges often offer certificates or associate's degrees for typists and word processors.

For those who do not pursue such formal education, temporary agencies will often train workers in these skills. Generally, it takes a minimum of three to six months of experience to become a skilled word processor.

Word processors must be able to type 45 to 80 words per minute and should know the proper way to organize such documents as letters, reports, and financial state-

ments. Increasingly, employers are requiring that employees know how to use various software programs for word processing, spreadsheet, and database management tasks.

Other Requirements
All typists and word processors need manual dexterity and the ability to concentrate. They should be alert, efficient, and attentive to detail. Because these employees must often work directly with other people, they need good interpersonal skills, including a courteous and cheerful demeanor. Good listening skills are important for transcribing functions of the typist.

■ Exploring
As with many clerical occupations, a good way to gain experience as a typist is through high school work-study programs. Students in these programs work part time for local businesses and attend classes part time. Temporary agencies also provide training and temporary jobs for exploring the field. Another way to gain typing experience is to do volunteer typing for friends, church groups, or other organizations and to create your own computerized reports.

■ Employers
Typists and word processors are employed in almost every kind of workplace, including banks, law firms, factories, schools, hospitals, publishing firms, department stores, and government agencies. They may work with groups of employees in large offices or with only one or two other people in small offices.

■ Starting Out
Business school and college students may learn of typing or word processing positions through their schools' placement offices. Some large businesses recruit employees directly from these schools. High school guidance counselors also may know of local job openings.

People interested in typing or word processor positions can check the want ads in newspapers and business journals for companies with job openings. They can apply directly to the personnel departments of large companies that hire many of these workers. They also can register with temporary agencies. To apply for positions with the federal government, job seekers should apply at the nearest regional Office of Personnel Management. State, county, and city governments may also have listings for such positions.

■ Advancement
Typists and word processors usually receive salary increases as they gain experience and are promoted from junior to senior positions. These are often given a classification or pay

scale designation, such as typist or word processor I or II. They may also advance from clerk-typist to technical typist, or from a job in a typing pool to a typing position in a private office.

A degree in business management or executive secretarial skills increases a typist's chances for advancement. In addition, many large companies and government agencies provide training programs that allow workers to upgrade their skills and move into other jobs, such as secretary, statistical clerk, or stenographer.

Once they have acquired enough experience, some typists and word processors go into business for themselves and provide typing services to business clients working from their homes. They may find work typing reports, manuscripts, and papers for professors, authors, business people, and students.

The more word processing experience an employee has, the better the opportunities to move up. Some may be promoted to word processing supervisor or selected for in-house professional training programs in data processing. Word processors may also move into related fields and work as word-processing equipment salespeople or servicers, or word-processing teachers or consultants.

■ Earnings

Workers with word processing experience generally receive higher salaries than those without it. In the federal government, beginning clerk-typists earned about $15,500 per year in 1997, while the average salary for all clerk-typists in the federal government was about $21,500. The range for typists and word processors employed in private industry was from $14,500 to $30,750 in 1996.

Typists and word processors occasionally may work overtime to finish special projects and may receive overtime pay. In large cities workers usually receive paid holidays, two weeks' vacation after one year of employment, sick leave, health and life insurance, and a pension plan. Some large companies also provide dental insurance, profit sharing opportunities, and bonuses.

■ Work Environment

Typists and word processors work 35 to 40 hours per week at workstations in clean, bright offices. They sit most of the day in a fairly small area. The work is detailed and often repetitious, and approaching deadlines may increase the pressure and demands placed on them.

Working with VDTs in improper lighting can cause eyestrain, and sitting at a workstation all day can cause musculoskeletal stress and pain. The computer industry is paying closer attention to these problems and is working to improve health and safety standards in VDT-equipped offices.

Another common ailment for typists and word processors is carpal tunnel syndrome, a painful ailment of the tendons in the wrist that is triggered by repetitive movement. If left unchecked, it can require corrective surgery. Proper placement of the typing keyboard can help prevent injury, and increased attention is now given to desks, chairs, and working spaces that accommodate the physical needs of workers in the best manner currently known.

Many typists and word processors work in temporary positions that provide flexible schedules. About 20 percent work part time. Some offices allow word processors and typists to telecommute from home, whereby they receive and send work on home computers via modems.

■ Outlook

Employment in the typing field is expected to decline through the year 2006 due to the increasing automation of offices. However, the sheer size of the occupation means that many jobs will become available for typists and word processors, especially to replace those employees who change careers or leave the workforce.

Technological innovations such as optical character recognition readers, which scan documents and enter their copy into a computer, are being used in more and more workplaces. Voice recognition technologies that enable people to enter text and data by speaking into a computer are also being developed. Such machines will reduce the demand for typists and word processors. Workers with the best technical skills and knowledge of several word processing programs have the best chances of getting hired.

■ For More Information

ABSSI is an international trade association that serves owners of business support, desktop publishing, and related services. Contact ABSSI for membership information:

Association of Business Support Services International
22875 Savi Ranch Parkway, Suite H
Yorba Linda, CA 92887-4619
Tel: 800-237-1462
Web: http://www.abssi.org

For information on certification, contact:

International Association of Administrative Professionals
PO Box 20404
10502 NW Ambassador Drive
Kansas City, MO 64195-0404
Tel: 816-891-6600
Web: http://www.iaap-hq.org

■ Related Articles

Business

Billing Clerks

Court Reporters

Data Entry Clerks

Real-Time Captioners

Secretaries

U.S. Fish and Wildlife Service Special Agents

▪ See Fish and Game Wardens

Umpires and Referees

▪ Overview

Umpires and referees ensure that competitors in athletic events follow the rules. They make binding decisions and have the power to impose penalties upon individuals or teams that break the rules.

▪ History

The history of sport goes back to the time of the ancient Olympic games and gladiator battles of Rome. Since gladiator battles were fights to the death, there were no rules to be observed and no need for umpires or referees to ensure fairness.

As athletics became more organized, if not less violent, rules were established and the need for umpires and referees to enforce these rules and regulations became necessary. Boxing, soccer, and rugby were the first sports to have trained officials. With the advent of professional sports such as baseball and basketball, officiating became a career option.

▪ The Job

Every sport has its own set of rules and regulations. Even the same game played on different levels may have its own distinct rules. For example, in professional basketball, the team in possession of the ball has 24 seconds to take a shot on goal. On the college level the shot clock is set at 45 seconds, and in the game played by most high school teams, there is no shot clock at all.

Sports officials are the experts on the playing field. They know all the rules for the sport they officiate. They observe players while the ball or puck is in play and penalize those who break the rules. They are the decision makers and the arbiters of disputes between the competing teams.

When an infraction of the rules is spotted by an official, the official blows a whistle to stop play. The penalty is communicated to the official scorer, the penalty is assessed, and play continues.

Major league baseball utilizes four umpires for each game. The *home plate umpire* works behind home plate and is responsible for determining whether each pitched ball is thrown within the strike zone. The home plate umpire also rules whether runners crossing home plate are safe or out, and must keep track of the ball/strike count on each batter.

Other umpires are responsible for the three bases. They decide whether runners are safe or out at their respective bases. *First* and *third base umpires* also must observe whether a ball, batted to the outfield, lands on the playing field within the foul line.

It is not uncommon for a single official to work a Little League game. When this is the case, the umpire generally stands behind the pitcher. The umpire is responsible for calling balls and strikes, keeping track of the number of outs and the ball/strike count, watching the foul line, and ruling on runners at the bases.

Three officials work National Basketball Association games. They are more active than baseball umpires. *Basketball referees* run up and down the court, following both the ball and the players. They must not only watch the ball but keep an eye out for illegal contact between players.

If three officials are supervising the game, one stands near the basket of the offensive team, another stands at the free throw line extended, and the third stands on the opposite side of the court (from the second official) half way between mid-court and the free throw line. Each official watches different parts of the court for infractions. For instance, the official near the basket makes sure that no offensive player stands inside the free throw lane for more than three seconds.

High school and college games have two or three officials. Grade school and amateur league games generally have two. Again, the rules may be slightly different, and the athletic ability may vary, but the game is still basketball.

Football games use between four and seven officials. Like other referees, football officials each have specific areas to observe. The referee, who is ultimately in charge, is positioned behind the offensive team. *Football referees* are responsible for

UMPIRES AND REFEREES	
SCHOOL SUBJECTS	Physical education Psychology
PERSONAL SKILLS	Leadership/management
WORK ENVIRONMENT	Indoors and outdoors Primarily multiple locations
MINIMUM EDUCATION LEVEL	High school diploma
SALARY RANGE	$5,000 to $70,000 to $181,000
CERTIFICATION OR LICENSING	Required by all states
OUTLOOK	About as fast as the average
DOT	153
GOE	12.01.02
NOC	5253
O*NET	34058L

Umpires must be able to make decisions quickly and decisively.

watching the offensive backfield for illegal movement before the ball is put into play, and they also communicate all penalties to the coaches and official scorer.

Another official observes the line of scrimmage, for off-sides penalties and marks the progress of the ball. The umpire stands on the defensive team's side, five yards off the line of scrimmage, and watches for illegal blocks in the line. Other officials stand in the defensive backfield and observe defenders and receivers for illegal contact or interference.

Hockey games have three officials who skate up and down the ice. The referee, who is in charge, stands between the other umpires and assesses penalties. The umpires call off-sides and icing violations. Off the ice, the penalty time keeper keeps track of penalty time served, and two *goal judges* determine whether shots on goal have eluded the goalie and entered the net.

■ Requirements

High School

If you are interested in becoming a sports official you should begin learning as much as you can about sports and their rules. You will also want to get in the physical shape necessary to keep up with the athletes during an event. The most obvious way to accomplish these goals is to participate in school sports.

In class, you will want to focus on English grammar and also other languages if you are interested in working as a baseball umpire or hockey official. Speech, debate, or theater courses will build your self-confidence and teach you the diction skills you need to be understood clearly.

Finally, sports brings together many kinds of people, and as an umpire or referee you must be diplomatic with

all of them. Classes in sociology, history, and psychology can help you learn about the different cultures and ways of thinking of people from all parts of the world.

Postsecondary Training

While umpires and referees are not required to attend four-year colleges or universities, many do have college degrees. Often sports officials are former college athletes who decided to pursue a career in sports in a nonperformance capacity. Obviously, attending college and participating in college athletics is an excellent way to reinforce your knowledge of a sport and its rules while receiving a solid education.

The International Association of Approved Basketball Officials has four schools that run each summer in different places in the United States. Here referees learn rules and work games at the players' camps that are held in conjunction with the schools. Officials for the National Football League must meet the requirements that enable them to become accredited association of football officials.

In almost all cases, officials must attend special training schools or courses. These can vary from the schools endorsed by the Major League's Umpire Development Program all the way to the training courses offered to officials in amateur softball. These schools and training courses can be contacted through professional and amateur leagues, college athletic conferences, and state interscholastic commissions. These organizations can also inform you of minimum age requirements (usually 18 and out of high school) and other criteria that vary between leagues and sports.

Certification or Licensing

The special training programs that umpires and referees attend act as their certification. Without these, they are not eligible to officiate. These courses may vary from those in the official training schools of professional umpires to those courses taken through a state interscholastic athletic commission for middle school volleyball officials.

Other Requirements

Different sports have different physical requirements. For example, to be a hockey official, one needs be an accomplished skater and should be in excellent health. General physical requirements include good vision, to some extent good hearing, and good physical health.

Sports officials must have good communications skills and the ability to make split-second decisions. Many calls that an official makes will be unpopular, so umpires and referees need courage to make the correct call and confidence to stand behind their judgment. An easily intimidated official won't last long in any league. Officials need the ability to remain cool under pressure. Often, games are played in front of large crowds, and fans can be vocal in their criticism of players, coaches, and especially sports officials.

Umpires and referees must also have a thorough understanding of the sport they officiate. Many are former college athletes. Sports officials need to be informed about changes to the rules. They keep informed by attending clinics and seminars sponsored by professional associations.

■ Exploring

A great way to find out if you enjoy being an umpire or referee is to officiate for a Little League team or at a summer camp. Try to locate a sports official in your area and set up an interview. Also you should continue to watch and participate in sports to learn more.

■ Employers

Sports officials are employed by professional and semi-professional leagues, sports organizations, youth leagues, and schools at all levels.

■ Starting Out

A person interested in becoming a referee or umpire should begin officiating Little League or amateur league games on weekends and at night. You may even want to volunteer your time. For a paid position, beginners need to pass a written examination and join the state association of officials for each sport they choose to officiate.

■ Advancement

The natural progression for umpires and referees is to begin by officiating young peoples' games and advance to amateur adults' contests. Those with talent and determination may move on to college games or professional minor leagues.

Many officials who would like to move to the professional level attend umpire or referee camps. Many of these camps are conducted by actual professional officials. These programs feature a rigorous review of rules and regulations and often include game situations.

The minor leagues in baseball are a testing ground for prospective umpires. On average, umpires spend six to eight years at the minor league level before they are even considered for a major league position.

■ Earnings

Umpire and referee salaries vary greatly, depending upon the sport and the level at which it is played. Typically, the closer an official gets to the top of a professional sports league, the higher the wages, but this is not always the case. For example, some college basketball referees might earn more money than a nonlead official in a less popular professional sport.

According to the Major League Baseball's Umpire Development Program, 1997 umpire salaries range from $2,000 per month in the Rookie League to $3,400 per month in the triple-A league to a starting annual salary of about $70,000 for a major league umpire. Major league umpires with considerable experience can earn as much as $181,000 a year. Professional basketball officials' salaries started at about $77,000 a year in 1997—according to an NBA spokesman—and rise significantly with experience.

Officials in the National Football League are considered part-time employees who are paid by the game and do not receive benefits. The league cites 1997 salaries as ranging from $2,100 to $4,000 per game depending on experience.

In professional sports, umpires and referees are typically given additional money for travel, hotel, and food expenses. These officials also receive extra payment if they are invited to work special events such as the World Series or Stanley Cup Finals. Football officials who work the Super Bowl, for example, are paid around $12,000.

Umpires and referees at the college, amateur, and youth levels are paid by the game. College officials earn between $200 and $800 per game, and high school and middle school officials earn considerably less. The Arizona State Interscholastic Athletic Commission, for example, cites officials' earnings as approximately $19 to $25 per game, depending upon the sport.

■ Work Environment

Professional officials work in front of huge crowds. Their judgments and decisions are scrutinized by the fans in the stadium and by millions of fans watching at home.

Professional football officials work one game a week, while baseball umpires may work up to six games a week. Some football stadiums are outdoors, and football officials may have to work through inclement weather. Baseball umpires may work outside also, but can stop the game because of rain.

Being an official at any level can be stressful. Officials must make split-second, unbiased decisions. Rulings are bound to be unpopular, at least to the team or player that is penalized, and even an eight-year-old Little Leaguer can be quite vocal.

Professional officials travel extensively throughout the season. They may be away from home for weeks at a time. Airplane flights, hotel food, and living out of a suitcase are some of the things that professional sports officials must endure.

At any level and with any sport, the work can be physically demanding. Baseball umpires must crouch behind the catcher to call balls and strikes. Basketball referees must run up and down the court, just as hockey officials must skate the rink. Football officials run the risk of colliding with heavily protected, helmeted players.

However, if you enjoy travel and can stand the verbal abuse from players, coaches, and fans, the job can be very rewarding. Actual hours spent officiating are relatively short. The duration of most games is less than three hours.

When an athlete's playing days are over, becoming an official is one way to maintain an active role in the sporting world. Most high school and junior high umpires and referees will tell you that they officiate not for the money, but because they enjoy it.

■ Outlook

The outlook for sports officiating depends upon the sport and the league worked. Umpires and referees are almost always needed at the youth, high school, and amateur levels, and people who are interested in supplementing their incomes this way or simply learning about the field of officiating should find plenty of opportunities for work.

In professional sports the market is much tighter. Travis Katzenmeir, an umpire for triple-A league baseball, explains, "In the lower minor leagues there's more turnover because people decide to leave the field, but the higher you go, it starts to bottleneck." Umpires in the major leagues rarely leave the job except to retire. In fact, during a 10-year period, the American League hired only 3 new umpires. When an opening does occur, an umpire moves up from triple-A baseball creating an opening for an umpire from double-A, and so on. Professional sports without minor leagues offer even fewer employment opportunities for officials at the professional level. The creation of new leagues and expansion teams such as baseball's 1998 Arizona Diamondbacks does occasionally offer additional job opportunities for professional sports officials.

The outlook for women sports officials has improved in with the creation of women's professional basketball leagues like the WNBA, offering many new positions to women officials, as well as coaches, trainers, and professional athletes. Additionally, in 1997, two women, Dee Kantner and Violet Palmer, became the first female referees to officiate NBA basketball games—a first for the all-male U.S. major sports leagues. Perhaps more openings for women officials will be created as the other leagues follow suit.

■ For More Information

Visit the MLUA Web site to ask umpires questions about their work, for information on training paths, and to access rules and measurements of the game:

Major League Umpires Association
Mellon Bank Center
1735 Market Street, Suite 3420
Philadelphia, PA 19103
Web: http://www.majorleagueumps.com/

The How To Become A Sports Official *section of the NASO Web site will help you learn how to become a sports official in the following fields: baseball, basketball, football, soccer, softball, and volleyball. NASO also offers a wide variety of publications for the aspiring sports official:*

National Association of Sports Officials
2017 Lathrop Avenue
Racine, WI 53405
Tel: 414-632-5448
Web: http://www.naso.org/

Contact IAABO for information on training schools, requirements, and other information for becoming a basketball official:

International Association of Approved Basketball Officials
12321 Middlebrook Road
Germantown, MD 20875
Web: http://www.iaabo.org/

The following professional umpiring schools are recognized by Major League Baseball for the Umpire Development Program:

Jim Evans Academy of Professional Umpiring
12741 Research Boulevard, Suite 401
Austin, TX 78759
Tel: 512-335-5959
Web: http://www.umpireacademy.com

Harry Wendelstedt School for Umpires
88 South Saint Andrews Drive
Ormond Beach, FL 32174
Tel: 904-672-4879
Web: http://webmaster.daytontrophy.com/umpireschool

■ Related Articles

Sports

Sports Statisticians

Uniformed Service Attendants

■ **See Baggage Porters and Bellhops**

University Professors

■ **See College Professors**

Upholsterers

■ **See Furniture Manufacturing Occupations**

Urban and Regional Planners

■ Overview

Working for local governments, *urban and regional planners* assist in the development and redevelopment of a city, metropolitan area, or region. They work to preserve historical buildings, protect the environment, and help manage a community's growth and change. Planners evaluate individual buildings and city blocks, and are also involved in the design of new subdivisions, neighborhoods, and even towns. There are over 29,000 urban and regional planners in the United States; most of them work for local government, while others work in the private sector.

■ History

Cities have always been planned to some degree. Most cultures, from the ancient Greek to the Chinese to the Native American, made some organized plans for the development of their cities. By the fourth century BC theories of urban planning existed in the writings of Plato, Aristotle, and Hippocrates. Their ideas concerning the issues of site selection and orientation were later modified and updated by Vitruvius in his *De architectura,* which appeared after 27 BC. The work helped create a standardized guide to Roman engineers as they built fortified settlements and cities throughout the vast empire. Largely inspired by Vitruvius, Italian theorists in the 15th century compiled enormous amounts of information and ideas on urban planning. They replaced vertical walls with angular fortifications in response to evolving methods of war, widened streets and opened up squares by building new churches, halls, and palaces, and generally focused on a symmetrical style that quickly became fashionable in many of the more prosperous European cities. Modern urban planning owes much of its impetus to the Industrial Revolution. A more sanitary environment was sought by the demolishing of slums, and new laws were developed to control new construction and monitor the condition of old buildings. In 1848, in Paris, Baron George Eugene Haussmann oversaw the destruction and replacement of 40 percent of the city's houses with new ones and the creation of new neighborhoods and park system. In England, in 1875, the Public Health Act allowed municipalities to regulate new construction, the removal of waste, and newly constructed water and sewer systems.

■ The Job

A planner assists in the development or maintenance of well-ordered and attractive communities. Working for a government agency or as a consultant, you'll be involved in integrating new buildings, houses, sites, and subdivisions into an overall city plan. This plan coordinates streets, traffic, public facilities, water and sewage, transportation, safety, and endangered or sensitive ecological regions such as wildlife habitats, wetlands, and floodplains. You'll also be involved in renovating and preserving historic buildings. You'll work with a variety of professionals, including architects, artists, computer programmers, engineers, economists, landscape architects, land developers, lawyers, writers, and environmental and other special interest groups.

Chris Wayne works as a planner for the city of Omaha, Nebraska, and is involved in redevelopment. His work involves identifying project sites—buildings that the planning department wants to redevelop—and going about acquiring the property. He must research the property to determine who owns it, then hire an appraiser to determine the worth of the building. The appraisal is then presented to the building's owner. The city may have to vacate the building once the property is purchased. "This involves interviewing the residents," Chris says, "to determine what's necessary for them to move. We determine what amount they'll be compensated." Various community programs assist in finding new housing or providing the tenant with funds for the move. Once the property has been vacated, the planning department accepts and reviews proposals from developers. A developer is then offered a contract. When demolition and construction begins, Chris's department must monitor the project and make the necessary payments.

Unused or undeveloped land also concerns you as an urban planner. You may help design the layout for a proposed building, traffic circulation, parking considerations, and the use of open space. You are also responsible for suggesting ways to implement these programs or proposals, including their costs and how to raise funding for them.

Schools, churches, recreational areas, and residential tracts are studied to determine how they fit into a plan of usefulness and beauty. As with the

URBAN AND REGIONAL PLANNERS	
SCHOOL SUBJECTS	Business English Government
PERSONAL SKILLS	Communication/ideas Following instructions
WORK ENVIRONMENT	Primarily indoors Primarily multiple locations
MINIMUM EDUCATION LEVEL	Bachelor's degree
SALARY RANGE	$30,700 to $45,000 to $63,300
CERTIFICATION OR LICENSING	Recommended
OUTLOOK	Little change or more slowly than the average
DOT	199
GOE	11.03.02
NOC	2153

Conceived as the ideal in small-town living, Celebration, Florida, opened in 1996. Never heard of a city having a grand opening? Leave it to Disney to "invent" a new town. Celebration is being built on 4,900 acres of land in north-west Osceola County, near Walt Disney World. Constructed in phases, the town will eventually have up to 8,000 residences. Homes are linked electronically, giving residents access to a network of telephone, video, and data services. Not only can you stay in touch with your neighbors through these links, but also with the Celebration School (with teachers trained at Celebration's own Teaching Academy), the Celebration Health Center, and Celebration Place, a 109-acre office park. With structures by pioneering architects, a well-designed golf course, and many parks and bike trails, some consider the town perfect, while others are put off by its "movie-set-like" design. Can a city be too carefully planned? You're limited in the style of house you can build, the number of pets you can keep in your home, and even the color of your drapes. But there are benefits to such careful design: The town has had only one reported crime since its opening—a car was stolen from someone's perfectly paved driveway.

other factors, specifications of the nature and kinds of buildings must be considered. Zoning, which regulates the specific use of land and buildings, is one aspect of the work of planning.

Some urban and regional planners teach in colleges and schools of planning, and many do consulting work. Planners today are concerned not only with city codes, but also with environmental problems of water pollution, solid waste disposal, water treatment plants, and public housing.

You may work in older cities or design new ones. Columbia, Maryland, and Reston, Virginia, both built in the 1960s, are examples of planned communities. Before plans for such communities can be developed, you must prepare detailed maps and charts showing the proposed use of land for housing, business, and community needs. These studies provide information on the types of industries that will be located there, the locations of housing developments and businesses, and the plans for handling such basic needs as transportation, water, and sewage treatment. After the charts have been analyzed, you design the layout in a form that will illustrate their ideas to others who will be involved, such as land developers, city officials, housing experts, architects, and construction firms.

The following short paragraphs list the wide variety of planners within the field.

Human services planners work to develop health and social service programs to upgrade living standards for those lacking opportunities or resources. They frequently work for private health care organizations and government agencies.

Historic preservation planners use their knowledge of the law and economics to help preserve historic buildings, sites, and neighborhoods. They are frequently employed by state agencies, local governments, and the National Park Service.

Transportation planners, working mainly for government agencies, oversee the transportation infrastructure of a community, keeping in mind local priorities such as economic development and environmental concerns.

Housing and community development planners analyze housing needs, studying neighborhoods to identify potential opportunities and problems that may help or hinder the positive growth of a neighborhood and its surrounding communities. Such planners are usually employed by private real estate and financial concerns, local governments, and community development organizations.

Economic development planners, usually employed by local governments or chambers of commerce, focus on attracting and retaining industry to a specific community. They communicate the presence of these resources to those in industry who select sites for plants, warehouses, and other major projects.

Environmental planners are advocates for the integration of environmental issues into building construction, land use, and other community objectives. They work at all levels of government and for some nonprofit organizations.

Urban design planners use their special knowledge of architecture and urban policy to link multiple facilities and the land that connects them into the larger community. Employers include large-scale developers, private consulting firms, and local governments.

Those who specialize in strategies for regional and national development are known as *international development planners.* They focus on topics such as transportation, rural development, modernization, and urbanization. They are frequently employed by international agencies, such as the United Nations, and by national governments in less developed countries.

■ Requirements

High School

You should take courses in government and social studies to learn about the structure of cities and counties. You'll need good communication skills for working with people in a variety of professions, so take courses in English composition and journalism. Drafting, architecture, and art classes will familiarize you with the basics of design. Become active on your student council so that you can be involved in implementing changes for the school community.

Postsecondary Training

A college education—with a major in urban and regional planning, architecture, landscape architecture, civil engineering, or public administration—is the minimum requirement for trainee jobs with most municipal or other government boards and agencies. Typical courses include geography, public administration, political science, law, engineering, architecture, landscape architecture, real estate, finance, and management. Computer courses and training in statistical techniques are also essential. Your school will direct you to internship opportunities with city planning departments.

For a career in planning, a master's degree in city or regional planning is usually needed. When considering schools, check with the American Planning Association (APA) for a list of accredited undergraduate and graduate planning programs. The APA can also direct you to scholarship and fellowship programs available to students enrolled in planning programs.

Certification or Licensing

Although certification is not a requirement, it is a valued credential that often leads to more responsible, better-paying positions. The American Institute of Certified Planners, of the APA, grants certification to urban planners who meet certain academic and professional requirements and successfully complete an examination. The exam tests a planner's knowledge of the history and future of planning, research methods, plan implementation, and other relevant subjects.

Other Requirements

Chris pursued a master's in urban studies because he was drawn to community development. "I was interested in the social interaction of people and the space they occupy, such as parks and plazas," Chris says. To be a good city planner, you should have design skills and a good understanding of spatial relationships. Good analytical skills will help you in evaluating projects. You must be able to visualize the relationships between streets, buildings, parks, and other planned spaces. You must be imaginative and possess vision in order to anticipate potential planning problems. Logic and problem-solving abilities are also important.

■ Exploring

Research the origins of your city by visiting the county courthouse and local library. There you'll find early photographs and maps of the city that can give you an idea of what went into the planning of the area. Study the development of your city and visit historic areas. Learn the histories of some of the old buildings. You may want to get involved in efforts to preserve buildings and areas that are threatened.

With the help of a teacher or academic advisor, you may be able to arrange a speech by a qualified planner or interview a planner to gain details of the job in a particular community. Another good way to see what planners do is by attending a meeting of a local planning commission, which, by law, is open to the public. Notices of meetings are usually published, but interested students can also call their local planning office for information.

■ Employers

Many planners take full-time work at the places they intern. Others look far and wide upon graduation, applying for jobs advertised nationally. Whereas opportunities used to be limited to city planning offices and consulting firms, planners are now finding work with state government and nonprofit organizations, as well. Planners work for agencies that focus on particular areas of city research and development, such as transportation, the environment, and housing. Urban and regional planners are also sought after by the United Nations and national governments of rapidly modernizing countries. Colleges and law firms also hire planners.

■ Starting Out

Experience in a planning office, an advocacy organization, or with a private planning, architectural, or engineering firm will be useful before applying to city, county, or regional planning agencies. Membership in one of the professional organizations is helpful in locating job opportunities. These include the APA (which publishes *JobMart* and maintains an online job database), American Institute of Architects, American Society of Civil Engineers, International City/County Managers Association, and the Engineers Council for Professional Development. The APA offers a discounted membership to college students; the membership includes a subscription to the student newsletter, along with information about internships.

Because most planning staffs are small, directors are usually eager to fill positions quickly. As a result, job availability is highly variable. Students are advised to research the field and send out resumes with their expected date of graduation even before they complete their degree requirements.

■ Advancement

Advancement takes place as the beginning assistant moves to more inclusive and responsible jobs within the planning board or department and to appointment as planner. The positions of senior planner and planning director are successive steps in some agencies. Frequently, experienced planners obtain advancement by moving to a larger city or county planning board, where they can become responsible for larger and more complicated problems and projects. Other planners may become consultants to communities that cannot afford a full-time planner. Some planners also serve as city managers, cabinet secretaries, and presidents of consulting firms.

■ Earnings

Earnings vary based on gender, experience, and the population of the city or town the planner serves. Although women still earn less than men in the profession, women's salaries are increasing faster than men's. The median salary for all urban and regional planners is about $45,300 according to the APA's 1995 salary survey. Urban and regional planners with less than five years' experience earned median salaries between $30,700 and $37,400. Those with between five and 10 years of service earned median salaries between $39,300 and $45,900. Planners with over 10 years experience earned median salaries between $52,100 and $63,300. Salaries for planning directors are considerably higher, ranging from $31,700 with five years or less experience to as high as $75,900 per year with 10 or more years of experience. The five states with the highest starting salaries are California, Connecticut, Washington, Hawaii, and New Jersey.

Because many planners work for government agencies, they usually have sick leave and vacation privileges and are covered by retirement and health plans. Many planners receive the use of a city automobile.

Consultants are generally paid on a fee basis. Their earnings are often high and vary greatly according to their reputations and work experience. Their earnings will depend on the number of consulting jobs they accept.

■ Work Environment

Conditions of work are good. As a planner, you'll spend a considerable amount of time in your office. However, in order to gather data about the areas you plan to develop, you will spend some time outdoors examining the land, structures, and traffic. Most planners work standard 40-hour weeks, but you must frequently attend weekend meetings or public forums with citizen groups, or meetings of town or city councils to explain your proposals.

You'll often work alone, but you'll be required to interact with land developers, public officials, civic leaders, and citizens' groups. You may also face opposition from interest groups representing those affected by your development proposals. Planners must have the patience needed to work with these disparate groups. The job may sometimes be stressful due to deadlines, project proposals, or the unpopularity of your proposals in both the public and private sectors.

■ Outlook

Opportunities will exist for graduates with professional city and regional planning training, but the market is small and highly competitive. The overall demand for city planners is expected to grow more slowly than the average through 2006. But the growth of the economy has helped planners as cities spend money to improve neighborhoods, develop subdivisions, and expand transportation departments. More communities will be turning to professional planners for help in determining the most effective way to meet the rising requirements for physical facilities resulting from urbanization and the growth in population. There will also be an increased demand for urban and regional planners to help fulfill the following needs: to zone and plan land use for undeveloped and nonmetropolitan areas; to assist with the planning of commercial development in rapidly growing suburban areas; to help redevelop the central cities; to assist in replacing old public facilities such as bridges, highways, and sewers; and to help to preserve historic sites and rehabilitate older buildings.

Factors that may affect job growth include government regulation regarding the environment, housing, transportation, and land use and development, such as the Clean Air Act, and the necessity of replacing the national infrastructure, including highways, bridges, and sewer and water systems. Other factors include the continuing redevelopment of inner-city areas and the continued expansion of suburban areas.

■ For More Information

To learn more about planning as a career and about accredited planning programs, contact:

American Planning Association
122 South Michigan Avenue, Suite 1600
Chicago, IL 60603
Tel: 312-786-6344
Web: http://www.planning.org

To learn about city management and the issues affecting today's cities, visit the ICMA Web site:

International City/County Management Association
777 North Capitol Street, NE, Suite 500
Washington, DC 20002
Tel: 202-289-4262
Web: http://www.icma.org

■ Related Articles

Government
Architects
City Managers
Congressional Aides
Federal and State Officials
Regional and Local Officials

Urologists

■ Overview

Urologists are physicians who specialize in the treatment of medical and surgical disorders of the adrenal gland and of the genitourinary system. They deal with the diseases of both the male and female urinary tract and of the male reproductive organs.

■ History

Medieval "healers" who specialized in the surgical removal of bladder stones could be considered the first "urologists," but due to his 1958 documentation of urethra, bladder, and kidney diseases, Francisco Diaz is the recognized founder of modern urology.

Advancements in urology came during the 19th century when flexible catheters were invented to examine and empty the bladder. In 1877, Max Nitze developed the lighted cytoscope, which is used to view the interior of the bladder. By the 20th century, diseases of the urinary tract could be diagnosed by X ray.

■ The Job

Technically, urology is a surgical subspecialty, but because of the broad range of clinical problems they treat, urologists also have a working knowledge of internal medicine, pediatrics, gynecology, and other specialties.

Common medical disorders that urologists routinely treat include prostate cancer, testicular cancer, bladder cancer, stone disease, urinary tract infections, urinary incontinence, and impotence. Less common disorders include kidney cancer, renal (kidney) disease, male infertility, genitourinary trauma, and sexually transmitted diseases (including AIDS).

The management and treatment of malignant diseases constitute much of the urologist's practice. Prostate cancer is the most common cancer in men, and the second leading cause of cancer deaths in men. If detected early, prostate cancer is treatable, but once it has spread beyond the prostate it is difficult to treat successfully.

Testicular cancer is the leading cause of cancer in young men between the ages of 15 and 34. Major advances in the treatment of this cancer, involving both surgery and chemotherapy, now make it the most curable of all cancers. Bladder cancer occurs most frequently in men age 70 and older, and treatment for it also has a high success rate.

Young and middle-aged adults are primarily affected by stone diseases, which represent the third leading cause of hospitalizations in the United States. Kidney stones, composed of a combination of calcium and either oxalate or phosphate, usually pass through the body with urine. Larger stones, however, can block the flow of urine or irritate the lining of the urinary system as they pass. What has become standard treatment today is called extracorporeal shock wave lithotripsy (ESWL). In ESWL, high-energy shock waves are used to pulverize the stones into small fragments that are carried from the body in the urine. This procedure has replaced invasive, open surgery as the preferred treatment for stone disease.

Urologists also consult on spina bifida cases in children and multiple sclerosis cases in adults, as these diseases involve neuromuscular dysfunctions that affect the kidneys, bladder, and genitourinary systems.

The scope of urology has broadened so much that the following are now considered subspecialties: pediatric urology, urologic oncology, and female urology.

■ Requirements

Postsecondary Training

To become a urologist you must first earn an M.D. degree and become licensed to practice medicine. (See *Physicians*) Then you must complete a five- or six-year residency in urology, of which the first two years are typically spent in general surgery, followed by three to four years of urology in an approved residency program. Currently, there are 116 approved residency programs.

Many urologic residency training programs are six years in length, with the final year spent in either research or additional clinical training, depending on the orientation of the program and the resident's focus.

The vast majority of urologists enter into clinical practice after completing their residency program. However, fellowships exist in various subspecialties, including pediatrics, infertility, sexual dysfunction, oncology, and transplantation.

Certification or Licensing

At an early point in the residency period, all students are required to pass a medical licensing examination administered by the board of medical examiners in each state. The length of the residency depends on the specialty chosen.

Certification requires the successful completion of qualifying written examination, which must be taken within three years of completing the residency in urology. The subsequent certifying examination, which consists of pathology, uroradiology, and a standardized oral examination, must be taken within five years of the qualifying examination. Certification by the American Board of Urology is for a 10-year period, with recertification required after that time.

Other Requirements

Urologists should like working with people and have a strong interest in promoting good health through preventive measures such as diet and exercise.

The urologist diagnoses and treats conditions of a very personal nature. Many patients are uncomfortable talking about problems relating to their kidneys, bladder, or genitourinary system. The urologist must show compassion and sensitivity to dispel the patient's fears and put him or her at ease.

Excellent communication skills are essential to patient-physician interactions. Urologists should be able to clearly articulate both the patient's problem and the recommended forms of treatment, including all of the options and their attendant risks and advantages. Because of their frequent consultations with other physicians, urologists also need to develop good working relationships with other medical specialists.

Urologists, like all surgeons, should be in good physical condition; they must remain steady and focused while standing for hours on their feet. Urologists who work in hospital trauma units should be prepared for the frenetic pace and tension of split-second decision making.

■ Earnings

According to a 1998 survey conducted by the American Medical Association, the average net salary of practitioners of internal medicine is about $185,700, but salaries may begin around $116,306. These figures pertain to doctors of internal medicine, and income for urologists may vary from these numbers. The average net pay for surgeons is about $275,200.

■ Outlook

Employment prospects for urologists are good. According to the *Occupational Outlook Handbook,* physicians' jobs are expected to grow faster than the average through 2006. The demographics of American society illustrate that the increase in the aging population will increase demand for services that cater, in large part, to them. With baby boomers aging, the need for qualified urologists will continue to grow.

■ For More Information

For additional information on becoming a urologist, contact the following:

American Medical Association
515 North State Street
Chicago, IL 60610
Tel: 312-464-5000
Web: http://www.ama-assn.org

American Board of Urology
2216 Ivy Road, Suite 210
Charlottesville, VA 22903
Tel: 248-646-9720

American Urological Association, Inc.
1120 North Charles Street
Baltimore, MD 21201
Tel: 410-727-1100
Web: http://www.auanet.org

■ Related Articles

Alternative Health Care
Health Care
Allergists/Immunologists
Anesthesiologists
Cardiologists
Dermatologists
Ear, Nose, and Throat Specialists
Epidemiologists
Gastroenterologists
General Practitioners
Geriatricians
Holistic Physicians
Neurologists
Obstetricians/Gynecologists
Oncologists
Ophthalmologists
Osteopaths
Pathologists
Pediatricians
Physicians
Podiatrists
Psychiatrists
Sports Physicians
Surgeons

User Support Specialists

■ **See Technical Support Specialists**

Utility Lineworkers

■ **See Energy Transmission and Distribution Workers**

Veterinarians

■ Overview

The *veterinarian,* or *doctor of veterinary medicine,* diagnoses and controls animal diseases, treats sick and injured animals medically and surgically, prevents transmission of animal diseases, and advises owners on proper care of pets and livestock. Veterinarians are dedicated to the protection of the health and welfare of all animals and to society as a whole.

■ History

The first school of veterinary medicine was opened in 1762 at Lyons, France, and it was a French immigrant who established the practice of veterinary medicine in the United States 100 years later. Veterinary medicine has made great strides since its introduction in this country, one advance being the significant reduction in animal diseases contracted by humans.

■ The Job

Veterinarians ensure a safe food supply by maintaining the health of food animals. They also protect the public from residues of herbicides, pesticides, and antibiotics in food. Veterinarians may be involved in wildlife preservation and conservation, and use their knowledge to increase food production through genetics, animal feed production, and preventive medicine.

In North America, about 80 percent of veterinarians are in private clinical practice. Although some veterinarians treat all kinds of animals, about half limit their practice to companion animals such as dogs, cats, and birds. Of the veterinarians in private practice, about 11 percent work mainly with horses, cattle, pigs, sheep, goats, and poultry. Today, a veterinarian may be treating llamas, catfish, or ostriches as well. Others are employed by wildlife management groups, zoos, aquariums, ranches, feed lots, fish farms, and animal shelters.

The remaining 20 percent of veterinarians work in public and corporate sectors. Many veterinarians are employed by city, county, state, provincial, or federal government agencies that investigate, test for, and control diseases in companion animals, livestock, and poultry that affect both animal and human health.

Veterinarians are utilized by pharmaceutical and biomedical research firms to develop, test, and supervise the production of drugs, chemicals, and biological products such as antibiotics and vaccines that are designed for human and animal use. Some veterinarians are employed in management, technical sales and services, and marketing in agribusiness, pet food companies, and pharmaceutical companies. Still other veterinarians are engaged in

research and teaching at veterinary and human medical schools, working with racetracks or animal-related enterprises, or working within the military, public health corps, and space agencies.

Veterinarians in private clinical practice become specialists in surgery, anesthesiology, dentistry, internal medicine, ophthalmology, or radiology. Many veterinarians also pursue advanced degrees in the basic sciences, such as anatomy, microbiology, and physiology. Veterinarians who seek specialty board certification in one of 20 specialty fields must complete a two- to five-year residency program and must pass an additional examination. Some veterinarians combine their degree in veterinary medicine with a degree in business (MBA) or law (JD).

Veterinarians are employed in various branches of federal, state, provincial, county, or city government. The U.S. Department of Agriculture has opportunities for veterinarians in the food safety inspection service and the animal and plant health inspection service, notably in the areas of food hygiene and safety, animal welfare, animal disease control, and research. Agencies in the U.S. Department of Agriculture utilize veterinarians in positions related to research on diseases transmissible from animals to human beings and on the acceptance and use of drugs for treatment or prevention of diseases. Veterinarians also are employed by the Environmental Protection Agency to deal with public health and environmental risks to the human population.

■ Requirements

High School

For the high school student who is interested in admission to a school of veterinary medicine, a college preparatory course is a wise choice. A strong emphasis on science classes such as biology, chemistry, and anatomy is highly recommended.

Postsecondary Training

The doctor of veterinary medicine (D.V.M.) degree requires a minimum of six years of college after graduation from high school, consisting of at least two years of preveterinary study that emphasizes physical and biological sciences and a four-year

VETERINARIANS	
SCHOOL SUBJECTS	Biology Chemistry
PERSONAL SKILLS	Helping/teaching Technical/scientific
WORK ENVIRONMENT	Primarily indoors Primarily one location
MINIMUM EDUCATION LEVEL	Medical degree
SALARY RANGE	$29,900 to $44,500 to $57,600
CERTIFICATION OR LICENSING	Required by all states
OUTLOOK	Faster than the average

veterinary program. It is possible to obtain preveterinary training in a junior college. Most preveterinary students, however, enroll in four-year colleges. In addition to academic instruction, veterinary education includes clinical experience in diagnosing disease and treating animals, performing surgery, and performing laboratory work in anatomy, biochemistry, and other scientific and medical subjects.

In 1997, all 27 colleges of veterinary medicine in the United States were accredited by the Council of Veterinary Medicine of the American Veterinary Medical Association (AVMA). Each college of veterinary medicine has its own preveterinary requirements, which typically include basic language arts, social sciences, humanities, mathematics, chemistry, and biological and physical sciences.

Admission to schools of veterinary medicine is highly competitive. Applicants usually must have grades of "B" or better, especially in the sciences. Applicants must take the Veterinary Aptitude Test, Medical College Admission Test, or the Graduate Record Examination. Fewer than half of the applicants to schools of veterinary medicine may be admitted, due to small class sizes and limited facilities. Most colleges give preference to candidates with animal- or veterinary-related experience. Colleges usually give preference to in-state applicants because most colleges of veterinary medicine are state-supported. There are regional agreements in which states without veterinary schools send students to designated regional schools.

Certification or Licensing

All states and the District of Columbia require that veterinarians be licensed to practice private clinical medicine. To obtain a license, applicants must have a D.V.M. degree from an accredited or approved college of veterinary medicine. They must also pass one or more national examinations and an examination in the state in which they plan to practice.

Some states issue licenses without further examination to veterinarians already licensed by another state. Approximately half of the states require veterinarians to attend continuing education courses in order to maintain their licenses. Veterinarians may be employed by a government agency (such as the U.S. Department of Agriculture) or at some academic institution without having a state license.

Other Requirements

Individuals who are interested in veterinary medicine should have an enquiring mind and keen powers of observation. Aptitude and interest in the biological sciences are important. Veterinarians need a lifelong interest in scientific learning as well as a liking and understanding of animals. Veterinarians should be able to meet, talk, and work well with a variety of people. An ability to communicate with the animal owner is as important in a veterinarian as diagnostic skills.

Veterinarians use state-of-the-art medical equipment, such as electron microscopes, laser surgery, radiation therapy, and ultrasound, to diagnose animal diseases and to treat sick or injured animals. Although manual dexterity and physical stamina are often required, especially for farm vets, important roles in veterinary medicine can be adapted for those with disabilities.

Veterinarians may have to euthanize (that is, humanely kill) an animal that is very sick or severely injured and cannot get well. When an animal such as a beloved pet dies, the veterinarian must deal with the owner's grief and loss.

■ Exploring

High school students interested in becoming veterinarians may find part-time or volunteer work on farms, in small-animal clinics, pet shops, animal shelters, or research laboratories. Participation in extracurricular activities such as 4-H are good ways to learn about the care of animals. Such experience is important because, as already noted, many schools of veterinary medicine have established experience with animals as a criterion for admission to their programs.

■ Employers

Veterinarians may be employed by the government, schools and universities, wildlife management groups, zoos, aquariums, ranches, feed lots, fish farms, or pet food or pharmaceutical companies. The vast majority, however, are employed by veterinary clinical practices or hospitals. Many successful veterinarians in private practice are self-employed and may even employ other veterinarians. An increase in the demand for veterinarians is anticipated, particularly for those who specialize in areas related to public health issues such as food safety and disease control. Cities and large metropolitan areas will probably provide the bulk of new jobs for these specialists, while jobs for veterinarians who specialize in large animals will be focused in rural, remote areas.

■ Starting Out

The only way to become a veterinarian is through the prescribed degree program, and vet schools are set up to assist their graduates in finding employment. Veterinarians who wish to enter private clinical practice must have a license to practice in their particular state before opening an office. Licenses are obtained by passing the state's examination.

■ Advancement

New graduate veterinarians may enter private clinical practice, usually as employees in an established practice, or become employees of the U.S. government as meat and poultry inspectors, disease control workers, and commissioned officers in the U.S. Public Health Service or the military. New graduates may also enter internships and residencies at veterinary colleges and large private and public veterinary practices or become employed by industrial firms.

The veterinarian who is employed by a government agency may advance in grade and salary after accumulating time and experience on the job. For the veterinarian in private clinical practice, advancement usually consists of an expanding practice and the higher income that will result from it or becoming an owner of several practices.

Those who teach or do research may obtain a doctorate and move from the rank of instructor to that of full professor, or advance to an administrative position.

■ Earnings

According to the American Veterinary Medical Association, newly graduated veterinarians employed by the federal government start at salaries of about $35,800 a year. The average yearly salary of veterinarians working for the federal government is about $57,600. For those in industry, the average yearly salary for veterinarians is about $44,500.

The earnings of veterinarians in private clinical practice varies according to practice location, type of practice, and years of experience. New graduates employed in the established private clinical practices of other veterinarians generally are paid an average of $29,900 a year. The average income of veterinarians in private clinical practice was $57,500 in 1995. Owners of private clinical practices must operate their practices as a small business. The average starting income for practice owners specializing in large animal care was $39,500 compared with an average income of $31,900 for veterinarians specializing in small animal care.

■ Work Environment

Veterinarians usually treat companion and food animals in hospitals and clinics. Those in large animal practice also work out of well-equipped trucks or cars and may drive considerable distances to farms and ranches. They may work outdoors in all kinds of weather. The chief risk for veterinarians is injury by animals; however, modern tranquilizers and technology have made it much easier to work on all types of animals.

Most veterinarians work 50 or more hours per week; however, about one-fifth work 40 hours per week. Although those in private clinical practice may work nights and weekends, the increased number of emergency clinics has reduced the amount of time private practitioners have to be on call. Large animal practitioners tend to work more irregular hours than those in small animal practice, industry, or government. Veterinarians who are just starting a practice tend to work longer hours.

A veterinarian gives a terrier his annual checkup

■ Outlook

In 1996, about 70 percent of the more than 58,000 veterinarians were employed in private clinical practice. The federal government employed about 2,000, mostly in the Department of Agriculture and the Public Health Service. The remainder were employees of industry or schools and universities.

Employment of veterinarians is expected to grow faster then the average through 2006. The number of pets is expected to increase slightly because of rising incomes and an increase in the number of people aged 34 to 59, among whom pet ownership has been highest in the past. Many single adults and senior citizens have come to appreciate animal ownership. Pet owners also may be willing to pay for more elective and intensive care than in the past. In addition, emphasis on scientific methods of breeding and raising livestock, poultry, and fish and continued support for public health and disease control programs will contribute to the demand for veterinarians. The number of jobs stemming from the need to replace workers will be equal to new job growth.

The outlook is good for veterinarians with specialty training. Demand for specialists in toxicology, laboratory animal medicine, and pathology is expected to increase. Most jobs for specialists will be in metropolitan areas. Prospects for veterinarians who concentrate on environmental and public health issues, aquaculture, and food animal practice appear to be excellent because of perceived increased need in these areas. Positions in small animal specialties will be competitive. Opportunities in large animal specialties will be better since most such positions are located in remote, rural areas.

Despite the availability of additional jobs, competition among veterinarians is likely to be stiff. First-year enrollments in veterinary schools have increased slightly and the number of students in graduate-degree and board-certification programs has risen dramatically.

■ For More Information

For more information on careers, schools, and resources, write to the American Veterinary Medical Association. In addition, check out the AVMA's Web page for career and education information, especially the "NetVet" link that provides access to information on specialties, organizations, publications, and fun sites.

American Veterinary Medical Association
1931 North Meacham Road, Suite 100
Schaumburg, IL 60173-4360
Attn: Education and Research Division
Tel: 800-248-2862 or 847-925-8070
Web: http://www.avma.org

For more information on veterinary careers and how to prepare for them, get in touch with the following:

Animal and Plant Health Inspection Service
U.S. Department of Agriculture
Butler Square West, 4th Floor
100 North Sixth Street
Minneapolis, MN 55403

NetVet
Web: http://netvet.wustl.edu/vet.htm

■ Related Articles

Animals

Animal Caretakers

Animal Shelter Employees

Veterinary Technicians

Zookeepers

Zoologists

Veterinary Technicians

■ Overview

Veterinary technicians provide support and assistance to veterinary doctors. They work in a variety of environments, including zoos, animal hospitals, clinics, private practices, kennels, and laboratories. Work may involve large or small animals, or both. Although most veterinary technicians work with domestic animals, some professional settings may require treating exotic or endangered species.

■ History

As the scope of veterinary practices grew and developed, veterinarians began to require assistants. At first the role was informal, with veterinary assistants being trained by the D.V.M.s they worked for. In the latter half of the 20th century, however, the education—and thus the profession—of veterinary assistants became formalized

■ The Job

Many pet owners depend upon veterinarians to maintain the health and well-being of their pets. Veterinary clinics and private practices are the primary settings for animal care. In assisting veterinarians, veterinary technicians play an integral role in the care of animals within this particular environment.

A veterinary technician is the person who performs much of the laboratory testing procedures commonly associated with veterinary care. In fact, approximately 50 percent of a veterinary technician's duties involves laboratory testing. Laboratory assignments usually include taking and developing X rays, performing parasitology tests, and examining various samples taken from the animal's body, such as blood and stool. A veterinary technician may also assist the veterinarian with necropsies in an effort to determine the cause of an animal's death.

In a clinic or private practice, a veterinary technician assists the veterinarian with surgical procedures. This generally entails preparing the animal for surgery by shaving the incision area and applying a topical antibacterial agent. Surgical anesthesia is administered and controlled by the veterinary technician. Throughout the surgical process, the technician tracks the surgical instruments and monitors the animal's vital signs. If an animal is very ill and has no chance for survival or an overcrowded animal shelter is unable to find a home for a donated or stray animal, the veterinary technician may be required to assist in euthanizing it.

During routine examinations and checkups, veterinary technicians will help restrain the animals. They may perform ear cleaning and nail clipping procedures as part of regular animal care. Outside the examination and surgery rooms, veterinary technicians perform additional duties. In most settings, they record, replenish, and maintain pharmaceutical equipment and other supplies.

Veterinary technicians also may work in a zoo. Here, job duties, such as laboratory testing, are quite similar, but practices are more specialized. Unlike in private practice, the *zoo veterinary technician* is not required to explain treatment to pet owners; however, he or she may have to discuss an animal's treatment or progress with *zoo veterinarians, zoo curators,* and other zoo professionals. A zoo veterinary technician's work also may differ from private practice in that it may be necessary for the technician to observe the animal in its habitat, which could require working outdoors. Additionally, zoo veterinary technicians usually work with exotic or endangered species. This is a very competitive and highly desired area of practice in the veterinary technician field. Currently there are only 50 zoo veterinary technicians working in the United States. There are only a few zoos in each state; thus, a limited number of job opportunities exist within these zoos. To break into this area of practice, veterinary technicians must be among the best in the field.

Another setting where veterinary technicians work is research. Most research opportunities for veterinary technicians are in academic environments with veterinary medicine or medical science programs. Again, laboratory testing may account for many of the duties; however, the veterinary technicians participate in very important animal research projects from start to finish.

Technicians are also needed in rural areas. Farmers require veterinary services for the care of farm animals such as pigs, cows, horses, dogs, cats, sheep, mules, and chickens. It is often essential for the veterinarian and technician to drive to the farmer's residence because animals are usually treated on site.

Another area in which veterinary technicians work is that of animal training, such as at an obedience school or with show business animals being trained for the circus or movies. Veterinary technicians may also be employed in information systems technology, where information on animals is compiled and provided to the public via the Internet.

No matter what the setting, a veterinary technician must be an effective communicator and proficient in basic computer applications. In clinical or private practice, it is usually the veterinary technician who conveys and explains treatment and subsequent animal care to the animal's owner. In research and laboratory work, the veterinary technician must record and discuss results among colleagues. In most practical veterinary settings, the veterinary technician must record various information on a computer.

■ Requirements

High School

A high school diploma is necessary in order to obtain the required training. High school students who excel at math and science have a strong foundation on which to build. Those who have had pets or who simply love animals and would like to work with them also fit the profile of a veterinary technician.

Postsecondary Training

The main requirement is the completion of a two- to four-year college-based accredited program. Upon graduation, the student receives an associate's or bachelor's degree. Currently, there are 65 accredited programs in the United States. A few states do their own accrediting, using the American Veterinary Medical Association (AVMA) and associated programs as benchmarks.

Most accredited programs offer thorough course work and preparatory learning opportunities to the aspiring veterinary

technician. Typical courses include mathematics, chemistry, humanities, biological science, communications, microbiology, liberal arts, ethics/jurisprudence, and basic computers.

Once the students complete this framework, they move on to more specialized courses. Students take advanced classes in animal nutrition, animal care and management, species/breed identification, veterinary anatomy/physiology, medical terminology, radiography and other clinical procedure courses, animal husbandry, parasitology, laboratory animal care, and large/small animal nursing.

Veterinary technicians must be prepared to assist in surgical procedures. In consideration of this, accredited programs offer surgical nursing courses. In these courses, a student learns to identify and use surgical instruments, administer anesthesia, and monitor animals during and after surgery.

In addition to classroom study, accredited programs offer practical courses. Hands-on education and training are commonly achieved through a clinical practicum, or internship, where the student has the opportunity to work in a clinical veterinary setting. During this period, a student is continuously evaluated by the participating veterinarian and encouraged to apply the knowledge and skills learned.

Certification or Licensing

Although the AVMA determines the majority of the national codes for veterinary technicians, state codes and laws vary. Most states offer registration or certification, and the majority of these states require graduation from an AVMA-accredited program as a prerequisite for taking the examination. Most colleges and universities assist graduates with registration and certification arrangements. To keep abreast of new technology and applications in the field, practicing veterinary technicians may be required to complete a determined amount of annual continuing education courses.

■ Exploring

High school students can acquire exposure to the veterinary field by working with animals in related settings. For example, a high school student may be able to work as a part-time animal attendant or receptionist in a private veterinary practice. Paid or volunteer positions may be available at kennels,

VETERINARY TECHNICIANS	
SCHOOL SUBJECTS	**Biology**
PERSONAL SKILLS	**Helping/teaching** **Technical/scientific**
WORK ENVIRONMENT	**Primarily indoors** **Primarily one location**
MINIMUM EDUCATION LEVEL	**Associate's degree**
SALARY RANGE	**$15,000 to $25,000 to $40,000**
CERTIFICATION OR LICENSING	**Required by certain states**
OUTLOOK	**Faster than the average**

A veterinary technician assists a veterinarian by holding a dog for easier examination.

animal shelters, and training schools. However, direct work with animals in a zoo is unlikely for high school students.

■ Employers

Veterinary technicians are employed by veterinary clinics and animal hospitals, zoos, schools and universities, and animal training programs. In rural areas, farmers hire veterinary technicians as well as veterinarians. Jobs for veterinary technicians in zoos are relatively few, since there are only a certain number of zoos across the country. Those veterinary technicians with an interest in research should seek positions at schools with academic programs for medical science or veterinary medicine. The majority of veterinary technicians find employment in animal hospitals or private veterinary practices, which exist all over the country. However, there are more job opportunities for veterinary technicians in more densely populated areas.

■ Starting Out

Veterinary technicians who complete an accredited program and become certified or registered by the state in which they plan to practice are often able to receive assistance in finding a job through their college's placement offices. Students who have completed internships may receive job offers from the place where they interned.

Veterinary technician graduates may also learn of clinic openings through classified ads in newspapers. Opportunities in zoos and research facilities are usually listed in specific industry periodicals such as *Veterinary Technician Magazine* and *AZVT News,* a newsletter published by the Association of Zoo Veterinary Technicians.

■ Advancement

Where a career as a veterinary technician leads is entirely up to the individual. Opportunities are unlimited. With continued education, veterinary technicians can move into allied fields such as veterinary medicine, nursing, medical technology, radiology, and pharmacology. By completing two more years of college and receiving a bachelor's degree, a veterinary technician can become a *veterinary technologist.* Advanced degrees can open the doors to a variety of specialized fields. There are currently efforts to standardize requirements for veterinary technicians. A national standard would broaden the scope of educational programs and may create more opportunities in instruction for veterinary professionals with advanced degrees.

■ Earnings

Earnings are generally low for veterinary technicians in private practices and clinics, but pay scales are steadily climbing due to the increasing demand. Better-paying jobs are in zoos and in research. Those fields of practice are very competitive, especially zoos, and only a small percentage of highly qualified veterinary technicians are employed in them.

About 70 percent of veterinary technicians are employed in private or clinical practice and research. Earnings for zoo veterinary technicians range from $17,000 to $35,000. Salaries in clinical or private practice range from $15,000 for recent graduates to $40,000 for experienced graduates working in supervisory positions. Earnings vary depending on practice setting, geographic location, level of education, and years of experience. Benefits vary and depend on each employer's policies.

■ Work Environment

Veterinary technicians generally work 40-hour weeks, which may include a few long weekdays and alternated or rotated Saturdays. Hours may fluctuate as veterinary technicians may need to have their schedules adjusted to accommodate emergency work.

A veterinary technician must be prepared for emergencies. In field or farm work, they often have to overcome weather conditions in treating the animal. Injured animals can be very dangerous, and veterinary technicians have to exercise extreme caution when caring for them. A veterinary technician also handles animals that are diseased or infested with parasites. Some of these conditions, such as ringworm, are contagious, so the veterinary technician must understand how these conditions are transferred to humans and take precautions to prevent the spread of diseases.

People who become veterinary technicians care about animals. For this reason, maintaining an animal's well-being or helping to cure an ill animal is very rewarding work. In private practice, technicians get to know the animals they care for. This provides the opportunity to actually see the animals' progress. In other areas, such as zoo work, veterinary technicians work with very interesting, sometimes endangered, species. This work can be challenging and rewarding in the sense that they are helping to save a species and continuing efforts to educate people about these animals. Veterinary technicians who work in research gain satisfaction from knowing their work contributes to promoting both animal and human health.

■ Outlook

The employment outlook for veterinary technicians is very good through the year 2006. Veterinary technicians are constantly in demand. Veterinary medicine is a field that is not adversely affected by the economy, so it does offer stability.

In 1996, there were 33,000 veterinary technicians employed in the United States. Currently, there is a shortage of veterinary technicians. In fact, there were 4,000 job openings for every 1,000 graduates in the mid-1990's. The public's love for pets coupled with higher disposable incomes will raise the demand for this occupation.

■ For More Information

For more information on careers, schools, and resources, write to the American Veterinary Medical Association. In addition, check out the AVMA's Web page for career and education information, especially the "NetVet" link that provides access to information on specialties, organizations, publications, and fun sites.

American Veterinary Medical Association
1931 North Meacham Road, Suite 100
Schaumburg, IL 60173-4360
Attn: Education and Research Division
Tel: 800-248-2862 or 847-925-8070
Web: http://www.avma.org

North American Veterinary Technician Association
PO Box 224
Battleground, IN 47920
Tel: 317-742-2216

Canadian Veterinary Medical Association
339 Booth Street
Ottawa, Ontario K1R 7K1 Canada
Tel: 613-236-1162
Email: mmcvma@magi.com

For more information on zoo veterinary technology and positions, contact:

Association of Zoo Veterinary Technicians
c/o Louisville Zoo
PO Box 37250
Louisville, KY 40233
Tel: 502-451-0440

■ Related Articles

Animals

Animal Caretakers

Animal Shelter Employees

Veterinarians

Zookeepers

Zoologists

Video, Video-Control, and Video-Robo Technicians

■ **See Broadcast Engineers**

Videotape-Recording Technicians

■ **See Broadcast Engineers**

Visual Marketers

■ **See Merchandise Displayers**

Vintners

■ **See Enologists**

Vocational Counselors

■ **See Career and Employment Counselors**

Volcanologists

■ **See Geophysicists**

Waiters

■ **See Restaurants and Food Service and Food Service Workers**

Waste Haulers

■ **See Refuse Collectors**

Wastewater Engineers

■ **See Wastewater Treatment Plant Operators and Technicians**

Wastewater Treatment Plant Operators and Technicians

■ Overview

Wastewater treatment plant operators control, monitor, and maintain the equipment and treatment processes in wastewater (sewage) treatment plants. *Wastewater treatment plant technicians* work under the supervision of wastewater treatment plant operators. Some technicians also work in labs where they collect and analyze water samples and maintain lab equipment.

■ History

Water systems and the disposal of wastes are ancient concerns. Thousands of years ago, the Minoans on the island of Crete built some of the earliest known domestic drainage systems. Later, the Romans created marvelous feats of engineering, including enclosed sewer lines that drained both rain runoff and water from the public baths. Urban sanitation methods, however, were limited. Garbage and human wastes were collected from streets and homes and dumped into open watercourses leading away from the cities.

These processes changed little until the 19th century. The health hazards of contact with refuse were poorly understood, but as populations grew, disease outbreaks and noxious conditions in crowded areas made sanitation an important issue. Problems worsened with the Industrial Revolution, which led to both increased population concentrations and industrial wastes that required disposal.

Early efforts by sanitation engineers in the 19th century attempted to take advantage of natural processes. Moderate amounts of pollutants in flowing water go through a natural purification that gradually renders them less harmful. Operators of modern wastewater treatment plants monitor the process that does essentially the same thing that occurs naturally in rivers to purify water, only faster and more effectively. Today's plants are highly sophisticated, complex operations that may utilize biological processes, filtration, chemical treatments, and other methods of removing waste that otherwise may allow bacteria to colonize (live in) critical drinking supplies.

Wastewater treatment operators and technicians must comply with stringent government standards for removing pollutants. Under the Federal Water Pollution Control Act of 1972 and later reauthorizations, it is illegal to discharge any pollutant into the environment without a permit. Industries that send wastes to municipal treatment plants must meet minimum standards and pretreat the wastes so they do not damage the treatment facilities. Standards are also imposed on the treatment plants, controlling the quality of the water they discharge into rivers, streams, and the ocean.

■ The Job

Wastewater from homes, public buildings, and industrial plants is transported through sewer pipes to treatment plants. The wastes include both organic and inorganic substances, some of which may be highly toxic, such as lead and mercury. Wastewater treatment plant operators and technicians regulate the flow of incoming wastewater by adjusting pumps, valves, and other equipment, either manually or through remote controls. They keep track of the various meters and gauges that monitor the purification processes and indicate how the equipment is operating. Using the information from these instruments, they control the pumps, engines, and generators that move the untreated water through the processes of filtration, settling, aeration, and sludge digestion. They also operate chemical-feeding devices, collect water samples, and perform laboratory tests, so that the proper level of chemicals, such as chlorine, is maintained in the wastewater. Technicians may record instrument readings and other information in logs of plant operations. These logs are supervised and monitored by operators. Computers are commonly used to monitor and regulate wastewater treatment equipment and processes. Specialized software allows operators to store and analyze data, which is particularly useful when something in the system malfunctions.

The duties of operators and technicians vary somewhat with the size and type of plant where they work. In small plants one person per shift may be able to do all the necessary routine tasks. But in larger plants, there may be a number of operators, each specializing in just a few activities and working as part of a team that includes engineers, chemists, technicians, mechanics, helpers, and other employees. Some facilities are equipped to handle both wastewater treatment and treatment of the clean water supplied to municipal water systems, and plant operators may be involved with both functions.

Other routine tasks that plant operators and technicians perform include maintenance and minor repairs on equipment such as valves and pumps. They may use common hand tools such as wrenches and pliers and special tools adapted specifically for the equipment. In large facilities, they also direct attendants and helpers who take care of some routine tasks and maintenance work. The accumulated residues of wastes from the water must be removed from the plant, and operators may dispose of these materials. Some of this final product, or sludge, can be reclaimed for uses such as soil conditioners or fuel for the production of electricity.

Technicians may also survey streams and study basin areas to determine water availability. To assist the engineers they work with, technicians prepare graphs, tables, sketches, and diagrams to illustrate survey data. They file plans and documents, answer public inquiries, help train new personnel and perform various other support duties.

Plant operators and technicians sometimes have to work under emergency conditions, such as when heavy rains flood the sewer pipes, straining the treatment plant's capacity or when there is a chlorine gas leak or oxygen deficiency in the treatment tanks. When a serious problem arises, they must work quickly and effectively to solve it as soon as possible.

■ Requirements

High School

A high school diploma or its equivalent is required for a job as a wastewater treatment plant operator or technician, and additional specialized technical training is generally preferred for both positions. A desirable background for this work includes high school courses in chemistry, biology, mathematics and computers; welding or electrical training may be helpful as well. Other characteristics that employers look for are mechanical aptitude and the ability to perform mathematical computations easily. You should be able to work basic algebra and statistics problems. Future technicians may be required to prepare reports containing statistics and other scientific documentation. Communications, statistics, and algebra are useful for this career path: such courses enable the technician to prepare

graphs, tables, sketches, and diagrams to illustrate surveys for the operators and engineers they support.

Postsecondary Training

As treatment plants become more technologically complex, workers who have previous training in the field are increasingly at an advantage. Specialized education in wastewater technology is available in two-year programs that lead to an associate's degree and one-year programs that lead to a certificate. Such programs, which are offered at some community and junior colleges and vocational-technical institutes, provide a good general knowledge of water pollution control and will prepare you to become an operator or technician. Beginners must still learn the details of operations at the plant where they work, but their specialized training increases their chances for better positions and later promotions.

Many operators and technicians acquire the skills they need during a period of on-the-job training. Newly hired workers often begin as attendants or operators-in-training. Working under the supervision of experienced operators, they pick up knowledge and skills by observing other workers and by doing routine tasks such as recording meter readings, collecting samples, and general cleaning and plant maintenance. In larger plants, trainees may study supplementary written material provided at the plant or they may attend classes where they learn plant operations.

WASTEWATER TREATMENT PLANT OPERATORS AND TECHNICIANS	
SCHOOL SUBJECTS	Chemistry Mathematics
PERSONAL SKILLS	Mechanical/manipulative Technical/scientific
WORK ENVIRONMENT	Indoors and outdoors Primarily one location
MINIMUM EDUCATION LEVEL	Some postsecondary training
SALARY RANGE	$17,420 to $34,736 to $53,678
CERTIFICATION OR LICENSING	Required by all states
OUTLOOK	Faster than the average
DOT	955
GOE	06.02.11
NOC	9424

A wastewater treatment plant operator oversees one of the largest treatment facilities in the Midwest at a master control station.

Wastewater treatment plant operators and technicians often have various opportunities to continue learning about their field. Most state water pollution control agencies offer training courses for people employed in the field. Subjects covered by these training courses include principles of treatment processes and process control, odors and their control, safety, chlorination, sedimentation, biological oxidation, sludge treatment and disposal, and flow measurements. Correspondence courses on related subject areas also are available. Some employers help pay tuition for workers who take related college-level courses in science or engineering.

Certification or Licensing

In most states, workers who control operations at wastewater treatment plants must be certified by the state. To obtain certification, operators must pass an examination given by the state. There is no nationwide standard, so different states administer different tests. Many states issue several classes of certification, depending on the size of the plant the worker is qualified to control. Certification may be beneficial even if it is not a requirement and no matter how much experience a worker already has. In Illinois, for example, operators who have the minimum state certification level are automatically eligible for higher pay than

those without any certification, although certification is not a requirement of hire.

Other Requirements

Operators and technicians must be familiar with the provisions of the Federal Clean Water Act and various state and local regulations that apply to their work. Whenever they become responsible for more complex processes and equipment, they must become acquainted with a wider scope of guidelines and regulations. In larger cities and towns especially, job applicants may have to take a civil service exam or other tests that assess their aptitudes and abilities.

■ Exploring

It may be possible to arrange to visit a wastewater treatment plant to observe its operations. It can also be helpful to investigate courses and requirements of any programs in wastewater technology or environmental resources programs offered by a local technical school or college. While part-time or summer employment as a helper in a wastewater treatment plant could be very helpful experience, such a job may be hard to find. However, a job in any kind of machine shop can provide an opportunity to become familiar with handling machinery and common tools.

Asking wastewater plant operators or technicians in your city if you can interview them about their job is a good way to learn about the job, and it may help you fulfill a requirement for a class paper or speech. Learning about water conservation and water quality in general can also be useful. Government agencies or citizen groups dedicated to improving water quality or conserving water can teach you about water quality and supply in your area.

■ Employers

While municipal wastewater treatment plants employ the majority of wastewater treatment professionals, there are other employers who need workers skilled in this field. Wastewater treatment plant operators and technicians may also find jobs for state or federal water pollution control agencies, monitoring plants and providing technical assistance. Examples of such agencies are the Army Corps of Engineers and the Environmental Protection Agency. These jobs normally require vocational-technical school or community college training. Other experienced wastewater workers find employment with industrial wastewater treatment plants, companies that sell wastewater treatment equipment and chemicals, large utilities, consulting firms, or vocational-technical schools.

■ Starting Out

Graduates of most postsecondary technical programs and some high schools can get help in locating job openings from the placement office of the school they attended.

Another source of information is the local office of the state employment service. Job seekers may also directly contact state and local water pollution control agencies and the personnel offices of wastewater treatment facilities in desired locations.

In some plants, a person must first work as a wastewater treatment plant technician before becoming an operator or working in a supervisory position. Wastewater treatment plant technicians have many of the same duties as a plant operator, but less responsibility. They inspect, study, and sample existing water treatment systems and evaluate new structures for efficacy and safety. Support work and instrumentation reading make up the bulk of the technician's day.

The Internet has become a useful resource for finding job leads. Professional associations, such as the Water Environment Foundation, offer job listings in the wastewater field as part of their Web site (http://www.wef.org). Such Web sites are a good place for someone getting started in the field as they also list internship or trainee positions available. Also, an Internet search using the words "wastewater treatment plant operator, or technician" will generate a list of sites that may contain job postings and internship opportunities.

■ Advancement

As operators gain skills and experience, they are assigned tasks that involve more responsibility for more complex activities. Some technicians advance to become operators. Some operators advance to become plant supervisors or plant superintendents. The qualifications that superintendents need are related to the size and complexity of the plant. In smaller plants, experienced operators with some postsecondary training may be promoted to superintendent positions. In larger plants, educational requirements are increasing along with the sophistication and complexity of their systems, and superintendents usually have bachelor's degrees in engineering or science.

For some operators and technicians, the route to advancement is transferring to a related job. Such jobs may require additional schooling or training to specialize in water pollution control, commercial wastewater equipment sales, or teaching wastewater treatment in a vocational or technical school.

■ Earnings

Salaries of wastewater treatment plant operators and technicians vary depending on factors such as the size of the plant, the workers' job responsibilities, and their level of certification. According to the 1998-99 *Occupational Outlook Handbook,* entry-level plant technicians and operators can expect to make at least $17,420 per year. Average earnings in the profession exceed $34,736 per year. Experienced

certified workers can make over $53,768 depending on the size of the plant and staff they supervise. In addition to their pay, most operators and technicians receive benefits such as life and health insurance, a pension plan, and reimbursement for education and training related to their job.

■ Work Environment

Most of the approximately 40,000 wastewater treatment plant operators in the United States are employed by local governments; others work for the federal government, utilities companies, or private sanitary services that operate under contracts with local governments. Jobs are located throughout the country, with the greatest numbers found in areas with high populations. In small towns, plant operators may only work part time or may handle other duties as well as wastewater treatment. The size and type of plant also determine the range of duties. In larger plants with many employees, operators and technicians usually perform more specialized functions. In some cases, they may be responsible for monitoring only a single process. In smaller plants, workers likely will have a broader range of responsibilities. Wastewater treatment plants operate 24 hours a day, every day of the year. Operators and technicians usually work one of three eight-hour shifts, often on a rotating basis so that employees share the evening and night work. Overtime is often required during emergencies.

The work takes operators and technicians both indoors and outdoors. They must contend with noisy machinery and may have to tolerate unpleasant odors, despite the use of chlorine and other chemicals to control odors. The job involves moving about, stooping, reaching, and climbing. Operators and technicians often get their clothes dirty. Slippery sidewalks, dangerous gases, and malfunctioning equipment are potential hazards on the job, but by following safety guidelines, workers can minimize their risk of injury.

■ Outlook

Over the next 10 to 15 years, employment in this field is expected to grow at a faster rate than average for all occupations. The growth in demand for wastewater treatment will be related to the overall growth of the nation's population and economy. New treatment plants will probably be built, and existing ones will be upgraded, requiring additional trained personnel to manage their operations. Other openings will arise when experienced workers retire or transfer to new occupations. Operators and technicians with formal training will have the best chances for new positions and promotions.

Workers in wastewater treatment plants are rarely laid off, even during a recession, because wastewater treatment is essential to public health and welfare. In the future, more wastewater professionals will probably be employed by private companies that contract to manage treatment plants for local governments.

■ For More Information

For current information on the field of wastewater management, contact:

American Water Works Association
6666 West Quincy Avenue
Denver, CO 80235
Tel: 303-794-7711
Web: http://www.awwa.org

For information on education and training, contact:

Coalition of Environmental Training Centers
c/o National Environmental Training Association
2930 East Camelback Road, Suite 185
Phoenix, AZ 85016
Tel: 602-956-6099

Environmental Careers Organization
179 South Street
Boston, MA 02111
Tel: 617-426-4375
Web: http://www.eco.org

The following is a professional organization monitoring developments in the field of wastewater management:

Water Environment Federation
601 Wythe Street
Alexandria, VA 22314-1994
Tel: 703-684-2452
Web: http://www.wef.org

■ Related Articles

Waste Management
Hazardous Waste Management Specialists
Hazardous Waste Management Technicians
Pollution Control Technicians
Recycling Coordinators

Watch and Clock Repairers

■ Overview

Watch repairers, or *watchmakers,* and *clock repairers,* or *clockmakers,* clean, adjust, repair, and regulate watches, clocks, chronometers, electronic timepieces, and related instruments. Watch and clock repairers work in department and jewelry stores, at home, or in repair shops. Currently there are approximately 7,000 watch and clock repairers in the United States.

■ History

Keeping track of time has always been important to people. Ancient devices for measuring and showing the passage of time included sundials, hourglasses, water dripping at a steady pace until it filled a container, and burning candles with regularly spaced marks on the side. The earliest mechanical clocks were built in Europe in the 1300s. Made of iron and driven by the energy of slowly dropping weights, they were so large and heavy that they were fitted into towers, and they could indicate the hours only approximately. Improvements in clock mechanisms made them smaller, and a few household versions of weight-driven clocks began to appear by the end of the 1300s.

Portable clocks and watches became possible in the early 1500s, when the coiled mainspring replaced weights as a means for driving the mechanism. Early watches were about four to five inches in diameter, three inches deep, and so heavy that they had to be carried in the hand. A long series of advances refined the size of watches and clocks and improved their performance. By 1809, a watch belonging to the Empress Josephine was small enough to be made into the first wristwatch, although wristwatches were not very successful for nearly another century. Among the many changes that improved clocks and watches were parts made of brass and steel, then later of special metal alloys, the introduction of the pendulum in clocks, and the invention of the hairspring to regulate the motion of the balance wheel in watches. More recently, electric and electronic devices have brought further miniaturization and helped increase timekeeping accuracy.

Until the 1800s, timepieces were made by hand, one by one, by skilled artisans. In the early United States, a few clockmakers copied European clocks of the era, and clock towers were built in city public places. Not many people owned watches prior to the 1800s. In that century, however, larger numbers of clocks and pocket watches were made using factory methods. Prices became more reasonable, and watches and clocks became popular as people led more active lives and traveled more. Today's watches and clocks are almost always mass-produced in factories, but workers skilled in adjusting and repairing their mechanisms are still needed for working on special timepieces.

■ The Job

Watches and clocks are complex machines with many small parts, and repairing them requires precision and delicacy. The ability to locate and correct defects is an important and necessary skill for watch and clock repairers. They employ a standard, systematic procedure to track down defects, sometimes using information from customers about the history and previous repairs of the timepiece. Some problems arise from incorrect replacement or improper fitting of parts. Careless pushing, pulling, or turning the winding device can also cause problems by making parts too tight or too loose, or permitting dust to enter the mechanism.

The first step is usually opening the case to examine the mechanism. Often with the aid of a magnifying eyeglass, or loupe, repairers check for defective parts and dirt and inspect the springs for rust and incorrect alignment. They may repair or replace such parts as the mainspring, hairspring, jewels or pivots, and escapements. With older timepieces, they may have to make parts in order for the device to function properly. They may clean the mechanism with a cleaning solution or ultrasonic sound waves. Timepieces that must be oiled need a delicate touch, for excessive amounts of oil, or oil in the wrong spots, can cause the mechanism to operate improperly. When the work is complete, the timepiece must be reassembled so that parts fit properly.

Repairers use a number of specialized tools and devices in their work. A timing machine is used to check the accuracy of timepieces. Watches and clocks that show erratic timekeeping are checked for magnetism and may be demagnetized in a demagnetizer. When diagnosing problems in electric and electronic timepieces, watch and clock repairers may use various meters and other testing equipment. They may also use hand tools, such as pliers, pilar files, pin vises, tweezers, turns, and lathes in their work.

Many watch and clock repairers, especially those who are self-employed or work in a retail store, also repair jewelry and sell items like clocks, watches, jewelry, china, and silverware. In large stores and shops they may have managerial or supervisory duties as well. Repairers who have their own shops often must order parts and merchandise, keep accounts, arrange for advertising, and perform other tasks required to maintain an efficient and profitable business.

■ Requirements

High School

A high school diploma is desirable for prospective watch and clock repairers. High school classes that would be good preparation for this career include technical/shop courses that introduce the use of various tools, and electronics classes to learn about circuits and electrical test equipment. Mathematics or accounting classes that teach business math and courses that help develop verbal communication skills are also beneficial.

Postsecondary Training

Few people learn this trade on the job. Instead, the best way to learn watch and clock repairing skills is to attend one of several schools of horology, which is the art of making and repairing timepieces. Their training programs typically take one to three years. Students receive instruction in disassembling and reassembling, cleaning and oiling, and replacing or repairing parts in various kinds of timepieces. They learn to use such devices as demagnetizers, lathes, and electronic timing equipment. Additional training may be obtained in servicing electronic watches, calendars, chronometers, and timers. They are also usually required to purchase a set of hand tools for their own use. After they complete their training period, watch and clock repairers may take refresher courses to learn about new products that come on the market.

Certification or Licensing

The American Watchmakers-Clockmakers Institute offers certification to watch and clock repairers based on a written examination and a practical test of repairing skill. The designations, Certified Watchmaker, Certified Master Watchmaker, Certified Master Electronic Watchmaker, Specialist, Certified Clockmaker, and Certified Master Clockmaker, are awarded to repairers who successfully pass the qualifying examinations.

Other Requirements

Watch and clock repairers need a combination of personal characteristics. They must have the ability to work independently with a high degree of precision. They need to be able to perceive tiny details in objects and make fine visual discriminations. They must have good manual dexterity, the finger sensitivity to feel small shapes, and steady hands so they can deftly place and work with small parts. They need orderly work habits and the ability to make judgments using set standards. Repairers who are in charge of their own shops need to be tactful, courteous, and able to communicate well with the public and employees. They also need at least a basic understanding of operating a business.

■ Exploring

You can begin learning about this field by getting a part-time job in a shop where

WATCH AND CLOCK REPAIRERS	
SCHOOL SUBJECTS	Mathematics Technical/Shop
PERSONAL SKILLS	Mechanical/manipulative Technical/scientific
WORK ENVIRONMENT	Primarily indoors Primarily one location
MINIMUM EDUCATION LEVEL	Some postsecondary training
SALARY RANGE	$16,000 to $30,000 to $50,000
CERTIFICATION OR LICENSING	Voluntary
OUTLOOK	Decline
DOT	715
GOE	05.05.11
NOC	7344

A watch and clock repairer displays some of the many types of timepieces he regularly works on.

watches and clocks are repaired and sold. Jewelry stores often hire high school or college students to work part-time during the holiday seasons.

Hobbies and technical courses that require dexterity and patience in using hand tools can provide another way of exploring similar activities and developing manual skills. Some people find out about their interest in detailed crafts when they learn to repair precision instruments while serving in the military.

■ Employers

Jewelry or department stores and service outlets employ watch and clock repairers. Watch and clock manufacturers also hire repairers to work in their service departments. Many people with these skills operate their own repair businesses either in a storefront or in their own homes.

■ Starting Out

Job seekers might check the listings for "jewelers" or "watch repair" in their local Yellow Pages and apply directly to any establishments that seem likely. Persons might also con-

tact watch manufacturers regarding job openings. Graduates of watch and clock repair training programs may get help finding a job from their school's placement office or through the American Watchmakers Institute. Finally, the beginning watch repairer should check local newspaper's classified ads for job openings in the field.

■ Advancement

Watch repairers who work in some stores and shops may be promoted to positions as supervisors or service managers. Experienced repairers can sometimes go into business for themselves by opening their own repair shop, and perhaps eventually expanding it into a retail store selling such items as jewelry and silver, as well as clock and watches. Some repairers get further training in engraving, jewelry repair, design, or stone setting. Such additional skills may open new avenues for advancement. Another possibility for some workers is to apply their precision skills in another field by moving to a job, for example, with a company that manufactures aircraft components with small parts. Such job changes, however, are likely to require additional training.

■ Earnings

Annual earnings for beginning watch repairers range from about $16,000 to $18,000. Experienced repairers may have earnings in the range of $30,000 to $50,000 a year. In some stores, part of their earnings is commissions on the items they service. Someone working 40 hours a week for a company or business can usually expect general benefits.

Repairers who operate their own businesses often earn considerably more than those who are employed by other businesses.

■ Work Environment

Watch and clock repairers work in a variety of settings, including at home or in a department store, shopping center, jewelry store, or repair shop. Work areas are typically clean, well lighted, and comfortable. Repairers often work individually and sit at a workbench much of the time. Because repairs consist of close work with fine tools and delicate instruments, some people experience eyestrain, especially at first.

Some repairers work a standard 40-hour workweek, while others work as much as 45 to 48 hours a week. Self-employed people may work longer hours, depending on the amount of business.

■ Outlook

The number of watch and clock repairers is expected to decrease in the coming years. One important factor in this decline is the mass production of inexpensive timepieces. Since many watches and clocks produced today cost as much or more to repair as to replace, owners tend to discard their old or broken items. Owners of expensive or antique timepieces will continue to have them repaired, maintaining a need for skilled workers in this field.

■ For More Information

For information on the field of watch making and repair, and a list of schools that teach it, contact:

American Watchmakers-Clockmakers Institute
701 Enterprise Drive
Harrison, OH 45030
Tel: 513-367-9800
Web: http://www.awi-net.org

■ Related Articles

Business, Personal, and Consulting Services
Electronics
Instrument Makers and Repairers
Jewelers and Jewelry Repairers
Silverware Artisans and Workers

Weavers
■ **See Textile Manufacturing Occupations**

Web Designers
■ **See Internet Content Developers**

Web Developers
■ **See Internet Content Developers**

Webmasters

■ Overview

Webmasters design, implement, and maintain World Wide Web sites for corporations, educational institutions, not-for-profit organizations, government agencies, or other institutions. Webmasters should have working knowledge of network configurations, interface, graphic design, software development, business, writing, marketing, and project management. Because the function of a webmaster encompasses so many different responsibilities, in a large orga-

nization, the position is often held by a team of individuals, rather than a single person.

■ The Job

Because the idea of designing and maintaining a Web site is relatively new, there is no complete, definitive job description for a webmaster. Many of their job responsibilities depend upon the goals and needs of the particular organization for which they work. There are, however, some basic duties that are common to almost all webmasters.

The webmaster, specifically site managers, first secures space on the Web for the site he or she is developing. This is done by contracting with an Internet service provider. The provider serves as a sort of storage facility for the organization's on-line information, usually charging a set monthly fee for a specified amount of megabyte space. The webmaster may also be responsible for establishing a URL (Uniform Resource Locator) for the Web site he or she is developing. The URL serves as the site's on-line "address," and must be registered with InterNIC, the Web URL registration service.

The webmaster is responsible for developing the actual Web site for his or her organization. In some cases, this may involve actually writing the text content of the pages. More commonly, however, the webmaster is given the text to be used, and is merely responsible for programming it in such a way that it can be displayed on a Web page. In larger companies webmasters specialize in content, adaptation, and presentation of data.

In order for text to be displayed on a Web page, it must be formatted using HyperText Markup Language (HTML). HTML is a system of coding text so that the computer that is "reading" it knows how to display it. For example, text could be coded to be a certain size or color or to be italicized or boldface. Paragraphs, line breaks, alignment, and margins are other examples of text attributes that must be coded in HTML.

Although it is less and less common, some webmasters code text manually, by actually typing the various commands into

WEBMASTERS	
SCHOOL SUBJECTS	**Computer science** **Mathematics**
PERSONAL SKILLS	**Communication/ideas** **Technical/scientific**
WORK ENVIRONMENT	**Primarily indoors** **Primarily one location**
MINIMUM EDUCATION LEVEL	**Some postsecondary training**
SALARY RANGE	**$25,000 to $35,000 to $100,000**
CERTIFICATION OR LICENSING	**Voluntary**
OUTLOOK	**Faster than the average**
DOT	**030**
GOE	**11.01.01**

the body of the text. This method is time-consuming, however, and mistakes are easily made. More often, webmasters use a software program that automatically codes text. Some word processing programs, such as WordPerfect, even offer HTML options.

Along with coding the text, the webmaster must lay out the elements of the Web site in such a way that it is visually pleasing, well organized, and easy to navigate. He or she may use various colors, background patterns, images, tables, or charts. These graphic elements can come from image files already on the Web, software clip art files, or images scanned into the computer with an electronic scanner. In some cases, when an organization is using the Web site to promote its product or service, the webmaster may work with a marketing specialist or department to develop a page.

Some Web sites have several directories or "layers." That is, an organization may have several Web pages, organized in a sort of "tree," with its home page connected, via hypertext links, to other pages, which may in turn be linked to other pages. The webmaster is responsible for organizing the pages in such a way that a visitor can easily browse through them and find what he or she is looking for. Such webmasters are called *programmers* and *developers;* they are also responsible for creating Web tools and special Web functionality.

For webmasters who work for organizations that have several different Web sites, one responsibility may be making sure that the "style" or appearance of all the pages is the same. This is often referred to as "house style." In large organizations, such as universities, where many different departments may be developing and maintaining their own pages, it is especially important that the webmaster monitor these pages to ensure consistency and conformity to the organization's requirements. In almost every case, the webmaster has the final authority for the content and appearance of his or her organization's Web site. He or she must carefully edit, proofread, and check the appearance of every page.

Besides designing and setting up Web sites, most webmasters are charged with maintaining and updating existing sites. Most sites contain information that changes regularly. Some change daily, or even hourly. Depending upon his or her employer and the type of Web site, the webmaster may spend a good deal of time updating and remodeling the page. He or she is also responsible for ensuring that the hyperlinks contained within the Web site lead to the sites they should. Since it is common for links to change or become obsolete, the webmaster usually performs a link check every few weeks.

Other job duties vary, depending upon the employer and the position. Most webmasters are responsible for receiving and answering email messages from visitors to the organization's Web site. Some webmasters keep logs and create reports on when and how often their pages are visited and by whom. Depending on the company, Web sites count anywhere from 300 to 1.4 billion visits, or "hits," a month. Some create and maintain order forms or on-line "shopping carts" that allow visitors to the Web site to purchase products or services. Some may train other employees on how to create or update Web pages. Finally, webmasters may be responsible for developing and adhering to a budget for their departments.

■ Requirements

High School

High school should take as many computer science classes as they can. Mathematics classes are also helpful. Finally, because writing skills are important in this career, English classes are good choices.

Postsecondary Training

As of today, there is no set advanced educational path or requirement for becoming a webmaster. While many have bachelor's degrees in computer science, liberal arts degrees, such as English, are not uncommon. There are also webmasters who have degrees in engineering, mathematics, and marketing. Not all webmasters have bachelor's degrees, however; some have two-year degrees, or a high school education only. Currently, most webmasters do not have formal, specific training in how to design Web sites.

Certification or Licensing

There is strong debate within the industry regarding certification. Some, mostly corporate CEOs, favor certification. They view certification as a way to gauge an employees skill and Web mastery expertise. Others argue, however, that is nearly impossible to test knowledge of technology that is constantly changing and improving. Despite the split of opinion, webmaster certification programs are available at many colleges, universities, and technical schools throughout the United States. Programs vary in length, anywhere from three weeks, to nine months or more; topics covered include client/server technology, Web development, programs, and software and hardware. The International Webmasters Association also offers a voluntary certification program.

Other Requirements

Webmasters should be creative. It is important for a Web page to be well designed in order to attract attention. Good writing skills and an aptitude for marketing are also excellent qualities for anyone considering a career in Web site design.

What most webmasters have in common is a strong knowledge of computer technology. Most people who enter this field are already well-versed in computer operating systems, programming languages, computer graphics, and Internet standards. When considering candidates for the position of webmaster, employers usually require at least two years of experience with World Wide Web technologies. In some cases, employers require that candidates already have experience in designing and maintaining Web sites. It is, in fact, most common for someone to move into the position of webmaster from another computer-related job in the same organization.

■ Exploring

One of the easiest ways to learn about what a webmaster does is to spend time "surfing" on the World Wide Web. By examining a variety of Web sites to see how they look and operate, you can begin to get a feel for what goes into a home page.

An even better way to explore this career is to design your own personal Web page. Many Internet servers offer their users the option of designing and maintaining a personal Web page for a very low fee. A personal page can contain virtually anything that you want to include, from snapshots of friends to audio files of favorite music to hypertext links to other favorite sites.

■ Employers

Webmasters are employed by Web design companies, businesses, schools or universities, not-for-profit organizations, government agencies—in short, any organization that requires a presence on the World Wide Web. Webmasters may also work as freelancers or operate their own Web design business.

■ Starting Out

Most people become webmasters by moving into the position from another computer-related position within the same company. Since most large organizations already use computers for various functions, they may employ a person or several people to serve as computer "specialists." If these organizations decide to develop their own Web sites, they frequently assign the task to one of these employees who is already experienced with the computer system. Often, the person who ultimately becomes an organization's webmaster at first just takes on the job in addition to his or her other, already-established duties.

Another way that individuals find jobs in this field is through on-line postings of job openings. Many companies post webmaster position openings on-line because the candidates they hope to attract are very likely to use the Internet for a job search. Therefore, the prospective webmaster should use the World Wide Web to check job-related newsgroups. He or she might also use a Web search engine to locate openings.

■ Advancement

Experienced webmasters employed by a large organization may be able to advance to a supervisory position in which he or she directs the work of a team of webmasters. Others might advance by starting their own business, designing Web sites on a contract basis for several clients, rather than working exclusively for one organization.

Opportunities for webmasters of the future are endless due to the continuing development of on-line technology. As understanding and use of the World Wide Web increase, there may be new or expanded job duties for individuals with expertise in this field. People working today as webmasters may be required in a few years to perform jobs that don't even exist yet.

■ Earnings

According to *U.S. News & World Report,* salaries for the position of webmaster range from $50,000 to $100,000 per year. The demand for webmasters is so great that some companies are offering stock options, sign-on bonuses and other perks, in addition to salaries from $80,000 to $110,000. While this may be true for those who are hired into an organization specifically to fill the position, it is not representative of the many webmasters who have merely moved into the position from another position within their company or have taken on the task in addition to other duties. These employees are often paid approximately the same salary they were already making. According to the 1998 Webmaster Survey, the majority of webmasters earn under $50,000. Nineteen percent of all webmasters earned from $25,000 to $40,999 annually; 17 percent earned less than $25,000.

Depending upon the organization for which they work, webmasters may receive a benefits package in addition to salary. A typical benefits package would include paid vacations and holidays, medical insurance, and perhaps a pension plan.

■ Work Environment

Although much of the webmaster's day may be spent alone, it is nonetheless important that he or she be able to communicate and work well with others. Depending upon the organization for which he or she works, the webmaster may have periodic meetings with graphic designers, marketing specialists, writers, or other professionals who have input into the Web site development. In many larger organizations, there is a team of webmasters, rather than just one. Although each team member works alone on his or her own specific duties, the members may meet frequently to discuss and coordinate their activities.

Because technology changes so rapidly, this job is constantly evolving. Webmasters must spend time reading and learning about new developments in on-line communication. They may be continually working with new computer software or hardware. Their actual job responsibilities may even change, as the capabilities of both the organization and the World Wide Web itself expand. It is important that these employees be flexible and willing to learn and grow with the technology that drives their work.

Because they don't deal with the general public, most webmasters are allowed to wear fairly casual attire and to work in a relaxed atmosphere. In most cases, the job calls for standard working hours, although there may be times when overtime is required.

■ Outlook

There can be no doubt that computer—and specifically on-line—technology will continue its rapid growth for the next several years. Likewise, then, the number of computer-related jobs, including that of webmaster, should also increase. The World Organization of Webmasters projects an explosion of jobs available through the year 2006—well over 8 million. The majority of webmasters working today are full time employees—about 86 percent according to the 1998 Webmaster Study, conducted by Collaborative Marketing. The newness of this job is reflected in the age demographics of webmasters—35 percent are between the ages of 26 and 35 (1998 Webmaster Study); and according to *Web Week,* 72 percent are in their first webmaster position. This indicates the attraction of the young to the Internet, and to better tap that market, a company's desire to fill webmaster positions with young computer-savvy individuals.

The 1998 Webmaster Study found this field to be currently male-dominated. However, there is great opportunity for women in this field. Many large companies, such as Wal-Mart, are looking for talented individuals who, according to a Wal-Mart webmaster (yes, female) "can combine a lot of technical knowledge with the ability to cooperate with people who don't know a lot of technology. Women can often be very good at that."

As more and more businesses, not-for-profit organizations, educational institutions, and government agencies choose to "go online," the total number of Web sites will grow, as will the need for experts to design them. Companies are starting to view Web sites as more than a temporary experiment, but rather an important and necessary business and marketing tool. Growth will be largest with Internet content developers—webmasters responsible for the information displayed on a Web site. The 1998 Webmaster Study predicts Internet content developers will become more sophisticated with their techniques and will significantly surpass the growth of the technical segment of webmasters.

One thing to keep in mind, however, is that when technology advances extremely rapidly, it tends to make old methods of doing things obsolete. If current trends continue, the role and role of webmaster will be carried out by a group or department instead of a single employee, in order to keep up with the demands of the position. It is possible that in the next few years, changes in technology will make the Web sites we are now familiar with a thing of the past. Another possibility is that, like desktop publishing, user-friendly software programs will make Web site design so easy and efficient that it no longer requires an "expert" to do it well. Webmasters who are concerned with job security should be willing to continue learning and using the very latest developments in technology, so that they are prepared to move into the future of online communication, whatever it may be.

■ For More Information

The Association of Internet Professionals represents the worldwide community of people employed in Internet-related fields.

Association of Internet Professionals (AIP)
9200 Sunset Boulevard, Suite 710
Los Angeles, CA 90069
Tel: 800-JOIN-AIP
Email: info@association.org
Web: http://www.association.org/index.html

For information on its newsletter, Webreference Update, *and information regarding its voluntary certification program, contact:*

International Webmasters Association
119 East. Union Street, Suite #E
Pasadena, CA 91103
Tel: 626-449-3709
Web: http://www.iwanet.org

For information on education and certification, contact:

World Organization of Webmasters
9580 Oak Avenue Parkway, Suite 7-177
Folsom, CA 95630
Tel: 916-929-6557
Email: info@world-webmasters.org
Web: http://www.world-webmasters.org/

■ Related Articles

Computer Hardware
Computer Software
Computers
Electronics
Internet
Computer Programmers
Computer Systems/Programmer Analysts
Computer Trainers
Desktop Publishing Specialists
Graphic Designers
Graphics Programmers
Hardware Engineers

Internet Content Developers

Internet Security Specialists

Software Designers

Software Engineers

Systems Set Up Specialists

Technical Support Specialists

Technical Writers and Editors

Wedding/Party Planners

■ Overview

From directing the bride to the best dress shops and cake decorators to pinning on the corsages the day of the wedding, *wedding/party consultants,* sometimes called *event professionals,* assist in the planning of weddings, receptions, and other large celebrations and events. These consultants generally have home-based businesses, but spend a great deal of time visiting vendors and reception and wedding sites.

■ History

Weddings have long provided good careers for musicians, photographers, florists, printers, caterers, and others. Even marriage "brokers" were once considered prominent members of some cultures—men and women who made their livings pairing up brides with grooms for nicely "arranged" marriages. Wedding consulting, however, has only emerged in recent years. In the years before wedding consultants, brides divided up responsibilities among cousins and aunts—a family got together to lick invitation envelopes factory-line style, a favorite aunt mixed batches of butter mints, a married sister with some recent wedding experience helped the bride pick a dress and china pattern. But usually it wasn't until after the event that the bride really had a sense of how to plan a wedding. Enter the first serious wedding consultants in the early 1980s. Recognizing how a bride can benefit a great deal from a knowledgeable guide, men and women hired themselves out as wedding and party experts. But it's only been the last few years that the major wedding magazines and publications have given serious consideration to wedding consultants. Now most wedding experts, even Martha Stewart, consider a consultant a necessity in planning a perfect and cost-efficient wedding.

■ The Job

Can't decide whether to have butterflies or doves released at your wedding? Want to get married on a boat, but don't know how to arrange it? Want a chef who will prepare your reception dinner table-side? Even if your requests run a little more mainstream than these, it can be difficult choosing reliable florists and other vendors, and staying within a budget. The average wedding costs close to $20,000 (including the dress), but many brides end up frustrated and disappointed with their ceremonies. Wedding consultants help brides save money and avoid stress by offering their services at the earliest stages of planning. They provide the bride with cost estimates, arrange for ceremony and reception sites, order invitations, and help select music. They also offer advice on wedding etiquette and tradition. Consultants then stay on call for their brides right through the ceremonies and receptions, pinning on flowers, instructing ushers and other members of the wedding parties, taking gifts from guests, and organizing the cake-cutting and bouquet toss.

When brides and their families seek out the services of Packy Boukis, owner of Only You Wedding and Event Consulting, she offers them "The Love Story," a full-service package of planning and organization. "I create a binder for the bride," Packy explains. "It includes a wedding schedule, the wedding party, a section for each vendor, a budget. Everything she'll need is in that book, and it's updated every four to six weeks." In these cases, Packy helps the bride with every step of the planning. She goes with the bride to visit each vendor, such as florists and photographers, to offer her advice and negotiate prices. Packy is also present at the rehearsal and the wedding to organize and see to the last-minute details, assisting in everything from floral arrangement to sewing on popped buttons. Packy has a full office in her home and works alone, with the exception of the wedding day when she has the assistance of a small staff and her husband. "My husband meets with the groomsmen," Packy says, "and makes sure the tuxes are okay."

Despite her involvement in the many different stages of a wedding's plan, Packy is quick to point out that each wedding is still very much the bride's own. "I show her three different vendors for

WEDDING/PARTY PLANNERS	
SCHOOL SUBJECTS	Family and consumer science
PERSONAL SKILLS	Communication/ideas Leadership/management
WORK ENVIRONMENT	Indoors and Outdoors Primarily multiple locations
MINIMUM EDUCATION LEVEL	High school diploma
SALARY RANGE	$22,000 to $50,000 to $100,000+
CERTIFICATION OR LICENSING	Recommended
OUTLOOK	Faster than the average
DOT	299
GOE	08.02.06

each category," she says. "I don't dictate; it's her choice." It is Packy's responsibility as consultant to make sure that the bride has a stress-free event, and to help the bride save money. Packy benefits from discounts on services, and accepts no commissions or rebates, therefore passing savings on to the brides.

In addition to full-service consulting, Packy offers smaller, less-expensive packages. The "First Date" package is simply a single consultation, while the "I Do, I Do" package includes only wedding day assistance with the plans the bride has already made herself. Packy has also formed a place for herself on the Internet, answering wedding-related questions on "Cleveland Live" (http://forums.cleveland.com/forums/get/wedding.html), in addition to hosting a wedding consultants chat on AOL, as ITWNPacky.

Though Packy will sell invitations from time to time, she doesn't market products. Some consultants, however, sell a variety of things from candles and linens to hand-calligraphed invitations to party favors. A consultant may even own a complete bridal boutique. Some consultants specialize in only "destination" weddings. They set up services in exotic locales, like Hawaii, and handle all the details for an out-of-town bride who will only be arriving the week of the wedding. Consultants also arrange for special wedding sites like historic homes, public gardens, and resorts.

A consultant can also introduce a bride to a number of "extras" that she may not have been aware of before. In addition to arranging for the flowers, candles, and cakes, a consultant may arrange for horse-and-carriage rides, doves to be released after the ceremony, wine bars for the reception, goldfish in bowls at the tables, and other frills. Some brides rely on consultants to meet difficult requests, such as booking special kinds of musicians, or finding alternatives to flowers. Weddings on TV and in the movies often inspire brides; a candlelit wedding on "Friends" in a condemned, half-demolished church sent wedding consultants scurrying to recreate the site in their own cities.

■ Requirements

High School

To be a wedding consultant, you have to know about more than wedding traditions and etiquette. Above all, wedding consulting is a business, so take courses in accounting and business management. A bride will be relying on you to stay well within her budget, so you'll need to be able to balance a checkbook and work with figures. A sense of style is also very important in advising a bride on colors, flowers, and decorations—take art courses, and courses in design. A home economics course may offer lessons in floral arrangement, menu planning, fashion, tailoring, and other subjects of use to a wedding planner.

Practically any school organization will offer you a lot of experience in leadership and planning. Also, join your prom and homecoming committees, and various school fund-raising events. You'll develop budgeting skills, while also learning about booking bands, photographers, and other vendors.

Postsecondary Training

A good liberal arts education can be valuable to a wedding consultant, but isn't necessary. Community college courses in small business operation can help you learn about marketing and bookkeeping. Some colleges offer courses in event planning. Courses in art and floral design are valuable, and you should take computer courses to learn how to use databases and graphics programs. Your best experience is going to be gained by actually planning weddings, which may not happen until after you've received some referrals from a professional organization. Various professional organizations offer home study programs, conferences, and seminars for wedding consultants. You should speak to representatives of the organizations to learn more about their programs, and to determine which one would be best for you. June Wedding, Inc., offers a training course available through the mail and at two community colleges. The Association of Bridal Consultants (ABC) has an apprenticeship program which links new members with established consultants. ABC also offers their Professional Development Program, a home-study program including courses in etiquette, marketing, and planning. The Association of Certified Professional Wedding Consultants have their own training program which addresses such topics as starting a business, and dealing with contracts and fees.

Certification or Licensing

Certification isn't required to work as a consultant, but it can help you build your business quickly. Packy received certification from June Wedding, Inc., an organization which also got her her first clients. Brides often contact professional associations directly, and the associations refer the brides to certified consultants in their area. Upon completing any of the training programs mentioned above, you'll receive some form of certification. Higher levels of certification exist for those who have been certified longer.

Other Requirements

From parties to vacations, Packy loves to organize things. "You should be creative," Packy advises, "and like to help people." Good people skills are very important—much of your success will rely on your relationships with vendors, musicians, and all the others you'll be hiring for weddings, as well as good word-of-mouth from previous clients. You should be good at helping people make decisions; moving clients in the right direction will be a very important part of your job. Patience is necessary, as you'll need to create a stress-free environment for the bride.

■ Exploring

Modern Bride, and other bridal magazines, publish many articles on wedding planning, traditions, and trends. Subscribe to a bridal magazine to get a sense of all the ins-and-outs of wedding consulting. Visit the Web sites of professional associations, as well as posting sites like Packy's at "Cleveland Live." Sites featuring questions and answers from professionals can give you a lot of insight into the business. A few cable networks feature series on weddings: "Wedding Story" on The Learning Channel depicts wedding planning documentary style; "Weddings of a Lifetime" on Lifetime Television broadcast the fantasy weddings of chosen couples.

For more hands-on experience, contact the professional organizations for the names of consultants in your area and pay them a visit. Some consultants hire assistants occasionally to help with large weddings. A part-time job with a florist, caterer, or photographer, can also give you a lot of experience in wedding planning.

■ Employers

Most consultants are self-employed. In addition to working for brides and other individuals planning large celebrations, consultants hire on with museums and other non-profit organizations to plan fund-raising events. They also work for retail stores to plan sales events, and plan grand-opening events for new businesses. Hotels, resorts, and restaurants that host a number of weddings sometimes hire consultants in full-time staff positions. Large retail stores also hire their own full-time events coordinators.

Consultants work all across the country, but are most successful in large cities. In an urban area, a consultant may be able to fill every weekend with at least one wedding. Consultants for "destination" weddings settle in popular vacation and wedding spots such as Hawaii, the Bahamas, and Las Vegas.

■ Starting Out

Packy worked for several years in other businesses before finding her way to self-employment. "But all my jobs," she says, "led naturally to consulting." Early on, she worked in her family's chocolate company, Mageros Candies, which gave her a strong entrepreneurial background. She holds an associate degree in business administration, and has worked as an executive secretary, and as a teacher. It was demonstrating magnetic windows for Sears that helped her develop valuable sales, presentation, and people skills. She has also worked for a bridal registry in a department store.

Many people find their way to wedding consulting after careers as events coordinators and planners, or after working weddings as caterers, florists, and musicians. If you have already developed relationships with area vendors and others involved in the planning of weddings, you may be able to start your own business without the aid of a professional organization. But if you're new to the business, it's best to go through a training program for certification. Not only will you receive instruction and professional advice, but you'll receive referrals from the organization.

With guidance, training, and a clear understanding of the responsibilities of the job, a wedding consultant can command a good fee from the onset of a new business. Start-up costs are relatively low, since you can easily work from your home with a computer, an extra phone line, and some advertising. You might want to invest in some basic software to maintain a database, to make attractive graphics for presentation purposes, and to access the Internet. Formal and semi-formal dress wear is also important, as you'll be attending many different kinds of weddings.

■ Advancement

As you gain experience as a consultant, you'll be able to expand your business and clientele. You'll develop relationships with area vendors that will result in more referrals and better discounts. With a bigger business, you can hire regular staff members to help you with planning, running errands, and administrative duties. Some consultants expand their services to include such perks as hand-calligraphed invitations and specially designed favors for receptions. Many consultants maintain Web sites to promote their businesses and provide wedding advice. Packy has already expanded her expertise to the World Wide Web and other media, providing interviews for *Modern Bride Magazine* and *The Wall Street Journal.* She would like to someday put together a packet of informative books for brides.

■ Earnings

Due to the fairly recent development of wedding consulting as a career, there haven't been any comprehensive salary surveys. Also, the number of uncertified consultants, and consultants who only plan weddings part-time, makes it difficult to estimate average earnings. Though consultants make between 10 to 15 percent of a wedding's expense, consultants generally charge a flat rate. Robbi Ernst, founder of June Wedding, Inc., has maintained a survey of consulting fees over the last 14 years. He places initial consultation fees at $275 to $425 per session, with a session lasting about three hours. A consultant may also be hired to oversee all the pre-wedding administrative details for between $1,000 and $2,000. A consultant who works the wedding day only, will charge between $1,200 and $1,800.

For a complete package, with assistance in the months before the wedding and up through the reception, a consultant will charge $3,000 or more. "These fees are based on educated and trained wedding consultants," Robbi says. "Our survey finds that people who have formally trained and certified can get these fees from the onset of their business if they are professional and know what they're doing."

These fees are based on consultants in metropolitan areas with populations of 500,000 or more. In a large city, an experienced consultant can realistically expect to have a wedding planned for every weekend. Because destination weddings are usually much smaller than traditional weddings, consulting fees are lower.

■ Work Environment

For someone who loves weddings and meeting new people, consulting can be an ideal career. Your clients may be stressed out occasionally, but most of the time they're going to be enthusiastic about planning their weddings. During the week, your hours will be spent meeting with vendors, taking phone calls, and working at the computer. Your weekends will be a bit faster paced, among larger crowds, and you'll get to see the results of your hard work—you'll be at the wedding sites, fussing over final details and making sure everything goes smoothly.

Your office hours won't be effected by weather conditions, but on the actual wedding days you'll be expected to get easily and quickly from one place to the other. Bad weather on the day of an outdoor wedding can result in more work for you as you move everything to the "rain site." One of the perks of wedding consulting is taking an active part in someone's celebration; part of your job is making sure everyone has a good time. But you'll also be expected to be present for weddings, receptions, and rehearsal dinners, which means you'll be working weekends and occasional evenings.

■ Outlook

There are currently four professional organizations devoted to furthering the careers of wedding consultants. This will result in more awareness of the career in the public, and therefore a more cautious clientele. Uncertified consultants will find it increasingly difficult to find work. With this increased career awareness, more community colleges will offer courses in wedding and event planning.

According to Robbi Ernst of June Wedding, Inc., the people getting married for the first time are older, better educated, and more sophisticated. They're paying for their own weddings and have more original ideas for their ceremonies. Also, more people are celebrating their anniversaries by renewing their vows with large events. Wedding consultants will want to capitalize on this trend, as well as expand into other ceremonies like bar and bat mitzvahs.

Wedding consulting is one of few career fields which will not likely be effected much by technology. Though fads and trends do change weddings slightly from season to season, wedding ceremonies are based on old traditions. Most brides like to adhere to wedding etiquette, and to have weddings similar to those they imagined as children. Desktop publishing may change the consultant's office somewhat, resulting in some consultants designing their own invitations. Consultants may even expand their areas by assisting brides over the Internet.

■ For More Information

Visit the June Wedding Web site for training and certification information:

June Wedding, Inc. (An Association for Event Professionals)
1331 Burnham Avenue
Las Vegas, NV 89104-3658
Tel: 792-474-9558
Web: http://www.junewedding.com

For information on home-study and professional designations, contact:

Association of Bridal Consultants
200 Chestnut Land Road
New Milford, CT 06776-2521
Tel: 860-355-0464
Web: http://www.trainingforum.com/ASN/ABC/index.html

For information on training programs, home-study, and certification, contact:

National Bridal Service
3122 West Cary Street
Richmond, VA 23221
Tel: 804-355-6945
Web: http://www.nationalbridalservice.com

For information on training programs, contact:

Association of Certified Professional Wedding Consultants
7791 Prestwick Circle
San Jose, CA 95135
Tel: 408-528-9000
Web: http://www.acpwc.com/

■ Related Articles

Business, Personal, and Consulting Services
Entrepreneurs
Bed and Breakfast Owners
Florists
Franchise Owners
Hotel Concierges

Weight Analysts

■ **See Mathematicians**

Welders

■ Overview

Welders operate a variety of special equipment to join metal parts together permanently, usually using heat and sometimes pressure. They work on constructing and repairing automobiles, aircraft, ships, buildings, bridges, highways, appliances, and many other metal structures and manufactured products.

■ History

Although some welding techniques were used more than 1,000 years ago in forging iron blades by hand, modern welding processes were first employed in the latter half of the 1800s. From experimental beginnings, the pioneers in this field developed a wide variety of innovative processes. These included resistance welding, invented in 1877, in which an electric current is sent through metal parts in contact. Electrical resistance and pressure melt the metal at the area of contact. Gas welding, also developed in the same era, is a relatively simple process using a torch that burns a gas such as acetylene to create enough heat to melt and fuse metal parts. Oxyacetylene welding, a version of this process developed a few years later, is a common welding process today. Arc welding, first used commercially in 1889, relies on an electric arc to generate heat. Thermite welding, which fuses metal pieces with the intense heat of a chemical reaction, was first used around 1900.

In the 20th century, the sudden demand for vehicles and armaments and a growing list of industrial uses for welding that resulted from the two world wars have spurred researchers to keep improving welding processes and also have encouraged the development of numerous new processes. Today there are more than 80 different types of welding and welding-related processes. Some of the newer processes include laser-beam welding and electron-beam welding.

■ The Job

Welders use various kinds of equipment and processes to create the heat and pressure needed to melt the edges of metal pieces in a controlled fashion so that the pieces may be joined permanently. The processes can be grouped into three categories. The arc welding process derives heat from an electric arc between two electrodes or between an electrode and the workpiece. The gas welding process produces heat by burning a mixture of oxygen and some other combustible gas, such as acetylene or hydrogen. The resistance welding process obtains heat from pressure and resistance by the workpiece to an electric current. Two of these processes, the arc and gas methods, can also be used to cut, gouge, or finish metal.

Depending on which of these processes and equipment they use, welders may be designated *arc welders, gas welders,* or *acetylene welders; combination welders* (meaning they use a combination of gas and arc welding); or *welding machine operators* (meaning they operate machines that use an arc welding process, electron-beam welding process, laser-beam welding process, or friction welding process). Other workers in the welding field include *resistance machine welders; oxygen cutters,* who use gas torches to cut or trim metals; and *arc cutters,* who use an electric arc to cut or trim metals.

Skilled welders usually begin by planning and laying out their work based on drawings, blueprints, or other specifications. Using their working knowledge of the properties of the metal, they determine the proper sequence of operations needed for the job. They may work with steel, stainless steel, cast iron, bronze, aluminum, nickel, and other metals and alloys. Metal pieces to be welded may be in a variety of positions, such as flat, vertical, horizontal, or overhead.

In the manual arc welding process (the most commonly used), welders grasp a holder containing a suitable electrode and adjust the electric current supplied to the electrode. Then they strike an arc (an electric discharge across a gap) by touching the electrode to the metal. Next, they guide the electrode along the metal seam to be welded, allowing sufficient time for the heat of the arc to melt the metal. The molten metal from the electrode is deposited in the joint and, together with the molten metal edges of the base metal, solidifies to form a solid connection. Welders determine the correct kind of electrode to use based on the job specifications and their knowledge of the materials.

In gas welding, welders melt the metal edges with an intensely hot flame from the combustion of fuel gases in welding torches. First, they obtain the proper types of torch tips and welding rods, which are rods of a filler metal that goes into the weld seam. They adjust the regulators on the tanks of fuel gases, such as oxygen and

WELDERS	
SCHOOL SUBJECTS	Physics Technical/Shop
PERSONAL SKILLS	Mechanical/manipulative Technical/scientific
WORK ENVIRONMENT	Indoors and outdoors Primarily multiple locations
MINIMUM EDUCATION LEVEL	Apprenticeship
SALARY RANGE	$16,000 to $30,000 to $45,000+
CERTIFICATION OR LICENSING	Required for certain positions
OUTLOOK	Little change or more slowly than the average
DOT	810
GOE	05.05.06

acetylene, and light the torch. To obtain the proper size and quality of flame, welders adjust the gas valves on the torch and hold the flame against the metal until it is hot enough. Then they apply the welding rod to the molten metal to supply the extra filler needed to complete the weld.

Maintenance welders, another category of welding workers, may use any of the various welding techniques. They travel to construction sites, utility installations, and other locations to make on-site repairs to metalwork.

Some workers in the welding field do repetitive production tasks using automatic welding equipment. In general, automatic welding is not used where there are critical safety and strength requirements. The surfaces that these welders work on are usually in only one position. Resistance machine welders often work in the mass production of parts, doing the same welding operations repeatedly. To operate the welding machine, they first make adjustments to control the electric current and pressure and then feed in and align the workpieces. After completing the welding operation, welders remove the work from the machine. Welders must constantly monitor the process in order to make sure that the machine is producing the proper weld.

To cut metal, oxygen cutters may use hand-guided torches or machine-mounted torches. They direct the flame of burning oxygen and fuel gas onto the area to be cut until it melts. Then, an additional stream of gas is released from the torch, which cuts the metal along previously marked lines. Arc cutters follow a similar procedure in their work, except that they use an electric arc as the source of heat. As in oxygen cutting, an additional stream of gas may be released when cutting the metal.

■ Requirements

High School

High school graduates are preferred for trainee positions for skilled jobs. Useful high school courses for prospective welders include mathematics, blueprint reading, mechanical drawing, applied physics, and shop. If possible, the shop courses should cover the basics of welding and working with electricity.

Postsecondary Training

Many welders learn their skills in formal training programs in welding, such as those available in many community colleges, technical institutes, trade schools, and the armed forces. Some programs are short term and narrow in focus, while others provide several years of thorough preparation for a variety of good jobs.

A high school diploma or its equivalent is required for admission into these programs. Beginners can also learn welding skills in on-the-job training programs. The length of such training programs ranges from several days or weeks for jobs requiring few skills to a period of one to three years for skilled jobs. Trainees often begin as helpers to experienced workers, doing very simple tasks. As they learn, they are given more challenging work. To learn some skilled jobs, trainees supplement their on-the-job training with formal classroom instruction in technical aspects of the trade.

Various programs sponsored by federal, state, and local governments provide training opportunities in some areas. These training programs, which usually stress the fundamentals of welding, may be in the classroom or on the job and last from a few weeks to a year. Apprenticeship programs also offer training. Apprenticeships that teach a range of metalworking skills, including the basics of welding, are run by trade unions such as the International Association of Machinists and Aerospace Workers.

Certification or Licensing

To do welding work where the strength of the weld is a critical factor (such as in aircraft, bridges, boilers, or high-pressure pipelines), welders may have to pass employer tests or standardized examinations for certification by government agencies or professional and technical associations.

Other Requirements

Employers generally prefer to hire applicants who are in good enough physical condition to bend, stoop, and work in awkward positions. Applicants also need manual dexterity, good eye-hand coordination, and good eyesight, as well as patience and the ability to concentrate for extended periods as they work on a task.

Many people in welding and related occupations belong to unions, including the International Association of Machinists and Aerospace Workers; the International Brotherhood of Boilermakers, Iron Ship Builders, Blacksmiths, Forgers and Helpers; the International Union, United Automobile, Aerospace and Agricultural Implement Workers of America; the United Association of Journeymen and Apprentices of the Plumbing and Pipe Fitting Industry of the United States and Canada; and the United Electrical, Radio, and Machine Workers of America.

■ Exploring

You may be able to arrange to visit a workplace where you can observe welders or welding machine operators on the job. Ideally, such a visit can provide a chance to see several welding processes and various kinds of welding work and working conditions, as well as an opportunity to talk with welders about their work.

■ Employers

Workers in welding occupations work in a variety of settings. About two-thirds of welders are employed in manufacturing plants that produce motor vehicles, ships, boilers, machinery, appliances, and other metal products. Most of the remaining welders work for repair shops or construction companies that build bridges, large buildings, pipelines, and similar metal structures. All welding machine operators work in manufacturing industries.

■ Starting Out

Graduates of good training programs in welding often receive help in finding jobs through their schools' placement offices. The classified ads section of newspapers often carry listings of local job openings. Information about openings for trainee positions, apprenticeships, and government training programs, as well as jobs for skilled workers, may be available through the local offices of the state employment service and local offices of unions that organize welding workers. Job seekers also can apply directly to the personnel offices at companies that hire welders.

■ Advancement

Advancement usually depends on acquiring additional skills. Workers who gain experience and learn new processes and techniques are increasingly valuable to their employers, and they may be promoted to positions as supervisors, inspectors, or welding instructors. With further formal technical training, welders may qualify for welding technician jobs. Some experienced welders go into business for themselves and open their own welding and repair shops.

■ Earnings

The earnings of welding trades workers vary widely depending on the skills need for the job, industry, location, and other factors. On average, welders and welding machine operators can expect annual earnings in the range of $16,000 to $29,000 or more. Highly skilled welders may have earnings ranging from about $26,500 to $45,000 and sometimes much more. In addition to wages, employers often provide fringe benefits, such as health insurance plans, paid vacation time, paid sick time, and pension plans.

■ Work Environment

Welders may spend their workday inside in well-ventilated and well-lighted shops and factories, outside at a construction site, or in confined spaces, such as in an underground tunnel or inside a large storage tank that is being built. Welding jobs can involve working in uncomfortable positions. Sometimes welders work for short periods in booths that are built to contain sparks and glare. In some jobs, workers must repeat the same procedure over and over.

Welders must wear protective gear and follow strict safety precautions.

Welders often encounter hazardous conditions and need to wear goggles, helmets with protective face plates, protective clothing, safety shoes, and other gear to prevent injuries. Many metals give off toxic gases and fumes when heated, and workers must be careful to avoid exposure to such harmful substances. Other potential dangers include explosions from mishandling combustible gases and electric shock. Workers in this field must learn the safest ways of carrying out welding work and always pay attention to safety procedures. Various trade and safety organizations have developed rules for welding procedures, safety practices, and health precautions that can minimize the risks of the job. Operators of automatic welding machines are exposed to fewer hazards than manual welders and cutters, and they usually need to use less protective gear.

■ Outlook

Over the next 10 years or so, overall employment in welding and related occupations is expected to change little. Most job openings will develop when experienced workers leave their jobs. However, the outlook varies somewhat by industry. In manufacturing industries, the trend toward increasing automation, including more use of welding robots, is expected to decrease the demand for manual welders and increase the demand for welding machine operators. In construction, wholesale trade, and repair services, more skilled welders will be needed as the economy grows, because the work tends to be less routine in these industries and automation is not likely to be a big factor. During periods when the economy is in a slowdown, many workers in construction and manufacturing may be laid off.

■ For More Information

American Welding Society
550 NW LeJeune Road
Miami, FL 33126
Tel: 800-443-9353
Web: http://www.aws.org/

International Association of Machinists and Aerospace Workers
9000 Machinists Place
Upper Marlboro, MD 20772
Tel: 301-967-4500
Web: http://www.iamaw.org/

■ Related Articles

Construction

Machining and Machinery

Automobile Collision Repairers

Ironworkers

Plumbers and Pipefitters

Sheet Metal Workers

Welding Technicians

Welding Technicians

■ Overview

Welding technicians are the link between the welder and the engineer and work to improve a wide variety of welding processes. They may supervise, inspect, and find applications for the welding processes. Some technicians work in research facilities where they help engineers test and evaluate newly developed welding equipment, metals, and alloys. Other welding technicians, who work in the field, inspect welded joints and conduct tests to ensure that welds meet company standards, national code requirements, and customer job specifications. These technicians record the results, prepare and submit reports to welding engineers, and conduct welding personnel certification tests according to national code requirements.

■ History

The origins of modern welding reach back thousands of years. Archaeological evidence suggests that primitive forms of welding were known even in prehistoric times. Ancient Egyptians practiced a form of welding similar to our gas welding in which they used a blowpipe and a flame from burning alcohol to heat the metal surfaces to be welded.

During the 19th century, new methods for joining two pieces of metal were developed, and existing methods were refined. Resistance welding was developed in 1857. In this method, the metal parts to be joined are pressed together and a surge of electrical current is sent through the metal at the point of contact. The combination of pressure and heat formed by electrical resistance results in the formation of a solid welded nugget that holds the pieces of metal together. This method was not perfected until 1886 because of the lack of sufficient electrical power.

Thermite welding, which fuses two pieces of metal by means of thermite (a mixture of aluminum and iron oxide), was first used in 1898. Arc welding, a process of fusing metal by means of heat generated from an electrical arc, was developed experimentally in 1881 and was first used commercially in 1889.

Gas welding uses the heat of burning gas, such as a mixture of acetylene and oxygen. Although oxygen was identified in 1774 and acetylene in 1836, the effect of joining the two gases was not discovered until 1895, when improved methods of commercial production of acetylene and oxygen were developed. The year 1903 marked the beginning of the commercial use of the oxyacetylene process in welding and cutting.

During the 20th century, these methods were further improved and dozens of new methods developed. Two other methods now commonly used are brazing and induction welding. In brazing, a filler metal is heated along with the metal surfaces and flows into a specially prepared joint. Induction welding uses an induction coil that generates heat and is very efficient for certain shapes such as small-diameter, thin-walled steel tubing.

■ The Job

The welding technician is the link between the welder and the engineer or production manager. Welding technicians fill positions as supervisors, inspectors, experimental technicians, sales technicians, assistants to welding engineers, and welding analysts and estimators.

Some beginning welding technicians are employed as *welding operators*. They perform manual, automatic, or semiautomatic welding jobs. They set up work, read blueprints and welding-control symbols, and follow specifications set up for a welded product.

As *welding inspectors*, welding technicians judge the quality of incoming materials, such as electrodes, and of welding work being done. They accept or reject pieces of work according to required standards set forth in codes and specifications. A welding inspector must be able to read blueprints, interpret requirements, and have a knowledge of testing equipment and methods.

Closely related to this work is that of the *welding qualification technician*. This person keeps records of certified welders and supervises tests for the qualification of welding operators.

Other welding technicians work as *welding process-control technicians*. These technicians set up the procedures for welders to follow in various production jobs. They specify welding techniques, types of filler wire to be used, ranges for welding electrodes, and time estimates. Welding technicians also provide instructions concerning welding symbols on blueprints, use of jigs and fixtures, and inspection of products.

Equipment maintenance and sales technicians work out of welding supply houses. They set up equipment sold by their company, train welding operators to use it, and troubleshoot for customers.

Welding technicians may also work as *technical writers*. In this position, they work closely with professional staff members to prepare reports and develop articles for technical or professional publications. Welding technicians may also work for in-house publications or trade magazines.

After more years of experience, welding technicians may be employed as welding analysts and estimators, welding engineering assistants, or welding equipment or product salespeople. *Welding analysts and estimators* analyze all the factors involved in a job, such as labor, material, and overhead, to determine what it will cost. *Welding engineering assistants* test welded metal parts, analyze design differences for a variety of welded structures, and determine welding's effects on a variety of metals. Some senior welding technicians may eventually advance in their companies to positions as welding supervisors, welding instructors, and welding production managers.

■ Requirements

High School

Interested high school students should have a good background in English, mathematics, physics, and chemistry. Courses that teach composition and communications skills are particularly important to the prospective technician. Shop courses also will prove helpful.

Postsecondary Training

Most prospective welding technicians should plan to complete a two-year associate's degree program. The U.S. Armed Forces also provide a welding technician training program.

Students with a concentration in welding technology should take comprehensive courses in welding practice or theory. They also need at least one course in applied physics—covering mechanics, heat, light, elementary electricity, materials, and metallurgy—to understand metals common in industry; basic metal production and fabrication techniques; and the structures, physical and chemical properties, and uses of metals.

Welding technicians should understand lattice structure, alloy systems, mechanical tests, and characteristics of strength, elasticity, ductility, malleability, and heat treatment. Elementary chemistry, which relates to metallurgy, is usually covered in metallurgical class and laboratory study.

Another area of training helpful to the welding technician is a course in metal shaping, forming, and machine-shop practice. Knowledge of drilling, tapping, reaming, shaping, and lathe and mill operation is useful. In addition, welding technicians should have some training in electronics. They may be called upon to read an electrical wiring diagram for a particular piece of equipment or to check the voltage on a machine. Courses in nondestructive testing also are helpful for the prospective welding technician.

Certification or Licensing

Welding technicians may qualify for certification as engineering technicians. In addition, they may be certified under any of the many certification programs conducted for welders; however, certification is usually not required for technicians who do not perform actual production welding.

Other Requirements

Welding technicians should enjoy working with their hands and doing research. They must be able to use drawing instruments and gauges, perform laboratory tests, and supervise and control machinery and test equipment. They are also required to collect data and assemble it into written reports. Because welding technicians work with management as well as with production personnel, they must have a sense of responsibility and the ability to get along with people.

■ Exploring

To observe welders or welding technicians at work, you may arrange to take field trips to manufacturing companies that use various

WELDING TECHNICIANS	
SCHOOL SUBJECTS	Physics Technical/Shop
PERSONAL SKILLS	Helping/teaching Technical/scientific
WORK ENVIRONMENT	Indoors and outdoors Primarily multiple locations
MINIMUM EDUCATION LEVEL	Some postsecondary training
SALARY RANGE	$18,000 to $38,000 to $60,000
CERTIFICATION OR LICENSING	Recommended
OUTLOOK	About as fast as the average
DOT	011
GOE	05.01.01
NOC	7265

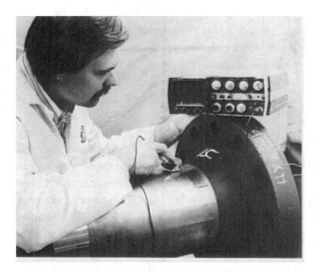

A welding technician performs an ultrasonic examination on a piece of tubing to ensure uniformity in the welding of the product.

welding processes to get an overall view of working conditions and the type of work performed.

Employers

Employment for welding technicians can be found in practically any industry: aircraft, appliances, armaments, automobiles, food processing plants, nuclear energy, radio, railroads, shipbuilding, structural engineering, and television.

Starting Out

Graduates of accredited engineering technology programs seldom have problems finding employment. Employers usually keep in close contact with these schools and often hire able students before graduation. Most graduates of two-year welding technician programs enter industry as welding operators or as assistants to welding engineers or welding production managers. This experience forms the foundation for future problem solving and job growth, allowing the graduate technician to apply both practice and theory.

Advancement

With experience, welding technicians become eligible for higher-paying jobs. Those who advance fastest have displayed a sense of personal initiative, especially in attending courses, seminars, and technical meetings that help broaden their knowledge and prepare them for more responsible positions.

With higher-paying jobs come greater responsibilities. Some welding technicians, for instance, become welding supervisors and take on the responsibility for assigning jobs to workers and showing them how the tasks should

be performed. They must supervise job performance and ensure that operations are performed correctly and economically. Other technicians become welding instructors, teaching welding theory, techniques, and related processes. Finally, some technicians advance to the position of welding production manager, responsible for all aspects of welding production: equipment, materials, process control, inspection, and cost control.

Earnings

The salary range for welding technicians varies according to the individual's function and level of education as well as the geographical location of the business. In general, however, starting salaries for welding technicians who are graduates of post-high school technical programs average $18,000 to $20,000 per year in industry. Salaries will increase with experience. Most graduates of technical or other recognized institutions offering technical training earn salaries that range from $24,400 to $30,400 per year after five years on the job. Those welding technicians in research and development earn an average of $48,000, while section heads earn between $58,000 and $60,000.

Work Environment

Welding technicians are employed by a variety of industries, ranging from aircraft manufacturers to heavy-equipment plants. Working conditions vary from performing tests in clean, well-lighted research and testing laboratories to laying pipeline in the extreme heat of the desert or the cold of Alaska.

In both training and responsibility, welding technicians occupy a position between the professionally trained scientist or engineer and the skilled trades worker. Although no position carries with it the promise of complete happiness, many welding technicians have found that this position offers them status and security, steady employment, and the opportunity to travel.

Outlook

There is an increasing variety of jobs open to welding technicians in industry. This is due to the great number of new inventions and technical processes that use an even wider variety of metals, alloys, and nonmetallic materials that can be joined by welding processes.

Most welding technicians work in industrial production settings; therefore, the actual number of welding technicians employed will be influenced by economic conditions. Anticipated modest industrial expansion through 2006, and increasingly complex modern technology might mean more demand for all kinds of engineering technicians, including welding technicians. This is especially true for those who search for and develop new and technically advanced products, equipment, and procedures.

The diversity of industries in which welding technicians work helps cushion them against threats to employment caused by economic downturns for a particular industry. If economic conditions, and hence employment opportunities, become unfavorable in one industry, there remain others that require the welding technician's training and experience.

■ For More Information

American Welding Society
550 NW LeJeune Road
Miami, FL 33126
Tel: 305-443-9353
Web: http://www.aws.org/

■ Related Articles

Construction

Machining and Machinery

Industrial Engineering Technicians

Welders

Wholesalers

■ **See Sales**

Wildlife Inspectors

■ **See Fish and Game Wardens**

Window Dressers

■ **See Merchandise Displayers**

Winemakers

■ **See Enologists**

Wireless Sales Workers

■ Overview

Wireless sales workers, also known as *cellular sales representatives* and *cellular* or *wireless salespersons,* work for wireless telecommunications service providers to sell wireless products and services to individuals and businesses. The products and services they sell may include cellular phones, cellular phone service, pagers, paging service, and various wireless service options. *Inside salespersons* work onsite at their employers sales offices, helping customers who come in to inquire about wireless service. *Outside sales workers* travel to call on various potential customers at their offices.

■ History

Although you may think of cellular phones as being a product of the late 20th century technology, they actually have their beginnings all the way back in the late 1800s. In 1895, an Italian electrical engineer and inventor named Guglielmo Marconi figured out how to transmit signals from one place to another using electromagnetic waves, creating the first radio. One of Marconi's first major successes came in 1896, when he was able to send signals over a distance of more than a mile. Marconi continued to improve and refine his invention. In 1897, he transmitted signals from shore to a ship at sea 18 miles away, and in 1901, he sent signals a distance of 200 miles. By 1905, many ships were regularly using Marconi's radio to communicate with the shore.

Radio evolved rapidly. By the mid-1920s, more than 1,400 radio stations were broadcasting programming all across America, and by the end of the 1940s, that number had grown to 2,020. Immediately following World War II, radio saw a period of especially rapid development and improvement. Sophisticated transmitting and receiving equipment played a key role in the exploration of space, and in 1969, astronauts on the Apollo mission used a very high-frequency radio communication system to

WIRELESS SALES WORKERS	
SCHOOL SUBJECTS	Business Speech
PERSONAL SKILLS	Communication/ideas
WORK ENVIRONMENT	Primarily indoors One location with some travel
MINIMUM EDUCATION LEVEL	High school diploma
SALARY RANGE	$35,000 to $68,000 to $110,000
CERTIFICATION OR LICENSING	None available
OUTLOOK	Much faster than the average

transmit their voices from the moon back to earth for the first time.

Cellular radio, which is essentially today's cellular phone service, was first tested in the United States in the 1970s. This system, a miniature version of large radio networks, was named "cellular" because its broadcast area is divided into units called cells. Each cell was equipped with its own radio transmitter, with a range of about 1 to 2.5 miles. As a mobile "radiophone" moved through this network of cells, its calls were switched from one cell to another by a computerized system. It was only possible to make calls within the area covered by the network of cells, however; once the radiophone was outside the cellular area, the connection was lost. First tested in Chicago and the Washington, DC, area, this cellular system was soon duplicated in other towns, both large and small throughout the United States. As more and more of the United States became covered with these networks of cells, it became possible to use cellular phones in more places—and these phones became increasingly widespread.

In order to use a cellular phone, one had to have two things: the phone itself and a subscription to a cellular service. Cellular service providers, much like traditional phone companies, signed users up for phone service to be billed on a monthly basis. Often, as part of the sign-up agreement, the new customer received a free or inexpensive cellular phone. As the availability of cellular service has expanded geographically, the number of people signing up for this service has increased dramatically. By 1998, more than 55 million Americans were signed up for cellular service. Cellular, or wireless, sales workers in communities across the United States have been the liaison between the cellular providers and the cellular users. They have been the workers selling the service, explaining its workings, and signing up these new users.

■ The Job

Wireless sales workers sell communications systems, equipment, and services to both businesses and individuals. The products they sell may be divided up into "hard" products—such as pagers or cellular phones—and "soft" products, such as cellular phone service, paging service, voice mail, or phone service options. Most wireless sales workers work for a cellular service provider, trying to persuade prospective buyers to sign up for that provider's phone service. In areas that are covered by two or more cellular providers, the salesperson may have to convince customers to use his or her provider, instead of the competition. In other cases, it is merely a matter of convincing the customer that he or she needs cellular service, explaining what the service provides, and doing the paperwork to begin a contract.

There are two categories of wireless sales workers. Outside sales workers visit prospective clients at their offices. These workers may make appointments in advance, or they may drop in unannounced and ask for a few minutes of the prospective customer's time. This practice is called "cold calling." Outside sales workers often only call on customers within a specific geographic "territory" that may be defined by their employers. The second category, inside sales workers, work in a cellular provider's offices, frequently in a customer showroom. These workers greet and help customers who come into the office to buy or inquire about wireless services.

There are several aspects of a wireless sales representative's job. The first is generating new customers. Sales workers develop lists of possible customers in many different ways. They may ask for referrals from existing customers, call on new businesses or individuals as they move into their assigned territory, or compile names and numbers from business directories or phone books. They may also attend business trade shows or expositions, or join networking groups where they can make contact with people who might be interested in signing up for their service. Once sales workers have their list of possible contacts, they may send out letters or sales brochures, often following up with a phone call and a request for an appointment.

The second aspect of the job is perhaps the most important. This involves talking with prospective customers about the company's services and products and helping them choose the ones that they will be happy with. In order to do this, the sales worker must have a thorough knowledge of all the company's offerings and be able to explain how these offerings can meet the customer's needs. Answering these questions may involve demonstrating the features of different phones or pagers, going over the pricing structures of various service plans, or explaining how the wireless service works and what its geographic limitations are. The sales worker must try to overcome any objections the customer might have about the products or services, and convince him or her to make the purchase. If the salesperson fails to "close the deal" on the first visit, he or she might follow up with more visits, phone calls, or letters.

A wireless sales worker's job usually involves a certain amount of paperwork. When a salesperson makes a sale, he or she may input the customer's billing and credit information into a computer, in order to generate a contract, explain the contract to the customer, and ask him or her to sign it. He or she may also do the paperwork necessary to activate the new customer's phone or pager. Sales workers may also maintain records on all their customers, usually in a computer database.

Many sales workers maintain contact with their customers even after they have made a sale. The salesperson may make a follow-up call to ensure that the customer's service or product is working properly and that he or she is satisfied. He or she may also check back periodically to see if the customer is interested in purchasing "upgrades"—new or improved services or products.

Because wireless technology changes so rapidly, learning about new products and services is an important part of a wireless sales worker's job. He or she may frequently attend seminars or training programs to keep current on the latest in wireless products, in order to be able to explain them to potential customers.

■ Requirements

High School
The minimum educational level needed to become a wireless sales worker is a high school diploma. To prepare for a career in wireless sales, you should choose high school classes that will help you understand and communicate with people. Courses in speech, English, and psychology are all good options for this. You might also want to take classes that help you understand basic business principles, such as business and math courses. Finally, it may be helpful to take some fundamental computer classes, in order to become familiar with keyboarding and using some basic software applications. Like virtually all other offices, wireless offices are typically computerized—so you will probably need to be comfortable operating a computer.

Postsecondary Training
Although there are no formal requirements, it is becoming more and more common for wireless sales workers to have a two-year or four-year college degree. Many employers consider a bachelor's degree in marketing, business, or telecommunications to be especially beneficial. In addition, because wireless services are so heavily dependent upon technology, some wireless sales workers enter the field with a technology-related degree.

Whether a new wireless sales worker has a college degree or not, there are likely to be aspects of the job and the company that he or she is not familiar with. Therefore, most wireless service companies provide training programs for their newly hired workers.

Other Requirements
Successful wireless sales workers have a combination of personal characteristics that allow them to do their jobs well. Perhaps the most important is the ability to connect and communicate with people; without these qualities, it is virtually impossible to be an effective salesperson. Wireless salespersons should enjoy interacting with people, feel comfortable talking with people they do not know, and be able to communicate clearly and persuasively. The ability to work in a high-pressure, competitive environment is also an important characteristic. Many wireless sales workers earn the majority of their income from commissions or bonuses. In addition, most workers are expected to meet monthly or quarterly sales goals that are set by the company. Successful sales workers should be able to handle the stress of working to meet these goals. Self-confidence is another essential quality of good sales workers. Any sales job will involve a certain amount of rejection from customers who are not interested or not ready to buy. Salespersons must be secure and confident enough to avoid letting this rejection affect them on a personal level. The willingness to learn and change is also highly important to success in this field because the industry is always changing.

■ Exploring
You can find out what it is like to be a wireless sales worker by visiting the offices of a local cellular provider. By talking with the sales staff and perhaps observing them as they work, you should be able to get a feel for what the day-to-day job entails. One of the best ways to find out firsthand if you enjoy selling is to find a summer or after-school job in sales. To learn more about wireless technology and the products available, visit your local library and see what books and magazine articles are available—or do some online research, if you have access to the Internet.

■ Employers
Most of the major telecommunications companies throughout the United States offer cellular service in addition to their traditional phone service. AT&T, Sprint, MCI, GTE, Ameritech, Bell Atlantic, Bell South, SBC Communications, and U.S. West all have wireless divisions—and, consequently, wireless sales staff. There are also many smaller wireless providers, such as United States Cellular, Nextel Communications, General Wireless, Telecom, Paging Network, and others. Each of these smaller providers also has a sales staff, although in many cases a much smaller one. These providers are located all throughout the United States, in virtually every medium-sized and large community. You should be able to find a list of them by asking your local librarian for help or by doing a keyword search on "wireless service providers" on the Internet.

■ Starting Out
To find a job in wireless sales, you should first determine which wireless service providers operate in your area. Check directly with these providers to find out if they have any openings, or send them a resume and cover letter. If you are willing to relocate, you might contact the national headquarters of each of the large wireless companies mentioned above to find out what jobs are available nationwide. Many of these companies even have Web sites that list current job openings. You might also keep an eye on local or regional

newspapers. Telecommunication companies, including wireless providers, frequently post job openings in the classified sections of these newspapers. If you have attended a college or university, check with your school's placement office to see if it has any contacts with wireless service providers.

Many wireless providers prefer to hire applicants with proven sales records. This may be especially true in cases where the applicant has only a high school degree. If you find that you are having difficulty obtaining a position in wireless sales, you might consider first taking another sales job—perhaps in electronic or communications equipment—to gain experience. Once you have proven your abilities, you may have better luck being hired for a wireless sales position.

■ Advancement

For most wireless salespersons, advancement comes in the form of increased income via commissions and bonuses. A proven sales worker might earn the title of *senior sales representative* or *senior account executive*. These workers may be given better territories or larger, more important accounts to handle. Some sales workers eventually move into managerial roles, as they expand in their capabilities and knowledge of the company. A sales worker might move into the position of *sales manager,* for example. In this position, he or she would oversee other salespersons, either for the entire organization or for a specific geographic territory. Another advancement possibility in larger companies is that of trainer. In the role of *sales trainer,* a sales worker would be responsible for developing, coordinating, and training new employees in sales techniques.

■ Earnings

For motivated and skilled salespersons, the pay for wireless sales can be quite good. Most companies offer their sales staff a small base salary, and incentive pay in the form of commissions, a bonus, or both. In some cases, the incentive pay can increase the salesperson's base salary by up to 75 percent. Because most salespersons earn the majority of their income through incentive pay, the income level depends greatly upon individual performance.

According to the 1998 *U.S. News & World Report's* "Best Jobs for the Future," the average beginning wireless sales worker might expect to earn around $35,000. A senior sales worker might earn around $68,000, and a top sales executive could make as much as $110,000. Wireless sales managers could expect to earn between $75,000 and $80,000.

Sales workers who are employed by most wireless companies receive a benefits package, which typically includes paid vacation, sick days, and holidays, and health insurance. Outside sales workers may be provided with a company car and an expense account to pay for food, lodging, and travel expenses incurred while traveling on company business.

■ Work Environment

Inside sales representatives work in comfortable customer showrooms. They usually have desks either in the showroom, or in a back office, where they can do their paperwork and perhaps meet with customers. While many sales reps work regular 40-hour weeks, Monday through Friday, it is not at all uncommon for these workers to work longer-than-average weeks. In addition, many wireless sales offices are open on weekends to accommodate customers who cannot come in during the week.

Outside sales workers may spend much of their time traveling to meet onsite with various potential customers. Unless a salesperson's territory is very large, however, overnight travel is uncommon. When not traveling, outside sales workers may spend time in the office, setting up appointments with customers, keeping records, and completing paperwork. Both types of sales workers spend the majority of their time dealing with people. In addition to customer contact, these salespersons often work cooperatively with service technicians and customer service staff.

■ Outlook

Job opportunities for wireless sales workers are expected to grow much faster than the average for all other occupations through the year 2006. The number of people signed up for cellular service rose by 11 million between 1996 and 1998—a 20 percent increase. The sales of pagers and paging service also grew during this time. These numbers are expected to continue to increase. Part of the reason for this growth is that technological advances are making cellular phones and pagers more effective and useful all the time. One of the most recent developments, a microwave-based digital communication technology, is especially expected to increase wireless phone use by offering better quality and range. Wireless service is also being increasingly used to transmit data as well as voice. Examples of wireless data communication include such applications as faxing and Internet access. In addition, new technology and widespread use of cellular services have driven the prices of cellular service down, making it an option for many people who previously couldn't afford it. All of these factors combined should spur the need for a growing number of wireless sales workers.

■ For More Information

For the latest on the wireless industry, job information, and information about Wireless Magazine, *contact or visit the Web site of:*

Wireless Industry Association
9746 Tappenbeck Drive
Houston, TX 77055
Tel: 800-624-6918
Web: http://wirelessdealers.com

Wireless Service Technicians

■ Overview

Wireless service technicians are responsible for maintaining a specified group of cell sites, including the radio towers, cell site equipment, and often the building and grounds for the sites. Most wireless service technicians spend their work time at various locations, visiting each of their cell sites as necessary.

■ History

The concept of cellular communication, as it is used today, was developed by Bell Laboratories in the late 1940s. However, it was based on a much older concept: using radio waves to transmit signals over distances.

Cellular radio, which is essentially today's cellular phone service, was first tested in two U.S. markets in the 1970s. This system, a miniature version of large radio networks, was named "cellular" because its broadcast area is divided into smaller units called cells. Each cell was equipped with its own radio tower, with a range of between 1 and 2.5 miles. As a mobile "radiophone" moved through the network of cells, its calls were switched from one cell to another by a computerized system. As long as the radiophone stayed within this network of cells, wireless communication was possible; once outside the system of cells, however, the connection was lost. After its initial tests in Chicago and Washington, DC, the cellular network was soon duplicated in other towns and cities. As more and more areas throughout the country became "covered" with these networks of cells, it became possible to use cellular phones in more places—and the use of these phones became increasingly widespread.

In 1981, the Federal Communications Commission (FCC) announced that the wireless industry would be regulated. By FCC orders, only 2 competing wireless service providers could be licensed to operate in each geographic market. The FCC also announced that they would begin licensing in 306 large metropolitan areas first. Licensing in rural service areas would come after the metropolitan areas. As licensing got underway and cellular service was provided in ever more areas, the number of wireless service users grew at a rapid pace. By the end of the 1980s, there were almost 4 million cellular subscribers in the United States. By 1992, there were more than 10 million users, 9,000 cell sites, and 1,500 cellular systems throughout the country.

Also in 1992, Ameritech began the country's first commercial trials of digital wireless technology. Digital wireless technology changed the voice to numeric computer code before transmitting it, providing better sound quality and clarity than the traditional, or analog, cellular technology, which carried the voice through radio waves. With continued improvements, digital technology is expected to eventually replace analog cellular phones.

The wireless industry experienced a major change in 1993, when the Omnibus Reconciliation Act was passed. This legislation opened up competition among wireless providers by allowing as many as nine wireless companies to operate in a single market, instead of the two that were previously allowed. With the rapid growth of wireless service throughout the United States, there has been an increased need for qualified, trained people to manage and service the equipment. Each cell site for each wireless carrier requires constant maintenance and troubleshooting to ensure that wireless coverage is not interrupted. The responsibility for maintaining this highly important and expensive equipment is the job of the wireless service technician—a key player in the wireless industry.

The Job

Wireless service technicians are sometimes also called *cell site technicians*, *field technicians,* or *cell site engineers.* These workers maintain *cell sites*—which consist of a radio tower and computerized equipment. Each cell site covers a geographic territory which varies in size. When a wireless call is made by someone within a particular cell site's geo-

WIRELESS SERVICE TECHNICIANS	
SCHOOL SUBJECTS	Computer science Physics
PERSONAL SKILLS	Mechanical/manipulative Technical/scientific
WORK ENVIRONMENT	Primarily indoors Primarily multiple locations
MINIMUM EDUCATION LEVEL	Associate's degree
SALARY RANGE	$35,000 to $45,000 to $53,000
CERTIFICATION OR LICENSING	None available
OUTLOOK	Much faster than the average

graphic territory, radio waves are transmitted to that cell site's antenna. The antenna picks up the radio waves and transmits them through cables to computerized equipment that is typically located in a building adjacent to the antenna. This equipment then "reads" the radio waves, turns them into a computerized code, and sends the information on to a "switching center." At the switching center, the call is transferred to its destination—which might be another wireless phone or a traditional, wireline phone.

The equipment at each cell site—the antenna and computerized equipment—are important pieces of the wireless telecommunications network. If a cell site stops functioning for some reason, wireless users within that site's coverage area may not be able to use their mobile phones. Since many people rely on these devices to receive or transmit important or emergency information, a lapse in coverage can be very serious. Wireless service technicians are responsible for maintaining and troubleshooting the equipment and operations of the cell sites. The majority of cellular communication is currently voice transmissions. However, wireless service is increasingly being used to transmit data, such as Internet access. The data transmission equipment may be a separate, peripheral part of the cell site equipment, and the technician is responsible for maintaining it as well.

Wireless service technicians typically perform both routine, preventive maintenance and troubleshooting of equipment that has malfunctioned. Routine maintenance might include scheduled visits to each cell site to check power levels and computer functions. Technicians often carry laptop computers, which contain sophisticated testing software. By connecting their laptop computers to the cell site equipment, technicians can test to make sure the equipment is functioning as it should. Wireless carriers may also have backup equipment, such as generators and batteries, at their cell sites, to ensure that even if the primary system fails, wireless coverage is still maintained. Technicians may periodically check this backup equipment to make sure it is functional and ready to be used in case of emergency. In addition to maintaining the actual cell site computer equipment, wireless service technicians may be responsible for routine and preventive maintenance of the radio tower, itself, and the building and grounds of the site. In many cases, technicians do not perform the actual physical maintenance on the tower and grounds themselves. Rather, they contract with other service providers to do so and are then responsible for ensuring that the work meets appropriate standards and is done when needed.

The frequency of the scheduled visits to individual cell sites depends upon the technician's employer and the number of sites the technician is responsible for. For example, a technician who is responsible for 10 to 15 sites might be required to visit each site monthly to perform routine, preventive maintenance. In some cases, these sites may be very near each other—perhaps within blocks of each other. In other cases, in less populated areas, the sites may be more than 20 miles apart.

When cell site equipment malfunctions, wireless service technicians are responsible for identifying the problem and making sure that it is repaired. Really, anything that goes wrong with the site is the engineer's responsibility. Technicians run diagnostic tests on the equipment to determine where the malfunction is. If the problem is one that can be easily solved—for example, by replacing a piece of equipment—the technician handles it. If it is something more serious, such as a problem with the antenna or with the local wireline telecommunications system, the technician calls the appropriate service people to remedy the situation.

In addition to routine maintenance and troubleshooting responsibilities, wireless service technicians may have a range of other duties. They may test the wireless system by driving around the coverage area while using a mobile phone. They may work with technicians in the switching center to incorporate new cell sites into the network and make sure that the wireless calls are smoothly transmitted from one cell to another.

■ Requirements

High School

If you are interested in pursuing a career as a wireless service technician, you should take high school classes that will prepare you for further schooling in electronics. Physics will provide the background necessary to understand the theory of electronics. Computer classes are also important because you need a strong understanding of computers, data communications, and operating systems.

Postsecondary Training

A two-year associate's degree in a technical field is the minimum educational level needed to become a wireless service technician. Many technicians obtain degrees in electronics or electronic technology. For these degrees, coursework would likely include both classes and laboratory work in circuit theory, digital electronics, microprocessors, computer troubleshooting, telecommunications, and data communications technology. Other students might opt for degrees in telecommunications management or computer science. Students working toward a telecommunications degree might take classes on such subjects as local area networks, advanced networking technologies, network management, and programming. Computer science courses might include such topics as programming, operating systems, computer languages, and network architecture. Although most wireless service technicians have two-year degrees, some may have four-year degrees in computer science, telecommunications, electronic engineering, or other, similar subjects.

Other wireless service technicians may have military training in electronics or telecommunications.

No matter what sort of educational background new technicians have, they have to learn about the specific equipment used by their employers. Most wireless carriers send their technicians through formal education programs, which are typically offered by equipment manufacturers. In these programs, new technicians learn the operating specifics of the equipment they will be maintaining. A new technician is usually given a smaller number of cell sites to manage when he or she first begins and may be paired with a more experienced technician who can answer questions and conduct on-the-job training.

Other Requirements

The ability to work independently is one of the most important characteristics of a good wireless service technician. Most technicians work on their own, traveling from site to site and performing their duties with little or no supervision. It is also important that technicians be highly responsible. The willingness to learn and to adapt to change is another key personality trait of successful wireless service technicians. The technology is always changing, so you constantly need to learn new equipment. You need to be interested in learning and growing. Finally, because so much of the job involves traveling between cell sites, it is vital that a technician have a valid driver's license and good driving record.

■ Exploring

If you think you might be interested in becoming a wireless service technician, you might first want to explore the ins and outs of electronics, which is a key part of the technician's job. There are numerous books on electronics and electronic theory, geared to various age levels. Check with your high school or local public library to see what you can find on this topic. In addition, many hobby shops or specialty science stores have electronics kits and experiments that allow young people to get some hands-on experience with how electronic circuits work.

To find out more about wireless communications specifically, you might again check for books or magazine articles on the subject in local libraries. You might also contact a wireless provider in your area and ask to talk with a cell technician about his or her job. Finally, a keyword search on the Internet might result in some useful information on the topic as well.

■ Employers

There are dozens of wireless service providers, both large and small, all over the United States. Anywhere that there is wireless service—that is, anywhere that you can use a cellular phone—there is a cell site, owned and maintained by a wireless provider. According to a 1998 Wireless Industry Survey by Moody's Investor Service, the largest wireless providers are AT&T Wireless Services, Inc.; Bell Atlantic Mobile; Sprint PCS; AirTouch Communications; BellSouth; GTE Wireless; Nextel Communications; Western Wireless; Geotek Communications; PrimeCo; PCS; and Omnipoint Communications. Most, if not all, of these companies have Web sites. Many even maintain a listing of available jobs on their site, or provide a phone number you can call to find out about current openings.

In addition to these major players, there are smaller wireless carriers sprinkled throughout the United States in virtually every medium-sized and large community. You should be able to find a list of them by asking your local librarian for help or by doing a key word search on "wireless service providers" on the Internet.

■ Starting Out

One of the best ways to start looking for a job as a wireless service technician is to visit the Web sites of several wireless providers. Many wireless companies maintain jobs sections on their sites, which list available positions. Another possibility is to browse through wireless industry publications, such as *RCR News* (Radio Communications Record), *Wireless Week*, *Telephony*, and *Wireless Review*.

Another way to find your first wireless technician's job is to look for and attend technical job fairs, expos, or exchanges. Because technically and technologically skilled employees are so much in demand, communities frequently have events to allow employers to network with and meet potential employees. Watch local newspapers for similar events in your community. Finally, an excellent source of job leads will be your college's placement office. Many wireless companies visit schools that offer the appropriate degree programs to recruit qualified students for employees. Some companies even offer a co-op program, in which they hire students on a part-time basis while they are still in school.

■ Advancement

In some companies, the natural path of advancement for a wireless service technician is becoming a *switch technician* or *switch engineer*. The switch technician works at the "switching center," which controls the routing of the wireless phone calls.

Another avenue of advancement might be to move into system performance. *System performance workers* strive to maximize the performance of the wireless system. They run tests and make adjustments to ensure that the system is providing the best possible coverage in all areas and that signals from the different cell sites do not interfere with each other.

■ Earnings

Because there is such a demand for qualified and dependable employees in the wireless field, the qualified wireless technician can expect to receive a good salary. According to the *U.S. News and World Report's 1998 Career Guide*, the entry-level technician might average around $35,000 annually. With a bit more experience and a proven record of success, he or she could expect to earn $45,000. At the high end of the salary scale, wireless service technicians can make as much as $53,000.

The job generally comes with other benefits as well. Many wireless companies provide their service technicians with company vehicles. Cellular phones and laptop computers, which technicians need to perform their work, are also common perks. Finally, most major wireless service providers offer a benefits package to their employees, which often includes health insurance, paid vacation, holiday, and sick days, and a pension or 401(k) plan.

■ Work Environment

Cell site technicians who are in charge of several cell sites spend their workweek visiting the different sites. Depending upon how far apart the sites are, this may mean driving a substantial distance. While the actual computer equipment is located inside a building at each cell site location, any work or routine checking of the radio tower requires outside work, in varying kinds of weather.

The management of cell sites is a 24-hour-a-day, 7-day-a-week business. If an alarm system goes off at 3:00 in the morning, a cell site technician must respond. The ability to access the system remotely from his or her laptop computer may save the technician an actual trip to the site. Because the sites must be maintained continuously, wireless service technicians are likely to sometimes work unusual hours.

Most wireless service technicians are not very closely supervised. They generally set their own schedules (with management concurrence) and work alone and independently. They may, however, have to work closely at times with other company employees to integrate new sites into the system, make modifications to the system, or troubleshoot problems.

■ Outlook

Job opportunities for wireless service technicians are expected to grow much faster than the average for all other occupations through the year 2006. The main reason for this increase is the growth of the number of cellular service users. Between 1996 and 1998, the number of people signed up for cellular service increased by 11 million—a 20 percent increase. The sales of pagers and paging service also grew during this time period.

There are several reasons for this growth in wireless users. Perhaps the most significant is the steady decrease in prices for cellular service. Since 1988, the average monthly bill for wireless service has gone from approximately $100 to approximately $40, according to the Cellular Telecommunications Industry Association. A second reason for the growth in users is that coverage areas are increasingly broad and comprehensive. As more and more cell sites are added, more and more parts of the United States have cellular service. Areas that previously had no wireless service are being covered—and consequently, more people have access to and use for cellular phones and pagers.

A third factor in the growth is the continuous improvement in cellular phones and services due to technological advances. One of the most recent innovations is a microwave-based digital communication technology called "personal communications services" (PCS). PCS is expected to increase wireless phone use by offering better quality and range. New technologies are also increasingly allowing people to transmit data as well as voice over wireless connections. Examples of wireless data communication include such applications as faxing and Internet access.

In addition to the growing number of wireless customers, recent years have also seen an increase in wireless companies. This growth was spurred by the Federal Communications Commission's partial deregulation of the industry in 1993, which allowed for as many as nine carriers in a geographic market. This competition has added a large number of technicians' jobs, and is expected to continue to do so.

■ For More Information

For job postings, links to wireless industry recruiters, industry news, and training information, contact or visit the Web site of:

Cellular Telecommunications Industry Association
1250 Connecticut Avenue NW, Suite 200
Washington, DC 20036
Tel: 202-785-0081
Web: http://www.wow-com.com

For the latest on the wireless industry, job information, and information about Wireless Magazine, contact or visit the Web site of:

Wireless Industry Association
9746 Tappenbeck Drive
Houston, TX 77055
Tel: 800-624-6918
Web: http://wirelessdealers.com

■ **Related Articles**

Wood Science and Technology Workers

■ Overview

Wood scientists and technologists experiment to find the most efficient ways of converting forest resources into useful products for consumers. Toward this end, they explore the physical, biological, and chemical properties of wood and the methods used in growing, processing, and using it. Wood science is conducted for both academic and industrial research and is carried out both in labs and on forest grounds. There are more than 2,500 wood scientists and technologists employed throughout the United States and Canada.

■ History

Wood is one of the oldest and most versatile raw materials, providing shelter, tools, furniture, and fuel from prehistoric times to the present. Since the technological revolution, scientists have found ways to treat and process wood in more innovative ways, which has allowed it to be used in many products—everything from plywood to wood plastics—that were unheard of only a few decades ago. From these efforts to find better ways of using wood, the field of wood science technology was developed. Experimentation during World War II marked its modern beginnings, and the field has advanced remarkably since then. Today, more than 5,000 different products use wood as their major raw material.

Before wood can be used in the making of these products, it must be processed. This can include drying, finishing, seasoning, gluing, machining, or treating for preservation. Wood scientists and technologists study these techniques, in conjunction with the chemical and structural properties of wood, to discover new ways to enhance and utilize wood's strength, endurance, and versatility.

Like metallurgy and plastics manufacturing, wood science is concerned with materials engineering. While wood is one of the earth's few renewable resources, it must be wisely grown, harvested, and used to maximize its benefit. Lumber companies have to plan when and which trees to harvest, and what types of trees to plant now for harvesting in 30 years, so as to get the greatest use of the timberlands. Manufacturers of wood products must use the most efficient methods of converting wood into useful products, so as to achieve the least amount of waste and greatest durability. Wood science helps to fulfill these goals, as it works toward more economical and efficient ways to satisfy people's need for wood products.

■ The Job

Some workers in wood science and technology are involved in research. They may work for large wood product firms, universities, or the government on various research projects, ranging from the development of new wood plastics to the designing of methods to cut wood without producing sawdust. Tim Murphy, project manager for Aspen Research Corporation, is one such researcher.

Tim's company is a contract research firm, which researches and designs products for other companies. Tim works in the forest products division, where he and his team of scientists and engineers take on various projects all aimed at making better use of wood products. "Primarily what we work with are engineered wood composites," Tim says. "In trying to develop a better product for our clients,

WOOD SCIENCE AND TECHNOLOGY WORKERS	
SCHOOL SUBJECTS	Biology Chemistry Mathematics
PERSONAL SKILLS	Mechanical/manipulative Technical/scientific
WORK ENVIRONMENT	Indoors and outdoors One location with some travel
MINIMUM EDUCATION LEVEL	Associate's degree
SALARY RANGE	$18,800 to $40,000 to $100,000
CERTIFICATION OR LICENSING	None available
OUTLOOK	Faster than the average
DOT	040
GOE	02.02.02
O*NET	24302C

we focus on a number of specific scientific challenges." Depending upon the product under development, Tim's team might try to enhance the wood's strength or impact resistance by adding fiberglass, adhesives, or polymers to the processed wood.

Another area of work in wood and science technology, which is similar to Tim's work, is manufacturing. This is the most diverse area of the field, with jobs encompassing product and process development, quality control, production control, engineering, personnel relations, and general management.

Some wood and science technology careers are in the area of technical service. *Technical service representatives* for wood industry suppliers use their knowledge of wood to enhance the efficiency of their clients' operations. They may work for a chemical company, a machinery manufacturer, or other service-oriented businesses. State and federal governments also hire workers in this capacity.

Specialists who work in these areas typically fall into one of three categories of workers: wood scientists, wood technologists or wood products engineers, and wood products technicians.

Wood scientists explore the chemical, biological, and physical properties of different woods. They try to find ways to make wood last longer and work better. They also look for faster, more efficient ways to turn wood into lumber, plywood, chemicals, paper, and other products. For example, they develop and improve ways to season or chemically treat wood to increase its resistance to wear, fire, fungi, decay, insects, or marine borers.

All wood must be dried before it can be put to any permanent use in construction or furniture. Wood scientists experiment with methods of drying or curing wood, firing it in kilns at different temperatures and for varying lengths of time, to find ways that will save energy and toughen the wood against warping and other defects.

Because of their thorough knowledge of the properties of different types of wood—pliability, strength, and resistance to wear—wood scientists are able to recommend which woods are most appropriate for certain uses. They can tell what hard and soft woods will make useful lumber and what fast-growing trees can be harvested for plywood and particle board.

While wood scientists often work in the research area of the industry, *wood technologists* work primarily for industry. Like scientists, they are also knowledgeable about the scientific properties of wood, but they look at the subject from a business perspective. These specialists work toward finding new ways to make wood products, with a minimum waste of wood, time, and money. Their jobs may combine responsibilities in areas that are usually considered the exclusive domain of either business or science, including materials engineering, research, quality control, pro-

duction, management, marketing, or sales. "In this field, you really have to want to be involved in both science and business," Tim says. "Normally, scientists don't have anything to do with business, so this is kind of an interesting blend."

In many ways, wood technologists carry on the work of the wood scientists, by investigating the differing qualities of woods. As employees of paper mills, sawmills, or plywood mills, they may test new kilns, test woods, or test new sawmill machines. They may cooperate with foresters who grow and harvest wood. If working for a wood products manufacturer, technologists may experiment with new methods of drying, joining, gluing, machining, and finishing lumber. In many cases, they also direct and oversee the activity of other workers, accumulate and analyze data, and write reports.

Wood technologists also work closely with their clients, who may be wood manufacturers or the buyers and distributors of wood products. If a sporting goods manufacturer is looking for light, resilient woods for making skis, for example, the wood technologist machines, treats, and supplies this wood. The technologist may even direct scientific research into new methods of improving the quality of wood for making skis. The wood technologist also knows how to test the wood for the qualities the buyer needs. New tooling machines may need to be designed, new processing techniques might need to be perfected, and workers may need to be hired or specially trained to accomplish the end goal. The wood technologist often coordinates all of these activities for both the company's purposes and the advancement of wood science.

Wood technologists often oversee the work of *wood products technicians,* who also add to the efficiency and profitability of their companies through their knowledge of wood and its properties. Wood products technicians operate kilns, plywood presses, and other machines used in the processing and treating of wood. They may also work in product testing and quality control, helping technologists and engineers overcome problems and expand the horizons of wood science.

Almost all careers in wood science and technology involve a substantial amount of paperwork. Project documentation, as with any scientific study, is extensive and constant. "The people on my team spend about 50 percent of their time actually in the lab, and the other half of the time on project communications, proposal writing, design layout, and process studies," Tim says.

■ Requirements

Because of the variety of work done in wood science, there are several academic paths that can be taken to prepare for a career in this field. Almost all of these jobs, however, require education after high school.

High School

Because careers in wood science and technology are heavily scientific in nature, you should take as many high school science classes as possible. Biology, chemistry, and earth sciences are likely to be especially helpful. Mathematics is another important focus area for career preparation. Many jobs in this industry are engineering jobs, which require a solid grasp of advanced math skills. Finally, because both written and oral communication plays such a role in scientific research, English and speech classes are good choices to help you develop these skills.

Postsecondary Training

A bachelor's degree is required for employment as a wood scientist or wood technician. Tim obtained both a bachelor's of science degree in wood science and production management and an associate's degree in natural resources. He received his degrees from the University of Minnesota, one of a number of colleges in the United States that offer degrees in wood science, wood technology, forestry, or forest products. Courses of study in these programs may include wood physics, wood chemistry, wood-fluid relationships, wood machinery, and production management. Degree programs in chemistry, biology, physics, mechanical engineering, materials science, or civil engineering can also be very useful if combined with courses in wood science.

For more advanced work as a researcher, a master's degree or doctorate is usually required. Advanced studies include such topics as pulp and paper science, business administration, production management, and forestry-wood sciences. Tim says that the majority of the researchers in his department have master's degrees. "Advanced education is common in the research end of the business," he says.

Apprenticeships used to be the most common method of training for wood products technicians, but today most earn a certificate or associate's degree from a two-year college. Their coursework in wood science includes the identification, composition, and uses of wood. It also covers wood design, manufacturing, seasoning and machining, and methods and materials for making wood products. Some business courses may also be included. Some students may wish to earn a two-year degree first and then transfer to another school to earn a bachelor's degree. "It's possible to get a job as a lab technician with an associate's degree," says Tim, "but the career path for those people is really pretty limited."

Other Requirements

According to Tim, the number one personal requirement for success in this field is the ability to communicate well. "You really have to be able to communicate quickly and effectively, both with your mouth and on paper," he says.

"You also need to have an enjoyment of the sciences and the desire to be in business."

The ability to understand and use scientific theory is important in this career, as is curiosity and persistence in your work habits. Finally, an interest in wood and conservation issues is a plus. Workers in this industry should be environmentally aware as their industry is contingent on the preservation and proper use of wood as a renewable resource.

■ Exploring

High school guidance counselors should be able to provide you with literature and information on careers in this field. If you live near a college that offers a wood science and technology degree, or near a logging industry or manufacturer of wood products, you may be able to talk with students, professors, or employees who can explain the field more fully. It may be even possible to find a part-time or summer job in the wood industry. Finally, any experience in working with wood and wood products will provide you with valuable insight and education. If there are woodworking classes offered in your high school or community, you might consider taking them. By working with wood, you can begin to understand the differences in wood types and how they respond to various kinds of woodworking procedures.

■ Employers

There are more than 2,500 wood scientists and technologists employed throughout the United States and Canada. Most are employed in private industry. Firms dealing with forest products, such as mills, manufacturers of wood products, suppliers to the wood products industry, forest products associations, and paper and pulp companies all hire these kinds of workers. Independent contract research firms, like Tim's company, may also be sources of employment. Universities and federal and state agencies, such as the Extension Service, hire wood science and technology experts to work on various research projects.

Geographically, careers in wood science and technology tend to be situated near large wood-producing forests and mills. Most wood science technologists work along the Eastern Seaboard, in the North Central States, in the Pacific Northwest, and in the southern states from Virginia to eastern Texas.

■ Starting Out

Tim feels that wood science and technology jobs are not hard for qualified applicants to come by. "I was at the University of Minnesota, and a company contacted me and hired me right out of the university," he says. "The companies really recruited us heavily."

This is not uncommon. Many forestry firms recruit new employees during visits to campus, and new graduates of wood science and technology programs often learn about employment opportunities through their colleges' career placement offices. Other sources of information are professional groups, which may maintain job referral or resume services, and trade magazines, which often carry want ads for job openings. Information on jobs with the federal government can be obtained from the Office of Personnel Management.

■ Advancement

Moving ahead in the wood science field depends on ingenuity, skills, and the ability to handle important projects. There is no typical career path, and advancement can come in the form of promotions, pay raises, and more important assignments. People with management skills may rise to become sales managers, division chiefs, or directors, although the size of the company often dictates the opportunities for advancement. Larger companies obviously offer more places within the organization, so advancement may be quicker than in a smaller company.

An advanced degree, such as a master's or a Ph.D., can be the ticket to advancement for those working in research; workers in this field may be granted permission to conduct independent research or be promoted to heads of research operations. Wood science and technology employees in the business area of the industry may find that additional schooling makes them better candidates for higher administrative positions. Wood products technicians may find that earning a bachelor's degree can help them move up to the position of wood technologist.

■ Earnings

Salary levels in the wood sciences depend on the individual's employer, experience, level of education, and work performed. According to the USDA Forest Products Laboratory, a wood science and technology worker with an associate's degree would earn a starting salary of approximately, $18,800. With a bachelor's degree a new employee might expect to make around $26,000, and with a master's, $32,000. A new employee who held a Ph.D. would likely earn $46,000. With advanced education and a great deal of experience, federal wood science and technology workers might earn up to $100,000 annually.

Workers in the private sector earn slightly higher starting salaries. According to recent data from the Society of Wood Science and Technology, an entry-level worker with a bachelor's degree could expect to earn around $35,000. With a master's he or she might earn around $42,000, and with a doctorate, $50,000. Wages for beginning wood products technicians are somewhat less, usually comparable to those for other types of technicians.

Usually wood scientists, wood technologists, and wood products technicians receive fringe benefits, including health insurance, pension plans, and paid vacations.

■ Work Environment

Depending on the type of work they perform, wood science specialists operate in a variety of settings, from the office to the open forest. Wood scientists and researchers work in laboratories and, if they are on university faculty, in classrooms. Their experimental work may take them to tree farms and forests. Wood technologists and technicians may work in offices, manufacturing plants, sawmills, or research facilities. Those technologists who are involved in sales often need to travel.

Work may be solitary or as part of a team, depending upon the position and the project. And workers in the lab may use a wide variety of equipment—anything from a table saw to a word processing program to a chemical analytical device, according to Tim.

These types of employees work a normal 40-hour week, but extra hours may be required in certain situations. Technologists who supervise technicians and other production workers may have to work second and third shifts. Administrators may also have to put in extra hours. Workers paid by the hour often get overtime pay, but salaried employees do not get extra monetary compensation for their extra hours.

Wood science and technology specialists have a difficult but rewarding job: applying scientific principles such as chemistry, physics, and mathematics to a commonplace raw material and finding new ways for society to use wood in more productive, efficient ways. Many who work in this field enjoy the challenge it presents and feel fulfilled by helping to better understand and more efficiently utilize one of the earth's most necessary resources.

■ Outlook

Wood technology is a relatively new science, with breakthroughs in products and technology occurring frequently. It is also a field in which the supply of qualified wood scientists and technologists is short of the demand. Therefore, the employment outlook for these workers in this field is expected to be very good.

The demand for wood products is increasing rapidly. At the same time, the costs of growing and harvesting timber and processing wood products are rising rapidly. Wood manufacturers need the skills of wood science specialists to keep their operations profitable and efficient and to help them compete with plastics manufacturers and the makers of other wood substitutes. "There's a lot of activity in this field right now because of the shortage of wood products," Tim says. "Companies are spending more money on product development in this area."

Conservation programs will affect the industry both positively and negatively. Pressure to reduce lumber harvests will continue to increase, particularly in threatened areas, such as the rain forest. Those pressures, however, will force increased study of ways to better utilize wood currently being harvested. "The main thrust of the industry right now is to use everything the tree has to offer," Tim says. "What we're trying to do is to optimize utilization of wood."

Although the employment outlook for wood science and technology workers is expected to be strong, it is heavily tied to the overall economy. Because the bulk of all forest products are used in the construction industry, a downturn in new construction means a downturn in all forest-related careers. "Our industry is tightly linked to the housing starts index," Tim says. "When those start to go down, you get nervous about your job. It can be a roller coaster ride with the economy."

■ For More Information

For a brochure or video on careers, or a listing of schools offering degrees in wood science and technology, contact:

Society of Wood Science and Technology
One Gifford Pinchot Drive
Madison, WI 53705-2398
Tel: 608-231-9347
Web: http://www1.fpl.fs.fed.us/swst

For a career packet and a listing of job opportunities and employers in the area of wood science and technology, contact:

Society of American Foresters
5400 Grosvenor Lane
Bethesda, MD 20814-2198
Tel: 301-897-8720
Web: http://www.safnet.org

■ Related Articles

Agriculture
Pulp and Paper
Wood
Biochemists
Chemists
Foresters
Forestry Technicians
Furniture Manufacturing Occupations
Logging Industry Workers
Paper Processing Occupations

Woodworkers

■ **See Furniture Manufacturing Occupations**

Writers

■ Overview

Writers are involved with expressing, editing, promoting, and interpreting ideas and facts in written form for books, magazines, trade journals, newspapers, technical studies and reports, company newsletters, radio and television broadcasts, and advertisements.

Writers develop fiction and nonfiction ideas for plays, novels, poems, and other related works; report, analyze, and interpret facts, events, and personalities; review art, music, drama, and other artistic presentations; and persuade the general public to choose or favor certain goods, services, and personalities.

■ History

The skill of writing has existed for thousands of years. Papyrus fragments with writing by ancient Egyptians date from about 3000 BC, and archaeological findings show that the Chinese had developed books by about 1300 BC. A number of technical obstacles had to be overcome before printing and the profession of writing evolved. Books of the Middle Ages were copied by hand on parchment. The ornate style that marked these books helped ensure their rarity. Also, few people were able to read. Religious fervor prohibited the reproduction of secular literature.

The development of the printing press by Johannes Gutenberg (1400?-1468?) in the middle of the 15th century and the liberalism of the Protestant Reformation, which helped encourage a wider range of publications, greater literacy, and the creation of a number of works of literary merit, helped develop the publishing industry. The first authors worked directly with printers.

The modern publishing age began in the 18th century. Printing became mechanized, and the novel, magazine, and newspaper developed. The first newspaper in the American colonies appeared in the early 18th

WRITERS	
SCHOOL SUBJECTS	English Journalism
PERSONAL SKILLS	Communication/ideas Helping/teaching
WORK ENVIRONMENT	Primarily indoors Primarily one location
MINIMUM EDUCATION LEVEL	Bachelor's degree
SALARY RANGE	$21,000 to $30,000 to $75,000+
CERTIFICATION OR LICENSING	None available
OUTLOOK	Faster than the average
DOT	131
GOE	01.01.02
NOC	5121

century, but it was Benjamin Franklin (1706-1790) who, as editor and writer, made the *Pennsylvania Gazette* one of the most influential in setting a high standard for his fellow American journalists. Franklin also published the first magazine in the colonies, *The American Magazine,* in 1741.

Advances in the printing trades, photoengraving, retailing, and the availability of capital produced a boom in newspapers and magazines in the 19th century. Further mechanization in the printing field, such as the use of the Linotype machine, high-speed rotary presses, and special color reproduction processes, set the stage for still further growth in the book, newspaper, and magazine industry.

In addition to the print media, the broadcasting industry has contributed to the development of the professional writer. Film, radio and television are sources of entertainment, information, and education that provide employment for thousands of writers.

■ The Job

Writers work in the field of communications. Specifically, they deal with the written word, whether it is destined for the printed page, broadcast, computer screen, or live theater. The nature of their work is as varied as the materials they produce: books, magazines, trade journals, newspapers, technical reports, company newsletters and other publications, advertisements, speeches, scripts for motion picture and stage productions, and scripts for radio and television broadcast. Writers develop ideas and write for all media.

Prose writers for newspapers, magazines, and books share many of the same duties. First they come up with an idea for an article or book from their own interests or are assigned a topic by an editor. The topic is of relevance to the particular publication; for example, a writer for a magazine on parenting may be assigned an article on car seat safety. Then writers begin gathering as much information as possible about the subject through library research, interviews, the Internet, observation, and other methods. They keep extensive notes from which they will draw material for their project. Once the material has been organized and arranged in logical sequence, writers prepare a written outline. The process of developing a piece of writing is exciting, although it can also involve detailed and solitary work. After researching an idea, a writer might discover that a different perspective or related topic would be more effective, entertaining, or marketable.

When working on assignment, writers submit their outlines to an editor or other company representative for approval. Then they write a first draft of the manuscript, trying to put the material into words that will have the desired effect on their audience. They often rewrite or polish sections of the material as they proceed, always searching for just the right way of imparting information

or expressing an idea or opinion. A manuscript may be reviewed, corrected, and revised numerous times before a final copy is submitted. Even after that, an editor may request additional changes.

Writers for newspapers, magazines, or books often specialize in their subject matter. Some writers might have an educational background that allows them to give critical interpretations or analyses. For example, a health or science writer for a newspaper typically has a degree in biology and can interpret new ideas in the field for the average reader.

Columnists/commentators analyze news and social issues. They write about events from the standpoint of their own experience or opinion. Critics review literary, musical, or artistic works and performances. *Editorial writers* write on topics of public interest, and their comments, consistent with the viewpoints and policies of their employers, are intended to stimulate or mold public opinion. *Newswriters* work for newspapers, radio, or TV news departments, writing news stories from notes supplied by reporters or wire services.

Corporate writers and writers for nonprofit organizations have a wide variety of responsibilities. These writers may work in such places as a large insurance corporation or for a small nonprofit religious group where they may be required to write news releases, annual reports, speeches for the company head, or public relations materials. Typically they are assigned a topic with length requirements for a given project. They may receive raw research materials, such as statistics, and are expected to conduct additional research, including personal interviews. These writers must be able to write quickly and accurately on short deadlines, while also working with people whose primary job is not in the communications field. The written work is submitted to a supervisor and often a legal department for approval; rewrites are a normal part of this job.

Copywriters write copy that is primarily designed to sell goods and services. Their work appears as advertisements in newspapers, magazines, and other publications or as commercials on radio and television broadcasts. Sales and marketing representatives first provide information on the product and help determine the style and length of the copy. The copywriters conduct additional research and interviews; to formulate an effective approach, they study advertising trends and review surveys of consumer preferences. Armed with this information, copywriters write a draft that is submitted to the account executive and the client for approval. The copy is often returned for correction and revision until everyone involved is satisfied. Copywriters, like corporate writers, may also write articles, bulletins, news releases, sales letters, speeches, and other related informative and promotional material. Many copywriters are employed in advertising agencies. They also may work for public relations firms or in communications departments of large companies.

Technical writers can be divided into two main groups: those who convert technical information into material for the general public, and those who convey technical information between professionals. Technical writers in the first group may prepare service manuals or handbooks, instruction or repair booklets, or sales literature or brochures; those in the second group may write grant proposals, research reports, contract specifications, or research abstracts.

Screenwriters prepare scripts for motion pictures or television. They select or are assigned a subject, conduct research, write and submit a plot outline and narrative synopsis (treatment), and confer with the producer and/or director about possible revisions. Screenwriters may adapt books or plays for film and television dramatizations. They often collaborate with other screenwriters and may specialize in a particular type of script or writing.

Playwrights do similar writing for the stage. They write dialogue and describe action for plays that may be tragedies, comedies, or dramas, with themes sometimes adapted from fictional, historical, or narrative sources. Playwrights combine the elements of action, conflict, purpose, and resolution to depict events from real or imaginary life. They often make revisions even while the play is in rehearsal.

Continuity writers prepare the material read by radio and television announcers to introduce or connect various parts of their programs.

Novelists and *short story writers* create stories that may be published in books, magazines, or literary journals. They take incidents from their own lives, from news events, or from their imaginations and create characters, settings, actions, and resolutions. *Poets* create narrative, dramatic, or lyric poetry for books, magazines, or other publications, as well as for special events such as commemorations. These writers may work with literary agents or editors who help guide them through the writing process, which includes research of the subject matter and an understanding of the intended audience. Many universities and colleges offer graduate degrees in creative writing. In these programs, students work intensively with published writers to learn the art of storytelling.

Writers can be employed either as in-house staff or as freelancers. Pay varies according to experience and the position, but freelancers must provide their own office space and equipment such as computers and fax machines. Freelancers also are responsible for keeping tax records, sending out invoices, negotiating contracts, and providing their own health insurance.

■ Requirements

High School

High school courses that are helpful include English, literature, foreign languages, general science, social studies, computer science, and typing. The ability to type is almost a requisite for all positions in the communications field as is familiarity with computers.

Postsecondary Training

Competition for writing jobs almost always demands the background of a college education. Many employers prefer you have a broad liberal arts background or majors in English, literature, history, philosophy, or one of the social sciences. Other employers desire communications or journalism training in college. Occasionally a master's degree in a specialized writing field may be required. A number of schools offer courses in journalism, and some of them offer courses or majors in book publishing, publication management, and newspaper and magazine writing.

In addition to formal course work, most employers look for practical writing experience. If you have served on high school or college newspapers, yearbooks, or literary magazines, you will make a better candidate, as well as if you have worked for small community newspapers or radio stations, even in an unpaid position. Many book publishers, magazines, newspapers, and radio and television stations have summer internship programs that provide valuable training if you want to learn about the publishing and broadcasting businesses. Interns do many simple tasks, such as running errands and answering phones, but some may be asked to perform research, conduct interviews, or even write some minor pieces.

Writers who specialize in technical fields may need degrees, concentrated course work, or experience in specific subject areas. This applies frequently to engineering, business, or one of the sciences. Also, technical communications is a degree now offered at many universities and colleges.

If you wish to enter positions with the federal government, you will have to take a civil service examination and meet certain specified requirements, according to the type and level of position.

Other Requirements

Writers should be creative and able to express ideas clearly, have a broad general knowledge, be skilled in research techniques, and be computer literate. Other assets include curiosity, persistence, initiative, resourcefulness, and an accurate memory. For some jobs—on a newspaper, for example, where the activity is hectic and deadlines short—the ability to concentrate and produce under pressure is essential.

■ Exploring

As a high school or college student, you can test your interest and aptitude in the field of writing by serving as a reporter or writer on school newspapers, yearbooks, and literary magazines. Various writing courses and workshops offer the opportunity to sharpen writing skills.

Small community newspapers and local radio stations often welcome contributions from outside sources, although they may not have the resources to pay for them. Jobs in bookstores, magazine shops, and even newsstands offer a chance to become familiar with the various publications.

Information on writing as a career may also be obtained by visiting local newspapers, publishers, or radio and television stations and interviewing some of the writers who work there. Career conferences and other guidance programs frequently include speakers on the entire field of communications from local or national organizations.

■ Employers

Nearly a third of salaried writers and editors work for newspapers, magazines, and book publishers, according to the *Occupational Outlook Handbook*. Writers are also employed by advertising agencies, in radio and television broadcasting, public relations firms, and on journals and newsletters published by business and nonprofit organizations, such as professional associations, labor unions, and religious organizations. Other employers are government agencies and film production companies.

■ Starting Out

A fair amount of experience is required to gain a high-level position in the field. Most writers start out in entry-level positions. These jobs may be listed with college placement offices, or they may be obtained by applying directly to the employment departments of the individual publishers or broadcasting companies. Graduates who previously served internships with these companies often have the advantage of knowing someone who can give them a personal recommendation. Want ads in newspapers and trade journals are another source for jobs. Because of the competition for positions, however, few vacancies are listed with public or private employment agencies.

Employers in the communications field usually are interested in samples of published writing. These are often assembled in an organized portfolio or scrapbook. Bylined or signed articles are more impressive than stories whose source is not identified.

Beginning positions as a junior writer usually involve library research, preparation of rough drafts for part or all of a report, cataloging, and other related writing tasks. These are generally carried on under the supervision of a senior writer.

Some technical writers have entered the field after working in public relations departments or as technicians or research assistants, then transferring to technical writing as openings occur. Many firms now hire writers directly upon application or recommendation of college professors and placement offices.

■ Advancement

Most writers find their first jobs as editorial or production assistants. Advancement may be more rapid in small companies, where beginners learn by doing a little bit of everything and may be given writing tasks immediately. In large firms, duties are usually more compartmentalized. Assistants in entry-level positions are assigned such tasks as research, fact checking, and copyrighting, but it generally takes much longer to advance to full-scale writing duties.

Promotion into more responsible positions may come with the assignment of more important articles and stories to write, or it may be the result of moving to another company. Mobility among employees in this field is common. An assistant in one publishing house may switch to an executive position in another. Or a writer may switch to a related field as a type of advancement: from publishing, for example, to teaching, public relations, advertising, radio, or television.

A technical writer can be promoted to positions of responsibility by moving from such jobs as writer to technical editor to project leader or documentation manager. Opportunities in specialized positions also are possible.

Freelance or self-employed writers earn advancement in the form of larger fees as they gain exposure and establish their reputations.

■ Earnings

In 1996, beginning writers and researchers received starting salaries of about $21,000 a year, according to the Dow Jones Newspaper Fund. Experienced writers and researchers are paid $30,000 and over, depending on their qualifications and the size of the publication they work on. In book publishing, some divisions pay better than others.

The salaries of technical writers are slightly higher than those of other professional writers. In general, the median beginning wage for those with a college degree is $28,600 per year. The salaries of experienced writers ranges from about $45,000 to over $67,000 per year. Earnings of those in administrative and supervisory positions are somewhat higher.

Technical writers working for the federal government average $47,400; other types of writers earn an average of $39,000 a year.

In addition to their salaries, many writers earn some income from freelance work. Part-time freelancers may earn from $5,000 to $15,000 a year. Freelance earnings vary widely. Full-time established freelance writers may earn up to $75,000 a year.

■ Work Environment

Working conditions vary for writers. Although the workweek usually runs 35 to 40 hours, many writers work overtime. A publication that is issued frequently has more deadlines closer together, creating greater pressures to meet them. The work is especially hectic on newspapers and at broadcasting companies, which operate seven days a week. Writers often work nights and weekends to meet deadlines or to cover a late-developing story.

Most writers work independently, but they often must cooperate with artists, photographers, rewriters, and advertising people who may have widely differing ideas of how the materials should be prepared and presented.

Physical surroundings range from comfortable private offices to noisy, crowded newsrooms filled with other workers typing and talking on the telephone. Some writers must confine their research to the library or telephone interviews, but others may travel to other cities or countries or to local sites, such as theaters, ballparks, airports, factories, or other offices.

The work is arduous, but writers are seldom bored. Each day brings new and interesting problems. The jobs occasionally require travel. The most difficult element is the continual pressure of deadlines. People who are the most content as writers enjoy and work well with deadline pressure.

■ Outlook

The employment of writers is expected to increase faster than the average rate of all occupations through 2006. The demand for writers by newspapers, periodicals, book publishers, and nonprofit organizations is expected to increase. Advertising and public relations will also provide job opportunities.

The major book and magazine publishers, broadcasting companies, advertising agencies, public relations firms, and the federal government account for the concentration of writers in large cities such as New York, Chicago, Los Angeles, Boston, Philadelphia, San Francisco, and Washington, DC. Opportunities in small newspapers, corporations, and professional, religious, business, technical, and trade publications can be found throughout the country.

People entering this field should realize that the competition for jobs is extremely keen. Beginners, especially, may have difficulty finding employment. Of the thousands who graduate each year with degrees in English, journalism, communications, and the liberal arts, intending to establish a career as writer, many turn to other occupations when they find that applicants far outnumber the job openings available. College students would do well to keep this in mind and prepare for an unrelated alternate career in the

event they are unable to obtain a position as writer; another benefit of this approach is that, at the same time, they will become qualified as writers in a specialized field. The practicality of preparing for alternate careers is borne out by the fact that opportunities are best in firms that prepare business and trade publications and in technical writing.

Potential writers who end up working in a different field may be able to earn some income as freelancers, selling articles, stories, books, and possibly TV and movie scripts, but it is usually difficult for anyone to be self-supporting entirely on independent writing.

■ For More Information

Information on writing and editing careers in the field of communications is available from:

National Association of Science Writers
PO Box 294
Greenlawn, NY 11740
Tel: 516-757-5664

This organization offers student memberships for those interested in opinion writing.

National Conference of Editorial Writers
6223 Executive Boulevard
Rockville, MD 20852
Tel: 301-984-3015
Web: http://www.ncew.org

■ Related Articles

Advertising and Marketing
Book Publishing
Broadcasting
Literary Arts
Newspapers and Magazines
Publishing
Telecommunications
Advertising Workers
Book Editors
Columnists
Editors
Foreign Correspondents
Magazine Editors
Newspaper Editors
Public Relations Specialists
Reporters
Research Assistants
Screenwriters
Technical Writers and Editors

Zoo and Aquarium Curators

■ Overview

Zoo and aquarium curators are the chief employees responsible for the care of the creatures found at zoos and aquariums; they oversee the various sections of the animal collections, such as birds, mammals, and fishes.

■ History

Ancient Sumerians kept fish in manmade ponds around 4,500 years ago. By 1150 BC, pigeons, elephants, antelope, and deer were held captive for taming in such areas as the Middle East, India, and China. In 1000 BC, a Chinese emperor named Wen Wang built a zoo and called it the Garden of Intelligence. Also around this time, the Chinese and Japanese were breeding and raising goldfish and carp for their beauty.

Zoos were abundant in ancient Greece; animals were held in captivity for purposes of study in nearly every city-state. In early Egypt and Asia, zoos were created mainly for public show, and during the Roman Empire, fish were kept in ponds and animals were collected both for arena showings and for private zoos. A fantastic zoo, with 300 keepers taking care of birds, mammals, and reptiles, was created in Mexico in the early 16th century by Hernando Cortes, the Spanish conqueror.

Zoo and aquarium professions as we know them today began to be established around the mid-18th century with the construction of various extravagant European zoos. The Imperial Menagerie of the Schönbrunn Zoo in Vienna, Austria, was opened in 1765 and still operates to this day. One of the most significant openings occurred in 1828 at the London Zoological Society's Regent's Park. The London Zoo continues to have one of the world's most extensive and popular collection of animals, with more than 8,900 examples of 1,200 species, including some of the rarest animals. The world's first public aquarium was also established at Regent's Park, in 1853, after which aquariums were built in other European cities. In the United States, P. T. Barnum was the first to establish a display aquarium, which opened in New York in 1856.

Today, curators have a host of responsibilities involved with the operation of zoos and aquariums. Although many zoos and aquariums are separate places, there are also zoos that contain aquariums as part of their facilities. There are both public and private institutions, large and small, and curators often contribute their knowledge to the most effective methods of design, maintenance, and administration for these institutions.

■ The Job

General curators of zoos and aquariums oversee the management of an institution's entire animal collection and animal management staff. They help the *director* coordinate activities, such as education, collection planning, exhibit design, new construction, research, and public services. They meet with the director and other members of the staff to create long term strategic plans. General curators may have public relations and development responsibilities, such as meeting with the media and identifying and cultivating donors. In most institutions, general curators develop policy; other curators implement policy.

Animal curators are responsible for the day-to-day management of a specific portion of a zoo's or aquarium's animal collection (as defined taxonomically, such as mammals or birds, or ecogeographically, such as the Forest Edge or the Arizona Trail); the people charged with caring for that collection, including *assistant curators, zookeepers,* administrative staff such as secretaries, as well as researchers, students, and volunteers; and the associated facilities and equipment.

For example, the curator in charge of the mammal department of a large zoo would be responsible for the care of such animals as lions, tigers, monkeys, and elephants. He or she might oversee nearly 1,000 animals, representing about 200 different species, and scores of employees and have a multimillion dollar budget.

Assistant curators report to curators and assist in animal management tasks and decisions. They may have extensive supervisory responsibilities.

Curators have diverse responsibilities and their activities vary widely from day to day. They oversee animal husbandry procedures, including the daily care of the animals, establish proper nutritional programs, and manage animal health delivery in partnership with the veterinary staff. They develop exhibits, educational programs, and visitor services and participate in research and conservation activities. They maintain inventories of animals and other records, and they recommend and implement acquisitions and dispositions of animals. Curators serve as liaisons with other departments.

Curators prepare budgets and reports. They interview and hire new workers. When scientific conferences are held, curators attend them as representatives of the institutions for which they work. They are often called upon to write articles for scientific journals and perhaps provide information for newspaper reports and magazine stories. They may coordinate or participate in on site research or conservation efforts. To keep abreast with developments in their field, curators spend a lot of time reading.

Curators meet with the general curator, the director, and other staff to develop the objectives and philosophy of the institution and decide on the best way to care for and exhibit the animals. They must be knowledgeable about the animals' housing requirements, daily care, medical procedures, dietary needs, and social and reproduction habits. Curators represent their zoos or aquariums in collaborative efforts with other institutions, such as the more than 80 American Zoo and Aquarium Association (AZA) Species Survival Plans that target individual species for intense conservation efforts by zoos and aquariums. In this capacity, curators may exchange information, negotiate breeding loans, or assemble the necessary permits and paperwork to effect the transfers. Other methods of animal acquisition coordinated by curators involve purchases from animal dealers or private collectors and collection of nonendangered species from the wild. Curators may arrange for the quarantine of newly acquired animals. They may arrange to send the remains of dead animals to museums or universities for study.

Curators often work on special projects. They may serve on multidisciplinary committees responsible for planning and constructing new exhibits. Curators interface with colleagues from other states and around the world in collaborative conservation efforts.

Although most zoo and aquarium curators check on the collection on a regular basis, they are usually more involved with administrative issues than animal husbandry. Much of their time is spent in meetings or writing email or on talking on the phone. "I value the times I get out to do rounds," said Mike Mulligan, curator of fishes at the John G. Shedd Aquarium in Chicago, Illinois. "It's amazing what you miss if you're not out there every day. You see snapshots rather than the natural progression. But the best part of my job is being involved in planning the future of the aquarium. It's very challenging and rewarding to be a player on the institutional level."

In addition to animal curators, large institutions employ curators whose responsibilities involve areas other than animal husbandry, such as research, conservation, exhibits, horticulture, and education.

■ Requirements

High School

High school students who want to prepare for careers in upper management in zoos and aquariums should take classes in the sciences, especially biology, microbiology, chemistry, and physics, as well as in mathematics, computer science, language, and speech.

Postsecondary Training

The minimum formal educational requirement for curators is a bachelor's degree in one of the biological sciences, such as zoology, ecology, biology, mammalogy, and ornithology. Course work should include biology, invertebrate zoology, vertebrate physiology, comparative anatomy, organic chemistry, physics, microbiology, and virology. Electives are just as important, particularly writing, public speaking, computer science, and education. Even studying a second language can be helpful.

Typically, an advanced degree is required for curators employed at larger institutions—many curators are required to have a doctoral degree. But advanced academic training alone is insufficient; it takes years of on-the-job experience to master the practical aspects of exotic animal husbandry. Also required are management skills, supervisory experience, writing ability, research experience, and sometimes the flexibility to travel.

A few institutions offer curatorial internships designed to provide practical experience. Several major zoos offer formal keeper training courses as well as on-the-job training programs to students who are studying areas related to animal science and care. Such programs could lead to positions as assistant curators. Contact the AZA for further information about which schools and animal facilities are involved in internship programs.

Other Requirements

Curators who work for zoos and aquariums must have a fondness and compassion for animals. But as managers of people, strong interpersonal skills are extremely important for curators, including conflict management and negotiating. Curators spend a lot of time making deals with people inside and outside of their institutions. They must have recognized leadership ability, good coaching skills, and the ability to create and maintain a team atmosphere and build consensus.

"I want the staff to be happy in their jobs, to feel a sense of fulfillment and accomplishment. That way the animals will be well cared for," said Anita Cramm, curator of birds at the Phoenix Zoo in Arizona. "I spend a lot of time talking to the keepers, brainstorming with them, responding to their problems. It's a very important part of all our programs."

Curators also need excellent oral and written communication skills. They must be effective and articulate public speakers. They need to be good at problem solving.

Curators should have an in-depth knowledge of every species and exhibit in their collections and how they interact. Modern zoo and aquarium buildings contain technologically advanced, complex equipment, such as environmental controls, and often house mixed-species exhibits. Not only must curators know about zoology and animal husbandry, but they must understand the infrastructure as well.

■ Exploring

Reading about animals or surfing the Internet, taking classes at local zoos and aquariums, or joining clubs, such as 4-H or Audubon, can help students learn about animals. Taking time to learn about ecology and nature in general will prepare students for the systems-oriented approach used by modern zoo and aquarium managers. "Tomorrow's curators need to develop an understanding of the complexity and interconnectedness of wild things and wild places," says Dennis Pate, senior vice president and general curator of Chicago's Lincoln Park Zoo.

Volunteering at zoos or aquariums, animal shelters, wildlife rehabilitation facilities, stables, or veterinary hospitals demonstrates a serious commitment to animals and provides firsthand experience with them.

Professional organizations, such as AZA and the American Association of Zoo Keepers, Inc. (AAZK), have special membership rates for nonprofessionals. Associate members receive newsletters and can attend workshops and conferences.

■ Employers

Because there are so few zoos and aquariums in the country (fewer than 200), most positions will be the result of turnover, which is low. While a few new zoos and aquariums may open and others may expand their facilities, the number of new curator positions available will be extremely low, particularly compared to the number of interested job seekers. The number of curators employed by each facility depends upon the size and budget of the operation and the range of animal types they house.

ZOO AND AQUARIUM CURATORS	
SCHOOL SUBJECTS	Biology Business Speech
PERSONAL SKILLS	Communication/ideas Leadership/management
WORK ENVIRONMENT	Indoors and outdoors Primarily one location
MINIMUM EDUCATION LEVEL	Bachelor's degree
SALARY RANGE	$20,000 to $40,000 to $79,000
CERTIFICATION OR LICENSING	None available
OUTLOOK	Little change or more slowly than the average
DOT	102
GOE	11.02.01
NOC	0212

Starting Out

The position of zoo and aquarium curator is seldom an entry-level job. Although there are exceptions, most curators start their careers as zookeepers or *aquarists* and move up through the animal management ranks.

"Learn as much as you can, and don't try to move up too quickly," advises Cramm. "Let the hands-on care teach you before you get into decision making. Once you're there, you can never go back."

Although the competition for zoo and aquarium jobs is intense, there are several ways to pursue such positions. Getting an education in animal science is a good way to make contacts that may be valuable in a job search. Professors and school administrators often can provide advice and counseling on finding jobs as a curator. The best sources for finding out about career opportunities at zoos and aquariums are trade journals (AZA's *Communiqué* or AAZK's *Animal Keepers' Forum*), the Web sites of specific institutions, and special-focus periodicals. Most zoos and aquariums have internal job postings. A few zoos and aquariums have job lines. People in the profession often learn about openings by word of mouth.

Working on a part-time or volunteer basis at an animal facility could provide an excellent opportunity to improve eligibility for higher-level jobs in later years. Although many curators have worked in other positions in other fields before obtaining their jobs at animal facilities, others began their careers in lower-level jobs at such places and worked their way up to where they wanted to be.

Moving up from a supervisory keeper position to a curatorial job usually involves moving out to another institution, often in another city and state.

■ Advancement

Curatorial positions are often the top rung of the career ladder for many zoo and aquarium professionals. Curators do not necessarily wish to become zoo or aquarium directors, although the next step for specialized curators is to advance to the position of general curator. Those who are willing to forego direct involvement with animal management altogether and complete the transition to the business of running a zoo or aquarium will set as their ultimate goal the position of zoo or aquarium director. Curators who work for a small facility may aspire to a curatorial position at a larger zoo or aquarium, with greater responsibilities and a commensurate increase in pay.

Advancing to executive positions requires a combination of experience and education. General curators and zoo directors often have graduate degrees in zoology or in business or finance. Continuing professional education, such as AZA's courses in applied zoo and aquarium biology, conservation education, institutional record keeping, population management, and professional management, can be helpful. Attending workshops and conferences sponsored by professional groups or related organizations and making presentations is another means of networking with colleagues from other institutions and professions and becoming better known within the zoo world.

■ Earnings

Salaries of zoo and aquarium curators are widely varied, depending on the size and location of the institution, whether it is privately or publicly owned, the size of its endowments and budget, and on the curators' responsibilities, educational backgrounds, and experience. Generally, zoos and aquariums in metropolitan areas pay higher salaries.

Generalizations can be made, however. Yearly salaries for curators range from as low as $20,000 to as high as $79,000 for general curators in major metropolitan areas; average earnings are about $40,000.

Most zoos and aquariums provide benefits packages including medical insurance, paid vacation and sick leave, and generous retirement benefits. As salaried employees, curators are not eligible for overtime pay, but they may get compensatory time for extra hours worked. Larger institutions may also offer coverage for prescription drugs, dental and vision insurance, mental health plans, and retirement savings plans. Private corporate zoos may offer better benefits, including profit sharing.

■ Work Environment

The work atmosphere for curators of animal facilities will always center on the zoo or aquarium in which they work. Curators spend most of their time indoors at their desks, reading email, talking on the phone, writing reports, meeting deadlines for budgets, planning exhibits, and so forth. Particularly at large institutions, the majority of their time is spent on administrative duties rather than hands-on interaction with animals. Like other zoo and aquarium employees, curators often work long hours tending to the varied duties to which they are assigned.

When the unexpected happens, curators get their share of animal emergencies. In difficult situations, they may find themselves working late into the night with keepers and veterinarians to help care for sick animals or those that are giving birth.

Celeste Lombardi, Living Collection Director at the Columbus Zoo in Ohio, told of an animal shipment that went awry. Two eight-month-old lions had been imported from South Africa through New York City on their way to Columbus when their connecting flight was delayed and then cancelled due to inclement weather. Concerned that the animals had already been crated with only water for 16 hours, Lombardi made numerous calls to arrange the services of an animal broker and to charter a plane, and, along with the assistant zoo director, stayed up until 3:00 AM when the lions finally arrived at their destination.

Curators are sometimes required to travel to conferences and community events. They might also travel to other zoos throughout the country or lead trips for zoo members to wilderness areas in the United States and abroad.

Despite the tedium and the long hours, zoo and aquarium curators derive great personal satisfaction from their work. "Ours is a family oriented business," said Lombardi. "People come to zoos to learn—whether they're kids or they're 90 years old. I feel that we're doing something good for the earth."

■ Outlook

There are fewer than 200 professionally operated zoos, aquariums, wildlife parks, and oceanariums in North America. Considering the number of people interested in animal careers, this is not a large number. Therefore, it is expected that competition for jobs as curators (as well as for most zoo and aquarium jobs) will continue to be very strong.

The employment outlook for zoo curators is not favorable. Because of the slow growth in new zoos and in their capacity to care for animals, job openings are not expected to grow rapidly. The prospects for aquarium curators is somewhat better due to planned construction of several new aquariums.

However, competition and low turnover rates will continue to squelch opportunities in these occupations. According to Pate, one area with greater growth potential than conventional zoos and aquariums is privately funded conservation centers.

■ For More Information

For information on careers, contact:

American Association of Zoo Keepers, Inc.
Topeka Zoological Park
635 Southwest Gage Boulevard
Topeka, KS 66606-2066
Tel: 785-273-1980
Web: http://aazk.ind.net/

American Zoo and Aquarium Association
Conservation Center
7970-D Old Georgetown Road
Bethesda, MD 20814-2493
Web: http://www.aza.org

For information regarding schools with animal management curricula, contact:

Friends University of Wichita
2100 W. University
Wichita, KS 67213
Tel: 316-295-5890 or 800-794-6945, x5890
Web: http://www.friends.edu/natsci/zoo.htm

Santa Fe Community College Zoo Studies Programs
3000 Northwest 83rd Street
Gainesville, FL 32606
Tel: 352-395-5604
Web: http://www.aazk.ind.net/aazk/SantaFe.html

Zoo and Aquarium Directors

■ Overview

Zoo and aquarium directors, or *chief executive officers,* are administrators who coordinate the business affairs of these centers. Like all executives, they have diverse responsibilities. Directors execute the institution's policies, usually under the direction of a governing authority. They are responsible for the institution's operations and plans for future development and for such tasks as fund-raising and public relations. They also serve as representatives of, and advocates for, their institutions and their entire industry.

■ History

Zoos and aquariums have undergone a revolution in recent times. Modern zoos are very different from the menageries of yesteryear, where the emphasis was on displaying and caring for as many species as possible for the amusement of visitors, with little concern for the context in which the animals were presented. Today's zoos and aquariums are built around habitat-based, multispecies exhibits designed to immerse the visitor in an experience simulating a visit to the wild places from which the animals came. The keeping and breeding of captive animals is no longer an end in itself, but a means of educating and communicating a strong conservation imperative to the public. The public has embraced this change, with visitor numbers rising steadily each year.

Along with this expanded public role has come a professionalization of the industry, marked by advances in animal husbandry, veterinary care, nutrition, and exhibit technology that have greatly improved the conditions under which animals are held. These advances have been costly, and the rise in operating expenses reflects these increased costs. Zoos and aquariums today are big business.

Traditionally, most zoo and aquarium directors came straight from the animal management staff, working their way up through the ranks from *zookeeper* or *aquarist* to *curator* to director. Some zoo and aquarium curators still become directors. However, the director's job has changed radically in the past 15 years, reflecting the overall maturity of the zoo and aquarium business. Directors no longer have direct responsibility for working with animals or managing the people who care for them. The director's role has broadened from animal management to overall management, with a focus that has shifted from internal issues to external ones. Rather than concentrate on day-to-day details of running the facility, the modern director must concentrate on the big picture.

■ The Job

Directors of zoos and aquariums are considered administrative personnel. Their job is like that of the president of a company or the principal of a school; that is, they are responsible mainly for the important business affairs of the institution.

Working under the supervision of a governing board, directors are charged with pulling together all the institution's operations, development of long-range planning, implementation of new programs, and maintenance of the animal collection and facilities. Much of the director's time is spent interfacing with the volunteer governing board to whom he or she reports and with departmental staff, who handle the institution's daily operations.

Directors are responsible for planning overall budgets, which includes consideration of fund-raising programs, government grants, and private financial support from corporations, foundations, and individuals. They work with the board of directors to design major policies and procedures, and they meet with the curators to discuss animal acquisitions, public education, research projects, and developmental activities. In larger zoos and aquariums, directors may give speeches, appear at fund-raising events, and represent their organizations on television or radio.

A major part of the director's job is seeing that his or her institution has adequate financial resources. Where zoos and aquariums were once funded largely by local and state governments, the amount of tax money available for this purpose is dwindling. Generally, zoos and aquariums need to generate enough revenue to pay for about two-thirds of their operating expenses from sources such as donations, membership, retail sales, and visitor services.

As zoos and aquariums endeavor to improve facilities for animals and visitors alike and to present the conservation message to the public in a more effective manner, renovation of existing structures and construction of new exhibits is on ongoing process. Directors spend much of their time working with architects, engineers, contractors, and artisans on these projects.

Directors are responsible for informing the public about what is going on at the zoo or aquarium. This involves interviews with the media, answering questions from individuals, and even resolving complaints. The director is the face—and the voice—that represents his or her institution to the public. In addition to being interviewed by journalists and other writers, directors do writing of their own for in-house newsletters and annual reports or for general circulation magazines and newspapers.

Although not directly involved in animal management within his or her own institution, the director may play a significant role in conservation at a regional, national, or international level. Directors work on committees for various conservation organizations, such as the more than 80 American Zoo and Aquarium Association (AZA) Species Survival Plans (SSP) that target individual species for intense conservation efforts by zoos and aquariums. They may be involved at a higher level of the AZA, working on such things as accreditation of other institutions, developing professional ethics, or long-range planning. Directors work with other conservation groups as well and may serve in leadership positions for them too.

As zoos and aquariums expand their conservation role from only the management of captive animals to supporting the preservation of the habitats those animals came from, directors are working with universities and field biologists to support research.

Within their own zoo or aquarium, directors may work with other volunteer boards whose purpose is to raise money. They attend numerous social gatherings, including fund-raising events for their institutions, and community events. Directors are constantly networking, always on the lookout for people who want to support their institutions in one way or another.

Because of their exposure and the public's fascination with animals, zoo and aquarium directors often become local or national celebrities.

Other directorial personnel include *assistant directors* and *deputy directors*. Like curators, these workers are responsible for a specific duty or department, such as operations, education, or animal management. They also manage employees, supervise animal care workers, and take care of various administrative duties to help the director.

■ Requirements

High School

Classes in English, speech, and business will help prepare you for management work. A background in biology and anatomy will help you understand the animals for which zoo and aquarium directors are ultimately responsible. Extracurricular activities for students interested in becoming zoo and aquarium directors should focus on developing leadership and communications skills.

Postsecondary Training

Students who aspire to upper-level management in zoos and aquariums should get a multidisciplinary education. As the director's job has evolved beyond a narrow animal management focus, so too has the career path to that job. While a knowledge of zoology is important for anyone interested in working at a zoo or aquarium, students should remember that experts in other areas of management can move into the director's chair.

A director's education and experience must be rather broad, with a solid foundation in animal management skills. Therefore, a good balance between science and business is the key to finding a position in this field. Directors need courses in zoology or biology as well as business courses, such as economics, accounting, and general business, and humanities, such as sociology.

Today, most directors have a master's degree; many at larger institutions have doctoral degrees. Directors continue their education throughout their careers by taking classes, as well as by reading and learning on their own.

Other Requirements

Zoo and aquarium directors are leaders and communicators. Inspiring others and promoting their institution are among their most important tasks. Their most important traits include leadership ability, personal charisma, people skills, and public speaking ability.

Directors need to be politically savvy. They interact with many different groups, each with their own agendas: the institution's governing board; its staff (animal management, operations, education, conservation, marketing, development, human resources, and so forth); local, state, and federal politicians; foundations; corporate and individual donors; members; schools; visitors; even animal rights organizations. Directors must be able to build bridges between these various groups and put together a consensus. They need to be flexible and open-minded without losing sight of their role as advocate for their institution.

Directors must have outstanding time management skills, and they must be willing and able to delegate. The best directors need to know their own weaknesses and hire people who can compensate in those areas.

"Too many people get into the business because they like animals," said Tony Vecchio, director of the Metro Washington Park Zoo in Portland, Oregon. "The zoo business is not just animals; it's all about people. Education may not be as exciting as breeding endangered species or supporting *in situ* research, but it is our best contribution to conservation."

Directors must be articulate and sociable. They must be able to communicate with people from all walks of life. Much of their time is spent cultivating prospective donors.

They must be comfortable with many different types of people, including those with wealth and power.

■ Exploring

Performing volunteer work at animal shelters is an excellent way to gain practical experience in caring for various types of animals. You could also attempt to get part-time jobs at zoos, kennels, pet stores, stables, veterinary facilities, or animal adoption facilities.

Professional organizations, such as the AZA and the American Association of Zoo Keepers, Inc. (AAZK), have special membership rates for nonprofessionals and allow them to attend workshops and conferences. Students interested in careers at zoos and aquariums should join these organizations to learn more about the field.

■ Employers

Since there are only approximately 200 zoos and aquariums in North America-and only one director for each—most people who aspire to this position will be forced to work in other positions (in zoos or aquariums, or in other businesses entirely) as they strive to fulfill their dreams. Even taking into consideration turnover (which is low) and the creation of new zoos and aquariums (which will be few), those sold on becoming zoo or aquarium directors face considerable challenges. The number of people interested in the field so far outweighs the available positions that zoos and aquariums are able to choose the cream of the crop.

■ Starting Out

The position of zoo and aquarium director is not an entry-level job. Achieving a position at this level requires focus, determination, ambition, and long-range career planning. Aspiring directors should set their goals high and constantly strive to do their best. This is not a career for someone unwilling to take the steps required to stand out above the crowd.

Although the competition for zoo and aquarium jobs is stiff, there are several ways to pursue such positions. Some animal facilities offer internships to students who are studying areas related to animal science and care; contact the AZA for further information about which schools and animal facilities are involved in internship programs. Other zoo and aquarium jobs can also start a student on the way to becoming a director.

The best sources for finding out about career opportunities at zoos and aquariums are trade journals (such as AZA's *Communiqué* or AAZK's *Animal Keepers' Forum*), the Web sites of specific institutions, and special focus periodicals. Most zoos and aquariums have internal job postings. Institutions seeking candidates for high level positions, such as the director's, sometimes use executive search firms. People in the profession often learn about openings by word of mouth.

Whatever your interest, you must pursue it within the zoo and aquarium setting. Among today's zoo and aquarium directors are people who began their careers in education, marketing, business, research, and academia, as well as animal management.

■ Advancement

The position of zoo and aquarium director is the top rung of the career ladder that many animal science students pursue. Because directors are considered high-level employees at animal facilities, if they wish to advance, they may consider moving from zoos to aquariums (or vice versa) or going on to a different field altogether. Or, if they work for a small facility, they may try to secure a position at a larger zoo or aquarium. Many young directors have established their reputations by rebuilding an institution with outmoded facilities or severe financial problems.

Although some directors may move about, the majority remain at the same institution, reflecting the strong identification of the director with the institution that he or she leads.

■ Earnings

Salaries of zoo and aquarium directors vary widely, depending on the size and location of the institution, whether it is publicly or privately owned, the size of its endowments and budget, and on the director's responsibilities, educational background, and experience. Generally, zoos and aquariums in metropolitan areas pay higher salaries.

Directors tend to be the highest paid employees at zoos and aquariums; the range of their salary is also broad, from $28,000 to more than $100,000 per year, with some directors at major institutions earning considerably more than that. Given the scope of their responsibilities, salaries are not very high.

Most zoos and aquariums provide benefits packages that include medical insurance, paid vacation and sick

ZOO AND AQUARIUM DIRECTORS	
SCHOOL SUBJECTS	Biology Business Speech
PERSONAL SKILLS	Communication/ideas Leadership/management
WORK ENVIRONMENT	Primarily indoors Primarily one location
MINIMUM EDUCATION LEVEL	Bachelor's degree
SALARY RANGE	$28,000 to $60,000 to $100,000+
CERTIFICATION OR LICENSING	None available
OUTLOOK	Little change or more slowly than the average
DOT	102
GOE	11.02.01
NOC	0212

leave, and generous retirement benefits. Larger institutions may also offer coverage for prescription drugs, dental and vision insurance, mental health plans, and 401(k) plans. Private corporate zoos may offer better benefits, including profit sharing.

Some directors supplement their regular salaries with income from books and paid public speaking engagements.

Work Environment

The zoo and aquarium director's job is very demanding and time consuming. The challenges of running a large, multifaceted institution never go away. All directors take work home with them, such as reading and correspondence; most have computers and offices in their homes.

Nonetheless, the daily responsibilities of directors of zoos and aquariums generally center on the facility in which they work. Directors tend to spend a great deal of time in their offices conducting business affairs. They attend a lot of meetings.

Directors are sometimes required to travel to conferences and community events. They might also travel to other institutions throughout the country or abroad to attend meetings of professional organizations and conservation groups or to discuss animal transfers and other matters. Often, directors lead groups on trips around the United States or to developing countries.

Outlook

There are fewer than 200 professionally operated zoos, aquariums, wildlife parks, and oceanariums in North America. Each of them employs only one director. Therefore, competition for jobs as directors is expected to remain very strong. Generally, the employment outlook for directors is not favorable. Because of the slow growth in the number of new zoos, job openings are not expected to grow. The continuing competition and low turnover rates will increasingly decrease the number of opportunities. The outlook for aquariums is somewhat brighter due to the planned construction of several new facilities.

For More Information

For information on careers, contact:

American Zoo and Aquarium Association
Conservation Center
7970-D Old Georgetown Road
Bethesda, MD 20814-2493
Web: http://www.aza.org

American Association of Zoo Keepers, Inc.
Topeka Zoological Park
635 Southwest Gage Boulevard
Topeka, KS 66606-2066
Tel: 785-273-1980
Web: http://aazk.ind.net/

Related Articles

Animals
Animal Caretakers
Animal Handlers
Animal Shelter Employees
Veterinarians
Veterinary Technicians
Zoo and Aquarium Curators
Zookeepers
Zoologists

Zookeepers

Overview

Zookeepers provide the day-to-day care for animals in zoological parks. They prepare the diets, clean and maintain the exhibits and holding areas, and monitor the behavior of animals that range from the exotic and endangered to the more common and domesticated. Zookeepers interact with visitors and conduct formal and informal educational presentations, sometimes assist in research studies, and depending upon the species, may also train animals.

History

Humans have put wild animals on display since ancient times. About 1500 BC, Queen Hatshepsut of Egypt established the earliest known zoo. Five hundred years later, the Chinese emperor Wen Wang founded a zoo that covered about 1,500 acres. Rulers seeking to display their wealth and power established small zoos in northern Africa, India, and China. The ancient Greeks established public zoos, while the Romans had many private zoos. During the Middle Ages, from about AD 400 to 1500, zoos became rare in Europe.

By the end of the 1400s, European explorers returned from the New World with strange animals, and interest in

ZOOKEEPERS	
SCHOOL SUBJECTS	Biology Computer science Speech
PERSONAL SKILLS	Helping/teaching Technical/scientific
WORK ENVIRONMENT	Indoors and outdoors Primarily one location
MINIMUM EDUCATION LEVEL	Bachelor's degree
SALARY RANGE	$14,000 to $27,000 to $40,000+
CERTIFICATION OR LICENSING	None available
OUTLOOK	About as fast as the average
DOT	412
GOE	03.03.02
NOC	6483

zoos renewed. During the next 250 years, a number of zoos were established. Some merely consisted of small collections of bears or tigers kept in dismal cages or pits. They were gradually replaced by larger collections of animals that received better care.

In 1752, what is now the oldest zoo, the Schönbrunn, opened in Vienna, Austria. Other European zoos followed. In the United States, the Central Park Zoo in New York City opened in 1864, followed by the Buffalo Zoo in New York in 1870, and Chicago's Lincoln Park Zoo in 1874.

Workers were needed to care for the animals in even the earliest zoos. However, this care probably consisted only of giving the animals food and water and cleaning their cages. Little was known about the needs of a particular species, for if an animal died, it could be replaced by another animal from the wild. Few zoos owned more than one or two animals of a rare species, so the keepers did not need to be involved in observations or research on an animal's lifestyle, health, or nutrition.

The modern zoo is a far cry from even the menageries of earlier eras. Today's zoos are still in the entertainment field, but they have assumed three additional roles: conservation, education, and research. Each of these roles has become vital due to the increasing pressures on the world's wildlife.

■ The Job

Zookeepers are responsible for providing the basic care required to maintain the health of the animals in their charge. Daily tasks include preparing food by chopping or grinding meat, fish, vegetables, or fruit; mixing prepared commercial feeds; and unbaling forage grasses. Administering vitamins or medications may be necessary as well. In addition, zookeepers fill water containers in the cages. They clean animal quarters by hosing, scrubbing, raking, and disinfecting.

Zookeepers must safely shift animals from one location to another. They maintain exhibits (for example, by planting grass or putting in new bars) and modify them to enhance the visitors' experience. They also provide enrichment devices for the animals, such as ropes for monkeys to swing on or scratching areas for big cats. They regulate environmental factors by monitoring temperature and humidity or water quality controls and maintain an inventory of supplies and equipment. They may bathe and groom animals.

Zookeepers must become experts on the species—and the individuals—in their care. They must observe and understand all types of animal behaviors, including courtship, mating, feeding, aggression, sociality, sleeping, moving, and even urination and defecation. Zookeepers must be able to detect even small changes in an animal's appearance or behavior. They must maintain careful records

of these observations in a logbook and file daily written or computerized reports. Often, they make recommendations regarding diet or modification of habitats and implement those changes. In addition, they assist the veterinarian in providing treatment to sick animals and may be called upon to feed and help raise infants. Zookeepers may capture or transport animals. When an animal is transferred to another institution, a keeper may accompany it to aid in its adjustment to its new home.

The professional zookeeper works closely with zoo staff on research, conservation, and animal reproduction. Many keepers conduct research projects, presenting their findings in papers or professional journals or at workshops or conferences. Some keepers participate in regional or national conservation plans or conduct field research in the United States and abroad.

Keepers may assist an animal trainer or instructor in presenting animal shows or lectures to the public. Depending on the species, keepers may train animals to shift or to move in a certain way to facilitate routine husbandry or veterinary care. Elephant keepers, for example, train their charges to respond to commands to lift their feet so that they may provide proper foot care including foot pad, and toenail trims.

Zookeepers must be able to interact with zoo visitors and answer questions in a friendly, professional manner. Keepers may participate in formal presentations for the general public or for special groups. This involves being knowledgeable about the animals in one's care, the animals' natural habitat and habits, and the role zoos play in wildlife conservation.

Keepers must carefully monitor activity around the animals to discourage visitors from teasing or harming them. They must be able to remove harmful objects that are sometimes thrown into an exhibit and tactfully explain the "no feeding" policy to zoo visitors.

Taking care of animals is hard work. About 85 percent of the job involves custodial and maintenance tasks, which can be physically demanding and dirty. These tasks must be done both indoors and outdoors, in all types of weather. In addition, there is the risk of an animal-inflicted injury or disease. Although direct contact with animals is limited and strictly managed, the possibility for injury exists when a person is working with large, powerful animals or even small animals that possess sharp teeth and claws.

Because animals require care every day, keepers must work weekends and holidays. They also may be called upon to work special events outside their normal working hours.

In large zoological parks, keepers often work with a limited collection of animals. They may be assigned to work specifically with just one taxonomy, such as primates, large cats, or birds, or with different types of animals from a specific ecogeographic area, such as the tropical rainforest or the apes of Africa. In smaller zoos, keepers may have more variety and care for a wider range of species.

■ Requirements

High School

Students planning a career in zookeeping should take as many science classes in high school as possible, including biology, ecology, chemistry, physics, and botany, coupled with mathematics and computer science is best. Courses in English and speech develop vocabulary and hone public speaking skills.

Postsecondary Training

Although practical experience may sometimes be substituted for formal education, most entry-level positions require a four-year college degree. Animal management has become a highly technical and specialized field. Zookeepers do much more than care for animals' bodily comforts: today's zookeepers are zoologists. They must be able to perform detailed behavioral observations, record keeping, nutrition studies, and health care. Their increased responsibilities make their role an essential one in maintaining a healthy animal collection.

Degrees in animal science, zoology, marine biology, conservation biology, wildlife management, or animal behavior are preferred. Electives are just as important, particularly writing, public speaking, computer science, education—even additional languages. Applicants with interdisciplinary training sometimes have an advantage. A few colleges and junior colleges offer a specialized curriculum for zookeepers. Those seeking advancement to curatorial, research, or conservation positions may need a master's degree. Animal care experience such as zoo volunteer, farm or ranch worker, or veterinary hospital worker is a must.

Smaller zoos may hire keeper trainees, who receive on-the-job training to learn the responsibilities of the zookeeper. Several major zoos offer formal keeper training courses, as well as on-the-job training programs, to students who are studying areas related to animal science and care; contact the American Zoo and Aquarium Association (AZA) for further information about which schools and animal facilities are involved in internship programs. Such programs could lead to full time positions.

Other Requirements

Some zoos require written aptitude tests or oral exams. Applicants must pass a physical exam, as keepers must be physically able to do such demanding work as lifting heavy sacks of feed or moving sick or injured animals.

Union membership is more common at publicly operated zoos, but it is on the rise in privately run institutions as well. There is no single zookeepers' union, and a variety of different unions represent the employees at various zoos.

Zookeepers must first and foremost have a fondness and empathy for animals. The work of the zookeeper is not glamorous. It takes a special kind of dedication to provide care to captive animals that require attention 24 hours a day, 365 days a year.

Keepers need excellent interpersonal skills to work together and to interact with visitors and volunteers. Strong oral and written communication skills are also required. They should be detail-oriented and enjoy paperwork and record keeping. They must be able to work well independently and as part of a team. Keepers rely on each other to get their jobs done safely. A calm, stable nature, maturity, good judgment, and the ability to adhere to established animal handling and/or safety procedures is essential. Being in a bad mood can interfere with concentration, endangering the keeper and his or her co-workers.

Keepers must have keen powers of observation. Often, exotic animals don't show that they're in trouble until it's too late. But with experience with different species and individuals, you learn to see those subtle little changes that indicate an animal is sick.

Due to the physical demands of the job, keepers must be physically fit. Psychological fitness is important too. Zookeepers have to be able to handle the emotional impact when animals with whom they have built a relationship go to another institution or die. They can't be squeamish about handling body wastes or live food items or dealing with sick animals.

■ Exploring

High school students can explore the field of animal care in several ways. They can learn about animals by reading about them and taking classes in biology and zoology. Most zoos have Web sites containing information about the institution and its programs and career opportunities, as well as about the industry in general. Hobbies such as birding expand the knowledge of animals.

Many institutions offer classes about animals and conservation or educational programs, such as Keeper Encounters, where students can learn firsthand what a zookeeper's job is like.

Some have part time or summer jobs that can give a good overview of how a zoo operates. Many zoos offer volunteer opportunities for teens, such as Explorers or Junior Zookeeper programs, which are similar to programs for adult volunteers, but with closer supervision. Most volunteer programs require a specific time commitment. Opportunities vary between institutions and run the gamut from cleaning enclosures to preparing food to handling domesticated animals to conducting tours or giving educational presentations.

Prospective zookeepers can volunteer or work part time at animal shelters, boarding kennels, wildlife rehabilitation facilities, stables, or animal hospitals. They may get a feel for working with animals by seeking employment on a farm or ranch during the summer. Joining a 4-H club also gives a person hands-on experience with animals. Experience with animals is invaluable when seeking a job and provides opportunities to learn about the realities of work in this field.

Professional organizations have special membership rates for nonprofessionals. Reading their newsletters provides an insider's look at what zoo careers are like. Attending local workshops or national conferences offers an opportunity to network and gather information for charting a career path.

■ Starting Out

The days when zookeepers were hired off the street and trained on the job are a thing of the past. Today, most institutions require a bachelor's degree. But "a classical education alone is not enough," according to Brian Rutledge, president and CEO of Zoo New England in Boston, Massachusetts. Practical experience working with animals is a must. This experience can involve volunteering at a zoo or wildlife rehabilitation center, caring for animals in a kennel or animal hospital, or working on a farm or ranch.

Part-time work, summer jobs, or volunteering at a zoo increases an applicant's chances of getting full-time employment. Many zoos fill new positions by promoting current employees. An entry-level position, even if it does not involve working directly with animals, is a means of making contacts and learning about an institution's hiring practices.

Occasionally zoos advertise for personnel in the local newspapers. Better sources of employment opportunities are trade journals (AZA's *Communiqué* or the American Association of Zoo Keepers, Inc.'s (AAZK) *Animal Keepers' Forum*), the Web sites of specific institutions, or special-focus periodicals. A few zoos have job lines.

Most zoos have internal job postings. People in the profession often learn about openings by word of mouth. Membership in a professional organization can be helpful when conducting a job search.

■ Advancement

Job advancement in zoos is possible but the career path is more limited than in some other professions requiring a college degree. The possibility for advancement varies according to a zoo's size and operating policies and an employee's qualifications. Continuing professional education is a must to keep current on progress in husbandry, veterinary care, and technology, and in order to advance.

Most zoos have different levels of animal management staff. The most common avenue for job promotion is from keeper to senior keeper to head keeper, then possibly to area supervisor or assistant curator and then curator. On rare occasions, the next step will be to zoo director. Moving up from the senior keeper level to middle and upper management usually involves moving out to another institution, often in another city and state.

Many zookeepers eschew advancement and prefer to remain in work where they have the most direct interaction with and impact on the animals.

■ Earnings

Most people who choose a career as a zookeeper do not do so for the money, but because they feel compassion for and enjoy being around animals.

Salaries vary widely among zoological parks and depend upon the size and location of the institution, whether it is publicly or privately owned, the size of its endowments and budget, and whether the zookeepers belong to a union. Generally, the highest salaries tend to be in metropolitan areas and are relative to the applicant's education and responsibilities. The zookeeper's salary can range from slightly above minimum wage to more than $40,000 a year, depending on the keeper's background, grade, and tenure and the zoo's location. Certain areas of the country pay higher wages, reflecting the higher cost of living there. City-run institutions, where keepers are lumped into a job category with less-skilled workers, pay less. On average, aquarists earn slightly more than zookeepers.

Most zoos provide benefits packages that include medical insurance, paid vacation and sick leave, and generous retirement benefits.

■ Work Environment

Cleaning, feeding, and providing general care to the animals are a necessity seven days a week, sometimes outdoors and in adverse weather conditions. The zookeeper must be prepared for a varied schedule that may include working weekends and holidays. Sick animals may need round-the-clock care. A large portion of the job involves routine chores for animals that will not express appreciation for the keeper's efforts.

Some of the work may be physically demanding and involve lifting heavy supplies such as bales of hay. The cleaning of an animal's enclosure may be unpleasant and smelly. Between the sounds of the animals and the sounds of the zoo visitors, the work setting may be quite noisy.

The zookeeper may be exposed to bites, kicks, zoonotic diseases, and possible fatal injury from the animals he or she attends. He or she must practice constant caution because working with animals presents the potential for danger. Even though an animal may have been held in captivity for years or even since birth, it can be frightened, become stressed because of illness, or otherwise revert to its wild behavior. The keeper must know the physical and mental abilities of an animal, whether it be the strength of an ape, the reaching ability of a large cat, or the intelligence of an elephant. In addition, keepers must develop a healthy relationship with the animals in their care by respecting them as individuals and always being careful to observe safety procedures.

Being a zookeeper is an active, demanding job. The tasks involved require agility and endurance, whether they consist of cleaning quarters, preparing food, or handling animals.

■ Outlook

Zoos hire more animal keepers than any other classification. But this is still a very small job pool. Approximately 350 zookeeper jobs become available each year in the United States. There are many more applicants than positions available. Competition for jobs is stiff in the nearly 200 professionally operated zoological parks, aquariums, and wildlife parks in North America.

As the preservation of animal species becomes more complicated, there will be a continuing need for zoo staff to work to preserve endangered wildlife and educate the public about conservation. The demand will increase for well-educated personnel who will be responsible for much more than simply feeding the animals and cleaning their enclosures. Zookeepers will need more knowledge as zoos expand and become more specialized. The amount of knowledge and effort necessary to maintain and reproduce a healthy animal collection will keep zookeepers in the front line of animal care.

■ For More Information

American Association of Zoo Keepers, Inc.
Topeka Zoological Park
635 Southwest Gage Boulevard
Topeka, KS 66606-2066
Tel: 785 273-1980
Web: http://aazk.ind.net/

For information on careers, contact:

American Zoo and Aquarium Association
Conservation Center
7970-D Old Georgetown Road
Bethesda, MD 20814-2493
Web: http://www.aza.org

ZooNet—All About Zoos
Web: http://www.mindspring.com/~zoonet/

ZooWeb
Web: http://www.zooweb.net/

■ Related Articles

Animals
Animal Caretakers
Animal Handlers

Animal Shelter Employees
Veterinarians
Veterinary Technicians
Zoo and Aquarium Curators
Zoo And Aquarium Directors
Zoologists

Zoologists

■ Overview

Zoologists are biologists who study animals. They often select a particular type of animal to study, and they may study an entire animal, one part or aspect of an animal, or a whole animal society. There are many areas of specialization from which a zoologist can choose, such as origins, genetics, characteristics, classifications, behaviors, life processes, and distribution of animals.

■ History

The first important developments in zoology occurred in Greece, where Alcmaeon, a philosopher and physician, studied animals and performed the first known dissections of humans in the sixth century BC. Aristotle, however, is generally considered to be the first real zoologist. Aristotle, who studied with the great philosopher Plato and tutored the world—conquering Alexander the Great—had the lofty goal of setting down in writing everything that was known in his time. In an attempt to extend that knowledge, he observed and dissected sea creatures. He also devised a system of classifying animals that included 500 species—a system that influenced scientists for many centuries after his death. Some scholars believe that Alexander sent various exotic animals to his old tutor from the lands he conquered, giving Aristotle unparalleled access to the animals of the ancient world.

With the exception of important work in physiology done by the Roman

ZOOLOGISTS	
SCHOOL SUBJECTS	Biology Chemistry English
PERSONAL SKILLS	Communication/ideas Technical/scientific
WORK ENVIRONMENT	Indoors and outdoors Primarily one location
MINIMUM EDUCATION LEVEL	Bachelor's degree
SALARY RANGE	$22,000 to $36,300 to $80,000+
CERTIFICATION OR LICENSING	None available
OUTLOOK	Faster than the average
DOT	041
O*NET	24308H

physician Galen, the study of zoology progressed little after Aristotle until the middle of the 16th century. Between 1555 and 1700, much significant work was done in the classification of species and in physiology, especially regarding the circulation of blood, which affected studies of both animals and humans. The invention of the microscope in approximately 1590 led to the discovery and study of cells. In the 18th century, Swedish botanist Carl Linnaeus developed the system of classification of plants and animals that is still used.

Zoology continued to develop at a rapid rate, and in 1859, Charles Darwin published *On the Origin of Species,* which promoted the theory of natural selection, revolutionized the way scientists viewed all living creatures, and gave rise to the field of ethology, the study of animal behavior. Since that time, innumerable advances have been made by zoologists throughout the world.

In the 20th century, the rapid development of technology has changed zoology and all sciences by giving scientists the tools to explore areas that had previously been closed to them. Computers, submersibles, spacecraft, and tremendously powerful microscopes are only a few of the means that modern zoologists have used to bring new knowledge to light. In spite of these advances, however, mysteries remain, questions go unanswered, and species wait to be discovered.

■ The Job

Although zoology is a single specialty within the field of biology, it is a vast specialty that includes many major subspecialties. Some zoologists study a single animal or a category of animals, whereas others may specialize in a particular part of an animal's anatomy or study a process that takes place in many kinds of animals. A zoologist might study single-cell organisms, a particular variety of fish, or the behavior of groups of animals such as elephants or bees.

Many zoologists are classified according to the animals they study. For example, *entomologists* are experts on insects, *icthyologists* study fish, *herpetologists* specialize in the study of reptiles and amphibians, *mammalogists* focus on mammals, and *ornithologists* study birds. *Embryologists,* however, are classified according to the process that they study. They examine the ways in which animal embryos form and develop from conception to birth.

Within each primary area of specialization there is a wide range of subspecialties. An ichthyologist, for example, might focus on the physiology, or physical structure and functioning, of a particular fish; on a biochemical phenomenon such as bioluminescence in deep-sea species; on the discovery and classification of fish; on variations within a single species in different parts of the world; or on the ways in which one type of fish interacts with other species

in a specific environment. Others may specialize in the effects of pollution on fish or in finding ways to grow fish effectively in controlled environments in order to increase the supply of healthy food available for human consumption.

Some zoologists are primarily teachers, while others spend most of their time performing original research. Teaching jobs in universities and other facilities are probably the most secure positions available, but zoologists who wish to do extensive research may find such positions restrictive. Even zoologists whose primary function is research, however, often need to do some teaching in the course of their work, and almost everyone in the field has to deal with the public at one time or another.

Students often believe that zoological scientists spend most of their time in the field, observing animals and collecting specimens. In fact, most researchers spend no more than two to eight weeks in the field each year. Zoologists spend much of their time at a computer or on the telephone.

It is often the case that junior scientists spend more time in the field than do senior scientists, who study specimens and data collected in the field by their younger colleagues. Senior scientists spend much of their time coordinating research, directing younger scientists and technicians, and writing grant proposals or soliciting funds in other ways.

Raising money is an extremely important activity for zoologists who are not employed by government agencies or major universities. The process of obtaining money for research can be time-consuming and difficult. Good development skills can also give scientists a flexibility that government-funded scientists do not have. Government money is sometimes available only for research in narrowly defined areas that may not be those that a scientist wishes to study. A zoologist who wants to study a particular area may seek his or her own funding in order not to be limited by government restrictions.

■ Requirements

High School

Those interested in zoology should begin by making certain that they get a well-rounded high school education. A solid grounding in biology and chemistry is an absolute necessity, but English is also important: Writing monographs and articles, communicating with colleagues both orally and in writing, and writing persuasive fund-raising proposals are all activities at which scientists need to excel.

Postsecondary Training

A bachelor's degree is essential for a zoologist, and advanced degrees are highly recommended, but no licensing or other certification is required, and there is no zoologists' union.

Academic training, practical experience, and the ability to work effectively with others are the most important prerequisites for a career in zoology.

Other Requirements

Success in zoology requires tremendous effort. It would be unwise for a person who wants to work an eight-hour day to become a zoologist, since hard work and long hours (sometimes 60 to 80 hours per week) are the norm. Also, although some top scientists are paid extremely well, the field does not provide a rapid route to riches. A successful zoologist finds satisfaction in work, not in a paycheck. The personal rewards, however, can be tremendous. The typical zoologist finds his or her work satisfying on many levels.

A successful zoologist is generally patient and flexible. A person who cannot juggle various tasks will have a difficult time in a job that requires doing research, writing articles, dealing with the public, teaching students, soliciting funds, and keeping up with the latest publications in the field. Flexibility also comes into play when funding for a particular area of study ends or is unavailable. A zoologist whose range of expertise is too narrowly focused will be at a disadvantage when there are no opportunities in that particular area. A flexible approach and a willingness to explore various areas can be crucial in such situations, and a too-rigid attitude may lead a zoologist to avoid studies that he or she would have found rewarding.

An aptitude for reading and writing is a must for any zoologist. A person who hates to read would have difficulty keeping up with the literature in the field, and a person who cannot write or dislikes writing would be unable to write effective articles and books. Publishing is an important part of zoological work, especially for those who are conducting research.

■ Exploring

One of the best ways to find out if you are suited for a career as a zoologist is to talk to zoologists and find out exactly what they do. Contact experts in your field of interest. Read books, magazines, and journals to find out who the experts are. Don't be afraid to write or call people and ask them questions.

Try to become an intern or a volunteer at an organization that is involved in an area that you find interesting. Most organizations have internships, and if you look with determination for an internship, you are likely to find one.

■ Employers

Zoologists are employed by a wide variety of institutions—not just zoos. Many zoologists are teachers at universities and other facilities, where they may teach during the year while spending their summers doing research. A large number of zoologists are researchers; they may be working for nonprofit organizations (requiring grants to fund their work), scientific institutions, or the government. Of course, there are many zoologists who are employed by zoos, aquariums, and museums. While jobs for zoologists exist all over the country, large cities that have universities, zoos, museums, and so forth will provide far more opportunities for zoologists than will rural areas.

■ Starting Out

Before you get your first job as a zoologist, you will need to have at least a bachelor's degree. For the best results, you will need a master's degree. It is possible to find work with a bachelor's degree, but it is likely that you will need to continue your education to advance in the field. Competition for jobs among those who have doctoral degrees is fierce, and it is often easier to break into the field with a master's than it is with a Ph.D. For this reason, many people go to work after they receive a master's degree and get a doctoral while they are working.

According to one zoologist, the best way to get your first job in zoology is to make contacts, particularly with qualified scientists who really know the field and know other people. "It's so competitive right now," he says, "that the personal contact really makes a difference."

You will be ahead of the game if you have made contacts as an intern or as a member of a professional organization. It is an excellent idea to attend the meetings of professional organizations, which generally welcome students. At those meetings, introduce yourself to the scientists you admire and ask for their help and advice.

■ Advancement

Higher education and publishing are two of the most important means of advancing in the field of zoology. The holder of a Ph.D. will make more money and have a higher status than the holder of a bachelor's or master's degree. The publication of articles and books is important for both research scientists and professors of zoology. A young professor who does not publish cannot expect to become a full professor with tenure, and a research scientist who does not publish the results of his or her research will not become known as an authority in the field. In addition, the publication of a significant work lets everyone in the field know that the author has worked hard and accomplished something worthwhile.

Because zoology is not a career in which people typically move from job to job, people generally move up within an organization. A professor may become a full professor; a research scientist may become known as an expert in the field or may become the head of a department, division, or institution; a zoologist employed by an aquarium or a zoo may become an administrator or head curator. In some cases, however, scientists may not want what appears to be a more prestigious position. A zoologist who loves to conduct and coordinate research, for example, may not want to become an administrator who is responsible for budgeting, hiring and firing, and other tasks that have nothing to do with research.

■ Earnings

A study conducted by the National Association of Colleges and Employers determined that beginning salaries in private industry in 1997 averaged $25,400 for holders of bachelor's degrees in biological science (including zoologists), $26,900 for those with master's degrees, and $52,400 for holders of doctoral degrees. According to the *Occupational Outlook Handbook,* the median annual wage for biological scientists in 1996 was $36,300, with the middle 10 percent earning between $28,400 and $50,900. In 1997, general biological scientists employed by the federal government earned an average salary of $52,100.

It is possible for the best and brightest of zoologists to make substantial amounts of money. Occasionally, a newly minted Ph.D. who has a top reputation may be offered a position that pays $80,000 or more per year, but only a few people begin their careers at such a high level.

The benefits that zoologists receive as part of their employment vary widely. Employees of the federal government or top universities tend to have extensive benefit packages, but the benefits offered by private industry cover a wide range, from extremely generous to almost nonexistent.

■ Work Environment

There is much variation in the conditions under which zoologists work. Professors of zoology may teach exclusively during the schoolyear or may both teach and conduct research. Many professors whose schoolyear consists of teaching spend their summers doing research. Research scientists spend some time in the field, but most of their work is done in the laboratory. There are zoologists who spend most of their time in the field, but they are the exceptions to the rule.

Zoologists who do fieldwork may have to deal with difficult conditions. A gorilla expert may have to spend her time in the forests of Rwanda; a shark expert may need to observe his subjects from a shark cage. For most people in the field, however, that aspect of the work is particularly interesting and satisfying.

Zoologists spend much of their time corresponding with others in their field, studying the latest literature, reviewing articles written by their peers, and making and returning phone calls. They also log many hours working with computers, using computer modeling, performing statistical analyses, recording the results of their research, or writing articles and grant proposals.

No zoologist works in a vacuum. Even those who spend much time in the field have to keep up with developments within their specialty. In most cases, zoologists deal with many different kinds of people, including students, mentors, the public, colleagues, representatives of granting agencies, private or corporate donors, reporters, and science writers. For this reason, the most successful members of the profession tend to develop good communication skills.

■ Outlook

According to the *Occupational Outlook Handbook,* the significant job growth that the field of zoology (and other fields of biology) experienced from the 1980s to the middle 1990s has slowed. There are still jobs available, but competition for good positions—especially research positions—is increasing. Much of the decrease in growth has been caused by government budget cuts. It is expected, however, that growth will increase in the early 21st century, spurred partly by the need to analyze and offset the effects of pollution on the environment. Those who are most successful in the field in the future are likely to be those who are able to diversify.

■ For More Information

SICB publishes American Zoologist, *and is an excellent source of information about all areas and aspects of zoology.*

Society for Integrative and Comparative Biology
401 North Michigan Avenue
Chicago, IL 60611-4267
Tel: 312-527-6697 or 800-955-1236
Web: http://www.sicb.org

AIBS is a good place to look for schools, internships, and job opportunities.

American Institute of Biological Sciences
1444 Eye Street, NW, Suite 200
Washington, DC 20005
Tel: 202-628-1500
Web: http://www.aibs.org

■ Related Articles

Animals
Animal Caretakers
Animal Handlers
Animal Shelter Employees
Veterinarians
Veterinary Technicians
Zoo and Aquarium Curators
Zoo and Aquarium Directors
Zookeepers

Photo Credits

14   John Elk, Tony Stone Images

17   Karl Weatherly, Tony Stone Images

22   Rich Frishman, Tony Stone Images

31   Barbara Filet, Tony Stone Images

34   Lawrence Migdale, Tony Stone Images

43   Charles Gupton, Tony Stone Images

70   Orkin Pest Control

72   Kindra Clineff, Tony Stone Images

78   John Lawlor, Tony Stone Images

86   Dow Chemical Company

91   David Tejada, Tony Stone Images

96   Phillips Petroleum

100   The Upjohn Company

104   Mathew Hohmann

108   Mitch Kezar, Tony Stone Images

116   Charles Gupton, Tony Stone Images

118   Mathew Hohmann

122   Ron Sanford, Tony Stone Images

126   Mathew Hohmann

128   Mathew Hohmann

132   Mathew Hohmann

135   Arthritis Foundation

140   Richard Shock, Tony Stone Images

152   American Airlines

159   Mathew Hohmann

162   Mathew Hohmann

171   Pipe Industry Fund

173   Mathew Hohmann

185   USDA

190   Robert E. Daemmrich, Tony Stone Images

200   Charles Thatcher, Tony Stone Images

204   Michael Rosenfeld, Tony Stone Images

207   Mathew Hohmann

214   Christopher Bissell, Tony Stone Images

224   Roger Tully, Tony Stone Images

258   Covenant Medical Center, Champaign, IL

273   Robert E. Daemmrich, Tony Stone Images

280   Mathew Hohmann

296   David Austen, Tony Stone Images

299   Waste Management

304   Robert E. Daemmrich, Tony Stone Images

308   Greg Pease, Tony Stone Images

315   Donald R. Downey

322   Chromo Sonm, Tony Stone Images

325   USDA-ARS

328   Stewart Cohen, Tony Stone Images

342   Stewart Cohen, Tony Stone Images

348   Charles Gupton, Tony Stone Images

360   Mathew Hohmann

368   Mathew Hohmann

375   Robert Kusel, Tony Stone Images

396   Bruce Ayers, Tony Stone Images

398   David J. Sams, Tony Stone Images

404   Steven Peters, Tony Stone Images

413   Martin Marietta Laboratories

419   Don Smetzer, Tony Stone Images

422   United Union of Roofers, Waterproofers, & Allied Workers

425   James Wells, Tony Stone Images

429   UPS

442   Robert E. Daemmrich, Tony Stone Images

450   John Coletti, Tony Stone Images

474   National Training Fund for Sheet Metal and Air Conditioning Industry

491   Gorham Textron

508   Hull House Association

Job Title Index

C